COMPARATIVE POLITICS

Domestic Responses to Global Challenges   FIFTH EDITION

Charles Hauss
George Mason University
Search for Common Ground

THOMSON
WADSWORTH

Australia • Canada • Mexico • Singapore • Spain
United Kingdom • United States

THOMSON
WADSWORTH

Comparative Politics: Domestic Responses to Global Challenges, **Fifth Edition**
Charles Hauss

Publisher: Clark Baxter
Executive Editor: David Tatom
Senior Development Editor: Stacey Sims
Assistant Editor: Rebecca Green
Editorial Assistant: Eva Dickerson
Technology Project Manager: Michelle Vardeman
Senior Marketing Manager: Janise Fry
Marketing Communications Manager: Kelley McAllister
Project Manager, Editorial Production: Candace Chen
Art Director: Maria Epes
Print Buyer: Barbara Britton
Permissions Editor: Stephanie Lee

Production Service: G&S Book Services
Text Designer: Ellen Pettengell
Photo Researcher: Kathleen Olson
Copy Editor: Michele Chancellor
Cover Designer: Brian Salisbury
Cover Image: Security Heightened in America, © Spencer Platt/Getty Images, Inc.; Democrats Unveil Immigration Reform Plan, © Joe Raedle/Getty Images, Inc.; First Day of School in Baghdad, © Paula Bronstein/Getty Images, Inc.
Cover Printer: Phoenix Color Corp
Compositor: G&S Book Services
Printer: R.R. Donnelley/Willard

Printed in the United States of America
2 3 4 5 6 7 09 08 07 06

For more information about our products, contact us at:
Thomson Learning Academic Resource Center
1-800-423-0563

For permission to use material from this text or product, submit a request online at **http://www.thomsonrights.com**. Any additional questions about permissions can be submitted by email to **thomsonrights@thomson.com**.

Library of Congress Control Number: 2004113633

Student Edition: ISBN 0-534-59053-5

Hardcover Edition: ISBN 0-495-09162-6

Thomson Higher Education
10 Davis Drive
Belmont, CA 94002-3098
USA

Asia (including India)
Thomson Learning
5 Shenton Way
#01-01 UIC Building
Singapore 068808

Australia/New Zealand
Thomson Learning Australia
102 Dodds Street
Southbank, Victoria 3006
Australia

Canada
Thomson Nelson
1120 Birchmount Road
Toronto, Ontario M1K 5G4
Canada

UK/Europe/Middle East/Africa
Thomson Learning
High Holborn House
50–51 Bedford Row
London WC1R 4LR
United Kingdom

Latin America
Thomson Learning
Seneca, 53
Colonia Polanco
11560 Mexico
D.F. Mexico

Spain (including Portugal)
Thomson Paraninfo
Calle Magallanes, 25
28015 Madrid, Spain

To Gretchen Sandles and Evonne Fei

CONTENTS

Chapter 14

Chapter 15

Chapter 16

LIST OF FIGURES

LIST OF TABLES

PREFACE

This is the fifth edition of *Comparative Politics*. Each time I agreed to revise the book I assumed that the new edition would be easier to update than the previous one.

Each time, I was wrong.

I especially thought that nothing could have been harder than preparing the fourth edition, which was written mostly in the aftermath of 9/11.

Wrong again.

The challenge this time had more to do with the structure of the book than with dramatic changes in the political world I had to cover, though the war in Iraq made updating the chapter on that country daunting to say the least. Instead, the task I faced was adding wholly new chapters on Iran and Nigeria and changing the "look" of the book as we moved to a full-color format. Even those countries whose political life had been reasonably calm during the preceding years underwent important changes. For instance, six had elections that led to new leadership teams in two of them.

Great Britain saw Prime Minister Tony Blair's popularity plummet largely because of his support for the war in Iraq, though he seemed certain to become the first Labour prime minister to win a third term in elections tentatively scheduled for about the time this book is published. France had the most unusual election in which President Jacques Chirac easily defeated the all but avowedly racist Jean-Marie Le Pen in a runoff election in 2002 that solidified the center-right's hold on power, perhaps for a decade or more to come. Germans reelected the government of Socialist Chancellor Gerhard Schröder by the narrowest of margins, but it continued to struggle in its efforts to revitalize an economy that has been anything but booming for a decade or more. The European Union added ten new members and is on the verge of passing a formal constitution. And, of course, the United States led the "coalition of the willing" into war with Iraq and reelected President George W. Bush after one of the most bitterly fought campaigns in recent history.

The current and former communist regimes kept changing as well. Russians overwhelmingly reelected President Vladimir Putin and added to his support in the legislature. Many observers are deeply worried, however, about Putin's administration efforts to centralize power and use it in arbitrary ways that remind some of how the Communist Party ruled before the Soviet Union collapsed. In China, an aging generation of leaders led by Jiang Zemin handed over power to a group led by party chair and president Hu Jintao who seemed even more committed than their predecessors to the economic reforms begun a quarter-century ago.

Perhaps the most surprising change came in India where the Congress Party scored an unexpected victory in 2004 and then, just as surprisingly, party leader Sonja Gandhi decided not to become prime minister. Iraq, of course, suffered the most devastating consequences in the war that toppled the regime governed by Saddam Hussein. This resulted in an American-led occupation of the country, which in turn sparked a bloody insurgency in much of the country. Politically, South Africa may have experienced the least amount of change with its leadership team remaining intact. However, like many poor countries, South Africa faces an HIV/AIDS infection rate that tops a third for people under thirty. Indeed, HIV/AIDS has become such an important issue almost everywhere in the world that each country chapter will feature a box on how it is dealing with the pandemic. Finally, Mexicans have discovered that electing a president who is not a member of the PRI in and of itself does little to help address the country's social and economic problems; President Fox never enjoyed much support in the legislature and had to cope with what we in the United States call gridlock.

In all, about a third of this book is brand new.

Nonetheless, I've tried to balance the same two overlapping and conflicting goals I focused on in the first four editions. On the one hand, I introduce the key concepts in our discipline. On the other, I focus on the major research findings and other evidence that I hope will grab and sustain my student-readers' attention.

Balancing the two is a challenge in any academic field. It is especially difficult in comparative politics, a field in which we academics, like everybody else, are struggling to make sense of the unprecedented acceleration of political change in the "real world." Our task is also difficult because most of us still base our teaching and writing on core concepts that have been around for forty years or more. Such ideas as political culture or the various dimensions of state power are still vital. However, we have not done as good a job of developing additional ideas that yield similarly powerful insights into the issues that have burst onto the political agenda in the past generation. These issues include democratization, the development of an increasingly interdependent international economy, and environmental decay.

Even when our concepts are up-to-date, comparative politics is difficult for students to master on purely pedagogical grounds. More than the other parts of political science, comparative politics requires students to constantly move back and forth between abstract concepts and an often-bewildering array of names, dates, places, and events.

I have therefore tried to write this book in a way that will help students navigate the confusing intellectual waters that make up comparative politics at the dawn of the new millennium. My hope is that students will come away from the course with a reasonable understanding of some of the most important general trends, an exposure to politics in a number of countries important both in their own right and because they help us see these broader trends, and a desire to dig more deeply into what is such a fascinating and exciting field.

In so doing, I have tried to accomplish three things:

- Write as timely a book as possible. Although I agree that historical sources of today's politics are extremely important and that the study of politics should not be a hostage of current events, we must acknowledge that we live in remarkable times. Indeed, we academics probably *should* be fixated on current trends because they seem to be putting so many of our concepts and so much of our conventional wisdom into question—something I have seen not only professionally as a teacher and as an author but also in my other life as an activist.

- Incorporate new theoretical concerns, including some that are not traditionally seen as part of comparative politics. The most important of these is captured in the book's subtitle. Political scientists have created what amounts to an intellectual fire wall between comparative politics and international relations. Although each has its own focus, we can no longer study one without including the other. We will understand less and less about any country's politics if we fail to explore the way international geopolitical, economic, cultural, and environmental factors constrain what the country's leaders and citizens can do.

- Make the alternation between the empirical and the theoretical as easy as possible. Because most readers of this book will be Americans, I have included a brief chapter on the United States that they can use as a frame of reference. Each chapter after the first has a series of features highlighting the comparative implications of the material in it. Each also has a section entitled "Critical Thinking Exercises" at the end that is designed to help students compare and think about general and theoretical issues. Each chapter includes dozens of relevant websites for further exploration of the topics and countries under consideration, in part because all students should learn how to use the Internet effectively, but more important, because I have found that students learn a lot about asking and answering their own questions by using the web. More pedagogical material and additional links can be found on the website created for this book at http://politicalscience.wadsworth.com/hauss05/. In trying to reach those goals, I frequently found myself going back to the sentence by Marcel Proust that I use to open Chapter 1: "The real voyage of discovery consists not in seeking new lands, but in seeing with new eyes."

This book and this course are both about seeing with new eyes. Even the most well-traveled student (or instructor, for that matter) will not have visited all the countries covered here. I certainly haven't. More important, even those who have traveled the most will not have learned all that much unless they have learned how to drop their intellectual, cultural, and political blinders and to see the places they have visited, the place they started from, and their own selves in a new light, one that allows them to question and reinterpret everything they previously took for granted.

Acknowledgments

Authors who write books this long that cover so much ground rack up massive intellectual debts to the people on whose evidence and ideas they have relied. I am no exception.

The debts start with the two friends who contributed the chapters on Japan and Iraq to earlier editions of the book. Roger Bowen and I started teaching introductory comparative politics together at Colby College in the late 1970s. Since then, we have both moved on—he is now president of the American Association of University Professors (www.aaup.org). We taught the course together for so long that it is hard to tell where his ideas end and mine begin. Guilain Denoeux joined our team at Colby (where he remains) during the Gulf War, when we introduced Iraq to our curriculum. He supported the war; I opposed it. More important, that our students could see us disagree with each other while obviously enjoying working together went a long way toward making the course a success.

I also have to thank colleagues at the two institutions where I have taught since leaving Colby—George Mason University in Virginia (www.gmu.edu/depts./pia) and the University of Reading in the United Kingdom (www.rdg.ac.uk/AcaDepts/lp). At George Mason, colleagues such as Scott Keeter, Jim Barry, Fran Harbour, Peter Mandaville, and Reuben Brigety have helped me improve my teaching and figure out the ever-more-complicated world of comparative politics and international relations. At Reading, Joel Peters, Barry Jones, Philip Giddings, Bob McKeever, and the rest of my colleagues took me in as a visiting scholar and professor for the three years my wife served on the staff of the U.S. Embassy. I owe Joel a special debt, not only because we are writing a book on international relations and doing some political work on reconciliation and conflict resolution together, but also because he taught me the finer points of cricket, soccer, and rugby—both codes.

Ken Wedding has been a good friend since we first started grading advanced placement exams together in the late 1980s. I am delighted that he has been able to work on the instructor's manual and website for this edition of *Comparative Politics,* and I'm hoping that we can work together even more now that he has retired from Hopkins High School.

I also owe a lot to colleagues at Search for Common Ground and elsewhere in the conflict resolution field who have helped me bring in some ideas and themes of that work to complement the traditional material of comparative politics. At Search, Roger Conner, Rob Fersh, Mary Jackstein, Tom Dunne, and Marie Williams have sharpened my thinking about consensus building in established democracies, while John Marks, Susan Collin Marks, Shamil Idriss, Sandra Melone, Carole Frampton, Rebecca Larson, and Michael Shipler have done the same for the prospects of reconciliation in other parts of the world where conflict has been far more violent. Outside of Search, I particularly want to thank members of the "Boulder Group" who meet at the base of Rocky Mountains to discuss what the group of senior practitioners who work there have been doing. The Boulder Group twice invited me to talk, first on my thoughts about Iraq just before the war began and then on the 2004 American election two days after it occurred. In the Boulder Group I start with Bernie Mayer and Peter Woodrow, both of whom were college housemates in the 1960s. Guy and Heidi Burgess have also gotten me involved in their online conflict resolution projects based at the University of Colorado (*www.beyondintractability .org* and *www.crinfo.org*). Of the other members of the group, Bill Ury and John Paul Lederach have given my thoughts inspiring criticism.

In addition, I need to thank a few people who have entered or reentered my life in the last three years. President Nancy Dye of Oberlin College not only accepted my invitation to be part of a Search for Common Ground delegation to meet with academic officials in Iran but invited me to campus to talk about Iraq and to teach for two weeks in 2004 when I had the eerie experience of living in an apartment, in a dorm, that was three doors away from my freshman room. Dick O'Neill—a childhood friend and retired Navy Captain who helps the Pentagon think outside the box—has forced me to think about the way national security concerns affect domestic politics. Finally, Dan Philpott of Notre Dame and Tom Gettman of World Vision have helped me see the expanding role that important questions of faith seem to play in political life.

I have also been able to draw on the criticisms of nearly thirty colleagues who have evaluated one edition or another of this book. Although I thank them all, I am particularly grateful to the instructors who were highly critical of earlier editions; I learned the most—and changed the most—because of them. The reviewers for this edition were Amir Abedi, Western Washington University; Paul S. Adams, University of Massachusetts–Amherst; Blaine David Benedict, Houghton College; Jean-Gabriel Jolivet, Purdue University; and Minion K.C. Morrison, University of Missouri–Columbia.

For earlier editions, the reviewers were Nozar Alaolmolki, Hiram College; Leslie Anderson, University of Florida; Steve D. Bollard, Western Kentucky; Alan D. Buckley, Santa Monica College; John M. Buckley, Orange Coast College; William E. Caroll, Sam Houston State University; Kristine K. Cline, Riverside Community College; Richard Deeng, Temple University; Jana Eaton, Unionville High School; Larry Elowitz, Georgia College; Edward Epstein, University of Utah; Joshua B. Forrest, University of Vermont; E. Gene Frankland, Ball State University; Kristina Gilbert, Riverside Community College; Michael Gold-Biss, St. Cloud State University; Phil Huxtable, University of Kansas; Amal Kawar, Utah State University; Michael Kenney, University of Florida; Frank P. La Veness, St. John's University; Clinton W. Maffett, University of Memphis; Margaret Martin, University of St. Thomas; Hazel M. McFerson, George Mason University; Marian A. L. Miller, University of Akron; Richard M. Mills, Fordham University; David J. Myers, Pennsylvania State University; Jeffrey R. Orenstein, Kent State University; Bradley Scharf, Seattle University; and Carrie Rosefsky Wickham, Emory University.

In addition, this book could not have seen the light of day without the talented team at Thomson Wads-worth. Publisher Clark Baxter convinced me to write the first edition of this book more than a decade ago. Clark gave me the freedom to do it my way while still teaching me the tricks of the trade he has learned in more than a quarter century in publishing. Our relationship has strengthened over the years to the point that I value him as a friend as well as a boss. David Tatom took over as the political science editor once Wadsworth acquired two other publishing houses, and he gave me firm grounding when my creative instincts took me too far. I also value David's friendship because we disagree about most political issues and enjoy discussing them, mirroring the kind of civility we stress in conflict resolution circles. Stacey Sims joined the team for this edition as development editor, which meant that she had the unenviable job of yelling at me all the times I fell behind schedule. Janise Fry, as usual, did a brilliant job not only of developing marketing material for the book but in motivating the wonderful Wadsworth sales staff to promote it. Michelle Vardeman came up with most of the ideas for the website that Ken Wedding and, to a lesser extent, I, then developed. Gretchen Otto made the production of the book as painless (for me, if not for her) as possible. Michelle Chancellor was by far the best copy editor I've ever worked with; any remaining typos or incomprehensible passages are my fault, not hers.

Finally, I have to thank the two women to whom this book is dedicated—my wife, Gretchen Sandles, and her daughter, Evonne Fei. Gretchen is an accomplished political scientist in her own right and has taught me most of what I know about the former Soviet Union. Now that she has retired from the federal government, we plan to do some writing together to help Americans rethink and expand what national security means in the post–cold war and post-9/11 world. Evonne's impending college tuition bills provided the impetus to begin the book. Her Christmas present to me the year I was finishing the first edition gave me the idea with which to end it. Now, she is a psychotherapist with an avid interest in politics and e-mails me articles she thinks I should read.

I had a wonderful time writing and revising this book, and I hope you find the same pleasure in reading it.

Falls Church, Virginia
March 2005

SUPPLEMENTS FOR INSTRUCTORS AND STUDENTS

Instructor's Manual and Test Bank

Prepared by Ken Wedding, contains chapter outlines, commentary, teaching suggestions containing web links and InfoTrac® College Edition sources, and student activities. The test bank includes multiple-choice, short answer, and essay questions.

Multimedia Manager with Instructor Resources CD-ROM

Including presentation tools and electronic instructor resources, this book-specific tool is a one-stop source that allows you to most effectively prepare for your course in a timely fashion. The CD-ROM contains Microsoft® PowerPoint® (lecture outlines, illustrations, charts, and graphs from the text itself); electronic transparencies from a selection of Comparative Politics texts, video clips, the Instructor's Manual and Test Bank, the Video Case Studies Instructor's Manual, and ExamView computerized testing—an easy-to-use assessment program.

ExamView®

Create, deliver, and customize tests and study guides (both print and online) in minutes with this easy-to-use assessment and tutorial system. ExamView offers both a Quick Test Wizard and an Online Test Wizard that guide you step-by-step through the process of creating tests, while its unique "WYSIWYG" capability allows you to see the test you are creating on the screen exactly as it will print or display online. You can build tests of up to 250 questions using up to 12 question types. Using ExamView's complete word processing capabilities, you can enter an unlimited number of new questions or edit existing questions.

Video for Comparative Politics

Short lecture launching clips get students interested in issues pertaining to comparative politics.

Comparative Politics Interactive Website

http://politicalscience.wadsworth.com/hauss05/

This book has a fully integrated website that links to major websites listed in the text and features chapters on Canada, Japan, and South Africa. Updates to countries discussed in the book will be posted to the website as events unfold.

The book companion website also offers a rich array of teaching and learning resources that can help students not only pass the Comparative Politics course but also excel in it! This website features the following for student study drill: chapter-by-chapter Learning Objectives, Chapter Outlines, chapter glossaries, audio flash cards, crossword puzzles, critical thinking questions and InfoTrac College Edition exercises from the book, web links, Interactive Maps with quizzing, "Comparing Constitutions of the World," and chapter quizzes.

Additional tools to help students better understand key concepts are available on the Comparative Politics Resource Center, offering a wealth of media products to enrich the teaching and learning experience. Accessed from the book companion website, the CPRC offers Video Case Studies, Microcase Exercises that allow students to manipulate real data and apply it to real-world situations, InfoTrac College Edition readings and assignments, Internet Activities, web links, and mapping exercises using the CIA factbook.

Part 1

INTRODUCTION

CHAPTER 1
Seeking New Lands,
Seeing with New Eyes

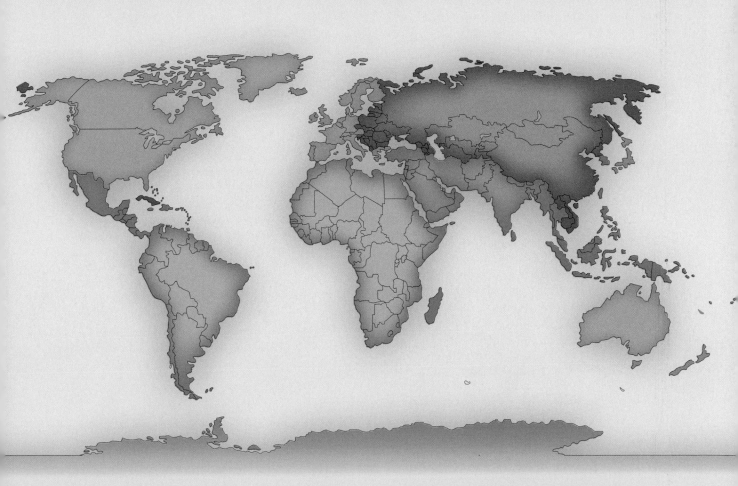

The voyage of discovery consists not in seeking new lands but in seeing with new eyes.

MARCEL PROUST

Chapter 1

SEEKING NEW LANDS, SEEING WITH NEW EYES

CHAPTER OUTLINE

- Dangers and Opportunities in a Changing World
- Leaders in Transition
- The State: One Focus among Many
- Comparative Politics
- Three Templates
- Five Themes
- Using This Book

Dangers and Opportunities in a Shrinking World

This book is based on three premises.

The first is all but obvious these days. Events taking place around the world affect us all.

The fact that we live in an interdependent world was driven home as clearly as it could possibly have been on 11 September 2001 when airplanes crashed into the twin towers of the World Trade Center in New York City and the Pentagon just outside of Washington, D.C. The cartoon that follows sums up how many people around the world felt that day. Before 9/11, many Americans thought that other countries and continents were far away. By noon on that warm and sunny fall day they knew the world and its problems were on their doorsteps.

Literally speaking, the cartoon is not accurate. The world and its oceans have not shrunk. Europe, Africa, and Asia are as far from the Americas as they were on 10 September 2001. However, our political, social, economic, telecommunications, and other systems have changed so much so fast that we ignore the problems of the rest of the world at our peril.

That, of course, is not only true of Americans. Citizens of more than twenty countries were among the nearly three thousand people killed at Ground Zero. At the end of 2004, captured Taliban and al-Qaeda fighters from Australia, the United Kingdom, and a number of Middle Eastern countries were still being held by American authorities at Guantanamo Bay, Cuba. In recent years, major terrorist attacks have occurred in France, Germany, Spain, Saudi Arabia, Kenya, Tanzania, Russia, Indonesia, Colombia, and more.

And for the purposes of this book, terrorism is but the tip of the political iceberg. We are tied into an increasingly interconnected world in ways that are so unremarkable we rarely think about them.

Just before writing this chapter, I put away my clean laundry. Knowing I was going to be writing about interdependence, I checked the labels. None of the shirts were made in the United States. Then I checked my ties, pants, and suit coats. Same thing. Labor costs are simply too high for companies to manufacture most clothes in the United States, Great Britain, France, Japan, or any other wealthy country.

The loss of jobs in the textile industry is part of a broader shift in manufacturing jobs to the poorer countries of South America, Asia, and Africa. Try as they might, governments have not been able to slow the trend of **globalization**[1] over the last fifty years.

---

[1] Terms in boldface can be found in the list of key terms at the end of each chapter and in the glossaries of concepts, people, acronyms, organizations, places, and events at the end of the book.

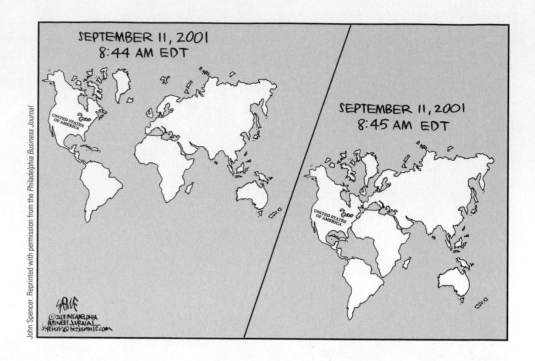

Consider the impact of the little-known African Growth and Opportunity Act (AGOA) that became U.S. law in 2000. The act reduced tariffs and other restrictions on 1,800 textile and other products imported into the United States from Africa. As such, it was designed to give manufacturers an incentive to open factories in the world's poorest continent. At that, it seems to have succeeded. The *New York Times* reports that it has helped to create tens of thousands of jobs in such countries as Kenya, Lesotho, and Uganda, where the women who work in the new textile mills are referred to as AGOA girls.[2]

The jobs, however, are a mixed blessing. The women who work in those factories do make more money than they could anywhere else. But the work is hard, in many ways reminiscent of American sweatshops of a century ago. Moreover, the jobs came with a cost. Most of the companies who opened these workshops were owned by South Asians who had closed more expensive operations in their home countries. Last, but by no means least, it is not certain that these jobs will last. The act itself is due to expire in 2008, and its provisions may run afoul of the World Trade Organization's rules on textiles that are due to take effect in 2005.

Comparative politics is mostly about much weightier issues than what we wear and where it is made. None-

theless, global shifts in the textile trade show us that what happens as far away as Uganda affects us all.

The second premise is harder to see in the politics surrounding AGOA. For that, it is best to return to 9/11, which may well prove to be the defining event of our time.

We live in a time of **crisis.** However, I do not intend to use that term the way it is typically employed in the West to convey a moment of great danger whether in the life of a family or of a country.

Of course, a crisis is about danger, as anyone who has been through either a divorce or the build-up to a war knows. Nonetheless, there is more to a crisis than "simply" a threat.

Physicians, for instance, refer to a medical crisis as that point in the development of a disease at which the patient will either live or die. It is, thus, a turning point when good as well as bad outcomes are still possible. The ancient Chinese broadened the idea of a crisis even farther by combining two characters to convey what we mean by the word "crisis." The first is danger; the second is opportunity. In other words, if handled well, a crisis also opens the door to new, often previously unthought of, possibilities.

The dangers associated with 9/11 and subsequent events are easy to see. But so, too, are the opportunities. To supporters of the Bush administration, they include passage of a series of laws designed to improve American security and the prosecution of the war on terrorism. To

---

[2] Marc Lacey, "U.S. Law Gives Africa Hope and Hard Jobs," *New York Times,* 14 November 2003, A1, 8.

Carmen Taylor/AP WideWorld Photos

The second World Trade Center tower, hit by a hijacked airplane on September 11.

some of Bush's opponents, the opportunities encompass the need to better understand Islam and to address the underlying causes of terrorism as reflected in the often asked question, "why do they hate us?"

In the pages that follow, we will not encounter many issues as threatening or as dramatic as 9/11. Nonetheless, we will encounter turning point after turning point in which politicians and average citizens had to make momentous decisions. Sometimes they succeeded, as when Charles de Gaulle and his followers created the French Fifth Republic in 1958. At other times we will find mixed results, as in the limited success Vicente Fox has had in Mexico since becoming the first president chosen from a party other than the Institutional Revolutionary Party (PRI) in more than seventy years. At still other times we will encounter abject failures as in Russia during the first few years after the Soviet Union collapsed in 1991.

Not every issue warrants being called a crisis. Indeed, much of politics is routine—and even rather dull. But the questions we focus on in comparative politics typically are fraught with implications. And in the final chapter I will make the case that there is also an integrated global crisis facing us all, rich and poor, young and old, North and South alike.

The third premise builds on the first two. Events in the news also remind us of how much and how fast our world is changing. A century ago, most of the world was ruled by colonial powers. A half century later, Germany and Japan were economically devastated by their defeat in World War II and were occupied and governed by the victorious Allied powers. A generation ago, Mexico's PRI ran the country without any serious opposition, Communists were firmly in power in the Soviet Union, and the apartheid government in South Africa seemed as invulnerable as ever. A decade ago, Japan was considered a threat to American and European prosperity, and its state was considered a model of how a government could steer a capitalist economy.

In 2005, there are almost no colonies left. The Soviet Union has disintegrated, and Communism in Eurasia is no more. South Africa's multiracial democracy has held three elections and seen its charismatic first president, Nelson Mandela, go into retirement. The PRI has lost its first election ever. Germany continues to struggle economically after nearly a half century of rapid growth that returned it to third place among the world's industrial powers.

It is at most a slight exaggeration to say, as some pundits do, that change is the only constant in our lives. And, in technological and some other areas of our lives, change is occurring at a dizzying, accelerating rate. To cite but one example, the president of Intel once said that computers would get twice as fast and powerful every eighteen months. Today it is occurring faster than that. The computer this book was written on was two thousand times more powerful than the first one I bought twenty years earlier—and cost hundreds of dollars less.

Comparative politics is but one of several academic disciplines you can turn to if you want to understand these and the other trends we will discuss in the pages that follow. As you will see, its focus is on domestic politics—that is, on what happens inside a country. To that end, this book and the course you are taking will introduce you to the ideas, findings, and techniques of comparative analysis.

Leaders in Transition

The rest of this chapter focuses on how comparative politics can help us understand political life around the world. However, because the concepts scholars use can be rather abstract, we will begin with a brief discussion of three of the more important national leaders who are likely to be out of office by the time the next edition of this book is published and whose careers illustrate the three premises discussed earlier.

Tony Blair (1953–) became prime minister of the United Kingdom of Great Britain and Northern Ireland in May 1997 when his Labour Party ended a string of four consecutive defeats in a landslide victory over the ruling Conservative (Tory) Party (www.number-10.gov.uk/output/page4.asp). The young and telegenic Blair took office amid a lot of hope and hype. He promised a wave of economic and constitutional reform, much of which he carried out. Observers began talking about a "cool Britannia" infused with a new sense of optimism and panache.

Labour won almost as sweeping a victory four years later. This time, however, the luster of Blair's first years had worn off. In fact, Blair won in large part because the Conservatives were even less popular than he was.

Support for Blair had eroded for many reasons. Many people objected to what seemed to be his obsession with maintaining total control over his party often with colleagues who made a series of dubious ethical decisions. Others objected to the fact that Blair was more pro-European than most British citizens and seemed likely to endorse adopting the euro as the country's currency. Yet others were dissatisfied with the relatively slow rate of economic growth that made it hard for the government to improve the National Health Service and other social programs.

Blair's woes only mounted after 9/11. He has been the United States' most loyal ally since then, as most British prime ministers have been since World War II. That did not get Blair into much trouble during the war in Afghanistan. However, he lost the support of a majority of his own party's supporters and the country as a whole when he took Britain into the war against Iraq without the support of the United Nations Security Council.

By the time President Bush paid a state visit to the United Kingdom in November 2003, Blair's support in the polls was at an all-time low. As we will see in Chapter 4, there was little or no chance that he would lose a vote of confidence in the House of Commons. Nonetheless, there were plenty of leading politicians in both the Labour Party and the opposition who called on him to resign.

On 31 December 1999, Boris Yeltsin made the surprising announcement that he was resigning immediately as president of Russia. According to the Russian Constitution, which had been written by Yeltsin to enhance his own power, Prime Minister Vladimir Putin (1952–) became acting president until new elections could be held (www.cnn.com/interactive/profiles/putin/putin.bio.html).

Before summer 1999, Putin was a virtual unknown. He had spent most of his career in the KGB, the Soviet

Blair leaves his residence at 10 Downing Street to attend the weekly Prime Minister's Question Time when he takes queries and comments from government and opposition Members of Parliament.

spy agency, before joining the city government of St. Petersburg in the mid-1990s. He moved to Moscow in 1996 and held a number of minor posts before being named head of the Federal Security Bureau (FSB), the KGB's successor organization. In August 1999, Yeltsin nominated Putin to be prime minister, the fourth person to hold the job that year.

Putin proved remarkably popular and effective. He got a lot of credit for his forcefulness in the renewed war with rebels in Chechnya. He also steered the new political party, Unity, to a surprisingly strong showing in the 1999 legislative elections and then won a decisive victory in the presidential elections in March 2000. Both Putin and his party won far more convincing victories in 2003 and 2004.

As was the case with Blair, Putin's success at the polls masks serious problems. Despite several years of relatively strong growth, the economy is still only a fraction of its Soviet-era size, and direct foreign investment is far below what Putin and his colleagues had hoped for.

Moreover, Putin spent much of his time in office in a struggle with a dozen or so wealthy "oligarchs" who had supported Yeltsin but came to oppose his successor. Many worried that Putin's strong-armed tactics with the oligarchs and with the rebels in Chechnya reflected a willingness to use Soviet-style repression rather than to rely on the rule of law.

Like Blair, Iranian president Mohammad Khatami (1943–) was first elected in 1997. Like Blair, he was seen as a moderate and a reformer who might loosen some of

Russian president Vladimir Putin with his predecessor, Boris Yeltsin.

Iranian president Mohammad Khatami (L) discusses political issues with Supreme Leader Ali Khamanei. Both wear black turbans indicating that they are clerics who are direct descendants of the Prophet Mohammad.

the controls imposed by the Islamic Republic following the 1979 revolution that overthrew the Shah's regime (abcnews.go.com/reference/bios/khatami.html).

Like his predecessors beginning with the Ayatollah Ruhollah Khomeini, Khatami is an Islamic cleric. But he also is a reformer. Khatami's government loosened some restrictions. Women are now allowed to wear skimpier veils. Men and women can hold hands in public. It is easier for some dissidents to make their points of view known in the media. On the other hand, there is widespread dissatisfaction with the lack of professional opportunities for young people, who make up the bulk of the country's population. The authorities are having a harder and harder time keeping Western ideas out of the country now that hundreds of thousands of people own satellite dishes. And, of course, outside pressure on Iran to reform its authoritarian rule has mounted ever since President George W. Bush included it in the "axis of evil" with Iraq and North Korea during his 2002 State of the Union Address.

Nonetheless, Khatami has had a rough time during his second term in office. Since Iran is one of the few theocracies in which religious leaders rule, Khatami has to share power with the supreme religious leader, Ayatollah Ali Hoseini Khamenei, who has to approve most major public policy initiatives. More generally, Khatami cannot count on the support of the conservative majority in the Majlis, or parliament.

The State: One Focus among Many

Seeing the three premises and three leaders allows us to look at the core issues in comparative politics. As is the case with most social sciences, political scientists do not agree on what the best focus of a text or course should be. I have chosen to organize this book around the evolution, structure, and performance of the state. Others have chosen to concentrate on public policy, the political economy, the role of average citizens, and the overall performance of the system as a whole. In fact, the focus an author chooses may not be all that important because all those other issues will get plenty of attention too.

I decided to focus on the state because it puts one of the most important questions in political life on center stage—the way scarce resources are allocated. That, in turn, means focusing on the single most important common denominator of political life—**power,** which is most often defined as the ability to get people or groups to do *what they otherwise would not do.* Those last six

words are key. They suggest that the exercise of power requires coercion. People typically have to be forced into doing things they don't want to do. The exercise of power does not always involve the use of physical force, but the threat of force is almost always there.

Politics is not exclusively about power. In the pages that follow, you will encounter plenty of people who have been driven to act politically for other reasons, such as the desire to help people or to create a fairer society. There are also newer definitions of power that strip the necessity of coercion from it. However, as things stand now, in most countries at most times, there is no escaping the connection between power and the ability to force adversaries to comply with one's wishes.

What Is the State?

The state is the first term in this book that we need to define with some precision. Many people use the terms *government, state, nation,* and *regime* interchangeably. In the case of some countries, like the United States, it may not be terribly misleading to do so. When we consider the former Soviet Union or Iraq before the 2003 war, however, treating the terms as synonyms can be extremely misleading:

- **Government** refers to a particular set of institutions and people authorized by formal documents such as a **constitution** to pass laws, issue regulations, control the police, and so on. For the moment, it is enough to note that the government rarely holds all the power available in a given country and, in some cases, can be far less influential than other actors. That is certainly true of what are referred to as failed states, in which the government lacks the ability to do much of anything in a society wracked by civil war. To a lesser degree, it was true of Mexico before Fox's election, when the PRI was far more important than government institutions.

- **State** is a broader concept that includes all the institutions and individuals that exercise power. One of Putin's main accomplishments has been the sharp reduction in the political clout of that shadowy group of oligarchs, who had had tremendous leverage during the Yeltsin years and were unquestionably part of the state.

- **Regime** refers to the institutions and practices that typically endure from government to government or, in American terms, administration to administration. This is, of course, a term that burst onto the political scene when President George W. Bush began demanding, and later enforced, a change in regime in Iraq. However, it should be noted that it is a concept political scientists have used for a half century or more.

- **Nation** is a psychological rather than an institutional concept. It refers to the cultural, linguistic, and other identities that can tie people together. Thus, the Chechens who want to secede certainly do not think of themselves as Russians. Indeed, as we will see in several chapters, a lack of national identity often reflects deep-seated ethnic and other divisions that can undermine support for any state, whatever institutional levers it may have for exerting power.

Types of States

All states are not alike. Some, like the United States, are large, rich, stable, and powerful. Others, like Somalia, are so poor, fragile, and weak that a "state" hardly seems to exist. The same is true as I write about Iraq, which may still be under American occupation when this book is published. About the only thing all states have in common is that what each state does—and doesn't—do matters for its own citizens and for many others who live outside its borders.

Unfortunately, political scientists have still not reached agreement about the best way to classify states. Despite all the changes since the end of the cold war, I have decided to stick with a traditional three-way classification:

- Industrialized democracies
- Current and former Communist regimes
- The third world

This way of dividing up the world is outdated. Nonetheless, because the industrialized democracies and the once-solid Communist bloc in particular have many historical and contemporary traits in common, it still makes sense to use this framework.

The **industrialized democracies** present us with a paradox. On the one hand, they have the most resources and, so, the greatest potential for creating and sustaining powerful states. Like Great Britain, most are wealthy and have at least reasonably effective and popular political institutions. As table 1.1 (also on the inside front cover) shows, the citizens of industrialized democracies enjoy standards of living similar to those of most Americans. Virtually everyone can read and write, and the infant mortality figures suggest that they enjoy at least basic health-care coverage.

On the other hand, these states also have the most built-in restraints on the exercise of power. Most of those limits on what leaders can do are laid out in constitutions and other laws. What the state can do is also determined to some degree by public opinion and by the re-

TABLE 1.1 Basic Data

COUNTRY	POPULATION (MILLIONS OF PEOPLE IN 1999)	AVERAGE POPULATION GROWTH 1990–1999 (%)	GNP PER CAPITA (US$)	GROWTH IN GNP 2001–2002 (%)	LITERACY (%)	INFANT MORTALITY (PER 1,000 BIRTHS)	AVERAGE LIFE EXPECTANCY
Canada	31	1.1	22,300	3.3	99+	7	79
China	1,281	1.2	940	8.0	91	36	72
France	59	0.5	22,010	1.0	99+	5	79
Germany	82	0.2	22,670	0.2	99+	6	77
India	1,048	1.9	480	4.4	61	83	45
Iran	66	2.6	1,710	5.9	70	35	70
Japan	127	0.5	33,350	-0.7	99+	5	77
Mexico	101	12.0	5,910	0.7	91	35	72
Nigeria	133	2.9	290	-0.9	67	110	52
Russia	144	0.3	2,140	4.3	99+	20	65
South Africa	44	2.1	2,600	3.0	86	83	49
United Kingdom	59	0.2	25,250	1.5	99+	7	77
United States	288	1.0	35,060	1.5	99+	7	77
High Income	965	0.7	26,310	1.3	99+	8	77
Low Income	2,495	2.1	430	4.1	64	107	60

Source: World Bank, *World Development Report*. www.worldbank.org. United Nations Development Program, *Human Development Report*. hdr.undp.org/reports/global/2004/. Iraq not included because data are incomplete.

Note: The World Bank and the UNDP do not put exactly the same set of countries into their poorest and richest categories. Therefore, the first, third, and fourth columns, which are based on the former, are based on slightly different calculation criteria from the others. That should not dramatically impact the findings, which would be stark whatever the criteria used.

sults of competitive elections that determine who the leaders are.

That paradox is reversed in the current and former **Communist** states. During their heyday, these states were extremely strong. The government controlled almost everything, from the schools to the press to the economy. Indeed, the term **totalitarianism** was coined to describe these and other states that sought complete control over their societies.

The collapse of Communism in the former Soviet Union and in Eastern Europe, however, demonstrated that repression and central control were not enough to keep these states strong indefinitely. Among the many causes of this historical turning point, we will focus on the failure of Soviet-style regimes to adopt innovative economic policies, which in turn reinforced the people's hostility toward a regime that suddenly lost most of its political teeth. There were many reasons for this failure. At or near the top of any list is the decision by the Soviet and Eastern European leaders to give their people more freedom in order to breathe new life into their economies. Once that happened, they could no longer rely on repression, and they lost the political "glue" that kept them in power.

The Chinese have followed a different path, implementing liberal economic reforms while retaining tight control over political life. So far, this strategy has "worked" in that the Chinese Communist Party (CCP) is still in power. However, most observers doubt that the CCP can continue stifling dissent indefinitely.

The **third world** is much harder to describe as a whole, which is hardly surprising given that it includes over 130 countries. Above all else, the third world is poor. Some third world countries are so impoverished that the average citizen has no more than $300 to $500 a year to live on. Table 1.1 shows just how wide the gap is between the industrial democracies and the forty-one poorest third world countries. Moreover, as the shortage of doctors, the large number of young people, and the high degree of illiteracy in the poorest countries suggest, third world governments face far more problems than the other two types of state. To make matters even worse, many still have not been able to forge states with functioning courts, bureaucracies, and other institutions people in the industrialized democracies take for granted. Many, too, have experienced military coups and other forms of political upheaval that have sapped a succession of regimes of the popular support vital to the long-term strength of any state.

There are exceptions to this otherwise gloomy picture—the **newly industrializing countries** (**NICs**), which have made great strides in breaking out of the trap of underdevelopment. The most famous are the Asian tigers—South Korea, Singapore, Indonesia, and Malaysia—as well as a few other Asian countries and, perhaps, Mexico, Brazil, and Chile. Although there is still some debate about what allowed these countries to grow so fast from the 1970s through the mid-1990s, every list of causes includes the way each state was able to build cooperative relationships with business and labor, albeit sometimes through force.

Strong and Weak States

We will also be asking why some states are stronger than others. Obviously, every state has tried to respond to the kinds of challenges faced by the three leaders discussed earlier. Just as obviously, there is tremendous variation in what these leaders have been able to accomplish.

The distinction between strong and weak states is one of the most controversial in comparative politics. In a textbook for an introductory course, however, we can use a fairly simple definition. **Strong states** take on more responsibilities and generally carry them out more effectively than do weaker ones. **Weak states,** by contrast, are less able to define and carry out policy goals.

Comparativists have not been able to reach many conclusions about the factors that determine how strong a given state is. The best we can do is to note that, when viewed over the long term, strong states are relatively wealthy, their regimes have widespread popular support, and their governing elites work reasonably effectively together. The use of repression can strengthen states in the short run. However, as events of the past two decades suggest, it may not be enough to sustain such states under today's social and economic conditions.

Basic patterns in state structure and power roughly coincide with the three types of states outlined earlier. In particular, the former Communist states could not adapt to the changing social and economic conditions they faced in the 1980s because their strength lay in their ability to maintain order, not innovate. Similarly, poverty, internal divisions, and other factors are part of the reason most third world countries have relatively weak states as well.

No state comes close to being able to do whatever it wants whenever it wants. If anything, most states are losing the ability to shape their own destinies in the light of globalization, which we will consider shortly.

Finally, we will spend a lot of time on the distinction between the state and regime. In particular, we will see that industrialized democracies are able to weather most crises because there is all but total acceptance of the regime that insulates it from such divisive protests as those of the new left of the 1960s and 1970s. We will also see that most other regimes lack that bedrock popular support and that dissatisfaction with the government of the day more easily spills over to the regime and even, in some cases, to the existence of the country itself.

Comparative Politics

Comparativists agree on very little. We do, however, have one point of view in common—a way of analyzing the political world. We are convinced that you can reach the most accurate and insightful conclusions by comparing two or more examples of the phenomenon you are interested in—in this case, states. In this text, we will use eleven states and one international organization as intellectual springboards for trying to understand political life as a whole.

Though political scientists compare in many different ways, we all start by asking two sets of questions about the phenomena that we are interested in:

- What are the key similarities and differences among them?

- How can we explain those patterns?

There is an extensive and often complex literature on what it takes to do comparative political analysis. In practice, however, it is quite easy to compare. When George W. Bush had to choose a running mate in 2000, he compared Dick Cheney with a number of other possible candidates and decided that someone with Cheney's vast experience, including service in the first President Bush's cabinet, would provide his ticket with the balance it needed. You, too, have undoubtedly done some serious comparing—for instance, in deciding which college or university to attend.

To see what comparative political analysis can do, consider the following simple example from the 2001 British general election. A total of 58 percent of registered voters cast their ballots. That one fact tells you very little about Britain or its political system. But the picture changes dramatically once you add two more pieces of information that allow you to compare Britain over time (it was the lowest turnout since 1935) and with another country (it is rare that much more than half of registered American voters vote in presidential elections). With those two pieces of comparative data, you can learn a lot more and can pose far more insightful questions about elections in general. For example, why is turnout in British elections normally higher than that in the United States? Why has it been declining in recent elections? What difference does turnout make? Does the fact that nearly three-fifths of the people voted make it easier or harder for Prime Minister Blair to meet the challenges he faces during his second term in office?

Three Templates

Comparative analysis can be a powerful tool. Comparison, however, is not powerful enough on its own to lead us to the kinds of overarching conclusions mentioned previously. We also have to know what to compare, what questions to ask, and which criteria to use in evaluating the evidence we uncover.

Most political scientists believe that theories best provide that focus. Unfortunately, comparative politics is not chemistry, physics, or microeconomics, each of which has a single theory or paradigm that structures everything from cutting-edge research to introductory textbooks. The best tools available to us are less powerful models that only allow us to see how the various components of a state are related to one another.

Think of models as equivalent to the templates for typical, routine tasks that computer companies provide when you buy new software. The three models that follow weave together most of the themes discussed so far in this chapter and so will help you organize the material in the rest of the book.

The Political System

The chapters on individual countries are organized around a model known as **systems theory.** (See figure 1.1.) Although most of the natural sciences are based on it, it is no longer very popular in political science. Nonetheless, it is more useful for our purposes than its intellectual competitors are because it allows us to see how a state's components interact over time and how nonpolitical and international forces shape what it can and cannot accomplish.

Systems theory revolves around five concepts: inputs, decision making, outputs, feedback, and the environment. **Inputs** are the ways average citizens and the groups they form engage in political life. David Easton, who adapted systems theory to political science, divided them into two types of activities: those that **support** and those that place **demands** on the state. Both come in many forms.

Individuals can act on their own by, for example, voting or writing a letter to the editor. However, most activity, especially that of a demanding nature, is channeled through two types of organizations: **interest groups** and **political parties.** Interest groups typically

▌FIGURE 1.1 The Political System

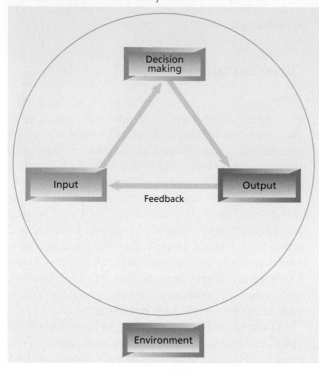

deal with a limited range of issues and represent a narrow segment of a country's population. Examples include trade unions, business associations, and environmental groups that organize and "lobby" around specific issues and other concerns. A political party, in contrast, tries to bring the interests of a number of groups together and to gain control over the government either on its own or in a coalition. A party need not build its support or power largely, or even primarily, through elections, as was the case in the former Soviet Union or when the Baath Party was in power in Iraq.

The conventional wisdom is that British interest groups are weaker than American ones because it is harder to lobby effectively in a parliamentary system than in a presidential one, something we will explore in the next three chapters. Nonetheless, the Labour Party has traditionally done well at the polls because of its close ties to the Trade Unions Congress, which helped form the party in the first place and is still an integral part of its organization. On the other hand, the opposition Conservative Party has close links to the major business and trade associations.

Sometimes demands go beyond the conventional "inside-the-system" activities of interest groups and political parties. Protesters, for instance, tried to disrupt President Bush's state visit to London in late 2003.

Chechen rebels have fought two wars in a thus-far vain attempt to win their independence from Russia. But there is no better example of "outside-the-system" protest than the attacks on 9/11. Analysts will long debate what motivated the nineteen hijackers and their supporters. However, there seems little doubt that their faith and their hatred of Western politics and policies led them to be willing to take not only their own lives but those of thousands of people in the World Trade Center, the Pentagon, and the four airplanes.

Political participation is also shaped by a country's **political culture,** or the basic attitudes people have toward each other, the state, and authority. A culture, in essence, reflects the impact of history on a society's beliefs.

In Great Britain, the legacy of feudalism remains (albeit faintly) in the willingness of some working-class voters to trust their "social betters" with roots in the aristocracy. The widespread support of Shiite Islam is an important value supporting the continued rule of the Islamic Republic in Iran. Russians' values today are in large part shaped by more than seventy years of Communist rule. Finally, the Chechen case also shows us that not all countries are homogeneous and that some have strikingly different subcultures.

Easton's second main concept, **decision making,** covers the same intellectual ground as the state, and thus does not need much elaboration here. It is enough to note that we will examine states from two main angles: the structure of their institutions and the values, skills, and personalities of their leaders. Institutions matter more in older, established regimes like Britain's even though it does not have a written constitution. That is less the case in a country like Iran, where the ruling clerics often do political end runs around the elected institutions they themselves created, or in Russia, where the institutions are barely a decade old. Each of the three examples presented earlier highlights the importance of leaders' values (Khatami's commitment to reform), skills (Putin's ability to consolidate power), and personality (Blair's ability to use the media effectively).

Inputs and decision making are important in their own right. However, their importance grows when we take the next step and explore what those decisions lead to—the system's **output** or **public policy.**

The most common type of policy regulates the behavior of individuals or organizations. Thus, Britain is struggling to find new ways of managing its aging railroads, which were sold to private owners under the Conservative governments of the 1990s.

Other policies redistribute resources, sometimes to such a degree that they alter a society's basic patterns of wealth and power. That, of course, has always been the goal of Marxists and other socialists. But even with the growing support for market economies, states are still heavily involved in distributional politics. In Iran, the authorities have channeled billions of dollars to companies and foundations they control in order to shape the way the country's economy modernizes.

Policies can also be symbolic. Under both Yeltsin and Putin, the Russian government has tried to build support for the symbols associated with the new state, including adopting a new national anthem. Even more obvious on this score is the fact that the Islamic Republic changed both Iran's flag and its national anthem when it came to power in 1979 to reflect its commitment to theological orthodoxy. By contrast, despite its long-standing disputes with the United States, it not only allowed a team of American wrestlers to compete in the world championships in Tehran in 1998, it encouraged its fans to cheer the team when it paraded around the arena waving the stars and stripes.

Systems analysis is also the most useful general model for our purposes because it incorporates **feedback,** which is the process through which people find out about public policy and the ways in which their reactions to it help shape the next phase of political life. Sometimes a decision directly affects an individual or group. More often, people only learn about a policy indirectly, either through the media or by word of mouth.

In each of the countries we will be covering in this book, the media play a powerful, and frequently quite biased, role in political life, either in supporting the state or in criticizing its policies. There are times, too, when people do not find out about state policies at all, which can result either from conscious attempts to keep these policies secret or from public apathy.

Feedback makes systems analysis particularly valuable, because it forces us to consider how a system changes over time. Too many of the other models political scientists use provide the intellectual equivalent of snapshots that show what a system is like during a relatively brief period. Focusing on feedback, however, draws our attention to how the entire system has evolved over the years, thus turning the snapshot into the intellectual equivalent of a videotape—and an extended-play one at that.

Here, of course, the media play a critical role. Britain's BBC (British Broadcasting Corporation) is renowned for the quality and impartiality of its coverage, though it has been criticized lately for what some see as its not so thinly veiled opposition to Blair's policies in Iraq. Similarly, Putin has been taken to task for his decisions to take away the licenses for all television stations that are not under government control. On the other end of the spectrum, the Iranian authorities are struggling to control access to television stations run by émigrés, which hundreds of thousands of people watch on nominally illegal satellite dishes.

The **environment** includes everything lying outside the political system. Systems are defined as being "bounded" or having an autonomous identity and organization. No system, however, is completely autonomous. All politicians and citizens must react to forces beyond their control. There are three types of forces that can limit—sometimes sharply—their ability to shape their own destinies.

The first is the impact of history discussed earlier. No country's history shapes exactly what happens today, but it does partially set the political stage, determining what is and is not likely to work. Thus, there is no way either Putin's government or Putin himself can escape the Communist past.

Second are the limits imposed by domestic social, economic, and physical conditions. Britain is densely populated, and traffic jams in major cities are unavoidable since many of the roads were built centuries before the car was invented. Therefore, its leaders have to pay more attention than their American colleagues do to mass transit, which is why the railroads in Britain are a major issue and why London recently imposed an $8 toll on every car that enters the center of the city.

Finally, and today perhaps most importantly, there are the global forces that arise outside a country's border. Sometimes their impact is hard to miss, as when British and American forces invaded and occupied Iraq. Other times they are subtler and far harder to document, as when global media conglomerates assume control of a country's television stations and other outlets. Sometimes they have massive consequences, as did the introduction of the euro in 2002. Other times the impact can be more limited, as was the European Court of Justice's 1995 decision overturning rules that limited the number of foreign players on a professional soccer team.

Historical and Contemporary Factors

Table 1.2 draws our attention to four types of forces that have largely determined the basic patterns of politics in all countries. The first row of the table highlights the historical forces that set the stage for the "dramas" of global political life today. Undoubtedly, the most important is **imperialism,** which led to the imposition of Western political, economic, and cultural institutions on the rest of the world. For example, although Iran was never formally colonized (as we will see later), the West had a profound and negative impact on its society and economy.

▌ TABLE 1.2 Factors Affecting the Development of States

	INTERNATIONAL	DOMESTIC
HISTORICAL	Imperialism	State and nation building
CONTEMPORARY	Globalization and the end of the cold war	Pressures from below

Opposition to Western influence, for instance, had a lot to do with the overthrow of the Shah in 1979. More generally, to this day, many former colonies are desperately poor and dependent on the policies and practices of the wealthy states and private corporations in the "north."

Imperialism was also important in determining how the state itself was formed and then spread around the world. In many respects, the modern state is a by-product of imperialism. Prior to the 1600s, the European monarchies were weak and decentralized. But the decision to expand abroad meant they needed more powerful states that could raise armies and feed, equip, and pay them.

State building never occurred smoothly. Everywhere, the power of the state grew at the expense of at least some of its citizens and left lasting scars. It was particularly difficult when one or both of two problems arose. First, when the state developed quickly, antagonisms arose toward a national government that all of a sudden demanded more of its people. Second, when minority ethnic, linguistic, or religious groups were forcibly incorporated into the emerging state, this tended to produce tensions that undermined the state's ability to govern.

The difficulties associated with state building have been particularly pronounced in the third world. Gaining independence usually involved an intense struggle with the old imperial power. When the conflict was especially prolonged or violent, as in Vietnam or Algeria, the new nation found itself physically and economically drained once it finally did gain its independence.

Moreover, when the imperialist powers carved up the Southern Hemisphere, they did so largely for their own reasons, ignoring traditional boundaries and lumping together groups that had historically been antagonistic toward each other. As a result, new states such as Angola, Afghanistan, and Nigeria faced deeply rooted ethnic tensions, which made it all but impossible for leaders to agree on anything.

As the second row in table 1.2 suggests, you cannot understand everything about political life today merely by putting it into historical perspective. If you could, there would be little reason to take a course such as this one or to want to change a world whose basic contours are already set!

The most important contemporary global force remains the **cold war** between the United States and the former Soviet Union. The two countries emerged from World War II as the most dominant powers on earth, ushering in an unprecedented period in which two superpowers alone shaped the destinies of almost every other country.

As the United States and the Soviet Union jockeyed for position, regional problems became global ones as well. When the superpowers' interests collided most directly, countries such as Vietnam, Nicaragua, and Afghanistan paid the price. Even such regional powers as Japan, Britain, Poland, Hungary, and the two Germanys saw their freedom to maneuver limited by the superpowers.

Now that the cold war is over, no one is quite sure how those international forces will play out. Some observers think supranational institutions like the United Nations or the European Union will play a larger, more constructive role in finding peaceful resolutions to the conflicts that still plague international and domestic political life. Others are more skeptical. Optimists thought the global shock wave caused by the attacks of 9/11 would unite the international community and go a long way toward eradicating terrorism once and for all. Pessimists worry that the subsequent wars and the upsurge in terrorist activities will only sow the seeds for more, bloodier violence in the future. No one, however, doubts that international political forces will remain an important determinant of domestic events around the world.

Since the Organization of Petroleum Exporting Countries (OPEC) oil embargo of 1973–1974 and the economic downturn that followed, we have become aware of another global force limiting what individual states can do—the **international political economy** (**IPE**), which is the term political scientists use to describe trade and other interactions that take place between countries. To some degree, the IPE is a legacy of imperialism. But as we are all painfully aware from the daily news reports about the loss of American factory jobs and the destruction of the Brazilian rain forest, the IPE has taken on a life of its own.

The countries that are suffering as a result of globalization are indeed in a difficult bind. How can the poorest nations break out of their poverty when those international dynamics are leaving them even further behind? How can countries as different as Mexico, Poland, and the United States solve their domestic problems when they owe billions of dollars to other governments and private financiers? How can a country like Brazil balance the needs of the environment with those of its impoverished citizens?

Finally, there is the traditional subject matter of comparative politics—what is happening within individual countries today. Because of what occurred in the past and because of what is taking place now outside their borders, few states are as fully masters of their own destinies as they were even a generation ago. Conversely, no state is completely at the mercy of globalization, although some states are better able to shape their future than others.

State, Society, and Globalization

We can work through the third template quickly because figure 1.2 covers many of the phenomena already discussed in this section. What makes this template different is its focus on the causal links among three key factors you can use to help stitch the pieces of this book together.

At least since Thomas Hobbes wrote in the seventeenth century, most political theorists have pointed out that individuals and the groups they form tend to seek ever more freedom and power. The more pessimistic of them have feared that people motivated by such self-interest would tear society apart if left to their own devices. Thus, like it or not, we have to create states to maintain order by keeping such centrifugal forces in check.

As a result, most political scientists believe that state and society exist in what they call an inverse relationship: For the power of one to increase, that of the other must be reduced. For example, when the Republicans

took control of both houses of Congress in 1994, they were convinced that the way to give average Americans more power was to limit the jurisdiction of what they believed was a far too dominant state. Similarly, the creation of the National Health Service in Great Britain in 1948 left doctors less free to practice medicine as they saw fit and left affluent patients less able to choose their own health-care options than they had been before.

Moreover, this inverse relationship seems to hold rather consistently across all types of political systems. Giving more power to Soviet citizens in the 1980s came at the expense of the state and contributed to its collapse. By contrast, there can be no clearer example of the way a state can limit people's freedoms than the rules the Iranian government imposed on what women could do and even what they could wear.

It also draws our attention to the way globalization is reshaping political life by reducing the real ability of states to make and implement economic policy. Although international institutions such as the European Union and the International Monetary Fund play a critical role in this respect, rarely can we pinpoint exactly how such influence is wielded, because these pressures are far subtler than those used by the U.S.-led coalition in the war against terrorism. Nonetheless, they are real and important enough that they may force us to change the ways in which we view global political life both as academics and as average citizens.

Even the more restrained analysts of globalization stress the degree to which states are losing influence, especially over the formation and implementation of economic policy. If current trends continue, we will soon have to develop wholly new intellectual models in which the line between comparative politics and international relations is blurred, if not eliminated altogether.

Five Themes

You will also find it easier to absorb the material in the chapters that follow if you keep five overarching themes in mind. All of them have been mentioned before, but they bear repeating here because they are excellent vehicles for helping you compare. For that same reason, there will be boxes on each of them in chapters to come to help you put the countries and types of regimes in a broader perspective. The first four of them will be featured in boxes and the fifth as the conclusion to the chapters on individual countries that follow.

First, as should already be clear, political life is filled

▌ **FIGURE 1.2** The Impact of Global and Domestic Forces on the State

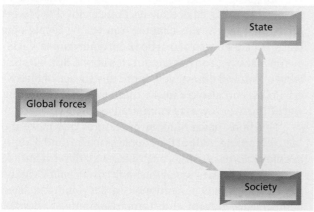

with conflict. The citizens, parties, and interest groups of a relatively stable country such as Great Britain differ sharply on a number of issues, including Northern Ireland, the European Union, and the future of the welfare state. In most other countries, the conflicts are even more intense and frequently erupt into violence, which threatens the very existence of regimes and even the states themselves. And, despite tremendous progress in methods of managing, preventing, and resolving conflict in recent years, there are typically at least thirty states in the midst of a civil war or other armed conflict at any time.

Second, there has also been a significant shift toward more democratic governments in the past decade or so. The end of the cold war ushered in new regimes in the former Soviet Union and Eastern Europe that at least hoped to become democratic. In the same vein, President George H. W. Bush used to delight in pointing out that 1990 marked the first year that all the countries in South America had democratically elected governments. However, as with globalization, the past few years have brought sobering news that **democratization** is not as easy as many had thought and hoped. Most of the newly created democratic regimes are fragile at best. Meanwhile, there still are plenty of ruthless dictators, and military coups remain a possibility in much of the third world.

Third, among the most important changes of the past quarter century has been the resurgence of capitalism and market economies as the preferred system for most of the world's political and business leaders. As recently as the late 1970s, Marxism and other forms of socialism still had a tremendous appeal. And, even in countries that were basically capitalist, economic theories that emphasized state coordination and planning still held sway. Since then, two things have happened that have tilted the balance toward less state involvement and a greater reliance on markets. The first was the declining performance of state-led and relatively autarchic policies in response to global and domestic economic pressures, which put a premium on innovation and other attributes that large organizations—public and private alike—rarely possess. The second was the crisis and then collapse of Communism in the Soviet Union and its allies, which left Marxism a highly unpopular political and economic ideology.

Fourth, globalization refers to the apparent "shrinking" of the world amid the simultaneous integration of our economic, social, environmental, and cultural lives. As such, it has probably been the most hyped concept in recent years. Some critics have cast doubt on how fast globalization is occurring and how interdependent the world really is. Nonetheless, as noted earlier, there is no denying that global forces increasingly constrain what even the strongest states can do. Therefore, no book on domestic politics would be complete without paying attention to globalization and the ways in which states and their citizens are coping with it.

Together, the first four themes lead to the fifth—the challenges most states face at the dawn of the twenty-first century. With few exceptions, states, their leaders, and their citizens are finding it ever more difficult to develop mutually acceptable and effective policies to cope with their problems, whether domestic or international in origin. Although comparativists still focus on the state as their key unit of analysis, researchers are beginning to question whether it remains the institution that is best able to cope with the problems we expect to face in the next millennium, an argument I will address in the final chapter.

Using This Book

You are at the beginning of what in one sense will be a typical introductory course with a typical textbook. To fully master the material, however, you will have to go beyond the typical, because you will constantly be confronted with controversial questions that do not have clear and obvious answers. What's more, many of them will have a direct bearing on your life for years to come.

In short, you will have to do more than merely memorize the notes you take in class or the key points you highlight throughout these pages. Courses that deal with new, complex, and controversial subjects succeed only when students stretch themselves to consider unsettling ideas, question their basic assumptions, and sift through evidence to reach their own conclusions. Therefore, if you are going to truly master the material, you have to take to heart the advice of the French novelist Marcel Proust that begins this chapter. You will be seeing new lands, because much of this book and your course will focus on places you do not know much about. But, if Proust is right, you will not get very far in this voyage of discovery unless you also try to see these lands through what will be the new "eyes" of comparative politics.

This book has a number of features that make the "active learning" side of the course as useful (and, I hope, as enjoyable) as possible, beginning with the structure of the book itself. The core of the book covers politics in the three kinds of states mentioned earlier—industrialized democracies, current and former Communist regimes, and the third world. Each part begins with an overview chapter that explores the key trends, theories, and ideas about that type of state. The rest of the part is devoted to case studies of countries that exemplify the different aspects of that particular type of state. The countries discussed in this book were chosen because they are important in their own right and because you can use them as intellectual springboards for reaching more general conclusions about the political trends (re)shaping our world. These countries are categorized as follows:

- Industrialized democracies: the United States, Great Britain, France, Germany, the European Union

- Current and former Communist regimes: Russia, China

- The third world: India, Iran, Iraq, Nigeria, Mexico

- Additional chapters on Canada, Japan, and South Africa can be found at the Book Companion Website: http://politicalscience .wadsworth.com/hauss05/

Because this book focuses on countries and individual instructors assign various subsets of them in their classes, it is hard to build comparative analysis into the text itself. However, the boxes on the four themes discussed will be explicitly comparative. So too will be the boxes on HIV/AIDS policy that will also appear in each country chapter. HIV/AIDS is an important issue in and of itself. But it is also a useful vehicle for comparative analysis, because the way a country has responded to the greatest health crisis in generations tells us a lot about how its political system as a whole operates.

I have also tried to write a timely book, but parts of it will be out of date before the book is actually published. So, each summer, I will post updates on the countries covered in the book on its companion website, which also includes general information on the countries and self-paced quizzes you can take to test your knowledge.

Key Terms

Cold war	Imperialism
Communist	Industrialized democracy
Constitution	Input
Crisis	Interest group
Decision making	International political
Demand	economy (IPE)
Democratization	Nation
Environment	Newly industrializing coun-
Feedback	tries (NICs)
Globalization	Output
Government	Political culture

Political party	Strong state
Politics	Support
Power	Systems theory
Public policy	Third world
Regime	Totalitarianism
State	Weak state

Critical Thinking Exercises

1 Much has changed since this book was finished in early 2005. Do the various assertions made in this chapter still make sense? In what ways? Why (not)?

2 Public opinion pollsters routinely ask whether people think the country is heading in the "right" direction or "is on the wrong track." If you were asked such a question about politics in the world as a whole, how would you answer? Why did you reach that conclusion?

3 Take your campus, community, or state, and analyze it using the three templates. What new insights did this exercise lead you to? What, if any, important facts, trends, or institutions were left out of the analysis?

4 Of all the concepts covered in this chapter, which do you think are the most and the least important? Why did you reach this conclusion?

5 You could interpret this chapter as arguing that it is becoming harder for governments to govern effectively. Do you agree? Why (not)?

Useful Websites

The Internet has become an essential tool for students of comparative politics. There are not many sites dedicated to comparative politics per se. However, the Internet is filled with information on specific countries, individuals, and issues. In particular, because so many newspapers, radio and television networks, and news services have gone online, it is easy to keep up with breaking news and evolving trends around the world.

That said, the Internet is increasingly hard to use because there are so many sites, and even the best search engines can catalogue only a tiny fraction of them. Therefore, I have created a companion website, which includes links to what I think are the best sites for the issues and countries covered in this book, updates on the countries, sources of statistical and other data, and quizzes on each chapter so you can gauge how well you have mastered the material. You can also e-mail me with questions about the book or issues that have arisen in your own course. It is located at:

http://politicalscience.wadsworth.com/hauss05/

Each chapter includes a section like this one with web addresses to portals and other general sites. Specific websites will be inserted in the text the first time an institution or individual is mentioned, as was the case with the brief biography of Putin earlier in this chapter.

There are other good resources for comparative politics. Here are three general sites that divide up the field in different but useful ways from the Universities of Colorado, Keele, and West Virginia, respectively:

sobek.colorado.edu/POLSCI/RES/comp.html

www.psr.keele.ac.uk/area.htm

www.polsci.wvu.edu/PolyCy/pscomp.html

The Internet also has dozens of sources providing basic data on countries that take you far beyond what can be covered in a single book and that include material on events occurring after this book was published. The CIA Factbook is a treasure trove of information about the world's countries and is updated quite frequently. The other three sources are the work of international "open source" teams of men and women willing to volunteer their time to provide general information about countries in general and elections in particular. The final one is a new commercial service that seems to rate sites but does not always include clickable links to them.

www.odci.gov/cia/publications/factbook/index.html

www.adminet.com

www.politicalresources.net

www.electionworld.com

political-science.designerz.com/political-science-comparative-politics.php

Finally, it is important to keep up with the news in any course on comparative politics and international relations. At this point, all of the world's major newspapers, news services, and broadcast media put much of their material on the web. Many, however, take the postings down after a week or two. The BBC and CNN do not and have searchable data based on their coverage, including items that never made it on air. That said, their coverage on third world issues is not great. Therefore, I also frequently look at One World, which is a good source for that part of the planet.

www.cnn.com

news.bbc.co.uk

www.oneworld.net

InfoTrac College Edition Sources

Bates, Robert. "Comparative Politics and Rational Choice Theory."

Burke, Johnny. "Rethinking Multiculturalism."

Hauss, Charles. "Duh, or the Role of IT in Teaching Comparative Politics."

Wiarda, Howard. "The End of the Great International Systems Debate."

Wilsford, David. "Getting Students to Think (Comparatively)."

Further Reading

Almond, Gabriel, and G. Bingham Powell. *Comparative Politics: System, Policy, and Process.* Boston: Little, Brown, 1978. Dated, but still the best presentation of the classic approach to comparative politics.

Ambrose, Stephen, with Douglas Brinkley. *The Rise to Globalism*, 8th ed. New York: Penguin Books, 1997. The best short volume outlining global history since World War II.

Basu, Amrita. *The Challenge of Local Feminisms.* Boulder, Colo.: Westview Press, 1995. The most comprehensive and readable book on women's issues, which have become important in comparative politics in recent years.

Chilcote, Ronald. *Theories of Comparative Politics.* Boulder, Colo.: Westview Press, 1993. A comprehensive review of the theoretical and conceptual schools of thought in comparative politics; written primarily for graduate students.

Friedman, Tom. *The Lexus and the Olive Tree.* New York: Farrar, Straus, & Giroux, 2000. The most influential and controversial book on globalization.

Huntington, Samuel P. *The Clash of Civilization and the Remaking of World Order.* New York: Simon & Schuster, 1996. A powerful but controversial book about the way cultural change is remaking the political world; by one of the most respected and conservative analysts, who has left his mark on this field since the early 1960s.

Lane, Ruth. *The Art of Comparative Politics.* Needham Heights, Mass.: Allyn & Bacon, 1997. One of the few recent books arguing that comparativists have made substantial progress.

Lichbach, Mark, and Alan Zuckerman, eds. *Comparative Politics: Rationality, Culture, and Structure.* Cambridge: Cambridge University Press, 1997. A fairly dense but important set of essays by political scientists writing from a number of perspectives.

Peters, B. Guy. *Comparative Politics: Theory and Methods.* New York: New York University Press, 1998. The one recent attempt to make sense of the entire field of comparative politics by one of the most prolific scholars of the past thirty years.

Soe, Christian, ed. *Comparative Politics: Annual Editions.* Guilford, Conn.: Dushkin/McGraw-Hill, published annually. A collection of recent articles from the press. Your best bet to stay up-to-date if you don't have access to InfoTrac®.

Steoan, Alfred. *Arguing Comparative Politics.* New York: Oxford University Press, 2001. A collection of essays by one of the few leading scholars in comparative politics willing to take on most issues and most regions.

Wilson, Frank L. *Concepts and Issues in Comparative Politics.* Upper Saddle River, N.J.: Prentice-Hall, 2002. An

excellent introduction to the basic ideas in comparative politics by one of the best writers in the field who, alas, died just after his book was published.

Zahariades, Nikolaos. *Theory, Concepts, and Method in Comparative Politics.* New York: Harcourt Brace, 1996. One of the few attempts to update the ideas of comparative politics since the 1960s.

Exploring EXPLORING THE WORLD WIDE WEB

This book comes with a website that complements the material presented in these pages. The website has hundreds of links to useful resources, updates on the countries written when important events occur, and quizzes you can take to gauge your progress.

The website lets you go deeper into some of the issues raised in the book. At the end of the first chapter of each of the first four parts of the book, I provide some guidelines for using the online resources for that section.

A study guide, developed by Ken Wedding, focuses on key issues raised in each chapter. In part 1 the focus is on key concepts in comparative politics and the degree to which the United States should (and should not) serve as our frame of reference.

Map exercises, also developed by Ken Wedding, will give you a better "feel" for what the various countries are like. The maps are based on the excellent series of outline maps that the CIA includes in its *World Factbook* (www.odci.gov).

Additional information supplements the "basic" data tables that begin each chapter. This information, like the tables themselves, is taken mostly from the *World Factbook*.

Constitutions and other key documents allow you to explore some of the formal political arrangements in the

countries covered in this book. For the United States, for instance, you might want to look at the highly ambiguous language of the Second Amendment, which lies at the heart of the dispute over gun ownership and control.

There are questions to ask in reading at least two Info-Trac College Edition articles per chapter. For chapter 1, you might want to think about a phenomenon I call the "parable of the frog" in assessing the state of comparative politics in the post-cold war teaching environment.

Perhaps the most distinctive part of the website is its incorporation of statistical and other data collected by my colleague and friend Michael LeRoy for his comparative textbook, which uses the MicroCase software package. Clicking on the MicroCase option on the book website will take you to its website (your internet connection must be on).

There you can do some simple mapping exercises and statistical analyses of selected variables drawn from his file of "global" data and national-level statistics. The examples we have developed can be done using the function that gives you maps depicting differences from one type of country to another. If you have had courses in statistics and research methods, you can use more advanced statistical techniques.

Instructions for using MicroCase are provided on the website.

Part 2

INDUSTRIALIZED DEMOCRACIES

*Democracy is the worst form
of government except for all the
others.*

WINSTON CHURCHILL

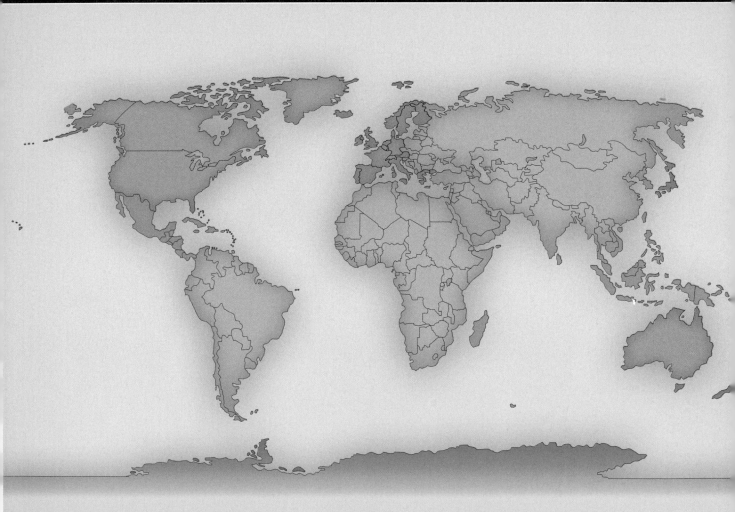

Chapter 2

THE INDUSTRIALIZED DEMOCRACIES

CHAPTER OUTLINE

- Four Elections
- Thinking about Democracy
- The Origins of the Democratic State
- Political Culture and Participation
- The Democratic State
- Public Policy
- Feedback
- Conclusion: The Worst Form of Government Except for All the Others?

The Basics: The Industrialized Democracies

REGION	DEMOCRACIES	CONTENDERS
Europe	Austria, Belgium, Denmark, Finland, France, Germany, Great Britain, Greece, Iceland, Ireland, Italy, Luxembourg, Malta, Norway, Portugal, Spain, Sweden, Switzerland, the Netherlands	Cyprus, Czech Republic, Estonia, Hungary, Latvia, Lithuania, Poland, Slovakia, Turkey
The Americas	Canada, the United States	Argentina, Brazil, Chile, Costa Rica, Mexico, most Caribbean Islands
Asia and the Pacific Islands	Australia, Japan, New Zealand	Philippines, South Korea, Taiwan
Africa		Botswana, South Africa

Four Elections

Every other chapter begins with a single example that serves as a springboard to the broader issues to be covered in the pages that follow. Here, however, I will start with a brief overview of the most recent elections in the four countries to be covered in Part 2. I do so because elections are one of the most important features of any **democracy.** But they will also show some of the important ways in which democracies differ from each other.

The United States

The presidential election of 2004 could not have been as close or full of tension as the one four years earlier when the Supreme Court finally made George W. Bush a winner after almost five weeks of lawsuits and recounts.

Nonetheless, the contest between President George W. Bush and Senator John Kerry went down to the wire. Although Bush won a clear victory in his quest for a second term and his Republican colleagues increased their majority in both the House of Representatives and the Senate, the election could easily have produced a Kerry victory. Indeed, many observers think that if the state of Ohio had not had a referendum on gay marriage on the ballot, Republican turnout would have been lower.

Kerry thus would have carried the state and won the presidency.

Great Britain

Unlike the United States, Great Britain and other parliamentary systems do not hold elections on a fixed schedule. Instead, the prime minister can dissolve the parliament at any time, thus prompting elections within a matter of weeks.

That is what happened in Britain in 2001. Prime Minister Blair's term still had a year to run when he announced that elections would be held that May. Blair calculated that he was likely to win an election then and that his popularity might plummet if he decided to wait until his five-year term was up.

He was right. Even though he and his government were both far less popular than when they were first elected in 1997, the opposition Conservatives were even more unpopular. As a result, the Labour Party won its second landslide victory in a row. Blair was thus in a position to be the first Labour prime minister to serve two full terms in office.

France

France is one of the few democracies that directly elects its president. Because of the then different lengths of their terms, presidential and legislative elections are rarely held at the same time. In 2002, elections for both were scheduled for the spring, and most observers expected the presidential race (held first) to be another close race between President Jacques Chirac and Prime Minister Lionel Jospin who had faced each other in 1995.

This was one the pundits got wrong. In all, seventeen candidates ran at the first ballot. To almost everyone's surprise, no one won even 20 percent of the vote. Even more shocking was the fact that far right wing (and some would say racist) Jean-Marie Le Pen edged out Jospin for second place and a spot in the runoff ballot two weeks later in which only the top two candidates could run. Jospin immediately resigned as prime minister. Chirac replaced him with his little-known ally, Jean-Pierre Raffarin.

The runoff produced one of the more remarkable votes in France's remarkable history. All the major candidates—including Jospin—supported Chirac. Not everyone was enthusiastic; nonetheless, Chirac won over 80 percent of the vote at the second ballot while Le Pen barely topped his first-round total.

Not surprisingly, when legislative elections were held the next month, the ruling Gaullist Party won a resounding victory winning 357 of 557 seats in the National Assembly. In between the two rounds of the presidential election, it had renamed itself the Union for the Presi-

Supporters of President Jacques Chirac await news of his landslide victory in 2002.

Jacques Brinon/AP/Wide World Photos

dential Majority (more recently named Union for the Popular Movement) and gained the support of many of the center-right parties that had previously maintained their independence from the Gaullists.

Germany

The German election in 2002 was almost as close as the one in the United States two years earlier. In 1998, a coalition government of Social Democrats (SDP) and Greens had been elected, the first time the environmentalist party gained membership in a government anywhere in the world. Chancellor Gerhard Schröder's government, however, struggled in dealing with a long-lasting economic slump at home and how it should react to September 11 attacks on the United States.

Many observers, then, expected the coalition to lose its bid for reelection. The election turned out to be a dead heat. The SPD and the opposition Christian Democrats (CDU) each won 38.5 percent of the vote. Because of the way seats in the Bundestag (Parliament) are allocated, the SPD ended up with three more than its rival. The final outcome of the election was determined by the fact that the Greens won 8.6 percent of the vote and fifty-five seats, slightly more than the Liberal Democrats (FDP) who were prepared to form a coalition government with the CDU.

So, Schröder and his allies found themselves back in power for a second term. But unlike Bush, who also held a razor-thin majority in the electorate and in Congress, Schröder could expect to see his legislative initiatives passed with a minimum of difficulty or delay.

Common and Not-So-Common Themes

There are two key common denominators to the recent electoral history in these four stories.

First, elections determine who governs in democracies. Sometimes—as in the United States in 2000—elections can be messy affairs whose results are in doubt for years to come. Nonetheless, one of the key principles of democracy is that the voters choose the men and women who will govern them in reasonably free and honest contests. There are concerns about fraud and voting irregularities in most countries (think of Florida in 2000), but on balance, elections in all these countries are run in far more open and corruption-free ways than we will see in the chapters on other countries in the next two parts of this book. And elections are just part of these systems that all guarantee basic personal and political freedoms. None do it perfectly, as the debates over the Patriot Act in

the United States and asylum seekers in Europe attest. Nonetheless, these countries stand in sharp contrast to, for instance, Russia, where there were deep doubts about both the honesty of the elections and commitment to democratic rights during the campaigns for the elections of 2003 and 2004.

Second, and more important, while the stakes of these elections were all very high, there were some critical issues that were not up for debate—but are in the kinds of countries considered in Parts 3 and 4. These elections were, in fact, bitterly contested. However, no one thought, for example, that the lawsuits and recounts after the U.S. election of 2000 could imperil the country's democracy. This is because in all four countries, the democratic regime is stable and secure. Voters may not like the politicians who govern them at a particular moment, but very, very few of them question the basic principles (constitutional and otherwise) political life is based on.

At the same time, these elections demonstrate that all democracies are not alike. Two differences among them will preoccupy us in this chapter and beyond. The first is that they do not all run their elections the same way. The United States and France elect their chief executives; Britain and Germany do not. The Germans elect half of their Bundestag using a system of **proportional representation** that gives each party the same percentage of seats that they got in the popular vote. The United States and Britain use a "first past the post system" that tends to favor the largest parties. France uses a hybrid two ballot system that allows many candidates to run in the first round but then encourages them to form alliances to support the top finishers in the second round.

The second difference, and the most important for American readers in particular, is that the United States is unique in having a presidential system with the separation and division of powers. As we will see later in the chapter, an American president cannot count on the support of members of his (so far they have all been men) party in Congress, even on the most important legislation. That, in turn, means that almost all legislation is the product of a series of compromises in which competing politicians and interest groups get some of what they want but also have to give some of what they hold near and dear. In parliamentary systems, the threat that a cabinet could lose a vote of confidence tends to produce far more disciplined voting among members of the majority party or coalition, which reduces the need for prime ministers to make the kinds of compromises that are the norm in the United States.

Thinking about Democracy

Freedom Forum is one of the most important non-governmental organizations monitoring how and if countries become democratic. The way it counts, as many as two-thirds of the countries in the world today are democracies because they guarantee some basic individual liberties and choose their rulers through reasonably free elections. However, democracy is about much more than elections, as those four vignettes attest. Indeed, as the editor of *Newsweek International* and political scientist, Fareed Zakaria, has argued, we may put too much emphasis on elections when trying to decide what makes a society democratic.[1] As he points out and as we will see in Parts 3 and 4, there are plenty of countries in the world today that hold reasonably free elections but have other characteristics that make observers reluctant to call them truly democratic.

In that sense, democracy is about relationships between the rulers and the ruled. Democracies vary tremendously in ways that go far beyond the differences in electoral systems discussed earlier in this chapter. And that is far more complicated than the rather simple notion that emerges from the two Greek words that are origins of the term itself—rule by the people.

In practice, democracy has proved to be anything but easy to define, let alone implement. In a literal sense, democracy cannot exist, because the people cannot rule. Even the small New England communities that still use the town meeting form of government are too large and have too many pressing issues for everyone to take part in making every decision. Instead, they have had to follow the path of all countries that claim to be democratic—adopting representative systems in which people select men and women to govern in their name.

In other words, democratic reality has always fallen short of the ideal. All observers acknowledge democracies compel their citizens to do things that they would rather avoid—pay taxes, serve in the military, drive at the speed limit, not drink alcohol before a certain age, and so on. All, too, have imperfect ways of holding elected officials accountable, which, after all, should be the essence of democracy itself.

To make matters even more complicated, observers like Zakaria claim that if we only define democracy with personal liberties like the freedom to vote, we can get ourselves in political as well as intellectual trouble. As we will see more clearly in the last half of the book, countries like the United States, Great Britain, France, and Germany have had more successful experiences with democracies because they have blended all the characteristics covered in the next few paragraphs, many of which are honored in the breach in other parts of the world. In this part, we will see the problems with defining democracy by the use of free elections alone when we consider Germany between the two world wars. After its defeat in 1918, Germany adopted one of the freest and most democratic constitutions in the world. Nonetheless, not even fifteen years later, Adolf Hitler and his Nazi Party rode the democratic process into power, allowing them to create one of the least democratic and most brutal regimes in history.

The Basics

There is no commonly accepted definition of what a democracy is. However, all serious observers include at least the first three features listed next. The last two are more controversial. They are also the ones that largely set the countries in Part 2 apart from those in Parts 3 and 4, and are probably less familiar to you.

Rights

Democracies guarantee basic individual freedoms of press, religion, association, and speech. Most observers are convinced that people cannot participate effectively in making the decisions that shape their lives unless those rights are guaranteed.

Different countries have expressed those rights in different ways. Many have enshrined them in their constitutions. For example, these and other rights are affirmed in the first paragraphs of the French Fifth Republic's constitution and in the Basic Law of Germany. Even where they are not included in a constitution, as in Great Britain (which does not have a written constitution), they are deeply ingrained in the culture.

These are not mere paper rights. The few restrictions placed on people's freedom are very much on the margins of political life. The French still have a law that allows the government to ban organizations whose goal is to overthrow the state. The Japanese constitution has a clause that permits the government to put the "public welfare" ahead of civil liberties if it believes that national security or other key policy goals are threatened. The French and German governments can declare a state of emergency and rule in what amounts to a dictatorial manner for a limited time. All these countries have police and intelligence agencies that have infiltrated organizations the government deemed subversive. The important point here, however, is that these provisions are rarely used and have had little impact on political life in

---

[1] Fareed Zakaria, *The Future of Freedom* (New York: W. W. Norton, 2003).

these countries since the end of World War II and, in some cases, longer.

Competitive Elections

At least as important as the basic right to civil liberties and the reliance on the rule of law is the requirement that the government be chosen through regular, free, and fair elections in which people can choose between two or more candidates and/or political parties. Simply holding elections is not enough. Mexico, for instance, has long held elections for all key offices, but few observers believe that the Institutional Revolutionary Party would have been able to stay in power from the late 1920s until 2000 had the contests been run honestly and fairly. The former Soviet Union and its Eastern Bloc allies also held elections, but voters had only a single candidate to vote for, who had been handpicked by the **Communist Party.** Other countries, such as Nigeria in 1993 or Panama in 1989, conducted elections, only to see the military reject the outcome and seize power.

The electoral and party systems in the industrialized democracies are not all alike. The United States is unique in having only two major parties, but the way Ralph Nader's candidacy affected the 2000 election results reminds us that this has not always been the case (www.ifes.org). More importantly, all other democracies have more than two parties that have an impact at the national level. In Great Britain and Germany, two major parties vie for power, but a number of smaller ones play a pivotal role in raising issues in both countries and in forming governing coalitions in the latter. In Japan, a single party has dominated electoral politics and governments since the 1950s, but it rarely comes close to winning a majority of the popular vote. France and the Scandinavian countries have five or more parties, but they fall into two blocs, one on the left and the other on the right, one of which normally wins each election. Israel and the Netherlands have as many as a dozen parties with seats in the national parliament.

These differences exist in large part because the industrialized democracies are divided along different lines, which reflect their histories, a point that will become clearer in the next five chapters. They also use different **electoral systems,** or ways of counting votes and allocating seats in their national legislatures. As discussed earlier, the United States, France, and Great Britain use single-member districts. Germany and most other European countries rely on some form of proportional representation in which parties win a number of seats roughly in keeping with their share of the vote.

Other things being equal, **single-member districts** make it relatively easy for major-party candidates to win

TABLE 2.1 Women in Parliament: Selected Countries

COUNTRY	ELECTORAL SYSTEM	PERCENTAGE OF WOMEN IN LOWER HOUSE
Sweden	Proportional	45.3
Netherlands	Proportional	36.7
Germany	Half proportional	32.2
United Kingdom	First past the post	17.9
United States	First past the post	14.3
France	Single member, two ballot	12.2

Source: International Parliamentary Union, www.ipu.org. Accessed 13 June 2004.

Note: These figures were accurate as of January 2004. Sweden and the Netherlands were added to the countries covered in the book to illustrate the range of results one finds.

and discourage the formation of new or, in American terminology, "third" parties. In proportional systems, parties do not have to win many votes to get into parliament. As a result, it is much easier for new parties to gain a toehold, and the countries with large numbers of parties typically use electoral systems with a strong proportional element.

One of the most discussed implications of electoral law in recent years is reflected in the number of women in national legislatures. As table 2.1 shows, women do not make up the majority of the members of the more powerful lower house of a national legislature anywhere. They come closest in countries that use proportional representation, while their numbers lag in those that use any kind of single-member district. In the latter, local party officials have the most say in determining nominations, and they tend to choose candidates who, they think, stand the best chance of winning. That usually means men. In proportional systems, national party elites have the most influence in choosing not only who is nominated but, more importantly, also who sits near the top of the party list, because those at the top have the greatest chance of getting elected. As a result, it is much easier for them to put large numbers of women in positions to win office.

The Rule of Law

Related to civil liberties is a reliance on the **rule of law,** which means that people are governed by clear and fair rules rather than by the arbitrary, personal exercise of power. What they can and cannot do is spelled out in constitutions and in ordinary laws. As a result, people can expect to be treated fairly by the government both in their routine dealings with the state (for example, in the way taxes are assessed) and on those rare occasions when they come up against it (for example, after being accused of a crime). The importance of the rule of law is actually easiest to see in its absence, which will be a common theme in Parts 3 and 4.

Civil Society and Civic Culture

The pathbreaking research on the role of political culture in democracies began in the late 1950s when Gabriel Almond and Sidney Verba conducted surveys in the United States, Great Britain, Germany, Italy, and Mexico. They concluded that stable democracies have a **civic culture** in which people accept not just the rules of the political game but the elites who lead them. Other pollsters have found that people in the United States and Great Britain, in particular, tend to be "joiners" who belong to many social and political groups, which ties them into their society, creates a **civil society,** and brings them into contact with people from a variety of social, economic, and political backgrounds.

With the upsurge of protest movements in the late 1960s, academic interest in civil society and civic culture waned. However, the past three decades have seen a decline in support for politicians and in interpersonal trust in the liberal democracies. Given that trend and the dozens of attempts to build democratic regimes elsewhere in the world, these ideas have returned to intellectual center stage. Although we do not fully understand how they operate, all the signs indicate that a civic culture and civil society psychologically bind people to their states, make it hard for "antisystem" protest to take root, and thus help make democracies resistant to sweeping change.

Capitalism and Affluence

Most—but not all—political scientists assume that democracy can only exist alongside an affluent economy based in large part on private ownership of the means of production. There is no denying that the industrialized democracies are the richest countries in the world. Most of their people live in cities, and almost all are literate. (See the table on the inside front cover.) Most have access to basic health care, which translates into a low infant mortality rate and high life expectancy.

Industrialized democracies are not all equally wealthy, of course. Great Britain's gross national product (GNP) is only two-thirds that of the United States. Some of the countries not included in this book (for example, Spain, Portugal, and Greece) are only about half as well-off as Britain. And not all provide the same services for their people, as reflected, for instance, in the United States' fairly high infant mortality rate, which actually surpasses that of some newly industrialized countries. Nonetheless, they are all dramatically better off than the countries we will consider in Parts 3 and 4.

Criteria for Democracy

There is no single, uniformly accepted set of criteria in determining whether a country is democratic. Of the five that follow, however, the first three are on virtually every list.

- Basic freedoms
- The rule of law
- Competitive, fair, and free elections
- A strong civil society and civic culture
- Capitalism and affluence

Scholars debate how, why, and if democracy needs affluence and capitalism. At the very least, there has been a historical connection between the rise of capitalism and the establishment of democracy. Although the causal connections are murky and hotly debated, it is true that, with only a handful of exceptions, only reasonably affluent and industrialized societies have been able to sustain governments that satisfy the other three criteria for an extended period of time. The example of India, Jamaica, and some of the countries in the "contenders" column of the Basics table that opens this chapter suggests that affluence, at least, may not be as important as some theorists have suggested. Nonetheless, given the political uncertainty in most of the "contender" countries and the historical link between capitalism and democracy, the focus in Part 2 is on countries in the industrialized world.

Which Countries Are Democracies?

Using these criteria, it is easy to identify at least twenty countries that are unquestionably democratic. As the chapter's Basics table suggests, most of them are in western Europe or in parts of the world Europeans colonized. The one obvious exception is Japan. All of these countries have met the five criteria for at least thirty years—which seems to be enough time for them to develop sufficient support for their democracies that there is little chance of their regimes collapsing.

It is not easy to make judgments about a few other countries in the "contenders" column. India has had a functioning democracy for a half-century, as have a few of the tiny Caribbean island states. None of them, however, meet the affluence criterion. Israel certainly is a democracy for its Jewish citizens, but it cannot be said to be one for the Arabs who live inside either its pre- or post-1967 borders. Some of the former Communist states may well be added to this list in the future, but they certainly cannot yet guarantee that basic freedoms will be tolerated or that elections will determine who governs. For the same reasons, most observers do not classify Chile, Argentina, Brazil, Turkey, South Korea, or Taiwan (Republic of China) as democracies.

Key Questions

In sum, the quotation from Winston Churchill, the introduction to recent elections, and the discussion of working definitions of democracy open the door to four questions that will preoccupy us for the rest of Part 2:

■ Why did democracy emerge in these countries?

■ Why did democracy become so remarkably durable in the second half of the twentieth century?

■ Why is there so much debate about public policy in the industrialized democracies at the dawn of the twenty-first century?

■ Why has that debate not gone one step farther and led many people to question their regimes or democracy itself?

The Origins of the Democratic State

You cannot make sense of politics in any country today without understanding its historical evolution (www.nipissingu.ca/department/history/muhlberger/histdem/index.htm). As we explore the origins of the industrialized democracies in this section, you will see three main conclusions that are important not only for these countries but also for the ones discussed in Parts 3 and 4.

First, the domestic concerns listed in the table on

■ **TABLE 2.2** Key Turning Points in the Development of Industrialized Democracies

CENTURY	TRENDS
Seventeenth	Emergence of the modern state
Eighteenth	First democratic revolutions
	Development of laissez-faire theory
Nineteenth	Industrial revolution
	Spread of voting and other democratic institutions
Twentieth	Further expansion of the vote
	Defeat of fascism and solidification of democracy in western Europe

The L Word

American students are often confused by the word *liberal.* In the United States, it refers to people who support the left and an interventionist government. Everywhere else in the world, however, it has almost exactly the opposite connotation — opposition to government interference in the economy and any other area in which individuals can make decisions for themselves. The term will be used in this latter sense in the rest of this book.

the inside front cover of the book (state and nation building, pressures from below) mattered far more than the international ones (imperialism, globalization) in their development. International concerns were important, of course. These countries fought countless wars, many of which strengthened their states, if not their democracies. On balance, however, the way in which these countries' leaders and their people handled a series of crises that were predominantly domestic in origin had a lot more to do with when, how, and why democracies emerged. That was less the case in the rest of the world, where international forces mattered more — especially the impact of the countries to be discussed here.

Second, it is impossible to disentangle the history of democracy from that of Europe and North America. Thus, we cannot determine with any certainty which of the characteristics discussed here are essential to democracy anywhere and which are peculiar to the European and North American experiences.

Third, democracy in these countries took a long time to develop. Leaders in the former Communist countries and the third world are trying to condense into a few short years what took centuries to develop in Europe, North America, and Japan. Although they might succeed, there is little historical evidence to suggest that they have a good chance of doing so.

The Origins of Democratic Thought

Modern democracy dates back only to the late eighteenth century. There were democracies in some of the ancient Greek city-states and in medieval Poland and Switzerland, but they do not warrant consideration here, because none involved states with either large populations or extensive civic responsibilities (see table 2.2).

By the late 1700s, the foundations of democracy had been building for at least two hundred years. With the rise of individualism, capitalism, and Protestantism, the emergence of the scientific revolution, and the exploration of the New World, new ways of thinking took hold whose roots lay in such diverse fields as Newtonian physics and Protestant theology. The innovative thinkers of the time believed that society is naturally composed of separate and autonomous actors who pursue their own interests and desires. For most of them, this "state of nature" was fraught with danger. They recognized that people freed of the shackles of feudalism and other social hierarchies would be more creative and productive. But they also realized that these people and the groups they formed would put new demands and pressures on the weak monarchies of the feudal period.

The most important of these theorists was **Thomas Hobbes** (1586–1679). He claimed that if people were left to their own devices, the competition among them would be so intense that it would lead to the "war of all against all." Therefore, to protect against anarchy, people had no choice but to give up some of their freedom to a large and powerful state, which he called the Leviathan.

Meanwhile, industrial capitalism became Britain's dominant economic system, which reinforced the shift toward more democratic government. Like the political liberals, the capitalists opposed a society still governed using feudal institutions and values. They began to demand a form of government that gave individuals free rein to pursue their economic interests. During the 1700s, their views crystallized as **laissez-faire** capitalism. Drawn from the French phrase meaning "allow to do," laissez-faire theory calls on government to stay out of economic life because the "invisible hand" of the market allocates resources far better.

In practice, the early liberal capitalists did not demand the abolition of government. They shared Hobbesian fears about the state of nature, especially as far as the lower classes were concerned. Therefore, most shared **John Locke**'s (1632–1704) notion that the state's role was to protect "life, liberty, and property."

The capitalists and their political allies added two key ideas to budding democratic thought. First, the state should be limited. Second, it should no longer try to prescribe what people do in all areas of life as had been the case under feudalism. Rather, it should be more of a referee whose job is to protect society from the arbitrary use of power and the excessive demands of the "mob" or the "dangerous classes."

Given the criteria laid out in the previous section, no country could have been called democratic in the early nineteenth century. All sharply limited the **suffrage** (the right to vote). For instance, no women and only a handful of freed African Americans could vote in the newly independent United States. In Britain, not even 5 percent of men had the franchise even after the passage of the Great Reform Act in 1832. What's more, the democratizing changes that occurred did not come quickly or easily, requiring massive protests in Britain and revolutions elsewhere.

Still, an important precedent had been set in those two countries: political power could no longer be monopolized by monarchs. Much of it had shifted into the hands of representatives who could, to some extent, hold rulers accountable and who were themselves accountable to the voters.

Even more importantly, the theorists and politicians who built the first democratic states opened a door that could not easily be shut. Over the next century, popular pressure forced the expansion of democracy in much of Europe and North America. Most countries were able to develop democracy under highly favorable international conditions. In 1815 the Congress of Vienna established a balance of power that left Europe largely free of war for the next century. The United States, Canada, Australia, and New Zealand were, if anything, even freer of outside interference.

More and more people gained the right to vote. Most white American males had it by the 1840s. All French men gained the franchise with the creation of the Second Republic in 1848. In Britain, the right of men to vote was gradually expanded, culminating in the Reform Act of 1918, which removed all property qualifications and income restrictions.

Eventually, the vote was also granted to women. In the United States, women won it with the ratification of the Nineteenth Amendment in 1920. An Act of Parliament did the same in Britain four years later. Women in France only got the vote after World War II, although there had been a female cabinet member before the war. The Swiss were the last industrialized democracy to grant women the vote in the early 1970s.

In the meantime, other opportunities for political engagement grew. Most American states passed laws enabling citizens to put proposed legislation on the ballot in a referendum. In France and Britain, laws limiting citizens' rights to form associations were abolished, permitting the growth of trade unions and other mass-based interest groups.

In much of Europe, popularly elected houses of parliament gained the all-important right to determine who governed. By the late 1870s, the two houses of the French parliament had stripped the presidency of all effective power. In 1911 the British House of Lords, which represented the hereditary nobility, lost the power to do anything more than delay the final passage of legislation. By the 1920s, cabinets everywhere in western Europe had become responsible to parliaments, with members remaining in office only as long as they retained the support of a majority in the lower house.

Building Democracies

Democracy was not built quickly or easily. In some of today's industrialized democracies, it was created gradually and without too much turmoil. In others, democracy was formed through a number of wrenching fits and starts that included periods of revolution and authoritarian rule in which democracy seemed a distant and often unreachable goal.

That said, in Europe and, to a lesser degree, North America, the way democracy developed was largely a result of the way countries and their rulers handled four great transformations over the last five hundred years or so:

- The creation of the nation and state itself
- The role of religion in society and government
- The development of pressures for democracy
- The industrial revolution

In places where democracy developed the earliest such as Great Britain and the United States, divisions over these issues were resolved relatively easily. This happened in part because their crises were spread out over a number of centuries, and the societies and leaders were able to reach closure on one crisis before the next one occurred.

The situation was very different in countries that had more trouble democratizing. There, the crises were not resolved in anything approaching a consensual manner, and they left deep **cleavages,** or social divisions. In France and Italy, conflict over the role the church should play in politics overlapped with controversies over whether the government should be democratic. Until the late 1800s, there was no unified Germany or Italy, which made it impossible for democracy to develop. Moreover, the fact that these deeply divisive issues remained unresolved meant that by the late nineteenth century the governments of the newly formed nation-states were dealing with all of them simultaneously.

These so-called late democratizers also found themselves in a more difficult position internationally. Germany, Japan, and Italy were newcomers to great power politics and found themselves lagging behind Britain and France militarily as well as economically. Desirous of power and prestige and fearful of invasion, leaders in all

British women demanding the right to vote in 1909.

three countries believed that they had to catch up with the other great powers as quickly as possible. They were also convinced that they could do so only if the state took the lead and forced the pace of development. Each therefore imposed strict limits on popular political rights. Adult males did get the vote, but real political power remained in the hands of the bureaucratic and military elites, which built industrial and military machines that rivaled those of Britain and France by the time World War I broke out.

After World War I, liberal regimes were established in much of central and eastern Europe, and Japan adopted a much more democratic constitution. Most of those states, however, quickly ran into trouble, giving rise to concerns about the dangers of excessive and disruptive popular participation. Extremist parties on the left and right won ever larger shares of the vote. Thousands of disgruntled workers and veterans took to the streets and formed private militias. Effective democratic government became all but impossible.

One after another, the new democracies turned to authoritarian leaders and **fascism**—the most important examples of which were Benito Mussolini in Italy and Adolf Hitler in Germany. These men and their parties won in large part because they built a strong popular base and came to power as part of an elected coalition government.

World War II marked the last watershed in the evolution of democratic theory and practice so far. The rise of fascism, the carnage of the Second World War, and the outbreak of the cold war led many to question whether average citizens were capable of sustaining democracy, especially in a country with a history like Germany's or Japan's. One group of scholars argued that there was a widespread "authoritarian personality" that left people vulnerable to appeals from communists and fascists. Others stressed the uneven development in countries that had to totally reconstruct their political systems after the war. Among other things, these included measures that made it more difficult for potentially disruptive parties to get their members into parliament and for divided legislatures to hamstring governments.

Second, a strong democratic state was in some respects a by-product of the cold war that began as World War II ended. Early on, Europe was its main "battleground." The Communist revolution in China then made Japan vitally important to the West as well. The United States sent billions of dollars in aid to help the European and Japanese economies recover and thereby block the spread of communism.

Political scientists and historians still debate how

Democratization

THE RECENT WAVE of democratization in the former Communist countries and in much of the third world has led political scientists to reconsider democracy's emergence in Europe and North America. Their conclusions are not all that encouraging for new and hopeful democracies.

Depending on how we count, it took generations, if not centuries, to create the first democracies. The history of democratization stretches back to the signing of the Magna Carta in 1215, and some people are convinced that it is still going on today, given that groups such as gays and lesbians are denied what they claim to be their full civil rights. Even with a more limited definition of what it means to be democratic, it took the Anglo-American societies at least three centuries to secure basic political rights for all their citizens.

What's more, democratization was a tumultuous process. There is a tendency to look upon the process as one of gradual and consensual reform. Compared to the political histories of most other countries, this may be true. However, even the United States and the United Kingdom have faced major upheavals, including a civil war and other prolonged periods of unrest, during which elites tried to hold onto their power.

However, we should also recognize that no real attempts were made to consciously create a democracy before the establishment of the Weimar Republic in Germany after World War I, and no successes were recorded until after World War II. Conditions may have changed enough and leaders in the new democracies may have learned enough that they can escape the problems that befell all but the most successful of the countries discussed in this chapter.

these various forces came together. But come together they did. Within a generation, democratic regimes were securely in place in "free world" countries that had so recently opted for some of the most brutally authoritarian regimes ever.

Political Culture and Participation

Obviously, the way people think and act is critical to the success—or failure—of a democracy. However, political scientists have reached some not-so-obvious conclusions about how those beliefs and actions can buttress—or undermine—democracies.

The Civic Culture?

After World War II, a number of political scientists turned their attention to the reasons for the collapse of democracy and the rise of fascism. Many of them ended up concentrating on political culture, most notably Gabriel Almond and Sidney Verba's in their landmark study, *The Civic Culture*. They contrasted the United States and Great Britain with Germany, Italy, and Mexico, emphasizing the importance of a culture in which democratic beliefs exist alongside a degree of political passivity. For example, they explored political efficacy—people's belief that they can do something about political decisions they disagree with. However, most of those surveyed also acknowledged that people rarely do so because they trust their leaders to do what is right.

The massive protests of the 1960s and 1970s soon undermined the more simplistic arguments linking a civic culture to democracy. Today, political scientists are returning to the role of political culture, albeit in a more nuanced way. There is no consensus yet in the scholarly community, but three conclusions from recent studies will prove important throughout Part 2.

First, in successful democracies, people have a deeply felt sense of **legitimacy** and accept the "rules of the game." Critical here is the distinction between the government of the day and the regime. As we will see in Chapter 4, even Britain had to cope with protests that reflected unprecedented anger toward the Labour government of 1974–79 and its Tory successor in the 1980s. However, there is no evidence that the protesters' ire extended beyond the Callaghan or Thatcher governments to the British constitutional order itself. Perhaps even more importantly, much the same is true of protests in countries that had not developed strong democratic regimes prior to the war. Thus, despite the massive protests of May and June 1968 that almost toppled General Charles de Gaulle's government, there was little talk of scrapping the Fifth Republic, and any inclinations to do so were long gone before the socialists finally won power thirteen years later.

Second, that feeling of legitimacy has remained despite a dramatic drop in most forms of political participation and in trust in most politicians. Only 58 percent of British voters bothered to go to the polls in 2001, the lowest figure since 1918. Turnout was particularly low in Britain's inner cities and among the young, of whom barely a third cast a ballot.

A panoramic view of the hundreds of thousands of nonviolent protesters at the 1963 March on Washington for civil rights.

Third, more recently, scholars such as Robert Putnam and Fareed Zakaria have forced us to consider more than just the values and assumptions of a political culture. Putnam, for instance, stresses the role of social capital, which reflects the degree to which a society has networks that build trust and cooperation, especially among people and groups who typically disagree with each other. Zakaria stresses the importance of attitudes of tolerance and institutions that instill a respect for the views and actions of others, because they can put a damper on the passions that people with strongly held views can bring to political life. Such ideas are hotly contested by other political scientists. Nonetheless, there is widespread agreement that a democratic culture consists not only of attitudes public opinion pollsters can measure but also of actions that tend to breed trust and cooperation.

Late Democracy/Strong State

There is a powerful theme lurking just below the surface in this discussion that will have a tremendous bearing later on in the book. Because they eschewed democracy in favor of "top-down" development, countries like Germany continued their tradition of a strong state into the democratic period after World War II. At that time (though not earlier), in combining democracy with a strong state, they spurred unprecedented economic growth and political stability that lasted until the early 1990s.

Political Parties and Elections

Democracies are different from other countries in large part because they give their citizens a wider variety of ways to participate in political life. None of them is more important than their involvement (or lack thereof) in the competitive elections that determine who fills the top offices in the government. And, with the exception of some local races in the United States, any analysis of elections and voting has to concentrate on **political parties,** the organizations responsible for contesting elections and forming governments afterward.

There is a bewildering array of political parties in the three democracies to be covered in Part 2. Most, though, have their roots in the cleavages left by the historical transformations discussed earlier. Not all countries were left with deep and lasting divisions. To the degree that they were, however, they left an indelible imprint by giving rise to the parties that have dominated electoral politics since the 1920s.

A few new parties have emerged in the past twenty years, which we will consider later. None of them, however, are strong enough yet to win elections or play a regular role in determining the composition of governments. In other words, if we are to understand the heart of the electoral process, we have to begin with the parties formed as a result of those four historical forces as outlined in table 1.2.

Parties are discussed along the traditional left-right spectrum. (See table 2.3.) Unlike most political terms, these two widely used ones do not have particularly revealing meanings. Their origins lie in the seating arrangements in the French parliament after the revolution of 1789, when deputies who favored radical change sat on the left of the speaker's rostrum and those who opposed it sat to his right. Since then, the meaning of the terms has evolved in the ways summarized in table 2.3.

On the **left** end are what remain of the communist parties. (See table 2.4.) They were formed in the aftermath of the Russian Revolution of 1917, when members of the more radical wings of the socialist parties quit and formed new organizations to support the Bolsheviks in Moscow. For most of the time since then, the commu-

TABLE 2.3 The Changing Meaning of Left and Right

PERIOD	LEFT	RIGHT
Eighteenth and early nineteenth centuries	Prodemocratic Anticlerical Promarket	Antidemocratic Proclerical Ambivalent on market
Industrial era	Prodemocratic Anticlerical For socialism and/ or welfare state	More prodemocratic Usual proclerical Less positive about welfare state, against socialism
Postindustrial era	Egalitarian, but qualms about welfare state and socialism as we know them Mostly globalist New social issues	Promarket capitalism Traditional values More nationalistic

TABLE 2.4 Main Types of Political Parties by Country

	TYPE OF PARTY					
COUNTRY	COMMUNIST	SOCIALIST	LIBERAL	CHRISTIAN DEMOCRATIC	CONSERVATIVE	OTHER
Great Britain	—	Labour	Liberal Democrats[a]	—	Conservative	Regional[b]
France	PCF	PS	[c]	[c]	UPM	Green National Front
Germany	PDS	SPD	FDP	CDU	—	Green National Front
Japan	JCP	DSPJ	—	—	LDP	Komeito

[a] Liberal to 1983, Liberal–Social Democratic Alliance 1983–87, Liberal Democrats 1988 on.

[b] Nationalist parties of Scotland, Wales, and Northern Ireland.

[c] The French Radical and Christian Democratic parties are no longer big enough to include here.

nist parties have been the most radical critics of capitalism and the strongest defenders of what they claim are the interests of the working class. Most were all-but-uncritical supporters of the Soviet Union during the cold war. Of the countries we will be covering, only France still has a significant Communist Party, and it has been in decline for years, a decline that has accelerated since the collapse of the Soviet Union.

Next are the **social democratic** parties. Like the communists, they also traditionally supported the **nationalization** of industry, extensive social welfare programs, and greater equality. Unlike the communists, however, the socialists rejected revolution and were harsh critics of the Soviet Union. Most moderated their positions during the post-war years and shed all but the most empty rhetorical references to Marxism and nationalization. Some people think that recent attempts, mainly by Tony Blair and his colleagues in the British Labour Party, to create a "third way" between socialism and capitalism might breathe new ideological life into these parties, but it is too early to tell. Only in the United States, Canada, and Japan have socialists not regularly been serious contestants for power.

In the center are parties known as either **liberals** or **radicals.** They gained their radical label in the nineteenth century when they did stand for fundamental change—the separation of church and state, a market economy, and democracy. The British Liberals were one of the two main parties until the 1920s, and the Radicals were France's most influential party under both the Third and Fourth Republics (1875–1958). Today, they appeal primarily to the wealthy and have no significant impact on who governs. The one major exception is the German Free Democratic Party (FDP). Although it has never done well at the polls, the FDP provided the votes either the Socialists or the Christian Democrats needed to form a governing coalition for all but three years between the creation in 1949 of the Federal Republic and 1998.

Countries that had deep and unresolved divisions over the relationship between church and state at one point or another have had explicitly religious, **Christian Democratic** parties that appealed primarily to Catholic voters. Some Catholics had qualms about democracy, and others advocated social reforms much like those backed by the social democrats. With the onset of the cold war, however, most Christian Democrats aligned themselves with the United States on foreign policy issues and with proponents of a capitalist economy at home. And they have been extremely influential, dominating governments in Germany and Italy for most of the postwar period. Indeed, France is the only country with a large Catholic population in which the Christian Democrats have been eclipsed by other right-of-center parties.

Britain, with very few Catholics, and Japan, with very few Christians, have not had major Christian Democratic parties. Instead, the **right** side of the political spectrum has been dominated by secular conservatives. Parties like the British Conservatives, French Gaullists, and Japanese Liberal Democrats are not all that different from the Christian Democrats except that they do not have a religious inspiration. American readers should note that they are not conservative in the sense that the term is used in the United States. They have not traditionally opposed state intervention in the economy. Indeed, as we will see in Chapters 5 and 6, they have developed effective mechanisms whereby the state works with private enterprise to stimulate growth.

Catch-All Parties

Some observers claim that democratic party systems today are not working very well because they have such old roots. As we will see in the chapters that follow, many have had a hard time adapting to the changes of recent years, especially the rise of new social movements and the globalization of the world economy.

In part, that reflects their adoption of more moderate positions for most of the past forty years. During the 1950s, political scientists began to notice a marked shift in public opinion toward the center. A combination of sustained economic growth, expansion of the welfare state, and escalation of the cold war undermined support for radical politics.

At first, the left was slow to respond. The British Labour Party and the German Social Democrats (SPD) clung to their traditional socialist appeals even though their electoral fortunes continued to sag. Gradually, however, a new generation of leaders moved these parties toward the center and led them to victory in the 1960s.

The changes on the right were less striking, but no less significant. Conservatives, too, had to respond to the emerging consensus about the welfare state. The British Conservatives, French Gaullists, and German Christian Democrats accepted the idea that government should provide extensive social service programs and actually expanded these programs when they were in office.

The moderation was so marked during the 1950s and early 1960s that some analysts began writing about the "end of ideology." They were convinced that sharp ideological divisions were a thing of the past and that

FIGURE 2.1 Political Participation in Flux: Two Versions

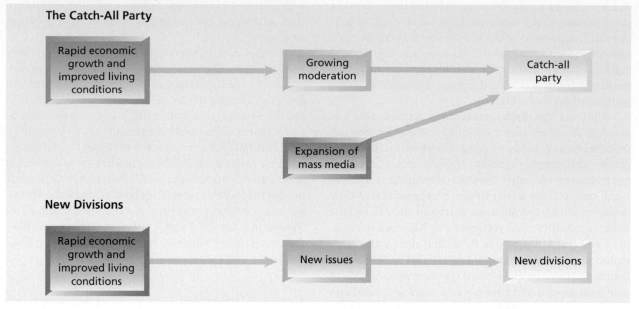

subsequent elections would be contests between similar teams of politicians.

Those ideological trends were reinforced by an even more dramatic change in the way election campaigns were conducted. By the 1960s, most people got most of their information about politics from television. Because it is impossible to say anything nuanced or detailed in a sixty-second news clip, the growing role of television accentuated the trend away from ideological appeals.

The issue-driven activists who dominated the old "mass parties" gave way to spin doctors who learned how to promote telegenic candidates. Parties no longer appealed only to their "own" portion of the electorate (for example, socialists to the working class) but now tried to reach out to everyone, and so were dubbed **catch-all.** (See the top half of figure 2.1.)

As we are about to see, events undermined the central claims of an argument that democracies were undergoing an end of ideology. However, the technological dynamics that led to the catch-all party have, if anything, intensified. There have been instances in which parties and candidates made major breakthroughs by stressing ideological themes, most notably in the victories of Margaret Thatcher in Great Britain (1979) and Ronald Reagan in the United States (1980). Yet even their campaigns featured slogans and video clips. Polls, focus groups, and other forms of market research have led party leaders to run campaigns that "sell" to undecided voters. How much these changes have sapped parties of the ability to take strong stands and thus help shape public opinion

for extended periods is still very much an open question. But the spread of media-based campaigns has heightened the cynicism many voters in democracies feel toward politicians.

New Divisions

The image of the party system summarized in table 2.4 is somewhat misleading because it implies that party systems were defined by cleavages that came into existence at the turn of the last century. The parties that have a realistic chance of winning most elections do have old and deep roots, but important changes are occurring on the fringes of the electoral mainstream that may have more dramatic consequences in the next few years.

Most visible is the growing differences between men and women. Women used to be more conservative than men. They were less likely to work outside the home and so were less exposed to the left-leaning influence of trade unions. They were also more religious and thus more heavily affected by the usually conservative clergy. As more women joined the workforce and were swept up in the feminist and new left movements of the 1960s and 1970s, some began to question their conservative views, especially those involving reproductive rights and the family. Many (though by no means all) began to realize that their interests lay with progressive parties. In the United States, this has led to the "gender gap" in which the Democratic vote among women can be as much as 20 percent higher than among men. In Britain, it prompted the Labour Party to field a slate of candidates in 1997 that led to the election of over a hundred female **members of parliament** (**MPs**).

Meanwhile, many men—especially those with limited professional skills—felt that their livelihoods and positions of dominance were under threat. Some made the opposite switch, abandoning traditionally left-wing parties to become "Reagan Democrats" in the United States, Thatcherites in Britain, and supporters of the racist National Front in France.

The gender gap is but the tip of a much larger, but poorly understood, political iceberg. For more than thirty years, Ronald Inglehart and his colleagues have been studying how the social and economic changes underlying **postindustrial society** are playing themselves out politically. (See the bottom half of figure 2.1.) Their theoretical assumption and research methods have been the subject of much controversy. Nonetheless, their empirical findings are so consistent that they unquestionably have tapped an important trend.

Inglehart uses the same starting point as the end-of-ideology theorists—rapid economic growth and improved living conditions—but then diverges sharply from them. From this perspective, the unprecedented economic growth of the past half-century has produced a new type of middle-class, **postmaterialist** voters. They are often the third generation to be raised in affluent conditions and can realistically assume that they will have productive and rewarding careers, and will not have to worry much about their economic security. As a result, they tend to focus on what Inglehart calls "higher-order" values, including job and personal satisfaction, self-actualization, and international understanding. In the process, postmaterialists have become far less conservative than earlier generations of affluent voters. In American terms, postmaterialists largely overlap with the "soccer moms" (and dads) who gained so much publicity for their support of President Clinton in 1996.

They have not become traditional leftists; most have serious qualms, for instance, about the welfare state and socialism. However, they supported the peace movements of the 1980s and, more recently, environmentalism, more than any other socioeconomic group in the electorate.

They are most likely to support the one type of new party that has had a significant impact—the **Greens.** Greens are best known for their strong stands against nuclear weapons and power and for their support of environmental causes. Party ideology goes a lot further to stress "deep ecology," or a world view based on the assumption that all life is interconnected. Green parties have done rather well in most of Europe, often ap-

Tony Harris/AP/Wide World Photos

Clare Ward, at twenty-four years old, the youngest of more than 100 women elected as Labour MPs on May 1, 1997.

proaching 10 percent of the vote, most of which comes from younger postmaterialists. They have had the greatest impact in Germany, where they have been in the parliament since 1983 and entered the governing coalition after the 1998 election. Before moving on, note that the Greens in the United States (at least as represented by the Ralph Nader campaign of 2000) are a very different phenomenon from what we find in Europe and do not fully reflect these trends either ideologically or demographically.

On the other end of the spectrum are older, less-educated people who have not benefited as much from economic growth. Indeed, in a high-tech world in which more and more low-skill jobs have been either automated or outsourced, these people feel most threatened by all the changes going on. As a result, the political priorities of these "materialists" include maintaining their own standard of living and national economic strength and security. Even though they may have been raised in left-wing families, many have moved rightward to parties that are hostile to women's and minorities' rights and that defend economic nationalism and "traditional values." They have, in short, become the conservatives of the new millennium.

Here, France's National Front is by far the most prominent example. As we saw in the introduction to this chapter, it routinely wins between 10 and 20 percent of the vote in most elections, and its leader, Jean-Marie Le Pen edged his way into the runoff ballot in the 2002 presidential election. Even in other countries in which the "new right" has not fared as well at the polls, it is typically more influential than its leftist counterparts even though they get the most attention from political scientists who study new social movements.

Realignment?

Do not read too much into the emergence of post-materialism or parties like the Greens or the National Front. If anything, they reflect just how slowly the individual parties and national party systems have been to respond to the social and economic changes that have swept through the industrialized democracies since the 1950s.

In other times of major change, the party system ultimately did respond. Existing or new parties took the lead by adopting strong positions on key issues, appealing to new segments of the electorate, and producing lasting changes in basic patterns of support for the parties and, hence, the government. In the United States, such realignments typically occurred in a thirty-two year, or eight-election, cycle.

Political scientists have been waiting for such a **realignment** to occur throughout the democratic world since the late 1960s. At most, two parts of it may have already occurred.

First, dealignment always precedes realignment. Before they are "free" to support new parties, voters have to sever the psychological ties that bind them to the ones they have traditionally supported. A massive amount of polling evidence suggests that rates of party identification have plummeted almost everywhere and that more and more voters are skeptical about what parties and politicians can or will deliver.

Second, as implied previously, the right has gone a long way toward redefining itself. Led by the likes of Thatcher and Reagan, it has staked out new positions on the economy, racial diversity, and national security. In so doing, they have kept some of their traditional voters in the fold while appealing to many of the newly conservative materialists. Nonetheless, many have moved so far to the right that they have a hard time winning elections now that the first generation of "new right" leaders have left the scene and their policies no longer have quite the appeal they did in the 1980s.

The left, by contrast, has had a much harder time redefining its image and appealing to a new coalition of voters who could propel it into office with a workable ideology and majority. But that may be changing. Beginning with Bill Clinton in the United States, more moderate politicians have taken over most of the leading left-of-center parties, including Tony Blair in Britain and Gerhard Schröder in Germany.

Interest Groups

The industrial democracies all have **interest groups** that seek to promote just about every point of view on just about every imaginable issue to the point that it is impossible for scholars to keep track of them all. As a result, political scientists have concentrated on trade unions, business groups, and other associations that are the most visible, use the most disruptive tactics, and/or have the greatest apparent influence.

In most countries, trade unions are now much weaker than they used to be. There are also new groups, including hundreds of organizations working on environmental issues, expanded rights for women and minorities (both for and against), and a host of foreign policy issues. Some are quite aggressive, such as the animal rights groups in England that disrupt fox-hunting parties and the export of chicken and sheep for slaughter on the Continent. Others are more conventional lobbyists who operate "inside the system," trying to translate their wealth and contacts into influence.

Because there are so many interest groups, it is hard to reach many firm conclusions about them. In the chapters that follow, we will concentrate on two broad themes about two main types of organizations. First, those that concentrate on economic issues and represent groups central to the country's economic future tend to have the most influence. Generally, business groups have more influence than unions do. Second, the nature of the relationship interest groups have with decision makers varies tremendously from country to country. In weaker states like the United States and Great Britain, civil servants and politicians try to keep their distance from interest group representatives. In Germany and France, there is a long history of open and close collaboration between interest groups and the state, which contributed heavily to the economic success of these countries from the end of World War II until the early 1990s.

Political Protest

The industrialized democracies all have protest movements that go beyond the activities of traditional interest groups. Some use violence. Some protests involve large numbers of people, as in the "events" of May and June 1968. Others involve only a handful of people, such as the vigil antinuclear protesters have maintained for years across the street from the White House. Some are national in scope, and others address issues of only local concern. Some come from the left end of the political spectrum, others from the right.

We will concentrate on two contrasting trends in the chapters that follow. First, there is plenty of protest, the angriest and loudest of which comes from groups that feel they are least well represented in the electoral process. Many pro-life activists in the United States believe they have no choice but to disrupt—and sometimes destroy—clinics where abortions are performed. Top business executives, however, rarely have to take to the streets to have their views heard.

Second, virtually none of it involves people who question the legitimacy of their regimes, let alone democracy itself. There are some such opposition groups on the fringes of the political system, but the Maoists and Trotskyites on the left and the American militias and Eu-ropean neofascists on the right have so little influence that they will rarely appear in the next four chapters.

The Democratic State

Elections, which determine who the leading policy-makers are, and the informal access provided by interest groups and political protest give the people in industrialized democracies more clout than their counterparts living under other kinds of regimes. But that power is by no means total. As noted earlier, democratic states do impose some limits on what people can do. In other words, democratic states have not been able to avoid the trade-off between the power of the state and that of society depicted in figure 1.2.

Presidential and Parliamentary Systems

The most important feature of the relationship between state and society in any liberal democracy is the way it handles representation between the government and the governed. To understand how that occurs and how it is reflected in public policy, we start by considering the differences between presidential and parliamentary systems. Both are based on the critical democratic principle that free and competitive elections determine who governs. However, they lead to very different kinds of outcomes.

Antiglobalization protesters marching from Annemasse, France to Geneva, Switzerland during the G-8 summit held in Evian, France in June 2003. The sign reads: Eight Deadly Sins: Globalization, Speculation, Exclusion, Corruption, Privatization, Manipulation, Lying, Contempt. Protesters clashed frequently with police in normally staid Geneva and caused millions of dollars in damage.

Antoine Serra/In Visu/CORBIS

It is actually somewhat misleading to speak of presidential systems in the plural, because there is really only one of them—the United States. As we will see in more detail in the next chapter, the drafters of the U.S. Constitution set out to create a state in which it would be very difficult for rulers to abuse their power or to act quickly and coherently. They made compromise the norm and rapid decision making difficult. By contrast, in parliamentary systems with a secure majority party or coalition, the prime minister rarely has to compromise as much as an American president, which allows their governments to act more quickly and decisively than any American administration.

The American president has to assume that if a bill he proposes actually is passed the final version will be very different from the one sent to Capitol Hill, because he has little leverage over what senators or representatives do. Once a bill is submitted, it must pass through a number of hurdles—subcommittees, committees, floor debate, and a conference committee—before it is sent on to the White House for the president's signature or veto. (See figure 2.2.) At each of those points the bill can be defeated once and for all. Even if it is not, it will almost certainly be drastically altered as members of Congress try to forge a compromise that will get the votes of a majority in each house. As that happens, the bill is normally sapped of much of the coherence in the original version.

Parliamentary systems operate very differently. A party that runs for election and wins a majority of the seats in parliament can take office and see the proposals in its program or platform passed virtually intact. Parliaments do have committees, debates, and votes. Unlike the American president, however, the prime minister has so much leverage over what happens at each of these stages that he or she can force proposed legislation through what is for all intents and purposes a compliant parliament.

As figure 2.3 suggests, power in parliamentary systems is fused, not separated. After an election, the parliament selects the prime minister, who is normally the head of the majority party or coalition of parties. The prime minister has not been elected by the country as a whole and in most countries is merely an MP.

The prime minister appoints the rest of the cabinet. Unlike the United States, most ministers (the exact proportion varies from country to country) are also members of parliament and retain their seats while they serve in the cabinet. Together, the prime minister and cabinet form what is known as the government.

The most important feature of a parliamentary system is the doctrine of **cabinet responsibility** to parliament. The government remains in office until the next

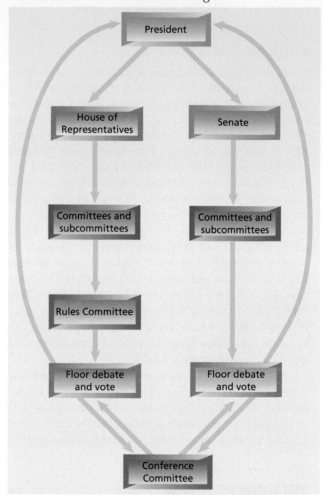

█ FIGURE 2.2 The President and Congress

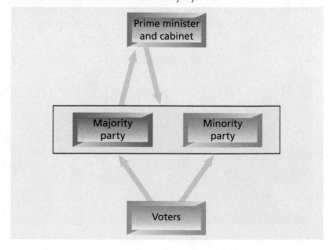

█ FIGURE 2.3 The Parliamentary System

election if and only if it retains the support of that majority on all major pieces of legislation. It also must keep its majority on **votes of confidence,** in which the parliament is explicitly asked to affirm its support for the government. If the government loses either of these types of votes, it must resign. At that point, either a new majority comes together within the existing parliament to form a government or the parliament is dissolved, leading to a new election within a matter of weeks.

In practice, when a prime minister has a clear majority, the government will not lose such a vote. Its members will stick together and support the government because the costs of not doing so are too high. The best a defeated government can look forward to is the uncertainty of an election. Breaking party discipline and bringing a government down can also destroy an individual member's career.

So, in a country like Great Britain, where the Labour Party won 413 out of 659 seats in the all-powerful House of Commons in 2001 (see table 2.5), Prime Minister Tony Blair can count on winning every key vote until the parliamentary term ends. Debates on the floor of the House of Commons are more heated than in the House of Representatives or Senate in the United States, but the legislative process rarely produces more than slight changes in the details of a bill, and then only if the government agrees.

The kind of protracted stalemate Washington suffers through at budget time each year rarely occurs in a parliamentary system with a firm majority. When Chancellor of the Exchequer Gordon Brown presented the Blair government's draft budget in July 1997, it contained a number of controversial proposals. Among other things, it called for a £4 billion ($6.5 billion) windfall profits tax on the recently privatized utilities and proposed using the money for a training and employment program for chronically unemployed young people. There had been a great deal of lobbying over the budget. But, unlike in the United States, most of it took place before the draft was unveiled. By the time Brown went before the House of Commons, all the important decisions had been made. In fact, the debate that day ended with the passage of a resolution that provisionally put the budget into effect.

▌ TABLE 2.6 The French Chamber of Deputies, 1951

PARTY	NUMBER OF SEATS
Communists	101
Socialists	106
Christian Democrats	88
Radicals	76
Independents and Peasants	95
Gaullists	120
Others	40

In other words, politicians face plenty of pressure in a parliamentary system, but to make a difference, lobbyists have to exert their influence before legislation is submitted to parliament. Otherwise, it is too late to have much hope of shaping the bill as it wends its way through the formal legislative process. Thus, because the majority party will consistently vote for legislation the government proposes, it can act quickly and coherently.

We need to insert an important caveat here. If there is no clear majority in parliament, a very different situation arises. As table 2.6 shows, six parties plus a smaller group of independents split the seats in the French Chamber of Deputies after the 1951 election. The parties held sharply different views, and their leaders disliked one another personally. Not surprisingly, they did not cooperate easily. As a result, every nine months or so, a cabinet would lose a vote of confidence or resign knowing that the next issue it had to deal with would do it in. For historical reasons to be discussed in Chapter 5, the premier could not dissolve the chamber and hold new elections. Instead, a new majority had to be cobbled together from the existing MPs. That cabinet, in turn, would fall once it had to deal with its first controversial issue, and the negotiations to form a new government would start all over again.

Under such circumstances, parliamentary systems yield anything but effective government. The Fourth Republic (1946–58) teetered from cabinet crisis to cabinet crisis and failed to meet any of the serious domestic or international challenges it faced. In the end, it lost most of its popular support and collapsed when a war of independence in colonial Algeria threatened to spill over to France itself.

In recent years, however, few parliaments have come close to being this divided. More often than not, elections have produced either a single party with a majority of its own or a **coalition** of parties that are close enough to one another ideologically to stay together for the duration of a parliamentary term as has been the case in Germany or France for most of the last half century or so. However, ideological fragmentation of this sort bedevils such countries as Israel and India today.

▌ TABLE 2.5 The British General Election of 2001

	LABOUR	CONSER-VATIVES	LIBERAL DEMO-CRATS	OTHER
SHARE OF THE VOTE (PERCENTAGE)	40.8	31.8	18.3	9.1
NUMBER OF SEATS	413	166	52	28

The Rest of the State

Governments today have to deal with highly technical issues that often call for a degree of expertise elected politicians rarely have. As a result, two sets of actors not included in figure 2.2 have come to play pivotal roles in most democracies—high-level civil servants in the **bureaucracy** and leading interest group representatives.

As first discussed by Max Weber, modern civil services are supposed to be the epitome of efficiency. Recruited and promoted on the basis of merit, bureaucrats are objective, scientific, and expert. Their behavior is governed not by ideology or personal whim, but by rules clearly laid out in law. They are supposed to be civil *servants*, working dispassionately for their political masters in the cabinet, whatever party happens to control it at the moment.

The realities of bureaucratic life are more complicated. In many countries, the civil service is able to attract highly educated and talented people, especially in Japan, Germany, and France, where a disproportionate number of the "best and brightest" begin their careers working for the state. That said, bureaucracies have rarely been able to reach the dispassionate and apolitical Weberian ideal. To varying degrees, civil servants have become important policymakers in their own right. However important their expertise may be, the bureaucrats' policy-making role is problematic from a democratic perspective because they are not elected officials and are thus difficult to hold accountable. That is especially true in countries where the business, bureaucratic, and political elites are so close that scholars speak of them as an **iron triangle.** (See figure 2.4.)

France and the United States represent the two extremes on this score. Americans are wary of any close cooperation among such groups. Federal bureaucrats, for example, cannot be employed by an organization that deals with the issues they worked on for two years after leaving government service. The doctrine of separation

▌ FIGURE 2.4 Elite Integration: Iron Triangles

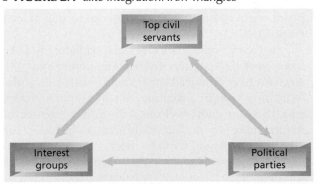

The Missing Link: The Courts

Readers in the United States, in particular, may be surprised by the absence of one institution in these pages—the courts. In few countries do the courts have the sweeping powers they do in the United States to rule not simply on individual cases but on the constitutionality of laws as well.

In the most extreme case, British courts lack any authority to exercise constitutional law. This is not so in the other countries to be covered in Part 2. As we will see in Chapter 6, the German Constitutional Court has made a number of important decisions, including on the legal status of a woman's right to abortion. Similarly, its French equivalent has gained power over the last twenty years or so. However, only in the United States are the courts a co-equal branch of government with the legislature and the executive.

of powers often makes it difficult for members of Congress and their staffs to get information from civil servants. And almost everyone looks askance at close relationships between interest groups and politicians, given long-standing concerns about big government and the possibility of corruption.

In France, cooperation among business elites, politicians, and bureaucrats is actively encouraged. Many ambitious French students decide to start their careers as civil servants by attending one of the prestigious *grandes écoles*, which train them for bureaucratic careers. After as little as ten years in the civil service, some bureaucrats leave the government through a process nicknamed *pantouflage*, which literally means putting on soft, cushy slippers. At that point, they either become politicians in one of the major political parties or top corporate executives. In other words, current and former civil servants with similar social backgrounds, educations, and early career paths lead the key governmental and private sector institutions.

Although no single factor can explain all the variation in the ways democratic states act, there is a clear distinction to be made among them along these lines. Those with the most **integrated elite,** like France, Germany, and Japan, have been among the most successful economically since the end of World War II. The countries that have resisted those trends toward interelite cooperation have had the most trouble, at least until the 1990s.

Those countries' economic woes and the U.S. resurgence of the 1990s suggest that these trends may not continue. Nonetheless, they are such an important part of democratic political life over the past half-century that they will draw considerable attention in the chapters on individual countries.

Public Policy

The Interventionist State

Orthodox economic theorists claim that the state should keep its hands off the economy. As they see it, properly functioning markets driven by the balancing effects of supply and demand provide the maximum possible wealth and efficiency at the minimum cost.

Markets, however, have never worked that well in practice, because two critical assumptions in economic theory have rarely been met. First, even the most ardent laissez-faire capitalists acknowledge that markets cannot effectively provide collective or public goods, such as a clean environment, a national defense system, or a general education. These are services that society as a whole may want, but it is not in any individual's or firm's self-interest to provide them. Second, markets will work at their best only if a number of conditions are met, including competition and the absence of concentrated wealth and power on the part of either capitalists or workers.

To make a long, complicated story short, the social and economic changes spurred by the industrial revolution made it more and more difficult to meet those criteria. A host of problems emerged, from pollution in industrial areas, to failing firms, to widespread poverty. Once it became clear that no one in the private or

Challenges to the Democratic State

There are no serious challenges to the existence of any of the major liberal democratic states. In the late 1960s and early 1970s, some observers argued that many of them were in trouble in the light of violent protests and terrorists attacks and the economic slump following the OPEC oil embargo. All have managed to weather those and other political storms, and with the end of the cold war, there are no major international threats to their survival, either.

charitable sectors could handle those problems, people turned to a more **interventionist state.**

All now offer a variety of social services, including these:

- Basic health care and education
- Subsidized and/or free education at all levels including universities
- Unemployment compensation
- Pensions and other programs for seniors

But there is considerable variation in what they actually do. The United States and Japan offer less, whereas the European states offer something approaching "cradle-to-grave" coverage.

The rightward drift during the past two decades has led many to question these programs. Britain and the

One of France's *écoles maternelles.* Programs such as these, which guarantees day care for all children from the age of two, are currently threatened by cutbacks in funding for the welfare state and the general reduction in state activity throughout the democratic world.

© Anthony Suau/Getty Images

United States, for instance, have recently passed welfare reform legislation that requires recipients to work or get job training. On balance, however, most of these programs remain extremely popular and have proved hard to cut back. To cite but one example, despite its antigovernment rhetoric, the Bush administration actually increased federal spending above and beyond the cost of the wars against terrorism and Iraq.

There is no such certainty with the rest of economic policy.

The industrialized democracies all have essentially capitalist economies because most businesses are privately owned. That should not mask the fact that they have been going through their most wrenching transformation since the industrial revolution.

The economic center of gravity has shifted away from manufacturing to the tertiary or service sector. Despite the demise of so many dot-com enterprises since 2000, the computer and information technology industries in general are increasingly at the heart of postindustrial society. As it has grown, millions of jobs in the automobile, textiles, and other heavy industries have been lost to either automation or the third world.

This transition is part of the globalization of economic activity. Academics and other observers debate just how quickly and extensively globalization is occurring. But a quick glance at the products in the room you are sitting in will tell you that we increasingly buy products and consume services that originate in countries all around the world. Because so much of what we use is imported and exported, and because so many of the companies that make those products are multinational and can move their operations as market conditions warrant, no government is as able as it was a generation ago to enact and implement its economic policies.

We will see this most clearly in Chapter 7 when we consider the European Union (EU), by far the most prominent international organization in the world today. With the introduction of the euro as a full-fledged currency in 2002, the EU has taken on even more of the trappings of a state and is probably more influential than any of its member governments in making economic policy.

At the domestic level, most governments have adopted more conservative, promarket policies in recent years. The collapse of Communism in eastern Europe, and the consensus that social democrats in Europe and liberals in the United States enjoyed little success in eliminating poverty, has given "antistate" forces more clout. In particular, governments have **privatized** much of the publicly owned sector, which, in some cases, amounted to as much as 20 percent of total

Economic Liberalization

Great Britain has led the way in privatizing state-owned industries. France and Germany have loosened their macro- and microeconomic coordination procedures to a lesser degree. Everywhere, tariffs and other barriers to international trade have been lowered, if not eliminated.

There is one important caveat here: Do not assume that the free market now reigns. States and the European Union for its members remain the most powerful economic factor in all the industrialized democracies. Great Britain, for instance, still heavily regulates the newly privatized industries. The albeit weakened iron triangles of France and Japan shock most American economists. And most provisions of the welfare state remain in place despite some changes in the way services are provided.

In short, free-market rhetoric has outpaced reality—at least so far.

production at the height of what the British call the collectivist years.

Foreign Policy

Important changes have been occurring in foreign policies as well. Events since the terrorist attacks on 9/11 have had a huge but differing influence on democratic states. But many of the changes began far earlier and may prove to have an even more lasting impact.

During the cold war, most leaders in the industrialized democracies followed the lead of the United States in making foreign policy. But there were exceptions to that rule. During Charles de Gaulle's presidency (1958–69), France charted an independent course in response to his desire to restore France's grandeur as one of the world's great powers. He pulled French troops from NATO, created the French nuclear arsenal, tried to serve as a broker between the superpowers, and defended what he saw as the rights of new states in the third world. De Gaulle's successors have echoed some of his nationalist themes, but, rhetoric aside, they have been far closer to the United States.

The end of the cold war ushered in a new era in international relations in which U.S. domination can no longer be taken for granted. To be sure, the United States is the world's only superpower. Moreover, almost all of the industrialized democracies followed Washington's lead on the major issues of the 1990s, including the Gulf War, the deployment of troops in Bosnia, and the bombing of Serbia in response to human rights violations in Kosovo. The dispute over the invasion of Iraq should not keep us from seeing how close the Western allies have been on most issues of national security, including how best to respond to the attacks of 9/11.

On other issues, however, the other industrialized democracies have always charted a more autonomous course. Again, the EU, which represents all of its member states in negotiating international economic agreements, is the best example of this. The EU and the United States have disagreed on a number of issues, including trade in agricultural products, such as genetically modified food, and environmental policy, most notably over whether the Kyoto Treaty limiting greenhouse gas emissions should be ratified.

Events following the terrorist attacks introduced new divisions in the democratic world. Virtually all the democracies supported American actions during the first stages of the war against terrorism in Afghanistan. Soon thereafter, disagreements began to appear, starting with widespread opposition, for instance, to the detention of prisoners at the U.S. naval base at Guantanamo Bay in Cuba. More importantly, France and Germany vocally opposed and joined Russia and China to deny American hopes to gain United Nations approval for its 2003 invasion of Iraq. The divisions began to heal once the United States found it needed the support of all of its allies as a result of the rising human and economic costs of its occupation of Iraq.

AFP/CORBIS

Foreign Minister Dominique de Villepin of France, one of the leading critics of U.S. policy during the preparation for the 2003 invasion of Iraq.

Globalization and the Liberal Democracies

THE LIBERAL DEMOCRACIES are the strongest states in the world—especially the larger ones discussed in the chapters that follow. In this sense, the figure on the inside front cover could well have been drawn with arrows "out" from them to reflect the way that they can shape global forces, especially on geopolitical or military issues.

But these countries still are affected by global forces in at least three key respects. First, their strengths are as much a function of their wealth and the clout wielded by their corporations as of their states. Second, despite that strength, international forces limit their ability to set and, even more so, implement economic policy. This is especially true for the twenty-five members of the EU, which is increasingly responsible for their economic policies. Third, because of their location and the consumption that accompanies their wealth, they are among the regions of the world most affected by environmental decay

How the future of Iraq and other international crises will affect the democracies is anybody's guess. At least one thing is clear, however. Foreign policy can no longer be excluded from the study of comparative politics, as it has been for most of the field's history. What happens outside a country's borders and how it, in turn, responds to those events, are simply too important for us to ignore. Foreign policy remains the focus of another part of political science—international relations. But with events like 9/11 and broader, long-term trends such as globalization, international relations in general and foreign policy in particular have "forced their way" onto the agenda of comparative politics.

Feedback

Although the term never appears in the classic texts, feedback has always been a key element of democratic theory. Given the importance of feedback, it is surprising how little research has been done on it. Nonetheless, it does seem safe to reach two conclusions about it.

First, for some people, it is getting ever easier to find out about politics at home and abroad. The telecommunications revolution has brought the world's news to our homes and has done so instantaneously. Some people argue that the television networks and even venerable newspapers such as the *New York Times* or the *Times* of London have "dumbed down" and are nowhere near as informative as they used to be. Nonetheless, people who are interested now have access to far more information. CNN is on twenty-four hours a day. You can buy the *New York Times* almost anyplace in the United States. Many people who spend a lot of time online now suffer from information overload because they can access most of the world's major newspapers, news services, and other material on the Internet.

Second, people view the world in their own terms, which may be quite different from those of either the politicians or the media moguls. For most people, one of those terms seems to be disinterest in what happens outside of their own country or region. It is no accident that American television news executives run longer local news programs than national newscasts and include less and less international news on their evening broadcasts. More and more people are tuning the political world out altogether. To some degree, this reflects what many feel is the cynical coverage by the media themselves, which has turned off millions. It may also partially be the result of the fact that, with the cable and satellite revolution, we can now watch reruns of *Seinfeld,* a soccer game from Spain, or the *Jerry Springer Show* instead of the news. But most of all, the declining interest has less to do with the media than with the general cynicism about and skepticism toward politics and politicians. In short, it probably isn't the messenger, but the message that is the problem.

Conclusion: The Worst Form of Government Except for All the Others?

Given what we have seen, it is hard not to agree with the first half of Winston Churchill's statement that begins this chapter. The industrialized democracies have obviously accomplished a lot. But, just as obviously, they face serious problems, some of which, at least, seem to be insurmountable.

The second half of the statement may be true as well, though you will have to take it as a leap of faith until you learn more about the countries covered in Parts 3 and 4. From that perspective, however serious as democracy's problems may be, they pale in comparison with those in the rest of the world.

In uneven and imperfect ways, democratic regimes achieve a series of balances better than any other type of government, at least over the long haul:

- Between the governors and the governed
- Between the political world and the rest of society
- Between unbridled capitalism and the interests of those who do not benefit (much) from it
- Between personal freedoms and the need to maintain order and forge coherent public policy

Key Terms

Concepts

Bureaucracy	Liberal
Cabinet responsibility	Member of parliament
Catch-all	Nationalization
Civic culture	Political party
Civil society	Postindustrial society
Cleavage	Postmaterialism
Coalition	Privatization
Democracy	Proportional representation
Electoral system	Radical
Fascism	Realignment
Integrated elite	Right
Interest group	Rule of law
Interventionist state	Single-member district
Iron triangle	Social democracy
Laissez-faire	Suffrage
Left	Vote of confidence
Legitimacy	

People

Hobbes, Thomas
Locke, John

Acronyms

MP

Organizations, Places, and Events

Christian Democratic parties
Communist parties
Greens

Critical Thinking Exercises

1 Much has changed in the democratic countries since this book was finished in early 2005. Does the analysis of democratic politics presented here still make sense? In what ways? Why (not)?

2 Public opinion pollsters routinely ask questions about whether people think the country is headed in the "right direction" or is "on the wrong track." If you were asked such a question about politics in the democratic countries as a whole, what would your answer be? Why did you reach that conclusion?

3 What are the main differences between presidential and parliamentary versions of democracy? What implications do those differences have for both policy making and democracy itself?

4 How did the "great transformation" of Western history help shape democracy?

5 How are the social and economic changes in these countries and in the world as a whole affecting the nature of and prospects for democracy?

6 What is postmaterialism? How important do you think it is for democracy today? Why do you reach this conclusion?

Useful Websites

There actually are not all that many websites that deal with democracy per se. That's partly because theorists do not use the Internet as comparativists do. It's also because few comparativists study all the democracies as a whole. Nonetheless, there are a few sites that can help sharpen your understanding of the ideas behind and the realities of democracy today.

The U.S. State Department has an excellent site that explores many of the issues raised in this chapter. Political Resources is a wonderful source for material on individual countries, while Election World has the most recent election results from every country in the world.

> **hypatia.ss.uci.edu/democ**
>
> **www.ned.org**
>
> **usinfo.state.gov/products/pubs/whatsdem**
>
> **www.politicalresources.net**
>
> **www.electionworld.org**

InfoTrac College Edition Sources

Barber, Benjamin. "Globalizing Democracy."

Bennet, W. Land. "The Uncivic Culture."

Clark, Elizabeth. "Why Elections Matter."

Dalpino, Catharin. "Does Globalization Promote Democracy?"

Dionne, E. J. "Why Civil Society? Why Now?"

Green, Daniel M. "Liberal Movements and Democracy's Durability."

Lovell, David. "Liberal Democracy and Its Critics."

Madeley, John T. S. "European Liberal Democracy and the Principle of State Religious Neutrality."

Putnam, Robert. "Bowling Together."

Scheuerman, William. "Liberal Democracy and the Empire of Speed."

Zakaria, Fareed. "The Rise of Illiberal Democracy."

Further Reading

Almond, Gabriel, and Sidney Verba. *The Civic Culture.* Princeton, N.J.: Princeton University Press, 1962; and Almond and Verba, eds., *The Civic Culture Revisited.* Boston: Little, Brown, 1979. The two best books on civic culture. They do, however, probably take the argument about the importance of culture a bit too far.

Barber, Benjamin. *Strong Democracy: Participatory Politics for a New Age.* Berkeley: University of California Press, 1984. A theoretical look at how to enhance participation to enhance democracy.

Dahl, Robert. *On Democracy.* New Haven, Conn.: Yale University Press, 1999. The most recent book by a scholar who has been studying what makes democracy "work" since the 1950s.

Fukuyama, Francis. *Trust: The Social Virtues and the Creation of Prosperity.* New York: Free Press, 1995. A good job of reinforcing the importance of culture, political and otherwise. By one of the most controversial and conservative analysts of the day, though many observers find his works overstated.

Held, David. *Democracy and the Global Order.* Oxford, U.K.: Polity Press, 1995. An argument that we have to rethink democracy in the light of globalization and other recent trends by a British theorist who is close to Tony Blair and his "third way." Not an easy read, but worth it.

Macpherson, C. B. *The Life and Times of Liberal Democracy.* New York: Oxford University Press, 1977. Like Dahl's work, a classic analysis of the way democracies work, though written from a more left-wing and democratic perspective.

Norris, Pippa, ed. *Critical Citizens: Global Support for Democratic Governance.* New York: Oxford University Press, 1999. An excellent collection of articles on the degree to which support for the regime holds in a number of democracies.

Putnam, Robert D. *Making Democracy Work.* Princeton, N.J.: Princeton University Press, 1993. Ostensibly only about Italy, a controversial book that provides the best recent analysis of the role of "social capital" and political culture in general.

Zakaria, Fareed. *The Future of Freedom.* New York: W.W. Norton, 2003. A thoughtful book about liberal as well as what he calls illiberal democracies. Worth considering for most of the countries covered in the rest of the book.

Perhaps the most striking feature of the recent political history of the United States is the stability of its basic institutions despite the stress of assassinations, war, racial strife, political scandal, and economic dislocation.

ALAN ABRAMOWITZ

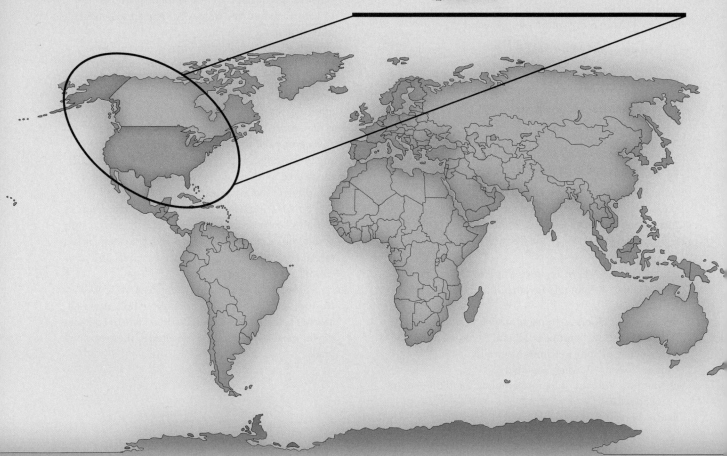

Chapter 3

THE UNITED STATES

CHAPTER OUTLINE

The Basics: The United States

Size	9,158,960 sq. km
Population	278,000,000
GNP per capita	$35,060
Ethnic composition	77.1% white, 12.9% black, 4.2% Asian, 1.5% Native American, 4.3% Other. (Note: The United States does not keep separate statistics on Hispanic-Americans, who can be of any race.)
Religion	56% Protestant, 28% Roman Catholic, 2% Jewish, 4% other, 10% none
Capital	Washington, D.C.
Head of state	President George W. Bush (2001–)

A More Normal Election

The United States experienced one of its closest and most controversial elections in 2000. The vote count dragged on well into the early morning hours after the election. Gradually, the exit pollsters called one state after another.

It all came down to Florida. Reports of voting irregularities had surfaced even before the polls closed. Early on, the pollsters "gave" the state to Vice President Al Gore. But around midnight it became clear that the state was too close to call. By 3 a.m. eastern time, George W. Bush led by more than 50,000 votes, with so few votes outstanding that he seemed to have a lock on the state. In fact, Vice President Gore called the Texas governor to concede the election.

But then, something remarkable happened. Almost every remaining vote came in for Gore. He retracted his concession. The battle had just begun, because whoever won Florida won the election. After more than a month of lawsuits, recounts, and ballots being shipped around the state, the U.S. Supreme Court finally stepped in to block Gore's last challenges, handing the election to Bush by well under a thousand votes.

Needless to say, the 2000 election was a traumatic event for most Americans, who were used to calm, tranquil voting, after which it was clear who had won and lost. Therefore, many deeply desired the 2004 contest to run more smoothly.

It did. Sort of.

If anything, the campaign was nastier than the one four years earlier. President Bush and his challenger, Massachusetts senator John Kerry, hurled personal and political potshots at one another, many of which referred to what each had done thirty-five years earlier during the Vietnam era. Indeed, the 2004 campaign may have been the most divisive and most expensive in American history.

But this time the results were clearer, according to most people. Turnout was higher than in any election in the last half century. It was particularly high in Ohio, which also had a referendum on gay marriage on the ballot. In the college town of Oberlin, for instance, the polls had to stay open until 11 p.m. to accommodate everyone who had showed up to vote three hours earlier. Victory or defeat in the electoral college came down to who won Ohio.

In the end, Bush won Ohio by more than two hundred thousand votes and won the total popular vote by just over 51 percent. Republicans also expanded their control of both the Senate and the House of Representatives.

Still, as in 2000, the United States was split right down the middle. Pundits talked about red and blue states, referring to the colors television analysts used on their maps on election night. Polls showed that a large number of Americans deeply disagreed on issues such as abortion, gun control, the war on terrorism, the economy, the role of religion in public life, and more.

In short, American politics was nasty during and after the 2000 election and it remained so four years later. But, as we will see in the rest of this chapter and the four that follow, democracy was not in jeopardy.

A bleary-eyed ballot counter in Broward County trying to determine how someone has voted.

AP/Wide World Photos

Thinking about the United States

If the first four editions are any indication, the vast majority of this book's readers will be Americans. Consciously or not, most of you will therefore use the United States as your intellectual starting point in analyzing the countries and concepts covered here.

There is nothing wrong with that if you keep one thing in mind. Political life in the United States is by no means the norm. In other words, to use the United States effectively as a frame of reference, you need first to take into account the ways in which it is different from other countries.

Readers who do not come from the United States would find its exclusion from a course and book on comparative politics perplexing. After all, the United States has long been the world's most powerful and affluent country. And for many, it has also become the most controversial given the way it has exercised its power in recent years.

This chapter on the United States is designed to meet the needs of both sets of readers. It is not as detailed as any of the chapters on the countries that follow. Since I assume that even non-American readers are reasonably familiar with the basics of American political life, my goal is to highlight the features that make American politics unusual, many of which would not be stressed in a course or a book that focuses on the United States alone.

In short, this chapter focuses on what academics call "American exceptionalism." All countries, of course, are unique. However, the United States is so different from most other countries in so many ways that it is, again, critical to underscore the peculiarities of its political life.

The United States has a **federal** system, in which the national government shares power with states, cities, counties, and other jurisdictions. In this case, states are responsible for determining how elections are held and votes counted. Washington only gets involved in setting some basic parameters, such as the requirement that presidential and congressional elections have to be held on the first Tuesday after the first Monday in November and that civil rights and other laws are upheld.

At the national level, the United States has a strong system of **checks and balances,** formally known as the **separation of powers.** The legislative, executive, and judicial branches all have unique powers, but rarely can one of them act on its own without oversight and approval from at least one of the others. That did happen in 2000 in Florida because the Supreme Court did not have to consult either the White House or Congress before issuing its decision that gave George W. Bush the presidency. On most policy matters, however, at least two of the three branches must reach an agreement.

That is one of the reasons most comparativists argue that the United States has a weak state. That might seem absurd at first glance, since the United States is so wealthy and exerts so much power on the world stage. However, the founders intentionally created a system that required politicians to compromise on almost every issue and that makes it hard for them to act in a rapid and decisive manner. As we will see, that also means that it is hard for American politicians to enact coherent policies that systematically address pressing social and economic issues.

The United States has also had an unusual history that spawned a distinctive political culture that, in comparative terms, grew out of a history in which political change has occurred gradually and incrementally. In particular, that culture includes widespread acceptance of the political "rules of the game." To be sure, the United States has had, and continues to have, its share of protest, including those over the way the 2000 election was conducted in Florida. However, virtually no one believes that the irregularities in the vote and the ambiguities in the recount rules require profound changes in the way the country is governed. Tom Brokaw put this well at 3:30 a.m. when NBC News went off the air after it seemed that Bush had finally won: "After months of bitter campaigning and a long night of partisan rhetoric, Americans can go to sleep comfortably because, unlike many other countries, we hold our elections with no need for tanks or even the police to keep order in the streets."

The Wrong Name

I have already misused the word "American" several times.

We in the United States use it as a shorthand word to describe our country and ourselves. We should not do so, since Canadians, Mexicans, Brazilians, Peruvians, and more are Americans, too.

Alas, our version of English has evolved in such a way that it is the only viable term we have to describe ourselves.

That, in turn, leads to two characteristics the United States shares at least with the other industrialized democracies. The first is a decline in civic engagement, not just in politics but in churches, community organizations, interest groups, and all the other bodies that make up **civil society**—and which, Harvard's Robert Putnam argues, are critical for a vibrant democracy.[1] The decline in such involvement has probably not been as great in those other countries as in the United States. Most, too, have not suffered through the same kind of "culture wars" that this country has. Nonetheless, there has been some decrease in trust in politicians and in political involvement in all the industrialized democracies.

That said, the dissatisfaction only goes so far. Chapter 1 drew the distinction between the government and the regime. In the United States and the other industrialized democracies, virtually everyone agrees that it is perfectly legitimate for citizens to criticize incumbent politicians and their policies. However, there is such widespread acceptance of the regime that the constitution and the institutions it created are almost never criticized. In Parts 3 and 4, you will see that one of the main differences between the industrialized democracies and the rest of the world is this powerful acceptance of regimes in the former, the absence of which dramatically raises the political stakes in most of the former Communist and third world countries.

The Making of the American State

American exceptionalism begins with the evolution of its state and the fact that the United States was able to handle the four major transitions dis-

[1] Robert D. Putnam, *Bowling Alone: The Collapse and Revival of American Community* (New York: Simon & Schuster, 2000).

cussed in the previous chapter with *relative* ease. The United States has faced its share of challenges, not all of which it met easily. Compared with those other countries, however, it has faced relatively few divisive issues and has been able to resolve most of those that did arise in ways that enhanced support for the regime, at least in the long run. Also, in comparative terms, the United States has been largely free of outside constraints (www.americanhistory.about.com).

Not everything has come smoothly. "Manifest destiny," or the expansion of the United States from coast to coast, occurred at the expense of the Native American population. North fought South in a civil war that was as bloody as any conflict ever up to that point. Industrialization was wrenching, too, especially for the waves of immigrants who lived in slums and worked in sweatshops.

Nonetheless, compared to most countries, the United States was fortunate, which is why the word "relative" is emphasized in the first sentence of this section. Only Britain established democratic institutions as smoothly, but that country was left with far more class conflict. No other regime enjoyed the wealth, power, and political support that allowed the United States to become the world's first superpower after World War II. (See table 3.1.)

By the early nineteenth century, rough agreement had been reached on the structure of the federal government and the strict separation of church and state. That consensus had its limits. The emerging democratic institutions did not allow women or African Americans to vote, except for a handful of freed slaves in the North. Moreover, the very existence of the republic was put in jeopardy by the Civil War, which, we often forget, the Confederacy nearly won. But, in a way, even the Civil War underscores the main point in this section. The states that seceded did not object to the type of state that had then been in existence for almost three quarters of a cen-

▍ TABLE 3.1 Key Turning Points in U.S. History

YEAR	EVENT
1781	Victory over the British in the Revolutionary War
1787	Constitutional Convention
1861–65	Civil War
1890	Passage of first antitrust act
1917	Entrance into World War I
1933	Beginning of the New Deal
1941	Entrance into World War II
1945	End of World War II; start of cold war
1964	Start of the "Great Society"

tury. Indeed, the one they created was more like the one they left than any other state in the world at the time.

The Constitutional Order

The most important event in the creation of what Seymour Martin Lipset once called the first new nation was the adoption of the Constitution in 1787 (the constitutions of the countries covered in this book are included on its companion website). Events before then certainly were important. However, given this chapter's goal of giving you a frame of reference, the critical starting point is the widespread acceptance of this document, which continues to shape American political institutions and culture to this day.

At the time, the new United States was in trouble. In the years after the Declaration of Independence was signed, the new country used the Articles of Confederation, which vested almost all power in the states. That should not be surprising, given that the thirteen colonies had staked their claim to independence on what they saw as the unjust, centralized, and arbitrary rule by King George III's England.

Quickly, however, the new country had to deal with problems that threatened to tear it apart. States imposed tariffs on each other that all but brought interstate trade to a halt. In every state, rural and urban interests—or factions as they were known—clashed, often violently.

By 1787 the state legislatures recognized that the situation had gotten out of hand and sent delegates to Philadelphia to amend the Articles. But they soon concluded that they could not solve the new country's problems by amending the Articles and so set out to create a new form of government altogether. The delegates then found themselves grappling with two goals that, according to the conventional wisdom of the time, were incompatible: centralizing power to overcome squabbling and incompetent state governments and continuing to protect against the arbitrary exercise of power. By the end of the summer, however, they had reached a series of momentous compromises and had written the Constitution.

To help persuade the states to ratify the Constitution, James Madison, Alexander Hamilton, and John Jay wrote a defense of the document in the now-famous *Federalist Papers* (www.yale.edu/lawweb/avalon/federal/fed.htm). Along with the diaries Madison kept during that long, hot summer and the Constitution itself, the Papers provide the key principles that remain at the heart of American politics to this day.

Of particular importance was the founders' novel

approach to what Madison called "the evils of faction" in *Federalist* #10. He argued that there was no way to avoid factions, as most democratic theorists of the time had hoped. From his perspective, they were a natural and inevitable outgrowth of an open society. The evils arose only in small units in which one group could dominate, leading to what Alexis de Tocqueville would call the "tyranny of the majority" a half-century later. Therefore, the best thing to do was to concentrate power in larger jurisdictions such as the national government. That way, there would be little chance that any single faction could dominate the entire system, obliging the large number of smaller ones to compromise with each other.

To make that happen, the founders created institutions that are radically different from those used in all other industrialized democracies. All the others have adopted a version of the parliamentary system, in which the legislature and executive are fused. (See Chapter 2 for details.) In particular, prime ministers can expect to see their proposed legislation enacted largely intact as long as they maintain a clear majority in parliament.

The American presidential system was designed to work in almost exactly the opposite manner. The founders understood that the United States would need a stronger central government than the Articles of Confederation allowed in order to control the evils of faction. However, they were equally convinced that they also had to find ways to make it as difficult as possible for the people who ran the new state to abuse their power. Instead, they wanted to make compromise and incremental change the normal method of policy making, through what is informally known as the system of checks and balances.

Shortly after the Constitution itself was ratified, Congress and the states passed the first ten amendments, the Bill of Rights, which added formal declaration of basic civil liberties and clarified some of the ambiguities in the relationship between the state and federal governments. For our purposes, the most important were the initial sixteen words of the first amendment, "Congress shall make no law respecting an establishment of religion, or prohibiting the free exercise thereof." Prior to independence, most states had official or established religions. Massachusetts and Connecticut were Puritan, Pennsylvania was Quaker, Maryland was Catholic, and most of the South was Episcopalian. There really was no way to establish a single faith as the official one. So, the framers decided to remove religion from formal political life, all the while guaranteeing "the free exercise thereof." The separation was never complete. Children prayed routinely in schools as recently as the 1950s. Pres-

> ### Democratization in the United States
>
> UNLIKE MANY of the other countries we will be considering, the United States did not consciously engage in democratization. In fact, most of the founders had serious doubts about democracy and the capacity of average people to make intelligent decisions about public life.
>
> Democracy grew as part and parcel of the evolution and conflicts of American political history. To cite but one example of how difficult it was, the Declaration of Independence included the statement that "all men are created equal."
>
> Then, alas, all men did not include African Americans and poor white men who did not have the right to vote or most other political freedoms. It would be a century and a half before "all men" came to include women and another half century before the last racial barriers to formal political participation were removed.
>
> If you listen to some activists for women's, minorities, or gay-lesbian-bisexual-transsexual-queer groups, we still may have a ways to go.

ident Bush's Faith-Based Initiative (to be discussed later in the chapter) was one of the most controversial bills sent to Congress during his first year in office. And to this day, more Americans practice their faith on a regular basis than in any other country in the industrialized world. Nonetheless, disputes over the relationship between church and state never had any real chance of undermining the regime created by the framers well over two hundred years ago.

Since the Founders

Even more unusual and remarkable than these ideas themselves is the fact that they continue to be the dominant ones in American political life more than two centuries later. A brief examination of some historical trends that have shaped both the continuity of and changes in the American system reveals that staying power.

The biggest crisis the United States has ever faced was the Civil War. After decades of grudging compromise over slavery and related issues, the Southern states no longer felt they could stay in the Union and seceded. For four years, "brother" killed "brother" in a war that ended with the defeat of the Confederacy and the assassination of President Abraham Lincoln.

For our purposes, it is even more important to see how the country rebuilt itself after the war. The North imposed a coercive regime to "reconstruct" the defeated South. Yet, within a decade, the former Confederate states had been readmitted to the Union. And, rather than bearing Washington the resentment many expected, white Southerners became the most patriotic and conservative segment of the population.

In the second half of the nineteenth century, the industrial revolution created tremendous concentrations of wealth and a host of problems in the burgeoning cities with their factories and slums. With these new developments came the first significant demands for an activist or interventionist state. But even here, the American approach was unusual. Rather than enacting extensive welfare programs or taking over industries, the United States passed a series of antitrust laws designed to break up monopolies and oligopolies. The goal then—and now—was to use government as a last resort and to emphasize the preservation of competitive markets with minimal government intervention.

Much the same can be said for policies toward the poor. The United States did adopt substantial social service and welfare programs as part of Franklin Roosevelt's New Deal during the Great Depression and of Lyndon Johnson's Great Society in the 1960s. Whatever we may think of those programs, they did mark a dramatic expansion of the American state at both the national and local levels. That should not keep us from seeing that these programs have always been less extensive and been viewed with more skepticism by the public than those in the other liberal democracies.

Perhaps most importantly of all, the United States never developed a powerful socialist party. Eugene Victor Debs did win almost a million votes in two presidential elections during the first two decades of the twentieth century. Other socialists won elections to a handful of local offices. Communists gained a toehold in some parts of the labor union movement during the Great Depression of the 1930s. But in comparative terms, the industrial revolution did not produce the kind of divisions it did in Europe, most notably because of the way the American political culture evolved, the topic we turn to next.

Finally, despite the many twists and turns of American political life, there is far more continuity than one finds in any other major country with the possible exception of Great Britain. Were the founders to rise from their graves today, they would find plenty of surprising and confusing things—television, public opinion polls, tight security at all federal buildings, and more. But their basic institutions and principles, especially the separa-

Economic Liberalization in the United States

THE UNITED STATES has not had to adopt reforms as sweeping as those of the other countries we will be covering to liberalize the economy, because it did not institute as many or as extensive intervention policies in the first place. Economic liberalism and "free market" capitalism developed hand in hand with many of the ideas the founders drew on during the Revolutionary War and the period of Constitution building that followed. Support for the idea that "the government that governs least governs best" has been part of U.S. political culture from the beginning, and most Americans have turned to a more active state only when other approaches to solving problems have failed. And, when Americans have done so, they have kept ideas akin to "curing the evils of faction" in mind and created programs to safeguard against anyone amassing too much power—as shown in America's penchant for antitrust and other antimonopoly legislation. This does not mean that the United States has a small state. It has grown dramatically, especially since the 1930s. However, Americans have always been reluctant to turn to the state and have been loath to give it the power to act quickly or coherently when establishing new public policies. That said, critics of the Bush administration, in particular, worried that its close links to major corporations in energy, telecommunications, and other industries brought the state and private sector dangerously close to each other.

tion and division of powers, remain intact and operate in ways they would easily recognize—and endorse.

The American People and Politics

Those historical patterns are reflected in how American citizens think and act politically today. However, as the global and domestic issues in the bottom row of table 1.2 have come to play a more prominent role, there have recently been some important changes that have both increased pressures "from below" and led to declining support for politicians and some political institutions, but not the regime itself.

The American Political Culture

The echoes of that unusual past are most evident in the American political culture. Systematic research on public opinion only began in the late 1940s. Still, scholars are

convinced that at least three trends in the American political culture can be traced back to the nineteenth century and the origins of the weak state.

First, with the exception of the years just before the
Civil War, no more than a tiny minority of Americans
have questioned the regime based on the Constitution of
1787. Americans do debate issues such as gay marriage
or the 2003 war in Iraq as heatedly as anyone, and, in recent years, distrust of politicians has reached alarming
levels. Yet it is political suicide to advocate rewriting the
Constitution, something the French have done eleven
times since the 1780s.

Second, almost all Americans accept the idea of a
weak state, even those who would like to see it add dramatic and expensive new programs such as a guarantee
of universal medical insurance. Indeed, American students have a hard time believing that most people in Germany or France think that a strong state is a good thing.

Third, **individualism** remains one of the most
widely held beliefs among all major groups in American society. Whatever the real chances of upward mo-
bility might be, most Americans still think anyone can
"make it" through hard work. More so, too, than most
Europeans, Americans are convinced that if someone
"fails" it is his or her fault. Therefore, there is little need
for the government to step in with extensive social service programs even though, as David Shipler has recently
argued, there are thirty-five million people in the United
States who are in poverty despite working on a regular
basis.

The net impact of this has been the paradoxical nature of what Gabriel Almond and Sidney Verba called a
civic culture.[2] Polls conducted since their research was
completed in the late 1950s have shown that Americans
are more convinced than their European or Japanese
counterparts that they could do something about a government action they objected to. Yet, even though plenty
of avenues for political involvement exist, few Americans
actually bother to become activists. To cite but one glaring example, barely half the eligible American population votes in most presidential elections, and only 39 percent turned out for the 1994 Republican congressional
landslide, figures that leave the United States with one of
the lowest turnout rates in the democratic world. Another team of scholars who wrote in the 1950s called this
state of affairs "functional apathy," because it meant that
average citizens put few pressures on their leaders, al-

[2] Gabriel Almond and Sidney Verba, *The Civic Culture: Political Attitudes and Democracy in Five Nations* (Princeton, N.J.:
Princeton University Press, 1963). Also see their *The Civic Culture Revisited* (Boston: Little, Brown, 1979).

▌ TABLE 3.2 Declining Trust in the United States

Question: How much of the time do you think you can trust
the government in Washington to do what is right—just about
always, most of the time, or only some of the time?

YEAR	PERCENT SAYING "ALL OR MOST OF THE TIME"	PERCENT SAYING "SOME OF THE TIME"
1964	76	22
1968	61	36
1972	53	45
1976	33	63
1980	25	73
1984	46	51
1988	44	54
1992	23	75
1996	25	71

Source: Adapted from Steffen W. Schmidt, Mack C. Shelly, and Barbara A.
Bardes, *American Government Today* (Belmont, Calif.: Wadsworth, 1997), 233.

lowing them more leeway to govern than did their equivalents in France or Italy.

The political difficulties of recent decades have
taken their toll on the American political culture. According to every indicator, faith in politicians and involvement in social and political life have declined dramatically. However, as Alan Abramowitz suggests in the
statement that begins this chapter, that dissatisfaction
has not led people to begin questioning the regime under
which they live. (See table 3.2.)

Some observers do worry that the rise of militias and
other extremist groups could be the tip of a much larger
political iceberg. For the moment, at least, they remain
"fringe movements," and fundamental constitutional reform has as little popular support today as ever.

Parties and Elections

As in most countries, the most common form of political participation in the United States is voting in the
most important national elections, those for the presidency and Congress. And as in the case of most of the issues covered in this chapter, Americans act quite differently from their counterparts in the other industrialized
democracies.

Americans are also unusual in their commitment
to the **two-party system** (www.rnc.org and www
.democrats.org). Only two parties have seriously contended for power since the end of the Civil War and Reconstruction. There have been several challenges to the
hegemony of the Democrats and Republicans, the most
recent of which was launched by maverick millionaire
H. Ross Perot in 1992 and 1996. However, one or both of
the main parties eventually adapted enough to undercut
the support of the "third" party that sought to replace it.

President George W. Bush and Senator John Kerry square off at the first presidential debate of the 2004 election campaign, held in September at the University of Miami (FL).

Joe Raedle/Getty Images

Many American political scientists think the United States needs a two-party system to ensure that the government functions smoothly, even though none of the other democratic countries we will be covering in Part 2 have ever had as few as two parties. Whatever the link between the number of parties and the process of government, no other democracy has seen such continuity in its party system.

The United States has had the same two dominant parties since before the Civil War, the Democrats and Republicans. But, before we examine them, it is important to understand that each of them has changed in many ways and at many times since the 1850s.

The Democratic Party is slightly older than the Republicans with a history dating from the 1830s. More often than not, it has tried to present itself as the party that better represents the "little man," beginning from its support for universal suffrage in the nineteenth century, its endorsement of the New Deal and Great Society reforms of the twentieth century, to its advocacy of women's and, to a lesser degree, gay rights in the last generation. The Democrats are more likely to propose expansion of social service programs and tax rates that tend to demand more of richer Americans.

The Democrats have not always been the more progressive or left-wing of the two parties. Most of the Progressives of late nineteenth and early twentieth centuries were Republicans. At that time, the base of Democratic support lay in the largely nonideological and corrupt urban machines that mobilized immigrant voters and the white, segregationist electorate of the "solid South." The New Deal and Great Society reforms of the 1930s and 1960s changed all that. Now, as many as 90 percent of African American voters routinely cast their ballots for Democratic candidates. And, as we will see in a moment, white Southerners, workers, and men disproportionately support the Republican Party.

The Republicans were created when a number of parties that opposed slavery and secession came together in the late 1850s. The first national election it contested under that name was in 1860 and brought Abraham Lincoln to power and served as the catalyst for the outbreak of the Civil War. When the war ended, Republican "carpetbagger" administrations were set up in the occupied Confederate states that went through a difficult period of Reconstruction. Those administrations won in large part because freed slaves voted for them. Most of the white voters became loyal Democrats in opposition to reconstruction. Within a generation, almost all African Americans had lost the vote with the passage of the "Jim Crow" laws establishing segregation in the South, where almost all blacks lived at the time.

The shifts after 1865 restored the party's traditional base of support among upper and middle-class Protestants in the northern half of the country. More often than not, that meant that Republicans supported business interests. At times, however, the elite would support reform as it did in the early twentieth century by pushing for the "good government" policies of the Progressive era, including the use of primary and recall election, merit-based civil service systems, and non-partisan local governments.

The Great Depression that began in 1929 cemented the party's position on the right. Because a Republican, Herbert Hoover, was president when the depression broke out and he did little to improve the state of the economy, the Republicans were blamed for the wretched conditions the country was experiencing. Republicans also opposed most of the progressive reforms initiated during Franklin Roosevelt's first two terms as they would again thirty years later under Lyndon Johnson.

The Republicans made one more ideological turn rightward beginning in the late 1970s with the rise of the "new right," which will be discussed in the section on social movements that follows. Here it is enough to note that with the emergence of Ronald Reagan, George H. W. Bush, and George W. Bush, very few moderate Republicans remain in either the House or Senate outside of the Northeast, having given way to "movement conservatives" who dominate the party's overall leadership.

Today, the two parties have very different regional and social bases. (See table 3.3.) Only about fifteen states and thirty House seats are normally considered to be competitive at most elections. The Democrats normally do best in the industrial Northeast and middle West as well as on the West coast. The Republicans have a virtual stranglehold on most of the South, agricultural Midwest, and the Rocky Mountain states. The Democrats do best among racial minorities and supporters of progressive goals that began to emerge in the 1960s, most notably civil rights and environmental protection. The Democrats also do well among people who consider themselves liberals and among people with qualms about U.S. foreign policy since 9/11. The Republican electorate

▌ TABLE 3.3 The 2004 Election

DEMOGRAPHIC GROUP/ISSUE POSITION	PERCENT VOTING FOR BUSH
Men	55
Women	44
Under 30 years old	45
Over 60 years old	54
White	58
Black	11
Hispanic/Latino	44
White Evangelical or Born-Again Christian	78
Gay, Lesbian, and Bisexual	23
Moral values mattered most	80
The economy or jobs mattered most	18
Terrorism mattered most	86
Health care mattered most	23
Approve of the war in Iraq	85

Source: Results of the 2004 election poll, adapted from *The New York Times*. 4 November 2004, P4.

is a mirror image of the Democrats'. The GOP wins the lion's share of the votes cast by poorer, rural, white, and Christian voters. It has even made huge inroads among working-class voters, who had been one of the most solid groups behind Democrats as recently as the 1960s.

As of this writing, the country is as evenly divided as at any point in recent history. The last three elections were among the closest in memory. In 2000, Gore won a half million more votes than Bush, but lost because of the quirks of the electoral college and the Supreme Court's decision in Florida. In 2002, the Republicans kept control of the House and regained a majority in the Senate, but their victories were wafer thin.

Most observers expected the 2004 race to be as competitive, if not as controversial, as the one in 2000. President Bush entered the campaign with strong support for his handling of the war on terrorism after 9/11, though the American public had significant doubts about the war in Iraq, especially given the insurgency that had broken out after Bush declared the "end to major combat." His domestic policies, however, were not nearly as popular as his war on terrorism, and most polls gave his opponent, Senator John Kerry, an edge on issues such as health care and education.

As in 2000, the race seemed to tighten as the election neared. In the week before the vote, Senator Kerry all but erased Bush's lead in the polls, and did so a few days earlier than Vice President Gore had four years earlier. The last few days of polling showed that Bush had reestablished his lead, but it was clearly going to be another close race.

The initial results leaked from the exit polls suggested that Kerry would win. Once the final results came in, however, it was obviously a Republican night. They won almost every Senate seat that was even somewhat competitive and increased their House majority by a handful of seats as well.

The presidential race was less one-sided. Bush did win the vast majority of the so-called "battleground states" that were deemed the key to victory for either candidate. No one knew who would win, though, until the results from Ohio came in. Turnout there was high. In the college town of Oberlin, so many students showed up at the polls in the early evening that the authorities kept the voting booths open until 11 p.m. In the end, Bush carried Ohio by more than 200,000 votes, probably because of the extremely large showing by evangelical Christians who flocked to the polls to vote in a referendum on gay marriage.

Bush and the Republicans viewed their victory as a mandate. After all, they not only kept the presidency but also strengthened their hold over both houses of Con-

Soccer Moms and NASCAR Dads

Two metaphors have emerged since the 2000 election to represent one core constituency in each of the parties' electorates.

Soccer moms (and dads) are affluent suburbanites. If they have children, they almost certainly play soccer. Soccer moms may have come from Republican families, but the fact that they tend to favor women's rights, environmentalism, and other progressive causes has contributed to the "gender gap" that has been a central feature of American political life for almost a generation.

NASCAR dads (and moms) are the soccer moms' social opposite. They tend to be white, rural, relatively poorly educated, and at most lower middle class (even though tickets for the 2004 Daytona 500 started at $95). Political scientists noted this demographic trend even before the "Reagan Democrats" phenomenon of the 1980s. They only got their NASCAR dads label recently and that was only because of the dramatic upsurge of interest in stock car racing as well as their tendency to support George W. Bush and other conservatives.

President Bush meets with NASCAR team owner Joe Gibbs. After this picture was taken, Gibbs returned to his former job as coach of the Washington Redskins.

AFP/Getty Images

gress. A closer look at the data reminds us that the United States remains deeply divided between what we have come to call "red" (Republican) and "blue" (Democratic) states. It seems unlikely that the Democrats can regain control of either house during this decade. Nonetheless, the president won just slightly more than 51 percent of the popular vote, one of the lowest totals ever for a president successfully seeking reelection.

The exit polls from election day reflect the divisions among Americans (see table 3.3). Men, older voters, evangelical Christians, and whites cast most of their votes for President Bush. Younger people, women, members of minority groups, gays and lesbians, and Jews voted overwhelmingly for Senator Kerry. Eighty-five percent of the people who supported the invasion of Iraq voted for Bush, but only twelve percent of those who opposed the war opted for the president. Attitudes about the state of the economy were almost the same.

Those divisions are increasingly important because of one other trend that has been reshaping the American electorate. For much of American history, voters have had a strong sense of party identification (www.umich .edu/~nes/nesguide/nesguide.htm). This meant that there were only relatively minor shifts in voting patterns from one election to the next because each party had the support of broad, yet distinct, coalitions of loyal voters. Thus, in the half-century following the New Deal, the Democrats won most of the votes from poor people and members of racial and religious minorities, and the Republicans did the same in rural areas and among the more affluent groups in the white community.

Much of that commitment and stability has evaporated since the civil rights movement and the Vietnam War. Party identification and voter turnout rates are both at an all-time low. Swings from one election to the next are bigger and more unpredictable than they used to be. The United States had a divided government during twenty-eight of the forty-one years from 1964 to 2005. In other words, at least one house of Congress was controlled by the Democrats during a Republican presidency, or vice versa. As table 3.4 shows, four of the last eleven presidential elections have featured a "third-party" candidate who won more than 5 percent of the vote.

American political parties have always been weak organizations. Historically that was the case because they were initially set up at the state level, and the center of gravity remained there well into the twentieth century. The United States is also the only major democracy in which the party organization is not primarily responsible for choosing its own nominees for office, especially for the highest office in the land. Instead, almost every state

■ TABLE 3.4 Recent Presidential Elections in the United States (Percentage of the Popular Vote)

YEAR	DEMOCRAT	REPUBLICAN	MAJOR INDEPENDENTS
1964	61.1	38.5	–
1968	42.7	43.3	13.5
1972	37.3	61.3	1.4
1976	50.1	48.8	1.0
1980	41.0	51.0	7.0
1984	40.8	59.2	–
1988	46.0	54.0	–
1992	43.2	37.7	19.0
1996	49.2	42.8	8.0
2000	48.3	48.1	3.6
2004	48.0	51.0	1.0

Democrats: Johnson 1964, Humphrey 1968, McGovern 1972, Carter 1976 and 1980, Mondale 1984, Dukakis 1988, Clinton 1992 and 1996, Gore 2000, Kerry 2004

Republicans: Goldwater 1964, Nixon 1968 and 1972, Ford 1976, Reagan 1980 and 1984, G. H. Bush 1988 and 1992, Dole 1996, G. W. Bush 2000 and 2004

Major independents: Wallace 1968, Schmitz 1972, McCarthy 1976, Anderson 1980, Perot 1992 and 1996, Nader 2000 and 2004

now uses primary elections, some of which are open to voters who are not even registered with one or another of the parties. What's more, once a new presidential nominee is chosen, he (so far they have all been men) takes all but total control of the party. Perhaps most importantly of all, the role of the media and of money in U.S. elections have turned the Democrats and the Republicans into the most catch-all of parties (see Chapter 2) in the world. Each election year, candidate images, sound bites on the news, and negative television ads seem to have a greater and greater impact on the way elections turn out.

Social Movements

There has also been a marked upsurge in protest and other "demanding" activity on the part of increasingly sullen elements of the public. Much of this activity takes place outside the traditional network of interest groups and political parties. In both the United States and the other industrialized democracies discussed in Part 2, three trends stand out.

The first was the emergence on the political scene of the **new left** in the 1960s. As in most liberal democracies, the "old left" consisted of voters and parties that sought more economic equality and protection for the interests of the poor. The new left added new issues, most notably the promotion of civil rights and opposition to the Vietnam War. Soon, other issues captured the attention of a core of mostly young activists, including the environ-

ment, feminism, and gay and lesbian rights. Throughout the industrialized world, these activists found broad support, some of which came from parts of the middle class that had never been associated with the left before.

By the early 1970s, however, support for the protest movements began to ebb. The new left itself has largely disappeared from the headlines. It remains important today primarily due to the "gender gap" and "soccer mom" phenomena that have left the Democrats with a huge lead among women because of the party's support for abortion rights, affirmative action, and other legacies of the 1960s. We also see it from time to time in the small but often violent protests against globalization and American foreign policy initiatives since 9/11.

Second, a **new right** has supplanted the new left as the most powerful dissenting force in American politics (though the same is not true in most of Europe). It is far more diverse than its left-wing equivalent ever was. Its most visible advocates are drawn from the roughly 20 percent of the population who consider themselves fundamentalist or evangelical Christians. It includes, as well, people who oppose legalized abortion, multicultural education, higher taxes, and the undermining of what they see as traditional American values.

Politically, the most important component of the American new right so far has been the "Reagan Democrats," who voted Republican during the 1980s and who have stayed with that party. These are mostly white, working-class men and women, whose parents and grandparents were at the heart of the New Deal Democratic coalition. Turned off by the new left and frightened by their own prospects in a rapidly changing economy, they initially drifted to the Republicans to vote for Richard Nixon and, of course, Ronald Reagan. They made up the lion's share of the "angry white men" who gained notoriety in the aftermath of the 1994 midterm congressional elections.

Third, there has been a groundswell of anger in American politics, as reflected in the spread of NIMBY (Not In My Back Yard) opposition to the location of unpopular facilities. In the Washington, D.C., area, opposition from people who lived near planned transportation projects has killed almost all of them with the net effect of worsening a traffic flow that is so bad that the *Washington Post* has a column three times a week called "Dr. Gridlock."

Although historians have a hard time quantifying such things, it does seem that the American people in general are placing more demands on their state than ever before. And this is occurring at a time, as we will soon see, when the state is having unprecedented diffi-

Conflict in American Politics

Examining political conflict in the United States is an ideal way to reveal the critical distinction between the government of the day and the regime.

The United States has seen major protest movements for civil rights for racial minorities, women, and gays on the left, and against abortion on the right. Although most of those efforts have been nonviolent, the United States is hardly immune from confrontation. Moreover, some of the individuals and organizers themselves have opted for violence as a strategy, as the Weathermen faction of the Students for a Democratic Society did in the 1960s and as a small number of antiabortion activists have done more recently in bombing clinics and killing doctors.

However widespread the confrontational and violent protests may be, the protesters rarely question the legitimacy of the regime set up by the founders over two hundred years ago. To be sure, some groups, such as the militias, advocate radical change in the constitutional framework. But there are few such people, and they have virtually no support in the population as a whole.

---

culties in responding to them. This may be the case even if, as some scholars suggest, overall rates of political participation in the population as a whole are going down.

These new trends regarding parties, voting, and social movements are one area in which Americans seem rather like their counterparts in other countries. To be sure, Vietnam was a more contentious issue in the United States than it was elsewhere. Similarly, of all the countries covered in Part 2, only the United States has seen the emergence of a religious right and the "culture wars" that have come in its wake. And, of course, Al Sharpton, Jerry Falwell, Rush Limbaugh, and Jane Fonda are quintessentially American figures. However, they have their equivalents in all the other countries covered in Part 2, and these broader shifts in the political tectonic plates are having the same unsettling effects everywhere.

The Weak American State

As discussed in Chapter 2, the United States has one of the weakest states of any of the industrialized democracies. Statements like that tend to confuse nonacademic observers, left and right alike. After all, with the collapse of the Soviet Union, the United States is the world's only superpower, which exerts its influence, seemingly, wherever and whenever it wants to.

This does not mean that the United States has a strong state for the kinds of domestic issues comparativists are most interested in. Compared with the other liberal democracies, the U.S. government has taken on fewer social and economic responsibilities. And it usually takes more time and is generally less effective than those other governments when it does act.

This weakness is no accident. It is, instead, a consequence of the system the founders created in 1787. As we saw earlier, they created a state in which multiple, overlapping levels of authority prevent any one person, group, or party from getting everything it wants and force all actors to seek compromise solutions to their problems.

The Legislative Process

To see the weakness of the American state, start by considering the way Richard Neustadt began his pathbreaking book on presidential power:

> **In the early summer of 1952, before the heat of the campaign, President Truman used to contemplate the problems of the general-become-president should Eisenhower win the forthcoming election. "He'll sit here," Truman would remark (tapping his desk for emphasis), "and he'll say, 'Do this! Do that!' And nothing will happen. Poor Ike—it won't be a bit like the Army. He'll find it very frustrating." Eisenhower evidently found it so.**[3]

Neustadt went on to show that there are very few things a president can make happen automatically. Rather, a president possesses the "power to persuade."

The president has to do more persuading than most democratic leaders because the rather fragmented American political institutions deny him the tools that facilitate executive leadership in parliamentary systems. Instead, the president is merely the most important person in a complex decision-making process. Along the way, decisions are made at many points, and the men and women involved have no compelling reason to go along with what the president wants.

Compared with other democratic heads of state, the president often has problems within his own administration. He makes over four thousand appointments to policy-making positions. By contrast, the British prime minister has barely a hundred political jobs to fill and is thus far more dependent on career civil servants. At first glance, this would seem to make the president extremely

---

[3] Richard Neustadt, *Presidential Power: The Politics of Leadership* (New York: Wiley, 1960), 9.

powerful. But if we probe just a little deeper, it is easy to see that having so many political appointees can be a mixed blessing.

To begin with, merely finding people to fill those positions is difficult and time consuming. A number of appointments go to people who are rewarded for political service to the president and his party. But many of them know little about the policy areas they will be working in—certainly less than their civil servant counterparts in France or Germany.

In short, the president has something decidedly less than a unified team working for him. Coordinating an administration and its policies is made all the more difficult by the fact that lines of authority are not clearly drawn. For example, three different departments and two agencies—the Departments of Defense, State, and Energy, and the CIA and the Arms Control and Disarmament Agency—have direct responsibility for developing policy to stop the proliferation of nuclear weapons. The Department of Commerce is also indirectly involved because it promotes American exports, including some technologies that could be used in a nuclear weapons program. Perhaps most telling of all, the creation of a single Department of Homeland Security required the merger of dozens of agencies housed in several different departments, ranging from Defense to the Treasury.

Once the executive branch reaches an agreement on proposed legislation, it has to overcome a far more imposing hurdle—Congress. It is in the interplay between legislators and the president that manifestations of the founders' fear of strong government are easiest to see.

The roots of congressional power lie in the multiple, independent decision-making points outlined in figure 3.1 (thomas.loc.gov). When a bill is submitted, it goes through a ceremonial "first reading" and is sent to the appropriate standing committees (and their subcommittees) of the Senate and House of Representatives, where most of the real work on a bill gets done. Many members of Congress serve on committees that deal with issues they know a lot about or that directly affect their districts. More importantly, the committees and subcommittees have large staffs with expertise on the subjects under their jurisdiction.

The first thing the committee has to do is decide whether to consider the bill. If it chooses not to, the bill dies. If it takes a bill on, it begins by doing research that often includes extensive hearings, some of which are televised on C-SPAN. If the president is lucky, the committee then "marks up" the bill. This is not, as the words may suggest, merely an editorial task. More often than not, major portions of the proposed legislation are eliminated and replaced with entirely new provisions. If the

FIGURE 3.1 The President and Congress

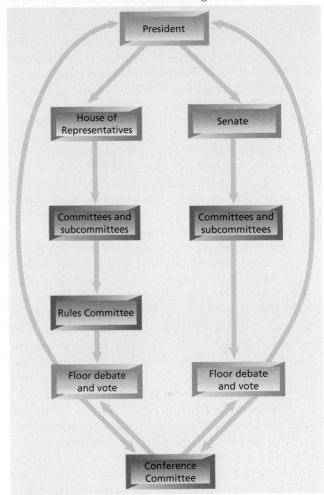

president is unlucky, the committee or subcommittee either declines to consider the bill or votes it down, both of which kill it.

The same thing can happen to the bill when and if it reaches the full House and Senate after favorable committee "reports." Once again, amendments can be made, and once again, a negative vote can kill it outright. The latter is what happened to the Clinton administration's health care initiative in 1994.

The House and Senate almost never pass identical versions of a bill. Therefore, if each passes a different version of the bill, those documents go to a conference committee of members from both houses whose job is to "iron out" the differences between the two. When and if the conference committee reaches an agreement, the bill is returned to both houses, either of which has another opportunity to kill it.

In principle, the same thing can happen in a parliamentary system. All have committees, floor debates, and votes, and parliamentary approval is required for most policy initiatives. The key difference between the United States and the other industrialized democracies is the degree of party discipline in the latter. A British prime minister can be all but certain that colleagues in the House of Commons from his or her party will support the government's proposed legislation. Because prime ministers can count on that majority, legislative programs are passed without any significant changes or delay.

However, American members of Congress do not have to vote along party lines. Research over the past forty years has uncovered five main factors that shape the way members vote. Some reflect the levers presidents have at their disposal. On balance, however, they show why presidents so rarely get what they want.

The first, of course, is the president. The White House Congressional Liaison Office regularly lobbies on Capitol Hill. Whenever a bill the president is especially interested in nears a final vote that might be close, the nightly news shows a parade of senators and representatives visiting the White House. The president cannot force members of the House or Senate to support him. What he can do, however, is to refuse to offer his own support for the members on other issues or even threaten to work to defeat them at the next election.

Second is the party, though it is by no means the most important factor as it is in parliamentary systems. Both parties have "whips" who try to convince members to vote the way the leadership wants. Toeing the line can help advance a member's career and can even bring leadership support for a bill he or she is interested in. Nonetheless, on almost every piece of legislation, a substantial number of representatives and senators do break ranks.

Third are the members' peers. No senator or representative can keep up with all the legislation pending before Congress. So, especially on matters of little interest to themselves or their constituents, they often defer to their colleagues who are experts or to those whose constituents would be affected.

Fourth is what the members' constituents want. All of them use their extensive staffs to keep track of constituent mail, the press back home, and other evidence of where voters stand on the issues. Many conduct polls. Even with all this information, members can never tell exactly what their constituents want, and some critics suggest that they tend to listen not so much to the population as a whole as to the people who donated the most money to their election campaigns. Still, there is an important link between member and constituency. Voters are not likely to elect someone who does not share community views about important local issues in the first

The United States and HIV/AIDS

As I noted in Chapter 1, each chapter will include a box on how that particular country has responded to HIV/AIDS both because the issue itself is important and because it often tells us a lot about broader political dynamics in that country.

The United States faced the AIDS epidemic earlier than most other countries. It also dealt with it in its early years primarily as a disease affecting gay men, which made it controversial indeed.

But, as the disease spread to reach most segments of the population and as American health care providers found ways to mute its effects for a decade or more, HIV/AIDS lost its place on the center of the domestic political stage.

It resurfaced as an important and divisive issue in American foreign policy shortly after George W. Bush took office in 2001. The administration pledged to add $15 billion over five years to total U.S. spending to help at least twelve of the world's poorest countries deal with the epidemic of HIV/AIDS (www.whitehouse.gov/infocus/hivaids/), a figure that was a marked increase over what the Clinton administration had done. Yet it was a controversial approach for two reasons. First, it bypassed the Global Fund to Fight AIDS, Tuberculosis, and Malaria (www.theglobalfund.org/en/). Second, it split the American AIDS community in two along what are known as ABC lines. Bush supporters pushed for programs that supported (A) abstinence from sex and (B) being faithful to your partner. Their opponents emphasized (C) providing condoms and other ways of preventing HIV infection.

place. And members tend to keep the people back home happy both by voting the "right way" and by providing services to their communities and constituents. As a result, although Congress as an institution may not be highly respected, individual members who choose to run are almost always reelected. Even in the anti-incumbent climate of 1994, over 90 percent of the incumbents who ran were reelected.

Finally, there are the members' own views. Americans expect senators and representatives to exercise their judgment at least on matters that are not extremely important locally. There are, however, some examples of members voting their conscience against their constituents' wishes—as, for example, the late Senator William Fulbright (D-Ark.) did in supporting civil rights legislation during the 1960s. The most obvious recent example is Senate Majority Leader Bill Frist (R-Tenn). Frist comes

On 22 May 2003, President Bush signed legislation authorizing up to $15 billion in additional funding to fight HIV/AIDS. With him are Rep. Tom Lantos (D–CA) and Sen. Bill Frist (R–TN)—the key legislative sponsors of the bill—and Secretary of State Colin Powell and Secretary of Health and Human Services Tommy Thompson. www.whitehouse.gov/infocus/hivaids/

Susan Walsh/AP/Wide World Photos

from a long family history of doctors and has emphasized health care as long as he has been in public life—he even carries his medical bag with him, which he has used to help people cope with emergencies on a number of occasions.

Americans derive some important benefits from a Congress whose members are willing and able to reshape legislation initiated by the executive. Constituency interests are considered far more in the United States than they are in parliamentary systems. Congress also provides far more effective protection against the abuse of power by the executive. But, as all those diverse forces enter into the process, whatever coherence there was in the original bill typically is sacrificed.

In other words, the American state usually cannot act either quickly or coherently even during those increasingly rare times when the White House and Capitol Hill are controlled by the same party. Instead, policy making tends to be slow and characterized by **incrementalism,** or limited, marginal, or minor changes. It is hard to see how it could be otherwise. There are simply too many decision-making points, and a group only has to win at one of them to block change.

This was true even in the aftermath of 9/11, when American politicians and citizens alike were more united than they had been in years. President Bush, for in-

stance, had to make a major compromise and agree that security officers at airports would become federal employees in order to get his airline security bill passed. And even though there was widespread agreement that the attacks and the recession that set in at about the same time required additional government spending, Congress adjourned that December without passing an economic stimulus package.

The Rest of the Weak State

The relationship between Congress and the presidency contributes more than anything else to making the American state weak. However, there are at least three other factors that make it weak and thus deserve our attention in passing.

First is the bureaucracy. Recall that the president appoints about four thousand people to policy-making and administrative positions. Some of them are experts in their field and have a wealth of experience inside and outside of government service. However, well trained or not, presidential appointees have to rely on senior civil servants to provide the technical expertise needed to draft most laws. Typically, civil servants who make it to the top of the government bureaucracy are experts in their fields, and because they retain their jobs from administration to administration, they provide a degree of continuity political appointees cannot. Recent research has shown that members of the Senior Executive Service are as well trained and hardworking as their European counterparts, who play a much more central role in policy formation. There, high-level civil servants are among the most respected people in the country, and there is widespread support for their involvement in policy making. However, the American bureaucrats are not widely respected in a culture that views government in general and civil servants in particular with disdain.

Second, the United States is rare in giving its courts wide-ranging powers of **judicial review.** The Supreme Court and lower federal and state courts can rule on the constitutionality of government actions. Judicial decisions and interpretations have often marked important turning points in the evolution of American public policy. The most striking examples in recent years have to do with civil rights. It was a Supreme Court decision (*Plessy v. Ferguson*) that initially upheld Southern laws segregating blacks and whites in 1896. Another decision almost sixty years later (*Brown v. Board of Education*) overturned the doctrine of "separate but equal" and also served as a major catalyst for the modern civil rights movement. Beginning in the 1980s, a more conservative Court issued a series of decisions that sharply limited the use of affirmative action (for example, *Adarand v. Peña* in 1995).

Third, the United States is a federal system, which means that Washington shares power with state and local governments. Most other liberal democracies have **unitary states** in which the central government—not the constitution—determines which powers are granted to subnational units. In the United States, state and local governments have more of the responsibility for education policy and have always had a lot of leeway in determining how social services programs are run. Among other things, that makes it difficult for the federal government to impose national standards.

Consensus Policy Making

There is one new policy-making arena in which the American state does not seem quite so fragmented or weak. The United States has been home to many organizations that promote the use of win/win conflict resolution and cooperative problem solving.

Until the 1990s, the use of these practices was limited largely to the corporate and nonprofit world. Today, however, there is growing interest in **consensus policy making,** which is quite different from **compromise,** the most common way decisions are reached in the United States. Consider an example used at a workshop I attended while writing this chapter. We were paired up and asked to role-play the atheist who sued a midwestern city to force it to remove a large monument with the Ten Commandments from the town square, and the mayor who wanted to keep it. My colleague and I decided to compromise and literally split the difference, keeping five commandments. Once the laughter stopped, we were asked to try to reach a consensus we could all be happy with. Most of the participants ended up with more creative outcomes, such as building additional monuments to other religious and spiritual traditions or moving the Ten Commandments to an equally prominent place on private land.

Since 1990, ten states have adopted consensus councils (though some use other names) to forge policies that go beyond compromise and meet everyone's goals. These bodies are adjuncts to the normal decision-making process. Composed of a broadly representative board of directors and a staff of trained conflict resolution and policy specialists, such a council works on issues referred to it, typically by a political leader. It convenes all the stakeholders in the issue and holds both open forums and private meetings until the participants agree on an outcome that meets all or most of their needs. That agreement then goes through the normal legislative or regulatory process, usually without much dissent since all the stakeholders have already accepted it.

These councils have shown remarkable promise. The North Dakota council enabled lawmakers to end an enduring logjam over the right to die. Montana's council reached a broadly accepted agreement on the normally contentious issue of hazardous waste disposal. In Delaware and California, consensus councils helped groups that had previously disagreed bitterly to find common ground on the use of the shoreline and coastal waters. In perhaps the most impressive accomplishment yet, a consensus policy-making process was used to ease the impact of floods in three states in the upper Midwest and in the Canadian province of Manitoba (www.policyconsensus.org).

Then, in 2001, Search for Common Ground, the world's largest conflict resolution organization, decided to bring the idea of a consensus council onto the national stage in two ways.

First, it convened a task force of prominent Americans of all political persuasions to create a federally chartered United States Consensus Council, modeled along the lines of those used in the states.

Second, in response to a request from Senator Rick Santorum and former Senator Harris Wofford, it convened a Working Group on Human Needs and the Faith-

The Weakening American State?

No one has done a definitive study of the strengthening or weakening of the American state in recent years. However, there is a rough consensus that it is not as effective as it used to be, if by that we mean it is less able to define policies that tackle social and economic problems in a reasonably consistent manner.

Other than globalization, there are two main reasons this is the case, reasons that reflect the domestic pressures cell of table 1.2. First, like all states, the American government now simply faces more issues that tax its resources in ways no one imagined even fifty years ago. If the critics are right, the United States may be worse off than some other countries (see the chapters on France, Germany, and Britain) because it continues to rely on institutions and practices designed two hundred years ago, when conditions were very different. Second, it probably also faces more pressures from below from a wider variety of groups than it did in previous generations. As research on social movements in Europe and North America has shown, this is not unique to the United States. However, because power is so fragmented in the United States, the government has had a relatively hard time trying to respond to those demands.

Based and Community Based Initiatives, which had proven to be one of the most controversial items proposed by the second Bush administration. The working group brought together thirty-five of the most prominent people involved in the debate on the initiative from all points on the political spectrum. The group members were able to reach agreements on most issues in the debate and to narrow their differences on those for which they could forge a full consensus. Senator Santorum then used their recommendations as the core of the CARE bill that was approved by the Senate but never came up for a vote in the House.

Public Policy

The American cultural qualms about an active state and the fragmented nature of its institutions has resulted in a government that does less than those in most of the other liberal democracies.

In recent years, the most widely discussed aspect of that limited involvement has been health care. Although Americans as a whole spend more on health care than anyone else, the United States is the only industrialized democracy that does not guarantee everyone basic coverage. Most middle-class and wealthy Americans get top-notch medical treatment because they can afford good insurance and can pay for care the policies do not cover. But more than forty million uninsured Americans have to fend for themselves, and perhaps as many with only minimal coverage get anything but high-quality health care. This disparity is one of the reasons at least twenty countries have a lower infant mortality rate than the United States.

It's not merely health care. Unemployment compensation and pension payments are lower. So, too, is the minimum wage. Publicly supported mass transit systems are almost never found outside big cities, and the passenger rail system is a shadow of its former self.

The government also does relatively little to coordinate economic policy. When it does, this usually involves cooperation among interest groups from a single industry and their supporters in Congress and the executive branch rather than the economy-wide strategies found in Germany and France. The Clinton administration started out doing more in that respect, especially during the late Ron Brown's tenure as secretary of commerce. However, the future of such programs is uncertain, given the opposition of many conservative Republicans.

There is also a widespread belief that when the government does act it usually does so inefficiently and sometimes corruptly. Federal and state programs are often divided up among dozens of agencies, which makes coordination difficult at best. To maintain its own control and supposedly to guard against corruption, Congress tends to micromanage federal agencies, often determining exactly how much money they can spend on computers or even what kinds of ashtrays they could buy (in the days when civil servants could still smoke in their offices). When applied to the private sector, such detailed and seemingly irrational regulations spawn complaints about a government that weighs too heavily "on the backs" of the people and their businesses. The Clinton administration sought to change things on this front with its "reinventing government" package of reforms designed to "steer the boat" of public policy rather than do the "rowing," or make every decision. So far, however, those proposals have done little more than provide intellectual justification for the dramatic downsizing of some federal agencies.

Feedback

Of all the countries covered in this book, the United States is the one on which the most research on feedback has been done. The results are mixed but are largely worrisome whatever one's ideological perspective. Although there has been an explosion in the number and type of media available, there has actually been a sharp decline in the quantity and quality of the political news most Americans pay attention to.

Readership of quality newspapers and magazines is down. Most people rely primarily on network television news for their political information, and the consensus among researchers is that network television does a less effective job of covering "serious" political news than it once did. To make matters even worse, fewer and fewer people are watching the news now that cable and direct satellite broadcasting give them dozens of other options during the slots the networks and local stations typically reserve for it.

Last but by no means least, American politicians are the acknowledged world masters at the art of spin-doctoring, or packaging their statements and actions in ways they think people will find most attractive, and often hiding the real import of the activity in the process. They do rely heavily on public opinion polls and focus groups, but one has to question how valuable these are for a public that is increasingly disinterested in political life and whose views are shaped by the spin doctors themselves.

Conclusion: American Exceptionalism

There is a lot missing from this chapter, including the differences between the House of Representatives and the Senate, the electoral college, and pressures for tax and campaign finance reform. Adding more material would take most readers—especially those who have had a course in American politics—more deeply into it than they need to go. And in so doing, it might obscure the key point being made here—that American exceptionalism is manifested in an unusually tranquil political history, supportive political culture, and weak or fragmented state.

Key Terms

Checks and balances	Individualism
Civic culture	Judicial review
Civil society	New left
Compromise	New right
Consensus policy making	Separation of powers
Federalism	Two-party system
Incrementalism	Unitary state

Critical Thinking Exercises

1 Much has changed in the United States since this book was finished in early 2005. Does the analysis of American politics presented in it still make sense? In what ways? Why (not)?

2 Public opinion pollsters routinely ask questions about whether people think the country is headed in the "right direction" or is "on the wrong track." If you were asked such a question about politics in the United States, what would your answer be? Why did you reach that conclusion?

3 Select a hotly debated domestic policy issue in the news and analyze it in light of the themes developed in this chapter. Is the United States having trouble solving it? Do you see evidence of the American cultural reluctance to use government to solve social and economic problems? Do you see evidence of the conflict between the legislative and executive branches? Other examples of the fragmentation or weakness of the American state?

4 Why has the United States been so stable? Is that stability likely to continue? To remain an asset?

Useful Websites

There are literally thousands of websites on politics in the United States. The White House and Thomas (run by the Library of Congress) provide gateways to the executive and legislative branches.

www.whitehouse.gov

thomas.loc.gov

The Supreme Court also has its own site, but, in my opinion, the one maintained by Cornell's Law School is better.

www.supremecourtus.gov

supct.law.cornell.edu/supct/index.html

Polling Report is the best online source for public opinion data. Vote Smart provides nonpartisan, unbiased information on pending issues to help voters make up their minds. The Public Agenda Foundation does much the same in analyzing policy issues themselves.

www.pollingreport.com

www.vote-smart.org

www.publicagenda.org

Three good sites on consensus policy making are Search for Common Ground (where I work), which has done the most work on controversial issues at the federal level; the Policy Consensus Institute, which concentrates on the states; and Public Conversations Projects, which brings average citizens together on such issues as a woman's right to choose or Mel Gibson's film, *The Passion of the Christ*.

www.sfcg.org

www.policyconsensus.org

www.publicconversations.org

InfoTrac College Edition Sources

Allin, Dana, et al. "The Democratic Party and Foreign Policy."

Fine, Terri Susan. "Presidential Nominating Conventions in a Democracy."

Glad, Betty. "When Governments Are Good."

Greenberg, Anna. "New Generation. New Politics."

Horowitz, Irving Louis. "The American Consensus and the American Conservative."

Nelson, Michael. "George W. Bush and Congress."

Pfiffner, James. "Recruiting Executive Branch Leaders."

Richardson-Osgood, Maria. "Bush's Faith-Based Legacy."

Karl Schonberg. "Global Security and Legal Restraint."

Further Reading

Ambrose, Stephen, with Douglas Brinkley. *The Rise to Globalism*, 8th ed. New York: Penguin Books, 1997. The best short volume outlining global history since World War II.

Dionne, E. J. *They Only Look Dead: Why Progressives Will Dominate the Next Political Era*. New York: Simon & Schuster, 1996. By one of America's most distinguished political journalists (who also holds a Ph.D. from Harvard), an exploration of why the left might be able to reassert itself in the next century.

Dionne, E. J., Gerald Pomper, and William Mayer, eds. *The Election of 2000: Reports and Interpretations*. Chat-ham, N.J.: Chatham House, 2001. The most recent in a series of excellent commentaries on U.S. presidential elections.

Hacker, Andrew. *Two Nations: Black and White, Separate, Hostile, Unequal*. New York: Scribner, 1992. A brief but comprehensive book on the sorry state of race relations in the United States.

Halstead, Ted, and Michael Lind. *The Radical Center: The Future of American Politics*. New York: Doubleday, 2001. A provocative new book on making dramatic policy changes from the middle of the political spectrum rather than the extremes.

Kuttner, Robert. *Everything for Sale*. New York: Twentieth Century Fund, 1998. A solid analysis of the strengths and weaknesses of the new conservative economics by one of the United States' leading left-of-center pundits.

Neustadt, Richard. *Presidential Power*. New York: Wiley, 1960. The classic book on the presidency. It has been republished in several new editions since then.

Nye, Joseph R., Philip D. Zelikow, and David C. King, eds. *Why People Don't Trust Government*. Cambridge, Mass.: Harvard University Press, 1997. An important volume contrasting interpretations of why trust in government and other key indicators of public political satisfaction are down.

Pfiffner, James. *The Modern Presidency*, 3d ed. New York: Bedford/St. Martin's Press, 1999. The best brief textbook on the American presidency.

Putnam, Robert D. *Bowling Alone*. New York: Simon & Schuster, 2000. The most thorough and most controversial book on declining civic engagement in the United States.

Shipler, David K. *The Working Poor*. New York: Knopf, 2004. The best recent work on poverty in the United States.

Tocqueville, Alexis de. *Democracy in America*. New York: Vintage Books, 1945. The classic account of American life by a French traveler and theorist, written in the 1830s.

The British happened to the rest of the world. Now the world happens to Britain.

ANDREW MARR

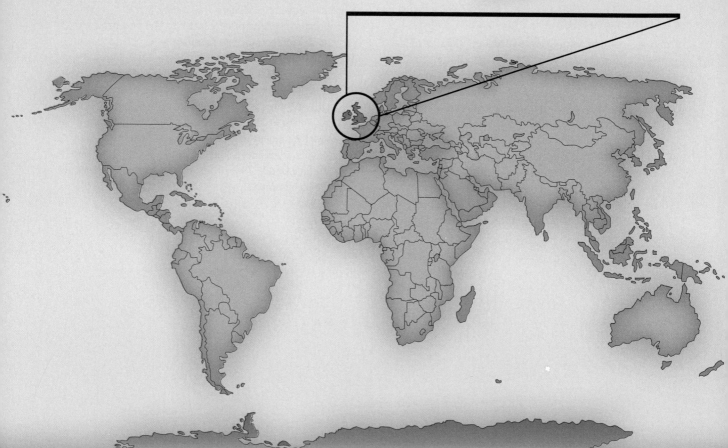

GREAT BRITAIN

CHAPTER OUTLINE

The Basics: Great Britain	
Size	244,820 sq. km (about the same size as California)
Climate	Mild, but over half the days are overcast or rainy
Population	59 million: 81.5% English; 9.6% Scottish; 2.4% Irish; 1.9% Welsh; 1.8% Northern Ireland; 2.8% West Indian, Indian, Pakistani and other
GNP per capita	$25,250
Currency	£1 = $1.80 (19 October 2004)
Ethnic composition	94.2% White, 5.8% other
Religion	Predominantly Anglican, but 9 million Roman Catholic, 1 million Muslim, 1.5 million other Protestant, 400,000 Sikh, 350,000 Hindu, 300,000 Jewish
Capital	London
Form of government	Constitutional monarchy
Head of state	Queen Elizabeth II
Head of government	Prime Minister Tony Blair (1997)

Tony's Tough Week

When **Tony Blair** (1953–) woke up on Monday 26 January 2004, he knew he was not going to have an easy week (www.number-10.gov.uk/output/page4.asp). Tuesday and Wednesday were going to be particularly tough as he faced events that could possibly bring down his prime ministry.

First, the House of Commons was to vote on a bill that would allow universities (all universities are state-run) to raise tuition for undergraduates to as high as £3,000 ($5,500) per year. This may not strike American students as a lot of money, but tuition had been free from the end of World War II until 1998 when a £1,000 fee was imposed. Poor students were given what amounted to scholarships. For everyone else, the fees amounted to long-term loans that graduates only paid back after their income reached a certain level.

Nonetheless, the bill was highly controversial, and as the vote neared it looked as if there might be enough defectors from Blair's **Labour** Party to defeat it. The new leader of the opposition **Conservative (Tory)** Party, **Michael Howard** (1941–) felt that the issue was central enough to Blair's official party platform that it should be considered a vote of confidence. Blair disagreed and

Ian Waldie/Getty Images

Dr. David Kelly arrives at Parliament to testify about allegations that the British government overstated the likelihood that Iraq possessed weapons of mass destruction. When his name was made public several weeks later, Kelly committed suicide.

probably would have held a separate vote of confidence had the tuition proposal failed.

In the end, Blair's proposal won by 316 to 311—Labour's overall majority was 161 seats at the time. Seventy-one Labour MPs (Members of Parliament) voted against their prime minister; another nineteen abstained, most of whom were opposed to the fee as well.

The next day saw the long-awaited publication of the Hutton Report. Hutton, one of the country's leading judges, had been called on to head an inquiry into the suicide of Dr. David Kelly, who had advised the government on Iraq's weapons of mass destruction programs and committed suicide in 2003 after the BBC publicly identified him.

Hutton was not asked to look into allegations that the Blair government had intentionally misled the country in the build up to the 2003 invasion of Iraq. However,

had Hutton found that the government had been involved in any sort of cover-up or in making Kelly's name public, Blair might have been compelled to resign.

In the end, the report was highly critical of the Ministry of Defense (its minister had already stepped down) but not Blair. It actually found more fault with the BBC for its sloppy editorial policies, which led the top two executives at the state-owned broadcasting service to resign.

Blair survived his tough week. And all the signs were that he would be able to govern effectively until the next elections, which have to be held by 2006 but will probably be called in spring 2005. That would make Blair the first Labour Prime Minister to govern for two full terms. Pollsters also predicted that Blair or another Labour leader would win the next election, although it would likely see its majority cut roughly in half.

Nonetheless, Blair's tough week provided new evidence that he was no longer the highly popular politician who took office in 1997 among talk of "Cool Britannia." Any hopes Blair had of becoming the president of the European Union when that office is created had already disappeared with his support of U.S. policy toward Iraq. His strong-handed rule of the Labour Party had tarnished his desired image as a new type of politician. He had become a politician "like the rest of them."

Thinking about Britain

Fifty years ago, Britain was included in comparative politics textbooks for four related reasons. First, it was the incubator, if not the originator, of liberal democracy. Second, that democracy evolved over a number of centuries in a process scholars call **gradualism,** which resulted in the post–World War II **collectivist consensus** in favor of a mixed economy and welfare state. Third, Britain had been one of the world's great powers over the past five hundred years and was still strong enough to warrant a permanent seat on the United Nations Security Council. Fourth, its political system was similar in many ways to those in other English-speaking countries, which made it an easy country to start with for most readers.

In Tony Blair's Britain, only the first and last of those reasons still hold. As we will see time and again in this chapter, Britain's ranking among the world's powers has been in gradual, but constant, decline for over a century. And in the 1970s, Britain's collectivist consensus evaporated in a wave of strikes and violence. In short, if Britain belongs in a book like this today, it is primarily because of its historical role—in particular for what it can tell us about the ways democracies develop.

Key Questions

As a result, this chapter will revolve around four themes that set the United Kingdom apart from other democracies. The first is gradualism. It is perhaps too charitable a term to use in describing a history that stretches back to the signing of the Magna Carta in 1215. Nonetheless, in comparative terms, Britain has suffered from less unrest and has had a more consensual history than almost any other country, which has helped smooth its transition to democracy over the past two hundred years or so. It did have to face the challenges of creating the nation-state, overcoming religious and class conflict, and undergoing democratization. However, unlike the countries on the Continent, it was able to spread these challenges out over a number of centuries and to largely resolve each of them before it had to meet the next.

Second, in some respects, Britain has had the most troubles of any of the major liberal democracies since the height of the collectivist period in the early 1960s. As table 4.1 shows, Britain's relative economic standing declined dramatically in the second half of the twentieth century. In 1939 it was the second-wealthiest country in the world, trailing only the United States. By the 1970s it had dropped out of the top ten, and in 2000 it ranked fourteenth.

Britain is by no means a poor country, as its per capita gross national product (GNP) of over $25,000 a year attests. However, its economic growth has lagged behind that of its major competitors for decades, something British tourists see whenever they visit France or Germany, where people enjoy a noticeably higher standard of living.

More important for our purposes are the political implications of the economic decline. No matter how you measure such things, the British are less masters of their destiny than they were a half-century ago, something the BBC's Andrew Marr pithily sums up in the quote that begins this chapter.

That brings us to the third trend—the way the conservative governments led by **Margaret Thatcher** (1925–) in the 1980s and early 1990s redefined British political life and spurred the renewal of support for free-market economics that has taken hold almost everywhere. Thatcher and her colleagues rejected most of the premises of collectivist politics and pushed the country in a dramatically different direction. Over the seventeen years that she and her successor, John Major, were in office, they privatized dozens of companies, reduced spending on social services, curbed the power of the unions, opposed further British involvement in Europe, and reasserted Britain's influence in global affairs.

To this day, the "iron lady" remains controversial. Her supporters are convinced that she saved the country from bankruptcy and social chaos. Her opponents claim equally vociferously that she took it to the brink of disaster and left it a far more heartless place, with a government that treats the disadvantaged with disinterest and even disdain.

The fourth theme of this chapter, of course, is the impact of Blair and "New Labour." During the Thatcher-Major years, Labour lost four consecutive elections in large part because it had veered too far to the left to have a chance of winning elections. After the second of those defeats in 1987, the party began an agonizing reassessment of its goals and strategies that eventually led to the selection of Blair as its leader in 1994.

Blair and his team embarked on a radical restructuring of the party organization and a redefinition of its goals to the point that it routinely came to be called "New Labour" as if it were a new party. Most notably, Blair shed the party's commitment to nationalized industry and state-based solutions to most of society's problems. Instead, he endorsed some of the Thatcherite commitment to a market economy, though tempered with a greater concern for equality and a desire to forge more cooperative "partnerships" linking business, labor, and the government. But, as we saw in the introduction to the chapter, much of the gloss is gone for Blair and his leadership, and there seems to be little chance of enacting major new reforms until after the next election.

The Basics

We have to start with something very basic indeed. What do all the different names used to describe this country actually stand for?

▌ TABLE 4.1 Britain's Decline: International Rank in GNP per Capita

COUNTRY	1939	1960	1974	1995	2000
United States	1	1	3	5	3
Great Britain	2	6	14	18	14

Source: Data for 1939, 1960, and 1974 from Walter Dean Burnham, "Great Britain: The Collapse of the Collectivist Consensus," in Louis Maisel and Joseph Cooper, eds., *Political Parties: Development and Decay* (Beverly Hills, Calif.: Sage, 1978), 274; data for 1995 from World Bank, *World Development Report 1996* (Oxford: Oxford University Press, 1996), 189; data for 2000 from www.worldbank.org, accessed 19 June 2001.

MARGARET THATCHER

Prime Minister Margaret Thatcher addressing the Conservative Party Conference in October 1984. This photo was taken shortly after a terrorist bomb exploded and nearly killed Thatcher in her bed.

Bettmann/CORBIS

Margaret Roberts was born in 1925 in Grantham, which has often been described as the most boring town in Britain. Her father owned a small corner grocery store and was a member of the town council. He imbued certain values on his daughter, including self-reliance, self-discipline, and a respect for tradition, all of which were reinforced by her experiences growing up during the Great Depression and World War II.

During the war, Roberts studied chemistry at Oxford, but she soon realized she was more interested in politics than science and so became a lawyer active in Conservative politics. Marriage to the wealthy banker Denis Thatcher allowed her to turn to politics full time. In 1959 she was first elected to a safe Tory seat in suburban London. In 1970 she was named minister of education, in which position she gained the nickname "Margaret Thatcher, milk snatcher" for eliminating free milk from school lunches.

After the Conservatives lost in 1974, she and a number of her colleagues abandoned their commitment to the collectivist consensus. Two years later, she was named leader of the Conservative Party and became prime minister when it won the 1979 election. Her eleven years in office made her the longest-serving prime minister in more than a hundred years. Her successor, John Major, named her to the House of Lords in 1993

Technically, this chapter is about the United Kingdom of Great Britain and Northern Ireland (U.K.). It is a title few people use other than in official communication. England is its historical core (see the map at the beginning of this chapter) and is where the Crown gradually solidified its hold on power centuries ago. Only later did the English conquer the Celtic fringes of their island—Wales and Scotland. The three are popularly referred to as Britain.

The U.K. also includes the six heavily Protestant counties of Northern Ireland. Their leaders chose to remain part of the U.K. when the rest of Ireland gained its independence in 1922. The status of Northern Ireland, or Ulster as Protestants call it, of course remains hotly contested, though many hope that the **Good Friday Agreement** of 1998 will pave the way toward political calm in the province.

It can get confusing. Scotland (but not Wales or Northern Ireland) has its own bank notes and legal system. England, Scotland, Wales, and Northern Ireland all have their own international soccer teams but play to-

gether in cricket and, sometimes, in rugby. It takes three years to get an undergraduate degree in England, but four in Scotland. To simplify things, I will follow conventional usage and use the terms Britain and U.K. interchangeably unless I am referring to a specific part of the country.

Barely the size of California, the U.K. has just over sixty million people, which makes it one of the most crowded countries in the world. The congestion is actually worse than the figures might indicate, because more than 70 percent of its people live in urban areas, the majority of which are located in a two-hundred-mile-wide band stretching from London in the south to Newcastle in the north. Put in other terms, almost half the country is open pastureland and home to tens of millions of sheep.

There are significant minorities in Wales and Scotland who want more autonomy, if not complete independence, from England, though virtually no one there condones the use of violence to achieve their goals. The Irish, by contrast, have not relied on nonviolent protest alone. Even with the 1998 peace agreement, some Catholic and Protestant extremists carry out bombings and drive-by shootings. In fact, the worst single incident during the thirty years of "the troubles" occurred when twenty-eight people were killed by a car bomb planted by a tiny Catholic terrorist group in Omagh in August 1998, four months after the Good Friday Agreement was signed.

Regional differences also overlap with religious ones. About two-thirds of the people belong to the Church of England. As an official, or "established," church, it receives funding and other support from the state. Twenty of its top leaders serve in the House of Lords. Other Protestant sects are strongest in the working class and in the Celtic minority regions. About 10 percent of the people are Catholic, most of whom either live in Northern Ireland or are residents of England, Scotland, and Wales with Irish roots.

Britain also is no longer an all-white country. At least 5 percent (and probably more, the statistics are unreliable) of the population is of African, Asian, or Caribbean origin. Racial issues have become politically significant over the past thirty years, especially among Conservative politicians, who call for an end to immigration and, at times, even the repatriation of Britain's nonwhite residents. As we will see later in the chapter, immigration, per se, is no longer the issue. Few people have been able to gain entry into the United Kingdom since the early 1990s other than as asylum seekers. But many of them became highly controversial after September 11 when some were alleged to be collaborators of al-Qaeda and the Taliban. Whether true or not, the reaction against those immigrants seems to have heightened the racism against nonwhites from a disturbingly large segment of the white population.

The British decline of the last half-century has left it the poorest of the major liberal democracies. That said, few of its people are poor by any reasonable definition of the term.

Despite cuts since 1979, the welfare state is still strong enough to guarantee basic health care, education, and pensions for everyone. There is very little homelessness. But other public services, most notably the country's extensive railroad system, are in need of massive investment.

The last decade has brought economically better times. The U.K.'s growth rate is among the highest and its unemployment among the lowest in Europe. Nonetheless, signs of the decline still exist. Most salaries are no more than two-thirds of what they would be in the United States. In the three years I lived in England in the late 1990s, most of my British colleagues, for example, had fewer clothes, older cars, smaller personal libraries, and slower computers than their counterparts in the United States.

Perhaps the most important economic characteristic of British life is social class. More than in most countries, you can tell peoples' backgrounds by their clothing, accents, and even the sports they follow (in England, rugby union is a middle- and upper-class sport; soccer and rugby league traditionally appealed to the working class). Many in the upper and middle classes have a degree of self-assurance that borders on arrogance, bred by generations of wealth and the education they received at one of Britain's prestigious private schools (to make things confusing for American students, the best of them are known as public schools).

The Evolution of the British State

Chapter 2 identified four great transformations that had a tremendous impact on political life in the industrial democracies over the past several centuries:

- Building the nation-state
- Defining the relationship between church and state
- Establishing liberal democracy
- Dealing with the impact of the industrial revolution

Each had a wrenching impact. As we will see in the next two chapters, most countries in Europe had to deal with two or more of them at the same time, never fully resolved any one of them, and ended up with deeply divided populations and political instability as a result.

By contrast, the British were basically able to deal with these crises separately. And, with the exception of the industrial revolution, Britain emerged from each with a rough consensus, avoiding the lasting divisions that left France and Germany with large numbers of antagonistic political parties. The one divisive issue that was left unresolved—class—did not lead to the intense conflicts found on the continent that would pit workers demanding revolution against an upper class fearfully holding onto its property and privilege.

This evolution was all the more remarkable because it occurred without recourse to a written constitution. The U.K. has a constitution, but it consists of laws and customs that never made it onto the statute books, which just about everyone accepts.

Put simply, it was this relative gradualism leading to consensus that allowed the British to move from one potentially divisive issue to another without provoking the lasting antagonisms that were so common elsewhere. Before moving on, be sure to note the importance of the term "relative" here. Britain's history has by no means been tranquil. But, as will be clearer after you read any of the remaining chapters, it has been calmer than most countries'. The relative ease with which it met these challenges was a major contributor to the consensus about institutions and practices that has marked the most tumultuous periods in its history.

The Broad Sweep of British History

The origins of the British state date back at least as far as 1215, when a band of nobles forced King John to sign the **Magna Carta.** (See table 4.2.) That historic agreement established that the king was not an absolute monarch. He was to rule in parliament and would need the consent of the nobility before imposing taxes or spending money. The Great Council, consisting of leading nobles and churchmen—the precursor of the current House of Lords—was created. As the thirteenth century wore on, the kings found that they could not meet state expenses with their personal revenues and called on the council to do so. Meetings took place wherever the king happened to be. The king and his ministers sat in the front, the nobility sat on benches facing them, and the commoners knelt in the back. After they heard the king's requests, the latter two groups met separately, which ultimately led to the creation of the two houses of the Parliament (britishhistory.about.com).

Over the next four centuries, a succession of kings brought most of England together in what was never more than a very loose and decentralized state. The English people did not have a sense of national identity, and the government institutions based in London lacked the power of a modern state. Still, there was an England, which was more than one could say for Italy, Germany, or, to some extent, France at the time.

In other words, when the events listed in table 4.2 hit in earnest during the sixteenth and seventeenth centuries, the British already had made major strides toward meeting two of them. The broad contours of the state already were set, and there was a rough understanding that the king had to share power with Parliament.

The sixteenth century brought the Reformation and the split between Catholics and Protestants that tore the Continent apart. In Britain, the Reformation left nowhere near as deep a scar. In part because he wanted to divorce and remarry, King Henry VIII broke with Rome and established the Church of England. It would be centuries before the British state tolerated other religions, and the division between Anglicans and Puritans would be one of the causes of the English civil war in the 1640s. Nonetheless, Henry's actions set in motion forces that would depoliticize the church and remove religion as a deeply divisive issue by the end of the seventeenth century.

England did experience two revolutions in the seventeenth century. They were, however, mild in comparison with what was happening on the Continent, and their resolution actually helped pave the way for parliamentary democracy.

During the civil war of the 1640s, Oliver Cromwell led a group of members of Parliament, businessmen, Puritans, and soldiers who overthrew the monarchy and beheaded Charles I. In 1660, Charles II was restored to the throne on the condition that he accept an expanded role for Parliament. Charles and his successors tried to reassert royal power and even flirted with Catholicism, which led to the Glorious Revolution of 1688 and the firm understanding that the king would henceforth be both Anglican and accountable to Parliament.

Royal prerogatives continued to disappear. The new king and Parliament agreed to a Bill of Rights, which made it illegal for the monarch to impose taxes or enforce any law without the consent of Parliament. In 1701, the Act of Settlement regularized procedures for succession to the throne and asserted that the king and queen had to govern Britain according to Parliament's laws. In 1707, Queen Anne failed to give her royal assent to a bill passed by Parliament, the last time any British monarch has done so. Shortly thereafter, King George I stopped attending cabinet meetings, a practice continued by his successors ever since. Later, people began to refer to Sir Robert Walpole as a prime minister, though it would be another two centuries before the title was mentioned in any laws. (There were less charitable terms used to describe him, including Man Mountain, the Norfolk Trickster, and Merlin the Wizard.)

When the American Revolution broke out, the king had become little more than the head of one parliamentary faction. He still appointed cabinet ministers, but

▌ TABLE 4.2 Key Events and Trends in British History

YEAR	EVENT
1215	Magna Carta signed
1532–36	Reformation; establishment of Church of England
1642–60	Civil war and Restoration
1688	Glorious Revolution
1701	Act of Settlement
Early 1700s	Emergence of prime minister
1832	Great Reform Act
1911	Reform of House of Lords
1928	Right to vote for all adults

they could not remain in office if they lost the confidence of Parliament. Although the king usually had the support of both houses, he could only be assured of it if a majority of the members of both houses felt he was ruling effectively and did not violate their de facto control over the budget.

In the nineteenth century, the rise of capitalism disrupted British life more than any of the other events discussed in this section. The industrial revolution and the imperialism that fed it brought untold wealth to the capitalists and to the country as a whole. But it was nowhere near as beneficial for the men and women who worked in the mills and mines.

Hundreds of thousands left the countryside to work in the unsafe factories and to live in the filthy, overcrowded cities so powerfully described in the novels of Charles Dickens. Trade unions were still illegal, but friendly societies, new denominations such as Methodism, and, most importantly, the great petition drives of the Chartist movement made it clear that the new working and middle classes were forces to be reckoned with.

Despite these rumblings from below, political life remained the preserve of a tiny elite. No more than 1 percent of all adult males were wealthy enough to vote. Parliament overrepresented rural districts, many of which were known as "rotten boroughs" because they had so few constituents that a single lord could control who was elected. Even the growing capitalist class chafed at being excluded from political power.

A number of movements demanding political change sprang up during the first third of the nineteenth century. Bands of workers and artisans known as Luddites broke into factories and smashed the machines. By 1810 the term *working class* was commonly used—and feared. Eventually, dissatisfaction with the status quo grew strong enough to force passage of the **Great Reform Act** of 1832. Despite its name, the reform was not all that extensive. Only about 300,000 more men gained the vote, and the aristocracy continued to dominate political life.

The small number of men added to the rolls should not lead you to underestimate the act's importance. Its passage showed that the British elite was willing to adapt to changing circumstances rather than cling to power and run the risk of widespread political disruption, if not revolution. It also gave the House of Commons new confidence in further curbing the power of the monarchy and aristocracy.

A second Reform Act in 1867 doubled the size of the electorate to nearly three million. In 1870 Parliament introduced the secret ballot. The Representation of the People Acts of 1884 and 1885 expanded the suffrage to

Democratization in Britain and the United States

BOTH BRITAIN and the United States have had comparatively peaceful histories. When crises did occur, they were typically resolved before the next major transformation loomed on the political horizon. Some were quite wrenching, most notably each country's civil war. However, in Britain, they were less divisive than conflicts on the Continent and, more importantly for our purposes, were largely resolved in that at least almost everyone accepted the outcome.

the point that working-class men constituted the majority of the electorate. By the early twentieth century, all men had gained the right to vote. Most women won the suffrage in 1918, and the vote was extended to all women ten years later.

After the 1867 reforms, the first modern political parties were formed by parliamentary leaders who needed to generate support from the newly enfranchised voters. The Conservative National Union, surprisingly, did quite well among the working class as well as the aristocracy, while the National Liberal Federation won disproportionate support among the middle class and in Ireland.

MPs were now dependent on massive party machines. Gradually, the party—that is, its leaders in Parliament—began to determine who would run for office and who would serve in cabinets. Strict party discipline was imposed on the MPs. In 1911 the House of Lords was stripped of its remaining power, marking the final step in the evolution of British parliamentary democracy.

A brief comparison with France should show just how much Britain had progressed. While Britain's parliamentary system was getting ever stronger, French democracy remained shaky at best. France had just suffered through the Dreyfus scandal, in which false accusations of treason against a Jewish army officer unleashed such passionate protests that the Third Republic nearly collapsed. Significant divisions over the role of religion and the nature of the state spawned antiregime parties that typically won a third of the seats in Parliament.

As noted earlier, only one of the four challenges was to have a lasting impact: the division of Great Britain into supporters of the Labour and the Conservative parties largely along class lines. And even that division paled in comparison with the class conflict taking place on the Continent. To cite but one example, in 1926 the **Trades Union Congress** (**TUC**) called for a general strike, and British workers walked off the job en masse. In France or

During the 1926 general strike, workers who walked off the job did not confront the police. Instead, they played football (soccer) together.

Hulton Archive/Getty Images

Germany, such a strike would have been accompanied by violent clashes between police and strikers. In Britain, instead of fighting, many of the policemen and strikers played soccer together to pass the time.

Workers' demands were by no means fully satisfied during the 1920s. However, their frustrations were increasingly channeled through the TUC and the Labour Party, which were both known for their moderation. By the 1920s, the Labour Party had surged past the Liberals and become the main competition for the Conservatives.

The Great Depression that began in 1929 hit Britain as hard as it did any European country except Germany, and had both political and economic consequences. For most of the next decade, no party had a clear majority in Parliament, and a succession of weak Conservative and Labour governments failed to ease the country's economic woes or to do much to meet the dangers posed by an ever more aggressive Nazi Germany. Two changes that were to reshape British politics after the war did occur despite the uncertainty of the 1930s. First, Labour solidified itself as the major alternative to the Conservatives. Second, the liberal or free-market wing of the Conservative Party was discredited because of its failure to solve the economic crisis brought on by the depression. In its place rose a new generation of Tory politicians

who were more willing to turn to the state in shaping the country's economic future and meeting the needs of the poor and unemployed.

The Collectivist Consensus

The period from 1945 until the mid-1970s is often portrayed as the golden era of British politics. (See table 4.3.) Leaders from both parties agreed on a variety of policy goals, including full employment, the provision of social services that guaranteed at least subsistence-level living conditions for all, cooperation with labor unions,

▌ TABLE 4.3 The Collectivist Years and Beyond

YEAR	EVENT
1942	Beveridge Report published
1945	Labour elected
1948	National Health Service created
1951	Conservatives return to power
1964	Labour returns to power
1972	Heath government forced into U-turn
1974	Labour wins two elections without a working majority
1979	Thatcher elected
1990	Thatcher resigns, replaced by John Major
1997	Blair elected

and active government intervention to secure economic growth.

Although the Liberal-Labour coalition government of 1906–11 did introduce minimal programs of unemployment and health insurance, the most important origins of the collectivist consensus lie in World War II. British fortunes had sagged during the first months of the war. Country after country fell to the Nazis. British troops were forced to withdraw from Europe. German planes by the thousands bombed London and the other major British cities. There were widespread fears of a German invasion, which would have been the first since 1066.

Finally, with defeat staring the U.K. in the face, Parliament called on Sir Winston Churchill to replace the ineffectual Neville Chamberlain as prime minister. Although his Conservative Party had a clear majority in the Commons, Churchill chose to head an all-party coalition. The opposition parties agreed to suspend normal politics—including elections—for the duration of the war. The Conservatives, in turn, agreed to establish a commission headed by the civil servant William Beveridge. Its task was to propose an overhaul of the social service system to be implemented after the Allied victory. When issued in 1942, the **Beveridge Report** called for a social insurance program in which every citizen would be eligible for health, unemployment, pension, and other benefits that would guarantee all Britons at least a subsistence income.

The elections of 1945, the first in ten years, were fought largely over the issue of social and economic reform. Both major parties endorsed the broad outlines of the Beveridge Report, although Labour was committed to going farther and faster in enacting its recommendations, as well as nationalizing a number of key industries.

Labour won a resounding victory, marking the first time it came to power with a parliamentary majority. Prime Minister Clement Attlee's government proceeded to turn the party program into legislation, which the House of Commons passed with only slight modification.

By 1949 the surge of reform had come to an end. Throughout Europe, the cold war sapped Socialist parties of their momentum. Furthermore, with recovery well under way, Labour decided to dismantle most of the planning boards that had brought government, the unions, and business together. Meanwhile, Labour's popular support began to wane. It barely won a majority in the 1950 elections, and when Attlee dissolved Parliament the following year, the Conservatives (**Tories**) returned to office.

One might have expected the party of capitalism to repeal the vast majority of Labour's reforms. In fact, it did not. The steel industry was privatized, and people had to pay a nominal fee for prescriptions and eyeglasses. Otherwise, the Conservatives retained the welfare state Labour had so greatly expanded in the first few years after the war.

In retrospect, the Conservatives' actions should not have come as much of a surprise. The party had supported most collectivist policies in 1945. During the election campaign that year, the debate between the parties had centered on the pace and extent of reform, not whether it should occur. In his first speech as leader of the opposition, Winston Churchill stated:

> It is evident that not only are we two parties in the house agreed on the main essentials of foreign policy and in our moral outlook on world affairs, but we also have an immense program, prepared by our joint exertions during the coalition, which requires to be brought into law and made an inherent part of the life of the people. Here and there, there may be differences of emphasis and view but, in the main, no Parliament has ever assembled with such a mass of agreed legislation as lies before us this afternoon.[1]

Electorally, the British populace remained divided along class lines. Normally, about 70 percent of the working class voted Labour, and an even larger proportion of the middle class voted Conservative. But ideologically, those differences were not very significant. Although the British did tend to support the party of their class, this did not lead them to hate either the other class or the other major party.

The two main parties routinely won over 90 percent of the popular vote and an even larger share of the seats in the House of Commons. It mattered little which party was in power. Each gradually expanded the role of the British state at almost exactly the same rate year in and year out. Elections were fought over slogans such as the Conservatives' "You Never Had It So Good" in 1959 or over Labour's claim that it would bring more modern management practices to government in 1964.

Many political scientists saw the collectivist years as the natural culmination of British political history, with its emphasis on class, consensus, and cooperation. Others saw them as providing a model of what modern liberal democracies could and should be like.

However, the collectivist consensus did not survive, because two conditions that had made it possible did not themselves endure. The consensus had existed in

---

[1] Quoted in Allen Sked and Chris Clark, *Post-War Britain: A Political History*, 3rd ed. (London: Penguin Books, 1990), 24.

part because steady economic growth allowed successive governments to meet popular policy demands. Also, British politics could be consensual only when there were not any deeply divisive issues.

The impact of the end of the collectivist consensus will be the focus of much of the rest of this chapter.

British Political Culture

At the height of the collectivist period in 1959, Gabriel Almond and Sidney Verba conducted about a thousand interviews in Britain, which they drew on in writing their landmark study *The Civic Culture*.[2] They painted a picture of a harmonious and trusting British public, and concluded that any effectively functioning democracy needed a culture much like the U.K.'s.

Critical analysis and subsequent events have led most political scientists to conclude that the British political culture is no longer as supportive as it once was and that a number of different types of cultures likely can sustain a democracy. (See, for instance, the online chapter on Japan at www.politicalscience.wadsworth.com/hauss5.) Nonetheless, the snapshot Almond and Verba took of Britain in the collectivist years goes a long way toward explaining why the British regime and democracy were not put in jeopardy during the crisis years of the 1970s and 1980s.

The Civic Culture and the Collectivist Years

The British people were not completely satisfied with their political lot. However, they probably were as content as any society in the twentieth century. There was virtually unanimous agreement that the political system based on parliamentary sovereignty and cabinet rule was legitimate. There were protests, such as those by the marchers who crossed the country to oppose nuclear weapons each year at Easter time. But, except for a tiny handful of communists and fascists, everyone acknowledged the government's right to govern.

The British were remarkably tolerant of each other and of the people who governed them. The quarter of the working class that regularly voted Conservative did so mostly out of a sense of deference toward people they believed to be their betters. Poll after poll revealed a public that trusted its politicians and institutions. Most British adults felt a sense of efficacy—that, as individuals, they could influence the political process. However, few people in Britain actually participated in ways that put demands on decision makers other than by voting, leading observers like Almond and Verba to conclude that democracies actually need a relatively inactive and uninvolved electorate!

The British also thought of themselves as patriotic, with flag-waving and national anthem-singing almost as widespread as in the United States. But even this patriotism was muted and did not lead to anything approaching jingoistic involvement abroad. This is most easily seen in the ease with which most people accepted the loss of Britain's colonial empire.

The Politics of Protest: Toward an Uncivic Culture?

In the 1970s, all that changed. More and more people expressed serious reservations about the collectivist consensus. Though the overwhelming majority of the population stayed on the sidelines, popular participation took on a decidedly confrontational tone and left many with the impression that Britain was becoming ungovernable.

Signs of dissatisfaction came from all points on the political spectrum. Northern Ireland, which had been rather peaceful, became anything but that after the introduction of British troops into the province in 1969 and "bloody Sunday" in January 1972, when thirteen Catholics were killed by British troops. The Irish Republican Army (IRA) and various Protestant paramilitaries escalated their campaigns of violence, including an attack that nearly killed Thatcher and the rest of the Conservative leadership at the party's annual conference in 1984.

Britain also had to come to grips with rather widespread racism. The Conservative and, later, Ulster Unionist (Protestant) politician Enoch Powell had built a career exploiting the fear and antagonism many British men and women felt toward Asians, Africans, and Afro-Caribbeans. The National Front, whose racism was at best thinly veiled, did well in local elections in working-class white neighborhoods adjacent to others with large minority populations. White toughs repeatedly attacked blacks and Asians, which periodically led to riots in London, Liverpool, Birmingham, and other smaller cities.

Here we can concentrate on the single most important example of heightened unrest that led to worries about Britain's becoming ungovernable: the new militancy of the unions and of many of their members. It should come as no surprise that workers grew more dis-

---

[2] Gabriel Almond and Sidney Verba, *The Civic Culture* (Princeton, N.J.: Princeton University Press, 1962).

Steve Millar

St. Ethelburga's was a medieval church and the smallest one in London. In 1993, it was leveled by an IRA bomb that killed one person and wounded more than fifty. The church has been rebuilt as a center for reconciliation where people of all faiths can find a safe place to discuss their disputes. www.stethelburgas.org

satisfied during the crisis years. By the mid-1980s, unemployment had topped three million, six times what it had been during the 1950s and 1960s. Workers who still had their jobs saw their standard of living eroded by inflation that regularly outpaced their annual raises.

The radicalization of the unions had begun during the 1960s and contributed heavily to the defeat of the Wilson, Heath, and Callaghan governments in the 1960s and 1970s. Strikes were larger and lasted longer. Often, workers struck without warning and without the authorization of union leaders. Workers also often called "secondary" strikes against other firms that their own company dealt with, thereby spreading the disruption caused

by the initial dispute. There was even violence at factory gates and mine pits.

The respective rigidities of Thatcher and the union leaders put them on a collision course that reached a peak during her second term. The government provided the pretext for such a collision in 1984 by passing a new Industrial Relations Act that obliged union leaders to poll their members using secret ballots before calling a strike and held them financially responsible for any illegal walkouts. On 1 March the Coal Board said that the Cortonwood mine in Yorkshire would be shut. Less than a week later, it announced that up to twenty more mines would be closed, with the loss of about twenty thousand jobs. The miners in the endangered pits put down their tools, and union leaders called for a nationwide strike without following the procedures outlined in the new legislation.

Both the striking miners and the government held firm for almost a year in a strike that was to cost the British economy about £3 billion. Finally, the miners gave up, and in March 1985 their local representatives narrowly approved a resolution to return to work.

The militancy of the unions was echoed in many other areas of political life. Many people felt that the Labour Party had been taken over by extreme radicals, called the "loony left" by the tabloid press. The peace movement actively opposed the deployment of U.S. cruise and Pershing missiles armed with nuclear warheads, which thousands of women tried to stop by blocking the entrance to the American base at Greenham Common for more than a year. More recently, environmental activists delayed construction of a bypass around the clogged nearby city of Newbury by living in the trees workers would have to cut down and building tunnels under the proposed path of the road.

Political scientists have discovered that all of the protests had a dual impact on British culture. On the one hand, the activists on the left and right helped create a far more polarized political system. The left believed that the capitalists were ruthlessly exploiting the working class. The right feared that the socialists, unions, feminists, and minorities were making Britain harder to govern and were undermining traditional values.

On the other hand, the vast majority of the populace did not take part in the protests and grew frustrated with the new confrontational politics. There was a general agreement that the left had gone too far in its demands on both domestic and foreign policy. Even Labour supporters came to doubt the new radicalism of the unions and their own party. As the 1980s wore on, there also was growing dissatisfaction with a right wing that was perceived to be too radical.

Joel W. Rogers/CORBIS

Environmental protesters opposing construction of a bypass around the city of Newbury in Berkshire.

The Civic Culture Holds

The protests also illustrate just how much British political culture did not change during the crisis. Indeed, in at least two respects, the British culture "held."

First, the dangers these protests posed proved rather fleeting, in large part because the Thatcher government met them head-on. To a large extent, it succeeded, which we can see by returning to the example of the trade unions. The Thatcher government viewed the 1984 miners strike as a showdown with the militant unions. Unlike earlier prime ministers of both parties, Thatcher was able to play on the growing dissatisfaction with union demands and the growing split between radicals and moderates within the union movement itself to bring the miners to their knees.

The defeat of the miners turned the tide. Since then, union militancy and membership have declined, and most of the radical leaders have been replaced by mod-

erates. The rhetoric and tactics of class war have largely disappeared.

The important point here is not that Thatcher was right or wrong. What matters is the impact her actions had on the British people. Together with the economic recovery of the mid-1980s, Thatcher's strong stands against the left helped sharply reduce the political tensions that seemed to imperil traditional British institutions and practices.

Second, and even more importantly, the analysts who predicted the end of the civic culture overstated the dangers the protest movements posed. Despite what the far left may have said or wanted, revolution was never on the horizon. The British public was too committed to established parliamentary institutions for that.

A 1979 review of the original conclusions about the civic culture did uncover some erosion in some of the indicators on which Almond and Verba had built their case twenty years earlier. In particular, given the common perception that the government had failed to solve many of the country's problems, the increased skepticism toward politicians and their motivations was to be expected.

But if we concentrate on the more general level that most students of political culture focus on, there is much less evidence that values changed. Dissatisfaction with recent governments simply has not translated into dissatisfaction with the regime.

Will There Always Be a Britain?

There may be one exception to the still civic culture. Since the late 1960s, identification with Britain as a whole has declined, especially among the Scots and the Welsh.

A 2000 poll asked people about the levels of authority they most identified with. Eighteen percent of the Scots said Britain, and 72 percent mentioned Scotland. The comparable figures for Wales were 27 percent for Britain and 81 percent for Wales. The English were split down the middle, with 43 percent mentioning Britain and 41 percent England. When asked about their lives twenty years in the future, 22 percent thought that the government in London would be the most important political institution in their lives—barely half the number that mentioned the EU.[3]

As we will see later in the chapter, there has been a resurgence of support for regional parties in Scotland and Wales, and the "British" parties have never fielded

---

[3] Andrew Marr, *The Day Britain Died* (London: Profile Books, 2000), 2.

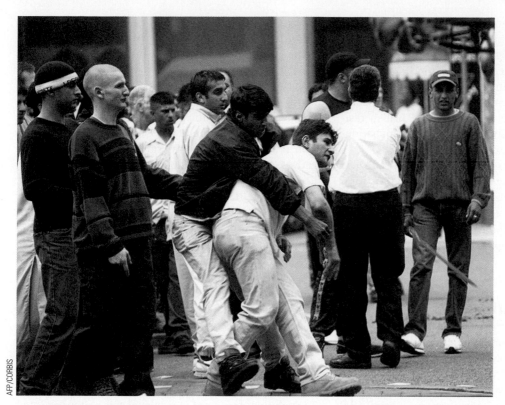

Rioting between white and Asian young people in Oldham, in 2001.

candidates in Northern Ireland. We will also see that, although the U.K. has long had one of the most centralized political systems in the democratic world, the first Blair government created regional parliaments in Northern Ireland, Scotland, and Wales. And the government floated trial balloons about regional assemblies in England as well, following the first direct election of a mayor of London in 1999.

No one is suggesting that the U.K. is going to fall apart or that there will be a fully independent Scotland any time soon. But many of the symbols and institutions that have held British culture together are losing their influence. There is no better example of this than the monarchy. The reigning king or queen has not had any real political power for more than a century. Nonetheless, the monarchy has been an important symbol of British unity and pride. But much of that pride has disappeared in the wake of scandals about the personal lives of many of the "royals," which culminated in the tragic death of Princess Diana in 1997.

This "new" country is reflected in the changing physical face of Britain—and most of the other major European countries. Britain is increasingly a racially diverse nation. Between 5 and 8 percent of the population is nonwhite, though most were born in the U.K. Even though the minority population pales in comparison with that of the United States, curry is probably the most popular food in the country, and most fish-and-chips shops are run by Chinese immigrants who also sell egg rolls and fried rice—not to mention curry. The success of the film, "Bend it Like Beckham," which features a racially mixed women's soccer team, is a sign of the progress that has been made in recent years.

Still, there are overt instances of racism, including the riots that shook a number of grimy industrial cities in the north in 2001 and led to racist candidates there winning over 5 percent of the vote in a number of local elections that June. As in the United States, young black men are more likely than their white contemporaries to be pulled over by the police "on sus" (racial profiling to Americans) and to be treated arbitrarily after an arrest. Perhaps most telling, a former cabinet member, Lord Norman Tebbitt, gained a lot of positive publicity when he said that citizens of Pakistani or Indian origin should not be considered truly British if they did not support the English cricket team when it played matches against their country of origin.

Last but by no means least, the British national identity is being undermined as a side effect of its involvement in the EU. Conservative **euroskeptics** ground their qualms about Europe as much in a feared loss of national distinctiveness as in doubts about the viability of the euro. They are probably fighting a losing battle as more and more Europeans come to work in the U.K. and more and more British spend time living and working on the Continent. Satellite and cable television services carry programming in multiple languages, and British residents can get any major European daily newspaper delivered to their door the next morning.

Again, there is little danger that the U.K. will collapse or even that the monarchy will disappear. Rather, for a growing number of people, the psychological ties that have bound the country together for generations are weakening, as has been the case ever since the British Empire began to disintegrate after the end of World War II.

Political Participation

Just as important in understanding both the long-term stability and short-term difficulties of any system are the ways in which people participate in political life. Over the past century or so, most of that participation in Britain has been through political parties and interest groups that pursue moderate policies and concentrate on class and economic issues.

Before the 1970s, the Labour and Conservative parties were the linchpin in British political stability as the primary architects of the collectivist consensus. After the war, one or the other won each general election with a firm parliamentary majority, and the victorious party treated the result as a mandate to carry out the policies laid out in its **manifesto,** or electoral platform. (See table 4.4.)

With the onset of the economic crisis in the 1970s, however, the parties, too, began to change. Both Labour and the Conservatives ended up deeply divided, with the balance of power in each drifting out toward ideological extremes. Some polarization occurred in all of the liberal democracies, though it went farther and faster in Britain than in most of the others. However, as in all of them, the shift toward extremism proved to be a passing phenomenon. By the end of the 1980s, Labour had joined the other social democratic parties in moderating its views, and Thatcher's retirement in 1990 and the Tory defeats in 1997 and 2001 have had the same effect on the Conservatives, although their "modernization" is still in its earliest phases.

In short, Labour and the Conservatives are now squarely catch-all parties whose primary motivation is winning elections. Their ideological positions still differ somewhat and remain important to the grassroots activists who attend the annual party conferences. However, the leaders have shown a willingness to sacrifice ideological purity for likely electoral gains. They are increasingly under the sway of spin doctors who, like their American counterparts, seem more like advertising executives than committed partisans.

The Conservatives

Though they are out of power as of this writing, we start with the Conservatives, because they were in charge for so much of the past century and a half that they have often been seen as the "natural party of government" (www.conservatives.com). They have won a majority of the elections since the late 1880s and have been in office about two-thirds of the time since World War II. That said, their inability to chart a new course after their defeats in the last two elections could consign the Tories to an extended period in opposition. That would be even more likely were Labour to introduce **proportional representation** for parliamentary elections, which they have put on and then taken off the agenda a couple of times since Blair took office.

The Conservatives were so successful for three main reasons, which began to evaporate during the Thatcher years. First, most Conservative leaders were pragmatic politicians who were flexible enough to change their policies when circumstances warranted. For example, the early-nineteenth-century Tories may well have wanted to maintain the elitist system in which only the wealthiest men could vote. But, by the time of the Chartist movement of the 1820s, they recognized that they would have to extend the suffrage. Similarly, it was the Conservative Party under Benjamin Disraeli that organized the first grassroots constituency organizations after the Reform Act of 1867 granted the vote to most working-class men.

▌ **TABLE 4.4** British Prime Ministers Since 1945

YEAR	PARTY	YEARS IN OFFICE
Clement Attlee	Labour	1945–51
Winston Churchill	Conservative	1951–55
Anthony Eden	Conservative	1955–56
Harold Macmillan	Conservative	1956–63
Alec Douglas Home	Conservative	1963–64
Harold Wilson	Labour	1964–70
Edward Heath	Conservative	1970–74
Harold Wilson	Labour	1974–76
James Callaghan	Labour	1976–79
Margaret Thatcher	Conservative	1979–90
John Major	Conservative	1990–97
Tony Blair	Labour	1997–

Second, because their roots lay in the nobility, conservative politicians tended to embody the values of noblesse oblige, or the responsibility of the elite to the less fortunate. As a result, the Conservatives did not historically champion the free-market economy and unbridled capitalism. To be sure, the party always included people like Thatcher who believed market forces should be strengthened. However, the party's most influential leaders stressed its responsibility for the poor and were willing to support a substantial welfare state, to use the government to maintain the health of a capitalist economy, and to accept the collectivist consensus after World War II.

Third, the Conservatives had a rather elitist but effective organization. The party maintained organizations in each constituency, most of which had a full-time paid "agent." Real power, however, lay in London and, ultimately, with the leader, who was also prime minister when the party was in power. There were no formal provisions for selecting the leader, who normally was secretly chosen by senior MPs. The leader, in turn, dominated the parliamentary party and the central office, which had veto power over whom local constituency organizations nominated to run for Parliament.

In the mid-1970s, the Conservatives adopted more open procedures for choosing new leaders that a new generation of market-oriented MPs who were hostile to the welfare state used to select Margaret Thatcher after Edward Heath led the party to two defeats at the polls in 1974. Thatcher and her colleagues preferred what they called the politics of commitment to the consensus building and pragmatism of earlier periods.

Thatcherism served the Tories extremely well through the 1980s. In large part because of its own difficulties, to be discussed shortly, Labour dumped the 1979 election into Thatcher's lap, beginning her eleven years in office. At first, she was obliged to include most of the senior party leaders in her cabinet, including many who did not share her objections to collectivist politics. Over the next few years, however, she gained more and more control over the party, forcing most of the moderates onto the sidelines and replacing them with ideological conservatives who also were personally beholden to her.

When Thatcher's popularity slipped and she was finally forced to resign in 1990, the challenge came not from the moderates, but from her erstwhile supporters who had come to see her as an electoral liability. They then chose her protégé, John Major (1943–). Though widely respected, Major proved to be a mediocre leader who neither appealed to the electorate nor bridged over the party's deepening divisions, especially over Europe.

Major resigned as party leader the day after the 1997 election and was replaced by the young but experienced William Hague. Since then, the party has had three leaders, all of whom were viewed as ineffective. In 2003, the party replaced Iain Duncan Smith with the veteran politician Michael Howard. Howard is part of the euroskeptic wing of the party, served in the cabinet under Thatcher and Major, and has a reputation for being abrasive.

The key to the Tory future probably lies in the way the party handles two issues. Given the fact that during only one month in 2003 and early 2004 did the Tories trail Labour by less than 8 percent in the most respected poll (www.mori.com), its future looks bleak indeed.

The first are its divisions over European integration. Although Thatcherism was initially defined by the prime minister's promarket and antiwelfare state positions, by the 1990s most of the Tory right came to be preoccupied with "Europe." They saw such developments as the **Maastricht Treaty,** which created the EU, and the creation of a single currency as serious threats to British sovereignty. (See Chapter 7.) Most of them objected to Major's decision to defer any decision on monetary union until a decision had to be made and were convinced that the party lost the election because of its indecisiveness. All the polls, however, suggest that the euroskepticism actually worsened the Tories' defeat in 1997 and will con-

AFP/Getty Images

Michael Howard, shortly after he was named leader of the Conservative Party in 2003.

tinue to undermine their popularity for the foreseeable future. Polls continue to show widespread doubts about adopting the euro. Nonetheless, few Britons share the depth of opposition to the EU one finds among the ardent euroskeptics who now control the party.

Second, and related, is its leadership and organization. As many as a third of its members are over 65. And the shrinking number of Conservative activists reflects the "hard right" views of the last three leaders. In other words, no matter how the party decides to choose its leaders (it has changed those procedures three times since Thatcher left office), it is likely to end up with someone who will have a hard time reaching out to the swing voters it would need to return to power.

Labour

For most of the past thirty years, it has been Labour, not the Conservatives, that has borne the criticism for being too extreme and out of touch with the electorate. But after four consecutive defeats and three leadership changes, the party moved back toward the center and become among the more modern and innovative parties in the industrialized world.

The Labour Party (www.labour.org.uk) was formed at the beginning of the twentieth century as an alliance of trade unions, independent socialist movements, and cooperative associations. Unlike the socialist parties we will encounter in subsequent chapters, Marxists had little influence on the party in its early years. Clause 4 of the original party program adopted after World War I did call for the nationalization of the "commanding heights" of British industry. Still, most observers were convinced that Labour had accepted the parliamentary system and the democratic rules of the game by the early 1900s, unlike many of its counterparts on the continent.

This was the case in large part because the unions dominated the party. Trade Unions Congress (TUC) members automatically join Labour as well unless they sign a form informing the union not to send part of their dues to the party. Because the trade unionists were more concerned with improving the lives of their members than with any doctrine, they were able to keep the party close to the center throughout most of its history. After losing three consecutive elections in the 1950s, many Labour leaders came to the conclusion that the party could never win a majority again if Clause 4 stayed in the party program or if it kept the few radical stands it had on controversial issues such as unilateral disarmament. Although it did not formally repudiate Clause 4 until after Blair took over the leadership, the party conference in 1959 did make it clear that socialism was at most a long-term goal for the party, not something it would implement were it to win the next election, which it did in 1964. (See table 4.5.)

The Labour government of 1964–70 was dominated by moderates in the parliamentary party. That moderation, however, would not survive the onset of the economic crisis. A new wave of union militancy pushed many in the party leftward, as did entry into the European Community (the predecessor to the EU) in 1972. Most importantly, the party's left wing gained support

▌ TABLE 4.5 British General Election Results Since 1945

YEAR	CONSERVATIVES VOTES	CONSERVATIVES SEATS	LABOUR VOTES	LABOUR SEATS	LIBERAL DEMOCRATS VOTES	LIBERAL DEMOCRATS SEATS	OTHER VOTES	OTHER SEATS
1945	39.8%	213	48.3%	393	9.1%	12	2.7%	22
1950	43.5	299	46.1	315	9.1	9	1.3	2
1951	48.0	321	46.8	295	2.5	6	0.7	3
1955	49.7	345	46.4	277	2.7	6	1.1	2
1959	49.4	365	43.8	258	5.9	6	1.0	1
1964	43.4	304	44.1	317	11.2	9	1.3	0
1966	41.9	253	47.9	363	8.5	12	1.6	2
1970	46.4	330	43.0	288	7.5	6	3.1	6
1974 (Feb.)	37.8	297	37.1	301	19.3	14	5.8	23
1974 (Oct.)	35.8	277	39.2	319	18.3	13	6.7	26
1979	43.9	339	37.0	269	13.8	11	5.3	16
1983	42.4	397	27.6	209	25.4	23	4.6	21
1987	42.3	376	30.8	229	22.6	22	4.3	23
1992	41.8	336	34.4	271	17.8	20	6.0	24
1997	30.6	165	43.2	419	16.7	45	9.7	30
2001	31.7	166	40.7	413	18.3	52	8.5	28

Note: Others consist almost exclusively of regional parties in Scotland, Wales, and Northern Ireland. Liberals includes Liberals up to 1983, Liberal–Social Democratic Alliance in 1983–87, and Liberal Democrats in 1992. The total number of seats varies from election to election, with a low of 625 in 1950 and 1951 and a high of 659 in 1997.

from activists first drawn to politics by the new left in the 1960s.

The shift leftward and the party's inability to control the newly radicalized unions led to its defeat in 1979. Rather than moderating its positions, the party moved even further to the left. It chose the radical Michael Foot to be its new leader. It also created an electoral college comprising members of Parliament, union officials, and rank-and-file activists to select new leaders, thus stripping power from the relatively moderate MPs. Meanwhile, seventeen of its most conservative MPs quit in 1981 and created the new Social Democratic Party, which we will discuss in the next section.

The party seemed dominated by its left wing, epitomized by the enigmatic Anthony Wedgwood Benn. Though from an aristocratic family (the Wedgwoods make some of Britain's finest china), Benn had gradually moved to the left during the 1970s and was now advocating a radical break from capitalism. He, not Foot, was Labour's most visible leader during the 1983 campaign, and together they led the party to one of its worst defeats ever. The party did so poorly that many observers thought that the **Alliance,** formed between the Liberals and Social Democrats, might replace Labour as the country's second largest party.

Had Benn not lost his seat that year, he might well have been chosen to replace the ineffectual Foot. Instead, the party turned to Neil Kinnock. Though on the left of the party, Kinnock was willing to put its electoral success ahead of ideological purity. The party made up some of its lost ground in 1987, but it still found itself 11.5 percent in votes and nearly 150 seats behind the Tories.

Over the next five years, Labour's moderation led to increased support in the polls. Nationalization of industry all but disappeared from the party program. The party also abandoned its commitment to unilateral nuclear disarmament, which had cost it dearly in 1983 and 1987.

Perhaps most importantly, like the American Democrats in 1992 or Labour itself in the early 1960s, party activists and leaders had grown tired of losing. As the next elections neared, Labour found new unity rooted in a common desire to defeat the Tories, which, in turn, reinforced the belief that it had to modify its stance. At the 1991 party conference, for instance, Clare Short, a left-wing MP and a member of Blair's cabinet until she quit to protest its policies on Iraq in 2003, won ringing applause for the following statement: Thatcher "should have been a short-term leader of the opposition. And that [she was not] is our fault. We have to be very grown-up, very serious and very honest about our politics. We all used to posture. This is deadly serious."

As election day neared, pollsters predicted either a Labour victory or, at least, a hung Parliament in which Labour would have the most seats but not an overall majority. When the votes were counted, Labour had lost an unprecedented fourth straight election.

This time, however, defeat did not splinter the party. Kinnock immediately announced that he would step down. Most party leaders were convinced that he had done a good job in creating a more credible image for the party and that it therefore had to continue with its more moderate policies. In any case, he was replaced by the widely respected and even more pragmatic John Smith.

The most dramatic shift in Labour politics came after Smith's sudden death in 1994. This time, Labour took a major risk by selecting the dynamic Tony Blair as his successor. Blair was only forty-one at the time. And he and his colleagues made it abundantly clear that they were planning to strip away all vestiges of the old—and loony—Labour left. Within a year, Clause 4 was gone. The party announced that it would keep many of the reforms of the Thatcher-Major era, including most of the privatizations of companies and the changes in the social service system. Blair even acknowledged that he had personally respected Thatcher's style, if not her policies. The power of the unions to control the party leadership was reduced even further, and most of the leftists were shunted onto the sidelines. In their place were younger and more moderate politicians who, like Blair, had few connections to the working class, let alone socialism.

The Blair government's actions will be discussed in depth in the section on public policy. Here, it is enough to build on his strengths and weaknesses as leader that were first raised in the introduction to the chapter.

There is no doubt that Blair has had moments when he has been remarkably popular. He is bright, personally engaging, and maybe the most effective British politician ever at using television to get his point of view across. There is no doubt either that the majority of British citizens saw his government as a welcome change to a Tory government that had grown stale, old, and, in many eyes, corrupt after eighteen years in office.

But there is little enthusiasm left for his prime ministry. His positions on issues ranging from Iraq to university fees have alienated even some of the Labour Party's staunchest supporters. His often iron-handed and seemingly arbitrary control of the party machinery has had a similar effect. Finally, the scandals that have brought down several of his closest colleagues and the government's failure to make inroads on such important policies as modernizing the public transit system or the National Health Service has cost it support among the moderates who flocked to the party in 1997.

TONY BLAIR

Owen Humphrey/AP/Wide World Photos

Tony Blair with his wife Cherie Booth.

Anthony Charles Lynton Blair became the youngest twentieth-century prime minister when Labour won its landslide victory in 1997.

Blair is not a typical Labour politician. He was born to an upper-middle-class family—his father was a law professor and led the local Conservative Party in Durham where the Blairs lived. Tony was educated at public (that is, private, in American terms) schools, including Edinburgh's Fettes, the most prestigious school in Scotland.

At Oxford, Blair largely avoided the hedonistic student life of the mid-1970s, though he did play in a mediocre rock group, Ugly Rumours, that disbanded after three performances. After graduation, he moved to London, where he practiced law and joined the Labour Party. In 1982, he ran and lost in a by-election. The next year, he was chosen for the safe seat of Sedgefield, near Durham, which he has represented ever since. Blair cast his lot with John Smith and other pragmatic party reformers early in his career, but he also did not alienate colleagues on the left. So, when Smith died, he won the party leadership surprisingly easily.

In 1980 Blair married Cherie Booth, whose father was one of the stars of *Till Death Do Us Part,* a 1960s sitcom that was the model for the American *All in the Family.* Booth is one of England's leading queen's counselors, or trial attorneys. The Blairs have four children.

Though often compared with Bill Clinton, there has never been a whiff of scandal about Blair's personal life.

There now seems to be little doubt that he will be able to hold on until the end of his term, which will probably come with elections in May 2005. As noted earlier, the Tories are still weak enough that Labour is expected to win handily again. At that point, only Margaret Thatcher would have served longer than Blair in the last one hundred years. It is not out of the question that Blair will turn over leadership of the party to his more taciturn ally in rebuilding the party and sometime rival in running it, Gordon Brown, who has served as Chancellor of the Exchequer throughout his time as prime minister. What happens then is anyone's guess.

The Liberal Democrats

The newest major party is the **Liberal Democrats** (www .libdems.org.uk). The party is a product of a merger of the Liberals (one of the country's original parties) and the **Social Democrats** (**SDP**). Britain has never had a true two-party system, but in the postwar period, Labour and the Conservatives dominated political life. The Liberals were the largest of the other parties, but the party never won more than fourteen seats between 1945 and 1979.

During the 1960s, Liberal leaders struggled to define a reform strategy that would situate their party between the increasingly ideological Labour and Conservative parties and provide a haven for the growing number of dissatisfied voters. Popular support for the Liberals did grow during the 1970s, although they were still able to only win a handful of constituencies. Most of their new voters were not confirmed Liberals. Instead, they were traditional Conservative or Labour supporters who felt that they could no longer vote for their traditional party but also could not bring themselves to vote for its main rival.

In 1981, four prominent leaders (known as the "gang of four") quit Labour to form the SDP. They assumed that millions of voters would follow them, and initial public opinion polls suggested they might be right. Quickly, however, it became clear that the SDP could not win on its own and would be consigned to a role much like that of the Liberals. At that point, Liberal and Social Democratic leaders decided to form the Alliance and run a single candidate in each district. The Alliance did well at the polls, winning about 26 percent of the vote in 1983, only two percentage points less than Labour.

But the new party fell victim to Britain's **first-past-the-post,** or winner-take-all, electoral system. Any number of candidates can run, and whoever wins the most votes wins the constituency even if she or he ends up far short of a majority. In other words, a minor party can win an impressive share of the vote, but if that vote is spread more or less evenly around the country, it can be all but shut out of Parliament. That is precisely what happened to the Alliance in 1983, when it only won twenty-three seats, or 3.5 percent of the total.

The Alliance itself proved difficult to maintain. The two parties had different traditions and different, but equally ambitious, leaders. Tensions mounted following its marginally worse results in 1987. The two leaderships decided to merge and create the Liberal Democratic Party. The merger was accepted by everyone except for a small faction headed by David Owen, who had been Labour's foreign minister and who would later be one of the leading negotiators seeking a solution to the civil war in Bosnia. Owen kept the SDP alive until a by-election in 1990, when it barely topped 150 votes, not even a third of the number captured by Lord David Sutch of the Raving Monster Loony Party. The SDP disbanded.

The new party and its leader, Paddy Ashdown, went into the 1992 election with high hopes. Unfortunately for them, it did even worse than the Alliance had, losing 20 percent of its vote and two of its twenty-two seats.

Since then, the party has turned its fortunes around in two key respects. First, it capitalized on dissatisfaction with the Conservatives to build a strong base in local government, where it has actually forced the Tories into third place. Then, in the run-up to the 1997 parliamentary election, it cast itself to Labour's left on a number of issues by advocating stronger environmental policies and an income tax hike to fund increased spending on health and education. That, plus some tactical voting in which Labour supporters cast their votes for a Liberal Democrat who stood a good chance of winning, led to a doubling of its representation in Parliament despite actually losing a few votes nationwide.

The Liberal Democrats' expectations continued to mount in 1997 and 1998, when Blair's government appointed some of their more prominent leaders to joint cabinet committees considering constitutional and electoral reform. But the party was dealt a serious blow in January 1999, when the highly popular Ashdown decided to retire. There was little reason to believe that Labour would support tactical voting again in the next election, especially once it failed to move forward on key Liberal programs, most notably a shift to proportional representation in parliamentary elections.

In fact, the party did even better in 2001, adding 1.6 percent of the vote and seven seats to its total. It did so because its new leader, Charles Kennedy, proved to be an excellent campaigner, and the party continued to attract middle-class and progressive voters who were turned off by Blair. Public opinion polls since 2001 have consistently shown the Liberal Democrats doing slightly better next time with predictions running between 20 and 22 percent of the vote.

Nonetheless, it is hard to see the Liberal Democrats making the kind of breakthrough the Alliance leaders had hoped for in the mid-1980s. Even given the Tories' terrible performance in the past two elections, they won almost twice as many votes as the Liberal Democrats, who are also still tremendously underrepresented in Parliament given their share of the poll.

Minor Parties

The rise in Scottish, Welsh, and Irish nationalism has also led to a moderate growth in support for regional political parties. In the 1970s, Plaid Cymru (Wales) and the Scottish National Party (SNP) each won seats in the House of Commons. In 1974, the SNP leapt ahead of the Tories into second place in Scotland.

After the 1974 election, the Labour government proposed **devolution,** which would give Scotland and Wales limited self-government. Both proposals were put to referendum, and both were defeated.

The regional parties' fortunes have ebbed and flowed ever since. In recent general elections, they have often come in second in their regions. They are strong enough to have shut the Conservatives out completely in Scotland and Wales in 1997 and to have limited them to a single seat in Scotland in 2001. However, the two parties combined won only ten seats in 1997 and nine in 2001.

Assemblies were created for Scotland and Wales after Labour's return to power, and the regional parties have come in second in the two elections held since then. In 2003, for instance, the SNP won 27 of 129 seats while Plaid Cymru took 12 of the 60 Welsh districts. It should be noted that both had done slightly better four years earlier and that there is no indication that their voters take the notion of secession from the United Kingdom seriously.

Regional parties have always dominated in Northern Ireland, because the "mainland" organizations never run candidates there. As a result, many analysts do not include the eighteen Northern Irish constituencies when covering a general election. Given the importance of the peace process, however, it is important to note, at least in passing, the fact that the balance of power swung in the direction of the province's more extreme parties in the 2003 provincial elections. Sinn Fein (the political wing of the IRA) and the Democratic Unionist Party (led by Protestant clergyman Ian Paisley) emerged as the largest parties in their respective communities, which has made governing the province and implementing the peace agreement all the more difficult.

Britain also has a host of truly minor parties that do little more than make campaigns more enjoyable for voters. Thus, the Natural Law Party based its 1997 and 2001 campaigns on the claim that the world's problems would be solved if we all learned to meditate and levitate. Similarly, independent cross-dresser Mrs. Moneypenny pranced around the stage while the results of the most hotly contested race in 1997, between former BBC correspondent Martin Bell and the Conservative (and corrupt) Neil Hamilton, were being announced.

The British Electorate

During the collectivist years, the British electorate was among the easiest to understand in the industrialized world. In those days, a single issue—social class—shaped the way most voters viewed the political world. (See table 4.6.) When a sample of voters was polled in 1963, 1964, and 1966, two-thirds identified with the same party in each of the three interviews. By contrast, only 22 percent of the French electorate did so in similar surveys. When the interviewers probed, they found that people identified themselves with parties primarily because of the positive connection they saw between "their" party and class.

The issues of the day, conversely, played a relatively minor role in determining either those long-term loyalties or the way people voted in a given election. At most, 2 or 3 percent of the electorate had clearly defined and consistent belief systems. No more than 25 percent had anything approaching a firm understanding of such central political concepts as the difference between left and right. And 75 percent of the electorate saw these concepts in ways that were no more sophisticated (though perhaps less graphic) than those expressed by a lubricating engineer in 1963:

> **Well, when I was in the army you had to put your right foot forward, but in fighting you lead with your left. So I always think that the Tories are the right party for me and that the Labour party are fighters. I know that this isn't right really, but I can't explain it properly, and it does for me.**[4]

In fact, people changed their opinions on such issues as British membership in the Common Market so frequently that pollsters wondered if most voters really had opinions at all on anything but the most visible and controversial matters.

That began to change in the decade before the 1979 election. At first, observers interpreted the Conservative victory as a vote against the radicalism and chaos of the Labour government rather than as a first stage in a more lasting realignment. There was little apparent support for most of Thatcher's policies in the polls, and certainly not the kind of support that could lead to a lasting shift in the way millions of people thought and acted.

Over the course of the next decade, however, a substantial number of workers and lower-middle-class voters did become loyal Tory voters. Nonetheless, by the early 1990s, the more marked trend was a substantial dealignment as voters grew disillusioned with both major parties. Thatcher and her policies did evoke powerful emotions, but ultimately they were largely negative, leading people to want to vote against her party rather than necessarily supporting Labour or the Liberal Democrats.

In other words, Labour did not win in 1997 or again in 2001 primarily because there was a massive and lasting increase in Labour Party identifiers. Rather, its two landslide victories can be explained more readily in terms of voters' "fatigue" with the Conservatives after eighteen years in office in 1997 and the extremely weak campaign run by William Hague and his team four years later.

Labour did regain some of the support it lost among manual workers in 1997 and 2001. (See table 4.6 again.) However, that statistic is misleading, because the size of the working class as a whole continues to decrease. That means that Labour cannot hope to win an election appealing primarily to it and must continue to build a consistent base of support in the growing middle class.

Indeed, there is evidence that Labour has done a

▌ **TABLE 4.6** The Changing Role of Class and Gender in British Politics (percentage voting Labour)

YEAR	WORKING CLASS	WOMEN
1974 (Oct.)	57	38
1979	50	35
1983	38	26
1987	42	32
1992	45	34
1997	58	49

Source: Adapted from Dennis Kavanaugh, *Thatcherism and British Politics: The End of Consensus,* 2nd ed. (New York: Oxford University Press, 1990), 168; Philip Norton, *The British Polity,* 3rd ed. (New York Longman, 1994), 91–92; and David Sanders, "The New Electoral Background," in *New Labour Triumphs: Britain at the Polls,* ed. Anthony King et al. (Chatham, N.J.: Chatham House, 1997), 220.

---

[4]David Butler and Donald Stokes, *Political Change in Britain,* 2nd ed. (New York: St. Martin's Press, 1976), 232.

good job of reaching out to some of what Inglehart called the postmaterialist voters, reflected here in the second column of table 4.6. No real gender gap has emerged in the U.K., perhaps because abortion has not been a serious issue in Britain. It has been legal since the 1960s, and few people want to see any change in the law.

If anything, women were slightly more likely to vote Tory than Labour ever since they won the right to vote in the 1920s. However, in 1997 and 2001, Labour worked hard to increase its support among women, especially in the middle class. That was clear not only in its manifesto but also in the number of young, professional women it nominated, the 106 of them who were elected in 1997 and 118 in 2001, and the high profile a number of women have had since the government took office (for a global list of the number of women in national parliaments, see www.ipu.org).

Interest Groups

Britain has hundreds of interest groups, ranging from the unions discussed earlier to the world's most organized group of backyard gardeners. Some of the groups are national, and others focus only on local concerns—as when the residents of Dover protested against a threatened French purchase of their port should the government privatize it.

Because votes in the House of Commons are normally foreordained conclusions, there is little of the lobbying one finds in the United States. Groups try to maintain good relationships with members of the House of Commons, including "interested" MPs who are acknowledged agents of a union or other group. Not surprisingly, however, the groups focus their activity on the people who actually make the decisions: ministers, party leaders, and senior civil servants. In short, their influence depends on being able to shape the drafting of a bill, not how it is dealt with on the floor of the House.

And, in a country in which the political parties have concentrated their appeals on class lines, not all groups have had levels of influence roughly comparable to their membership or other resources. Two groups, in particular, wield disproportionate influence because of their close links to the major parties—the TUC with Labour and the **Confederation of British Industry** (**CBI**) with the Conservatives.

Britain actually has over three hundred trade unions that enroll about 38 percent of the workforce, down from 53 percent in 1979. About 90 percent of all unionized workers are affiliated with the TUC (www.tuc.org.uk).

The business sector is not as monolithic. As in the United States, there are trade associations for most industries. Chambers of commerce promote business interests in their communities. The CBI is the most important of these groups, with a membership that includes more than 250,000 companies and trade associations (www.cbi.org.uk). Although most of the CBI's members are small companies, the vast majority of its income comes from large firms with over a thousand employees, and these companies dominate it.

All governments increasingly have to consult with interest groups. They have information and expertise that civil servants have to draw on in crafting legislation. Even more importantly, the government needs their cooperation in implementing new laws, something the Heath administration learned to its regret when the TUC refused to comply with the Industrial Relations Act of 1971.

During the collectivist years, the government also included the TUC and CBI when developing most economic policy in what were known as tripartite or **corporatist** arrangements. They and other groups were officially brought into the deliberations of a number of agencies, including the National Economic Development Council (NEDC), Health and Safety Executive, and Commission for Racial Equality.

Relations between the state and interest groups have changed dramatically since then. The Thatcher government effectively froze the unions out of decision making. And, despite Labour's long-standing links to the TUC, it, too, has distanced itself from the unions and has sought, instead, to solidify its relationship with dynamic corporations, especially in the high-tech industries, since Blair took office.

The British State: Enduring Myths and Changing Realities

In 1867, Walter Bagehot (1826–77) published *The English Constitution*. Much like Alexis de Tocqueville's *Democracy in America*, Bagehot's book is still read not only as a classic historical document but also as a source of useful insights into politics today for two main reasons.

First is the very fact that he analyzed the British constitution. That may not seem like a big deal to people from other liberal democracies, but it is for Britain because it does not have a written constitution. What Bagehot pointed out was that Britain indeed had one composed of acts of Parliament, understandings, and traditional practices that everyone agreed to follow.

Second, Bagehot drew a distinction between what he called the "dignified" and the "real" parts of the Brit-

▌TABLE 4.7 The British and American States

FEATURE	UNITED KINGDOM	UNITED STATES
Basic constitutional arrangements	Unwritten Unitary Fusion of powers Relatively strong	Written Federal Separation of powers Relatively weak
Executive	Dominant Recruited from Parliament	Power to persuade Recruited every-where
Legislature	Mostly debating Party voting	Making laws Coalition-based voting

ish constitution. The dignified side included the monarchy and other institutions that no longer had much impact on day-to-day political life. Instead, he argued, the real power in the English constitutional system lay with the House of Commons. (See table 4.7.)

The Monarchy and the Lords: Still Dignified?

The monarchy and the **House of Lords** have duties and responsibilities that give them quite a bit of visibility. But it is safe to say that they have no real impact on what the government does.

Officially, there are four types of lords (www.parliament.the-stationery-office.co.uk/pa/ld/ldhome.htm). Until 1958, all lords were hereditary peers. They came from the traditional nobility, whose ancestors were made lords for service—meritorious and otherwise—to the Crown. Sons inherited seats from their fathers. A 1999 law stripped the hereditary peers of their membership except for a small group of ninety-two of them who were elected by their colleagues to remain.

About six hundred of the seven hundred current members of the lords are life peers. A 1958 law authorized the monarch (but, in practice, the prime minister) to elevate people to the Lords for exemplary service in politics, business, or other walks of life. Their peerages end with their deaths and are thus not inherited by their children. The five archbishops and about twenty other church officials are also lords. Finally, the law lords serve as Britain's highest court of appeals. However, unlike the U.S. Supreme Court, they cannot rule on the constitutionality of acts of Parliament. The House of Lords does have to approve all legislation. However, various agreements reached over the centuries have stripped it of the power to do anything more than delay enactment of a

bill by a few months. It did use that power to effectively kill the government's plan to outlaw foxhunting in the last days of the first Blair government. But it cannot do even that on legislation included in the government's election manifesto.

In late 2001, a royal commission outlined the government's plans for a new upper house with about 550 members that would be partially elected but largely appointed. In early 2003, the parliament was presented with seven options for implementing that plan. It rejected all of them. The government went back to the drawing boards, and no new proposals had come forward by mid-2005 when these lines were written.

The monarchy is even less powerful. Theoretically, the monarch still rules "in Parliament." (See figure 4.1.) This means that Queen Elizabeth II names the new prime minister and the rest of the cabinet. They all then have to kneel before her to take their oaths of office. She opens each session of Parliament by reading a speech from the throne outlining "her" policies for the upcoming term. Finally, a bill only becomes law when she gives her royal assent (www.royal.gov.uk).

In practice, the monarch has no such powers. She does not determine who joins a cabinet or whether to agree to legislation. And her speech from the throne is written by the prime minister.

For many, the monarchy today is an embarrassment. The House of Windsor has been embroiled in scandals involving the failed marriages and highly publicized affairs of Prince Charles and his siblings. The tragic death of Diana, Princess of Wales, in August 1997 and

▌FIGURE 4.1 Decision Making in Britain

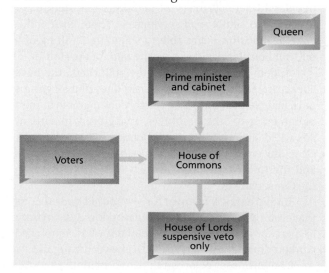

the tremendous outpouring of grief it engendered only added to the royal family's woes.

Parliamentary Sovereignty—Sort Of

In Bagehot's eyes, the **House of Commons** (www .parliament.uk/about_commons/about_commons.cfm) was sovereign because it was the body that determined who governed and which laws would be passed. Parliament officially retains those powers. However, as critics of the British state are quick to point out, the Commons as a whole is no longer a particularly powerful body. Instead, real influence lies with the leadership of the majority party and, increasingly, in the nonelected bodies that grew in importance during the more than a decade and a half of uninterrupted Tory rule.

To see that, however, we have to start with the House of Commons and the discussion of parliamentary systems presented in Chapter 2 and figure 4.1 The Commons currently has 659 MPs. (The exact number changes slightly each time the country is redistricted.) Like members of the U.S. House of Representatives, MPs represent single-member districts and are elected in first-past-the-post elections. There, the similarity between the two systems ends. The MPs are not expected to represent their constituencies' interests in the way members of Congress do. They do not even have to live in their districts, and the national party organization will frequently "parachute" leading politicians into safe seats (as with Blair in 1983), all but guaranteeing that they will be re-elected time and time again.

From 1995 to 1998, I lived just outside of Henley-on-Thames, site of the world-famous regatta and one of the most solidly conservative constituencies in the country. The MP was Michael Heseltine, long one of the most prominent Tories, who served as deputy prime minister during the last two years of the Major government. Few of my British friends knew if Heseltine lived in the district (he did not, though his mother did). And even fewer of them cared, because they understood that MPs are not primarily elected to reflect the views and preferences of the "folks back home."

The key to British politics is the **parliamentary party,** as its delegation in the House of Commons is known. The leader of the majority party becomes prime minister and can almost always count on the support of his or her parliamentary colleagues. The head of the largest minority party becomes leader of the opposition and appoints the **shadow cabinet,** whose members monitor and criticize the actions of their equivalents in the government. The party leaders are senior politicians who enjoy the ideological and personal support of the other MPs in their party. As such, they are quite different from most recent American presidential candidates, who

The first televised session of the House of Commons in 1989. Many parliamentary debates and question periods are now televised on C-SPAN in the United States.

REX USA Ltd.

got that far because of their personal bases of support and built careers largely outside of Washington. In Britain there is only one road to the top—through the parliamentary party.

Thatcher's and Blair's careers are typical. Elected to Parliament at age thirty-three in 1959, Thatcher spent her first decade on the **backbenches,** as the seats reserved for MPs who are not part of the leadership are known. She was appointed to her first cabinet post eleven years later. Only such a veteran could seriously aspire to the leadership of a party in reasonably good shape, a post that came six years later. Similarly, Blair was only thirty when he was first elected. Because Labour was in disarray, young politicians like Blair could rise through the ranks more quickly, and by the time his predecessor, John Smith, died, Blair had held a number of important positions in the shadow cabinet. Still, he had spent eleven years in the House before he became party leader and had fourteen years experience before moving into 10 Downing Street.

The prime minister selects the rest of the cabinet (most of whom are officially called secretaries of state), along with about seventy other junior ministers. All are members of Parliament. All but two members of Blair's cabinet are members of the House of Commons. The only exceptions are Lord Chancellor and the Leader of the House of Lords who must be chosen from the upper house.

As in the United States, each cabinet minister is responsible for a department or portfolio, such as foreign affairs, the Exchequer (economics), or defense. Men and women are appointed to cabinet positions that roughly correspond to their positions in the party's power structure, which are not necessarily ones that reflect their interests or talents. Consequently, ministers are even less likely to be experts in the area they are responsible for than are their American counterparts. Each minister also has two or three other MPs who serve as junior ministers, usually coordinating relations with the bureaucracy and Parliament.

Unlike in the United States, the cabinet is governed by the principle of **collective responsibility,** remaining in office as long as the entire government retains the support of its parliamentary majority. Moreover, individual ministers must publicly support all cabinet decisions, including those they disagree with. If not, they are expected to resign, as Clare Short and former Foreign Minister Robin Cook did over Iraq.

The cabinet introduces all major legislation. Once it proposes a bill, a highly charged adversarial process unfolds as the bill wends its way through Parliament. Debate in the House of Commons is among the most acrimonious in the world, which is reflected in the very architecture of its chamber in the Palace of Westminster. Most legislatures are laid out in a semicircle, with the speaker's podium in the center. In Britain the government and opposition face each other on benches that, tradition has it, are separated by the distance of two drawn swords.

Members hurl political charges and personal insults at each other. They often shout so loud that the person who has the floor cannot be heard, while the speaker pounds the gavel and screams "order, order" to no avail. Sessions are especially heated when an important bill is being debated and when ministers appear to answer whatever questions opposition MPs and their own backbenchers ask of them.

The intensity of parliamentary debate, however, should not lead you to conclude that it actually matters very much. Because of the way parliamentary systems work, as discussed in Chapter 2, as long as one party has a majority in Parliament, it is virtually assured of getting its bills passed.

Of the 213 bills proposed by the Thatcher and Major governments in the 1987–92 Parliament, 202 passed. And 6 of the remaining 11 probably would have been approved as well had the House of Commons had time to get to them before the 1992 election. Backbench pressure sometimes forces the government to modify or even withdraw a bill, but that almost never happens on what it considers to be major legislation.

There are exceptions when a significant number of the government's backbenchers vote against something as happened in the votes on tuition rates and Iraq. So many members defected that Labour cannot realistically hope to discipline them other than blocking their promotion off the backbenches in the short run. But, it should also be noted that such incidents are few and far between. Even more importantly, there is strong, if anecdotal, evidence that many disgruntled MPs decided to vote for the government or abstain because they were not willing to put the life of the government in jeopardy.

There are "free votes" in which members can do as they choose, which governments sometimes use when their own party is divided. For instance, in 1995 Prime Minister Major allowed a free vote on the recommendation of the Nolan Commission, which sought to force MPs to make public how much money they made as consultants to organizations with political interests. Sometimes, too, the government agrees to accept amendments from its backbenchers. However, all major legislation and even significant amendments to key bills are deemed votes of confidence, and the government wins because the majority's MPs have no real leeway in determining how to vote.

MPs are officially notified that such a vote will take place when they receive a **three-line whip.** Physically, this is a simple note from the party whips, underlined three times, stating that a vote will take place at a stated time. But the MPs know what it means. When it is time for the vote or a division (the MPs literally divide and go into two rooms, one for those in favor of a bill and the other for those against it), the prime minister can count on more than enough support for the bill to pass.

Backbenchers' influence is limited, too, by the way the House of Commons is organized. It does not have the kind of committee system in which members and their extensive staffs develop expertise in a given policy area. Members of the Commons have at most one or two full-time staffers, compared with an average of eighteen for members of the U.S. House of Representatives. Their office budgets are barely a fourth that of an American representative.

Despite their power, British governments rarely act rashly or irresponsibly. The decision to proceed with new legislation usually comes only after an extended period of study and debate. The discussions that culminated in the 1948 act that established the National Health Service began in the mid-1930s, when major flaws in the old insurance system began to receive serious attention. It was another decade before the government **white paper** on the subject was issued, in 1944. Four more years elapsed before the bill was passed. More recently, Thatcher's program of privatizing nationalized industries and other assets did not appear out of thin air but had been under scrutiny by the Conservative Party and economists for years.

Furthermore, when governments do blunder, there are ways, however imperfect, in which disgruntled MPs can respond. For example, when British and French troops occupied the Suez Canal in 1956 after it had been taken over by the Egyptian government, Conservative MPs continued to support Anthony Eden's government, which easily survived a vote of confidence. It was clear, however, that Eden's actions had cost him the confidence of his own party. Sensing that, he resigned the following year, citing his declining health. In fact, he did not resign because of his health—he lived until 1977—but because enough Conservative MPs had exerted behind-the-scenes pressure that Eden realized he had to leave. The same thing, of course, happened to Thatcher in 1990 and could happen to Blair if his popularity continues to slide.

But, on balance, the government does get what it wants. As Andrew Marr put it:

> Government backbenchers can, at rare moments, exercise some leverage on the general drift of the executive policy which can, from time to time, help change the world beyond Westminster. But most of the time, frankly, it's more like children shouting at passing aircraft.[5]

Cabinet Government?

Because all important legislation originates with the cabinet, its plans and objectives are a constant source of rumor. Speeches by ministers (especially at the annual party conferences), their appearances before the House of Commons during question time, and the interviews they grant the early morning *Today* show on BBC radio or the late evening *Newsnight* on television can be moments of great political drama.

That said, cabinet government is becoming something of a myth. As in most countries, cabinet meetings are held in secret, and only a brief official announcement of what was decided is issued at the end of each week's session. Nonetheless, we have learned a good deal in recent years about how the cabinet operates through numerous leaks (at which British politicians seem particularly adept) and the often revealing memoirs of former ministers, most notably Richard Crossman. He also was a political scientist and journalist who held a number of offices in the 1964–70 Labour governments.

Crossman was one of the party's leading theoreticians and hoped to head one of the major ministries. However, because of his relatively low position in the party hierarchy, he ended up as minister of housing, a position he was neither particularly interested in nor qualified for. Nonetheless, Crossman came to office committed to fulfilling the goal for his ministry laid out in the party's manifesto: constructing 500,000 new housing units during its term in office. He assumed, too, that he would simply inform his civil servants of that goal, and they would say, "Yes, minister," and begin drawing up the legislation and plans to implement it. But, as the sitcom of the same name shows, "yes, minister" often means exactly the opposite. Officially, the civil servants are there to do what their title suggests—serve their minister. In reality, they possess so much more experience and have so much more leverage over the bureaucracy than the minister does that they often have a lot more to

[5] Andrew Marr, *Ruling Britannia: The Failure and Future of British Democracy* (London: Michael Joseph, 1995), 115.

The Cabinet

The cabinet is the most important political institution in Britain for all the reasons discussed in the body of the text. However, it is different from the American cabinet in two critical respects. All ministers and secretaries of state must also be members of the House of Commons or the House of Lords. Second, the prime minister is free to combine, break up, or create new ministries in keeping with the fact that the United Kingdom does not have a written constitution. In fall 2004, the following were the ministries whose heads were part of the cabinet (translations for American readers are provided in those cases when it is not obvious what the ministry's jurisdiction is): Prime Minister; Deputy Prime Minister; Chancellor of the Exchequer (Treasury); Foreign and Commonwealth Affairs Home Secretary (justice and police); Environment, Food, and Rural Affairs; Transport; Health; Chancellor of the Duchy Lancaster (no formal duties; minister without portfolio); Northern Ireland; Defense; Trade and Industry; Women; Culture, Media, and Sport; Chief Whip; Education; Chief Secretary to the Treasury; Leader of the House of Commons; Leader of the House of Lords; Constitutional Affairs; International Development; Work and Pensions (www.number-10.gov.uk).

---

say about what happens. In this case, they told Crossman it was impossible to build that many new homes so quickly. Despite everything Crossman tried, he could not get them to change.

More importantly for Crossman, instead of experiencing the excitement and power that would come with making the "big decisions" about his country's future, he found himself preoccupied with seemingly never-ending public relations functions and paperwork. Meanwhile, Prime Minister Harold Wilson and the handful of ministers closest to him were making important decisions and then presenting them to the cabinet as a whole as faits accomplis. Ministers like Crossman, who were not part of the inner circle, had a say only on issues that affected their own ministries, not on the broader issues of national policy that had drawn them into public service in the first place. If anything, that trend has accelerated with Blair, who has relied more heavily on personal advisers than on his cabinet.

In sum, many analysts today argue that Britain has prime ministerial government, since the holder of that office has tremendous sway over what the state does. Some even argue that Blair has tried to make the prime minister more presidential, at least during his first government. He took all but total control of the Labour

Party, kept ideological rivals in the party out of the cabinet, and used his personal popularity to build support for his policy agenda. In his second term, as his popularity ebbed, he seemed more prime ministerial—governing with colleagues and having to deal with disputes inside his own party. Nonetheless, there is little doubt that the prime minister is no longer *primus inter pares* or the first among equals as the office was initially intended to be.

The Rest of the State

The rest of the British state is nowhere near as important. Nonetheless, there are three areas that deserve at least some attention here.

First is the weakness of the British bureaucracy compared to its equivalents on the Continent and in Japan. There, top civil servants believe that it is their role to help forge cooperative arrangements that allow the state to coordinate much of the economic policy making for public and private sectors alike.

Most British senior civil servants do not think of themselves as formulators of policy. Instead, they consider themselves primarily as administrators and believe that the cabinet should determine public policy. At most, their job is to flesh out the details of proposed legislation, keep the politicians from committing major mistakes, and ensure that policy gets carried out once passed by Parliament.

The civil service has also long been dominated largely by white male "mandarins" who were recruited and promoted on the basis of their general intellectual ability and seniority. Since the 1990s a number of reforms have been made, most notably the creation of a Senior Civil Service in 1996. It consists of about 3,900 people and is about half the size of the American Senior Executive Service. About a third of its members are technical experts, not generalists. By 1999, 17 percent were women and almost 2 percent members of racial minorities. Both figures were growing rapidly. Senior civil service pay is determined on the basis of merit rather than time in service. It is, however, too early to tell how and if the SCS will change the way the civil service operates.

Second, during their eighteen years in office, the Tories diluted cabinet and parliamentary sovereignty by assigning more and more responsibilities to two types of nonelected bodies. First are regulatory agencies, which are supposed to oversee the newly privatized companies, most of whose names begin with "Of." Thus, Oftel deals with telecommunications, Ofwat with water, and Ofsted with standards in education.

In addition, there are now more than 7,700 QUANGOs, or quasi-autonomous nongovernmental organizations, which are roughly equivalent to independent U.S. agencies such as the Environmental Protection Agency. During the 1960s and 1970s, Conservative and Labour governments alike decided to "hive off" many regulatory, commercial, and cultural functions to these bodies. QUANGOs were set up, for example, to coordinate the development of new towns, to regulate health and safety at the workplace, and to develop human resources. Some of them, like the British Mint, were not very important politically. Others, like the Consultative Panel on Badgers and Tuberculosis or the Welsh Office Place Names Advisory Board, rarely raise a political eyebrow. But some, like the Commission for Racial Equality or the University Grants Committee (which funds universities), have had some of the most controversial assignments in British politics.

Third, the courts have never had a policy-making role. The settlement ending the Glorious Revolution of 1688 forbade judges from going beyond the merits of a particular case or ruling on the constitutionality of an act of Parliament. Although that is still technically the case, a new generation of more activist judges is stretching that centuries-old policy to its limits. In 1991 a judge overturned the law that did not allow men to be tried for raping their wives. Two years later, another ruled that doctors do not have to keep brain-dead patients alive if their condition is irreversible. And in 1995 the country's most powerful judge publicly criticized Home Secretary Michael Howard's plans to require stiffer sentences for repeat offenders.

Public Policy: The Thatcher and Blair Revolutions

Their supporters often call Margaret Thatcher's and Tony Blair's public policies revolutions. By the standards we will see in later chapters, this is an overstatement. However, Thatcher used her "politics of conviction" to produce dramatic change, most notably in British economic life. It is too early to determine how much Blair's government can or will accomplish. Nonetheless, the fact that the Labour Party has accepted **privatization**—the selling off of state-owned companies—and much of the rest of the core of Thatcherism while trying to give it a more humane and egalitarian face does mark at least a profound break with its past.

While this is true of domestic policy, continuity has been the norm internationally. Both have sought to maintain the U.K.'s "special relationship" with the United States; both have made the U.K. the least European of Europe's major powers.

Economic Liberalization in Britain

NOT SURPRISINGLY, Britain is usually held up as the model of economic liberalization among the industrial democracies. When Thatcher came to power, the government owned or controlled a large part of the economy. By 1997 it had sold off more than fifty major businesses with well over a million employees. In short, the U.K. went further and faster toward privatization than any of its major competitors.

It also went further in adopting liberal (in the European sense) values. Sir Keith Joseph, who was the intellectual architect of the privatization, once said that trying to get a state-owned firm to act like a private one was like trying to "make a mule into a zebra by painting stripes on its back."[a]

[a] Quoted in Daniel Yergin with Joseph Stanislaw, *The Commanding Heights: The Battle Between Government and the Marketplace That Is Remaking the Modern World* (New York: Simon & Schuster, 1998), 122–123.

Domestic Politics

In 1919 the Labour Party committed itself to **nationalization,** or state ownership, of the "commanding heights" of the economy. In addition, it planned to place much of the rest of the economy under government control through planning and to pass the benefits on to the working class and others, thereby creating a more equal and just society. This pledge had little impact on public policy because Labour never had a majority in Parliament until after World War II. After the 1945 election, Labour set up planning boards with wide-ranging authority and nationalized dozens of key industries, especially those that provided public services but that were no longer profitable.

By the 1960s, most of the nationalized industries performed poorly and required massive subsidies. Attempts by successive Labour governments to plan the key industrial sectors of the economy were deemed abject failures that left the greedy and disruptive unions more powerful than ever. The welfare state was proving increasingly expensive, especially the National Health Service (NHS), which provided free health care to all but was terribly underfunded. Overall government spending grew to over 40 percent of GNP in the late 1970s.

Therefore, Thatcher wanted to sharply reduce the role of the state and privatize as many of the nationalized industries as possible. In Thatcher's first term, eight major firms were sold, including British Petroleum (BP), British Aerospace, Cable and Wireless (Telecommunications), long-distance trucking, sugar refining, and the ports. She also allowed most council (public) housing tenants to purchase their homes. During the rest of her years in power, shares in British Leyland, British Gas, British Airways, British Telecom, the jet engine division of Rolls-Royce, and the Jaguar and Rover automobile companies were sold. Under Major, the water distribution system, buses, electricity generation, and even parts of the NHS and the British Broadcasting Corporation (BBC) were sold to private owners.

Privatization proved extremely popular in the short term. As the council houses were gobbled up, home ownership soared to 60 percent of the total population during Thatcher's first term alone. Though most of the shares in the privatized firms were bought by institutional investors, 2.2 million citizens bought into British Telecom and 4 million did the same with British Gas. In the short run, privatization gave the government a needed infusion of capital, adding £70 billion (well over $100 billion) to the British treasury by the end of 1988.

More generally, the Thatcher governments tried to strengthen the role of market forces in shaping the economy. Government subsidies to industry were cut. Firms were encouraged to modernize and to reduce "redundant" labor, even though that meant the number of unemployed rose to over three million. Taxes that hit the wealthy the hardest were slashed to generate more money for investment. In their place, taxes on cigarettes, alcohol, and gasoline that disproportionately affected the poor were raised.

Thatcher's and Major's policies remain highly controversial. Even the Conservatives' severest critics, however, agree that they used the levers of state power quite effectively in producing one of the most dramatic policy changes in modern British history.

This is less clear for the other centerpiece of Thatcherite economic policy—rolling back the welfare state. As the critics saw it, the income support and other policies put in place, usually with the support of earlier Tory governments, wastefully handed out money without giving people the ability to pull themselves out of poverty.

Unlike the nationalized industries, most of the social services programs were quite popular, and attempts to reduce them met with stiff resistance. Still, the government cut back on programs that help single parents, university students, and the unemployed. The delivery of many social services has been privatized, including the hiring of prison guards.

More than a decade has passed since Thatcher was forced out of office, but her policies and legacy remain

Political Theater

One of the most controversial policies of the Thatcher and Major governments was the privatization of industries. Most controversial of all was the 1994 breakup of British rail into what the *Washington Post* described as "25 train operating companies, each using trains owned by three other companies operating on infrastructure—tracks and stations—owned by yet another firm." (10 March 2004, C4).

Almost everyone acknowledges that the rail system has deteriorated since privatization.

In early 2004, the hottest ticket in London's theatre district was David Hare's *The Permanent Way.* At first glance, a play in which people mostly talk about the decline of train service might seem horribly dull. However, the dialogue between actors who play owners, customers, employees, and others in the rail system had audiences riveted.

Even Michael Portillo, the Conservative minister who oversaw the sale of the rail system had to acknowledge the play's power. After seeing a performance, he told the *Washington Post*, "I don't suppose that mine was the only dry throat in the theater, or that only former Tory ministers were having difficulty swallowing."

controversial. To her supporters, she saved the British economy by bringing both inflation and unemployment under control and by creating a more dynamic private sector. To her detractors, she created new problems and exacerbated existing ones by widening the gap between rich and poor and by allowing public services to deteriorate.

Blair's policies are no less controversial. To his supporters, he is charting a **third way** that combines the best aspects of the socialist goals commitment to equality with a market economy. To his detractors inside the Labour Party, he is a flashy politician who has sold out the left and created something they sneeringly refer to as "Thatcher lite."

Blair joined Bill Clinton in the United States and Chancellor Gerhard Schröder in Germany in offering a new kind of progressive public policy that is neither on the right nor the left as those terms have been defined for several generations. In theory, these policies retain the social democratic goals of a more just and egalitarian society but do so in a way that fits the realities of a post-industrial society in an interdependent world. In so doing, they draw on a number of sources, including traditional social democratic thought, Green values, aspects

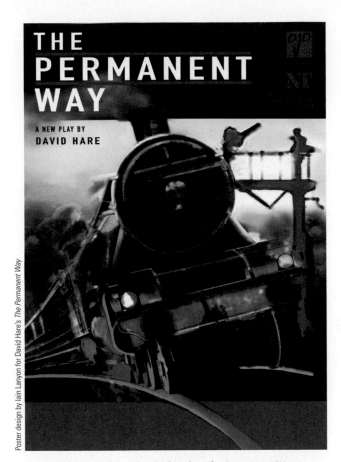

Poster design by Iain Lanyon for David Hare's *The Permanent Way*

The promotional poster for the hit play, *The Permanent Way.*

of management theory, and, in Blair's case, Christian ideals.

Blair and his colleagues have no plans to roll back Thatcher's and Major's reforms. Indeed, in some ways, they have out-Thatchered Thatcher. In one of the first acts of Blair's government, it gave the Bank of England the power to set interest rates without consulting the government. Perhaps most telling of all, government spending as a percentage of GNP actually shrank. The first Blair government pledged not to raise taxes for the life of the parliament or to increase spending above the levels set by the Conservatives for two years. They have actually privatized some more services, including failing local education authorities. The second Blair government plans to privatize part of the London Underground to raise much-needed revenue and allow more private enterprise in the NHS to improve the quality of care.

It has also taken some less significant steps to transform the welfare state from a system that merely provides benefits to one that gives recipients skills to find meaningful jobs and, thus, places some responsibility on them. In one of its most controversial actions, the government agreed to retain a Conservative policy that reduces grants to lone parents (mostly single mothers) who refuse to take jobs. Its most sweeping reform does the same to unemployed people under age twenty-five who do not get either a job or job training.

Curiously, the statistics tell a very different story from Labour's frankly Thatcherite rhetoric. The first Blair government actually was able to redirect quite a bit of money to the poor and to public services. In part, that reflected the booming economy, which generated more tax revenues than the government had expected. But, as the following examples suggest, the government made some important policy changes.

The most impressive accomplishment involved the welfare-to-work scheme, now known as the New Deal. Of the 250,000 chronically unemployed young people, three-quarters found and kept jobs for at least three months after they finished their training. The program was then expanded to serve single mothers and older people. All in all, it cost the government about $7,000 for each job created, less than it spent for a year on welfare payments.

The poorest retirees saw their incomes grow by at least 3 percent per year. The overall impact of fiscal reform was to increase the income of the bottom two-fifths of the population by 8 percent (the rich saw next to no change). Especially after the self-imposed spending limit ended, the government was able to devote significantly more money to education and the NHS, and those figures seem certain to go up further during Blair's second term.

The Blair government has pledged to continue reforms aimed at helping the poor and improving public services in its second term. It campaigned on a promise to add ten thousand teachers, twenty thousand nurses, and ten thousand doctors. In October 2004, it raised the minimum wage to £4.85, or nearly $8 an hour.

But it is fair to say that almost all of the most important and potentially progressive initiative came during the first Blair government before the decline in his personal popularity set in. In the first three years of his second government, only two major initiatives stand out. The first is the widely unpopular tuition increase discussed in the introduction to this chapter.

The second is far more innovative, although it is as much the work of the new London city government as it is of Blair's cabinet. London was one of the most congested and polluted cities in the world. As of 17 February 2003, drivers entering the city center were assessed a toll of approximately $8. The scheme has already reduced traffic congestion dramatically and is now paying for itself. Within ten years it is expected to generate over $2 billion, which will used for investment in the country's dilapidated mass transit network (www.cfit.gov .uk/congestioncharging/factsheets/london/index.htm). Similar plans have been introduced in Durham and are being considered in cities like Reading where I could walk the three miles from my wife's office to mine faster than I could drive it during rush hour.

Foreign Policy

Not even a century ago, the United Kingdom was the world's greatest power. Today it is among a handful of "second tier" countries whose influence pales in comparison with that of the United States. In the changed international environment since the end of World War II, Britain has seen its empire disappear, and government after government has sought to redefine its global role. After the end of decolonization in the 1960s, British foreign policy has focused on two divisive issues that also tell us a lot about the way politics in that country works —its engagement with an integrating Europe and what leaders on the left and right alike see as its "special relationship" with the United States.

Europe

At least for the long term, the most important foreign policy issue facing the country is Europe because it will have the greatest impact on British domestic politics in ways and for reasons that we will consider in Chapter 7. Europe is particularly important here because the British are as divided as any European society about how they should deal with their increasingly unifying continent. That ambiguity is reflected in their country's geography. It is little more than twenty miles from Dover in Kent to Calais in France, a distance that high speed trains span in fifteen minutes. But, for many in Britain, the English Channel is the psychological equivalent of an ocean separating them from people on the continent who are not like them at all. The fact is, however, that Britain is a part of a European Union whose decisions have more impact on the British economy and other aspects of life than those made in London.

At this point, there are two issues regarding Europe that seem likely to spark debate in Britain for years to come. Should it join the European Monetary Union and abandon the pound for the euro? Should it ratify the draft constitution for the European Union that will take it closer to be something like a united states of Europe?

Debate over Britain's role in Europe is nothing new. The government decided not to join the Common Market when it was established in 1957. When it tried to

Britain and HIV/AIDS

Britain has been one of the leaders in the worldwide effort to reduce the spread of HIV and AIDS.

HIV and AIDS is not a particularly controversial issue at home because the National Health Service provides all infected individuals with the medications they need. What's more, effective educational programs have helped reduce the spread of the HIV infection considerably.

It is Britain's engagement internationally that is most striking for our purposes. The government has pledged to spend hundreds of million of pounds to help bring the spread of the disease to a halt by 2015. Unlike the United States, however, the British have not chosen to set up their own programs. Rather, they are channelling their funds primarily through the Global Fund for AIDS, Tuberculosis, and Malaria (www.dfid.gov.uk/mdg/hivaidsfactsheet.asp).

join in the 1960s, its application was vetoed twice by France's President Charles de Gaulle. Georges Pompidou, de Gaulle's successor, was less hostile toward the British, and it was allowed to become a member in 1972 over the objection of many Britons, especially those in the Labour Party. The first referendum in the country's history, held in 1975, determined that the U.K. would stay in, and virtually all politicians came to accept that position.

But that was all they accepted. Thatcher's wing of the Conservative Party consistently opposed any further expansion of the European Community's (as it was then known) powers. The British government reached compromises that allowed it to agree to the Single European Act (1986) and Maastricht Treaty (1991). However, the party's rhetoric increasingly reflected the views of the euroskeptics whenever European decisions or initiatives seemed to threaten British sovereignty.

Anti-European sentiment has grown each time the EU did something that seemed to limit British sovereignty. For instance, the EU ruled that the British violated the human rights of IRA terrorists killed in Gibraltar, and it banned the worldwide export of British beef as a result of "mad cow disease."

For fifteen years, the most controversial issue has been the single currency. The Maastricht Treaty laid out a timetable that would bring qualifying countries into a single monetary system (EMU) in 1999 and replace their currencies with the euro in 2002. But the Major government negotiated an "opt-out" clause, which meant that

Britain would not have to join if the government of the day did not want to.

Most British voters opposed joining the EMU in both 1997 and 2001. Nonetheless, Conservative intransigence on European issues in general and internal party divisions contributed heavily to its two drubbings at the polls.

By contrast, the Labour leadership strongly supports most aspects of the EU. Initially, the party was more hostile to Europe than were the Conservatives. In the 1975 referendum, most prominent Labour officials opposed British membership and campaigned on the "no" side. Gradually, however, the vast majority of Labour leaders and members made their peace with the European Community and then the EU. By the time Blair became leader, almost everyone enthusiastically supported both adding new countries and giving new powers to the EU.

The one notable exception has been the single currency. In part because of the uncertainties about the economic logic of joining the EMU and in part because of the state of public opinion, Labour campaigned in 1997 on a pledge not to join during the life of the parliament elected that year. By 1999, however, Blair and his colleagues confirmed most observers' suspicions by announcing that they would make a decision during the first two years of the next parliament. If five economic conditions were met, the government would then recommend entering the EMU and hold a referendum on it. When the new cabinet was sworn in, the best guess was that the government would try to "soften" public opinion on the euro in preparation for such a referendum. If anything, however, public opinion has turned even more against the euro, and there is little chance of a referendum until after the next election—if then.

That the proposed constitution is controversial is more surprising. A commission headed by former French President Valéry Giscard d'Estaing spent the first years of this decade drafting a document that would formalize the powers and responsibilities of the Union, especially once the ten new members joined in 2004. Among other things, the draft called for the creation of a European president. Before the war in Iraq, it was widely assumed that the job would be offered to Blair. However, as we will see in the next section, Blair's strongly pro-American stance on Iraq has made him unacceptable to colleagues, especially in Germany and France. And it also soon became clear that most British voters had doubts about the constitution, which proved to be controversial throughout the Union. Even though there was no legal necessity for doing so, Blair said that his government would submit the constitution to a referendum, which, at this point, would almost certainly doom it to defeat.

Globalization and Great Britain

BRITAIN PROBABLY provides the best illustration of the impact of globalization on an industrialized democracy.

In most ways, the quote from Andrew Marr that begins this chapter tells it all. Britain, which once "ruled the waves," finds itself increasingly buffeted by forces from beyond its shoreline. The most obvious is the EU, which has had a direct impact on so many areas of Britain's life, from economic policy to the composition of its sports teams. Perhaps most important—although harder to pin down—is the role of economic forces in other countries. Thus, 99 percent of British automobile production is by companies not headquartered there. The U.K. is a major site for direct foreign investment, in large part because the wages of its industrial workers are so low. And, with the spread of satellite and cable technologies, the British increasingly watch television networks that are owned by foreigners and that run programs mostly made abroad.

In the long term, however, such opposition to further European integration seems like a rear-guard effort and a lost cause. Even though the U.K. does not use the euro, most of its companies conduct business in it. Consumers can have bank accounts and be paid in euros. And it's more than just the currency or the constitution. When I taught at the University of Reading in the late 1990s, fully 20 percent of our students came from other European countries. Today, almost a third of the faculty comes from outside of the U.K. The village we lived in had at least one family from all of the EU member states at that time other than Luxembourg. Our satellite television service had almost as many German as English language channels.

Iraq

Blair has taken his country to war more times than any prime minister in British history. That Britain joined in the first Gulf War in 1991 was not surprising. After all, both it and the United States had conservative governments. Besides, Iraq's invasion of Kuwait was an unambiguous violation of international law. It was also hardly surprising that Blair supported the United States after the terrorist attacks of 9/11 given his country's experience with terrorism during the "troubles" in Northern Ireland. Last, but by no means least, the United States has stronger ties to the U.K. than to any other European government.

None of that makes the British decision to support the United States and send the second largest contingent of troops to Iraq in the war that began in 2003 easy to understand. Blair and President George W. Bush have almost nothing in common. Indeed, Blair is widely known for his respect for and close relationship with former President Clinton with whom he helped develop the idea of the third way.

Nonetheless, from the beginning of the preparation for the war with Iraq, Blair stood behind Bush and the special relationship. The two leaders took all but identical positions, including on the claims made about Iraqi weapons of mass destruction, most of which now seem to have been in error. The British backed the United States at the United Nations and in discussions with Germany and France, who led the European opposition to the war. And Blair made it clear from the beginning that Britain would send troops to be part of the so-called coalition of the willing. About fifteen thousand British troops were deployed to Iraq for the 2003 invasion; once the regime fell, they were given primary responsibility for security and reconstruction near the southern city of Basra (for more on the war, see Chapter 14).

For our purposes, the domestic political ramifications of Blair's position are the most important. From the beginning, a majority of the British population opposed the war, including the overwhelming majority of Labour voters. In the summer of 2003, only 32 percent of the population approved of the way Blair was handling the situation in Iraq; 56 percent opposed his policies (www .mori.com/polls/2003/iraq4-top.shtml). Blair was never in any danger of losing a vote of confidence over the war, since the Tories supported British involvement. Nonetheless, support for Blair's policies have continued to decline as the situation in Iraq itself has worsened and in the aftermath of Dr. Kelly's death and the Hutton inquiry discussed earlier in this chapter.

Blair's popularity continued to plummet for the rest of 2004 and early 2005, when this book went to press. Nevertheless, nothing suggests that he would lose a vote of confidence or be forced from office because of dissatisfaction with his policies.

Feedback

As in all the industrialized democracies, a majority of people get most of their information about political life from the mass media. Britain's television and radio networks and printed media, however, are quite different from those found in the United States. To begin with, they are far more centralized, with most political information coming from national newspapers and television and radio stations.

England has eleven main daily newspapers, all of which are edited in London and distributed nationally. Scotland, Wales, and Northern Ireland have their own papers, but the London dailies are available there as well. Five are "quality" newspapers known as broadsheets. The *Guardian* and *Independent* usually support Labour, the *Times* and *Telegraph* almost always endorse the Tories, and the *Financial Times* is aimed at the business community. Each has the kind of high-quality and in-depth coverage American readers find in the *Washington Post* or *New York Times*. Together, the broadsheets sell about two million copies a day.

The rest are tabloids whose political coverage is much more superficial and whose tone is often scandalous and even racist. The *Mirror* normally supports Labour but opposed the war in Iraq, including publishing a faked picture supposedly showing the abuse of prisoners by British soldiers. The others are traditionally Conservative. In 1997, however, the *Sun*, which is the most widely read paper in Britain, switched camps and endorsed Labour. In all, the tabloids sell about ten million copies a day.

There are local daily papers, most of which are published in the afternoon. They do not, however, cover much national news, and their political influence is largely limited to local issues.

British television news is also rather different from its American equivalent. To begin with, there is very little local news on television—at most half an hour a day. Conversely, the five networks carry their national news programs at different times, so you can watch it at 6:00, 7:00, 8:00, 9:00, 10:00, and 10:30 every evening. BBC Radio 4's news programs are also widely listened to and have a greater impact than their equivalents on National Public Radio in the United States. Although British networks tend to be impartial, that is not necessarily true of individual journalists. Interviewers are known for the grillings they give politicians, especially those thought to be arrogant or to be withholding information. Some interviewers, including John Snow, the most popular anchor, openly display their personal views from time to time.

Conclusion: Blair's Legacy and British Democracy

As Labour nears the end of its second term, Blair and his colleagues face more problems than ever.

Prime Minister Blair meets President Bush before the formal start of the 2004 G–8 Summit in Sea Pines, Georgia.

As the above photograph of Blair and President Bush shows, in contrast with the one on p. 86, the prime minister has aged considerably in his (at that time) seven years in office. His will be the first Labour government to serve two full terms in office. The polls in mid-2004 showed that the party still had about a ten point lead over the Conservatives, which would give it a majority of about 70 if those figures hold until the next election.

But the lustre of the young, witty, and telegenic prime minister is gone. Blair is seen as a normal politician, and a manipulative one at that. His own party chafes under what can only be called his authoritarian control over the Labour organization and his disdain for colleagues who disagree with him. In June 2004, the party came in third in elections for local governments in England and for the European parliament. While these were not important contests for national leadership and probably do not have any implications for the next parliamentary election, they are a sign of how far his popularity has plummeted.

Any hope of a third way that truly brings sweeping social reform is gone. So, too, is any serious likelihood of British adoption of the euro in the foreseeable future. There have been enough scandals that touched many people close to Blair that his government is seen as no less sleazy than the Tory one it replaced. Blair's legacy is likely to include dissatisfaction with missed opportunities for social reform at home and his inability to prevent a war very few British citizens wanted.

Perhaps only one thing is clear. Even Blair's harshest critics do not argue that he has done or could do significant damage to British democracy. Its institutions are too strong and the regime as a whole has rock-solid support from the population. As we will see in many of the rest of the chapters in this book, that is not a case we can make for many countries.

Key Terms

Concepts

Backbenchers	Manifesto
Collective responsibility	Nationalization
Collectivist consensus	Parliamentary party
Corporatism	Privatization
Devolution	Proportional representation
Euroskeptic	Shadow cabinet
First-past-the-post	Third way
Gradualism	Three-line whip
Magna Carta	White paper

People

Blair, Tony
Howard, Michael
Thatcher, Margaret

Acronyms

CBI
SDP
TUC

Organizations, Places, and Events

Alliance	House of Lords
Beveridge Report	Labour Party
Confederation of British Industry	Liberal Democratic Party
	Maastricht Treaty
Conservative Party	Social Democratic Party
Good Friday Agreement	Tories
Great Reform Act	Trades Union Congress
House of Commons	

Critical Thinking Exercises

1 Much has happened since this book was finished in early 2005. Go to the library or the Internet and catch up on recent events in Britain. Does the argument made in this chapter still hold? Why (not)?

2 Public opinion pollsters routinely ask questions about whether people think the country is headed in the "right direction" or is "on the wrong track." If you were asked such a question about Great Britain, what would your answer be? Why did you reach that conclusion?

3 Of all the countries we consider, Great Britain is the only one without a written constitution. Yet most scholars agree that the British constitutional system is among the strongest in the world. How can that be?

4 British political development is often described in terms of gradualism. Why did that occur? How is it reflected in British political life today?

5 Many people argue that social class is less important in British political life than it was a generation or more ago. Do you agree? Why (not)?

6 How does the parliamentary system enable British governments to act quickly and decisively?

7 The British economy is often said to be in decline and the country has had more than its share of protests in recent years. Yet there has been little or no pressure for fundamental political change. How can that be?

8 The Conservatives under Thatcher and Major and now Labour under Blair have scaled back the state's economic role. Why has that happened? What impact has it had?

Useful Websites

There are dozens of good Internet gateways on aspects of British politics. The following three are among the best. The first is the U.K. Politics page, which has the widest variety of links as well as a subscription service. The second is run by *UKPOL,* a print magazine. The third is managed by the British Politics Group, which is based in Cincinnati, Ohio.

www.ukpolitics.org.uk

www.ukpol.org.uk

www.uc.edu/bpg

The most complete public opinion data are found on the site of Britain's biggest polling firm, MORI.

www.mori.com

All of the quality British newspapers are online. However, none of them are as useful for readers of this book as the BBC's site, which has every story it has run since it went online.

news.bbc.co.uk

The prime minister's office has an excellent portal for government ministries, including the fascinating e-envoy's office, which is using the web to empower people. Direct .gov is a well designed entry point for people seeking services and jobs from the government. You can also watch

the weekly debate when the prime minister goes to the House of Commons for Question Time from C-SPAN's website. You will have to navigate a bit around the C-SPAN site since its layout changes frequently.

www.number-10.gov.uk

www.e-envoy.gov.uk

www.direct.gov.uk

www.cspan.org

InfoTrac College Edition Sources

Allmendinger, Philip, and Mark Tewdwr-Jones. "New Labour, New Planning? The Trajectory of Planning in Blair's Britain."

Berrington, Hugh. "Election Report: After the Ball Was Over."

Curtis, Mark. "The Ambiguities of Power: British Foreign Policy Since 1945."

Johnson, Nevil. "The Judicial Dimension in British Politics."

Miller, John. "Breaking Up Britain: A Kingdom No Longer Required."

Morgan, Kenneth. "The Historical Roots of New Labour."

Nairn, Tom. "Scotland, the Blair Project, and the Zombie Factor."

Renton, Michael. "Examining the Success of the British National Party, 1999–2003."

Wheatcroft, Geoffrey. "The Tragedy of Tony Blair."

Further Reading

Beer, Samuel. *British Politics in the Collectivist Age* and *Britain Against Itself: The Political Contradictions of Collectivism.* New York: Norton, 1982. An examination of the origins and workings of politics during the collectivist era and the reasons it came under pressure during the crisis, respectively.

C-SPAN. *Commons Sense: A Viewer's Guide to the British House of Commons.* Washington, D.C.: C-SPAN, 1991. A short booklet to help viewers understand the parliamentary debate that C-SPAN has regularly televised since 1990. Probably the best short source on the House of Commons.

Feigenbaum, Harvey, Jeffrey Henig, and Chris Hamnett. *Shrinking the State: The Political Underpinnings of Privatization.* Cambridge: Cambridge University Press, 1998. A thoughtful analysis of privatization in the U.K., the United States, and France.

Hennessy, Peter. *The Prime Minister.* New York: Palgrave/St. Martin's 2000. An encyclopaedic but readable account of all post-war prime ministers and what made some more effective than others.

Kavanaugh, Dennis. *Thatcherism and British Politics: The End of Consensus,* 2nd ed. London: Oxford University Press, 1990. Of all the books on the Thatcher period, the only one that is easy for a nonspecialist to understand, although written from the perspective of a political scientist.

King, Anthony, et al. *Britain at the Polls 2001.* Chatham, N.J.: Chatham House, 2001. The most recent in an excellent series of anthologies on British elections.

Marr, Andrew. *Ruling Britannia: The Failure and Future of British Democracy.* London: Michael Joseph, 1995. A good argument for the need for political and even constitutional reform, given new pressures at home and abroad, by one of Britain's top political journalists. Also very funny.

Marr, Andrew. *The Day Britain Died.* London: Profile Books, 2000. Based on a television series by the BBC's chief political correspondent, an exploration of the centrifugal tendencies in British political, cultural, and social life.

Pimlott, Ben, and Nirmalo Rao. *Governing London.* New York: Oxford University Press, 2002. The best analysis of the new metropolitan government in London. Unfortunately written before the tolls on driving in the city went into effect.

Rentoul, John. *Tony Blair.* London: Warner Books, 1996. Though written before the 1997 election, still by far the best biography of Blair. Also gives first-rate insights into the workings of the Labour Party and British politics in general.

Solomos, John. *Race and Racism in Contemporary Britain,* 2nd ed. London: Macmillan, 1995. The most comprehensive of the many books on racism in the U.K., and one of the few available in the United States.

Toynbee, Polly, and David Walker. *Did Things Get Better? An Audit of Labour's Successes and Failures.* London: Penguin Books, 2001. A comprehensive and in some ways surprising assessment of the first Blair government's public policies, by two left-of-center journalists.

My roommate's father was visiting last weekend and asked what my major was. When I said French and government, he told me that was a contradiction in terms.

COLLEGE STUDENT

FRANCE

Paris

Lyons

Bordeaux

Marseilles

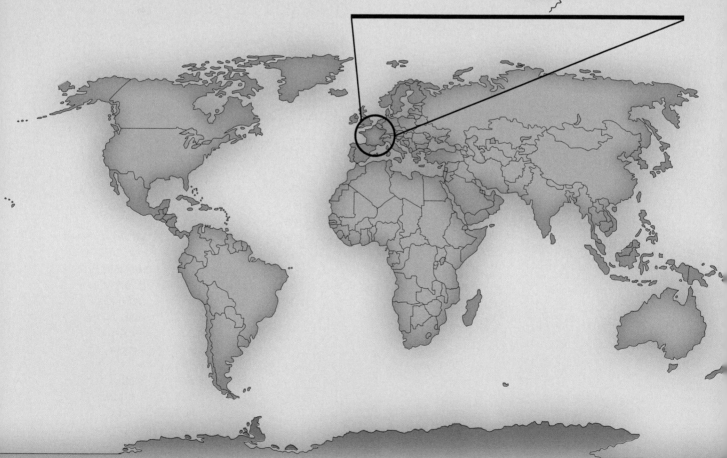

FRANCE

The Basics: France

Size	547,030 sq. km (more than two times the size of the U.K.)
Climate	Mild, but much warmer along the Mediterranean coast
Population	59 million
GNP per capita	$22,010
Currency	1.29€ = US$1
Ethnic composition	Over 90% white, but with substantial minorities of African, Middle Eastern, Asian, and Caribbean origins
Religion	90% Catholics, with small minorities of Protestants, Jews, Muslims, and atheists
Capital	Paris
Form of government	Fifth Republic (1958)
Head of state	President Jacques Chirac (1995)
Head of government	Prime Minister Jean-Pierre Raffarin (2002–)

Not a Contradiction in Terms

Every other chapter in this book begins with a statement by an eminent politician, political scientist, or journalist. This one starts with one by an undergraduate who came to my office one day twenty years ago to talk about a conversation she had had with her friend's roommate's father.

And every other chapter begins with a short story or anecdote that serves as a jumping off point for the analysis of the country as a whole. This one begins with a remarkable change that began almost half a century ago that remains the defining characteristic of French politics to this day.

When he went to college in the 1950s, my student's roommate's father's statement made sense. The average French government lasted nine months and accomplished little. The Fourth Republic, which had only been created in 1946, teetered on the brink of collapse and would not survive the decade. Pundits still make comments like this about France, most recently as part of criticisms of its government's refusal to support the U.S.-led war in Iraq in 2003.

However, it is hard to make the case that "French" and "government" are a contradiction in terms today. In fact, since the creation of the **Fifth Republic** in 1958, France has gone through a series of transformations that made political life there similar to that in such countries as Great Britain or Germany.

As we will see later in the chapter, the Fourth Republic collapsed in 1958 when its leadership could not put down two revolutions in colonial Algeria. The politicians reluctantly turned to **Charles de Gaulle,** who had been the leader of French resistance against the Nazis in World War II, led the interim government after its Liberation, and then resigned in protest against the adoption of the ineffective new republic.

De Gaulle agreed to take power again only if he were given the authority to revise the constitution, which he did by creating the Fifth Republic. For the next decade, de Gaulle served as president and ruled as what Harvard's Stanley Hoffmann called a heroic leader whose personality and past accomplishments enabled him to act largely as he wished. De Gaulle resigned in 1969, and his four less charismatic successors—**Georges Pompidou, Valéry Giscard d'Estaing, François Mitterrand,** and **Jacques Chirac**—all led France through an unprecedented period of political stability. Only once (1962) did a government lose a vote of confidence, and even that was welcomed by the government because it made possible a referendum on the direct election of the president and, then, the Gaullists' winning the first clear parliamentary majority in modern French history. Politicians are ably supported by senior servants who are graduates of the **École nationale d'administration** (ENA—National School of Administration) or one of the other *grandes écoles*. The politicians and civil servants have helped turn France into one of the most prosperous countries in the world, ranking only behind the United States, Japan, and Germany in economic might.

To be sure, there are important differences between France and the other industrialized countries. Its people probably take to the streets in political protest faster and more often than their counterparts elsewhere. The country endured two months of sustained strikes and demonstrations in 1968 that almost toppled de Gaulle and has had a half dozen other shorter and smaller, but still substantial, protest movements since then.

Nonetheless, in the first years of the twenty-first century France's regime seems as stable and secure as any in the world. There is no better way to see that than in the unusual pair of elections that took place in 2002.

Because of a quirk in the electoral calendar, presidential and legislative elections were both held that spring. The presidential election was expected to be a duel between outgoing Prime Minister **Lionel Jospin** and President Chirac, who had squared off against each other seven years earlier. In all, sixteen candidates ran at the first ballot. Everyone expected Chirac and Jospin to come in first and second and then be the only candidates allowed to run at the decisive second ballot two weeks later. In a shocking upset, the all but avowedly racist **Jean-Marie Le Pen** of the **National Front** (Front National; **FN**) edged out Jospin yielding a race between a moderate conservative and a politician whose commitment to democracy was doubted by many. In the end, Jospin joined all mainstream politicians in supporting Chirac, who won by a four-to-one margin. When legislative elections were held a month later, the devastated left did as poorly as it had at any point since the early 1960s. The bland prime minister, **Jean-Pierre Raffarin,** returned to office with one of the largest majorities in history.

The two election campaigns provided high political drama. Four years before the election, Le Pen went so far as to call on the French not to support their national soccer team in the 1998 World Cup because it had too many nonwhite players. The prospects of a Le Pen presidency frightened many, but the results demonstrated that there was no chance a politician with such extreme views could get elected. France is the only major democracy in which someone with ideas like Le Pen's could win close to one-fifth of the vote. But the 2002 elections were no more a threat to the regime than the even more controversial one in the United States two years earlier.

France's political life can be peculiar at times. Where else could the use of machines that clean up after dogs be a major issue in the capital city's mayoral campaign? But it shares perhaps the most important strength of a liberal democratic regime as discussed in Chapter 2—rock-solid support for the regime and constitution.

Thinking about France

Key Questions

When my student's roommate's father's statement is juxtaposed with the realities of the last quarter century or more of French politics, four obvious questions arise:

- Why did it take so much longer for a stable democratic regime to take hold in France?

- How did de Gaulle's changes to the country's institutions and social, political, and economic processes contribute to the creation of an effective industrial democratic state?

- What is the impact of the influential elite whose roots lie in the bureaucracy?

■ Why has the French economy proven more resistant to reform over the past ten to fifteen years than that of the British?

The Basics

France is a large country by European standards. It has slightly less than sixty million people, just about the same number as Britain. But France has about 550,000 square miles of territory, almost two-and-a-half times that of Britain. As a result, France has more open space and less congested cities.

France is also relatively homogeneous. Almost everyone speaks French. There are still noticeable local accents, and some older people speak Breton, Occitan, or a regional dialect of French. The spread of radio and television, however, has made standard Parisian French as widely used and understood as English is in Great Britain.

Almost 90 percent of the population is at least nominally Catholic, leaving France with no sizable religious minorities. The Catholic population, however, is not very devout. No more than 10 percent of them attend mass on anything approaching a regular basis. Roughly 2 percent of the country is Protestant and 1 percent is Jewish. Perhaps as much as 8 percent of the population—mostly recent immigrants from former French colonies and their children—are Muslim.

The other important factor contributing to France's homogeneity is the way Paris dominates this highly centralized country. Depending on exactly where one draws the boundaries, the Paris region contains between a quarter and a third of the total population.

Paris is the country's cultural, political, economic, and communications core. Almost all corporations and government agencies have their headquarters there. Road and rail systems were built with Paris as their hub. Paris has long been a thriving metropolis, whereas the major provincial cities were dull and drab, leading one observer to call them the "French desert" in the 1960s. Even now, there are plenty of "turboprofs" who teach at provincial universities but refuse to move from Paris, even though they have to commute as much as eight hours each way on France's high-speed trains.

Throughout this chapter, we will encounter examples of that centralization of French life. Here, it is enough to consider two remarkable examples.

France is one of the few countries in the world with an official agency that determines which new words can be added to its language. In recent years, it has struggled to keep foreign—mostly English—words out. People may well want to refer to a one-man show, disc jockey, or hit parade, but the High Commission for the French Language insists on *spectacle solo*, *animateur*, and *palmares*. The commission has fined American Airlines for issuing English-language boarding passes at Charles de Gaulle Airport and has hauled a furniture store owner into court for advertising his showroom rather than his *salle d'exposition*.

The second example is a tradition that has only recently been abandoned. Until the early 1990s, the government insisted that children be given the name of a saint or a figure from classical history in order to receive the extensive benefits it offers families. Breton, Occitan, and German names were forbidden. Richard Bernstein of the *New York Times* tells of a friend whose first and middle names were Mignon Florence, which was double trouble. Not only was Mignon not on the list of approved names, but the people at the registry office were convinced that, as a girl, she should have been Mignonne. Later, her teachers insisted that she spell her name that way. Officially, she had to be Florence, which she remained until the rules were relaxed when she was an adult.[1]

Despite its long-standing reputation as an economic backwater, France is an affluent country. Most French families enjoy a standard of living roughly equivalent to that in the United States. American salaries are a bit higher, but the French make up for that with guaranteed health care, university tuition that still costs under $200 a year, and a day-care system integrated into the public schools and open to all children over the age of two.

France is a leading technological and economic power. There are more French than German firms in the world's top twenty. The French make the world's fastest trains, the TGV (*trains à grandes vitesses*), which can travel comfortably at more than two hundred miles an hour. The French play a leading role in Airbus, which makes state-of-the-art jumbo jets, and Arianespace, which now surpasses NASA in commercial space ventures.

Not everyone has benefited equally from what journalist John Ardagh called the "new French revolution." Three relatively disadvantaged groups, in particular, stand out. First are those mostly older people who are too poor to move out of their isolated villages or dingy urban apartments. Second are women, who have yet to make as much political or professional progress as their counterparts in the United States. Third are members of minority groups, who are still largely stuck with the jobs

---

[1] Richard Bernstein, *Fragile Glory: A Portrait of France and the French* (New York: Penguin Books, 1900), 110ff.

whites are not willing to take and who are discriminated against in ways reminiscent of the American South before the civil rights movement.

The Evolution of the French State: Centuries of Turmoil

Transformation and Division

Comparativists typically cite Great Britain as the model of a state that evolved relatively smoothly over several centuries. They turn to France to illustrate a rather different, but far more common, historical pattern—that state building can be a long and wrenching process. That can be seen first in the fact that France has had eleven regimes since the revolution that began in 1789. The United States and Great Britain have had one each. (See table 5.1.)

To see why that was the case, it makes sense to do the same thing we did for Britain and use the top row of the table on the inside front cover to explore how France was affected by the great transformations that shaped European history. In France, the conflicts generated by those transformations were largely left unresolved, leaving deep scars that continue to affect French politics today. France did not continually have to confront the specter of revolution. Nonetheless, in comparative terms, it had far more trouble than Great Britain did in dealing with the challenges it faced over the past few centuries (europeanhistory.about.com/od/France/).

The first transformation led to the formation of France itself. It did not leave France with a deep ideological split, but it did give rise to one of its most powerful political traditions, centralization. As in Britain, there was an entity we could identify as France by 1500. It had a government headed by a king, but its power was limited, especially the farther one went from Paris.

France could not, however, remain as isolated as the British Isles were, and it could not avoid the wars of religion and national expansion that ravaged Europe. One French response was to create a strong and centralized state, which many historians date from the reign of the "Sun King," Louis XIV (1643–1715).

The revolution of 1789 cemented this tradition of centralized government in Paris. Some of the revolutionary groups wanted to drastically scale back Paris's power. By 1792 they had lost out to the Jacobins, who were, if anything, greater centralizers than the Bourbon monarchs they replaced and who strengthened the state beyond the monarchs' wildest expectations. The country was divided into departments controlled from Paris, which made France the most uniformly and effectively administered country in early-nineteenth-century Europe. But it also led many to view the state as a distant and arbitrary geopolitical stone wall that frustrated them everywhere they turned.

The other three transformations left France deeply divided and also added to the alienation caused by centralization.

Historically, the dispute over the role of religion and the relationship between church and state has had the most disruptive impact. Even though the overwhelming majority of French people are Catholic, this does not mean that they have the same views about their church.

The church traditionally was closely allied with the monarchy. Many of the best-known leaders of the *ancien régime*, such as Armand Jean du Plessis Richelieu, Jules Mazarin, and Jean-Baptiste Colbert, were cardinals as well as ministers to the king. The revolution of 1789, therefore, not only overturned the monarchy but also made the official political role of the church a controversial issue indeed.

During the nineteenth and twentieth centuries, the religious question divided France into an **anticlerical** left that advocated the total separation of church and state and a proclerical right that believed the church should play a leading role in a restored monarchy. In the 1890s and early 1900s, the decisions to separate church and state and thus undermine ecclesiastical wealth and power provoked such resistance from proclerical groups that the Third Republic was nearly toppled.

Debates over the role of the church no longer jeopardize the regime. Nonetheless, they remain important. To this day, the few remaining practicing Catholics are the social group most likely to vote for the parties of the center and right.

Disputes about the nature of the regime overlapped those about the role of the church. France has one of the oldest and strongest democratic traditions in the world.

■ **TABLE 5.1**   French Regimes since 1789

YEAR	REGIME	YEAR	REGIME
Until 1792	Bourbon Monarchy	1851–70	Second Empire
1792–1804	First Republic	1875–1940	Third Republic
1804–15	First Empire	1940–44	Vichy Regime
1815–30	Bourbon Restoration	1944–46	Liberation Government
1815–48	July Monarchy	1946–58	Fourth Republic
1848–51	Second Republic	1958–	Fifth Republic

It was in France in 1789 that a declaration of the rights of man was first included in an official government document. Subsequent constitutions expanded the definition of human rights beyond the minimum political rights to include such "social" ones as the right to a job and social security. France was also the first country to extend the right to vote to all men, following the revolution of 1848.

But, unlike Britain, France was unable to adopt democracy one step at a time with the acquiescence, let alone the support, of the traditional elite. Instead, it came in lurches, many of which did not last. Prior to 1958 France always had major groups that opposed democracy in any form. Moreover, the democratic regimes it adopted were not very effective for reasons that will become clear shortly. It has only been with the widespread acceptance of the Fifth Republic that we can speak of the definitive victory of democracy in France.

The final transformation—the industrial revolution and the class conflict it spawned—also affected France in more complex and divisive ways than it did Britain. As with democracy and religion, social class provoked deep and lasting conflict. Many workers supported the social democrats who, like Labour in Britain, believed that fundamental change in social and economic life could be achieved by working through the parliamentary system. Others preferred more radical socialists, who argued, instead, that meaningful change could only occur through a revolution. After 1920 that division was reflected in the split between a reformist **Socialist Party (PS)** (SFIO until 1969 and PS since) and a **Communist Party (PCF),** initially inspired by the Bolshevik revolution in Russia.

Also unlike Britain, the procapitalist forces were divided. Most small manufacturers, merchants, and farmers had qualms about the industrial revolution. They used free-market rhetoric to help protect the traditional economic system under which they prospered. Because these business-oriented groups that resisted change often were in power, capitalists who wanted to modernize and industrialize did not endorse laissez-faire. Rather, they argued that concerted state action was needed to overcome the market's biases toward stability, a point of view that would not prevail until after World War II when it became the cornerstone of economic policy making under the Gaullists.

Traditional Republican Politics: A Vicious Circle

In trying to understand the complicated evolution of French politics, we can limit our attention to the Third and Fourth Republics and concentrate on key themes rather than historical details. Political life during those

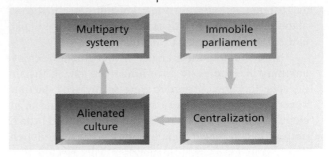

FIGURE 5.1 Traditional Republican Politics in France

years can best be seen as a political vicious circle of four interlocking problems as summarized in figure 5.1.

The ideological divisions left by the four transformations spawned six major "political families" of roughly equal size. The 1951 election, summarized in table 5.2, was typical and allows us to see how the many parties reflected the conflicting points of view found in French society.

As noted earlier, the Socialists and Communists, which represented the two halves of the socialist tradition, had been bitter rivals ever since the PCF split from the SFIO. Much like the SFIO, the Catholic Popular Republican Movement (MRP) supported the welfare state and European integration, but the two found it hard to work together given their sharp disagreement over church-related issues.

The **Radicals** were nineteenth-century radicals, which meant that they believed in liberal democracy, anticlericalism, and free-market capitalism. The Independents and Peasants shared many of the Radicals' economic views but were staunchly proclerical. Finally, the **Gaullists** were the most recent manifestation of a strand of public opinion that demanded strong leadership. Although such beliefs had their roots in monarchism and Bonapartism, the Gaullists claimed to be solid republicans. They simply wanted to replace the Fourth Republic with a better one!

The existence of so many antagonistic parties made the second component of the vicious circle—a deadlocked parliament—all but inevitable. As in all parliamentary systems, the president was little more than a

TABLE 5.2 Seats in the French Chamber of Deputies, 1951

PARTY	SEATS	PARTY	SEATS
PCF	101	UDSR	23
SFIO	106	IOM	17
MRP	88	Independents and Peasants	95
Radicals	76	Gaullists	120

figurehead. Real power was shared by the parliament and cabinet. As in Britain, the prime minister and the rest of the government were drawn from the members of parliament and had to retain their confidence.

Unfortunately, the French were never able to achieve anything like the party government we saw in Britain. Because the French parties were so divided, elections never produced a majority. Instead, cabinets had to include members of three or four parties that had little or nothing in common. Often, tiny parties like the Independents from Overseas (independent MPs elected from French colonies) held the balance of power. Virtually any issue of consequence would split the coalition so that every nine months or so the government would lose its majority and be forced to resign. The ensuing cabinet crisis would last until the parties could resolve their differences on the issues that brought the old government down and form a new one. That cabinet, in turn, would survive until it had to confront the next difficult issue. As a result, most of France's pressing problems remained unsolved.

The president and prime minister were denied the one constitutional device that might have broken the deadlock—dissolving parliament and calling for new elections. Marshall Macmahon, the first president of the Third Republic, had called for elections in 1877, hoping they would yield a monarchist majority. Instead, the republican parties won a resounding victory and forced Macmahon to resign. From then on, there was an unwritten rule that neither the president nor the prime minister could dissolve parliament before its term ended.

The Macmahon fiasco and other episodes convinced politicians that people with lofty goals were dangerous. Reform-minded leaders were routinely passed over when it came to forming cabinets. The kingmakers preferred politicians whom they could count on, which meant those who were happy with the deadlocked system.

The effects of the ideological divisions were compounded by yet another problem—politicians' willingness to sacrifice just about everything else to advance their own careers. According to most political scientists, they used ideological rhetoric as little more than a veneer to hide the self-serving behavior and corruption that dominated political life. Many current and potential ministers were willing to sabotage any cabinet—including those they served in—and to destroy any politician's reputation to enhance their own prestige and power.

Last but by no means least, there was a "negative" consensus on what social and economic policy should be like, which Stanley Hoffmann called the republican synthesis that sustained a stalemate society. The dominant centrist politicians represented the most traditional elements of the population—the peasantry and the petite bourgeoisie of the small towns. Although these politicians could rarely agree on what to do about the "big issues," they had little trouble seeing eye-to-eye on what France should *not* do. They accepted society as it was and rejected the idea that government should be used to foster modernization.

In the absence of effective parliamentary government, what power there was devolved onto the third cog of traditional republican politics, the bureaucracy. The effects of extreme centralization and inflexibility in the bureaucratic system as a whole rippled throughout society. Educational standards, for example, were set in Paris. A uniform curriculum was used by all schools to prepare students for national examinations that determined whether they passed. Individual teachers, students, and parents had little or nothing to say about what happened in the schools.

Centralization had much to do with the final component of the vicious circle—an alienated political culture rooted in the revolutionary tradition. Political scientists did not gather systematic evidence on French values until the 1960s. Nonetheless, everything we know suggests that the French were as alienated and ideologically divided as any mass public in the industrialized world.

Unlike the British, the French frequently questioned the regime's basic structures and practices. Many were defensive individualists, convinced that they had to protect themselves from government officials and all other outsiders, who, they "knew," were out to do them in. Few people believed they could redress their grievances by working through the parties or parliament. Similarly, the bureaucracy seemed closed to input from below. So, the French suppressed their anger and hostility until something triggered an explosion.

This was not merely a feature of national politics. What Michel Crozier called the "bureaucratic phenomenon" was the defining characteristic of an entire society that was built around centralized, insensitive institutions. Students, for instance, chafed under the rigid rules of the national education system, but they grudgingly accepted a classroom experience they disliked as long as they felt that the teacher was doing a good job preparing them for the exams. If, however, the students felt that a teacher was not doing a good job, it was a different story. Then the students might suddenly break out into a wild demonstration or *chahut* (from the words for "screaming cat"), which William Schonfeld graphically described:

> **Students might constantly talk with one another, get up and walk around the room whenever they feel like it, and if the teacher should call on them to respond to a question, they would answer disre-**

Democratization in France

FRANCE'S DIFFICULTIES in building any kind of legitimate state, let alone a democratic one, illustrate just how fortunate the United States and Great Britain have been.

By 1900, both the United States and Great Britain had states with broadly based support. The basic contours of democracy were established as well, although it would be a generation before women could vote in either country and sixty years before most American blacks could do so.

In France, the Third Republic was teetering on the brink of collapse. Though it weathered the crises of the moment, the Third Republic survived only because, as Georges Clémenceau put it, it was the form of government that divided the French the least. And, although it survived, it accomplished very little, which is one of the reasons France developed the reputation epitomized by the statement that begins this chapter.

spectfully—e.g., Teacher: "When you mix two atoms of hydrogen with one atom of oxygen, what do you get?" Pupil: "It rains," or "merde." Or the students might jeer at the teacher in unison, call him nasty names and run around the classroom. In certain classes, wet wads of paper will be thrown across the room, landing and then sticking on the wall behind the teacher's desk. Or there might be a fistfight, with the winner ejecting the loser from the room, while the other pupils stand around cheering for one or the other of the pugilists. With some teachers, the students might bring small glass sulfur bombs into class, which would be simultaneously broken, creating such a stench that the teacher is usually driven into the hall while the pupils stay in class, happily suffering the odor. Finally, students might bring a tent, camping equipment, and food into their class and, during the lesson, set up the tent, prepare lunch for each other, and then eat it—the teacher being powerless to help.[2]

Ultimately, that alienation fed back into the party and parliamentary morass to complete the vicious circle. The political psychologist Nathan Leites titled one of his books about parliament under the Fourth Republic *The House Without Windows.* The main section of the parliament building actually is windowless, but he chose the image to reflect the widespread conviction that politi-

cians didn't care about the country, its problems, or its people.

The windowlessness went in both directions. As far as we can tell, the French people did not try to look in all that often either. Even though they complained about the irresponsible politicians and their ideological squabbles, they consistently reelected the MPs who got pork barrel legislation through and couldn't get the bureaucracy to move on an individual's or a community's problems. In so doing, they made it impossible for the government to govern effectively.

From the Fourth to the Fifth Republic

Though characterized by deadlock and inertia, the traditional republican system had its share of accomplishments. The church-state issue receded from center stage. Even though governments came and went with mind-boggling speed, there was more governmental stability than one might expect at first glance. Cabinets were, after all, variations on the same theme, because most of the same parties and politicians appeared in government after government.

None of this should obscure the basic point. Government after government failed to meet France's pressing policy problems, which came to a head again after World War II.

Following its liberation from German occupation in 1944, France did have one brief flirtation with effective government. The old political guard had been discredited by the depression of the 1930s, the defeat by Germany, and collaboration with the Nazis. Few people, thus, wanted to go back to the status quo ante. The provisional government headed by de Gaulle nationalized major industrial and financial firms and established a planning commission to supervise economic recovery. Even the bureaucracy changed with the establishment of the ENA to train civil servants committed to democracy and modernization.

Unfortunately, it was to be a very brief flirtation. When the politicians finally agreed on a constitution for the **Fourth Republic,** it proved to be virtually a carbon copy of the one used by the Third. De Gaulle resigned in protest.

The history of the Fourth Republic was a sorry one indeed. The mismatch between an unchanging, ineffective government and a society with mounting unsolved problems proved to be even more serious than it had been before the war. At home, successive governments could do little to build the social infrastructure needed for a rapidly urbanizing population. Abroad, the pressures were even more intense, especially from

[2] William Schonfeld, *Obedience and Revolt* (Beverly Hills, Calif.: Sage, 1976), 30–31.

CHARLES DE GAULLE

© Hulton Archive/Getty Images

President Charles de Gaulle casting his ballot in the 1962 parliamentary elections at Colombey-les-deux-églises, where he lived during the Fourth Republic and where he died after resigning as the Fifth Republic's first president.

Charles de Gaulle (1890–1970) was one of the most prominent and influential leaders of the twentieth century. He began his career in the army, where he built a reputation as a visionary who urged his superiors (while often irritating them) to modernize their armaments to meet the growing challenge from Nazi Germany.

Despite the fact that he was largely unknown outside of military circles, de Gaulle led the resistance against Nazi occupation during World War II and headed the Liberation government from 1944 to 1946. He then retired because the politicians refused to heed his calls for a strong executive.

Brought back to power during the Algerian crisis in 1958, de Gaulle created the Fifth Republic. He led France for the next eleven years until he resigned following a defeat in a referendum on minor constitutional reforms. De Gaulle died the following year, but his new regime was firmly in place as the first stable and popular democracy in France's long and troubled history.

The Charles de Gaulle Institute and Foundation maintains an excellent website on the general and his legacy. Unfortunately, it only has a tiny portion of its material available in English, which some would argue is to be expected (www.charles-de-gaulle.org).

the colonies, which were beginning to clamor for their independence.

By the mid-1950s, support for politicians was at an all-time low. Young people were so turned off that they did not even bother to learn who their leaders were. Thus, one public opinion poll showed that 95 percent of the men drafted into the army in 1956 knew who had won the Tour de France bicycle race that year, but only 17 percent could identify the prime minister.

Although domestic problems received the most attention, it was a foreign policy crisis that brought the Fourth Republic's short life to an end. Throughout the postwar period, France had struggled vainly to hold onto its empire. In 1954, a revolution broke out in Algeria, where the majority Arab population demanded independence. By 1958, many of the minority French settlers were in revolt as well, blaming the Parisian government for failing to put down the Arab insurgency.

In spring 1958 the Fourth Republic's seventeenth

prime minister resigned. It soon became clear that the next man to hold the job would be the little-known Pierre Pflimlin, who was expected to begin negotiations with the Algerian Arabs.

That proved to be the last straw for the army and the white colonists. On the night of 12–13 May, soldiers seized power in Algiers. Rumors quickly spread that the military was preparing to invade the mainland and topple the Fourth Republic. Finally, on 1 June, the politicians turned to de Gaulle, who agreed to become the Fourth Republic's final prime minister on the condition that he be given extraordinary powers not only to deal with the rebellion but also to revise the constitution. (See table 5.3.)

Despite their agreement, most politicians expected de Gaulle to be a typical heroic leader. On several other occasions, the parliament had turned to exceptional men to deal with crises and then had gotten rid of them as soon as the immediate danger passed. And they had

▌ TABLE 5.3 Key Events in French Politics since 1958

YEAR	EVENT
1958	Creation of the Fifth Republic
1961	End of Algerian War
1962	Referendum on direct election of president
	First parliamentary majority elected
1965	De Gaulle reelected
1968	"Events" of May and June
1969	De Gaulle's resignation
1970	De Gaulle's death
1973–74	OPEC oil embargo
1981	Mitterrand and Socialists elected
1986	First period of cohabitation
1988	Mitterrand reelected
1993	Second period of cohabitation
1995	Chirac elected
1997	Socialists' return to power
2002	First scheduled simultaneous election of parliament and president

every reason to expect the same would happen with de Gaulle. He was already sixty-eight years old. Even after the 1958 elections, he had at most reluctant support from the politicians in parliament, most of whom were waiting for him to leave so they could return to business as usual.

De Gaulle proved them very, very wrong. When he left office in 1969, a wholly new republic had been put in place, one that was strong and stable enough to confound the skeptics and survive the departure of its charismatic leader. The details of this republic will be the subject of the rest of this chapter.

French Political Culture: From Alienation toward Consensus

Stereotypes about French culture abound. The French are arrogant and rude. They love to argue. Their erratic and deadly driving habits are indicative of a broader unwillingness to accept discipline and order. Somehow all that leads to the massive waves of strikes and demonstrations that have occurred on and off throughout French history.

Whatever the cause, there is no question that the French were more divided and less "civic" than the British or Americans until the 1970s. The past thirty years, however, have brought a dramatic lessening of the ideological tensions that had been so divisive and damaging. Widespread protests still occur, but, on balance, we can safely say that the success French governments have had since 1958 is now mirrored in popular attitudes and beliefs. Put in other terms, virtually no one now talks about

moving on to a Sixth Republic, let alone another monarchy or empire. The alienation that remains is no worse than the dissatisfaction one encounters in the most stable of democracies.

Taming Political Protest

Return for a moment to the distinction between the government of the day and the regime as a whole, which was drawn in Chapters 1 and 2. Public opinion polls conducted in the United States and Great Britain since the 1950s suggest that, however intense opposition might be to a Blair or a Bush, it stops there. No more than a handful of British or American citizens would be willing to overturn the regime and the constitutional order.

By the mid-1970s, the French had come to resemble the British and Americans in that respect. Two-thirds of the population claimed to have confidence in the president's judgment, and a similar number believed that elections make politicians pay attention to what average citizens are thinking. Trust in government has fluctuated a good bit since then and has been a bit lower since the 1990s. Still, the French public does seem to be as willing to trust its politicians and institutions as are the people in any other industrialized democracy. (See table 5.4.)

The turning point as far as support for the regime is concerned probably occurred in the late 1960s. In May 1968, a massive wave of strikes and demonstrations paralyzed the country. Many observers (including this writer) interpreted the **events of May** as evidence of a new kind of alienation, which many of us thought could imperil both capitalism and the Gaullist regime. We may have been right about the anger of the moment, but not about its enduring implications.

The movement started innocently enough. Facilities at the suburban branch of the University of Paris in Nanterre were not very good. Students also chafed under

▌ TABLE 5.4 Support for the Fifth Republic

Question: "The Constitution of the Fifth Republic went into effect in 1958. If you had to render a judgment on how its institutions have functioned since then, would you say that they have functioned well or not functioned well?"

YEAR	FUNCTIONED WELL	NOT FUNCTIONED WELL
1978	56%	27%
1983	57	25
1992	61	32
2000	71	21

Note: Nonresponses excluded.

Source: Adapted from Olivier Duhamel, "Confiance institutionnelle et defiance politique: la démocratie française," in *L'état de l'opinion 2001*, ed. Olivier Duhamel and Philippe Méchet. (Paris: Editions du Seuil, 2001), 75.

strict rules regarding dormitory life at what had been billed as France's first American-style campus.

Their first significant protest occurred at the dedication of the campus swimming pool on 22 March. There was nothing unusual about the demonstration—other than the fact that the students threw the dean into the water. What mattered was the way the university authorities tried to discipline the students. Because the university administration was so centralized, the hearing on their actions took place not in Nanterre, but at the Sorbonne in the Latin Quarter. While it was going on, a small group of students staged a support demonstration for what was now known as the 22 March movement in the courtyard. For the first time in centuries, the police entered the Sorbonne. Their action provoked nightly demonstrations, which were violently repressed by the police. As the security forces continued to overreact (at least in the eyes of most middle-class people), support for the students grew.

On the night of 10–11 May, students erected barricades reminiscent of earlier revolutions. The police responded ever more violently. By the end of the night, leaders of the major trade unions and other left-leaning interest groups had realized that they had the same adversary as the students—the Gaullist state. Finally, the unions and the left-wing parties decided to join in by staging a march on 13 May.

After the rally, students took over the Sorbonne and other buildings in the Latin Quarter. Acting without the authorization of union leaders, workers started occupying factories around the country. Within days, France was at a standstill. By the middle of the month, approximately eight million people were on strike, and more than two million had already taken part in at least one demonstration.

The protesters were concerned about the centralization of power under the Gaullists. Along with personal attacks on de Gaulle (*Dix ans, ça suffit!*—Ten years, that's enough!) came demands for increased participation, freedom of speech, decentralization, labor reform, and improved quality of life. **Autogestion,** or a participatory, decentralized form of self-managed socialism, became a rallying cry for much of the noncommunist left.

The government and the regime held, however. At the end of May, de Gaulle used one of his new powers (see the section on the state) and dissolved the National Assembly. The Gaullists, playing on growing public fear of disorder, won by a landslide in the legislative elections that finally put an end to the crisis in late June.

To some degree, the "events" were typical of traditional forms of protest in France. However, they were qualitatively different in many key respects that point to changes in the political culture that were probably already well under way.

The diverse groups came together in that massive movement because they could see that they had a common adversary in the state. The spontaneity and size of the protests reflect the breadth and depth of dissatisfaction that was anything but trivial or traditional. It had taken a decade, but now the "losers" had finally come to realize that the effective new regime required a new form of opposition that included criticism not just of the issues of the day but of the overall centralization of power under the Gaullists.

Conversely, it is just as important to notice that virtually no one questioned the legitimacy of a republican form of government in general or the Fifth Republic in particular. Even the most outspoken advocates of autogestion saw it as part and parcel of a democratic regime. Most of the veterans of the movement I interviewed in 1972 simply assumed that the sweeping policy changes they struggled for could be realized without altering the institutional arrangements of the Fifth Republic in any appreciable manner.

After 1968, alienation itself began to abate for a number of reasons. François Mitterrand took over and rejuvenated the Socialist Party in 1971. It began to champion many of the themes the students and workers had raised in 1968, including autogestion, women's rights, the plight of immigrant workers, and the environment. In the process, it became one of the world's most dynamic political parties, attracting many who had been in the streets in 1968 and, in essence, channeling the conflicts growing out of the protests into conventional political life.

Meanwhile, the Gaullists learned many of the lessons of 1968, too. Parliament passed reforms in the wake of their electoral victory in June that gave universities a degree of autonomy, raised the minimum wage by 35 percent, and expanded workers' benefits by, for instance, giving them a fifth week of guaranteed, paid vacation.

Perhaps most important of all was the continued rapid economic growth that contributed to a visible improvement in the standard of living of almost all French families. The improvements continued during Valéry Giscard d'Estaing's presidency (1974–81), even though the rate of economic growth slowed considerably as a result of the OPEC oil embargo and the recession it sparked.

In the 1980s, the most important factor in the erosion of alienation undoubtedly was the election of Mitterrand and his Socialist parliamentary majority in 1981. It marked the first time there had been a real shift in who

The evolution of conflict in France demonstrates the importance of the difference between the government and the regime more clearly than anything we have seen so far. Before 1968, protest against the government, its leaders, and its practices easily spilled over into opposition to the regime as well. As a result, French politics had a degree of instability and fragility rarely seen in the United States or Great Britain.

Since then, however, the stakes of political life have lowered appreciably. As in most stable and effective democracies, just about everyone takes the regime for granted and accepts its legitimate right to govern.

Given the countries we have covered so far, this may not seem like a very important or surprising point. However, in Parts 3 and 4, we will see that such support and legitimacy are very much the exception rather than the rule.

governed France since the foundation of the Fifth Republic, which is an important turning point in the history of any regime. Right-wingers had worried that a PS-PCF coalition would be dangerous. Yet the smooth transition to Socialist rule further established the legitimacy of the regime. The sense that the political stakes were no longer

all that high was reinforced after the 1986, 1993, and 1997 elections, when left and right had to cohabit and govern together, and did so surprisingly effectively.

By that time, doubts about the Fifth Republic had largely evaporated. As table 5.4 shows, most Frenchmen and -women thought that the institutions of the Fifth Republic were working well by the end of the 1970s, a belief that has only strengthened since then as the traditional divisions between left and right and between working class and bourgeoisie have declined in significance.

New Divisions

This does not mean that French politics lacks ideological divisions and the protest movements they can spawn. Although the existence of the Fifth Republic is no longer in jeopardy, France is divided on two overlapping issues that tap the postmaterialist values discussed in Chapter 2—race and Europe.

As noted earlier, France has a significant minority population, drawn mostly from its former colonies in Africa and Asia. Until the economic downturn of the 1970s, few people objected to their presence. Rather, many welcomed the immigrants, who gladly took low-paying or unpleasant jobs the French no longer were interested in doing.

That is not the case today. Many of the immigrants

The multiracial and multicultural French soccer team celebrating its victory in the 1998 World Cup. Many hoped that the victory would help ease race relations in France.

Luca Bruno/AP/Wide World Photos

and their French-born children have not assimilated, sparking the resentment of traditionalists and nationalists. Although there is less immigration than there was a generation ago, many who are now entering France are doing so as political refugees at a time when, long before September 11, terrorism led many to equate immigration with violence. More importantly, there is resentment against nonwhites who hold jobs or receive funds from France's ample social service programs at a time when unemployment and the budget deficit have both been at near record levels for more than a decade.

The manifestations of these trends extend far beyond the 10–20 percent of the vote the National Front (discussed later in this chapter) has won in most elections since the 1980s. But we should not make too much of the new French racism. There are probably as many people who oppose all forms of racism and who welcome a more multicultural and diverse France. Many people, too, hope that the continued success of France's multiracial soccer team since the 1998 World Cup victory will help ease tensions. Still, such people have been far less visible and influential both on the streets and at the ballot box.

European integration became a divisive issue for the first time with the referendum on the Maastricht Treaty on European Union. As with racism, the fault lines cut across the traditional ideological camps. Similarly, opposition to further integration is concentrated in the same social and economic groups that see themselves as most threatened by competition from "foreign" workers. We will defer discussing these divisions until Chapter 7 on the European Union itself.

Political Participation

Patterns of political participation in France are quite different from those in most other European countries. Although it is hard to measure such things, the French probably protest more—or at least more colorfully—than their counterparts elsewhere on the continent. And their party system has changed more often and more drastically than most. It is also going through yet another period of uncertainty and transition, as evidenced by the unusual 2002 presidential and legislative elections. Nonetheless, there is little in this section to suggest that the stability of the republic is in jeopardy.

Renewing the Party System

From the late 1960s onward, many political scientists argued that political parties had "failed." As we noted in Chapter 2, they had become catch-all organizations bet-

ter suited to running slick campaigns than at generating either fresh ideas or strong, enduring support.

The first signs that those arguments were somewhat overstated for France came in an obscure article published in 1988 on how French parties "refused to fail."[3] The political scientist, Frank Wilson, argued that over the preceding thirty years, the French parties and party system had gotten stronger. Instead of the fragmentation reflected in table 5.2, the party system revolved around coalitions on the left and right, each of which was centered on two major parties. From 1962 on, one or the other of them won a majority of seats in the National Assembly and the presidency. The parties took relatively clear stands. The major parties were led by men (the first prominent women only took on senior leadership positions in the socialist party in the 1990s) who were political fixtures for a quarter century or more.

To be sure, these are catch-all parties whose spin doctors can massage the media with the best of their British or American colleagues. A visit to the governing Union for a Popular Movement (UPM) usually has some attacks on the left and a brief overview of what the government is doing (www.u-m-p.org). But it also contains an online shop where you can buy pens (including one that glows in the dark), t-shirts, coffee mugs, ties, and other products all adorned with the party's unusual logo of a half red and half blue tree.

The Majority

Any analysis of the party system obviously has to start with the Gaullists. The generic term Gaullist is used in most of the chapter because the party has repeatedly changed its name. Under de Gaulle and Pompidou, its title always included the terms "union" and "republic." After Chirac took over in 1974, it became the **RPR (Rally for the Republic).** In 2002, it became the Union for a Presidential Majority for the election campaign. Afterwards, it renamed itself the Union for a Popular Movement.

In 1958, there was not an official Gaullist party. The general disliked parties and dissociated himself from them after the first Gaullist organization failed to win the 1951 legislative elections. De Gaulle's disdain for parties is reflected in the fact that none of its names have ever included the term "party."

In 1958 it was hard to tell what being a Gaullist meant, because a wide variety of politicians ran in the election, claiming to be an ally of the new republic's

---

[3] Frank L. Wilson, "When Parties Refuse to Fail: The Case of France," in *The Future of Political Parties.* Ed. Kay Lawson. (Princeton, N.J.: Princeton University Press, 1988), 503–532.

■ TABLE 5.5 Parliamentary Elections, 1958–97: Major Parties Only

YEAR	PCF VOTES[d]	PCF SEATS	PS[a] VOTES	PS[a] SEATS	CENTER[b] VOTES	CENTER[b] SEATS	GAULLISTS[c] AND ALLIES VOTES	GAULLISTS[c] AND ALLIES SEATS	NATIONAL FRONT VOTES	NATIONAL FRONT SEATS
1958	19.1%	10	15.5%	47	41.0%	215	17.6%	212	–	–
1962	21.8	41	12.5	66	26.5	84	36.4	269	–	–
1967	22.5	73	19.0	121	12.6	41	37.7	242	–	–
1968	20.0	34	16.5	49	10.3	33	43.7	354	–	–
1973	21.2	73	20.4	101	12.4	31	34.5	261	–	–
1978	20.5	86	24.7	117	–	–	43.9	274	–	–
1981	16.2	44	37.6	281	–	–	40.0	150	–	–
1986	9.7	35	31.85	210	–	–	42.0	274	9.9%	35
1988	11.3	27	35.9	276	–	–	37.7	258	9.8	1
1993	9.2	23	20.3	70	–	–	39.5	460	12.4	0
1997	9.9	37	28.6	282	–	–	39.5	257	15.1	1
2002	4.8	21	24.1	140	–	–	38.5	386	11.3	0

Note: Different sources provide somewhat different figures, especially for the earlier elections, when it was often difficult to tell which party an individual candidate represented, especially when it came to second-ballot alliances.

[a] SFIO before 1971. Includes parties allied with the Socialists, usually the left wing of the radicals.

[b] Includes MRP, Moderates, Radicals not allied with the SFIO, and other centrists not part of the Gaullist coalition.

[c] Includes both the Gaullist Party and, after the 1962 election, Giscard's Party, both of which kept changing their name from election to election.

[d] First-ballot vote only.

architect. (Legislative and presidential election results since 1958 are summarized in tables 5.5 and 5.6.) By the mid-1960s, the Gaullists had created the first disciplined conservative party in French history. Since then, the Gaullists have regularly won about a quarter of the vote, distributed fairly evenly among all segments of French society. They like to refer to themselves as the majority. While they and their allies have never won a majority of the votes, they have been in power either on their own or with the Socialists during periods of cohabitation throughout the Fifth Republic except for 1981 to 1986 and 1988 to 1993.

The Gaullists claim to be above ideology. Nonetheless, three themes have stood out throughout their history. First is an unwavering commitment to the legacy of General de Gaulle and the republic he created. Second, of all the French political parties, the Gaullists have focused their appeal and their organization most around a single leader from de Gaulle to Pompidou and, now, to Chirac for an unprecedented period of forty-five years. Third, of all the major European center-right parties, the Gaullists have been the slowest to adopt the rhetoric and reality of market capitalism, something we will see in the section on public policy later in this chapter.

The UPM scored two massive victories in 2002. The presidential landslide was not surprising once Le Pen edged out Jospin for a spot on the runoff ballot. The UPM went into the legislative elections a month later with a lot of momentum and a surprising popular leader, interim Prime Minister Raffarin. Meanwhile, the PS was in shock

following Jospin's defeat and immediate resignation after the first ballot and, therefore, ran a listless campaign. Together, that produced the second largest majority in the history of the Fifth Republic.

The UPM did not keep its popularity long. The economy slumped, taking the approval ratings of Chirac and Raffarin with it. The Gaullists lost badly in the 2004 elections for the European parliament when the Socialists made up almost all of their lost ground from two years earlier. Although the elections have little or no bearing on domestic politics, Chirac reshuffled the cabinet, in particular promoting the popular Nicolas Sarkozy, who is widely expected to be the Gaullist presidential candidate in 2007 unless Chirac decides to run again at age 77.

The second member of the conservative coalition that dominated the Fifth Republic during its first twenty-three years got its start when the minister of finance, Valéry Giscard d'Estaing, split with most moderate politicians and supported a 1962 referendum on the direct election of the president. Giscard then formed his own small party, the Independent Republicans (RI), which did well enough to provide the Gaullists with the first stable parliamentary majority in the legislative elections that followed later that fall. After Giscard's defeat for re-election in 1981, the RI merged with a number of other moderate parties to form a loose coalition known as the **Union for French Democracy (UDF)** (www.udf.org). Most UDF leaders supported Chirac in 2002 and then joined the UPM. A small rump group supported François Bayrou, who came in fourth with 6.8 percent of the vote.

▌TABLE 5.6 Presidential Elections, 1965–95: Major Candidates Only (in percentages)

YEAR	COMMUNISTS[a]	SOCIALISTS[b]	CENTER[c]	GISCARDIEN[d]	GAULLIST[e]	NATIONAL FRONT[f]
1965						
First ballot	–	32.2	15.8	–	43.7	–
Second ballot	–	45.5	–	–	54.5	–
1969						
First ballot	21.5	5.1	23.4	–	43.8	–
Second ballot	–	–	42.4	–	57.6	–
1974						
First ballot	–	43.2	–	32.6	15.1	–
Second ballot	–	49.2	–	50.8	–	–
1981						
First ballot	15.3	25.8	–	28.3	17.9	–
Second ballot	–	51.8	–	48.2	–	–
1988						
First ballot	6.7	34.1	–	16.5	19.9	14.4
Second ballot	–	54.0	–	–	45.9	–
1995						
First ballot	8.5	23.5	–	19.0[g]	20.8	15.2
Second ballot	–	47.4	–	–	52.6	–
2002						
First ballot	3.4	16.2	–	6.8	19.9	17.8
Second ballot	–	–	–	–	82.2	17.8

[a] Jacques Duclos in 1969, Georges Marchais in 1981, André Lajoinie in 1988, and Robert Hue in 1995 and 2002.

[b] François Mitterrand at all elections except 1969, when it was Gaston Defferre, and Lionel Jospin in 1995 and 2002.

[c] Jean Lecanuet in 1965, Alain Poher in 1969.

[d] Valéry Giscard d'Estaing in 1974 and 1981, Raymond Barre in 1988.

[e] Charles de Gaulle in 1965, Georges Pompidou in 1969, Jacques Chaban-Delmas in 1974, and Jacques Chirac in 1981 through 2002.

[f] Jean-Marie Le Pen.

[g] Raymond Balladur was actually a second Gaullist candidate.

The party did not even reach 5 percent of the vote in the legislative elections, and its twenty-one deputies normally support the government.

The Left

The third of the major parties offers the best evidence about the success enjoyed by the party system until recently. The old SFIO had been one of France's strongest political parties during the first half of the twentieth century. However, it went into a prolonged decline after World War II, which left it with barely 5 percent of the vote in 1969 (www.parti-socialiste.fr).

When Mitterrand took over and renamed it the PS two years later, the party underwent a remarkable recovery. It began to champion autogestion and other issues first raised in 1968 in a way that appealed to a broad cross-section of the electorate. Within a decade it was in power and has vied with the Gaullists for first place in every election since then, other than the presidential race in 2002.

Mitterrand succeeded in part because he broke with socialist tradition and adopted an electoral strategy centered on an alliance with the PCF. In 1972, the two parties signed a Common Program of Government that they pledged to enact if they won the next legislative elections. Although they fell just short of victory the next year, the left regained all the ground it lost in 1968 and clearly established itself as a viable alternative to the Gaullists.

Mitterrand also nearly defeated Giscard in 1974. However, the Communist-Socialist coalition foundered afterward. In 1977, the parties failed in their attempt to update the Common Program. The next year, their squabbling cost them what had at first seemed a sure victory in the legislative elections.

Largely because of the economic difficulties facing the Giscard government, Mitterrand finally won the presidency in 1981. The PS also won a massive majority in the National Assembly in the elections held after Mitterrand dissolved parliament. But the economic difficulties did not go away, which forced the government to abandon its leftist goals (see the public policy section), and the party's standing in the country dropped dramatically. The PS went into the 1986 election knowing it was going to lose its majority. Still, it remained France's strongest party, with almost 32 percent of the vote.

During the first **cohabitation** period that followed, in which one party controls the presidency and the other controls parliament, Mitterrand was able to portray himself as a national leader above the partisan fray. He then capitalized on this in his surprisingly easy reelection in 1988. As in 1981, he immediately dissolved the National Assembly, and the PS came within a few thousand votes of again winning an outright majority.

At that point, the Socialists' fortunes began to plummet once more. The party had no clear policy agenda to offer voters, and nothing it tried seemed to work, especially in reducing the skyrocketing unemployment rate.

Moreover, the party now had a serious leadership problem. The old and terminally ill Mitterrand was a lame duck. The party did quite badly in 1993, losing close to half its vote and three-quarters of its seats. All the signs indicated that it would do poorly in the 1995 presidential race, since it had trouble even finding a candidate. Jospin, however, proved to be a more successful campaigner than anyone expected, and the party began yet another recovery.

The recovery continued with the surprising victory by the PS in the snap election of 1997. However, the party has not gone through anything like the kind of renewal we saw in Blair's Labour Party in Britain. As noted earlier, the PS was thrown into disarray by its disastrous showing in 2002. Its new leader, François Hollande, has done rather well since then. However, regaining some of its 2002 losses has more to do with the problems facing the UPM than with the PS's own strengths, since it is still having a hard time defining its positions on many key issues.

More importantly, barring some unimaginable change in the country as a whole, the PS will not be able to win a majority of the vote on its own. Therefore, it will continue to have to rely on Greens, Communists, and other small leftist groups to have a chance of forming a parliamentary majority.

The final established party, the PCF, is the only one that existed in anything like its current form before 1958 (www.pcf.fr). It was born on Christmas night 1920, when a group of socialists who supported the Bolshevik revolution in Russia split from the SFIO. The PCF struggled until the depression, when its willingness to cooperate with the SFIO and the Radicals in the Popular Front of the mid-1930s helped swell its ranks. It gained support as well during World War II, when it spearheaded the domestic resistance against the Nazis.

From then until the late 1970s, the PCF prospered, normally winning between 20 and 25 percent of the vote. But few of its voters were committed Marxists. Rather, the PCF thrived because it gained a disproportionate share of the country's large protest vote and had a well-organized subculture within the working class.

Despite the prosperity of the postwar years, the party stuck with its traditional demands for revolution, nationalization of industry, and a sweeping redistribution of wealth. It was able to get away with its dated positions because the SFIO was in even worse shape. But when the PS began to change and the PCF did not, the party found itself in deep trouble. Its vote slipped below 10 percent in most local and national elections in the late 1980s, and its membership declined by as much as half. The collapse of communism in Europe only made matters worse. The party reached its lowest point in 2002 when two Trotskyist candidates outpolled the PCF's Robert Hue. Its survival has been in question for a decade. At this point, however, the party seems likely to hang on, though more as a party of working-class protest than as one committed to Marxism-Leninism.

The National Front

Only one wholly new party has gained a prominent place for itself under the Fifth Republic—the FN (National Front) (www.frontnational.com). The Front is the most recent incarnation of an antidemocratic, far-right tradition in French politics that dates back to 1789. But, in most respects, it is a new party whose appeal is based largely on fears of immigration, the "dilution" of French nationality and culture, and, now, European integration.

The party was founded in the 1970s as an outgrowth of one of France's small neofascist organizations. Later in the decade, it was taken over by Jean-Marie Le Pen (1928–), who had briefly been a deputy in the 1950s.

The FN did poorly at the polls until 1983, when it won control of the town hall in Dreux, a city about sixty miles west of Paris with a large immigrant population. The next year, the FN won 11 percent of the vote in the elections for the European parliament. It has won between 8 and 18 percent of the vote in most elections since then. In other words, it had done well enough that its total vote in 2002 did not come as a surprise, only the fact that Le Pen came in second.

Its share of the vote is volatile because France conducts elections differently than most Westernized democracies. As we will see, the electoral system used in parliamentary elections discriminates against new, small, and extremist parties like the FN. That does not happen in elections for the European Parliament or the French presidency, in which the Front has done consistently well, scoring about 15 percent throughout the 1990s.

Le Pen himself is a colorful character who has been known to make outrageous statements, including one challenging whether the Holocaust ever happened. But, on balance, the party has done a good job of presenting

Jean-Marie Le Pen, head of the National Front, addressing a press conference during the 1993 election campaign.

AP/Wide World Photos

its racist ideas with a more acceptable profamily and patriotic veneer. As a result, it has been able to make inroads in most socioeconomic groups, especially those whose security is most threatened by the changes sweeping the Western world. Typical are the views of an unemployed twenty-five-year-old man:

> When I go abroad I have no problem at all with foreigners. I respect their differences and their rules. But not all foreigners here have respect for our rules! It's a problem of integration. There should be special places for them to live—ghettos in the city which will offer everything so people can live in a community with others who speak their own language.[4]

Some thought that the National Front had fallen into what they hoped would be a long decline in the late 1990s. For some time, Le Pen and his chief deputy, Bruno Mégret, had fought over whether the party should forge electoral alliances with the mainstream right-wing parties. The two were also rivals for control of the party, with attention focused on what would happen once Le Pen left the political scene. The last straw came with preparations for the elections to the European parliament in

1999. Le Pen was initially banned from running as punishment for having earlier struck a rival candidate. He insisted first that his wife, not Mégret, head the Front's list of candidates and then that Charles de Gaulle, the general's grandson, be placed ahead of Mégret. Early in 1999, Mégret forced a schism and led his forces out of the party to form a rival organization.

But the split did not hurt the FN much. Mégret won only 2.3 percent of the vote in the presidential election, and his party did not even reach half that total in the legislative elections.

While the FN seems to have a solid core of voters, it is not likely to have a major policy-making impact. The electoral system makes it all but impossible for the party to win seats in the National Assembly for reasons that will become clear shortly. But, it is neither likely to make major gains at the polls nor be invited to join a coalition government with the UPM.

Minor Parties

France also has a number of small parties of little political significance. For instance, it has two main groups of Greens and three small parties to the left of the communists that regularly compete for a combined 5 or 6 percent of the vote. There are also "flash" parties that burst onto the scene for an election or two and then fade away. Some can be intriguing, such as the oddly named Ex-

---

[4] Mary Dejevsky, "Les évenements," *Independent Magazine.* 4 November 1994, 14.

treme Center Party that ran four candidates in 1967 or Hunting, Fishing, Nature, Traditions, which has contested every election in this century.

Exploring these groups in any detail would not add much to your understanding of French politics. Nine of the sixteen candidates in 2002 won under 5 percent of the vote. Thirteen parties won under 4 percent of the vote and eighteen seats in the new Assembly, and they only won those seats because of alliances with the PS or UMP.

Why These Changes Happened: The French Electoral System

There are many reasons the French party system changed so dramatically in the 1960s. In all likelihood, the unusual electoral system used in all post-1958 elections except 1986 was the most important.

Under the Fourth Republic, France used a form of **proportional representation** that gave each party the same share of seats in parliament that it won at the polls. As a result, it was easy for small parties to win seats, which reinforced the fragmentation and division among the parties.

The Fifth Republic uses a **single-member district, two-ballot system** (*scrutin uninominal à deux tours*). The country is divided into districts as in Britain or the United States. Any number of candidates can run at a first ballot, and if one of them wins a majority, she or he wins the seat. If not (which is usually the case), a second ballot is held one week later. Any candidate winning at least 12.5 percent of the vote at the first ballot can run at the second. A candidate who does well enough to continue can decide to withdraw and support another candidate she or he thinks has a better chance of winning.

Therein lies the significance of this unusual electoral system. In 1958, a single candidate represented pro-Gaullist forces on the second ballot in most districts. Because Communist and Socialist candidates often remained in the race, the Gaullists won a much higher share of the seats than their number of votes would otherwise have indicated. In 1962, the Communists, Socialists, and other left-wing parties realized that, by competing with each other on the second ballot, they were making Gaullist victories that much easier. So they, too, began to cut deals on a district-by-district basis whereby only the candidate who had the best chance of winning remained at the second ballot.

By 1967, both the left and the right had reached such agreements nationwide. Since then, almost all second-ballot races have pitted a single left-wing and a single conservative candidate against each other.

The shift toward two coalitions was reinforced by the similar system used for presidential elections. Anyone who gets a mere handful of nominations from local officials can run on the first ballot. If a candidate wins a majority of the vote on the first ballot, the election is over. However, no candidate has ever come close to winning half the vote, and so a second ballot has always been required. Unlike legislative elections, *only* two candidates can stay in the race, thereby magnifying the trend toward a more bipolar and consolidated party system.

Early on, the electoral system put the squeeze on the centrist parties, like the MRP and the Radicals, that had dominated the Fourth Republic. These parties' voters realized that they would have to choose between left and right on the second ballot, and so, as early as 1962, began voting for one or the other of them in the first round as well. The centrist parties vainly tried to stem the tide, but by 1974 they had disappeared as a viable political force. Today, the same system hurts the National Front and, to a lesser degree, the more radical of the Greens. There is no structural impediment against running at the first ballot; however, the only candidates who are affiliated with the two broad coalitions have a reasonable chance of getting elected.

Parity: A Victory for Feminism?

The French municipal elections of 2001 were the first to be contested following passage of a constitutional amendment that requires parties to run slates of candidates with equal numbers of men and women—the so-called **parity law** (www.info-france-usa.org/atoz/gdr _pol.asp#1). For some, passage of the constitutional amendment in 1999 and enabling legislation in the two years that followed amounted to a major victory for women. For others, it was a sign of weakness because, without it, women would never gain any meaningful political impact.

The presence of women in politics had increased in 1995 when the new prime minister, Alain Juppé, appointed twelve women to his cabinet. But, as a sign of lingering sexism, they were immediately dubbed the *juppettes*—French for "miniskirt." Then, in an attempt to solidify his right-wing support, Juppé dismissed half of them (apparently referring to them as "old biddies"), in so doing inadvertently generating even more support for the movement for parity.

The movement for parity began slowly and only received significant public attention in 1997 when 577 activists issued the Manifesto of 577 calling for a parity democracy. The National Assembly has 577 members; 289 of the signatories were women and 288 were men. Eventually, over 90 percent of the population supported the idea, at least in principle.

Then the Socialists and their allies won the 1997 Assembly election. They already included more women in their parliamentary delegation than the right ever had. Prime Minister Jospin appointed a number of women to key positions, including Martine Aubry, who headed a superministry on employment, social security, and health. The government also quickly introduced the constitutional amendment on parity that went into effect two years later, after attempts to block it by the more conservative Senate failed.

France's overall track record on women and politics is mixed. It was the first country to grant the vote to all men (1848) but one of the last to give it to any women (1946). In the 1993 National Assembly election, fewer women were elected than in 1946. Even after a small surge in 1997 and 2002, only 12.2 percent of Assembly members were women, which left France next to last in Europe and in sixty-third place worldwide, between Chile and Slovenia. The figure was that low because the parity law only applies to elections run under proportional representation, which is not used for the country's most important contests.

Interest Groups

It is hard to reach firm conclusions about French interest groups. France was long thought to be a country in which people did not join them, although the evidence now suggests that they are as likely to do so as their counterparts in Britain or the United States.

Despite the legacy of 1968, only about 10 percent of the population belongs to an environmental group, and an even smaller percentage belongs to the antinuclear or the peace movement. France's organized women's movement is among the weakest in Europe. Racial minorities are also poorly represented in the interest group arena.

Political scientists have paid quite a bit of attention to the trade unions, perhaps because of the contentious role they have played in much of French history. The unions assert that about 25 percent of all nonagricultural workers belong to one or another of them, but most observers think that the true figure is closer to 10 percent. Moreover, there is no equivalent to the British TUC, which brings together most individual unions into a single peak association.

Instead, French unions are fragmented. Three unions compete for members in most factories and offices. The **CGT** (Confédération Générale du Travail), the largest union for most of the twentieth century, is affiliated with the Communist Party. Since the mid-1960s,

however, its position has been challenged by the **CFDT** (Confédération Française Démocratique du Travail). The CFDT began as a Catholic union, but dropped its links to the church and moved dramatically to the left during the 1970s. It now has close ties to the PS, though it has moved toward the center in recent years and even supported the Raffarin government's legislation to stiffen the requirements before a retiree could receive a maximum pension. **Force ouvrière** (Workers' Force) broke away from the CGT at the beginning of the cold war. It was then the most moderate of the three, but it has become more aggressive in recent years. It, too, has reasonably close ties with the PS.

Separate unions exist for teachers and most professional groups, including business managers. Even students have unions. France also has large and active groups representing small business owners, employers, farmers, and almost any commercial group one can imagine.

Until the 1980s, the unions were one of the most radical forces in French political life. In the 1960s, for instance, the CGT demanded the nationalization of all major industrial firms, a ban on layoffs without retraining for the workers involved, and a reduction in the work week without a cut in salaries. In the early 1970s, the CFDT added support for autogestion to its list of demands. That was not mere rhetorical militancy: From 1963 through 1973 (even excluding 1968), an average of 2.5 to 3 million workdays were lost to strikes each year.

After the economic downturn of the mid-1970s, levels of union membership and militancy have both sagged. The CGT has dropped its demands for more nationalization and mandatory retraining. For the CFDT, autogestion has become a slogan with little or no meaning.

Since 1995 the unions have been more active. That year, a massive wave of strikes and demonstrations forced the government to roll back some of its plans to cut social services and raise taxes. In 1997 unions occupied some offices in opposition to the Socialist government's failure to move fast enough in creating jobs for the eighth of the workforce that was unemployed. From time to time, truck drivers engaged in wildcat strikes that brought parts of the country's commercial life to a halt for as long as a week or two. However, on balance, the unions are struggling to protect the gains made for their members over the years and are, at most, a disruptive force rather than a potentially revolutionary one. But France now loses fewer days to work stoppages each year than Spain, Italy, or Great Britain.

There is one exception to this picture of divided and weakening interest groups—big business. As we will see in the next section, business leaders have had such easy

JOSÉ BOVÉ

© Reuters NewMedia Inc./CORBIS

The best symbol of the French tradition of outside-the-system protest today is José Bové. A veteran of the "events" of 1968, Bové abandoned the bourgeois professional career that awaited him and moved to a farm in southern France where he raises goats and makes Rocquefort cheese.

In the 1970s he was part of a successful protest to keep the French army from taking over the stark but beautiful Larzac plateau. In the 1980s he participated in Greenpeace's campaign to stop French nuclear testing and led a group of his fellow farmers who plowed up part of the land near the Eiffel Tower in opposition to EU farm pricing policies. In the 1990s he became one of France's leading critics of globalization. That led him to the activities that got him the most notice and notoriety—vandalism at McDonald's restaurants. He labeled them symbols of American cultural imperialism, not to mention sellers of food that offended French culinary traditions.

José Bové (at the back), outside one of the many McDonald's restaurants where he has led protests.

access to the upper levels of the civil service and to elected officials that it has often been hard to tell where the influence of one ended and that of the other began. Their impact is not exerted primarily through their main association, MEDEF (Movement of French Enterprises—www.medef.fr), but through those informal ties that link them to politicians and civil servants that we will be exploring shortly.

The French State

As we saw in the historical section of this chapter, France is the home of the modern state, though it fell on hard times after the revolution of 1789. De Gaulle's return to power marked a return to that strong state. The regime he created has turned out to be both more ambitious and more effective than anything we saw in Great Britain or the United States. In part, this reflected the adoption of a constitution that gave new powers to the president and prime minister while limiting those of the parliament. In part, it also reflected something that will become clearer in the next chapter on Germany—the importance of informal but extremely close relationships between the public and private sectors in ways not spelled out in the constitution. That said, at the end of this section and in the one on public policy to follow, we will also see that the French state in the first years of the twenty-first century is not as strong as it was under the Fifth Republic's first presidents for three reasons.

A New Constitution for a New State

Recall that the twin revolts in Algeria left the Fourth Republic's political leaders with a tough choice—either succumb to a likely military coup or bring de Gaulle back to office. Because he understood that the politicians really had little choice in the matter, de Gaulle was able to strike a tough bargain.

He demanded emergency powers that allowed him to rule with minimal interference from parliament for six months while revising the constitution. He appointed the noted lawyer **Michel Debré** (1912–96) to head the commission to revise the constitution. Debré's group quickly decided not to amend the existing document but to start from scratch and create a new Fifth Republic.

Debré had long been an admirer of British party government, which enables prime ministers to see their policy initiatives enacted because the government has a disciplined majority in parliament. Debré assumed, however, that the French were too divided to ever elect a British-style majority. Therefore, the drafting committee set out to write a constitution creating institutions that would give the executive the same leverage the British cabinet gets through the election of a majority in the House of Commons. Those provisions fell into two main categories (www.elysee.fr/ang/instit/text3_.htm).

First, the president would be a lot stronger. He (so far, they have all been men) could use emergency powers to rule as a de facto dictator for up to six months (Article 16) and to call a referendum (Article 11) on matters related to the "organization of governmental authority." The constitution also listed the powers of the president ahead of those of the cabinet and parliament, thereby sending a signal that the office was to take on new importance and could even exercise the most draconian of all measures—dissolving parliament and calling for new elections.

The stronger presidency was also evident in the way elections for the office were to be held. Under the Third and Fourth Republics, the two houses of parliament met together to choose the president for a seven-year term. The president could not be removed by a vote of confidence and was thus beyond the reach of parliament. Fearing a potentially strong president, the parliament routinely chose elderly, incompetent, and/or unambitious men to hold what was, at most, a ceremonial position (www.elysee.fr/ang/index.shtm).

Now, the president was to be elected by an electoral college of more than eighty thousand voters. The members of both houses of parliament were included in the college. Their influence, however, was dwarfed by that of representatives of local and departmental councils, who made up nearly 98 percent of its membership. But this system was used only once. Following an assassination attempt on de Gaulle's life in 1962, the voters approved a referendum that made the president directly elected by the people.

The second set of changes was designed to strengthen the government as a whole while weakening the lower house of parliament, the **National Assembly.** The framers retained the central feature of any parliamentary system—cabinet responsibility to parliament. But, to reduce the likelihood that France would lapse back into "revolving-door prime ministers," the constitution included a number of provisions that strengthened the government's hand in legislative-executive relations (www.assemblee-nat.fr/english/index.asp).

For example, the new cabinet no longer had to submit to a vote of investiture, which gave it the parliament's formal endorsement before it took office. Similarly, it could not be defeated in a vote of confidence unless the opposition won an absolute majority of all MPs, not a simple majority of those present and voting, as had been the case since 1875. These may seem like minor differences, but under the Fourth Republic, several potential cabinets lost those initial investiture votes, and almost half were defeated by relative, not absolute, majorities.

The **incompatibility clause** (Article 23) required members of parliament to give up their seats once appointed to a cabinet. No longer could cabinet members undermine a government they served in, knowing they had their seats in the legislature to fall back on.

The National Assembly was not allowed to either raise the expenditures or lower the tax rates proposed in the government's budget. The government also could demand a **bloc vote** in which the Assembly was not allowed to make any amendments to a bill but had to vote for or against the government's draft as a whole. The government could even determine when the parliament met and what its agenda would be. Much economic and foreign policy was placed in a "domain of regulation," which meant that the government could rule by decree, without parliamentary approval.

Although the constitution sought to shift the balance of power from the parliament to the executive, it really did not make clear whether the president or prime minister would dominate. That question was resolved with de Gaulle's first act as president—appointing Debré as prime minister. (See table 5.7.) Debré was neither a popular politician nor a member of the elite that had guided France for three-quarters of a century. He was clearly de Gaulle's lieutenant, always doing what the president wanted, including resigning when the general thought the time had come in 1962. De Gaulle and Debré appointed a number of bureaucrats and other people from outside parliament to the first cabinet, yet another action the established politicians took as an insult.

In those first years, de Gaulle used all the new powers the constitution gave him. Presidential power and

TABLE 5.7 French Presidents and Prime Ministers since 1958

YEAR TOOK OFFICE	PRESIDENT	PRIME MINISTER
1959	Charles de Gaulle	Michel Debré
1962		Georges Pompidou
1968		Maurice Couve de Murville
1969	Georges Pompidou	Jacques Chaban-Delmas
1972		Pierre Messmer
1974	Valéry Giscard d'Estaing	Jacques Chirac
1976		Raymond Barre
1981	François Mitterrand	Pierre Mauroy
1984		Laurent Fabius
1986		Jacques Chirac
1988		Michel Rocard
1991		Edith Cresson
1992		Pierre Bérégovoy
1993		Edouard Balladur
1995	Jacques Chirac	Alain Juppé
1997		Lionel Jospin
2002		Jean-Pierre Raffarin

autonomy from parliament were strengthened in two referenda on Algerian independence through which de Gaulle gained popular approval for a policy he could never have gotten through the Assembly. He invoked emergency powers after the failed coup attempt. As mentioned earlier, the general went to the people in 1962 with a constitutionally questionable referendum that made the president directly elected by the people, which made his mandate far broader than that of any party or other politician.

The constitution mentioned a "reserved domain" in which the president would predominate without specifying what it included. Within the first few years, de Gaulle made it clear that the reserved domain involved anything he thought was important, as he intervened in just about every policy-making area—domestic and international. From the beginning, the system functioned as de Gaulle and Debré intended, with the executive dominating a National Assembly that was normally as compliant as the British House of Commons. The president's and prime minister's tasks were made much easier when the unexpected began happening in 1962 and the electorate regularly supported a clear majority.

Most of the president's real power rests on the fact that he is directly elected. The president can also draw on a much larger personal staff than the British prime minister. Currently, the Elysée staff numbers over seven hundred and includes the president's closest advisers, many of whom are drawn from France's remarkable civil service, which we will encounter shortly.

France's Dual Executive

France is the only major Western democracy in which the two top executive offices are powerful *and* can be occupied by members of different parties. The current leaders tell us a lot about political dynamics in France.

Born in Paris, Chirac attended both the prestigious *Institut d'études politiques* and the even more prestigious ENA. After graduation, he served on the personal staff of Prime Minister Georges Pompidou, and he was appointed to his first ministerial position in the mid-1960s. Only in 1967 did he begin his own elective political career, winning a parliamentary seat in the region his family had originally come from. In the 1970s he became leader of the Gaullist Party and was elected prime minister (1974–76) and mayor of Paris (1977–95). He ran unsuccessfully against François Mitterrand in 1981 and 1988 before winning the presidency in 1995. Though he often uses free-market rhetoric, he is a Gaullist and thus expects the state to play a major role in sustaining French political, military, and diplomatic power.

Chirac appointed Jean-Pierre Raffarin (1948–) interim prime minister after Jospin resigned when the first ballot results for the 2002 presidential election were announced. Raffarin lost the interim status after the legislative elections that June. Though Raffarin is a veteran and well-liked politician, he was virtually unknown to the general public when he was appointed. His father had been a cabinet member. Raffarin attended a state-run business school rather than ENA (see the next box) and has generally been a strong supporter of small businesses. He worked in public relations in the 1980s before entering politics on a full-time basis. After that he served in the European parliament, was president of his home regional council in the southwest, and was minister for small business during the government of Alain Juppé from 1995 to 1997.

Throughout the Fifth Republic, about a third of all cabinet members have been recruited from the bureaucracy. Chirac's case is representative. He began his career as a civil servant and worked on the staff of a number of ministers in the early 1960s before being appointed agriculture minister in one of Pompidou's first governments. Only later, in 1967, did he run for electoral office.

A smaller number of ministers are recruited from outside government altogether. Pompidou, for instance, became prime minister after a career as an investment banker. Similarly, Bernard Kouchner joined one of the later Mitterrand governments after building a worldwide reputation as head of Doctors without Borders (*Médecins*

French president Jacques Chirac (right) and former prime minister Lionel Jospin.

Reuters/CORBIS

sans frontières), a group of physicians that provides humanitarian aid in war-torn areas.

All presidents and prime ministers have availed themselves of the power to issue decrees and otherwise avoid dealing with parliament. The decisions to build the first atomic bomb in the 1950s and 1960s, as well as the one to test such bombs in 1995, were made without consulting parliament.

When parliament has been involved, it has normally voted as routinely along party lines as the House of Commons. As in Britain, backbench revolts have occasionally stymied governmental initiatives. These incidents are rare, however, as the president and prime minister have almost always been able to prevail. Indeed, the best book on economic planning through the 1970s devotes only a two-page chapter to parliament's role because it has had so little influence over one of the most important aspects of policy making in early Fifth Republic France.

The machinery has worked a bit less smoothly during the three periods of cohabitation. There were some fears that the system might fall into a Fifth Republic version of parliamentary gridlock when Mitterrand first faced a Gaullist parliament in 1986. However, the two sides quickly worked out a reasonably effective modus vivendi, through which the parliamentary majority controlled most domestic policy, which has been the norm during the three periods of cohabitation.

Finally, the **Senate** is slightly more influential than the British House of Lords, though that is not saying much. Its members are indirectly chosen by electoral colleges composed overwhelmingly of local elected officials. Its districts are based on the state's cantons (counties) and give small towns and rural areas a disproportionate number of seats, which means that conservatives have an overwhelming majority.

The Senate frequently objects to government proposals, especially those that conflict with the interests of the members' largely rural constituents. However, the Senate has not been, and cannot be, a serious obstacle to the government. If the National Assembly and Senate do not agree on a bill, a joint committee is established, and if no agreement is reached, the government determines which body's version of the bill will prevail. (See figure 5.2.)

■ FIGURE 5.2 The Legislative Process in France

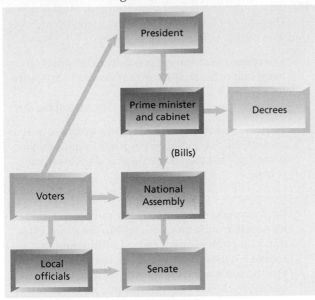

The Integrated Elite

There is an obvious question to ask given what we have seen so far. If its legislative-executive mechanisms work in much the same way as Britain's, how can the French state be stronger?

The answer lies in the distinction between the government and the state drawn in Chapter 1. Recall that the state involves all the people involved in making key decisions, not all of whom are formally governmental officials.

For France, that means extending our analysis to the bureaucracy, which has been the linchpin of the strong state since 1958. In Chapter 4, we saw that the British civil service plays a limited role in coordinating economic and other policy making. In France, however, not only are civil servants themselves powerful, but former bureaucrats dominate the political parties and big business, and serve as the glue holding a remarkably integrated elite together.

Their influence begins with their education at the ENA and other **grandes écoles.** These are specialized and highly selective institutions of higher education whose mission is to train high-level civil servants. Young men and women from France's most privileged families tend to do best on the entrance exams because of the educational and other privileges they enjoy throughout their lives. Until recently, a majority of the ENA's students were graduates of a half dozen leading Parisian *lycées*

The ENA

There is no other school in the world comparable to the École nationale d'administration (National School of Administration) (www.ena.fr/E/).

Created after World War II, the ENA was designed to train a new generation of civil servants committed both to democracy and the use of the state to spur economic growth. Although it is a small institution that admits about a hundred new students per year and has fewer than five thousand living graduates, it has cast its net over all areas of French life.

The first generation of ENArques reached the peaks of their careers at about the time de Gaulle returned to power. They thus began dominating the key branches of the civil service, orienting them toward goals of grandeur and growth—goals they shared with the Gaullists. Then they started moving out of the bureaucracy and into key positions in politics and business. Although the ENArques gained more fame—and criticism—under the Gaullists, they actually have made up a larger share of officials in most Socialist governments. In any case, they form a large proportion of top business executives than political leaders.

(high schools), and as many as a third come from families in which their fathers (but rarely their mothers) were themselves top-level civil servants.

The sway of the ENArques extends far beyond the civil service. Grandes écoles graduates only owe the state ten years of service and in some cases can buy their way out earlier. Then they can resign and move into big business or politics. Thousands of them have done so in a process known as **pantouflage**—literally, "putting on soft and cushy slippers." As noted earlier, many prominent French politicians are ENA graduates. The ENArques play at least as important a role in French business. Well over half of the chief executive officers of the largest French firms in both the public and private sectors are former civil servants. Because so many of them share the same background, training, and values, this integration of the elite facilitated coherent decision making throughout the first quarter-century the Gaullists and their allies were in power.

The connections survived when the left came to power in 1981. There is no question that the government-business links were stronger under the Gaullists. Nonetheless, the Socialists attract more than their share of ENArques as well, including three of their six prime ministers. The Socialists also drew heavily on former

FIGURE 5.3 The Iron Triangle

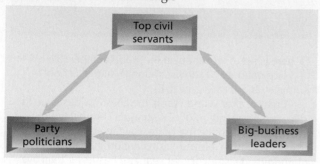

ENArques to head the industries they nationalized, and many of them have moved on to key positions in the private sector.

In the United States, observers often talk about an **iron triangle** of interest group lobbyists, bureaucrats, and members of Congress who dominate policy making in a given area. (See figure 5.3.) The French version of it is far stronger.

With the new institutions and Gaullist control of them, the Fifth Republic was able to engage in far more systematic planning. Paris, for example, underwent massive gentrification. Real estate speculators bought up old buildings that housed workers, small shopkeepers, and artisans, and replaced them with expensive office and apartment complexes. Businesses and families were displaced by the thousands and forced into dreary, working-class suburbs that one urban activist referred to as "people silos." Some suburban public housing complexes were so cheaply constructed that interior walls only went about three-quarters of the way to the ceiling. New suburbs with tens of thousands of inhabitants had few cafés or other public places for people to gather.

The same story was repeated for other policy areas. Immigrant workers, small merchants, farmers, students at regular universities, and the elderly fared poorly under the Gaullists. The winners did a remarkable job of turning French political and economic life around, but the way they "won" left France an even more unequal society than it had been in 1958.

The shift toward more centralized, bureaucratic, and elitist decision making is by no means unique to France. As all industrialized societies have grown more complex and more dependent on expertise, more and more decision-making power has moved to the upper reaches of the bureaucracy.

What is unique to France is the speed with which that process occurred and the way in which it limited the power of those outside the integrated elite. In interviews

with Ezra Suleiman, bureaucrat after bureaucrat tried to put their power in the best possible light. Most claimed that they did not have this kind of relationship with any interest groups. As three of them put it:

> The contact with groups is mostly to inform them, to explain to them. It's true that they can't influence policy.
>
> —*Ministry of Industry*

> We always consult. It doesn't mean we listen, but we consult. We don't always reveal our intentions. We reveal only as much as we think it is necessary to reveal.
>
> —*Ministry of Education*

> First, we make out a report or draw up a text, then we pass it around discreetly within the administration. Once everyone concerned within the administration is agreed on the final version, then we pass this version around outside the administration. Of course, by then it's a fait accompli *and pressure cannot have any effect.* [emphasis added]
>
> —*Ministry of Industry*[5]

They did not ignore people they considered "serious"—the representatives of big business and others who shared their vision of economic growth—that is, individuals like themselves. They simply did not consider them to be interest groups. In so doing, they felt comfortable claiming that they did not consult with such groups in any meaningful and, in their eyes, inappropriate way. But they were still able to work closely with those organizations and individuals who shared their conceptions of France's future. This is hardly surprising, given that the partisan and business leaders they did take seriously mostly started their careers in the civil service and shared the bureaucrats' background, training, and worldview.

Although the evidence is indirect, it certainly seems that these men and women understood that they had a choice: Either they could devote their resources to economic growth and national grandeur, or they could succumb to what they saw as the petty and selfish demands of the "nonserious." And there was no question in their minds which they should choose.

Consequently, workers were not able to communicate to key decisionmakers that they were among the most exploited people in Europe. Immigrants were not able to do much about either the racism or the horrible living and working conditions they had to put up with.

[5] Suleiman, *Politics, Power, and Bureaucracy in France* (Princeton. N.J.: Princeton University Press, 1974), 335–336.

The Socialists did try to address some of these issues when they first came to power in 1981. New admissions procedures were established to make it easier for working-class and underprivileged youths to get into the ENA and the other grandes écoles. This was supplemented in 1997 by a limited affirmative action program for students from a number of impoverished Parisian suburbs. Similarly, in a symbolically important step, the ENA campus was moved from the heart of Paris to Strasbourg. In the current business climate that stresses the importance of small business and entrepreneurial skills, schools like ENA have lost some of their lustre. Still, on balance, one has to be struck by the continuity, not the change, in the bureaucratic impact on national government since de Gaulle's return to power.

Local Government

We can see the declining but still critical centralization of power in France by shifting our attention away from Paris and briefly exploring local government.

Two French terms tell us a lot about what that centralization was like. First, until 1981, the closest the French came to an American governor for its ninety-six departments was the **prefect.** Unlike the American governor, who is elected, the prefect was a national civil servant, appointed by the minister of the interior. Moreover, tradition had it that prefects should not be from the department they ran and were rotated out after two or three years so they would not get too close to the local population. The second is the *tutelle,* or oversight, the prefects and the administration as a whole exercised over local governments. Virtually all local decisions, down to the naming of schools or streets, not to mention municipal budgets, had to be approved by the prefect's office in advance.

By the 1970s this extreme centralization had become a serious burden. There were simply too many things that had to be done locally for the central bureaucracy to control. Moreover, even if they did not make many decisions, local governments had grown in size because of the policies they had to implement, which gave the mayors considerable leverage over the prefect. Local power was reinforced because of a peculiar French policy that allows people to hold more than one elected office. Mayors of most major cities were simultaneously members of parliament and even cabinet ministers.

Socialist mayors chafed under the *tutelle,* and they convinced the PS to make decentralization a critical plank in the party's program during the 1970s. When the Socialists finally won in 1981, decentralization was the first major reform to work its way onto the statute books. The *tutelle* was abolished, though it was later restored for the smallest towns, which actually needed the support services the prefectural offices provide. Among other things, cities and towns (communes) gained control of urban planning, the departments assumed jurisdiction in the administration of welfare, and the regions got responsibility for economic planning. The heads of the elected departmental and regional councils are at least as important as the prefects were. The central government now issues block grants to fund long-term investment programs and gives local authorities the revenues from the annual automobile registration fees. Communes also have the freedom to set real estate and other local tax rates.

The Courts

The Fifth Republic has a large and strong judiciary, headed by the *Cour des comptes,* which is the country's chief financial investigator, and the *Conseil d'état,* which has jurisdiction over the state and its actions.

These are not, however, bodies that exercise judicial review and thus rule on the constitutionality of laws or other governmental acts. As in Britain, the Third and Fourth republics' tradition of parliamentary sovereignty meant that the courts were not granted any such power.

The constitution of 1958 created the Constitutional Council with the power to supervise elections and rule on the constitutionality of bills passed by the Assembly before they formally become law. This council is composed of nine judges who serve staggered nine-year terms. Three each are appointed by the president and the leaders of the two houses of parliament. Under de Gaulle, the council was little more than a political joke. The one time it tried to assert its power, by finding his decision to hold a referendum on the direct election of the president unconstitutional, de Gaulle simply ignored its judgment and forged ahead.

In the 1980s, however, the council began to play a more assertive role. For the first few years of the Mitterrand presidency, it was still dominated by judges appointed by conservatives, and it forced the Socialists to modify a number of their reforms—among other things, dramatically increasing the compensation to the former owners of nationalized firms. After 1986, the new conservative government faced a court with a Socialist majority, which overturned four of the fourteen laws that would have sold off much of the state sector.

One should not, however, draw too many parallels between the French and the American or even the German courts, which we will cover in the next chapter. The French courts' powers are far more limited both by the constitution and by tradition.

The Changing Role of the State

So far, this chapter has revolved around a single theme—the growing stability and acceptance of the Fifth Republic and its strong executive. We have to add one qualifier that is important not only for France but for most of the other industrialized democracies as well.

There has been no appreciable erosion of support for the French regime, nor have its institutions changed in any significant way. In fact, the most important reform of the past generation—the reduction in the president's term from seven to five years—will probably not change the nature of the office at all.

However, the presidency and the other institutions have weakened in ways that have not reached the statute books and that often do not draw much public attention. Each is more pronounced in France than in Britain because the French state entered the last decades of the twentieth century so much stronger than its counterpart across the Channel. Three aspects of those changes stand out.

First, France has a stronger civil society. As Vivien Schmidt put it, the traditional vision of politics in France was that

> the state would lead, society would follow. [Now], the state is no longer so sure of its leadership capacity [and] society is no longer so willing to be led.[6]

French interest groups are no stronger than they were thirty years ago. However, French society has changed in ways that make it hard for the state to run roughshod over a population that is more sophisticated and more sceptical about politicians and their actions.

Second, in the 1960s the historian Arthur Schlesinger coined the term *imperial presidency* to describe the growing powers of whoever occupied the White House. The term is even more appropriate for describing the French presidency in the first half of the Fifth Republic.

Much of the public policy we will cover in the next section grows out of a tradition of "heroic" decision making by an individual leader such as de Gaulle or the cohesive elite of ENArques and their allies. According to most interpretations, they were able to use the levers provided by the Fifth Republic to take bold new policy initiatives in the economy and in foreign affairs.

In recent years, however, there has been less demand or need for such heroic policy making. Instead, France has had a different and less dramatic style of leadership, most notably expressed in the declining clout of the presidency since the middle of the Mitterrand years.

There are several reasons for this shift. First and foremost, between 1986 and 2002, France had ten years of cohabitation in which one coalition controlled the National Assembly and had to govern with a president from the other side of the political spectrum. Under those circumstances, no one political camp could dominate. In addition, since the PS abandoned policies designed to produce a "rupture with capitalism" two years after Mitterrand won his first presidential election, neither the left nor the right has supported proposals for profound change. Thus, the PS and its allies have not "modernized" themselves as much as Blair's Labour Party, and the Gaullists have resisted the whole-scale adoption of liberal values we saw in Thatcher's and Reagan's governments. Finally, Mitterrand and Chirac have been decidedly "unheroic" individuals. Like Mitterrand before him, Chirac is immensely talented. However, their ages (Mitterrand was seriously ill for most of his second term) and the scandals that reached into the Elysée sapped them both of any hopes of leading the country in a profoundly different direction. Indeed, it is hard not to notice how little policy change there has been in the last twenty years—regardless of who was in office.

Third, France is increasingly subject to global forces. The French interventionist state worked from the 1950s through the 1970s because it could largely control the country's economy. France was by no means autarchic. Nonetheless, it was able to enact policies that reshaped the French economic and social landscape.

This is far less true today. As we will see in more detail in the rest of the chapter, France is like other states in that it is less and less master of its own destiny. This is an outgrowth of the world's headlong shift toward globalization. National boundaries simply matter less than they used to in determining the flow of goods and services. In France, at least a third of the gross domestic product comes from foreign trade. Sometimes it is hard to see this effective loss of national sovereignty because it is at least one step removed from most people's daily lives. But for the twenty-five members of the EU, the decline of the state has a concrete, legal base. As we will see in Chapter 7, the EU has gradually added to its powers since it was formed in 1957. At this point, it certainly is more important than the states as far as economic policy

---

[6] Vivien Schmidt, "The Changing Nature of State-Society Relations in the Fifth Republic," in *The Changing French Political System.* Ed. Robert Elgie. (London: Frank Cass, 2000), 14.

making is concerned, especially since the introduction of the euro in 2002.

Public Policy: The Pursuit of Grandeur

The 1958 constitution gives Fifth Republic leaders powers to make policy in ways that their predecessors could only have dreamed of. The emergence of the integrated elite in the 1960s gave them even more leverage, allowing the Gaullists to restore French power at home and abroad in pursuit of what the general called **grandeur.** Since the late 1970s, however, his successors on the left and right alike have enjoyed far less success, which we will see in three policy areas—the economy, assimilating the nonwhite part of the population, and international relations.

Economic Policy

In the eighteenth century, the French coined a word to describe state management of a capitalist economy—*dirigisme.* Between 1789 and 1958, however, republican governments were reluctant to use the policy levers at their disposal to modernize the country. The failures of the 1930s and 1940s changed all that.

Les Trentes Glorieuses

From the end of World War II until the recession sparked by the OPEC oil embargo of 1973–74, France enjoyed a period of unprecedented economic growth, which one historian called *les trentes glorieuses* (thirty glorious years). Economists have yet to separate out the effects of the various forces that propelled France into this economic prosperity. However, the policies pursued by the Gaullists during their brief period in power after the Liberation in 1944 and then after 1958 have to be near the top of any list of causes of that postwar boom.

The provisional government nationalized a number of firms, including the Renault automobile company and the three largest savings banks. De Gaulle also created the General Planning Commission to speed the recovery by bringing business leaders and civil servants together to help rebuild such key industries as electricity generation, cement production, and the railroads. Meanwhile, a number of business leaders realized that they had to modernize, which they decided could best be done by cooperating with the bureaucrats.

Although the economic growth continued under the Fourth Republic, the political connections between the public and private sector were not as strong. Most political leaders were opposed to *dirigisme* or too weak to pursue it.

That changed when de Gaulle returned to power. From 1958 until 1973, the economy, on average, grew more each year than it did during the entire interwar period, a rate that outstripped all its main competitors except Japan. Changes occurred most rapidly in large firms, which could become competitive in world markets for products such as automobiles, heavy durable goods, intermediate machinery, electronics, and chemicals.

During the 1960s, the government helped broker the creation of hundreds of bigger and more efficient firms. During the 1950s, companies worth a combined 85 million francs merged with each other. By 1965 the net value of firms that merged had leapt to 1 billion francs, and by 1970 to 5 billion francs. Typical of the change was the consolidation of five relatively weak automobile companies into two then highly profitable giants—Renault and Citroën-Peugeot.

In the late 1950s, not one of the world's most profitable hundred firms was French. By 1972 France had sixteen of them, whereas West Germany had only five.

The economic growth also had a human side that went beyond the statistical indicators. The improved standard of living was easy to see in the new houses and cars and even the changed diets that have produced a generation of taller, thinner people. The *hypermarché* (a combination supermarket and department store created a quarter century before Wal-Mart) all but wiped out the quaint but inefficient corner shops in most urban neighborhoods.

This economic growth did not appear out of thin air. The emergence of the modern French economy was in large part a result of the policies and procedures introduced by the Gaullists. De Gaulle understood that, as with everything else that could lead to grandeur, the state had to play a prominent role in managing the economy.

The Gaullists and the rest of the iron triangle were committed to the long-term development of the French economy. In part, they hoped to create firms that would be competitive enough to withstand competition from foreign firms at home and to win France a larger share of markets abroad. They hoped, too, that modernizing these industries would have spillover effects throughout the economy.

They relied primarily on discretionary tax and investment credits, subsidies, and other state funds to encourage the formation of those larger and more competitive firms. Five giant corporations received about half of the subsidies granted in the mid-1970s, a figure that reached 80 percent by the end of the decade. In all, an average of 2.7 percent of GNP went to support industry. Under Giscard, the government's explicit goal became the creation of one or two large firms in each industrial sector to produce potential "national champions" that could lead in world markets.

The argument being made here is not that there was a one-to-one correspondence between elite integration and economic success, but rather that there was a strong connection between this increasingly integrated, self-conscious elite's policies and economic prosperity. Their attention was selective, focusing on high-growth industries that they assumed would make French firms leaders in global markets for the rest of the century.

Other advanced industrialized countries enjoyed similar successes in the years after the end of World War II. But the countries that relied most heavily on market forces—including Great Britain and the United States—did not perform as well for most of that period. Rather, those that used the state in a concerted way to devise a reasonably coherent and consistent set of economic policies that limit the disruptive aspects of market forces did far better. Each country followed a unique path, but all involved increasing the cooperation among public and private sector elites and diminishing the role of "traditional" political forces, including legislatures and political parties.

Decline

The French economy went into a tailspin after 1973 and the OPEC oil embargo. Since then, France frequently has been outperformed by most of its European competitors, and when compared with *les trentes glorieuses,* conditions seem discouraging indeed. (See table 5.8.)

Industrial growth dropped to an average of 1 percent per year. Unemployment topped 10 percent for most of the 1980s and 1990s, with France losing an av-

erage of 150,000 industrial jobs per year. Inflation, too, averaged over 10 percent per year from the mid-1970s until the mid-1980s before it was finally brought under control.

Industrial disasters replaced the success stories. Shipbuilding all but collapsed. Steel was in so much trouble that the government had to restructure the industry in the late 1970s and then was forced to take it over altogether in the 1980s. The French automobile companies saw their share of the European market cut by a third while the number of imported cars grew by more than half.

Under Giscard, the government tried to reduce state intervention so that market forces could shape the future growth of a strong economy. The recession after the first oil embargo, however, forced Giscard and Prime Minister Raymond Barre to redirect the substantial state investment to industries that they felt would most likely be national champions in a global market, especially in the third world.

Economic conditions stabilized in the mid-1980s, and there have been brief periods of sustained growth and improved standards of living. Nonetheless, France has never come close to achieving anything like those thirty years of profound economic change again.

From Nationalization to Privatization

For the last twenty years, attention has shifted to government ownership rather than its management of the economy. As noted earlier, the government **nationalized** a number of public utilities and other businesses after World War II. A second wave of nationalizations occurred after the socialists' first victory when the government bought the country's nine largest firms. The new nationalization put the government in control of about 60 percent of France's industry and even more of its investment capital. The elite, in short, would have increased leverage in shaping the economy as a whole and, in Mitterrand's terms, in "reconquering the domestic market."

But the Socialists quickly had to abandon their goals. Within a year, France found itself facing rapidly growing unemployment and inflation rates. The budget deficit skyrocketed in large part because many of the newly nationalized firms lost money. In 1983, the Socialists did a U-turn, adopting a policy of economic austerity and abandoning all talk of further radical reform.

In the first cohabitation period, the Chirac government largely controlled economic policy. The government announced that sixty-five nationalized firms would be sold. Before the 1987 stock market crash brought those efforts to a halt, the government sold off fourteen

▌ **TABLE 5.8** The French Economy in Decline (in percentages)

YEAR	UNEMPLOYMENT	GROWTH IN GDP
1979	5.9	3.2
1981	7.4	1.2
1983	8.3	1.7
1986	10.4	2.5
1988	10.0	4.5
1993	11.7	2.9
1995	11.7	2.0
1998	11.5	0.3
2001	12.2	0.3

Source: Adapted from David Cameron, "Economic Policy in the Era of the EMS," in *Remaking the Hexagon,* ed. Gregory Flynn, (Boulder, Colo.: Westview Press, 1995), 145, and *Economist,* 10 Feb. 1999, 134.

companies, including eight large conglomerates. Subsidies for private industry were slashed. More emphasis was placed on regional economic planning and on the development of small and medium-sized businesses.

By 1988, a rough consensus had emerged on both the left and right. Since then, **privatization** has been the norm. While the Gaullists have sold state assets more quickly and more often, the Socialists have presided over the partial privatization of such high visibility companies as Air France and France Telecom.

That said, neither the left nor the right has moved as far toward reliance on market forces as has Labour, let alone the Conservatives, in Britain. The Gaullist government passed a law authorizing the privatization of another seventeen companies in 1993. However, only about half of them had been sold off by the time of the 1997 election. Since then, privatization has continued on an intermittent basis, normally when international competition seemed to require it.

But we should not confuse French privatization with what happened in Great Britain under Prime Ministers Thatcher and Major. The Gaullists' rhetoric may evoke the importance of a market economy. However, their actions reflect the, albeit diminished, legacy of *dirigisme*.

The most obvious difference is the fact that the French have not privatized most public utilities for which there is what the economists call a natural monopoly. The generation and distribution of electricity and gas, the railroads, and postal service remain publicly owned. The utilities that have been privatized, including the telephone system and airlines, faced international competition and thus had to function like conventional capitalist firms, regardless of who owned them. As of 2000, more than a quarter of the workforce was still employed by the state.

The key characteristic of French privatization is that the government or its political allies retain de facto control of many of the new companies through what is called a *noyau dur* (hard core) of stock. Sometimes, the government itself retains an ownership share. Thus, France Telecom was not allowed to bid for the cell phone contract in postwar Iraq because the state still held more than a 5 percent stake in it. Sometimes the state made sure that "friends" in the business community gained a controlling interest. Sometimes it refused to allow foreigners to buy any stock in a privatized company, claiming doing so would jeopardize national security.

Last but by no means least, the state has intervened to influence the way some of these firms evolved. Under Jospin, the government used its traditional financial levers to try to convince three banks to merge and create a single entity that could compete with British, German,

and American financial giants. In 2004, the government bailed out the industrial giant Alstom (which, among other things, builds the high speed trains) to prevent its takeover by Siemens.

In short, the new consensus to reinforce the private sector and use the market more fell far short of the one that emerged in Britain. Thus, Harvey Feigenbaum, Jeffrey Henig, and Chris Hamnett have labeled British privatization systematic because the Thatcher and Major governments truly believed in it and sold off every nationalized firm they could. By contrast, they consider French privatization to be pragmatic, conducted not out of principle but because selling off state assets would either help an individual firm or bring in needed funds to the state's coffers.

Still, it is safe to say that the state plays a less dominant role today than it did a quarter century ago. There are at least two reasons why that is the case.

First, as in the United States and the United Kingdom, the leading force behind the growth that began in the late 1990s was the new and relatively small firms in the high-tech sector. Very few ENArques are found in that part of the business community, though a growing number of graduates of other grandes écoles are choosing to become entrepreneurs rather than work for the big companies in either the public or the private sector. At best, the government's role here is indirect, most notably in subsidizing rail service or helping to build industrial parks, the most important of which is in the new city of Sophia-Antipolis, which is rapidly become France's Silicon Valley.

Second, the economy is being shaped more and more by European and global financial dynamics. In 2000, there were 119 leveraged buyouts of French firms. Some of the purchasers were foreign, such as the British Candover company, which bought the giant French frozen food company Picard Surgelés. Even more frequently, the financing of these deals was arranged by European venture capitalists looking for firms that would be more dynamic and flexible. In the case of the bank merger mentioned earlier, the government failed in large part because the shareholders of one of them opposed the idea and began looking for a British or German bank to merge with instead. In exchange for allowing the state to subsidize Alstom, the EU insisted that the government force the company's directors to sell some of its assets.

The bottom line is clear. France has to operate in an economy in which national borders matter less and less, and a goal like Mitterrand's to take back control of the domestic market becomes more and more implausible. Since the 1990s the French have invested almost $300 billion abroad per year, and foreigners invested

Economic Liberalization in France

France's record on liberalization is the most ambiguous of any of the industrialized democracies covered in this book.

The right has embraced privatization rhetorically. But its actions while in office have been less clear-cut, most notably in maintaining the state's continued stake in most of the privatized corporations. The left has not gone as far as Labour in Britain or the German SPD in making its peace with a market-driven economy, and the Jospin government sold off only those firms it had to for international economic reasons. There are few signs that there will be major changes made by the Gaullist government elected in 2002.

There are many reasons this is the case. Among the most important is the role the "state with a capital S" has played not only in day-to-day political life but also as a very symbol of what it means to be French. In other words, just as "that government that governs least governs best" is an integral part of American political culture, the strong state is at the heart of France's. And, so far at least, it has proved difficult for liberals to overcome.

As one of its leading left-of-center analysts put it:

> The French are not simply afraid of losing the safety net provided by the welfare state; they fear that the retreat of the state could undermine their sense of collective purpose. Although most French people complain about the state, they are proud of its achievements and seem to accept financial burdens that in other countries, less preoccupied with their sense of "grandeur," would be considered excessive.[a]

[a] Jean-Marie Guéhenno, "The French Resistance," *Prospect* (London), June 1998, 32.

---

about $200 billion in France. Those investments account for about 30 percent of France's jobs and 40 percent of its exports.

The Politics of Headscarves

Like all of its neighbors, France has become a country of immigrants. For the last several centuries, it has welcomed both political refugees and people simply looking to improve the quality of their lives. Until recently, most of those immigrants were white and, more importantly, adopted French values and culture rapidly.

The most recent wave of immigrants are not white. Many have refused to "become French." Many have not even learned to speak the language. They have also arrived in far larger numbers than their predecessors.

What is important for our purposes is how the French government deals with the tensions that inevitably arise when a country's population changes so dramatically and so rapidly. That policy has been rather ambiguous, at times seeming to support the interests of immigrants and their children, at times seeming to harm them. The one common thread to them all is a firm basis in the traditions of centralization and egalitarianism that can be traced back to the French revolution.

On the one hand, the French government has insisted that immigrants enjoy the same rights and privileges as native-born French men and women once they become citizens. Blatant acts of racism have been dealt with harshly by the judiciary.

On the other hand, the French tradition of egalitarianism has kept governments on the left and right alike from introducing policies that would address some of the specific problems faced by nonwhites precisely because politicians believe they have to treat all French people the same way. For instance, it was only in the last few years that any of the *grandes écoles* introduced affirmative action policies that would add more members of minority groups to their student bodies. There are currently no nonwhite members of parliament elected from France proper, and only a handful of members of minority groups have served in a cabinet during the Fifth Republic.

The often unstated goal of most policies is to encourage the immigrants and their children to assimilate fully into French society. The most telling example involves what students are allowed to wear to school. As is the case in the United States or Great Britain, Muslim girls started wearing head scarves to school in large numbers during the 1990s. But what was routinely accepted in the United States and Great Britain was not tolerated in France.

The separation of church and state has been an all but universally accepted principle since 1906, when the French government cut all ties to the Catholic Church. That principle led a number of school administrators to forbid girls from wearing head scarves, arguing that it brought religion into the schools. A number of Muslim girls were expelled from school and went instead to private Muslim academies, which are not recognized by the government. Many Muslims were, not surprisingly, incensed because no such effort was made to keep Christians from wearing crosses.

The issue came to a head on 17 December 2004 when President Chirac announced a plan to introduce

On 20 December 2003, protestors rallied against the ban on conspicuous religious garb in schools.

AP/Wide World Photos

legislation that would ban "conspicuous" religious symbols from the schools. Small crosses or stars of David would be allowed, but not yarmulkes or head scarves. In an attempt to gain support for the plan, Chirac made the Algerian-born deputy minister Hanifa Cherifi his spokesperson on the issue. Public opinion polls found that almost 60 percent of the public supported the ban and a similar one that already existed for civil servants. The bill on the schools easily passed the National Assembly in February, with 494 votes for it, 36 against it, and 31 abstentions.

The law by no means settled the issue. Three days after Chirac's declaration, massive protests were held around the country in which, among other things, girls marched wearing red, white, and blue headscarves. The law only reinforced the anger many Muslims feel toward a society they believe treats them as second-class citizens.

Foreign Policy

Nothing about France is more controversial than its foreign policy. American observers, in particular, have been critical of what they see as an irrational and unacceptable streak of independence in its international relations beginning with de Gaulle's flamboyant search for grandeur down to its refusal to support the United States in its decision to go to war with Iraq in 2003.

What I will try to show here, however, is that there has been little about French foreign policy that has been irrational. Rather, French presidents from de Gaulle to Chirac have tried to pursue what they saw as their national interest, a national interest that has periodically been at odds with that of the United States or Great Britain.

The Gaullist Years

Prior to 1914, France was one of the world's great powers. It had the largest and best-equipped army in Europe, and its empire was second only to that of Great Britain.

Over the next thirty years, France's position deteriorated rapidly. It emerged from World War II with its economy in tatters, its political leadership in disrepute, and its fate largely in American hands. Almost immediately thereafter, it faced the first in a series of colonial wars that pointed to the demise of its empire by the middle of the 1950s.

De Gaulle was able to stem that decline. His political philosophy and sense of mission were based on restoring France to its "proper" place among the world's major powers. The general believed that all countries have an inherent national interest akin to what the eighteenth-century political theorist Jean-Jacques Rousseau meant by the "general will." Grandeur was thus the successful pursuit of that national interest, thereby maximizing the country's power and prestige. Moreover, a more assertive and independent foreign policy would help restore the sense of unity and pride the French had lost under the Third and Fourth republics.

De Gaulle is frequently criticized for excessively nationalistic, bombastic, and even dangerous policy initiatives. The general, however, was neither a romantic nor a utopian. Rather, he used the available institutional levers and his own charisma in the unbending but normally pragmatic pursuit of grandeur. De Gaulle's pragmatism was not of the kind one normally expects in foreign policy. His was leadership designed to produce as much symbolic and substantive change as possible.

There is no better example of the mix of symbol and substance in Gaullist foreign policy than the decision to create the French nuclear arsenal. De Gaulle had no illusions that it would make France the equal of the United States or the former Soviet Union. He did hope that having even a small nuclear arsenal would give the country a larger role in major international decisions involving the superpowers and the countries caught between them. Most importantly, the bomb was to be a symbol of France's newly rediscovered influence, leading people to develop a sense of pride and unity that he was sure would spill over into other policy areas.

De Gaulle's desire to free France of American tutelage had a similar motivation. Throughout his decade in office, de Gaulle made it clear that France would no longer blindly accept American cold war policy. He rejected proposals by Presidents Eisenhower and Kennedy to integrate French forces more fully into the NATO command, because this would have meant relinquishing part of French sovereignty. In 1964 and 1965, he responded favorably to Soviet overtures about improving Franco-Soviet relations. The next year, de Gaulle withdrew French forces from NATO control and, while speaking at the Kremlin, advocated cooperative relations between France and the Soviet bloc.

That same desire to maximize French power animated policies on European integration. De Gaulle accepted the principle that the countries of Western Europe would have to cooperate more if they were to meet the challenge posed by the growing impact of American capital and industry on the Continent. Therefore, de Gaulle firmly supported the elimination of tariff barriers and the provisions of the Treaty of Rome (which created the European Economic Community in 1957) that worked in France's interest.

There were limits, however, to how much cooperation he would accept. As someone interested in grandeur and France's own problems, he opposed a multinational, integrated, homogeneous Europe, preferring one based on sovereign states cooperating in ways beneficial to France (and, when possible, its partners as well). Consequently, he opposed British entry into the Common Market, as well as anything else he felt might lead to a loss of French influence.

If de Gaulle is seen as a visionary nationalist, Georges Pompidou is commonly portrayed as a moderate pragmatic practitioner of realpolitik. In fact, Pompidou continued the quest for grandeur, though he did it through more conventional political and diplomatic means. Pompidou did not engage in the kinds of flamboyant actions de Gaulle was so famous for. That wasn't his style. Because he had firmer parliamentary support than de Gaulle did in the early 1960s, and because France's position in the world had improved substantially, he didn't have to. He was able to continue de Gaulle's foreign policy using the more conventional tactics the general himself had come to rely on during his last years in office.

However more cooperative and malleable Pompidou may have been, he did not compromise on the central tenets of Gaullist grandeur. He never considered integrating French forces into NATO. There was never any question of abandoning nuclear weapons or submitting them to international control. The French government continued trying to play its self-defined role as an intermediary between East and West, most notably doing what it could to settle disputes in Indochina and the Middle East.

After the OPEC Oil Embargo

President Pompidou died just months before the OPEC oil embargo of 1973–74 and the worldwide recession it helped spark. For the rest of the century, French foreign policy was noticeably less successful as the "inward" arrows of the figure on the inside front cover grew more powerful.

French rhetoric often struck the independent and anti-American tones of the Gaullist years. All parties agreed that the country should keep its nuclear arsenal. And there were areas in which it continued to go its own way, most tragically in Rwanda, where French policy contributed to the genocide that claimed 10 percent of the country's population in 1994. Socialist officials were critical of what they saw as U.S. cultural hegemony and have been at the forefront of efforts to limit American imports—including curved bananas, under the pretext that straight ones (grown in former French colonies) are better.

But overall, France adopted a foreign policy in line with those of the other major Western powers. Support for the EU in general and the euro in particular were at its core.

As we will see in Chapters 6, 8, and 9, the events that led to the end of the cold war and the collapse of communism in Europe took almost everyone by surprise, including the French. As the Soviet Union began to change and the peoples of Eastern Europe mounted the movements that overthrew their regimes, France was only a bit player in that remarkable political drama.

This is most evident in the negotiations surrounding perhaps the most dramatic and least expected event—the reunification of Germany in 1990, which we will explore in more detail in the next chapter. As one of the four powers that occupied Germany after World War II, France was involved in the "four-plus-two" negotiations that led to formal approval of this dramatic development. The emphasis, though, should be on "formal," because real decisions were made by the two superpowers and the two Germanys.

The post–cold war period saw French leaders of the left and right trying to find their place in a world adrift in a sea of political uncertainty. The French were actively involved in most of the international crises of the 1990s, most notably the first Gulf War (see Chapter 14), the efforts to stop the fighting in the former Yugoslavia, and the campaign to combat terrorism following the attacks on the World Trade Center and the Pentagon.

But France has not been able to play the kind of role it did at the height of the cold war, when it wielded an influence greater than one might expect from a country with its geopolitical resources. Evidence of the strength of forces beyond French control is even more striking when it came to Europe. After de Gaulle's retirement, politicians of all ideological stripes came to see greater European involvement as critical for France's development.

A number of critical choices were made by French governments, especially during the Mitterrand presidency, but two in particular stand out. Each reflects a decision made by France, but each also reveals a Europe in which decision-making power was shifting away from Paris and other national capitals.

The first was Mitterrand's decision to appoint his former finance minister, Jacques Delors as president of the European Commission in 1984. As we will see in more detail in Chapter 7, Delors was the chief architect of the expansion of what is now the EU to then fifteen members and the leading force behind the Single European Act and the Maastricht Treaty.

The second was the broader decision to make Europe France's top foreign policy priority in the post–cold war years. Early on, this was widely seen as an attempt to dilute the power of a unified Germany, which had emerged as both the largest and the wealthiest country in western Europe. But by 1991, the Socialists, many of whom had once been quite skeptical of the EU, had become its strongest supporter, seeking Europe-wide solutions to such problems as the fighting in the former Yugoslavia.

At first, all the signs were positive. France was now the strongest proponent of the movement to deepen and broaden European institutions. It parlayed its presence in Europe into expanded markets for its goods and a vehicle to help strengthen its currency.

As the 1990s wore on, however, the European gambit failed to solve France's long-term problems, especially its high unemployment rate. More importantly, as support for European integration disintegrated, France found itself facing more problems no matter who was in control in Paris. And some of the positions it took struck foreign observers as churlish, if not downright silly. In the negotiations for a new GATT (General Agreement on Tariffs and Trade), France insisted on protection for its farmers, who then accounted for less than 5 percent of the population, and on its right to limit the number of American movies and television shows shown in France.

But many of its problems were real. High unemployment rates were becoming the rule, not the exception, especially among the young and less skilled. By contrast, even with problems of its own, which we will address in the next chapter, Germany had solidified its position as Europe's most powerful country.

Tensions reached a peak over French ratification of the Maastricht Treaty in 1992. When it was signed, all leading French politicians supported the treaty, and it was assumed it would pass easily, even after the Constitutional Council ruled that it had to be put to the people in a referendum. When the vote was held, the French came within a whisker of turning it down.

European integration turned out to be the lightning rod for the dissatisfaction with the politicians and the economy that had been building for years. Moreover, the treaty, and all the other issues that eddied around it, divided the three major parties in ways quite reminiscent of the American debate over NAFTA (North American Free Trade Agreement) early in the Clinton administration.

Prominent Gaullists, Socialists, and Giscardiens found themselves on both sides of the issue. The opposition included not only some mainstream politicians but members of the PCF and the National Front—unusual political bedfellows, to say the least.

Perhaps most importantly, what looks like a set of willful choices by French governments since Pompidou's day may actually have done little more than acknowledge the existence of changes that were already taking place and that would have altered French political and

❚ TABLE 5.9 France and the Global Economy

YEAR	EXPORTS AS PERCENTAGE OF GDP	IMPORTS AS PERCENTAGE OF GDP
1962	12	11
1974	20	22
1980	22	23
1992	23	22
1999	26	24
2002	27	25

Source: Data for 1962–92 from David Cameron, "Economic Policy in the Era of the EMS," in *Remaking the Hexagon,* ed. Gregory Flynn (Boulder, Colo.: Westview Press, 1995), 121; data for 1999 from www.worldbank.org, accessed 20 July 2001; data for 2002 from www.undp.org, accessed 15 November 2004.

economic life whatever the politicians had done. As table 5.9 shows, international trade is a much more important part of French life today than it was even a generation ago.

The table presents raw statistics, but they have real meaning in people's lives. The fact that imports and exports account for more than 20 percent of French consumption and production affects everyone. It means that more people eat McDonald's burgers, drive Nissans, and, shockingly, drink Italian or German wine. By the same token, France's prosperity is ever more dependent on its ability to sell Renaults, Airbus jets, and cheese abroad. It also means that people who lack the education or skills to shift from the dying heavy industries to more high-tech ones are losing out and, not surprisingly, are getting angrier and angrier.

Iraq

Criticisms of French foreign policy in the United States and Great Britain reached a new peak in 2002 and 2003 because of its opposition to the American-led war in Iraq. As noted earlier, France had participated in the first Gulf war and supported the United States after the terrorist attacks of 9/11.

But the second war with Iraq was another story. France was by no means the only country to oppose what it saw as a rush to war by the Bush administration. Russia and China joined France, which meant that three of the five permanent members of the United Nations Security Council refused to authorize the use of force. The European Union, too, was divided. Of the major members, France and Germany opposed the war, while Britain, Italy, and Spain supported it.

France, however, was the object of the most condemnation from the United States. Sales of French wine and cheese plummeted. Some of New York's most fa-

French Fries and French Toast

One of the silliest reactions to France's position on Iraq was a boycott of French fries and French toast endorsed by many leading Congressional Republicans.

It turns out that the French do not call them French fries. Just *frites.* They were most likely invented in Belgium. French toast is named for an eighteenth century tavern owner in Albany, New York, who first served the cholesterol-laden delicacy. I used to make it for French friends, when I could find white bread and maple syrup—neither of which are commonly sold in French stores.

This was not the first time Americans used language for political purposes. During World War I, hamburgers and frankfurters become salisbury steak and hot dogs. The Danish do not eat Danish pastry. Russians "play" pistol roulette, not Russian roulette. The list goes on and on.

mous French restaurants had to close because of a diners' boycott.

On closer inspection, the French position does not seem all that irrational or, frankly, all that critical of American policy (www.france.diplomatie.fr/index.gb .html). As late as his New Year's Eve address to the French people on 31 December 2002, Chirac advised that their sons and daughters could be heading into war.

What Chirac and the other critics of U.S. policy insisted on was allowing inspectors to finish their work and determine once and for all if Iraq had weapons of mass destruction. Of course, there were other issues involved. France had closer commercial and diplomatic ties to Iraq than the other major Western powers, similar to ties the United States had had to Iraq during the Reagan administration. Many in France also felt insulted when Defense Secretary Donald Rumsfeld made statements that seemed to belittle France, its power, and its values.

From the beginning, France made it clear that it welcomed a regime change in Iraq. What they objected to was the way the United States managed the run up to the war and the occupation after Saddam Hussein's regime fell (again see Chapter 14).

Before the war, France and others insisted that weapons inspectors be allowed to complete their work before any decision was made. It is not clear if Chirac would have ever endorsed an invasion, but, in retrospect, it seems that his government understood more clearly than the Bush administration that Iraq's weap-

Globalization and France

RECENT FRENCH GOVERNMENTS have taken relatively ambiguous positions on globalization. Most notably, they have tried to promote international rules that would restrict the number of foreign television programs and movies allowed into the country. But they have also been among the most resolutely European. In particular, they recognize that France's economic success is inextricably intertwined with that of the EU and have thus been among the strongest supporters of the single currency and other attempts to deepen integration. Conversely, public opposition to the EU and other "foreign" influences has risen noticeably since the mid-1990s

ons of mass destruction program had been all but completely shut down.

Again, the point is not to question whether the war in Iraq was appropriate or not. Rather, the key here is that the French reacted out of what they perceived to be their national interest, something they have done consistently throughout the history of the Fifth Republic.

Feedback

In most respects, the French media resemble the British. The printed press is dominated by Parisian-based dailies, which are sold throughout the country. Each of them has a distinctive political slant. Some are very good, especially *Le Monde,* which is widely considered to be one of the world's four or five best newspapers. Television news, too, is based primarily on nationwide channels rather than networks built on locally owned and controlled stations.

There are some important differences. The tabloid press has a much smaller circulation and more limited influence than in Britain. France also has three high-quality weekly news magazines, each of which takes a different political line. Finally, until the early 1980s, the government routinely influenced the content and tone of television news. That changed once Giscard's government began privatizing television and Mitterrand's administration decided to adopt a more hands-off policy. As in most countries, with the spread of cable and satellite television systems, France has seen the launch of dozens of niche program providers. The most recent is

Pink TV (www.pinktv.fr). It is not the first gay-oriented station in the world, but it is the first one projected to turn a profit.

One of the quirks of French political life is that pollsters are not allowed to publish their findings in the week before an election. They can and do carry out surveys for parties and candidates. However, the law prevents them from making the money and getting the exposure they would otherwise obtain through contracts with the print or audiovisual media. Pollsters have always found ways to partially get around the law by publishing their results abroad; in 1997 they also began posting their findings on the Internet using foreign-based websites.

Conclusion: A Remarkable Turnaround

France has experienced a remarkable political turnaround since the creation of the Fifth Republic. At the time, few observers expected it to last, let alone thrive. Many wrote books and pamphlets discussing why it was bound to collapse and outlining what form they thought the next republic should take.

The new republic was blessed with a remarkable leader with a proven track record as a reformer. However, even this was no guarantee that it would succeed. Indeed, this book is filled with examples of countries in crisis that also had leaders with plausible ideas for fundamental reform. All too often, neither those leaders nor their ideas got a chance, and if they did, they failed in their efforts to produce change.

The Liberation government of 1944–46 in France provides one such example. Even more striking is the Gorbachev era in the former Soviet Union, in which the failure to carry through with an ambitious reform package led to the collapse of one of the world's two superpowers. (See Chapter 9.) In other words, relatively peaceful, successful, and profound reforms are the exception rather than the rule.

Political scientists have yet to do many comprehensive and comparative studies of such periods of dramatic but nonrevolutionary change. Any attempt to lay out a theory of why they occur is premature at best. Nonetheless, the history of the shift to the Fifth Republic contains three ingredients we probably would expect to find in any such transition.

First, the old regime has to be in a particular type of crisis. Obviously, it has to face deep and enduring problems such as those we saw for the Third and Fourth republics. It just as obviously has to confront a wrenching, immediate trauma like the Algerian uprising, which forces the issue of the very survival of the regime onto center stage. Conversely, the political situation cannot have degenerated to the point that substantial numbers of respected leaders think revolution or some other violent alternative to the status quo is the only possible course.

Second, the transition needs strong leadership. Often, this involves a charismatic individual like de Gaulle who can mobilize average citizens and elites across much of the ideological spectrum. It also probably requires a broader leadership that can build an enduring coalition that includes not only opponents of the old regime but also at least some of its critical supporters, something the Gaullists were able to do at the polls.

Finally, any transition has to have a certain amount of luck. As noted in Chapter 1, political scientists seek regular and rational patterns in the events and trends they study. In fact, life cannot easily be put into such neat packages, and this is especially true at times like these. In this case, the transition from the Fourth Republic to the Fifth was certainly facilitated by a number of what could almost be considered accidents of history, including these:

- The fact that France (unlike Italy, which was in similar circumstances at the time) had a de Gaulle to turn to
- De Gaulle's survival of the 1962 assassination attempt
- Having the new generation of ENArques—instead of party politicians, few of whom shared the Gaullist commitment to growth and grandeur—ready to step into leadership positions

Key Terms

Concepts

Anticlerical	Pantouflage
Autogestion	Parity law
Bloc vote	Prefect
Cohabitation	Privatization
Dirigisme	Proportional representation
Grandeur	Single-member district,
Incompatibility clause	two-ballot system
Iron triangle	*Tutelle*
Nationalization	

People

Chirac, Jacques	Giscard d'Estaing, Valéry
De Gaulle, Charles	Jospin, Lionel
Debré, Michel	Le Pen, Jean-Marie

Mitterrand, François	Raffarin, Jean-Pierre
Pompidou, Georges	

Acronyms

CFDT	PCF
CGT	PS
ENA	RPR
FN	UDF

Organizations, places, and events

Communist Party	National Assembly
École nationale	National Front
d'administration	Radicals
Events of May	Rally for the Republic
Fifth Republic	Senate
Force ouvrière	Socialist Party
Fourth Republic	Union for French
Gaullist	Democracy
Grandes écoles	

Critical Thinking Exercises

1. Much has changed since this book was finished in early 2005. Does the analysis of French politics presented here still make sense? Why (not)?

2. Public opinion pollsters routinely ask questions about whether people think their country is heading in the "right direction" or is on the "wrong track." If you were asked such a question about France, how would you answer? Why did you reach this conclusion?

3. Democracy did not develop as quickly or as smoothly in France as in the United States or Great Britain. Why do you think that was the case?

4. French political culture is no longer as alienated or divided as it once was. Explain the changes.

5. Some political scientists argue that French political parties refused to fail in the 1960s and 1970s but are in more trouble today. Why is that the case?

6. The French state has a more integrated elite than do its British or American counterparts. How did that develop? What difference does it make?

Useful Websites

There are fewer English websites on France than on Britain or the United States. Gradually, however, organizations are adding English versions of their French ones. In the body of the chapter's text, I have included a few French-only sites. Those listed here are all in English.

There are two American-based sources for links to political topics in France. The first is a project run by a consortium of librarians. The second is an off-shoot of H-France, a listserv for scholars working on things French.

www.library.uiuc.edu/ala/alawess/index.html

www3.uakron.edu/hfrance

There are surprisingly few ways of getting news on France in English. The best source is:

www.French-News.com

The best, though still limited, English-language source on public opinion polls is run by the firm CSA.

www.csa-tmo.fr

The President's Office site is a good entry point for websites from most government offices and agencies.

www.elysee.fr

The Tocqueville Connection is a project of U.S.-Crest, a nonprofit organization based in the Washington, D.C., metropolitan area that focuses on enhancing dialogue between France and the United States.

www.ttc.org

InfoTrac College Edition Sources

Beland, Daniel, and Randall Hansen. "Reforming the French Welfare State."

Haase-Dubose, Danielle. "Sexual Differences and Politics in France Today."

Jack, Alex. "Why the French Really Are Different."

Miguet, Arnaud. "The French Elections of 2002."

Perry, Sheila. "Thirty Years of French Political Television."

Piketty, Thomas. "Economic Inequality in France."

Safran, William. "Pluralism and Multiculturalism in France."

Vaisse, Justin. "American Francophobia Takes a New Turn."

Wawro, Geoffrey. "Our Special Correspondent: Letter from France."

Further Reading

Allwood, Gill, and Khursheed Wadia. *Women and Politics in France: 1958–2000.* London: Routledge, 2000. A fine overview of the role women play (and don't play) in French politics.

Ardagh, John. *France in the 1980s.* New York: Penguin Books, 1987. An encyclopedic account by a journalist fascinated with the social and economic transformations that have occurred since World War II.

De Gaulle, Charles. *Memoirs of Hope and Renewal.* New York: Scribner, 1971. A look at the postwar years and his reshaping of France.

Elgie, Robert, ed. *The Changing French Political System.* London: Frank Cass, 2000. An excellent anthology by some of the best French, British, and American academic analysts of French politics.

Feigenbaum, Harvey, Jeffrey Henig, and Chris Hamnett. *Shrinking the State: The Political Underpinnings of Privatization.* Cambridge: Cambridge University Press, 1998. A thoughtful analysis of privatization in Great Britain, the United States, and France.

Flynn, Gregory, ed. *Remaking the Hexagon: The New France in the New Europe.* Boulder, Colo.: Westview Press, 1995. A volume that brings together some of the best European and American authors working on France.

Hauss, Charles. *Politics in Gaullist France: Coping with Chaos.* New York: Praeger, 1991. A focus on the large-scale transformations of the Gaullist years.

Jack, Andrew. *The French Exception: France—Still So Special?* London: Profile Books, 1999. The most thoughtful book on French politics by a journalist in recent years.

Marcus, Jonathan. *The National Front.* New York: New York University Press, 1995. The best single source on the National Front by the BBC World Service's defense correspondent.

Sa'adah, Anne. *Contemporary France.* Boulder, Colo.: Rowman and Littlefield, 2003. The best available overview of French history by a political scientist.

Tiersky, Ronald. *François Mitterrand: The Last French President.* New York: St. Martin's Press, 2000. A provocative biography that casts a broader argument about the declining power of the French president and state.

Timmerman, Kenneth R. *The French Betrayal of America.* New York: Crown, 2004. An important, but to my mind, a wrong-headed view of how France has systematically undermined American interests over the years.

Germany's reemergence as a world power has been driven by no one and no cult but by many Germans pulling together in an elaborate democracy and market economy.

NICO COLCHESTER

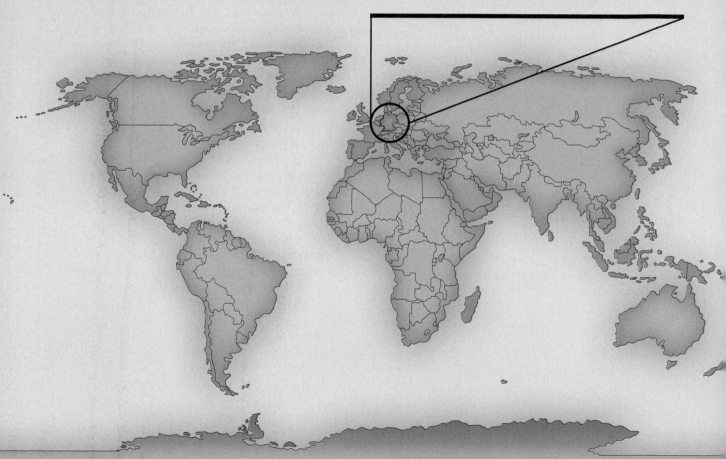

Chapter 6

GERMANY

CHAPTER OUTLINE

The Basics: Germany

Size	356,910 sq. km (about two-thirds the size of France)
Population	82 million
GNP per capita	$22,670
Currency	1.29€ = US$1
Ethnic composition	91.2% German; of the largest remaining groups, 2.5% Turkish, 1.0% Yugoslav
Religion	38% Protestant, 34% Catholic, 2% Muslim, remainder unaffiliated or undeclared
Capital	Berlin
Form of government	Federal republic
Head of state	Horst Köhler (2004–)
Head of government	Gerhard Schröder (1998–)

A Telling Snapshot

In June 2001, Chancellor **Gerhard Schröder** of Germany got a gift from a long-lost cousin—a photograph of his father. Getting a picture of your father from relatives is rarely a politically interesting event. In this case, it was in at least two respects.

First, Schröder had never known his father, who was killed a few months after Schröder was born in 1944. In fact, this was probably the first picture of his father he had ever seen.

It showed Corporal Fritz Schröder in his Nazi uniform, with a swastika on the helmet. He looked just like his son had at that age. Schröder knew that his father was a low-ranking enlisted man who had been forced into the army like most men of his generation. But the photo forced the younger Schröder, like all Germans of his generation, to come to grips with his personal links to Germany's horrid past.

The Holocaust and other atrocities of the thirteen-year Nazi era are now more than a half-century in the past. Almost no one who took an active part in them is still active in political life, because they are all in at least their late seventies. Nonetheless, Germany and the Germans cannot escape a history that makes its political life very different from what we saw in Britain, France, or the United States.

Reuters/CORBIS

Chancellor Gerhard Schröder.

Second, the photograph was politically interesting because it came from a cousin Schröder did not know existed. Like many German families, his had been separated by the postwar division of Germany and the subsequent creation of the Federal (West German) and Democratic (East German) republics. And like many families, the Schröders in the west lost contact with the Schröders in the east. The eastern cousins were able to establish connections with their famous western cousin shortly after he became chancellor, as the Germans call their prime minister. They could do so only because the end of the cold war meant that Germany was no longer divided into two separate countries. In other words, the Schröders' experience, again, was like that of many families in that, in the chancellor's words, "Now the fall of the Iron Curtain has become personal as well as political. I have to find a relationship to people I had not believed existed." [1]

The differences between the two Germanys is the leading issue facing the country today. The economic gap between them remains immense. More than a decade after unification, unemployment stands at 17 per-

cent in the east, a full 10 points higher than in the west. This was the case even after the federal government and Western firms had pumped close to $200 billion a year into the east.

But as Schröder's experience shows, the real gap may be in the Germans' heads and hearts more than in their pocketbooks. It turns out that his cousin, Renata Gritzke, had worked for the Stasi, East Germany's notorious intelligence agency. She—and about 40 percent of her fellow East Germans—still vote for the **Party of Democratic Socialism (PDS),** the renamed and more moderate Communist Party. By contrast, her cousin the chancellor is a moderate who is trying to forge the same kind of "third way" policies as Tony Blair and Bill Clinton in the 1990s.

Thinking about Germany

Traditionally, introductory courses in comparative politics have not included Germany. But it is hard to leave it out today. It is, after all, one of the world's leading political and economic powers. Furthermore, it is important for comparative analysis. Germany has been so successful in recent years largely because it has been able to combine a functioning liberal democracy with a strong state. Thus, it is an important country to consider given the overarching themes of this section of the book.

The Basics

Germany is the strongest country in Europe. Its eighty-two million residents make it by far Europe's most populous country—unless one counts Russia as wholly European. Its GNP per capita of roughly $23,000 makes the **Federal Republic of Germany** one of the world's richest countries. Germans who earn noticeably less than that average are covered by Europe's most extensive social service system, which makes it all but impossible for them to have to endure the kind of poverty, homelessness, or treatable ill health that is common in many other industrialized democracies.

Germany's wealth is all the more remarkable given the devastation of World War II, which left the country in ruins. The Federal Republic turned the economy around so far and so fast that its system, dubbed **Modell Deutschland** (the German Model), was widely seen as an approach for other countries to emulate.

The country has its share of problems. The five *länder* (states) inherited from East Germany in 1990 remain far poorer than the rest of the country. It is there, too, that

---

[1] Roger Cohen, "Schröder, Like Germany, Looks Harder at the Past." *New York Times.* 2 July 2001, A1, A6.

A right-wing rioter tossing a firebomb at a hostel for asylum seekers in Rostock, Germany.

© Reuters NewMedia Inc. /CORBIS

racist attacks have occurred most frequently and that neo-Nazi organizations have enjoyed the most support.

Schröder's government also faces economic problems that, curiously, grew out of its past success. Only a country with West Germany's assets could have easily taken on the challenge of unification. Moreover, as we will see, the system of cooperative labor-management relations and extensive social services, which helped build Modell Deutschland in the first place, leaves the economy less flexible and dynamic than many of its competitors today.

When all is said and done, we should not make too much of these problems. Germany has done something no other industrialized democracy has had to even contemplate—incorporate sixteen million people whose standard of living was at most a quarter of its own, and do so virtually overnight, with minimal political or social disruption. Germany's position among the three wealthiest countries in the world is not in jeopardy. Instead, most observers assume that it will overcome any short-term difficulties and remain one of the world's leading political and economic powers. And, as we will also see, much of the key to that success lies in the pragmatic and careful approach to political life evoked by the late Nico Colchester in the statement that begins this chapter.

Finally, Germany is as socially diverse as France or Britain. However, it was only in 2000 that immigrants who were not ethnic Germans could become citizens without waiting for fifteen years and that children of foreigners living in Germany could be naturalized once their parents had been in Germany legally for eight years.

Key Questions

We could ask the same basic questions about the stability of democracy in Germany that we did for Britain and France, and to some degree we will. But the Schröder family history gives us a first glimpse at how much higher the political stakes have historically been in Germany and how much they have been lowered since the end of World War II. Any discussion of the country, then, has to focus on what scholars call the **German question,** which is really a series of questions:

■ Why did it take Germany so long to unite, and how did that delay affect German behavior once it did come together under Prussian rule in the 1870s?

■ Why did Germany's first attempt at democracy give way to **Adolf Hitler** (1889–1945) and his **Nazi** regime, which were responsible for the deaths of Fritz Schröder and millions more?

■ How did the division of Germany and other events after World War II help create the remarkably prosperous and stable democratic Federal Republic of Germany in the west but also the stagnant and repressive **German Democratic Republic (DDR)** in the east?

- Why did unification occur with the end of the cold war in Germany, and what new challenges has it posed for what is now the largest and richest country in Europe?

Because the first three questions have had such sweeping implications for Germany and much of the rest of the world, we will spend more time on the historical material here than in the preceding two chapters. Once we examine how the Federal Republic was created and became a stable and legitimate regime, we will turn to the kinds of "normal" political issues we focused on for Britain and France while considering that final question. Even though there is some uncertainty on that score, we will see that the economic and cultural difficulties brought on by unification have been handled using the conventional tools of an established democracy.

Germany does have right-wing, antidemocratic protest movements. Since unification, most of the neo-Nazi and skinhead groups have focused their hatred on immigrants, asylum seekers, and other foreigners. However, their influence is limited, and despite an occasional breakthrough at the state level, none of them have shown any signs of breaking the 5 percent barrier parties needed to gain representation in the Bundestag, or lower house of parliament.

Put simply, Germany now faces the same kinds of political, social, and economic problems we find in all major industrialized democracies. Democracy is as strongly established in Germany as it is anywhere. To refer again to that key distinction made in Chapter 1, its regime is as secure as any.

The Evolution of the German State: The German Questions

In 1945, no serious observer would have dreamed that Germany could become so rich, so stable, and so democratic so quickly. The country was defeated, dismembered, and treated as a pariah by the rest of the world (europeanhistory.about.com/cs/germany).

Yet succeed it did. If we are to understand that turnaround and the development of a democratic Germany, we actually have to start much earlier and explore why there have been so many "German questions" over the centuries.

Unification and the Kaiser's Reich

In Chapters 4 and 5, we saw that the state and nation developed roughly in tandem in Great Britain and in France. This was not the case in Germany. Domestic and international pressures kept Germany divided until 1871, a delay that has had tremendous implications for political life there ever since, especially its ability to sustain a democracy.

During the early Middle Ages, Germany had one of the most advanced political systems in Europe. It was more united than most "countries" by a single government, the Holy Roman Empire, which some Germans call the First Reich. More than most, too, Germans were unified around a common culture and language—or at least closely related dialects.

By the middle of the thirteenth century, however, any semblance of political unity had disappeared when the German part of the Holy Roman Empire disintegrated into hundreds of principalities. The Reformation deepened those divisions as local princes lined up on both sides of the split between Catholics and Protestants. They fought the Thirty Years' War (1618–48)—the bloodiest conflict the world had ever seen, but one that did not produce a clear winner or loser. As a result, Germany remained a patchwork of tiny states, some Catholic, some Protestant. The religious conflict did, however, reinforce the authoritarianism of most of the rulers, Catholic and Protestant alike.

The first tentative steps toward German unification occurred late in the seventeenth century in the eastern province of Brandenburg, which became the Kingdom of Prussia in 1701. Under Frederick I (ruled 1640–88), Frederick Wilhelm I (ruled 1688–1740), and Frederick the Great (ruled 1740–86), Prussia gradually gained control of more and more territory. By the end of the eighteenth century, it was one of Europe's great powers, and also one of its most conservative. Lacking wealth and natural resources, the Prussians had to rely on discipline, thus strengthening authoritarian values that were under increasing pressure to the west. (See table 6.1.)

Prussian expansion was brought to a temporary halt by the Napoleonic Wars. But by the time they ended, Napoleon's campaigns had served to consolidate many of the smaller states, especially in western Germany. The Congress of Vienna in 1815 continued that trend, leaving thirty-eight German states, of which only two, Prussia and Austria-Hungary, had the size and resources to conceivably unite Germany.

TABLE 6.1 German Regimes since 1871

YEAR	REGIME
1871–1918	Second Reich
1919–33	Weimar Republic
1933–45	Third Reich
1949–	Federal Republic
1949–90	German Democratic Republic

Under the skilled, if often ruthless, leadership of Chancellor **Otto von Bismarck,** Prussia won wars against Denmark, Austria, and France between 1864 and 1870. At that point, Bismarck had brought all the German states other than Austria under Prussian control. In 1871, these states "asked" the Prussian king, Wilhelm I, to become emperor, or *kaiser,* of a new Reich.

The new German state was very different from France or Britain. To begin with, it was more deeply divided. The religious disputes of the preceding three centuries had left a country split not only between clericals and anticlericals but between Catholics and Protestants. Germany's democrats found themselves sharply at odds with the dominant Prussian elite. With the introduction of universal male suffrage, the **Social Democratic Party (SPD)** became the largest party, but it had no real influence, because the new parliament was all but powerless.

Bismarck and his colleagues responded to the disruptive potential of these cleavages by extending the Prussian constitution to the entire country, thereby creating a strong, authoritarian regime. For its first twenty years, the Second Reich was dominated by Bismarck. After he left office in 1890, the government was controlled by the Kaiser, the Junkers, and other nobles in the bureaucratic, military, and civilian elites.

Although all men could vote, Germany was far from democratic. The Reichstag (parliament) did not control the budget, nor were the chancellors and their cabinets answerable to it. The leadership resisted the prodemocratic forces that were gaining strength and thus laid the seeds for greater conflict down the line.

The newly unified Germany also lagged behind Britain and France economically and militarily. Although the industrial revolution was well under way in parts of the country, unification had been sparked by the predominantly rural Prussians. Germany lacked an independent entrepreneurial class and the kind of heavy industry needed to produce such weapons as machine guns and massive metal warships.

The political leaders realized that they had to modernize its military and economy as rapidly as possible. As they saw it, Germany could not afford the time it would take if they relied on market forces. Instead, they devised a new way of developing an industrialized capitalist economy directed by the state, sometimes called a revolution from above. The government worked with the traditional elites in the nobility and the military to force the country to industrialize so that it could compete militarily and economically with its European rivals.

Germany changed at an unprecedented pace. By the end of the nineteenth century, a modern army and navy had transformed Germany into a global power that ri-

valed Britain and France. Militarization, in turn, required the construction of huge industrial centers, specializing in the production not only of weapons but of manufactured goods, including railroads, chemicals, and telephone and telegraph equipment. The production of both iron and steel, for instance, grew more than 700 percent between 1870 and 1910.

In Britain and, to a lesser degree, France, the impetus for the industrial revolution had come "from below," from capitalist entrepreneurs operating largely on their own, independent of the state. Both countries also took substantial, if less than complete, steps to incorporate the working class and other underprivileged groups into the political process. Perhaps most importantly, both reinforced parliamentary rule, thereby curbing the arbitrary power of elites not elected by the people.

Little of that happened in Germany. Instead, the Prussian-based elite clung to power. It introduced social insurance programs to try to gain the support of the working class. It also passed a series of antisocialist laws and repressed the growing union movement, which left an unusually alienated and potentially revolutionary working class. By 1890, the SPD had become Germany's largest political party, and the trade union movement affiliated with it enrolled millions of members.

Imperial Germany was what scholars call a **faulted society.** On one side of the political fault line were the elites; on the other were the powerless and increasingly angry masses. On the one hand, the elites pursued policies that were transforming German society; on the other, they resisted accepting the political consequences of those social and economic changes. Indeed, the failure of the elites to adapt to the changed conditions of the late nineteenth and early twentieth centuries led some observers at the time to expect a civil war.

An important fault line also was present in Germany's relationship with the rest of Europe. There was no easy way to fit a newly powerful and ambitious German state into the elaborate and fragile international system created at the Congress of Vienna. Germany's imperial aspirations were mostly thwarted—at least in German eyes. It did take over a few colonies, but its empire was far smaller than those of the Netherlands, Belgium, and Portugal, let alone Great Britain and France.

Just like their geological namesakes, geopolitical fault lines ultimately produce geopolitical earthquakes. In this case, the European balance of power finally crumbled early in the twentieth century. A variety of open treaties and secret pacts pitted Germany and the weakening Austro-Hungarian and Ottoman empires against Britain, France, and Russia. Then in 1914, a Bosnian Serb nationalist assassinated the heir apparent to the Austro-

Hungarian throne. That isolated act by a single individual acting on his own culminated in the outbreak of World War I, a war no one wanted, but one that no one could prevent.

At first the war went well for Germany. Hopes for victory in a matter of weeks, however, gave way to a bloody stalemate. By the end of the war, more than eight million people were dead, more than half of them civilians.

At home, Germany was torn apart. The left increasingly opposed the war. At the other end of the spectrum, nationalist groups began blaming the left and the Jews for Germany's woes.

On 6 November 1918, the military-led government initiated a program of political reforms. Three days later, the kaiser was forced into exile, and the monarchy was replaced by a hastily organized group of politicians who declared Germany a republic. Two days later, Germany surrendered.

Weimar and the Rise of Hitler

The next spring the **Weimar Republic** (named for the town where its constitution was drafted) was created. It never had a chance.

The constitution transformed Germany from one of Europe's most authoritarian countries into one of its most democratic overnight. The traditional political and bureaucratic elites were stripped of almost all their power. Instead, authority was vested in a reformed Reichstag to which the cabinet was answerable. Elections were conducted using **proportional representation,** which gave parties a share of the seats equal to their percentage of the vote. This made it easy for extremist parties to get their foot in the parliamentary door and left Weimar with a far more fragmented and polarized party system than France's Third Republic.

Few politicians gave the new republic their wholehearted support. Most socialists did so until the very end. More radical leftists, however, wanted nothing to do with the new republic and attempted revolutions in 1919 and 1920. Although they were put down rather easily, the revolutions drove a deep wedge between the increasingly moderate SPD and the new Communist Party (KPD).

On the right, many traditional elites and millions of average Germans could not bring themselves to accept that their country had been defeated because of its own weakness and ineptitude. Rather, they looked for scapegoats. Dozens of small, antidemocratic nationalist groups formed, laying blame for the defeat on "non-German" forces, including Jews, socialists, and the politicians who had both sued for peace and created the Weimar Republic. They, too, attempted a number of coups.

The terms of the Treaty of Versailles that formally ended the war magnified the frustrations on the right. U.S. President Woodrow Wilson had called for a "just and lasting peace" sustained by a powerful League of Nations. The British and French, however, insisted on a far more vindictive settlement. The size and composition of the German army were severely restricted, and the Allies imposed a strict system of **reparations** that forced Germany to pay for the costs of the war. The payments worsened an already serious economic crisis. Inflation skyrocketed, unemployment tripled, and the purchasing power of those who kept their jobs was reduced by as much as two-thirds. Especially hard hit were the veterans who had survived four years of hell at the front only to return to a social, political, and economic hell at home.

The fact that the same politicians who had surrendered in 1918 also agreed to the treaty's terms reinforced the right wing's hostility toward Weimar. In 1919, the three parties that most strongly supported the new republic—the SPD, the Catholic Zentrum (Center), and the mostly Protestant and liberal People's Party (DDP)—won over three-quarters of the vote. In the next two elections, they saw their share of the vote drop to the benefit of the Communists on the left and the Nazis and German National People's Party (DNVP) on the antidemocratic right.

Antitreaty protest reached a new peak in early 1923. That November, the little-known Adolf Hitler and his equally little-known party, the Nazis or **NSDAP** (National Socialist Democratic Workers Party), attempted their first putsch. It failed miserably. Many Nazi leaders were arrested. Hitler himself spent nine months in prison, where he wrote his infamous *Mein Kampf.*

As the economy rebounded temporarily, support for the extremists began to wane. Better news came from abroad, too, as the Allies agreed to a series of measures that reduced reparation payments.

The calm did not last. In 1929, the bottom fell out of the German economy after the New York stock market crash. Unemployment leapt from 6.3 percent in 1928 to 14 percent in 1930 and 30 percent two years later. No German family was spared.

The Great Depression and the resulting political tensions came at a time when effective government was most needed and least attainable. The three main Weimar parties had seen their share of the vote drop below 50 percent. In other words, at a time of crisis, German government fell further into the trap of immobilism than anything we saw in France.

The parliamentary stalemate was broken in 1930, though not in a way that would strengthen the republic.

ADOLF HITLER

Adolf Hitler, reviewing Nazi forces.

Adolf Hitler was born in Austria in 1889. Prior to 1914 he was a ne'er-do-well who had dreams of becoming an artist, although his biographers say he had little or no talent. He joined the German army in World War I, experienced the horrors of trench warfare, and eventually was wounded.

Hitler came back to a weakened and dispirited Germany. Like so many of his generation, he could not accept a German defeat as anything but the result of a conspiracy. By the time he got out of prison after his failed 1923 putsch attempt, he had woven together an appeal that focused on frustrated nationalism and on the widespread hatred of the republic, the Jews, and the left.

During the course of the next decade, Hitler used his impressive oratorical and organizational skills to build support for the Nazi Party. After it came to power, he began systematically wiping out all opposition, creating a totalitarian state, and taking the aggressive steps that would ultimately lead to World War II and the Holocaust.

Hitler died in his bunker during the final days of the war.

Chancellor Heinrich Brüning knew he had no chance of gaining a parliamentary majority that would support his policies. Therefore, he convinced the aging President Paul von Hindenburg to invoke the emergency powers provision of the 1919 constitution that allowed the government to rule by decree.

The parliamentary elections two months later confirmed the legislative paralysis. The Weimar parties won barely 40 percent of the vote. Meanwhile, the Nazis continued their growth, earning nearly 15 percent, almost double their total from two years before.

The temporary expediency of emergency rule became permanent. For three years, right-wing politicians pursued an orthodox economic strategy that emphasized fiscal responsibility and deflation. As President Herbert Hoover discovered in the United States, such policies only worsened the depression.

What happened in the streets was at least as important as what happened in governmental offices. As V. B. Berghahn put it, there was a "tense atmosphere of perpetual conflict."[2] The Communists, the SPD, and the Nazis all had massive popular organizations, which waged battles against each other and against the police, who were powerless to stop the violence.

Support for the regime continued to ebb. By the time elections were held again in July 1932, the anti-system parties had won over 40 percent of the vote, a figure they would nearly match when Germans went back to the polls in November.

The big winners were the Nazis. After the fiasco in 1923, Hitler realized it would be far easier to come to power electorally. For the next decade, he dedicated his demagogic skills and the party's organization to that effort.

The Nazis' fortunes sagged during the relative calm of the mid-1920s, but when the depression hit, the Nazis were ready. Their popularity took off, especially among small-town and lower-middle-class Protestants. By 1932, the NSDAP had become Germany's largest party, and Hitler had made a surprisingly successful showing against President Hindenburg in that year's presidential election. Even more importantly, the party's influence in the streets had grown to the point that its SA (*Sturmabteilung*) was the largest and most ruthless of the partisan "armies."

By the end of the year, Germany had reached a turning point. Brüning and his successor, Franz von Papen,

---

[2] V. B. Berghahn, *Modern Germany: Society, Economy, and Politics in the Twentieth Century,* 2nd ed. (New York: Cambridge University Press, 1987), 11.

had accomplished next to nothing despite the continued use of emergency powers. Moreover, they were unable to maintain order in the streets as the balance of political power shifted from the moderates to the extremists, both left and right. Finally, the politicians had to make a choice, and on 30 January 1933, they invited Hitler to become chancellor and to form a government.

Most conservative politicians assumed that they would be able to tame Hitler by bringing him into office and then getting rid of him once the immediate crisis had passed. However, in conjunction with the more mainstream right-wing parties, Hitler controlled a majority in the Reichstag. He used that majority to pass legislation that created the most repressive and reprehensible regime in history.

The Third Reich

Within weeks of taking office, Hitler began dismantling the Weimar Republic. On the night of 7 February, the Reichstag building was set ablaze. Hitler blamed the communists, even though the Nazis themselves were responsible for the fire. The Nazi-controlled police began arresting communists the next day. New parliamentary elections were held less than a week later. Even though the NSDAP fell short of an absolute majority, it won enough seats to allow passage of the infamous Enabling Act on 23 March, which provided the legal basis for the creation of the Third Reich.

Before the end of 1933, trade unions and all political parties other than the Nazis were banned. Germany withdrew from the League of Nations. The next year Hitler declared himself **führer** as well as chancellor, at the same time abolishing the presidency and most of the remaining Weimar institutions. Universal military service was reinstated. The infamous Nuremberg laws were passed, which removed Jews from all positions of responsibility and began the officially sanctioned anti-Semitism that would end with the appalling "final solution" and the death of over six million Jews.

Hitler and his henchmen proved to be remarkably persuasive leaders, using the new media of radio and cinema to reach, seduce, and mobilize millions of Germans. Nazi organizations blanketed all areas of German life. Even the 1936 Olympics were organized to show off the new Germany.

To undo the "damage" of 1918 and 1919 and restore Germany to its "rightful" place among the world's powers, the Nazis looked far beyond German soil. Hitler's notion of Aryan superiority meant that all other nationalities were inferior to and so should be ruled by Germans.

Moreover, as the world's superior race, the Germans needed more space, or living room (*lebensraum*).

Germany rearmed and set its sights first on neighboring countries with a substantial German population and then on the rest of the world. In 1936, Hitler remilitarized the Rhineland along the French border, violating the Treaty of Versailles. Two years later Germany annexed Austria and intervened in the Spanish civil war on the side of Generalissimo Francisco Franco's neofascist forces. Later in the year, it laid claim to the Sudetenland, a region in the new country of Czechoslovakia that was predominantly German. Germany's actions caught Britain and France unprepared, and at the Munich conference of 1938, Prime Ministers Neville Chamberlain and Edouard Daladier acceded to Hitler's demands in what has since come to be called appeasement. Despite Hitler's success at Munich, German ambitions were not satisfied. In March 1939, its forces occupied the rest of Czechoslovakia. In August it signed a nonaggression spact with the Soviet Union in which the two countries pledged not to attack each other and secretly planned the dismemberment of Poland, Lithuania, Latvia, and Estonia.

Germany's aggression finally met resistance when it invaded Poland on 1 September. Two days later France and Britain declared war on Germany. The Second World War had begun barely twenty years after the First World War had ended.

For more than two years, German successes on the battlefield suggested that Hitler may have been right in proclaiming the Germans the master race and his a thousand-year Reich. Poland and the rest of eastern Europe were quickly overcome. The German blitzkrieg shifted to the west, defeating Belgium, the Netherlands, and France in a matter of weeks. In 1941, the Germans attacked the Soviet Union, laid siege to Leningrad, reached the outskirts of Moscow, and penetrated 1,500 miles into Soviet territory. In all of Europe, Britain was the only major power to hold out.

When the Soviet Union and the United States entered the war on the Allied side, German fortunes began to sag. At the battle of Stalingrad in the winter of 1942–43, the Soviet army finally halted the German advance and launched a counterattack that would last until the end of the war in 1945. At about the same time, Allied troops invaded Sicily and began their slow, steady drive up the Italian peninsula. Allied planes began an air assault on the German homeland that would leave the country in ruins. The final straw came with the Allied D-day invasion of the beaches of Normandy in France on 6 June 1944. On 30 April 1945, Hitler committed suicide.

Eight days later, the German general staff surrendered unconditionally.

The thousand-year Reich was over twelve years after it began.

Occupation and the Two Germanys

With the end of the war, the four main Allied powers occupied Germany, Italy, and Japan. Although the circumstances of the defeat and occupation varied somewhat from country to country, the Allies were committed both to avoiding the "mistakes" of Versailles and to crafting stable democracies.

Given what we have seen so far, that must have seemed a daunting, if not impossible, challenge. However, it is what happened in all three.

To some degree, the defeated countries turned inward as people tried to come to grips with the values that had produced fascist governments. In so doing, some key politicians were able to draw on the less-than-successful, but still significant, experiments with democracy all the defeated countries had conducted before the fascists came to power.

All benefited from the occupation in three ways. First, the victorious powers helped restructure the political systems, most notably by barring former fascists from holding political office and by writing new constitutions. Just as important was the massive financial aid provided to rebuild the economies and, with it, confidence in the political system. Finally, the cold war gave the United States and its allies all the more reason to do what they could to ensure that stable, effective, and democratic governments survived.

Germany was split into four zones, each occupied by one of the Allied nations, France, England, the United States, and the Soviet Union. The Western powers would have liked to have turned Germany into a strong democratic regime right away, but they were convinced that authoritarian values were too deeply engrained. Therefore, they removed Nazis from leadership positions, and the most nefarious of them were tried and executed. Even more importantly for the long run, the Western powers realized they would be better off if they helped rebuild Germany rather than add insult to injury by imposing reparations and other policies like those of the 1920s. Food, clothing, and other forms of Western relief aid poured into the three western zones. The educational system was reformed in an attempt to build more support for democratic values. Tentative steps were taken to reestablish the German government as well. Potential leaders who had not been tainted by involvement with

And Iraq?

In American and British discussions about the reconstruction of Iraq after the overthrow of Saddam Hussein and his Baath party, parallels were often drawn with the German, Japanese, and Italian experience after World War II.

In those countries, democracy took hold surprisingly quickly and surprisingly easily. Why should Iraq be any different, asked politicians such as President Bush and Prime Minister Blair.

The differences between Iraq and these other cases are, in fact, enormous and, as we will see in Chapter 14, do not augur well for democracy in Iraq.

For our purposes, two of them stand out. First, there was widespread agreement in all three of the defeated Axis powers that their governments had been to blame for the war and, in many cases, they actually welcomed American and other occupiers. Second, all three of those countries had had substantial experience with early forms of democracy before the fascists took over in the 1920s and 1930s.

the Nazis were identified. Anti-Nazi political parties and trade unions were allowed to reorganize. Limited authority over education, welfare, and other policy areas was given to the new states into which the three western zones were subdivided.

In 1947, the Soviets began systematically imposing Stalinist governments on the countries in their sphere of influence and the cold war began. This led to a shift in Western policy toward Germany. Strengthening recent enemies so they could become allies became more important than the long-term goals of de-Nazification and cultural change.

The purge of former Nazis came to an end, and some of them with limited involvement in the Third Reich were allowed to hold bureaucratic and teaching positions. Attempts to break up the prewar cartels that had supported Hitler and to democratize the German economy also were halted.

The Western powers sped up the political integration of their three zones. At the London Conference in January 1948, the three occupying powers began implementing currency reform that would bring the three economies closer together and drafting what would become a new constitution.

Pressure for the creation of a Western state increased six days after the currency reform went into effect. The Soviets imposed a land blockade on Berlin, which was deep inside their zone of occupation. The

▌ **TABLE 6.2** German Chancellors since 1948

YEAR	NAME	PARTY
1948–63	Konrad Adenauer	CDU
1963–66	Ludwig Erhard	CDU
1966–69	Kurt Georg Kiesinger	CDU
1969–74	Willy Brandt	SPD
1974–82	Helmut Schmidt	SPD
1982–98	Helmut Kohl	CDU
1998–	Gerhard Schröder	SPD

West responded with an airlift that kept the besieged city supplied until May 1949. During the blockade, a Constituent Assembly met to draft a constitution, which was completed three days after the blockade was lifted. Because they assumed it would be in place only temporarily until Germany was reunited, the drafters called it the **Basic Law,** not a constitution. Bonn became the "provisional" capital city. On 14 August the first postwar elections were held. The **Christian Democratic Union (CDU),** the successor to the prewar Zentrum, and its leader, the antifascist mayor of Cologne, **Konrad Adenauer** (1876–1967), won a slim plurality of the votes. (See table 6.2.)

Chancellor Adenauer then put together a coalition of his CDU, the liberal **Free Democratic Party (FDP),** and a number of regional parties. On 23 September 1949 his cabinet was accepted by the Allied High Command, signaling the birth of the Federal Republic.

Few expected much of the new republic. The cold war loomed over German politics. Within weeks of the ratification of the Basic Law, the strictly Stalinist DDR (German Democratic Republic) was established in the East. Moreover, there was no guarantee that the economic recovery would continue, especially given that the new republic had to assimilate more than ten million refugees from countries that had come under communist rule. Everyone acknowledged, too, that there had not been enough time to progress very far in changing German values. Most observers had doubts about how deeply democratic roots had been sunk in a country that had so recently embraced one of the most authoritarian regimes ever. Finally, there was little or no enthusiasm for building a democracy based on a regime that had been largely imposed by outsiders.

But that is precisely what happened.

Building a Democratic Germany

For fourteen years, Adenauer and the CDU gave the country strong leadership around which new political institutions and a modernized economy could be built. Throughout that period, Adenauer dominated political life without ever facing a serious challenge to his authority from the opposition either in parliament or in the streets. Moreover, the CDU and its FDP allies forged links with the business, industrial, bureaucratic, and even union elites, thereby producing the greatest period of growth Germany had ever seen, dubbed the economic miracle. (See table 6.2.)

Crucial to the renewal of German political and economic life was Adenauer himself. He had been a leader of the Catholic Zentrum Party during the Weimar Republic and had impeccable anti-Nazi credentials. That made him an obvious person for the Allies to turn to in seeking leadership for the new Germany.

Adenauer was widely respected and, like his contemporary in France, Charles de Gaulle, used that reputation to gain broader support for the new regime. Under his leadership, the CDU and its allies won four elections in a row. Like most politicians of his day, he was skeptical about how democratic Germany could be in the late 1940s and early 1950s. Therefore, he centralized power as much as possible in the chancellor's office, forging a system that has been called **chancellor democracy** ever since.

With his finance minister, Ludwig Erhard, Adenauer used the new political system to help forge the unprecedented economic growth mentioned earlier. When Adenauer was finally urged into retirement at age eighty-six, he left the same kind of legacy as did de Gaulle—stability that made domestic and foreign policy success possible.

Adenauer was succeeded by Erhard, who generally was given credit for the economic miracle. Erhard, however, was not an effective chancellor and took the blame for the first postwar recession, which occurred during his three years in office. During the recession, the neo-Nazi **National Democratic Party (NPD)** began to make major gains and threatened to cross the 5 percent barrier, raising concerns about continued German susceptibility to right-wing extremism.

In 1966, Erhard resigned and was replaced by another Christian Democrat, Kurt Georg Kiesinger. This time, the coalition was formed not with the FDP but with the SPD in a **grand coalition** of the two largest parties. They came together, among other things, to end the recession and, with it, the NPD threat. Moreover, with the 1967 **Law for Promoting Stability and Growth in the Economy,** the two parties committed themselves to policies designed to produce balanced growth that would benefit all of German society. In other words, a broad consensus about social and economic policy was added to the stability achieved during the Adenauer years. Indeed, that consensus and the ways that it has been implemented ever since set Germany apart from Britain and France, as we will see throughout the rest of this chapter.

After elections in 1969, a new coalition between the SPD and FDP was formed, removing the CDU from office for the first time. Under the leadership of **Willy Brandt** and then **Helmut Schmidt,** the SPD enacted modest social reforms and opened up relations with the communist world. Far more importantly, the socialist leaders demonstrated their commitment to working within the broad consensus established during the grand coalition years. The government also was able to withstand terrorist attacks at home and the economic shock of the OPEC oil embargo in the 1970s with remarkable ease.

In the early 1980s, however, the Schmidt government encountered increasing difficulties. The SPD's left wing pulled it in one direction, and the increasingly conservative FDP pushed it in the other. Finally, in 1982, the FDP decided to quit the center-left coalition and ally once again with the CDU. On 1 October the Schmidt government lost a vote of confidence. Because of the rules on **constructive votes of no confidence** (see the section on the German state), the Bundestag immediately selected **Helmut Kohl** to be the new chancellor. Because the Bundestag was not dissolved when the FDP switched camps, no new elections were held. Kohl agreed to early elections the next year, which the CDU-FDP won easily, the first of its four consecutive victories.

Kohl's sixteen years in office reflected how far German politics had come since the war. We will discuss all these issues in more detail later in the chapter. However, the following examples illustrate the pragmatism and stability in German political life during the 1980s:

- Kohl's government did not follow Reagan's and Thatcher's lead and shift dramatically toward a more market-oriented economy. Rather, Kohl largely retained the social market economy that reflected the society-wide consensus on balanced growth. Among other things, it ensured that workers would receive generous social benefits and encouraged the trade unions and corporate executives to cooperate with each other. In so doing, Kohl kept Germany in its position as one of the three leading economies in the world.

- The government did not overreact to the cultural and political shock waves that occurred following the election of Green Party members to the Bundestag in 1993. Instead, Germany became an environmental leader. Tough laws mandate the recycling of 80 percent of all cardboard and plastics and 90 percent of all aluminum, glass, and tin. Ger-

Democratization in Germany

HISTORIANS AND political scientists still debate why democracy took root so much later in Germany than in the United States, Great Britain, or France. In the end, we will probably never be able to sort out the reasons, because the various factors overlap so much.

There was little in German history before 1945 to suggest that it could democratize so quickly. Its divided and authoritarian past, as well as the ill-fated effort to introduce a democratic regime after World War I, discredited democracy far more than in countries like France, where it had also had its share of troubles.

After the Second World War, however, a combination of international and domestic factors made effective democracy possible. The three occupying countries in the West avoided the mistakes they made after World War I, helping to rebuild rather than cripple their former enemy. More importantly in the long run, many Germans themselves "turned inward" and sought their own ways of avoiding the forces that had led to the creation of the Third Reich.

Just as remarkable was the smooth political integration of the DDR into the Federal Republic after 1990. Despite forty more years of authoritarian rule, people in the East had had extensive exposure to Western media and, of course, benefited from the remarkable wealth the Federal Republic could offer to ease the transition.

In other words, the German experience probably offers few guidelines for other countries to follow. None have either the luxury of extensive outside support or the time to rethink national priorities that so aided Germany from 1949 onward.

many also agreed to reduce its greenhouse gases more than it was later required to do by the provisions of the Kyoto Treaty on climate control.

- Even though he came to office without any experience in international relations, Kohl had an even greater impact on foreign policy than he did on domestic affairs. He skillfully guided Germany through a difficult decade that began with renewed superpower tensions but concluded with the unexpected end of the cold war. Germany remained one of the strongest advocates of European integration and became one of the chief architects of the Single European Act, the Maastricht Treaty, and the euro. Kohl also spearheaded attempts to forge a common policy on such difficult issues as the fighting in the former Yugoslavia. Most importantly of all, Kohl skillfully engineered the later stages of the reunification of Germany in the months after the collapse of the Berlin Wall and then the DDR.

We could go on and consider the details of Kohl's remarkable sixteen years in office and what has happened since his defeat. But this would add little to what should be a clear picture by now. The issues facing Germany since the 1980s are little different from those in any stable democracy. It has plenty of problems, but the durability and legitimacy of its regime are not in question.

Creating a Democratic Political Culture

In their attempts to figure out why German politics changed so dramatically and so quickly, many political scientists focused on its political culture, where the evidence of a transformation is overwhelming . As noted earlier, at the end of the war, most analysts were convinced that the values that had made the Third Reich possible were deeply rooted in German society. According to the conventional wisdom, the Weimar Republic failed in large part because it was a "republic without republicans." Even the most sympathetic observers, who believed that the overwhelming majority of Germans had not openly supported the worst aspects of Nazism, found them guilty of having silently accepted Hitler's Reich and not having done anything about its excesses when such opportunities were open to them. No one put those sentiments more eloquently than Pastor Martin Niemöller, writing while in a concentration camp in 1944:

> First they came for the Communists, but I didn't do anything, because I wasn't a Communist.
> Then they came for the Jews, but I didn't do anything, because I wasn't a Jew.
> Then they came for the trade unionists, but I didn't do anything, because I wasn't a trade unionist.
> Then they came for the Catholics, but I didn't do anything, because I wasn't a Catholic.
> Finally, they came for me, and there wasn't anyone left to do anything.

In the immediate postwar years, there were ample signs that the antidemocratic and authoritarian culture persisted. Various anti-Semitic and neo-Nazi organizations appeared, and many veterans openly expressed their continued desire for a strong military. Early public opinion polls indicated that many Germans still preferred authoritarian forms of government and could conceivably support Nazi-like movements at some point in the future.

The first elections confirmed those fears. Turnout was low, primarily because the young *ohne mich,* or "count me out," generation wanted nothing to do with politics.

Creative artists explored the German soul, trying to discover how the nation that had produced Beethoven and Hegel could also give rise to Hitler and Goebbels. The conclusions most of them reached were hardly encouraging. In his novel *Dog Years,* for instance, Günter Grass gives 1950s German teenagers special eyeglasses that allow them to see what their parents had done during the war, which led many of the teens to have nervous breakdowns or commit suicide.

Even after the Bonn republic began to take hold, skepticism remained. Observers worried that support for the system was dependent on continued economic growth and that hard times could bring new antidemocratic movements.

Some of those concerns were confirmed empirically in 1959 when Gabriel Almond and Sidney Verba found substantial differences between German and British or American values, which they thought did not augur well for German democracy.[3] Very few Germans took pride in their political institutions. They were less trusting of authority figures and felt less able to influence decision making than their British or American counterparts. In trying to explain why Germans held these views, Almond and Verba pointed to German history and to the continued authoritarian nature of their schools and families.

Twenty years later, Almond and Verba gathered a group of scholars to reconsider their conclusions in the light of more recent data. They realized that the earlier depiction of German culture no longer held. Instead, Germany now had the kind of civic culture they claimed was democracy's best attitudinal underpinning.

There are still signs of rigidity. In his wonderfully insightful study of post-unification Germany, the *Washington Post*'s Marc Fisher describes a number of them. Many rules and regulations are amazingly strict and, even more amazingly, are obeyed.[4] Germans cannot, for instance, mow their lawn between 1:00 and 3:00 p.m. because this might disturb a napping neighbor. Other rules sharply curtail how long stores can be open in the evenings and on weekends (though these have been relaxed) and even how long workers can take for their *pinkelpause,* or bathroom break. Laws even prescribe

---

[3] Gabriel Almond and Sidney Verba, *The Civic Culture: Political Attitudes and Democracy in Five Countries* (Princeton: Princeton University Press, 1962) and their edited volume, *The Civic Country Revisited* (Boston: Little, Brown, 1979).

[4] Marc Fisher, *After the Wall: Germany, the Germans, and the Burden of History* (New York: Simon and Schuster, 1995).

what Germans must put at the beginning of the messages on their answering machines.

One should not make too much of such rules, however quaint and irksome they can be for visitors from more informal societies. The fact is that, as far as political values are concerned, Germans have more in common with their counterparts in other industrialized societies than these laws might lead one to believe.

According to a typical poll conducted in 1977, only 7 percent of the public could imagine voting for a new Nazi party. Well over 90 percent now routinely endorse the idea that Germany needs a democratic form of government with a multiparty system. Germans are as supportive of democratic practices as citizens anywhere. Although it is hard to draw conclusions across national lines on the basis of spotty comparative research in which different questions are asked, the conclusions about Germany itself are rather striking. (See table 6.3.)

The German people clearly believe that the Federal Republic is legitimate. The nation has the kind of strong, general support that characterizes the British and American political cultures. Moreover, Germans tend to see political participation as a way to affect decision making rather than simply as a social obligation.

There are some blemishes on the German culture. More than other Europeans, Germans do not favor an equal political role for women. There also has been a resurgence of racist, anti-Semitic, and even neo-Nazi activity since unification, especially in the east.

Obviously, any such behavior is reprehensible at best, but we should not overstate its importance. In 1992, authorities estimated that there were no more than 1,500 active neo-Nazis and 50,000 sympathizers in the entire country, many of whom are better thought of as violent hooligans than as ideologically sophisticated extremists. Of all the people arrested for their participation in racist attacks, 70 percent are men with little education. Many seem more angry about their personal prospects as a result of unification and the influx of hundreds of thousands of immigrants than they are committed to right-wing extremism. What's more, the parties that espouse neo-Nazi themes are nowhere near as successful in Germany as the National Front is in France.

The obsession with the nondemocratic fringe kept political scientists from giving another important cultural trend its due until quite recently—the postmaterial values discussed in Chapter 2. Polls throughout the 1990s showed that fully a third of the electorate could be classified as postmaterialists, which is far more than the European average and three times the German figure for 1970.

Those views are most evident in support for environmental causes. One 1991 poll showed that 87 percent of the people in the West and 82 percent of those in the East believe that the environment should be a top priority for government and industry.

Postmaterialism has also had its clearest political impact in Germany. Well over 80 percent of all postmaterialists vote for the SPD or the **Greens,** the first party in the world to gain widespread support on the basis of this "new politics."

Postmaterialists are frequent participants in citizens' initiatives as well. In sharp contrast to the conventional view of a population that shuns voluntary participation, thousands of locally based, issue-oriented groups have sprung up in recent years to oppose the storage of nuclear waste, expand kindergarten space, support recycling programs, improve the conditions of immigrant workers, and so on.

There is one final area in which the German political culture has changed. The overwhelming majority of Germans have come to accept their geopolitical status. Most are profoundly antimilitarist and endorse the government's leading role in the EU, NATO, and other international organizations. Many scholars are convinced that Germany's new pacific (if not pacifist) culture is one of the reasons it has not sought to assert its newfound power militarily even though it has participated in peace-keeping and peace-building operations in Kosovo and Afghanistan—actions that the Constitutional Court ruled in 1994 were legal.

Political scientists have pointed to three broad reasons why the political culture has changed so dramatically in barely fifty years.

The first and most obvious is that the Federal Republic has worked. As we saw with the Fifth Republic in France, the Federal Republic's success has had an impact on the way people assess it.

Second, there has been considerable change in two of the major "agents" of political socialization. Under Allied pressure, the states began teaching civics during the

▌ **TABLE 6.3** Germans and Democracy
(percentage agreeing)

	1980	1983	1989
THE PRESENT NATIONAL GOVERNMENT PROTECTS OUR BASIC LIBERTIES.	89.5	81.6	79.0
THE POLITICAL SYSTEM AS A WHOLE IS JUST AND FAIR.	87.6	86.8	77.0

Source: Adapted from Dieter Fuchs, "Trends of Political Support in the Federal Republic of Germany," in *Political Culture in Germany,* ed. Dirk Berg-Schlosser and Ralf Rytlewski (London: Macmillan, 1993), 249.

Conflict in Germany

The most important conclusion to reach about conflict in Germany is that it is not very intense. Germany certainly has social movements and individuals who do not believe that the Federal Republic should continue in its current form. For the moment, the most prominent of them are the neo-Nazis on the right. But it should be remembered that the left spawned a number of terrorist groups in the 1960s and 1970s, the most violent of which—the Red Army Faction—only decided to disband in 1998.

Political scientists have not done the kind of research that would allow us to say with any precision whether extremist groups are more or less problematic in Germany than in the United States, Great Britain, or France. Still, there is nothing to suggest that these or any other groups will constitute a serious threat to the legitimacy of the Federal Republic in the foreseeable future.

Critics are quick to point out that the Nazis themselves started out as a small band of hooligans whom no one took seriously. However, there is one important difference between Weimar and the Federal Republic. In Germany today—as in the United States, Great Britain, and France—virtually everyone agrees that the regime is legitimate and the people as a whole will not support movements that call for radical constitutional change, democratic or otherwise.

---

occupation years and have included it in their curricula ever since. The right-wing bias of the prewar teacher corps has disappeared. Similarly, the impact of the "authoritarian father" has declined. Child-rearing patterns have been liberalized, and, as in all industrialized democracies, the family is less important in most people's lives in general.

Finally, and perhaps most importantly, we are now two generations removed from the Nazi era. Fewer than 10 percent of those in the current electorate reached adulthood during either the Weimar or the Nazi periods, and even the current generation of political leaders only experienced Nazism and the war as teenagers.

Political Participation

As we saw earlier, the fragmented and ideologically polarized parties were a major problem in the Weimar Republic and played a substantial role in its demise. Many observers expected that to be the case in the Federal Republic as well. By the mid-1950s, however, Germany had developed what many observers have called a two-and-a-half-party system. The CDU and SPD have been the dominant parties, never winning less than 74 percent of the vote since the 1949 election. (See table 6.4.) During this period, the FDP has won between 5.1 percent and 12.8 percent of the vote—thus earning the half-party designation. And, except for the years from 1957 to 1961, the grand coalition period (1966–69), and the present, the FDP has provided either the CDU or the SPD with the seats needed to form a parliamentary majority. Only one new party, the Greens, has been able to overcome the 5 percent barrier nationwide and win seats in the Bundestag on a consistent basis. The formerly communist PDS did so in 1998 as well with a strong showing in its eastern strongholds, but even these developments have not altered the basic logic of a system that has worked effectively since 1949.

Parties and the Electoral Process

More than is the case in any other country covered in this book, the Basic Law puts political parties in a privileged position. It gives them official status and assigns them the role of "forming the political will." The major parties play a central role in nominating judges, university professors, television and radio station managers, and directors of firms ranging from the big banks to local public transit authorities. Public financing provides about 30 percent of the roughly $100 million each major party spends during each election campaign. The government also helps fund charitable foundations each party runs to provide aid and assistance to the developing world and to help find peace between Israel and Palestine.

Perhaps the most important provision of the Basic

▮ TABLE 6.4 German Election Results since 1949 (percentage of vote)

PARTY	1949	1953	1957	1961	1965	1969	1972	1976	1980	1983	1987	1990	1994	1998	2002
CDU/CSU	31.0	45.2	50.2	45.3	47.6	46.1	44.9	48.6	44.5	48.8	44.3	43.8	41.5	35.2	38.5
FDP	11.9	9.5	7.7	12.8	9.5	5.8	8.4	7.9	10.6	7.0	9.1	11.0	6.9	6.2	7.4
SPD	29.2	28.8	31.8	36.2	39.3	42.7	45.8	42.6	42.9	38.2	37.0	33.5	36.4	40.9	38.5
Greens	–	–	–	–	–	–	–	–	1.5	5.6	8.3	3.9	7.3	6.7	8.6
PDS	–	–	–	–	–	–	–	–	–	–	–	4.4	2.4	5.1	4.7

Law is Article 21, which created a dual system for electing the Bundestag, designed to minimize the number of new and small parties. Half the seats are elected in 299 single-member districts, as in Britain and the United States. Any number of candidates can run, and whoever wins the most votes takes the seat. This makes it easy for the SPD and CDU to convince people that casting a ballot for a new, fringe, or extremist party means that they are wasting their vote. Indeed, they routinely win all the single-member districts in the old West Germany and lose only a handful of seats to the PDS in the East.

Voters also cast a second ballot in which they choose from lists of candidates representing each of the parties. Seats are then allocated proportionally to all parties that win over 5 percent of the vote. Thus, because the FDP won 7.4 percent of the vote in 2002, it got that proportion of seats in the Bundestag for a total of 47. The second ballot is also used to make any adjustments necessary from the constituency races so that each party's total Bundestag representation equals its share of the proportional vote, which meant that 304 candidates were elected on this side of the ballot in 2002. Here, the 5 percent barrier has worked extremely effectively, dooming a number of parties that won seats in 1949 to extinction in the 1950s and keeping all claimants but the Greens and the PDS out thereafter.

The parties themselves also changed. During the Weimar era, the German parties were known for their ideological rigidity and for their millions of dedicated grassroots activists. During the 1950s, however, continued rapid growth and affluence undermined support for left-wing radicalism, while the very success of the regime did the same for neo-Nazism on the right. In other words, divisive ideological issues disappeared and the voters flocked toward the center and away from extremist positions, left or right. To maintain their share of the vote, first the CDU and then the SPD had to follow suit.

Each became a catch-all party in order to appeal to the increasingly moderate voters. The parties had to water down their ideologies. The number of ideologically motivated activists diminished, forcing the parties to shift their organizational tactics and rely more on leaders who were effective campaigners on television. Because television news stories rarely last more than a couple of minutes, parties had to sacrifice the complexities of a sophisticated belief system for slogans that would fit into sound-bite journalism.

In this sense, the major parties are very different in that, instead of focusing their attention on a particular group, they literally try to "catch" all voters. The SPD no longer sees itself as primarily a working-class party, but appeals to progressive members of the middle class as well. The CDU no longer woos only Catholics as the Zentrum did, but also tries to attract support from all Germans who care about religion and traditional values.

The Christian Democrats

The CDU has been by far the most powerful party in the Federal Republic both before and after unification (www.cdu.de).

Officially, the CDU is two distinct parties. The CDU exists in every state other than Bavaria, where it cooperates with a local partner, the CSU (Christian Social Union). During the 1970s and early 1980s, there was some tension between the two, because the CSU was noticeably more conservative than its larger partner. After the death in 1988 of the CSU's leader, Franz Joseph Strauss, however, the tensions abated, and we can treat the two as if they are a single party.

After World War II, Adenauer and the other surviving Zentrum leaders chose not to re-create a party whose appeal would be limited to Catholics and, thus, to less than half the population. Instead, they decided to form a more broad-based organization that would apply basic Christian principles to political life. At first, this included a clear commitment to social justice. The Ahlen Program of 1947 called for egalitarian social reforms and even the nationalization of some industries. The CDU also agreed to the codetermination law in 1951 (see the policy section), which gave workers' representatives seats on the boards of directors of large firms in the coal and steel industries.

The early CDU, however, was pulled in two contradictory directions. On the one hand, Catholic thought had long stressed social solidarity and, with it, programs for the poor and the otherwise disadvantaged. On the other hand, because it drew most of its support from practicing believers who tended to be rather conservative, the party had rather strong right-wing inclinations.

Adenauer and his colleagues quickly resolved those tensions by forging a centrist and pragmatic party that focused more on winning elections than on doctrinal principles. As Germany came to be the flash point in the cold war, and as the United States grew increasingly disenchanted with progressive social and economic policies, the CDU's support for conservatism at home and a pro-American foreign policy increased.

After the shift from Adenauer to Erhard in 1963 and the economic slowdown in 1965, the CDU did not fare as well. Finally, in 1969, the party lost control of the government. For much of the next thirteen years, it floundered. It had never developed either a large mass membership or a strong central organization. Instead, power within

HELMUT KOHL

Fritt Reiss/AP/Wide World Photos

A 1998 campaign ad by the CDU playing on Kohl's size (hence the elephant) and Lake Wolfgang, his favorite holiday spot, and trying to capitalize on the importance of continuity and stability.

Helmut Kohl (1930–) was the longest-serving chancellor in the history of the Federal Republic. He was also the first to have come of age after World War II and the Third Reich.

Other than that, his career was fairly typical. After graduating from university, he began his political career within the CDU organization in his home state, Rhineland-Palatinate. Following the party's loss to the SPD in the 1972 Bundestag elections, Kohl was chosen leader of the party. At the time, few expected much of a man known for his pragmatism, an expectation that was reinforced by the CDU's defeat again in 1976. But, as so often happens in politics, events transformed Kohl and his career. The collapse of the SPD–FDP coalition brought him to power in 1982. At the end of the decade, he skillfully guided the Federal Republic through unification and then was a major player in the strengthening of the EU with the Maastricht Treaty two years later. Kohl is a remarkably unpretentious man, known to prefer vacationing at home, watching television while wearing his Birkenstocks. He is also an extremely large man who, with his wife, has published a cookbook of traditional (and fatty) German dishes.

the party remained primarily in the hands of the state parties and their leaders. Following the CDU's defeat at the polls in 1972 and 1976, the party's drift was compounded by a deep ideological struggle between its right wing, headed by Strauss, and the moderates, increasingly dominated by the young Helmut Kohl, minister president of the state of Rhineland-Palatinate.

In 1978, the party broke with its pragmatic practices and issued a vague new program calling for "renewal" on the basis of more traditional values and market-oriented economic policies. In 1980, however, the party suffered its third straight defeat—this time with Strauss as its candidate for chancellor—and power within it swung back toward Kohl and the moderates.

Kohl was never as dynamic a leader as the other two great conservative heads of state of his generation—Ronald Reagan and Margaret Thatcher. He also never supported their hopes for a radical shift toward smaller government and a more powerful market. But he didn't have to. His first decade in office was marked by a dramatic economic upturn that allowed the government to maintain popular support without questioning the status quo.

From 1990 on, Kohl's support was based largely on his successful handling of German unification. To the

surprise of many, Kohl proved an effective negotiator both with authorities in the DDR and with the victors from World War II, who had to sign off on any agreement to unify the two Germanys. He also was largely responsible for pushing through economic policies that directed hundreds of billions of dollars in aid to the five former East German states.

By the middle of the 1990s, however, the costs of unification had become clearer, and the CDU saw its support drop. It probably held on in 1994 only because the SPD ran a lackluster campaign. Finally, as we saw earlier, the CDU's and Kohl's string of successes ended in 1998.

Kohl's legacy will not be an altogether positive one. In 1999, he was implicated in a financial scandal. The CDU had accepted millions of dollars in illegal contributions, and Kohl acknowledged personally taking at least $1 million, though he refuses to name the donor. As of mid-2001, the CDU has paid over $1 million in fines and had to forego at least $20 million in state funds. Kohl's reputation for honesty is in tatters, and the party's image as the embodiment of the best in traditional German values is in jeopardy.

When first chosen in 2000, it seemed that the CDU's new leader, **Angela Merkel** (1955–), might lead the party out of the political wilderness. Hers is an interesting story. Her father was a Lutheran minister who chose to move to and preach in East Germany when Angela was a baby. Angela was educated in the East German state system and eventually earned a Ph.D. in physics. Because of her father's profession, however, she was never able to get an appropriate post under the Communists and was a member of the small CDU in the east before the fall of the Berlin Wall. She quickly emerged as one of the most popular and effective party leaders. When Kohl's designated successor, Wolfgang Schäuble, was forced to resign as party leader, she was chosen to replace him—the first woman and the first easterner to reach the top of the political world in the Federal Republic.

Known for her wit and independence, Merkel was one of the first CDU leaders to break with Kohl once news of the illegal payments broke. Initial reaction to her was positive, but as the 2002 election drew near, serious concerns were aired about her lack of experience, especially in economic policy making. And, in April 2001, she, too, had to admit involvement in obtaining questionable funds. Therefore, in January 2002, Merkel decided not to try for the nomination to run against Schröder that fall. Instead, the party opted for the more charismatic and more conservative premier of Bavaria, Edmund Stoiber. Merkel remains head of the CDU organization and is the presumptive challenger to Schröder in 2006.

As table 6.4 shows, the CDU pulled almost even with the SPD in 2002, winning only three fewer seats. Since then, it has made even bigger gains in state and European Parliament elections and defeated the SPD in some of its traditional strongholds. Were elections to be held early, the CDU would almost certainly win. However, the polls also show that most voters doubt that the Christian Democrats would govern any more effectively than the Social Democrats. Moreover, in 2001, surveys showed the CDU had a significant lead, which evaporated during the last few months before the election the next year.

The Social Democrats

The SPD historically has been the Federal Republic's second strongest party (www.spd.de/servlet/PB/menu/1010237/index.html).

Although the SPD has been in office twice (1969–82 and 1998–), it has outpolled the CDU in only two elections. The SPD has lagged behind the Christian Democrats in large part because it has not been as successful in becoming and remaining a catch-all party. To some degree, this reflects the SPD's early postwar history. It was led by men who had survived the Third Reich as prisoners, exiles, or members of the small underground resistance. Most were supporters of the prewar party's commitments. None were revolutionaries or even doctrinaire Marxists, but most shared leader Kurt Schumacher's support for nationalization of major industrial firms.

The SPD's failure to seriously threaten the CDU's hold on power touched off a heated internal debate over its basic principles, much like the one over Clause 4 in Britain's Labour Party. In 1959, matters reached a head when the moderates won a majority at the annual conference at Bad Godesberg and dropped all references to Marxism and the nationalization of industry from the party's program.

At about the same time, politicians from the Schumacher generation left the political scene, to be replaced by younger and more pragmatic leaders, most notably the mayor of West Berlin, Willy Brandt. The party made significant progress in the 1961 and 1965 elections. Its fortunes continued to improve when the CDU brought it into the Grand Coalition to help thwart the far right and end the country's first postwar recession. Socialist ministers performed well, and the party demonstrated its acceptance of capitalism with its ringing endorsement of the 1967 law on balanced growth.

The SPD took control of the government when the FDP decided to form a coalition with it rather than the CDU after the 1969 election, even though the Socialists, again, had come in second. Rather than embarking on a bold program of social reform, Brandt stressed "continuity and renewal." In fact, his greatest accomplishment came not in expanding socialism but in improving relations with the Soviet bloc, for which he won the Nobel Peace Prize.

When Brandt was forced out of office in 1974 as the result of an espionage scandal, he was replaced by the even more moderate Helmut Schmidt. With the exception of the codetermination system (to be discussed shortly), social reform all but ground to a halt as Germany struggled to cope with the turbulent economic conditions of the post-OPEC years. Schmidt's moderation earned him the respect of leaders around the world, but it opened deep divisions within his own party. The economic problems and the ideological infighting cost the SPD 4 percent of the vote in 1980. Still, it was able to form another government with the FDP. But, in the one example of a lost vote of confidence in the Federal Republic's history, the FDP put the Schmidt government out of its misery two years later.

The next sixteen years spent in opposition were difficult for the SPD. It lost four consecutive elections, which allowed commentators and voters alike to begin thinking of the CDU as the "natural party of govern-

GERHARD SCHRÖDER

Gerhard Schröder is not just the first SPD chancellor in sixteen years. His election also marks an important generational shift in German politics.

Born in 1944, he is the first chancellor not to have experienced the Nazis or World War II. He is also the first in recent memory to have been born into poverty, his father having been killed in the war shortly before Schröder was born.

Like many baby boomer politicians, Schröder began his career on the far left of the SPD in the late 1960s. Unlike many of his wealthier comrades, Schröder never questioned the party's commitment to social democracy and reformist strategies. Like his American contemporary, Bill Clinton, Schröder's views moderated during the 1970s and 1980s, and he rose to prominence as a popular and successful state governor.

Unlike Clinton or any other ambitious American politician, Schröder has been married four times.

ment." The Socialists' problems were magnified by the CDU's popularity because of unification.

Meanwhile, the Socialists shot themselves in the political foot. They were slow to support unification, and some of the party's leading intellectuals actually opposed it until the last moment. Moreover, the party contested the 1994 election under a rather lackluster leader, Rudolph Scharping, who became chancellor-candidate only after a scandal forced his predecessor to withdraw.

The SPD did begin to turn things around in 1995. Scharping was replaced by the more dynamic, if more left-wing, Oskar Lafontaine, the popular chief minister of Saarland. Though Lafontaine had led the party to its 1990 loss, he was widely seen as a breath of political fresh air. Under his leadership, the party began to modernize.

Then, in 1997, Gerhard Schröder (1944–) burst onto the political scene. Dubbing himself Germany's Tony Blair, he openly wooed the middle class and the business community and gained massive media exposure—and popular support. At that point, Lafontaine stepped aside, and Schröder became the party's candidate for chancellor.

Although his personal views are quite similar to Blair's, traditional social democrats have a stronger influence in the SPD than in Labour, and the country's social service and social market economic policies are far more popular and effective than in Britain. Last but by no means least, the SPD has to keep the support of its coalition partners, the environmentally oriented Greens, whom we will encounter shortly.

Its participation in the NATO bombing of the former Yugoslavia in 1999 marked the first time that a postwar German government had taken part in a military operation. The Greens' impact has been felt most strongly in an environmental tax that added about 30¢ per year to the price of a liter of gasoline through 2003. Similarly, in 2000, the government passed a law making it possible for roughly half of the 7.3 million non-German residents to gain citizenship. In 2001, it announced that it would not support any further reforms of the labor market or initiate any further tax cuts until after the 2002 election.

Since then, the government has launched an ambitious program of economic reforms, Agenda 2010, which we will discuss in the section on public policy that follows. The government was also a vocal critic of American policy in the run-up to the Iraq war, though the tensions between Berlin and Washington have eased considerably since then.

The Free Democratic Party

The FDP has always run a distant, but surprisingly influential, third behind the CDU and SPD. Although it often comes close to falling below the 5 percent barrier, the FDP derives its strength from the fact that it has been needed to form all but three of the governments since 1949 (www.fdp.de/portal).

Like the CDU and SPD, the FDP had "ancestors" in Weimar, when there were a number of predominantly middle-class, Protestant parties that called themselves liberal. But theirs was an economic more than a political liberalism, which left them in an ambiguous position during Hitler's rise to power.

The postwar FDP has been more consistently liberal on political issues, valuing personal responsibility, individual freedom, and respect for the rights of others over what it sees as the collectivist tendencies of the SPD and CDU. Mostly, though, the FDP carved a niche for itself as the party its two larger rivals needed to form a government. In that role, the FDP has provided the Federal Republic with a number of important leaders, including, most recently, Hans-Dietrich Genscher, who was foreign minister from 1974 until 1992.

The FDP has struggled since unification and following Genscher's retirement. Its standing in the polls improved somewhat since its lowest points in 1994 and 1998, but mostly because disgruntled CDU supporters said they might vote for it out of disgust with Kohl's financial scandal, not because they supported the FDP per se. In an attempt to make a comeback, the party named Guido Westerwelle, a thirty-nine-year-old lawyer, its leader and Cornelia Pieper, a forty-two-year-old easterner, its secretary-general. There is no reason to believe, however, that dynamic new leadership can turn the FDP into a challenger for power.

The Greens

In 1983, the Greens became the first new party to break the 5 percent barrier and enter the Bundestag. The Greens are also Germany's most intriguing and least understood party. To many people, members are still seen as weird and, perhaps, even dangerous, an image fostered by their early deputies' insistence on wearing jeans and sporting shaggy beards to work (www.gruene.de).

The Greens *are* different. Until 1991, for example, Greens elected to office were expected to resign and be replaced by colleagues halfway through their terms so that they could never let power go to their heads.

However, the image is also seriously off-target because there is something serious and important about the Greens and their philosophy. The success they have enjoyed in Germany and several other European countries is no fluke. It reflects the inability of established parties to devise widely accepted solutions to the new problems facing their countries. Moreover, the research on postmaterialism indicates that there is a far larger pool of potential supporters than the Greens have yet been able to tap.

The Greens' ideology is based on deep ecology, or the belief that all of life, and thus all of our problems, are interconnected. Pollution, militarism, sexism, homophobia, poverty, and the like are part of a single general crisis that can only be addressed through an equally general and radical shift to a worldview that puts the good of the planet and humanity first (see Chapter 17).

The Greens scored major breakthroughs in the 1983 and 1987 elections. However, they were in deep trouble in the early 1990s. Even more than the SPD, they suffered because of their qualms about rapid unification. More importantly, the party itself was split, with the more radical *fundis* gaining influence at the expense of the more pragmatic *realos*. After the 1994 election, however, the pragmatists gained the upper hand. The most plausible scenario for beating the CDU was a "Red-Green" coalition with the SPD, which the party had entered into in several state governments. Also, frustrations that grew out of always being on the fringes led party moderates like **Joska Fischer** (1947–) to question their own (and the party's) more radical pasts.

Therefore, the Greens reached an agreement with the SPD to form a coalition and to serve in it for the length of the next parliament if the two parties won the 1998 election. Although it raised concerns in many other Western capitals, Fischer became foreign minister. It is hard to gauge the Greens' impact on the government because they are very much the junior member of the coalition. The stiff gasoline tax undoubtedly would not have been passed had the Greens not been in government. The same may be true of the law making it easier to gain German citizenship.

More important here is the fact that the Greens have continued their movement toward moderation. In particular, like many individuals and organizations with roots in the new left of the 1960s, the Greens reluctantly abandoned their pacifism and supported the Allied war effort in the former Yugoslavia following ethnic cleansing in Kosovo in 1999 and in Afghanistan following the attack on the World Trade Center and the Pentagon two years later. The Greens have also become staunch supporters of the EU.

The Party of Democratic Socialism

The Greens are no longer the only "new" party to have made it into the Bundestag since the 1940s. The PDS was created out of the ashes of the Socialist Unity Party (SED, the Communist Party) that ruled the DDR until its collapse (www.pds-online.de).

The SED had been one of the most rigid and out-of-date of all the communist parties in cold war Eastern Europe. From 1949 until 1989, it monopolized political power in the DDR. (See Chapter 8.) As the DDR collapsed, the SED tried to reform itself, among other things changing its name to the PDS. It also chose a new leader, Gregor Gysi, who was well known for defending dissidents under communist rule—and who is now deputy mayor of Berlin.

In 1990 the PDS benefited from a one-time rule that allocated proportional representation seats separately in the east and west. In 1994 it survived only because it won a number of single-member districts in working-class districts in the Berlin metropolitan area.

Most observers doubted the PDS could win seats again. However, it confounded the pundits by getting nearly 20 percent of the vote in the old DDR and thus topping 6 percent nationwide in 1998. It fell short of the 5 percent barrier in 2002 and only won two single-member seats. In 2004 it was in a governing coalition with the SPD in one of the old East German states and in the city of Berlin.

But we should not read too much into the PDS's success. For one thing, it is a purely regional party. Although it does well in the old DDR, it struggles to reach 1 percent of the vote in the west, where only 3,000 of its 95,000 members live. More importantly, like most of the "reformed" communist parties in eastern Europe, the PDS is by no means a throwback to the Marxist-Leninist organizations that ran the old communist regimes with an iron fist. The party does accuse the federal government of favoring the west and business interests over those of the east and of labor. But neither the party nor its members advocate anything like a return to the DDR, and most seem to have made their peace with democracy, if not modern capitalism.

The Far Right

Throughout its history, the Federal Republic has had to deal with right-wing parties that, in one way or another, appealed to some of the same traditions as the Nazis. As we saw earlier, the NDP came close to breaking the 5 percent barrier in 1966 before its support evaporated.

Since unification, there has been another flurry of support for the far right, given the pressures of unification and immigration. A number of small parties have done reasonably well in state and local elections, including one that won over 5 percent in one of the eastern states in 1998. However, the far right did not come close to the 5 percent barrier in the national elections that year, reinforcing the belief that it is not a serious force in German politics.

Interest Groups

As we will see in the discussion of corporatism, German interest groups play a more important role in policy making than their British or French equivalents. Surprisingly, however, there has not been very much detailed research on them, so we cannot say for sure if it is their strength that has led them to be included or if their inclusion has, instead, contributed to their strength.

Unlike France, Germany has a relatively large and unified labor movement. About two-thirds of all industrial workers and over 40 percent of the total workforce are unionized. The overwhelming majority of workers belongs to the **Federation of German Labor (DGB).** The DGB is an umbrella association representing seventeen unions, each of which organizes a single industrial sec-

Double Standards

For understandable historical reasons, observers have been reluctant to label Germany or other countries such as Japan democratic and have been quick to voice concerns about incidents involving the far right in both countries. Although there are plenty of reasons to worry about such events, we should also be careful not to use a double standard and hold these countries to higher criteria than we use for others with fewer historical blemishes. All democracies have imperfections—including Germany. But, as this chapter has suggested, Germany's are no more (or less) worrisome than those we find in the United States or Great Britain, the countries that are usually portrayed as the paragons of democratic virtue.

tor. As such, it is better able to coordinate union activity or even speak with a single voice than is the more decentralized TUC in Britain.

The organization of the business side is a bit more complicated. The two largest groups—the Federal Association of German Employers (BDA) and the Federation of German Industry (BDI)—both represent smaller associations of business groups organized on geographical and industrial lines. Although it is harder to determine membership rates for business associations than for trade unions, a large proportion of businesses belong to one or the other of these organizations. In addition to the BDA and BDI, there are quasi-public chambers of commerce and industry (DIHT) that promote business and also provide job training and certification services for the government.

Both business and labor have close ties with the political parties. Union officials hold important positions in the SPD and in its Bundestag group. Agricultural and business interests have a similar relationship with the CDU. Members of parliament from these groups tend to dominate their parties' delegations on the Bundestag committees that deal with their interests. Church groups also have a significant impact on the CDU, helping to explain why West Germany banned abortion unless a doctor certified that the woman's life was in danger.

Interest groups in other areas are nowhere near as strong or as well connected politically. As noted earlier, a lot of locally based citizens' initiatives were important building blocks for the early Greens. Also, a number of protest groups emerged in East Germany in the late 1980s, but most of them have fallen by the wayside.

The German State: A Smoothly Functioning Democracy

From the mid-1960s until its recent economic difficulties, observers praised what they called the "German model." Put simply, the state was built on a nationwide consensus and close cooperation with business and labor to forge consistent economic growth, the benefits of which were enjoyed by virtually everyone.

To some degree, that success reflects the formal institutions created by the Basic Law in the late 1940s (www.bundesregierung.de/en/Federal-Government/Function-and-constitutional-ba-,10206/Basic-Law.htm). Just as important, however, are more informal arrangements that political scientists call **corporatism,** in which the government and key interest groups work behind closed doors to forge integrated economic policies. Rarely are the supposedly vital actors in a democracy—political parties and elected officials—central players in them. Moreover, corporatist practices are never spelled out in constitutions, and only rarely are they even mentioned in laws. But they are important, because the countries that have most fully adopted corporatist practices are the ones that were most successful economically from the end of the Second World War into the 1990s.

Chancellor Democracy

Before turning to those corporatist arrangements, we have to see how the conventional side of the German state works. Any such discussion must begin with the chancellor. (See figure 6.1.) As in other parliamentary systems, the chancellor started out literally as the "prime" minister, the first among what were supposed to be equally powerful members of the cabinet. During the twentieth century, however, the powers of prime ministers everywhere grew so dramatically that all notions of being first among equals disappeared.

This was done by design when the Federal Republic was created. The conflicting and overlapping jurisdictions of the chancellor and president had been among Weimar's many flaws. The framers of the Basic Law did not want to eliminate the dual executive in which the largely ceremonial functions of a head of state (president) and the actual control of the government (chancellor) are in separate hands. At the same time, they wanted to make it clear that the chancellor held the real executive power (www.bundesregierung.de/Federal-Government/-,10147/Chancellor.htm).

Executive and legislative power are fused. The chancellor and most members of the cabinet also are members of the Bundestag, and remain in office either as long as they have the confidence of the parliamentary majority or until their four-year terms end. Because of the powerful link between cabinet responsibility and party discipline in parliamentary systems, German chancellors have been able to see most of their policy proposals enacted without much interference from the Bundestag (but see the section on the Bundesrat that follows).

There are some differences between the role of the chancellor in Germany and that of the prime minister in other parliamentary systems. One is the unusual power the Basic Law grants to that office. In particular, Article 65 gives the chancellor the power "to determine the guidelines of policy" and to assume responsibility for defining the government's policy, resolving differences within the cabinet, and proposing virtually all major legislation.

The chancellor is subject to a constructive vote of no confidence. The opposition can throw a government out only if it simultaneously agrees on a new one to take its place. As a result, the chancellor is far less vulnerable than prime ministers in most parliamentary systems. In fact, this is one of the reasons most of the Greens who opposed German involvement in the war against terrorism did not vote no confidence in Schröder's government in November 2001.

His power is reinforced by a large Chancellor's Office with over five hundred employees. A staff that large gives the chancellor the opportunity to coordinate the entire executive. Indeed, each Monday, the head of the Chancellor's Office (who holds cabinet rank) meets with the top civil servants in each department to do just that.

German governments are also more streamlined than most. Although the cabinet is of average size, most

▌FIGURE 6.1 Policy-Making Processes in Germany

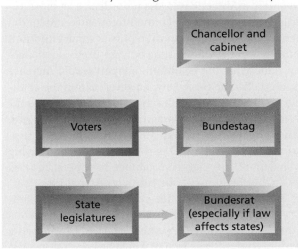

departments have only the minister and one other po-litical appointee. In all, only about 8 percent of all Bun-destag members (as opposed to 17 percent in Britain's House of Commons) serve in the government, thereby giving the chancellor considerably more flexibility in choosing a leadership team. Ministers tend to serve un-usually long terms in a single department and can thus develop more expertise than their British or French counterparts. Erhard, for instance, was economics min-ister from 1949 until he became chancellor in 1963. Sim-ilarly, Hans-Dietrich Genscher was foreign minister for nearly twenty years.

Much of the administrative work of cabinet minis-ters in France or Britain is conducted either by the states or by independent agencies. Cabinet ministers are, thus, free to spend more time planning rather than imple-menting public policy.

The chancellor, however, is not as powerful as the French president. The chancellor cannot, for instance, go to the public with a referendum, and the emergency powers available to the government are harder to invoke and far more limited. There is no German equivalent to the sweeping domain of regulation that allows the French government to rule by decree in many policy areas.

The chancellor's power is also less personalized. As in Britain, there is little room for an "outsider" to make it to the top on the basis of his or her personal popular-ity, despite Schröder's meteoric rise prior to the 1998 election. Previously, at least, chancellor candidates pro-gressed through their party's ranks, like British prime ministers, in careers in which negotiation and coalition building were among the most valued skills.

The Bundestag

Like most legislatures in parliamentary systems, Ger-many's lower house, the **Bundestag,** has the formal power to pass legislation and select the prime min-ister (www.bundestag.de). In practice, real power lies elsewhere. Because the chancellor is responsible to the Bundestag, he can expect his majority to hold up on any crucial vote, thus minimizing the actual impact the members of parliament can have on most legislation.

That does not mean that the Bundestag is powerless. Although the comparative evidence is sketchy at best, the Bundestag probably is a bit more powerful than the lower houses in Britain or France.

For one thing, the Bundestag can play a pivotal role in determining who becomes chancellor. The peculiari-ties of the provisions of the constructive vote of no confi-dence have made it a significant (though not the most powerful) actor on a number of occasions when the par-

Sven Kaestner/AP/Wide World Photos

The old Reichstag building in Berlin, which became the new Bun-destag building when the German capital was moved there from Bonn in 1999. The new illuminated dome, designed by a British architect, is a sign of how much more "European" Germany has become.

liamentary arithmetic was less than clear. The most im-portant came in 1972, when the Brandt government did not have the popular support to pursue some important domestic reforms. Polls showed that if elections were held right away the coalition's support would increase substantially. The Basic Law, however, allows the chan-cellor to dissolve the Bundestag only if he loses its confi-dence and no alternative majority exists to take its place. Brandt engineered that outcome by retaining the sup-port of almost every SPD and FDP deputy, but having seventeen of the eighteen cabinet members abstain, leaving the government one vote shy of a majority.

The Bundestag also has a far more powerful com-mittee system than either the British House of Commons or the French National Assembly. There are twenty-one standing committees, each of which has several specialized subcommittees that discuss all pending legislation. Committee members and chairs are chosen on a proportional basis from each of the parties. Because individual members' votes are not made public, party discipline not as strict in the committees than it is on the floor of the house.

The legislative committees are, however, considerably less powerful than their American equivalents. It is virtually impossible, for example, for them to drastically revise or kill a piece of legislation. Nonetheless, the committees propose amendments on most legislation, many of which are accepted by the government and the entire Bundestag.

The third source of Bundestag power lies in its organization. As in France and Britain, the Bundestag elects a speaker (president) and a broader leadership group, the Council of Elders, that is responsible for organizing its schedule. In the Bundestag, however, comparatively more power is given to the party groups. Individual members have larger staffs to draw on for both clerical and research assistance, which allows them to develop something like the experience and expertise of many American senators and representatives.

The Bundesrat

The most unusual aspect of the Federal Republic's legislative system is the **Bundesrat.** (www.bundesrat.de; this site was in transition in late 2004. From the homepage, click on "English" and it should guide you to the English version.) Most upper houses have lost any real power to affect either the composition of the government or the content of legislation.

That is not the case with the Bundesrat. This unusual upper house gives the sixteen states direct representation in the national government. The framers of the Basic Law saw it as yet another institution that could reduce the possibility of any future Nazi-like regime emerging by limiting the power the national government could exert, whoever ran it.

Each state has between three and six votes in the Bundesrat (depending on state population), and there are a total of sixty-nine members. Officially, the state governments are represented by cabinet members. In practice, the demands of running a state are so great that they normally send senior civil servants instead.

Like most upper houses, the Bundesrat has no impact on the composition of the cabinet. Similarly, it can only delay enactment of laws that would not have a direct impact on the states. However, the Bundesrat must approve all "consent" legislation that affects the *länder,* which accounts for more than half of all bills that come

TABLE 6.5 Bundesrat Delegations: Summer 2004

COALITION	NUMBER OF STATES	TOTAL SEATS
CDU led coalition or in power on its own	9	41
CDU with SPD	2	7
SPD with Greens, PDS, or FDP		

before it. When the two houses disagree, the Bundesrat convenes a Mediation Committee composed of members of both houses that tries to iron out the differences. Given the string of SPD losses since the 2002 Bundestag election, the Mediation Committee was split down the middle after a series of state elections in 2004, which meant that the government could not get critical legislation passed without the support of some CDU-dominated states.

The Bundesrat has vigorously defended state interests without being an exceptionally partisan or disruptive force. For most of the Federal Republic's history, the two houses have been dominated by the same coalition of parties, and so there have been few ideological disputes. In late 2004, the SPD was in a decided minority in the Bundesrat, as table 6.5 shows. The SPD on its own or in alliance with one or another of the other left or center parties was in power in five states with only 21 of the 69 total votes. The opposition actually controlled 41 votes in a total of nine states. Finally, two states with 7 votes had governments run by coalitions that combined the SPD with the CDU.

The Federal System

The Bundesrat is but one part of an unusual constitutional system for a parliamentary-based government. Most other countries, including Britain and France, are unitary states in which virtually all power is derived from the central government. The Basic Law, by contrast, divides responsibility between the national and state governments.

The national government has sole responsibility for matters that transcend state boundaries, such as foreign policy, defense, issues involving German citizenship, economic policy, transportation, communication, and property rights. Everything else—including civil and criminal law, the organization of associations, broadcasting, welfare, mining, industry, banking, labor, education, highways, and health—is left to the states. The states also administer most federal law and have some leeway in determining how they do so.

But, as in other federal systems, the balance of

power has long been tilting toward the national government. Most of the important policy issues, including those we will focus on in the next section, are predominantly federal in nature. And even for many of those that are not federal issues, such as the mass media, the highways, and welfare programs, the federal government has imposed more uniform rules and procedures from state to state than one finds in the United States.

Over the years, the most important role of state politics has been as a source of national-level leaders. Kohl, Strauss, Brandt, and Schröder all rose to prominence first at the state level. That is quite different from the situation in France or Britain, where the careers of major national leaders are shaped almost exclusively in Paris and London, respectively. In the mid-1990s, the state governments in Germany were also important because they provided opportunities to try out different types of coalitions that could eventually replace the CDU-FDP at the national level.

The Civil Service

Although German legislators have larger staffs than their French or British counterparts, they, too, are ill equipped to deal with the technical issues facing most governments today. As a result, bureaucrats are playing an increasingly influential role in policy making, as well as implementation.

Upper-level civil servants have long had a powerful, though not always positive, impact on German politics. In the early years of the Second Reich, only the chancellor was a political official. All the other members of the cabinet were drawn from the upper ranks of the civil service. In the Weimar period, the bureaucracy remained extremely conservative and was recruited primarily from the nobility. Most senior civil servants actively and voluntarily cooperated with the Nazis.

It was hardly surprising that de-Nazifying and democratizing the bureaucracy became one of the Allies' highest priorities after the war. In all, about 53,000 civil servants were purged before the British, French, and American authorities realized they needed a strong administrative service if the new republic they were creating was to get off the ground. With the onset of the cold war, the de-Nazification and democratization programs quickly ended. As a result, there was considerable continuity in both the operations and personnel of the prewar and postwar civil service.

The new civil service, however, differs significantly from the old one. Most notably, it is decentralized. Only about 10 percent of the top civil servants, or *Beamten*, work for the federal government.

AIDS in Germany

Germany's AIDS policy is among the most advanced in the world. By the early 1990s, the government and the insurance system had developed programs not only to treat all people infected with HIV but also to conduct an intensive national education program to reduce the spread of the disease. As a result, the 2002 infection rate was 22.8 per million people, the lowest in Europe. That said, there has been a slight increase in the number of new infections per year, primarily among homosexual men, largely because there has been a decline in condom use and because the previously successful education programs now have less money to spend.

Germany has also been a leader in funding international HIV/AIDS programs both through its own international development agency and, now, through the Global Fund to Fight AIDS, Tuberculosis, and Malaria. Between 1998 and 2003, German funding for international AIDS work leapt from $20 million to over $300 million per year. That money is used to provide free condoms in over twenty countries and combines with other German programs on general education, poverty reduction, and economic growth (www.dw-world.de/dw/article/0,1564,1392365,oo.html).

Federal bureaucrats do relatively little administrative work, most of which is the responsibility of their counterparts at the state level. Instead, federal civil servants spend most of their time drafting legislation and regulations for their partisan bosses. Most civil servants accept their political role far more readily than do their British or American counterparts. Many, in fact, are open party members or sympathizers. Some have moved on to political careers.

The civil service as a whole has largely escaped the daily battles of partisan politics, but there are two significant exceptions. In the aftermath of student protests and terrorist attacks in the late 1960s and early 1970s, the SPD government passed laws that severely restricted the entry of alleged radicals into the civil service at all levels, especially among the ranks of teachers and social workers. And after unification, many Communist officials were purged in the east, especially in the education and foreign ministries.

The Constitutional Court

Like the civil service of which they were a part, most judges before 1945 were conservatives who actively supported the Third Reich. In attempting to minimize the chances of a Nazi revival, American advisers advocated a revamped judiciary that would be more politically neutral but that could also buttress the new democracy.

The most important part of the judicial system they and the framers of the Basic Law created is the **Constitutional Court.** Its two chambers, or "senates," each have eight judges who serve nonrenewable twelve-year terms. Half are chosen by the Bundestag, and half by the Bundesrat. In each house, a two-thirds vote is required, which means that to be elected any judge has to be acceptable to members of both major parties. In other words, although most of them have as clear a political identity as any U.S. Supreme Court justice, they have to have more broad-based support and thus more moderate views than many of the justices nominated by recent U.S. administrations.

The court has wide-ranging powers. It can hear cases involving the constitutionality of state and federal law. Through the process of abstract review, an issue can go directly from the parliament to the court without any legal proceedings ever being started.

The court has had a hand in almost all important policy areas involving all aspects of the Basic Law, including these:

- Ruled that the Communist Party and the neo-Nazi Reichs Party were illegal under the provisions of the Basic Law concerning political parties (1952)

- Determined that the Adenauer government could not establish a second, nationally directed television network because the Basic Law gives states responsibility for the media (1961)

- Upheld the treaty with the DDR that was the cornerstone of Brandt's opening of relations between the Federal Republic and the countries of the Soviet bloc (1973)

- Largely upheld the provisions designed to keep "radicals" out of the civil service and required new federal and state employees to affirm their loyalty to the Federal Republic (1975)

- Overturned the liberal abortion law passed by the SPD-FDP government (1975)

- Upheld the codetermination law that gives workers nearly half the seats on the boards of directors of large firms (1979)

- Determined that the first elections in the newly unified Germany had to be conducted using a modified version of the two-tiered electoral system with separate allocation of seats in the west and east (1990)

- Made almost all abortions illegal (1993)

Corporatism

Corporatism is the last—and perhaps most important—component of the policy-making process. It is not mentioned in the Basic Law. Nonetheless, as in many countries, such informal procedures can be more influential than any constitutional provisions in determining what actually happens in political life.

The word *corporatism* itself is one of the most controversial in modern political science. Its origins lie in nineteenth-century Catholic thought. It was later used by the fascists to describe the sham legislatures they created in which major interests or "corporations" were supposedly represented. In other words, when scholars first began using corporatism to describe close relationships between the state and interest groups, their very choice of terms conveyed the strength of their reservations about such arrangements.

Scholars also have not used the term very precisely. There are dozens of definitions of corporatism, most of which revolve around the broad cooperation of highly centralized business and union organizations with the government in setting economic policy. Typically, corporatist negotiations take place behind closed doors, and neither political parties nor backbenchers have much of a role in them. Rather, cabinet members and high-level civil servants serve as brokers to help the interest groups reach agreements, which are then accepted as binding by everyone involved.

Germany has used corporatist procedures more than any of the other countries covered in this book. That said, they were used on an official basis only when the SPD was first in government and helped orchestrate the **Concerted Action** meetings that brought business, government, and labor together from 1966 until 1977. Concerted Action was originally instituted by the CDU-SPD grand coalition as part of its efforts to end the Federal Republic's first recession. Over the next three years, groups met annually to reach national agreements about wage and price increases, broad macroeconomic and social policy issues, and the landmark 1967 law on balanced growth. Once the CDU went into opposition and the post-OPEC economic slump hit, the discussions became more acrimonious and less productive. They were scrapped in 1977 when union officials refused to participate following the decision by several industrial associations to challenge the codetermination law (to be discussed shortly) before the Constitutional Court.

Since then, there has been far less formal corporatist decision making, especially at the macroeconomic level. One should not, however, make too much of its decline because, on balance, the most important practices have always been based on informal ties between the bureaucracy and the business community. Indeed, it is often said that the Economics Ministry sees itself as the *Anwalt,* or attorney-spokesman, for industry. The ministries' planning staffs cooperate with business and labor in trying to determine what their goals could and should be for the next five years or more. Because the states administer most federal policy, they also collect most of the data. Therefore, when federal civil servants need information, they often simply turn to the business associations with which they have developed close relationships over the years.

Informal corporatist arrangements also build on the consensus that exists between business and labor on basic economic priorities. At first, the DGB shared the SPD's desire for socialism. However, as the "economic miracle" unfolded, the unions, too, made their peace with capitalism and began concentrating on demands for a bigger share of the expanding economy for their members instead.

Labor's biggest contribution today comes through Germany's unique system of **codetermination,** which gives unions half the seats on the boards of directors of all companies with more than two thousand employees. The workers' representatives are not quite as powerful as those named by the owners. The law reserves one of the union seats for someone representing management employees and automatically gives the chair of the board to ownership.

Codetermination is but one part of a relatively peaceful system of labor-management relations that has endured throughout the postwar period. Unions traditionally have been willing to sacrifice short-term wage gains in exchange for job security and long-term corporate growth, from which they benefit. All firms have works councils that bring employees and management together to discuss job-related issues. Elaborate rules exist that help regularize and harmonize worker-management relations, including one that requires bosses to send flowers to any employee who has been out sick for more than six weeks.

Thus, codetermination is part of a system of industrial relations that is less adversarial than that found in any other liberal democracy. Although there has been some tension between the two sides over the years, union-management relations are usually cordial and cooperative. One union official who serves on the board of a major corporation put it this way:

> It is true that relations have become a little more conflictual nowadays, owing to lower growth and higher unemployment. But basically, we still believe that it is by cooperating with management, rather than fighting it, that we stand the best chance of securing better pay and working conditions—and the results prove it. What is more, as we see it, our obligation is not just to our own members or to other workers but to German society as a whole, where we must play an active role in upholding democracy and the rule of law. We're part of the establishment and proud of it. We're certainly not revolutionaries; we do not want to overthrow capitalism but to reform it from inside, in a more "social" direction, within the social market economy.[5]

Finally, until recent changes shook up the industry, Germany's banks helped set and coordinate economic policy. The three main private banks—Deutsche, Dresdner, and Commerz—owned about 10 percent of all the stock in Germany's leading industrial and commercial firms. For example, Deutsche Bank controlled more than a quarter of the German-held stock in Daimler-Chrysler. It had a similar stake in fifteen other major companies. In addition, depositors give the banks their proxies for their individual shares, leaving the banks with de facto control of almost all major firms. Thus, a relatively small number of bank officials could work with a similarly small number of colleagues in the public sector to coordinate much economic policy.

Many observers also argued that the **Bundesbank** was Germany's most powerful political institution until the EU's central bank took over many of its functions in 1998. Technically not part of the government, the bank worked closely with the cabinet for fifty years following its formation in 1948. In particular, it single-mindedly sought to use interest rates and other financial levers to keep inflation down and thereby help the country avoid one of the main problems that led to the collapse of the Weimar Republic. It is widely assumed that German influence will ensure that the new European Central Bank plays a similar role now that the euro has replaced the deutsche mark and other national currencies.

But corporatism is a mixed blessing. Though less so than was the case under the fascists, corporatist systems underrepresent labor. Compared with what we saw in France or Britain, labor has fared rather well in Germany. But even so, it has only approached being an equal partner during the first few years the SPD was in power in the early 1970s.

Labor is not the only group to get short shrift. The consensus and the neocorporatist arrangements are limited to issues of industrial and economic growth. Groups concerned with issues such as women's rights, immigrant workers, and the growing elderly population,

---

[5] Cited in John Ardagh, *Germany and the Germans: After Unification* (New York: Penguin Books, 1991), 125.

which emerged with postmaterial politics and citizens' initiatives beginning in the 1970s, are not part of the corporatist system.

Chapter 2 outlined two versions of liberal democracy. The American presidential system makes it relatively easy for organized groups to influence the decision-making process between elections. The fusion of legislature and executive in parliamentary systems provides a sharper link between party programs and the policies the government enacts, making elections themselves an effective way for a majority of the public to voice its opinions and, in turn, shape subsequent public policy making.

Corporatism poses problems for either version. Decision making takes place behind closed doors and involves bureaucrats, not the elected officials over whom the voting public has some degree of control.

None of this is to say that Germany and other relatively corporatized countries are not democratic in the sense most political scientists use the term. However, the realities of corporatism reveal one of the great trade-offs of German politics today. There is little question that these cooperative arrangements have helped Germany become one of the world's leading economic and political powers, something we will see in more detail in the rest of the chapter. Yet that success has come at the cost of substantial popular participation in the setting of economic policy.

Public Policy: Modell Deutschland

One of the key themes of this chapter is embedded in the quote that begins it. The Federal Republic has succeeded in large part because it has rarely adopted dramatic reforms, its leaders preferring instead to take incremental steps on the basis of an all but society-wide consensus.

We can see that by turning to two policy areas that reflect both the success the regime has enjoyed for more than a half century and also the challenges it faces today that put those accomplishments in doubt. The first, not surprisingly, is the economy, which was at the heart of Germany's rebirth after the war but is equally at the heart of its difficulties in the early twenty-first century. The second—and related—issue is the ease with which it incorporated the former East Germany despite the social, political, and economic costs that came with unification.

The Social Market Economy

Germany has not always been one of the world's richest countries. In 1951, GNP per capita stood at $500 a year, or about a fourth that of the United States. By the end of the 1980s, it had drawn even with the United States on most major economic indicators. Only Japan's economy has grown at a faster pace since the end of World War II. And, unlike during the interwar years, Germany was able to keep its inflation and unemployment rates among the lowest in the world.

As was the case with the Gaullists in France, domestic public policy has not been the only cause of this remarkable track record. Germany's recovery got a needed boost from $4.4 billion in Marshall Plan aid and the influx of fourteen million refugees from the East who helped keep labor costs down. Since the late 1940s, Germany has done well, too, because its companies produce high-quality goods that are in demand in the international marketplace. This is why, for instance, BMW and Mercedes-Benz sell far more cars in Japan than Cadillac does.

Still, the state has played an extremely important role in Germany's turnaround. Since the 1950s, the government has followed remarkably consistent and successful economic policies, which were formalized in the 1967 law that obliges the state to pursue policies that maintain stable prices, full employment, adequate growth, and a positive balance of trade.

More than French policymakers, the German elite understood that the route to economic growth lay in international trade and investment more than through attempts to capture a larger share of a relatively small domestic market. As a result, Germany had Europe's most globally oriented economy well into the 1990s. It exported more goods and services than any other country in the world on a per capita basis. Its exports accounted for more than a quarter of all trade within the EU. Its currency dominated the EU for two decades and, in many respects, is the foundation on which the euro has been built.

The key here is not so much economic performance as the consistent role of the state in promoting it, which we can see by considering the last two alternations in power—the beginning of the Kohl and Schröder governments.

Margaret Thatcher, François Mitterrand, and Helmut Kohl took office in the aftermath of the second oil shock of the 1970s, which was a period of sluggish and intermittent growth. As we saw in the last two chapters, Thatcher and Mitterrand enacted sweeping reforms they thought would help their countries cope with these deteriorating conditions.

Under Kohl, by contrast, there was more continuity than change. Rather than embarking on a radical Thatcher-esque restructuring of the economy, Kohl advocated minor reductions in government spending to make more funds available for private investment in order to re-create one of the conditions that had led to the economic miracle of the pre-OPEC years.

Also, unlike the British and French policies, Kohl's seemed to work. By 1986 the budget deficit had been cut by two-thirds, and inflation had been all but eliminated. Industrial production increased by an average of 15 percent per year. The fact that half of Germany's exports were bought by its European partners made it the country that benefited the most from the creation of the single European market.

That economic success can perhaps best be seen in the standard of living its citizens enjoy. The average industrial worker makes about $30 per hour in wages and nearly as much again in fringe benefits and social services. Most workers also earn the equivalent of another month's wages in annual Christmas bonuses. Until France passed its thirty-five-hour work week, the Germans worked the shortest hours and enjoyed the most vacation time (forty-two working days a year) in Europe. Most are able to afford large cars, which they drive as fast as they want on the country's superhighways that effectively have no speed limits.

Since the early 1990s, Germany's performance has not been as impressive. In part, that reflects the economic costs of unification, which we will consider shortly. In part, too, the last decade has seen some of Germany's past strengths turn into weaknesses.

Germany's economic growth rate has been among the lowest in Europe since unification because of the burden that came with incorporating the East (see the next section). Additionally, a combination of high wages and laws making it hard for companies to restructure themselves in any meaningful way has left Germany with what has essentially been a stagnant economy for the last decade.

The Schröder government has tried to find a way out of that dilemma by drawing both on the German past that stresses economic cooperation and Blair's success in strengthening market forces in his "New Labour" governments in Britain. In 2003, the government introduced a sweeping plan known as **Agenda 2010,** which is designed to sweep away many of the rules and regulations that have made many German products uncompetitive in the increasingly global market.

The main goal of the reforms is to make it easier for companies to hire and fire workers. Unemployed people will see their benefits reduced after their first year out of work. They will face even further cuts if they refuse to take most jobs offered to them. Unemployment and other welfare benefits will be combined, thereby reducing total payments people receive and giving them even

Liberalization in Germany

LIBERALIZATION POLICY in Germany can be broken into two components. In the West, there has been relatively little liberalization, because the government owned relatively little of the economy. Although the two main state-owned industries—Deutsche Post and Deutsche Telekom—are being privatized, the key issue in Western Germany is not the ownership of industry, but the intricate system of regulation, which remains largely in place.

The situation is very different in the East. There, the regime owned virtually the entire economy before it collapsed (see Chapter 8). Unlike some of the other former Communist countries in Eastern Europe, however, Germany quickly reached a consensus on the need to privatize state-owned firms as soon as possible, a task that it accomplished by the middle of the 1990s.

more of an incentive to return to work. On the other side of the coin, employers will get significant tax cuts and have to pay somewhat smaller social security taxes in the hopes that more people will get at least part-time jobs and more small businesses will be created.

It is by no means certain that Agenda 2010 will succeed. This is always a concern when a government attempts to implement dramatic reforms in what is increasingly an international economic system. The government also cannot even be sure that the reforms will pass parliament, since the opposition controls the Bundesrat, as we saw earlier. Nonetheless, these are the most far-reaching proposals put forward by a German government since the 1967 law on balanced growth. And, if they succeed, it will be in large part because the government and opposition reached an agreement on the best way to move forward.

Unification

Most chapters in this book include a section on foreign policy as one of the ways to demonstrate the state in action. Foreign policy is important in Germany, especially now that it is by far the most powerful country in Europe. However, I chose to focus on unification instead in this chapter for three reasons.

First, unification has significantly slowed Germany's economic growth and raised the possibility of serious political disruption. Second, even though Germany has had a hard time coping with the social and economic

Crowds scaling the Berlin Wall following the DDR announcement that it would no longer restrict travel to the west.

implications of unification, it is likely to make the country even stronger in the long run. Finally, unification provides yet another example of German adaptation to changing circumstances.

The Basic Law was not called a constitution because the Federal Republic's founders expected that the two Germanys would eventually be reunited. For forty years, leading politicians in the West (but not those in the DDR) consistently called for unification, but no one realistically expected it to happen until the remarkable events of 1989 unfolded.

As we will see in more detail in Chapter 8, reform movements swept through Poland and Hungary that spring, culminating in the Hungarian decision to dismantle the barbed wire "iron curtain" along its border with Austria. An average of five thousand East German "vacationers" a day streamed across the border past not-very-diligent border guards. In September, Hungary gave up even the pretence of policing the border. The DDR then closed its border with Hungary, but East Germans anxious to head West found another way out through Czechoslovakia.

On 25 September 1989, the first of what turned out to be weekly mass rallies demanding political reform took place in the East German city of Leipzig. In October, the DDR celebrated the regime's fortieth anniversary, which Soviet President Mikhail Gorbachev attended. During his visit, it became increasingly clear that the East German regime was in deep trouble and could not meet either domestic demands or Soviet pressures for a German equivalent of *perestroika* and *glasnost.*

Shortly thereafter, the Communist Party's elite forced the aging and intransigent Erich Honecker to resign and replaced him with the younger, but still hardline, Egon Krenz. Krenz could do nothing to stop either the protests or the flood of DDR citizens fleeing to the West. On 9 November, Krenz gave in. All travel restrictions were lifted, and that evening, people began tearing down the Berlin Wall. Krenz resigned, and his successor, Hans Modrow, began planning free elections for the spring. The Federal Republic's parties moved into the East and took over the campaign.

Only then did Kohl seriously back rapid unification. He apparently first raised the idea in a telephone conversation with Krenz two days after the wall came down. From then on, Kohl's goal was to incorporate the DDR into the Federal Republic as five new states, under Article 2 of the Basic Law rather than through Article 146, which would have required the negotiation of a whole new constitution subject to a referendum. He also proposed that the all-but-worthless East German marks be exchanged for deutsche marks on a one-for-one basis. Finally, he insisted that newly united Germany remain in NATO and the EC.

At that point, rapid unification still seemed unlikely given Soviet objections to a unified Germany's membership in NATO. But even those objections were quickly overcome. In March 1990, Kohl's supporters won an overwhelming victory in the East's first and only free election, which made negotiations with the West far easier. Meanwhile, with strong encouragement from the first Bush administration, the Soviet government agreed to join "four plus two" talks, which brought the four former occupying powers and the two Germanys to the bargaining table.

By early summer 1990, the two Germanys agreed to merge their economies on 1 July. In September, the Soviets agreed to German membership in NATO after the Germans formally accepted the boundaries drawn after World War II and committed themselves to spending $8 billion to send the 340,000 Soviet troops stationed in East Germany back to Russia, build housing for them, and retrain them for civilian jobs. On 4 October the two countries were politically united. In December, Bundestag elections were held throughout the country that confirmed the CDU in power.

Before continuing, it is worth underscoring the most important point here. Most of the steps that made unification possible were taken in East Berlin and Moscow rather than Bonn. When the federal government acted decisively, it did so on the basis of a broad consensus. Only the Greens and a handful of intellectuals, including the novelist Günter Grass, opposed unification. The SPD preferred a slower pace using Article 146, but it still supported the idea of unification. In short, as in domestic policy, the German government acted reactively more than proactively and took bold steps only after achieving a broad consensus.

Unification, however, presented new challenges that could not be met using the incremental policy making that German governments had used since the 1960s. Almost everything in the East was substandard—workforce training; environmental conditions; the highway, rail, and telecommunications infrastructure; factory equipment; and housing. Only 7 percent of DDR households had a telephone, and there were only a few hundred lines that could handle international calls—including those to the Federal Republic. Per capita income in the East was a quarter that in the West, and productiv-

ity was a third that of the Federal Republic. Economists estimated that it would take up to $100 billion to modernize the rail system alone and determined that no more than 20 percent of Eastern enterprises could survive in a competitive market economy.

Therefore, the Federal Republic adopted policies to make the transition as rapid as possible, even if doing so would cause hardship in the short run. A new agency, the *Treuhandanstalt*—or **Treuhand** for short—was created to supervise the privatization of East German firms. Until they could be sold, the state-owned industries were subjected to the same market forces operating in the West, including the possibility of unemployment for workers and bankruptcy for the firm. All Western wage, social service, and labor laws took effect immediately, except for the granting of a year's protection from unemployment for workers in the largest factories.

The economic results were painful indeed. A year after unification, industrial production in the East was down by 70 percent. Unemployment had risen to 3.5 million in a workforce of 8.5 million. The Treuhand discovered that it could not easily sell off antiquated industries even though the federal government offered a 40 percent tax credit for firms that invested in the East. Even when buyers could be found, they faced colossal challenges. BASF, for instance, bought a reasonably modern Eastern chemical firm only to discover major environmental problems, a 74,000-person workforce that would have to be cut in half, and a management filled with former Communist Party apparatchiks. What's more, there was not much of a market for the factory's goods, because its primary outlet had been the former Soviet Union, which could no longer pay for the chemicals.

More than a decade after unification, the East remains an economic burden for the West. The federal government has sent an average of over $100 billion a year to the East in aid and subsidies—the equivalent of 40 percent of the former DDR's GNP. This has had a tangible impact on Westerners' lifestyles, because the government imposed a 7.5 percent increase in the income tax and what amounted to a 55¢ per liter additional tax on gasoline.

In the late 1990s, however, economic conditions in the East began to improve. Having sold off all the viable companies, the Treuhand was disbanded. By 2000 unemployment had fallen to 17 percent, only 10 percent more than in the West. Per capita income had topped $16,000 a year, almost twice what it was at the time of unification.

Integrating the East is not merely an economic challenge. Although most DDR citizens had been able to watch television shows and listen to radio broadcasts from the West for many years, they were largely isolated from the political and, even more, the cultural trends that remade the West after 1945. Most had never experienced a market economy or lived in a democracy, and have had a hard time adapting to both. There has been a backlash against the loss of guaranteed housing, employment, and other services that were eliminated.

Perhaps the most important long-term obstacle to effective unification is what many Germans call the "wall in the mind." Other terms used to describe the difficulties in combining the *ossis* (people from the East) and *wessis* (people from the West) include "united but not together" and "sharing a bathroom with a stranger." Most observers are surprised at how different the two societies had grown despite having been separated for only forty-five years. Westerners are increasingly resentful of the economic costs of unification, which has come at the cost of their own standard of living. On the other side of the psychological border, a 2000 poll found that only 16 percent of the *ossis* felt "solidarity" with their fellow citizens in the West.

Feedback

Like their counterparts in Britain and France, Germans have access to a variety of sources of information about politics. Also like their counterparts, few take much advantage of them.

Germany's newspapers have surprisingly small circulations. The five main "quality" dailies sold only 157,000 to 405,000 copies a day at the end of 1997. As in Britain and France, they each have clear, traditional political leanings. However, as the 1998 election neared, the *Frankfurter Allgemeine Zeitung* (known to friends and foes alike as *FAZ*) was unusually critical of the Kohl government it had long supported. The CDU has also been able to count on support from the Axel Springer media empire, with its high-quality daily *Die Welt* and Germany's main tabloid, *Bild*. But they, too, were more critical of Kohl in 1998, perhaps sensing that their readers were ready for a change. Finally, most of the six major weeklies have been more critical of the CDU than they were in the mid-1990s.

Germans have more locally produced television options than people in Britain or France do. Subscribers to the ASTRA satellite system (cable is much less developed than direct satellite broadcasting in Europe) can receive upwards of twenty German-language stations. The most popular private station (SAT 1) was more supportive of

Globalization and Germany

SO FAR, GLOBALIZATION has affected Germany less than the other European democracies. Despite the costs of unification, its companies and its currency (until the launch of the euro) remain the strongest in Europe. That said, Germany is by no means immune from global pressures. In particular, its high labor costs make its goods increasingly hard to sell abroad. And some of its legal restrictions have forced its companies to do some cutting-edge work abroad. For example, the Basic Law and constitutional court decisions have made the destruction of embryos for stem cell research illegal. This does not mean that German firms do not engage in that research; they simply do it in Britain or France, where there are no such restrictions.

Kohl than the state-owned ones (ARD, ZDF) were, and it is widely believed that it played a major role in the CDU's reelection in 1994. There is an all-news channel and another channel that resembles C-SPAN, but they are not very popular. The one event that usually draws a large audience is the so-called "elephant round table," or debate among the party leaders, which occurs in the last few days before a Bundestag election.

Conclusion: Democratization

Throughout the rest of the book, we will be asking why some countries develop stable, flourishing democracies and others do not. Germany's remarkable history since 1945 provides two insights to keep in mind as we examine countries that have had a more troubled experience.

First, Germany suffered a traumatic defeat in World War II. That loss and the horrors of the Third Reich as a whole forced millions of Germans to question many of their basic values. As a result, German culture changed from stressing authoritarian values to endorsing a democratic society as rapidly as any in history. This may not be possible in other countries facing similar situations.

Second, and more encouraging for other countries, democracy began to take hold before the cultural change had begun. During the economic miracle, people started to accept democracy because it worked. It provided them with tangible benefits—most notably, the prosperity and security offered by the social market economy.

Key Terms

Concepts

Agenda 2010
Basic Law
Chancellor democracy
Codetermination
Concerted Action
Constructive vote of no
  confidence
Corporatism

Faulted society
Führer
German question
Grand coalition
Länder
Modell Deutschland
Proportional representation
Reparations

People

Adenauer, Konrad
Bismarck, Otto von
Brandt, Willy
Fischer, Joska
Hitler, Adolf

Kohl, Helmut
Merkel, Angela
Schmidt, Helmut
Schröder, Gerhard

Acronyms

CDU   FDP   PDS
DDR   NPD   SPD
DGB   NSDAP

Organizations, Places, and Events

Bundesbank
Bundesrat
Bundestag
Christian Democratic
  Union
Constitutional Court
Federal Republic of
  Germany
Federation of German
  Labor
Free Democratic Party
German Democratic
  Republic

Greens
Law for Promoting
  Stability and Growth
  in the Economy
National Democratic Party
Nazis
Party of Democratic
  Socialism
Social Democratic Party
Treuhand
Weimar Republic

Critical Thinking Exercises

1. Much has changed since this book was finished in early 2005. Does the analysis of German politics presented here still make sense? Why (not)?

2. Public opinion pollsters routinely ask questions about whether people think their country is heading in the "right direction" or is on the "wrong track." If you were asked such a question about Germany, how would you answer? Why did you reach this conclusion?

3. Democracy in Germany developed much more slowly and far more tumultuously than in France, let alone the United States or Great Britain. Indeed, Germany's difficulties extended far beyond Nazism and the Third Reich. Why was that the case?

4. How does Germany's troubled history still affect its political culture and the rest of its political life today?

5. The current German party system is very different from the one that existed under the Weimar Republic. What historical and institutional factors contributed to those changes?

6. How do federalism and corporatism make decision making in Germany different from what we find in other democracies?

7. How has the operation of the German state contributed to its economic success throughout the postwar period and also to its difficulties since 1990?

8. Why has unification proved to be more of a burden than many expected in 1990?

Useful Websites

There are three good entry points to German politics on the web, though none of them are as good as the portals for most of the other countries covered in this book. The Dartmouth College library has an excellent one on German studies in general. The editors of H-Net, a collection of listservs for scholars, maintain a set of links on German issues, including politics. Finally, Professor Russell Dalton of the University of California-Irvine has an excellent but brief set of links he has chosen for his own students.

www.dartmouth.edu/~wess

www2.h-net.msu.edu/~german

www.democ.uci.edu/democ/dvita.htm

The German government provides a gateway to the chancellor's office and government agencies, most of which have material in English as well as German.

www.bundesregierung.de/en

There are two good sources of news about Germany. The first is from the English language feed of Deutsche Welle, one of the country's leading radio and television broadcasters. The other is provided by the German Embassy in Washington.

www.dw-world.de/dw/0,1595,266,00.html

www.germany-info.org

Debatte is an academic journal that deals with contemporary German affairs. Some of its articles and issues are available on the publisher's website. Go there and follow the directions.

www.tandf.co.uk/journals/arenas.asp

InfoTrac College Edition Sources

Camerra-Rowe, Pamela. "Agenda 2010: Redefining German Social Democracy."

Duffield, John S. "Political Culture and State Behavior: Why Germany Confounds Neorealism."

Fuchs, Dieter, and Robert Rohrscheider. "Postmaterialism and Electoral Choice Before and After German Unification."

Kwon, Heyeong-ki. "The German Model Reconsidered."

(No author listed). "Schröder's Upset Victory."

Patton, David. "The Rise of Germany's Party of Democratic Socialism."

Ramet, Sabrina P. "Religion and Politics in Germany Since 1945."

Ritter, Hennig. "What is Left and What is Right in Germany."

Seeleib-Kaiser, Martin. "A Dual Transformation of Germany's Welfare State?"

Yoder, Jennifer. "West-East Integration."

Further Reading

Almond, Gabriel, and Sidney Verba. *The Civic Culture: Political Attitudes and Democracy in Five Nations.* Princeton, N.J.: Princeton University Press, 1963. The classic study of political culture, including significant doubts about German commitment to democracy.

———, eds. *The Civic Culture Revisited.* Boston: Little, Brown, 1979. A volume that includes substantial data on the way German culture changed during the 1960s and 1970s and became more "civic."

Ardagh, John. *Germany and the Germans: After Unification,* rev. ed. New York: Penguin Books, 1991. An encyclopedic look at modern Germany, with an emphasis on culture and economics rather than on politics.

Ash, Timothy Garton. *The Magic Lantern: The Revolution of '89 Witnessed in Warsaw, Budapest, Berlin, and Prague.* New York: Random House, 1990. One of the best journalistic accounts of the events that swept through Eastern Europe in 1989.

———. *The File.* New York: HarperCollins, 1997. A chilling look at East Germany through Garton Ash's attempt to see his own Stasi file.

Berghahn, V. R. *Modern Germany: Society, Economy, and Politics in the Twentieth Century,* 2nd ed. New York: Cambridge University Press, 1987. A historical overview that provides the best link among political, social, and economic trends.

Bering, Henrik. *Helmut Kohl.* Washington: Regnery, 1999. The best of the few biographies of Kohl in English, although many readers will find that it lavishes too much praise on him.

Blumenthal, W. Michael. *The Invisible Wall: Germans and Jews, a Personal Exploration.* Washington, D.C.: Counterpoint, 1998. A thoughtful volume by the former secretary of the treasury during the Carter administration.

Bracher, Karl Dietrich. *The German Dictatorship.* New York: Praeger, 1970. Still perhaps the best and most accessible analytical study of the Hitler years.

Fisher, Marc. *After the Wall: Germany, the Germans, and the Burden of History.* New York: Simon & Schuster, 1995. An analysis of contemporary Germany by the *Washington Post*'s correspondent. Especially good on ethnic issues.

Goldhagen, Donald. *Hitler's Willing Executioners.* New York: Random House, 1997. An extremely controversial book that argues that most Germans cooperated willingly with the Third Reich.

Grimond, John. "The Burden of Normality: Germany: A Survey." *The Economist,* 6, February 1999. An almost book-length overview of German politics and economics.

Marsh, David. *Germany and Europe: The Crisis of Unity.* London: Heineman, 1994. The most comprehensive book on the impact of unification for Germany and the EU, by the editor of the *Financial Times.* Marsh is also the author of a book on the Bundesbank.

Parkin, Sarah. *The Life and Death of Petra Kelly.* New York: Pandora/HarperCollins, 1994. A biography of the Greens' most prominent leader, and also a solid analysis of the party itself. Written by one of the founders of the British Greens.

Roberts, Geoffrey. *Party Politics in the New Germany.* London: Pinter/Cassell, 1997. The best of the few recent academic books looking at the "big picture" of German politics.

> *Over the longer term, the institutions and powers of the [Union] will continue to expand and certain policy-making powers, heretofore vested in the member states, will be delegated or transferred to, or pooled and shared with, [Union] institutions. As a result, the sovereignty of the member states will increasingly and inevitably be eroded.*
>
> **DAVID CAMERON**

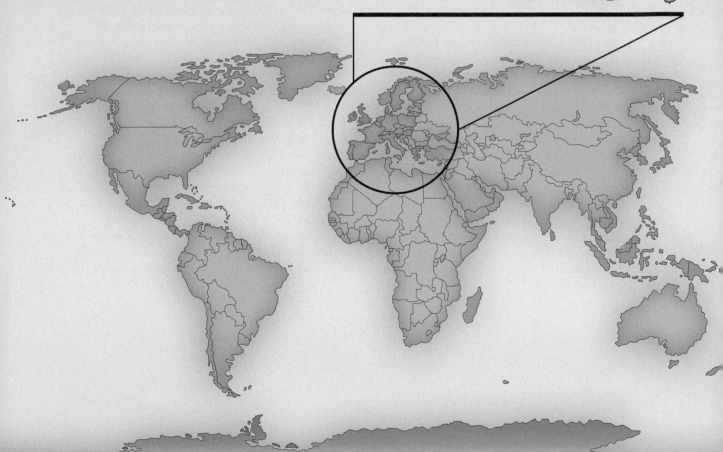

Chapter 7

THE EUROPEAN UNION

CHAPTER OUTLINE

- You Say You Want a Constitution?
- Thinking about the EU
- The Evolution of the EU
- Political Culture and Participation in the EU
- The European State?
- Public Policy in the EU
- Feedback
- Conclusion: A Balance Sheet

The Basics: The European Union

COUNTRY	DATE OF ACCESSION
Belgium, France, Germany, Italy, Luxembourg, Netherlands	1957
Denmark, Great Britain, Ireland	1972/73
Greece	1981
Portugal, Spain	1986
Austria, Finland, Sweden	1995
Cyprus, Czech Republic, Estonia, Hungary, Latvia, Lithuania, Malta, Poland, Slovakia, Slovenia	2004

You Say You Want a Constitution?

The Beatles' 1968 path-breaking "White Album" included two versions of their song "Revolution" (www.lyricsdepot.com/the-beatles/revolution.html). It was a call to young radicals like this author to rethink their commitment to profound political change. They chastised us for focusing on the need to reform our countries' constitutions and institutions rather than changing our ways of thinking instead.

Almost forty years have passed since the White Album was released. Two of the Beatles have died. The political revolution they worried about in Europe and North America has long disappeared from any serious observer or activist's political agenda. But constitutions and institutions have not.

After two years of difficult negotiations, the leaders of the twenty-five members of the European Union reached an agreement on a constitution for the world's most powerful international organization (european-convention.eu.int). It would replace a number of treaties and other agreements the member states had reached since 1957.

As we will see in more detail later in the chapter, the more than five hundred page constitution will not dra-

European leaders congratu-
late each other after agreeing to draft a constitution.

Yves Herman /CORBIS

matically alter how the European Union goes about its work. What matters most is that the leaders are using the term "constitution" rather than "treaty" to describe it. In the past, major steps forward for the EU had taken the form of treaties, which are documents agreed to by sovereign states. The constitution at least symbolically suggests that the EU is taking on more of the attributes of a state itself, another point we will return to later.

As of this writing, it is by no means certain that the constitution will ever become official. Each state must approve it. In a sign of how far the EU has to go to become a state, each country will use different mechanisms to vote on it and will do so at different times over a six-month period. Thus, Ireland, the United Kingdom, and Denmark will use a referendum. Germany will have a vote in the Bundestag because the Basic Law makes no provision for referenda. Even more importantly, the EU leaders have not taken the Beatles' notion to change our minds all that seriously. There is, in other words, a good chance that at least some of the countries will vote "no" in referenda.

In short, this is a chapter about an important, evolving, but still incomplete Union. It is one of the very few international organizations that has enforceable powers over sovereign states. As I suggested in the three previous chapters, this is particularly true of economic policy that is determined more by the EU than by the member states' governments. But it is far less true of almost all other policy matters, including foreign affairs and defense where the countries have struggled to find common ground on controversial issues as in the breakup of Yugoslavia and the U.S.-led war against Iraq.

Thinking about the EU

As was the case with Great Britain, we have to start by clarifying what we will discuss in this chapter. Uncertainty over which name to use—not to mention all the accompanying acronyms—can make studying the EU confusing indeed (europa.eu.int /comm/ enterprise /construction /faqbase /faqhome.htm). In this chapter, four different names will be used:

- The **European Economic Community (EEC),** established by the Treaty of Rome in 1957
- The **Common Market,** a term informally applied to the EEC and still sometimes used today
- The **European Community (EC),** adopted in 1965 once its functions expanded beyond economics

■   The **European Union (EU),** the name of all the institutions gathered under the EC's umbrella according to the 1991 Maastricht Treaty on European Union (TEU)

Who's In? Who's Out?

In 2004, the EU grew to twenty-five member states. France, Germany, Italy, Belgium, the Netherlands, and Luxembourg signed the Treaty of Rome and became charter members in 1957. Britain, Ireland, and Denmark entered on New Year's Day 1973. Norway had also been invited to join, but its voters decided not to in a referendum the previous year. Greece joined in 1981, and Spain and Portugal followed suit five years later. Finland, Austria, and Sweden became members in 1995. Cyprus, the Czech Republic, Estonia, Hungary, Latvia, Lithuania, Malta, Poland, Slovakia, and Slovenia were admitted in 2004. Applications from four more states are pending. That leaves only Norway and Switzerland among the major European countries with no current interest in "acceding" to the EU.

The member countries have more than 450 million residents, or roughly 170 million more than the United States. Their combined gross domestic product for 2000 was about $700 billion more than that of the United States, though in terms of average purchasing power, the Europeans had only about two-thirds of the average American's disposable income. Still, the EU is an economic powerhouse, generating about 30 percent of all international trade. (See table 7.1.)

The EU also has many of the trappings of a state. Its flag of fifteen yellow stars on a blue background flies from official buildings. This is also a common logo in advertisements, and you can get it emblazoned on t-shirts and umbrellas (I have one of each). The EU has three active capital cities, with various government offices headquartered in Brussels, Luxembourg, and Strasbourg (France). Most major world powers have an embassy in Brussels that is dedicated to relations with the EU. The EU embassy is typically larger and more prestigious than the one to Belgium itself. And with the introduction of the **euro,** the EU has one of the most important attributes of a state—its own currency.

The New Europe

The 2004 expansion probably marked the most important change in the history of European integration in at least three ways. First, if nothing else, adding ten countries all at once will force significant changes in the way the Union is governed. Second, before 2004, all the states that joined were established democracies with reasonably prosperous economies. Even the poorest of the fifteen—Greece, Portugal, and Spain—had GDPs of about two-thirds the Union's average. Of the ten new members, only a handful are even close to half of that average. Finally, all but Malta and Cyprus had been ruled by Communists until barely a decade ago and are thus making the rough transitions to democracy and capitalism that we will focus on in Part 3 of this book. In the short term, at least, this expansion will be harder politically and economically than earlier ones.

The expansion has also led to more discussion of what some call a "multi speed" Europe in which countries participate in the Union to varying degrees. That had already begun in the 1990s when some states were allowed to opt out of social policies and of the elimination of internal border controls. Even more importantly, three states decided not to adopt the euro. A number of policies, including the free flow of labor throughout the union, will not apply to the new members for a number of years. There is a certain logic to allowing states to participate in some, but not all, EU functions.

Three Pillars

As the history of its name suggests, many people mistakenly think of the EU as an economic organization. Although it is true that it began as a trading bloc, its founders always intended it to be much more than that. Since its creation, the EU has expanded to include other powers, together known as the **three pillars,** or spheres, of activity:

■   The traditional involvement in trade and other economic matters

■   Cooperation in justice and home affairs (JHA)

■   The desire to create a **Common Foreign and Security Policy (CFSP),** which is the most visionary and controversial aspect of the EU today

▌TABLE 7.1 The EU and the United States

	THE EU	THE UNITED STATES
Population in millions	456	288
GDP in millions of euros	2,549	2,419
Imports as percent of GDP	.25	.15
Exports as percent of GDP	.27	.10

Source: Various pages from epp.eurostat.cec.eu.int, accessed 18 November 2004.

Functionalism

Functionalism is a theory of international organization developed most prominently by David Mitrany in 1943. Its proponents believe that the best way to develop a body like the EU is to go step by step or expand function by function.

The EU does not exactly fit functionalist theory because its growth has come more in fits and starts than Mitrany and his colleagues hoped or expected. Nonetheless, we will see later in this chapter that success in one area "spilled over" into additional members and additional powers for the European institutions.

Key Questions

Long ago, political scientists erected an intellectual firewall between comparative politics and international relations. The former deals with politics within states and the latter with the interactions among them.

In retrospect, it never made sense to treat the two parts of the discipline separately. States have always had to deal with problems arising outside their borders. Similarly, domestic political dynamics have always factored heavily in determinations of what states can do internationally.

Whatever the situation was in the past, it is all but impossible today to keep international relations out of comparative politics and vice versa, which is, after all, the idea behind this book's subtitle. Nowhere is this easier to see than in the EU and the way it limits what its member states can do in formulating economic and other policies. Those issues lurked below the surface in the last three chapters, and now we will address them directly by asking the same basic questions of the EU that are being posed for nation-states:

- How and why did the EU emerge?
- What is its political culture, and how does it shape the way people participate in its political life?
- What are its main decision-making bodies?
- What are its critical public policy initiatives?
- How do the European people learn about and react to that policy?

This chapter will also be more than merely another description of a governing body. It will also provide a first glimpse at the trends indicating that we are entering a new period in political history in which the nation-state may no longer be the only, or even the primary, unit we should focus on. It is very much an open question whether the EU and other **supranational** organizations will gain more power, and it is highly unlikely that they will replace the nation-state in the foreseeable future. Nonetheless, the EU forces us to think of political life as a multilevel phenomenon that crosses the traditional divide between international relations and comparative politics.

That said, do not read too much into the pages that follow. Despite its statelike attributes, the EU is far from being a state. For one thing, it lacks the monopoly over the legitimate use of force that, most political scientists argue, makes a state a state.

What's more, movement toward a more integrated Europe has not occurred at a steady pace. Rather, it has progressed in a series of fits and starts, with bursts of growth followed by longer periods of stagnation filled with doubt and criticism. This holds both for the **broadening** (adding new members) and the **deepening** (adding new powers) of European institutions.

The Evolution of the EU

As we saw in Chapters 3–6, it took centuries of often protracted conflict to create the modern state. This has not been the case for the EU. Rather, European integration is a recent phenomenon that has been all but exclusively the handiwork of political, technical, and economic elites (www.eu-history .leidenuniv.nl).

Not Such a New Idea

The idea of uniting Europe has been around at least since ancient Roman times. Leaders from Julius Caesar to Adolf Hitler tried to make it happen through force, but without lasting success.

In the aftermath of World War I, some politicians and intellectuals began to look to international organization as a possible solution to the wars that had wracked the continent for centuries. When the League of Nations was created and many countries signed the Kellogg-Briand Pact, which formally abolished war, groups of young activists began organizing support for a united Europe, which they also assumed would be a peaceful Europe.

The outbreak of World War II put an abrupt end to their efforts. In the longer term, however, the war only

JEAN MONNET

Jean Monnet giving a radio address on European Union.

Jean Monnet (1888–1979) was a remarkable man. In his long career, he was everything from a brandy salesman to the primary architect of both the French economic planning system and European integration. In a professional life that spanned two world wars (which, perhaps not coincidentally, he could not fight in because of ill health), he came to see the need to replace the carnage resulting from trench warfare and blitzkrieg with a new kind of transnational economic cooperation.

After World War II, he dedicated his energies to reconstruction and peace through planning and integration, which he saw as inseparable parts of the same whole. Among the few official positions he held was president of the European Coal and Steel Community from its founding until 1955. He spent the next twenty years trying to create a true United States of Europe. Monnet died at age ninety (so much for ill health) without seeing his broader dream realized but having left an indelible mark on his continent and the world.

strengthened the Europeanists' cause. Resistance movements developed in the countries the Germans occupied. Most were led by people who had few ties to the discredited prewar regimes, anticipated the creation of new and improved institutions once the fighting ended, and realized that Europeans simply could not afford to keep fighting each other. (See table 7.2.)

A small group of them met in neutral Switzerland to discuss a document that called for a supranational government directly responsible to the European people. It

▌ TABLE 7.2 Key Events in the Evolution of the EU

YEAR	EVENT
1951	Creation of ECSC
1957	Treaty of Rome signed
1967	Creation of EC
1972	First expansion
1981	Admission of Greece
1985	Single European Act passed
1986	Portugal and Spain admitted
1991	Treaty of Maastricht signed
1995	Austria, Finland, and Sweden admitted
1997	Treaty of Amsterdam signed
1998	Twelve countries agree to join EMU
2001	Treaty of Nice signed
2002	Euro launched
2004	Ten new members added

would have its own military, which would replace the national armies. An international court would settle disputes between national governments.

By the end of the war, the Europeanists had split into two camps. Whereas the federalists wanted to create that Europe-wide government, the functionalists preferred acting in one area (that is to say one function) at a time, building momentum for further integration along the way.

As it turned out, neither side got its way. The outbreak of the cold war in the late 1940s made security the paramount issue on both sides of the iron curtain. The tensions between East and West magnified the need to reconstruct the war-ravaged economies and strengthen the new regimes in Germany, France, and Italy. Conventional politicians returned to center stage, eclipsing Europeanist visionaries like **Jean Monnet** in France and **Paul-Henri Spaak** in Belgium.

Nonetheless, the first important steps toward integration did occur in the late 1940s as an unintended byproduct of the early cold war. The United States decided that it would not allot **Marshall Plan** aid to individual governments. Instead, it chose to distribute the money through the OEEC (Organization for European Economic Cooperation), the predecessor to today's OECD (Organization for Economic Cooperation and Development). The OEEC had limited powers and thus did not satisfy either the federalists or the functionalists. Still, it was a start on which further integration could be built.

For the rest of the 1940s, little else happened on the economic front. The cold war and the need for military cooperation led to the creation of NATO in 1949. More importantly for our purposes, to the degree that attention was paid to nonmilitary integration, the assumption was that key leadership would have to come from Britain, still Europe's leading power. But such leadership was not forthcoming.

This does not mean that the supporters of European integration gave up. In 1949, they succeeded in forming a Council of Europe that would represent the various governments. The council had little power, given that each government could veto anything it proposed. But it did provide an opportunity for national leaders to meet, and it began developing one of the key components of the later EU: an organization representing individual governments for both consultation and decision-making purposes.

The following year, Foreign Minister Robert Schuman of France issued a plan (actually written by Jean Monnet) for a supranational authority for the coal and steel industries. The two industries were chosen because they were critical to any modern economy, had been damaged heavily in the war, and were an obvious place to attempt more cooperative endeavors.

Negotiations moved swiftly, in part because Britain was not involved and because Christian Democratic and other politicians who shared pro-European views occupied key posts in most of the governments involved. France, West Germany, Italy, Belgium, Luxembourg, and the Netherlands signed a treaty establishing the **European Coal and Steel Community (ECSC).** It laid out provisions for a single market for the two products through the gradual elimination of tariffs and other barriers to trade. The treaty also created four institutions that remain, in only somewhat altered form, at the core of the EU today:

- A High Authority composed of representatives selected by the national governments who served as the administrative body for the ECSC at the supranational level

- A Special Council of Ministers, consisting of cabinet members from the individual governments charged with making policy for the ECSC

- A Court of Justice to resolve disputes arising between the ECSC and national governments or companies

- A Common Assembly consisting of delegates chosen by the national parliaments

The new community also had a degree of autonomy, because it was funded directly from fees levied against individual companies.

It is important to underscore two points here. First, these initial steps toward European integration had more to do with the cold war than with the purported benefits of cooperation. The United States believed that it needed an economically and politically strong Western Europe to help contain communism, and thus supported most early efforts at European integration, including the creation of the ECSC. Second, however small and tentative these steps may have been, the creation of the ECSC did involve the transfer of some aspects of national sovereignty to a supranational body.

The ECSC was not an overnight success. Almost immediately, member governments began squabbling over which language to use and where to locate its offices. The High Authority quickly discovered that eliminating tariffs and quotas would not be enough to create a truly common market. Still, the ECSC did live up to the functionalists' most important expectation—that support for the ECSC would expand into other sectors of the economy. By the middle of the decade, plans involving agriculture, the military, and transportation were on the table.

In mid-1955, the foreign ministers of the six member countries formed a committee headed by Paul-Henri Spaak to explore further options. In its report of March 1956, it called for a common market and an integrated approach to the new industry of nuclear power. Spaak's group then drafted the **Treaty of Rome,** which was signed by the six governments in 1957.

This treaty established two bodies—the European Economic Community (EEC) and the European Atomic Energy Commission (Euratom). Its most important provisions called for the elimination of all internal tariffs and the creation of common external ones over a period of twelve to fifteen years.

The EEC had essentially the same institutional structure as the ECSC. The High Authority was renamed the **Commission** and was assigned responsibility for representing supranational interests and for administering the EEC. Though given few formal powers, it was assumed that the Commission would also be the major source of new policies.

The **Council of Ministers** was the organ of the national governments and had to approve all policy initiatives. In those days, its members were the relevant cabinet ministers from the member states, and it met when needed. Most importantly, if a state decided it had a strong interest in an issue before the Council, it could veto it, thus requiring unanimity before the EEC could take any major step. Only a few relatively minor kinds of proposals could be passed through a system of **qualified majority voting,** which will be described later in the chapter.

The treaty increased the size of the renamed **European Parliament** and gave it the power to review activities of the Commission and Council. Nonetheless, it remained the weakest of the four main European institutions.

The **European Court of Justice (ECJ)** had seven members, one named by each government and the seventh chosen by the other six. Like members of the Commission, the justices were no longer under the direction of their own governments after their appointment. The court was responsible for seeing that the EEC itself, the member governments, and their private corporations abided by the provisions of the Treaty of Rome.

During its first decade, the EEC's primary challenge was the removal of tariffs as called for in the treaty, which it accomplished ahead of schedule. It also decided to streamline its institutions by merging the EEC and Euratom into the new European Community (EC) in 1967.

Creating the Common Market

Even in its early years, the EEC was beset by a dilemma that has been at the heart of European integration ever since: How much power should be given to the supranational institutions, and how much should remain in national hands as represented by the Council?

The difficulties came to a head in 1963 when France vetoed Denmark's and Britain's applications for membership. At a press conference, President Charles de Gaulle announced that he was for a *Europe des patries*— a Europe based on nation-states—and that Britain was not sufficiently European to join. Then, in the "empty chairs" crisis of 1965–66, the French government boycotted all decision-making sessions, which, given the unanimity rule, paralyzed the entire organization.

De Gaulle's successor, Georges Pompidou, was a far more committed European. He did not block applications from Britain, Ireland, Denmark, and Norway, which were approved in January 1972. But the Norwegian electorate then voted against joining, which meant that the EC grew to only nine members. The organization expanded again in the 1980s when Greece, Spain, and Portugal were added. It reached a total of fifteen in 1995

when Austria, Finland, and Sweden joined. Progress was made on functional fronts as well. Cyprus, the Czech Republic, Estonia, Hungary, Latvia, Lithuania, Malta, Poland, Slovakia, and Slovenia were admitted in 2004.

In terms of functions, the **Common Agricultural Policy (CAP)** was created in 1966. The **European Monetary System (EMS),** with its "snake," or band, in which all member currencies floated against each other, was initiated in 1972. The EC reached a broad-based trade-and-aid agreement with most third world countries. Members of the European Parliament were chosen in direct elections beginning in 1979. The workings of the Council were made more routine with the establishment of the **Committee of Permanent Representatives (COREPER)** from the member states.

At the same time, problems began to loom on the horizon. The generation of visionary, functionalist leaders who had played such a vital role in the creation of the ECSC and the EEC left the political scene. Their replacements were far less committed to further European integration. Their hopes also ebbed as a result of the economic slump following the OPEC oil embargo of 1973–74. As the EC proved no more able to spark continued economic growth than the individual nation-states, people began to talk about "eurosclerosis" rather than further integration.

Meanwhile, the EC itself encountered two roadblocks. First, the elimination of internal tariffs was not enough to create a single, common market. The free movement of goods and services was impeded, for example, by the regulations and standards individual governments used for industrial products or by procurement policies that required state agencies to purchase goods and services from domestic sources. Second, there had been little of the spillover effect the EC's founders had expected, and thus little new support for further economic or political integration above and beyond the expansion of its membership.

It had also become clear to a growing number of business and economic leaders that the EC would have to become more dynamic if the European economies as a whole were to take off again. That realization began a process of consultation and negotiation that eventually led to the Single European Act and the Maastricht Treaty.

The first step toward further integration came with a report prepared under the direction of Prime Minister Leo Tindemans of Belgium in 1976. Tindemans called for monetary and economic union, a common defense and foreign policy, and a joint industrial development program. Though nothing came directly from the Tindemans Report, it set an agenda for the next fifteen years.

JACQUES DELORS

Jacques Delors is generally considered the second most important person in the evolution of the EU, trailing only Jean Monnet.

Born in 1925 in a working-class neighborhood of Paris, Delors was unable to attend university because of both World War II and his father's demand that he go to work. He thus started his career as a clerical worker in a Parisian bank and came to politics through his Catholicism and the trade union movement.

From the 1950s on, he was involved in attempts to redefine what it meant to be on the left. At times this led him to work with groups to the left of the Communists, and at others to serve as an adviser to Gaullist ministers. In 1981, President Mitterrand appointed him minister of finance, from which position he was largely responsible for the U-turn of 1983 that ended the Socialists' radical reforms. Two years later, he went to Brussels as president of the Commission.

He retired after two terms and resisted attempts to draft him as the Socialist candidate for president of France. He remains an avid soccer fan. His daughter, Martine Aubry, was slated to be the next leader of the French Socialist Party until her surprise defeat in the 2002 legislative elections.

Former president of the European Commission Jacques Delors at a press conference in 1989.

© Reuters/Bettmann/CORBIS

Pressures to move forward were intensified when Hans-Dietrich Genscher and Emilio Colombo, the foreign ministers of Germany and Italy, respectively, issued their own report advocating the strengthening of European institutions.

Progress was accelerated, too, by the appointment of **Jacques Delors** as president of the Commission in 1985. Delors had been France's minister of finance and one of President Mitterrand's closest advisers. The appointment of someone of that stature reflected the new life being breathed into European integration.

All those efforts culminated in the Council's passage of the **Single European Act (SEA)** in December 1985. Although the Council did not go as far as some had wanted, its actions in three areas widened the scope of the EC's powers at the expense of national governments.

First and foremost, the SEA introduced provisions for the completion of what is now called the internal market. As noted earlier, the abolition of internal tariffs and quotas did not remove all barriers to trade. In all, the

Commission estimated that rules and regulations would have to be written in at least three hundred areas before there could be truly free trade of goods and services across the borders of the member states. The Commission estimated that it would take seven years to draft and ratify all those documents, thus creating the popular image of "Europe 1992."

Second, the SEA introduced a number of changes in the way the EC was run. The most important of these was a sharp cutback in the use of the **unanimity principle.** After 1985, unanimity would be needed only when determining whether new members should be admitted and when embarking on wholly new policy initiatives. Otherwise, the EC would employ the easier qualified majority procedures.

The final provisions of the SEA dealt with political cooperation. It regularized the semiannual summit meetings of the national leaders and the links between the Council and the Commission and European Parliament (discussed later in the chapter). The SEA also called for more cooperation in determining foreign policy in general and national security policy in particular, though it did little to specify exactly how that should take place.

The SEA by no means unified the EC. It remained primarily an economic union that had little or no authority regarding social, environmental, and political issues. In most ways, national sovereignty had not been challenged. Even in the economic arena, the all-important issue of monetary and financial integration had barely been addressed.

The drive toward further deepening occurred while the bureaucrats were filling in the details of the SEA. Delors continued to symbolize the enthusiasm many felt about the new Europe. The events that swept the Continent in 1989 made a strong Europe all the more desirable. Power was increasingly defined economically while Eastern Europe would need billions of dollars to make the transition from communism to capitalism. Finally, the departure of Margaret Thatcher in 1990 removed the leader who was most skeptical of further expansion of the EC's power, which she had labeled "eurononsense."

This momentum led to the signing of the **Maastricht Treaty** in December 1991. The treaty gave what was now officially called the European Union authority to act in new areas, including monetary policy, foreign affairs, national security, fisheries, transportation, the environment, health, justice, education, consumer protection, and tourism. It also formally established the idea of three pillars and European citizenship, which means that people can work in any member country and vote in European parliamentary and local elections. All but Britain agreed to harmonize their labor relations and social service policies. In an attempt to appease the concerns of many national politicians, the treaty also endorsed the principle of **subsidiarity,** which holds that the EU should only act in areas in which policy goals cannot be achieved by national or subnational governments and are more likely to be reached at the supranational level. Most importantly, it committed the EU to the single currency and central bank.

For most of the rest of the 1990s, the EU fell on harder times. Europe suffered a serious recession, which reinforced qualms about the EU and put talk of further deepening on hold. The costs of German unification, the EU's inability to end the fighting in the former Yugoslavia, internal divisions over most major issues, and uncertainties about the euro reinforced the sense of "eurosclerosis" similar to that in the years before Delors moved to Brussels.

Ironically, the EU's troubles began with the Maastricht Treaty itself. At first, everyone assumed it would be ratified easily. However, the Danish voters rejected it in a referendum, and ratification debates dragged on in Britain and Germany. Despite the support of all mainstream politicians, a referendum on the treaty barely squeaked through in France. Great Britain and Denmark eventually did ratify it, but only after provisions were approved that would allow them to "opt out" of the social chapter and single currency.

The EU also had trouble finding a leader to succeed Delors, whose second term as president of the Commission ended in early 1995. After a long process that included a British veto of everyone else's first choice, Belgian Prime Minister Jean-Luc Dehaene, the members chose a little-known former prime minister of Luxembourg, Jacques Santer. Although a committed European, Santer lacked Delors' charisma and clout, and his selection was widely seen as a sign that few major initiatives would be forthcoming under his leadership.

The leadership situation was muddied with publication of the European Parliament's study of mismanagement and corruption by the Commission in March 1999. No individual commissioners were accused of wrongdoing. Nonetheless, all twenty commissioners decided to resign, provoking what many thought would be a major setback.

In practice, the crisis turned out to be nothing of the sort. Within days, an agreement was reached. The outgoing commission would stay in office in a caretaker capacity, much as a cabinet that lost a vote of confidence would in any of the member states. A week later, the fifteen governments agreed on a successor to Santer—former Italian prime minister Romano Prodi, who would take over with a full complement of new commissioners when the old one's term expired at the start of 2000.

The EU also adopted two new treaties, whose impact we will explore in more detail in the sections on governance and public policy. A 1997 treaty extended the Schengen agreement, which eliminates most border controls inside the EU, and gave the EU more responsibility over legal matters, including issuing residence permits to immigrants, determining asylum procedures, and promulgating directives on judicial cooperation across borders. Most importantly, the Amsterdam accord acknowledged that the EU viewed NATO as the dominant security organization in Europe while reinforcing its desire to chart its own foreign policy in other areas, including the creation of a rapid deployment force to use in humanitarian emergencies.

At the December 2000 summit, the leaders of the member states reached an agreement, which they signed in early 2001. The **Treaty of Nice** is vital because it opened the door to the enlargement of 2004 and future expansion. It also outlined provisional plans for reforming the EU's institutions so they could function effectively with as many as thirty members, including the possibility of enacting a constitution.

Political Culture and Participation in the EU

The chapters on individual countries all have extended sections on political culture and participation. This one does not simply because they are not (yet) very important to politics in the EU in at least two respects.

First, it is hard to even speak of a European political culture. There is little widespread identification with "Europe." As will become clearer through counterexamples in the chapters on the former Soviet Union and the third world, in countries with stable, legitimate regimes, most people have a strong sense of national identification.

Although there is growing recognition that the EU plays an important role in people's lives, there are still very few people for whom the statement "I am a European" is anywhere near as important as "I am French" (or German, or whatever). Younger, better-educated people who have traveled extensively are the most "European," but even they tend to put their national identity ahead of any transnational one.

Second, the key organizations linking people to the state have not put down very deep roots at the European level. Parties in the European Parliament are organized along transnational lines (for example, socialists from all twenty-five states form a single group and sit together). Other than that, partisan life remains almost exclusively national in orientation. Voters tend to use national issues and criteria in making up their minds about how to vote in European elections. That was never clearer than in the 2004 elections for the European Parliament, when almost every governing party suffered a huge defeat due to national political reasons that had little to do with Europe.

Most interest groups, too, remain nationally oriented, even those that maintain lobbying operations in Brussels. Some trade organizations have successfully worked across national lines, but they are almost exclusively businesses run on a Europe-wide basis to begin with. Most other groups, especially trade unions, have found it difficult to present a common front either in their protests in the streets or their "inside-the-system" efforts with the Commission.

The lack of intensive public involvement in the EU has given rise to what critics call its **democratic deficit.**

Conflict and Democratization in the EU

IT SAYS SOMETHING about the EU in comparison with the countries covered in Part 2 that we can treat the topics of conflict and democratization in the EU so quickly.

The EU has always been of primary interest to elites. Although its institutions provide some opportunities for public involvement, it does not have the formal mechanisms for public accountability we find in democratic states. And, of course, it incorporates a much larger population.

That said, the EU provokes surprisingly little interest—and hence conflict—among its citizens. This may change as the euro makes the EU an inescapable part of everyone's life. Also, any further deepening of the EU's powers likely will require greater involvement and more active support from rank and file voters.

It is entirely possible that the perceived lack of democracy will generate public protests in the not-so-distant future. As the EU's powers expand, as it has to cope with the political and economic differences between its old members and its new ones, and as it tries to figure out how to create a multispeed Europe, conflict between citizens and elites could emerge.

With nearly 500 million citizens, the EU's population is exceeded only by those of China and India. What's more, these citizens have at most an indirect role in determining who sits on its most important decision-making bodies. A growing number of Europeans are coming to resent the power of EU institutions and their own seeming inability to hold them accountable—something we have seen in most recent national referenda, in which the anti-European vote has been much higher than most analysts expected.

The lack of European-ness is also indirectly reflected in the mass media, through which people learn about political life at the national and supranational level. Attempts have been made to create everything from Europe-wide soap operas to political newspapers. The only real success story is Eurosport, a satellite TV provider that sends out a single video feed of mostly second-tier events with audio channels in all the major languages. There are two different television systems—PAL (used in Britain, Germany, and the Netherlands, among others) and SECAM (used in France and Spain most notably). Viewers with televisions that use one cannot watch programs on the other, even with dishes that can reach satellites serving stations using both standards. Although people can get all the major European newspapers in most cities and can have them delivered to their homes, the fact remains that these papers are all nationally based.

One of the key causes of the lack of European identification and the failure to create European political institutions is the language gap. All official documents are published in twenty languages. Many Europeans speak a second or even a third language, but there is no common language that more than 20 percent of them are comfortable using. Further, that language is English, and there is strong resistance in France and elsewhere toward adopting it or any other single tongue.

The European State?

This section begins with a question mark, because political scientists debate whether the EU is a state. Most argue that it is not, because it lacks an army and a police force to maintain order and ensure that the rule of law is enforced. That said, the EU has many other features of a state. It has formal institutions that do the same things as the ones we saw in Britain, France, and Germany—enact laws and issue decrees that are binding on the member states, their citizens, and their corporations.

The best way to get past the debate is to view the EU in terms of what international relations scholars call "multilevel governance." From that perspective, the EU has some of the characteristics of a state, but not all of them. More importantly, the degree to which it is "state-like"—or, conversely, the degree to which the member states retain the bulk of their power—varies from time to time and issue to issue. In particular, the EU is most like a state in exercising sovereign power in the economic pillar. However, the states still wield most of the power in major new initiatives and in the few remaining policy areas in which unanimity is required.

The Commission

The most *European* institution is the Commission. The word *European* is emphasized here because the Commission has been the most important body in sustaining and expanding the EU's authority. The responsibility for actually making the most important decisions lies elsewhere, but the Commission initiates most new programs and is responsible for implementing them once they are enacted.

Until 2004, the Commission had twenty members who served renewable five-year terms. Britain, France,

TABLE 7.3 Presidents of the European Commission

START OF TERM	NAME
1958	Walter Hallstein
1967	Jean Rey
1970	Franco-Maria Malfatti
1972	Sicco Mansholt
1973	Francois-Xavier Ortoli
1977	Roy Jenkins
1981	Gaston Thorn
1985	Jacques Delors
1995	Jacques Santer
2000	Romano Prodi
2004	Jose Manuel Barroso

Germany, Italy, and Spain each had two commissioners. Traditionally, one of them comes from the governing party or coalition, and the other from the opposition. The other ten countries had one commissioner each.

With the 2004 expansion, the Commission was expanded to twenty-five members, one from each country. Once more countries are added, the total number of commissioners will be reduced to twenty, with states sending members on a rotating basis.

Commissioners are nominated by their home governments and are approved by qualified majority voting in the Council. One commissioner serves as president and, in recent years, has been the most visible leader in all the European institutions. (See table 7.3.)

Once on the Commission, the members swear an oath of allegiance to the EU and are not supposed to take instructions from their national government. Most commissioners are prominent politicians in their home countries, and their independence of the home country is often questioned. For example, the British commissioner who took office in October 2004 is Peter Mandelson, one of Prime Minister Tony Blair's closest friends and advisors. At times, the European orientation of the commissioners has posed problems, as when Margaret Thatcher refused to reappoint Lord Cockfield because he had been the architect of the detailed plans to implement the Single European Act (SEA), which the British prime minister did not like.

The Commission is the permanent executive of the EU. It supervises the work of the twenty-two directorates-general and eight services, which roughly correspond with the purview of a traditional national cabinet. (See table 7.4.) Each directorate is managed by a commissioner, who is, in turn, aided by a senior European civil servant and a small personal staff.

The Commission supervises the work of about 2,500 high-ranking civil servants and another 20,000 staff members. Some of these men and women are on loan from their national governments, but the overwhelming

▌ **TABLE 7.4** Directorates–General of the European Union as of 2004

Agriculture	External Affairs
Competition	Development
Economic and Financial Affairs	Enlargement
Education and Culture	External Relations
Employment and Social Affairs	Taxation and Customs
Energy and Transport	Union
Enterprises	
Environment	
Fisheries	
Health and Consumer Protection	
Information Society	
Internal Market	
Joint Research Center	
Justice and Home Affairs	
Regional Policy	
Research	
Taxation and Customs Union	

Thierry Tronnel /CORBIS

Jose Manuel Barroso

majority are permanent EU employees on career tracks reminiscent of the French ENArques and the German *Beamten*.

The Commission is also important in the policy-making process. On a day-to-day basis, its primary job is to make rules that spell out the details of European policy, as in the more than three hundred documents it had to draft to put the principles of the SEA into effect. Commission drafts immediately have the force of law in some minor and technical policy areas. Otherwise, its drafts have to be approved by the Council and the Parliament.

The Commission's most important job is the initiation of proposed legislation or directives. The Treaty of Rome and later agreements gave it the exclusive right to put new policy proposals on the EU's agenda. Although agenda setting is by no means the same as the ability to pass legislation, the Commission has used this power to become the driving force behind the initiatives that strengthened the EU's supranational authority.

The Commission may indeed resemble a national cabinet, but we should not push that analogy too far. In particular, because its members are chosen by twenty-five quite different governments, there is far more diversity and disagreement than we would expect in a national executive.

The Commission inevitably reflects the personality, style, and preferences of its president. Under Delors, the Commission assembled a staff of dynamic young civil servants who helped push through his agenda, often against the wishes of reluctant fellow commissioners, let alone national governments.

Perhaps in response to Delors' impact, the governments of the member states (especially Great Britain) were reluctant to choose a successor who would be anywhere near as prominent or dynamic. Neither of his first two successors, Jacques Santer and Romano Prodi, had that kind of dramatic impact, and it is hard to tell if the next president of the Commission, **Jose Manuel Barroso** will be able to restore its prominence (ue.eu.int).

The Council

If the Commission represents the growing supranational nature of the EU, the Council of Ministers demonstrates the continued power of the states. The Council now consists of two institutions. The presidency of each rotates from country to country every six months. That government's representative chairs each Council meeting, represents the EU at diplomatic functions, and makes all its public pronouncements. That system will change with ratification of the constitution. At that point, the presidency will be assumed by a troika (from the Russian word for three) of countries serving eighteen months each, with one leaving every six months. It is hoped that this arrangement will give more continuity to the presidency. The constitution would also create a separate (and largely symbolic) President of the European Union and a Foreign Minister who would take responsibility for the current work of the commissioners in charge of external affairs.

The various ministers and other representatives of the national governments meet as needed to make policy decisions. The foreign ministers meet monthly as the General Affairs Council, as do the finance ministers in Ecofin (Economic and Financial Council). For other meetings, each government designates one of its members to attend, determined by the issue on the agenda. For instance, when the Council dealt with the mad cow disease crisis in the second half of the 1990s, the governments sent their agriculture ministers. The work of the Council is supported by the COREPER (Committee of Permanent Representatives), a group of national civil servants who work in Brussels for their national governments.

In addition, the national chief executives meet every six months as the European Council. Sometimes these meetings are simply opportunities for general discussions. But they have also become the forum at which major new initiatives and reforms to the treaties that gave rise to the EU and its institutions are adopted. The European Council was the body that approved the adoption of the constitution in July 2004.

The Council is at the heart of the EU's legislative process. The Commission initiates most EU legislation, but its proposals become law only after they have been passed by the Council. Since passage of the Single European Act, the Council has to share most of its decision-making power with the Parliament and Commission (see figure 7.1) and can override parliamentary objections only if it acts unanimously. Nonetheless, its approval is needed for any new legislation.

▌ TABLE 7.5 Size and Voting Power in the EU: 2004

COUNTRY	POPULATION IN MILLIONS	SEATS IN EUROPEAN PARLIAMENTS	VOTES IN QUALIFIED MAJORITY VOTING
Germany	82.0	99	10
United Kingdom	59.4	78	10
France	59.1	78	10
Italy	57.7	78	10
Spain	39.4	54	8
Poland	38.6	54	8
Netherlands	15.8	27	5
Greece	10.6	24	5
Czech Republic	10.3	24	5
Belgium	10.2	22	5
Hungary	10.0	22	5
Portugal	9.9	22	5
Sweden	8.9	19	4
Austria	8.1	18	4
Slovakia	5.4	14	3
Denmark	5.4	14	3
Finland	5.2	14	3
Ireland	3.7	13	3
Lithuania	3.7	13	3
Latvia	2.4	9	3
Slovenia	2.0	7	3
Estonia	1.4	7	3
Cyprus	0.8	6	2
Luxembourg	0.4	6	2
Malta	0.4	5	2

▌ FIGURE 7.1 Decision Making in the EU

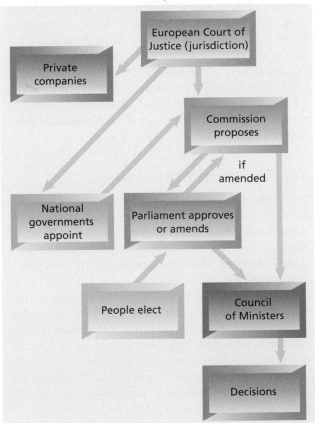

The unanimity principle that often paralyzed the EEC early in its history has been eliminated except with regard to the most dramatic new initiatives and the addition of new members. Otherwise, the Council uses qualified majority voting. Each country is assigned a number of votes in rough proportion to its share of the EU population, which it casts as a bloc. (See table 7.5.) Of the current 124 votes, 88 are needed to create a qualified majority. Therefore, 37 are enough to block new initiatives. The system tends to overrepresent the smaller countries to keep large states from dominating, but it is difficult to pass legislation without the support of two or three of the big countries.

This cumbersome system was one of the obstacles to the adoption of the constitution. Once it is ratified, a majority will be defined as a vote in which at least 55 percent of the states representing at least 65 percent of the total EU population supports a proposal. In practice, the full European Council rarely votes, but operates by consensus instead.

The European Court of Justice

The EU has a powerful judiciary. A Court of First Instance hears cases in much the way a superior court in the United States or Crown court in the United Kingdom does. There is also a Court of Auditors that deals with the EU's finances. And the Amsterdam and Nice treaties have provisions for the creation of specialized courts to deal with highly technical issues in narrow subject areas (www.curia.eu.int/en/transitpage.htm).

But we can restrict our attention to the European Court of Justice (ECJ). Its decisions have frequently made major expansion of the EU's authority possible. Even more importantly, its actions have limited national sovereignty in favor of the EU's institutions. As such, it has more sweeping powers than the judiciaries in all but a handful of the world's states.

Each government appoints one member to the ECJ. The court rarely meets with all of its judges presiding. Instead, it sits in smaller "chambers" for all but the most important cases. It also has nine advocates-general who aid it in its work. No votes or dissenting opinions are published.

The ECJ has a broad jurisdiction and hears over four hundred cases in a typical year. The Council, Commission, and Parliament can challenge each others' actions. Member states can contest EU laws and regulations. Individuals and firms can sue the EU. However, states can bring cases against each other only if the claimant can show it has been directly harmed. Over the years, the court has overturned actions by all the EU institutions, all member states, and hundreds of private companies and individuals.

Early on, the ECJ decided that it practiced constitutional law, which meant that its decisions would have more clout than those of traditional international tribunals or most national courts, which lacked the power of judicial review. This authority is based on the court's assertion that, in ratifying the Treaty of Rome and subsequent accords, the states relinquished some of their sovereignty. The court has consistently held that European law (as passed by the Council) and regulations (as promulgated by the Commission) take precedence over national law. In other words, when the two come in conflict, it is EU law that is upheld and enforced.

Among the most important and illustrative of the court's decisions was the Cassis de Dijon case of 1979 that opened the legal door to both the SEA and Maastricht. Cassis is a liqueur that, when combined with white wine, makes the smooth, sweet, and potent drink known as kir. It is made only near the city of Dijon in France. A German firm wanted to import cassis, but the national government banned it on the grounds that under German law it contained too little alcohol to qualify as a liqueur but too much to be considered a wine. The court found for the importer, ruling that if cassis met French standards for a liqueur it should qualify under Germany's as well and that bans based on such arbitrary differences constituted an illegal barrier to trade. The court thereby introduced the idea of "mutual recognition," which holds that, except under the most unusual of circumstances, member states must recognize the standards used by other countries. This meant that the Commission could avoid the hugely cumbersome task of harmonizing standards across national lines and simply assert that, if one national government ruled that a good or service met its standards, it had to be accepted by all of them.

A more recent ruling with broad (if less political) ramifications came in 1995. Jean-Marc Bosman, a mediocre Belgian soccer player whose contract was expiring, wanted to move to a new team in France, much like a free agent in American sports. But his old team and the Belgian football authorities denied him the right to do so. Bosman took his case to the ECJ, arguing that the so-called transfer restrictions violated the provisions of the Maastricht Treaty regarding the free movement of labor within the EU. The court ruled in Bosman's favor and, in one fell swoop, threw out not only the rules restricting the freedom of players to move but also the ones limiting the number of foreigners who could play for a team at any one time. The wealthiest teams in England, Spain, Italy, and Germany immediately went on spending sprees, signing up players from around the EU. The impact of the decision was obvious to anyone who watched London's Chelsea play Rome's Atalanta in the 2000–2001 Champions League. Chelsea did not have a single player who was born or raised in the United Kingdom on its starting team. What it did have was more Italians (four) than Atalanta!

The European Parliament

One reason that scholars and politicians worry about the democratic deficit is that the Parliament is by far the weakest institution in the EU. As we saw earlier, the ECSC had a Common Assembly, which was renamed the European Parliament with the formation of the EEC (www.europarl.eu.int).

Part of its weakness lies in its original composition. Until 1979, members of Parliament, or MEPs, were chosen by national governments. Thus, they tended to act as emissaries from their states, docilely voting as the leadership back home wanted.

Since then, the MEPs have been directly elected, and the powers of the Parliament have grown. The SEA also gave the Parliament more influence by creating a co-

The European Parliament meeting in its new building in Brussels. The EP actually meets in both Brussels and Strasbourg, France. Note the large number of empty seats, which is typical of EP sessions.

operation procedure—now known as **codecision**—for most legislation. It obliges the Council and Commission to consult the Parliament in two stages. First, when the Commission proposes a new initiative, the Parliament must give its opinion on it. If the Council agrees with the Parliament, the proposed directive (which will be called a law under the Constitution), is adopted. If not, the Parliament must be consulted again, at which point one of three things can occur:

- If the Parliament agrees or takes no action within three months, the Council's bill is adopted

- If the Parliament proposes amendments, they must be considered by the Commission within a month

- If the Parliament rejects the Council's position outright, the Council can only adopt the initiative if it votes to do so unanimously

The architects of the SEA and the Maastricht Treaty understood that the powers of the Parliament would have to be increased if the EU were to achieve widespread legitimacy. Thus, the Parliament now has the right to approve all nominees to the Commission and can remove the entire Commission if a vote of censure passes by a two-thirds margin. The Parliament also has to approve the budget.

As it did for the Council, the Treaty of Nice makes provisions for changes in the size of Parliament and spells out the number of seats each country will have.

The total size of the body eventually will rise to a permanent 732 seats. Because most of the new member states will join during the life of the Parliament elected in 2004, it is assumed that the number of seats will actually break the 732 barrier as even more members join, most likely in 2007. The total number will drop back to 732 with the 2009 election.

The Complexity of EU Decision Making

Policy making in the EU is more complex and confusing than in any of the individual countries we have considered so far for two main reasons. First, the EU has to reconcile the interests of its twenty-five member states with those that transcend national boundaries. Second, the various EU institutions are even more fragmented and independent of each other than those in the United States, where the separation and division of power makes coherent decision making difficult.

The EU's steps forward have occurred when the interests of the major nations and its own institutions coincide as they did in the months leading up to the signing of the Maastricht Treaty. When those interests diverge—as has often been the case since Maastricht—it becomes more difficult for European integration to proceed.

This complexity is also a reflection of the fact that the EU is still being built, which makes it quite different from the national states covered in the rest of Part 2. In some areas (for example, trade), European institutions and practices are fairly well developed; in others (for example, defense and social policy), they are not.

Next Steps?

Assuming the constitution passes, the European Union will have reached a political "plateau" from which further broadening or deepening seem unlikely for the foreseeable future.

Bulgaria, Romania, and Turkey have applications pending, and they may be allowed to join in 2007. There is little question that other countries in the former Soviet Union or former Yugoslavia would like to enter the EU as well, but even the three states with pending applications may have a hard time qualifying. The criteria laid out in the 1997 **Treaty of Amsterdam** require:

- Establishment of a functioning and stable democratic regime

- Adoption of a market-oriented capitalist economy

- Acceptance of the *acquis communautaire,* the eighty thousand pages of laws and regulations already on the EU's books

Further deepening seems even more problematic. There undoubtedly will be some tinkering to strengthen the internal market and perhaps even expand the Schengen provisions, which eliminate internal borders and harmonize judicial systems. The Constitution could add some new institutions that would streamline EU decision making.

However, the next truly important step in building what could potentially be a "United States of Europe" would be the commitment to a common foreign and security policy—the third pillar of the post-Maastricht EU. As noted at the beginning of the chapter, the EU is committed to that on paper. But establishing a common foreign and security policy has not been easy, to say the least.

Some progress has been made. The EU is creating a rapid deployment force that could intervene in humanitarian disasters such as those that devastated the former Yugoslavia in the 1990s. It has also made great strides in determining how it can coordinate its activities with NATO, the OSCE, and other bodies whose membership overlaps with, but is the same as, the EU's.

However, as the debates within Europe over the war in Iraq showed us, the European states view their national interests differently. France and Germany, most notably, opposed the United States. The United Kingdom, Italy, and Spain supported the Bush administration,

though Spain pulled out after a socialist victory at the polls following the 11 March 2004 terrorist attack there. In other words, in areas like foreign policy where deepening has not progressed as far as it has with the economy, national governments and their desires are likely to trump community-wide ones for decades to come.

The EU and National Sovereignty

For the purposes of a comparative politics course, the most important question to ask about the EU is whether it could supplant the state as the primary actor determining public policy and the broader ways in which people are governed. Here, too, the answer is ambiguous.

It is tempting to follow the lead of most international relations experts and argue that the EU has not undermined national sovereignty. This certainly is true if we focus on questions of national security and the "high politics" that have long been at the heart of that branch of political science.

However, if we focus instead on economic or social policy, the EU seems a lot more powerful. In those areas, its powers certainly limit the freedom of member states to make and enforce their own policies.

The study of the EU can become quite complex, and exploring its powers in many areas requires mastering a welter of acronyms and technical detail. To avoid that confusing detail yet still illustrate the main point here, consider two policy areas dealing with food. These issues may not seem all that important but they do reveal the kinds of day-to-day power the EU can exercise over its members.

The first involves chocolate. As part of its goal of creating a single market, the EU has devised common standards for thousands of goods and services. In 1973 it therefore issued Directive 73-241 on the "harmonization" of chocolate recipes. As one British observer put it:

> **This directive was drawn up in the early, heady days of European integration, when European leaders believed that all products must be harmonised in every member state if the single market was to operate properly. All food had to be made to the same specification. Drawing up a European chocolate recipe meant agreeing on rules on such ingredients as vegetable and cocoa fat. Directive 73-241 declared that chocolate shall be: "the product obtained from cocoa nib, cocoa mass, cocoa powder and sucrose, with or without added cocoa butter, having, without prejudice to the definition of chocolate vermicelli, gianduja nut chocolate and converture chocolate, a minimum total dry cocoa solids**

content of 35 percent—at least 34 percent of non-fat cocoa solids and 18 percent of cocoa butter—these weights to be calculated after the weight of the additions provided for in paragraph five and six have been deducted.[1]

Chocolate became a problem because candy manufacturers in Britain and a few other countries did not meet those standards, and British consumers liked their chocolate with less cocoa nib. After a brief tiff, the European bureaucrats allowed the British to "opt out" of these requirements, and there was something of a two-tiered chocolate market for the next twenty years.

In the mid-1990s, the chocolate controversy reared its ugly head once again. French and Belgian chocolatiers claimed that inferior and cheaper British candy was undermining their markets. They threatened to go to the ECJ and demand a ruling forcing the British companies to use the term "vegolate" instead. The court put an end to the case by invoking the mutual recognition principle to allow the British to continue selling their products as chocolate.

Second, in one of the most controversial recent moves, the EU banned the export of British beef in 1996. Over the previous decade, thousands of British cows had come down with BSE, known to most citizens by its nickname—mad cow disease. In March 1996, the British government published research findings that linked BSE with Creutzfeld-Jakob disease (CJD), which is fatal to humans. The announcement touched off a furor on both sides of the English Channel. Within days the Council voted to ban the sale of British beef first in the other fourteen EU countries and then in the rest of the world. The British government was furious, because no more than fifteen people had come down with CJD. Moreover, British agriculture minister Quentin Hogg (the pundits had great fun with his name) vainly tried to devise a plan to slaughter up to a million cows in an attempt to eradicate the disease and the political and public reaction to it. Meanwhile, governments on the Continent began insisting on instituting every safeguard imaginable before allowing British beef back on the market.

Negotiations dragged on into 1999, even though there was virtually no chance that anyone could actually contract CJD. Nonetheless, politicians on the Continent, leery of public opinion at home, kept the ban in place. Finally, when the cull of the herds had been completed so that no cow born before 1996 could enter the food chain, the Commission lifted the ban.

---

[1] Sarah Helm, "The Woman From Mars," *Prospect (UK).* March 1996, 21.

Public Policy in the EU

The EU has pursued a wide range of policies, from supporting research on high technology to sponsoring student exchanges. Here, we will focus on two of them that illustrate what the EU has done in a more general way than the debate over chocolate or beef—the creation of an integrated internal market and the Common Agricultural Policy (CAP). The two also highlight what are seen by most observers as the EU's greatest accomplishment and its greatest failure.

The Internal Market

The EU's most significant achievement has been the creation of what is, for all intents and purposes, a single internal market. Economics has always been a top priority for the EU, because its architects assumed that economic cooperation would be the lynchpin to all other policy goals.

The most important policy and strategy for creating the single market has been the removal of tariffs and other barriers to trade. The Treaty of Rome began a decade-long process of elimination of all internal tariffs. The Single European Act (SEA) did the same for the remaining obstacles.

Most of those barriers were technical in nature, but also very easy for the average consumer to see. Truckers, for example, could spend hours filling out paperwork or having their cargoes inspected before they were allowed to enter another country. Although it may be hard to believe, such administrative rules and regulations added as much as 10 percent to the cost of transporting goods across national borders.

Similarly, each country imposed its own standards of quality on goods sold in its market, which frequently blocked imports from other EU countries despite the elimination of all tariffs. The same held for professional licenses, which meant that doctors, lawyers, beauticians, and so on could work only in the country in which they were trained. National governments erected barriers to free trade by following procurement policies that gave the edge to domestic firms whose sales accounted for nearly 10 percent of the EU's total production of goods and services.

The SEA was designed to eliminate internal border checks, although this practice has not been fully implemented because of a few countries' fears regarding immigration and drug trafficking. Most goods that meet the standards of one country are assumed to meet the standards of all—as in the case of the chocolate/vegolate

Liberalization in the EU

THE EU HAS long been a champion of liberal economic policies. It has never had to deal with privatization directly, because it has never owned any businesses. Moreover, it has rarely urged member states to sell off the ones they own.

That said, it has regularly pushed for more open and competitive economies, which, of course, is in the very nature of a common market. Throughout its history, it has pursued antimonopoly policies that would be familiar to Americans who have studied their country's antitrust laws. In recent years, it has required states to cut subsidies to their companies, especially state-owned monopolies such as national airlines and telecommunications systems.

dispute. The same is now true for most professional licenses—though not for lawyers, reflecting the continued differences among national legal systems. Financial institutions are free to invest and loan money throughout the EU.

The reasons for moving to a fully open internal market were most clearly laid out in a report for the Commission prepared by the economist Paolo Cecchini in 1988. His study predicted that these and other policies would lead to increased private investment, higher productivity, lower costs, and reduced prices. European industry, in turn, would be more profitable, stimulating more growth, jobs, and government revenue.

In the short run, "Europe 1992" fell short of those expectations. The recession of the early 1990s slowed growth everywhere. Cecchini could not have anticipated the political changes that would sweep Europe and divert billions of dollars from the EU and its member states eastward. Still, there seems to be little question that the removal of all barriers in the long term had the kind of impact the framers of the SEA had in mind.

This impact is evident in the explosion of transnational enterprises facilitated by the easing of these restrictions. The EU is not always a major actor in these endeavors, but the opening of the market itself has made the ones described here and dozens of others feasible in the first place. Airbus, for example, is a joint effort on the part of French, German, Spanish, and British companies that make commercial jet airplanes and now is Boeing's only serious competitor. In the automobile industry, Fiat forged close links with Peugeot, and in 1999 Ford bought Volvo. In 1985 the Commission established Eureka, a joint research and development program aimed

at creating technologies to compete with Japanese and U.S. firms in computers, telecommunications, and other high-tech areas. By 1991 the Commission had funded over five hundred projects involving more than three thousand companies in nineteen European nations.

The internationalization of European firms within the EU seems to have led them to be more aggressive globally as well. The most notable example is the tremendous increase in European investment in the United States. To cite but a few prominent examples, Renault bought Mack Trucks; Michelin acquired Uniroyal Goodrich, making it the largest tire manufacturer in the world; and Britain's Martin Sorrell purchased two of America's largest advertising agencies, the Ogilvy Group and J. Walter Thompson, and public relations giant Hill and Knowlton.

For our purposes, though, the important thing to understand about the policies creating the single market is that they have had a tremendous impact on both European governments and their citizens. States now have far less control over what is made and sold within their borders. Of course, policy differences remain from country to country. Britain, for example, still imposes higher taxes on liquor than France and has strict rules regarding the import of pets into the country. Such examples aside, the national governments have ceded much of their control over microeconomic policy.

The single market has expanded the options available to consumers. German supermarket shoppers can now purchase French wine, Italian pasta, and Spanish oranges more cheaply than before the trade barriers came down. French consumers find that Rovers, Fiats, or Volkswagens are now as affordable as Renaults, Citroëns, or Peugeots. In the early 1990s, thousands of unemployed British construction workers fled their recession-plagued country and found work rebuilding the infrastructure of the former East Germany.

Monetary union proved to be the key to the further integration of the European economy. From the Treaty of Rome on, the more visionary European leaders looked to monetary union as the next big step toward a more integrated Europe. To see why, think about what the United States would be like if the states had their own currencies. It would be all but impossible for the federal government to coordinate economic policy, and it would be costly and complicated for companies to carry out transactions across state lines.

Monetary union, however, was a long time coming. The first significant steps were taken in 1979 with the creation of a European Monetary System (EMS) with two broad features. First, it created the European Currency Unit (ECU), which was used in international business transactions. A consumer could not withdraw ECUs from a bank and use them to buy, say, an MP3 player. The ECU existed purely for accounting purposes and enabled companies to avoid paying commissions charged for converting funds from one currency to another. It also established the Exchange Rate Mechanism (ERM), whereby all the currencies floated together in global markets. In its "snake," no currency was allowed to move more than 5 percent above or below the ERM average. If a currency was heading in that direction, the national central banks would intervene in financial markets to bring it back into line.

The reforms did help. The ECU simplified business dealings and reduced the substantial costs that accompany frequent currency conversions. The ERM gave a degree of predictability to European financial markets so that, for example, Fiat in Italy could be reasonably certain how many francs or pesetas, as well as how many lire, it could get for its cars.

The actual creation of a single currency took another twenty years. The key is not simply that the national currencies were replaced by the euro in 2002. Additionally, the **European Monetary Union (EMU)** gives the EU and its new central bank powerful levers they can exert over national governments.

Previously, governments determined their own fiscal and monetary policies—in particular, setting basic interest rates for lenders and savers. Now that power has largely been transferred to European authorities, who set a common rate for countries with economies as diverse as Germany's and Poland's.

So far, debate on the EMU has focused largely on whether it makes sense economically—an issue far beyond the scope of this chapter. Here, it is enough to see that it will have a tremendous impact on the balance of political power in at least two ways. First, it will strengthen the EU as a whole, because the euro is already one of the world's three leading currencies along with the dollar and the yen. Second, it provides yet another area in which national governments are de facto ceding some of their sovereignty to a supranational body over which they will have relatively little day-to-day control.

This is one of the reasons opposition to the EMU grew during the mid-1990s. For many political leaders, especially in Britain, the local currency is an important symbol of national pride, and abandoning it is seen as an unacceptable loss of national sovereignty.

Perhaps most importantly, now that the EMU is in place, there may be no going back. Nothing in political life is irreversible or permanent, but it is difficult to imagine the twelve initial members abandoning the euro and reintroducing their own currencies. The same is true for the ten countries that joined the EU in 2004.

The single market has not benefited all Europeans. Increased competitive pressures have forced hundreds of inefficient firms into bankruptcy, leading to at least temporary unemployment for their workers.

Nonetheless, there is little doubt that the EU has made a considerable contribution to economic growth since 1957. Among other things, a 1999 Commission report suggested that the single market was responsible for creating as many as 900,000 jobs, adding as much as 1.5 percent to per-capita income, reducing inflation by a similar amount, and increasing trade in goods and direct foreign investment in the EU by about 15 percent each.

Its contribution may be even more important in some less visible policy arenas, as we saw in the discussion of the Bosman ruling. I was fortunate enough to live and teach in England from 1995 to 1998. Because of the EU, I was able to have any major European newspaper delivered to my doorstep each morning. According to the owner of the corner store that supplied the papers, citizens of fourteen of the then fifteen member states were living in our village of less than three thousand residents. Because EU students pay the equivalent of in-state tuition anywhere in the Union, I had students in my classes from France, Greece, Spain, Finland, Denmark, Germany, Portugal, Ireland, Italy, and Belgium, as well as the United Kingdom, which made teaching highly enjoyable.

The Common Agricultural Policy

Not everything the EU has done has been successful. The Common Agricultural Policy (CAP), in particular, is now the subject of virtually universal criticism. *The Economist* went so far as to call it the "single most idiotic system of economic mismanagement that the rich western countries have ever devised."[2]

The CAP reflects two important political dynamics. First, it demonstrates how pressure put on member states can lead to policies that tend to impede a free market and that also make the EU resistant to change. Second, we will see that some of the more recent reforms to the CAP have been forced on the EU by the Global Accord on Trade and Tariffs (GATT) and the World Trade Organization (WTO), which are, of course, even larger international organizations.

In the 1950s, there were about fifteen million farm-

---

[2] Cited in Helen Wallace and William Wallace, eds., *Policy-Making in the European Union.* 4th ed. (Oxford: Oxford University Press, 2000), 182.

ers in the six countries that created the EEC. Although their numbers were declining rapidly, they were still a major political force, especially in France, where they lobbied persuasively to keep small, inefficient family farms alive. Meanwhile, countries with small agricultural populations needed to import food and wanted to keep prices as low as possible.

Not surprisingly, agriculture was a divisive issue from the beginning and almost destroyed the EEC in the early 1960s. The members finally reached a compromise in 1966 and created the CAP and its two main components. First, it took steps to modernize inefficient farms so that they could be more competitive in the European market. Second, to ease the fears of farmers whose livelihood was threatened by that modernization, the EC established the European Agricultural Guidance and Guarantee Fund (EAGGF), which gave them subsidies and guaranteed the purchase of surplus goods at artificially high prices.

Over the years, the modernizing side of the CAP went by the wayside. Payments to farmers, however, consumed more than half of the EC budget. By the early 1970s, food prices in Europe were two to four times higher than they would have been had they been determined by market forces. Imposition of CAP provisions in Britain was a major source of that country's objections to the EC's overall budgetary process. In 1991 alone, the EC purchased 25 million tons of cereal grains, 800,000 tons of butter, and 700,000 tons of other dairy products. Pundits joked about its butter mountains and wine lakes.

The CAP was also a major stumbling block in the Uruguay round of the GATT negotiations, which led to the creation of the WTO. American objections to the EAGGF payments almost led to a trade war between the United States and Europe in 1992 even though the United States still heavily subsidized its own farmers at the time. In the end, the EU and the other parties reached a compromise in which the Union agreed to scale back subsidies and guaranteed payments by about a third. Nonetheless, the continued political clout of farmers' groups kept the CAP alive, leaving Europe with an extremely inefficient agricultural sector and burdening the EU's budget in the process.

The CAP will not, however, be able to survive the 2004 enlargement given the number of farmers in most of the new member states. Therefore, the decision was made not to extend it to them. In addition, some modest reforms have been proposed for the fifteen Western members. Most notably, the EU is moving toward "decoupling" or ending the link between what farmers produce and the amount of money they receive as subsidies. Instead, they are slated to receive a one-time payment

Globalization and the EU

THE EU IS one of the best vehicles we have for illustrating the impact of globalization and regionalization.

It is, of course, a major architect of both. Critics have properly noted that European economies and cultures would have opened up to some degree without the EU. There can be little doubt, however, that it has sped up the flow of people, information, goods, and money within its borders. It has generally been a major advocate for liberalizing trade as well.

It also demonstrates that even the strongest powers are vulnerable to global pressures.

that would presumably give them the resources either to compete in the market or leave agriculture altogether.

Finally, it should be noted that there is one other pressure on the CAP that reflects the impact of global pressures on the EU. Its agricultural subsidies have been sharply criticized by the World Trade Organization. Although the EU's policies have received the most attention in the United States (such as its refusal to allow the import of curved bananas), Europe is facing legal pressure and could eventually be subject to sanctions by the WTO if it does not reduce the subsidies provided under the CAP.

Feedback

Feedback in the EU illustrates the importance of things that do *not* happen in political life. Put simply, there is very little feedback because of the way the EU is structured and the way people participate (or don't, as the case may be) in it.

As noted in the section on its origins, the EU has always been primarily of interest to elites—and until now, only economic ones at that. Polls routinely show that people pay little attention to the politics and policies of the EU. Turnout in European elections is usually much lower than in national ones. Coverage of the EU in the press is spotty and, as in most of political life, concentrates on its problems, not its accomplishments. There is, for instance, only one English-language weekly that concentrates on the EU, and it struggles to survive. When people are drawn to events in the EU, they tend to focus on the often demagogic claims about "faceless bureaucrats" in Brussels stealing their power. By contrast, as also noted earlier, very few people think of themselves primarily as Europeans, even though the number of people living, working, and even marrying across national borders is growing rapidly.

This lack of feedback overlaps with the notion of the democratic deficit. Critics properly point out that the size of the EU, as well as the fact that the European Parliament has relatively few and weak mechanisms for enforcing accountability, makes it difficult for average people to have much of an impact on decision making within it. In other words, the perceived lack of political clout magnifies the sense of distance and disinterest evident in most polls.

Conclusion: A Balance Sheet

On balance, it is hard not to be optimistic about the EU on two levels. First, it has made a major contribution to the peace and prosperity that Western Europe has enjoyed since the end of World War II. Obviously, no one factor can account for this, and scholars are still trying to determine just how important the EU and its predecessors have been. Nevertheless, it is impossible to deny the EU's role in turning Western Europe into what Max Singer and Aaron Wildavsky have called a "zone of peace," in which war has become virtually impossible. It will be another major accomplishment if, working with NATO and other bodies, it can extend that zone eastward.

Second, it has demonstrated that the nation-state is not the end point in political evolution as many realists in international relations believe. Jacques Delors once claimed that EU policies determine, or to some degree shape, 80 percent of social and economic policies enacted in European capitals. Although that may be an overstatement, the EU certainly has more power than the states in a number of critical policy-making arenas. In the language of international relations, the EU provides concrete evidence that states can and do cede some of their sovereignty to international organizations.

Key Terms

Concepts

Acquis communautaire	Qualified majority voting
Broadening	Subsidiarity
Codecision	Supranational
Deepening	Three pillars
Democratic deficit	Unanimity principle

People

Barroso, Jose Manuel	Monnet, Jean
Delors, Jacques	Spaak, Paul-Henri

Acronyms

CAP	ECJ	EMU
CFSP	ECSC	EU
COREPER	EEC	SEA
EC	EMS	

Organizations, Places, and Events

Commission
Committee of Permanent Representatives
Common Agricultural Policy
Common Foreign and Security Policy
Common Market
Council of Ministers
Euro
European Coal and Steel Community
European Community
European Court of Justice
European Economic Community
European Monetary System
European Monetary Union
European Parliament
European Union
Maastricht Treaty on European Union
Marshall Plan
Single European Act
Treaty of Amsterdam
Treaty of Nice
Treaty of Rome

Critical Thinking Exercises

1 Much has changed since this book was finished in early 2005. Does the analysis of EU politics presented here still make sense? Why (not)?

2 Public opinion pollsters routinely ask questions about whether people think their country is heading in the "right direction" or is on the "wrong track." If you were asked such a question about the EU, how would you answer? Why did you reach this conclusion?

3 Given what you learned in Chapters 4–6, why would European integration have seemed appealing to so many people after World War II?

4 What is the democratic deficit? Why does it exist? What difference does it make for the EU today? For possible expansion tomorrow?

5 What do the terms *broadening* and *deepening* mean? Track them both through the evolution of the EU and its predecessors.

6 In what ways does the EU limit what its member states can do?

7 How do member states limit what the EU can do?

8 What are the prospects for further broadening and deepening of the EU in the next few years?

Useful Websites

The EU's website is an excellent portal to everything the Union does—and the information is available in more than twenty languages.

www.europa.eu.int

Many of the academic centers that focus on the EU have websites with good collections of links to other on-line EU material. Among the best are the European Union Studies Association and the libraries at the University of California-Berkeley, the University of Pittsburgh, and the New York University Law School.

www.eustudies.org

www.lib.berkeley.edu/doemoff/gov_eu.html

www.library.pitt.edu/subject_guides/ westeuropean/wwwes/

www.jeanmonnet.org

European Voice is the only weekly newspaper on the EU and is published by *The Economist*. Its website provides the most comprehensive, up-to-date information about things European.

www.european-voice.com

There are many "euroskeptic" websites that are highly critical of the deepening and broadening of the EU. The first site listed is the most comprehensive of them. The second has links to many other similar sites.

www.eurofaq.freeuk.com

www.euro-sceptic.org

 InfoTrac College Edition Sources

Biscoe, Adam. "European Integration and the Maintenance of Regional Cultural Identity."

Calleo, David. "Transatlantic Folly: NATO v. the EU."

Gibson, James, and Gregory Caldeira. "Changes in the Legitimacy of the European Court of Justice."

Hix, Simon. "Elections, Parties, and Institutional Design: A Comparative Perspective on European Democracy."

Jordan, Andrew. "The Europeanization of National Government and Policy."

Kupchan, Charles. "The Rise of Europe."

Shepherd, Mark. "The European Parliament."

Warleigh, Alex. "Better the Horse You Know? Synthetic and Confederal Understandings of European Unification."

Weidenfeld, Werner. "The Euro and the New Face of the European Union."

Zahariades, Nikolaos. "Rethinking European Integration in the Competition Domain."

Further Reading

Bellamy, Richard, and Alex Warleigh. *Citizenship and Governance in the European Union*. New York: Continuum, 2002. A theorist and EU specialist look at the overlap (or lack thereof) between the way the EU is run and the way average citizens respond to it.

Dinan, Desmond. *An Ever Closer Union: An Introduction to the European Community*. 2nd ed. Boulder, Colo.: Lynne Rienner, 1999. The most comprehensive survey of European integration and its impact up to and beyond Maastricht.

Moravschik, Andrew. *The Choice for Europe*. Ithaca, N.Y.: Cornell University Press, 1999. The best overview of EU history through Maastricht.

Reid, T. R. *The United States of Europe*. New York: Penguin, 2005. A very extensive overview of post-Maastricht events by a very thoughtful—and very funny—journalist at the *Washington Post*.

Rosamond, Ben. *Theories of European Integration*. Basingstoke (UK): Palgrave, 2000. A look at the EU through the lens of various theories of integration and international relations.

Ross, George. *Jacques Delors and European Integration*. New York: Oxford University Press, 1995. An insider-like account of the workings of the Commission by one of the leading U.S. experts on French politics, to whom Delors gave unprecedented access late in his presidency. Not the easiest read, but probably the most insightful book on the EU ever written.

Sbragia, Alberta M., ed. *Euro-Politics: Institutions and Policymaking in the "New" European Community*. Washington, D.C.: Brookings Institution, 1992. An anthology that includes articles on most of the critical issues facing the EU; especially strong on the causes and consequences of the Single European Act.

Schmitter, Philippe. *How to Democratize the European Union . . . and Why Bother?* Boulder, Colo.: Rowman & Littlefield, 2000. A fairly abstract but powerful argument by one of the leading political scientists working on democratization.

Urwin, Derek W. *The Community of Europe: A History of European Integration Since 1945*, 2nd ed. New York: Longman, 1995. A short, comprehensive overview of how the EU evolved.

Wallace, Helen, and William Wallace, eds. *Policy-Making in the European Union*, 4th ed. Oxford: Oxford University Press, 2000. A mammoth and technically detailed look at how the EU makes policy in general.

Exploring
EXPLORING THE WORLD WIDE WEB

Parts 2–4 end with brief discussions of how you can use the website that accompanies this book to deepen your understanding of comparative politics. You can use the study guide, map exercises, and the other materials to go further than the book does in exploring individual countries. These brief passages in the book focus on how you can use the website to understand the similarities and differences among the countries covered in each part of the book—in this case, the industrialized democracies.

For parts 2–4, the MicroCase exercises operate on two levels. First, they help you see how the types of countries covered in each part differ from the others. Thus, for part 2, the MicroCase data show you that the industrialized democracies both are wealthier and enjoy more political freedom than either the former communist countries or those in the third world. Because they also use different electoral systems and vary on other political criteria, they differ in terms of how many people bother to vote and how many women there are in their national legislatures.

The website also contains the constitutions of all the countries covered in part 2 except for Great Britain, which, of course, does not have a written constitution. After reading them, note the political features stressed in each chapter that are not covered in the constitution. Ask yourself how or why those "nonconstitutional" practices and procedures came into existence and remain an important part of political life.

Of all the InfoTrac College Edition articles listed, two are particularly important as you think about the cultural underpinnings of democracy. The first is E. J. Dionne's 1997 article "Why Civil Society? Why Now?" In it, this award-winning political scientist and journalist reviews the literature on why such cultural norms are so important. Just as I was putting the finishing touches on the book, Robert Putnam published "Bowling Together," which looks at how reactions to the events of September 11 have helped restore political confidence and trust in the United States, at least in the short run. Dionne and Putnam cover only the United States in their articles; however, both have implications for all democracies and are thus worth your serious attention here.

Part 3

THE CRISIS OF COMMUNISM

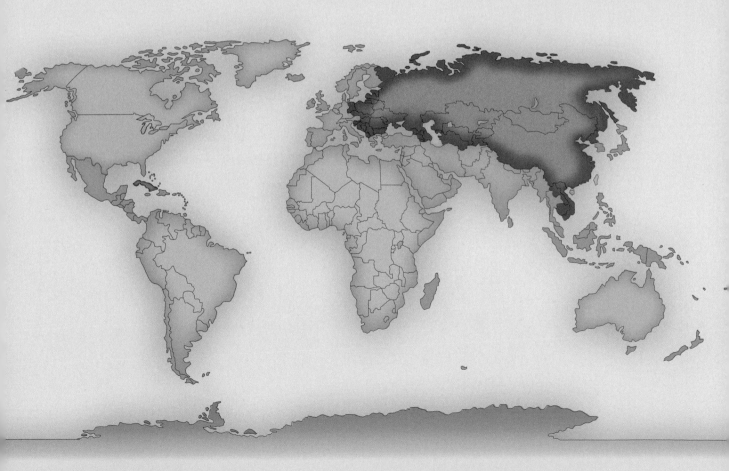

Socialism cannot exist, no matter where, contrary to the will of the people.

GEORGI ARBATOV

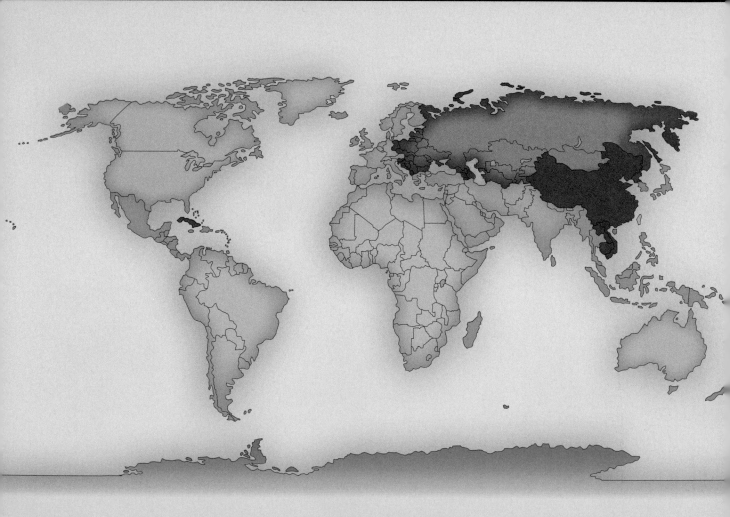

CURRENT AND FORMER COMMUNIST REGIMES

The Basics: Current and Former Communist Regimes

COUNTRY	POPULATION IN MILLIONS	GDP PER CAPITA IN PURCHASING POWER PARITY UNITS (US$)	ECONOMIC GROWTH, 2003 OR MOST RECENT AVAILABLE YEAR	PERCENTAGE OF POPULATION FROM MINORITY GROUPS
Albania	4	4,500	7	5
Armenia	3	3,500	10	7
Azerbaijan	8	3,400	11	10
Belarus	10	6,100	7	19
Bosnia	4	6,100	4	52
Bulgaria	8	7,600	4	16
Cambodia	13	1,900	5	10
China	1,300	5,000	9	8
Croatia	5	10,600	4	10
Cuba	11	2,900	3	NA
Czech Republic	10	15,700	3	19
Estonia	1	12,300	5	35
Georgia	5	2,500	6	30
Hungary	10	13,900	3	10
Kazakhstan	15	6,300	9	46
Korea (North)	23	1,300	1	0
Kyrgyzstan	5	1,600	7	35

(continued)

The Basics: (*continued*)

COUNTRY	POPULATION IN MILLIONS	GDP PER CAPITA IN PURCHASING POWER PARITY UNITS (US$)	ECONOMIC GROWTH, 2003 OR MOST RECENT AVAILABLE YEAR	PERCENTAGE OF POPULATION FROM MINORITY GROUPS
Laos	6	1,700	5	32
Latvia	2	10,200	7	42
Lithuania	4	11,400	9	20
Macedonia (FYROM)	2	6,700	3	36
Moldova	4	1,800	6	35
Mongolia	3	1,800	5	5
Poland	39	11,100	4	3
Romania	22	7,000	5	10
Russia	144	8,900	7	18
Serbia and Montenegro	11	2,200	2	32
Slovakia	5	13,300	4	14
Slovenia	2	19,000	2	8
Tajikistan	7	1,000	7	35
Turkmenistan	5	5,800	23	15
Ukraine	48	5,400	9	22
Uzbekistan	26	1,700	3	20

Source: CIA Factbook, www.odci.gov. Accessed 29 November 2004.

Good Bye, Lenin

Germans are not normally known for their comedy films. Certainly not ones about politics.

But, in 2003, Wolfgang Becker issued *Good Bye, Lenin!* The film begins in 1989 just before the wave of demonstrations brought down the Berlin Wall and took East Germany's Communist regime with it.

A young man, Alex, finds himself in the middle of one of the protests and gets arrested. He actually was not demonstrating, just chasing a pretty girl. Nonetheless, his mother, Katrina, sees him arrested as she walks by the site on her way to a party. It turns out that Katrina is one of the most ardent supporters of the Marxist-Leninist regime and is appalled by what seems like her son's political indiscretion.

Before Alex has time to explain what happened, Katrina suffers a heart attack and slips into a coma. When she regains consciousness many months later, Germany has been unified under the leadership of Chancellor Helmut Kohl as part of the Federal Republic of Germany (West Germany). To complicate matters further,

Katrina's doctor tells Alex that any serious shock could kill her, including news that the DDR is no more.

So, Alex does everything humanly possible to convince his mother—who is confined to her apartment—that East Germany still exists. He has friends make fake television and radio broadcasts, including one that seems to show disgruntled residents of West Berlin crossing the wall to move to the East, when, of course, exactly the opposite had occurred. He comes up with ingenious explanations for why his mother can hear what she thinks are illegal Western broadcasts through her poorly sound-proofed walls. Katrina eventually wanders out of the house and sees ads for BMWs and Coke. Alex convinces her that Coca-Cola is a Communist invention and that ads for BMWs are there because so many Westerners have moved to the East to avoid crime and inequality.

Of course, *Good Bye, Lenin!* is based on a preposterous plot line. That said, there is substantial *ostologie* or nostalgia for aspects of life in East Germany and in the other former Communist countries.

Few people have any desire to return to the repression of Communist rule. Nonetheless, many people miss the security the party-state provided, including low rents, guaranteed employment, and free health care. In the former East Germany, upwards of a quarter of the population is unemployed (including Alex, whose television repair business collapsed after unification). Life is particularly hard for older people on pensions, anyone on a fixed income, and people with little education and few job skills.

Yet, reformed Communist parties now do well at the polls in almost all former Communist countries, and have even won elections many of them. They do well because they speak effectively to so many of the "losers" of the transitions from Communist rule.

There are signs that significant progress is being made. Eight former Communist countries joined the European Union in 2004. Many have also seemingly turned an economic corner and are recording rapid rates of growth that are beginning to be translated into improved standards of living. There have been very few protests against the reformed systems, particularly in the countries that have seen democratic institutions take root the most.

But there are also places where conditions are far worse than in the former East Germany. Bloody wars have been fought in what used to be Yugoslavia and in a number of the former Soviet republics. Central Asia remains mired in poverty and has governments that are almost as authoritarian as the Communist states they replaced. In fact, most of them are led by the same men who ran the country before the USSR collapsed.

Thinking about the Current and Former Communist Regimes

Writing about Communism in the early twenty-first century is like trying to shoot at a rapidly moving and even more rapidly shrinking target. Twenty years ago, President Ronald Reagan used American fears of Communism as a major campaign theme in his landslide victory over Walter Mondale. Barely seven years later, the Soviet Union—Reagan's "focus of evil in the world"—had collapsed.

Reagan could hardly be blamed for a lack of foresight. At the time, no serious observers predicted that the Soviet Union and its allies would abandon Communism in a few short years.

After World War II, the cold war between the industrialized democracies and the Soviet bloc dominated world politics. By the 1980s, however, it had become clear that the Communist regimes were neither as strong

nor as ruthless as the alarmists had argued in the 1950s and 1960s. Most of the Eastern European countries had been rocked by protest movements. Even the Soviet Union had loosened some of its more repressive policies. Factional disputes had divided the Chinese Communist Party on several occasions. Nonetheless, virtually everyone assumed that the Communist regimes would remain in power and that the cold war would continue indefinitely.

But then, the impossible occurred. The unraveling of the Communist world began shortly after the selection of **Mikhail Gorbachev** as general secretary of the Communist Party of the Soviet Union (CPSU) in March 1985. Terms like *perestroika* and *glasnost* became almost as familiar to Americans as baseball and apple pie. New York department stores sold pieces of the Berlin Wall and shoddy Soviet consumer goods as the latest trendy fads.

"Gorbymania" was not to last, however. The reforms he introduced opened a political Pandora's box. By the end of 1989, every Communist regime in Eastern Europe had disintegrated. Then, less than a year after being named *Time*'s "man of the decade," Gorbachev and his Soviet Union were gone.

The transition from Communist rule has been anything but smooth. Each of the Eastern European and former Soviet states declared itself a democracy. But each found that creating a regime that bore more than a fleeting resemblance to those covered in Part 2 is easier said than done. Meanwhile, they also had to accomplish something that had never been done anywhere before—shift from a centrally planned command economy to one dominated by private ownership in a reasonably free market.

The news is not all bleak, of course. The countries that have joined NATO and the European Union have made major progress on both the political and economic fronts. Poland, Hungary, the Czech Republic, Slovakia, Slovenia, Lithuania, Latvia, and Estonia have all held at least three competitive elections and seen power shift from government to opposition, indicators most political scientists take to be signs of a strengthening democracy. Similarly, those countries have all experienced a period of sustained growth since their economies bottomed out in the middle of the 1990s.

China, North Korea, Cuba, and a few others remain nominally Communist. With the exception of North Korea and Cuba, however, these countries did adopt sweeping economic reforms that outstripped anything Gorbachev anticipated when he spoke of perestroika. To be sure, the Communist Party remains securely in control in those countries. But their societies seemingly have

Paul B. Davies

little in common with the socialism Karl Marx and Friedrich Engels (discussed later in this chapter) predicted a century and a half ago. For example, despite their supposed commitment to egalitarian policies, as well as Marx's opposition to the way women were treated under capitalism, Communist regimes never saw fit to promote more than a handful of women to top leadership positions.

More and more analysts are also coming to the conclusion that it will be all but impossible for these regimes to remain Communist. Even if their regimes survive, they almost certainly will face growing pressure from below, as evidenced, for instance, by the upsurge of interest in the Falun Gong sect in China and the authorities' stern reaction, which we will consider in Chapter 10.

Thinking about Communism

As with the liberal democracies, there is some ambiguity about which countries should be considered in Part 3. The criterion used here is simple, however. The thirty-three countries highlighted in the map at the beginning of this chapter were all part of one of the sixteen states that once employed a **Marxist-Leninist** regime.

The most important of them, by far, was the Union of Soviet Socialist Republics (USSR), or Soviet Union. The first Communist regime came to power there as a result of the October revolution of 1917 and the civil war that followed. Only in Mongolia did a Communist regime come to and stay in power between the two world wars. After World War II the Soviet Union imposed regimes that were all but carbon copies of its own on Poland, Czechoslovakia, Romania, Bulgaria, Hungary, and the eastern part of Germany—these countries became known in the West as **satellites** of the Soviet Union. Communist regimes came to power on their own in Yugoslavia and Albania. None of these countries has a Communist regime today.

Most of the other Communist countries were in Asia, as are all but one of the remaining ones. The settlement that ended World War II divided Korea. The northern half became the Democratic People's Republic of Korea, a Communist country. The Chinese Communist Party won its civil war against the Nationalists in 1949, thus bringing the world's most populous country into the Communist camp. Also after World War II, a Communist insurgency broke out in the French colony of Indochina. After the French were defeated in 1954, Indochina was split into four independent countries: Laos, Cambodia, and North and South Vietnam. Of the four, only North Vietnam was Communist at the time. Another two decades of fighting ensued in which half a million U.S. troops could not defeat the Communists. By 1975 Marxists were in power in Laos, Cambodia, and a united Vietnam. Laos and Vietnam still had Communist regimes as of this writing.

The last country on the list is Cuba. It was granted its independence after the Spanish-American War in 1898. For the next sixty years, the United States was for all intents and purposes in charge of a country whose government was officially in the hands of a series of weak and corrupt dictators. The last of them, Fulgencio Batista, was overthrown by revolutionaries led by **Fidel Castro** in 1959. Relations with the United States quickly deteriorated, and Cuba became a Soviet ally and adopted Marxism-Leninism in 1961.

Several other countries are sometimes included in lists of Communist regimes, such as Nicaragua, North Yemen, Angola, and Mozambique. These countries all had distinctly left-wing governments at one point or another. However, they are not included here because they never fully adopted Marxist-Leninist principles.

The Leninist State

The first and most important characteristic these countries had in common was a form of leadership devised by **Vladimir Lenin** for the prerevolutionary Bolshevik Party in Russia. We will explore its characteristics in detail later in this chapter and the next. Here, it is enough to note two things.

First, the Communist Party completely controlled political life. In a few countries, other parties were allowed to exist, but they were mere pawns of the Communists. The party dominated the government, the media, the economy, the educational system, and most social and leisure time activities. The parties were run according to the principle of **democratic centralism.** But that meant that they were democratic in name only and were in reality ruled by a tiny group of party officials at the top of the hierarchy.

Second, until the late 1950s, the Soviet Union controlled the entire Communist world. New Communist regimes not only adopted Marxism-Leninism but submitted to Moscow's leadership in determining how their countries were run.

In the late 1950s, however, the Communist world began to splinter. The Chinese leaders came to oppose a Soviet Union they found too moderate and complacent. The two states soon became bitter enemies, and their troops occasionally fired at each other along their four-thousand-mile-long border. Still, most Communist regimes remained loyal to Moscow until the very end, even though all experienced periods in which dissenters went public with their opposition, often capturing the attention of the rest of the world in the process.

Command Economies

Until the late 1980s, the Communist countries also relied on a **command economy,** in which the government owned almost all industrial enterprises and retail sales outlets. Only in Poland and Yugoslavia was much private farming allowed to continue. (See table 8.1.) The economies were managed by a party-dominated state planning committee (Gosplan in the Soviet Union). It devised detailed blueprints for what was to be produced, exported, and sold, typically for a five-year period. Individual enterprises, run by managers appointed by the party, were then issued instructions about what to produce and how to produce it.

Early on, central planning helped produce rapid growth. By the 1950s, some of the Communist countries were among the world leaders in the production of steel, ships, and other heavy industrial goods. Major improvements were made in the average person's standard of living. Homelessness was eliminated in Eastern Europe, and starvation in China.

However, by the late 1980s the benefits of centralized planning had evaporated, and the Communist countries found themselves in deep economic trouble. Plan-

▌ TABLE 8.1 The Collectively Owned Portion of the Economy in 1967 (in percentages)

COUNTRY	AGRICUL-TURAL LAND	INDUSTRIAL PRODUCTION	RETAIL SALES	NATIONAL INCOME
Bulgaria	99	99	100	95
Hungary	94	99	99	96
Poland	15	100	99	76
East Germany	95	88	79	94
Romania	91	100	100	95
Czechoslovakia	90	100	100	95
Soviet Union	98	100	100	96
Yugoslavia	16	98	NA	77
Weighted average	92	99	98	95

Source: Adapted from Bernard Chavance, *The Transformation of Communist Systems: Economic Reform Since the 1950s,* trans. Charles Hauss (Boulder, Colo.: Westview Press, 1994), 28.

ning and coercion could help stimulate growth in the early stages of industrialization, but they were of little or no use when it came to the vitally important high-tech sectors of the economy for reasons that will become clear later. The macroeconomic problems were reflected in the people's poor living conditions. To be sure, most people were far better off than their parents or grandparents had been. However, everything from housing to health care was mediocre at best—a fact that was driven home to the millions of people who gained access to Western mass media or who met Western tourists visiting Eastern Europe or the USSR.

Key Questions

Later in the chapter, we will explore exactly how and why the crisis of Communism hit. For now, simply note that it did occur and that it forced these countries to all but completely change their political course. In other words, the stakes of political life in the current and former Communist countries are much higher than anything we saw in Part 2.

As noted earlier, the Eurasian countries are in the midst of a social, political, and economic transition for which there are no real precedents. Their leaders are simultaneously trying to build a democratic state on the ashes of the old Leninist one, a market economy based on private ownership, and a new culture stressing such values as individualism and personal initiative, which have never been prominent features in their cultures.

Any one of those challenges would be difficult enough. Together, they have proved all but impossible to overcome. Almost all highly trained people more than forty years old in these countries have been touched by the Communist past, which leaves many of them politically and socially suspect. The collapse of the Leninist state has unleashed new political forces. Millions of people are impatient with the pace of reform. Old ethnic and other antagonisms have been rekindled. And all this is happening without as much Western economic aid as many in these countries had expected.

The stakes are different, but no lower, in the countries that still cling to the Leninist model—and "cling" is probably the most telling verb to use in describing them. All are engaged in a high-risk political balancing act. All have acknowledged the need for economic reform. However, all have resisted political reform and have tried to retain unfettered Communist Party rule. As we will see in Chapter 10 on China, most observers do not think this state of affairs can continue indefinitely. Further, they believe that if these Communist parties hold on to power they will have to adopt significant democratizing reforms as well.

Studying the current and former Communist countries also requires us to shift intellectual gears. We will ask many of the same questions posed in Part 2:

- What contemporary and historical, domestic and international forces shaped their development?

- How are decisions made in these countries?

- What role do average citizens play in policy making?

- What are their public policies?

- How is political life affected by global forces?

But we will also have to ask some new questions:

- How could regimes that seemed so strong collapse so quickly?

- Why have some Communist systems survived?

- What are the political implications of economic reform in countries that have kept Communism and in those that have abandoned it?

- Why are they all facing much more serious domestic and global challenges than any of the countries covered in Part 2?

Socialism, Marxism, Leninism

As the Communist regimes aged, socialism in general, and Marxism and Leninism in particular, mattered less and less to their leaders and people alike. However, both because the three doctrines gave rise to these governments and because they were so fre-

quently misunderstood by critics in the West, it is still important to consider them here.

Socialism

Historians have traced the origins of socialism back to the radical Levelers of the seventeenth-century English Civil War, who advocated social, political, and economic equality. And, as you would expect with an idea that old, there are dozens of interpretations of what socialism means, making it impossible to present any single, universally accepted definition here. For the purposes of an introductory course, it is good enough to think of **socialism** as having four characteristics.

First, socialists believe that capitalism and the private ownership of the **means of production** are flawed. They are convinced that private ownership leads to unacceptable levels of inequality. Not all socialists are persuaded that the central government has to control the entire economy. Nonetheless, all believe that representatives of the people as a whole, and not a small group of capitalists, should determine how the economy is run.

Second, most liberals are satisfied if a society can achieve equality of opportunity, which theoretically offers everyone the same chance to succeed. Socialists go further and demand substantial equality of outcome as well. They believe that, to be truly "free to" do the things that capitalist and liberal democratic societies offer, people must also be "free from" hunger, disease, and poverty.

Third, socialists are convinced that democracy as practiced in liberal, capitalist society is too limited. Most believe that the personal freedoms and competitive elections that are at the heart of liberal democratic theory are vital. However, they would extend democracy to include popular control over all decisions that shape peoples' lives, most notably at work.

Finally, socialists claim that providing for public ownership and control of a substantially more egalitarian society will improve human relations in general. In one way or another, all are convinced that capitalism keeps most of us from reaching our potential. In other words, if we could remove the fetters of capitalism, we would all be better off.

Marxism

Since the late nineteenth century, socialists have been divided into two main camps. The first includes the various social democratic parties that play such a major role in the industrialized democracies discussed in Part 2.

KARL MARX

Karl Marx.

Karl Marx was born in 1818 in Trier, Germany, to a family of wealthy, assimilated Jews. While a university student, Marx was exposed to the democratic and revolutionary ideas sweeping Europe at the time. In the early 1840s, Marx moved to Paris, where he worked for a number of fledgling radical journals. He started reading British capitalist economic texts, as well as the philosophy that had so stimulated him while a student. He also met **Friedrich Engels,** the son of a rich industrialist and author of one of the first detailed accounts of what factory life was like.

As revolutions swept Europe in 1848, Marx and Engels began writing about a new version of socialism that was later to be called Marxism or **communism.** Their ideas were first set out in a tract, *The Communist Manifesto,* that they published that winter. Over the next forty years, the two wrote dozens of volumes, the most important of which was Marx's three-volume historical and theoretical study of capitalism, almost always referred to by its German title, *Das Kapital.*

They believe that social and economic change can and must be achieved by working through a democratic, representative system. Here we will concentrate on the second camp, consisting of parties and politicians who believe that significant political and economic progress can occur only through revolution, based on principles derived from the writings of **Karl Marx.**

As with socialism in general, there is no universally accepted interpretation of Marxism. What follows is a brief version of the theory that stresses its key principles, most of which ended up being honored in the breach by those leaders who thought of themselves as Marxists.

Like most intellectuals of his generation, Marx believed that societies passed through stages, evolving from primitive groups of hunters and gatherers and eventually culminating in the industrial society he lived in. Indeed, what set Marx apart from most socialists of his time was his understanding that industrial capitalism is but one (irreversible) step along the path of social development.

Marx also agreed with the German philosopher Georg Hegel, who believed that societies shift from one stage to another in a wrenching process he called the **dialectic.** Societies do not change in fundamental ways as a result of incremental reform. Rather, major shifts occur only when their basic values and principles are challenged and new ones are adopted.

Unlike Hegel, Marx believed that progress occurs as a result of changes in the distribution of economic power, which he called **historical materialism.** Any society can be broken down into social classes determined by who owns—and who doesn't own—the means of production or the key institutions through which wealth is created.

Thus, according to Marx, progress occurs as a result of conflict between these classes. He was convinced that the ruling class had to exploit the rest of the population who did not control the means of production and that the relationship between them constituted the economic **base** of any society. (See figure 8.1.) Any society based on private ownership also has built-in **contradictions,** because people will not long accept being exploited and will eventually rise up in opposition. To

▌FIGURE 8.1 Base, Superstructure, and Contradictions, According to Marx

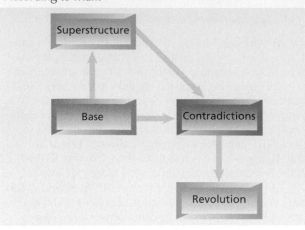

▌FIGURE 8.2 The Role of Money in Feudalism and Capitalism

In feudalism:
    C–M–C
In capitalism:
    M–C–M'
    M' = M + profit
But Marxist theory also holds:
    M' = total value of the labor that went into making
        the commodity
    M' = wages paid + profit
    Or, wages = labor value − profit = exploitation
Legend:
C = commodity, M = money

slow the rise of rebellion, the owners create a **super-structure** of other institutions, such as the state or religion. The former runs the bureaucracy, police, and army to maintain law and order, while the latter offers false hopes and expectations. It is from Marx's discussion of the superstructure that we get two of his most commonly cited statements: "Religion is the opiate of the masses" and "The executive of the modern state is but a committee for managing the common affairs of the whole bourgeoisie." But, said Marx, with time the oppressed would be able to organize, rise up, overthrow their oppressors, and usher in a new pattern of class relations.

From Marx's perspective, capitalism was a step forward, because it replaced feudalism with a system that had capital at its core. Under feudalism, the wealthy use money primarily as a vehicle to buy the commodities—goods and services—they want (the C and M of figure 8.2). For example, they sell grain or wine and use the

money to buy clothes or spices. In capitalism, the pursuit of money becomes the driving force. Capitalists are less interested in the goods and services they produce or can purchase than in the money they can make from a transaction M', which placed the profit motive at the heart of the economy for the first time.

This pressure to make a profit also makes capitalism exploitative by its very nature. Here Marx drew on one of his most controversial assumptions. He was convinced that the real worth of any good, as well as the price capitalists could sell it for, equalled the value of the labor that went into making it (also M' in figure 8.2). The problem was that the price capitalists set for their commodities had to include both the wages they paid their workers and their own profit. This meant that capitalists had to pay workers less than they deserved if they wanted to make money.

According to Marx, the constant need to open new markets to make more profit would, in turn, lead to alternating periods of booms and busts. (See figure 8.3.) As capitalism expanded and competition intensified, more and more businesses would fail as weaker capitalists proved unable to deal with the competitive pressures of the market. As that happened, the **bourgeoisie,** or capitalist class, would grow smaller and smaller, while the working class, or **proletariat,** would swell until it included the vast majority of the population.

As in any society based on inequality, workers would resent their exploitation. Their alienation and, later, class consciousness would be enhanced by two of capi-

▌FIGURE 8.3 Expansion and the Collapse of Capitalism

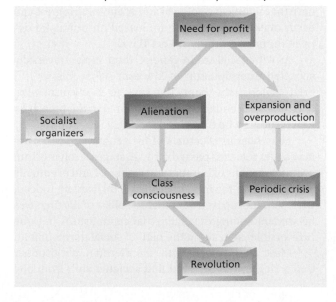

talism's own innovations—the spread of mass education and the political freedoms of liberal democracy.

Marx assumed that the contradictions of capitalism could only be resolved through revolution. However, he did not expect a long and bloody struggle. Instead, he thought that once the proletariat grew to such a size, a wave of strikes and demonstrations would lead to the overthrow of the bourgeoisie with a minimum of violence. Marx also believed that the revolution could not be confined to one country but would spread around the capitalist world.

The revolution would be followed by a transitional period that, unfortunately, he chose to call the "dictatorship of the proletariat." The means of production would be taken over and run collectively, the cultural vestiges of capitalism would be destroyed, and resources would be redistributed in an egalitarian manner.

Afterward, society would move into communism. At this point, there would be no need for government or any other part of the superstructure because people would no longer be exploiting each other. Instead, they would work freely and efficiently because they were freed of the fetters of ownership and lived in a society organized by Marx's famous dictum "from each according to his abilities, to each according to his needs."

Marxism-Leninism

As an evolutionary thinker, Marx believed that socialist revolutions would first occur in advanced industrialized societies. Unfortunately for Marxists, that is not where revolutions inspired by Marx's ideas took place. Rather, they came to power in countries in which industrialization and capitalism had not developed very far. All had small working classes and socialist movements, and most had repressive governments that made the organization of broadly based socialist movements impossible.

To come to power in these circumstances, Marxists had to adopt a very different strategy. Although there was considerable variation in the way Marxists won in these sixteen countries, all relied heavily on an organization and strategy first developed by Lenin to help the Marxists adapt to the poverty and repression in Russia during the first years of the twentieth century.

Even though Marx's theory seemed to rule out the possibility of Marxism taking root in countries like Russia at the time, many intellectuals there were drawn to it. At first, orthodox Marxists urged patience, arguing that no Marxist revolution was possible until Russia became industrialized and democratic. Others, led by Lenin, were unwilling to wait for history to take its "natural" course.

▌ **TABLE 8.2** Key Events in the Evolution of Communist Regimes

YEAR	EVENT
1917	Bolshevik revolution in Russia
1924	Death of Lenin
	Stalin begins consolidation of power
1945–47	Start of cold war
	Communists seize power in Eastern Europe
1949	Chinese Communists come to power
1950	Start of Korean War
1953	Death of Stalin
1956	Secret speech and de-Stalinization
	Revolt in Hungary
1959	Castro comes to power in Cuba
1975	End of Vietnam War, solidification of Communist rule in Indochina

Lenin got the Russian Social Democratic Party to adopt a new strategy based on a highly disciplined, hierarchical organization of professional revolutionaries. Lenin called his model "democratic centralism," but as we will see in more detail in the next chapter, there was next to nothing democratic about it. The leadership would run the party with an iron hand and would brook next to no dissent. (See table 8.2.)

At the time Lenin developed his ideas, they had virtually no impact because he and most of his **Bolshevik** colleagues were living in exile and had little popular support inside Russia. Yet, within fifteen years, the Bolsheviks had seized power, and Lenin was convinced that they had done so because they had relied on democratic centralism.

The tactics developed to pull off a revolution in a society very different from the one that Marx envisioned now became the model the Bolsheviks used to structure their new regime. Most historians now argue that Russia's adoption of Lenin's hierarchical organization and the control over society it allowed made the attainment of Marxist goals of human liberation and democracy all but impossible. Too much power was concentrated in too few hands.

Stalinism

After the Bolsheviks took power, they established a regime that they expected would preside over Marx's dictatorship of the proletariat and guide the transition from capitalism to socialism. However, something very different—and very tragic—occurred instead.

The authoritarian features of communism became the regime's defining characteristic after the 1917 revolution. To some degree, the authoritarianism, if not the totalitarianism, was an outgrowth of Lenin's democratic centralism. However, most political scientists assign the primary responsibility for the degradation of communism to **Joseph Stalin** and his dictatorial control over the world communist movement from the mid-1920s until his death in 1953.

It was in studying this period that Western scholars coined the term **totalitarianism.** Stalin and his colleagues used the party, the mass media, and campaigns of terror to subjugate the population and then mobilize the people in pursuit of the leadership's goals. The **party state** became as close to totalitarian as imaginable.

I could go on and present statistical and other "hard" evidence about those regimes. However, as is often the case with emotionally charged material, it is easier to illustrate this point by turning to a piece of fiction, George Orwell's *Animal Farm.*

Orwell was part of a generation of young European intellectuals who were drawn to Marxism in the 1920s and 1930s. But Orwell soon became disillusioned with Stalin's dictatorial and opportunistic policies, which he criticized in his writing for the rest of his life.

In *Animal Farm*, the animals rise up and throw off the yoke (literally and figuratively) of human oppression. Initially they are inspired by an ideology that reads a lot like Marxism and is embodied in the anthem "Beasts of England," which Orwell tells us was sung to a tune somewhere between "La Cucaracha" and "My Darling Clementine."

Soon, however, things turn sour. The old revolutionary leader dies shortly after the revolution just as Lenin did. The pigs, the animal Orwell not coincidentally chose to represent the Communist Party, assume more and more power over the other animals. Then a struggle for power breaks out between the two leading pigs. Snowball (based on Leon Trotsky), the more orthodox "Marxist," believes that the revolution must spread to all the farms and beasts of England. In the end, he loses out to the dictatorial Comrade Napoleon, who, like both his namesake and Stalin (on whom he is based), is more interested in power for power's sake than in any lofty goals.

In the book, the subtle complexities of Marxist ideology give way first to the Seven Commandments and then to the simplistic slogan "Four legs good, two legs bad." And "Beasts of England" is replaced by a new anthem, "Comrade Napoleon," which adulates the leader. The pigs lord their power over the other animals, and become more and more like their prerevolutionary oppressors: "All animals are equal, except some are more equal than others." The pigs violate the Seven Commandments by sleeping in beds and drinking alcohol. Orwell ends the novel with a scene in which the pigs are in a house drinking and playing cards with a group of men, their sup-

posed "class" enemy. The other animals look in on the game from outside:

> As the animals outside gazed at the scene, it seemed to them that some strange thing was happening. What was it that had altered in the faces of the pigs? Clover's old dim eyes flitted from one face to another. Some of them had five chins, some had four, some had three. But what was it that seemed to be melting and changing? Then, the applause having come to an end, the company took up their cards and continued the game that had been interrupted, and the animals crept silently away.
>
> But they had not gone twenty yards when they stopped short. An uproar of voices was coming from the farmhouse. They rushed back and looked through the window again. Yes, a violent quarrel was in progress. There were shoutings, bangings on the table, sharp suspicious glances, furious denials. The source of the trouble appeared to be that Napoleon and Mr. Pilkington had each played an ace of spades simultaneously.
>
> Twelve voices were shouting in anger, and they were all alike. No question, now, what had happened to the faces of the pigs. The creatures outside looked from pig to man, and from man to pig, and from pig to man again; but already it was impossible to say which was which.[1]

Expansion

As noted earlier, Marx expected that once revolution broke out, it would soon spread. To speed up that worldwide uprising, two Workingmen's International groups were created to coordinate the actions of the world's Socialist parties. During World War I, the second of them failed to keep most socialists from joining the war effort and made no contribution to the Russian Revolution of 1917.

Lenin thus felt justified in claiming that the Bolsheviks should lead the world revolutionary movement. Within months of seizing power, he and his colleagues established a **Third International,** or **Comintern,** to spread revolution, Bolshevik style. Most Socialist parties split (see the discussion of the origins of the French Communist Party in Chapter 5), with the more radical wing supporting the Bolsheviks.

But the revolution did not spread as either Marx or Lenin had expected. A few attempts to establish Bolshevik regimes were made in 1919 and the early 1920s, but they were quickly put down. By the time Stalin had so-

---

[1] George Orwell, *Animal Farm* (New York: Harcourt Brace, 1946), 128.

lidified his power, it was clear that no such revolutions were likely to occur in the foreseeable future. Instead, the new, weak Soviet state was vulnerable to pressures from the hostile countries that surrounded it.

Stalin then inaugurated a new phase in Soviet policy dubbed "socialism in one country." The first and foremost goal of the Soviet government, and of all other Communist parties that belonged to the Third International, was to help the world's one Marxist regime survive, even if that meant slowing the prospects for revolution in other countries.

Following the end of World War II, communism did expand, though not in the way Marx had anticipated. As the war drew to a close, resistance forces dominated by Communists drove the Germans and their collaborators out of Albania and Yugoslavia and established Marxist-Leninist regimes. Between 1945 and 1947, the Soviets imposed Communist regimes on the rest of Eastern Europe. In China, North Korea, Indochina, and Cuba, Communist regimes were the result of domestically inspired revolutions.

No matter how they came to power, all these regimes were patterned after the Soviet party state. Even where Communists came to power on their own, they acknowledged Soviet leadership and patterned their own new government on Moscow's.

De-Stalinization

Stalin died in March 1953. He was replaced by a group of men who had been his colleagues and henchmen. Surprisingly, they ushered in a period of relaxation and, to some degree, reform that came to be known as **de-Stalinization.**

Cracks in the supposedly impenetrable totalitarian wall first came to light in **Nikita Khrushchev**'s 1956 secret speech to the Twentieth Congress of the CPSU, which documented many of the atrocities committed under Stalin in gory detail.

Political controls in some areas of intellectual life were loosened. Works critical of Stalin were published and widely discussed. Universities became politically and intellectually exciting places for their students, including Gorbachev, Yeltsin, and most of the 1980s generation of reformers. There were, however, limits to what the reformers could openly discuss. Stalin was the only acceptable figure people were allowed to attack, and criticism of the current leadership, Lenin, or the party's monopoly on power remained strictly forbidden.

The Soviets cracked down whenever they felt that events in their own country or in Eastern Europe were getting out of hand. In 1956 reform Communists came to power in Hungary and planned to create a multiparty system and leave the Soviet-imposed **Warsaw**

Protestors demolishing symbols of Soviet rule during the Hungarian uprising of 1956. Here a bust of Stalin is being used to hold a street sign.

AP/Wide World Photos

Pact alliance. Meanwhile, thousands of people demonstrated in the streets of Budapest and other Hungarian cities. Finally, Soviet troops intervened, overthrowing the government of Imre Nagy and replacing it with one headed by Janos Kadar, known to be loyal to the Soviet leadership.

Things had gotten too far out of hand for Khrushchev's conservative colleagues, who forced him from office in October 1964. He was replaced by a collective leadership team headed by **Leonid Brezhnev,** whose hostility toward change would not only characterize his seventeen years in power but would contribute heavily to the demise of Eurasian communism.

This point is worth underscoring. Less than half a century after the Bolshevik revolution, the Soviet Union and most other Communist regimes had been taken over by an aging generation of leaders more committed to stability than to change. The new leadership could not, however, put a halt to two trends that were to become ever more prominent in the quarter-century before the crisis of communism began in earnest.

First, there was no longer a monolithic world communist movement. As early as the late 1940s, Albania and Yugoslavia had effectively broken free from Soviet control. By the 1960s the same was true for the non-European Communist regimes.

Second, although it was difficult to see at the time, Brezhnev and his colleagues had come to power at a moment when their countries needed to change—and change dramatically. That, however, was not something they were prepared to consider, as we will see shortly.

The Marxist-Leninist State

By the mid-1960s, governments that ruled in the name of Marx had drifted far from the egalitarian goals outlined earlier. Instead, political, economic, and other forms of power were concentrated in the hands of a few elite party leaders. Constitutions in the Soviet Union and elsewhere gave the party the leading role in government and society, which meant that it, and not the government, held a monopoly on decision-making power.

The Party State

Political scientists thus emphasize what they call the party state in which the former was far more powerful than the latter. The critical institutions were its **secretariat** and **Politburo.** (The exact titles varied from country to country and from time to time.) The most important individuals were the **general secretary** and the members of the Politburo, who functioned as the equivalent of the prime minister and cabinet in a parliamentary system. Typically, the politburo was the main decision-making body, while the secretariat managed the party's internal affairs. In most countries, the top leaders were members of both bodies. There was a formal government, and most important party leaders served in both. But it was always their party "hat" that prevailed. The parliament, cabinet, and other institutions were little more than a rubber stamp for decisions made in the party, which the government then implemented.

The party had extremely powerful leaders. Ironically, Marx had tried to downplay the role individuals play in shaping history, stressing instead the impact of broad historical and economic forces. Lenin, too, resisted attempts to turn himself into a hero. Yet, shortly after Lenin died, Stalin and his supporters transformed him into a symbol that some observers believe was equivalent to a god. As Orwell pointedly shows in *Animal Farm*, Stalin became the center of an even greater **cult of personality.** After Stalin, Marxist leaders maintained various types of collective leadership in which a number of people shared power. Nonetheless, the prominence of a Fidel Castro, Mao Zedong, or even Mikhail Gorbachev suggests that general secretaries continued to amass substantial power well into the twilight of communism.

The party always relied on democratic centralism. Leaders at one level co-opted those who served under them. Appointments to key positions, included in a list known as the *nomenklatura,* had to be approved by the Central Committee staff. All real debate within the parties was forbidden, and rank-and-file members had no choice but to carry out the decisions made by leaders above them in the hierarchy.

The Communist Party was the only institution that mattered. Anyone desiring a successful career had to be a loyal and active party member. Almost every child joined the party-dominated Young Pioneers, the equivalent of the Boy Scouts and Girl Scouts in the United States. Young men and women with any ambition at all joined the Communist Youth League, from which adult party members were recruited. The party determined where high school and university graduates were sent to work. Trade unions, women's groups, and even stamp-collecting societies were under party control. Most important of all, the Communist Party presided over a command economy, which determined what goods and services would be produced, where they would be sold, and how much they would cost. It is no wonder that Western observers called these regimes totalitarian!

There was some variation from country to country. Communist control was never quite as absolute in Eastern Europe as it was in the Soviet Union. Demonstrations against Communist rule took place as early as 1953 in East Germany. Major protest movements were put down in Poland and Hungary in 1956, but they reappeared with the reform movement in and subsequent Soviet invasion of Czechoslovakia in 1968. After that, the focus turned to Poland, where a series of protest movements culminated in the rise of the independent trade union **Solidarity** in 1980–81, the first time a Communist regime officially acknowledged the existence of an independent political organization. There were also some economic reforms in Eastern Europe—most notably, experiments with market mechanisms in Hungary.

China followed yet another path. Unlike most other parties, the Chinese Communist Party (CCP) had always been able to maintain a good deal of autonomy, largely because it spent the 1930s and 1940s fighting a guerrilla war and was often beyond Moscow's reach. After coming to power, the CCP followed the Soviet line until 1956. However, because **Mao Zedong** and the other top Chinese leaders objected to de-Stalinization and the other Soviet reforms, they began adopting their own, more revolutionary policies.

The CCP also became divided into factions that opposed each others' policies over the next twenty years. At times, the left, increasingly associated with Mao himself, was dominant and led the country in what it called a revolutionary direction, most notably in the chaotic and violent **Cultural Revolution,** which lasted from 1965 into the 1970s. When the more orthodox faction was dominant, the leadership adopted more moderate, Soviet-style policies focusing on industrial development.

Within two years of Mao's death in 1976, the moderates, led by **Deng Xiaoping,** took control. Deng and his colleagues began a program of dramatic economic reforms that we will explore in more detail in Chapter 10. Here it is enough to note that, however much economic reform they have countenanced, Chinese elites have never tolerated any changes that threatened the party's stranglehold on power.

The Graying of Communism

It is impossible to overstate how much the Marxist-Leninists changed in the half century following the Bolshevik revolution. Revolutionary leaders gave way to the likes of Leonid Brezhnev with his love of cowboy movies and German luxury cars. Purges were replaced by what the Soviets called "trust in cadres" that all but ensured party officials would retain their jobs as long as they didn't cause trouble. Leaders who forced their countries to change were replaced by "machine" politicians intent on maintaining their own power and the perks of office. At best, the Communist leaders of the 1970s and 1980s were old men like Brezhnev, desperately clinging to power (and life) as the times continued to pass them by. At worst, they were venal and corrupt, like the members of the Ceausescu family, who oppressed the impoverished Romanian people to get castles, personal armies, and Swiss bank accounts for themselves—all somehow justified in the name of Marx.

Even if they had wanted to, it is doubtful that these leaders could have used the party state to produce the kind of economic change that should have been on their agendas. Charles Lindblom likened these centralized authoritarian regimes to our thumbs.[2] If you think about it, you realize that the thumb is best suited for crudely pushing things, whereas the other four fingers are better suited for doing more subtle, delicate, and complicated work. Lindblom suggested that in the earlier stages of industrial development political "thumbs" are good enough. At that point, a country needs more cement, railroad track, electric wire, and other relatively low-tech commodities. These can be manufactured by unskilled workers, including those who are forced to follow orders. Although most historians now doubt that the collectivization of agricultural and forced industrialization were the best ways to bring the Soviet Union into the twentieth century, there is no denying that such authoritarian mechanisms got the job done, if brutally.

However, a more modern, technologically sophisticated economy requires organizations and skills that are more like political "fingers." Take, for example, a television. Unlike a tub of cement, a modern television has many complicated parts, from the remote control to the picture tube to the electronic circuitry inside the box. Workmanship and quality control are extremely important. If the frequency emitted by the remote control or the wiring or the circuitry is just a little bit off, the television won't work. This is something a "thumb"-based economy is not very good at.

Most importantly, moving toward "fingers" would undoubtedly have meant loosening many political as well as economic controls and abandoning the two defining elements of Communist societies: the party state

---

[2] Charles Lindblom, *Politics and Markets* (New York: Basic Books, 1977).

and the command economy. In this sense, the party state became an increasingly ineffective way to run a country. To be sure, the party retained its monopoly over who the decision makers were and what policies they adopted. And the party kept the secret police and other repressive agencies well staffed and equipped. However, leaders in all these countries found it ever more difficult to control their societies. People were better educated, and this led them to seek more control over the decisions that shaped their lives. Moreover, the influx of Western tourists and mass media made it clear to millions of people that the propaganda they heard from their own governments was wrong. People in the West were much better off than they were.

Their societies increasingly paid the cost for the lack of fingers. Growth rates dropped precipitously. The economic woes were most serious in the sectors in which fingers were most needed, such as light industry, research and development, and consumer goods. The downturn was reflected in a poor standard of living that left everyone in the Communist world lagging further and further behind people in the West. Most Soviet families, for instance, still lived in tiny, shoddily built apartments, often sharing kitchens and bathrooms with other families. People throughout the Communist world had money, but there were not enough goods to satisfy the pent-up demand. The waiting list for cars was so long that used cars cost more than new ones simply because they were available.

Even the military, the most efficient sector of the Soviet economy, lagged behind. Soviet submarines were much noisier, and therefore easier to detect, than American ones. The United States developed reliable solid fuels for its missiles in the 1960s; it is not clear whether the Soviets ever did. Soviet nuclear warheads were larger than American ones because they had to be; Soviet missiles were a lot less accurate, and so larger bombs were needed to get a "kill" if the missile landed considerably off target.

When Brezhnev died in 1982, Communist regimes were facing ever more serious problems that imperiled the very principles on which they were based. The external problems were easiest to see. Rapid technological change, the development of global financial and commercial markets, and more rapid rates of growth, not only in the West but in parts of the third world, were leaving the Communist countries in an ever-deepening economic bind. Meanwhile, a renewed cold war "forced" the Soviets to spend even more on defense at a time when the costs of doing so spiraled. The domestic challenges were harder to see. Nonetheless, these societies were changing, and many people, especially the young, were

chafing under continued repressive rule, as the plotline of *Good Bye, Lenin!* attests.

The Crisis of Communism: Suicide by Public Policy

Reform: Too Little, Too Late

In retrospect, it is easy to see how fragile these regimes had become. At the time, however, most observers assumed that the party state was here to stay. As evidence of its continued clout, the Soviets invaded Afghanistan in 1979, and the Polish government was able to impose martial law and drive Solidarity underground two years later.

Perhaps trying to blind themselves to the inevitable, the party states refused to change. The Soviets continued to select leaders from the same old generation, picking Yuri Andropov to succeed Brezhnev, and then Konstantin Chernenko when Andropov died fifteen months later. With the exception of Poland, the Eastern European countries all had general secretaries who had taken office in the 1960s. Only China was engaging in any kind of reform, but its aging leaders were carefully limiting reform to economics, not politics.

In 1985, however, European Communism's final act began. (See table 8.3.) When Chernenko died, the Soviet Central Committee had no choice but to turn to the next generation and appointed Mikhail Gorbachev as general secretary. Gorbachev was by no means responsible for everything that happened in the Communist world afterward. Nonetheless, he was the catalyst who unleashed the forces that brought about unprecedented and unexpected change.

When Gorbachev came to power, he was known to be something of a reformer, but no one expected him to go anywhere near as far as he did. After all, he had risen through the ranks of the Soviet Communist Party and

▌ TABLE 8.3 Key Events in the Crisis of Communism

YEAR	EVENT
1956	Hungarian uprising
1968	Prague Spring in Czechoslovakia
1980–81	Emergence of Solidarity in Poland and imposition of martial law
1985	Gorbachev chosen general secretary of CPSU
1988	Opening of iron curtain in Hungary
1989	Collapse of communism in Eastern Europe Democracy movement in China
1990	German unification
1991	Disintegration of Soviet Union

had triumphed because he had gained the support of old-guard politicians.

Quickly, however, Gorbachev began replacing the older generation with younger men and women. Together, they introduced reforms that they hoped would revitalize Communism. In the end, the political forces they unleashed killed it instead.

These four types of reforms will be discussed in detail in the next chapter:

- **Glasnost,** or more openness in the political system
- Democratization, beginning with the introduction of elements of competition to the way the Communist Party was run
- **Perestroika,** or economic restructuring, including a degree of private ownership
- New thinking in foreign policy, especially improved relations with the West

It is important to emphasize that when the Soviet leadership initiated these reforms they certainly did not expect them to destroy Communism. That they would prove fatal to Communism as we knew and feared it only became clear when the spirit of reform reached Eastern Europe and hit a political roadblock.

There, the elderly party leaders resisted implementing glasnost, perestroika, and democratization. East Germany's Erich Honecker went so far as to forbid the press to carry stories about the changes taking place in the Soviet Union.

But Honecker and his colleagues would not be able to maintain the Brezhnevite status quo for long. There were pressures for change from abroad, most notably and ironically from the Soviet Union itself. Gorbachev and his supporters in the Soviet leadership had decided that they no longer had to keep an iron grip on Eastern Europe. The security value of the "buffer states" had declined in a world in which nuclear missiles could fly over Eastern Europe and strike the Soviet Union in a matter of minutes. In fact, Eastern Europe had become such a financial burden on the Soviet Union that, at the height of the popularity of the *Star Wars* films, an American political scientist titled an article on Soviet–Eastern European relations "The Empire Strikes Back."

By 1988 the Soviet Union was eager to see change in Eastern Europe, though certainly not the total collapse of Communism. Gorbachev continued to push the region's recalcitrant leaders to reform. It was even clear that the Soviets were willing to consider modifications in their relationship with Eastern Europe.

Changes within Eastern Europe itself were at least as important. To varying degrees, these countries were suf-

---

Conflict and Democratization in the Communist World

SOME KEY DIFFERENCES between the industrialized democracies and the current and former Communist regimes become easy to see in considering the role of conflict and democratization in each.

In Part 2 we saw that democracies have taken firm root—albeit often after centuries of turmoil—and that conflict is viewed as a normal part of political life.

In the countries covered in Part 3, however, almost all forms of conflict were suppressed throughout the Communist period. All had some dissident movements, but rarely did they reach beyond a tiny proportion of the population or threaten the regime. The collapse of Communism in Eurasia and the changes in what remains of the Communist world have brought much of the conflict that lurked just below the surface into the open. Indeed, as the twenty-first century begins, many of these countries have more conflict than they can effectively handle and still build a democracy or market economy.

Thus, if there are parallels to the Western democracies, it is to France or Germany of the early 1900s, when their regimes were anything but stable and legitimate in large part because of protests coming from literally dozens of groups.

---

fering from the same economic problems as the Soviet Union. More importantly, the cultural changes discussed earlier had progressed further in the more economically advanced countries of Eastern Europe. Moreover, none of the Eastern European regimes (save, perhaps, Albania) had ever succeeded either in completely suppressing dissent or in achieving even the limited degree of legitimacy found in Brezhnev's Soviet Union.

1989: The Year That Changed the World

The revolution began in Poland. In 1988 Solidarity reappeared, stronger than it had been when General Wojciech Jaruzelski imposed martial law in December 1981. His government was quickly forced into "round table" negotiations with Solidarity and other non-Communist organizations. Out of those discussions came an agreement to hold elections in which some seats would be reserved for the Communist Party and others freely contested. Solidarity won a resounding victory in the competition for open seats, and in August the Communists agreed to give up power, the first time that had ever happened anywhere. Jaruzelski stayed on temporarily as president, but the Catholic intellectual Tadeusz Mazo-wiecki held the more powerful position of prime minister in a Solidarity-run government that dismantled the command economy within months.

The next to fall was Hungary, where the first liberal economic reforms had been implemented in the mid-1960s. By the late 1980s, reformists within the Communist Party had grown strong enough to replace Janos Kadar, whom the Soviets had put in power in 1956. The new leaders dismantled the iron curtain along the Austrian border. They also roundly criticized the Soviet invasion of 1956 and the Hungarians who had cooperated with the USSR. They even stopped calling themselves Communists. Finally, the leadership agreed to free elections in April 1990, in which anti-Communists won an overwhelming majority.

Opening the border in Hungary inadvertently sparked more sweeping changes. East German tourists vacationing there crossed the open border into Austria and then moved on to West Germany. Even though the Warsaw Pact required them to keep the border closed, the Hungarian government did nothing to stop the escapees, claiming that its commitment to human rights was more important than the provisions of an outdated political and military alliance. By the fall of 1990, thousands of people were fleeing to the West every day.

Meanwhile, protest movements in East Germany sprang up, and pressures continued to mount until the unthinkable happened. On 9 November 1989, jubilant Germans smashed open the Berlin Wall, and people from both sides celebrated together. The most visible sign of the Cold War disappeared.

The pace of change continued to accelerate. The East German government agreed to free elections in spring 1990, which Christian Democrats with strong ties to their colleagues in West Germany won handily. By that time, German unification as a part of NATO, which had seemed impossible a year before, was inevitable.

The quickest to fall was the Czechoslovak government headed by Gustav Husak, whom the Soviets had installed in power in 1968. The Soviet invasion of Czechoslovakia in August of that year was a brutal response to the peaceful reform movement dubbed the "Prague Spring." Anti-Soviet demonstrations broke out again during the late 1980s. Hundreds of thousands jammed Wenceslaus Square in Prague on a daily basis. Finally, in 1989, the previously powerless legislature reacted to public pressure and chose Vaclav Havel—who had been in jail less than a year before—to be the new president. Even more remarkably, the legislature elected the liberal Communist leader of the 1968 "Prague Spring," Alexan-

© Reuters/CORBIS

One of many people who took a turn at knocking down the Berlin Wall.

der Dubcek, to be its own head. When elections were finally held in June 1990, the reforms were confirmed when the Communists came in a distant third.

Only in Romania did the revolution turn violent. That country had been ruled by Nicolae and Elena Ceausescu as little more than a personal fiefdom since the mid-1960s. Even as the Romanian people were forced to starve so that the country could pay off its international debt, the Ceausescus built monuments to themselves. Elena Ceausescu had herself named head of the Academy of Sciences and awarded herself a doctorate even though she had the equivalent of a fourth-grade education. The Ceausescus also controlled the largest and most ruthless secret police in Eastern Europe, the Securitate.

The first protests took place in the provincial city of Timisoara on 17 December 1989. Securitate forces fired into the crowd, killing hundreds. A civil war broke out, with the Securitate and other forces loyal to the Ceausescus on one side and much of the army and armed citizens on the other. Within a week the government had been overthrown. The Ceausescus fled but were soon captured. On Christmas day they were executed. By the end of the month, Securitate opposition was crushed, and a regime headed by the reform Communist Ion Iliescu was in power.

These successful and largely nonviolent revolutions were not the only earthquakes to hit the Communist world in 1989. Economic reforms in China were beginning to show some promising results. Political reform, however, was not forthcoming. In early 1989, pro-democracy protests broke out as a group led by students occupied the symbolic heart of Chinese politics—**Tiananmen Square** in downtown Beijing.

In May 1989, Gorbachev became the first Soviet leader since the start of the Sino-Soviet split to visit Beijing. As in Eastern Europe, Gorbachev served as a lightning rod for reformers. Massive, adoring crowds greeted him wherever he went, giving more and more support to the pro-democracy movement. The crowds kept growing. As they did, hopes for any kind of peaceful end to the protests evaporated. The government began assembling troops around Beijing. During the night of 3–4 June, they stormed the square, killing as many as a thousand students and others who were still there. After martial law was imposed, China was widely criticized as the most repressive of the Communist regimes.

In 1990 the focus of attention shifted back to the Soviet Union, where centrifugal forces were tearing the country apart. The Communist Party had already given up its legal monopoly on power. New organizations were cropping up at every imaginable point along the political spectrum. The new Congress of People's Deputies and Supreme Soviet were turning into real legislative bodies. Groups demanding sovereignty and, sometimes, total independence emerged in each of the fourteen non-Russian republics. In many of them, ethnic antagonisms escalated into violence that bordered on civil war.

At the party congress in the summer of 1990, **Boris Yeltsin** led fellow radical reformers out of the Communist Party. Meanwhile, Gorbachev increasingly turned to conservative leaders within the military and security apparatus to keep himself in power even though advisers such as former foreign minister Eduard Shevardnadze kept warning of a right-wing coup. By April 1991, the Baltic republics (Lithuania, Latvia, and Estonia) were clamoring for independence. The economy was on the brink of collapse.

Finally, the most impossible of impossible events occurred. On 19 August 1991, military and security service leaders attempted a coup against Gorbachev at his villa in the Crimea. For nearly four days, Gorbachev was held hostage, and his wife apparently was psychologically abused by men he had put in power. In Moscow, Yeltsin, his most vocal critic, led the opposition in the streets that toppled the plotters. On 22 August, Gorbachev returned to Moscow and to what he thought was power.

The coup proved to be the last straw. The Baltic republics gained their independence. Every remaining Soviet republic declared itself sovereign. Yeltsin emerged as the most powerful politician. Finally, in December, leaders of most of the republics agreed to form the Commonwealth of Independent States. Gorbachev was not even invited to the founding meeting. On 31 December, he resigned the presidency of a country that no longer existed.

The Remnants of the Communist World

In early 2005 there were only five Communist countries left—China, North Korea, Vietnam, Laos, and Cuba. Far less attention has been paid to the reasons Communist regimes survived in these countries than to the reasons they collapsed in Eurasia. The limited research on the subject has, however, pointed to three main reasons.

First, each of their parties remains willing to use force. One of the remarkable aspects of the events in Eastern Europe and the Soviet Union was that the police and the army (that is, the party) were not willing to fire on their own people. With the exception of Romania, only a handful of people died in the revolutions, and those deaths were inadvertent. In these other countries, however, the regimes have been more willing to resort to force.

Second, these countries are poorer and less open to outside influences than was the Soviet bloc. In other words, the cultural developments discussed earlier had not progressed anywhere near as far. To be sure, Chinese students and members of the middle class were beginning to demand "discos and democracy," as journalist Orville Schell put it, but they constituted only a tiny proportion of the total population.

Recent reports hint that some children of members of the Cuban elite have grave reservations about the regime. However, there are only a handful of these people, whereas there were thousands of young "new thinkers" beginning to build careers and exert political influence in the Soviet Union during the 1980s. Similarly, the American press has given such spectacular events as Elian Gonzalez's case and the defection of star baseball players a lot of attention but have probably overstated the degree to which they reflect widespread dissatisfaction with the regime. The key issue for Cuba is what will happen when Castro finally leaves the scene.

Third, these countries had been outside the Soviet Union's orbit for quite some time before 1989. Cuba and Vietnam were Soviet allies and, in many ways, were dependent on the USSR economically and militarily. However, the Soviets exerted relatively little influence on the way local Communists ruled. They also had little desire or ability to force their leaders to adopt perestroika or glasnost. Thus, during his April 1989 visit to Cuba, Gorbachev had no success in convincing Castro to reform, nor were there any demonstrations in the streets of Havana as there would be throughout the rest of the Communist world that spring, summer, and fall.

Transitions

There was a good bit of optimism in the first heady days after the collapse of Communism in Eastern Europe and the Soviet Union. Given the demonstration of "people power" in 1989, many thought it would be relatively easy for those countries to make the transition to a market economy and democratic government. Those hopes gave way to widespread pessimism following a wave of strife and civil war, weak leadership, and further economic deterioration.

Conditions have improved in most of those countries since then. With a few exceptions, their economies hit rock bottom and began to recover, though they still have a long way to go. Many have relatively stable and democratic governments. Nonetheless, in only a handful of cases can we safely say that major progress has been made toward either democracy or capitalism.

To see how difficult the first stages of the economic side of the transitions were, consider table 8.4, which is based on data gathered and analyzed by the World Bank for the period 1989–95. None of these countries had it easy. Groups 1 and 2 are made up mostly of the former satellite countries and Baltic republics from the Soviet Union. Though they did the best, their economies shrank, and they suffered from an inflation rate that saw prices at least double each year through the mid-1990s.

Groups 3 and 4 consist of the other twelve former Soviet republics, including Russia. Their economies declined by as much as 10 percent per year, which meant that in 1995 some of them produced only half the goods and services they had before the collapse of the USSR. Inflation rates were typically in the 500 percent range, which meant that prices went up fivefold each year. Even more remarkable than the economic statistics are those on life expectancy. In Russia, the average man could expect to live ten years less than he would have a decade earlier because of the failing social welfare, health care, and economic systems.

The World Bank also identified a subset of these four groups—countries that were severely affected by ethnic conflict. Before we proceed, note two things about that row of the table. It includes neither Russia, because the fighting in Chechnya had yet to begin, nor Bosnia, because neither the World Bank nor local authorities could gather reliable statistics. The wars in those countries not

▌ **TABLE 8.4** Economic Change in Former Communist Countries, 1989–95

COUNTRY OR TYPE	AVERAGE GDP GROWTH	AVERAGE INFLATION (PERCENTAGE)	LIBERALIZATION INDEX	CHANGE IN LIFE EXPECTANCY (YEARS)
Group 1	−1.6	106.0	6.9	0.7
Group 2	−4.2	149.2	4.7	−0.2
Group 3	−9.6	466.4	3.4	−4.4
Group 4	−6.7	809.6	2.0	−1.6
Countries affected by regional tensions	−11.7	929.7	3.9	0.5
China/Vietnam	9.4	8.4	5.5	2.1

Notes: Chinese data are for the entire reform period (1979–95) and include Vietnam for the liberalization index.

Group 1: Poland, Slovenia, Hungary, Croatia,* Macedonia,* Czech Republic, Slovakia

Group 2: Estonia, Lithuania, Bulgaria, Latvia, Albania, Romania, Mongolia

Group 3: Kyrgyz Republic, Russia, Moldova, Armenia,* Georgia,* Kakakstan

Group 4: Uzbekistan, Ukraine, Belarus, Azerbaijan,* Tajikistan,* Turkmenistan

Countries with an asterisk (*) are among those severely affected by regional tensions. The table does not have data on Bosnia and Yugoslavia (Serbia and Montenegro) because of the continuing war there.

Source: Adapted from World Bank, *From Plan to Market: World Development Report 1996* (Washington, D.C.: World Bank, 1996), 18, 33.

Liberalization in the Current and Former Communist World

LIBERALIZATION IN GENERAL and privatization in particular have been very popular policies since the collapse of Communism in Eurasia. In fact, the process began somewhat earlier in China, Hungary, and Yugoslavia.

These countries also provide us with a classic example of how theoretical predictions and empirical realities do not always jibe. In this case, the now-dominant liberal economic theory tells us that freeing markets, decentralizing control of an economy, and transferring ownership from state to private hands should do tremendous good.

However, the situation on the ground has never been quite so rosy. In countries in which **shock therapy** has been fully implemented, we have seen tremendous growth in the disparities between the winners and losers of economic reform. In most countries, as well, political pressures have forced governments to slow the pace of reform to some degree, and resentment against change has sparked the limited left-wing resurgence noted at the beginning of this chapter.

---

only disrupted the economies, as shown in this table, but also made effective government—let alone a transition to democracy—impossible.

Finally, contrast these groups of countries to those in the final row—China and Vietnam, the two remaining Communist regimes that have reformed their economies the most. Instead of the decline we see for the rest of the countries in the table, the Chinese economy grew by an average of nearly 10 percent a year, which meant that overall output doubled during that same period.

(Relative) Success: Eastern and Central Europe

All the former Communist countries that have been admitted to the European Union or NATO are found in the first two rows of table 8.4. There is no commonly accepted explanation of why they have succeeded more than the others. However, a glance at the experience of Hungary gives us a good look at the kinds of trends political scientists stress the most.

First, Hungary is ethnically homogeneous. Almost 90 percent of its population is ethnically Hungarian. The largest minority are the often ill-treated Roma (or gypsies), but they make up less than 5 percent of the population.

Second, Hungary's economy is doing relatively well. It grew by almost 3 percent in 2003. Although the gap between rich and poor is growing, GNP per capita is almost $14,000 per year, or about 40 percent of that in the United States. One indicator of Hungary's growing affluence is that 70 percent of the population owned a cell phone by the end of 2003.

Third, and perhaps most importantly, the Hungarian transition occurred so smoothly in part because many reform-minded Communists and opposition leaders cooperated with each other in a process political scientists call **pacting.** Among other things, that made it relatively easy for the former Communists to turn themselves into a Western-style social democratic party that has won two elections since 1989 and to establish something approaching a consensus on economic policy with their former opponents.

Thus, both democracy and market capitalism are taking root in Hungary and the other reasonably successful post-Communist states in Eastern Europe. In Hungary's case that can be seen in the fact that the left and the right have each won two elections since 1989 and the transition from left to right and back to left again has goon smoothly each time. Ideological tensions between left and right are quite high, but most observers think they are no more intense than those in the United States between Democrats and Republicans in the aftermath of the 2000 and 2004 presidential elections.

Troubled Transitions: The Former Soviet Union

The case of Russia and most of the former Soviet Republics is a different story. With the exception of the Baltic states (Latvia, Estonia, and Lithuania), these countries have had a much harder time making the political and economic transition. Like Russia, most have had several elections. However, the best we can say about these elections is that several have been relatively free and fair contests. However, very few of them resulted in a genuine shift in power in which a party or coalition that was once in opposition took office. All, too, suffer from corruption because an elite cadre of former Communists has not only entrenched itself in political power but has enriched itself by gaining control of the countries' leading enterprises, whether they remain in public hands or have been privatized. We will defer dealing with these difficulties in any detail until the next chapter.

Ethnic Conflict

The first President Bush used to enjoy noting that the forty-five years between the end of World War II and the collapse of Communism marked the longest period in recorded history without a war in Europe. Unfortunately, that period lasted only forty-five years.

By the early 1990s, sporadic fighting had broken out in a number of the former Soviet republics. It began even before the USSR collapsed with the conflict between Armenia and Azerbaijan over the predominantly Armenian enclave of Nagorno-Karabakh within Azerbaijan.

For our purposes, it is most important to note two conflicts that have had a devastating impact on the peoples caught up in the fighting. The former Yugoslavia has experienced five wars since the breakup of the country in 1991. Only the first one, over the independence of Slovenia, resulted in few casualties and caused little damage. By contrast, upwards of 250,000 people were killed and millions more were turned into refugees during the struggle in Bosnia-Herzegovina, which also introduced the notion of ethnic cleansing into the world's political vocabulary.

The wars between Russia and rebels in Chechnya have been even more devastating. Antagonism toward Russians in the tiny, mostly Muslim region of Chechnya has existed since it was incorporated into Russia in the early nineteenth century. But bloody fighting erupted when Russia put down a first bid for independence in 1994–96. After two years of fighting, tens of thousands were dead, the city of Grozny had been leveled, and no settlement had been reached. The war broke out again shortly after Vladimir Putin became Russia's prime minister in 1999. This time the Russians were able to defeat the rebels more handily, but only after thousands of civilians and rebels had been killed. Sporadic fighting continues more than five years after the war supposedly ended and has included the world's deadliest terrorist attack since 9/11.

What's Left of Marxism?

North Korea and Cuba have kept their orthodox Marxist-Leninist systems, and their people have paid the price. Their countries are among the poorest in the world, and there have been reports of mass starvation in North Korea.

In contrast, the others have embraced economic reform to the point that countries such as China and Vietnam have mixed economies in which the private sector is far more dynamic than the remaining state-owned industries. In fact, the shift toward capitalism

---

Globalization and the Communist World

PRIOR TO the 1980s, global trends did not affect Communist countries as much as they did the democracies covered in Part 2. However, globalization did have a bearing on them then—and has an even more powerful impact today—in two broad ways.

First, global forces were at least indirectly responsible for the crisis of communism that is at the heart of this chapter. The Communist countries certainly had their internal problems. However, they might well have survived had they not faced increased economic pressures from, and a renewed arms race with, the West.

Second, international influences have left their current states in a weakened position, economically and otherwise. As we will see with the Russian economy in the next chapter, the triumph of capitalism has given Western bankers, industrialists, and politicos unprecedented influence over the internal affairs of most of these countries. And that impact is not merely economic, as the popularity of Western cultural icons from CNN to Coca-Cola to Barbie dolls attests. To cite but one admittedly trivial example, you can buy *matroshka* dolls (multiple dolls within dolls) in Moscow's open-air markets with likenesses of the Clinton family (including Monica Lewinsky), the Simpsons, and the New York Yankees.

---

and the popularity of the growing consumer culture is so pronounced that there is little of Marxist egalitarianism left.

The one remaining aspect of Marxism-Leninism is the continued political monopoly enjoyed by the Communist parties in these countries. As we will see in Chapter 10, the Chinese Communists have cracked down whenever any signs of political dissent appeared, and, so far, most Chinese citizens have been willing to accept economic reform without political liberalization. However, many observers are convinced that it is only a matter of time before a significant number of people demand political as well as economic change.

Feedback

When political scientists wrote about the totalitarian nature of Communist regimes, they invariably included the media in their list of characteristics. Technologically, the media in the Communist bloc were never the equal of those in the West. The party also controlled them hook, line, and sinker. Every newspaper, magazine, and book printed, as well as all television and radio outlets, were controlled by the party. What's more, anything printed or broadcast was subject to prior censorship. Meanwhile, the authorities kept Western media out.

That started to change in the 1980s. Advances in communication technology made it more difficult to keep Western influences out. Then, during the Gorbachev years, there was a noticeable loosening of controls in the Soviet Union and, to a lesser degree, in Eastern Europe. Since then, the printed press has been just as open as in the West and, given the nature of political and economic life, even more contentious. Even in Russia, where the state still dominates the main national television channels, viewers have little trouble finding criticism of the status quo in newspapers and on the radio.

There are cracks in the party's protective armor in the countries that have kept their Communist regimes. The protesters in Tiananmen Square were able to coordinate their activities in part because of faxes they received from Chinese students abroad, and the CCP is now struggling to limit access to satellite television and the Internet. Similarly, Cuba's isolation is less than complete, something U.S. sports fans discovered when they learned that 1998 World Series star Orlando Hernandez (El Duque) of the New York Yankees had watched his half-brother Livan's exploits for the Florida Marlins on television beamed from the United States before deciding to make his own escape from the island.

Conclusion: The End of an Era

Those of us who are old enough to have lived through the height of the cold war "knew" that the Soviet Union and its allies would be competitors with and adversaries of the West for the indefinite future. The superpower rivalry seemed to be the most important and most dangerous relationship in international political life.

By contrast, most students reading this book will have been under the age of ten when the Berlin Wall came down. In other words, Communism and the cold war will be at best foggy memories. The defining role that they played for the first forty-five years after World War II will seem like a historical relic.

Nonetheless, it is important for young people today to understand that period for two reasons. First, as we saw in Part 2, the cold war rivalry played a major role in

determining the way the liberal democracies evolved. We will see this again in Part 4 when we consider the third world. There, the competition between the United States and Soviet Union not only helped determine what kind of regimes emerged but also, tragically, exacerbated existing regional conflicts and escalated them into some of the bloodiest wars in history.

Second, we cannot understand politics in the former Communist world today without exploring the Communist past itself in depth. This is true not only of a country like Russia, which is struggling to shed itself of Communist institutions and values, but also of the few remaining Communist regimes, like China, in which the nature of its Marxist past limits its ability to enact and implement reforms within the framework of the party state.

Key Terms

Concepts

Base	Means of production
Bourgeoisie	*Nomenklatura*
Command economy	Pacting
Communism	Party state
Contradictions	Perestroika
Cult of personality	Proletariat
Democratic centralism	Satellite
Dialectic	Shock therapy
Glasnost	Socialism
Historical materialism	Superstructure
Marxism-Leninism	Totalitarianism

People

Brezhnev, Leonid	Lenin, Vladimir
Castro, Fidel	Mao Zedong
Deng Xiaoping	Marx, Karl
Engels, Friedrich	Stalin, Joseph
Gorbachev, Mikhail	Yeltsin, Boris
Khrushchev, Nikita	

Organizations, Places, and Events

Bolsheviks	Secretariat
Comintern	Solidarity
Cultural Revolution	Third International
De-Stalinization	Tiananmen Square
General secretary	Warsaw Pact
Politburo	

Critical Thinking Exercises

1 Why did Marx think that socialism could emerge only after capitalism? What difference did it make that Marxist regimes first took power in such countries as Russia and China?

2   What is democratic centralism? How did it—and other factors—give rise to what are often called totalitarian regimes?

3   Following the death of Stalin and the ouster of Khrushchev, the Soviet Union and its allies developed regimes that are sometimes referred to as party states. What does that mean?

4   Why did the crisis of Communism set in during the 1980s? Why couldn't the party states in Eurasia cope with it?

5   Why are the post-Communist regimes having such a hard time developing either a democratic government or a successful market economy?

6   What is the likely future of the remaining Communist regimes? Why do you reach that conclusion?

 ## Useful Websites

Because Communism collapsed in Eurasia just as the Internet was becoming even a minor factor in our lives, there are not as many good sites on it as one would like. Both Marxists.org and the Australian National University maintain archives with many of the basic documents in Marxist history.

www.marxists.org

www.anu.edu.au/polsci/marx

My colleague Bryan Caplan of George Mason University's Department of Economics runs a highly critical "Museum of Communism" website.

www.gmu.edu/depts/economics/bcaplan/museum/marframe.htm

About.com's site on Communism no longer seems active. However, it still has dozens of good short articles on events from the twentieth century.

history1900s.about.com/cs/communism/

Transitions Online and Radio Free Europe/Radio Liberty both provide regular news feeds on post-Communist countries.

www.tol.cz

www.rferl.org

St. Francis Xavier University in Canada has an excellent program in post-Communist studies, including a website with some of its scholars' own writing and a great group of lists.

www.stfx.ca/pinstitutes/cpcs/

 ## InfoTrac College Edition Sources

Barber, Benjamin. "An Epitaph for Marxism."

Chirot, Daniel. "The Lessons of 1989."

Crowley, Stephen. "Explaining Labour Weakness in Post-Communist Eastern Europe."

Gilman, Antonio. "The *Communist Manifesto* 150 Years Later."

Kennedy, Michael, and Naomi Galtz. "From Marxism to Postcommunism."

Kluegel, James, and David Mason. "Political Involvement in Transition."

Mayer, Tom. "The Collapse of Soviet Communism."

Further Reading

Ash, Timothy Garton. *The Magic Lantern.* New York: Random House, 1990. The best general account of what happened in Eastern Europe in 1989, by someone who witnessed most of it first-hand.

Chavance, Bernard. *The Transformation of Communist Systems: Economic Reform Since the 1950s.* Trans. by Charles Hauss. Boulder, Colo.: Westview Press, 1994. The only brief overview of Communist political economy and efforts at reform that carries into the early 1990s.

Dawisha, Karen. *Eastern Europe, Gorbachev, and Reform.* New York: Cambridge University Press, 1990. The best academic treatment of domestic politics in Eastern Europe in the years before 1989.

Diamond, Larry, and Marc F. Plattner, eds. *Democracy After Communism.* Baltimore: Johns Hopkins University Press, 2002. A generally excellent collection of articles drawn from the *Journal of Democracy,* which means they were written for a general more than a scholarly audience.

Lindblom, Charles. *Politics and Markets.* New York: Basic Books, 1977. A rather dense, theoretical, and dated book, but also one of the first to identify the limits to what could be accomplished with a command economy.

Mason, David S. *Revolution in East Central Europe: The Rise and Fall of Communism and the Cold War,* 2nd ed. Boulder, Colo.: Westview Press, 1997. An outstanding overview of why Communism came to power in Eastern Europe, why it collapsed, and why the countries in that region have had such trouble since then.

Nolan, Peter. *China's Rise/Russia's Fall.* London: Cassell/Pinter, 1997. The only good book contrasting the reforms in the two countries; makes an unusual, left-of-center argument.

Przeworski, Adam, et al. *Sustainable Democracy.* New York: Cambridge University Press, 1995. By a group of twenty-one prominent social scientists; an exploration of what we know about democratization, drawing on the experiences of southern Europe, South America, and Eurasia.

Tucker, Robert C., ed. *The Marx and Engels Reader,* 2nd ed. New York: Norton, 1984. Among the best of the many collections of Marx's and Engels' basic works.

World Bank. *World Development Report: From Plan to Market.* New York: Oxford University Press, 1997. A report on liberalization in the "transitional" economies; heavy going, but informative.

*Autocratic leadership existed in
Russia for many centuries, changing
only its ideological colors and
method of legitimization.*

LILIA SHEVTSOVA

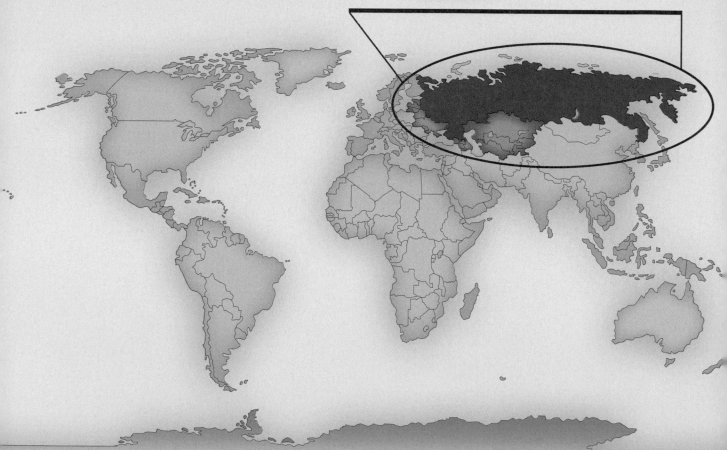

Chapter 9

RUSSIA

CHAPTER OUTLINE

The Basics: Russia

OFFICIAL NAME	RUSSIAN FEDERATION
Size	17,075,200 sq. km (roughly 1.75 times the size of the United States)
Climate	Subarctic in much of the country
Population	144 million
Currency	26.53 rubles = $1
Ethnic composition	81.5% Russian, 3.8% Tatar, 3% Ukrainian, 11.7% Other
Life Expectancy	Men 60, Women 73
Capital	Moscow
President	Vladimir Putin (1999)
Prime Minister	Mikhail Fradkov (2004)

Guilty until Proven Guilty

On 24 October 2003, two busloads of heavily armed police officers stormed a private airplane while it was being refuelled in Novosobirsk. They promptly arrested its main passenger, **Mikhail Khodorkovsky** (1963–), who controlled Yukos, Russia's largest oil company. At the time, Khodorkovsky was the wealthiest person in Russia with about a billion dollars of assets in his own name and control of at least ten times that amount in companies and stock. Rumor had it that his empire accounted for 7 percent of the government's total tax revenue.

Khodorkovsky was one of the dozen or so oligarchs who had risen to positions of prominence and wealth during the 1990s because they had been able to capitalize on the privatization of formerly state-owned enterprises. They were able to do that in large part because of their close relationship with President **Boris Yeltsin,** who ran the country from the collapse of the Soviet Union in 1991 until his surprise resignation on 31 December 1999.

Some of the oligarchs quickly ran afoul of Yeltsin's hand-picked successor, **Vladimir Putin** (1952–). The two most powerful of them, Boris Berezovsky and Vladimir Gusinsky, had already been forced into exile. Khodorkovsky, however, resisted the pressure from the government even after he was arrested and charged with seven

Mikhail Khodorkovsky in the cage he was kept in during his trial.

AFP/Getty Images

crimes, including the alleged failure of Yukos to pay as much as $4.5 billion in taxes.

There is little doubt that the oligarchs had used their connections to engage in massive insider trading and unethical and illegal business practices. All had some connections to organized crime.

But Khodorkovsky was widely seen as the most honest oligarch. So his incarceration in solitary confinement with minimal access to his attorneys and business colleagues was roundly criticized at home and abroad. When his trial began in July 2004, Khodorkovsky was forced to stand in a cage for the duration of each day's proceedings, as the accompanying photo shows. Even more ominously, the headline in the *New York Times* that morning was "guilty until proven guilty," because the court and its procedures were so rigged that there was no realistic chance that he could be found not guilty.

For Putin's critics, this was just the tip of the iceberg. There is no doubt that Putin's leadership has brought much-needed stability to Russia or that the worst of its economic freefall that began in the 1980s is over. Nonetheless, the attacks on the oligarchs, the emergence of a new group of oligarchs loyal to Putin, the takeover of all the national television networks, and a presidential and parliamentary election in which Putin and his allies faced only token opposition led academic observers and activists alike to raise new doubts about Russia's chances

for developing an effective democracy. Some critics even argued that Putin was trying to recreate a state almost as powerful as the old Soviet regime, through which he had built his own career.

Thinking about Russia

Khodorkovsky's wealth, power, arrest, and trial illustrate one the most important themes of this chapter and the rest of the book. The stakes of politics in Russia and the other countries we will be considering are much higher than those in any of the states covered in Part 2.

It is not because Russia has business leaders with questionable ethics or corrupt politicians. There are cases of politicians and business executives in every country covered so far that have been brought down for their financial excesses or lapses in legal judgment.

What makes Russia different is that the actions of Putin, Khodorkovsky, and hundreds of others carry far more risks than those of anyone we have seen so far on at least two levels. The one Westerners focus on most often is the economy, which saw its production cut virtually in half in the first decade after Communist rule. Second is Russia's transition from totalitarian rule to democracy, which is proceeding with difficulty—at best. Indeed, since Putin came to power, most outside observers believe that Russia has become less democratic, not more.

Russia's problems are not just political. To get a glimpse of the problems Russia confronts, we will start with three "basics" about the country and its society.

The Basics

Diversity

The **Russian Federation** is the world's largest country, stretching across eleven time zones. Although Russia only has about half the population of the former Soviet Union, it is still the sixth most populous country in the world, trailing only China, India, the United States, Indonesia, and Brazil.

Russia is also blessed with an abundance of natural resources, including oil, natural gas, and precious minerals, though many of these resources lie under permafrost. That is not surprising given that the Russian Federation is also one of the coldest countries on earth. Almost all its territory lies above the forty-eighth parallel, which separates the United States from Canada. St. Petersburg has six hours of dim sunlight in January. Kotlas, in the northern region of Arkhangelsk, has a growing season of about forty-five days, which makes raising even radishes difficult. If you spend time in Russia in January, the weather forecast will become boringly monotonous— *sneg ne bolshoi*—snow, but not much.

For our purposes, the most important thing to note about Russia and the other fourteen former Soviet states is their diversity. As table 9.1 shows, Russia's population, for instance, is only 82 percent Russian, and twelve of the others are even more ethnically diverse. All but Armenia have sizable Russian minorities, which has heightened demands from nationalists inside the federation to re-create the Soviet Union in what they call the **near-abroad.**

As the ethnic strife of the past few years suggests, the Soviet Union was anything but a melting pot. Unlike immigrants who came to the United States voluntarily (other than slaves, of course), most of these groups were forced into the Russian Empire prior to the Communist revolution or into the USSR afterward.

Although most non-Russian groups retained their culture and language, the Soviet regime kept a lid on ethnic protest until the late 1980s. But the reforms of the late 1980s allowed minority groups to voice their dissatisfactions, and by 1991 each republic had declared some form of sovereignty or independence from central rule. Most experienced substantial violence. In some places, ethnic tensions have gotten worse since the collapse of the So-

▌ TABLE 9.1 Ethnic Composition of the Former Soviet Republics

COUNTRY	POPU-LATION (MILLIONS)	TITULAR NATIONALITY (PERCENTAGE)	MAIN MINORITIES (PERCENTAGE)	
Russia	147.0	82	Tatars	4
Ukraine	51.5	73	Russians	22
Uzbekistan	19.8	71	Russians	8
Kazakhstan	16.5	40	Russians	38
			Ukrainians	5
Belarus	10.2	78	Russians	13
Azerbaijan	7.0	83	Russians	6
			Armenians	6
Georgia	5.4	70	Armenians	8
			Russians	6
			Azeris	6
Tajikistan	5.1	62	Uzbeks	23
			Russians	7
Moldova	4.3	65	Ukrainians	14
			Russians	13
Kyrgyzstan	4.3	52	Russians	22
			Uzbeks	12
Lithuania	3.7	80	Russians	9
			Poles	7
Turkmenistan	3.5	72	Russians	9
			Uzbeks	9
Armenia	3.3	93	Azeris	2
Latvia	2.7	52	Russians	35
Estonia	1.6	62	Russians	30

Source: Based on 1989 census.

viet Union. Fighting over the mostly Armenian enclave of Nagomo-Karabakh in Azerbaijan, for example, has continued on and off since 1988. The three Baltic republics passed legislation restricting the ability of ethnic Russians and other "foreigners" who lived in the republics at the time of independence to achieve Lithuanian, Latvian, or Estonian citizenship. The ethnic strife continues to this day, mostly in the on-again, off-again war between Russia and rebels who seek independence in Chechnya.

Poverty

Russia is also much poorer than any of the countries we have covered so far. It is the only major country in the world in which life expectancy is declining, for reasons that have little or nothing to do with HIV/AIDS. A typical urban family lives in a three-room apartment, does not own an automobile, and may not even have a telephone. Living conditions in the countryside are worse. Household tasks take at least twice as long as in the West, because stores are poorly organized and few families have washing machines, microwaves, and other labor-saving devices that are standard in Western homes. Table 9.2 summarizes some recent statistical data on the declining

■ TABLE 9.2 Economic Decline in Russia, 1990–97
(All figures in millions of tons unless otherwise noted.)

PRODUCT	1990	1997
Meat	6.6	1.4
Butter	0.8	0.3
Canned goods (billions of cans)	8.2	2.2
Salt	4.2	2.1
Bread	16.2	8.9
Pasta	1.0	0.5
Footwear (millions of pairs)	385.0	32.0
Silk (millions of square yards)	1,051.0	134.0
Coats (millions; later figure is 1992)	17.2	2.3
Cement	83.0	26.6
Beer (millions of gallons)	874.0	655.0
Watches and clocks (millions of units)	60.1	5.0
Refrigerators (millions of units)	3.8	0.1
Vacuum cleaners (millions of units)	4.5	0.6

Source: Adapted from the *Washington Post,* 14 Nov. 1998, A16.

The Stakes of Russian Politics: A Lighter View

As the Soviet Union was falling apart in late 1991, the *Economist* ran a tongue-in-cheek contest, asking its readers to suggest names for the new country that would be replacing it. Here are some of the more revealing—and humorous—answers:

- ■ RELICS—Republics Left in Total Chaos
- ■ PITS—Post-Imperial Total Shambles
- ■ COMA—Confederation of Mutual Antagonism (Its people would be called Commies)
- ■ UFFR—Union of Fewer and Fewer Republics

production of basic goods most Russian citizens and corporations rely on in their daily lives.

The Environment

Russia is an environmental nightmare. Most Americans are familiar with the disaster at Chernobyl (in today's Ukraine) in 1986. It was the worst accident ever to occur at a nuclear power plant and devastated hundreds of square miles of farmland. Scientists predict that upwards of thirty thousand people will die over the next three generations as a result of cancer and other diseases caused by radiation from the plant.

But Chernobyl is only the tip of the iceberg. The Soviet and Russian governments have dumped dozens of spent, leaking, and dangerous nuclear reactors from submarines into the ocean. More than seventy million people in the former Soviet Union live in cities where it is unhealthy to breathe the air. Three-quarters of their surface water is polluted. A water diversion project led to the shrinking of the Aral Sea by dozens of miles, and the salt left behind when the water evaporated has destroyed the soil that is now on the surface.

Air and water pollution in the city of Kemerevo, where the environment probably is too dirty to be cleaned up, is all too typical. Its residents have three times the average incidence of chronic bronchitis, kidney failure, and diseases of the endocrine system. In one particularly filthy neighborhood, 7 percent of the children born in 1989 were mentally impaired, more than three times the national average. In the small city of Karabash, the foundry emits the equivalent of nine tons annually of sulfur, lead, arsenic, tellurium, and other pollutants for each man, woman, and child.

Key Questions

On one level, the key questions to ask about Russia are the same as those laid out in Chapter 1, including how its state evolved, what it is like today, and how it deals with domestic and international pressures. However, given the differences between Russia and the countries covered in Part 2, we will also have to spend more time on the historical material and then focus on the uncertainties and difficulties that emerged during Yeltsin's presidency and that have continued under Putin.

- ■ How and why did the Soviet Union collapse?
- ■ How did its legacy affect the way Russia has evolved?
- ■ Will Putin and his colleagues be able to continue to strengthen and stabilize the Russian state?
- ■ In so doing, will they also be able to make the regime more democratic and legitimate?
- ■ Can they build stronger and more broadly accepted institutions if the economy continues to founder?
- ■ How will Russia adapt to its new international role in which it remains a major power in some military arenas but is increasingly buffeted by global economic forces beyond its control?

The Evolution of the Russian State

The Russian Federation is a new state, and it is therefore tempting to begin this section by discussing the events that led up to its creation following the collapse of the Soviet Union. However, it would be a mistake to do so. Perhaps even more than was the case for the countries covered in Part 2, Russia's past weighs heavily on its present. If nothing else, most leading politicians were active members of the **Communist Party of the Soviet Union (CPSU),** and all Russian adults lived the bulk of their lives under Soviet rule.

Therefore, this section actually has to be somewhat longer and more detailed than its equivalents in previous chapters. Not only do we have to examine the basic trends in Russian and Soviet history before 1991, we have to dig more deeply into the institutions and power bases of the once-powerful state that collapsed so quickly and so unexpectedly (www.departments.bucknell.edu/russian).

The Broad Sweep of Russian History

Accounts of Russian history normally begin with the ninth-century Kievan Rus, which was centered in today's Ukraine. The Kievans were but one of many Slavic tribes that occupied a wide arc stretching from the former Yugoslavia (which literally means "land of the southern Slavs") northward and eastward to Siberia, which the Kievans and their Russian successors gradually took over.

Russia's evolution was not as easy or as peaceful as that last sentence might suggest. Time and time again, Russia was invaded and overrun. However, by the early nineteenth century, it had solidified itself as one of Europe's major powers and had occupied most of the lands that would become part of the Soviet Union a century later.

This does not mean that Russia remained one of Europe's great powers for long, because it had missed out on most of the transformations that reshaped Western Europe from the 1500s onward. The tsars remained absolute monarchs. There was no Reformation, leaving Russia dominated by an Orthodox Church with strong ties to the autocracy. Individualism, the scientific revolution, and the other intellectual trends that played such a key role in the West had next to no impact on Russia.

There were periods of reform. Peter the Great (ruled 1682–1725) introduced ideas and technologies from the West, just as Mikhail Gorbachev did three centuries later. From then on, Russia always had elites, dubbed "Westernizers," who looked elsewhere for ways to modernize their country. Just as important, though, were the Slavophiles, who were convinced that Russian traditions were superior to anything in the West and who fought to keep foreign influences out.

Consequently, Russia lagged behind the other European powers. As is so often the case, the stark realities of

TABLE 9.3 Key Events in the Origins of the Soviet State

YEAR	EVENT
1854	Start of the Crimean War
1881	Assassination of Tsar Alexander II
1904–05	Russo–Japanese War
1905	First revolution
1914	Outbreak of World War I
1917	February and October revolutions
1921	End of civil war, formal creation of Soviet Union
1924	Death of Lenin

Russia's situation were driven home by a relatively minor event—its defeat by Britain and France in the Crimean War of 1854–55. That defeat set political forces in motion that would culminate in the revolution of 1917. (See table 9.3.)

Prelude to Revolution

As we saw in Chapter 8, Marx expected a socialist revolution to occur first in one of the industrialized capitalist countries. There, a tiny bourgeoisie would exploit an increasingly large, educated, and organized proletariat that would eventually rise up and overthrow its oppressors.

Instead, it took place in a Russia that had little in common with the more advanced societies Marx had in mind. Three overlapping differences between the expectations of Marxist theory and the realities of life in Russia go a long way toward explaining why the Bolshevik revolution occurred, and then why the USSR turned out as it did.

Backwardness

The term *backwardness* is value laden and pejorative. However, it does describe Russia in the second half of the nineteenth century (history1900s.about.com/library/world/blxrussia.htm).

At that time, Russia had a tenth of the railroad lines of Germany or France. To the degree that Russia was beginning to industrialize, its factories were owned either by the government or by foreigners, so it did not develop the class of independent capitalists Marx had thought was so important. As late as the 1860s, most Russians were serfs who were, for all intents and purposes, slaves of their feudal lords. At the end of the century, over 90 percent of the people still lived in the countryside. Most urban workers were illiterate and had not developed the organization and sophistication Marx expected of a mature proletariat.

Failed Reform

Russia also adopted few of the democratic reforms we saw in eighteenth- and nineteenth-century France and Britain. Indeed, groups that advocated individualism or limits on the autocracy had no choice but to be revolutionaries. There were no "inside the system" ways of effectively pressing for change.

In the aftermath of Russia's defeat in the Crimean War, the new tsar, Alexander II (ruled 1855–81), realized that Russia was lagging too far behind the West and began a series of belated but limited reforms. Serfs were liberated. Some forms of censorship were relaxed. Universities and the civil service were opened to commoners. Alexander was on the verge of introducing a constitution that would give about 5 percent of the male population the right to vote when he was assassinated in 1881.

Political reform came to a halt under his son, Alexander III (ruled 1881–94). State-led industrialization continued, but this tsar was a reactionary who reinforced the autocratic state at the same time that the power of kings and lords was disappearing in the West.

A Weak State

This does not mean that Russia had a strong state. In fact, during the reign of the last tsar, Nicholas II (ruled 1894–1917), the state grew weaker and weaker in every respect other than its ability to infiltrate revolutionary movements.

Russia's weakness was especially evident in its dealings with the rest of the world. The Russian elite continued to think of their country as a great power. The fact that it was not was driven home as a result of the disastrous Russo-Japanese War and World War I. In 1904, Russia attacked Japan, in part to quell dissent at home. The Russians assumed they would win easily, but they were routed by the Japanese. Their remaining pretenses to great power status were shattered in World War I, when Russian troops on horseback were mowed down by the dramatically better trained and better-equipped forces of Germany and its allies.

Lenin and the (Wrong?) Revolution

Not surprisingly, a growing number of Russians found the political and economic situation to be intolerable. Because the state maintained its secret police and banned all reformist groups, the ranks of revolutionaries swelled with dissidents of all stripes, many of whom were forced into exile.

By the 1890s, these dissidents included small groups of Marxists. They were actually among the least revolutionary because, as orthodox Marxists, they assumed that Russia would have to first go through capitalism before a socialist revolution was possible.

Early in the 1900s, however, one of the exiled Marxists, **V. I. Lenin** (1870–1924), reached a conclusion that was to affect Russian politics until the Soviet Union collapsed. As he saw it, the situation in Russia was so bad that the country could not wait until the conditions for a Marxist revolution were ripe.

In the pamphlet *What Is to Be Done?* (www.fordham .edu/halsall/mod/1902lenin.html), Lenin outlined plans for a new type of revolutionary organization. He argued that only a small, secretive, hierarchical party of professional revolutionaries could hope to succeed. To thwart the secret police, the party would have to be based on what he called **democratic centralism.** Discussion and debate would be allowed before the party decided to do something. However, once a decision was made, everyone would obey it without question. Leaders at the top would coopt officials to run lower-level organizations, which, in turn, would not be allowed to communicate with each other. All party members would be known by pseudonyms. All of these measures were designed to make it hard for the secret police to infiltrate what Lenin expected would be an efficient machine.

At a congress of the Social Democratic Party held in 1903, there was a spirited debate over Lenin's ideas, which led to the famous split between the **Mensheviks** and **Bolsheviks.** The former, advocating a more orthodox Marxist approach, barely lost on the key vote to Lenin's supporters, who came to be called Bolsheviks—a term that simply meant they were the larger faction.

Like the party itself, their disagreements had little practical impact, because most socialist leaders were in exile and had minimal support among the masses at home. But the Bolsheviks' prospects improved dramatically over the next fifteen years, not so much because of anything they did but because the tsarist regime continued to weaken. A spontaneous revolution broke out in 1905 in the wake of the Japanese debacle. Although the tsar was able to put it down and solidify his power in the short run, the state turned out to be even more fragile than it had been before the war began.

The autocracy finally collapsed in 1917 as Russia staggered toward defeat in World War I. The tsar was replaced by a **provisional government** that, in turn, found itself unable to withstand a counterrevolution by tsarist forces without the help of the Bolsheviks. Finally, in the fall, Lenin decided that the time had come. On the night of 7 November, Bolshevik troops overthrew the provisional government. For the first time anywhere, Marxists had succeeded in taking over a government.

The revolution was by no means over. Although the

V. I. LENIN

Lenin addressing Communist activists and soldiers in Red Square, 1919.

© Bettmann /CORBIS

Lenin was the chief architect of the Bolshevik revolution and first leader of the Soviet Union.

He was born Vladimir Ulyanov in 1870. His father was a successful bureaucrat, and young Vladimir seemed destined for a prominent career himself until his brother was arrested and hanged for his involvement in a plot to assassinate the tsar. Vladimir entered university shortly thereafter and began studying law, but was quickly expelled and sent into exile for his own political beliefs. He spent those years near the Lena River, from which he derived his pseudonym. While in his first period of exile, he became a Marxist. He finished his studies independently and was admitted to the bar in 1891. Lenin spent the rest of the 1890s organizing dissidents in St. Petersburg and was in and out of jail until he was sent into exile again in 1900.

Lenin returned to Russia after the tsar was overthrown, and led the Bolsheviks' seizure of power in the October revolution. But he never fully recovered from an assassination attempt that left him with a bullet in his shoulder and another in his lung. He suffered three strokes during 1922 and 1923, and died in 1924.

Bolsheviks quickly took control of most of the cities, they had little support in the countryside and faced opposition from dozens of other groups. In the Constituent Assembly elected on 25 November, they won only 168 of the 703 seats.

Despite the Bolsheviks' lack of popular support, Lenin was not prepared to yield. He allowed the assembly to meet once in January 1918 and then closed it for good, dashing hopes for a democratic outcome. Meanwhile, the Bolsheviks accepted the Brest-Litovsk Treaty with Germany, which cost revolutionary Russia 32 percent of its arable land, 26 percent of its railroads, 33 percent of its factories, and 75 percent of its coal mines. As industrial production dropped to a third of its 1913 level, thousands of workers fled the cities. No one knows how many froze or starved to death.

Civil war broke out in 1918. A poorly organized group of forces loyal to the tsar and the provisional government joined with other revolutionary factions in an attempt to topple the new Bolshevik regime.

The Bolsheviks responded by reinforcing democratic centralism, laying the groundwork for the CPSU's domination of all aspects of life. They created the **Cheka,** their first secret police, to enforce discipline within the party. At the same time, the Bolsheviks had to bring back members of the old elite to run the factories and the new Red Army. Because the Bolsheviks did not trust them, they assigned loyal political commissars to oversee what the officers and bureaucrats did.

In 1921, the Bolsheviks finally gained control of the entire country. Once their rule was secure, they formally created the USSR. The Communist Party was given the leading role in policy making and, in fact, supervising everything that happened in the new country. The overlapping party and state hierarchies from the civil war were maintained along with democratic centralism.

234

In the early 1920s, the Soviet Union was not yet the totalitarian dictatorship it would become under Stalin. There were still open debates within the party. There was also a lively cultural and artistic world in which dissenting views were frequently raised. Stringent wartime economic measures were relaxed under the New Economic Policy (NEP), which encouraged peasants, merchants, and even some industrialists to pursue private businesses.

Stalin, Terror, and the Modernization of the Soviet Union

Just before he died in 1924, Lenin wrote a political "testament" in which he criticized the Bolshevik leadership. He singled out Leon Trotsky (1879–1940) and **Joseph Stalin** (1879–1953), warning that neither should be allowed to take over the party.

To make a long and complicated story short, Lenin's wishes were not heeded. After an intense factional fight, Stalin won control of the party—and hence the country. Few people had expected him to replace Lenin. He was not part of the group of exiled intellectuals who dominated the Bolsheviks before the revolution. Instead, he stayed at home to work with the underground party, among other things robbing banks to raise money for it. After the revolution, Stalin was put in charge of the party organization. From that position, he was able to surpass his more visible rivals because, in a party in which all leaders are coopted, he determined who was appointed to which positions.

The quarter-century that Stalin ruled the Soviet Union was one of the most painful periods in all of history. (See table 9.4.) In what is often called the second revolution, as many as twenty million Soviet citizens lost their lives—far too often for little or no reason.

▌ **TABLE 9.4** Key Events in the Evolution of the Soviet State

YEAR	EVENT
1927	Solidification of power by Stalin; socialism in one-country speech
1929	Beginning of collectivization campaign
1934	First major purges and show trials
1939	Nonaggression pact with Germany
1941	German invasion of Soviet Union
1945	End of World War II, beginning of cold war
1953	Death of Stalin
1956	Twentieth Party Congress and Khrushchev's secret speech
1964	Ouster of Khrushchev
1982	Death of Brezhnev

Industrialization

Stalin is typically—and accurately—portrayed as one of the most vicious men ever to lead a country. There was, however, a degree of macabre rationality to some of what he did. The Soviet Union was in trouble. Hopes of global revolution had given way to a resurgence of right-wing governments in countries surrounding the USSR, something that Stalin was to call "capitalist encirclement." Whoever was in charge, the world's first socialist state had to respond decisively. To see that, consider this excerpt from one of his speeches:

> **To slacken the tempo would mean falling behind. And those who fall behind get beaten. But we do not want to be beaten. No, we refuse be beaten. One feature of the history of old Russia was the continual beatings she suffered because of her backwardness. She was beaten by the Mongol Khans. She was beaten by the Swedish feudal rulers. She was beaten by the Polish and Lithuanian gentry. She was beaten by British and French capitalists. She was beaten by Japanese barons. All beat her because of her backwardness. We are fifty or a hundred years behind the advanced countries. We must make good this distance in ten years. Either we do it or we shall go under.**[1]

Stalin forced his beleaguered country to industrialize. In so doing, he committed some of the worst excesses of his rule. But a plausible case can be made that, if Stalin hadn't pursued something like the policies described here, the Soviet Union would not have survived.

Before turning to the issue of forced industrialization, we should acknowledge that no country has ever been able to create a modern industrial economy painlessly. This is especially true of states that lag far behind their competitors and want to close that gap quickly. Adopting a laissez-faire approach seems to condemn these countries to decades of "catch-up economics." They therefore often conclude—and perhaps rightfully so—that their only option is to force their society to industrialize as quickly as possible.

Stalin adopted a two-pronged strategy.

First, because the Soviet Union had only one real resource—human labor, which was concentrated in the countryside—Stalin decided to restructure rural life. Farmers were herded onto gigantic, supposedly more efficient, collective and state farms. The peasants who were no longer needed in the countryside were relocated to the cities to work in the factories that were being built at breakneck speed. The government planned

---

[1] J. V. Stalin, *Problems of Leninism* (Moscow: International Publishers, 1953), 454.

JOSEPH STALIN

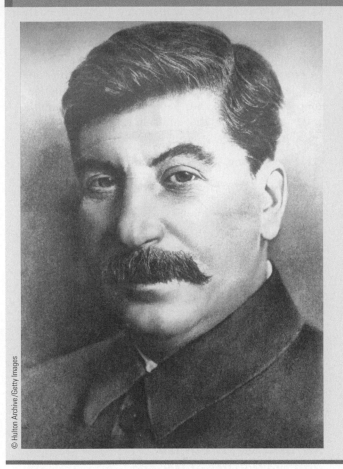

© Hulton Archive /Getty Images

Iosif Dzhugashvili was born in the Georgian town of Gori in 1879. Unlike Lenin, he was of humble origins. His mother was a maid, and his father an alcoholic and abusive shoemaker. As an adolescent, he entered a seminary, but he abandoned his studies in 1899 to become a full-time revolutionary.

Stalin followed Lenin into the Bolshevik wing of the Social Democratic Party, but unlike most of his influential colleagues, he spent the years before 1917 in Russia, organizing the party underground. During those years he took the pseudonym "Stalin," for "man of steel."

During the revolution and civil war period, Stalin was given more and more responsibility for the "nationality question" and for party organization. Despite alienating Lenin because of his "rude" behavior, Stalin was able to outmaneuver his competitors and seize all but complete control of the country by 1927.

Most historians are convinced that Stalin suffered from a series of psychological problems that contributed to making his regime one of the most brutal in history. He died in 1953.

Joseph Stalin in 1929, shortly after he had consolidated power and begun the brutal collectivization campaign.

to sell the surplus food the new factory-like farms produced abroad to raise desperately needed hard currency. The government accomplished this with violence the likes of which the country had never seen. In a matter of months, more than nine million peasants were forced to move to the cities. At least that many more who resisted collectivization were sent to forced labor camps, where most of them perished. An unknown number were killed on the spot.

Second, the agricultural surplus and other resources were used to spark the industrialization and modernization of the Soviet economy. Stalin initiated this through an ambitious **five-year plan** that called for at least doubling the production of such goods as coal, oil, pig iron, steel, electricity, and cloth between 1928 and 1932. The Central State Planning Commission (**Gosplan**) set goals for the entire economy. Individual ministries then turned them into specific quotas for each factory and farm to ful-

fill. As in the rural areas, people who resisted the state's plans were treated brutally. Although the plan fell short of its most ambitious goals, the Soviet Union industrialized as rapidly as any country in history, though at a tremendous human cost.

Foreign Policy

There was a similar pattern to Soviet foreign policy under Stalin. Lenin had created the **Third International,** or **Comintern,** to spearhead what he expected to be a worldwide revolution, Soviet style. By the time Stalin solidified his power, however, the revolutionary tides had ebbed. Instead, capitalist forces seemed to threaten the very existence of the world's first socialist state.

Therefore, in the late 1920s Stalin reversed the course of Soviet foreign policy and called for "socialism in one country," something no orthodox Marxist would have dreamed possible. Over the next twenty-five years, this policy led the Soviet Union and the global communist movement through what must seem like a contradictory series of shifts. At first, Stalin prohibited Communist parties elsewhere from participating in antifascist coalitions that might, for instance, have kept the Nazis from taking power in Germany. But once he realized how serious the fascist threat was, Stalin switched direction in 1934, endorsing popular or united fronts in which communists cooperated with just about anyone who opposed fascism. In 1939 the Soviets reversed course once again, signing the infamous nonaggression pact with Nazi Germany. It was to last less than two years. The Germans invaded the Soviet Union in 1941, at which point Moscow joined the British-led Allies, which would include the United States after the attack on Pearl Harbor. Almost as soon as the war ended, however, tensions between the Soviet Union and the West escalated into what became the cold war, prompting yet another U-turn in Soviet policy.

The Purges

Stalin's economic and foreign policies made some macabre sense. Obviously, they had horrible consequences for millions of people, but the Soviet Union did industrialize, and it did survive. In fact, by the time Stalin died, the Soviet Union had become one of the world's two superpowers.

It is impossible, however, to find any such logic behind the **purges.** In the 1920s, the party conducted limited purges to eliminate opportunists and others who joined in the aftermath of the revolution. Later in the decade, Stalin forced Trotsky and most of his other leading rivals out of the party. But from the early 1930s on, the pace of the purges picked up and had no credible link, however twisted, to the country's economic development.

In 1933, the party held a congress, which Stalin called the "Congress of Victors," to celebrate the completion of the collectivization campaign. At that meeting, Sergei Kirov, the young party leader in Leningrad, actually won more votes than Stalin in the election of the new Central Committee. In December 1934, Kirov was assassinated at his office, apparently on Stalin's orders.

Nonetheless, Stalin ordered the arrest of anyone "involved" in Kirov's assassination, which set off a wave of arrests, torture, show trials, and executions that touched the lives of millions of innocent Soviet citizens. By the end of the decade, 5 of the 9 Politburo members, 98 of 139 Central Committee members, 1,108 of the 1,966 delegates to the 1933 party congress, and half the army officer corps had been killed. A series of show trials took place at which most of the old Bolshevik leaders confessed to crimes they did not commit and then were summarily executed.

The purges and executions were carried out all the way up and down the party hierarchy. They drained the party of many of its enthusiastic members and qualified leaders, including in the secret police, many of whose own leaders found themselves on trial for their lives.

In this nightmarish environment, virtually the only way people could express their feelings was through humor. Consider, here, one "report" of a conversation between two prisoners that sums up just how absurd and horrible the purges were:

> **Prisoner One: What's your sentence?**
>
> **Prisoner Two: Twenty-five years.**
>
> **Prisoner One: What for?**
>
> **Prisoner Two: Nothing.**
>
> **Prisoner One: Don't lie. You only get five years for nothing in our country.**

In the larger prisons, the authorities executed an average of seventy people per day. Millions of average citizens were sent to the gulag, or network of concentration camps. People were given five- to eight-year sentences merely for having a "socially dangerous" relative. Very few survived that long.

No wonder political scientists came to call the Soviet Union totalitarian.

Khrushchev, Brezhnev, and the Politics of Decline

In March 1953, Stalin suffered a fatal stroke. Like Lenin, he died without designating a successor, and a number of men jockeyed for control. This time the dozen or so top politicians apparently agreed that no one should ever be allowed to amass the kind of power Stalin had and that the Soviet Union should, instead, be governed by some form of collective leadership.

Within two years **Nikita Khrushchev (1894–1971)** emerged as the most influential of those leaders. Khrushchev was a typical Communist of his generation. Drawn to the party by the revolution, he had risen to the top during Stalin's rule and was involved in some of the regime's most brutal activities.

Under his leadership, the basic institutions of the party state remained intact. Nonetheless, Khrushchev proved to be a reformer both at home and abroad.

Most importantly, he brought the worst excesses of Stalinism to a halt. The first clear sign that politics was changing came on the night of 24–25 February 1956, when Khrushchev called the delegates to the CPSU's **Twentieth Party Congress** back for a special session. For three hours he held his audience spellbound with his famous **secret speech** in which he detailed many of Stalin's crimes. After the speech, which did not remain secret for very long, censorship and other political controls were loosened. More open political debate made university campuses exciting places to be and left an indelible mark on that generation of students, which included Gorbachev and Yeltsin. Khrushchev also sought to decentralize economic decision making and to revitalize the flagging agricultural sector. The Soviet Union retained its cold war hostility toward the West but also sought to relax tensions through a policy he called "peaceful coexistence."

Always controversial, Khrushchev barely survived an attempt to oust him in 1957. Many of his colleagues believed that his reforms went too far in eroding central party control and Soviet prestige. More importantly, few of the reforms worked. As social and economic problems mounted, so did opposition to his rule.

For many, the Cuban missile crisis of 1962 proved to be the last straw. That August, U.S. reconnaissance planes discovered that the Soviets were preparing to deploy nuclear missiles in Cuba, a country ninety miles south of Florida that had recently passed into the Soviet camp. Two months later, President John F. Kennedy imposed a naval blockade to prevent the ships carrying the missiles and other material from reaching Cuba. World War III was a very real possibility. Eventually, the ships turned around, and the Soviets dismantled the bases.

Khrushchev's critics in Moscow saw Cuba as a humiliating defeat and as yet another example of what they branded his "harebrained schemes." Two years later they succeeded in removing him from office.

Khrushchev was replaced by a group of leaders, many of whom had been his protégés. The most important of them was **Leonid Brezhnev** (1906–1982), who served as general secretary of the Communist Party until his death in 1982. Under Brezhnev the reforms ended, and the leadership took as few risks as possible in both domestic and foreign affairs.

By the time Brezhnev and his colleagues took power, the Soviet Union already faced serious economic problems. (See the discussion of "thumbs" and "fingers" in Chapter 8.) In the years that followed, things only got worse. By the early 1980s, overall economic growth slipped to 3 percent per year, or barely 60 percent of the goal laid out in the Tenth Five-Year Plan (1976–80). In some sectors, the figures were even worse—only a fifth of planned increases in coal and chemicals, barely a third in steel and consumer goods, and only half in agriculture.

The Brezhnev leadership did introduce some limited economic reforms. However, little progress was made because anything more than piecemeal change would have threatened the two central elements of the Soviet system that dated back to Lenin's time: the party's monopoly on power and the centrally controlled economy. The Brezhnev generation was not willing to modify either.

Instead, it clung to power. By the beginning of the 1980s, the average age of Politburo members was about seventy. And when Brezhnev finally died in 1982, power was transferred to other members of the old guard—Yuri Andropov and Konstantin Chernenko—both of whom died within months of taking office.

Economic conditions continued to deteriorate. In the 1980s, economic growth averaged less than 1 percent per year. Even though people had more disposable income, there were not enough consumer goods to meet pent-up demand, and those goods that were available were shoddily made. To cite but one example, the few people fortunate enough to own cars took their windshield wipers with them when they parked. Otherwise, they would be stolen.

The *Economist* summed up this period brilliantly in its rather snide obituary on Brezhnev:

> **The death of Leonid Brezhnev was the only major innovation he ever introduced into Soviet political history. In life, he stood for the status quo—as firmly as a man can stand when he is in fact walking slowly backward on a conveyor belt that is moving slowly forward beneath his feet. Brezhnev, a solid machine man, was put in to reassure the frightened hierarchs that the experimenting would stop. In this he was remarkably successful. He did not just stop the clocks, but turned some of them back. Defying Marx, he virtually halted the evolution of Soviet society in its tracks. But the country, which was intended to be ruled by the Brezhnev men after Brezhnev's death, presumably with the aim of immortalizing his immobilism, had been changing under them despite all their efforts; and the world in which it must live has been changing too. His legacy in foreign as in domestic policy is a set of concepts which were old when his reign began eighteen years ago. In Brezhnev's Russia, only one thing was kept entirely up to date: its military hardware. The most appropriate monument for him would be a multiwarhead nuclear missile linked to a stopped clock.[2]**

---

[2] "Brezhnev's Legacy." *The Economist.* 13 November 1982, 7–8.

When Chernenko died in March 1985, there was no one from the Brezhnev generation left. Someone younger had to take over, and Gorbachev was the obvious choice.

Although there were signs that he was not cut from the same political cloth as members of the Brezhnev-Andropov-Chernenko generation, no one expected change to come as quickly as it did. In 1984, Serge Schmeman of the *New York Times* reported an incident that hinted at just how uncertain things were. That December Gorbachev was sent on a mission to London. He was already in line to replace Chernenko, who was clearly in failing health. The assumption was that the trip would provide some insight into the next leader of the Soviet Union.

Schmeman began his report with Gorbachev's departure from Moscow. Gorbachev, dressed in a somber gray suit, shook the hands of his equally somberly dressed colleagues who had come to see him off. His wife, Raisa, went up the back ramp into the plane, out of public view. When they arrived in London, however, they emerged from the airplane together, wearing colorful Western-style clothes, and enthusiastically greeted the crowd.

Which, Schmeman wondered, was the real Gorbachev?

The Collapse of the Soviet State: The Gorbachev Years

Schmeman's question was answered quickly. **Mikhail Gorbachev** (1931–) proved to be a dedicated reformer and one of the twentieth century's most influential leaders. In the end, however, he failed in large part because he was either unwilling or unable to take on the party state. Because his reforms went a lot further than those of the Khrushchev years, he provoked fierce opposition within the party hierarchy. However, his reforms probably could never have sparked the revitalization of the Soviet society and economy he sought because they did not go far enough in challenging the party and its stranglehold on power. The end result was the rapid polarization of Soviet politics and, with it, the country's demise.

The Party State

The Soviet Union Gorbachev inherited was dominated by the CPSU and its massive organization, whose members amount to about 10 percent of the adult population. It was, for all intents and purposes, the same as the state and was therefore the only political body that counted. Until 1988 all important decisions were made by senior party leaders. Party officials were responsible for over-seeing the actions of every individual and institution. For all but those at the very top, the party was a massive bureaucratic machine whose primary task was to ensure that the policies made by the elite were carried out. Most leading journalists, military officers, factory managers, teachers, and even athletes were required to be party members. Few, however, joined out of a sense of commitment to building a society based on Marxist ideals. Rather, most entered one of the four hundred thousand or so primary party organizations for a far more pragmatic reason—the CPSU was the only route to success in almost every sector of Soviet society.

Until the late 1980s, the party structure remained the same as it had been since the 1920s. (See figure 9.1.) The primary party organizations reported to city or regional committees that, in turn, reported to provincial units. Fifteen union republic party organizations were above the provincial units.

Atop it all were the national party organs. In principle the most important—but in practice the least influential—was the party congress, normally held every four years. Until the final one in 1990, however, party congresses were little more than rubber stamps that ratified decisions made by the party elite. Much the same could be said of the **Central Committee,** which had about three hundred members, many of whom lived and worked outside of Moscow.

Real power was concentrated in two small groups that the Central Committee officially appointed but that were really self-perpetuating bodies. The **Politburo** (normally 12–15 members, with another 5–6 nonvoting, candidate members) acted much like a cabinet in a parliamentary system. The **Secretariat** (usually about 25 members and a staff of about 1,500) oversaw the work of the entire party apparatus. There was considerable overlap in the membership of these two bodies, and the general secretary served as both head of the Secretariat and chair of the Politburo.

The continued reliance on democratic centralism meant that leaders at one level determined who ran things at the level below them in the hierarchy. This allowed the elite to perpetuate itself by choosing people it could count on for all important positions. Its control over the entire organization was exercised through the *nomenklatura*—lists of important positions and people qualified to fill them, both of which were maintained by the Secretariat. As a result, the arrows in figure 9.1 that suggest "upward" influence are misleading. Because of this continued use of the system Lenin created to wage and win a revolution, the leadership maintained total control over who was appointed to official positions and, therefore, also over the decisions it cared most about.

▌FIGURE 9.1 The Communist Party of the Soviet Union

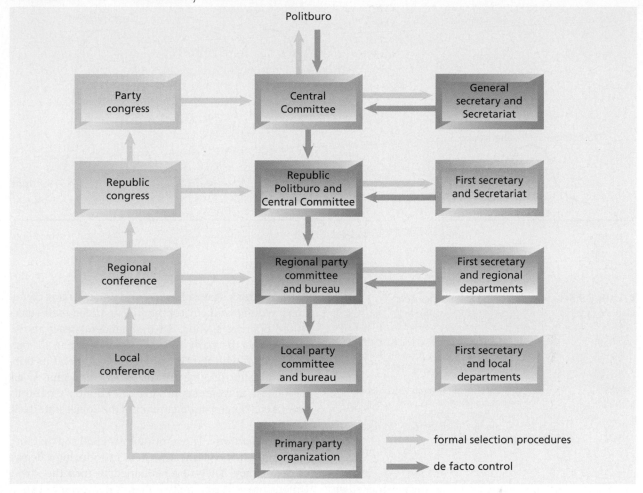

Reform

Gorbachev and his colleagues came to power understanding that the Soviet Union had to change. Economic growth had all but ground to a halt, and the country was falling behind the West in almost every way imaginable.

Therefore, they introduced four sets of reforms designed to reinvigorate Soviet society. What the reforms actually did, however, was polarize both the elite and society as a whole. (See figure 9.2.) Gorbachev took over a country in which only a tiny proportion of the population—the party elite—was politically relevant, and there were only minor differences of opinion within it. The reforms dramatically expanded both the number of people trying to influence decision making and the range of opinions voiced in those debates. As the 1980s wore on, Gorbachev found himself trying to govern from the ever-shrinking center. That would have been a challenge under the best of circumstances, but Gorbachev also be-

came quite tentative in his own decision making, especially once it became clear that the party itself was the major roadblock. (See table 9.5.)

Glasnost Gorbachev and his colleagues understood that they could not breathe new life into Soviet institutions without changing the country's political culture. At most, Soviets granted the party state a grudging sense of legitimacy. More often than not, they accepted the status quo because there was little or nothing they could do about it. A country that would be more innovative and take more risks economically would have to start by creating a culture that stressed similar values.

The first of the reforms, **glasnost** sought to do so in what turned out to be the most counterproductive of Gorbachev's new ideas. The term is derived from the Russian word for voice and is best translated as "openness." It had occasionally been discussed by earlier So-

■ FIGURE 9.2 The Changing Soviet Political Landscape

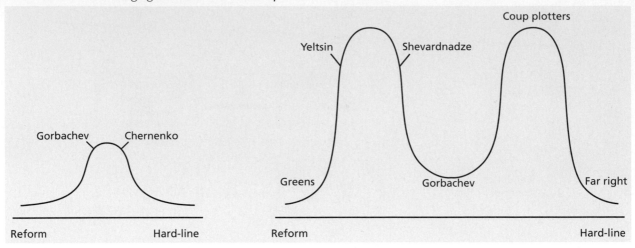

■ TABLE 9.5 Key Events in the Gorbachev Years

YEAR	EVENT
1985	Gorbachev becomes general secretary of CPSU
1986	Chernobyl; first summit with President Reagan
1987	Intermediate nuclear forces agreement; Yeltsin removed from office
1988	Special party conference; Reagan visits Moscow
1989	First somewhat competitive elections; collapse of communism in Eastern Europe
1990	Final CPSU congress; Yeltsin resigns from party
1991	Failed coup attempt; collapse of USSR

viet leaders but only made it onto political center stage after the 1986 Chernobyl nuclear power plant disaster. After a few days of typical Soviet secrecy, the government began making everything about the accident public and even allowed foreign experts in to care for people who had been exposed to radiation.

From then on, the system opened up dramatically. The old Soviet aphorism—"Everything that isn't explicitly permitted is forbidden"—was turned on its head. Censors stopped reviewing most works before they were published. The heavy-handed control over the mass media was lifted. Some conservative newspapers and magazines remained, but the press and airwaves were filled with material that was critical not only of the Soviet past but also of the current leadership.

Glasnost did not, however, create the kind of tolerant, Western-style political culture Gorbachev had in mind. Instead, it allowed people to vent seventy years' worth of frustrations. Rather than a more energized and enthusiastic population, the Soviet Union faced ever larger and more radical protests on a number of fronts.

Workers struck against low pay and poor working conditions. Women and environmentalists added their voices to the political agenda. An independent peace movement urged the party to move even faster in its rapprochement with the United States and to end its crippling invasion of Afghanistan. Most important of all, nationalist movements among the country's minority groups challenged the legitimacy of the Soviet state itself.

Democratization   The reformers also realized that they could not pursue glasnost without introducing a degree of democracy. They never planned to turn the Soviet Union into a Western-style liberal democracy. This is hardly surprising, given that even the most radical reformers were products of the system and that most of them—including Gorbachev himself—thought of themselves as committed Marxists. Therefore, movement on democratization came more slowly but included two important steps.

First, the reformers removed Article 6 from the Soviet constitution, which had defined the party as "the leading and guiding force of Soviet society and the nucleus of its political system, of all state organizations and political organizations." As early as January 1987, Gorbachev hinted that there could be changes in the party's monopoly on power. Formal proposals were made in June 1988 at a special party conference called to discuss democratization and economic reform. Plans were announced to strengthen the presidency, a position Gorbachev assumed that September.

Second, Gorbachev announced that there would be a new parliament, the Congress of People's Deputies, which would be chosen through partially free elections.

MIKHAIL GORBACHEV

© Peter Turnley/CORBIS

Former Soviet president Gorbachev speaks on his return to Moscow following the failed coup attempt in 1991.

Mikhail Gorbachev was born in 1931 near Stavropol in the Crimea. His father was a tractor driver, and Gorbachev himself worked on a collective farm while a teenager. At eighteen he was already a committed and respected member of the Komsomol, or Communist Youth League, when he entered Moscow State University to study law. Like many of his generation, he was deeply affected by de-Stalinization, which, some say, convinced him as early as the 1950s of the need for reform.

Gorbachev returned to the Stavropol region, where he quickly moved up the party ranks. He was no radical. But like many of his colleagues in out-of-the-way parts of the country, he implemented some innovative reform—in his case in agricultural administration—that earned him national attention and a seat on the Politburo in 1980.

Gorbachev was never willing or able to wholly break with the traditional party state, which ultimately led to his and his country's undoing. Since 1991 he has headed the Gorbachev Institute, which works for human rights and world peace along the lines of the "new thinking" he championed while in office. He made an attempt at a political comeback in the 1996 presidential election but won less than 1 percent of the vote (www.gorby.ru/en/default.asp).

When the elections were held, many of the liberal reformers gained a lot of publicity. However, people concerned that Gorbachev was moving too fast and going too far won more of the seats.

In short, Gorbachev did make the regime somewhat more democratic. He did not, however, mount a frontal assault on the CPSU. If anything, he was hoping to strengthen it by forcing it to reform and modernize. Nonetheless, the main consequence of his actions was to intensify apprehension and opposition from party members to his right.

Perestroika   As noted earlier, Gorbachev inherited a rapidly deteriorating economy. Soviet factories were archaic and were rendered even less productive by a workforce that neither worked very hard nor cared about the quality of what it produced. The service industries were in shambles, and people who could afford to do so turned to the black market to get their cars repaired or to obtain decent food. The massive state and collective farms were so poorly run that a third of the harvest spoiled or was lost between harvest and market. Last but not least, the peculiar nature of the Soviet currency and the country's arcane foreign trade laws kept the USSR from participating in the increasingly important international economy.

At first, there were few signs that Gorbachev contemplated radical economic reform. In his first two years in office, he tried to make improvements within the party state system by increasing the discipline of Soviet workers—for instance, clamping down on the sale of alcohol. As the crisis deepened and his incremental reforms failed to bear fruit, Gorbachev and his advisers decided that nothing short of **perestroika,** or a total restructuring of the economy, would restore the Soviet Union to world prominence or improve the living conditions of its citizens. They realized that such a restructuring necessarily involved relinquishing much of the party state's economic power to the market and promoting private ownership, individual initiative, and decentralized decision making.

Although much of perestroika never made it onto the statute books, by the late 1980s the leadership had taken five broad initiatives:

■ Proposing a Law on State Enterprises to introduce market mechanisms into the parts of the economy that would remain under state ownership

- Passing the Law on Cooperatives authorizing the existence of some small, privately owned companies, mostly in the service industries

- Initiating agricultural reforms that would eventually allow farmers to lease, if not own, their land

- Introducing price reforms so that people paid market value for goods and services

- Easing restrictions on joint ventures with foreign firms

We will never know if those reforms would have turned the Soviet economy around, because they were never fully implemented. Like democratization, they faced resistance from much of the party hierarchy, whose power they threatened. Moreover, the ever more indecisive Gorbachev team never even got to the point of proposing a full-fledged package of reforms. By the time they came close to doing so, it may have already been too late to satisfy the demands of an increasingly politicized and impatient population.

Foreign Policy   Gorbachev will be remembered most positively for his role in ending the cold war. One of his first acts was to declare a unilateral moratorium on nuclear testing, which was followed by more dramatic initiatives. There was a strong dose of self-interest behind those proposals from a leader who understood that his country was overburdened by defense expenditures that consumed at least a quarter of its GNP.

Gorbachev was the most visionary international leader of his time. Thus, in his remarkable speech to the United Nations General Assembly in December 1988, he talked hopefully about interdependence and a new world order of countries able to solve their differences peacefully. This is not the place to review those actions in any detail because they fall in the domain of international relations. Here it is enough to note that they provoked considerable opposition at home from people who feared that they would undermine the Soviet Union's position as one of the two most powerful countries in the world (www.gci.ch/GreenCrossFamily/gorby/gorby.html).

Crisis and Collapse

By the time Communism collapsed in Eastern Europe, the Soviet Union had become a political tinderbox. In the two years between the fall of the Berlin Wall and the disintegration of the Soviet Union, the state grew weaker and its society more divided. By 1990, rumors of an impending coup were rife. In response, Gorbachev strengthened presidential powers and elevated hard-

liners to prominent posts in the military and the security apparatus.

On 12 June 1991, Yeltsin was elected president of the Russian Republic, enabling him to claim that he had a broader mandate and that his rule was more legitimate than Gorbachev's. Five days later, the head of the **KGB** issued an ominous warning against carrying out liberal reforms "dreamed up across the ocean." On 24 July, Gorbachev reached an agreement with the presidents of ten of the fifteen republics that would have given them considerable autonomy in most areas of domestic policy making. The Union Treaty was to be signed on 20 August after Gorbachev returned from vacation.

At 6 A.M. on 19 August 1991, TASS (the Soviet press agency) announced that Gorbachev was ill and had been replaced by Vice President Gennadi Yanayev, who, along with seven other hard-liners, had seized government and party offices in Moscow and other major cities. Gorbachev and his family were taken into custody. Troops occupied critical locations in Moscow and other cities.

Most politicians were slow to respond to the coup. Yeltsin, however, opposed it from the outset. He immediately went to the Russian White House in Moscow (the seat of Russian government), which was surrounded by troops. Overnight, he galvanized opposition to the rebellion. Within forty-eight hours it had become clear that the coup was poorly planned by desperate leaders who knew that the signing of the Union Treaty would have meant the end of the Soviet Union as they knew it. The coup collapsed and Gorbachev returned to Moscow, claiming he would continue to rule as before.

In fact, business as usual could not continue. The Union Treaty was put on hold indefinitely as the Soviet Union continued to disintegrate. By September the Baltic republics had broken away, and in December the leaders of eleven of the remaining twelve republics agreed to form the Commonwealth of Independent States. By the end of the month, Gorbachev had resigned his position as president of a country that no longer existed.

Between Dictatorship and Democracy

One of the best recent books on Russian politics bears the apt title, *Between Dictatorship and Democracy*.[3] At first, many people were hopeful that the new country would make a rapid and smooth

---

[3] Michael McFaul, Nikolai Petrov, and Andrei Ryabov, *Between Dictatorship and Democracy: Russian Post-Communist Political Reform* (Washington: Carnegie Endowment for International Peace, 2004).

© Reuters NewMedia, Inc. /CORBIS

Boris Yeltsin, standing on an armored personnel carrier and rallying the crowd opposing the coup against Gorbachev in 1991.

transition to democracy. That is not what happened. The rest of the 1990s were traumatic times, as reflected in the troubled presidency of Boris Yeltsin. Yeltsin resigned on the very last day of the twentieth century, and since then political life has stabilized considerably under the leadership of Russia's second president, Vladimir Putin. However, Putin has achieved that stability by undermining some of the tentative steps Russia had taken toward democracy in the first decade after the breakup of the Soviet Union.

Birth Pangs

Most of the post-Soviet republics got off to a shakier start than did the new regimes covered in Part 2. To begin with, they did not make as clean a break from the old order. The new republics began their lives using Soviet-era institutions, and most were led by politicians who had forged their careers within the Communist hierarchy. In Russia, Yeltsin's team had to govern along with a parliament that had been elected in 1989 and was still dominated by men and women who had been loyal party activists.

The Russian people had never lived under a democracy. In contrast, although Germany and Japan had hardly been successful in their first attempts at democracy, they had "untainted" politicians to call on, established organizations that could serve as the starting point for new political parties and interest groups, and

millions of individuals who had voted in competitive elections. Russia did not. (See table 9.6.)

What's more, economic conditions sank to a level no one could have imagined under the Communists. Ethnic conflict, which had been bad enough before 1991, intensified after the Soviet collapse. Russians also had to deal with the humiliating reality that they were no longer a superpower and, even worse, had been stripped of territories and peoples—some of which they had controlled for centuries. Even more humiliating and contentious for some was the fact that the Russian gov-

▌ **TABLE 9.6** Key Events in Russian Politics since 1991

YEAR	EVENT
1991	Yeltsin elected Russian president
	Failed coup
	Collapse of USSR
1992	New state called Russian Federation
1993	Referendum supports most reforms
	Coup attempt
	First parliamentary elections
	New constitution
1994	Drift rightward accelerates
	Outbreak of war in Chechnya
1995	Yeltsin's second heart attack
	Second parliamentary election
1996	Presidential election
1997	Expansion of NATO
1998	Economic collapse
	Two prime ministers sacked
2000	Putin assumes presidency
2004	Putin reelected

BORIS YELTSIN

© Laski Diffusion/Getty Images

Boris Yeltsin's first public appearance after suffering his second heart attack in less than a year.

Boris Yeltsin was born in Siberia in 1931. Like most Soviet leaders of his generation, he was well educated, beginning his career as a civil engineer. He soon turned to full-time party work and rose through the ranks in the city of Sverdlovsk, which has since returned to its pre-Communist-era name of Ekaterinburg.

Yeltsin was brought to Moscow in 1985 and put in charge of the Moscow party organization (a prize position) and made a member of the Politburo. He soon became one of the country's most outspoken and radical reformers. For instance, he openly criticized party leaders for their privileged and lavish lifestyles. In 1988, Gorbachev felt he had gone too far and Yeltsin was stripped of all his major party and state posts. In 1990, Yeltsin quit the Communist Party at what turned out to be its final congress. The next year, he was elected president of the Russian Republic, which had previously not been a particularly important post. But with his personal popularity and the position he took in opposition to the August 1991 coup, Yeltsin soon became the most powerful politician in the USSR as it collapsed and then in the new Russian Federation.

He was less successful as president. His years in office were marred by economic difficulties, ethnic unrest, corruption, and, of course, questions about his own health and sobriety.

---

ernment seemed to have to beg for aid from the same Western governments that so recently had feared Soviet military power.

The hard-line holdovers turned into the new regime's conservatives. They obviously did not advocate free-market capitalism along the lines of conservatives in Great Britain or the United States. Rather, they were conservative in the sense that they resisted the reforms proposed by the Yeltsin administration, preferring instead to reestablish the old system and possibly to reintegrate the lost republics back into Russia or to re-create the USSR itself.

Meanwhile, the old Communist Party reinvented itself as the **Communist Party of the Russian Federation (CPRF),** the details of which we will cover later. New political groupings, most notably the Liberal Democrats, led by Vladimir Zhirinovsky, sprang up as well, defending various versions of traditional, Soviet-style geopolitical and economic goals. On the other end of the spectrum, radical reformers, most of whom started off in the Yeltsin camp, formed an opposition and clamored for **shock therapy** in the economy. This Western-inspired policy

emphasizes the selling off, or **privatization,** of state-owned industry and macroeconomic policies designed to bring the rampant inflation under control, and dramatic shifts toward a democratic regime.

As 1993 wore on, the tensions continued to mount. By summer, Yeltsin's team apparently realized that it had made a mistake in trying to implement meaningful economic and political reforms with a Communist-era political system. Therefore, it proposed a new constitution, which met stiff resistance from many parliamentary and regional leaders. On 21 September Yeltsin issued Decree 1400, which dissolved the Congress of People's Deputies and announced new legislative elections for 12 December.

This proved to be the last straw for his opponents, who took the decree as "proof" that the president was trying to create a personal dictatorship. For the next two weeks, hundreds of people, including many parliamentary leaders, occupied the White House. Yeltsin countered by sending troops to surround the building and by cutting off its heat, water, and electricity. The crisis reached a peak on 3 October, when supporters of the occupiers stormed the militia barricades and then attacked the mayor's office and the main television and radio complex.

In sharp contrast to what he had done in 1991, Yeltsin ordered the troops to attack the Russian White House. The occupiers proved no match for the troops and soon surrendered, but not before at least a hundred people were killed and the White House was heavily damaged. The leaders were hustled out of the building and arrested.

At that point, Yeltsin decided to add a new draft constitution to the ballot for the planned elections in December. The constitution was approved, but to his embarrassment, conservative parties won by far the most seats in the **State Duma,** the lower house of the new parliament.

In other words, despite removing the coup's plotters from active politics and gaining support for the new constitution, Yeltsin faced the same kind of political deadlock as Gorbachev. For the next two and a half years, the president and parliament remained at loggerheads. If anything, the conservatives grew stronger and obliged the president to drop more and more of his reformist goals and advisers. Meanwhile, Yeltsin's declining personal popularity and deteriorating health sapped the executive of its strength. The pace of economic and other reform slowed. Intense fighting broke out between the central government and separatists in the southern republic of Chechnya. More important for the long term were the preparations for the legislative and presidential elections that were to be held in December 1995 and June 1996, respectively.

But those elections did little to resolve the differences between Yeltsin and the Duma, which remained under opposition control. The president had had to bring former general Alexander Lebed and other conservatives into his coalition. In short, the high-stakes political stalemate continued in only slightly modified form.

Conditions only deteriorated for the rest of Yeltsin's abbreviated second term. As we will see in more detail later, the bottom fell out of the economy in 1998, and there was growing concern with the political and economic clout of the "family"—the people in Yeltsin's inner circle. So, there was something approaching a collective sigh of relief when Yeltsin quit.

Putin and Stability

Yeltsin's surprise resignation made Vladimir Putin acting president. When Yeltsin named him prime minister earlier that August, Putin was a virtual unknown. He had spent the bulk of his career in the KGB and had then served in the office of St. Petersburg's mayor after the collapse of the Soviet Union. Putin's personal popularity soared that fall because of what seemed like the successful prosecution of the second war in Chechnya, and it soon became clear that Yeltsin was grooming him to be his successor. Putin also proved to be an effective politician steering the newfound Unity Party to a victory in the 1999 parliamentary elections and then winning the presidency the following March without even requiring a runoff election.

Since then, Putin has had a much greater impact on Russian politics than anyone expected, which we will consider in detail in the rest of this chapter. For now, it is enough to note two things. First, despite the country's lingering social, economic, and political problems, its institutions are far stronger than they were when Putin took office. Second, in building up the power of the Kremlin and other parts of the central government, Putin has undermined important aspects of democracy, albeit without removing basic freedoms or eliminating competitive elections.

Political Culture and Participation

The evidence regarding Russian political culture and participation is difficult to assess for two reasons. First, open and voluntary political participation is a novel phenomenon, and it is often difficult to determine what peoples' intentions are when they get involved. Second, public opinion polling is also quite new, so we have relatively little reliable data about what the Russian people think and do politically.

Nonetheless, the available evidence points to a pair of paradoxical conclusions. On the one hand, there is reason to believe that most Russians want a democratic regime. On the other, their voting patterns and other political behavior suggest that they are not happy with the way their regime is currently working (www.russiavotes.org).

Political Culture

As is the case with most aspects of Russian politics, its political culture forces us to shift gears, because it has so little in common with those in the liberal democracies. Most people in the industrialized democracies believe that their regimes are legitimate, which contributes to political stability and helps sustain the system during tough times.

This is not the case for Russia. To the degree that we understand it, Russian political culture is shaped by the widespread frustration and hostility felt by its people.

VLADIMIR PUTIN

AFP/Getty Images

Vladimir Putin and George W. Bush at their first summit in Crawford, Texas, in November 2001.

Vladimir Putin was born in Leningrad (now St. Petersburg) in 1952. His family was not particularly well off, and Putin describes himself as having had a troubled youth until he started competing in judo, which has been a passion for him ever since.

In 1975, he graduated from the Leningrad State University with a degree in law. He then joined the KGB where he held a number of posts in Germany and the Soviet Union until he left to work for the Leningrad city government in 1990. There, he became a protégé of its mayor, the prominent reformer Anatoly Sobchak. Putin seems to have helped Sobchak flee the country after he was accused of corruption.

In 1996, Putin was brought to Moscow to help run the Kremlin's administrative office. There, he seems to have captured the attention of Yeltsin's "family" of inner circle of politicians, including his all-powerful daughter, Tatyana Dyachenko. In March 1999, he effectively was given control of the Federal Security Bureau (FSB), the successor to the Soviet era KGB. On 9 August 1999, he was named prime minister and automatically became acting president when Yeltsin resigned.

Putin was very well received initially. President George W. Bush, for instance, stated that he had stared into Putin's eyes and seen the soul of a man he could trust at the press conference ending their first summit in 2001. Assessments of Putin have been more mixed since then given difficulties at home and disagreements with other countries over Iraq and other foreign policy issues.

It could hardly be otherwise. Russians have never been governed by a regime that enjoyed widespread legitimacy. When people were finally given the opportunity in the late 1980s to participate somewhat freely and to express their views, it was the anger built up over centuries of imperial rule and seventy years of Soviet control that burst to the surface.

The shift to a drastically different regime does not mean that the underlying culture has changed. The limited available evidence points to a number of values that have carried over from the Soviet—and in some cases the tsarist—periods. There is, for instance, widespread suspicion of those in positions of authority. Most Russians, especially those who did relatively well under the old system, still seem to want the state to provide critical services, hand down directives, and take the initiative in important social, political, and economic issues.

Surveys conducted by the New Russia Barometre project since 1993 show that most Russians prize the freedoms they have gained since the end of the Communist era. Solid majorities support freedom of speech and

the right to vote, and see them as among the key accomplishments of the Russian Federation. Similarly, three-quarters of all Russians typically tell the pollsters that the regime is better than the old Communist one as far as respecting individual rights is concerned. And voter turnout is reasonably high. Only 50.6 percent of eligible voters participated in the 1993 Duma election following the failed coup attempt. But the turnout in national elections since then has only once dropped below 60 percent, which is 10 percent higher than the rate of participation in a typical American presidential contest.

Less clear is Russians' support for the broader values that tend to yield social capital and, with it, deep and ongoing support for a democratic regime. Russians have low expectations of the government—expectations most people believe it rarely meets. In addition, one poll found that only 9 percent of one sample thought that "people like me" had more power in the mid-1990s than under Gorbachev; 45 percent claimed that the reverse was true. One 1998 poll showed that Russians trusted the army and the church more than any other institutions, but

▮ TABLE 9.7 Russian Attitudes about Democracy (percent of respondents agreeing with the following statements)

ISSUE	1995	1997	2000
Democratic procedures are a façade	73.1	74.4	74.5
Democratic procedures are indispensable	56.0	51.0	47.8
Public participation is important	23.4	18.8	23.8
Ordinary citizens have no role to play, only politicians do	66.1	70.3	66.4

Source: Adapted from Michael McFaul, Nikolai Petrov, and Andrei Ryabov, *Between Dictatorship and Democracy: Russian Post-Communist Political Reform.* (Washington: Carnegie Endowment for International Peace, 2004), 276.

Conflict in Russia

As in most of the formerly Communist countries, there is much conflict in Russia and has been since Gorbachev removed the political lid with glasnost in the late 1980s. Unlike the industrialized democracies, however, much of the protest is aimed not just at individual politicians and their policies but at the regime as well.

There is surprisingly little violence in the conflict at the mass level, other than in Chechnya. However, dozens of politicians, journalists, human rights activists, and business leaders have been assassinated.

these figures only hovered around one-third. As table 9.7 suggests, few Russians think they can make much of a difference. What's more, there are signs that support for democracy may be eroding, at least in some respects.

There are important demographic changes occurring that indicate that Russian culture may become more democratic over time. In particular, young, urban, and well-educated people support the new regime and liberal values far more than their older, rural, and poorly educated counterparts. But if such a shift occurs, it will take place over the course of the next generation or two, not the next year or two.

And the concerns are not simply seen in public opinion polls. Perhaps even more important—and even harder to pin down—is the weakness of Russia's civil society. As we have seen in other chapters, a strong civil society is important because it helps build legitimacy *and* the belief that people can have an impact on the policy decisions that have to be made by elites.

One of the best indicators of the strength of a civil society is the status of its interest groups. Here, the signs are not encouraging.

Russia has the same kinds of interest groups and other social organizations we found in Part 2. However, they tend to be weaker and less independent of the state. If anything, the regime has made it harder for groups to organize or try to exert their influence. The most glaring example of this is the way the state has used cumbersome registration procedures to deny legal status to as many as half of the existing environmental, religious, and regional organizations. Indeed, the situation is so bleak that Michael McFaul and Elina Treyger concluded, "civil society's ability to influence political outcomes on a national scale seems to have been greater during the last years of the Soviet era than it is today. Russian civil

society is weak, atomized, apolitical, and heavily dependent on Western assistance for support."[4]

This sense of alienation is reflected, too, in the low rates of involvement in interest groups. This holds for trade unions, women's groups, and other associations that have links to Communist-era bodies, as well as those that were created from scratch after 1991. The one possible exception to this trend toward alienation is the growing number of strikes among miners, teachers, industrial workers, and others who often go months without getting paid. Even here, however, the unions that supposedly represent the interests of those workers are small and have had at best a limited impact on economic policy making.

Political Parties and Elections

Perhaps even more worrisome is the status of Russia's electoral and party systems. As we saw in Chapter 2, these are vital to the health and stability of any democratic regime. Russia's situation is problematic on two very different levels.

First, through the post-Communist period, it has what the scholars conducting the New Russia Barometre (NRB) polls call a "floating" party system. In most stable democracies, voters choose from essentially the same parties from election to election. And, because the individual parties do not change their positions all that much from one ballot to the next, most voters develop loyalties to one or another of them in what political scientists call "party identification." One NRB study found that only

[4] Michael McFaul and Elina Treyger, "Civil Society," in McFaul, Petrov, and Ryabov, *Between Dictatorship and Democracy,* 135–6.

22 percent of Russians had any party identification, in contrast to over 80 percent in Britain and the United States. This stability, in turn, allows parties to play a vital role in linking people's preferences to the parties' actions as they organize governments and make policy decisions.

There are few signs that this pattern of partisan and electoral behavior is developing in Russia. Instead, as all the tables in this section will show, there is little continuity in either the parties that contest elections or in the voters' reactions to them. Indeed, the Russian party system is more fluid than any other we will consider in this book. This fluidity, in turn, contributes to the broader uncertainties about Russian politics.

Second, there are clear signs that Putin wants to reshape the party system so that it can be more easily manipulated, if not outright controlled, from the center. There are no indications that he has any desire to end competitive elections, and there is little evidence of the kind of voting fraud that we will see, for instance, in Chapter 16 on Mexico.

Nonetheless, since he came to power in 1999, the government has taken effective control of all the television stations, which it has used to assiduously promote Putin and his policies. Before the 2003 legislative election, he forced a law through the Duma which made it all but impossible for small parties without nation-wide support to even get on the ballot. Then, as these lines were being written, he announced plans to abolish the single-member district half of the electoral system (see discussion in the text that follows).

All this has been done in the name of stability and even of antiterrorism. However, giving the Kremlin more control over the information people can get or the options people have when they go into the voting booth can hardly be seen as a good sign for democracy.

Elections

Russians' first opportunity to vote in a reasonably free election came in the referendum of 1993. Early that year, the conflict between the still-reformist administration and the increasingly conservative Congress of People's Deputies came to a head. Boris Yeltsin invoked special powers and called for a referendum in which the people were asked if they supported his rule and economic reforms and if they favored early elections for president and the Congress.

Yeltsin got clear but not overwhelming majorities in support of his presidency and economic policies. Voters rejected early presidential elections but supported them for the legislature. However, the turnout was so low that Yeltsin did not get the absolute majority he needed to call

new legislative elections. Moreover, only about a third of the eligible voters actually supported either Yeltsin or his policies. In short, the referendum results did little more than set the stage for the events that culminated in the unsuccessful coup attempt that fall.

Russians' second opportunity to vote was a referendum on the new constitution held simultaneously with the State Duma elections in December 1993. As in the spring, barely half the voters turned out, and barely half of those voting supported the government's initiative. Since then, Russians have voted in seven national elections—four for the Duma (1993, 1995, 1999, and 2003) and three for the presidency (1996, 2000, and 2004).

The Duma elections are run under the same basic system used in Germany. There are 450 seats, half of which are elected by proportional representation and half in single-member districts. In the proportional half of the ballot, seats only go to parties who win at least 5 percent of the vote nationwide. In the single-member district half, whoever wins the most votes in a district wins it.

Presidential elections follow the French pattern. Any number of candidates can run on a first ballot, and if no one wins a majority in that first round of voting, the top two vote getters compete in a runoff two weeks later.

The dual system for choosing Duma members, in particular, has worked very differently from the similar one in Germany. There, in every election in the past fifty years, the major parties have won just about as many votes in the proportional representation and the single-member district contests, which means that the parliamentary delegations accurately reflect the parties' overall support. In Russia, anywhere from 60 to 110 independents have been elected from the single-member districts, most of whom before 2003 were beyond the control of national party leaders. Herein lies the importance of the proposed elimination of the single-member districts. Doing so would create Duma delegations that are much easier for party leaders—and the Kremlin—to control.

More generally, there is nothing stable about Russian parties and elections. (See tables 9.8 and 9.9.) Indeed, the most striking thing is that only three parties have run candidates in all the Duma elections. Overall, the four parties saw their share of the vote slip from nearly half in 1993 to barely a quarter in 2003 (see the next section).

The presidential elections do not show much more stability. (See tables 9.10 through 9.12.) To be sure, some of the same candidates have run in more than one election, and some of them are easily identified as members of one of the national political parties. Of concern here is

▌TABLE 9.8 Elections to the Russian Duma, 1993, 1995, and 1999

PARTY	PERCENTAGE OF LIST VOTE			SEATS ON PARTY LIST			SEATS IN SINGLE-MEMBER DISTRICTS		
	1993	1995	1999	1993	1995	1999	1993	1995	1999
Communists	12.35	22.30	24.29	32	99	67	32	58	55
Women of Russia	8.1	–	–	21	–	4	3	–	–
Liberal Democrats	22.79	11.18	5.98	59	50	17	11	1	2
Our Home Is Russia	–	1.13	–	–	45	–	–	10	7
Unity	–	–	22.32	–	–	64	–	–	9
Yabloko	7.82	6.89	5.93	20	31	17	13	14	5
Russia's Democratic Choice	15.38	–	–	40	–	–	56	9	–
Union of Right Forces	–	–	8.52	–	–	24	–	–	5
Fatherland All Russia	–	–	13.33	–	–	36	–	–	32
Party of Russian Unity and Accord	6.76	–	–	18	–	–	9	1	–
Democratic Party of Russia	5.5	–	–	14	–	–	7	–	–
Others and independents	–	–	–	–	–	–	60	103	110
Against all	4.36	3.60	–	–	–	–	–	–	–

Note: Includes only parties that broke the 5 percent barrier.

▌TABLE 9.9 The 2003 State Duma Election

PARTY	VOTE (PERCENT)	SEATS
United Russia	37.6	222
Communists	12.6	51
Liberal Democrats	11.5	36
Rodina	9.0	37
Yabloko	4.3	4
Union of Right Forces	4.0	3
Independents	21.0	94

Note: The "others" were all elected from single-member districts. Many have since rallied to United Russia.

▌TABLE 9.10 The Russian Presidential Election of 1996

CANDIDATE	PERCENTAGE OF FIRST-BALLOT VOTE	PERCENTAGE OF SECOND-BALLOT VOTE
Boris Yeltsin	35.3	53.8
Gennady Zyuganov	32.0	40.3
Alexander Lebed	14.5	–
Grigori Yavlinsky	7.5	–
Vladimir Zhirinovsky	5.7	–
Others	2.2	–
Against all	1.5	4.8

▌TABLE 9.11 The Russian Presidential Election of 2000

CANDIDATE	PERCENTAGE OF VOTE
Vladimir Putin	52.94
Gennady Zyuganov	29.21
Grigori Yavlinski	5.80
Anan Tuleev	2.95
Vladimir Zhirinovsky	2.70
Other candidates	2.58
Against all	1.88

▌TABLE 9.12 Presidential Vote, 2004

CANDIDATE	VOTE (%)
Vladimir Putin	71.2
Nikolai Charitonov	13.7
Sergei Glaziev	4.1
Others	6.7
Against all	4.3

how strongly the major media outlets weighed in on behalf of Yeltsin in 1996 and Putin in both of his campaigns, which led many outsider observers to suggest that these were anything but fair and honest campaigns.

Each presidential campaign has been less competitive than the one before it. Only the first election required two ballots to determine a winner. In contrast, France has always needed two ballots, as have most of the other Eastern European countries that have adopted a similar system for electing a president. The 2004 election in Russia was particularly problematic. Putin's obvious strength coming out of the Duma elections made the results a foregone conclusion. As a result, other potentially serious candidates withdrew from the contest. The Communists ran an unknown who came in a very distant second. Rodina ran its founder (and reported Putin protégé) Sergei Glazev, who came in an even more distant third. Putin won with almost three quarters of the vote.

The Political Parties Today

Table 9.9 presents the results of the 2003 election separately from the three earlier ones because it is important to see just how much the system changed during the first Putin administration. For the first time, a single party scored an overwhelming victory and assured the president of a massive majority in the Duma. All the signs are that that party, **United Russia,** will dominate political life for years to come. The only question, then, is how—or if—the other parties can restructure themselves into a viable democratic opposition.

United Russia is not like any of the political parties considered in Part 2 in that it is not defined primarily by its stance on divisive issues. Rather, it is what observers of Russian politics call a party of power created not so much to defend policy proposals or ideological positions as to promote the interests of the current leadership. It is also not the first party of power. In 1995 then–Prime Minister **Viktor Chernomyrdin** created **Our Home Is Russia.** It, too, was short on ideological positions and existed largely to support Chernomyrdin and his entourage. When he was forced to resign in 1998, the party's fortunes plummeted. It won only 1.2 percent of the vote and five single-member districts in 1999. It did not survive to run in 2003.

United Russia was formed for the 1999 Duma election, when it was known as Unity. Its specific origins are shrouded in secrecy, but all signs indicate that it was put together by oligarch Boris Berezovsky and other members of the Yeltsin "family." It had minuscule support in the polls until Putin's popularity began to soar because of his forceful prosecution of the war in Chechnya. Three months after its creation, Unity came within a single percentage point of the Communists, even though it won only nine single-member districts—which is to be expected for a new organization. It later merged with **Fatherland—All Russia** and took on its new name.

Early on, Putin publicly kept his distance from the party. By the time of the 2003 and 2004 campaigns, there was no longer any pretense of his staying above the political fray. In fact, the most critical observers think he is planning to reshape the party system from the top so that the middle-of-the-road United Russia will be well placed to defeat competitors on the left and on the right.

That assumes, of course, that United Russia survives Putin's departure. As we will see, a Russian president can only serve two terms, and he is thus due to leave office in 2008. In early 2005, there were rumors that the constitution would be changed or some other device found (e.g., formally creating a new country by merging with Belarus) for Putin to stay in power. It is also possible that the Putin team can build up the party's organization so it can thrive under a new leader. That said, building such an organization from scratch is not going to be easy.

Until 2003, the Communist Party had been the most effective party in Russia. It is the only one to have a viable organization throughout the country, which allows it to do such things as conduct door-to-door election campaigns. More importantly, its support steadily increased until it earned nearly a quarter of the vote in the proportional half of the election in 1999. Its leader and presidential candidate, **Gennady Zyuganov,** came in second in the first two presidential elections.

Like the reformed Communist parties in Eastern Europe, the CPRF is not a carbon copy of the old Stalinist machine. The new party counts few prominent Communists from the old days among its leaders. Zyuganov comfortably plays his role as leader of the parliamentary opposition and has tried to portray the party more in Social Democratic terms as an organization that wants to protect the social and economic interests of Russia's poor.

Nonetheless, the party is far less reformist than its counterparts in Eastern Europe. Zyuganov himself was a staunch opponent of Gorbachev-era reforms and headed a shady "national salvation front" that seemed to want to restore the Soviet Union after it fell apart. He also was quoted as saying that the army should combat "the destructive might of rootless democracy," and he served on the editorial board of a conservative and often anti-Semitic newspaper. Like many former Communists, Zyuganov and his colleagues have adopted nationalistic positions that include sometimes not-so-veiled references to expand the Russian Federation's border into the near-abroad. In the 1996 campaign, Zyuganov and the CPRF took a harder line against economic reform than before, advocating a return to more state ownership and central planning. They have also called for the retention of the collective and state farms created under Stalin. During the 1998 economic crisis, they advocated a slowdown in the pace of economic reform and the breakup of the monopolies and oligopolies created since 1991, which we will discuss shortly.

The Communists undoubtedly are the best-organized party in Russia today. This is the case because they can draw on the thousands of middle- and lower-level party officials from the old CPSU. One asset they do not have, however, is the property formerly owned by the CPSU, which was all transferred to the state.

The CPRF's influence probably peaked in 1995 when, along with other antireform factions, it held enough seats to have de facto control of the Duma and block many of Yeltsin's legislative measures. The CPRF and those other groups lost support in 1999, and Zyuganov's inability to win more than a third of the vote suggested that the party was unlikely to come to power on its own or as part of any easily foreseeable coalition.

The 2003 and 2004 elections brought even more bad news. It saw its share of the Duma vote cut almost in half. Most of its losses went to a new left-of-center party, Rodina, that had been created by former Communists (and some say with the active support of the Kremlin). No

An angry woman confronting Liberal Democratic Party leader Vladimir Zhirinovsky during a Duma debate on Russia's relationship with NATO in September 1995.

AP/Wide World Photos

prominent Communist was willing to run in a campaign everyone knew would lead to a landslide victory for Putin. The lacklustre candidate who filled in for Zyuganov won little more than a third of the votes the Communists tallied four years earlier.

Russia also has two parties that are typically considered reformist because they have been reasonably consistent supporters of efforts to forge a democratic state and a market economy. Together, they account for no more than a quarter of the electorate. Only one of them, Yabloko, has run in all three Duma elections.

Yabloko is the most consistent and persistent of the reformist parties. Yabloko (Russian for "apple") is an acronym for its three founding leaders, Grigori Yavlinsky, Yuri Boldyrev, and Vladimir Lukin. Only two of these leaders, Yavlinsky and Lukin, are still with the party. Of the reformist parties, it has taken the strongest stand not only in support of democracy but also for the retention of some form of welfare state, which makes it most like the Social Democratic parties considered in Part 2. It is also the party that does the best among intellectuals, who were prominent supporters of Gorbachev's reforms. Yabloko's vote has dropped by one percentage point in each of the Duma elections. Its leader, Yavlinsky, announced that if the party did not win at least 6 percent of the vote in 1999 he would not run for president in 2000. It didn't, but he ran anyway—coming in a disappointing

third and further harming his own reputation and that of the party.

The **Union of Right Forces** was created by another group of reformers who were more firmly committed to promarket policies than Yabloko. The most prominent of them, **Yegor Gaidar** and Anatoly Chubais, had been key architects of privatization and economic policy in general in the early Yeltsin years. When their previous party, Russia's Choice, failed to break the 5 percent barrier in 1995, Gaidar realized that he had to build a broader coalition. The new Union of Right Forces hinted that Putin supported its economic plans and was therefore able to score a respectable 8.5 percent of the proportional vote in 1999. The party's use of the word "right" in its name does not mean it is right-wing. Rather, the Russian term it uses, *pravikh*, has the same root as *pravda*, or "truth." Thus, "right" is used by Gaidar and his colleagues to suggest that they have the right or correct answers to Russia's political and economic problems.

Both parties face uncertain futures—at best. Their leaders have failed to find a durable audience outside the intellectual communities in the big cities. Both also fell below the 5 percent barrier in 2003 and kept a tiny foothold in the Duma only because they won a handful of single-member districts. There were rumors that the authorities doctored the vote count so that both "failed" to reach 5 percent. More importantly, if the single-member districts are abolished, these two parties would probably have to merge in order to survive.

Finally, Russia has a number of political parties that can only be viewed as antidemocratic—or worse. The most prominent of them has been the **Liberal Democrats,** headed by the enigmatic, and some say dangerous, **Vladimir Zhirinovsky.** Almost everything about him is murky. Despite his frequently anti-Semitic ravings, he is of Jewish origin. Some think he was formerly a KGB agent paid to infiltrate Jewish and dissident organizations during the 1970s and 1980s.

There is no debating one thing. He is a loose cannon whose often-frightening rhetoric struck a chord with a significant proportion of Russia's most alienated voters. Since he burst onto the scene in 1993, he has, among other things, done the following:

- Hinted that he would use nuclear weapons on Japan
- Advocated expanding the Russian border all the way to the Indian Ocean
- Invited French racist politician Jean-Marie Le Pen to a ceremony marking his twenty-fifth wedding anniversary
- Blamed Western governments and businessmen (in his case, it is always men) for the collapse of the Soviet Union
- Attacked just about every reformist politician in Russia (for instance, alleging that Yeltsin is in power only because of the CIA)

The Liberal Democrats have no local organization to speak of, which is the main reason the party was able to capture only one single-member constituency in 1995. The party's fortunes have declined since then as Russians have grown tired of Zhirinovsky's positions and antics. The party was technically ruled unconstitutional for the 1999 election and had to reformulate itself as the Zhirinovsky Bloc. It saw its vote decline to a bare 6 percent in 1999, and then Zhirinovsky won only 2.7 percent of the vote in 2000 but rebounded to nearly 12 percent four years later. Nonetheless, at the very least, it is safe to say that Zhirinovsky and the Liberal Democrats have passed their peak and, for the moment at least, are not a significant factor in day-to-day politics.

A Balance Sheet

The Russian party system is likely to remain in flux. Given the impermanence of the parties and the fragmentation of the system, it is hard to imagine how Russia could develop a system anything like those we saw in Britain, France, or Germany in the foreseeable future

unless United Russia can establish itself as a dominant centrist party.

The difficulties go far beyond election returns or party platforms. To illustrate this, consider the following television ads, which ran during the 1995 Duma campaign. Only Our Home Is Russia had anything approaching slick, Western-style commercials with rapidly changing and reassuring images backed by neutral-but-not-bland synthesized music. The other ads ranged from unprofessional to incompetent—to the degree that it was often hard to tell what the ad and the party were for. Some simply showed "talking heads," and even they were unable to keep within the time allotted to them. Some of the less-than-serious parties, of course, had less-than-serious ads. An ad for the Beer Lovers' Party (0.62 percent of the vote) started with two old women looking disapprovingly at a drunken man staggering along a muddy path, a bottle of vodka sticking out of his pocket. One woman said to the other: "This is not an acceptable way to drink." Immediately the scene shifted to three men at a picnic on a sunny day, drinking beer. One said to the others: "This is an acceptable way to drink."

The Ivan Rybkin Bloc (Rybkin was the outgoing speaker of the Duma, although his party only won 1.11 percent of the vote) ran one ad showing a conversation between two cows in which one (Ivan) tried to explain justice to the other by asking if (s)he had ever seen butter made from milk or eaten it. It ended with the first cow eating a slice of bread covered with butter and saying that they would all have butter with their bread if Rybkin was reelected. The Communists ran a simplistic piece in which they showed horror scenes from the Russian past and asked: "Who will stop this?" The answer was obvious. Yabloko had one of Isaac Newton (though the ad said it was Lord Byron) getting hit by an apple falling from a tree.

The two most bizarre ads were made by the Liberal Democrats. The first showed a couple watching television in bed. Former Soviet leader Leonid Brezhnev came on; they said he was boring. Then came Gorbachev, and they said they had seen all that before. Finally it was Zhirinovsky's turn, and this time they said that this was more interesting even as their body language made it clear that watching more television was not on their agenda for the rest of the evening. The second ad took place in an upscale nightclub. After the singer finished her act, she was lured back onstage for an encore that was a much more upbeat song with the refrain, "Without you, this would be boring; Vladimir Wolfovich [as Zhirinovsky is commonly known], you turn me on."

The quality of television ads has improved noticeably since 1995. However, the state's all but complete

HIV/AIDS in Russia

Most health experts think AIDS is a time bomb waiting to go off in Russia. No one knows for sure, but about a million people were infected with the HIV virus at the end of 2004. Most had gotten the disease either from shared needles or from sexual contact with prostitutes. The World Health Organization estimates that the number will rise to somewhere between five and fifteen million by 2020 if steps are not taken now.

AIDS has not received much public attention yet in Russia for two reasons. First, only four thousand people had died from the virus as of mid-2004. Second, because most people with HIV are either drug users or customers of the sex industry, many think it is a taboo subject.

In 2004, only 1,800 people were being given antiretroviral drugs. That number was expected to reach 7,000 in 2005. The minimum number needing the full cocktail of drugs was expected to top 70,000 that year.

www.avert.org/ecstatee.htm

---

control of the mass media has kept the opposition parties weak and strengthened Putin's hand in ways that cannot be considered favorable to democracy.

The Russian State

Each of the countries examined in the remainder of this book has one major difference from those discussed in Part 2. They all have constitutions specifying how offices are structured, bills are passed, rights are ensured, and the like. However, those constitutions matter less than they do in any of the industrialized democracies. In the case of Russia, as in the other countries we will consider, it is just as important to recognize that certain institutions, some of which are not mentioned in the constitution, probably wield more power than the State Duma, cabinet, or any other legally authorized body. And it is a more fluid kind of power, determined as much by who holds which offices and what resources they have at their disposal as by the rules laid out in the constitution or any other legal document (www.constitution.ru/en/10003000-01.htm).

The Presidency

Given Russian traditions and the rocky relations between President Yeltsin and what was then still the Supreme Soviet, it came as no surprise when he wrote a constitution for a regime based on a strong presidency in 1993, much like the one in France. Indeed, there was every reason to believe that, were it to adopt a conventional parliamentary system, Russia would have been even more divided and difficult to govern than France's Fourth Republic (www.kremlin.ru/eng/).

As we have already seen, the president is directly elected for a four-year term in a two-ballot system. Any candidate who gets a million signatures (which could be bought for a dollar apiece in 2004) can run on the first ballot. If a candidate gains a majority at the first ballot, he or she wins outright, as was the case in 2000. If, however, no one wins more than half of the votes cast, the first- and second-place candidates meet in a runoff two weeks later.

The president is all but completely independent of the Duma. There are provisions for impeaching the president, but it is extremely difficult to do so, as Yeltsin's opponents learned when they tried to impeach him shortly after the constitution was adopted. The president appoints the prime minister and the other cabinet members. (See table 9.13.) The Duma can reject the president's choice, but if it does so three times, the president can dissolve the Duma and call for new elections. Thus, in 1998, Yeltsin fired Prime Minister Sergei Kiriyenko and tried to bring Viktor Chernomyrdin back in to replace him. The Duma voted the former prime minister down twice. It took the threat of new elections before the deputies and president agreed on a compromise candidate, Yevgeni Primakov.

The president can issue decrees that have the force of law in many policy areas. More importantly, the president runs an administration that is extremely centralized. Since the mid-1990s, authority has been concentrated in the **power ministries**—defense, foreign affairs, interior (including the police), the State Security Bureau (FSB), and an informal body known as the Security Council.

At least since Chernomyrdin was replaced, the prime minister has exercised little independent authority, and the incumbent when these lines were written,

▌ **TABLE 9.13** Russian Presidents and Prime Ministers

PRESIDENT	PRIME MINISTER
Boris Yeltsin (1991–1999)	Boris Yeltsin (1991–1992)
	Yegor Gaidar (Acting 1992–1993)
	Viktor Chernomyrdin (1993–1998)
	Sergei Kiriyenko (1998)
	Yevgeni Primakov (1998–1999)
	Sergei Stepashin (1999)
	Vladimir Putin (1999)
Vladimir Putin (2000–)	Mikhail Kasyanov (2000–2004)
	Mikhail Fradkov (2004–)

Mikhail Fradkov, is little known outside of the country. Government ministries are free to act more or less on their own as far as implementing policy is concerned. Nonetheless, for reasons that will become clearer when we look behind the scenes, they are not very good at implementing policy.

The Oligarchs

Some people think that the real power in Russia is held by a tiny group of tycoons who have profited immensely from privatization and who have used their wealth to gain political leverage. The power of these **oligarchs** became clear toward the end of Yeltsin's first term in office when analysts began criticizing what they thought was the undue influence of what they came to call the "family"—a small circle of relatives and advisers who controlled access to and had tremendous influence over the president (www.cdi.org/russia/johnson/7033-4.cfm).

The most important member of the family undoubtedly was Tatyana Dyachenko, Yeltsin's younger daughter. And there is no doubt as well that Yeltsin's family made millions of dollars through shady deals, if not outright corruption, which led Putin to grant them all amnesty from possible prosecution in one of his first steps as acting president.

Although the Yeltsins have left the scene, the oligarchs haven't. No one outside the Kremlin knows exactly how many of them there are, how they made their money, or how much influence they have. Nonetheless, no one thought it was an outrageous overstatement when **Boris Berezovsky** declared in 1997 that he and six other businessmen controlled over half of Russia's GNP. Like Yeltsin's "family," the oligarchs undoubtedly gained much of their wealth through shady deals, if not outright corruption. They also have sent much of their wealth abroad; in fact, they may have exported more capital from Russia than has been invested there by foreign businesses since 1991. What's more, they all have close, if not well-documented, ties to the Russian mafia.

Berezovsky's case is typical. Born in 1946 to a Jewish family that was part of Moscow's intellectual elite, Berezovsky earned a Ph.D. in mathematics and electronics, and then joined the prestigious Academy of Sciences, where he specialized in developing computerized management systems. He used his contacts to launch his first business during the Gorbachev years, and by the time the USSR collapsed, he was a major trader in automobiles, oil, gas, and the nationalized airline Aeroflot. As we will see in the section on public policy, the Yeltsin government virtually gave away shares in the nationalized industries it inherited. Berezovsky and the other oligarchs capitalized on this odd form of privatization to gain control over thousands of companies. Berezovsky ran companies in dozens of sectors but exercised the most influence through his media holdings, including two of the most respected newspapers and the most widely watched television network, ORT.

It is no exaggeration to say that Yeltsin owed his reelection in 1996 to Berezovsky and the other oligarchs. Not only did they contribute vast sums of money, they controlled all the major media outlets, whose campaign coverage was extremely biased. They also are largely responsible for the creation of Unity and for Putin's meteoric rise.

However, Putin's relationship with some of the oligarchs has been extremely bumpy, and three have had dramatic clashes with the president. First was Vladimir Gusinsky. After his television network, NTV, openly condemned Putin, Gusinsky was arrested for corruption, and control of NTV was handed over to the still state-owned natural gas monopoly, Gazprom. After being released on bail, Gusinsky moved abroad. Berezovsky, too, ran afoul of Putin and joined Gusinsky in exile in late 2001. Finally, of course, there is Mikhail Khodorkovsky, whose arrest and trial begin this chapter.

The downfall of these three oligarchs does not mean that their power has been more widely distributed. Rather, they have been replaced by other oligarchs who head other massive corporations such as the petrochemical giants, Lukoil and Sibneft. The only difference is that the new oligarchs are loyal to Putin.

The Parliament

Until 1999 the parliament was the main counterweight to the presidency and, as such, frequently was a lightning rod in the intensely conflicted Yeltsin years. That does not mean, however, that the parliament has ever been all that powerful. In fact, the 1993 constitution was written in a way to minimize its likely impact.

As is the case in most of the democratic world, the parliament consists of two houses. The upper house, the **Federation Council,** has two members from each republic and region. But, like most upper houses, it can do little more than delay the passage of legislation. If anything, its power has diminished further since its members became for all intents and purposes presidential appointees.

The lower house, the State Duma, is elected much like the German Bundestag. The Duma itself is a fairly wild place by Western standards. Deputies scream at each other and walkouts are common, as are fistfights. By 1995 eighty-seven candidates either had been convicted of felonies or were under indictment.

Democratization in Russia

ALTHOUGH INSTITUTIONS MATTER, focusing on them can obscure the most important point about Russia's fledgling democracy. Constitutional provisions and the rule of law pale in comparison with what political scientists call the "personalization of leadership" around Yeltsin, Putin, and other top leaders.

Perhaps it should not come as a surprise that a man who spent the first thirty-five years of his professional life clawing his way up the Communist Party hierarchy would find it natural to create a "top–down" style of leadership when the going got rough. Nonetheless, by the time of the 1996 election, it was clear that neither Yeltsin nor any of his leading rivals could be said to be committed democrats. Indeed, all the major candidates favored maintaining the personalization of power around a strong presidency in ways that are not likely to strengthen democratic institutions or the rule of law.

There is little evidence that things on this extremely important but hard-to-measure front have changed appreciably during Putin's tenure in office.

More important for our purposes is the fact that the Duma does not have much real power. It cannot, for example, force the executive to enforce laws it passes, and it has only limited influence over the budget. In theory, the Duma has to approve presidential appointments, but Yeltsin was known to keep nominees in "acting" positions for upwards of a year. Most importantly, the Duma has no effective ability to cast a vote of no confidence and force a prime minister and cabinet out of office. It also can do little to remove a president.

As table 9.9 showed, the Communists and other opponents of reform controlled the Duma following the first two elections. They used that base to block many policy proposals requiring legislative approval and to keep reformist nominees from taking or holding onto office. With the emergence of United Russia, however, the role of the Duma has changed. Putin and his cabinet now have the kind of disciplined parliamentary majority we find in Britain's House of Commons. In practice, the majority is much larger than that table suggests, since most of the independents elected in the single-member districts have affiliated themselves with the majority. That means that the Duma now eagerly passes all of Putin's major legislative initiatives, including laws that reduced the power of the republics and regions, restructured the party system, and reduced taxes.

The Bureaucracy

The Yeltsin team would have preferred purging the bureaucracy of the officials who had been the glue to the old Communist system, especially those in policy-making and security positions. In practice, however, they could not do so because the country lacked trained personnel to take their place. Consider education, for example. The old regime had relied heavily on the schools in its attempts to shape public opinion and create a docile population. Teachers were expected to support the party line. The curriculum and textbooks presented official party positions not only in the mandatory courses in Marxism-Leninism but also in the examples used by textbook writers to teach first-graders reading or arithmetic. As much as they might have liked to, government officials lacked the resources to replace all those teachers and books.

In areas such as the Foreign Ministry and the various agencies that replaced the KGB, many top officials lost their jobs. However, even in those organizations, there are many people left from the old days whose loyalties are by no means certain (and who can therefore be used to staff the plots of post–cold war spy novels).

There is some concern today about the impact of the security services, most notably the Federal Security Bureau (FSB), which is the main body that replaced the Soviet-era KGB. This is the case because of Putin's background. He spent his entire career in the KGB during the Soviet era, was brought to Moscow in part to run the FSB, and has appointed a number of security officials to top posts in his government. The security services also may be influential because it has *kompromat,* or compromising material, on all leading officials, including Putin. (See figure 9.3.)

❚ FIGURE 9.3 Decision Making in Russia

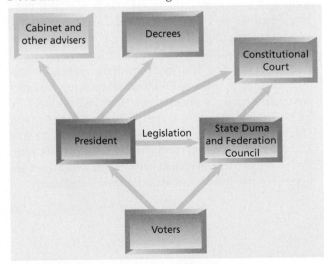

The Judiciary

Prior to 1991, the Soviet judiciary was little more than a cog in the party machine. The situation was not as bleak as it had been under Stalin. Nonetheless, the legal system lacked the provisions that sustain an independent and impartial judicial system and the rule of law.

The new Russian republic has tried to rebuild a judicial system that invariably found defendants guilty and historically relied on "show" trials in high-profile cases. Most notably, it established a Constitutional Court to deal with cases involving legal principle. Similarly, there is now a Supreme Court that serves as a final court of appeal in criminal, civil, and administrative cases. Both have been reasonably active. The Constitutional Court, for example, played a major role in determining how the 1993 referendum was conducted. More importantly, both courts have been highly politicized because their judges are named by the president and by the heads of the two houses of parliament, respectively, each of whom is reluctant to appoint anyone he cannot count on.

In the long run, what happens in everyday judicial life—given the many abuses that occurred during the Soviet years—may prove to be more important. And despite the difficulty in retraining the entire legal profession and/or recruiting a new generation of attorneys, considerable progress has been made. Although sixty-five thousand people claimed they were illegally detained in 1994, fully a third of them were released from jail on the basis of a court order. A few defendants who were falsely accused have won cash settlements from the state prosecutor's office. There have even been a few hundred jury trials—the first since 1918. Still, the Russian government faces an uphill struggle on this and many other fronts. To cite but one example, in 1995 there were only twenty-eight thousand prosecutors and twenty thousand independent attorneys, most of whom were trained under the very different Soviet legal system.

Most important of all is the degree to which the judiciary can contribute to the rule of law, which is still frequently violated. That begins with the spectacular examples, such as the way Khodorkovsky's arrest and trial were handled. But it goes deeper. Basic civil liberties are by no means guaranteed, especially outside the major cities. Even everyday interactions between the people and the state are often conducted outside the law with, for instance, the widespread expectation that bribes are needed or the still pervasive underpayment of taxes.

The Federation

On paper the Soviet Union was a federal system formed by union republics that had joined it voluntarily. The constitutions adopted over the years guaranteed certain political and cultural rights to the republics. There were even provisions outlining procedures for seceding from the USSR.

But these provisions existed only on paper. Until the Gorbachev years, party leaders in Moscow determined policy for the subnational units, just as they did everything else. This changed, however, in the late 1980s. Pent-up hostilities in the non-Russian republics, and then in Russia itself, erupted and proved to be one of the most important reasons the USSR disintegrated.

Some observers thought that the creation of fifteen new countries would ease the ethnic tensions. However, because none of the new republics is anywhere near homogeneous, most have faced serious internal difficulties.

The Russian Federation is no exception. In some instances, most notably Chechnya, the Russian government has been no more successful than its Soviet predecessor in quelling ethnic unrest. However, on balance, it has been able to defuse much of the pressure from the regions.

The minority population consists of hundreds of ethnic groups, the largest of which, the Tatars, makes up only 4 percent of the total. Russia has basically kept the complex maze of regions delineated along ethnic lines that it inherited from the Soviet Union. There are twenty-one autonomous republics and sixty-eight other bodies with various titles that are defined as "subjects of the federation."

Relations between Moscow and many of the republics and regions were quite tense in 1992. Tatarstan declared itself a sovereign state. Leaders in what was then Checheno-Ingushetia refused to carry out Russian laws. Fighting in Georgia spilled over into the Russian republics in the north Caucasus. The situation was by far the worst in Chechnya, where civil wars raged from 1994 to 1997 and 1999 to the present, cost well over one hundred thousand lives, and took a terrible toll on the government's legitimacy at home and abroad.

Chechnya may prove to be the exception rather than the rule. In the aftermath of the 1993 coup attempt in Moscow, the overall situation began to improve. There was a growing awareness in most of the autonomous republics that full independence was not a viable option. Only Tatarstan and the impoverished Bashkyria had more than three million people; eleven had fewer than one million.

As a result, the government has negotiated a nation-

Mourners following the 2004 attack by Chechen rebels on a school in Beslan, which killed hundreds of children.

AFP/Getty Images

wide Federation Treaty and a series of bilateral agreements with eight of the republics. Komi, for example, was granted special powers to deal with its environment, which had been heavily contaminated by wastes from the petrochemical industry. Yakutia won concessions allowing it to keep profits from the sale of its diamonds and other minerals. The tiny but once independent Tyva gained the right to secede. Other such agreements have been worked out to give more autonomy to the forty-nine provinces not defined in ethnic terms, most of which are in the more highly populated western third of the country.

But there may be trouble ahead for these subjects of the federation. Putin has also pushed through reforms designed to weaken the power of the republics' and regions' governors. Many of them had turned their jurisdictions into personal fiefdoms, all but ignoring Moscow's policies and regulations. So, in May 2000, Putin established seven new "federal districts" between the national government and republics and regions, each of which is headed by a presidential representative. The Federation Council also has been weakened. Another new law gives the president the power to remove a governor if he or she refuses to harmonize local law with national policy or the constitution. Finally, Putin issued a plan to have the governors appointed by the president and only ratified by the regional assemblies.

The Military

In studying Russia, we also have to consider an institution that was ignored in Part 2 but that will feature prominently in the rest of this book—the military. Under the Soviets, the military was not actively involved in politics, other than in trying to increase its piece of the budgetary pie.

So far, this has largely been true in post-Communist Russia as well. Yeltsin survived the 1993 coup attempt because the troops he called on were loyal to the regime. They attacked the Russian White House even though one of the leading conspirators, Vice President Alexander Rutskoi, was a former air force general and one of the few heroes of the Afghanistan war.

However, many commentators are worried that the military might not stay out of politics. Yeltsin needed support from another prominent former general, Alexander Lebed, to win in 1996. Since then, the military (unlike the intelligence services) have not been actively involved in politics. However, there have been rumors of frustration within the military. This is hardly surprising in a country whose past influence was largely a function of its military might, which disappeared virtually overnight. Officers are worried, too, because so many of their comrades are suffering economically. Thousands of serving officers are not being paid and have been forced to moonlight in other jobs to make ends meet.

Public Policy

Not surprisingly, the Yeltsin and Putin governments have struggled to define and implement public policy. Although this has been the case in all the former Communist countries, Russia has had a particularly hard time, as we saw, for instance, in table 9.4.

The Economy

By far the most important, and the most problematic, policy area is the economy. To see why, simply recall how economic deterioration contributed to the collapse of the Soviet Union.

The new Russian leaders faced a dual challenge. First, how would they shift from a centrally planned economy in which the state owned virtually everything to one based on private ownership and a freer market? Second, how could they ensure that the fruits of these changes—when and if they came—would be shared by all Russians?

Yeltsin and his team were initially committed to sweeping economic reform as the only viable response to the appalling conditions they inherited. However, like everything else in the former Soviet Union, actually carrying out reform was easier said than done. To begin with, there were no historical examples of transitions from centrally planned to market economies for them to draw on. Add to that Yeltsin's own personal lack of decisiveness, perhaps magnified by his many illnesses, and the result was a government that was usually unwilling and unable to follow any consistent economic policy.

Post-Communist economic policy initially revolved around the struggle between two groups. The reformers, including most professional economists, stressed the importance of a rapid and complete shift to a market economy. Their preferred policy was shock therapy, but even its strongest advocates acknowledged that it would have tremendous costs in the short term.

The conservatives wanted to proceed much more slowly. They stressed the fact that the laissez-faire approach has not been all that successful in the West, where all countries have had to turn to a welfare state to help cushion the impact of capitalism's uneven development on the less fortunate.

Proponents of the two approaches were not distributed randomly in Russian society. On the one hand, almost all reformers were in the Yeltsin camp and have never gained much support either in the parliament or the country as a whole. The first Dumas, on the other hand, were dominated by the rejuvenated Communist Party and others who preferred a "go slow" approach.

Conservatives were not the only obstacle facing the reformers. Given the domination of the Communist Party over education prior to 1991, most reformist economists, like former acting Prime Minister Yegor Gaidar, were self-trained and inexperienced. Therefore, in a move that provoked criticism at home and in the West, the reformers drew on a relatively unrepresentative group of Western neoclassical economists who urged them to move rapidly to a free-market economy, whatever the costs to people and enterprises in the transition.

In 1991 and 1992, deteriorating economic conditions, the popularity of Yeltsin and his administration, and the as-yet untested but theoretically elegant predictions of the professional economists tilted the balance toward shock therapy. This led the first Yeltsin governments to emphasize privatization, which took two forms.

The first occurred spontaneously, mostly among small firms in the service sector. About 95 percent of the restaurants, shoe repair stores, gas stations, barber shops, and other such businesses that existed before 1991 quickly gained private owners, usually the men and women who managed them under the Communists. Other people formed upwards of twenty thousand small firms, also mostly in the service sector.

Such "bottom-up" privatization would not have worked for the gigantic industrial enterprises that dominated the Soviet economy. Potential individual investors could not come up with anywhere near the capital to buy these firms. And most were of dubious value because they would have had to be gutted and completely restructured before they could turn a profit. As a result, the government adopted a different approach to privatizing them, using a system of vouchers made available to the public. In 1992, all citizens got a voucher worth 10,000 rubles (then about $25), which they could sell, use to buy stock in privatized companies, or invest in larger funds that bought and managed shares in those companies. Most chose the third option, which means that these new bodies, which are roughly equivalent to American mutual funds, have become the owners of most of the stock that was offered for sale on the open market.

Shares were also made available to the firms' managers—in other words, to men and women who had been part of the old Communist elite. The new owners/managers have thus enriched themselves and, in the process, have strengthened their links to the new state, which is not exactly what the orthodox economists had in mind when they urged the government to privatize.

Finally, shares in most enterprises being privatized were offered to foreign investors. At first there was relatively little interest because the companies were inefficient (at best) and because Russian law limited how much of a stake foreigners could have in companies. After 1993, however, the investment and legal climates both improved, and foreigners pumped an average of $100 billion per year into Russia over the next five years. Outside investors, for instance, own about 90 percent of the shares of AO Volga, which produces a third of Russia's newsprint. The privatized firm is managed by Germans, who are changing its operations so that it can export more of its product to markets where it might earn more profits.

Do not equate privatization with success for radical economic reform. Simply taking enterprises out of public ownership does not necessarily mean creating a competitive market economy. In part because managers were able to gain control over so many companies and because investment funds bought up most of the vouchers, there is a tremendous concentration of wealth in the Russian economy, which led to the creation of the powerful oligarchs and their conglomerates.

Even shock therapy's strongest supporters acknowledge that in the short term it caused many people to lose their jobs or see their incomes shrink. However, few expected Russia to suffer as much as it has. The Russian economy deteriorated tremendously, with overall production declining by an average of more than 6 percent per year during the 1990s. The decline was particularly pronounced in heavy industry, which had been the mainstay of the old Soviet economy.

To cite but one example, the giant Uralmash heavy machinery factory has lost more than twenty thousand jobs and come close to being shut down because there was no longer any real market for its products. Eventually Uralmash was swallowed up by one of the new conglomerates and is a thriving company today, because it makes tools used in the booming oil industry (see discussion later in this chapter).

The changes can be seen most graphically in the amazing decline in the value of the ruble. Under the Soviets, the ruble was not a convertible currency, because the government artificially fixed the value of a ruble at $1.60. When I was there in 1986, people could buy and sell rubles on the black market at about 20 rubles for a dollar. In mid-1997 it took 5,500 rubles to get a dollar, and when these lines were written in late 2004, it took nearly 30,000. (In practice, it was 30 to a dollar, because the Russians had introduced a new ruble that was worth 1,000 of the old ones on which these values were calculated.)

There were signs that the economy had reached rock bottom in 1997, but the country was shaken the next year by its worst financial crisis yet. The government had borrowed billions of dollars after 1991. For a variety of complicated economic reasons, Russia could not pay its debt and for all intents and purposes defaulted on the loans.

Liberalization in Russia

RUSSIA IS OFTEN cited as a good example of liberal economic policy in action. After all, virtually all enterprises are now in private hands, and, at least since 2000, the economy is booming.

However, it isn't that simple.

Privatization has not brought with it a competitive market, which is a key component of any liberal approach to economics. Rather, large conglomerates—many of which are run by oligarchs—control an immense share of the economy where there is no competition to speak of.

There are some signs of change. Russia now has about thirteen thousand people with MBA degrees who seem to be heading primarily toward new and more entrepreneurial businesses. For instance, the country's leading cell phone provider is not part of one of the conglomerates. Similarly, a Yale MBA started Russia's first American-style drug store, 36.6, the "normal" temperature in centigrade.

The stock market lost half its value and the ruble by two-thirds. Two prime ministers were fired because they could not end the crisis. Finally, new loans and a new stabilization package imposed by Western governments and the International Monetary Fund slowed the decline.

Since then, there have been some promising economic trends. The value of the ruble has stabilized. Growth rates have averaged more than 5 percent since then and reached almost 7 percent in 2004. The upturn is most visible in the new middle class, which numbers at least five million people. Russia also currently has more billionaires than any other country, and Muscovites buy more luxury cars than residents of any other city. Moscow's Mega Mall is the most visited shopping center in Europe. Overall, consumer spending was up by about 20 percent in 2004 over 1997 levels.

But, we should not make too much of this upturn for three reasons.

First and foremost, it is not clear how much of a role the state has played in fostering it. There is no question that the stability of the Putin years has made the country more attractive to foreign investors, but it is difficult to see any direct connection between government policies and the better economic performance.

That is the case, in part, because of the second cause for concern. Most of the improvement can be attributed to a single industry—petroleum. Because oil prices have skyrocketed since the late 1990s and because Russian supplies are stable and reliable, its petrochemical sector is booming. In 2003, oil and related products accounted for $76 billion in exports, or about half of the goods and services Russian firms sold abroad. While this sector is likely to continue to prosper for the foreseeable future, it is by no means certain that the glut of petrodollars will be used to strengthen other sectors of the economy.

Third, most Russians continue to suffer. The average person still makes about $250 a month, which makes buying a Mercedes or shopping at Ikea impossible. The World Bank estimates that about 20 percent of the population lives in absolute poverty, which means their incomes fall below subsistence levels. Some Russian think tanks put the figure at closer to 30 percent. That's another way of saying that the bulk of the benefits from growth have gone to people near the top of those large conglomerates. In fact, it is estimated that they spirited about $24 billion dollars out of the country in 2003, a capital flight roughly equal to four times the amount of money foreigners invested in Russia that year.

Foreign Policy

One might have expected Russia to have similar difficulties with its foreign policy. After all, at the beginning of 1991 it was one of the world's two superpowers. A year later it was no more than a relatively minor player in international affairs and a supplicant for economic aid. To make matters even worse, it had to develop relations with fourteen states that had been part of the Soviet Union and that many Russians still felt were rightfully part of their country.

The Russians have occasionally given observers in the West reason for concern about their foreign policy. The ravings of politicians like Vladimir Zhironovsky have received a lot of attention in the press and among right-wing politicians on both sides of the Atlantic. Yeltsin's occasional anti-American statements and more frequent diplomatic gaffes worried people who saw him as the West's biggest hope for stability. And Russia unquestionably has been less than vigilant about the movement of nuclear technology across its borders and the disposal of nuclear waste.

Still, on balance, Russian foreign policy has been largely pragmatic. Rhetoric aside, Yeltsin and his team adapted to their status as a middle-level power, developed reasonable relations with their neighbors, and began putting as much emphasis on economic as on geopolitical issues in their foreign policy. We can see this if we focus on relations with the United States.

It was hard for both Russian and American foreign policymakers to adapt to the new post-Communist world. American leaders in the first Bush and the Clinton administrations, however, took for granted that the United States needed to maintain a positive working relationship with the new Russian state. At first they felt that way because there was genuine enthusiasm about Yeltsin and his role in the collapse of Communism. However, as Yeltsin's flaws became more obvious, American and European leaders sought to distance themselves from him even as they realized that the alternatives were worse.

They were not worried that Russia would pose the same kind of threat to the United States and its allies that the Soviet Union had. Indeed, the United States and Russia reached a series of agreements to dismantle more than a third of their nuclear arsenals and stop targeting each other. Moreover, the Russian government was so poor, and morale in the army was so low, that it could no longer be thought of as having a fighting force that could have an impact far beyond its borders.

Rather, the United States and its allies worried that instability in the region and aggression from Russia could exacerbate already difficult situations in such places as Chechnya, Yugoslavia, and Moldova, and even as far away as the Indian subcontinent. Furthermore, they had to pay some attention to the fears of post-Communist leaders in Eastern Europe, who were not convinced that Russia had given up all its designs over them.

As a result, the United States and Russia have had a sometimes tense and sometimes cordial relationship in which the Americans have normally cast their lot with Moscow despite some very important sources of friction. U.S. support for Russia has included the following:

- Aid in dismantling Russian nuclear equipment
- Incorporation of Russia as a permanent member of the G-7 (now, of course, G-8) annual summit
- Provision of substantial economic aid and investment from the public as well as the private sector
- Training and other assistance in developing democratic institutions

Under Putin, Russian-American relations have been something like a political roller coaster ride. They took an unexpected turn for the better after the events of September 11. The Russians realized that they shared concerns about terrorism with the Americans when it emerged that al-Qaeda personnel had fought in Chechnya and that Chechens had participated alongside the Taliban during the war in Afghanistan. Washington, in turn, realized that it needed to use bases in several of the former Soviet republics, most notably Uzbekistan, all of which were heavily dependent on Moscow for their defense. Not only did the United States and Russia cooper-

Globalization in Russia

VISITORS TO MOSCOW and St. Petersburg can be forgiven for thinking that globalization has taken firm root in Russia. Western chain stores and offices, gleaming new shopping centers featuring luxury goods, and thousands of BMWs and Mercedes are hard to miss.

But globalization's impact is more muted than those first appearances might suggest in two ways. First, there is less foreign investment in the country as a whole than in most countries Russia is normally compared with. Thus, in 2004 foreigners invested about $7 billion in Russia compared to almost $55 billion in China. Second, few people outside the biggest cities are enjoying the benefits (or enduring the consequences) of globalization.

ate in the initial stages of the war on terrorism, but their overall relations improved. In particular, the two countries moved closer to an agreement on changes to the Anti-Ballistic Missile Treaty that would allow the United States to move forward with its plans for a missile defense system.

In early 2002, however, the relationship began to sour. Among other things, the Russian government did not share the American perception that Iran and Iraq should be considered potential targets in the next stages of the war on terrorism. Russia joined France and China in blocking United Nations Security Council approval for the armed intervention in Iraq. It should be pointed out, however, that even though Putin was as critical of the Bush administration as the Chirac government was, Russia never drew the kind of ferocious criticism the United States levelled at France.

As of this writing, U.S.-Russian relations are much improved. Some American officials criticized Putin's move to further centralize power in the Kremlin. But there has been no talk in Washington of sanctions or any other retaliatory actions.

Feedback

Putin has perhaps been most severely criticized for reasserting state control over the central organs of the mass media. Before Gorbachev came to power, the Communists controlled everything that was legally printed, published, or broadcast. There was a tiny underground, or *samizdat,* press, but its circulation numbered in the tens of thousands, at most.

Almost overnight, there was a revolution in the media that Soviet citizens had access to. The world's most closely state-controlled media became its most contentious. By 1988, almost anything that could be said was being said on the airwaves. New newspapers, magazines, and journals were published, many of which were critical of everything and everyone.

After 1991, the major media outlets passed into private hands. Not surprisingly, the most influential (and profitable) of them came under the control of the oligarchs. For instance, the two leading national television networks were run by Berezovsky and Gusinsky. And in Russia today, it is television that counts, because newspaper circulation has plummeted given the rising cost of newsprint, journalists' salaries, and the like. Similarly, people with Internet access can get news from other, independent sources, but the best estimate is that well under 5 percent of the population is online.

Television's impact became abundantly clear in the 1996 presidential campaign. As we saw earlier, Berezovsky and the other oligarchs orchestrated Yeltsin's re-election campaign largely by manipulating what was (and was not) presented on their channels.

While there was some criticism of the obviously biased media, television did not become a major issue until the two network-owning oligarchs turned on Putin. He was able to use the power of the Kremlin to force them out of the television industry even before they were forced into exile. Ownership of the networks was transferred to other conglomerates sympathetic to the Putin administration. What that has meant is that the Kremlin has taken de facto control of television news, which is nearly as one-sided as it was before Gorbachev came to power.

Conclusion: Half Empty or Half Full

Of all the countries covered in this book, Russia comes closest to reflecting the cliché about whether the glass is half empty or half full. This is the case because, even after more than a decade of transition, it is impossible to predict whether Russia will develop a stable democracy and a prosperous market economy.

On the "half empty" side are all the problems laid out in this chapter. Indeed, after analyzing the industrialized democracies in Part 2, it is hard not to be pessimistic given Russia's social, economic, and political difficulties, many of which have worsened since the breakup of the Soviet Union.

But we should not ignore the "half full" aspects of Russian life. It has had seven reasonably fair and competitive elections. There was a successful transition of power from Yeltsin to Putin. The oligarchs are slightly less powerful. There are signs that the economy has started to recover.

Nonetheless, there really is only one conclusion we can reach about Russia, one that will apply to many of the other countries we consider in the rest of this book. The transitions to democracy and market capitalism are rarely easy.

Key Terms

Concepts

Democratic centralism	Perestroika
Glasnost	Power ministries
Near-abroad	Privatization
Nomenklatura	Purges
Oligarch	Shock therapy

People

Berezovsky, Boris	Lenin, V. I.
Brezhnev, Leonid	Putin, Vladimir
Chernomyrdin, Viktor	Stalin, Joseph
Gaidar, Yegor	Yeltsin, Boris
Gorbachev, Mikhail	Zhirinovsky, Vladimir
Khodorkovsky, Mikhail	Zyuganov, Gennady
Khrushchev, Nikita	

Acronyms

CPRF
CPSU
KGB

Organizations, Places, and Events

Bolsheviks	Mensheviks
Central Committee	Our Home Is Russia
Cheka	Politburo
Comintern	Provisional government
Communist Party of the Russian Federation	Russian Federation
	Secret speech
Communist Party of the Soviet Union	Secretariat
	State Duma
Fatherland–All Russia	Third International
Federation Council	Twentieth Party Congress
Five-year plan	Union of Right Forces
Gosplan	United Russia
Liberal Democrats	Yabloko

Critical Thinking Exercises

1 Much has changed since this book was finished in early 2005. Does the analysis of Russian politics presented here still make sense? Why (not)?

2 Public opinion pollsters routinely ask questions about whether people think their country is heading in the "right direction" or is on the "wrong track." If you were asked such a question about Russia, how would you answer? Why did you reach this conclusion?

3 The Soviet Union was often referred to as a "party state" ruled under "democratic centralism." What do those two terms mean? How did they shape the USSR? How did they contribute to its collapse?

4 How did the history of tsarist Russia and the Soviet Union contribute to the difficult beginnings of the new Russian Republic?

5 In this book, you have encountered a number of influential individuals. How would you compare Boris Yeltsin's or Vladimir Putin's impact with any one or two of those other leaders?

6 Russia is having a hard time establishing effective institutions, democratic or otherwise. Why do you think this is the case?

7 Russia recently faced a serious problem of "gridlock" between a conservative and Communist-dominated State Duma and a more reformist executive. How did that affect its ability to enact economic and other reforms?

8 Today, it could be argued that the Russian president has too much influence both because of the powers granted him by the Constitution and the weakness of the opposition in the State Duma and elsewhere. How has that affected politics since Putin came to power?

9 If you were hired as a consultant to an American (or other Western) firm thinking of investing in Russia, what would your advice be?

Useful Websites

Due to the shaky state of the Russian economy, many of the promising Internet portals created there a few years ago have fallen by the wayside. The best English-language entry point for Russian news and political sites is European Internet. Another good source of news is the Open Society Institute.

www.einnews.com/russia/

www.omri.cz

Because of the difficulties Russians are having maintaining their own sites, especially their English-language mirrors, the best entry points to things Russian are probably those maintained by U.S.-based Russian studies centers, especially those at the universities of Michigan, Pittsburgh, and Washington.

www.umich.edu/~iinet/crees

www.ucis.pitt.edu/reesweb

depts.washington.edu/reecas/

There are still a number of organizations doing analytical work and NGOs helping Russian develop. Two of the best are the Jamestown Foundation and the Initiative for Social Action and Renewal in Eurasia, with roots on the right and left wing, respectively.

www.jamestown.org

www.isar.org

Finally, the Carnegie Endowment for International Peace held a major international conference on "Russia—Ten Years After" in 2001, which is probably the single best source in print or online on the transition.

www.carnegieendowment.org

Further Reading

Aron, Leon. *Yeltsin: A Revolutionary Life.* New York: St. Martin's Press, 2000. Perhaps the best biography of Russia's first president.

Dawisha, Karen, and Bruce Parrott. *Russia and the New States of Eurasia: The Politics of Upheaval.* New York: Cambridge University Press, 1994. Though a bit dated, still the most comprehensive review of the issues facing Russia and the other former Soviet republics.

Gorbachev, Mikhail S. *Perestroika.* New York: Harper & Row, 1987. Despite what has happened to his reputation since then, an important and revealing book, especially about the reasons behind perestroika and new thinking.

Herspring, Dale, ed. *Putin's Russia: Past Imperfect, Future Uncertain.* Lanham, Md.: Rowman and Littlefield, 2005. Not quite as well integrated as the McFaul volume, this is still an excellent and readable collection of essays.

Hough, Jerry, and Merle Fainsod. *How the Soviet Union Is Governed.* Cambridge, Mass.: Harvard University Press, 1979. The definitive text. Even though the Soviet Union is no more, this book is well worth reading because you cannot understand the post-Communist transition without understanding what came before.

Kampfner, John. *Inside Yeltsin's Russia: Corruption, Conflict, Capitalism.* London: Cassell, 1994. The best of the journalistic accounts of the post-Soviet period.

Mackenzie, David, and Michael W. Curran. *A History of the Soviet Union.* Belmont, Calif.: Wadsworth, 1991. One of the best of the brief textbooks on the entire Soviet period.

McCauley, Mary. *Russia's Politics of Uncertainty.* Cambridge: Cambridge University Press, 1997. The most detailed and perceptive work yet published on the actual workings of Russian politics. Focuses on federal-republican relations.

McFaul, Michael, Nikolai Petrov, and Andrei Ryabov, *Between Dictatorship and Democracy: Russian Post-Communist Political Reform.* Washington: Carnegie Endowment for International Peace, 2004. An excellent collection of integrated essays written by McFaul and a number of leading Russian experts.

Nolan, Peter. *China's Rise, Russia's Fall: Politics, Economics, and Planning in the Transition from Stalinism.* Houndsmill, U.K.: Macmillan, 1995 (distributed in the United States by St. Martin's Press). Probably has better coverage on China, but a good exploration of the uncertainties caused by the "stop-start" pattern of Russian reform.

Shevtsova, Lilia. *Putin's Russia.* Washington: Carnegie Endowment for International Peace. 2003. A very good overview of Putin's first term written by one of Russia's leading political scientists.

Von Laue, Theodore. *Why Lenin? Why Stalin?* Philadelphia: Lippincott, 1971. A relatively old book, but still the best short source on why the revolution turned out as it did.

White, Stephen, Richard Rose, and Ian McAllister. *How Russia Votes.* Chatham, N.J.: Chatham House, 1997. The first systematic study of Russian voters from 1991 on; also puts the country into a comparative perspective.

Black cat, white cat, what does it matter as long as the cat catches mice?

DENG XIAOPING

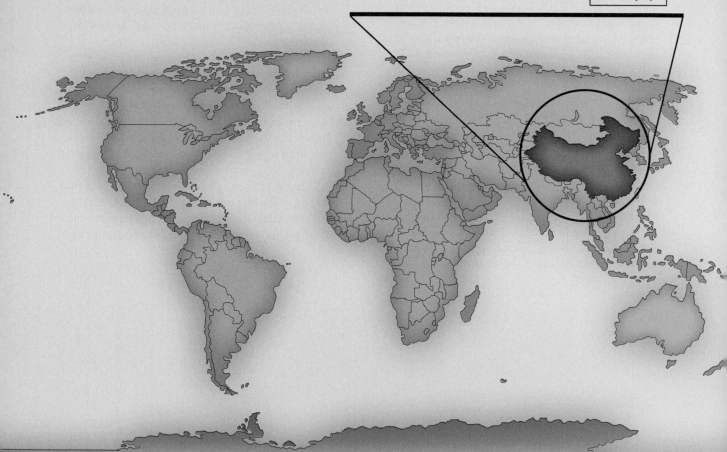

Chapter 10

CHINA

CHAPTER OUTLINE

The Basics: China	
Size	9,595,960 sq. km (a bit smaller than the United States)
Arable land	10%, down by one-fifth since 1949
Population	1.28 billion
Population growth rate	1.1%
GNP per capita	$940
Currency	8.28 yuan renminbi = $1
Life expectancy	72
Ethnic composition	92% Han Chinese
Capital	Beijing
Head of State	President Hu Jintao (2003)
Head of Government	Prime Minister Wen Jiabao (2003)

Hu's on First [1]

One of the largely correct conclusions political scientists reached about Communist countries is that they did not have a normal or routine way of choosing new leaders. Typically, the General Secretary (or whatever his title was at the time) stayed in power until he died, and his death was followed by some sort of power struggle that could drag on for years. In practice, most Communist countries developed procedures whereby the party's senior leadership selected the next person in charge with a minimum of conflict, as we saw in the last chapter following the deaths of Brezhnev, Andropov, and Chernenko.

Still, the consolidation of power by **Hu Jintao** (1942–) in fall 2004 marked one of the smoothest transitions in any Communist country ever. Not everyone had expected it to be that easy (news.bbc.co.uk/2/hi/asia-pacific/2404129.stm).

---

[1] Serious baseball fans will understand that this section's subtitle refers to Abbott and Costello's riotous and absurd routine, "Who's On First?" www.baseball-almanac.com/humor4.shtml. Who is on first. What plays second. Because is in left field. I leave the rest to your imagination. Or your browser.

Hu had been named Chairman of the **Chinese Communist Party (CCP)** in 2002 and President of the People's Republic of China in 2003. Though little known outside the country, Hu had risen steadily through the CCP's ranks after moving from his first career as an engineer into full time party work for its youth league.

Hu was only sixty (young by Chinese standards) when he was selected. What's more, most observers thought that his predecessor, **Jiang Zemin** (1926–), would try to keep control of key decisions as his predecessors had done with him. Jiang had been forced to officially retire, because a president can now serve a maximum of two five year terms. Jiang kept his position as head of the **Central Military Commission** (**CMC;** www .globalsecurity.org/military/world/china/cmc.htm).

But, in one of the most closely guarded secrets in a country where secrecy is the norm, Jiang announced his retirement on 19 September 2004. Jiang and Hu were shown live on television together meeting and greeting delegates who were attending the party's central committee plenary session in Beijing.

The news was also a surprise because there had been rumors for some time that the two leaders clashed frequently. Hu is more reform-oriented and seeks to work by building consensus more often than Jiang did.

Most observers thought that Jiang was also angling to have some of his key supporters gain positions on the

Chinese Names and Terms

Issues involving the Chinese language can easily confuse readers and thus should be clarified at the outset.

Chinese names are always rendered with the family name first. In other words, George Walker Bush would be written or spoken Bush George Walker.

Failure to remember this can be embarrassing. For example, the first time President Harry Truman met Chiang Kai-shek, he reportedly greeted him, "Glad to meet you Mr. Shek."

There are also two primary ways of transliterating Chinese terms. Almost everyone writing about China uses the pinyin system its leaders prefer. People in Taiwan and Hong Kong still use the Wade–Giles version. I have used pinyin for all names and terms other than those associated with Taiwan and the Nationalists who fled to Taiwan.

Politburo, CMC, and other important governing bodies. In fact, he failed to do so. Therefore, his retirement and other personnel changes announced during that meeting almost certainly mean that Hu will be able to govern with minimal opposition from other top party leaders, perhaps for the rest of his full ten-year term in office.

Outgoing president Jiang Zemin and new president Hu Jintao at the 2004 Plenum of the Central Committee of the CCP.

Li Xueren / XineHua/CORBIS

Thinking about China

The Basics

China's most important characteristic is its size. The **People's Republic of China (PRC)** is by far the world's most populous country, with nearly 1.3 billion people, or more than one-fifth of the world's population. The government has engaged in largely successful attempts to limit population growth. Some 74 percent of women of childbearing age use contraceptives, compared with only 5 percent in Myanmar (formerly Burma) and 35 percent in India. Nonetheless, a baby is born somewhere in China every two seconds, and estimates now suggest that the Chinese population will reach 1.5 billion in the next fifty years.

China's huge population is stretching the country's limited natural resources. In all there are only about two acres of land—or one-eighth of the Asian average—per person, and only one-fourth of that is arable. There is also a severe water shortage for both human consumption and irrigation. And the limited land and water are being gobbled up by new housing and industrial development at an alarming rate.

Unlike the former Soviet Union, China has a relatively homogeneous population. A total of 92 percent of the people are Han, or ethnically Chinese. The rest of the population consists of far smaller groups, but with the exception of the Tibetans and the Uygers minority nationalities have not been politically important.

Although there is a single written Chinese language, there are tremendous differences in the way it is spoken. Someone who speaks only Mandarin, for instance, cannot understand Cantonese and other southern dialects. Gradually, however, Mandarin is becoming the lingua franca and is now spoken by almost all educated people.

The two characters the Chinese use to denote their country (middle kingdom), as well as one of the ones they use for foreigners (barbarians), tell us much about their country. Some sense of national superiority is a part of every culture, but in the case of China, it has played an especially important role. Though less so than in Tokugawa Japan, Chinese leaders closed themselves off from outside influences for much of the last millennium. Until early in the twentieth century, for instance, examinations that tested a student's ability to memorize Confucian texts were used to determine entry into the all-important civil service. More recently, the leadership's concerns about Western cultural influences were reflected in the 1983 "antispiritual pollution campaign" that attacked people who used makeup or listened to rock and roll. As the consumerism of modern capitalism sweeps so much of the country, the leadership worries that the traditional—and implicitly superior—Chinese values will be lost and the country harmed as a result.

China remains a very poor country despite all the progress that has been made since 1949. Per capita income is about $780 a year, a figure substantially below that of Mexico. However, it is more than four times higher when measured in terms of purchasing power parity, which some think is a better indicator of actual living conditions. That said, the Taiwanese standard of living is substantially higher than the PRC's, which is probably more important than any statistic to many Chinese citizens.

Despite the continued overall poverty, the Chinese have made remarkable strides in overcoming the country's social and economic ills. Life expectancy has leaped to 72 years, far above the Asian average. Three-quarters of the population is literate, compared with the Asian average of 40 percent. Only 6 percent of Chinese babies—compared to 30 percent of India's—are born dangerously undersized. For the past decade or so, China also has enjoyed a remarkable economic boom. In the mid-1990s, before the Asian economic crisis hit, the Chinese economy grew by an average of about 8 percent per year, and industrial production increased by close to twice that rate.

The recent growth has thus produced millions of newly rich Chinese men and women, though they make up only a tiny proportion of the total population. In the countryside prosperous peasants really should not be called "peasants" anymore because they may employ dozens of workers, earn hundreds of thousands of dollars a year, and drive luxury cars. The newfound wealth is even more evident in the cities. The middle class can shop at Benetton or eat in the world's largest McDonald's. And cellular phones and pagers have become status symbols.

Key Questions

Hu Jintao and his colleagues govern a China that is still nominally Communist, but is very different from what we saw in the last years of the Soviet Union under Gorbachev. The reformists in the former Soviet Union went a long way toward opening up their political system but foundered in their attempts to implement perestroika. The growing economic frustrations and the greater opportunities for people to participate politically combined with ethnic and other tensions put so much pressure on the regime that it collapsed.

The CCP's leaders, in contrast, have limited their reforms to the economy and have maintained their tight grip on political life. On those rare occasions when they have allowed a modicum of free expression, they have clamped down as soon as the protests began to threaten the party's authority—as in **Tiananmen Square** in 1989 or with the public demonstrations of the Falun Gong since the late 1990s.

In the medium to long term, the question is whether the party can keep doing this. There are already signs that it is having trouble recruiting talented young members and that its organization is atrophying. More importantly, the economic reforms are transforming the lives of millions of people, who are growing used to making their own choices in the marketplace. So far, most Chinese have been willing to accept policies that limit their freedom to economic matters, but there is reason to believe that they will eventually demand political power as well. It is by no means clear that the party will be able to hold off such demands save, perhaps, by giving the **People's Liberation Army (PLA)** a substantial role in maintaining order.

Because only a handful of Communist countries are left, what happens in China will go a long way toward determining the future of Marxism in general. It is very much an open question whether any Marxist-Leninist regimes will survive. Moreover, as the Chinese experience of the 1980s and 1990s suggests, we will have to ask whether societies that maintain Leninist states but allow their economies to become ever more capitalistic will bear any real resemblance to the type of egalitarian and classless society Marx envisioned.

From these broad concerns flow four more specific questions we will concentrate on here:

- Can the Chinese leadership realistically hope to limit the impact of the outside world to the economy? As the Chinese people learn more about other cultures and have more money to spend, won't they begin to demand political freedoms as well?

- Will the state continue to be able to put down protests like the one in Tiananmen Square in 1989, especially if they become larger or more violent?

- What will happen if the CCP continues to have trouble recruiting talented and dedicated members who could become its future leaders?

- Hu Jintao and his colleagues are popularly referred to as the "fourth generation" of leaders. How might they change Chinese political life?

The Evolution of the Chinese State

As was the case with Russia, we cannot understand the reformist policies in China today or, for that matter, the more than half-century of Chinese Communist Party (CCP) rule without considering the impact of the country's past. We will see that its distinctive version of a Marxist-Leninist state is in part an outgrowth of historical trends that made China less-than-fertile ground for anything approaching orthodox Marxism. As in the Soviet Union, the CCP's commitment to Marxism was not one of the most important reasons it came to power. Indeed, as was also the case in the USSR, those other reasons go a long way toward explaining why China evolved as it did after the revolution.

The Broad Sweep of Chinese History

The historical roots of contemporary Chinese politics go back nearly three thousand years to the teachings of Confucius and other ancient scholars whose ideas have had a remarkable influence on culture (and hence politics) to this day. (See table 10.1.) Commonly thought of as a religion in the West, **Confucianism** is actually more a code of social conduct that revolves around a few key principles. People should accept their place in the social hierarchy, and the living should respect their ancestors, women their husbands, children their fathers, and every one their social and political superiors (orpheus.ucsd .edu/chinesehistory).

The Chinese also developed the world's first large and centralized state in the third century before the birth of Christ. The militaristic Qin (from whom the English word *China* is derived) defeated most of the other regional kingdoms and established a single unified empire covering most of modern China. The Qin emperors were able to mobilize thousands of people to build canals, roads, and the first parts of the Great Wall.

The Qin and subsequent dynasties succeeded in large part because of the remarkable bureaucratic system. Two thousand years before Europeans even considered a civil service based on merit, the Chinese had a well-established system of examinations through which a bureaucracy that served the emperor was recruited. By the fourteenth century, at least forty thousand bureaucrats were responsible for collecting taxes and administering imperial law throughout the country. The civil servants often competed with local landlords who had their own armies. Nonetheless, the imperial bureaucracy was an indispensable part of a state that had to support more

■ TABLE 10.1 Key Events in the Origins
of the People's Republic of China

YEAR	EVENT
551 BC	Birth of Confucius
221 BC	Start of Qin dynasty
1644	Start of Qing dynasty
1839–42	Opium War
1894–95	Sino-Japanese War
1898	Imperial reforms begin
1911	Overthrow of the Qing dynasty
1919	May Fourth Movement
1921	Formation of the CCP
1925	Death of Sun Yat-sen
1927	KMT attack on CCP
1931	Japanese invasion of Manchuria
1934–35	Long March
1949	CCP victory; KMT flees to Taiwan

than forty cities of over one hundred thousand people, including several of more than a million as early as the seventeenth century.

When China had effective emperors in place, things went well. However, this was not always the case. China went through cycles in which a dynasty declined, rebellions broke out, and, eventually, a new group solidified its hold on the national government, creating a new dynasty. In all, there were twenty-five of these dynastic changes in the two thousand years leading up to the collapse of the last dynasty, the Qing, in 1911.

The Qing was, in fact, a Manchurian dynasty that took over in 1644. Quickly, however, the Qing adopted the Chinese language and customs, and ruled through the traditional imperial processes.

By the end of the eighteenth century, however, the Qing had entered a period of decline. The population was growing faster than agricultural production, leaving an overstretched peasantry and an often hungry urban population. Peasant rebellions broke out over much of the country. More important were the cultural blinders that led the Manchus to look upon Chinese traditions as superior and to ignore the industrial revolution and the other trends that were transforming the West.

Early in the nineteenth century, Europe came crashing in anyway. Though China never became a colony, European and American missionaries, traders, and soldiers gained considerable control over its affairs. The British, who had been smuggling opium into the country, defeated China in the first Opium War (1839–42). The country was then opened up to missionaries and merchants. During the 1850s the loosely coordinated Taiping rebellion (led by a man who claimed to be Jesus' younger brother) broke out.

During the rest of the century, all the major European powers moved in. A few areas, like Hong Kong, passed directly into European hands. More often, the Europeans took effective control of much of coastal China and imposed the principle of **extraterritoriality,** which meant that their law, not China's, applied to the activities of the Europeans.

The Chinese were humiliated. The government lost any semblance of authority, and the once proud and powerful civilization saw itself under the sway of Christians and capitalists. Parks in Shanghai, for instance, often carried the sign "No dogs or Chinese allowed."

Things came to a head after the Sino-Japanese War of 1894–95. Japan had been even more isolated from events in the West, but once Admiral Matthew Perry arrived in 1854, the Japanese embarked on a rapid and successful program of modernization. Even though the Chinese continued to look upon their neighbor to the east as a second-rate power, Japan was rapidly becoming one of the world's mightiest nations. After winning the war and seizing control of Taiwan and Korea, Japan gained concessions within China itself, thereby joining the Western powers in their de facto imperial control of much of the country.

By the end of the century, Chinese leaders belatedly realized that they had to change. The educational system, for instance, was still based on the traditional Confucian curriculum, which left China without the industrially and scientifically trained elite it would need to meet the challenge from the West.

The traditional examinations were discarded. Young people were sent abroad to learn about what **Chen Duxiu,** later one of the founders of the CCP, called "Mr. Science and Mr. Democracy." Dissatisfaction with the imperial system grew. Young people adopted Western dress and Western values. Movements calling themselves democratic began to organize.

During the Hundred Days' Reform of 1898, the emperor issued decrees designed to modernize the education system, the economy, the military, and the bureaucracy. Instead, the reforms provoked resentment from the elite and were halted almost immediately following a coup that sent the emperor to prison and doomed any hopes of a Chinese equivalent of the Japanese Meiji Restoration.

Some reform efforts did continue. But as in tsarist Russia, they came far too late. In fact, all the reform proposals did was further reveal China's weaknesses and heighten opposition to the imperial system. Universities that had so recently educated loyal Confucian scholars were now turning out revolutionaries.

A Failed Revolution

As was the case in Russia at the same time, China had more than its share of revolutionaries. Between May 1907 and April 1911, there were eleven failed military coup attempts launched by the followers of **Sun Yat-sen** alone.

Sun (1866–1925) was one of the first Westernized intellectuals and one of the first Chinese people to be photographed wearing Western clothes. While still in his twenties, he decided that the situation in China was so grim that he became a full-time revolutionary. In 1895 he was exiled for his role in an abortive plot against the government and spent most of the next sixteen years abroad, raising support for a series of failed coup attempts. In 1905 a group of radical students in Tokyo elected him head of the Revolutionary Alliance, which soon became the **Kuomintang (KMT),** or **Nationalist Party.**

On "double ten" day (10 October 1911), yet another rebellion broke out, this time in the city of Wuhan. Much to their surprise, the conspirators drove the governor-general from the city and took it over. In Denver at the time, Sun decided to stay in the United States and finish his fund-raising tour rather than return to China for what he assumed would be another failure. This time, however, the rebellion spread throughout the country without a single shot being fired. When Sun finally returned in December, it was to take over as president of the new Republic of China.

As in Russia, toppling the old regime was one thing, and building a new one to take its place quite another. The empire had fallen not because the revolutionaries were so strong, but because it was so weak.

The revolutionaries had only their nationalism and their opposition to the imperial system in common. Within months their differences came to the fore, and central authority began to crumble once again. Unlike in Russia, however, it would be another forty years before a new regime was firmly in place.

In an attempt to save the revolution, Sun gave way to a **warlord,** General Yuan Shikai. Yuan was briefly able to bring the country together under what amounted to a personal dictatorship, but his own imperial pretensions simply spawned more rebellions. All hopes to unite China around a strong, authoritarian leader collapsed when Yuan died suddenly in 1916.

From then on, there was a central government nom-inally under KMT control. In reality, it never had control over much of the country. Instead, power devolved to dozens of warlords, who ran the regions they controlled with only the slightest concern for doing what the KMT wanted or for modernizing the country. In short, the political situation remained as volatile as it had been a generation earlier.

The next major transition came in 1919 after the publication of the Treaty of Versailles. Like Japan, China had entered World War I on the Allied side on the assumption that Wilsonian principles of democracy and national self-determination would lead to the end of imperialism. Nothing of the sort happened. The German concessions were simply transferred to other Allied powers.

This proved to be the last straw for alienated, well-educated young Chinese. The day the treaty's provisions were announced, thousands of students took to the streets. Their **May Fourth Movement** quickly sounded broader themes—against Confucianism, the education system, and the family. Magazines like Chen Duxiu's *New Youth* gained a wide following among this generation, which was even more frustrated by China's failure to modernize. After May Fourth, the students and their supporters grew more political, but this particular movement, like so many before it, was poorly organized and gradually lost momentum.

China Stands Up

It was not surprising that many young people would turn to Marxism. Even though Marx argued that socialism could only develop after capitalism, his ideas seemed to speak to the oppressed everywhere. What's more, Lenin had incorporated imperialism into Marxist analysis, and the radicalized Chinese students could easily relate to the Soviets' struggle against the Western European powers.

In 1921 twelve delegates, representing fifty-seven members, met to form the CCP, first headed by Chen Duxiu. The party was composed almost exclusively of young intellectuals, and, like the rest of the international Communist movement, it quickly fell under Moscow's direct control.

The KMT, too, drew inspiration from the Bolsheviks, who, in turn, were convinced that the Nationalists were the faction Moscow should cast its lot with in China. KMT officers were trained by the Soviets, including **Chiang Kai-shek,** who would take over the party after Sun's death in 1925. Mikhail Borodin, the Comintern's agent in China, ordered the CCP to merge with the KMT to unify the country.

Meanwhile, the Communists' influence expanded

among industrial workers in the big cities in the south and became a major force within the KMT. Tensions between the CCP and the Nationalists mounted as the Communists grew in strength and numbers, but overall the center of gravity in the KMT shifted rightward. Chen and some of the other leaders urged an end to the united front, but Moscow prevailed.

Along with its Communist supporters, the KMT launched the Northern Expedition in 1926 in another attempt to unite the country under a single national government. Support for the CCP continued to mushroom. Workers threw open the gates of a number of cities as Communist forces approached. Chen advocated arming workers and peasants under CCP leadership, but Borodin demurred again.

The conflict between the CCP and KMT finally came to a head in April 1927, when Kuomintang forces attacked their supposed CCP allies in Shanghai. Nationalist troops slaughtered thousands of CCP members, including most of the leadership. Of the fifty thousand CCP members in early 1927, only five thousand, including Chen Duxiu, survived.

Just before the attack, one of the few party members from a peasant background, the little-known **Mao Zedong** (1893–1976), had published a short pamphlet reporting on what he had found in his native Hunan province. Mao argued that, given China's overwhelmingly rural population and the KMT's control over most cities, the revolution had to be based on massive mobilization in the countryside and conducted as a guerrilla war.

Because of his peasant background and the time he had spent in the countryside during the 1920s, Mao was better able than the other surviving CCP leaders to draw two key lessons from the Shanghai massacre. First, revolution in China was not going to come through spontaneous uprisings in the cities. Second, it would take years to organize the only kind of revolution that could work: one based on the peasantry.

Ignoring Borodin's orders, Mao launched his first attacks on the city of Changsha that fall. This Autumn Harvest Uprising was quickly put down, and the CCP leadership as a whole was slow to come around to Mao's views. Mao persisted anyway, establishing the first "base camp" along the Hunan-Jiangxi border.

The KMT responded by launching a series of campaigns to "exterminate the communist bandits." CCP forces survived the first four campaigns, but during the fifth they were surrounded by a massive force of KMT troops. Mao realized that conventional warfare was bound to fail, so in October 1934 a small group of Communist soldiers launched a diversionary counterattack

© Hulton Archive/Getty Images

Mao Zedong and Zhou Enlai during the Long March.

while the bulk of their forces, numbering about one hundred thousand, broke through the KMT cordon to the west.

Mao's bedraggled troops then embarked on what became the **Long March,** which lasted almost a year. The CCP forces fought skirmishes every day and full-scale battles every few weeks against either the pursuing KMT or local warlords. The fighting and the difficulties of the march itself took a horrible toll. Only 10 percent of the troops who started out were still alive when the army arrived in Yanan in October 1935. Among the dead was one of Mao's sons.

Ironically, the Long March proved to be a stunning success for the CCP. All along the way, the party organized. Members talked about a China based on justice and equality. Unlike the bands of marauding soldiers who had come and gone over the centuries, they treated the peasants well. No men were conscripted, and no women were abused. The CCP paid for the food and supplies it took. Where the CCP gained control, large estates were broken up and the land given to the peasants. Taxes were reduced, and the arbitrary power of the landlords was eliminated.

In January 1936 the Politburo elected Mao chairman of the CCP, a post he would hold until his death in 1976. With this move, all notions that a Marxist revolution could be based on a large, urban proletariat disappeared. Although Mao always paid homage to Lenin, gone, too, was the Leninist notion that a revolution could be carried out by a small vanguard party. In its place was the more populist **mass line,** which Mao described at length in 1943:

> In all practical work of our Party, all correct leadership is necessarily "from the masses, to the masses." This means take the ideas of the masses (scattered and unsystematic ideas) and concentrate them (through study turn them into concentrated and systematic ideas), then go to the masses and propagate and explain these ideas until the masses embrace them as their own, hold fast to them and translate them into action, and test the correctness of these ideas in such action. Then once again concentrate ideas from the masses and once again go to the masses so that the ideas are preserved and carried through. And so on, over and over again in an endless spiral, with the ideas becoming more correct, more vital, and richer each time.[2]

Note that the Chinese revolution bore even less resemblance to Marx's expectations than the Russian one did. Certainly, the CCP leadership was inspired by Marx's analyses, and Mao's writings were always couched in Marxist terms. Nonetheless, the CCP took even greater liberties with Marxism than the Bolsheviks did. The Chinese Communists made a remarkable contribution, turning Marxism into a philosophy that appealed to millions of peasants in Asia, Africa, and Latin America after 1949. Still, the fact that China was even more backward than the Russia of 1917 meant that the kind of transition to socialism that Marx had in mind (based on the redistribution of the resources of an affluent society) was impossible.

There was yet another reason the CCP ultimately won: its resistance against Japanese aggression. After 1895 Japan joined the countries with imperial designs on China, which generated considerable resentment, in particular among the Chinese intellectual community. Japanese troops invaded Manchuria in 1931, and by 1935 they had taken control of much of northern China, including well over half of the country's industrial base.

Chiang Kai-shek knew that the Chinese army was not capable of beating the Japanese, and so he retreated

Evolution of the Chinese State in Comparative Perspective

UNLIKE IN THE FORMER Soviet Union and most of Eastern Europe, Communists came to power in China as a result of a massive popular revolution. However, this does not mean they did so in a way Marx anticipated.

Rather, the revolution succeeded because the CCP could appeal both to the oppressed peasants and to people from other walks of life who wanted to resist the Japanese occupation. As a result, the CCP took China even further from orthodox Marxist expectations than the Soviets did. Over the years, the country was characterized by reliance on the mass line, emphasis on rural development, the central role attached to culture and ideology, and factionalism within the CCP itself.

It was thirty years before the party's leaders decided that those approaches could not pull the country out of deeply rooted poverty and weakness. Thus, it was only after the death of Mao Zedong in 1976 that the first tentative steps toward economic, but not political, reform were taken.

to the south while trying to build a modern, more competitive army. During the Long March, however, the CCP decided that it would fight the invaders, something it set out to do as soon as the Yanan camp was established.

In late 1936 a group of disgruntled generals took Chiang Kai-shek prisoner. Communist leader **Zhou Enlai** (1899–1976) was consulted and called for Chiang's release in order to form a new united front to fight the Japanese. From 1937 to 1945, the KMT and CCP were ostensibly allies once again. In practice, however, the KMT was always ambivalent about both forming a united front and fighting the Japanese. As a result, the CCP got most of the credit for spearheading the resistance, which helped expand its base of support. Adding nationalism and anti-imperialism to its message of social justice, the CCP became quite appealing in almost every social milieu.

The Communist army grew from eighty thousand in 1939 to about nine hundred thousand regular troops and two million reserves by 1945. The CCP also gained considerable administrative experience in the one-fifth of the country it controlled.

Still, when World War II ended, the KMT seemed way ahead. Its army was much larger, and it received millions of dollars of aid from the United States, whereas Stalin had done little to help the CCP. But in early 1946 the disciplined Communist army, headed by **Lin Biao,** gained control of Manchuria and started moving south.

---

[2] Mao Zedong, "Some Questions Concerning Methods of Leadership," *Selected Works* 3 (Beijing: Foreign Language Press, 1943): 119.

By the end of 1947, guerrilla war had given way to full-scale conventional combat, and the tide was turning in favor of the CCP.

Less than two years later, the KMT forces had been routed. Only a few scattered troops were still fighting when Chiang and the Nationalist leadership fled to Taiwan. In October 1949 the Communists proclaimed the creation of the People's Republic of China (PRC). The victory marked the end of one of the darkest periods in Chinese history, something Mao eloquently noted in a speech a week before the PRC was born:

> The Chinese have always been a great, courageous, and industrious nation; it is only in modern times that they have fallen behind. And that was due entirely to oppression and exploitation by foreign imperialism and domestic reactionary government. Ours will no longer be a nation subject to insult and humiliation. We have stood up.[3]

Factionalism

As we saw in the chapters on France, Germany, and Russia, the creation of the current regime does not mark the point at which we should stop examining its history. Rather, it makes sense to continue our discussion up to the point at which a degree of stability and continuity in political decision making and policy implementation was achieved.

In China that took thirty years. In the interim, leadership shifted back and forth between more moderate, orthodox leaders and radicals who wanted to take the country toward socialism as quickly as possible. Twice, during the Great Leap Forward and the Cultural Revolution, the radicals under the leadership of Chairman Mao took the country to the brink of disaster. It was only with the death of Mao that the moderates gained control of the party and state and set the country on the path of reform, which it has followed to this day. (See table 10.2.)

Then and now, the Chinese system closely resembled the Soviet state Gorbachev inherited, at least on paper. The CCP has a legal monopoly on political power and dominates all areas of policy making and implementation. It is also based on **democratic centralism,** which theoretically means that internal disagreements are kept to a minimum, if they are allowed to exist at all.

The CCP, however, was never able to escape those internal disagreements and, at times, has actually had loosely organized **factions** supporting different ideological viewpoints and leaders. When the political pendulum has swung most widely between them, the struggle has led to attacks on key party and state institutions. It also has propelled groups such as regional leaders and the military onto political center stage. Most importantly, the struggle often led to the personalization of power around the "supreme leader"—even more than in the Soviet Union after Stalin's death.

The CCP did not start out divided. From 1949 until the late 1950s, what differences existed between leaders had virtually no impact on party life or the country as a whole. Mao Zedong commanded the support of the entire party. Moreover, no one in the CCP questioned the assumption that they would establish a Soviet-style Marxist-Leninist regime, just as in every other Communist country in the world.

So, the CCP announced a First Five-Year Plan in 1953 that channeled more than half the available investment funds into heavy industry. As in the Soviet Union, the heaviest burdens fell on the peasants, who were driven into ever larger units and forced to sell their grain to the state at predetermined prices. Meanwhile, a constitution was promulgated in 1954 that centralized power even further and led to a rapid expansion of both state and party bureaucracies.

The PRC also quickly established an international role squarely within the Soviet-dominated world Communist movement. In 1950, without any apparent input from the Chinese, North Korean troops invaded the southern half of the Korean peninsula and occupied Seoul. The United States was able to convince the United Nations (the Soviets boycotted the Security Council on the day of the crucial vote, and Taiwan still held the Chinese seat) to send UN troops dominated by the United States into Korea. The Chinese had little option but to

▌ TABLE 10.2 Key Events in Chinese History since the Revolution

YEAR	EVENT
1949	CCP takes power
1956	De-Stalinization in Soviet Union begins
1956	Hundred Flowers Campaign
1957	Great Leap Forward
1960	Demotion of Mao Zedong
1965	Beginning of Cultural Revolution
1972	Opening to United States
1976	Deaths of Zhou Enlai and Mao Zedong; formal end of Cultural Revolution
1978	Democracy Wall
1983	Anti-spiritual pollution campaign
1989	Democracy Movement and Tiananmen Square
1997	Reversion of Hong Kong to PRC
1997	Death of Deng Xiaoping
2003	Hu Jintao becomes president

---

[3] Cited in Witold Rodzinski, *The People's Republic of China: A Concise History* (New York: Free Press, 1988), 13.

MAO ZEDONG

Mao Zedong addressing the masses shortly after taking power.

Mao was different from the sophisticated intellectuals who led the CCP in its early years. His father was a fairly successful peasant who ran his family with an iron fist. Mao began working in the family's fields at the age of six, but because his father wanted to make certain that at least one of his children could read and write enough to keep the books, he sent his son to school. The young Mao was an excellent student and graduated from teacher's training college in 1918. He then moved to Beijing, where he took a job at the university library under Li Dazhao, who, along with Chen Duxiu, was to found the CCP. Mao experienced May Fourth in Beijing and soon returned to his home region and began organizing.

Mao might never have become a major CCP leader were it not for the tragedies that hit the party in the 1920s and 1930s. The 1927 attack by the KMT forced the CCP to consider a peasant-based strategy—an approach that was confirmed by the Long March. Mao's leadership of the party was only once seriously questioned in the forty years between the end of the Long March and his death.

As more information has been gathered about Mao's personal life and the disruption of the Cultural Revolution, assessments of his historical role have become far more critical. Nonetheless, he certainly will always be thought of as one of the most influential Marxist analysts and political leaders of the twentieth century.

support their fellow Communists in the north. As the UN troops approached the Yalu River, separating China and North Korea, the PRC sent in its troops—with substantial Soviet military aid—and fought until the end of the war three years later.

This Soviet phase of the PRC's history was not to last long, however. Serious qualms about the Soviet Union and the relevance of the Soviet model lurked just below the surface.

Nikita Khrushchev's "secret speech" in 1956 brought these concerns into the open. In it, he admitted that there could be multiple "roads to socialism," thereby opening the door for the CCP to pursue its own strategy. However, the Chinese leadership found the rest of the speech highly disconcerting. Its attack on Stalin's **cult of personality** did not sit well with a leadership that stressed Mao Zedong's thoughts and actions. More importantly at the time, the new openness of the world Communist movement gave the CCP leadership an opportunity to vent its resentment toward the Soviets, which had been building since the days of Borodin.

Within months the Chinese and Soviets were taking verbal potshots at each other. Mao referred to Khrushchev's reforms as "goulash communism" that was taking Soviet-bloc countries further and further from Marxist goals. Most of the time, however, the early Sino-Soviet debate was couched in elliptical terms—with the Chinese attacking the Yugoslavs when they really meant the Soviets, and the Soviets doing the same thing with the Albanians, the only European Communist Party to ally with the PRC.

By the end of the decade, the Soviet Union had withdrawn all its advisers and cut off its economic and military aid to the PRC. During the late 1960s and the 1970s, there were skirmishes on the long border separating China and Siberia. It was only in the late 1980s, with the rise of reformist leaders in both countries, that any substantial steps were taken toward healing this **Sino-Soviet split.**

For our purposes, the split was important because it allowed the CCP to develop its own policies and address its own problems. The most important of these problems was the factionalism that developed around both ideology and, eventually, the role of Chairman Mao. From 1956 until the 1980s, Chinese politics was little more than a battle between two factions: the Maoists and the more moderate or orthodox Marxists.

The first open signs of the rift came with the **Hun-**

dred **Flowers Campaign** in 1956. Intellectuals were given considerable freedom to express themselves, much as in the "thaw" in the Soviet Union. Far more than the Soviets, the CCP traditionally relied on **campaigns** in which the party sought to mobilize the masses to meet its goals, which have ranged from eliminating flies and other pests to reshaping Chinese culture. In this campaign Mao used a traditional phrase—"Let a hundred flowers bloom and a thousand points of view contend"—in urging the people to speak their minds. They did just that in ways that soon worried Mao and the wing of the leadership that crystallized around him.

The Hundred Flowers Campaign was quickly brought to an end. The following year, Mao and his supporters moved in the opposite direction and called for a **Great Leap Forward,** through which the Chinese were to make rapid progress in the transition to socialism and communism. The campaign was based on the assumption that they could do so if and only if the Chinese people threw all their energies into the effort. Therefore, the move toward collective agriculture was accelerated. An attempt was made to incorporate everyone in the process of industrialization—for instance, by building small backyard furnaces on the collective farms. Intellectuals, who in Mao's eyes had become suspect during the Hundred Flowers Campaign, were expected to engage in manual labor that would bring them closer to the people. More generally, Maoists took the "red" side in the **red-versus-expert** debate in which the factions disagreed about the relative importance of ideological and technological factors in China's development.

The Great Leap Forward turned out to be a disaster. Industrial production declined precipitously. Experimental programs, like the one that called on farmers to build their own smelters, were abject failures. The situation in the countryside was particularly chaotic, and in the hard winter of 1958–59, at least a million people starved to death.

As the evidence about the failure of the Great Leap Forward began to pour in, the debates within the party heated up. Leading the charge was Peng Dehuai, head of the People's Liberation Army (PLA) and a Politburo member, who wrote a letter to Mao in July 1959 attacking the campaign. An enlarged Politburo met later that month to consider Peng's criticism. Mao threatened to go to the countryside and start another revolution if Peng's views prevailed, and he was able to summon up enough support to have Lin Biao take Peng's place as head of the PLA.

Mao's victory was short-lived. Within a year he had been forced to give up his position as chairman of the PRC and lost much of his influence in both the party and

AP/Wide World Photos

Chinese accused of being "capitalist roaders" being paraded through Beijing in 1967 during the Cultural Revolution.

state bureaucracies. The more moderate wing of the leadership, led by **Liu Shaoqi,** who was named Mao's successor-designate, and **Deng Xiaoping,** reembarked on a more gradual and orthodox policy of industrial development during the first half of the 1960s.

For our purposes, understanding the issues in the debate is less important than the fact that it was occurring at all. It marked the first time that Mao's leadership had been questioned, paving the way for the **Cultural Revolution** that was to do so much damage to the CCP and to China as a whole.

Scholars are still debating what drove Mao to embark on the Cultural Revolution. For someone who had been the architect of a popular revolution, there was good cause for concern in the early 1960s. The CCP was becoming increasingly bureaucratic and showed signs of developing the kind of conservative elitism that we saw in the Soviet Union during the Brezhnev era. Furthermore, there was a whole new generation of young people who had not experienced the trauma or the exhilaration of the revolutionary struggle. In short, Mao feared that China was becoming too self-satisfied and flabby.

The psychiatrist and historian Robert Lifton was the first of many observers to add Mao's aging and its effects on his personality to the factors leading to the Cultural Revolution. To such analysts, Mao mixed together concerns about his own mortality with those about the revolution that had been his life for almost a half-century. Another historian put it more bluntly and pejoratively: "Not only did his arrogance increase, his vanity did as well."

In the end, we will never know how much of Mao's decision was a rational political response to the situation after the Great Leap Forward or how much of it was a quirk of an increasingly quirky personality. Nonetheless, almost immediately after his demotion, he turned to the main source of power he had left—the PLA.

With its support, Mao launched the Socialist Education Movement in 1963, which returned ideology and mobilization to center stage. Meanwhile, Lin Biao used his position as head of the PLA to create a cult of personality around Mao that dwarfed anything orchestrated by Stalin and his henchmen. Every imaginable accomplishment was attributed to Mao. His position in Marxist philosophy was equated with that of Marx and Lenin and enshrined as what came to be called Marxism–Leninism–Mao Zedong thought. The ridiculous turned to the absurd when news stories about the seventy-year-old Mao swimming six miles in an hour appeared on the front page of the PLA's daily newspaper.

In March 1966 Mao stepped up the pressure by attacking the Beijing party apparatus. Peng Zhen, then head of the Beijing party, was dismissed. In May 1966 Professor Nie Yuanzi put up the first *dazhibao,* (big-character poster) at Beijing University, urging revolutionary intellectuals to "go into battle" against the party bureaucracy. University officials quickly tore it down, but a few days later Mao publicly endorsed it.

Professor Nie's poster brought the conflict within the party into the open. Liu and Deng realized that their positions were in jeopardy and counterattacked. They organized work teams to go to the universities to criticize Nie and Mao and to enforce discipline.

Their efforts failed. University and middle-school students formed groups of **Red Guards** to carry on the work of the Cultural Revolution. Within weeks they had paralyzed the nation's educational system. With Mao urging them to attack party members who also were **capitalist roaders** (those accused of opposing Mao), many of the Red Guards turned into vigilantes and vandals. Meanwhile, Mao attacked the CCP as "capitalist bureaucrats." In August 1966 Liu was officially labeled "the leading person in authority taking the capitalist road" and Deng "the number two person in authority taking the capitalist road." Liu, Deng, and thousands of others were arrested and sent either to prison or to the countryside. Liu would be the most famous of the countless thou-

sands of Chinese citizens who died in this campaign. Deng (who was already in his mid-sixties) was forced to work as a machinist on a collective farm; one of his sons was either pushed or fell from a seventh-story window and has been confined to a wheelchair ever since (www .morningsun.org/library).

New radical groups emerged around the country. Most famous was the Shanghai commune, organized by three relatively unknown men—Zhang Chunqiao, Wang Hongwen, and Yao Wenyuan—who were quickly promoted to positions of national prominence and who joined Mao's wife, **Jiang Qing,** in eliminating anything Western and nonideological from the theaters and airwaves.

Revolutionary "seizures of power" took place all over the country. Jiang urged her Red Guard faction to use weapons to defend themselves if need be. They did just that. Sometimes the violence was clearly aimed at political targets, but on all-too-many occasions, the young people were simply settling old scores or lashing out randomly at anyone who struck them as a symbol of the "bad" China.

Although it is hard to fathom just how disruptive the Cultural Revolution was, Harvard's Ross Terrill provides one insightful anecdote. It turns out that even trained circus horses were stripped of their lives of luxury and sent to work in the countryside. One group of horses was sent to a commune near a military base, where they worked dutifully until the bugles began to play, when

ZHOU ENLAI

Z hou was born in 1899. Unlike Mao's family, Zhou's was part of the gentry, and his father had passed the traditional Confucian exams that determined entry into the bureaucracy. Like many privileged young people of his generation, Zhou went to Japan to study and returned to participate in the May Fourth Movement. He later continued his studies in France, where he became a Marxist.

Zhou's charm and sophistication enhanced the CCP's reputation with foreigners and Chinese intellectuals alike. Once the PRC was established, Zhou became prime minister, a post he held until his death. He was a conciliator, the one leading politician who held the respect of both factions and could, at times, build bridges between them.

Unfortunately, Zhou contracted cancer in the early 1970s and knew he would not live much longer. Still, he was able to gain enough support to launch the four modernizations and bring Deng Xiaoping back into the leadership.

Premier Zhou Enlai meeting and dining with President Richard Nixon's envoy, Henry Kissinger.

---

they returned to the equine version of the capitalist road and performed a few of their old dance steps.[4]

By late 1967 it was clear even to Mao that things had gone too far, and he called on the PLA to restore order. Red Guards were to merge into "three-in-one" committees with the PLA and politically acceptable CCP members. But in a country that large, in which conditions were so chaotic, the disruption continued.

Moreover, the party continued to tilt dramatically to the left. Of the more moderate leaders, only Zhou Enlai remained. To make matters even more complicated, Lin Biao, who had been designated Mao's successor after Liu's fall, attempted a coup in 1971. Although details have never been made public, Lin had either come to oppose the Cultural Revolution or had grown tired of waiting his turn to replace Mao. Along with his wife, son, and other supporters from the PLA, Lin hatched a plot to kill Mao. The plot failed, and Lin perished in a plane crash while trying to escape to the Soviet Union.

By then, order had been restored, and the chaos of the Cultural Revolution was largely over. The **Gang of Four**—as Jiang, Zhang, Yao, and Wang came to be known—still controlled cultural and educational affairs. The economy and administration, however, began to

take center stage, and all but the most dedicated Maoists realized that China could not afford the disruption it had experienced in the late 1960s. This meant that the country's leading administrator and survivor, Zhou Enlai, became more influential.

In 1973 Zhou announced that China would concentrate on the **four modernizations**—agriculture, industry, science, and the military—that have been the focus of the country's official policy goals ever since. Although already terminally ill, Zhou was still politically strong enough to bring Deng Xiaoping back from exile to become deputy prime minister later that year.

In January 1976 Zhou died. On 25 March a Shanghai newspaper accused him of having been a capitalist roader—an accusation that evoked a tremendous response. Memorial wreaths began to appear in Tiananmen Square, and massive demonstrations were held in his honor, until they were finally broken up by the authorities on 4 April.

When Mao died the following September, the mourning paled in comparison. His positions in the party and government were taken over by Hua Guofeng, a political unknown who proved unable to end the struggle between Deng and the Gang of Four. In the short run, it seemed the Maoists would be the winners. Deng was demoted again, and Hua tried to drape himself in Mao's political mantle, even combing his hair the way

[4] Ross Terrill, *China in Our Times* (New York: Simon and Schuster, 1992), 65.

the chairman had in order to emphasize the physical resemblance between the two men.

Hua, however, was no friend of the Gang of Four. As a regional party official responsible for security in the late 1960s, he had seen the impact of their policies firsthand. Moreover, he realized that Jiang coveted his position. Therefore, he brought Deng back from political obscurity yet again and arrested the Gang of Four.

The Cultural Revolution was finally over, but its legacy remained. For a decade, scientific and industrial development had been put on hold. In addition, a generation of students had been unable to go to school, so the country lost their potential contributions to social, economic, and cultural development. Perhaps most importantly of all for the long term, the Cultural Revolution heightened the already substantial cynicism among large segments of the Chinese population.

Since Mao's Death

Factionalism did not disappear with Mao's death. However, the conflict since then has not been as intense or disruptive.

By 1978 Maoism had been effectively destroyed with the arrest of the Gang of Four and the removal of Hua Guofeng from office. Ever since, power has been in the hands of party officials who had been moderates before the Cultural Revolution; many had also been among its victims. Not surprisingly, they have downplayed ideological goals and embarked instead on what has now been more than two decades of reform featuring the introduction of private ownership and freer markets in much of the Chinese economy. They have done little, however, to open up the political system. In fact, they have quickly and harshly brought the few even vaguely liberalizing political reforms to a halt as soon as any signs that they might challenge the party's hegemony have appeared.

The post–Cultural Revolution leadership has been more unified than at any time since the mid-1950s. Still, there has been considerable division within it over the nature and pace of reform.

One group has favored moving toward a market economy as quickly and as fully as possible. It was also reasonably open to political as well as economic reform. Because its most visible leaders during the 1980s—Hu Yaobang and Zhao Ziyang—were believed to be Deng's protégés, outside observers often saw him as part of this faction. The other group centered on leaders who had more qualms about the disruptions reform can cause and so backed less sweeping change and was more willing to clamp down on dissent.

Deng's role in this was always obscure, given that he championed both economic reform and continued party control. His critics called him part of a "wind faction" that changed its direction with each shift in the political breeze. Whatever the details of what happened, by the 1980s disruptive factionalism disappeared most of the time as the moderate reformers and moderate hardliners found ways to coexist. That coexistence will be the subject of the rest of this chapter.

Political Culture and Participation

In previous chapters, political culture and participation were treated separately following the logic discussed in Chapter 1. Cultures generally reflect generations of political and other developments in the values of people living today. These values, in turn, help determine what those people do (and don't do) politically.

In China the link between the two is far more complicated, and they feed off each other in ways we in the West are not accustomed to. Chinese political culture reflects the same long-term impact of history on people's values and assumptions about politics. However, as the discussion of the Cultural Revolution suggests, the culture itself has been politicized, especially when the Maoists were in power and actively tried to reshape it. Moreover, as in the Soviet Union before Gorbachev's time, the party has actively tried to manipulate political participation.

As with most of Chinese politics, much has changed since the death of Mao. Cultural campaigns are largely a thing of the past, and there are even competitive political campaigns in local elections in rural counties. However, it still makes sense to think of political culture and participation as more of a seamless web than we did for any of the liberal democracies covered in Part 2.

A Blank Slate? A Cultural Revolution?

Mao's greatest failures had their roots in his misunderstanding of his own people. He correctly realized that Chinese values would have to change if he and his colleagues were to succeed in implementing Marxist ideals. However, he incorrectly assumed that it would be relatively easy to do so. Shortly after coming to power, Mao wrote:

> The two outstanding things about China's 600 million people are that they are "poor and blank." On a blank sheet of paper free from any blotches, the freshest and most beautiful characters can be writ-

ten, the freshest and most beautiful pictures can be painted.[5]

For those in the Maoist faction, cultural change was the top priority because they believed that socialist institutions could only be built by a people committed to socialist values. Most orthodox and moderate party leaders differed only in degree, arguing that cultural change was but one of a series of priorities and ranked below economic growth in importance.

Unfortunately, it is very hard to determine how much Chinese political culture changed—if at all. Cultures are always difficult to chart, because they include values and assumptions that people rarely think about and that represent what amounts to their political "second nature." Political culture has always been documented using public opinion polls and more in-depth observations of what people think and do by journalists and anthropologists. In China, public opinion polling is in its infancy, and very few of the published results touch on issues of culture and change. We have access to some first-rate anthropological studies and journalistic accounts, but even these barely scratch the surface of a complex question about a complex society. Therefore, everything that follows in this section should be read with even more skepticism than usual.

In one sense, Mao was right about the Chinese people being a blank slate. Prior to 1949, Chinese peasants, who made up the overwhelming majority of the population, were not politically involved other than paying taxes and getting caught up in the occasional war. Politics was something that concerned the landlords and magistrates, a view reinforced by Confucian values stressing group loyalty, conflict avoidance, and acceptance of one's place in the social hierarchy.

But this does not mean that they had no political values. We also know from the history of dynastic change and peasant rebellions that this neo-Confucian culture did not always "work." Violent uprisings occurred for much the same reasons they did in other countries with a tradition of peasant unrest. Generally, people tolerated the system. However, if a large number of peasants in a given area came to the conclusion that the local scholar-gentry elite was not performing adequately, respect for authority disappeared, and pent-up anger erupted into violence.

There is considerable evidence that much of this cultural tradition has persisted into the Communist period. Studies carried out in some isolated rural areas suggest that peasants still generally defer to the authority of local leaders and that loyalty was rather easily transferred from the pre-1949 elites to CCP officials. Thus, many students and intellectuals who were "sent down" to the countryside during the Cultural Revolution expressed surprise at the willingness of the peasantry to accept them, even though they did not contribute much labor and stretched scarce local resources.

Reports persist, too, of the sense of resignation and the sullen anger that seem always to have been a part of peasant, and now working-class, attitudes in China. During the immediate post-revolutionary, Great Leap Forward, and Cultural Revolution periods, there were numerous accounts of peasants using the official ideology of the campaign as a cover to settle old scores with other peasants or former landlords. Some research on the events since the Democracy Movement of 1989 uncovered what can only be called urban thugs, who used demonstrations as a pretext for vandalism and intimidation. Finally, the Western press includes periodic reports of isolated protest movements, especially in ethnic minority and other rural areas. Most have been quickly put down, often with some violence on the part of the authorities.

The early CCP tried to replace this inherited culture with a value system based on four main elements:

- *Collectivism.* Chinese culture has traditionally revolved around group loyalties to one's family or village. The CCP wanted to see that loyalty transferred to a broader and more inclusive institution—the party and state. From at least the time of the Hundred Flowers Campaign on, however, this transition clearly has been an especially hard one for intellectuals and others who are increasingly tempted by individualism as the society and economy modernize.

- *Struggle and activism.* Traditional values revolved around harmony and acceptance of the status quo. As part of Mao's notion of the mass line, the CCP wanted the Chinese people to participate in what the leadership understood would be a bumpy transition to socialism. However, the party also saw participation not as something people did for themselves but as part of the collectivist goal of serving the people and fighting selfish tendencies.

- *Egalitarianism and populism.* Hierarchy was one of the key organizing principles in Chinese society prior to 1949. The CCP tried to end what it saw as the irrational subordination not only of the working class and peasantry but of women and younger

---

[5] Cited in Terrill, *China in Our Times*, 1.

people as well. Even recent policies that have created an extremely wealthy minority of the population are justified as leading to a more egalitarian future. Abolishing hierarchy does not, however, lead to a more individualistic society, but rather, again, to one in which people voluntarily serve the country as a whole. It should be pointed out that the CCP also reinforced hierarchical traditions with its imposition of a Leninist-Stalinist-style party state, which certainly minimized the degree to which egalitarian or populist goals could be reached or even pursued.

- *Self-reliance.* Finally, the Chinese tried to break with the traditional values that left most people dependent on the elite, waiting for instructions and leadership from above. Instead, the CCP tried to convince people that together they could control their own destinies. Over the years, self-reliance has taken on many forms, from the extreme, failed campaign for self-sufficiency during the Great Leap Forward to the ongoing efforts to modernize China with as little interference from abroad as possible.

Especially in the early years, the party relied on two main techniques for speeding up cultural change. The first was the state domination of all key agents of political socialization except for the family. As in the former Soviet Union, the CCP has total control over the education system and the mass media. Even today, the party uses the schools and media for overt political education. It even tried to undermine the power of the family by shifting many child-rearing activities to the *danwei,* or **unit**—the basic body assuring work, housing, and welfare to which most urban Chinese were assigned before economic reforms took hold.

The CCP also relied on mass campaigns more than the Communist parties did in what used to be the Soviet bloc. From the 1950s through the 1970s, the CCP initiated countless campaigns to rid the country of physical and social "evils," from flies to homosexuality. The great movements, from the Hundred Flowers Campaign to the Cultural Revolution itself, were efforts in which party leaders argued that success hinged on maximum participation for two reasons. First, in the absence of a large, trained, and reliable bureaucracy, the people were normally needed to implement any kind of sweeping new reform. Second, and more important for our purposes, the campaigns included political study sessions in which people were brought together to discuss the problem at hand and some relevant texts by Mao, and

thereby deepen their understanding of and commitment to Marxism–Leninism–Mao Zedong thought.

Typical of the Maoist-era campaigns was the Socialist Education Movement, launched in 1963. After the failure of the Great Leap Forward, Mao was deeply concerned about what he believed to be the corruption and demoralization of rural party **cadres** or full-time party members. Mao and his followers prepared a statement about rural conditions that required cadres to participate in productive labor. As in most campaigns, this document was discussed in study groups around the country, and Maoist sympathizers used it to foster popular criticism of the cadres and to put pressure on them to adopt a more Maoist point of view.

Neither the campaigns nor the broader efforts to create a "new socialist man" were very successful. There was a lot of cynical and self-interested participation in them. Many of the seventeen million young people sent down during the Cultural Revolution came to resent their exile and the system that sent them there, as did the peasants whose lives were disrupted by their arrival.

These efforts, however, do seem to have been far more successful than their equivalents in the former Soviet Union. There, for example, university students were required to take courses in Marxism-Leninism, but these were treated as boring requirements by both the faculty who taught them and the students I saw who slept or knitted through the classes. In China, a far larger proportion of the party members who led the "education" and the average citizens who "learned" from them appeared to have taken those exercises more seriously. As a result, the CCP probably did succeed in forging a regime that was seen as legitimate by most elements in Chinese society, at least until the Cultural Revolution.

Even the Democracy Movement of 1989 worked on the assumption that democratic institutions could *and should* be built within the existing socialist order. Unlike many of their counterparts in the Soviet Union and Eastern Europe, the students who first occupied Tiananmen Square cast their demands in patriotic terms, arguing that socialist democracy required the elite to be open to criticism from the people.

We should not make too much of either the CCP's commitment to cultural change or the degree of legitimacy it enjoyed. The limits to the progress it has made can easily be seen in its failed attempts to "reinvent" one of the most important lingering aspects of traditional thought and action: the role of women. Of all the countries covered in this book, the PRC made the most concerted efforts to improve the status of women. Women played a vital role in the revolution, prompting Mao to stress how they "held up half the sky." The 1950 Law on Marriage and other early decrees gave women legal equality and outlawed a series of traditional practices, including foot binding.

The CCP has not engaged in this kind of consciousness raising and gender reform since Mao's death, except for its largely successful campaign to keep families from having more than one child. As in the former Soviet Union, women in China continue to occupy secondary positions in everything from the politics of the household to the politics of the Politburo. In fact, only a few women have played a significant role in the CCP elite, most of whom were the wives of even more prominent men, including Mao and Zhou.

And now there are signs that the condition of women may actually be worsening. Women are being discriminated against more in hiring, housing, and the distribution of land. At a recent job fair to recruit government officials, fully 80 percent of the positions were open only to men. Women who are hired are routinely required to promise that they will not marry for at least three years. Women are again being bought and sold as wives, a practice that had been outlawed in the 1950s.

The party has also drastically scaled back its efforts to reshape public opinion and the political culture since the death of Mao. Deng's sense of pragmatism, according to which the people were exhorted to "seek truth from facts," left little room for the kind of ideological education Mao favored. The party has loosened its controls somewhat in recent years, allowing a wider range of views to be expressed in the media and schools and, more importantly, allowing foreign music, films, and news into China on a scale that would have been unimaginable a generation ago.

Some party leaders are deeply concerned that the spread of Western pop culture and personal computers is creating a population more concerned with self-interest than collectivism. The modernization of the country opens the door to a greater diversity of interests, and some of the new groups, such as the urban entrepreneurs and international traders, are beginning to band together, if for no other reason than to express their professional interests. As the number of people who work outside the centrally planned economy continues to grow, the unit is becoming less and less of a factor in their lives.

In some respects, then, the cultural unity that may have existed before the Cultural Revolution has disappeared. We have no way of knowing how much dissatisfaction there is with either the party elite or the regime as a whole. What is clear is that there are pockets of discontent scattered throughout the country—among young intellectuals and business executives who have been "winners" during the reform years, and among manual workers, poor peasants, and ethnic minorities whose conditions have at best barely improved.

Do not, however, equate this discontent with a commensurate increase in active and potentially disruptive dissent. Although there is more open protest than there was a generation ago, it undoubtedly lags behind public opinion. More importantly, most recent protests occurred among poorly organized groups that have not been able to come together to pose any sort of serious challenge to the authorities.

To see why this is the case, we have to take a step back from the current situation and consider how Communist regimes in China and elsewhere traditionally orchestrated participation "from above."

Participation from the Top Down

People studying comparative politics in the West often conclude that political participation is largely from the bottom up. In the industrialized democracies, most of the participation we focus on takes place because individual citizens choose to get involved, typically to express their point of view on who should govern or what policies they should adopt.

This was not the case in the former Communist regimes of the Soviet bloc, nor is it the case in China today. The Chinese authorities include democracy and the mass line in their rhetoric. And average citizens actually participate in political life more than their counterparts in the West. However, little of that involvement actually plays a role in shaping public policy. Rather, some political scientists call it "mobilized" participation because the CCP determines what people should do and then turns them out to meet the regime's goals.

Although they are sometimes consulted before decisions are made, their typical activity involves carrying out policies that have already been approved farther up the political hierarchy. This was especially true during the Maoist years, during which the campaigns mentioned earlier were a routine fact of life. Politics affected all aspects of people's lives. Almost everyone in urban areas was assigned to units, which were dominated by local party representatives. Much the same was true of the people's communes in rural areas, which were much like state and collective farms in the Soviet Union.

Between 6 and 10 percent of the adult population belongs to the CCP, which is actually a rather high proportion by Western standards. Again, we should not read too much into this, because most party members do political work that is determined by the cadres, who outrank them. Most of their work, too, involves the routine implementation of policy decisions made by their superiors. And, as in the former Soviet bloc, many people join the party because it is the one and only way to get ahead in all areas of Chinese society.

There is less top-down activity now than there was during the Maoist years. As noted earlier, major campaigns are a thing of the past. The party has had trouble recruiting reliable and competent members now that private enterprise holds out opportunities to gain wealth and influence. Finally, the units are far less influential; in fact, many urban residents are no longer part of a unit at all, but instead find work, housing, and other services in the open market. In rural areas, the communes have been abolished and replaced with what amounts to private farms and looser forms of social control, both of which will be described later.

From the Bottom Up?

There is also some fragmentary evidence that some Chinese engage in more of the kinds of political participation we focus on in the West. The most important is based on elections in rural areas in which more than one candidate has been allowed to run since 1987. The CCP is still the only organization that can nominate candidates; nonetheless, voters often now have choices for members of the governing bodies that replaced the People's communes. Economic liberalization has also given people more of an ability to make the decisions that shape their economic lives, which, if Western theorists are correct, could be translated into demands for more influence over their political lives as well (www.chinaelections .org/en).

Those rural voters have been the subject of some empirical research. Polling is in its infancy in China, but surveys conducted in Beijing and in four rural counties in the late 1990s have shown that substantial numbers of people engage in voluntary political activity, some of which puts demands on policymakers.

In the rural poll, respondents were asked if they had done any of the following:

- Attended local party meetings
- Attended official village meetings
- Worked with others to help solve a local problem
- Expressed their opinion to a party cadre

TABLE 10.3 Political Participation in Rural China

NUMBER OF ACTIVITIES	ALL FORMS (PERCENTAGE)	DEMANDING FORMS ONLY (PERCENTAGE)
0	41	66
1	31	22
2 or more	28	12

Source: Adapted from M. Kent Jennings, "Political Participation in the Chinese Countryside," *American Political Science Review,* 91 (June 1997), tables 2 and 3.

- Tried to contact and influence a local government official

The results, summarized in table 10.3, surprised the American scholars who helped direct the research. In fact, the numbers compare quite favorably with those in Western democracies, though we should take Chinese polling results with a hefty grain of salt.

Moreover, with but one exception, the same factors contribute to participation in China as in the West. For example, men participate more than women; young people are less active than their elders; and, as in most countries, the more educated people are, the more likely they are to be involved in political life. The one somewhat worrying difference is that CCP members are much more likely to get involved than the rest of society, which may limit the importance of this small rural groundswell of political participation for the future.

These changes have been concentrated in the countryside because the authorities have concluded that they can experiment with somewhat competitive elections there without incurring the risks they would in the cities. Since 1987, the Party has allowed a growing number of local elections to include more than one candidate, albeit all chosen by the local CCP cadres.

Dissent

During the last few years there have been reports of strikes by factory workers and peasants, as well as demonstrations by Tibetans, Uygers, and other ethnic minorities. Few of these events were anything but short-term, local movements. In fact, the skimpy evidence available to us suggests that the party rarely hesitated to put them down—with force if need be. That said, there have been three coordinated movements since the late 1970s. Although the regime ultimately repressed them as well, aspects of each indicate that the regime may not be as powerful as some of its critics believe (www.chinasite.com/dissident.html).

Democracy Wall

First came the **Democracy Wall** effort of 1978. Initially, Deng and his colleagues allowed a degree of political freedom after they replaced Hua Guofeng and the other holdover leaders from the Cultural Revolution. With government approval, people put up big-character posters, first on the so-called Democracy Wall in downtown Beijing, and then elsewhere in the country. Many were simply critical of how socialism was being implemented. Others went further and advocated a wider variety of reforms, ranging from freedom of speech to a multiparty system.

The man who became the most prominent of the dissidents, **Wei Jingsheng,** then a twenty-five-year-old electrician, wrote about democracy as the fifth modernization to accompany Zhou and Deng's four. Wei went further than anyone else had in openly criticizing the party and its leadership. For instance, he wrote:

> We hold that people should not give any political leader unconditional trust. Does Deng Xiaoping want democracy? No, he does not. We cannot help asking: What do you think democracy means? If the people do not have a right to express their views freely, how can one speak of democracy? If refusing to allow other people to criticize those in power is your idea of democracy, then what is the difference between this and what Mao euphemistically called the "dictatorship of the proletariat"?[6]

Soon, Deng's patience ran out, and the government prohibited all posters and publications that criticized socialism. The leaders were arrested, including Wei, who was sentenced to fifteen years in prison.

The Democracy Movement

For the next decade, visible dissent came only from isolated individuals, most notably the world-renowned astrophysicist **Fang Lizhi,** who is now living and teaching in exile in the United States. Fang was a brilliant physics student who graduated from Beijing University at the age of twenty and who was immediately assigned to work for the prestigious Academy of Science's Institute of Modern Physics. He later taught at the University of Science and Technology. Though he thought of himself as a loyal party member, he got into political trouble during the

Great Leap Forward and the Cultural Revolution. Fang was able to keep his job, but he could only publish his scholarly works under a pseudonym and was never allowed to occupy the administrative posts his colleagues elected him to.

Beginning in 1978, Fang took advantage of his professional reputation and the relaxed political controls to begin speaking out on broader political issues. For example, he included the following remarks in a 1985 speech:

> There is a social malaise in our country today, and the primary reason for it is the poor example set by Party members. Unethical behavior by Party leaders is especially to blame. This is a situation that clearly calls for action on the part of intellectuals. We Communist Party members should be open to different ways of thinking. We should be open to different cultures and willing to adopt the elements of those cultures that are clearly superior. We must not be afraid to speak openly about these things. In fact, it is our duty.[7]

Like many other intellectuals, Fang soon ran afoul of the authorities and was silenced for most of the 1980s. In 1989 the situation changed dramatically with the emergence of the **Democracy Movement,** the first large, reasonably well-organized protest movement against the CCP and its policies.

As with the demonstrations in 1976, the Democracy Movement began with spontaneous protests following the death of a respected reformist leader—Hu Yaobang. Within hours of his death, big-character posters appeared on the walls of Beijing University. That evening, the highly connected graduate students in its Department of Communist Party History bicycled into Tiananmen Square to place a wreath in his memory. Two days later, five hundred students marched to Tiananmen Square to lay more wreaths. Each new day brought larger and more militant demonstrations. The police did not intervene.

Within a week, younger students had come to dominate the movement. Unlike the graduate students, they had few memories of the Cultural Revolution, took the new openness for granted, and assumed that they could take the protest to a new level. On the night of 21–22 April, ten thousand of them marched into the square—and stayed. A day later, their ranks had swelled to one hundred thousand.

On 27 April the students planned another massive

[6]Orville Schell, *Mandate of Heaven* (New York: Simon and Schuster, 1994), 29.

[7]Orville Schell, *Discos and Democracy* (New York: Anchor Books, 1989), 131–33.

march. This time the government tried to block them. The students marched anyway, and their courage inspired an estimated two hundred thousand Beijing residents to join them.

At that point, both the government and the students were still looking for a mutually acceptable solution, but the two sides ended up talking past each other. In early May the movement spread beyond Beijing to other major cities. Journalists defied party discipline and began reporting what they saw. The students who remained in the square proved to be an embarrassment during Gorbachev's visit to Beijing by disrupting planned events and by making it clear that they were inspired in large measure by the political reforms undertaken under his leadership in Moscow. The demonstrations continued after he left. A small group of students began a hunger strike. On 17 May an estimated two million people filled Tiananmen Square in the largest demonstration since the Cultural Revolution,

On 20 May, however, the students' leaders realized that they could not apply further pressure on the government without dropping their commitment to nonviolence. Meanwhile, the hard-liners began a counterattack, seizing control of the party leadership. By the end of the month, they had replaced Zhao with Jiang Zemin, the mayor of Shanghai, who was reputed to be squarely in their camp.

The standoff continued for two more weeks. Finally, on the night of 3–4 June, troops loyal to Yang Shangkun, president of the PRC and head of the family that dominated the PLA, stormed the square. No one knows how many people were killed, but estimates run as high as four thousand. Many student leaders fled the country. Even though they took no part in the movement, Fang Lizhi and his wife had to take refuge in the American Embassy, where they remained for almost a year before being allowed to emigrate. In the days and months after the crackdown, the hard-liners solidified their hold on power and made the open expression of dissent impossible. Most movement leaders were either arrested or escaped into exile.

Falun Gong

The most serious challenge in recent years, and the most revealing response by the authorities, has come from a most unusual source—**Falun Gong.** Falun Gong is one of those organizations that is hard to fit into Western conceptual schemes.

On one level, it is merely a version of *qigong,* which is a set of physical exercises that practitioners believe lead to spiritual and physical well-being. On another level, it is inspired by Buddhism and thus has many aspects of a religion. On yet another level, the very fact that it exists as an autonomous organization with as many as fifty million practitioners means that the party leaders view it with caution—at best.

Falun Gong was founded in 1992 by a minor railway official, Li Hongzhi, who had no particular expertise in either spirituality or religion. Nonetheless, the movement and its program of exercise and meditation quickly took hold—especially among middle-aged, middle-class Chinese, many of whom had been victims of the Cultural Revolution and many of whom were not thriving as a re-

AP / Wide World Photos

Students at Beijing's Central Academy of Fine Arts putting the finishing touches on the "Goddess of Democracy," modeled after the Statue of Liberty.

sult of the most recent economic reforms. The movement also spread through its effective use of the Internet. Although its sites are no longer accessible in China itself, Falun Gong adherents abroad now e-mail material from the sites, which Chinese can routinely receive online (www.falundafa.org or www.faluninfo.net).

As long as Falun Gong adherents simply went to parks to perform their exercises, the regime tolerated them. However, on 25 April 1999, ten thousand of them held a peaceful demonstration in Tiananmen Square. By mid-2000 Falun Gong had held more and larger illegal rallies. Falun Gong members claimed that their meetings were not political at all. The authorities viewed things otherwise, just as they have any attempt to create an independent body that lies outside their monopoly of sources of political power. That July they outlawed Falun Gong, claiming it was an "evil cult."

Falun Gong does have some cultlike tendencies, and its belief that ritualistic exercise and meditation can cure disease is certainly unusual by Western standards. Nonetheless, it is part of a venerable Chinese spiritual tradition whose beliefs are no more dangerous or cultish than those of, for instance, Christian Science.

Nonetheless, the authorities cracked down. Li Hongzhi went into exile and now runs the movement from New York. The party responded by sending at least five thousand members to labor camps for "reeducation" and arrested several hundred more. A few dozen members committed suicide while in prison.

For our purposes, the key to Falun Gong is not what it does or does not believe in. Rather, it lies in the way the authorities respond to it. As the religious sociologist Richard Madsen puts it, "Any organization like Falun Gong, no matter what the content of its ideology, would be a threat to the communist regime."[8] The fact is, a well-organized group beyond the control of the party is an obvious source of concern for the party elite, who know that the CCP itself is nowhere near as powerful or popular as it once was.

In other words, Falun Gong, in and of itself, might prove to be nothing more than a passing fad. However, the party elite seem to believe it sets a dangerous precedent. If they allowed it to continue to grow and take positions different from their own, however bland and benign those positions might be, other more political and more challenging organizations might look at Falun Gong's relative freedom and demand the same for themselves. So, all the signs suggest that the party leaders believed they had no choice but to crack down.

---

[8] Richard Madsen, "Understanding Falun Gong," *Current History* 99 (September 2000).

Democratization in China

CHINA IS ONE of two or three countries covered in this book (Iraq and possibly Iran being the others) in which we cannot realistically talk about democratization. Western journalists and human rights advocates seize on whatever evidence they can find of hostility to the CCP, such as the 1998 attempt by dissidents to register their own opposition party, as signs of prodemocratic sentiment. In fact, there is little or no evidence to suggest that any significant democratization is occurring "below the surface."

What is less clear is what will happen in the long term. Political scientists are not naïve enough to assume that the emergence of capitalistic forces in the economy will necessarily lead to democratic political movements as well. What's more, the regime still seems to be able to quash embryonic movements that spring up, such as the attempt to register the independent Democratic Party. Still, it's by no means certain that the regime will be able to stave off such efforts in the future or that it won't try to preempt them with gradual, pragmatic reforms of its own.

The Party State

There has been one common denominator in Chinese politics since 1949—domination by the CCP. Despite all the forces that are changing the face of China, the party remains quite close to the Leninist model laid out in Chapter 8 and has been able to resist pressure for political reform. There are, however, some ways in which today's CCP is different from that model, as well as reasons to believe that the party is weakening (www.chinatoday.com/org/cpc).

Like all other Communist parties that joined the Comintern in the 1920s, the CCP endorsed democratic centralism and the rest of the Bolshevik organization. This means that, although the People's Republic of China (PRC) has a government and a constitution, the most recent version having been adopted in 1982, the state is not really where power lies. Despite some minor exceptions, which we will encounter later in this section, the party still calls all the political (if not the economic) shots.

The PRC is officially governed by a massive National People's Congress of well over two thousand members. But like the Supreme Soviet prior to Gorbachev, the congress meets infrequently and serves primarily as a rubber stamp for decisions made elsewhere. Similarly, the president and prime minister are powerful primarily because they hold positions atop the CCP, not because of their formal government offices.

The only significant structural difference between the PRC and other Communist governments is the somewhat larger role given to provincial and local authorities in China. Even that should hardly be surprising given China's size and its relatively poorly developed communications infrastructure.

As in the former Soviet Union, real power lies in the party. The 1982 constitution dropped Article 2, the PRC's equivalent of the Soviet Article 6, which gave the party a monopoly on power. This made little difference in practice, given Deng's continued endorsement of party control.

The CCP enrolls a slightly smaller proportion of the total population than did the Communist Party of the Soviet Union (CPSU). However, it is still a huge organization. Its more than sixty-six million members means that the CCP is bigger than all but twenty-two countries! The dominance of the party unit in determining where people lived and worked into the 1980s gave it at least as much control as the CPSU had before the reforms of the Gorbachev era.

A New Kind of Party?

The new generation of pragmatic leaders has tried to change the party's composition. Increasingly, they are trying to recruit university graduates and technicians whose expertise, and not their class background or ideological commitment, is seen as necessary if the party is to lead the way toward further modernization. This explains the importance of opening the economy to the private sector, as discussed at the beginning of the chapter.

Twenty years ago, the party would have had little difficulty finding these types of dedicated members and future leaders because party membership was the one and only way to reach the top of Chinese society. Now, this has begun to change. With private businesses employing more and more well-educated young people, the CCP is no longer the only "game in town," and the party is finding it harder and harder to recruit the kinds of cadres it wants.

This helps explain why the party announced in 2001 that it would allow capitalists to join. In fact, party offi-

cials estimated that already 113,000 of the 64.5 million members owned businesses. But they had all formed their firms after they had joined the party. Three years later it was estimated that between a quarter and a third of all Chinese entrepreneurs were CCP members.

Some hard-liners objected. A regional party official said that "if these people really join the party they will use their strength to first seize power within the party and to change the party's nature." Another put it far more bluntly: "Capitalists in the Communist Party? You've got to be kidding."

Party membership remains a requirement for a political career. However, for many apolitical young people who are more concerned with making money, there is no need to belong to the CCP. For them the often petty administrative work new party members are assigned can be an unnecessary burden. Nonetheless, there seems to be no turning back for a party that will have to adapt to China's changing social and economic realities if it is to survive.

The Road to Power

The CCP leadership still controls all major appointments in the government and in the party itself. Like the CPSU, it has a **nomenklatura.** The Chinese were among the first Communist governments to separate party and state leadership below the national level. In practice, however, this has yet to make much difference, because the party elite still controls appointments to both.

Power is officially lodged in the party congress, which normally meets every five years and ratifies the **Central Committee** to manage party affairs until its next session. Practically speaking, the Congress and Central Committee are powerless. As in the old Soviet Union, neither body has much influence. Democratic centralism still operates. Party Congress delegates are co-opted from above, and the meetings themselves have done little more than ratify decisions already made by the elite.

The Central Committee, too, exercises little day-to-day power. Unlike the former CPSU, there is not much continuity in its membership, with a turnover rate of about 50 percent at each of the most recent congresses. The Central Committee is a massive body that meets only a few times a year because well over half its members live outside Beijing. Although these plenums have often been the site of acrimonious debate over most of the major policy initiatives taken since 1978, the final decisions are invariably made higher up.

As was the case in the CPSU, power is concentrated in the very small political elite, at the heart of which is the

❚ FIGURE 10.1 Decision Making in China

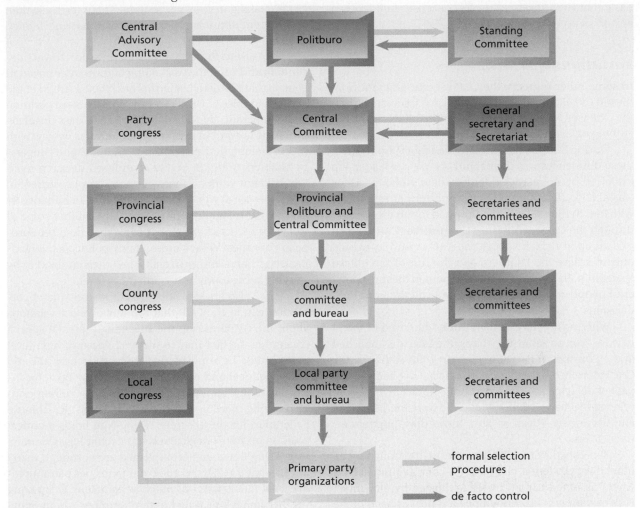

Politburo, usually composed of about twenty members, all of whom are senior party leaders. The Politburo includes top state officials as well, such as the premier or the chair of the State Planning Commission. Unlike the CPSU, the Politburo's day-to-day work is the responsibility of its smaller **Standing Committee.** (See figure 10.1.)

We (perhaps) gained a unique glimpse into the inner workings with the publication of the *Tiananmen Square Papers* in early 2001.[9] Three prominent American sinologists were given copies of what they were told were transcripts of secret meetings of the party's leadership during the Tiananmen crisis in 1989. Initially, the three doubted that the documents were authentic. However, after months of study and queries of colleagues around the world, they decided that they probably were legitimate and decided to publish them. The papers reveal a leadership that was deeply divided between reformers and hard-liners, though it is safe to say that similar transcripts from meetings during the first days of the Cultural Revolution would show far more acrimony. In the end, Deng Xiaoping had the last word and cast his lot with the hard-liners and their desire to force the students and their supporters out of Tiananmen Square. No one knows how much debate there is on more normal political issues. The one thing we can say with a reasonable degree of certainty is that the dominant leader does seem able to have his will prevail if he voices his viewpoint

---

[9] Liang Zheng, Andrew Nathan, Perry Link, and Orville Schell, eds., *The Tiananmen Square Papers: The Chinese Leadership's Decision to Use Force against Their Own People—In Their Own Words* (New York: Public Affairs, 2001).

strongly enough. That said, the conventional wisdom has it that Hu Jintao is more of a consensus builder than any of his predecessors.

Variations on a Theme

In some other respects, the CCP is quite different from the old CPSU. Those differences help us understand why the CCP went in such a novel direction following the beginning of factionalism.

During Deng's years in power, the most important of these differences was the behind-the-scenes leadership exercised by the party's elderly leaders. Although Deng was able to urge his colleagues into formal retirement with him in the 1980s, they continued to run the country through the **Central Advisory Committee (CAC),** which was set up in 1982. In theory, the CAC ostensibly existed only to advise the Politburo and the rest of the official leadership. In fact, its members remained the most powerful people in the country and made all the important decisions.

With most of its members either deceased or too ill to work even on a part-time basis, the CAC was abolished at the Fourteenth Party Congress in 1992. Although the CAC, therefore, existed for only a decade, it had the impact of delaying the real assertion of power by Jiang and other so-called first-line leaders who were then widely—and accurately—seen as little more than puppets for their elders.

The constitution prohibits presidents from serving more than two terms, and Jiang's second expired in 2003 when, as noted earlier, he was replaced by Hu Jintao. Hu's elevation to his third important post as head of the Central Military Commission occurred just before these lines were written, so it is too early to tell how he will lead now that he faces little or no opposition.

There are also growing signs that the party's organization is neither as rigid nor as powerful as the Leninist model or figure 10.1 might suggest. Among the most important evidence of this is the erosion of the party organization itself. China has a long history of highly centralized bureaucratic rule, which meant that the Leninist party was by no means wholly out of line with tradition. If anything, such practices have been reinforced under the CCP, with its emphasis on the top twenty-five to thirty-five officials and the "core leader" at any one time. As in the old Soviet bloc, these officials have been able to concentrate power through their personal networks and the *nomenklatura* system. These general tendencies are probably even more pronounced in China with its sys-tem of *kou,* or policy gateways, which coordinates decision making in four key sectors—party organization, government administration, state security, and foreign affairs.

Conversely, there are powerful pressures toward decentralization and the weakening of the party's power in general that Kenneth Lieberthal has labeled "fragmented authoritarianism." Until recently, both Chinese tradition and democratic centralism led people to pass unsolved problems upward in the party hierarchy. As we saw with the distinction between political "thumbs" and "fingers" in Chapters 8 and 9, highly centralized decision making does not work all that well in a complex society in which people at the "bottom" have to take initiative or act quickly. It should also be remembered that some of China's provinces have more people than do most European countries. What's more, many politicians, including Deng, Jiang, and Hu, established their credentials by working successfully at the provincial level.

There also are growing signs of nepotism and corruption within the CCP that top any of the revelations about the CPSU during the Brezhnev years. Of special concern is the fact that so many children of high-level party cadres have positioned themselves near the top of the political and economic hierarchies. Take, for instance, Deng Xiaoping's five children. Deng Pufang, crippled during the Cultural Revolution, heads the Chinese Federation for the Disabled. Deng Nan holds a critical position on the State Science and Technology Commission. Deng Lin is an accomplished artist, though many believe that the $20,000 she commands per painting reflects her family name as much as her talent. Deng Rong was her father's secretary and interpreter, whom many believe had the most influence over the aging leader. Finally, Deng Zhifang holds an American Ph.D. and is one of China's top young entrepreneurs.

The strength of these families opens the door to a far broader, but harder to document, concern—corruption. The press is filled with reports of new millionaires living luxuriously at least partially as the result of illegal activities. Bribes are an accepted part of doing business in the new China. Corruption within the police force is known as the "three chaoses"—for the acceptance of bribes, the unauthorized imposition of fines, and the illegal sharing of license and other fees by the men and women who collect them.

Finally, there is the PLA. As we saw in Chapter 9, the Soviet army stayed away from political controversies until the 1991 coup, at which time it proved incapable of intervening politically in any kind of unified manner. The

HU JINTAO

Luke Frazza/AFP/Getty Images

Hu Jintao with U.S. president George W. Bush and Nigerian president Olusegun Obasanjo.

Hu Jintao became Chair of the CCP in 2002, President of the People's Republic in 2003, and head of the Central Military Commission in 2004.

Hu's elevation marks a major turning point in Chinese politics. Born in 1942, he is the first leader to have come of age after the revolution. Like many leaders of his generation, he first joined the Communist party's youth league while studying engineering at the height of the Cultural Revolution. Also, like many of his contemporaries, he began his career as a provincial technician working for the Ministry of Water Conservancy and Power.

Because of his successes at the local level, he rose quickly up the ministry ranks and moved into full-time party work during the 1980s when, among other things, he led Beijing's repressive administration of Tibet.

In 1992, he moved to Beijing and became a member of the seven-person Standing Committee of the Politburo. Though little known outside of China at the time, Hu gained the support of his colleagues and emerged as the obvious first member of the "fourth generation" of leaders to take over the party and the country. He has always been reluctant to state his views too strongly. For instance, he once said that political success "requires resolve, attention to concrete matters, and courage making decisions."

PLA, in contrast, has been an important political actor since the Long March. At that point, the party and the army were one and the same. Many party leaders, including Deng Xiaoping, started their careers in the PLA, and army leaders have always held prominent positions in the CCP leadership. Membership on the party's Central Military Commission has similarly been a sign of political power within the CCP as well as the PLA.

The PLA became part of the factional struggles in the 1960s, beginning with the purge of its leader, Peng Dehuai, who had openly criticized Mao's policies during the Great Leap Forward. Under Lin Biao, the PLA played a vital role in planning the Cultural Revolution and then restoring order once the campaign got out of hand.

The PLA was far less political in the years between Lin Biao's death and the Democracy Movement of 1989. During the 1980s the army was as divided as the party as a whole. Some leaders sided with the reformers. Press reports during the spring of 1989 suggested that the PLA was so deeply split that units controlled by the rival factions came close to fighting each other. In the end, most of the leading PLA officers came down on the side of the hard-liners.

The PLA is important because it has an independent power base of its own. It is far less subject to control through the normal mechanisms of party oversight than was the case for the old Soviet army. And it has had a tremendous vested interest in the future of economic reform because it runs dozens of enterprises, some of which have been converted from military to consumer-oriented production and some of which have been accused of using what amounts to slave or sweatshop labor.

Public Policy: Perestroika without Glasnost

Since the late 1970s, the CCP has followed a political and economic strategy that is almost exactly the opposite of the one we saw in Gorbachev's Soviet Union. There the CPSU loosened political controls but dithered when it came to economic reforms. The combination of political liberalization and frustration with the accelerating economic decline opened the political floodgates that destroyed the USSR.

Ever since Deng solidified his hold on power, the CCP did the opposite. As we have just seen, there have

DENG XIAOPING

Bettmann/CORBIS

Deng Xiaoping in 1985—as usual, smoking a cigarette.

Like Zhou Enlai, Deng was born into an elite family and spent his youth studying the Confucian classics. In 1920, at the age of sixteen, he went on a work-study program to Paris, where, among other things, he joined the European branch of the CCP that Zhou had formed, worked in a factory, and developed a life-long love of croissants. Later in the 1920s, he again studied in Paris.

On his return to China, he joined Mao in his effort to organize in the countryside and took part in the Long March. He became a leading military figure within the CCP, and by the 1940s was political commissar of the PLA.

After the CCP came to power, he held a number of positions in the party hierarchy and gradually cast his lot with Liu Shaoqi and others seeking a more pragmatic approach to economic policy. For this he was purged during the Cultural Revolution and, again, following Mao's death.

He returned to office for a third time in 1978 and guided Chinese political life until his death. He actually never officially held a high position (he was never more than vice premier of China and vice president of the Chinese Bridge Club), but like many of his generation, he exercised power from behind the scenes. He resigned from his last government position in 1989, made his last tour of the country in 1992, and died from Parkinson's disease in 1997.

been no significant openings of the political system. However, economic policy has changed so much that it is difficult to speak of China as a socialist state.

Economic Reform

The economy is the centerpiece of any socialist country's public policy. Concern about inequality sparked support for socialism in the first place, and socialist policymakers of all stripes have accorded the state a more central role in economic management than we find in the capitalist societies with the strongest *dirigiste* (managed economy) traditions.

In China today, we also have to focus on the economy, because Deng and his colleagues led the country away from socialist principles, albeit always rationalizing their actions in the name of socialism. In so doing, they presided over one of the most dramatic periods of growth in world history, which some analysts believe will make China one of the world's leading economic powers in the near future.

When Mao died, China's economy was not in good

shape, though it was doing better than might have been expected given the political turmoil of the Cultural Revolution. Industrial production had grown by an average of 9 percent per year from 1957 to 1976, and most factories were not targeted during the upheaval. During normal times, no one starved, and everyone had access to at least elementary education and rudimentary health care.

There were signs, however, that China would soon face many of the same problems the Soviet Union did during the Brezhnev years—a shortage of investment in everything but heavy industry, a slow rate of technological innovation, an emphasis on the quantity rather than the quality of production, the inability to respond to consumer preferences, supply bottlenecks, irrational prices, and insufficient food production. China had poor communication and transportation networks. The shortage of trained managers had been worsened by the Maoist policy of recruiting cadres on the basis of class background and ideological stance rather than professional qualifications.

Most importantly, China remained one of the world's poorest countries and had made only minor steps toward improving the living conditions of its people. The problems were, if anything, worse in China than in most other poor countries. Mao had all but completely closed off the country, limiting foreign trade to the single city of Guangdong (Canton). No foreign aid or loans were accepted.

The first signs of change came in 1972, when Zhou Enlai announced that China would pursue the four modernizations. It would be another six years before the leftists would finally be defeated and Deng Xiaoping would solidify his hold on power.

Since then, the CCP has enacted a series of sweeping reforms guided by three very non-Marxist principles:

- Private property can play a useful role in a socialist economy.

- Market forces should be used to allocate goods and services and to determine prices.

- Material incentives, including higher wages, personal profit, and the accumulation of wealth, should be the main way to boost productivity and efficiency.

Some Western observers have read too much into the specific reforms to be discussed shortly. The CCP has not come close to fully endorsing capitalism and has yet to introduce reforms in the entire economy. Instead, as implied by the statement that begins the chapter, the party has, above all else, been pragmatic in two ways. First, it has been reluctant to go too far, too fast. Whenever reforms threatened to do so, the party slowed things down most recently by raising interest rates in October 2004. Second, it has avoided reforms that would be likely to threaten its hold on power. Thus, as we will see, it has barely begun restructuring the massive state-owned industries that still employ two-thirds of the urban workforce because doing so could unleash massive protests.

In other words, both for its own sake and for that of overseas investors, the CCP has sought to create a climate of stability. And, so far, it has been quite successful in this. (See table 10.4.)

▌ TABLE 10.4 Economic Growth in China: Annual Rates of Change (percentage)

SECTOR	1980–1990	1990–1999
Gross domestic product	10.2	10.7
Agriculture	5.9	4.3
Industry	11.1	14.4
Services	13.6	9.2
Exports	11.5	12.2

Source: *World Bank, World Development Report, 1998, 1999, 2000,* www.worldbank.org, accessed 28 Oct. 2001

HIV/AIDS in China

China was not a country that responded early and constructively to HIV/AIDS. When the epidemic first broke out in the 1980s, the Chinese authorities did little because the disease was widely viewed as one that affected gay men, and the CCP did not even acknowledge that homosexuality existed in their country.

In the last decade, the situation has changed appreciably. In 1994, the number of reported HIV cases per year topped 1,000 for the first time. By the end of the decade, it had reached 8,000 per year, and today it hovers around 10,000. Of course, there are still many cases that go unreported. The infection rate rose for two main reasons—an unsafe, often tainted blood supply and the expansion of the sex trade into cities and regions with large numbers of foreign workers and visitors. The Chinese authorities also had to come to grips with HIV/AIDS as a result of its inability to effectively handle the 2004 SARS outbreak, which showed them just how quickly diseases can spread today.

By 2004, the government had allocated close to $100 million for HIV/AIDS prevention and treatment. Despite that increase in funding, the programs will have a limited impact because the country's public health infrastructure is so weak.

Agriculture

Though it receives the least attention today, the first (and arguably most important) reforms came in agriculture. During the 1980s, the Maoist-era communes were dismantled and replaced by the household responsibility system. The party divided collective farms into small plots, which were worked by families that, for all practical purposes, owned their land. The state also reduced the amount farmers had to sell to it and allowed the market to determine almost all agricultural prices.

The agricultural reforms proved highly popular and successful. Production increased by more than 10 percent per year during the 1980s. Some former peasants are now extremely well off, especially those who live in areas in which they can readily sell their produce in the burgeoning urban markets. Overall, the gap between urban and rural standards of living has been cut by about 30 percent.

Private Enterprise

Even more dramatic has been the development of private businesses, some owned by the Chinese themselves and others primarily owned by foreign investors. Indeed, it is the growth of this sector that has led observers to claim that China will soon become one of the world's major economic powers.

The reforms started slowly, and the regime moved gradually until it was clear that private enterprise would contribute to its broader goal of modernization. As in the former Soviet Union, privately owned enterprises started out as small, service-oriented firms mostly in the retail trades. Until the late 1980s they accounted for less than 1 percent of industrial output. Today their earnings are greater than those of the state-owned enterprises.

Since then, however, the private sector has begun to boom. The original legislation restricted private firms to eight employees, a figure that has never been seriously enforced. In 1988, the National People's Congress officially created a new category of "private business" to regulate the somewhat larger firms outside the state sector.

In 1980 there were only 1,500 entrepreneurial firms in all of China; a decade later there were about 400,000. Urban co-ops, service organizations, and rural industries together employ about two-thirds of all nonagricultural laborers. Privately owned village industries alone employ at least one hundred million people, more than the entire public sector. Most importantly, the private firms are far more dynamic and profitable than the state-owned ones, and thus attract the attention of the reformers, who are, above all else, interested in maximizing the rate of economic growth.

In some areas, opening things up to private industry has led to dramatic improvements in the way people live. In late May 1992, the *Washington Post* reported on the village of Lanchang near Hong Kong and its entrepreneurial leader, Chen Hai, who at age fifty-six had taught himself to read and write. Then, when the opportunity presented itself, he opened a factory that makes tin cans. Chen became tremendously wealthy and began driving a Mercedes around town. The 250 people who worked for him were each making about $5,000 a year, or more than sixteen times the national average.

There was some concern that the hard-liners would slow the pace of economic reform in the wake of the events in Tiananmen Square in 1989. By mid-1992, however, it had become increasingly clear that Deng Xiaoping was throwing his lot in with the reformers. That summer, after visiting a steel factory, he complained that the party had not adequately responded to calls for more rapid economic change. Local officials seized the opportunity, and even horse-racing tracks were privatized. More importantly, private enterprises increasingly provide the high-quality goods that China needs if it wants to sell widely in the global market.

The key to the initial success of the reforms—and a guide to its cautious nature—is the way the leadership opened the economy to foreign investment. Even before Mao's death, the autarkic policies were eased. Foreign aid and investment came to be seen as ways of speeding up modernization. To facilitate—and control—foreign entry into the Chinese market, four **Special Economic Zones (SEZs)** were created in 1979. In these regions, foreign investors were given preferential tax rates and other incentives. Five years later, Hainan Island and fourteen more cities became SEZs as well. By the mid-1990s, market mechanisms and foreign investment had spread to most of urban China, blurring the distinction between the SEZs and the rest of the country.

Joint ventures have been established in dozens of industries and have turned China into a leading exporter of textiles and other low-tech products. It has also made some, albeit more limited, progress in developing high-tech goods, including rockets for launching satellites.

Typical of the new breed of private companies is Huawei Technologies based in Shenzen, one of the original SEZs. The company was founded in 1988 by a former sergeant in the PLA. At the time, it merely sold telephone equipment made in Hong Kong. Today, it makes world-class computer routers and telecommunications switches and competes effectively with global giants, Cisco, Siemens, and Alcatel. It employs twenty-two thousand people, and its 2004 sales were expected to top $5 billion, almost half of it coming from overseas.

By contrast, the state-owned enterprises (SOEs) have lagged behind. Most have been monopolies and models of inefficiency. However, in the late 1990s the authorities began to issue new rules requiring the SOEs to operate more under market conditions, which streamlined some of their operations. This trend toward increased efficiency will continue as China phases in World Trade Organization regulations. The one thing that does not seem to be on the agenda is the wholesale privatization of the SOEs. In October 2001, the government announced that it planned to sell about $3 billion worth of stock in them, but this amounts to only a tiny fraction of the still-nationalized sector of the economy.

The fallout from Tiananmen Square never extended to foreign investors. Investment grew steadily—from about $5 billion in 1987 to $27 billion in 1993 to $60 billion in 1999. Over half of it came from Hong Kong, Macao, and other overseas Chinese communities. Taiwan, which is still officially at war with the mainland, accounts for about 10 percent of the investment, as does South Korea, which has also had a hostile political relationship with the PRC.

Altogether, the reforms have sparked one of the longest periods of rapid economic growth in history.

From 1980 to 1999, GNP quadrupled, although the rate of growth slowed somewhat to "only" 7.2 percent in 1999. In 2004, it was back up to almost 10 percent.

On a more tangible and personal level, most people eat better because better-quality food is available, often at lower prices than before the reforms. Some eighty million peasants have been able to leave the land and take more lucrative jobs in new rural enterprises. The urban standard of living has not improved as much, but most city dwellers still are noticeably better off than they were before Mao's death.

The reforms have also led to some problems that seem likely to pose political as well as economic difficulties in the future. Unofficial estimates put the unemployment rate at close to 20 percent in the cities, and that figure is almost certain to rise when and if the market reforms are extended to heavy industry. There are now tremendous regional inequalities, given that four-fifths of foreign investment has gone to the coastal provinces. There are class disparities as well. Millions of peasant and merchant families have become amazingly rich by Chinese standards. However, the 40 percent of the population on fixed incomes saw their income drop precipitously for most of the late 1980s and early 1990s until inflation was brought under control.

Moreover, it is commonly believed that only the *guanxi* (people with connections) benefit to any significant degree from the reforms. Such beliefs cannot be supported by hard evidence, though the frequent anecdotal reports about official corruption suggest that they contain more than a grain of truth.

In any case, the very success of the reforms is worsening China's already fragile environment. Even its successful population control program is waning; the birth rate has already risen 0.2 percent since the 1980s, which will add another fifteen million people each year. Increased agricultural production and industrialization have cost the country more than a million acres of arable land a year. Peasants who are trying to maximize their income have turned to cash crops such as tobacco instead of following their traditional rotation practices, which replenished the soil with needed nutrients.

And despite all the reforms, China remains a desperately poor country. In all it accounts for only 5 percent of the world's output of goods and services despite having 23 percent of its population. A typical worker makes barely more than his or her Indian counterpart and only one-tenth that of someone in Taiwan. Put in other terms, the average Chinese factory worker annually earns only half the cost of a color television or one-sixtieth that of a Jeep produced there.

Finally, some observers are not convinced that it is

Liberalization in China

WESTERN JOURNALISTS often hold China up as an example of how helpful it can be to shift to a market economy. Although such benefits are easy to see, we should also point out that China has not made the transition from a planned to an open economy as quickly or as fully as many of the Eastern European countries. There has been no shock therapy, and Western economic theorists have had little or no influence on Chinese decisionmakers.

Rather, the leadership has shifted toward a market economy in a series of gradual and measured moves. Some of the steps—for example, the family responsibility system in agriculture, the first privately owned "cooperatives" in the service sector, and the creation of the original SEZs—were risky. But none is likely to prove riskier than the one the leadership is still resisting—privatizing the "commanding heights" of the economy, most of which are still state-owned.

truly or fully becoming an economic giant. Companies like Huawei aside, most Chinese firms still rely on imported technology. More than half of the country's exports are sold by foreign-dominated firms. Given China's rigid and hierarchical political system, it has been hard for firms to expand beyond a regional basis.

Foreign Policy

Chinese foreign policy has also undergone profound changes that have brought the country closer to the international mainstream. As in domestic policy, there have been significant exceptions to this trend, such as the military exercises China engaged in that seemed to threaten Taiwan in early 1996 and the protracted dispute with Washington after a U.S. spy plane was shot down over Hainan Island in 2001. And the Chinese government still resists international pressure to improve its human rights record. Nonetheless, on balance, China has integrated itself into the world diplomatic and, especially, economic communities in ways no one could have realistically imagined as recently as the early 1970s.

For most of the time Mao Zedong was in power, the PRC pursued the kind of foreign policy Marxist theory would lead us to expect of a Communist country that saw itself as one of the leaders of the world revolutionary movement. At least rhetorically, the PRC supported third world militants who fought against the vestiges of colonialism. China was one of the founders of the nonaligned movement and championed national liberation struggles that sought independence from their colonizers throughout the third world. Despite its own limited resources, the PRC provided substantial development assistance to a handful of the most radical of the new third world states. China also was the first less developed country to deploy nuclear weapons, and it consistently has been a major supplier of arms, especially in the Middle East.

Not surprisingly, the PRC consistently attacked the United States and other capitalist powers for trying to maintain their political and economic hold on the third world even after those nations achieved independence. Given its role in Korea, Vietnam, and elsewhere, and its failure to recognize the PRC, the United States was a frequent target of Chinese criticisms. Most of the time, this conflict was purely rhetorical. Only in 1958 did the two countries come even close to war, during the dispute over Quemoy and Matsu, two tiny islands in the Taiwan Straits.

The Chinese reserved their harshest attacks for their supposed ally, the Soviet Union. The relationship between the world's two largest Communist countries had never been smooth. After World War II, the Soviets supplied the CCP with only minimal aid—far less in value than the resources they took from northern China as the war was ending.

The rivalry came to the fore in the late 1950s when the Chinese decided that the Soviets had turned their backs on Marx and revolution. Tensions between the two reached a peak in 1969 when the rhetorical battles escalated into skirmishes along their border. Sino-Soviet relations remained highly strained until the collapse of the USSR.

Under Mao, Chinese foreign policy could best be described as autarkic for two main reasons. First, the Chinese assumed that they would continue to face a hostile world and would not be able to get significant help from the outside. Second, the Maoist model provided an alternative approach to development. If the party was able to mobilize the masses, China could modernize using its own resources.

By the 1970s, both of those assumptions had been proven false, something best seen in China's relations with the United States. The Cultural Revolution taught the leadership something it probably should have learned from the Great Leap Forward: Mass mobilization and commitment to socialism were not the way to industrialize the country. Also, geopolitical realities had changed. In particular, President Richard Nixon and Secretary of State Henry Kissinger were willing to overlook ideological differences if they could forge alliances that advanced what they took to be America's national interest. China, in short, presented such an opportunity because of its hostility toward the Soviets.

Signs that things might improve began to appear in the early 1970s. A young American graduate student, John Strong, was allowed into the country to claim the body of his recently deceased aunt, Anna Louise Strong, who had spent most of the period since the 1930s in China as a "friend" of the revolution. In 1972, an American table tennis team played in China, lending its name to what soon came to be called "Ping Pong diplomacy." Later that year, Kissinger made a secret trip into China while visiting Pakistan. At that meeting, he, Zhou, and perhaps Mao reached a quick agreement that the two countries could and should reestablish relations. Before the year was out, President Nixon had visited China and, virtually overnight, two of the world's worst enemies became practically the closest of friends.

Relations between the two countries continued to improve. The United States reversed its long-standing opposition to PRC membership in the United Nations. Formal diplomatic relations were resumed during the Carter administration. Currently, no non-Asian country has more invested in China than the United States, and only Japan has more extensive bilateral trade.

Relations between China and the United States have not been perfect. U.S. leaders have been highly critical of China's human rights record. Critics were most vocal in the aftermath of the Tiananmen Square clampdown, but the rhetorical decibel levels have risen almost any time Washington had to make a decision regarding trade or other relations with China.

However, there have been recent signs that Chinese-American relations could improve. To begin with, entry into the WTO will force China to open its markets more for outside investment, including from the United States. What's more, the decision to grant Beijing the 2008 Olympics will bring pressure to open its political and social systems. If this happens, it should satisfy some of Beijing's critics in Washington. Finally, the events of September 11 drew the two countries somewhat closer together because of the Chinese concern that al-Qaeda and other militants were training potential terrorists among China's Muslim minority groups.

It is not simply Chinese-American relations that have normalized since the end of the Cultural Revolution. China has successfully negotiated the return of Hong Kong from Britain and improved relations with most of its neighbors. Given the size of its army and the sophistication of its weapons, China is certain to remain a regional, if not a global, military power. And if China is able to permanently overcome the regional economic crisis that started in 1997 and to continue anything like its current rate of growth, it will become a global economic force as well.

Indeed, China is now so deeply integrated into the global economy that it is hard to imagine how it could isolate itself again. What's more, as we have seen at numerous points in this chapter, this involvement is fraught with implications for Chinese domestic politics. Millions of people have been drawn to Western values and living conditions as a result of their own travel abroad, their contacts with foreigners visiting China, or, most commonly, their exposure to Western media.

Feedback

There is probably no better indicator of the limits to liberalization in China than the regime's continued control of the mass media, which are the primary ways people learn about political events. As in the Soviet Union before Gorbachev came to power, the party determines who is on the air, what is written in the newspapers, and so on. Some journalists did speak their minds in the weeks before the 1989 crackdown in Tiananmen Square, but they all subsequently lost their jobs. As noted earlier in the chapter, a few independent journals have been able to publish for brief periods, but their circulation was always extremely small.

The best evidence that the CCP is trying to hold onto these levers of power lies in its policies regarding information technology. In 1989, students used fax machines to keep in touch with each other and with their colleagues studying in the West. Since then, people have tried to feed information into China via the Internet and satellite TV. Until recently, however, the regime has been remarkably successful at blocking access to foreign-based political websites, and private citizens are technically not allowed to own satellite dishes. As recently as 2002, an Internet service provider was convicted for piping political news into the country via e-mail, which is not susceptible to the filtering technology that keeps people from accessing websites. But change is afoot, most notably in a deal announced in October 2001 that grants AOL–Time Warner the first franchise for a foreign company to operate a cable system in the country. One recent report also suggested that most of the eighty million Internet users have found ways to circumvent the blocks that supposedly keep them away from foreign sites.

Globalization in China

CHINA IS OFTEN held up as the political "poster child" for globalization.

No other country has moved so strongly or so quickly onto the global economic stage. Its foreign trade has increased at a faster rate than the economy as a whole, which itself is growing extremely rapidly. Some argue that China will become one of the world's economic giants long before the middle of this century.

It's not just the economy. About a million Chinese have studied at Western universities and returned. Western pop culture can be found in all cities—often in bootleg versions. Some Chinese films have become cult hits in the West.

But it must be recalled that only a small portion of the Chinese population is part of this immersion in global markets and culture. And the regime still tightly restricts access to political information and opinions coming from the outside.

Conclusion: Kadan or Communism?

The dramatic changes that have swept through the Communist world since 1989 have abundantly demonstrated that political scientists are not very good at predicting concrete events. This does not mean, however, that we cannot at least anticipate broad future trends.

In this sense, China provides us with a good illustration of the reasons most Marxist-Leninist regimes collapsed and the few remaining ones face uncertain futures. The pressures from an ever more sophisticated and impatient population, and these countries' increasing inclusion in global economic and cultural life, weakened all Communist states. Some, like the Soviet Union, collapsed in part because the CPSU proved unwilling or unable to apply enough force to stay in power. In China, however, repression has helped keep the CCP in power, at least for now.

But the genie probably cannot be kept in the bottle forever. The Tiananmen Square crackdown in 1989 showed that desperate leaders can still suppress dissident movements, even ones with widespread mass and elite support. Nevertheless, it seems highly unlikely that such movements can be suppressed indefinitely. In part, this reflects the social changes that are leading to a more educated, sophisticated, and ultimately demanding population. Even more, it reflects one of the most important lessons to be learned from the experiences of either China or Poland during the 1980s. Despite the harsh repression by the elites, reform movements reappeared in both countries. Each time the movement grew stronger until, in the Polish case, Solidarity was able to defeat the Communist Party altogether even as Chinese tanks were rumbling into Tiananmen Square.

The "thumbs" of the command economies in the few remaining Communist countries are also imperiled. Again, we do not know precisely what their economic future holds. No one knows if socialist goals of equality, justice, and dignity can be attained using a market-based economy. No one knows either how far Communist elites are willing to go in sacrificing their political and economic power in exchange for economic growth. All we can conclude—and it is a very important conclusion—is that they will have to move away from "thumbs" and toward "fingers," a move that will have political as well as economic repercussions throughout these societies.

As with protest from below, the obsolescence of command economies has two sources. First, domestic changes have eroded all the ways in which central planning worked in the earlier stages of development. Second, and in the long run more important, the global economy has had an inescapable impact on these systems. For good or ill, as long as they retain centralized planning, the Communist regimes are simply not going to be competitive in the world marketplace.

Again, Communist regimes such as the one in China may hang on. But if they do, they will have to be very different from the powerful ones that hostile analysts once called totalitarian. We could continue to examine more statistics and other "hard" evidence that illustrate these points. However, in closing, it might make more sense to consider three news stories about China from the mid-1990s.

The first is a 1995 report on two illegal fads. It seems that dogs have become a big status symbol in Beijing ("puppies for yuppies," the *Economist* calls it). A pedigreed dog can cost as much as $4,500, even though dog ownership is technically illegal. Dogs and their wealthy owners are so "in" that there are reports of poor people being turned away from (human) hospitals while medical doctors treated dogs whose "parents" were paying customers. Satellite dishes are banned, too. But this does not keep hundreds of thousands of people from buying them. There is no sign that people get them primarily to watch CNN or the BBC's World Service. Rather, the World Cup and MTV seem to be far more popular. But as was the case in Eastern Europe, entertainment can be just as subversive as hard news.

Second, paradoxically, is a spontaneous, popular cult of personality for the late Chairman Mao. Bus and cab drivers place portraits of the chairman on their dashboards. Mao pins from the Cultural Revolution have become collectors' items. Drunken middle-aged men sing disco versions of old political songs in karaoke bars. Artists and entrepreneurs are raking in profits from the brisk Mao portrait sales.

Drivers put up the portraits because they are convinced that doing so protects them from accidents. One taxi driver said that Mao was like a god to him and likened the former leader's picture to the statue of the Buddha he had in his home. Although it may seem peculiar to see drunken businessmen singing Maoist songs in Western-style bars, it certainly does not augur well for a return to either Marxism or Maoism. If these were the values of China's citizens in the 1990s, it seems hard to imagine how the country could be forced back into the austerity of Mao suits and Maoist politics.

Finally, consider the Kadan (the closest Chinese equivalent of Cardin) Model Training School. Apparently, the school has a long waiting list of young people willing to pay the princely sum of $42 a semester to strive for a new version of the Chinese dream—wealth and fame. Such private training schools that teach everything from modeling to accounting to foreign languages have sprung up around the country to meet the demands of a growing generation of young people who are aware of the outside world and want to be a part of it. The modeling schools, of course, have a unique Chinese twist. Both men and women stagger around trying to learn how to walk in high heels. Still, all the aspiring models share a common goal that one male student expressed well: "I came because I have a dream. I love this. I would love to travel around the world and be the best model of the century."[10]

Key Terms

Concepts

Cadre	Faction
Campaign	Four modernizations
Capitalist roader	Mass line
Confucianism	*Nomenklatura*
Cult of personality	Unit
Democratic centralism	Warlord
Extraterritoriality	

---

[10] James Steingold, "China in High Heels: A Wobbly School for Models," *New York Times*, 8 August 1990, A5.

People

Chen Duxiu	Jiang Qing	Sun Yat-sen
Chiang Kai-shek	Jiang Zemin	Wei Jingsheng
Deng Xiaoping	Lin Biao	Wen Jiabao
Fang Lizhi	Liu Shaoqi	Zhou Enlai
Hu Jintao	Mao Zedong	

Acronyms

CAC	KMT	PRC
CCP	PLA	SEZ
CMC		

Organizations, Places, and Events

Central Advisory Committee	Kuomintang
Central Committee	Long March
Central Military Commission	May Fourth Movement
	Nationalist Party
Chinese Communist Party	People's Liberation Army
Cultural Revolution	People's Republic of China
Democracy Movement	Politburo
Democracy Wall	Red Guard
Falun Gong	Red versus expert
Gang of Four	Sino-Soviet split
Great Leap Forward	Special Economic Zone
Hundred Flowers Campaign	Standing Committee
	Tiananmen Square

Critical Thinking Exercises

1. Much has changed since this book was finished in early 2005. Does the analysis of Chinese politics presented here still make sense? Why (not)?

2. Public opinion pollsters routinely ask questions about whether people think their country is heading in the "right direction" or is on the "wrong track." If you were asked such a question about China, how would you answer? Why did you reach this conclusion?

3. How did Maoism and the Chinese revolution differ from Marxist thought and from Leninism and the Soviet revolution? What difference did this make for the evolution of the PRC?

4. Mao once claimed that the Chinese people were a "blank slate" whose political culture could easily be remade. Did he and his colleagues succeed in doing so? Why (not)?

5. The CCP dominates political participation in China. Why is this the case? Can the party survive?

6. The PRC is the last major country left that relies on democratic centralism and the Bolshevik model of a Communist party. What are the pressures on the CCP to change? Do you expect it to follow the example of the former Soviet Union and collapse? Why (not)?

7. China has reformed its economy but not its political system—perestroika without glasnost. Has it worked better than reform in the former Soviet Union? Why (not)?

Useful Websites

The Internet itself in China is controversial, because the Chinese authorities have tried to block access to overseas sites that carry material critical of the PRC. That is becoming increasingly difficult as the number of regular Internet users approaches 10 percent of the adult population and enterprising web surfers find ways to get around the firewalls the CCP's censors create.

The government itself has created a portal with links to state agencies that have English language sites, which was about half of them in early 2005.

www.china.org.cn/english

There are also a number of non-Chinese portals that include daily feeds from the Chinese and foreign press. The two best of them is the Canadian-based China Today and Asia Source, which is produced by the American Asia Society.

www.chinatoday.com

www.asiasource.org

There are also may universities and think tanks that maintain good resources on Chinese politics and society, including links to other good sites. The University of Heidelberg in Germany continues to operate the Virtual Library site on China. London's Royal Society for International Affairs (informally known as Chatham House) not only has links but reports emanating from its highly respected China project. Finally, Professor William Joseph of Wellesley College has one of the largest and most frequently updated sites on China.

sun.sino.uni-heidelberg.de/igcs

www.chathamhouse.org.uk/index.php?id=272

www.wellesley.edu/Polisci/wj/China/chinalinks .html

Finally, there are some far more specialized sites. The China Leadership Monitor publishes regular reports and updates on the country's leaders. Chinese military power does the same for national security issues.

www.chinaleadershipmonitor.org

www.comw.org/cmp

 *InfoTrac College Edition Sources*

Chandler, Clay. "Inside the New China."

Economy, Elizabeth. "Don't Break the Engagement."

Fewsmith, Joseph. "The Politics of China's Accession to the WTO."

Gilboy, George. "The Myth Behind China's Miracle."

Madsen, Richard. "Understanding Falun Gong."

Moore, Rebecca. "China's Fledgling Civil Society."

Nathan, Andrew J. "The Tiananmen Papers."

Williams, Harry. "Socialism and the End of the Perpetual Reform State in China."

Zweig, David. "China's Stalled Fifth Wave."

Further Reading

Blecher, Marc. *China against the Tides: Restructuring through Revolution, Radicalism, and Reform.* London: Pinter, 1997. The best recent overview of Chinese politics since the revolution, written by one of the few scholars who is still even somewhat sympathetic to socialism and Mao Zedong.

Feinberg, Richard E., John Echeverri-Gent, and Friedemann Müller. *Economic Reform in Three Giants.* Washington, D.C.: Overseas Development Council, World Policy Perspectives, No. 14, 1990. An overview of economic reform in the former Soviet Union, plus China and India. There are better books on the Chinese economy, but this is the only good one that puts it in comparative perspective with other countries considered in this book.

Gilley, Brian. *Tiger on the Brink: Jiang Zemin and China's New Elite.* Berkeley: University of California Press, 1998. A biography of the former Chinese leader; also a first-rate analysis of Chinese politics in the post-Deng era.

Harding, Harry. *China's Second Revolution: Reform after Mao.* Washington, D.C.: Brookings Institution, 1988. The best overview of the economic reforms and the reasons the party adopted them, although dated in places.

Lampton, David. *Same Bed Different Dreams: Managing U.S.-China Relations 1989–2000.* Berkeley: University of California Press, 2001. Although focused on foreign policy, a valuable resource on Chinese domestic politics as well.

Liang Zheng, Andrew Nathan, Perry Link, and Orville Schell, eds. *The Tiananmen Square Papers: The Chinese Leadership's Decision to Use Force against Their Own People—In Their Own Words.* New York: Public Affairs, 2001.

Lieberthal, Kenneth. *Governing China: From Revolution through Reform.* New York: Norton, 1995. A comprehensive overview of Chinese politics that is especially good at illuminating the informal power relations that may well be more important than the formal rules and procedures.

Lifton, Robert Jay. *Revolutionary Immortality: Mao Tse-tung and the Chinese Cultural Revolution.* New York: Norton, 1976. A biography of Mao by this generation's leading psychological analyst of political affairs.

Nathan, Andrew. *China's Transition.* New York: Columbia University Press, 1997. Mostly a collection of essays by an American academic who has long criticized the CCP for its human rights record. Unlike Blecher's book, it is quite hostile to the Beijing regime.

Nolan, Peter. *China's Rise, Russia's Fall: Politics, Economics and Planning in the Transition from Socialism.* Basingstoke, U.K.: Macmillan, 1995. A first-rate comparison of Chinese and Russian reform that emphasizes the gradualism, pragmatism, and stability of the former.

Saich, Tony. *Governance in China.* London: Palgrave, 2004. The best new overview of Chinese politics, including many of the author's personal experiences over the last thirty years.

Schell, Orville. *Mandate of Heaven.* New York: Simon & Schuster, 1994. This author is one of the best American journalists working on China. As with most of Schell's work, this is especially good on issues involving the economy and human rights.

Snow, Edgar. *Red Star over China.* New York: Random House, 1938. The best account of the early years of the revolution, written by an American who spent much of that period with the CCP and Mao.

Terrill, Ross. *China in Our Times.* New York: Simon & Schuster, 1992. An overview of Communist Chinese history that also shows how one observer's views of the country changed along with its politics.

Exploring
EXPLORING THE WORLD WIDE WEB

Studying the current and former communist regimes requires the most straightforward comparative analyses in this book, which you can do in some depth with the material on the website. First, you need to see how the communist regimes (past and present) differed from the other main types of states discussed in parts 2 and 4. Second, you have to compare China and the few other remaining communist countries with those that abandoned Marxism-Leninism after 1989.

For part 3, it makes sense to start with the MicroCase example, which is described on the website. You can examine the ways in which these countries differ from the liberal democracies and third world societies politically, socially, and economically. In general, you will see that they occupy a middle position—not as democratic, wealthy, or calm as the established democracies, but facing far less trouble than many third world countries on all of those indicators. In considering the differences among the current and former communist countries, you will see that their post-1989 experiences have all been difficult. Most saw their economies shrink during the 1990s, and many of them experienced ethnic strife. However, you will also see that their political experiences have not by any stretch of the imagination been the same. For instance, they have very different types of political regimes today.

The text recommends quite a few general articles on Marxism from InfoTrac College Edition. One of the most useful is Benjamin Barber's "An Epitaph for Marxism," which he wrote in 1995. In it, he tries to make the case that social democracy, if not Marxism itself, remains a viable ideological option in most societies. Do you agree? Why (not) given what have you learned about Russia, China, and Marxist theory?

Finally, the website has the constitutions of the People's Republic of China and the former Soviet Union. Even a casual reading of them will show you how little they tell us about how political life is/was played out in these countries. Given what you learned in part 3, why are the constitutions such poor guides to day-to-day political events?

Part 4

THE THIRD WORLD

Decisions made in Washington are more important to us than those made here in Dar es-Salaam. So, maybe my people should be allowed to vote in American presidential elections.

JULIUS NYERERE,
FORMER PRESIDENT, TANZANIA

Chapter 11

THE THIRD WORLD

CHAPTER OUTLINE

The Basics: Contrasts between the Richest and Poorest Countries

	LIFE EXPECTANCY (YEARS)	ADULT LITERACY (PERCENTAGE)	GROSS DOMESTIC PRODUCT PER CAPITA (PPP)	HDI SCORE[a]
Poorest	59.1	63.6	2,349	0.557
Richest	77.4	97.0[b]	28,741	0.94

[a] HDI (Human Development Index) is a statistical measure converting the information from the first three columns in the table to ranges from 0 (least developed) to 1 (most developed).

[b] This figure is from the 1999 report, which is the most recent one to have included that information. Presumably the adult literacy rate is even higher today.

Source: United Nations Development Program, *Human Development Report: 2004.* www.undp.org/hdro.

Coltan and Politics

On 12 August 2001, the *New York Times Magazine* included a seemingly minor story about coltan mining in a game reserve in the eastern region of the Democratic Republic of Congo (DRC) (www.nytimes .com/2001/08/12/magazine/12COLTAN.html?ex=99888 8435&ei1).[1]

Coltan contains tantalite, a heavy metal used to make a powder that is a critical component of such high-tech devices as cell phones, PDAs, and video game players. Mining coltan is not difficult. People pick away at streambeds and sift the muck they dig up in washtubs until the coltan settles to the bottom. At the height of the coltan market, the price soared from $30 to $400 per pound. Miners could make as much as $80 per day—in a country in which most people have to survive on less than $1 per day.

But coltan mining is a mixed blessing. It is technically illegal in that part of the DRC because it does tremendous damage to the ecosystem of the Opkapi Faunal Reserve and the Kahuzi-Biega National Park. The elephant population has been wiped out, and the number of gorillas has been cut in half. Several other species that

---

[1] Blaine Harden, "The Dirt in the New Machine." *New York Times Magazine,* 12 August 2001, 35–39.

can only be found in this region are in danger of extinction. The mining has given rise, as well, to camps in which unscrupulous merchants provide provisions and prostitutes, both at outrageous prices.

To make matters worse, the downturn in the global high-tech economy in 2000 and 2001 dramatically reduced demand for coltan and cut the price miners received by 90 percent. Thus ended the new-found wealth of several thousand families, all of whom returned to the abject poverty they had experienced before the market peaked.

Most importantly, profits from the mining contributed to the civil war that pitted rebels in the east against a national government based well over a thousand miles away in Kinshasa. In all, 2.5 million people have died since the fighting began in 1998, though not all of those deaths can be attributed to the issues surrounding coltan. At the height of the war and of the coltan market, exporters paid rebel authorities a $15,000 fee and 11 percent of their income in "taxes." The Rwandan army, which supports the rebels, made an estimated $250 million from its participation in the coltan trade. At the time the *New York Times Magazine* article appeared, a cease-fire had been in place for over a year, but the government had no real authority in the eastern region, and the combatants had made little progress toward a lasting peace.

Coltan is obviously not as important as many of the issues used to begin chapters in this book. Nonetheless, in a few brief pages, Blaine Harden identified five of the most important issues facing the **third world** today, all of which we will return to in the rest of this chapter and in the five country studies that follow.

The first issue is poverty. The table on the inside front cover provides bone-chilling statistics. Over a billion people—one-fifth of humanity—live in utter poverty in countries where the average person makes no more than a dollar a day. In the West, we take safe drinking water, indoor plumbing, a nutritious diet, and adequate health care for granted. But they are all very much the exception to the rule in the third world. What's more, for Africa at least, the gap between the rich Northern Hemisphere ("north") and the poor Southern Hemisphere ("south") is actually widening. Note that for the purposes of this discussion, I will refer to the developed, Western nations as "north" and the underdeveloped nations as "south." This is common terminology in political science, although it is not completely accurate. Australia and New Zealand are in the Southern Hemisphere, but are not considered underdeveloped, and China and India, which are underdeveloped, are located in the Northern Hemisphere.

The second issue is globalization. Neither the people

of the eastern DRC nor the Congolese government are masters of their own destiny. Indeed, in Part 4 we will see just how important the impact of the global forces alluded to in this book's subtitle are.

Most third world countries spent an extended period of time as colonies, which destroyed much of their preexisting social, economic, political, and cultural life. Like most African countries, the DRC gained its independence in the 1960s, but the influence of the north did not end. The United States helped plan the assassination of its first president, Patrice Lumumba, and then supported his corrupt and dictatorial successor, Mobutu Sese Seko, who ruled for more than thirty years. And, as the coltan example suggests, northern multinational corporations (MNCs) and financial institutions still have a tremendous impact on the local economy—if nothing else, by determining the prices paid for the raw materials most third world countries export.

The third issue is the existence of weak states. Many of the poorest third world countries have what northern analysts call **failed states,** because the national government cannot maintain law and order or provide basic services throughout the country. In the DRC, the national government has little or no presence in the east. There aren't any roads that allow people to travel across the country, and there is not a single radio or television station that can be heard everywhere. Not every third world country has a failed state by any stretch of the imagination. However, with very few exceptions, the third world countries are far weaker than those covered in either Part 2 or Part 3.

The fourth issue is ethnicity. The fighting that has taken such a heavy toll on the DRC and so many other countries has several causes. High on any list is the divisions between ethnic groups forced to live in the same jurisdictions by their colonial rulers, who often drew arbitrary boundaries for their own purposes. In the case of the DRC, the impact of ethnicity is particularly tragic because the fighting began in the late 1980s as a by-product of civil wars in Burundi and Rwanda. There, Tutsi and Hutu refugees, fleeing what could only be called genocide, ended up in massive camps in what was then still Zaire and other neighboring countries. The influx of refugees heightened the resentment of their fellow Tutsi and Hutu, as well as members of other ethnic groups, toward the dictatorial regime of Mobutu Sese Seko in Kinshasa.

The final issue is the environment. The eastern part of the DRC has a number of environmental threats looming on the horizon—in this case the shocking decline in the elephant and gorilla populations. More often than not, these threats are part of a broader danger to the world's ecosystem. To cite but two examples, around the world, species are becoming extinct at more than a thousand times the natural rate, thus depriving the world of plants and animals that could well provide new medicines or otherwise help meet human needs. Similarly, the destruction of rain forests and the expansion of deserts both contribute to global climate change that could jeopardize much of human existence in the decades to come. But, as the journalist Robert Kaplan has most pointedly shown us, environmental decay combines with poverty, ethnic tensions, and a weak state to create a political tinderbox in much of the third world, which he labels "the coming anarchy." In his words,

> **It is time to understand "the environment" for what it is: *the* national security issue of the early twenty-first century [because] an increasingly large number of people will be stuck in history, living in shanty-towns where attempts to rise above poverty, cultural dysfunction, and ethnic strife will be doomed by a lack of water to drink, soil to till, and space to survive in.**[2]

We do not have to go as far as Kaplan does in predicting unprecedented levels of political violence and crime in the third world. Nonetheless, as we will see throughout Part 4, unmet human needs contribute both to worsening environmental conditions and to heightened conflict.

Thinking about the Third World

It is easy to convince students in countries like the United States that they should understand politics in other liberal democracies, because doing so can tell them a lot about their own country and its institutions, values, and problems. At first glance, it is less obvious why we should worry about the third world, because countries like the Democratic Republic of Congo (DRC) have so little in common with the West.

In fact, the third world is vitally important to us all. As we will see in more detail in the final chapter, we live in an interdependent world in which everything that happens affects everyone and everything else. Nowhere is this easier to see than in the speed with which the United States and its allies launched massive attacks against Afghanistan in the weeks following the 9/11 terrorism attacks.

But there is another, perhaps more important, rea-

[2] Robert Kaplan, *The Coming Anarchy: Shattering the Dreams of the Post–Cold War World* (New York: Random House, 2000), 19, 23.

What's in a Name

Academics argue about everything, including terminology. Sometimes these debates help clarify matters; sometimes they don't. Debates over what to call the third world have been particularly intense and also not particularly helpful.

Over the years, each of the following terms have been in vogue: *developing, underdeveloped, less developed, third world,* and *the south.* All were tried as part of the search for a term that would convey the plight of most of these countries but do so in a nonpejorative manner. The situation has only gotten more complicated as some of them have managed to achieve a degree of economic success, giving birth to such new terms as NICs (newly industrializing countries) and the fourth world.

I have decided to stick with the most commonly used term—the third world. It was coined more than a half-century ago by a French analyst who wished to distinguish the countries shaking off colonial rule from the Western democracies (first world) and the members of the Soviet bloc (second).

son. To a degree few of us in the West want to acknowledge, the third world has also been a place where the rich countries exported their problems and waged their battles. It was in the third world that Europeans and Americans established most of their colonies. More recently, almost all the wars during the cold war and post–cold war periods have occurred in Asia, Africa, or Latin America.

The events of 9/11 also drove home the fact that many of these conflicts have a direct impact on life in Europe and North America. This is true only in part because the north is subject to attack by terrorists today and may also be vulnerable to attacks by more conventional forces tomorrow.

Even before 9/11, the third world was important because we in the north are also dependent on it. Most of our natural resources and more and more of our relatively unsophisticated manufactured goods come from there. As the **Organization of Petroleum Exporting Countries (OPEC)** oil embargo of 1973–74 and the periodic oil price shocks since then have shown, when third world commodity producers are able to band together, they can wreak havoc on northern economies.

In short, we ignore the third world at our peril. The failure to take the third world and its problems seriously has kept us from seeing two critical trends. First, we have been slow to acknowledge the role of the rich and powerful countries in creating and sustaining its economic and political woes in the third world. Second, we have been even more reluctant to come to grips with the fact that few third world countries can solve their problems without significant support from the north.

The Basics

As with the move to Part 3, you will have to shift intellectual gears to fully understand political life in most of the third world. Although few of these countries are going through the wrenching changes we saw in Russia, the stakes of politics are, if anything, higher in the third world because of their poverty, weak states, environmental threats, and ethnically based conflict.

Poverty

The third world is one of the most controversial subjects studied by political scientists today. Indeed, we cannot even agree on what to call this part of the world, let alone which countries to include in it. In practice, however, most of the definitions and lists of countries overlap significantly because they all have one key criterion in common—poverty.

The third world includes the world's poorest countries and three-fifths of the global population—three-fourths if we include China. As the map at the beginning of this chapter shows, it covers all of Africa and Latin America and much of South and Southeast Asia. GNP per capita in the richest countries is almost sixty times larger than in the poorest, which also have almost four times as many people. The richest countries consume nearly twenty times more energy than the poorest. A quarter of the people in the third world have to get by on less than $1 a day, including 2.5 million people in the capital city of the DRC alone.

In the United States, only about 10 out of every 1,000 babies die in infancy. For the world as a whole, that number is 75 out of 1,000, and for Africa, it is 113.

The average Congolese woman will live to age 51, and the average man to only 46. In the third world as a whole, the lack of access to safe drinking water is the most important—and avoidable—cause of death for more than forty thousand children daily. The United States does not even bother gathering this statistic on its population.

There is one doctor for every five hundred Americans, as opposed to one for every twenty-five thousand people in the DRC. As is the case with almost every indicator of social and economic well-being, Africans face the most appalling medical situation. Indeed, as table 11.1

TABLE 11.1 Estimated AIDS Cases and Deaths at the end of 2003

REGION	ADULTS AND CHILDREN LIVING WITH HIV/AIDS (IN MILLIONS)	ADULT INFECTION RATE (%)	DEATHS OF ADULTS AND CHILDREN IN 2003 (IN MILLIONS)
Sub-Saharan Africa	25.0	7.5	2.2
East Asia	0.9	0.1	0.04
South and Southeast Asia	6.5	0.6	0.46
Eastern Europe and Central Asia	1.3	0.6	0.049
Western Europe	0.58	0.3	0.006
North Africa and Middle East	0.48	0.2	0.024
North America	1.00	0.6	0.016
Caribbean	0.43	2.3	0.035
Latin America	1.6	0.6	0.084
Worldwide total	37.8	1.1	2.9

Source: Adapted from www.avert.org/worldstats.htm. Accessed 13 Sept. 2004. Reprinted with permission from AVERT.

shows, the AIDS epidemic is more widespread in Africa than anywhere else. Of the estimated forty million people infected with HIV worldwide, fully twenty-five million are in Sub-Saharan Africa. Between 1981 and 2003, twelve million children in that part of the world were orphaned because they lost both of their parents to AIDS. Because governments and people there cannot afford the "cocktails" of medicines that are keeping many HIV-infected patients alive in the West, death rates dwarf those in any other region of the world.

In Africa and Asia, fewer than 40 percent of the people can read and write. Yet most of these countries have to cope with a "brain drain," as highly educated young people emigrate to Europe and North America because of the widespread unemployment among university graduates at home.

It is not just in the poorest third world countries that people suffer. In South Korea and Brazil the infant mortality rate is, respectively, three and six times that of the United States. In each of these countries, only three-fourths of the people have access to drinkable water, and there are only about one-third as many physicians on a per capita basis as in Europe and the United States.

There is no commonly agreed-on measure of the level of a country's wealth or development. GNP, for example, has properly been criticized for missing the noneconomic side of a country's quality of life. This chapter's basic table, therefore, presents the scores on the United Nations Development Program's **Human Development**

Index (HDI), which combines data on GNP with that on literacy and life expectancy. The fact is, however, that the same depressing picture of the third world emerges no matter which of the available indices we choose.

In the least developed countries, almost 70 percent of the rural population lives below the poverty line. For the third world as a whole, more than a third of the rural population does not get enough to eat. And the number of poor people in the countryside has increased by 40 percent over the past quarter-century.

Most third world countries lack anything approaching a diversified economy. They tend, instead, to rely on the export of a few primary commodities, such as oil in Iraq and Nigeria, or coffee and cotton in Nicaragua. Often, prices for these commodities fluctuate wildly, and when they fall sharply, there is little hard currency available to pay for food, manufactured goods, or other needed imports. Because their own money is not considered acceptable by northern banks and companies, they have to use dollars, euros, yen, and pounds to pay for those imports.

The expansion of world trade has brought with it unprecedented levels of debt. At the height of the international **debt crisis** in the late 1980s, Argentina owed northern banks and governments over $60 billion. For Brazil and Mexico, that figure was well over $100 billion. At the end of the 1990s, the third world owed northern banks, governments, and international financial institutions more than $2.8 trillion, or more than $400 per person. In the mid-1990s countries as diverse as Brazil, Cameroon, Guatemala, India, Kenya, and Madagascar all paid more in interest on their loans than they did on social services. (See table 11.2.)

To make matters even worse, the prospects for catching up to the advanced countries are not very good. Although the **newly industrializing countries (NICs)** and some others have done quite well in recent years, per capita GNP in all the low- and middle-income countries is less than 10 percent of that in the countries covered in Part 2. And perhaps most depressing of all, because the poorest and richest countries both grew at a rate of 2.4 percent per year during the 1990s, the gap between them has not narrowed at all.

Environmental Threats

The difficulties facing the third world are magnified by its rapidly growing population. The population in the poorest countries is increasing at three-and-a-half times the rate in the richest ones. Even this figure underestimates the problem because population growth is exponential; it builds on itself like compound interest on a savings account. At 0.6 percent, it will take 120 years for the population of the richest countries to double, a rate they can easily absorb given projected rates of economic growth. At 2 percent, which is the norm in the poorest countries, it will take less than thirty-five years for the population to double. In the DRC, where the annual increase tops 4 percent, it will not even take a generation. Egypt, with its already overstretched economy and ecosystem, adds a million people to its population every nine months.

Poverty and population growth are combining to produce an ecological time bomb. Population growth puts demands on environments that over the centuries have often provided little more than a marginal existence. Poverty, in turn, has made people desperate, willing to trade the future of the environment for food for themselves and their families today. Thus, many—perhaps most—of the people who slash and burn the trees in the Amazon rain forests are peasants who can provide for their families only by farming that land. In Asia and Africa, about 15 percent of the land has been severely damaged. Everywhere, development is putting marginally adequate water supplies and irrigation systems at risk. In short, throughout the third world, human action is threatening what environmentalists call the **carrying capacity** of the land.

Ethnicity and Conflict

These problems have been compounded by racial, linguistic, ethnic, and religious conflict. This is especially true in Africa and Asia, where the colonial powers paid little or no attention to traditional alignments when they drew boundaries during the nineteenth century, most of which are still in use. This is less true in the Americas, though almost all those countries have significant minorities of "Indians" and people of African descent.

When political scientists started studying the third world in the 1950s, most of them assumed that the spread of the mass media and Western culture would gradually erode people's attachment to what were viewed as "primitive" identities.

▌ **TABLE 11.2** Debt as a Proportion of GNP (in percentages)

REGION	1981	1991	1998
Sub-Saharan Africa	28.6	107.9	71.8
East Asia and Pacific	16.9	28.2	84.8
South Asia	17.0	35.6	29.0
Middle East and North Africa	31.0	58.8	34.7
Latin America and Caribbean	35.5	41.3	69.0

Source: Data for 1981 and 1991 adapted from R. J. Barry Jones, *Globalization and Interdependence in the International Political Economy* (London: Pinter, 1995), 159. Data for 1998 from World Bank, *World Development Report, 2000,* www.worldbank.org, accessed 9 Nov. 2001.

Put simply, they were wrong. In the past few decades, quite the opposite has happened. If anything, these identities have become much more important, both in and of themselves, and as a source of conflict within and between countries. There will be plenty of examples of ethnic identity and conflict to follow, but none rival the genocide in Rwanda.

On 6 April 1994, an airplane carrying the presidents of Rwanda and Burundi was shot down, killing all aboard. This incident set off waves of violence between the majority Hutu and minority Tutsi populations in both countries, which Philip Gourevitch chillingly describes in the opening of his award-winning book on the genocide:

> **Decimation means the killing of every tenth person in a population and in the spring and early summer of 1994 a program of massacres decimated the Republic of Rwanda. Although the killing was low-tech—performed largely by machete—it was carried out at dazzling speed; of an original population of about seven and a half million, at least eight hundred thousand were killed in just a hundred days. Rwandans often speak of a million deaths, and they may be right. The dead of Rwanda accumulated at nearly three times the rate of Jewish dead during the Holocaust. It was the most efficient mass killing since the atomic bombings of Hiroshima and Nagasaki.[3]**

Rwanda is not alone. At any time, there are twenty to forty wars being fought in the third world, almost all of which have ethnic origins. Although few societies have had to deal with conflict anywhere near as bloody as that in Rwanda or Burundi, all are bitter and intense. In Sierra Leone, rebels asked tens of thousands of men they captured a simple question: "Long sleeves or short?" Then they cut off that person's arm at the elbow or the wrist, depending on how he answered.

Globalization

The final defining characteristic of the third world is the role global forces continue to play in shaping what citizens and leaders alike can do. As the book's subtitle suggests, global forces are limiting states' ability to maneuver. This is especially true of the third world for the reasons former Tanzanian president Julius Nyerere pithily laid out in the sentence that begins this chapter.

It may be an exaggeration to say that decisions made in Washington, D.C., are more important to Tanzanians than those made in Dar es-Salaam, their capital city. Tanzania *is* a sovereign country that passes its own laws, is-

Langevin Jaques/CORBIS Sygma

One of the many mass graves to be found in Rwanda . . . and in other places where ethnic conflict has disrupted the peace in the third world.

sues its own decrees, and reaches its own judicial decisions. However, what happens in places like Tanzania is largely determined elsewhere—sometimes by force, and other times as a result of subtler and often unintended consequences of actions by power holders in our increasingly interdependent world.

These relationships are hard to document, and their impact varies from country to country and from time to time. Nonetheless, they cannot be ignored, however incomplete our understanding of them may be.

Whether they like it or not, almost all third world countries are now being integrated into the global economic and cultural systems. However, they are not being brought in as equals.

The most obvious of these links are economic. In the section on public policy later in the chapter, we will explore how third world governments try to cope with global economic forces. Here, we will look only at the common difficulties most of these countries face.

---

[3] Philip Gourevitch, *We Wish to Inform You That Tomorrow We Will Be Killed with Our Families: Stories from Rwanda* (New York: Farrar, Straus and Giroux, 1998), frontispiece.

If the World Had 100 People

The World Game is an educational organization that helps people understand what it means to live in an interdependent world. Its college version involves laying a massive map of the world on a gymnasium floor on which 100 people make some basic decisions about allocating the world's natural and human resources. The basic characteristics of these 100 people reflect current global demographic trends:

- 51 are female
- 57 are Asians
- 14 are from the Western Hemisphere
- 70 are non-White
- 30 are Christian
- 70 are illiterate
- 50 suffer from malnutrition
- 80 live in substandard housing
- 6, all from the United States, own half the wealth
- One has a college education
- None owns a computer

 www.worldgame.org

Formal colonialism is long gone. However, the former colonial powers still have considerable economic leverage. In the 1970s and 1980s, radical social scientists popularized the idea of **dependency** to describe a situation in which the legal ties of colonialism gave way to informal mechanisms of economic control. Such ideas are far less popular in academic and political circles today than they were a generation ago. The shifting tides of political fashion, however, have not changed the reality of third world economic weakness and first world economic strength.

Multinational corporations (MNCs) headquartered in the north still dominate the more modern sectors of the economy. (See table 11.3.) Such companies have always repatriated the lion's share of their profits back to their home countries. In recent years, they have tended to relocate operations that require the lowest-skilled labor and produce the most pollution to the third world. To be sure, many of the people who work for these companies are better off than they would have been otherwise, and most MNCs do contribute to local economic growth. At the same time, however, these countries are ever more at the mercy of institutions and events outside their bor-

■ TABLE 11.3 The Leading Multinational Corporations by Country of Origin

COUNTRY	NUMBER OF MNCS	COUNTRY	NUMBER OF MNCS
Japan	21	France	2
United States	13	South Korea	2
Germany	6	Italy	2
Great Britain/Dutch		Switzerland	1
joint venture	2	Great Britain	1

Source: Adapted from "The Fortune Global Five Hundred: The World's Largest Corporations," *Fortune*, 4 Aug. 1997, F1–F12.

ders. The largest of these companies are massive, controlling resources that make them richer than many third world countries themselves. And, as the table also shows, they all have their headquarters in Western Europe, North America, Japan, and South Korea. MNCs are often criticized for exploiting the workers and other resources they use in the third world. In recent years, however, many have adopted corporate responsibility policies that guarantee above market wages, protect the local environment, and help build the local infrastructure (see, for instance, www.timberland.com/timberlandserve/timberlandserve_index.jsp).

Some countries have been able to retain a substantial degree of control, especially over their natural resources. The most obvious and spectacular example of this was the OPEC cartel, which forced worldwide oil prices sharply upward in the 1970s and brought untold riches to the member nations. But OPEC is very much the exception to the rule of economic as well as political power concentrated in the north.

Finally, there has been a marked shift in global economic preferences that began prior to the end of the cold war and that has accelerated since then. As we saw in Parts 2 and 3, almost all northern governments, multinational companies, and independent agencies have opted for liberal, market-oriented development strategies, which the third world countries have "had" to adopt as well. The word *had* is in quotes because no one put a gun to the head of third world officials. Nonetheless, as we will see in the country chapters that follow, they had little choice but to open their borders to trade and investment from abroad, export goods for which there is a niche in the global market, and reduce public ownership and other forms of state intervention.

Supporters of this approach, known as **structural adjustment,** assume that in the long run third world countries will find areas of comparative advantage that spark sustained growth. In the shorter term, however, these trends are widening the gaps between the rich and poor within these countries, and between themselves and the countries of the more affluent north.

Just as important, though perhaps even harder to pin down, is the growing spread of a common culture, also dominated by the north and especially by the United States. Such ties have existed since colonial times, with the spread of Western religions and languages figuring most prominently in what many in the third world see as the cultural subjugation of their peoples.

Key Questions

We will use the same basic framework developed in figure 1.1 in the next five chapters on the third world. However, as this discussion has already suggested, we will have to go farther and ask three more questions that help us understand why so many third world countries face such serious difficulties:

- Why are global forces so much more influential in the third world?
- Why are third world societies so divided?
- Why are many states in the third world so weak?

Including so many countries in one category masks dramatic differences, which have led some observers to question whether any label like the "third world" still makes sense. Some of these countries are so poor that any discussion of their political or economic conditions can bring tears to the eyes of even the most dispassionate observer. Other countries, especially the NICs, have actually made tremendous strides in recent years and are as well off as Spain or Portugal were a generation ago.

Five countries will be covered in the chapters that follow—India, Iran, Iraq, Nigeria, and Mexico. They were chosen to reflect the range of issues facing the third world as a whole. They also demonstrate some of the most important differences within the third world in terms of political systems and economic conditions. However, because the five constitute only a tiny fraction of the third world's states, we have included a chapter on South Africa on the website that accompanies this book.

The Evolution of Politics in the Third World

Imperialism and Its Legacy

With but a handful of exceptions, the modern states of Africa, Asia, and Central and South America all have their most important roots in **imperialism.** Almost all of them were ruled by white men from Europe and North America. Even the few countries that retained their legal independence were not able to escape the corrosive effects of northern economics and culture.

From the sixteenth through the nineteenth centuries, statesmen, entrepreneurs, missionaries, and adventurers flocked to the Americas, Africa, and most of Asia in pursuit of the three *G*s: god, gold, and glory. In virtually every case, the colonizers looked down on the cultures they encountered and ignored the wishes of the people they subjugated. Boundaries were drawn to suit the colonizers' wishes—boundaries that often divided existing political units and lumped traditional adversaries together.

There were three distinct phases to European colonial expansion. The first came in the sixteenth and seventeenth centuries, when the Portuguese, Spanish, Dutch, British, and French carved up the Americas. These countries also established beachheads in Africa to support their expanding commercial networks in India and the Americas, including the infamous slave trade. The second wave came mostly in the nineteenth century, when the forts and trading posts were transformed into full-blown colonies in Africa and much of Asia. The third came after World War I when the allies divided up the remnants of the Ottoman Empire. (See table 11.4.)

The colonizers were convinced that they had encountered primitive peoples. This prompted the arrogance of what Rudyard Kipling called "the white man's burden," according to which everything Western was superior while everything in the indigenous culture was inferior:

> Take up the white man's burden,
> Send forth the best ye breed,
> Go bind your sons to exile
> To serve your captives' need
> To wait in heavy harness
> On fluttered fold and wild,
> Your new-caught, sullen peoples
> Half devil and half child.

Given this arrogance and these cultural blinders, the imperialists undermined some highly sophisticated civilizations—the Aztecs, Incas, and Mayans in the Americas; the great kingdoms of precolonial Africa; and the various cultures of India and China. Most of the new colonies had relatively unsophisticated **subsistence economies.** They were not affluent societies, but most produced enough food and other goods to meet basic survival needs.

But the colonizers wanted their newly acquired pos-

■ TABLE 11.4 Key Events in the History of the Third World

YEAR	EVENT
1450 on	Exploration and then colonization of the "new world"
1600 on	Slave trade
1776	United States declares independence
1810–30	Most of Central and South America gains independence
1867	India formally taken over by British government
1880s	"Scramble for Africa"
1919	German colonies pass to Allied powers as League of Nations mandates
Late 1940s	India and other countries gain independence
1960s	Most remaining colonies gain independence
Mid-1970s	Portuguese African empire collapses
1997	Hong Kong reverts to China

sessions to turn a profit. Therefore, they introduced commercial agriculture based on one or a handful of crops to be exported back to the home country. The Central American countries became known as "banana republics" because of the way United Fruit and other North American companies concentrated production. Massive coffee and tea plantations were built in the Central Highlands of Kenya. Cotton was sent back to factories in Britain, destroying long-established Indian spinning and weaving industries. Most tragically of all, regions that had previously been self-supporting now had to import food and other vital commodities.

Minerals, oil, and other natural resources were added to the colonies' list of exports, and eventually there was some industrialization. But the general situation remained the same. Decisions about what to grow, mine, or build were mostly made in Europe and North America. The profits mostly went there as well.

These common trends notwithstanding, there was also a great deal of variation in European and North American colonialism, which largely coincided with the time a given region was taken over. In most of the Americas, the colonists gained control of relatively sparsely settled lands and then proceeded to wipe out most of the indigenous population. Where large numbers of native peoples survived, they were integrated into the dominant Spanish or Portuguese cultures. There also was, of course, the forced relocation of millions of Africans, brought to the Americas and Caribbean islands as slaves.

During the nineteenth century, colonization primarily occurred in Africa and South Asia. There, the colonial powers encountered a more serious "numbers problem." Because there were many more Africans and Asians than Europeans, the colonial powers could not hope to govern their new conquests alone. Therefore, they had to incorporate growing numbers of "locals" into a system of government that the British called **indirect rule.**

Independence

There were also three waves of decolonization. The first began during the 1770s, when the thirteen colonies in British North America became the United States, and spread through most of the rest of the Western Hemisphere over the next half century. In every one of these cases, however, it was not the native peoples—the directly colonized—who rose up and won their independence, but the descendants of the colonizers who had migrated from Europe.

Although one author has described the United States as the "first new nation," most accounts of this first wave of decolonization are restricted to the Spanish and Portuguese colonies in the Caribbean and in Central and South America. Independence came early there in large part because of the growing domestic weakness of Spain and Portugal, which left them unable to maintain their hold over the colonies.

As Chapter 16 will make clear, these revolutions settled little. Most of the newly independent countries suffered at least another century of turmoil in which rival elites vied for power. Meanwhile, they remained on the bottom rung of the capitalist world economy, with Britain and the United States taking over Spain's and Portugal's economic role and managing the trade of food and other primary products and, later, low-quality industrial goods. Many nominally independent Central American states soon had to deal with the United States as a military as well as an economic power, because it sent in the Marines whenever it felt that its financial or security interests were imperiled.

The second wave was also limited to a single region—the Middle East. After World War I, the Ottoman Empire collapsed, and some countries gained at least nominal independence. Others, such as Iraq, passed to British or French control, though most of them had become somewhat independent before World War II broke out.

The third wave occurred during the second half of the twentieth century. By the beginning of World War II, there was substantial anticolonial sentiment in most of Asia and Africa, the best known of which was the nonviolent protest movement led by Mohandas Gandhi in India. As we will see in the next chapter, Gandhi and his allies pressured the British into agreeing to grant India its independence after the war in exchange for its at least tacit support during the war. Despite some false starts, the British lived up to their word, and India and Pakistan became independent states within the British Commonwealth of Nations in 1947.

Over the next quarter-century, most of the remaining colonies gained their independence. Sometimes the colonial powers hung on, and independence required a protracted revolutionary struggle, as in Vietnam and Algeria. Other times independence came rather easily, as in Nigeria. By the late 1970s, this second wave of decolonization was all but complete. Today, Europe and the United States have only a few tiny outposts left.

In a few former colonies, such as India, Israel, Vietnam, and Algeria, independence occurred following a protracted struggle that engaged much of the population. When freedom did come, these new states found themselves with a large proportion of their populations committed to the new regime, which was run by the same groups that had led the struggle against colonial rule. This unity eroded with time, but it gave these countries a host of advantages to start with, including a well-trained and respected elite that enjoyed quite a bit of legitimacy.

Most of the other former colonies were not so fortunate. By the late 1950s, it had become clear to most Europeans that their colonial empires could not last. Although independence itself therefore came easier in most of Africa and the Middle East, its very ease obscured problems that were to plague these countries almost immediately thereafter. In particular, they lacked either the trained leadership or the unity and commitment on the part of much of the population that figured so prominently in India's nonviolent Congress or Algeria's violent National Liberation Front. In fact, as we will see in the chapter on Iraq, independence often came without any significant development of national identity. The new leaders had support only among either the small Westernized elite or their own regional or ethnic constituencies. In other words, they took over countries that had weak institutions and limited support from the population as a whole, both of which were to quickly worsen once the exhilaration of independence wore off.

Postcolonial Problems

At first, there was tremendous optimism about these new countries. Most had well-trained and internationally respected leaders presiding over institutions patterned after those in London, Paris, and Washington. Political scientists and political leaders assumed that what they mistook as the enthusiasm of the newly independent peoples, along with aid from the outside, would lead to a rapid improvement in the quality of life and the development of strong and democratic states.

This is not what happened. Almost all of the new governments degenerated into military, single-party, or other forms of authoritarian rule. Many faced bloody civil wars when the antagonisms between the ethnic groups the colonial powers had forced to live together came to the political surface. Regional conflicts often turned into proxy battles between the superpowers, thereby worsening an already difficult situation.

In many former colonies, ethnic, religious, linguistic, and racial tensions disrupted political life and eroded what little sense of national identification and commitment had been built during the years before independence. Far from being helpful, northern governments and businesses imposed their economic, and sometimes political, will. Meanwhile, the lack of experience of the new leaders and shortage of resources available to them made maintaining order difficult and made reaching broader social and economic goals nearly impossible. Under the circumstances, it is hardly surprising that the business elite, political leaders, military officers, and others who felt they had much to lose proved willing to toss out the seemingly democratic institutions most of these countries inherited from their erstwhile colonial masters.

Political Culture in the Third World

In Part 2 we saw that a political culture based on a common identity, shared values, and sense of legitimacy plays a vital role in sustaining the established liberal democracies. In Part 3 we saw how hard it is for the former Communist countries to develop similar attitudes and beliefs. Here, we will encounter even starker evidence of what happens when a country's political culture includes divisions over basic attitudes about the country and the rules of the political game.

Identity

We cannot blame colonialism for all of the problems with political culture in the third world, especially as colonial rule recedes into history. However, imperialism remains an important long-term cause of the lack of a national identity.

In Part 2 we saw that most people in the liberal democracies define themselves politically first and foremost in national terms. In large part because of the way the colonial conquerors established borders in Africa and most of Asia, this is a hard thing for people there to do.

In West Africa, for instance, different ethnic groups live in what amount to bands stretching east and west and that parallel the Atlantic coast. In the 1880s and 1890s, however, the Europeans established colonial boundaries that ran from north to south, thereby splitting many ethnic, religious, and linguistic groups into several jurisdictions.

In other words, most third world countries are artificial entities, with little or nothing that psychologically holds their inhabitants together. To be sure, soccer fans have been treated to the antics of wildly enthusiastic Nigerians at recent World Cups and Olympics. However, international soccer is one of the few things that lead them to think of themselves as Nigerians. More often, their political views are derived from their regional or ethnic identities.

Ethnic and Other Divisions

The lack of a common national identity is a major cause of the divisions that have wracked most third world countries. Preexisting ethnic divisions, worsened by the colonial powers' arbitrary drawing of national boundaries, have exacted a terrible cost by diverting scarce resources that could otherwise be used for economic and social development. Dozens of African countries have suffered through bloody civil wars. Even where wars have not occurred, there has been intense conflict, as we will see in all five of the country chapters that follow.

When political scientists first began studying the third world in earnest in the late 1950s, many expected that these predominantly rural and poor societies would give way to Asian, African, and Latin American versions of the industrial democracies. With time, the argument went, education and urbanization would lead people to become more aware of the world and to take on Western values and aspirations.

However, the hoped-for cultural change failed to materialize. Then, as ethnic conflict erupted in much of the third world, political scientists began to explore the resilience of the supposedly weak, "traditional" societies.

Among other things, they found that many institutions reinforcing older values persisted. For example, many countries still have strong informal **patron-client relations** that have their roots in feudalism. As in Europe during the Middle Ages or in the Mafia today, people are tied together in hierarchical relationships in which they have mutual responsibilities and obligations. Lords, bosses, and patrons are more powerful than their clients. Nonetheless, all are tied together through financial, military, and cultural bonds, that have proven remarkably hard to break in most parts of the third world.

Similarly, the assumption that the new nations would become more secular as they modernized has proved unfounded. If anything, religion has become more important and divisive. To some degree, these conflicts pit Christians against adherents of the religions the colonists and missionaries found when they arrived. Such is the case in much of West Africa, where ethnic conflicts are frequently exacerbated by antagonisms between Christians along the coast and Muslims in the interior. In other cases, such as India, the conflict is between religious, ethnic, and linguistic groups that have been at odds for centuries. Finally, contrary to what scholars initially expected, there has been a tremendous upsurge in **fundamentalism,** especially among Muslims who fear that modernity in the guise of Westernization is a threat to what they hold dear and is anything but a step forward.

In some instances, most notably in the Middle East, political cultures have evolved in ways that have left people and leaders strongly preferring *not* to develop along Western lines. The Islamic Republic that has ruled Iran since the 1979 revolution that overthrew the shah is in many respects a rejection of everything Western and modern. The shah's grandiose industrial and commercial projects and his increasingly cosmopolitan society have given way to more traditional customs, including the strict application of Islamic law and the removal of women from much of public life.

It's not just Iran. Throughout the Muslim world, for instance, women are once again wearing the veil that is widely viewed in the West as a symbol of their lower status in Islamic society. More generally, Muslim peoples are coming to see their religion and the broader values and lifestyle it embraces, as something to have pride in, and even as something far superior to industrialization, democracy, and Western culture.

In short, rapid change can be a disruptive force. This is true not only in the third world. As we saw in Part 2, many people are struggling to keep up with the technological revolution and with other economic changes sweeping the industrialized democracies. However, social and economic change has been particularly disruptive in the third world precisely because so many of the "new" ideas are Western and thus at odds with traditional values. Also, many of the social and economic developments require the shedding or, at best, alteration of long-standing practices.

Although it is hard to generalize, no doubt one of the by-products of cultural change has been additional demands placed on governments. To some degree, this simply reflects the fact that more people have the time and skills needed to organize politically and to put pressure on whoever is governing them. To some degree, too, it reflects the fact that changing social, economic, and political conditions have touched raw political nerves. Worldwide, new groups have been spawned all along the political spectrum—if it makes sense to speak of a single political spectrum—including many that want to slow down and others that want to speed up the pace of change. In turn, groups have formed within elites that are increasingly committed to retaining the status quo and, with it, their own power and privileges.

To make sense of these rather abstract points, briefly consider two examples, the first of which we will return to in more detail in the next chapter. In India, a Hindu is born into one of four castes or into the so-called untouchables. These groups, in turn, are subdivided into smaller communities, or *jati*, usually on the basis of their members' traditional occupation (for example, grocer, tanner, or teacher).

The traditional communities remain important despite the many attempts to remove at least the worst of the discriminatory practices untouchables have been subjected to merely because their ancestors held jobs in which they dealt with animals, dead people, or human excrement. As India has become more urbanized and industrialized, the historical link between *jati* and profession has declined, and some of the restrictions it imposed on people (whom they can marry or who can prepare their food) are no longer as important. However, caste and *jati* remain extremely significant politically, because the patron-client and other relationships that keep them so strong are also the mainstays of the political party organizations at the all-important state level.

In other words, some Hindus have modified some of their cultural norms because they have had to. After all, it is very hard to tell the *jati* of the cooks who prepare their food when they fly on an airplane! But these values have not disappeared. In some politically important respects, they are, if anything, stronger in ways that tend to deepen divisions and hinder the prospects for either national unity or democracy.

The second example, of course, is the terrorist attacks on the World Trade Center and the Pentagon on 11 September 2001. These obviously did not reflect a traditional division within a state. Rather, they forced us all to confront just how far some people are prepared to take their hatred of the United States and Western civilization. Analysts are still debating how much U.S. foreign policy toward Israel, for instance, led to the attacks and how much they reflect what Samuel Huntington has called a "clash of civilizations." Although it will probably be years before political scientists and historians reach a

Conflict in the Third World

The first and most obvious conclusion to be drawn from this chapter is that there is more conflict in the third world than in either the liberal democracies or most of the current and former Communist countries. In many cases, conflict targets not only the government of the day and its policies but also the regime. In some, the existence of the nation-state itself is put in jeopardy. The conflict is all the more remarkable because, in the more authoritarian countries, protesters run a major risk by signing a petition, let alone taking to the streets.

Not all third world countries are revolutions or civil wars waiting to happen. Still, even in the most stable of them, such as India, deaths during election campaigns are common enough that they rarely draw more than a passing note in the press.

consensus on the causes of 9/11, these kinds of factors have to be in the explanatory mix of such tragic events and of contemporary terrorism in general.

A Lack of Legitimacy

Finally, few third world regimes enjoy much legitimacy. There is little of the tolerance of, trust in, or satisfaction with the regime we find in the liberal democracies. It remains an open question whether a democracy needs such a culture. (Also see the conclusion to this chapter.) But clearly the cultural shifts, as well as those in the patterns of political participation we are about to discuss, have heightened *in*tolerance, *mis*trust, and *dis*satisfaction.

Political Participation in the Third World

We can divide political participation into two main types: activities that provide support for the authorities, and those that place demands on them. In Part 2 we saw that people in the industrialized democracies resort to the kinds of demands that could threaten the existence of the regime only under the most unusual of circumstances. What's more, they frequently engage in "supportive" participation that, at least indirectly, bolsters the regime. There may not be a lot of political content to such acts as singing the national anthem before a baseball game. Nonetheless, such symbolic forms of participation reflect the widespread support accorded the state, if not the specific men and women who are in office at the time.

Political participation is very different in most of the third world. There are political parties, like Mexico's PAN, that try to forge broad coalitions around a few key ideological positions. Similarly, India has trade unions, women's movements, and other interest groups reminiscent of those in the industrialized democracies.

However, do not read too much into such examples. Even in countries with reasonably open political systems, there is less of the balance between supporting and demanding participation than we find in the industrialized democracies. Over the years, such countries have come to face more and more pressure "from below" that has led to massive waves of protest, if not revolution itself.

In those countries with authoritarian regimes, the patterns of political participation are more reminiscent of what we saw in the former Soviet Union. In the West, we tend to think of participation as a "bottom up" phenomenon, in which citizens participate voluntarily in order to have their views heard by those "above" them. But this is not always the case in the third world. In countries with single-party or military governments, much of the participation comes from the "top down." For example, in Iraq before and after the first Gulf War, there were large demonstrations in support of the Iraqi government's intransigence vis-à-vis the United States, but most commentators wrote them off because they were orchestrated by Saddam Hussein's regime.

It is a mistake, however, to write such participation off as merely cynical manipulation of the masses by the elite. Like the demonstrations in favor of Chairman Mao Zedong at the height of China's Cultural Revolution, such activities often reflect genuine enthusiasm and add to the commitment of the people involved.

Similarly, there are many examples akin to the Chinese Communist Party's campaigns in which the state mobilizes people in an attempt to implement policies that its weak and unreliable bureaucracies cannot handle. These, too, may be portrayed as cynical and manipulative efforts by the state, as in the literacy campaigns of the Iraqi and Nicaraguan governments in the 1980s. In other cases, however, even the most skeptical of analysts acknowledge that such campaigns can have a significant and positive impact. Nigeria has few programs it can point to for building bridges across communal lines. However, its Youth Corps sends teams of young people for voluntary service in economic and other developmental projects outside their home states. If nothing else, people in the regions where the volunteers work gain some presumably positive exposure to members of groups they may have antagonistic relations with politically.

Patron-client relations are also more important in the third world than in the countries considered in Parts 2 and 3. We will see that they are an even more central element of politics in the third world, in large part because capitalism and the accompanying changes have not gone as far as political scientists first thought they would in destroying traditional social structures. Thus, Mexico's Institutional Revolutionary Party (PRI) remained in power for more than seventy years not because of its ideology or accomplishments but because it built a client-based machine that could turn out (and, if need be, manufacture) the vote through the distribution of jobs and other benefits. Similarly, it has been a long time since India's Congress Party was nationalist or socialist in orientation or ideology. It, too, survives largely as an organization of ambitious politicians tied together by their desire for power. In perhaps the most blatant example of "clientelism," there were so many members of the Iraqi elite from Saddam Hussein's hometown that the government decreed that people should no longer include the part of their names that indicated where their family was from, thereby making the number of al-Tikritis in the ruling circles less obvious.

Perhaps most importantly of all is the degree to which political participation is based on **communal groups.** As has been the case with much of political life in the third world, political scientists have sought non-pejorative terms to describe these trends. Terms like *parochial* or *tribal*, which were once in vogue, have now been rejected in favor of less telling but more neutral ones like *communal*.

Whatever term we use, much of political life revolves around religious, ethnic, linguistic, racial, and other "communities." To be sure, there is some of that in the West, including the all-but-total loyalty of African Americans to the Democratic Party in the United States. However, such trends pale in comparison with what we will see in the third world.

For instance, it is very hard to assemble a table of Indian election returns like the ones given in Part 2 because only three parties run candidates nation-wide. Instead, much of the vote goes to parties that operate only in the single state where their linguistic or religious constituency is clustered. Similarly, the strongest opposition to the former regime in Iraq came from the Kurdish and Shiite communities, which objected not so much to Saddam Hussein's religious or foreign policies as to the fact that their people had been systematically discriminated against after the Baath Party took power in 1969. Even in relatively homogeneous Mexico, the rebellion in the

316 Part 4 The Third World

southernmost and poorest state, Chiapas, which broke out in early 1994, has ethnic overtones in that many rebels apparently come from Indian groups that have never been assimilated into the dominant Spanish culture.

There is one final form of political participation that political scientists are just beginning to pay attention to—the role of **nongovernmental organizations (NGOs).** As their name suggests, NGOs are unofficial bodies that operate in third world (and other) countries, though many of them are organized internationally and are actually composed of people who are not from the country they are active in. The most visible NGOs, such as *Médecins sans Frontières* (Doctors without Borders) and Save the Children, are not very political. They concentrate instead on humanitarian relief during what are euphemistically called "complex emergencies." Increasingly, however, even the most apolitical NGOs are recognizing that their work invariably brings them into political life. Those that concentrate on development or conflict resolution gladly acknowledge their political role. For countries in which both the state and the formal international community lack resources and credibility, NGOs can play a vital role in efforts to modernize the economy or build civil society from the grassroots level up.

Weak States

In Parts 2 and 3, the industrialized democracies and the current and former Communist regimes were defined in large part in terms of institutional features they shared. There are no such political common denominators for the third world. In fact, we can identify five main types of states found there.

Types of States

Democracies

There are a handful of established liberal democracies in the third world. In addition to India, the list includes Costa Rica, most of the island nations in the Caribbean, and several of the smallest and newest African states.

Some observers add a few others, like Mexico, that have maintained some features of democracy. But Mexico cannot be said to guarantee basic individual freedoms, competitive elections, or the rule of law. Similarly, many of us would like to label South Africa as democratic, given the remarkable changes there since Nelson Mandela's release from prison in 1990. However, it is far from certain that its multiracial democracy will survive the many social and economic problems facing the country.

Many countries have taken steps toward democracy since the late 1980s. Indeed, 1990 marked the first time that every country in South America had a government chosen through reasonably free and competitive elections. Democratization has occurred more slowly in Africa and most of Asia, but moves in that direction are occurring there as well.

We will return to the issue of democratization at the end of this chapter and as a central theme in the country chapters to follow. Here, it is enough to note that democratic regimes of the sort discussed in Part 2 are very much the exception to the rule and that most of those that do exist are fragile to say the least.

Single-Party Regimes

Most of the new nations initially adopted liberal constitutions with multiparty systems patterned after those of their colonizers. Few of them, however, lasted.

Especially in Africa, the struggle for independence was typically dominated by a single movement, which became the most powerful party after the transfer of power. Often, this group quickly abandoned the liberal democratic constitution and made itself the only legal party.

In some cases, there were elaborate and plausible justifications for such a move. Former president Nyerere of Tanzania likened competitive party systems to a soccer game in which a lot of energy was expended for only a goal or two—energy a new and poor country like his could not afford. More often, the shift to a single-party regime was little more than a power play by one faction in the country's elite, often representing a single ethnic or religious group.

In Tanzania, attempts were made to provide for democracy within the Tanzanian African National Union (TANU) in ways that resemble primaries with the Democratic or Republican parties in the United States. In most countries, however, the single party has amounted to little more than political window dressing for a dictatorship.

None of the countries considered in the rest of Part 4 currently has a classic single-party regime. Iraq's started that way under the Baath Party, but as Saddam Hussein consolidated his personal power, the party per se lost influence. Similarly, in Mexico, although other parties existed, the Institutional Revolutionary Party (PRI) controlled the Mexican state and dominated policy making for almost the entire twentieth century before it was finally defeated in 2000.

Military Regimes

Multiparty regimes have also frequently succumbed to military coups. Even though wars between states have been relatively rare in the third world (there were very

Sani Abacha, military leader of Nigeria from 1993 to 1998.

simply maintain law and order or enrich themselves. During the late 1970s and early 1980s, many political scientists and other observers believed that, for good or ill, these were the only kinds of regimes that could start third world countries on the road to development. By the end of the decade, however, such governments were in trouble everywhere. Economic growth slowed, making the uneven distribution of its benefits a more significant political issue. Protest over economic conditions combined with opposition to human rights abuses to create powerful movements that removed the military from power throughout South America and, to a lesser degree, in the rest of the third world.

Personal Dictatorships

Perhaps the most tragic form of government in the third world is personal dictatorship, such as those run by the Somozas in Nicaragua, Mobutu Sese Seko in Zaire, Muammar Gaddafi in Libya, Ferdinand and Imelda Marcos in the Philippines, or, the case we will consider in detail in Chapter 14, Saddam Hussein in Iraq. Sometimes, these rulers came to power through military coups. At other times, they were able to consolidate their control over the country after (more or less) open elections. Almost always, they were able to stay in control because one of the superpowers was convinced that they were vital allies in the cold war.

The Somozas of Nicaragua are a painfully typical example. For all intents and purposes, the United States put the "dynasty's" founder, Anastasio Somoza, into power. A succession of administrations had believed that this tiny Central American country was vital to U.S. national security interests and so had periodically sent the Marines in to keep people it opposed from taking over. During the 1930s, the Marines were used to help defeat a rebellion led by Augusto Cesar Sandino, whose primary goal was to force the United States out of his country.

Afterward, the Americans made the young Somoza head of the country's National Guard, in large part because he had been educated in the United States and spoke English fluently. Thus began four and a half decades of arbitrary and often brutal rule by the first Somoza and by his two sons, Luis and Anastasio. The Somozas did not tolerate any opposition to their rule, and routinely killed dissidents. The National Guard was given free reign to strong-arm political opponents and engage in a wide variety of corrupt activities, including prostitution and gambling. The Somozas stuffed their own pockets. By the 1970s, they owned the country's airports, electrical system, cigarette and match companies, a Mercedes-Benz dealership, and as much as half of the land. After the 1972 earthquake that devastated the capital city

few in South America, for instance, during the twentieth century), the military has been involved politically everywhere. The military has seen itself as having a dual role: to protect the country not only from external threats but also from civil unrest. From the military's perspective, multiparty regimes have turned chaotic far too often. Throughout Africa and South America, the twin fears of instability and Communist insurrection led the military to seize power time and time again. Consider Nigeria. Under its first two republics (1960–66, 1979–83), the political parties were organized almost exclusively along ethnic lines, making effective government all but impossible. The ensuing instability prompted the military to intervene to quell ethnic protest and political corruption. As has often been the case elsewhere, not only has the military overthrown civilian governments, but one group of soldiers has overthrown another on five occasions there as well.

Some military leaders have tried to do more than

of Managua, Anastasio Somoza kept most of the millions of dollars in **foreign aid** sent to rebuild the city, claiming that the weather was warm, so people really didn't need houses.

The Somozas are all too typical of this kind of ruler. Mobutu built dozens of palaces for himself even though a third or more of his people were starving. After her husband was overthrown, people around the world were shocked by Imelda Marcos's collection of thousands of pairs of shoes. Dozens of former dictators have, like former Haitian ruler Jean-Claude Duvalier, led lives of luxury in exile after being forced out of power.

Relatively few of these rulers made it to the end of the twentieth century. The Somozas, for example, were finally overthrown in 1979 by revolutionaries inspired by the memory of Sandino. "People power" brought the Marcoses down eight years later. Mobutu was forced into exile and died in 1997. Unfortunately, their successors have not had an easy time of it. Typically, the new leaders took office only to find the treasury looted, the country's natural resources depleted, and the people extremely impatient. In other words, the dictators' impact on their countries continued long after they were thrown out of office.

Failed States

In the regions of the third world states most affected by communal violence, we can no longer speak of sovereign states. In fact, observers are beginning to speak of failed states instead, because the government has lost the ability to exercise the most basic functions. All have governments and officials, but they resemble the Wizard of Oz more than a leader of an effective state. Once we get past the uniforms and the trappings of office, we can see that the leaders are little more than figureheads for a state that at best can control only a tiny fraction of its crime- or war-torn country.

For reasons of space, we will not cover any examples of failed states in this book. However, some observers are convinced that Mexico and India could fall apart if conditions continue to deteriorate. In other words, we will see some of the dynamics that have led to the collapse of governments in such countries as the Democratic Republic of Congo (DRC), Burundi, Rwanda, and Somalia in the chapters to follow.

States and Power

Of the three types of countries considered in this book, those in the third world face the most daunting problems and so are most in need of a reasonably strong state. But few have one.

At first glance, this might come as a surprise. After all, the stories we see in the news often stress the apparent power of these authoritarian rulers. This certainly was the case in accounts of Saddam Hussein after the invasion of Kuwait in 1990, the Nigerian regime that executed Ken Saro-Wiwa and other environmental activists in 1995, and, most recently, the Taliban in Afghanistan.

But few third world states have been able to do much more than maintain law and order by suppressing dissent, and many have not even accomplished that. There are some exceptions, such as in India, whose state-sponsored "green revolution" has improved agricultural output so much over the past generation that the country no longer has to import food. Far more common, though, is the disheartening history of Nigeria, where the average citizen is worse off than forty years ago despite the billions of dollars the government has earned from the sale of oil.

In the chapters that follow, we will see evidence of this weakness in three overlapping ways. The first is as a by-product of their poverty. No government in a country with a GNP of $500 per year will have much money to devote to education or health care. The lack of resources also leaves such a country with a weak infrastructure because it cannot afford to pave roads or lay cables for modern telecommunications systems.

More than just a lack of money is involved. In the poorest countries, the government may not "reach" everyone in the ways we in the north take for granted, including enforcing the law and collecting taxes. And these states are often short on human resources. For example, at the time of independence, there were only thirteen university graduates in all of what is now the DRC. Although there have been marked advances in education, life expectancy, and other areas of social life, none of these countries benefit from the kind of highly trained workforce that could produce the coalitions of business, government, and bureaucratic elites that have been so important in Europe, Japan, and elsewhere.

Second, many third world countries have had trouble developing regimes that last for more than a few years. As we saw in Parts 2 and 3, it takes both time and a degree of political success to develop strong institutions that are not dependent on the power or personality of individual leaders. Time allows people to establish routines and expectations for the institutions that govern them. Success helps build legitimacy.

But this has not happened in most of the third world. In part, the failure to develop effective states reflects the fact that most African and Asian countries are still new. More importantly, all have had to face heavy demands in a very short time frame. Thus, many people expect what happened over two or three centuries in the West to be squeezed into two or three decades. Put simply, people run out of patience with states that are not providing results fast enough.

Weak institutions are a particular problem in countries that have had a personal or military dictatorship for an extended time. For reasons we do not fully understand, these kinds of leaders tend not to concentrate on building institutions that will function effectively after they depart the scene.

Third, many third world countries with weak states are also plagued by widespread corruption, which extends far beyond the loss of scarce resources that leaders like the Marcoses, Somozas, Duvaliers, or Saddams spirit out of their countries. The corruption often extends far into the bureaucracy, especially in countries that lack a strong legal system and other institutions that could keep state employees in check. Thus, in Nigeria, civil servants are frequently referred to as "lootocrats" or "kleptocrats."

Public Policy: The Myths and Realities of Development

Given the poverty described earlier, it is hardly surprising that attempts to foster and speed economic development have been at the heart of most public policy making in the third world. It should also come as no surprise that the inability to make much progress on this front is seen as yet another example of the weakness of most third world states.

Timing is vital here. Economic and political development in Western Europe and North America took the better part of three centuries. In the few cases in which it happened more quickly (for example, Imperial Germany and Meiji Japan), it still took decades and required stiff repression.

Most third world countries—including those in Latin America that have been independent since the nineteenth century—embarked on their own developmental odysseys only recently and under much less promising circumstances. Britain, France, and the United States industrialized at a time when they also were the world's dominant economic and military powers, and thus were largely free to marshal needed resources as their leaders saw fit. Quite the opposite is the case in the third world today. Most countries are playing a game of political and economic catch-up in which they lag way behind the north and have few opportunities to close the gap.

To make matters even more difficult, there is no agreement about what "development" itself means. Some observers argue that it involves creating an urban, industrial economy that would turn, say, India or Mexico into a carbon copy of Germany or Japan. Others doubt that there is such a "linear" or common path to development and that third world countries will have to come up with their own ways of sustaining growth, adding to their wealth, and improving their people's standard of living. And, in recent years, some observers have questioned how much third world countries should be allowed to develop given the pressures economic growth places on our fragile ecosystem.

In any case, third world countries have adopted two general development strategies. The first—**import substitution**—was most popular from the 1950s into the 1980s. Since then, it has been all but completely abandoned for the more capitalist-oriented structural adjustment.

Import Substitution

Import substitution was designed to do just what the term suggests. If a country could replace expensive imported products with goods made locally, it would conserve more of its hard currency and other scarce resources, which could then be used to speed up development of its own industrial base.

It is easiest to see why such approaches were popular by first exploring **dependency theory,** which suggests why countries were eager to pursue what amounted to economic nationalism. Dependency theorists divide the world in two. On one side are the wealthy, capitalist nations of the north. On the other are the poor, underdeveloped third world countries that remain victims and de facto colonies of the north, whatever their legal status. In other words, dependency theorists focus on the economic rather than the political implications of imperialism and stress how the regions that became the third world were forced into the global capitalist system.

From this point of view, capitalists restructured local economies for the worse. Instead of encouraging them to grow food or manufacture commodities for domestic consumption, the imperial powers forced their colonies to produce a few raw materials for export: coffee and tea in Kenya, bananas in Guatemala, copper in Chile, and so on. In turn, first the colonies and then the new nations provided markets for the north's finished goods, which earned massive profits for the already rich countries.

Dependency theorists do not deny that there has been considerable industrialization and economic development in the third world in recent decades. Rather, they argue that such development has left the third world

A woman being carried away from the explosion of the Union Carbide chemical factory in Bhopal, India.

C. Zlotnik / Woodfin Camp & Associates

even more dependent on the north than ever before. The latter's banks and governments provide aid, but they invariably attach strings to it. These same institutions have issued loans that have left many third world governments owing hundreds of billions of dollars they cannot afford to repay. Northern corporations decide much of what is to be produced and ensure that the lion's share of the profits go back to their headquarters and shareholders.

Most third world countries are left with narrowly based economies that are highly vulnerable to the vagaries of the international market. The industrial development that has taken place there benefits only a tiny proportion of the population and has often left everyone else worse off. Foreign investment is increasingly oriented toward industries the northern countries no longer want because they degrade the environment or cost too much in workers' salaries and benefits. Most importantly, decision-making power remains overwhelmingly in foreign hands.

Leaders who accepted all or part of this explanation adopted policies that sought to reduce such dependency by strengthening their economy and their own control over it. Most tried to develop a manufacturing base independent of the multinationals in such vital areas as steel, automobiles, clothing, and agricultural equipment. This involved, among other things, erecting tariff and other barriers that made it more difficult for foreign goods and businesses to penetrate their mar-

kets. This way, they could protect their own fledgling manufacturers from competition from cheaper and higher-quality imports. Most set up publicly owned or controlled companies, often called **parastatals,** through which the government could steer the development of a domestic industrial base.

Of the countries covered here, India most consistently pursued import substitution. For the first thirty-five years after its independence in 1947, it enacted high tariffs and passed other laws that made it hard for foreign companies to invest there and impossible for them to buy more than a minority share in an Indian corporation. Available resources were concentrated on Indian manufacturers, most of which were government owned or controlled. The goods they made were rarely competitive in open markets, which meant that India could not export much and that its overall growth rate remained low, but at least it controlled its own development, however limited that development was.

Many countries stuck with import substitution well into the 1980s. By then, however, two things had happened that undermined support for it just about everywhere.

First, it had become clear that the countries using it were growing far more slowly than those that had aggressively tried to build niches for themselves in global markets. In India, it was derisively known as the "Hindu rate of growth"—steady, but far too slow.

It was at about this time that observers began noticing the NICs and their often spectacular development record. Indians, for instance, had to acknowledge that they were now far worse off than the Taiwanese, who had been as poor as they were in the 1940s. In short, India may have charted its own development. The problem was that there was just too little of it.

Second, geopolitical changes all but forced third world countries to become more active participants in the global economic system. The most important events in this respect, again, were the OPEC-induced "price shocks" of 1973 and 1979. Most third world countries traditionally have had to import not only oil but dozens of other products that are made using petroleum and its by-products. And they have had to pay for these goods in dollars or other **hard currencies.** At best, this meant that they had to export more to earn that money, which, in turn, implied meeting global price and quality standards. At worst, they had to borrow even more from northern banks, governments, and agencies, which left many of them so deeply in debt that there seemed no way they could ever pay back even the interest on the loans, let alone the principal.

In other words, dependency theory may have taken scholars and policymakers a long way toward explaining why the third world was in such dire economic straits. Indeed, the debt crisis and the other post-OPEC difficulties reinforced many of its conclusions about the power of the north.

It did not, however, help the third world countries develop policies that would actually work. Then, when conditions worsened in the 1980s, and the end of the cold war removed socialism as an attractive option for leaders around the world, the political momentum shifted toward a dramatically different approach to development.

Structural Adjustment

Currently, most economists and political scientists prefer the more conservative approach to economic growth known as structural adjustment. According to its proponents, the global capitalist market is not the problem but the solution. They are convinced that import substitution was a disaster and believe that the third world's best chance of developing lies in integrating itself into the global economy as quickly and as fully as possible. This can be achieved by following a mix of policies designed to open up the domestic economy to imports and investments, reduce government spending and national debt, slash inflation, restore macroeconomic equilibrium, and sell off state-owned enterprises. Few third world governments have eagerly embraced structural adjustment. However, most have been convinced, and in some cases

Downtown Seoul, South Korea. Countries like South Korea— the so-called NICs—have made a lot of economic progress.

compelled, to do so by northern governments and the international financial institutions, as will be discussed in the next two sections.

Studies conducted by the World Bank, among others, divided the third world according to the degree to which countries were "outward" or trade oriented. Contrary to dependency theory's predictions, the countries that traded the most—that is, the countries that played by the rules of the capitalist economic game—grew the fastest. From 1973 to 1985, these countries grew, on average, 7.7 percent per year overall and 10 percent per year in manufacturing. By contrast, the least trade-oriented states grew by only 2.5 percent overall and 3.1 percent in manufacturing.

The evolution of South Korea is instructive. Prior to the Asian economic crisis beginning in 1997, it grew at a rate that exceeded even Japan and was one of the most trade-oriented countries in the world. At first, the growth was concentrated in low-quality, low-tech industries in ways that mirrored what the dependency theorists would lead us to expect. During the 1970s, however, the nature of that growth changed. Korean companies started making steel, automobiles, and electronic goods, and became major players in global markets.

There are many reasons why the South Korean economy boomed that had little to do with structural adjustment, including its then-strong and often repressive state. Nonetheless, high on any list of explanations for its success has to be the way Korean companies, with the encouragement of the state, learned to operate effectively in international markets.

Structural adjustment's supporters tend to exaggerate its benefits and ignore its shortcomings, including the fact that it does little to help the plight of the poor. Nonetheless, they are correct in their basic assertion that the countries that grew the most in the 1980s and 1990s were those that, as the term itself suggests, adjusted their policies to the realities of global economic conditions.

Structural adjustment may not be the panacea its supporters think it is. However, there is no escaping the fact that it is now being followed almost everywhere. As with any major shift in public policy, there are many reasons leaders throughout South America, Africa, and Asia have turned to structural adjustment. None, however, is more important than the fact that most loans and aid have been made contingent on its adoption.

The International Financial Institutions

The **International Monetary Fund** (**IMF;** www.imf.org), the **World Bank** (www.worldbank.org), and the **World Trade Organization** (**WTO;** www.wto.org) have been critical forces in the shift toward structural adjustment in the third world. The three are often called the Bretton Woods organizations because the first steps toward creating them occurred at a 1944 meeting at that New Hampshire resort.

Originally the institutions were designed to spur economic recovery and stabilization in the war-torn countries of Europe and Asia. However, as Europe recovered and as more and more countries gained their independence, the focus of the three organizations turned to the third world and, to a lesser degree, the current and former Communist countries.

In recent years these organizations have also become controversial. Each of their major meetings since the protests against the WTO in Seattle in 1999 has been disrupted by demonstrators who accuse them of everything from destroying the environment to reinforcing poverty and sexism in the third world and beyond (www .50years.org).

The World Bank (officially the International Bank for Reconstruction and Development) is the largest—and perhaps the least well understood—of the three. Today, the Bank primarily makes loans and also issues a smaller number of direct grants to developing countries. Some of its funds come from member countries, but most now come from the private financial market. The Bank is controlled through a system of weighted voting in which the countries that contribute the most funds (the richest countries) have by far the greatest influence. Early on, the Bank supported many large-scale industrial projects that were consistent with import substitution. But as the Bank has moved increasingly into the private financial sector, it has also made more of its loans along strictly commercial lines. This orientation is one of the reasons antiglobalization critics have attacked the Bank's policies. However, its supporters point to changes in the

The first major protest against the WTO and globalization in Seattle. Dozens more have since been held.

John G. Mabanglo/AFP/Getty Images

Liberalization in the Third World

STRUCTURAL ADJUSTMENT IS, in fact, little more than another term for liberalization. Unlike in the former Communist countries, however, the emphasis in the third world has not been primarily on privatizing publicly owned corporations. This has occurred in countries like Mexico, which had a large and inefficient state sector. But most international banks and agencies have insisted that third world leaders get their countries' macroeconomic life in order in two other ways—reducing inflation and cutting the national debt. Doing so, it is argued, will enable these countries to participate more effectively in the international economy.

This may make good sense from the perspective of classical economics. But it is less clear whether these countries can use structural adjustment either to catch up with the north or to close the gap between their own rich and poor citizens by enacting such policies.

Finally, it has to be stressed that few countries have adopted structural adjustment policies voluntarily. There are exceptions—for example, Chile under General Augusto Pinochet. For most countries, however, liberalization has been urged on them by northern governments, banks, and agencies that made adopting structural adjustment a precondition for receiving further aid and other forms of support.

Bank's family of institutions, including the creation of units to promote the environment, postconflict reconstruction, environmental protection, and the reduction of poverty.

The IMF, by contrast, is far more unambiguously in the structural adjustment camp. It was created at the same time as the World Bank, and the headquarters of the two organizations are located next to each other in Washington, D.C. The IMF was originally designed primarily to stabilize international monetary flows at a time when other currencies were fixed to the value of the U.S. dollar, which, itself, was determined to be worth $35 per ounce of gold. In the early 1970s this system collapsed, and the role of the IMF shifted to that of lender of last resort for troubled economies in the third world and, later, the former Soviet bloc. It is governed in roughly the same way as the World Bank, though the rich countries have even more voting power in the IMF. In recent decades the IMF has insisted on **conditionality,** or the acceptance of structural adjustment and other policy-related "conditions," before granting a country a loan. Thus, far

more than the World Bank, it has been directly responsible for the often grudging adoption of these policies, something we will see most clearly in Mexico and Nigeria.

The WTO is the newest of the three organizations. Originally, the negotiators at Bretton Woods hoped to create a permanent institution that would work to reduce tariffs and otherwise open up international trade. For reasons we do not need to get into here, that organization was not created at the time. Instead, the far looser General Agreement on Tariffs and Trade (GATT) was formed in 1947. Its original agreement and subsequent "rounds" of negotiations gradually lowered tariffs and eased other restrictions on trade around the world. Finally, the leaders of over 130 countries agreed to form the permanent WTO in 1994 and granted it powers to enforce rules that would further free trade and resolve commercial disputes among member states. In other words, the WTO, too, is a strong supporter of structural adjustment and related policies. With China's and Taiwan's accession to membership in 2001, all the world's major economies other than Russia are members of the WTO.

Foreign Aid

Long before the colonies began declaring their independence after World War II, it was clear that the third world would not be able to develop on its own. Therefore, the leading industrial nations—which, of course, included the leading colonial powers—realized that they would have to help out.

The same sort of naïve assumptions we saw regarding state building also existed for economic development. The hope was that a limited amount of money and material aid would lead to what analysts at the time called an economic "takeoff" that would propel these countries to modern industrialized capitalist economies.

But this was to happen only to a tiny handful of NICs. There are many reasons for this, a number of which have to do with the internal politics of the countries themselves. Much, though, also is a function of the way the distribution of foreign aid has evolved since the 1950s.

There are several types of foreign aid. Northern governments make some grants and loans directly to third world governments. In recent years, international agencies have become more involved, most notably in providing loans both for long-term investment and to help countries work their way out of the **debt trap.** In a sense, multinational corporations also offer a form of aid when they invest in the third world and create jobs and other indirect economic benefits. Finally, the past few years have seen a growing role for nonprofit NGOs, some of which have been attempting to counter what they see as the negative impact of aid from these other sources.

Foreign aid as we know it today began with the Colombo Plan. Signed in 1950, it committed the British government to providing developmental assistance to its former colonies in South and Southeast Asia. Soon, the United States (1951) and Japan (1954) signed on. Since then, most of the industrialized democracies have been providing some developmental assistance, which at one point they have agreed should equal at least 0.7 percent of their GNP each year.

However, few of the industrialized democracies come close to reaching that goal. As table 11.5 shows, only five of the world's richest twenty-two countries reached that 0.7 percent goal in 2003, all of whom are fairly small and can thus have only a limited impact. The United States is the world's largest donor in absolute terms, and its contributions have increased since the terrorist attacks of 2001. Nonetheless, it ranks last in the column that measures the share of GNP it contributes. And the top four recipients of U.S. aid in 2003 were Egypt, Russia, Israel, and Pakistan, who were chosen because of their strategic importance to Washington more than their actual economic need. But it should be pointed out that all the major donors concentrate their aid on former colonies and other countries deemed critical to their national interest.

To be fair, table 11.5 does not include sources of aid and investment that come from the private sector. Reliable statistics on that score are only available for the United States where corporations and NGOs provide at least twice the amount of aid made available by the government.

There are also serious criticisms of the nature of the aid itself that parallel those of the international financial institutions. Too much, it is said, goes for large-scale industrial projects that cannot be readily maintained and operated using domestic resources. Similarly, little of the aid is used to help people in the recipient countries develop the skills and other resources that will help them achieve some degree of self-sustained development, thereby reducing the need for aid. Recipient countries are expected to use the grants or loans to buy material or hire consultants from the donor country. Also, a surprising amount of the aid is aimed not at civilian but at military development, whose benefits for the economy as a whole are limited. Finally, once all financial transfers and other economic costs (such as agricultural subsidies in northern countries), the third world probably contributes more to the affluence of the industrialized democracies than vice versa.

Microcredit

There is one promising sign in what has so far been a relatively disheartening saga—**microcredit.** Some people in the third world have established their own small-scale financial institutions that enable them to determine and implement more of their own development policies and thus avoid the problems associated with foreign aid. In one form or another, each of these financial institutions tries to mobilize local people to control their own resources, which, in turn, can be used to help finance others.

The best known of these institutions is Bangladesh's Grameen Bank (www.grameen-info.org). The bank was founded in 1976 by Muhammad Yunus, an economics professor at Chittagong University. Unlike most Western experts, Yunus was convinced that average Bangladeshi peasants could use banking services to create businesses they could run and profit from themselves.

The Grameen Bank's principles are simple and clear. As Yunus put it recently:

> Their [the peasants'] poverty was not a personal problem due to laziness or lack of intelligence, but a structural one: lack of capital. We do not need to

■ TABLE 11.5 Foreign Aid: The Major Donors, 2003

COUNTRY	OVERSEAS DIRECT ASSISTANCE (IN MILLIONS OF DOLLARS)	OVERSEAS DIRECT ASSISTANCE (AS PERCENTAGE OF GNP)
Norway	2,043	0.92
Denmark	1,747	0.84
Netherlands	3,377	0.81
Luxembourg	143	0.80
Sweden	2,100	0.70
Belgium	1,877	0.61
Ireland	510	0.41
France	7,337	0.41
Switzerland	1,297	0.38
United Kingdom	6,166	0.34
Finland	556	0.34
Germany	6,694	0.28
Canada	2,209	0.26
Spain	2,030	0.25
Australia	1,237	0.25
New Zealand	169	0.23
Portugal	298	0.21
Greece	356	0.21
Japan	8,911	0.20
Austria	503	0.20
Italy	2,393	0.16
United States	15,791	0.14

Source: Adapted from www.oecd.org.

Muhammad Yunus with a typical group of Grameen Bank clients.

Grameen Communications

teach them how to survive: they know this already. Giving the poor credit allows them to put into practice the skills they already know. And the cash they earn is then a tool, a key that unlocks a host of other problems.[4]

The Grameen Bank lends money only to destitute people. By mid-2004 the bank had 3.7 borrowers located in more than two-thirds of Bangladesh's. Ninety-four percent of its clients are women because they are better credit risks than men. To obtain a loan, a person has to pass a test on how the bank works and has to join a group of fellow borrowers who provide support, but also, if necessary, apply pressure to the borrower to repay the loan. The bank does not provide business training, but it does expect its borrowers to abide by "sixteen decisions," including a pledge to send their children to school and not to pay dowries when their daughters marry. Loans are for a year and may be renewed and extended for up to five years. Repayments are made at weekly meetings in which eight to ten of the loan groups gather.

In one typical case, a villager could not afford to feed her three children and her blind, unemployed husband. After overcoming her husband's objections, she passed the bank's test, got her loan, and bought a calf. Within a

year, she used money from the sale of the calf to pay off the loan. She then took out another loan, with which she bought another calf and land for banana plants. Within five years, her farm had grown to include a rice paddy, goats, ducks, and chickens. Her family has three meals a day, and she can even consider sending her children to high school. As she told a British reporter, "You ask me what I think of Grameen? Grameen is like my mother. She has given me new life."

This is not an isolated example. A World Bank study found that over 95 percent of Grameen loans were repaid on time. Even more impressively, within five years, half of the borrowers were above the poverty line, and another quarter were close. The Grameen Bank's operations have expanded, too, and it now gives $300 home mortgages to families who have taken out and repaid at least three loans. It also has begun giving its village leaders cell phones, which serve as the only local pay phones. And, in 1999, the bank became Bangladesh's leading Internet service provider—on the profits from its cell phone business.

Most of the countries in the world now have some type of microcredit projects, including the United States. In 2001, over 2,600 people from 137 countries met in Washington for the first Microcredit summit (www .microcreditsummit.org). U.S. senator Hillary Clinton and World Bank president James Wolfensohn shared the stage with women from around the world who had

---

[4]Quoted in Alan Jolis, "The Good Banker," *Independent on Sunday Magazine.* 5 May 1996, 15–16.

taken major strides in improving their living conditions through microcredit programs. Attendees pledged to reach 100 million of the world's poorest people by 2005.

Feedback

Feedback occurs in very different ways in the third world—ways that reflect many of the broader themes of this chapter.

Because of poverty, relatively few people have access to television, which has become the primary source of political information in the rest of the world. Indeed, in 1985, when an American peace group wanted to do a global televised presentation of its annual awards, it encountered what seemed to be an insurmountable obstacle. Tanzania, where one of the recipients lived, had no television at all. And it's not just television. Whereas two out of three Americans have access to the Internet at home, in the third world that figure comes closer to one in three thousand. In fact, a major breakthrough occurred in the 1990s for the world's poorest people who do not have electricity when a British inventor developed an affordable radio that used a hand crank to generate its own power.

Many third world countries also do not have a free press available to their citizens who can read and/or afford to buy a newspaper or magazine. The authoritarian regimes, in particular, are quite effective when it comes to censoring the news or, in the case of Mexico, limiting the ability of newspaper owners, should they be too critical, to obtain such vital supplies as newsprint.

As a result, patron-client networks and other "traditional" institutions provide critical feedback "services" in the third world. In the process, the patrons reinforce

Talking Drum Studio has had a major impact on reducing ethnic tensions now that most fighting has ceased in Sierra Leone.

Courtesy of Talking Drums Studio/Search for Common Ground

Globalization and the Third World

WESTERNERS OFTEN THINK of globalization in their own terms. For the optimists, it is bringing unprecedented riches, instant communication, and affordable global travel. For the pessimists, it is eroding working-class jobs and harming the environment.

When we shift our attention to the third world, the picture looks less clear—from either an optimistic or pessimistic perspective. Globalization is drawing more and more people into international networks, commercial and otherwise. However, there are still upwards of a billion people whose lives are barely touched by global forces. Moreover, a case can be made that globalization is contributing to a growing gap between rich and poor, and is reinforcing traditional values and religions, thereby sparking conflict the third world can ill afford.

their own strength, as well as the dependency of their clients on them.

Last but by no means least, the mass media have often been used to foment ethnic conflict, most notably in the lead up to the 1994 genocide in Rwanda. Some NGOs like Search for Common Ground have tried to counter those trends by producing radio programs that document interethnic healing in deeply divided societies.

Conclusion: Democratization

A generation ago, an introductory chapter on the third world would have ended with a recap of its economic and/or environmental woes. It would have been even more depressing than this one, given the rampant and deepening poverty, the debt crisis, and environmental degradation. Today, those problems remain, and most of them are as serious as they ever have been. Nevertheless, we can end this chapter on a slightly more upbeat note.

For the past decade or so, the most exciting trend in the third world has been democratization. In 1990, all the Latin American countries south of Mexico had a democratically elected government—the first time this had ever happened—and most have kept those regimes. The Nigerian military has turned control of the country over to a third republic, and a few other African governments are experimenting with competitive elections, the first time the momentum had swung in that direction since the early 1960s. A number of the previously authoritarian regimes in East Asia have taken substantial, though still incomplete, steps toward democracy, including the Philippines and South Korea.

Democracy may well be taking root in places that were as far from it as one could imagine a decade or so ago. South Africa, in particular, has made remarkable strides in moving from apartheid to majority rule. Most remarkably, the core leaders of the old Afrikaner regime made their peace (albeit reluctantly) with the African National Congress and served in the government of former president Nelson Mandela for two years before quitting in May 1996. As we will see in the online chapter, the fledgling South African democracy has made great strides with its Truth and Reconciliation Commission and has survived Mandela's retirement.

For over a decade, political scientists have been focusing more of their attention on why some democracies survive and thrive while others do not. Although they are far from reaching anything like definitive conclusions, they have come to six preliminary conclusions that offer some reason for hope.

First, much will depend on the attitudes and behavior of average citizens, many of whom are less than forgiving toward dictatorial regimes that have done little or nothing to improve basic standards of living. The experience of South Africa today and India over most of the past half-century suggests that people may come to support a regime and temper their own demands not out of a general commitment to democracy but because they are convinced that it is working. In other words, short-term pragmatic considerations, which states may actually be able to do something about, can be as important in building a basis for democracy as the forging of the more difficult-to-achieve sense of commitment to the abstract principles and procedures underlying it. After all, in poll after poll, many Americans reject some of the provisions in the Bill of Rights when asked about them on their own rather than as amendments to the Constitution. This suggests that democratic principles are not always deeply supported in the north.

Second, for this kind of "pragmatic support" to build, the state has to be reasonably effective. One of the misreadings of contemporary and historical trends that has come with the rightward shift in recent years has been the assumption that if the state merely "gets out of people's lives" things will improve. But the historical record reviewed in Part 2 reveals something quite different. Democratic regimes succeeded in part because their states were capable of making tough decisions about the allocation of resources, the shape of institutions, and the handling of disorder.

Third, timing is important. The first years in the life of any regime are critical because it is new and fragile. Therefore, it does seem to be the case that if a democracy can get through the first few elections and, as we saw with France's Fifth Republic, survive the transition from the first government to the opposition, it is usually much stronger and more likely to endure.

Fourth, there is a link between democracy and capitalism. However, it certainly is not as simple or as automatic as the strongest advocates of structural adjustment would lead us to believe. Markets are not natural phenomena but have to be created and sustained, reinforcing the importance of a reasonably strong state. Also, the purported benefits of markets do not come quickly—if they come at all—whereas, as the history of all democratic regimes suggests, people tend to be impatient and to expect dramatic improvements in the short run. There is also evidence that democracy may have a good chance of succeeding only after societies have reached a certain level of wealth. The most recent research has put that figure at a per capita income of about $5,000 per year, which is well above what most third world states can dream of.

Fifth, for all the reasons discussed earlier, international factors will become more and more important as the world continues to "shrink." (See Chapter 17.) There is growing awareness that northern policy toward the south should be made with more long-term goals regarding development and democracy in mind, which might mean sacrificing some shorter-term profits and/or market share. However, there are stronger signs that the shift toward market-based policies will continue, which might actually worsen conditions for most people in the politically all-important short run.

Finally, we should definitely *not* expect the democracies that might emerge in the third world to resemble those in the West. As we saw in Part 2, the Western democracies developed as a result of a long historical process that cannot be replicated because conditions are so dramatically different today. Indeed, it may well be that democracy in the third world will not be much like what we saw in Part 2 at all.

Key Terms

Concepts

Carrying capacity	Dependency theory
Communal group	Failed state
Conditionality	Foreign aid
Debt crisis	Fundamentalism
Debt trap	Hard currency
Dependency	Human Development Index

Imperialism

Import substitution

Indirect rule

Microcredit

Newly industrializing
   country

Parastatal

Patron-client relations

Structural adjustment

Subsistence economy

Third world

Acronyms

HDI	NGO	OPEC
IMF	NIC	WTO
MNC		

Organizations, Places, and Events

International Monetary Fund

Multinational corporation

Nongovernmental organization

Organization of Petroleum Exporting Countries

World Bank

World Trade Organization

Critical Thinking Exercises

1 Much has changed since this book was finished in early 2005. Does the analysis of the third world presented here still make sense? Why (not)?

2 Public opinion pollsters routinely ask questions about whether people think their country is heading in the "right direction" or is on the "wrong track." If you were asked such a question about the third world, how would you answer? Why did you reach this conclusion?

3 The chapter asserts that global forces have been more influential in the third world than in the countries covered in Parts 2 and 3. Do you agree? Historically? Today? Why did you reach this conclusion?

4 Many third world countries have had trouble building a sense of national identity or other cultural values that could lend legitimacy to their states. Why is this the case?

5 Most third world countries have weak states. What does this concept mean? Why are weak states so common in the third world?

6 Development has been the most important issue in most third world countries. What does this concept mean? Why have we seen such a sweeping change from import substitution to structural adjustment in recent years? What kind of impact has this change had?

7 Political violence and conflict are common in the third world. Why? How do the conflict and protest differ from what we find in the rest of the world?

8 Democratization is on the agenda of most third world countries. Should we be optimistic or pessimistic about it? Why did you reach this conclusion?

Useful Websites

There are not all that many websites on the third world, per se. There are, however, many good ones that touch on much of what is covered in this chapter. The best of these is the new site on globalization created by the Center for Strategic and International Studies in Washington.

> **www.globalization101.org**

The Virtual Library also has good sites on sustainable development and on microcredit.

> **www.ulb.ac.be/ceese/meta/sustvl.html**
>
> **www.gdrc.org/icm/**

The Center for World Indigenous Studies focuses on the status of ethnic minorities in the third world. The Third World Network is a good, left-of-center source for news and analysis on development issues.

> **www.cwis.org**
>
> **www.twnside.org.sg**

Many international organizations and NGOs issue regular reports filled with analysis and data, including the World Bank, the United Nations Development Program, and the World Resources Institute.

> **econ.worldbank.org/wdr/**
>
> **www.undp.org/hdro**
>
> **www.wri.org**

InfoTrac College Edition Sources

Acker, J. "Gender, Capitalism, and Globalization."

Adelman, Carol. "The Privatization of Foreign Aid."

Krueger, Anne. "First World/Third World."

Landolt, M. K. "Misconstructing the Third World."

Leftwich, Andrew. "Bringing Politics Back In: Towards a Model of the Developmental State."

Maynes, Charles William. "America's Fading Commitments."

Mitchell, Michael. "Explaining Third World Democracies."

Randall, V. "Using and Abusing the Concept of the Third World."

Wolfensohn, James. "The Other Lives."

Yunus, Muhammad. "Empowerment of the Poor (Grameen Bank)."

Further Reading

Dickson, Anna K. *Development and International Relations: A Critical Introduction.* Oxford: Polity Press, 1997. A valuable resource. Don't be put off by "international relations" in the title. Because the two fields overlap so much, this is as useful in comparative politics and the one source that truly tries to assess the various theories, including those focused on here.

Easterly, William. *The Elusive Quest for Growth.* Boston: MIT Press, 2001. An exploration of how the conventional wisdom and policy on development have evolved over the years, and the costs associated with those changes, by a leading World Bank economist.

Ellwood, Wayne. *The No-Nonsense Guide to Globalization.* London: Verso, 2001. Though written from an explicitly antiglobalization perspective, a book worth reading by us all because it contains one of the best short descriptions of what globalization entails and why it is happening.

Fisher, Julie. *Non-Governments: NGOs and the Political Development of the Third World.* West Hartford, Conn.: Kumarian Press, 1997. By far the best source on NGOs, by a woman who combines the insights of an academic with the enthusiasm of an activist.

Haynes, Jeff. *Third World Politics: A Concise Introduction.* London: Blackwell, 1996. A basic text organized conceptually that goes beyond the basic issues to get at such themes as gender and the environment.

Huntington, Samuel P. *The Clash of Civilizations: Remaking the World Order.* New York: Simon & Schuster, 1996. A highly controversial book, by one of the most respected (and conservative) analysts of the third world, that focuses essentially on cultural arguments in anticipating the next round of global conflict, domestically and internationally.

Isbister, John. *Promises Not Kept: Poverty and the Betrayal of Third World Development.* 6th ed., Bloomfield, Conn.: Kumarian Press, 2003. The best overview of the dilemmas facing third world countries trying to develop economically and politically.

Kaplan, Robert. *The Coming Anarchy: Shattering the Dreams of the Post–Cold War.* New York: Random House, 2000. A depressing, journalistic account of looming conflict and its implications. This book is a collection of short essays, but interested readers with time would do well to consult his longer *The Ends of the Earth.*

Migdal, Joel S. *Strong Societies and Weak States: State-Society Relations and State Capabilities in the Third World.* Princeton, N.J.: Princeton University Press, 1988. Although limited in its geographical scope, a useful discussion of the idea of strong and weak states in ways that amplify the central theme of this chapter.

Przeworski, Adam. *Sustainable Democracy.* New York: Cambridge University Press, 1995. Probably the best book written so far on the subject. Actually written by a committee of twenty-one well-known social scientists who combine a lot of important ideas about democratization and economics in the "east" and "south" into 112 pages. A difficult read, but well worth it.

Sorenson, Georg. *Democracy and Democratization.* Boulder, Colo.: Westview Press, 1993. Part of an outstanding series of books on international relations written for undergraduates. This one is more about comparative politics issues and is probably the most readable book on democratization, including in the West. It does, however, frame the issues a bit differently from the way they are presented here.

Taras, Raymond, and Rajat Ganguly. *Understanding Ethnic Conflict: The International Dimension.* New York: Longman, 2002. An excellent overview of the way ethic conflict hinders many countries in the third world and beyond.

World Bank. *World Development Report.* Published annually, the best single source of statistics on development issues as well as a topic considered in depth each year.

As Indian citizens, we subsist on a regular diet of caste massacres and nuclear tests, mosque breakings and fashion shows, church burnings and expanding cell phone networks, bonded labor and the digital revolution, female infanticide and the NASDAQ crash, husbands who continue to burn their wives for dowry and our delectable stockpile of Miss Worlds. What's hard to reconcile oneself to, both personally and politically, is the schizophrenic nature of it.

ARUNDHATI ROY

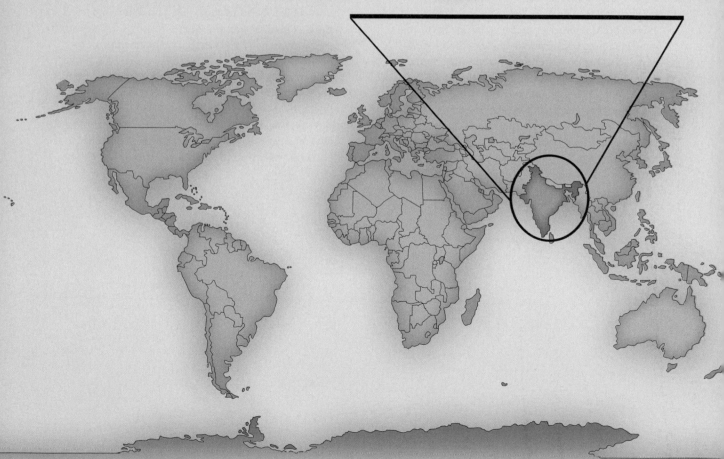

Chapter 12

INDIA

CHAPTER OUTLINE

The Basics: India

Size	3,287,590 sq. km (about 1.3 times the size of the United States)
Population	1.04 billion; growing at the rate of 1.9% per year
GNP per capita	$480
Currency	45 rupees = $1
Ethnic groups	72% Indo-Aryan, 25% Dravidian, 3% other
Religion	81% Hindu, 12% Muslim, 2% Christian, 2% Sikh, 3% other
Capital	New Delhi
Head of State	President Abdul Kalam (2002–)
Head of Government	Prime Minister Manhoman Singh (2004–)

Who Gives a Dam?

On 18 October 2000, the Indian Supreme Court allowed authorities in the state of Gujarat to continue construction of the Sardar Sarovar Dam in the Narmada River valley (see the map on the preceding page). In April 2004, enough work on the project had been done that the dam's generators began feeding electricity into India's woefully inadequate electrical grid. When completed it will be an impressive structure—almost 137 meters (460 feet) tall—and will irrigate 1.8 million hectares (over 4.3 million acres) of land. It is also but one of about thirty large dams planned for that region of India (www.narmada.org/sardarsarovar.html and www.sardarsarovardam.org).

For their supporters, the big dams will bring unprecedented economic growth and prosperity to the world's second-most-populous country, and also one of its poorest. Half of India's population lies below one of the most widely used measures of poverty—surviving on less than a dollar a day. According to this same measure, a third of the world's poor live in India. The water from the dams could be used to irrigate fields to boost crop output on the region's arid land, and the electricity they generate would provide energy for new factories and offices in a country that is developing a modern industrial sector.

The Sardar Sarovar Dam also has many opponents.

The Sardar Sarovar dam, which has been the source of much controversy in India in the decade since construction began.

Robert Nickelsberg/Time Life Pictures/Getty Images

Criticisms range from the devastating effects such dams will have on the daily lives of poor peasants to broader worries linking them to the corrosive impact of globalization. If the critics are to be believed, more than thirty million people have been displaced by the construction of big dams in the past decade. The Sardar Sarovar Dam alone will force a half million people to move from villages that will be flooded. Despite the legal requirement to do so, no plans have been made to resettle about half of them. Most of those affected will come from the so-called untouchables and people of tribal origin, who are outside the caste system but probably even worse off than the untouchables.

India's economic growth occurred as the country opened its economy to international trade and investment, as called for by proponents of structural adjustment (see Chapter 11). Tariffs have been slashed and other restrictions on imports eliminated. Dams themselves have become a big business worth $40–45 billion per year, and most of that money comes from multinational corporations. Opponents of the dams, however, question the alleged benefits of this kind of investment and outline scenarios in which large multinational agricultural firms will undercut the livelihood of poor peasants, just as other foreign firms are siphoning off market shares for Indian cars and other manufactured goods.

There have been bigger political stories in India in recent years, including the surprise victory by the Congress Party in the 2004 election and the even more surprising decision by **Sonia Gandhi** to decline the post of prime minister. But more than anything else, the dams introduce us to the key dilemma that India and many other third world countries face. How can a country develop without harming either the welfare of its people or its physical environment?

Thinking about India

The controversy surrounding the Sardar Sarovar Dam is very different from the vignettes used to begin the chapters in Parts 2 and 3. That's because India and the other countries discussed in Part 4 are very different from those we explored in the first two-thirds of this book. In other words, as Chapter 11 implied, studying India in particular and the third world in general means shifting gears once again to consider widespread poverty, ethnic conflict, and weak states, as well as the far more disruptive impact of globalization.

The Basics

A Nation of Contrasts

As the chapter-opening quote by Arundhati Roy (a leading opponent of the Sardar Sarovar Dam) suggests, India is a land of stark contrasts and contradictions. Depending on your perspective, it is one of the most backward or one of the most promising countries on earth. It is one of the poorest countries, yet it is also the world's tenth-largest industrial power. Only the United States and Russia have more scientists and engineers. About 60 percent of Indians are illiterate, yet rural India is connected by a network of satellite stations that have brought television to more than 80 percent of its 700,000 villages. At home, its people seem reluctant to work hard and take risks, yet Indians abroad are known for their business acumen.

Politically, India was the home of the world's most famous and influential pacifist, yet it has one of the largest armies in the world and is one of but ten countries (as far as we know) to have developed nuclear weapons. India was a founder of the nonaligned movement that tried to avoid taking sides during the cold war. Yet it has also fought several wars with Pakistan, its neighbor and fellow nuclear power, imposed an economic and military blockade on Nepal, and sent fifty thousand troops to protect the Tamil minority in neighboring Sri Lanka.

Size and Diversity

The other striking thing about India is its size and diversity. Only China has more people. Seven of its states each have more inhabitants than Britain or France. Despite its family planning program, India adds the equivalent of Argentina to its population each year, and in 2000 it topped a billion people.

India's population is also among the most diverse in the world, which is most evident to outsiders in the languages its people speak.

Nearly 60 percent of the population speaks one of the Indo-Aryan languages used mostly in northern India. Of them, about half speak Hindi. However, even though these languages are related, people who speak Hindi, Bengali, or Gujarati do not fully understand each other. The 30 percent of the people who live in the south mostly speak one of the Dravidian languages, which are completely different from those used in the north. About 5 percent of the people (mostly Sikhs) speak Punjabi, an offspring of Persian and Urdu, the dominant language of Pakistan.

The constitution lists fourteen official "principal languages." (See table 12.1.) In fact, the situation is much more complicated, because there are hundreds of dialects subsumed in these linguistic families, and as many as one hundred million people speak languages that do not figure on the list in any form. As in much of South Asia and Africa, the only language educated Indians have in common is English. Thus, the language of the colonizer has become the lingua franca in much of business and government.

The government has drawn the twenty-five state and seven union territory boundaries so that each has

TABLE 12.1 India's Principal Language Groups

LANGUAGE	PERCENTAGE OF POPULATION	WHERE SPEAKERS ARE CONCENTRATED
Assamese	1.4	Assam
Bengali	7.6	West Bengal
Gujarati	4.9	Gujarat, Bombay
Hindi	38.6	Bihar, Haryana, Himachal Pradesh, Rajasthan, Uttar Pradesh, Delhi
Kannada	3.9	Karnataka
Kashmiri	0.5	Jammu and Kashmir
Malayalam	3.8	Kerala
Marathi	7.2	Maharashtra
Oriya	3.3	Orissa
Punjabi	2.7	Punjab
Tamil	6.5	Tamil Nadu
Telegu	7.9	Andhra Pradesh
Urdu	5.2	Most Hindi-speaking regions

Source: Adapted from Robert W. Stern, *Changing India* (New York: Cambridge University Press, 1993), 19.

a dominant language and culture. Nonetheless, they all have large minorities that have played a significant and often violent role in local as well as national political life.

India also has three main religious groups. Slightly over 80 percent of the population is Hindu, but each major regional/linguistic group practices a different version of the religion. Approximately 10 percent are Muslim, but they run the full range of belief from fundamentalists to highly assimilated and secularized people who have, for all intents and purposes, stopped practicing their religion. Most of the rest are Sikhs. This religion has at its roots an attempt to blend Hindu and Muslim traditions emphasizing peacefulness and other-worldliness, but Sikhs are now known for their ferocious fighting ability and their dissatisfaction with their status in Punjab.

Like language, religion has been politically important since the Muslims first arrived as part of the **Mughal** conquest more than five hundred years ago. Independent India came into existence amid communal violence as millions of Muslims tried to escape India for Pakistan and millions of Hindus fled in the other direction. In the 1980s, the most difficult problem involved Sikhs, who sought their own homeland and who saw the national government attack their holiest shrine, the Golden Temple at Amritsar, and kill thousands of their most militant leaders. Since then, violence has most often occurred along religious lines, as in the case of the conflict over the temple/mosque site at **Ayodhya,** which we will examine in more detail later. Here, it is enough to note that the attempt by Hindus to build a new temple there led to riots in which thousands of Hindus and Muslims were killed throughout the northern part of India.

Language and Politics

As is the case in many third world countries, Indians speak many languages, and there is no common one they all understand. Hindi is the most widely spoken, but most speakers of other languages opposed its use in commercial and official communication so strongly that there were anti-Hindi riots in much of the south in the 1960s. As a result, the language of the colonial power—English—remains the lingua franca, although several prominent leaders do not speak it.

The role of English also reveals a lot about the elite domination of political life in India since colonial times. According to one recent count, about thirty-three million Indians speak English, which makes it the third largest English-speaking country in the world after the United States and the United Kingdom. However, that number also represents less than 4 percent of the total Indian population, and almost all English speakers are highly educated, wealthy, and influential.

Finally, India is divided along **caste** lines. Historians trace the caste system back nearly four thousand years, when in all likelihood the lighter-skinned Aryans established it to minimize "mingling" with the darker-skinned Dravidians. There are four main castes. The Brahmans historically were the priests and the most prestigious caste, the Kshatriyas were rulers and soldiers, and the Vaisyas were merchants. These three upper castes are often referred to as "twice born," reflecting the belief that they are further along in the Hindu cycle of death and reincarnation. The lowest-caste Sudras traditionally were farmers but did "respectable" enough work to warrant their inclusion in the caste system. Below them are the **untouchables,** or *dalits,* who are outside the caste system altogether because their ancestors were sullied by their occupations as scavengers and collectors of "night soil." About 8 percent of the populations are "tribals" who do not use the caste system; about that same number are part of even smaller ethnic groups that were never a part of this unusual system.

Each caste, in turn, is broken into hundreds of sub-castes known as *jati.* The castes and *jati* have elaborate rules for most social situations, including such things as what clothes to wear and what food to eat. Until very recently, people rarely broke out of their caste's restrictions.

The constitution officially abolished the status of outcaste and outlawed discrimination against untouchables and tribals. In practice, caste remains a volatile political issue. Discrimination against those at the bottom of the hierarchy is still as pervasive as racism is in the United States or Western Europe. In summer 1990, for instance, Prime Minister V. P. Singh proposed reserving about a quarter of all new positions in the civil service for members of the lower or "scheduled" castes in an Indian version of American affirmative action. The proposal so incensed upper-caste young people that they staged demonstrations at which some burned themselves alive.

Poverty

The most important fact of life in India is poverty. It is so widespread and has proved so difficult to reduce that we will devote much of the public policy section to it. As the table on the inside front cover shows, India's average per capita GNP is barely over $300 per year, making it the poorest country covered in this book. Despite recent gains, the gap between India and other countries that started out as poorly as it did, such as China, continues to grow.

The statistics are remarkable. One Indian baby in ten will die before reaching the age of one, and overall life expectancy is only about fifty years. For most people, health care is rudimentary at best. Although the "green revolution" of the 1960s all but eliminated mass starvation, most Indians eat a diet that does not quite meet the minimal caloric intake needed for a healthy life. And in 1998, a doubling in the price of onions took millions of people to the brink of starvation and cost the then-ruling **Bharatiya Janata Party (BJP)** control of three states.

The statistics tell only part of the story of Indian poverty. The cities are crowded and filthy, something that Indo-Caribbean and Nobel Prize–winning writer V. S. Naipaul put powerfully when describing his arrival in Bombay during only his second visit to India in the late 1980s. Things have not changed much since then:

> Traffic into the city moved slowly because of the crowd. When at certain intersections, the traffic was halted, the pavements seethed all the more, and such a torrent of people swept across the road, in such a bouncing froth of light-weight clothes, it seemed that some kind of invisible sluicegate had been opened, and that if it wasn't closed again, the flow of road-crossers would spread everywhere, and the beaten-up red buses and yellow-and-black taxis would be quite becalmed, each at the center of a human eddy.
>
> With me in the taxi were fumes and heat and din. Bombay continued to define itself: Bombay

flats on either side of the road now, concrete build-ings mildewed at their upper levels by the Bombay weather, excessive sun, excessive rain, excessive heat; grimy at the lower levels, as if from the crowds at pavement level, and as if that human grime was working its way up, tidemark by tidemark, to meet the mildew.[1]

Key Questions

Because India is the first country considered in detail in Part 4, this section has to do two things—outline general questions to ask of all third world countries along with specific ones about India.

- What are its political origins?
- How do people participate politically?
- How is it governed?
- How has it coped with poverty and unemployment?

Like most of the third world, India suffered from centuries of occupation and colonization, first under the Mughals and later under the British.

India's experience with imperialism was typical in many ways. Foreigners made all the decisions that mattered, which, among other things, served to destroy much of its economic base.

However, in other ways, it was unusual. The British never directly ruled the entire country. Moreover, they allowed a massive independence movement to develop following the creation of the **Indian National Congress** in 1885. As a result, the Indian regime that gained its independence in 1947 had widespread popular support and experienced leaders who were committed to democracy. That group of leaders, headed by the first prime minister, **Jawaharlal Nehru,** gave the country a generation of stability that deepened popular support for democracy and that has helped the country survive more serious conflict since the late 1960s.

India has been able to sustain its democracy in large part because its citizens supported it, especially during the country's critical formative years. Although we have to ask why this was the case, it is more important today to probe why there has been so much more protest in recent decades than there was during the heyday of Congress's rule under Nehru.

Then Congress was what political scientists call an inclusive party that found a way to appeal to people of all socioeconomic backgrounds and political beliefs. Once

Nehru's daughter, **Indira Gandhi,** became prime minister two years after her father's death in 1964, the party system began to fragment. National opposition parties, including the predecessors of the BJP, began to gain strength by appealing to narrower segments of the electorate. More importantly, regional parties began scoring impressive victories, often winning control of state governments and electing up to half of the members of the lower house of parliament from "their" state. The fragmentation has not just been electoral. As noted earlier, communal violence has been widespread since the late 1970s. Violent protests and riots occur on a regular basis, and disaffected members of minority ethnic groups assassinated both Indira Gandhi and her son **Rajiv Gandhi,** who also served as prime minister.

The obvious question to ask in terms of how India is governed is whether or not Indian democracy is cut from the same political cloth as the version we saw in Part 2. On paper, the answer is an obvious yes. India's institutions were patterned closely on Britain's parliamentary system and have changed surprisingly little since independence.

In practice, however, democracy there has some decidedly Indian characteristics. They start with the dominant role Congress has played for most of India's history as an independent country. Under Indira Gandhi and her successors, Congress transformed political life by centralizing political power to the point that the Indian state can now be more repressive and certainly is more corrupt than anything we saw in Part 2.

Finally, we have to ask why India's public policy has become so much like that in the rest of the third world. From independence until the late 1980s, India was one of the world's strongest supporters of import substitution and of the autarkic strategy of industrialization it led to. Since then, however, India has adopted the more liberal policies of structural adjustment, although it has done so more gradually and grudgingly than has Mexico, as we will see in Chapter 16.

The Evolution of Indian Politics

The Weight of History

As we have seen throughout this book, one cannot understand politics in any country without first coming to grips with how it evolved over time. (See table 12.2.) Most third world countries are relatively new as independent states. But the impact of history is, if anything, more extensive in the third world because of the additional factor of colonialism, which touched all areas of life there

---

[1] V. S. Naipaul, *India: A Million Mutinies Now* (New York: Viking, 1991), 1.

▌ TABLE 12.2 Key Events in Indian History
Prior to Independence

YEAR	EVENT
Circa 1000	Beginning of Islamic impact
1556–1605	Mughal unification of much of the subcontinent
Circa 1600	First significant European impact
1707	Start of Mughal decline
1857	Sepoy mutiny
1858	Government of India Act
1885	Formation of Congress
1919	Jallianwala Bagh massacre
1920	Gandhi's first *satyagraha* campaign
1930	"March to the Sea" against the salt tax
1937	Elections
1939–45	World War II
1947	Independence

but did not figure prominently in most countries covered in Parts 2 and 3.

In India's case, this means going back more than three thousand years. As early as 1500 BC, light-skinned Aryans from the north began developing what became the Sanskrit language, Hindu religion, and caste system. Many of the classics of Indian literature and culture antedate the birth of Christ. During the third century AD, the Mauryan Empire was able to unite almost the entire subcontinent during the reign of Ashoka, who remains an inspiration to many Hindus today.

Until AD 1000 or so, Indian culture flourished. More literary classics were written, and Buddhism spread through most of Asia.

The last thousand years have been a different story. For all but the past fifty years, most of India was dominated by outsiders.

In the centuries after the death of the Prophet Muhammad, Muslim armies set out to conquer and convert the world. They got as far west as Spain and were gaining ground in France when they were beaten at the battle of Tours. Their influence extended all the way to the Atlantic coast of Africa. And, most importantly for our purposes here, the Muslims moved east as well, reaching well beyond India to the Philippines.

Beginning in the tenth century, Muslims made inroads into India. Although the Persian-based Mughals were able to gain control of most of India by the middle of the fifteenth century, there was nothing approaching a central government for the subcontinent.

In 1526 some of the regional rulers turned to Babur, a descendant of the great Mongol warrior Chinghiz (Genghis) Khan. Babur took Delhi and was named the first padishah, or Mughal emperor, of India. It was only after the accession of Babur's grandson Akbar in 1556 that the Mughals consolidated their rule. Through a combination of negotiation and force, Akbar united most of the subcontinent and built an elaborate and efficient bureaucratic system. This system was far superior to anything in Europe at the time and allowed the Mughals to run a country that already had over one hundred million inhabitants.

The Mughals never managed to subdue all their opponents and almost always faced violent opposition, either from rival Muslim claimants to the throne or from Hindus and Sikhs struggling to regain control over their own land. More importantly for the long run, the Mughals never tried to change mass values, including religion, outside of their bastions in the north. As a result, Islam remained a minority religion, and the Mughals adapted to local conditions and became every bit as much Indian as they were Muslim. Among other things, they did not seek to eliminate the caste system. In fact, because many *jati* seem to have converted to Islam en masse in an attempt to improve their social and economic lot in life, there are some castes in the Indian, Bangladeshi, and Pakistani Muslim communities.

Toward the end of the seventeenth century, the last of the great Mughals, Alamgir, dedicated the last quarter-century of his life to uniting the entire subcontinent. He assembled an army of unprecedented proportions and traveled with it in a "moving capital" that was thirty miles in circumference and had five hundred thousand "residents." On average, one hundred thousand people died during each year of the campaign, which ultimately ended with the Mughals' conquest of the bulk of India in 1707. It proved, however, to be a Pyrrhic victory. Alamgir himself died two years later, leaving an overextended empire that quickly fell prey once again to infighting among the Mughals and opposition from the countryside.

British Colonialism

Ultimately, the greatest threat to Mughal rule came from a new source: Europe. Portuguese traders had established a beachhead in India as early as 1498. By the middle of the eighteenth century, British and French merchant companies, supported by private armies, operated from coastal bases. Gradually, the British emerged as the most powerful of the European forces in India, largely because of their victories in wars fought back in Europe.

From its base in Calcutta, the **British East India Company** began to expand its influence. It should be

The Endfield mutiny.

The Mary Evans Picture Gallery/London

stressed that this first stage in the British takeover was not carried out by its government, but by a private corporation—albeit one with strong state support. Thus, the architects of British colonial rule stressed profit rather than political conquest. At that time, the colonizers were more than willing to allow local rulers to remain in power if they helped the company's commercial operations. Indeed, its policy was to find or, if necessary, create a class of leaders who would be loyal to Britain and who could themselves profit from the trading networks the British established.

By the early nineteenth century, the company had spread itself too thin. There were years when it lost money and could not pay its debts to the Crown. Meanwhile, it also lost its monopoly over British trade to a new generation of merchants who undermined the weaving industry of Bengal by sending Indian cotton to the new factories in Manchester.

In so doing, they magnified the anger many Indians already felt, which led the British to take more and more territory under their military "protection." Tensions boiled over in 1857 when the British introduced the Enfield rifle for use by its army, which included a large number of Indian soldiers. The rifle used grease from cows and pigs, which offended Hindus and Muslims respectively. In the first anticolonial mutiny, they killed a number of British soldiers, freed some prisoners, and captured Delhi at the cost of hundreds of British lives, including women and children.

The British fought back with what Stanley Wolpert calls "terrible racial ferocity."[2] Although the outcome was never in doubt, the British wreaked a savage vengeance on the Indian population, destroying the bridges that had been built between themselves and the Indian population. The mutiny also proved to be the death knell for the peculiar mix of state and private colonization.

On 2 August 1858, the British Parliament passed the **Government of India Act,** which transferred all the company's powers directly to the Crown. As the map in figure 12.1 shows, the British never took direct control of the entire country, but even in the areas where "princely states" continued to exist, the British called the political shots. The British raj was an elaborate bureaucratic system that relied heavily on the cooperation of the Indian elite. It could hardly have been otherwise, given that the Indian population outnumbered the British by more than ten to one. Indeed, this was a problem colonial rulers faced everywhere, as we will see with colonial rule in Nigeria and the puppet monarchy in Iraq.

At the top of the raj hierarchy was a secretary of state in the British cabinet in London who was responsible

[2] Stanley Wolpert, *A New History of India,* 3rd ed. (New York: Oxford University Press, 1989), 237.

FIGURE 12.1 British India circa 1900

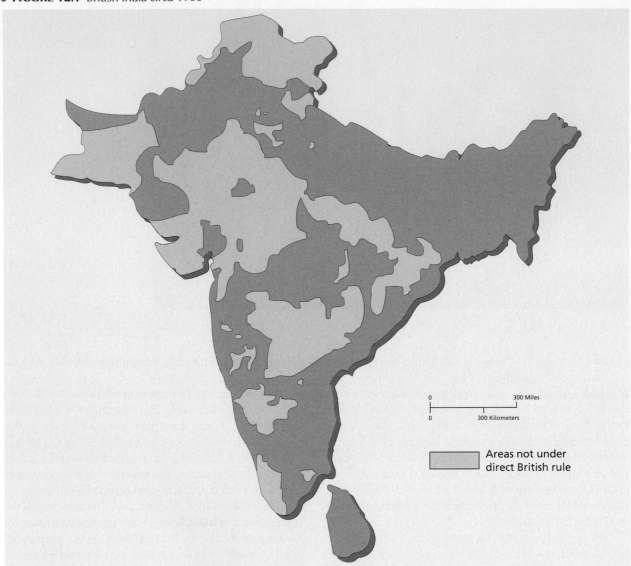

Areas not under
direct British rule

for Indian affairs. He, in turn, appointed a viceroy who served in India, usually for five years. The administration was dominated by the **Indian Civil Service,** which, despite its name, was chosen on the basis of competitive examinations given only in London until 1923.

The Struggle for Independence

As was the case throughout the empire, British colonial rule in India planted the seeds of its own destruction. Its oppression of the Indian people and, ironically, its use of Indian elites in business, education, civil administration, and the military created an ever growing body of people who objected to the raj. What makes India unique is the way this opposition to colonial rule came together in a mostly unified and nonviolent movement that achieved independence very early and that endowed the new state with a consensus its first generation of leaders could use to get the country off to a good start.

Opposition to British rule continued after the Enfield mutiny. By the 1880s, a group of well-educated, upper-caste Indians began talking about **swaraj,** or self-rule. Some were merchants who had benefited from British rule. Others were intellectuals who had discovered their Hindu or Muslim roots while receiving a British education.

Their frustrations with colonial rule came to a head in 1883 when the British enacted a new law that actually was designed to aid Indians by allowing some of them to serve on juries that tried Europeans. The one hundred thousand or so British then living in India forced the government to back down. As Wolpert, again, put it:

> **It soon became painfully clear to more and more middle-class Indians, however, that, no matter how well intentioned or powerful individual Englishmen might be, the system they served was fundamentally unresponsive and hostile to many basic Indian needs, aspirations, and desires.**[3]

In December 1885, seventy-three Indians met in Bombay to form the Indian National Congress. The Congress advocated swaraj and demanded that Indian Civil Service exams be given simultaneously in India as well as England so that Indians would have a better chance of gaining admission to the increasingly powerful service.

Meanwhile, the British raj became more ruthless and arbitrary. Costly wars were fought to conquer and then retain land on the frontiers of the subcontinent in what is now Myanmar (Burma), Afghanistan, and Tibet. Then, in 1905, the British decided to split Bengal into two.

This action infuriated the nationalists, leading Congress to launch its first widespread protest movement, a boycott of British imports. The polite petitions and requests of Congress's first twenty years turned into the first steps of what would be a nationwide, nonviolent revolutionary movement. By 1908, imports had been cut by more than a quarter. Indians, instead, started buying the more expensive *swadeshi* (of our country) cloth woven in new factories in Bombay and in other northern cities.

The British responded by arresting and prosecuting hundreds of Congress leaders, which further incensed younger activists, many of whom now turned to violence. The adoption of what could only be called terrorist tactics split Congress and enabled the British to gain the upper hand.

World War I fueled hopes for independence among Indian leaders. Most agreed to support the British war effort on the assumption that doing so would enhance their chances for freedom. More than a million Indian soldiers served in the British army.

Those hopes were quickly dashed, however. Proposed political reforms died in the British House of Lords. Meanwhile, Indian soldiers were being killed by the thousands in distant lands while the economy suffered from the loss of its huge markets in Germany. To make matters worse, Indian troops, including Muslims, were used in the invasion of parts of the Ottoman Empire. The end of the war brought anything but the hoped-for transfer of power to Indian hands. All political meetings were banned, and in April 1919 troops led by Brigadier R. E. H. Dyer opened fire without warning on a group of Hindus at Jallianwala Bagh, killing four hundred and wounding more than one thousand. At that point, thousands more Indians joined the movement, demanding outright independence.

For the next twenty years, the Indian independence movement was to be dominated by Congress and its remarkable leader, **Mohandas Karamchand Gandhi** (1869–1948). In the early 1920s, Gandhi led a massive boycott of British goods that landed hundreds of Congress leaders in jail. By the end of 1921, it was clear that the boycott was not going to lead to independence any time soon. Frustration with the Gandhian approach set in, which led to violence between Hindus and Muslims that would culminate in the partition of the subcontinent into two countries in 1947.

Meanwhile, Gandhi was sent to prison, where he served two years of a six-year term. After his release, Gandhi pulled back from active politics for the rest of the decade, claiming that India was not ready for a nonviolent movement.

Despite the failures of the 1920s, two important breakthroughs had occurred. First, until then Congress had been a movement of intellectual upper-caste leaders. Gandhi's personal integrity, simple life, and political strategy brought the broad masses of the Indian population into the struggle for independence. Second, new leaders emerged within the Congress who added a more modern approach to Gandhi's traditional spiritualism. Most important of these was the young, British-educated Brahmin Jawaharlal Nehru, who by the end of the 1920s was already mayor of Allahabad and was exploring ways of combining socialist ideas with satyagraha and ahimsa.

The independence movement took on new life in early 1930 when Gandhi proclaimed a salt boycott. Salt was one of the few commodities all Indians needed, and it had been heavily taxed by the British. Gandhi and seventy-eight colleagues began a two-hundred-mile march to the sea, where they would gather salt as a symbol of their resistance against the British. The sight of the tiny sixty-one-year-old, half-naked man leading his band inspired millions of other Indians and led to yet another wave of arrests that included both Gandhi and Nehru.

---

[3] Wolpert, *New History*, 56.

MOHANDAS GANDHI

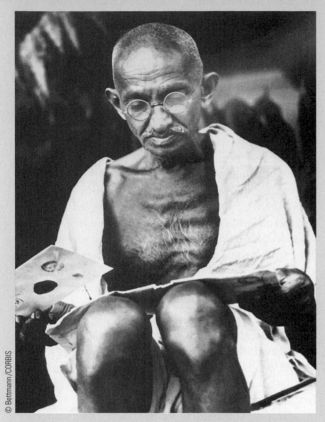

Mohandas Gandhi in the simple clothing he always wore, even when, as in this case, he was meeting with top British officials.

© Bettmann /CORBIS

Mohandas Karamchand Gandhi was born in 1869. His family was reasonably upper caste, and his father was the chief minister in a small, unimportant princely state.

Like many privileged and ambitious Indians of his day, Gandhi studied law in England. He then spent twenty years in South Africa, where he served as a lawyer and as the informal political leader for the large Indian community there. In 1914 he returned to India and began pressing for independence. By 1920 he was already a prominent Congress leader, and in the aftermath of the violence of the immediate postwar years, the other leaders made him their de facto leader, in part because he had such a broad appeal based on his commitment to nonviolence.

Gandhi was a remarkable man whose views, power, and impact cannot readily be summarized in a few sentences. He was one of the few truly charismatic leaders of the twentieth century, whose power stemmed not from his personality or oratory but from his conduct, in which every action was based on humility and principle.

Gandhi was a devout Hindu. Despite his worldly success, first as a lawyer and then as a political leader, he lived the ascetic life of a Hindu *sadhu*, or holy man, wearing only plain white robes made of cloth he spun and wove himself. Gandhi and his family lived in rural communities known as ashrams, where they forswore almost all modern (that is, Western) human pleasures.

Personally, Gandhi rejected all forms of violence. Moreover, he realized that, given the British war machine, there was no way India could win its independence through the use of violence.

In its place, Gandhi offered a radically new strategy based on two Hindu concepts—satyagraha (holding fast to truth) and ahimsa (nonviolence toward all forms of life). Instead of violence, Gandhi offered fasts, boycotts, and marches. Instead of consumption of British goods, Gandhi offered self-reliance, especially the use of only homespun cloth.

Because of his spirituality and devotion, he was known as the Mahatma, or holy one.

Talks between the British and prominent Indians soon began, but Congress was excluded, which led to even more support for the opposition. Gandhi launched one of his famous fasts. More demonstrations occurred, culminating in the Government of India Act of 1935, which expanded the franchise and enabled Congress to take over eight provinces two years later.

The experience of governing frustrated Gandhi, Nehru, and their allies. In particular, they proved unable to maintain any semblance of intercommunal unity as Hindu and Muslim nationalists grew further and further apart.

World War II was to bring an end not only to British rule but also to Gandhi's dream of a united and peaceful India. When the war broke out, most Indians seemed to be either apathetic or vaguely supportive of the Allied cause. Gandhi led thousands of protesters in a campaign demanding that the British "quit India." A few of his former rivals in Congress even collaborated with the Nazis, forming an Indian National Army that fought against the British.

The British sent a high-ranking delegation to stabilize the situation on the subcontinent, which everyone now acknowledged would gain independence after the fighting ended. However, negotiations between Congress and the Muslim League broke down, which also made it likely that colonial India would be divided into Hindu and Muslim states.

Talks about how to partition India began in earnest right after the war but got nowhere during 1945 and 1946. In February 1947, Prime Minister Clement Attlee told Parliament that Britain had decided to relinquish power to "responsible Indian hands" by June of the following year. He dispatched Lord Louis Mountbatten, the dashing commander of British forces in Southeast Asia during the war and Queen Victoria's great-grandnephew, to be the last viceroy and to supervise the transition to independence.

Within weeks of his arrival, violence broke out throughout the country. Mountbatten helped convince the key Indian leaders that the creation of a separate Muslim Pakistan was inevitable. Only Gandhi refused to accept partition and roamed the country trying to quell the rioting. But the inevitable came sooner than anyone expected. By the summer of 1947, Great Britain, the Indian National Congress, and the Muslim League agreed to make about 80 percent of colonial India part of a new and independent India and turning the rest into Pakistan, itself divided in two parts in the northwestern and northeastern (now Bangladesh) corners of the subcontinent.

Even though the new countries were to be overwhelmingly Hindu and Muslim, respectively, as many as fifty million people were caught within the borders of the "other" country. Within days, most of them started to migrate in both directions. The outbursts of communal violence that accompanied the refugee movement continued beyond 15 August 1947, the day India and Pakistan both formally gained their independence.

All this happened over Gandhi's objections. He began yet another fast to try to get people to end the violence. From almost everyone's perspective, however, Gandhi and his ideals were a thing of the past. The demands of governing independent India seemed to call for more pragmatic leaders such as Nehru. Gandhi accused Congress of corruption and its leaders of engaging in power politics. He even went so far as to demand that the venerable old organization be dissolved.

Meanwhile, because of his support for all Indians, including outcastes, Muslims, and Sikhs, Gandhi had earned the enmity of militant Hindus. At dusk on 30 January 1948, a member of one of those groups assassinated him while he was on his way to lead a prayer meeting. That evening, Nehru announced during a national radio broadcast that "the light has gone out of our lives and there is darkness everywhere." Though Nehru was only talking about one man, his words were prophetic, be-

▌ **TABLE 12.3** Key Events in Indian History since Independence

YEAR	EVENT
1947	Independence
1950	Constitution goes into effect
1964	Nehru dies, replaced by Shastri
1966	Shastri dies, replaced by Indira Gandhi
1975	Emergency Rule begins
1977	Emergency Rule ends; first non-Congress government
1979	Congress returns to power
1984	Indira Gandhi assassinated; Rajiv Gandhi succeeds her
1989	Second non-Congress government
1991	Rajiv Gandhi assassinated; P. V. Narasimha Rao becomes prime minister
1996	Congress suffers its worst electoral defeat; BJP comes in first
1998	BJP elected; nuclear weapons tested
1999	BJP government reelected
2004	Congress returns to power

cause the assassination also marked the death of Gandhi's principles. (See table 12.3.)

The New Republic

The movement for Indian independence was not as unified, principled, or nonviolent as Gandhi would have wanted. However, it did have two legacies that helped the Nehru-led republic maintain its democratic regime and make progress on a number of social and economic fronts in its first twenty years of independence. In fact, no other third world country has started with so much working in its favor.

Because of the tactics Congress followed and because the independence movement lasted so long and developed as it did, there was a strong sense of national identity. This identification with India was a highly positive one, which for most people probably was as important as any religious, ethnic, caste, or linguistic attachment. People had little trouble thinking of themselves as both Indian and, say, a lower-caste Hindu, which was rarely the case in the new countries of Africa and Asia.

The new country had a strong and popular political party in charge. In the early elections, Congress got the lion's share of the votes and seats in the **Lok Sabha** (lower house of parliament). Even more importantly, because of the way the independence movement had developed, Congress also set about forging coalitions with other parties and organizations as part of the consensus building that was at the heart of Nehruvian values. (See table 12.4.)

Congress sought to be an inclusive political party. As we will see later, although the party had opposition, it also included groups representing all the major ideo-

▌TABLE 12.4 Indian Prime Ministers

NAME	YEARS IN OFFICE
Jawaharlal Nehru	1947–64
Lal Bahadur Shastri	1964–66
Indira Gandhi	1966–77
Morarji Desai	1977–79
Charan Singh	1979–80
Indira Gandhi	1980–84
Rajiv Gandhi	1984–89
V. P. Singh	1989–90
Chandra Shekhar	1990–91
P. V. Narasimha Rao	1991–96
H. D. Deve Gowda	1996–98
Atal Bihari Vajpayee	1998–2004
Manhoman Singh	2004–

logical and social groups in Indian society. Thus, when problems arose, Congress was able to take positions that would appeal to the disaffected groups, if not co-opt them into the party altogether.

Centralization and Fragmentation

Indian political life has changed dramatically since Nehru died in 1964. This is why the historical section of this chapter includes some quite recent events. Indeed, some observers argue that it has changed so much that we can almost think of it having created a new regime in the 1990s even though the basic institutions have changed little, if at all.

This starts with the concentration of power in fewer and fewer hands under Indira Gandhi (1917–84). Nehru was one of the last preindependence stalwarts, and there was no obvious candidate to succeed him. The Congress party machine leaders—known as the **Syndicate**—turned to Lal Bahadur Shastri. However, he never gained more than the grudging support of his fellow Congress leaders and had not left much of a mark on political life when he died suddenly in 1966.

This time, conflict between the party's left and right wings became public. In the end, the conservative Syndicate chose Nehru's daughter, Indira Gandhi (no relation to Mohandas), to be prime minister. As a woman with little political experience, they assumed that she would be more manipulable than any of the other contenders.

Perhaps because she had begun her political career at the top, and so had never developed strong ties to average Indians or to local political elites, Gandhi adopted an authoritarian leadership style that alienated many of her colleagues. Within a matter of months, Congress split when the business-oriented **Morarji Desai** formed a rival faction.

After an election victory in 1971, Gandhi announced a series of bold new economic policies. Land was given to the peasantry, coal mines were nationalized, and harsh new taxes were imposed on the rural and industrial elite. The Fifth Five-Year Plan called for the "removal of poverty" and the "attainment of self-reliance."

Not everyone was happy with Gandhi's policies or her heavy-handed rule, which included appointing her son Sanjay as head of the new state automobile enterprise, thereby catapulting him onto political center stage. Protests against inflation and corruption within Congress became more frequent and strident. Desai became the focal point of an increasingly unified opposition.

Then, on 12 June 1975, the Allahabad High Court found Gandhi guilty of two counts of illegal campaign practices during the 1971 election. Technically, Indian law required her to resign, but Gandhi gave no indication that she planned to do so. Politicians around the country urged her to step aside temporarily until her legal predicament was resolved. She did nothing of the sort.

Instead, on 26 June, Gandhi invoked the constitution's provision for **Emergency Rule.** Civil liberties were suspended. Press censorship was imposed. Twenty-six political groups were banned, and all major opposition leaders were arrested. In July, the remaining MPs passed a law extending the Emergency indefinitely, enacted constitutional amendments that banned any legal challenges to it, and retroactively cleared Gandhi of any wrongdoing. Parliamentary elections were "postponed" a year until 1977.

Democracy was in jeopardy. Then, on 18 January 1977, Gandhi suddenly ended Emergency Rule, released all political prisoners, and called for national elections in March.

The opposition that bore the brunt of the repression under emergency rule was now more united than ever around Desai, the Gandhian socialist Jayaprakash Narayan, and other anti-Indira leaders at both the national and state levels. Their new **Janata** Party beat Congress by 10 percent in the popular vote and won an overwhelming majority of the seats in the Lok Sabha.

But the Janata coalition was a "negative" majority united only in its opposition to what one historian has called the "Indira Raj." Within two years it collapsed. New elections were held, which Congress won, bringing Indira Gandhi back to power in 1979 after only two years in opposition.

Gandhi's second term in office was just as tumultuous as her first. Hopes for radical economic reform disappeared. Many states elected legislatures hostile to central rule, and in a number of cases Gandhi dissolved

THE NEHRU CLAN

© Bettmann /CORBIS

Jawaharlal Nehru, India's first prime minister, holding his grandson Rajiv Gandhi on his knee. Gandhi eventually succeeded his mother and became the third family member to hold India's highest office.

No democracy has ever had one family exert as much influence as the Nehru–Gandhi clan in India.

The patriarch, Jawaharlal Nehru, was one of the two most important leaders of the independence movement, and he also served as prime minister during the new country's first, critical years. His daughter, Indira, was as influential (although often less constructively so) from the time she became prime minister in 1966 until her assassination in 1984. At that point, her elder son, Rajiv, became prime minister, but only because his younger brother Sanjay had been killed in an airplane crash.

The Nehru–Gandhi clan has been out of office since Rajiv's assassination in 1991. His Italian-born widow, Sonia, became leader of the Congress Party in 1999. That year, she presided over its third consecutive defeat at the polls. In 2004, she led the party to victory and then surprised the country by declining the prime ministry. Her political future—and that of her children—is uncertain.

those governments and replaced them with officials loyal to her.

Her biggest problem was the increase in ethnic hostility toward central rule, especially in Punjab. As we will see in more detail later, there was growing and widespread protest from Sikhs who had begun demanding independence from India and who often used violence in pursuit of their political aims.

In May 1984, Indira Gandhi imposed martial law in Punjab. The next month Indian troops attacked the Golden Temple in Amritsar, leaving it in ruins and killing hundreds of militant Sikh activists. Finally, on 31 October, Sikh members of her own bodyguard assassinated the prime minister, setting off yet another wave of violence with Hindus taking revenge against Sikhs living outside of Punjab.

Indira Gandhi's domination of Indian politics for nearly a generation remains a subject of controversy to this day. There is, however, one point on which her supporters and critics agree. Gandhi ended Congress's role as a consensus builder. Instead, she centralized power within the party, driving out politicians who either re-jected her vision of India's future or who balked at the concentration of power in her hands. And, as a result, for the first time in Indian history, a strong opposition was created that was capable of winning elections.

Indira Gandhi had been grooming her son Sanjay to succeed her, but he was tragically killed in an airplane accident. Therefore her other, and previously apolitical, son Rajiv (1944–91) became the heir apparent. No one was surprised when he became prime minister and immediately called for new elections while sympathy for his mother remained high. Rajiv proved to be an effective campaigner, building support around his youth and his image as "Mr. Clean" in an otherwise corrupt political system. Congress won an unprecedented 80 percent of the seats in the Lok Sabha.

Congress's victory marked the entry of a new generation of leaders into Indian politics. Rajiv Gandhi and his closest advisers were young, well-educated, Westernized, and affluent. They did not share the older generation's commitment to economic planning and democratic socialism, but instead were highly impressed with the market economies in the Western countries they had studied and worked in. At first, then, they seemed to be ideal candidates to implement an Indian version of structural adjustment.

In his five years in office, Gandhi did introduce the first market-oriented reforms. However, his reputation for honesty was undermined by the Bofors scandal in which the government and the Congress party machine were implicated in a kickback scheme in their dealings with a Swedish arms manufacturer. Moreover, to keep itself in power, the government had to resort to the same kind of centralizing tactics that had gotten Indira Gandhi into so much trouble.

In 1989 Rajiv Gandhi's term came to an end. Congress was still the only party with a truly national base, but it could not beat another loose opposition coalition, the **Janata Dal.** As in 1977, the Janata Dal was a classic "negative coalition," brought together in common opposition to the incumbent government but with little or no agreement about what it should do when it won.

Coalition Politics

In one key respect, the 1989 election marked the last major turning point in Indian politics. With it, Congress lost its traditional role as a hegemonic party because it could no longer build consensus. Since then, India has been governed by broad-based coalitions because no national party has any realistic chance of winning either a majority of the vote or a majority of the seats in the Lok Sabha. Further, the balance of power is held by politicians with regional, ethnic, or caste bases of support, a point we will return to in the section on political parties.

The Janata Dal coalition elected in 1989 lasted only months, and after two more weak governments fell, early elections were scheduled for 1991. The polls again showed that Congress was in trouble, though no single party mounted a serious challenge.

In the middle of the two-week voting period, however, Rajiv Gandhi was assassinated by Tamil extremists. The elections were postponed, and Congress desperately sought a new leader. Rajiv's Italian-born wife, Sonia, turned down an offer to head Congress and keep the dynasty alive. Thus, the party had to turn to the seventy-year-old former foreign minister **P. V. Narasimha Rao** (1921–), a long-time party loyalist.

When the elections were finally completed, Congress won, though it fell sixteen seats short of an overall majority. The BJP came in second, well ahead of the Janata Dal and the regional parties. Narasimha Rao proceeded to form a coalition government with a few of the minor parties. No one expected the new government to do very well given the problems it inherited. Surprisingly,

Democratization in India

INDIA IS ONE of the few third world countries that has been able to sustain a democratic regime for an extended period of time.

The reasons for this are not clear, largely because we do not understand all that well how democratization works in general. Nonetheless, two main factors seem to stand out. First, India's independence movement and first governments were able to build a strong sense of national identification and support for the new state. Second, despite the difficulties of recent years, the government has functioned reasonably well and has avoided the kind of serious centrifugal conflict that has disrupted political life in so many other third world countries.

---

however, it lasted its entire five-year term, during which time it accelerated the pace of economic reform. It was not, however, a strong government. It was tainted by corruption (Narasimha Rao was sent to jail after he left office) and internal bickering, and it did little to address the country's problems other than by opening up its economy. It was thus hardly surprising that Narasimha Rao and Congress went down to such a crashing defeat in 1996.

As had been the case the other two times Congress lost, a divided coalition won in 1996. This time the erstwhile opposition turned to H. D. Deve Gowda (1933–), a little-known politician from the southern state of Karnataka, who was the first prime minister who did not speak Hindi.

Like all of his non-Congress predecessors, Deve Gowda headed an unwieldy coalition consisting of thirteen political parties. Therefore, no one was surprised when it collapsed after less than a year, as did the government of his successor, Inder Gujral.

Early elections were held again in 1998, which cemented coalition politics, though with a new and—for some—worrisome twist. This time the BJP came in a strong first and was able to form a government with twelve other parties under Prime Minister **Atal Bihari Vajpayee** (1924–). Many observers feared that the BJP would stress its fundamentalist Hindu roots and deepen the divisions and intolerance that had marked Indian politics for the preceding generation (also discussed shortly). However, Vajpayee and his colleagues understood that they had to govern from the center, both to retain the support of their coalition partners and to have any hope of gaining new voters for the BJP.

Congress was able to convince enough of the BJP's partners to defect that the BJP lost a vote of confidence by one vote in March 1999. When early elections were held yet again in September, the BJP's coalition increased its support in the Lok Sabha following a disastrous showing by Congress, now lead by Sonia Gandhi. Vajpayee was able to put together an even broader coalition of twenty-four parties that allowed it to remain in office until the end of the parliamentary term in 2004.

That year, Congress scored a surprising but limited victory. Forty-two parties won at least a single seat. The two leading parties barely won half of the 543 elected seats (two members of the Anglo-English community are appointed). Prime Minister **Manhoman Singh** became head of a coalition of thirteen parties, only five of which have ten or more members of parliament.

© Reuters NewMedia Inc./CORBIS

A yogi with his head buried in the sand on a busy street in the center of Calcutta's business district. India is known for its blend of the "traditional" and the "modern."

Political Culture

The historical section of this chapter was longer than most, because it was only in the past few years that the basic contours of contemporary Indian politics were set. This means that we have already seen some of the key themes in Indian politics and that the remaining sections can be shorter than their equivalents in most other chapters.

As far as political culture is concerned, this long history combines with the diversity of India in two ways that might seem contradictory at first glance. On the one hand, the growing identification with region, caste, and religion has spawned considerable conflict, some of which has turned violent. On the other hand, ever since independence, there has always been widespread identification with and support for the Indian regime. A decade or so ago, many observers thought that the growing intolerance might tear India apart. Now, however, there is general agreement that Indian democracy is secure.

We will explore these two points in the rest of this section, and each will appear in one form or another in the rest of the chapter. Keep in mind, however, that because public opinion polling is not very well developed, it is easier to see these points in what we know about the way Indians act than in the way they think.

Challenges to Culture and Country

As we saw earlier, Indira Gandhi's eighteen years in and out of office marked a major turning point in Indian politics as consensus and coalition building gave way to more centralized power and adversarial politics. This new political style has been echoed in a culture marked by division and conflict.

By far the most important manifestation of this has been the rise of regional identification and, with it, periodic demands for the creation of new states along ethnic or religious lines and even for secession from India itself. This topic is important enough that we will defer dealing with it until the section on public policy. Here, it is enough to note that in such different regions as Assam, Kashmir, Tamil Nadu, and Punjab, the growth in ethnic and regional identification has presented the central state with serious challenges since the 1970s. In the late 1990s, according to one study, as many as 200 of India's 534 districts (the administrative unit below the state level) were experiencing intense conflict.

Next to the growth of regional identification, the most disruptive force has been the rebirth of religious fundamentalism, especially among Hindus. As remarkable as it may seem, many Hindus think of themselves as an oppressed group, even though they make up over 80 percent of the total population. Politically organized Hindu groups have existed since the formation of the **Rashtriya Swayamsevak Sangh (RSS)** early in the twentieth century. The RSS and similar organizations have become an important and troubling force on the Indian political landscape. In some states, Hindu groups are pressing for reforms that would put the secular commitment of the country's founders into question, including special provisions on divorce and other legal issues for Muslims. Because the growth of Hindu nationalism has been inextricably intertwined with the meteoric rise of the BJP, we'll defer dealing with it, too, in more detail until we cover the party system.

Last but by no means least, we cannot ignore the continued importance of caste. Although the constitution and subsequent legislation banned discrimination against *dalits* (formerly the untouchables) and other backward castes and tribes, caste continues to have a major impact on people's daily lives—from what they do for a living to whom they vote for.

Recall that the fifty thousand or so castes and *jati* (subcastes) are social structures that reflect centuries-old social, racial, and economic divisions. For Hindus, caste is not merely a social category one is born into. It has a religious side as well that carries with it duties and devotions commensurate with one's position in the hierarchy. Caste can still spark protest if members believe that their interests are in jeopardy. For instance, the creation of the reserved-places scheme (a kind of affirmative action) for untouchables, members of scheduled tribes, and lower castes touched off massive protests among the upper castes, which included the ritual suicide of hundreds of young Brahmins. More recently, a mere typographical error led to rioting. An official document included "Gond-Gowari" instead of "Gond, Gowari," which legally meant that there was no Gowari caste eligible for the set-aside jobs. Furious Gowaris protested in the state of Maharashtra where most of them lived. By the time the rioting ended a few weeks later, at least 113 Gowaris had died.

Support for the Regime

At the same time, there is compelling evidence that most Indians are actually satisfied with the regime in New Delhi. To see this, note that India has held thirteen national and countless state and local elections since 1947, and only once—during Emergency Rule—did the democratic process fail to hold. In that case, the Indian people repudiated Indira Gandhi and Congress at the first possible opportunity.

Elections are remarkable events. Every time Indians go to the polls, it is the largest event ever organized by humans. Turnout has averaged 57 percent in each national election, which is roughly comparable to that in the United States. But in India, over half the electorate cannot read enough to comprehend a ballot and has to rely on a well-established set of pictures to identify which party and candidate they prefer. In fact, the poorest Indians vote at a rate three times that of the national average.

Generally, poorly educated Indians are remarkably well informed about the issues and the politicians before they go to the polls. In a survey conducted in the mid-1990s, almost 7 in 10 respondents thought that parties and elections made government function better, as opposed to only a little more than 4 in 10 in 1971. Similarly, 6 in 10 agreed that voting made a difference, and, again, the poorest voters were disproportionately likely to take that point of view.

Indian voters have a penchant for electing movie stars, former bandits, and politicians who had previously been convicted of corruption. That said, they also have reelected only about half of the incumbents in most recent elections, compared with an average of about 90 percent in elections for the U.S. House of Representatives.

Most political scientists are convinced that this supportive side of Indian political culture exists because of the way Indian democracy was created and has evolved since independence. Dozens of events, from the way independence was forged to India's ability to build and test nuclear weapons, have added to the pride most Indians feel for their country. Perhaps more than any other mass public in the world today, they have no trouble combining a positive identification with the nation-state and those with their caste, religion, or ethnicity.

Congress's remarkable leadership in the years before 1947 did a lot to create both this sense of Indian identity and the consensus regarding certain broad public policy goals before independence was achieved. In short, nation building occurred along with and, in some ways, even ahead of state building.

This undoubtedly helped India survive the first years after the communal strife of partition, when many observers doubted that an egalitarian democratic political system could be grafted onto a society that was both deeply divided and rigidly hierarchical. Some observers, too, thought that elements of Hindu culture, including its emphasis on harmony, pluralism, and spiritual rather than worldly matters, helped smooth the process. Whatever the exact constellation of causes, there is considerable evidence that by the late 1960s India had developed the kind of political culture that helps sustain democracy in Britain and the United States.

The Challenge of Modernization

There is one other cultural question looming on the horizon that is typical of many rapidly changing countries in the third world. How will India's culture evolve as the country's economy grows and develops more of a Western-style middle class?

There is some evidence that Indians will adapt quite easily.

The best estimate is that there are more than one hundred million Indians who can today afford such

HIV/AIDS in India

HIV/AIDS is a serious problem, but does not yet pose a crisis in India. About four million people were infected in 2002, but that number had risen dramatically from just a few thousand a decade earlier. Although a small proportion of the total population, only South Africa had more cases of HIV/AIDS, and by 2001, India had more than a million AIDS orphans.

Addressing the epidemic is difficult for at least three reasons. As we will see in all third world countries with a large population of people who are infected, the cost of treatment and prevention is prohibitive, even if the Indian government had decided to spend more than the $40 million of its own resources it had committed. Second, the nature of the outbreak of HIV/AIDS varies dramatically from state to state. In some areas, it is largely spread by the sharing of hypodermic needles, in others, through the sex trade, and still others through conventional heterosexual sex. Finally, as the coordinator of one NGO put it, "how do you talk about HIV/AIDS to someone who does not know the basics about health and hygiene?" (www.avert.org/aidsindia.htm. Accessed 11 November 2004.)

things as a car or cable/satellite television. Middle-class Indians have become the world's biggest market for blenders, which they use to grind the chilis and other spices they need to make their traditional dishes. Similarly, it seems to take only about six weeks to train English-speaking Indians to sound as if they are from Birmingham, England, or from Birmingham, Alabama, so that they can work in call centers that handle routine requests for businesses in Europe and North America.

As rural India has become wealthier, more and more consumer goods have become available. Younger people are, of course, the ones most attracted by these new luxuries. This does not mean, however, that traditional values have disappeared. For example, even though the government ruled dowries illegal years ago, many couples who clamor for Western products still submit to arranged marriages with dowries that can top $6,000 and include a television, refrigerator, or motor scooter.

But there are worrisome signs as well. In most parts of India, boy babies still are prized whereas girls are seen as a burden (not only because their parents will have to pay those dowries to get them married). Medical care for girls has always been worse because parents don't seek medical treatment as often for girls. If there is a food shortage, boys are more likely to be fed and girls more likely to be allowed to starve. The now widespread use of

ultrasound tests for pregnant women has added a new twist to the discrimination against girls. There are only about 850 live births of girl babies for every 1,000 boys, because parents are far more likely to choose to abort a fetus if they know it is a girl.

It is too early to tell what the overall impact of economic growth on cultural values will be. There have been some protests against the presence of Western institutions, including, surprising as it may seem, Coca-Cola's sponsorship of international sporting events. However, there has been little of the open and visceral rejection of Western culture we see in much of the third world, including among the overwhelming majority of India's 150 million Muslims.

Political Participation

The overlap among and tensions between ages-old traditions and modern democratic practices extend beyond the political culture to the day-to-day behavior of India's people and the organizations they form. As in any long-standing democracy, this, in turn, means focusing on political parties and elections. As we explore political participation here, you will see yet again the interplay between the two and the challenges they pose.

The End of the Congress System

There are a handful of democracies in which a single party has dominated political life for an extended period of time—the Social Democrats in Sweden since the depression, the Christian Democrats in postwar Italy, and, of course, the LDP in Japan.

Congress was one of them. Although never able to win an outright majority at the polls, it routinely took advantage of India's British-style single-member-district electoral system and the division of its opponents to win overwhelming majorities in the Lok Sabha until the onset of coalition politics in 1989.

Congress was successful then for the same reasons it had been prior to independence. Paradoxically, it both stood by its basic principles and proved to be remarkably flexible in dealing with allies and potential adversaries.

Of all the liberal democracies covered in this book, India is the one in which class has played the least important role, even during Indira Gandhi's most radical years. Rather, the Indian party system and politics in general involve many different, overlapping cleavages. As a result, a party that hopes to win enough votes to govern has to be able to balance the interests and demands

Indian election officials counting the vote in May 1996. Because so many Indians are illiterate, ballots have pictures as well as words to identify each candidate's party affiliation.

Saurabh Das/AP/Wide World Photos

of enough of the groups spawned by India's many divisions to forge a majority coalition in the Lok Sabha.

Nehru's Congress party did that extremely well. However, the fragile balance that gave the party its hegemonic power was not to survive the leadership struggle after the unexpected death of Prime Minister Shastri in 1966.

As we have seen, Indira Gandhi challenged the Syndicate and won, but her victory had tremendous costs for Congress. Over the next decade, the Congress system fell apart in three ways. Its share of the vote declined, its organization deteriorated, and it faced new opposition. (See table 12.5.)

The decline began with the 1967 elections in which Congress's majority in the Lok Sabha was reduced to 54 percent. Congress also lost six states, in every case as a result of its inability to respond to local pressures.

▌ **TABLE 12.5** Congress's Share of the Vote and Seats in the Lok Sabha, 1952–1991

YEAR	PERCENTAGE OF VOTE	NUMBER OF SEATS
1952	45.0	364
1957	47.8	371
1962	44.7	361
1967	40.8	283
1971	43.7	352
1977	34.5	154
1980	43.7	353
1984	48.1	415
1989	39.5	197
1991	36.0	226

Those defeats, combined with the first signs of Gandhi's heavy-handed leadership, provoked the first post-independence split within the party. Gandhi was unwilling to become a pawn of the powerful Congress factional leaders. Her relationship with them worsened, and the tensions erupted during the 1969 election for the largely symbolic presidency. Against the wishes of the Syndicate, Gandhi supported the incumbent, V. V. Giri, who was running as an independent. The Syndicate then threw her out of the party. Congress MPs, however, voted overwhelmingly in her favor.

Despite her personal victory, the party split, ironically, during the one-hundredth anniversary of Mohandas Gandhi's birth. Now there were two Congress parties: the Syndicate's Congress (O, for organization) and Indira Gandhi's Congress (I, for Indira). Congress (I) now lacked a working parliamentary majority, and the Gandhi government stayed in power only through the support of former opposition parties, including the Communists and Tamil nationalists.

In 1971, Gandhi dissolved the Lok Sabha and called for new elections. In the campaign, it became clear that Congress (I) was going to be a new kind of party in at least two respects. First, it ran on a far more radical platform to appeal to the poor and disadvantaged, especially the scheduled castes, youth, and Muslims. Second, the party was personalized around Gandhi's rule in ways never before experienced in Indian politics. Not only did Gandhi centralize her power in the new party, but the opposition made her the focal point of its campaign, with the slogan *Indira hatao* (Indira out of power) as its centerpiece.

Gandhi confounded the experts by winning 44 percent of the vote and 352 of 518 seats. State legislative elections the following year gave Congress (I) even wider margins of victory. Gandhi and Congress (I) won in large part because the opposition was so divided and ineffective, which was also typically the case in other countries in which a single party dominated for a long period of time.

From that point on, Gandhi's behavior as prime minister and as head of the Congress (the other faction soon disappeared, so we can drop the [I]) contributed to the collapse of the system. Perhaps the most damaging of her actions was the imposition of Emergency Rule. Almost as important was the prominence given her younger son, Sanjay, who was widely viewed as little more than a power-hungry young man. Sanjay pushed such controversial policies as family planning and forced sterilization. He also controlled access to his mother, the "household" of personal advisers to the prime minister, the Youth Congress, and much of the government's repressive apparatus.

In 1977, Gandhi made yet another of the mistakes that typified her final decade. She decided to end the Emergency and hold new elections on the assumption that she would win again.

This time she got it wrong. There was widespread opposition to the Emergency, her policies, and Sanjay's style. More MPs quit Congress, including Jagjivan Ram, a senior cabinet member, Congress leader, and the most prominent untouchable in political life. Meanwhile, Morarji Desai forged the Janata Party, a coalition of four opposition groups.

Congress was routed, dropping to 34.5 percent of the vote. Both Indira and Sanjay Gandhi lost their seats. Janata and its allies won a clear majority with 298 MPs.

Desai's government brought Indira Gandhi to trial and sent her to prison for a brief period. Quickly, however, it became clear that nothing held Janata together other than its desire to drive Gandhi from office. By 1979 the coalition had fallen apart, and the following year Prime Minister Charan Singh realized his minority government could not survive and called for new elections.

For the first time, an Indian election had turned into a personalized contest focused on the three main candidates for the prime ministry: Singh, Ram, and Gandhi. This time support swung to Congress, which won about 43 percent of the vote and an overwhelming two-thirds majority in the Lok Sabha. As in 1972, victory at the national level was followed by more victories at the state level.

But all was not well with Congress. Gandhi had taken the party even further to the left. She also insisted on personal loyalty to herself, her family, and the rest of her inner circle. After Sanjay died in June 1980, Indira Gandhi tapped her elder son, Rajiv, who until that point had shown no interest in national affairs.

Rajiv Gandhi quickly took to political life, and by 1982 he had established himself as his mother's likely successor, a role he took on following her assassination. He hoped to modernize the country by breaking away from many of the traditional political practices and economic policies Congress had followed since independence in favor of a more pragmatic approach emphasizing modern management systems. Indeed, Rajiv used the one-hundredth anniversary of the founding of Congress in 1885 to launch an attack against what the party had become, at least implicitly criticizing both his mother and the remaining party oligarchs.

As we will see in the policy section, most of those reforms never got off the drawing board. Rajiv Gandhi suffered a series of defeats in state elections. Moreover, the new government faced unprecedented challenges from dissidents in a number of states. Finally, Gandhi's reputation for honesty wore off as his government was implicated in scandals much like those that had tarnished his mother's reputation.

In short, Rajiv Gandhi and his advisers quickly realized that, despite the magnitude of their victory in 1984, their hold on power was tenuous at best. They stopped taking risks in terms of both policy making and reforming the Congress Party. In fact, by 1989 Rajiv was running Congress in much the same way his mother had done—with an iron fist. Further, the party itself had lost virtually all the enthusiasm for and commitment to social change that had characterized it during his grandfather's time.

The deterioration of Congress's fortunes has continued since the death of Rajiv Gandhi, despite the surprisingly effective leadership initially exercised by Narasimha Rao. But, as we saw earlier, he could not stem the public's dissatisfaction with the party, and it went down to another crushing defeat in 1996.

The defeat and corruption charges he was facing forced Narasimha Rao from the party leadership. He was replaced by seventy-eight-year-old Sitaram Kesri. Kesri was responsible for bringing down the Gujral government, which forced the 1998 elections in which Congress saw its seat total decline once again. It lost despite the fact that Rajiv's widow, Sonia, finally joined the party and campaigned actively on its behalf.

Sonia Gandhi then became party president and led its 1999 election campaign. But everything went wrong that possibly could have. The fact that she was born and raised in Italy (though she became an Indian citizen in 1983) cost her votes. So, too, did a series of tactical blun-

▌ TABLE 12.6 Seats in the Lok Sabha:
Major Parties and Their Allies, 1996–1999

PARTY GROUP	1996	1998	1999
Congress and allies	139	148	134
BJP and allies	186	251	296
United Front	111	97	—
Others	98	51	107

Note: The first three rows include only major political parties and minor parties that had firm alliances with them. Other winning candidates are included in the "others" category. Also, seven seats were not filled following the 1999 election.

ders that convinced many voters she would not be as effective a leader as the BJP's Vajpayee. (See table 12.6.)

Much to the surprise of most observers, Sonia Gandhi proved to be an outstanding campaigner during the 2004 election campaign and led her party to victory without dramatically altering its decade-old stance as a secular organization in favor of economic reform. That election is important enough that we will consider it separately after discussing the other parties in the system.

The BJP

Fifteen years ago the BJP would not have featured prominently in a book like this. It had topped 10 percent of the vote in 1989 and won eighty-five seats, but few serious observers thought it could do much better, let alone become India's largest party (www.bjp.org).

Although the BJP itself is a rather new party, its roots lie in the revival of organized Hindu fundamentalism that began with the formation of the RSS in 1925. It was a disgruntled RSS member who assassinated Mohandas Gandhi in 1948. In the 1950s and 1960s, the RSS led campaigns opposing the slaughter of cows, the presence of Christian missionaries, and other alleged evils.

It also had a political party, the Jan Sangh, that won more than 7 percent of the vote only one time and was part of the Janata coalition that won in 1977 but lost two years later. Jan Sangh left Janata and ran on its own under the new BJP label in 1984, winning exactly the same percentage of the vote as in 1971.

In fact, the party was beginning to score major breakthroughs in the northern "cow belt," where it had won control of four states during the 1970s. There, it did particularly well among young men from upper castes who felt threatened by affirmative action and other programs they believed would undermine their social status and economic power.

The BJP's symbolic breakthrough occurred as the result of a clash centered on the disputed Babri mosque/temple in the northern city of Ayodhya. The building that stood there had been a mosque that some Muslims claim had been built by the first Mughal conqueror, Babur,

Evidence of the destruction at the Ayodhya mosque/temple, which has been in dispute between Hindus and Muslims for a generation.

Doug Curran/AFP/Getty Images

Bal Thackeray, along with other right-wing Hindu activists, at a meeting during the 1996 election campaign in which the Hindu BJP party came in first.

during the sixteenth century. Some devout Hindus disputed that claim, arguing that the site was the birthplace of one of their major gods, Lord Ram, which made it one of the holiest places in that tradition (news.bbc.co.uk/2/hi/south_asia/1844930.stm for a Hindu perspective and islam.about.com/library;weekly/aa030302a.htm for a Muslim one).

Not surprisingly, the building had long been a source of contention between Hindus and Muslims. For most of the past century or so, however, a modus vivendi had been worked out in which Muslims used it on Fridays and Hindus were free to pray there during the rest of the week.

Controversy broke out in 1986 after a judge's ruling closed the building to everyone. The rapidly growing Vishwa Hindu Parishad (VHP), or Worldwide Hindu Brotherhood, which made the freeing of such properties its highest priority, entered the scene. It routinely gathered one hundred thousand devout Hindus along the banks of the river next to the temple/mosque. Within two years, the VHP had mustered enough support to convince a judge to open the facility to Hindus. This, in turn, led to Muslim counterprotests. In one typical 1989 incident, a riot broke out after the VHP announced that it would add on to the building using specially consecrated bricks. More than 150 people were killed.

Later that year, Congress was defeated and replaced by a government that convinced the VHP to postpone construction of the new addition. Pressures around

Ayodhya then eased until a Hindu mob destroyed the mosque and started building a new temple in December 1992.

The violence soon spread far from Ayodhya. Hindu revivalist movements, such as the Shiv Sena in Mumbai (formerly Bombay), took to the streets, demanding vengeance and attacking individual Muslims who obviously had nothing directly to do with the situation in Ayodhya. At least 1,700 died in Bombay alone.

The BJP and related organizations had thus built a base of support reminiscent of France's National Front. Its leaders had taken extreme positions and used what can only be described as thinly veiled racist rhetoric.

Most notorious on that score has been the BJP's ally the Shiv Sena and its leader, Bal Thackeray, cartoonist and former gang leader (www.shivsena.org). Thackeray is now mayor of Mumbai, the most important politician in Maharashtra, and a vital cog in the BJP machine. He rose to power by, among other things, refusing to allow Kentucky Fried Chicken to open restaurants in his state of Maharashtra because there had been some minor health code violations in KFC restaurants elsewhere in the country. It was hard, however, to raise too much of a fuss about a restaurant using excess amounts of MSG or having a dead fly in the batter when street vendors in the same neighborhood were selling cucumbers soaked in water that came from open sewers. Thackeray's supporters charged (with some degree of accuracy) that the grain needed to raise KFC's chickens would be better put to use directly in feeding people. Most observers, though, were convinced that his real anger was rooted in the fact that the chain was foreign and that its parent company, PepsiCo, did business in Pakistan.

It is easy to not take such actions seriously. However, Shiv Sena and other groups loosely affiliated with the BJP are responsible for widespread violence against Muslims, Sikhs, Christians, and other minorities. They maintain paramilitary organizations, some of which are armed and can mobilize tens of thousands of activists for major protests such as those over Ayodhya.

The BJP also has a strong nationalist streak. Some of its more extreme leaders have argued against economic reforms because they will open the country up to foreign economic and cultural influences. And few analysts who were familiar with the BJP were surprised when the Vajpayee government tested nuclear weapons in 1998, given that doing so had long been a part of the party's platform.

In power, however, the BJP proved to be far more moderate, in large part because it had to be in order to retain the support of its coalition partners. Vajpayee's government continued the liberal economic reforms to be detailed later in the chapter. It did not propose legislation that would make India into a Hindu country or in any significant way undermine the commitment to secularism expressed in the constitution. In fact, it took a strong nationalist stance only in regard to relations with Pakistan (including its testing of nuclear weapons) and the related issue of Kashmir. But even there, the BJP did not act in dramatically different ways from what a Congress-led government would probably have done. What's more, although its hostility toward Pakistan is real, this did not keep Vajpayee and his colleagues from supporting the U.S.-led war against terrorism in which Pakistan has played a central role.

The Other Parties

It is difficult to cover all the other Indian political parties in an introductory text because there are so many of them. Forty of them won 216 seats in 2004. Indeed, there are so many of them and they change so frequently that it is impossible to present the kind of tables used in earlier chapters to document election results. What's more, almost all of them operate within a single state or appeal to only a single ethnic, linguistic, or religious group. This is true even of those whose name or ideology might suggest a national appeal.

Things have not always been this way. Under Nehru, several opposition parties enjoyed nationwide support, including the Communist Party of India and the Socialists on the left and the Jan Sangh and Swatantra on the more traditionalist right. As noted earlier, however, Congress had factions of its own with similar beliefs. Further, Congress found it fairly easy to adopt at least some of the opposition's goals, as in the redrawing of the boundaries so that each major linguistic group was predominant in at least one state.

During the 1960s, however, more and more politicians left Congress to form new parties, of which only the regional ones ever truly prospered.

More importantly, these politicians went through a radical transformation of their own. Most were arrested during Emergency Rule, which only served to harden their opposition. It also led them to the realization that, whatever their many differences, they had to work together. As a result, most of the former Congress politicians, plus some of the others from the original opposition, formed Janata in 1977. However, as we saw earlier, these groups had only one thing in common—opposition to Congress.

These parties can be divided into two main types:

- *The remnants of the traditional left.* Two parties call themselves Communist. The traditional, orthodox Communist Party of India (CPI) has seen its support dwindle to under 3 percent of the national vote. The more radical Communist Party of India—Marxist (CPM) has support primarily in the state of West Bengal, where it is the largest party. There are also some even weaker Socialist parties. In practice, these are all regional parties with no illusions about winning votes nationwide. Their support, however, is needed to keep the Singh government elected in 2004 in power.

- *Regional parties.* Every state that has been subject to ethnic, linguistic, or religious unrest has spawned at least one political party that claims to speak for those interests, including the Akali Dal in Punjab, the DMK and AIADMK in Tamil Nadu, the National Conference in Jammu and Kashmir, and the Telegu Desam in Andhra Pradesh.

By 2004, most of these groups had aligned themselves as part of coalitions with either Congress or the BJP, which won 67 and 37 seats respectively from them. Another 74 members of the Lok Sabha were elected from the extremely loose All India Forward Bloc, another coalition with 74 members.

The Election of 2004

As the 2004 election neared, all the signs pointed to a fourth straight victory by the BJP and its partners in the National Democratic Alliance. Vajpayee's government

Cricket and the 2004 Election

The passions of Indian politics were on center stage during the winter of 2004 when India began a series of six five-day cricket test matches of six hours each (with additional time for lunch and tea) in Pakistan (usa.cricinfo.com/link_to_database/ARCHIVE/CRICKET_NEWS/2004/MAR/105572_WAC_24MAR2004.html).

This sport, bequeathed to the subcontinent by their common British colonizer, produces more excitement and more animosity than any American Super Bowl or NCAA Final Four. Analogies are often drawn between cricket and war, since both can only have one winner and must thus have one loser (critics of cricket lament that wars often do not last as long as a test match, which they think drags on interminably).

The 2004 test series turned out to be quite different. To be sure, Indian and Pakistani fans painted their faces and cheered against each other as vehemently as ever. However, the hundreds of thousands of Indian fans who travelled to Pakistan for the matches (there were thirty games) found an unexpected welcome from Pakistanis once they left the stadiums.

Overall, cricketers are trying to build bridges between the two countries. In 2003, they fielded a joint team to play (and wallop) New Zealand in a one-day exhibition match. Two of their national stars had a daily program during a recent series when India played (and was walloped by) Australia.

had muted some of its more nationalistic stands. Polls showed it had gained support among all groups other than the Dalits, scheduled tribes, and Muslims who had always been put off by what most of their voters saw as Hindu fundamentalism. The government even expected to benefit from India's victory against archrival (in sports as well as politics) Pakistan in that winter's test match series in cricket.

Moreover, Congress seemed to be in trouble. Sonia Gandhi trailed Vajpayee in the polls when Indians were asked to state a preference about the two leaders. Having spent most of the last decade out of office, Congress no longer attracted the best and most ambitious political leaders, many of whom even defected to the BJP.

But Congress found a winning issue by appealing to the three hundred million people who lived in chronic poverty. While attention focused on the lucky few people who, for instance, got high tech jobs outsourced from the West, they numbered barely a million at a time when nine million young people entered the workforce each year, most of whom ended up unemployed. Gandhi and her party appealed to this largely rural bloc of voters who passed below the pundits' and pollsters' radar screens. When the votes were counted, Congress and its formal allies won thirty-two more seats than the BJP total, but fell short of a majority. (See table 12.7.) Because it could count on support from the Left Front, Congress immediately set out to form a new government. The only surprise was Sonia Gandhi's decision not to take the prime ministry, which left the job to Manhoman Singh, who

Indian and Pakistani cricket fans seek reconciliation during the 2004–2005 Test Match series.

Scott Barbour/Getty Images

TABLE 12.7 The Indian Election, 12 November 2004

PARTY	VOTE (%)	SEATS IN LOK SABHA
BJP	22.2	138
BJP allies	13.1	47
Congress	26.8	145
Congress allies	7.8	70
Left Front	7.6	59
Minor parties and Independents	22.5	78

had been the architect of Congress' first economic reforms in the early 1990s and to whom we will return later.

Interest Groups

Because India has been a functioning democracy for more than fifty years, it has the range of interest groups we saw in the countries covered in Part 2—and then some. However, this does not mean that interest groups in India look and act the same as those in the West.

India has an extensive labor movement that seeks to organize and improve the lot of mostly manual workers. India, in fact, has more than twenty-five thousand unions because the labor law allows any group of seven or more workers to organize one. However, only about ten million people—a tiny fraction of the labor force of nearly four hundred million—are unionized. Moreover, the unions themselves are fragmented. Most major unions are extensions of political parties rather than autonomous organizations such as the American AFL-CIO or French CFDT. Congress controls the Indian National Trades Union Congress (INTUC). The All-Indian Trades Union Congress (AITUC) is associated with one of the Communist parties, and the Congress of Indian Trades Union (CITU) is linked to the other. What's more, few of the unions seem to be gaining strength. The one exception to that may be the Bharatiya Mazdoor Sangh (BMS), which is associated with the BJP.

The unions have a limited impact, too, because they primarily cover workers in the "organized" sector of the economy, in which people are employed for cash wages. Virtually unrepresented are the poorest people, who work in the "informal economy" and who are more desperately in need of help. Perhaps most importantly, when unions have chosen to strike, they have rarely been able to overcome the resistance of the state or private employers.

Similarly, India has no shortage of business associations. The most important of these is the Federation of Indian Chambers of Commerce, which represents some forty thousand enterprises. Unlike the unions, business groups do not have formal ties to parties but have historically supported the conservative wing of Congress and its right-wing rivals. Individual business leaders also gain some leverage because of the substantial contributions they make to individual candidates.

Business, like the unions, has not been particularly powerful in India. This reflects, in part, the traditional Brahmin disdain for business. It also grows out of Congress's preference for socialist policies in the years before Rajiv Gandhi came to power. Most importantly, business traditionally has been weak because the modern sector of the economy has been dominated by the state. This is changing as India opens up its economy (see the public policy section), but it is too early to tell how large a base of entrepreneurs the country is generating and how they will ally themselves politically.

Both business and labor are far less important than the religious, linguistic, and ethnic groups that have gained newfound influence over the past quarter-century. To see this, consider a single example—protest in Assam.

Assam is a poor state in the northeastern part of the country. During the 1950s and 1960s, its fortunes improved when the tea it produces became a significant money maker in global markets. But its economy was always fragile, and native Assamese never constituted more than a bare majority of the state's population.

In the 1970s, tensions began to mount after significant numbers of Hindus and Muslims fled into the state from war-ravaged and even more impoverished Bangladesh. Not surprisingly, there was widespread concern among the Assamese that they would be a minority in their own state. Thus, the 1970s saw the emergence of a number of organizations that sought to mobilize Assamese worried about the state's future.

In 1978, eleven organizations came together to form the All Assam Gana Sangram Parishad (AAGSP), or Popular Movement Front. The AAGSP protested the continued immigration of Bengalis, from both India and Bangladesh. The All Assam Students' Union even went so far as to demand the expulsion of all foreigners.

The issue was hardly new. Attempts to block the immigration of Muslim Bengalis dated back at least to 1926. But it was a particularly charged issue in the 1970s when the redrawing of Assam's borders reduced the state in size.

The various groups launched a campaign to remove non-Assamese from the list of registered voters, a figure some estimated to be seven million. They also organized massive protest movements that all too frequently

Conflict in India

At first glance, it might seem as if India's democracy is threatened by conflict that, for example, kills at least a thousand people during each election campaign.

In practice, however, the conflict is not that serious. In part, this reflects the size of the Indian population.

More importantly, the conflict does not have as serious implications as the disputes we will see in the next two chapters, largely because even the most outspoken critics of the current government accept the basic "rules of the game" in India.

■ **FIGURE 12.2** Decision Making in India

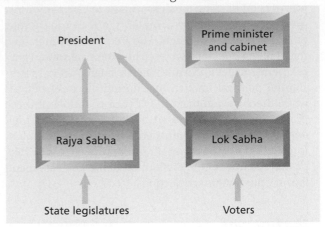

launched savage attacks on Muslim Bengalis. In February 1983, a crowd of about 12,000 Assamese killed an estimated 1,400 Bengalis in what has come to be known as the Nellie Massacre. In all, well over 10,000 people died before an agreement was reached in early 1985 between the Assamese leadership and Rajiv Gandhi's government. There is less violence now, but a number of farmers and business leaders have raised private armies because neither the central nor the state government can ensure law and order.

Today, however, it is not at all clear how far such protest movements can or will go. Thus far, the violence has been contained in the sense that it has not led to serious calls for a new regime or the breakup of India itself. Whether this remains the case is anybody's guess, especially if the recent pattern of weak coalition governments and sociopolitical fragmentation continues.

The Indian State

India has more than its share of problems, most of which are typical of those facing the third world in general. It is unique, however, in that it has kept its democracy alive—if not always flourishing—for more than a half-century. If nothing else, this means that the section on formal state institutions will be longer and more detailed than the comparable ones on Iran, Iraq, Nigeria, and Mexico, where the personality of individual leaders is often more important than institutions in determining what the state does.

India's democracy has endured in large part because Indians have adapted European institutions and practices and have created a political hybrid that in some

ways very much resembles and in others markedly differs from British-style parliamentary democracy. (See figure 12.2.)

The Constitution

Like the leaders of most of the new states in Asia and Africa, India's founders gained independence under a system they inherited from their colonial masters. They confirmed that legacy when they wrote their own constitution, which went into effect in January 1950 (indiacode .nic.in /coiweb /welcome.html).

It is not a carbon copy of the British constitution. For one thing, it is written. Indeed, with nearly four hundred articles and eight schedules, the Indian constitution is one of the longest in the world. And because it can be amended by a simple majority vote in both houses of parliament, it is among the easiest to change.

The constitution defines India as a secular republic, guaranteeing a degree of freedom to the roughly 20 percent of the population that is not Hindu. It also guarantees an extensive list of individual civil liberties and forbids discrimination along religious, caste, racial, and gender lines.

However, the constitution also allows the prime minister to exercise emergency powers during a crisis. These provisions have been used only the one time, in 1975. During the nearly two years of Emergency Rule, the constitution was drastically amended. After the 1977 elections, however, the Desai government repealed most of those amendments and limited the conditions under which emergency powers could be used to an invasion from abroad or an armed rebellion at home.

As with most recently formed states, India has no

king or queen. Instead, a president plays the symbolic role of head of state, much as we saw in Germany. Most presidents have readily accepted their secondary role; the exception is Zail Singh, who frequently complained that Rajiv Gandhi failed to keep him informed about government policies and plans. The president has had a substantial political impact only during the brief periods when there was no majority party or coalition. At those times, the president played the role expected of him, helping find a prime ministerial candidate who might forge a majority coalition or, if that proved impossible, paving the way for the dissolution of the Lok Sabha and for new parliamentary elections.

Parliament

As in Britain, the key to power in India lies in the lower house of parliament, the Lok Sabha. All but 2 of its 545 members represent single-member constituencies (those two are appointed by the president) in which elections follow the same kind of **first-past-the-post,** or winner-take-all, system used in the United States and Great Britain. It should be noted, though, that, given the size of the Indian population, the average MP represents 1.5 million people (indiaimage.nic.in).

The upper house, or **Rajya Sabha** (House of the States), has 250 members. Of those, twelve represent the artistic and intellectual community, and are appointed by the president. The rest are elected by the state legislative assemblies, making the Rajya Sabha much like the Bundesrat in Germany in the way it is chosen, though it is nowhere near as powerful.

Nominally, the president appoints the prime minister, but in reality he has little or no leeway, because the prime minister must be the head of the majority party or coalition in the Lok Sabha (parliamentofindia.nic.in). As in Britain, the prime minister appoints the other members of the Council of Ministers, all of whom must already be members of parliament or must win election to it in a by-election within six months. Of the council members, the prime minister will invite some twelve to eighteen to join the cabinet. And, because a group even that size can be ungainly, there is normally a smaller group of cabinet members and other informal advisers (for example, the "household" of Indira Gandhi's years) who wield the most power.

The decision-making process is very similar to that in Britain. The cabinet initiates almost all significant legislation (pmindia.nic.in). Other business, including private-member bills, receives less than a day's attention per week when the Lok Sabha is in session.

Bills receive the same three readings they do in Brit-

ain, with the most important being the second, when the Lok Sabha votes on the principles of the legislation after it has been examined by the relevant committee. Voting is almost always along party lines, which all but ensures that the government's legislative proposals are passed, except during periods when there is no clear majority.

Party discipline in the Lok Sabha has not been quite as strict as it is in Britain's House of Commons because the parties themselves are often in flux. Thus, traditionally, it was not uncommon for an individual MP to quit his or her party and join a new one during the middle of a term. These defections caused so much uncertainty at both the federal and state level that recent legislation requires MPs who quit their party to leave parliament as well unless one-third of their delegation joins them. Not surprisingly, these rather draconian rules have led to a sharp reduction in the number of defections and to less uncertainty in the Lok Sabha.

Once passed by the Lok Sabha, a bill is sent to the Rajya Sabha. If the two houses do not agree, a variety of consultative mechanisms are used in an attempt to iron out the differences. If they don't work, the two houses meet together and vote on the bill—a vote the Lok Sabha invariably wins, given its more than two-to-one size advantage.

On balance, though, the Lok Sabha is even weaker than the House of Commons as a legislative body. To begin with, there is far more turnover. In recent elections, as many as half the MPs were elected for the first time, which leaves the Lok Sabha with fewer experienced members than in most liberal democracies. Even more than in Britain, MPs lack the staff, offices, and other facilities that would enhance their ability to assume an effective oversight role. Finally, and most importantly, the opposition has been so fragmented that it has been hard for it to effectively utilize question time and other mechanisms that give oppositions elsewhere a modicum of leverage over the majority party and the executive.

The Bureaucracy

Another British inheritance that is a cornerstone of the state is the **Indian Administrative Service (IAS),** which sits atop the country's gigantic bureaucracy. The British established the Indian Civil Service in the nineteenth century, and over the last half-century of colonial rule, more and more positions in it were filled by Indians.

After independence, the service was renamed, but little else changed. The Union Public Service Commission (www.upsc.gov.in) supervises annual examinations through which about 150 extremely talented young men and women are admitted into the IAS and a few other top civil service corps. In all, this bureaucratic elite has about four thousand members and thus constitutes but a tiny fraction of a civil service that employs something approaching fifteen million people.

The rest of the civil service is a different story. Below the IAS level, the bureaucracy is generally seen as overstaffed and inefficient. Although bureaucrats have job security, their salaries are quite low. Many, therefore, tend not to work very hard. Many take bribes. Informal groups of fixers and brokers act as intermediaries (paid, of course) between average citizens and the bureaucracy. For instance, it is often only through these intermediaries that villagers gain access to development assistance. In short, in contrast to the impersonal, legally structured civil services in the advanced industrialized democracies, power in the Indian civil service—and hence in the effectiveness of policy implementation—revolves around personal connections, which are typically based on family, caste, or religion.

Federalism

The British were never able to bring all of India under a single, centralized government. And their successors never tried. A series of "reorganizations" since the constitution went into effect have left India with twenty-eight states and seven union territories, the boundaries of which have been drawn so that the major linguistic groups each predominate in one of them (indiaimage.nic.in/states.htm). Some of the states are the size of a major European power.

Each has a government patterned after the national one. A governor appointed by the central government is the official head of state. Real power, however, is supposed to lie with a state legislature (bicameral in some but not all states) and a council of state ministers responsible to the lower house. The exact names of these bodies vary from state to state and language to language.

What matters here is not how these state governments are structured or what powers they do or do not have. Rather, the states are of interest because they demonstrate the importance of caste and other informal social relationships in political life.

At first, Congress dominated at the state level as well, not losing control anywhere until 1967. Since then, its support has declined even more rapidly in the states than in New Delhi. But even this picture is misleading, because much of state politics is not about ideological issues. Rather, the competition is mostly between factions based on **patron-client relations.**

Patrons can be party, caste, or religious leaders (they, of course, overlap), who offer their clients jobs, infrastruc-

tural projects, or other benefits in exchange for votes. Local patrons tend to be clients of more prominent leaders who weave the networks together into what are all but ideology-free factions. Above all, factional leaders want and need to win in order to obtain the resources and benefits that keep their clients loyal. So, they can seem quite fickle, casting their lot with one party or leader today but shifting to another tomorrow as a result of their constant calculations about how best to maximize their power and influence. Robert Stern has described this process well for Congress, though his analysis also applies to most of the other parties:

> **Parties or factions, unburdened by ideological commitment, inclined to promote middle-class welfare, purposeful primarily in winning elections and positioned to deliver the goods to its voters, the Congresses have patched together their pluralities and majorities from India's vast heterogeneity. Here from one village, there from another. Here from one jati or jati subgroup, there from their rivals. From a state coalition here that depends on the support of dominant and twice-born jatis, from another there dependent on the support of other backward classes. The myriad, separate cost-benefit calculations that have held the Congresses together in fragments and factions can, however, undo them in fragments and factions. Factions want to know what's in it for them.[4]**

The combination of factional politics with growing linguistic, religious, and ethnic tensions has also made most states hard to govern. Few elect clear and disciplined majorities to their lower houses, which means that state governments have often been unstable. Moreover, all-too-many factional leaders have condoned the use of violence, engaged in corruption, and relied on organized criminals (it is worth noting that *thug* is one of many English words of Indian origin) in seeking power.

In part to maintain their own power, central governments controlled both by Congress and its opposition have been increasingly willing to suspend normal state politics and to use Article 356 of the Constitution and impose **Presidential Rule,** the state-level equivalent of the federal emergency powers. For example, the Narasimha Rao government imposed it on Bihar at the end of March 1995. To some degree, this represented an attempt to restore order in a state that had seen more than its share of violence. Its non-Congress state administration was still in office despite passing the end of its five-year term and still had not appropriated money for civil servants' sala-

---

[4] Robert Stern, *Changing India* (New York: Cambridge University Press, 1991), 189.

ries and other vital government expenditures. To some degree, though, the move was a rather blatant attempt by the central government to influence the direction of a state in which the local Congress was all but certain to lose the elections that were about to be held. The incumbent chief minister, of course, complained loudly, not on ideological grounds but on the grounds that Congress and the BJP were supporting higher-status castes against the *dalits* and lower-ranking *jati*, which were critical components of his government's coalition.

In December 2003, the federal and state governments reached an agreement that should sharply curtail the use of this practice. The prime minister agreed to apply it as a last resort only if constitutional mechanisms had completely broken down. The government would also have to get prior agreement from the Lok Sabha and fully explain its reasons for resorting to presidential rule.

Public Policy

The continuity of India's democracy may be unusual by third world standards. The travails it has encountered with its public policies are not.

As is the case in most of the third world, the weakness of India's state is evident in virtually any policy area in which the domestic and global forces summarized in the figure on the inside front cover come into play. Lacking economic and other resources to start with, India faces increasing pressures from "below" in its own society and from the outside, most notably as the global economy impinges ever more closely on it. In India's case, the two sets of pressures are easiest to see in successive governments' attempts to confront ethnic, linguistic, religious, and caste-based conflict and to speed up economic growth.

Confronting Communal Violence

The issue of ethnic conflict crops up in a number of places in this chapter, as it will throughout Part 4. What is important to see at this juncture is that the violence and the state's reaction to it created a situation in which such conflict has become an all-but-permanent part of the Indian political landscape and has contributed to the rise of the BJP and the regional parties. Alternatives involving, for instance, strengthening federal institutions, which seemed plausible a generation ago, would now be much harder to implement, given the resentments that have built up over the years. In other words, India will all but surely face serious ethnic tensions for years to come in large part because of the policies pursued by national

and, to a lesser degree, state governments since Indira Gandhi's time.

In the first years after independence, Indian governments did fairly well in settling communal conflict short of violence because they followed two key principles, the second of which is less important today. First, all governments have been committed to maintaining the unity of India. Second, the government tried to work out accommodations with linguistic groups desiring more autonomy. However, given its commitment to India as a secular state, the leadership was unwilling to allow religious groups to stake territorial political claims. Although specific policies have varied from state to state and group to group, it is safe to say that, on balance, the net effect of public policy since the mid-1970s has been to exacerbate—not ease—ethnic, religious, and linguistic tensions.

During the Nehru years, Delhi redrew some state borders so that each major linguistic group would have a state it could govern. Once those states were created and/or restructured in the mid-1960s, however, the government faced an impasse, because the remaining issues generally involved conflict within individual states, pitting the majority linguistic or religious group against a minority or, as in Assam, minorities. Moreover, these more difficult issues emerged at the same time that the Congress's majority was eroding. Therefore, unlike in the 1950s and 1960s, the party had to pay more attention to holding onto its core electoral constituencies, which included key groups that were hostile to further accommodation with minorities.

Ethnic conflict worsened under Indira Gandhi, with her contradictory desires to control as many states as possible but to do so with as weak leaders as possible. As Paul Brass put it, the

> relentless, unprincipled intervention by the center in state politics has been the primary cause of the troubles in Punjab and elsewhere in India since Indira Gandhi's rise to power. A structural problem arises from the tensions produced by the centralizing drives of the Indian state in a society where the predominant long-term social, economic, and political tendencies are towards pluralism, regionalism, and decentralization.[5]

It needs to be recognized, therefore, that the flourishing of local communal violence has been enhanced since Nehru's death by the political uses to which it has been put in competitive politics at the national and state

---

[5] Paul Brass, "The Punjab Crisis and the Unity of India," in *India's Democracy: An Analysis of Changing State-Society Relations.* Ed. Atul Kolhi (Princeton: Princeton University Press, 1990), 212.

levels and by the entrenchment of an ideology of the secular state that, in its tolerant face, justifies pluralist practices but can also be used to condemn minority demands as a danger to national unity and the integrity of the Indian state.[6]

To see the general patterns of ethnic conflict and the way public policies contributed to it, we will focus on Punjab and Kashmir.

Punjab

Punjab lies along the Pakistani border to the west of New Delhi. The original state of Punjab was ethnically mixed. In 1951, a little over half of its sixteen million people were Hindus, but it also had the country's largest concentration of Sikhs. By the 1960s, they were the only large ethnic group that did not have its own state (www.sikhnet.com).

Negotiations to create a majority Sikh state were complicated by the fact that they are a religious as well as a linguistic group, and granting them a state would call the commitment to a secular India into question. Nonetheless, an agreement was finally reached to split Punjab, creating a new state with the same name whose population was about 60 percent Sikh. Some difficulties remained, including the status of Chandigarh, which was to serve as a shared capital for Punjab and the other new state. Still, most people expected this to be another of the largely successful settlements that had marked the history of ethnic conflict in India up to that point.

This was not to happen. Observers are still having a hard time disentangling all the reasons protest increased. Most, though, cite two main factors.

The first was the social and economic changes that swept Punjab and left many members of its Sikh majority dissatisfied. Punjab had been one of the poorest regions in the country. However, the state-sponsored "green revolution" (discussed shortly) and the hard work of thousands of Punjabis had turned it into one of the richest.

As this happened, some Sikhs began to fear that their traditional culture and values would be lost, while others remained dissatisfied with the resolution of the issues remaining after the state borders were redrawn. To make a long story short, a new generation of militants emerged, the most audacious of whom was a young cleric, **Jarnail Singh Bhindranwale.**

Most Sikhs rejected the extremists' call for an independent Kalistan or Sikh state. Nonetheless, tensions mounted as more Sikhs came to demand a larger slice of the political and economic pie, including, for instance, a greater share of water from the rivers that flowed through the state. Moreover, a Sikh party, the **Akali Dal,** mounted a serious challenge to what had been Congress domination of state politics. Finally, employing a strategy that has become quite common in the third world, Bhindranwale and other leaders used the mass media to spread their message, including their growing hatred of a central government that they thought was ever more pro-Hindu and anti-Sikh.

Second, after Indira Gandhi took office, the government became far less accommodating. And after the creation of the new Punjab, the government rejected further Sikh demands. Gandhi never dealt gently with people who disagreed with her. She took a particularly hard line toward Punjab because the Sikhs and the Akali Dal had been among the most vocal opponents of Emergency Rule.

As support for the Akali Dal grew in the late 1970s, Congress actually tacitly supported Bhindranwale and other Sikh extremists who were critical of the party. But this support backfired on Congress once it returned to power.

During the late 1970s, tensions mounted. More and more Sikhs endorsed the Anandpur Sahib Resolution of 1973, which apparently called for a dramatic transfer of power away from New Delhi to the states ("apparently" because the resolution was never actually written down, and the people who were there disagree about exactly what was included in it). More importantly, a growing number of Sikhs launched attacks against Hindus, some of whom assaulted Sikhs as well. Meanwhile, Bhindranwale and other extremists gained more and more influence, especially among young men.

In 1981, Bhindranwale was accused of murder. When, two years later, it seemed as if the government might finally take him into custody, Bhindranwale and his supporters occupied the Golden Temple in Amritsar, the Sikhs' holiest shrine.

In a typically opportunistic move, Indira Gandhi overthrew the elected Akali Dal state government, imposed Presidential Rule, and sent one of her most trusted lieutenants to oversee the arrest of the alleged terrorists. Despite Presidential Rule, violence continued. Clashes between Sikhs and Hindus threatened to undermine Congress's electoral base among Hindus outside Punjab, who were frustrated by the government's inability to protect their coreligionists. Congress also had lost any meaningful contacts and relationships within the Sikh community that it might have used to defuse the increasingly tense situation.

In March 1984, the All India Sikh Student Federation (AISSF) was abolished. One hundred fifty companies of

---

[6]Paul Brass, *The Politics of India Since Independence* (New York: Cambridge University Press, 1990), 202–203.

The Golden Temple, the holiest shrine in the Sikh religion. It was the site of a bloody 1984 attack by government forces against nationalist rebels.

Kapoor Baldev/Sygma/CORBIS

police troops were stationed in Punjab, including ninety at the Golden Temple alone. In response, AISSF members occupied more temples and turned them into arms warehouses and sanctuaries. Meanwhile, in neighboring Haryana, Congress chief minister Bhajan Lal at the very least condoned organized mob violence against Sikhs who lived in his state.

Finally, in June 1984, Gandhi ordered troops to storm the temple. Bhindranwale, at least five hundred of his supporters, and eighty-three soldiers were killed. The surviving Sikh leaders, including most prominent Akali Dal officials, were arrested. Sikh soldiers in other units mutinied and rioted in the most serious breach of army discipline since independence.

Then, in October, Sikh members of her own security detail assassinated Gandhi. The assassination was followed by nights of rioting in which Hindus killed hundreds of Sikhs in Delhi and other cities—individuals who, of course, had had nothing to do with Gandhi's murder or, for that matter, Sikh nationalism. Last but not least, Rajiv Gandhi won his landslide victory at the polls in part because he appealed to Hindu chauvinism in ways no Congress politicians ever had before.

In short, Indira Gandhi behaved very differently from her father, who typically took powerful politicians from the states and incorporated them into the national elite. His daughter did everything possible in Punjab and elsewhere to undercut powerful local politicians and to replace them with weak chief ministers who were personally and politically beholden to her. When the crisis

came and unifying leadership was needed both in New Delhi and in Chandigarh, it was not there.

As was the case in most public policy areas, Rajiv Gandhi set out to do things differently. Almost immediately upon taking office, he began negotiations with the Akali Dal government. The two sides eventually reached an agreement that, among other things, would have returned Chandigarh to Punjab and given the state some control over the vital water resources its farmers claimed they needed.

By 1987, however, Rajiv Gandhi had backed down. He played the Hindu trump card in the 1989 campaign in ways designed to maximize his party's support among orthodox Hindus, who were expected to be the swing vote and thus the key to victory. On television, Congress frequently showed footage of Indira Gandhi's funeral pyre with a sobbing Rajiv standing nearby, the implication being that the Sikhs were to blame. In his own constituency, he was challenged by his brother's widow, Maneka, herself half Sikh. One of Congress's most widely used slogans during the campaign was "the daughter of a Sikh, traitor to the nation." Put simply, his Hindu constituents throughout northern India were not prepared to go along with such sweeping concessions to the Sikhs.

During the 1990s, the violence continued, albeit at something less than the levels of the early 1980s. The situation in Punjab was so intense following Rajiv Gandhi's assassination during the 1991 campaign that elections there had to be put off for months. On 1 March 1993, police officers killed Gurbachan Singh Manochabal, head of the significantly named Bhindranwale Tiger Party of Khalistan. Extremist Sikhs are generally held responsible for an 11 September 1993 car bomb attack on Maninder Singh Bitta, president of the ruling Congress Party's youth wing and himself a Sikh. He escaped with minor injuries, but eight people were killed and at least thirty-five seriously wounded. On 31 August 1995, a bomb killed Punjab's chief minister, who, despite being a Sikh, had allowed the police to torture and kill militants and their families.

In the last few years, support for Sikh independence has diminished considerably. Indeed, the most significant protests of the early 2000s in the state came from the BJP, which objected to special benefits supposedly given to Sikhs. Sikh nationalists as such did not launch counterdemonstrations, and the whole question of secession has disappeared from mainstream politics, though many Sikhs remain resentful of what they claim to be several hundred thousands of their compatriots who have been killed by Indian authorities and as many as fifty thousand who have been imprisoned since 1984.

Kashmir

Today, the most serious communal conflict is in Jammu and Kashmir, whose status has been in dispute since independence. It was one of the princely states that was not officially under British rule. The leaders of those states had to choose to join either India or Pakistan. Geography made that choice easy in most cases.

That decision was anything but easy for what became the state of Jammu and Kashmir, which lies in northwestern India along the Pakistani border (www.jammu-kashmir.com/index.html). Like much of India, it is quite diverse ethnically, but it has a substantial Muslim majority, which would lead one to expect that it would have gone to Pakistan. However, its prince was a Hindu who leaned toward joining India. In the months after independence, Pakistani troops invaded part of the state and forced the maharajah to flee. He then asked for support from Indian troops, at which point the state joined India. Nehru's government agreed to hold a referendum on which country the state should definitively join, but it was never held because Pakistan continued to occupy part of it.

War broke out again in 1965, and Jammu and Kashmir were battlegrounds in the 1971 war that led to the independence of Bangladesh. After the 1971 war, the two sides agreed to a de facto division of the state into regions controlled by India and Pakistan on each side of the last positions their troops had occupied, now dubbed the Line of Control.

Over the next few years, opposition to remaining part of India grew among Muslims. Some wanted to join Pakistan, and others wanted to create their own country. Tensions reached a peak when many Muslims concluded that the 1987 state election had been rigged against them.

At about the same time, some militant Muslims went to Pakistan where they were trained as fighters—many Indians would say terrorists. In 1989, the most recent wave of fighting broke out when militant Muslims and allies from abroad (mercenaries to the Indians) started launching attacks on Indian targets. According to Indian sources, over thirty-five thousand people have been killed since then. The Pakistanis put the number at seventy thousand. One count in 1996 found ninety-four armed groups operating in the Kashmir Valley alone. Some 350,000 Indian troops were based in the state and faced an equally large force of Pakistanis in the land they occupied and just across the border in Pakistan proper.

The two sides could not even agree on who did what. Pakistan claimed that it gave only "moral and diplomatic support" to the Kashmiris, and India accused Pakistan of sponsoring "cross-border terrorism." One thing is clear. During the 1990s and the first years of the twenty-first century the opposition became more Islamic than nationalistic and began attracting other *jihadis* who had fought against the Soviets in neighboring Afghanistan.

The outside world paid relatively little attention to the on-again/off-again fighting in the region until India and Pakistan both tested nuclear weapons in 1998. At that point, observers realized that the fighting in this disputed state could lead to a devastating regional nuclear conflagration. This was readily apparent in May 1999, when Indian artillery began shelling Pakistani positions across the Line of Control, claiming that the government of Pakistani President Nawaz Sharif had infiltrated regular troops into the region, a charge that was vehemently denied. Tensions were defused when Pakistan submitted to pressure from the United States and redeployed some of its troops.

Jammu and Kashmir made the world's headlines after the attacks of September 11. Pakistan quickly agreed to become a major force in the U.S.-led coalition against terrorism. Tensions with India remained high, however. This led the Vajpayee government to accuse the government of General Pervez Musharraf, who had seized power in a 1999 coup, of hypocrisy. On the one hand, it claimed to oppose the terrorism of al-Qaeda and the Taliban. On the other, it continued to support it in Kashmir.

The worst fighting in more than a year began in October 2001 when India started shelling Pakistani positions. Tensions mounted ever further following an attack on the Indian parliament building in December, for which Vajpayee's government blamed Pakistani and Kashmiri militants. For the rest of 2001 and the first weeks of 2002, rarely a day went by without at least one violent death. More troops massed along the Line of Control, and yet another war between India and Pakistan seemed possible. Tensions eased a bit when President Musharraf said that he would not allow terrorists to operate from Pakistani soil.

A brief flurry of hope occurred in late 2003 and early 2004 when both governments floated peace proposals as part of a general rapprochement between the two countries. Neither proposal succeeded. The most important source of optimism today is the work of Indian and foreign NGOs who have been working to get the two sides to the negotiating table.

The most impressive of these has been run by the Washington-based International Center for Religion and Diplomacy (www.icrd.org/projects.html#kashmir). Since 2001, it has sent teams of clergy and laypeople to Kashmir to work on both sides of the Line of Control. By the summer of 2004, it had conducted reconciliation seminars that more than three hundred local Muslim, Hindu, and Buddhist leaders have attended. It helped some of those young men and women establish reconciliation centers in Jammu and Srinagar, which are the winter and summer capitals of the state respectively. Perhaps most importantly of all, it identified and helped train a group of leaders who are interested in build bridges between the two communities.

In early 2005, the two governments also forged some small and largely symbolic agreements, the most important of which established bus lines that would carry people across the line of control. This may not seem like a major step forward, but any agreement after more than a half century of frustration has to be taken as a serious move by both sides.

Stimulating the Economy

The saga of the Sardar Sarovar Dam used to begin this chapter raises a lot of questions about Indian politics, including issues of caste, regionalism, and the often distant and insensitive behavior of central government policymakers. But the main reason I chose to discuss the dam is that it squarely demonstrates India's shift toward structural adjustment and the controversy surrounding it.

Prior to the mid-1980s, Indian governments pursued import substitution and central planning of a largely state-owned and -controlled economy to spur growth and reduce poverty. Since then, a combination of outside pressures and domestic frustration with what the Indians themselves often called the "Hindu rate of growth" has led Rajiv Gandhi and his successors to reconsider the social-democratic goals and practices that their predecessors had taken for granted. Though less dramatically than Mexico (see Chapter 16), India has opened its economy to the global market. So far, growth has increased by between 4 and 7 percent a year since the mid-1990s, but no major dent has been put in the poverty rate and other social problems.

Indian economic policy from independence through the 1980s was not an abject disaster. There was enough growth to create a new middle class. The **green revolution** introduced high-yield crops that all but eliminated famine, if not hunger and malnutrition. In some technological areas, India is a world leader. It has tested nuclear weapons and medium-range ballistic missiles, and its computer software is among the best in the world. Further, India has been among the most successful third world countries in using modern telecommunications technology to reach the residents of its villages, who would otherwise be isolated from the outside world.

On balance, however, the Indian economy has not fared very well, especially when compared with countries like South Korea, which were almost as poor as India at the end of World War II. Table 12.8 presents comparative data on economic growth for India and some other third world countries in the mid-1980s that had roughly equal economic conditions in the mid-1950s.

Two seemingly contradictory trends emerge from these data. India's economy grew by an average of nearly 2 percent per capita per year during that period. The growth was concentrated in the industrial sector of the economy, which the import substitution policy made the top priority. But India did not do very well in relative

Courtesy International Center for Religion and Diplomacy

Next-generation Kashmiri leaders discussing reconciliation at a seminar organized by the International Center for Religion and Diplomacy.

▌ TABLE 12.8 Selected Economic Indicators: India and Comparable Countries before Structural Adjustment

COUNTRY	GNP 1987 ($)	AVERAGE ANNUAL GROWTH 1965–87 (PERCENTAGE)
India	300	1.8
Brazil	2,020	4.1
China	290	5.2
Indonesia	450	4.5
Mexico	1,830	2.5
Pakistan	350	2.5
South Korea	2,690	6.4
Thailand	850	3.9
Turkey	1,210	2.6

terms. Of the countries included in the table, none had a slower rate of growth, and only China had a lower GNP per capita. India's economic plight seems all the worse because a number of countries that were equally poor in the early 1950s far outperformed it. Average income in South Korea then (and now) was about ten times what it was in India, and in Hong Kong, the figure was more like twenty-five times.

Poverty

This relative failure is not simply a statistical artefact. It has had tangible and politically significant costs, most notably the inability of the Indian government to do much to alleviate the wrenching poverty in which so much of its population lives.

Despite its slow but steady growth, the government has been able to accomplish very little if for no other reason than the size and rapid growth of India's population. Most mainstream scholars today estimate that at least 300 million Indians are poor, a number greater than the total population of every country on earth except for China. Of the 20–30 million Indians born each year, well over half are born into poverty.

One recent study defined poverty Indian-style as not having access to adequate food, clothing, and shelter. By that standard, about one-sixth of the population lives in what is called "ultrapoverty," because their incomes fall more than 25 percent below the level needed to obtain those basics. Many of the poor are homeless; the best-off live in substandard housing, with dozens of families crammed into teeming tenements. Many are malnourished, and those who do get the minimum daily caloric intake needed to sustain a healthy life survive primarily on grains. A missed day or two of work can leave a family without money for food. Health care for the poor is virtu-

ally nonexistent, and life expectancy for those in poverty barely tops fifty.

Poverty, of course, is not randomly distributed. The lower castes and *dalits* are most likely to be poor. There are still about six hundred thousand families of outcaste origin who make a living, such as it is, emptying latrines and chamber pots. Poverty is worse in rural areas (41 percent poor, 20 percent ultrapoor) than in urban areas (34 percent and 16 percent, respectively). There are thousands of villages without potable drinking water.

Women bear the heaviest costs of poverty. In poor families, they are responsible for all household tasks, which in rural areas can include the time-consuming and physically draining search for firewood. In urban areas, women are much less likely to receive health care or an education than are men. In the states of Bihar and Rajasthan, for instance, about 38 percent of the population is literate. Overall, not even one-fourth of India's women are literate, and in the poorest, rural areas, only about 2 percent of all women can read and write, thus depriving them of one of the skills they could use to pull themselves out of poverty.

The government has enjoyed some success in reducing poverty. Between 1970 and 1990, the poverty rate was cut by about one-fourth. Still, as a result of continued population growth, the number of poor people actually increased during those same years.

The government also devised a number of successful and innovative approaches to help people improve their lives. The Integrated Rural Development Program (IRDP) was created to give villagers low-level technology and new skills. For instance, in a number of villages, "night soil" gatherers were taught how to harness the methane contained in human waste to generate electricity to fuel small-scale industrial facilities. In all, the IRDP reached about twenty-seven million rural families, spending an average of about $500 on each. But this gave no more than 10 percent of the rural poor the ability to escape poverty—assuming the program worked perfectly, which, of course, it did not.

Finally, although the government has had some success in reducing poverty, its record pales in comparison with most other large third world countries. India has been able to reduce the size of the population below the poverty line by about 1 percent per year, which is better than Colombia, Morocco, and Sri Lanka have done. But most other countries that started at similar rates of development have done far better, including Indonesia, which is reducing its poor population by about 2.5 percent per year. On another indicator of poverty—reducing the mortality rate for children under five—India ranks last in this same sample of countries. It has been able to reduce the number of children who die before reaching the age of five by almost 2 percent per year, but Morocco and Colombia both top 5 percent.

The Nehruvrian Model and India's Economic Woes

India's continued poverty obviously has many causes, the most important of which is the broader economic policy of import substitution pursued from 1947 until the mid-1980s. Nehru and his colleagues had been deeply influenced by the British Fabian movement and its moderate and democratic version of socialism. This led them to focus on a strong public sector to steer development and to generate a more just and egalitarian society.

The Industrial Policy Resolution of 1948 called for a mixed economy, with government ownership of all munitions, atomic energy, and railroad enterprises. The resolution also gave the government the sole right to start new ventures in such key sectors as iron and steel, telecommunications, aircraft, and shipbuilding. Eighteen other industries were to remain in private hands, but subject to government control and regulation.

Under the leadership of one of Nehru's closest advisers, P. C. Mahalanobis, these "commanding heights" of the economy were to be managed using five-year plans that were more controlling than the French but less so than the Soviets' before Gorbachev. At the heart of the system was what the Indians call the **permit raj,** an elaborate system of tariffs, licenses, and other regulations that kept most imports out and made the ones that did get in so expensive that next to no one could afford them. In so doing, it protected publicly and privately owned firms alike, which continued making the same old products in the same old way and earning the same all-but-guaranteed rate of profit year after year.

Over time, most Indian business leaders came to accept the planning system because it guaranteed reasonable profits and an advanced standard of living for those working in the modern sector of the economy. Wages in the protected sector averaged about 70 percent higher than those in the rest of the country.

High tariffs and other regulations also protected domestic industry. In 1985, rates ranged from 107 percent on capital goods to 140 percent on most manufactured products. In addition, most industrial goods could be imported only by what the government called "actual users." But even that was not always possible, because, for instance, automobile, truck, and bus manufacturers were not allowed to import tires.

There is little question that these economic policies met their initial goals, as India did become reasonably self-sufficient. In 1984 the import of finished goods accounted for only 8 percent of its GDP, compared with an average of over 19 percent in other third world countries. India developed a substantial industrial base with limited interference from or obligations to other countries.

But isolation also had its costs. The absence of internal competition was one of many causes of corruption and inefficiency. More importantly, the economy did not benefit from the capital, technology, and other resources more trade could have provided—admittedly, at the cost of considerable domestic control. Most importantly of all, the Indian economy was falling ever further behind those of many other third world countries.

Liberalization

Most economists supported India's desire to maintain its economic independence. But by the early 1980s there was a growing consensus that import substitution and related policies were retarding overall growth by depriving the economy of the stimuli a more open market could provide.

Since then, India has gradually opened its economy and adopted other promarket policies supported by international financial institutions and multinational corporations. It has not done so as quickly as Mexico, nor has international pressure on it to change been as direct. Nonetheless, India's policies in the new century are a far cry from what they were when Rajiv Gandhi took office in 1984.

There are many reasons Gandhi began to tilt the balance away from state ownership, planning, and control. In part, the new policies reflected his own background, which included university study in the West and a career that began in business. In part, they grew out of forces in the global economy that inflicted a heavy price on countries that tried to resist the trend toward more open markets and relatively unrestricted international trade.

In contrast, countries like South Korea were growing far more rapidly because they took advantage of some niches in the emerging global marketplace. This is not to say that their economies were trouble free, but following international economic trends seemed to bring them significant economic payoffs. Rajiv Gandhi and his youthful colleagues wanted to take India in that same direction. During his five years in office, reforms were implemented incrementally. The forces behind liberalization gained even more support after 1989 and the col-

Liberalization in India

INDIA HAS GRADUALLY liberalized its economic policy, although government approval is needed for most direct foreign investment and the elaborate system of rules and regulations of the permit raj remain largely in place for the big corporations protected during the years of important substitution. Thus, foreigners may own as much as three-fourths of the shares in a privately owned bank but only 20 percent in those that are publicly traded.

Central to this gradual process of liberalization has been current Prime Minister Manhoman Singh (1932–). The Oxford educated economist was named Minister of Finance in 1991 after a long career in academe and the civil service. After leaving office, he served in the largely ceremonial Rajya Sabha and was a powerful behind the scenes advisor to Congress' economic policy makers. As noted earlier, he was a surprise choice when his colleagues in Congress chose him to be prime minister in 2004. After their presumptive selection, Sonia Gandhi decided not to take the position.

AP/Wide World Photos

Prime Minister Manhoman Singh, the surprise choice to lead the government following Congress' surprise victory in 2004.

lapse of the Soviet bloc. Reform efforts peaked early in the Rao government, in which reformers like Manhoman Singh and P. Chidambaram (with his Harvard MBA) were given the key economic ministries.

Recently, barriers to outside investment have been cut on the assumption that capital and competition from abroad will give a much needed boost to domestic industries that stagnated under the protection of import substitution. Overall, an average of about $4 billion a year in direct foreign investment poured into India since the 1990s. By contrast, there was only $13 million of it in 1981 and $121 million in 1989. The government has sold parts of many state-owned industries, including the automobile manufacturer, Maruti Udyog, which is partially owned by Suzuki. And both Air India and Indian Airlines are scheduled for privatization. Much of the foreign investment comes from Indians living abroad.

The most visible change has come in information technology. Because its economic borders historically were so closed, India had not developed a competitive domestic computer industry even though it had long been a world leader in software development. With the newly open economy, it offered outside investors a pool of skilled and low-paid labor, and it held out the promise

of a massive new market at some point in the future. "Silicon valleys" have developed around Bangalore in the south and Hyderabad in the north.

In 2003, there were about two hundred thousand professional jobs in information technology in the Bangalore area alone. About one-fourth of all outsourced offshore jobs from the United States ended up in India's high-tech sector.

The government has also encouraged more exports so that India can earn hard currency to buy the goods it has to import. Throughout the 1990s, exports grew at the rate of 20 percent per year, although the country still imports about $20 billion worth of goods and services more than its exports. The biggest growth area, not surprisingly, was in information services. Overall exports of electronic goods and services grew by a factor of five from 1997 to 2003. For computer software, exports grew by almost eight times during that six-year period.

The government has also steered some of its revenues from taxes on the new firms to address the isolation of poor villages. Pilot programs have been conducted in some desperately poor regions near Bangalore in which solar power is introduced and people are trained to use telephone and computer systems. The knowledge center in the town of Embalm brought more than six hundred new users to the Internet, which saved them significant amounts of time and money that they would have had to expend on travel to find out such basic things as market prices for their crops.

India has not gone as far in terms of economic reform as some of the other third world countries because of domestic political pressures. Recall that the Gandhi and Narasimha Rao governments were not terribly popular and were beholden to traditional politicians and conservative social groups within Congress. As a result, as the costs of economic reform mounted for everyone from the poor to the economically powerful, their governments backed down. Further, the two coalition governments that succeeded them were far weaker and were all but paralyzed as far as economic reform is concerned. Finally, the BJP continued the process of reform, but it has not been willing to speed it up, especially when it comes to eliminating the permit raj. Still, in early 2004, the government issued new rules allowing foreigners to own as much as 74 percent of private banks, petrochemical countries, and scientific and other scholarly journals.

It is too early to tell how much more open the economy will be under the Singh government elected late in 2004. However, the fact that Singh himself was one of the architects of the initial liberalization projects in the 1990s indicates that the rules and regulations that limit the role of market forces will continue to be weakened, and possibly even eliminated.

Feedback

As befits its tumultuous and divided political system, India has a lively mass media.

Even though barely half of the population is literate, India has over two thousand daily newspapers, which are among the cheapest in the world. The papers, of course, are published in dozens of languages, and twelve million out of each day's circulation of sixty-eight million are in English. The papers cover the entire political spectrum, and many of the best papers have well-respected reputations for their investigative journalism. Although political news dominates the printed press, the fastest

Globalization in India

INDIA IS OFTEN portrayed in the English-speaking world as one of the most striking examples of how globalization can reshape a country. That has especially been the case in the last five years with the growth of its "silicon valleys" and the export of many Western technology jobs to them.

However, it should be noted that India as a whole has not been all that deeply affected by these globalizing developments. To cite but one example, its overall import and export totals are only about one-eighth of the Chinese.

growing newspapers are the ones that concentrate on financial news; their circulations have tripled since the introduction of economic liberalization.

Until recently, television and radio were completely state owned. Since the mid-1990s, however, cable and satellite television have been introduced, and one journalist estimates that more than three hundred million people have access to one or the other. These people can now watch both the BBC World News and Rupert Murdoch's Star service, and thus get differing perspectives on political events. A nationwide network of satellite dishes brings television service to most villages, although it is often the case that the whole community watches together on its one receiver.

Conclusion: Democracy in India and the Third World

However serious its difficulties, India is not likely to suffer the fate of the Soviet Union or Yugoslavia, or even see its democracy succumb. It is risky to predict anything during these times of such rapid and unanticipated political change. Nonetheless, this conclusion seems warranted if we place India in a broader comparative and theoretical perspective.

Over the past decade, political scientists have spent a lot of time investigating why some democracies succeed and others collapse. Although these studies are controversial, two themes appear time and time again in the research. First, the more legitimate the regime is, the less likely it is to collapse. Second, the more effective the government is, the more likely it is to retain that legitimacy and, more generally, to survive. These may not seem like particularly profound conclusions, but if we shift from abstract theory to two comparisons, the reasons we can be reasonably optimistic about India's political future become clearer.

In examining the Soviet Union and the broader collapse of Communism in Europe, we saw the dramatic interplay between policy failure and the loss of legitimacy. We may lack systematic evidence that would allow us to directly compare their experiences with India's, but the impressionistic indications available to us reveal a very different situation in the latter. The Indian government has been more successful in at least some policy areas (for example, liberalization) than any European Communist regime was. And, although its population is increasingly angry and polarized, most Indians still view the regime as legitimate. Perhaps most importantly, there is not the kind of repressed rage ready to erupt when political straitjackets are removed, as happened when glasnost was instituted in the Soviet Union and Eastern Europe.

The other comparison is between India and the rest of the third world. No matter how dire India's situation might have seemed in this chapter, it is in relatively good shape on two levels. First, India's economic performance and, more importantly, its economic potential are both superior to most of what we will see in Mexico, Iran, Iraq, and Nigeria. Second, its regime has been more effective and retains more legitimacy than most others, some of which are wracked with basic divisions over whether the country itself should even exist.

Whether India is a relative success or a failure in comparative terms should not obscure the most important points for American or European students to learn about this or most other third world countries. First, these are incredibly poor countries that lack some of the basic resources and amenities we take for granted, such as primary education, rudimentary health care, safe drinking water, and shelter. Second, poverty is but one of many factors that make these countries much harder to govern, whatever the strengths or weaknesses of the people who end up trying to lead them.

Key Terms

Concepts
Caste
Dalit
Emergency Rule
First past the post

Jati
Patron-client relations
Permit raj
Presidential Rule
Swaraj
Untouchable

People
Bhindranwale, Jarnail Singh
Desai, Morarji
Gandhi, Indira
Gandhi, Mohandas
Gandhi, Rajiv
Gandhi, Sonia
Narasimha Rao, P. V.
Nehru, Jawaharlal
Singh, Manhoman
Vajpayee, Atal Bihari

Acronyms
BJP
IAS
RSS

Organizations, Places, and Events
Akali Dal
Ayodhya
Bharatiya Janata Party
British East India Company
Government of India Act
Green revolution
Indian Administrative Service
Indian Civil Service
Indian National Congress
Janata
Janata Dal
Lok Sabha
Mughal
Rajya Sabha
Rashtriya Swayamsevak Sangh
Syndicate

Critical Thinking Exercises

1. Much has changed since this book was finished in early 2005. Does the analysis of India presented here still make sense? Why (not)?

2. Public opinion pollsters routinely ask questions about whether people think their country is heading in the "right direction" or is on the "wrong track." If you were asked such a question about India, how would you answer? Why did you reach this conclusion?

3 India is one of the very few third world countries to have sustained a democracy for an extended period of time. Why do you think this is the case? Do you think India is likely to survive well into the twenty-first century?

4 The independence movement in India was one of the largest and most unified in what became the third world. How did that help the new Indian government to get off to a successful start?

5 India is one of the most ethnically and religiously diverse countries in the world. How has that affected its political life since independence?

6 The Indian political system has long revolved around the Congress Party. The party has slipped badly at the polls in recent years. How has that changed Indian politics?

7 India used to follow import substitution as strictly as any country in the third world. Over the past ten to fifteen years, however, it has moved toward structural adjustment and the open market. Why did this change occur? How has it altered Indian political and economic life?

Useful Websites

As one might expect of a country with such a large high-tech community and such a large diaspora, there are several good portals on Indian affairs, all of which have links to political sites and news feeds. Among the best are:

www.outlookindia.com

www.indiainfo.com

Asianinfo.org is a general site, but it is more focused on making information on Asia (including India) available to the rest of the world.

www.asianinfo.org/asianinfo/india/politics.htm

The Indian government maintains an excellent site for access to information about the parliament, federal agencies, and most state governments.

Indiaimage.nic.in

Finally, there are some good sites on Indian politics, including the Virtual Library, Professor Gene Thursby's collection, and an India-based site that has material on elections, parties, and public opinion polls.

www.india.com.ar

www.clas.ufl.edu/users/gthursby/ind/politics.htm

www.indian-elections.com

InfoTrac College Edition Sources

Bouton, Marshall M. "India's Problem Is Not Politics."

Chibber, Pradeep. "Who Voted for the BJP?"

Cohen, Stephen P. "India Rising."

Lijphart, Arend. "The Puzzle of Indian Democracy."

Nayer, Balda Raj. "Globalisation and India's National Autonomy."

Ninian, Alex. "The Indian General Election of 2004."

Raman, A. S. "Politics in India."

Root, Hilton. "A Liberal India: The Triumph of Hope over Experience."

Sarkar, Tanika. "Women in South Asia."

Schaffer, Teresita. "Indian Democracy after 52 Years."

Swamy, Arum. "India in 2000: A Respite from Instability."

Further Reading

Brass, Paul. *The Politics of India Since Independence.* New York: Cambridge University Press, 1990. The most detailed of the texts on Indian politics. It is especially good on ethnic issues.

Das, Gundcharan. *India Unbound.* New York: Knopf, 2000. A personal and analytical account of India's economic and political transformations by one of the country's leading entrepreneurs.

Gupta, Bhabani Sen. *Rajiv Gandhi: A Political Study.* New Delhi: Konark, 1989. A highly critical but also highly insightful biography that takes Gandhi up to the end of his term as prime minister.

Gupte, Pranay. *Mother India: A Political Biography of Indira Gandhi.* A powerful and critical biography by the former *New York Times* reporter in India.

Hansen, Thomas. *Wages of Violence: Naming and Identity in Postcolonial Bombay.* Princeton: Princeton University Press, 2001. A systematic analysis of ethnicity in Bombay, written by a social anthropologist.

Jeffrey, Robin. *What's Happening to India?* 2nd ed. London: Macmillan, 1994. A book primarily about Sikhs and Punjab, but of more general interest as well.

Khilnani, Sunil. *The Idea of India.* London: Penguin Books, 1997. A powerful essay on politics and life in India by a young British political scientist.

Kohli, Atul. *India's Democracy: An Analysis of Changing State-Society Relations.* Princeton, N.J.: Princeton University Press, 1990.

———, ed. *Democracy and Discontent: India's Growing Crisis of Government.* New York: Cambridge University Press, 1990. Two works that focus on ethnicity and other problems imperiling Indian democracy.

Roy, Arundhati. *Power Politics.* Boston: South End Press, 2001. An impassioned plea against dams, globalization, and their impact on India by a leading architect and writer who gained notoriety after this book was published for criticizing the war against terrorism in Afghanistan.

Schofield, Victoria. *Kashmir in Conflict: India, Pakistan, and the Unending War.* New York: I. B. Taurus, 2003.

Thakur, Ramesh. *The Government and Politics of India.* London: Macmillan, 1995. The best textbook on Indian politics.

Varadarajan, Siddharth, ed. *Gujarat: The Making of a Tragedy.* New Delhi and New York: Penguin, 2002. An in-depth analysis of why Gujarat joined Kashmir as one of the two most explosive states in recent years.

Wolpert, Stanley. *A New History of India,* 3rd ed. New York: Oxford University Press, 1989. The best single-volume history of India.

*Your task is very difficult. Not even
Iranians understand Iran.*

ANONYMOUS IRANIAN PROFESSOR

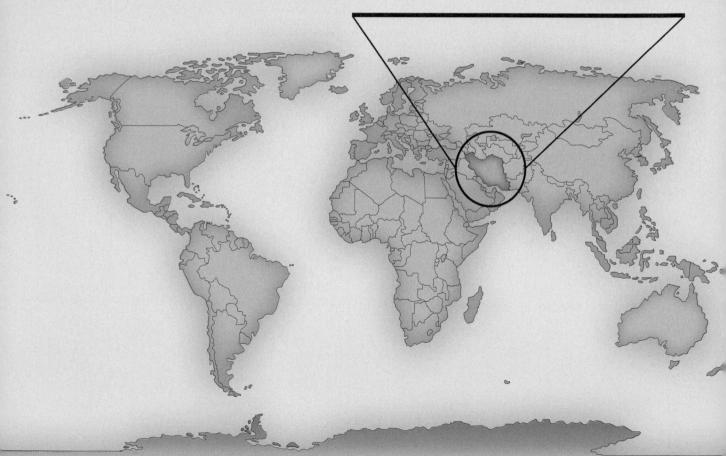

Chapter 13

IRAN

CHAPTER OUTLINE

The Basics: Iran

Size	1,648 sq. km. Roughly the size of Alaska
Population	68.3 million
Age distribution	29% under 15 years old
Infant Mortality	44.2 children per 1,000 births
HIV/AIDS rate	<0.01%
Ethnic distribution	Persian (51%), Azeri (24%), Kurds (7%), Arabs (3%), Others (15%)
Religion	Shiite Muslim (89%), Sunni Muslim (9%), Other (2%)
GNP per capita	$6,800
Growth GNP	7.6%
Poverty rate	40% (estimate)
Literacy rate	79%
Currency	6,906 rial = $1 (2002)

Teaching Lolita in Tehran

There was a minor controversy in American publishing circles when Azar Nafisi's book, *Reading Lolita in Tehran*, was published in 2003.[1] Any book about Lolita is bound to be contentious because Vladimir Nabokov's plot revolves around the manipulative sexual relationship between a middle-aged man and a thirteen-year-old girl.

But *Lolita* is especially controversial in Iran where the conservative clerics who have been in charge of the country since the 1979 revolution have imposed some of the world's most extensive limits on what women can and cannot do. Indeed, Nafisi herself lost two university appointments in part because she refused to follow rules that required her to cover her head if not wear a body-covering **chador** when she appeared in public.

Nafisi is like many Iranian intellectuals of her generation. She received a PhD in American literature from the University of Oklahoma in 1979. Again like many of her contemporaries who studied in the United States, Nafisi was an active opponent of the regime of **Mohammed Reza Shah** and eagerly returned home when it was over-

---

[1] Azar Nafisi, *Reading Lolita in Tehran* (New York: Random House, 2003).

Three Iranian girls wearing the traditional chadors wait for the arrival of Iranian President Mohammad Khatami to a pro-reform rally at a mosque in northern Tehran Tuesday, 5 June 2001. Elections were scheduled for 8 June. Part of the word "Independence" is written on the left.

Enric Marti/AP Wide World Photos

thrown and replaced by the Islamic Republic led by the **Ayatollah Ruhollah Khomeini.**

But, like many of her friends and colleagues, Nafisi soon soured on the theological and other restrictions imposed by the *mullahs* who ran the new regime and almost immediately led it into a deadly war with neighboring Iraq that lasted from 1980 to 1988 and settled next to nothing.

The book chronicles her growing disenchantment with the regime and her agonized decision to leave Iran for the United States again, where she now teaches at Johns Hopkins School of Advanced International Studies in Washington, D.C. But *Reading Lolita* is not about Nafisi's political journey alone. Instead, it focuses on an informal course she taught to a group of seven women students in her home after she resigned from her second university post. The students read and discussed a number of American novels, including *Lolita*. And, as one would expect, the discussion went far beyond the novels and included a growing amount of time spent on political repression in Iran, especially as it affected women.

Some of the issues the women faced will strike young Western readers as bizarre. Nafisi begins the book by contemplating two pictures, one of her students entering her house wearing their chadors. The other was taken a few minutes later when they had removed the required total-body cover to reveal colorful, Western-style clothes.

But it was more than the politics of clothing. The young women could get in trouble if any of their hair was exposed in public because it might tempt men. By that same logic, one of the women was suspended from school for running up the stairs when she was late for class because part of her leg could have been exposed and that would have tempted her male classmates. It was hard for the young women to establish relationships with men, because they were not allowed to be alone with members of the opposite sex who were not close relatives. A couple of the women had spent time in prison for their political activities and beliefs. Many of them seriously contemplated leaving the country. Almost everything that young people in the West take for granted—listening to rock music, watching R-rated films, and going to the beach—could land an Iranian woman in jail. In perhaps the most remarkable story for most Westerners, no women were allowed to attend the soccer game between the United States and Iran in 1999. There are rumors that women snuck in anyway, wearing baggy coats, no makeup, and turbans to cover their hair. Women who played sports had to do so in their chadors, which made it all but impossible for them to be competitive, say, on the basketball court.

Nafisi also makes it clear that the politics of gender in Iran is more complicated than Western stereotypes might suggest. First, many women—especially poorly educated, working-class women—gladly accept the chador and all the other restrictions put on them. What's more, a higher proportion of women work in Iran than in any other predominantly Muslim country, including hundreds of thousands who hold professional and even political jobs.

Nafisi's account, finally, suggests why Iran is one of the two most controversial countries covered in this book, especially for Americans. Iran has been controversial for more than a quarter century since the 1979 revolution, which overthrew a monarchy that had been a staunch ally of the United States. Shortly thereafter, a small group of students and other young people occupied the American embassy and held 61 of its employees hostage for 444 days, only releasing them on the day President Ronald Reagan was inaugurated. Since then, Iran has been accused of supporting terrorists in the Middle East and beyond. And, most recently, President George W. Bush included it in his "axis of evil" during his 2002 State of the Union Address, singling it out again for its alleged support of terrorism and its attempt to build a nuclear arsenal.

We will not be ducking the controversies that swirl around Iranian politics in the pages that follow. However, as with the status of women, its political life is far more nuanced than the rhetoric that has been the norm in the speeches of American presidents from Jimmy Carter through George W. Bush. The revolution is nowhere near as militant as it was in its early years. In particular, a new generation of more moderate leaders wielded considerable influence after Ayatollah Khomeini died in 1989 until the 2004 elections. Indeed, Iran has more proto-democratic features than most of the other major states in which Muslims constitute a majority.

And perhaps most importantly of all, at least until the 2004 election for the parliament (*majlis*), the Iranian leadership seemed to sincerely want to improve relations with the United States and the rest of the West. But it should be pointed out that the United States was highly skeptical of the trial balloons from Tehran, as we will see in more detail later in the chapter.

Iran did not, for instance, support Iraq in either of its two wars with the United States, a country Khomeini had labeled the "great Satan." In September 2003, Foreign Minister Kemal Kharrazi signaled that his government was prepared to permit nuclear weapons inspectors, had arrested al-Qaeda operatives who fled into its territory, and shared the same basic priorities that the United States had for rebuilding Iraq.[2] To be sure, Kharrazi was one of the leading moderates in the Iranian leadership, and he and his colleagues were locked in a political

struggle with more conservative colleagues, especially members of the clergy, which culminated in their defeat in the 2004 legislative election and will probably lead to a similar result in the presidential contest in 2005 when current president **Mohammad Khatami** has to step down.

Iran: The Basics

Persia versus Iran

Iran is one of the world's oldest countries, although it was known by its earlier name, Persia, until 1935. In one form or another, a country with one or the other of those names has existed for more than 2,500 years since it was created by its first great emperors, Darius and Cyrus.

The name Persia comes from the region's dominant linguistic group who speak Farsi. **Reza Shah,** the first of the two **Pahlevi** monarchs, changed the country's name to Iran, a term whose origins are the same as "Aryan," which he wanted to underscore as a critical part of the country's origins.

Over time, modernizers like the Pahlevis stressed the country's Persian roots over its more recent affiliation with the Shiite sect of Islam (to be discussed in the next section). That, of course, changed with the Islamic revolution, which turned the emphasis back to religion.

That said, Iran is not an overwhelmingly Persian country, since they make up barely half of the population. Almost a quarter are Azeris. The rest come from a number of ethnic groups, none of which make up more than 8 percent of the population, including Kurds and Arabs. This ethnic diversity is reflected in the fact that not even three in five Iranians speak Farsi or one of its dialects.

Shiite versus Sunni

As already noted, Iran is an Islamic republic that is governed according to Muslim principles implemented largely by clerics. As such, it is one of the few theocracies left in the world today, where the **Sharia** (Muslim law) is far more influential than, say, in Nigeria, which will be covered in Chapter 15.

As is the case with all of the world's major religions, Islam has been divided into rival sects over the centuries. Most Muslims are **Sunnis** who make up the majority of the population in every Muslim country other than Iran.

Iran, instead, is dominated by **Shiites** who are widely (and often mistakenly) viewed as the most militant and fanatical believers in their faith. The origins of the Sunni /

[2] Glenn Kessler, "Iran Signals Readiness to Cooperate." *Washington Post*, 25 September 2003, A18, A26.

Shiite split date from the early years of Islam. When the Prophet Muhammad died in 632, he had not designated a successor to head the rapidly expanding empire he had created. Almost immediately, his followers split into two groups. Those who became Sunnis felt that the most prominent members of the community should select the new leader, or caliph, on the basis of personal attributes such as piety, wisdom, morality, leadership ability, and competence. Others, however, contended that the leadership of the Islamic community should stay in the prophet's family. They also believed that Muhammad had designated his cousin, son-in-law, and close companion, Ali, to be his successor. They were called Shiites, a word derived from the expression "Shi'at Ali," or "the partisans of Ali."

Although the Sunnis won the argument, Ali himself was eventually elected to the caliphate in 656 after the death of Uthman, the third caliph. However, Muawiyah, Uthman's nephew and governor of Syria, refused to accept this choice. Eventually, Muawiyah prevailed and established the Damascus-based Umayyad dynasty (661–750).

The Shiites never recognized Umayyad rule, continuing to claim that only the descendants of Ali had the right to govern the Islamic community. In 680, Ali's second son, Hussein, led a group of his followers in an armed uprising against Umayyad rule. Hussein was defeated and killed at Karbala in what is now southern Iraq.

The story of Hussein's defeat lies at the heart of Shiite culture, especially its emphasis on martyrdom. The defeat also widened the gulf between Sunnis and Shiites. In the following centuries, what initially had been limited to a disagreement over who should succeed the prophet became a full-fledged religious and political schism that continues to be felt throughout the Muslim world.

Contemporary shiism stands out from its more widely practiced rival in two main ways for our purposes. First, it has an established clergy and stresses the importance of theological training among those who reach the top of the Shiite hierarchy, the ayatollahs. Second, as is often missed by Western observers, Shiites have long tolerated and even encouraged debate over the interpretation of key principles from the Quran, Hadith, and Sharia.

Iran is the only major Islamic country in which Shiites constitute an overwhelming majority of the population. As a result, Iran was the only country governed by Shiites in late 2004, though they will dominate the transitional government elected in January 2005 in Iraq, as well, because Shiite Arabs outnumber both Sunni Arabs and Kurds, most of whom are also Sunnis (see Chapter 14).

A Note on Transliteration

Rendering Iranian terms in English is a problem as it is for all countries included in this book that do not use the Roman alphabet. It is particularly difficult in the case of Iran because scholars, the U.S. government, journalists, and others use multiple conventions in transliterating names and terms. I have chosen not to use the system favored by most scholars and government officials, because names, in particular, are shown in complicated forms. Therefore, unlike the case in other chapters, I have decided to adopt the transliteration scheme used by the *New York Times, Washington Post,* and other Western press services that is far simpler and, frankly, easier to follow.

Conventional interpretations of Shiism overstate the sect's **fundamentalism.** Most of the Muslims who have attacked Western targets over the last thirty years have been Sunnis, not Shiites. Before the Islamic Revolution of 1979, the Shiite clergy largely shunned politics, arguing for an Islamic equivalent of the Western principle of separation of church and state. Last but by no means least, Shiism is not monolithic. In fact, the community has actively encouraged debate between leading clerics about the true meaning of the faith, which has made the Shiite community as intellectually open as any major religious group in the world.

Since the Iranian revolution and the rise of terrorism, many in the West have used the term **fundamentalist** to refer to groups like the Iranian leadership. Observers latched onto that term as they struggled to make sense of why millions of people were turning to traditional interpretations of religion after years in which the trend had been toward a more secular and Western approach to life.

More recently, some scholars have stopped using the term fundamentalist because it tends to blend together too many very different viewpoints. The term was initially coined to describe American Protestants who chose to use a literal interpretation of the Bible.

In that sense, Osama bin Laden, the Taliban, and many of the early leaders of the Islamic revolution in Iran could be considered fundamentalists. However, many, including the reformers in Iran, are better thought of as **Islamicists** who are trying to find a way to blend the tenets of their faith with the needs and complexities of a modern, industrialized, and globalizing world.

The same should probably be said for another commonly used label, fanatics. It is true that many of the people we will encounter in this chapter hold extreme views and, like many of their colleagues throughout the Muslim world, are deeply angry about the impact of the West in general and the United States in particular. But, fanaticism is a pejorative word, one that could be used to describe anyone who deeply espouses and publicly demonstrates unusual beliefs.

Personally, I do not use either word because I find that they make it hard to see either the complexities of life in a country like Iran, throw us off course when trying to understand a regime like the one Saddam Hussein led in Iraq for almost a quarter century, and make it hard not to fall into the use of what the psychologists call the **image of the enemy** in which we view people we disagree with as completely evil and unacceptable.

I am as critical of anyone of the intolerance, violence, and brutality that has been carried out in the name of "god the most compassionate." However, terms like fundamentalist and fanatic obscure a lot of trends we need to understand if we are to deal with these vitally important challenges.

Persia versus Shiism

In short, Iran has two powerful traditions, Persia and Shiism. Over the last century, its leadership has fought over which one would be the most important in shaping political life.

As we will see in the section on Iranian history that follows, the Pahlevis and other modernizers wanted to downplay the role of Islam and thus stressed the more secular aspects of Persian history, ranging from the poetry of its intellectuals to the world-famous wine made from Shiraz grapes. By contrast, the clergy emphasized the country's Shiite tradition and the role of faith, especially in the impoverished rural areas of the country and, later, in the slums of Tehran and other big cities.

The revolution of 1979, of course, marked a victory for those who favored the Muslim tradition. It remains to be seen, however, if their victory will last.

Social and Economic Conditions

Iran has tremendous economic potential because it sits atop almost 100 billion barrels of proven oil reserves. Even though some countries refuse to buy oil from Iran, it still produces almost four million barrels of oil a day, much of which is sold on the global market.

However, oil has not produced the level of wealth

Arab and Muslim

Westerners often make the mistake of equating Arabs and Muslims. They are definitely not one and the same.

Arabs are an ethnic group that constitutes the bulk of the population from Morocco in the west to Iraq in the east. Not all Arabs are Muslims. Large numbers of Lebanese and Palestinians, in particular, are Christians, as was Tariq Aziz, one of the leaders of Saddam Hussein's regime in Iraq.

And by no means are all Muslims Arabs. Most Iranians are Persians who have a different heritage from Arabs and do not speak Arabic. Overall, Islam spread as far as Western Africa (see Chapter 15 on Nigeria) and the Philippines. In fact, the countries with the largest Muslim populations, India and Indonesia, have no Arabs to speak of.

one finds in Saudi Arabia, Kuwait, and the other oil-producing states on the Persian Gulf. Hard statistics are hard to come by, but the CIA estimates that GDP per capita is only about $7,000 a year. What's more, the distribution of income and wealth is highly skewed with a rather small upper middle class and as much as 40 percent of the population that lives in poverty. As we will see later in the chapter, President Khatami's government sought to introduce market reforms to make the economy more efficient and remove the structural problems created both under the shah and under the early years of the Islamic Republic. Iran has also lost some of its brightest, best-educated, young professionals who have emigrated for political and/or economic reasons since the 1970s.

Finally, it should be noted that Iran has the youngest population of any country covered in this book. In the early years of the Islamic Republic, the leadership encouraged people to have as many children as possible to boost the size of the country's population. As a result, 29 percent of all Iranians are under 15, and 23 was the median age for the population as a whole. Because the population explosion has been an unexpected burden on an economy with an inflation rate of about 15 percent, the government has encouraged the use of birth control to limit the expansion in the number of young people. The emphasis on youth is also reflected in the fact that authorities lowered the voting age to 15, which is almost certainly the youngest in the world.

Iranians showing the marks on their fingers after voting in 2004.

AFP/Getty Images

Key Questions

To understand Iran, we need to explore key questions that arise for every country in the third world. But, in so doing, we will also see issues that are specific to Iran and, at most, a handful of other countries.

■ Why is Iran having a hard time developing its economy? Why is that the case, in particular, despite the fact that it has so much oil and other natural resources?

■ Why is Iran one of the few countries left in the world that is run by its religious leaders? How does the isolation it has experienced since the 1979 revolution affect the way its government is structured and limit the prospects for democracy?

The Evolution of the Iranian State

Before Islam

Key features in the politics of Iran today have important roots that go back more than 2,500 years. (See table 13.1.) While we do not have the time or space to discuss that entire history, there are key themes we have to highlight from the thousand years before the Arabs conquered the country and converted Iranians to Islam. That is the case because there has been an independent country called Persia or Iran occupying much of the territory of the cur-

rent state for almost all that time (www.iranchamber.com/history/historic_periods.php).

Those origins are both religious and political in nature. They begin with the Prophet Zoroaster who lived sometime between the ninth and seventh century BC and created one of the world's first monotheistic religions, which took root among most of the people in what is now Iran. The political evolution began somewhat later and dates from the accession of Cyrus the Great to the Persian throne of Medes in 550 BC. At the time, the people who lived on the Fars (whence the name Persia) were taking up agriculture and moving into fixed settlements that required protection. By the time he died in 521, Darius had expanded the Achaemenian Empire as far as parts of today's Bulgaria and Greece in the northwest, Libya in the southwest, and India and Pakistan in the east. It wasn't just the size of the empire. Cyrus and

▌ **TABLE 13.1** Turning Points in Iranian History before 1900

YEAR	EVENT
550 BC	Cyrus comes to power
332 BC	Defeat by Alexander the Great
560 AD	Accession of Khosrow I
638 AD	Arab victory, introduction of Islam
1219 AD	Invasion by Mongols
1501 AD	First safavid shah named
1896 AD	Assassination of Nasir ed-Din Shah

The ruins of the ancient city of Persepolis

his successors Darius and Xerxes drew on Zoroastrian traditions that required just rulers to establish a positive working relationship with those they governed. In other words, they could not rule solely by force.

Their great power was not to last, however. In 332, the Macedonian Alexander the Great defeated the Persians and occupied their large and glorious capital, Persepolis.

Shortly after Alexander's death, the nomadic Parthians—an Aryan tribe (whence the name Iran)—began to settle in the area and adopted Persian culture. By 163 BC, they were able to establish enough power to wall Persia off from the Roman Empire and restore a degree of independence. The Parthians stayed in power for almost four hundred years until their rule disintegrated in tribal fighting. The struggle culminated not in a war but in a personal struggle between the last Parthian, Adravan, and his challenger, Ardeshir. Once the latter killed the former, he was able to establish the Sassanian dynasty that ruled Persia from 208 to 637. Most importantly for our purposes, like the Parthians, the Sassanians adopted most of what was now a millennium-old Persian culture and style of rule. That said, one of their key innovations was to begin calling the rule *shahinshah,* or King of Kings.

The last of the great Sassanian shahs, Khosrow I, took power in 560. He restored Persian power and began to move its influence and borders westward again. He also built a new capital at Ctesiphon where the floor of his immense palace was covered with a remarkable, ninety-foot-square carpet, dubbed the "spring of Khosrow."

The Arrival and Consolidation of Islam

Khosrow's power would not last long either. The Christian Byzantines fought back and forced Khosrow to flee in 626, which effectively shattered the Sassanian state.

But it would not be the Byzantines who would dominate Persia. At that same moment, a new religion, Islam, was taking root on the Arabian Peninsula. Following the prophet's death on 8 June 632, his followers fanned out in all directions to convert people to the new faith. Previously, Persians had never had any reason to fear the relatively underdeveloped Arabs. Thus, when their far larger and far better-equipped army faced the Muslims at Qadisiya just west of the Euphrates in present-day Iraq, they expected a swift and easy victory. After four months of negotiations, the battle began in 637 and the dispirited Sassanian troops crumbled. The next year, the Arabs occupied Ctesiphon. In a sign of things to come, they shipped the Spring of Khosrow back to Mecca where they cut it into pieces.

Incorporating Islam into Persian culture was not very difficult given the Zoroastrian beliefs in a single god and the struggle between good and evil. However, Persians had a hard time adjusting to the fact that they were now a far less important power and that their tradition of strong kings had been undermined because Persia became subordinate to the temporal and spiritual leaders of Arabic-based Islam. Persians helped make the Islamic Middle East one of the cultural centers of the world during the early centuries of the last millennium. However, Persia itself fell into decline in part because Islam downplayed the role of kingship, which had been at the heart of its culture since the time of Cyrus and Darius.

As we saw earlier, the Islamic world split between Shiite and Sunni in the first decades after the prophet's death. However, it would be eight hundred years before the Persians became the first people to accept Shiism en masse—and then only following another debacle that would shape Persian values for centuries to come.

In 1219, the Mongol army led by Chinghiz (Genghis) Khan overran Persia. Among other atrocities, the

Mongols decapitated and disemboweled every resident of Naishapur, then one of Persia's intellectual centers. Chinghiz's grandson, Hulagu, returned to rampage in Persia forty years later and remained to rule much of the region as an independent Mongol territory. The last invasion from the northeast came under Tamarlane, who called himself a Tatar rather than a Mongol, in 1394. These repeated invasions gave birth to an understandable fear of outside intervention that has endured ever since.

During this time, some Iranians developed the sufi mystical tradition in which holy men whipped up religious frenzy throughout the region, promising that the faithful would reach communion with God. One of the sufi orders, the Safavid, came to the fore under Junayd who also turned it from a religious into a political movement. In 1501, forces loyal to his grandson, Ismail, took control of the city of Tabriz and proclaimed their leader, **shah.** Ismail and his followers fought back repeated attacks from the Sunni Ottoman Empire founded by the Mongols. As they solidified their rule over a land that is about 20 percent larger than today's Iran, they also turned to Shiism, in part to set themselves apart from the Ottomans and Arabs.

For the next four hundred years, the Safavid and, later, Qajar, dynasties combined the traditional Persian commitments to strong kingship with Shiite beliefs in faith and obedience to rule the country. Unlike earlier periods, however, their approach to governing produced stagnation, not the kind of growth and domination that had been so much a part of Persian history in early centuries.

During that time, the Persian kings came to emphasize the authoritarian nature of their rule. To cite but one example, Abbas Shah was convinced that his closest advisors were conspiring against him. So, he ordered one of his sons killed in 1615 and another blinded six years later. His successors may not have been quite as ruthless. Nonetheless, they continued a system in which monarchs with absolute power dominated a hierarchical society in which religion was central and social and economic change all but impossible to achieve. Authoritarian rule was reinforced by Shiism, which provides tremendous respect to the most learned scholars, especially those who are descendents of the prophet.

Yet the combination of the tradition of Persian kingship and Shiite Islam produced a strain in the country's culture that called for charismatic leadership from the king but required that his rule be just and in keeping with religious and other traditional beliefs. By the end of the nineteenth century, the inability of generations of kings to live up to that ideal did the traditional line of dynasties in.

They were not wholly without accomplishments. If nothing else, they were one of the few rulers in what we now call the third world who were able to prevent direct colonial rule. The Qajars, in particular, were able to put together a reasonably integrated state by building networks of local warlords and potentates out of which grew at least a rudimentary sense of national identity.

Nonetheless, by the late nineteenth century, Persia found itself, like many other cultures in Asia and Africa, torn between its own traditions and the growing pressures from the West. Iran never became a colony. That does not mean, however, that pressures from the West had a minor impact.

To begin with, many middle-class Iranians studied and later did business in Europe and North America. Foreign companies developed a presence in the country long before oil became its leading product, often as a result of direct grants or concessions handed to them by the Qajars. Russian military advisors provided the only semblance of training and discipline to the army. Most importantly of all, the military and economic power of the West drove home just how weak the Qajar dynasty had become.

Opposition to the regime built throughout the society. Orthodox Shiites objected to secularization. The *bazaaris,* or small businessmen who worked the country's many marketplaces, wanted the opportunity to make more money while reducing competition from outsiders. The growing secular middle class wanted political reforms that would lead to the rule of law, if not to democracy itself. (See table 13.2.)

The last decade of the nineteenth and first decade of the twentieth centuries were troubled years for Iran. There were protests against almost all aspects of Qajar rule, including an extremely unpopular ban against smoking tobacco. In 1896, the aging (and most thought incompetent) Nasir ed-Din Shah was assassinated.

The most important of the protests was the **Constitutional Revolution** of 1905 to 1911. It succeeded at first

▐ **TABLE 13.2** Iran: 1900–1979

YEAR	EVENT
1905	Start of Constitutional Revolution
1911	End of Constitutional Revolution
1925	Reza Khan becomes shah
1941	Mohammad Reza Pahlavi becomes shah
1953	Overthrow of Mossadeq government
1979	Islamic Revolution

because it promised all things to all people, including firming up the legal status of Islam, strengthening the state, instituting economic reforms, and codifying the legal system. On 12 January 1906, a huge protest convinced Muzaffar ed-Din Shah to dismiss his prime minister, give up absolute rule, and call the first equivalent of a parliament.

Unfortunately, the situation degenerated in the months that followed, culminating in June when soldiers fired on demonstrators and killed a cleric. As many as twenty thousand protesters then fled inside the walls of the British embassy. But the situation was thrown into turmoil again when the shah died and was replaced by his son, Muhammad Ali, who was described by one American advisor as "perhaps the most perverted, cowardly, and vice-ridden monster that had disgraced the throne of Persia in many generations."[3] The king finally dismissed his prime minister, created the Majlis, and accepted the constitution of 1906.

In the end, the secularized and Westernized portion of the Iranian population was the most pleased with the constitutional reforms. By 1907, proclerical forces were already attacking the constitution in the Majlis, insisting, for instance, that a council of clerics get the right to review all legislation passed by the parliament.

In the meantime, the Russians and British had divided the increasingly ungovernable country into two zones of influence. On 23 June 1908, Russian-led troops attacked and destroyed the Sepahsalar Mosque, which had been the symbolic home of the protest movements of the preceding two years. For the next three years, Russian troops reinforced those of the shah until 24 December 1911 when the shah dissolved the Majlis.

The Last Shahs

The defeat of the Constitutional Revolution by no means restored the shah to power. He controlled Tehran and a few other cities, but tribal leaders ran the rest of the country, to the degree that it was run at all.

British influence increased as well. Following its navy's decision to switch from coal to oil to fuel its ships, Iran's oil became a vital resource. As a result, the British all but formally occupied the southern part of the country and the Russians the north, leaving Iranians in de facto control of a narrow strip in the center that did not include Tehran or most other major cities.

---

[3] W. William Schuster, *The Strangling of Persia*, cited in Sandra Mackey, *The Iranians: Persia, Islam, and the Soul of a Nation* (New York: Plume, 1996), 149.

CORBIS Sygma

Reza Khan Shah and Mohammed Reza Shah at the former's coronation

If anything, the situation deteriorated even further after the Bolshevik Revolution when Marxists briefly set up a Soviet Republic in the Gilan region of northern Iran. This produced a massive nationalist reaction that, in the short run, led to the defeat of the Marxist republic and, in the longer term, produced the first serious nationalist movement in modern Iranian history.

Central to that nationalism was a mid-level officer, Reza Khan, who would establish Iran's final dynasty a decade later. Born in 1878, Reza Khan quickly rose in the ranks of the Cossack troops (named for their Russian leaders), becoming their leader in the city of Hamadan. After defeating the Soviet republic, he led three thousand Cossacks into Tehran and occupied it. He also subdued many of the tribal leaders who were still in charge in most of rural Iran. The British, meanwhile, were convinced that this tall, tough soldier could bring order to the country and threw their support behind him. For the next four years, Reza Khan was the de facto leader of the country, but it was only on 31 October 1925 that he had himself crowned shah and chose the dynastic name, Pahlavi, after the language spoken before Persia was defeated by the Arabs.

The first Pahlavi shah took power in the name of nationalism and Shiism. However, he soon turned his back on Islam and focused his attention on modernizing his hopelessly poor and weak country. The shah set out to change the Iranian landscape. His government built the first national railroad system, introduced the first modern factories, and expropriated land from rural elites. The Majlis continued to exist, but it did little more than rubber-stamp decisions made by the monarch.

Perhaps most importantly of all, the shah turned on the clerics. He took two steps of powerful symbolic importance to orthodox Muslims; women were no longer allowed to wear the veil and men had to shave their beards. He closed religious schools, replacing them with free, state-run institutions that stressed science and other modern topics.

The Pahlavi regime also stressed the country's Persian origins and its historical glories before the arrival of Islam. He even changed the name of the country from Persia to Iran on the dubious historical claim that it was the legitimate name, since it was the one used under Cyrus and Darius.

Reza Shah also played the traditional Iranian "game" of protecting its territorial integrity through a complicated pattern of international alliances. In the 1930s, because of his support for the Nazis' "Aryan" policies, he cast Iran's lot with Germany. After Germany attacked the Soviet Union in 1941, the British decided that they could not run the risk that the Iranian oil fields could come under Nazi control. Therefore, on 25 August 1941, the British navy captured southern Iran and the Soviets marched into the north. Saying he could not remain at the head of a country under foreign occupation, the shah resigned less than a month later and went into exile.

Assessments of his generation in power are mixed. There is little doubt that Reza Shah brought much-needed social and economic change to a country he seemed to treat as a personal fiefdom. That said, he definitely lost touch with most of people, provoking widespread anger because he failed to live up to the Persian tradition of just rule.

Mohammad Reza Shah replaced his father. Born in 1919, the new shah was not quite twenty-two years old and was thought to be a playboy who preferred dancing and drinking in Europe to the affairs of state. And, indeed, the new shah did little to alter his reputation for the first twelve years he sat on the Peacock Throne.

The new shah faced three challenges once World War II ended. Surprisingly, the easiest came when diplomatic pressure from the United States and United Kingdom led the Soviets to withdraw from northern Iran.

In 1949, the growing Communist party (Tudeh) tried to assassinate him. One bullet hit his cheekbone and emerged under his nose. Three more went through his hat. Somehow he survived.

His political survival was even more severely challenged from 1951 to 1953 when the charismatic **Muhammad Mossadeq** was prime minister. Over the shah's objections, the prime minister led a campaign to nationalize the Anglo-Iranian Oil Company (AIOC) of which the British owned 51 percent. AIOC was a visible symbol of the degree to which foreigners controlled the country. To cite but one example, Iran earned more from the export of carpets than it did from much more valuable oil. Mossadeq himself was part of a broad coalition of political groups known as the National Front, which included many of the early nonreligious leaders of the Islamic Republic as well as the more politicized clerics of the time.

On taking office, he ordered all British employees of AIOC out of the country. Because Iran did not have workers who could run the production and refinery facilities, chaos ensued. In July 1952, the Majlis granted Mossadeq emergency powers in a law including nineteen clauses enumerating areas in which he was authorized to act. The nineteenth was simply "et cetera."

In practice, Mossadeq overstretched his capacities when he lost the support of the clerics and his appeal to the Tudeh. He also generated opposition when he dissolved the upper house of the parliament, suspended the supreme court, confiscated royal property, and expanded the scope of martial law. The shah then tried to fire the prime minister, who refused to resign.

At that point, the United States intervened largely through the actions of Kermit Roosevelt (son of President Theodore Roosevelt), who was CIA station chief in Tehran. Fighting broke out, killing at least three hundred. The shah fled to Rome. Finally, the United States succeeding in forcing Mossadeq to resign, which paved the way for the shah to return.

The coup against Mossadeq was at most a short-term and pyrrhic victory for the United States and the shah. It would only contribute to the anti-Western and anti-American sentiments that would boil over during the revolution of the 1970s and in the early years of the Islamic Republic. In other words, the return of the shah to power laid the groundwork for his defeat a quarter century later.

Some observers think that the shah took his survival as a sign that he had a divine right to rule and to do so in

MOHAMMAD REZA SHAH

AP/Wide World Photos

Mohammad Reza Shah, the last Pahlavi king, was born in 1919, two years before his father became ruler of Iran. He received his initial education in Switzerland but later graduated from a military academy in Tehran.

His first years on the throne were marked by turmoil. Communists tried to assassinate him in 1949. In 1951, he fled the country and the reform government of Muhammad Mossadeq and could only return after the CIA orchestrated a coup d'etat that forced the nationalist prime minister from office.

By the 1960s, the shah had solidified his rule and embarked on the white revolution, aimed to continue the secularization and modernization begun by his father. He provoked even more opposition from both the secular left and the religious right and was forced from office and the country in 1979. He died of cancer the following year (persepolis.free.fr/iran/personalities/shah.html).

A soldier bends to kiss the feet of Mohammed Reza Shah as he leaves the country in 1979

an absolutist manner. He also ruled in a way that reflected his lack of trust, even in men who were supposedly his most valued advisors. As he did, he provoked more intense opposition than his father had ever seen.

It began with his alienation of the Shiite clerics. Despite the stereotypes that have arisen since the 1979 revolution, most Shiite scholars and clergymen have traditionally shunned politics, especially those who teach at such centers of the faith as Qom in Iran and Najaf in Iraq.

That changed in the 1960s once the shah instituted the **white revolution** and created the notoriously brutal **SAVAK** to enforce his rule. The white revolution began in 1963 and was a revolution in name only. It was yet another attempt to both modernize the country and increase the shah's power. As was the case under his father's rule, the clergy were an important target of the reforms, including giving the peasants land that belonged to the clerics and reducing their impact on daily life. Again, women's rights were extended and the train-

ing and equipment provided for the growing military were upgraded.

SAVAK was formed in 1957; it is a Farsi acronym for Intelligence and Security Organization of the Country. It not only arrested and tortured dissidents at home, but it spied on and even killed students and others living abroad who deigned to oppose the shah.

But the most important change in the 1960s and 1970s came from the religious community, especially from Ayatollah Khomeini. Khomeini had long been one of the leading clerics in the spiritual center of Qom. The tall, austere Khomeini built his reputation and his charisma largely because he was seen as a religious leader who was above politics and was exceptionally learned in the legal aspects of Islam. By the time he gained the title of ayatollah in 1960 he was still not actively involved in political life.

The white revolution proved to be the last straw for Khomeini. Given the regime's opposition to Islam, he ar-

AYATOLLAH RUHOLLAH KHOMEINI

AP/Wide World Photos

Ayatollah Khomeini addresses an audience in the airport building in Tehran, Iran, 1 February 1979, after his arrival from 14 years of exile.

The Ayatollah Ruhollah Khomeini was born in 1902 in the isolated town of Khomein. As was the norm in those days, he did not have a last or family name, something Reza Khan Shah only imposed on the country in 1926 at which point Khomeini became known as Ruhollah Mustafavi. His father, also a cleric, was killed when Ruhollah was a baby, and the boy (whose name means "soul of God") reportedly finished his first reading of the Koran when he was only seven.

In Shiism, an ayatollah has reached the highest level of spiritual awareness. Those who are descended from the prophet are allowed to wear a black turban; others wear a white one. In Iran, they also use their hometown as their family name, which is why he became known as Ayatollah Khomeini rather than Mustafavi.

Khomeini emerged as a leader for two main reasons. First, he developed the notion that senior clerics had the obligation and right to rule in order to maintain the Islamic nature of Iran because of their spiritual expertise. Second, he became one of the leaders of the opposition to the increasingly secular regime of the shah, especially after Khomeini was forced into exile, first in Iraq and later in France.

As Supreme Leader of the Islamic Republic, Khomeini struck a stern and often angry pose in both his dealings with his own people and with the United States. After his death in 1989, his successors adopted more moderate policies, although Iran is still often seen as an adversary by many in the West, especially in the United States (www.asiasource.org/society/khomeini.cfm).

gued that one could no longer separate state and religion and that clerics had an obligation to see to it that Islamic principles were upheld in Iran. In so doing, he shifted the center of gravity of opposition to the shah from the secular left to the followers of orthodox Shiite Islam.

The repression followed quickly. On 22 March 1963, the shah's troops broke into the most famous theological school in Qom and killed two unarmed students. The students who escaped immediately went to Khomeini's house, because he was already the symbolic heart of the opposition. When he went to preach at that school on 3 June, power throughout Qom was cut off by the authorities. The next day, Khomeini joined the ranks of over sixty clerics who had been arrested. Muslims rioted after his arrest, and it took the imposition of martial law in a number of cities to end the disturbances.

Khomeini was released from prison the following spring. The shah and his supporters tried to convince him to stay out of political life, but he always gave his new but standard response, "all of Islam is politics." In November 1964, he was arrested again, put on an airplane, and sent into exile in Iraq. For the next fifteen years, his teaching and preaching galvanized opposition to the shah. Even though his actions were ignored by the official media, his supporters were able to smuggle in audiotapes of his messages, which circulated among the faithful throughout the country.

More than religion was involved in the downfall of the shah. In fact, the unintended consequences of land reform may have done him the most harm. Most peasants were illiterate and ill-prepared to run the farms they were given. Many, for instance, had to take out huge loans that they could not repay, lost their land, and ended up flocking to the cities where they lived under appalling conditions in the slums of South Tehran and other urban areas. Tehran's population doubled in the 1970s, and city dwellers reached half the total population of the country in 1979. In other words, the overall rapid rate of economic growth, the foreign investment, the skyscrapers and mansions built in North Tehran provided an illusion about how successful and popular the shah was.

But the shah failed to see that his reforms and his power were little more than an illusion. He became increasingly distant from the population as a whole, continued with his economic reforms, and concentrated more and more power in his own hands. All opposition political parties were abolished. The SAVAK kept track of the opposition at home and abroad and is widely believed to have assassinated a number of leading dissidents living at home and abroad and tortured thousands at its infamous and enormous Evin Prison.

The regime also got into trouble because of its alliance with the United States. With the overthrow of Mossadeq, the United States and the CIA became the main focus of anti-imperialist sentiment. Yet the shah forged a close alliance with the United States and used its newfound oil wealth (after the OPEC oil embargo quadrupled prices in 1973–4) to buy billions of dollars worth of weapons. Americans doing business in Iran did not help their country's image since they acted as if they ruled the country and failed to even notice that their drinking and/or sexual openness insulted the sensitivities of many Iranians.

The Islamic Republic

The rest of the chapter will deal with the institutions and policies of the Islamic Republic. However, because there are so many misconceptions about it, especially since the death of Ayatollah Khomeini, it is important that we review its history. But, because everything covered in this section will reappear in the second, more analytical half of the chapter, we can do so quite briefly.

Some scholars talk about three periods or even three republics that coincide with the three men who have dominated political life in postrevolutionary Iran. (See table 13.3.) That will likely turn to four periods when President Khatami leaves office about the time this book is published.

The first, not surprisingly, covers the decade when Khomeini was **Supreme Leader.** Despite the initial popularity of the revolution and Khomeini himself, these were not easy years.

To begin with, the coalition of individuals, groups, and organizations that toppled the shah was too diverse to govern. Early on, Khomeini made declarations about having an open government in which the clerics might not play the dominant role. He also ruled with prominent politicians who had opposed the shah and did not share his conception of an Islamic state, including Abolhassan Bani-Sadr and Sadeq Gotzbadeh.

Quickly, and in ways reminiscent of Stalin's or Saddam's purges (see Chapters 9 and 14), people from every other major political faction were purged and removed from office. Some prominent politicians, including Bani-Sadr, were accused of crimes and executed, as were thousands of supporters of rival political movements ranging from the Communist Party (Tudeh) to moderate Muslims.

By the early 1980s, there was little doubt that Khomeini had created an Islamic republic. Members of the laity continued to hold important positions in the Majlis, the bureaucracy, and the executive. However, all decisions that mattered were made by senior clerics. Khomeini's power was reinforced by three of the most important events of his decade in power.

The first was the 444-day occupation of the U.S. embassy by a group of young Islamic militants, often described as students, that began on 4 November 1979. Students had occupied the embassy earlier and been denounced by both Khomeini and the revolution's secular leaders, which led them to withdraw.

After the first occupation, the United States allowed the dying shah to enter the country for medical treatment. That act deepened anti-American sentiment and led to the second occupation of the embassy. This time, Khomeini and other hard-line leaders gave the action their tacit approval.

The occupation had a dual impact. It, first, deepened the divide between Washington and Tehran, which has been hostile—at best—ever since. Second, it made it easier for Khomeini and his allies to remove more moderate and secular leaders from power. Virtually none of them remained in prominent positions by the time the hostages were released the day President Ronald Reagan was inaugurated in 1981.

The second event was the long and brutal war Iran fought with Iraq between 1980 and 1988. Ayatollah Khomeini was not the only ruler to come to power in the region in 1979. That year, the long-time second in command in Iraq, Saddam Hussein forced his mentor and predecessor from power in Iraq (see the next chapter). The two new rulers viewed each other as threats to both their respective regimes and to their hopes for hegemony in the troubled Persian Gulf region and the Middle East as a whole (www.crimesofwar.org/thebook/iran-iraq-war.html).

The eight years of fighting turned into little more than a stalemate. The front lines barely moved inside the borders of either country. Yet by the time the two sides accepted a cease-fire there were more than five hundred

▌ **TABLE 13.3** Key Events in the Islamic Republic

YEAR	EVENT
1979	Khomeini becomes Supreme Leader
1980–88	War with Iran
1989	Death of Khomeini
1997	Election of Khatami
2004	Victory by conservatives in Majlis election

An Iranian protester sets fire to a United States' flag, while other demonstrators give a clenched fist salute during an anti-American protest in Tehran, Monday, 5 November 1979. The demonstration came after students stormed the United States Embassy in Tehran and held the staff hostage against the deportation of the former Shah of Iran from the United States.

Mohammad Syad/AP/Wide World Photos

thousand killed and wounded on each side. The war also solidified American hostility toward the Islamic republic, which led it to give at least indirect support to Saddam's regime, something most U.S. policymakers came to regret following the Iraqi invasion of Kuwait in 2000.

Most scholars add a third trend to this first period. The dangers imposed by the war led Khomeini and his colleagues to increase the level of repression against potential as well as real opponents. On one level, that introduced new institutions like the Revolutionary Guards, which sought to supplant the less-than-loyal military inherited from the shah. Even more worrisome is the fact that the regime imprisoned and/or executed thousands of people in an attempt to solidify support for the regime and its fight with Iran.

The second period coincides with the death of Ayatollah Khomeini and the election of **Ayatollah Hashemi Rafsanjani** (1934–) as president. While **Ali Khamenei** (1939–) replaced Khomeini as supreme leader (a post he still holds), the balance of power shifted to the more moderate Rafsanjani. He had been one of the clerics who led the Islamic revolution to its consolidation of power in the early 1980s. He had also been seriously wounded in an assassination attempt. What's more, Khamenei was not a senior religious leader and lacked the moral authority Khomeini had.

Unlike Khomeini, Rafsanjani is a pragmatist who wanted to concentrate on Iran's mounting domestic policy concerns. Chief among them was reforming the slumping economy hurt both by the theological commitments of the new regime and the costs of the war with Iraq, which included a major boycott by the United States and some of its allies.

Rafsanjani had widespread support because he had the backing of the vast majority of the conservative clerics. In 1989, for instance, he won with over 95 percent of the vote; four years later, he won more than two-thirds of the ballot in his bid for reelection.

Khameini is far more conservative and has tried to keep the spirit of the revolution and the purity of the theocracy alive. He has consistently made statements, for instance, that are far more hostile to the United States and Israel than the two presidents who served with him.

That said, there was relatively little political reform under Rafsanjani. There were some changes made to the constitution in 1989 that slightly shifted the balance of political power away from the clerics. Significant reform only came under his successor, Mohammad Khatami who was elected in 1997 when Rafsanjani was barred from seeking a third term.

Although a cleric himself, Khatami was widely known as a moderate who had, among other things, fought against censorship when he was a newspaper editor. During his election campaign, he supported more rights for women and members of religious and ethnic minority groups and stressed the importance of strengthening civil society. Therefore, many observers expected him to lose to the more conservative cleric, Nadeq Nuri, who

Former president Moham-
mad Khatami

Peter Blakely/CORBIS SABA

had been the speaker of the majlis and had the implicit support of Khamenei.

In fact, the election was a landslide, with Khatami winning more than two-thirds of the vote and almost four times that gained by Nuri. Reformists did even better in the 2000 legislative election, winning 189 of the 290 seats in the majlis. When Khatami ran for reelection the next year, he won 78 percent of the vote against what amounted to only token opposition from nine other candidates, only two of whom won more than 1 percent of the vote. Khatami and the reformist legislators fared particularly well among women and young people, which were the social groups who chafed the most under authoritarian rule and a stagnating economy.

During the first six years of his presidency, Khatami introduced a number of reforms. It became easier for people to organize political groups, there was less censorship of the press, and some open protests were permitted. The government also began to try to improve relations with the United States and other (less antagonistic) Western powers, and even allowed inspections of its nuclear facilities by the International Atomic Energy Agency.

What might turn into a very different fourth period began in 2003 when Khamenei and his more conservative colleagues began to reassert the influence of those who favored retaining the goals and values of the first years of the Islamic republic. In particular, forces loyal to the clerics struck back at the limited political reforms of the first Khatami years. For example, armed thugs oper-

ating with government support routinely attacked demonstrators. Most importantly of all, the clerics refused to allow about 2,500 moderates and reformists to run in the 2004 majlis election, thereby guaranteeing a conservative landslide. The same is likely to occur when Khatami has to step down in 2005, which will ensure conservative dominance at least through 2008.

The People and Politics

As is the case with all of the chapters on individual countries in this book, my primary goal is to describe and explain basic patterns in their political systems. This chapter has a second, and more focused, goal. For most of the quarter century since the overthrow of the shah, Western observers have portrayed Iran as a ruthless dictatorship, something President George W. Bush encapsulated in his famous "axis of evil" State of the Union speech in 2002.

What I will try to show is that the realities of Iranian political life are far more nuanced. To be sure, the banning of reformist candidates in the 2004 majlis election reminds us that the Islamic republic has often been extremely repressive and illiberal. However, we will now also see that it has provided far more opportunities for public participation and has allowed far more debate and division than popular depictions of Iran in the West might lead us to expect.

No one has defined this complex situation better than the British political scientist, Ali Ansari:

> Far from the monolithic totalitarian state described by some commentators, Iran's politics reflect an intensely complex, highly plural dynamic characteristic of a state in transition that incorporates the contradictions and instabilities inherent in such a process. Democratizing moderates confront authoritarian conservatives; a secularizing, intensely nationalistic society sits uneasily next to the sanctimonious piety of the hard line establishment.[4]

Political Culture

For all practical purposes, political scientists and other scholars have not been able to do field research in Iran since 1979. Among other things, that means that there are tremendous gaps in what we know about the country, especially its political culture, which could only be analyzed through in-depth and direct observation of the link between people's core beliefs and their political behavior.

That, of course, has not kept academics and journalists from speculating about this vitally important topic. Nonetheless, any statement that tries to assess the importance of particular values with any degree of precision needs to be taken with many grains of intellectual salt.

One thing is clear: Iran does not have a homogeneous political culture. Its history has left the Iranian people quite nationalistic, perhaps increasingly so. Both its long history as an independent country and its troubles of the last century have given Iranians a stronger sense of national identity than most people in the third world. After that, any sense of homogeneity disappears in a welter of somewhat overlapping subcultures, the size and importance of which are hard to define.

The division into subcultures is even true of religion. Although most Iranians are Shiites, they approach their faith in a number of ways. A goodly number of people support the conservative and even puritanical version of Islam adopted by the clerics who proved victorious after the overthrow of the shah. But there is also an Islamic left, which is best reflected today in the reformist groups to be discussed shortly. Finally, there are Iranians like Azar Nafisi and most of her students who are secular and do such forbidden things as drink alcohol, wear makeup, and watch foreign television shows and films, albeit in the privacy of their own homes.

The religious subcultures also overlap with ones that grow out of the country's social and economic divisions. Orthodox Shiites are found most commonly in rural and poor areas. The bazaaris or small businessmen have mostly cast their lot with clerics like Rafsanjani who have supported them, for instance, against foreign investment. Well-educated and affluent Iranians are most likely to have had ongoing contacts with the West and to be secular.

The most significant wild card in Iranian culture will be how today's youth evolves. Three in ten Iranians today are under fifteen; almost two-thirds of the population is under thirty. These people have at most hazy memories of the revolution and its early years. Instead, they have grown up in difficult economic times in which about half of the younger members of the workforce are unemployed at any one time. The protest movements that have burst onto the scene on several occasions since the mid-1990s have been composed all but exclusively of dissatisfied young people of all social classes, but especially of university students.

Most surprising of all to critics of the regime, Iran is one of the most liberal countries in which Muslims dominate politics. As we will see in the next two sections, some dissent is allowed most of the time and Iranians vote in regular, reasonably fair, and competitive elections, although the degree to which they are fair and competitive has varied considerably over the twenty-five years.

These differing and even conflicting values are reflected in Iranian attitudes toward the United States. Many Iranians despise the United States—and the West as a whole—for the way it treated Iran and its resources until the overthrow of the shah and for its opposition to the regime's politics since then. But others are fascinated by American culture, especially those aspects of it that are formally forbidden by the clerics.

Protest and Challenges to the Islamic Republic

Unlike Iraq, Iran has had an often vibrant and visible opposition for much of the last quarter century. As we saw, the coalition that overthrew the shah was quite diverse, and it took several years before the clerics could completely solidify their rule and remove most members of the Islamic left from office.

But other perspectives never disappeared, and by the mid-1990s significant protest movements began to occur. Most notable were two "spasms of unrest"[5] in

---

[4] Ali Ansari, "Continuous Regime Change from Within," *Washington Quarterly* 26 (Autumn 2003), 53.

[5] "Thanks, but Please Don't Support Us: Iranian Protest." *The Economist,* 21 June 2003, 38.

Iranian protesters burn a U.S. flag during demonstrations outside the former U.S. Embassy in Tehran, Iran Friday, 3 November 2000, marking the twenty-first anniversary of the overtaking of the U.S. Embassy in 1979.

Vahid Salemi/AP/Wide World Photos

1999 and 2003. Both were brutally put down by the regime, which arrested thousands of young people, some of whom were tortured.

There is some uncertainty about how large the 1999 protests were. Their supporters claim that the students and their allies gained control of some cities for two days. What is clear is that tens of thousands of students at most of the country's universities held rallies at which both Khatami and Khamenei were criticized for their failure to enact pro-democratic reforms. Then, on 9 July, the authorities allowed a group of what can only be called thugs to attack a dormitory. At least one person was killed and several others were hurled out of fourth-story windows. Larger protests followed in the next few days, but they quickly lost momentum as the regime made it clear it would use arrests and the vigilantes to quell the protests.

The 2003 demonstrations started in a more mundane way as students complained about the high costs of tuition. But they evolved in two respects that were quite different from those of four years earlier. First, they began to draw working-class youth who were frustrated by unemployment and poverty, which is the lot of as many as 40 percent of the population. Second, they gained a lot more international attention, both from the Bush administration and from the television and radio stations set up by the Iranian exile community in southern California where about a half million of them live. Again, the government quickly cracked down.

We should not read too much into these protests. The Bush administration and the émigrés may see them as signs of an imminent revolution, but there is no reason to believe that is the case. There is no organized democratic movement in Iran. The links between the university students and other young people are limited. And, while the few available public opinion polls show widespread support for reform, almost everyone wants it to occur within the framework of the system created in 1979. Indeed, most dissidents who have been interviewed by Western television networks and newspapers insist that their country has been through too much turmoil since the revolution, and any regime change would almost certainly make a bad situation worse.

Elections and the Prospects for Democracy in Iran

When I teach about Iran, my students are most surprised by the fact that Iran has one of the freest electoral systems in the Middle East. Far more common are countries such as Saudi Arabia, which has had no elections at all, or Kuwait, where the suffrage is strictly limited.

Iranians have voted in eight presidential and seven Majlis elections since the revolution. All citizens over 15 are eligible to vote.

There are also dozens of political parties, most of which are tiny and poorly organized. In 2004, an authoritative website (www.electionworld.org) listed thirty-four of the parties with their websites but put them all in the "minor party" category. In practice, Majlis candidates run their own campaigns as what Americans would call independents, but they make it clear where they stand in relation to the broad ideological groupings in the population as a whole, most of which deal with the pace and extent of political reform they support.

The weakness of the parties is an all but inevitable outgrowth of the fact that there are still clear limits on who can play an active role in political life. They are also weak because of the way Majlis elections are conducted.

The country is divided into twenty-eight constituencies, which are allocated a certain number of seats on the basis of their populations. Candidates who wish to run propose their name to a subcommittee of the Guardian Council. In the run-up to the 2004 election, 8,157 people indicated they were willing to run for the 290 seats in the seventh Majlis. The committee then determined who should be allowed to run using criteria developed in the constitution and later electoral laws. Some are straightforward. Candidates must be over 30 but under 75 and those running for the first time must have the equivalent of a university degree. Men who were already members of the Majlis before the current law went into effect can continue to run and serve. They also must have a "belief in and commitment in practice to Islam and the sacred system of the Islamic Republic of Iran." In 2000, the Guardian Council interpreted that rule quite loosely, which allowed many popular reformists to run and win. Four years later, they required positive proof of faith, which led to the disqualification of most reformists, including many of those who had served in the sixth Majlis.

Iranian elections cannot be considered democratic because the unelected Guardian Council has to approve all candidates. In some elections, it has simply screened out candidates who were too radical in one form or another and those who had no chance whatsoever of winning (including more than two hundred hopefuls for the 1997 presidential race). In the 1992 and 1996 elections, the council kept about a third of those who wanted to run off the ballot. In 2000, it was far more lenient, only doing so for 11 percent of the candidates, including only a handful of prominent reformers. The 2004 contest was a different story altogether. Almost three thousand candidacies were blocked, including those of many prominent reformers. Some only learned their fate less than two weeks before the election. Reformist incumbents (including those who might have won) resigned from the Majlis in protest and urged their supporters to boycott the elections. Not surprisingly, that led to the conservative landslide discussed earlier and will probably lead to the demise of the **Second of Khordad Movement,** named for the day President Khatami was first elected.

Elections are held on a nonpartisan basis. Voters only see a ballot with a long list of names without any partisan identification when they show up at the polls. Furthermore, the official election campaign is only a week long. Many typical campaign tactics in the West (e.g., putting up posters) are forbidden. Candidates are allowed to hand out campaign literature but no piece of paper can be larger than roughly 4 by 6 inches. Candidates are allowed to circulate lists of colleagues they support, which help voters reach decisions.

Voting occurs in two rounds. Any candidate who gets at least 25 percent of the vote at the first ballot is declared a winner. That was the case for three quarters of the seats in 2004. A second round is held several months later for the undecided seats for which only the top two remaining candidates can run.

The 2004 election did not bode well for democracy. All but sixty-four seats were decided at the first round, and the vast majority of the victors were conservatives. Nationwide, turnout was put at 51 percent, but it was much lower in the urban areas where the reformists have the most support. Thus, barely a quarter of the residents of the Tehran metropolitan area voted, and the conservatives swept all thirty seats. The most reliable estimate is that the reformists elected as few as thirty candidates.

The 2005 presidential election was expected to be much like the one for the Majlis the year before. As of early March 2005, no candidate had formally declared an intention to run even though the vote was less than three and a half months away. The reformists tentatively planned to present a ticket with outgoing President Khatami's brother as vice presidential candidate. However, in an interview with CBS News' *60 Minutes* on 27 February 2005, he was all but certain that the Guardian Council would keep them off the ballot. Earlier in the year, the Guardian Council overturned a court ruling that women who met all the qualifications for the presidency should be allowed to run by interpreting that the Constitution only permitted male candidates.

As the election neared, most of the speculation centered on the head of the Guardian Council and former president, Ayatollah Rafsanjani. In an interview with *USA Today*, Rafsanjani said it was time for new leaders to emerge. However, he said, if that did not happen by early May, he would consider running.

At this point, there is no political party of any sort that officially supports the conservative clerics. After the revolution, they created the Islamic Republican Party, which was a bastion of militant supporters of the new regime, but it was disbanded at Khomeini's urging in 1987. The closest the conservatives have to a party is the *ruhaniyat* or Militant Clergy Association. Its members include former President Rafsanjani and Ali Akbar Nadeq Nuri, a former speaker of the Majlis who lost to Khatami in 1997.

Conflict in Iran

Iran has been beset by conflict for a century or more. In the first years of the twenty-first century, much of the conflict revolves around the differences between religious conservatives and reformers. Reformers probably have more public support, especially among young people. However, conservative clerics control enough of the country's critical political positions that they were able to ensure a landslide victory in the 2004 Majlis election and will likely do the same when the presidency is contested before this book is published in 2005.

There are, of course, specific issues Iranians debate, ranging from what clothing is appropriate for women to wear to its relations with the West. But the bottom line is that they all reflect the divisions over the role Islam should play in Iran a quarter century after the Islamic Republic was created.

It had earlier abolished the National Front and other groups that were part of the revolutionary coalition. Some of them, including the Communists (*Tudeh*) and the Islamic *Mujahadin e-Qalq* still exist underground but have at most a limited impact. There are, of course, dozens of political parties and other organizations in the exile community that dream of a return to open political activity inside Iran.

There is one possible exception to this rule. After his election, Khatami and his supporters organized the **Second of Khordad Movement,** named for the date in the Iranian calendar when he was elected in 1997. It is a loose coalition of seventeen groups that supported his presidency and reform. It was remarkably effective in 2000 when candidates affiliated with it won 189 seats (two-thirds of the total number of parliamentary seats) and in 2001 when Khatami was reelected. However, it did extremely poorly in 2004 because many of its candidates and incumbents were denied the right to run, and, as noted earlier, it seems likely its candidates will be kept off the 2005 presidential ballot as well.

The Iranian State

The only partially democratic nature of Iranian politics is even easier to see in the way its state operates. We can do so briefly, because many of its features have been discussed already.

The new leadership wrote a constitution shortly after taking power in 1979. Some significant amendments were added in 1989 (e.g., abolishing the prime minister's office), but its basic features have remained the same since the revolution (www.salamiran.org/Iran Info/State/Constitution/).

On the one hand, by allowing elections using universal suffrage to elect the Majlis and president, it is by far the most democratic constitution Iran has ever had. On the other hand, it was written to ensure that ultimate authority rested in the hands of senior Shiite clerics through a series of unelected and often repressive institutions. Over the years, the clerics have certainly lost some prestige and possibly some of their power. The 2004 election, however, suggests that they have no intention of going into a permanent political decline. Indeed, how the balance between the elected and authoritarian elements of the state evolves will largely determine the political direction the country takes.

The order in which this section is written is a telling statement about Iranian politics. Had it been written in 2000, the elected parts of the state might have come first. Many signs indicated that the rule of law and other aspects of democracy were gaining support under the leadership of President Khatami. But writing in the aftermath of the 2004 Majlis election, it is clear that Supreme Leader Khamenei, the Guardian Council, and other unelected and more conservative parts of the Iranian state have reasserted their influence and that the future of reform and of the elected parts of the state are very much in doubt.

The Unelected Elements

For all intents and purposes, Iran has two chief executives. On the one hand, there is an elected president, which will be discussed shortly. On the other, there is a **Supreme Leader,** a senior cleric named for life by another senior cleric, who has veto power over almost everything elected officials want to do.

The rationale for this position lies in the writings of Ayatollah Khomeini. As his opposition to the shah intensified, Khomeini added political recommendations to his preachings, most notably in a series of nineteen lectures he delivered in Najaf, Iraq, in early 1970. These were subsequently published as *Velayat-e Faqi* or **The Guardianship of the Jurist.**

As noted earlier, for most of the history of Shiism, its clerics shunned any form of direct political involvement. Most argued that until the twelfth imam reappears it is inappropriate for members of the clergy to take part in mundane political affairs.

Khomeini, in other words, made a major shift in Shi-

AYATOLLAH ALI KHAMENEI

Vahid Salemi /AP/ Wide World Photos

Supreme leader Ayatollah Ali Khamenei

Supreme Leader Khamenei was born in the provincial city of Mashhad in 1939 and began his theological studies in elementary school. At eighteen he moved to the holy city of Najaf in Iraq, but returned to Qom the following year to continue his studies under Khomeini and others.

He joined the growing Islamic resistance to the shah in the early 1960s and was arrested with many others in 1963. After his release, he continued to teach and preach. He was arrested again in 1977. After his subsequent release, he helped found the Combatant Clerics Association, which became the Islamic Revolutionary Party after the fall of the shah.

Following the assassination of President Muhammad Ali Rajai in 1981, Khamenei was elected to that post with about 95 percent of the vote. He was named an ayatollah in early 1989, which made him eligible to replace Khomeini when he died later that year.

ite thinking by arguing that the senior clerics had a moral responsibility to provide leadership in political as well as religious matters. Because he carried with him the ethical concern about faith and justice, the jurist would be a more legitimate ruler than anyone drawn from the secular community.

The Supreme Leader is appointed by the **Assembly of Experts,** a body of senior clerics who are elected by the people. The leader then serves for life. Not surprisingly, the charismatic Khomeini was the dominant personality in the entire political system for the decade he served. At first, Khamenei had much less power and prestige. As is almost always the case for leaders who follow a charismatic figure, they cannot conceivably command their predecessor's authority. That was especially true of Khamenei, who was a relatively minor cleric at the time of his selection. In fact, he was only made an ayatollah a few weeks before Khomeini's death, and his appointment drew some criticism from more senior colleagues. By the end of the 1990s, his prestige had grown and, more importantly, he became the focal figure for conservatives who resisted the reformist movement that was based among President Khatami's supporters.

The Supreme Leader has immense power. He controls the military, much of the media, the judiciary, and the clerical hierarchy. Both Khomeini and Khamenei have been willing to speak out on any issue they deemed

important and thus largely set the agenda for the country as a whole.

The most important collegial body is the **Guardian Council.** It consists of six senior clerics appointed by the Supreme Leader and six judges named by the Majlis from a list compiled by the Supreme Judicial Council who are appointed by the Supreme Leader.

In short, the Council is composed primarily of men who support the conservative and theocratic elements of the regime. It has to approve all legislation and has blocked reform proposals on numerous occasions. One example was when they vetoed the loosening of restrictions on the media in the late 1990s. It also has to approve all candidacies for presidential and majlis elections. As noted earlier, it was the body responsible for barring more than 2,500 candidates from running in 2004, thereby ensuring the conservative landslide. While the council is one of the more conservative components of the state, it does not always live up to that reputation. In May 2004, it approved a bill that would ban the use of torture in Iranian prisons, which had been widely used in the first years after the revolution and has not been uncommon in recent years, if statements by dissidents are to be believed.

There have been frequent conflicts between the majlis and the Council. To help smooth out any differences, Khomeini created the **Expediency Council** in

Democratization in Iran

THE UNCERTAINTIES about democratization in Iran are reflected in the two types of state institutions.

On the one hand are the offices that are directly elected by the people that seemed to be gaining in importance under President Khatami. On the other hand, however, with the resurgence of the conservative clerics before and after the 2004 election, nonelected and nondemocratic institutions regained their central place in Iranian politics. It seems likely that these institutions will keep their influence until the next round of elections are held, if not longer. It is not clear, however, if that can remain the case indefinitely.

TABLE 13.4 Presidents of Iran since 1979

NAME	YEARS IN OFFICE
Abolhassan Bani-Sadr	1979–80
Muhammad Ali Rajai	1980–81
Ali Khamenei	1981–89
Hashemi Rafsanjani	1989–97
Mohammad Khatami	1997–2005

1988. It is a senior advisory board whose members are appointed by the Supreme Leader for five-year terms. All major factions are included, but Khamenei's followers currently have an overwhelming majority.

It meets with the leaders of the other two bodies and generally tries to anticipate procedural and other problems not foreseen by the constitution. The fact that it is currently headed by former President Rafsanjani suggests it is important indeed, even if its formal powers are not all that clearly defined. For instance, it tipped the scales in the Council of Guardians' favor after the Majlis had refused the list of jurists it could choose from in determining its six members.

The last of the unelected institutions is the judiciary. In addition to the kinds of criminal and civil courts one finds in most countries, Iran also has clerical courts with vast powers not only to adjudicate but also to prosecute cases involving Islam.

The constitution adopted a highly restrictive version of Sharia or Islamic law to apply. Offenses such as adultery or homosexuality could lead to the death penalty. The courts could impose stoning or amputating fingers as punishment. Initially, at least, banks were not allowed to charge interest. The courts have loosened up a bit as the regime has solidified, but it is still one of the major conservative forces in the country.

The Elected Institutions

Since the death of Ayatollah Khomeini, the most visible politician in day-to-day politics has been the president. For reasons noted earlier, there could well be a shift away from presidential power if conservatives win that post in 2005.

The president is directly elected. As is the case for all senior elected offices, candidacies have to be approved by the Council of Guardians. Unlike the situation for the Majlis, the council has mostly only removed candidates who had no realistic chance of winning. That said, there has really only been one competitive election, in 1997 when Khatami won in what many thought was an upset.

Between 1979 and 2005, Iran had five presidents. (See table 13.4.) The first two are barely worth mentioning. Abolhassan Bani-Sadr, an Islamic leftist, was removed from office by Khomeini within a year of taking office. He remains a part of the opposition living in exile. He was succeeded by Muhammad Ali Rajai who was assassinated the following year.

Since then, three clerics have been president—Khamenei, Rafsanjani, and Khatami. It also seems likely that the next president will be one as well. However, as Khatami has shown, not all leading clerics are as conservative as the group that brought Khomeini to power.

The Routinization of Charisma

A century ago, Max Weber introduced the term **charisma** into the social sciences. In invoking a concept with powerful religious overtones, Weber wanted us to realize that there are a few political leaders who have remarkable personal gifts that lead people to follow them all but unquestioningly. That was certainly the case for Ayatollah Khomeini and several other leaders we encountered in earlier chapters.

However, Weber also warned that charisma was the most fleeting form of rule that rarely survived the initial leader's departure from the political scene. As we saw in Chapter 5 on France, a few leaders have been able to "routinize" their charisma so that less-magnetic successors could govern almost as effectively. So far, that seems to be the case in Iran as well.

That said, it should be pointed out that the generation of clerics and lay politicians who were swept to power along with Khomeini are disappearing from the political scene. Anyone who studied with Khomeini in Qom, for instance, would now be well into his sixties.

SHIRIN EBADI

The Nobel Peace Prize winner and human rights lawyer, Shirin Ebadi

Hasan Sarbakhshian/AP Wide World Photos

The hopes for human rights and an improvement in the status of women in Iran were given a major and unexpected boost when Shirin Ebadi was named the Nobel Peace Prize winner for 2003. She was a surprise pick, since Ebadi was little known outside of Iran and British bookies, at least, expected the gravely ill Pope John Paul II to win the award.

Ebadi is, however, widely known in Iran. She was the first female judge in Iran but was forced to resign after the 1979 revolution. Since then, she has been a champion for human rights and democracy. After being forced out of the judiciary, she became a professor and set up an organization that tried to reform laws on inheritance and divorce and defended dissidents, and she was banned from practicing law in 2000 for her activities.

The Nobel Prize committee said during the announcement of her award, "As a lawyer, judge, lecturer, writer and activist, she has spoken out clearly and strongly in her country, Iran, and far beyond its borders." And, in a rare political statement, the committee also made it clear that its choice was designed to aid the movement for democracy and human rights in Iran.

In the first hours after the announcement, no mention of Ebadi's honor was made in the state-run Iranian media.

When informed of her award, Ebadi said, "I'm a Muslim, so you can be a Muslim and support democracy. It's very good for human rights in Iran, especially for children's rights in Iran. I hope I can be useful."

Whether the next generation will be able to sustain the authority the clerical leadership still holds is anybody's guess.

Public Policy

In the next chapter, we will see that Saddam Hussein's three wars all but destroyed the Iraqi government's hopes of pursuing any coherent domestic public policies. While Iran was certainly hampered by the costs of its war with Iraq and from its isolation by much of the West, it has been able develop and (to a considerable degree) implement social and economic policies at home and, with somewhat less success, abroad.

Faith and Gender

During the 1990s, Samuel Huntington created a wave of controversy with his idea of a **clash of civilizations.** As he saw it, the post–cold war world would not be tranquil because it would give rise to conflict between the world's

HIV/AIDS in Iran

One of the more surprising aspects of Iranian politics is the official attitude toward AIDS.

Its infection rate is not very high, only topping twenty thousand in 2002. And, until then, its conservative regime rarely even addressed the pandemic publicly.

However, in May 2002, health minister Hossein Malek-Afzali acknowledged that the country had at least eighteen thousand infected citizens and sharply criticized his colleagues, who had not discussed the issue for the first twenty years after the revolution.

He and other experts acknowledged that at least three thousand Iranians had died of AIDS, which has mostly been spread among the more than 2.5 million drug addicts who share needles. Since 2002, public awareness campaigns about the epidemic have been launched, as have programs aimed to protect health-care professionals from inadvertent infection.

major cultural traditions. As he saw it, too, none would be more difficult than that between the Muslim world and the West. The terrorist attacks of 2001, the wars in Afghanistan and Iraq, and the renewed hostilities between Israelis and Palestinians only led to more interest in Huntington's thesis.

Most political scientists, however, believe that his argument is too simplistic. From their perspective, none of his "civilizations" are coherent culturally nor do their states act uniformly in international politics.

Nonetheless, if there is a country that comes close to meeting what Huntington had in mind, it is Iran. It is one of only a handful of countries in the world that is run by religious leaders. Nowhere is their impact clearer and change more ambiguous and the prospects for reform more uncertain than in their policies regarding women.

As we saw in the introduction to this chapter, the regime has enacted policies that even antifeminists in the West would find unacceptable. To cite but one more example, when the United States played Iran in an international soccer match several years ago, more than 100,000 people attended. All were men. Female fans were not allowed because the authorities felt that would lead to sexual temptation.

Women who commit adultery can legally be stoned to death. After a divorce, men almost always gain custody of the former couple's children.

But as is the case with almost everything in this chapter, the status of women is much more complicated than one might think at first glance. Women only make up about 10 percent of the labor force, but that is a higher percentage than in most other countries in the Middle East. As of 2001, female students outnumbered men in Iranian universities.

And, as part of the broader reform movement, restrictions on what women can wear—and do—have been relaxed in recent years. Women have figured out ways to modify their manteaus (the required coats) so that they reflect the shapes of their bodies and have slits that run up most of the length of their legs. Many young women wear gauze scarves that cover their heads but let their coiffed hair be seen. Unmarried men and women can now be seen together in public—even holding hands. Women have been known to disguise themselves as men and sneak into soccer matches.

The Economy

Perhaps the most important issue for the long-term future of the Islamic republic is the weak state of the economy. Iran is by no means a poor country. Its per capita income of almost $7,000 a year in purchasing parity makes it about as wealthy as Mexico or Russia.

But that figure masks a number of serious problems. Much of that wealth is the result of a single industry—oil. Iran has 7 percent of the world's proven oil reserves and only Russia has a larger untapped supply of natural gas. The spike in oil prices after the 9/11 terrorist attacks is largely responsible for Iran's growth rate that has stood at about 6 or 7 percent during the first years of this century. As is true in Russia and Nigeria as well, dependence on the export of a single commodity is not a recipe for economic success in the long term.

What's more, the oil boom has not helped address the poverty, inflation, and youth unemployment discussed earlier in the chapter. To find work for all of its young people, Iran needs to add 800,000 jobs a year, a figure it has never come close to reaching. The standard of living of most Iranians is below what it was in 1979. The inflation rate routinely hovers around 10 percent. Even oil production is only about two-thirds what it was under the shah.

The economy has problems for two reasons that are currently beyond the government's control. It still suffers from the cost of its war with Iraq (see the next chapter). And, while some Western countries have expanded their trade ties with Iran, the United States has reinforced its sanctions, thus depriving the country of what had been its leading economic supporter under the shah.

There are also some public policy concerns shared by analysts of almost all ideological stripes. They do not

Liberalization in Iran

OF ALL THE COUNTRIES covered in this book, Iran has the smallest private sector operating all or mostly beyond the control of the state.

The government itself does not own that much of the economy, but its control of the bonyads and other seemingly private enterprises leaves it with a dominant economic position.

That said, Iran does have a long tradition of private enterprise, though many of its entrepreneurs fled after 1979. If the leadership allows the economy to open up more to foreign investment, the involvement of the Iranian diaspora and others could give a major boost to what is a largely moribund economy.

agree on what the problems are or what should be done about them, but they do agree that the state's economic priorities for the last quarter century have been largely misguided.

Especially during periods when the conservative clerics have been dominant, the economy has not been at the top of the leadership's list of priorities. When asked by an assistant about the difficult state of the economy, Ayatollah Khomeini once said, "this revolution was not about the price of watermelons."

In short, economic growth and prosperity have never been the most important goal of the conservatives. And the conservative government wields impressive economic clout. Depending on how one counts, the state owns and/or controls as much as 80 percent of the Iranian economy, far more than is the case in any other country covered in this book. Iran's private sector was never a model of either efficiency or transparency under the shah.

After 1979, the new leaders confiscated the property of the shah's family and almost every other industrial leader who had cooperated with the old regime. Those resources were turned into **bonyads,** a form of Islamic charity that the clerics control. The evidence is sketchy, but it seems certain that the bonyads are corrupt money losers for the most part. Ultimate responsibility for what they do and how they operate rests with the Supreme Leader, not the marketplace.

The leadership has also been reluctant to open the economy to outside investment or involvement in any form. In 2002, the government signed a contract with a Turkish firm to run the Imam Khomeini International

Airport in Tehran. When the company arrived to set up operations, they found that the government had decided to break their contract, arguing that foreign management of the airport would be an insult to Iranian national honor. Two years later, following the conservatives' electoral victory, the Majlis passed legislation making it harder for foreign firms to invest in Iranian enterprises.

Some of the leaders are seen as more economically pragmatic than others. Among those thought to be the most open to economic reform is former president Rafsanjani. In other words, if he or someone close to him replaces Khatami, the regime just might open up its economy more than it has so far.

Iran and the United States: Axis of Evil?

Iran and the United States have sharply different interests and pursue seemingly incompatible goals in their foreign policies. Iranian hostility toward the United States dates since at least the 1953 overthrow of the Mossadeq government, which was partially orchestrated by the CIA. It intensified along with opposition to the shah who was widely seen—and resented—as a tool for Washington's cold war politics. For many Iranians, the Carter administration's decision to allow the shah to come to the United States for medical treatment was the last straw.

But Iranian hostility toward the United States has other roots. Today, many of the conservative clerics think the United States would like nothing more than to remove them from office. Under Republican and Democratic administrations alike, American governments have never minced words in objecting to Iranian support for the Palestinians and its belief that the state of Israel should not be allowed to exist.

There have been three particularly difficult periods in Iran's relations with the United States. The first period coincides with the occupation of the American embassy that began on 4 November 1979. Not surprisingly, the hostage crisis infuriated most Americans and their government, an anger that was reinforced by Iranian action and rhetoric during the fifteen months the standoff endured. It was at this time that Khomeini and his colleagues' language was most inflammatory, including calling the U.S. government the "great Satan." Even its few humanitarian gestures, such as releasing the women and people of color it held, were accompanied by self-serving and anti-American statements. The authorities reacted to the failed attempt by American forces to rescue the hostages in mid-1980 as yet more evidence of Washington's evil designs on Tehran. Finally, many saw Iran's timing by releasing the hostages the day President Ronald

Reagan was inaugurated as a sign of their hatred of President Carter whose chances for reelection were destroyed by a crisis he seemed unable to solve.

Iranians also demonstrated their profound dislike of the United States during an eight-year war with Iraq (the war itself will be discussed in more detail in the next chapter). The United States never officially supported Iraq and never harbored any illusions about the nature of Saddam Hussein's regime. Nonetheless, its antipathy toward Iran led the Reagan administration to rebuild its relationship with Iraq, much of it done, ironically, by the same Donald Rumsfeld who would be the chief architect of Saddam's defeat two decades later. Khomeini's government kept up its anti-American rhetoric especially during the second half of the war in response to two American actions it found particularly reprehensible. First, the United States "reflagged" Kuwaiti and other tankers that shipped oil from the Middle East to the West in 1986. The tankers allowed American flags to fly on the ships, which meant that they could and would be defended by the U.S. Navy. When some of the tankers were attacked, the U.S. Navy fought a series of skirmishes with the small Iranian fleet. Then, as the war was drawing to a close in the summer of 1988, the USS Vincennes mistakenly shot down an Iranian airliner killing all 290 people aboard.

The one exception to this track record of hostility was the secret negotiations and deals between the United States and Iran that Americans know as the Iran-Contra affair. Officially, the United States claimed it would never negotiate with terrorists and was pressuring its allies not to supply arms to Iran. However, in a series of secret deals, the United States supplied Iran with missiles and other arms initially to win the release of Americans held hostage in Lebanon and later to provide funds for the Contras fighting a civil war in Nicaragua, which Congress had explicitly banned. When the affair became public in 1987, President Reagan claimed he was hoping to build support from moderates with the Iranian regime. There is little evidence that there was serious division on American policy with the Iranian elite.

The third episode came in the aftermath of the terrorist attacks on the United States on 11 September 2001. This time, relations deteriorated largely because of decisions made in Washington rather than in Tehran.

In fact, under the Clinton administration, relations between the United States and Iran had actually eased a bit despite the fact that the United States passed a law in 1995 that prohibited American companies and their subsidiaries from doing business with Iran. The United States indicated its approval of the reform efforts made by President Khatami and urged his government to go farther and faster.

But after 9/11, President Bush sought to link Iran to al-Qaeda and the world terrorist network, even though there was little evidence of any link between the two. If anything, Iran played a minor, but constructive, role in the defeat of the Taliban in Afghanistan and did nothing to oppose the war that toppled Saddam Hussein's government. Its diplomats even tried to defuse tensions between the American occupation forces and supporters of radical Shiite clerics in spring 2004. Nonetheless, President George W. Bush included Iran with Iraq and North Korea in the "axis of evil" in his 2002 State of the Union address and stepped up his anti-Iranian rhetoric, especially regarding its nuclear energy and weapons program and its alleged support for terrorist activities carried out by Hezbollah, Hamas, and Islamic Jihad against Israel (www.whitehouse.gov/news/releases/2002/01/20020129-11.html).

Evidence on both accusations is mixed. There is little doubt that Iran has supported Shiite and some other opponents of Israel, including providing funds and training for some groups that commit acts of terrorism. That said, its links to al-Qaeda are far less certain and probably not very extensive. To begin with, most al-Qaeda members are Sunni, not Shiites. Furthermore, some Iranian officials suggested that they helped the United States by closing its borders so alleged terrorists could not cross into Iran and even turned over a few that had somehow managed to do so.

There is similar ambiguity about its nuclear weapons program. There is no doubt that Iran has long been working to enhance its nuclear capacities, including developing the ability to produce enriched plutonium that would be needed for manufacturing weapons. The Iranians, however, claim that the program is only designed to provide electricity. The United States is skeptical because given its vast oil and natural gas reserves, it is hard to see why it needs nuclear energy. Tensions eased a bit in late 2004 when the British, French, and German governments convinced Iran to suspend its enrichment activities. Even though Iran initially agreed to the suspension, its acceptance was always conditional.

The United States responded skeptically and in a way that suggested it still planned to do what it could to stop Iran's nuclear program and do so unilaterally, if need be.

In February 2005, tensions eased a bit again. At a summit of NATO leaders in Europe, President Bush announced that it was preposterous for people to think that the United States had plans to attack Iran. But he almost

Globalization and Iran

IRAN IS ONE of two countries in which globalization is not primarily an economic issue. To be sure, the government is eager to encourage foreign investment and to see restrictions on its sales abroad end, especially given the dramatic rise in oil prices since the start of the Iraq war in 2003.

However, it is probably the case that its overall isolation from the rest of the world will prove a more vexing problem. If the conservatives regain control of the presidency in 2005, that will probably lead to more radical rhetoric, if not more radical policies, toward the West. That said, the authorities will have a harder and harder time keeping Western influences out of the country, influences that have already had a profound impact on at least young members of the middle class.

---

immediately qualified that remark by saying all options remained on the table at some point in time.

On his return from the summit, the president sent out trial balloons suggesting that the U.S. might join the European effort to use economic and other incentives to convince Iran to abandon any plans that could lead to nuclear weapons, although analysts close to the Bush administration voiced doubts that a diplomatic solution could work.

Iran's response was similarly mixed. It insisted it had the right to enrich uranium for what it continued to claim was a nuclear energy program. And, within days of the NATO summit, it signed an agreement with Russia that would provide Iran with precisely the kind of uranium the United States and the major European powers were most worried about.

Relations between the two countries are bad because they have conflicting values and interests. They are also bad because both sides have engaged in a practice psychologists call the image of the enemy. One side views the other in stereotypical terms, typically stressing only what it sees as the negative characteristics of the other. Enemy images are also frequently exaggerated in their attribution of criticisms of one's adversary. Use of terms like "axis of evil" or "the great Satan" only deepen already deep divisions and lead to misperceptions and mistakes in judgment about the other side's behavior and the intentions underlying it. Most importantly of all, when both sides invoke the image of the enemy, each waits for

the other to take the first steps to improve the relationship, which means that it almost never happens.

At this point, the Bush administration is probably engaging in more of this form of behavior than the Iranian government. It has had almost nothing positive to say about events in Tehran, and in so doing has missed such important trends as Iranians' understandable concerns about ensuring their national security in a hostile world.

There has been one area in which some progress has been made through what the conflict resolution community calls "track-two" diplomacy. Such negotiations involve private citizens who have no official authority and cannot represent their governments in discussions that could lead to binding treaties or other agreements. Instead, track-two processes can involve people with close ties to decision makers or simply try to improve the relationships between people in the societies involved at a time when formal, traditional diplomatic initiatives are not likely to prove fruitful.

There was, in practice, very little track-two contact between Americans and Iranians before the late 1990s. It was very difficult for people to get permission to visit the other country, and there were relatively few contacts between people from the two societies, except from Iranian émigrés who were for the most part vocal opponents of the Islamic republic.

The first significant opportunities for track-two work began after newly elected President Khatami called for a "dialogue of civilizations." Search for Common Ground, an organization founded with the purpose of finding cooperative rather than adversarial ways to resolve conflict, has been a leader in those efforts ever since (www.sfcg .org). In 1998, it arranged for the U.S. national wrestling team to participate in a major international tournament, the first time the American flag had been displayed by Americans in Iran since before the hostage crisis. The American athletes were greeted warmly by the Iranian athletes and by the huge crowd that turned out for the event—wrestling is one of the two most popular sports in Iran.

Since then, other athletic opportunities have been seized, including a soccer match between the two national teams that was watched by over 100,000 fans, all men. Search for Common Ground has also arranged exchanges of scientists, filmmakers, and artists, arranged for the Iranian ambassador to the United Nations to meet with two leading Republican members of Congress, and helped host an Iranian cultural festival and the visit of a leading ayatollah to Washington. In 2004, at the request of Iranian officials, Search for Common Ground

An American and an Iranian wrestle at a 1998 international tournament in Tehran. The American wrestlers were able to participate in the event because of the work of Search for Common Ground, the world's largest NGO working on conflict resolution.

Atta Kenare/AFP/Getty Images

sent a group of American educators to Tehran to begin planning student exchanges. If visas can be arranged, the first exchange will involve student musical groups from Oberlin College and Tehran University in 2006.

Nonetheless, there is little real hope for a dramatic improvement in U.S.-Iranian relations in the near future. Iran's leaders for the next decade or two will all have spent part of their adult lives under the shah and will have a hard time overcoming resentment toward the United States first nurtured during those years. Washington is also unlikely to make conciliatory moves if it thinks it has a chance of undermining the regime and until Iran drops its opposition to the existence of Israel.

That said, there is one very strong force that could lead to a gradual accommodation as it already has with much of Europe. As we saw in an earlier section, Iran faces serious economic problems that it can only hope to meet with a hefty dose of foreign investment. And that is not going to happen as long as its relations with the West are weak and as long as its political and economic decision-making systems remain as closed as they have become since 1979. It will be no easy task for future Iranian leaders to reconcile their concern with national security and Islamic values with more openness toward a globalizing economy, but the pressures are nudging even the conservatives around Khamenei in that direction.

Feedback

Iran's official media are all but completely controlled. The country's television and radio stations are all owned and run by the state, and the clerics have an obvious vested interest in their programming.

At times, the government has allowed critics to publish newspapers and magazines. But they tend to crack down whenever these publications are perceived to have gone too far. Since 2000, it has shut down nearly 120 of them, and virtually no dissenting periodicals were being published in late 2004.

Conclusion: Uncertainty

There is more uncertainty about the future of politics in Iran than in any of the countries we have considered so far in this book.

One seemingly minor example from the summer of 2004 suggests just how hard it is to predict anything about Iran these days. Just six years before, the American wrestling team discussed earlier participated in an international championship in Tehran, a visit that was taken as a sign that the government was seeking an opening to its long-time enemy in Washington. But just before the opening ceremony at the 2004 Olympics, two-time world judo champion, Arash Miresmaeili, announced that he would forfeit his opening match against an Israeli judoka, thereby giving up any chance of winning an expected gold medal. Miresmaeili minced no words, "Although I have trained for months and was in good shape I refused to fight my Israeli opponent to sympathize with the suffering of the People of Palestine and I do not feel upset at all."[6]

Some of that uncertainty is domestic in origin. There is every indication that the power struggle between the orthodox and moderate factions of the clergy will continue. What is not clear is who is likely to win. The conservatives will almost certainly win back the presidency in 2005. However, the reformers are too numerous and too influential to give up and disappear.

The other major uncertainty is external. No one knows how U.S.-Iranian relations will change as a result of the 2004 U.S. presidential election. President Bush did not indicate that there would be any significant changes in American policy during the first weeks after he was reelected. And the departure of Secretary of State Colin Powell from the administration suggested that hardliners would have a more prominent role over the following four years. Yet the agreement with the French, British, and German governments to suspend its nuclear enrichment program sent a different message—that Iran might be more willing to cooperate with the West, especially if economic aid is increased.

Key Terms

Concepts

Chador	Islamicists
Charisma	Shah
Fundamentalism	Sharia
Guardianship of the Jurist	Shiite
Image of the enemy	Sunni

People

Khamenei, Ayatollah Ali	Rafsanjani, Ayatollah Hasemi
Khatami, Mohammed	
Khomeini, Ayatollah Ruhollah	Shah, Mohammed Reza
	Shah, Reza
Mossadeq, Mohammed	

Acronyms

SAVAK

---

[6]Michelle Kaufman, "Politics, Not Sport, Come First for Iranian Athlete." *Washington Post,* 16 August 2004, D12.

Organizations, Places, and Events

Assembly of Experts	Pahlevi dynasty
Bonyad	Second of Khordad
Constitutional Revolution	Movement
Expediency Council	Supreme Leader
Guardian Council	White Revolution
Majlis	

Critical Thinking Exercises

1 Much has changed since this book was finished in early 2005. Does the analysis of Iranian politics presented here still make sense? Why (not)?

2 Public opinion pollsters routinely ask questions about whether people think their country is heading in the "right direction" or is on the "wrong track." If you were asked such a question about Iran, how would you answer? Why did you reach this conclusion?

3 How did Western imperialism shape Iranian political life before, during, and after the revolution?

4 Why did the clerics emerge as the dominant political force in Iran? How have they been able to stay in power for so long?

5 What is the evidence for and against claims that Iran is somewhat democratic? Which do you find more compelling?

6 What are the most important difficulties facing Iran domestically? Do they pose a threat to the regime?

7 What impact does the United States have on Iran? Is it a threat to the regime?

8 If, as expected, a conservative cleric wins the 2005 presidential election, what impact do you think it will have on Iranian politics?

Useful Websites

There are not a lot of reliable websites that provide information on Iran. The Iranians themselves have very few sites with information in English, and most Westerners treat them with skepticism since they are directly or indirectly controlled by the government.

However, there are four Western sites that provide good sets of links to sites on Iran as well as news feeds on a daily basis. MERIP (The Middle East Research Information Project) is a somewhat left-of-center publication. The website includes its own material plus op-ed pieces and other items that originally appeared elsewhere. Columbia University's School of International and Political Affairs also tries to assemble online information on Iran and the other seven countries that border the Persian Gulf. Iran Focus is one of many sites that provides in-depth news on the country. Finally, the Iran Chamber is one of the best general portals for information on Iranian life in general and not just politics.

> www.merip.org
>
> gulf2000.columbia.edu/iran.shtml
>
> www.daraee.com/iran.html
>
> www.iranfocus.com/modules/news
>
> www.iranchamber.com

The president's office maintains a small website that may be the only official site in English other than that of the official news service.

> www.president.ir/eng/

Search for Common Ground maintains a website not only on its own initiatives on U.S.-Iranian relations but most other track-two projects currently underway.

> www.sfcg.org

InfoTrac College Edition Sources

Abdo, Geneive. "Iran's Generation of Outsiders."

Ansari, Ali. "Continuous Regime Change from Within."

Brumberg, Daniel. "Dissonant Politics in Iran and Indonesia."

De Bellaigue, Christopher. "Iran's Last Chance for Reform?"

Kazemi, Farhad. "The Precarious Revolution: Unchanging Institutions and the Fate of Reform in Iran."

Keddie, Nikki. "Women in Iran Since 1979."

Molavi, Afshin. "Buying Time in Tehran: Iran and the China Model."

Sariolghalam, Mahmood. "Understanding Iran: Getting Past Stereotypes and Mythology."

Further Reading

Brumberg, Daniel. *Reinventing Khomeini: The Struggle for Reform in Iran.* Chicago: University of Chicago Press, 2001. An intriguing analysis of how Khomeini's political persona was created and how competing politicians have tried to adapt it since his death.

Keddie, Nikki. *Modern Iran: Roots and Results of Revolution.* New Haven: Yale University Press, 2003. Probably the best book on Iran by an academic historian, covers the period from the late eighteenth century to the present.

Mackey, Sandra. *The Iranians: Persia, Islam, and the Soul of a Nation.* New York: Plume, 1996. The best single overview of the broad sweep of Iranian history and culture.

Nafisi, Azar, *Reading Lolita in Tehran.* New York: Random House, 2003. A stunning look at gender and politics in contemporary Iran through the lens of a small, informal American literature seminar run by a former Iranian professor.

Pollack, Kenneth. *The Persian Puzzle.* New York: Century Books, 2004. By the provocative author of one of the best books on why the United States should have gone to war with Iraq. He argues the opposite here.

Roy, Olivier. *The Failure of Political Islam.* Cambridge: Harvard University Press, 2001. This controversial book argues that the attempt to build a political agenda on the basis of Islamic principles cannot consistently be done. Covers much more than Iran.

Sciolino, Elaine. *Persian Mirrors: The Elusive Face of Iran.* New York: Touchstone, 2000. The most readable overview of Iran written by the veteran *New York Times* correspondent who has spent a lot of time covering Iran.

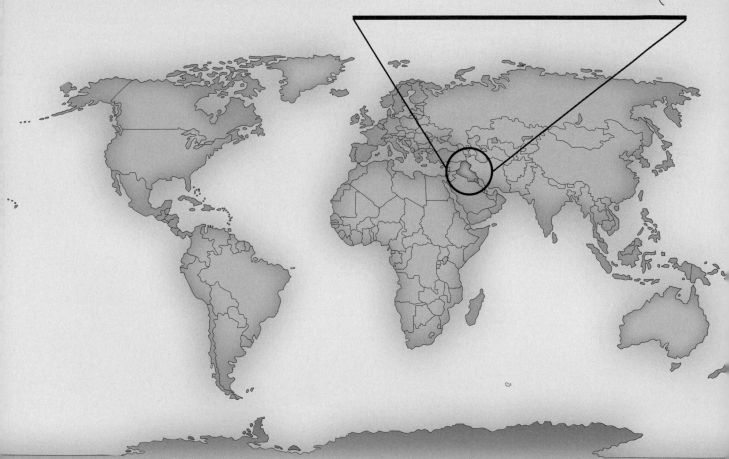

Tasting the blood of collaborators is better than that of occupiers.

STATEMENT BY AN UNIDENTIFIED
GROUP OF INSURGENTS, JUNE 2004

Chapter 14

IRAQ

with Guilain Denoeux

The Basics: Iraq

Size	437,009 sq. km. Roughly twice the size of Idaho
Population	25.4 million
Ethnic Groups	Arabs (about 75%), Kurds (about 20%), Other (about 5%)
Religious Groups	Shiite Muslims (60–65%), Sunni Muslim (30–35%), Other, (3–7%)
Currency	1,522 dinars = $1 (1 March 2005)
Capital	Baghdad
Prime Minister	Ibrahim al-Jaafari

Before We Begin

This will be the most inconclusive and controversial chapter in *Comparative Politics.*

It will be inconclusive because the war is still being fought, and the transition to a new form of government has a long way to go. It will be controversial because people inside the country and abroad still disagree very strongly about the proper path that should be followed in this deeply troubled country.

That said, this chapter may not be quite as controversial as you might think. Because its focus is on the domestic politics of Iraq, I will not spend a lot of time discussing the more controversial aspects of the American-led invasion of 2003 and will instead focus on the domestic politics of Iraq and how they led to the confrontation that destroyed Saddam Hussein's regime and so much of the country he ruled for a quarter century.

What a Difference a Year Can Make— In Either Direction

On 12 December 2003, American troops found and arrested a bedraggled **Saddam Hussein** hiding in a hole in the ground near his hometown of Tikrit.

Saddam Hussein is led into a courtroom on Thursday, 1 July 2004, at Camp Victory, a former Saddam palace on the outskirts of Baghdad.

Karen Ballard/AP/Wide World Photos

By that time, most of the members of his leadership team had either been arrested or killed, including his two sons who died earlier that year in a shootout with American troops in Baghdad.

A year earlier, Saddam was firmly in control. Iraq was in the midst of a diplomatic showdown with the United States that, many think, started the day of the 9/11 terrorist attacks in New York and Washington. That day, most Westerners thought the United States would attack unless he capitulated. Few outside the United States thought he would even consider not doing so. They were right.

A year later, Saddam was in prison. His country was in turmoil. After a brief invasion, U.S.-led forces toppled the Iraqi regime in April 2003, which led to President George W. Bush's decision to declare that "major combat operations" were over.

It was, of course, nowhere near as simple as that. Almost immediately, an insurgency against the United States and its allies in Iraq broke out. On the first anniversary of Saddam's capture, more than one thousand Americans were dead, most having been killed after the supposed end of major combat. That total topped 1,500 during the first week of March 2005.

The resistance came from many sources. There were undoubtedly some foreign fighters, perhaps including some who had been recruited to al-Qaeda both before and after 9/11. Most, however, seemed to be Iraqis, especially Sunni and Shiite Arabs whose positions had been undermined following Saddam's defeat, albeit in very different ways.

Six weeks after the first anniversary of Saddam's capture, Iraq held its first even reasonably fair election ever. The result, however, was a forgone conclusion. Groups close to the United States and the provisional authority it put into place that represented the country's Shiite majority (to be discussed shortly) won and took on the responsibility of writing a new constitution and creating a new regime. It would then go out of existence when the new regime takes over, which was planned for the end of 2005.

Yet those elections had little in common with those we saw in Part 2. There were entire provinces where it was not safe for people to vote. Governors, local police chiefs, and other officials had been assassinated in the weeks leading up to the voting.

In short, Iraq is different from all the other countries covered in this book. War-torn. Occupied. In ruins.

So this chapter will be different, too. It will look at how the country got into this devastating position and what that tells us about authoritarian regimes, the potential for democratization, and the realities of globalization in the post-9/11 world, especially how international forces can totally reshape domestic politics.

Thinking about Iraq

If we went back in time and conducted a poll in July 1990, we undoubtedly would learn that most Westerners did not know who Saddam Hussein was, let alone where Iraq was located on a world map.

Ever since, Saddam Hussein and his country have been on center stage. The sudden upsurge of interest in a hitherto little-known country began because of Iraq's invasion of its small, oil-rich neighbor Kuwait on 2 August 1990. In an unprecedented display of cooperation, most of the world community, including both superpowers and several Arab states, denounced Iraq's actions and demanded its withdrawal. After Iraq refused to do so and the United Nations approved an international military response, President George H. W. Bush ordered the international coalition he led into the **Gulf War,** which resulted in the defeat of Iraq on the battlefield but not the overthrow of Saddam's regime.

Twelve years later, President Bush's son, George W. Bush, led a much smaller coalition of states into another war with Iraq. It seemed to end just as quickly and just as decisively. But as we saw, this time, while the United States succeeded in toppling Saddam Hussein's regime, it also unleashed an Iraqi resistance that bogged down American and other occupying troops and reminded many observers of the American involvement in Vietnam in the 1960s and 1970s.

The Basics

Any discussion of Iraqi politics must begin with the legacy of more than thirty years of brutal rule by the **Baath Party** and the man who was its undisputed leader from 1979 until 2003, Saddam Hussein. As in Stalin's Soviet Union, a totalitarian regime was established by a narrowly based party that claimed to speak for the masses but that, in fact, represented little more than a tiny group of political activists who were never able to develop much genuine popular support.

Individual and minority rights were subordinated to the "needs" of the state, which the party claimed it represented. Dissenters were systematically denounced as "traitors" and "enemies of the state," and the most prominent of them were executed after a series of well-publicized mock trials that succeeded in instilling massive fear of the regime.

However, as in any country, we cannot understand Iraq's politics without first considering some of the country's social and economic features. Again, as in any country, those characteristics give rise to many of the political issues Iraq faced during Saddam Hussein's years in power and the difficulties it confronts today.

Economic Potential

One of the tragedies of Iraqi politics is that its current plight was far from inevitable. Different policy choices would have led to a very different outcome, including prosperity for most of the Iraqi population.

By third world standards, Iraq has tremendous resources. There are over 100 billion barrels of oil (one barrel holds forty-two gallons) under its soil, which represents 15 percent of all known Middle Eastern reserves. Only Saudi Arabia has more. Many geologists believe that Iraq has more undiscovered oil than any other Middle Eastern country. Thus, in 1987 it was estimated that Iraq would not run out of oil for another 140 years at production levels prevailing at the time.

Iraq also has significant agricultural potential, despite a southwestern region that is a desert and the high salt content of the soil elsewhere. There are surprisingly fertile areas in the Kurdish regions of the north and along the banks of the Tigris and Euphrates rivers, which provide ample water for irrigation and the generation of electricity.

Iraq's other major resource is its population. With more than twenty-five million people, it is relatively large, especially when compared with Saudi Arabia and the smaller Gulf states, and can therefore support a diversified and integrated economy. Moreover, Iraq's labor force is relatively skilled and well educated by regional standards.

As a result, Iraq could easily be an economically successful country. In fact, in the mid-1970s, following the world-wide quadrupling of oil prices, many observers predicted that it would soon emerge as the economic powerhouse of the Arab world.

Although some of this new-found wealth was used to modernize the country's infrastructure and provide Iraqis with an enhanced standard of living, the staggering increase in oil revenues mostly enabled the regime to gain access to sophisticated devices of political control and to build up the military.

Diversity

Iraq's population is more than 95 percent Muslim. Behind this apparent homogeneity, however, lies a sharp distinction between **Sunni** and **Shiite** Muslims and Arabs and **Kurds.**

Iraqi population figures are notoriously inaccurate. Nonetheless, the best guess is that approximately 60 percent of the population is Shiite and approximately 35 percent is Sunni, with the majority of the Sunni being Kurds.

The origins of the Sunni-Shiite rivalry date back to the dawn of Islamic history. The prophet Muhammad died in 632 without having designated a successor to head the rapidly expanding Islamic empire he had created. Almost immediately, his followers split into two groups. The one that became the Sunnis believed that the most prominent members of the community should select the new leader, or caliph, on the basis of personal attributes such as piety, wisdom, morality, leadership ability, and general competence. Others, however, contended that the leadership of the Islamic community should stay in the prophet's family. They believed that Muhammad had designated his cousin, son-in-law, and close companion, Ali, to be his successor. They were called Shiites, a word derived from the expression *Shi'at Ali,* which means "the partisans of Ali" (www.arches.uga .edu/~godlas/home.html).

Although the soon-to-be Sunnis won the argument, Ali himself was eventually elected to the caliphate in 656 after the death of Uthman, the third caliph. However, Muawiyah, Uthman's nephew and governor of Syria, refused to accept this choice. Eventually, Muawiyah prevailed and established the Damascus-based Umayyad dynasty (661–750).

The Shiites never recognized Umayyad rule and continued to claim that only the descendants of Ali had the right to govern the Islamic community. In 680 Ali's second son, Hussein, led a group of his followers in an armed uprising against the forces of the Umayyad dynasty. Despite his bravery and courage, Hussein was defeated and killed at Kerbala in what is now southern Iraq.

The story of Hussein's defeat lies at the heart of Shiite culture, especially its emphasis on martyrdom. To the Shiites, who rapidly became the most important minority sect within Islam, the battle of Kerbala symbolizes worldly injustice and the triumph of the forces of evil over the forces of good. More significantly, the defeat widened the gulf between Sunnis and Shiites. In the following centuries, what initially had been limited to a disagreement over who should succeed the prophet became a full-fledged religious and political schism that continues to be felt throughout the Muslim world.

In addition to the Sunni-Shiite split, Iraqis are also divided into two main ethnic groups—Arabs and Kurds. (See figure 14.1.) About 75 percent of Iraq's population is Arab—that is, speaks Arabic and identifies with the Arab heritage. The Kurds, who represent 20 percent of the population, speak Kurdish, which has nothing in com-

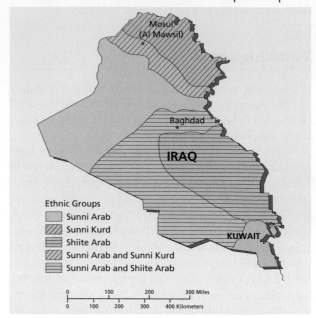

■ FIGURE 14.1 Distribution of Ethnic Groups in Iraq

mon with Arabic. Kurds also have their own history and modes of social and political organization. Indeed, they have less in common with Iraq's Arab majority than with other Kurdish communities in Turkey, Iran, Syria, and the former Soviet Union.

Key Questions

As noted in Chapter 11, most third world countries struggle with three related problems—economic development, ethnic tensions, and limited prospects for democratization. These are key issues in Iraqi politics as well.

However, given the discussion so far, it should be clear that we need to focus more on other questions. In particular:

- How were Saddam Hussein and the men around him able to create such a powerful regime?

- How were they able to sustain it despite all the setbacks of the two decades before the 2003 war?

- What are the likely outcomes following the war that began in 2003 and the tumult that followed it?

The Evolution of the Iraqi State

In European liberal democracies, the development of the state was mostly an indigenous process that spanned hundreds of years. Consequently, when the twentieth century began, most Europeans already thought of themselves as belonging to a "nation"—a group of people bound together by a common history, a shared culture, a sense of collective identity, and a willingness to live together

By contrast, few third world countries are more than a half-century old in their current form, and their boundaries were often arbitrarily drawn and imposed by imperialist powers. As a result, countries like Iraq have had to simultaneously address both state and **nation building** under less than auspicious circumstances.

Iraq's Origins

Urban civilization first developed some six thousand years ago in the city-states of Sumer in what is now southern Iraq (www.al-bab.com/arab/countries/iraq/history.htm). The Sumerians were the first to invent writing by drawing pictures on clay tablets, and they made important contributions to irrigation methods, literature, mathematics, architecture, metal working, transportation (they built the first wheeled chariot), and astronomy (they produced the first reasonably accurate calendars). Their successors added to those accomplishments—most notably, the Babylonians, who produced the Code of Hammurabi, the first complete legal framework. After Mesopotamia was incorporated into the Muslim empire during the seventh century, the region's fame and prosperity reached new heights. Baghdad was the seat of the Abbassid dynasty (750–1258), during which time Islamic civilization reached its peak while Europe still lived in the Dark Ages.

Given its strategic location on the eastern flank of the Arab world and its all but defenseless border, Iraq was always coveted by foreign powers that sought to dominate the region. Its period as one of the leading cultural centers in the world came to an end when the Mongols invaded and destroyed Baghdad in 1258 and slaughtered 100,000 Iraqis. A century and a half later, in 1394, the invading Tatars reportedly built a pyramid with the skulls of their unfortunate victims in the small provincial town of Tikrit, where some 543 years later Saddam Hussein was born.

Even this brief overview should illuminate the distinguished history of the area that is now Iraq. Yet Iraq as a distinct political unit is barely eighty years old. Until World War I broke out, "Iraq" was merely a region of the **Ottoman Empire.**

In 1914, the already weakened Ottoman authorities made what turned out to be a disastrous choice when they entered World War I, siding with Germany and the Austro-Hungarian Empire against France, Britain, and Russia. During the war, the Ottoman Empire collapsed,

TABLE 14.1 Key Events in Iraqi History

YEAR	EVENT
1919	Treaty of Versailles, giving Britain mandate over Iraq
1932	Nominal independence
1958	Overthrow of monarchy
1963	First, short-lived seizure of power by Baath Party
1968	Definitive seizure of power by Baath Party
1979	Saddam Hussein takes control

which gave Britain and France the opportunity to divide its former Arab provinces between themselves. They created entirely new countries, the borders of which were drawn to fit Britain's and France's colonial ambitions and did not reflect the distribution of religious, ethnic, and linguistic groups or the wishes of the populations involved. Iraq was one of these new countries. (See table 14.1.)

In 1916, when most of the Arab world was still under Ottoman control, British officials struck a deal with a group of Arab leaders. In an attempt to facilitate the allied war effort, they promised they would support the creation of one large, independent Arab state after the war if the Arabs rose up in rebellion against the Ottomans. The Arabs lived up to their side of the bargain, but the British did not. By 1920 Arabs found themselves living in separate countries under regimes installed and controlled by either France or Britain. Understandably, the Arabs felt bitter and betrayed.

The British created a constitutional monarchy in Iraq, a political system entirely alien to the area's customs and traditions. They then added insult to injury by selecting a foreigner to be Iraq's first king. **Faisal I** was a member of the prestigious and pro-British Hashemite family, whose roots lay not in Iraq but in the western part of what is now Saudi Arabia.

From the beginning, therefore, the Iraqi government lacked legitimacy. It also had to contend with the heterogeneity of Iraq's population. When the British created Iraq, they brought together disparate ethnic, religious, and tribal groups, none of whom considered themselves "Iraqi" nor wanted to become part of the new country. In fact, some of the communities artificially stitched together by the British had a long history of mutual distrust and hostility. Thus it was not easy to forge a cohesive political community out of a patchwork of rival groups that shared neither a common heritage nor a willingness to live together.

During the 1920s and 1930s, the task of the new regime was made even more difficult by the presence of rebellious Kurdish and Shiite tribes and by traditional feelings of distrust toward any central authority.

Independent Iraq

In 1932 Iraq formally became independent, although British advisers continued to exert tremendous influence over the kingdom. The minority Sunni Arabs have controlled every regime since Iraq gained its independence. Their domination reflects a legacy of the Sunni-ruled Ottoman Empire, which systematically discriminated against Shiites. It continued under the monarchy, when Shiites and Kurds were forced into the new state against their will.

After twenty-six years under the monarchy, a group of military officers overthrew the regime but retained Sunni domination. In retrospect, the demise of the monarchy appears all but inevitable, considering its consistently narrow base of support, the poor quality of the men at the helm, their perceived subservience to British interests, and their unwillingness or inability to reduce glaring social inequalities and to reach out to a rapidly growing and politicized middle class.

The decisive element in the downfall of the monarchy was the spread of pan-Arab, socialist ideologies in the army's ranks. Riding a wave of popular discontent, Arab nationalist officers, led by General Qasim, organized a successful coup and in 1958 established the first republican regime in the country's short history. It proved to be a republic in name only. The country was ruled by heavy-handed army officers for most of the first decade after the overthrow of the monarchy. In 1963 the Baath Party overthrew the officers then in power, but was itself forced out in a matter of months.

In July 1968 the Baath came back to power. This time, the Baathists were determined to stay in control, and they rapidly moved to eliminate everyone else from positions of influence. (See table 14.2.)

Eleven years later, Saddam Hussein forced his predecessor, **Ahmad Hassan al-Bakr,** into retirement. He announced his ascension to the presidency at a meeting of the Central Committee of the Baath party at which almost a third of its members were summarily executed.

Afterward, he consolidated his own power along with that of the party to the point that it was all but impossible to separate the two, as we will see in the rest of this section. The dictatorship of the Baath Party gave way to personal rule, and the state became little more than a tool Saddam Hussein, his family, and the rest of his entourage used to reinforce their hold on the country.

Political Culture and Participation

Iraq's history produced a culture that political scientists believe hinders the development of a stable, effective, and popular regime, let alone a democracy. Even without

TABLE 14.2 Key Events in Iraq since the Baath Took Power

YEAR	EVENTS
1968	Baath Party seizes power
1970	Government signs autonomy agreement with Kurds
1972	Kurdish autonomy agreement collapses; war breaks out in north between Baghdad and Kurdish separatists
1975	Iran and Iraq agree on Kurds and Shatt al-Arab waterway Kurdish uprising collapses
	Deportation and resettlement of Kurds
1979	Saddam Hussein becomes president
1980–88	Iran-Iraq War, including use of chemical weapons against Kurdish civilians
1990	Invasion of Kuwait, Operation Desert Shield
1991	Gulf War
	Uprisings among Shiites and Kurds
1995	Saddam's son-in-law and former minister of industry, Hussein Kamel al-Majid, defects to Jordan
	Referendum gives Saddam Hussein another term
1996	Hussein Kamel al-Majid is pardoned, returns to Iraq, is killed
	Saddam launches attack on Kurdish enclave in north
	Assassination attempt on Saddam's son, Uday
1998	Most recent crisis between Iraq and the West over UN weapons inspections
	Four-day bombing campaign of Iraq by American and British forces
1999	Continued U.S. and U.K. bombing in response to Iraqi violations of 1991 cease-fire terms
2003	U.S.-led invasion topples Baath regime.

the years of repression under the Baath, Iraq would have had a hard time creating any sense of national unity, let alone a commitment to democracy.

Cultural Pluralism

As in most of the third world, religious and ethnic divisions acted as a brake on the development of an Iraqi national identity. Instead, older, parochial identities thwarted government efforts to promote any sense of Iraqi nationalism. After all, Iraq originally was little more than an artificial conglomerate of tribes, clans, and religious and ethnic groups that lived in isolation from one another for centuries, had no tradition of political cooperation, and shared a long history of mutual distrust and hostility.

The sharply differentiated religious and ethnic communities were reluctant to give up their distinctive character for the benefit of an Iraqi identity concocted by

British colonial officers. Although religious and ethnic cleavages did not always preclude cooperation between Sunnis and Shiites or between Arabs and Kurds, they did make the process of nation building more difficult than in any of the other third world countries considered in this book.

The Baath regime understood the need to defuse tensions among Iraq's ethnic and religious communities. Accordingly, it tried to convince Iraqis that a common identity rooted in the country's Mesopotamian heritage transcends its religious and ethnic divisions. Its propaganda portrayed modern-day Iraqis as direct descendants of the ancient Sumerians, Akkadians, and Babylonians. In addition, it invested huge sums of money in the rebuilding of Babylon and in archaeological excavations intended to retrieve the country's pre-Islamic past.

However, these efforts failed because many Iraqis continued to identify themselves primarily with their clan, ethnic, and religious groups. This is by no means uncommon in the third world, but in Iraq, the way in which parochialism has played itself out at both the mass and elite levels put exceptional burdens on the former regime and seem likely to do so for whatever government comes next.

That means that the differences between Kurds and Arabs and Shiites and Sunnis are a central element in Iraqi political culture. Those differences surged to the surface in the months after the U.S.-led invasion in 2003, but have been part of the country's political landscape for many generations.

The inability of Arabs and Kurds to coexist peacefully has always been a major problem for Iraq's leaders. Given the development of a Kurdish nationalist movement at the turn of the twentieth century and the lip service paid by the Great Powers to the principle of self-determination after World War I, the Kurds had hoped that the postwar settlement would see the establishment of a Kurdish state. Instead, the Kurds found themselves spread across the borders of Turkey, Iraq, Iran, Syria, and the former Soviet Union.

Most Kurds never accepted the crushing of their nationalist aspirations. Consequently, their relationship with successive Iraqi governments has been stormy. Kurdish uprisings have punctuated Iraqi political life since the mid-1920s. In turn, the Iraqi central authorities have always seen Kurdish aspirations for autonomy as a threat to the country's very existence. The fact that Kurdish insurgents were supported by Iran, the United States, and other outsiders did little to ease the tension between them and Iraq's Arab majority. Thus, at the height of the Iran-Iraq War, one of the two main Iraqi Kurdish organizations, the **Patriotic Union of Kurdistan (PUK),** coop-

Barry Iverson / Woodfin Camp & Associates

A group of Kurdish rebels showing off a captured Iraqi airplane after the first Gulf War.

erated with the Iranian army and helped it seize a number of villages in Iraqi Kurdistan.

Much of the blame for Arab-Kurdish hostility also lies with a succession of Iraqi governments that never made a sincere effort to meet even limited Kurdish demands. In 1970, for instance, Kurdish leaders and Saddam Hussein reached an agreement granting administrative autonomy to Iraqi Kurdistan, the teaching of Kurdish in schools, the use of Kurdish as the official language in the north, and the increased representation of the Kurds in state institutions. Within a year of signing the agreement, however, it had become clear that the Baath leadership had no intention of living up to its provisions. And, as many Westerners learned for the first time in the run up to the invasion of Iraq, the authorities in Baghdad used chemical and biological weapons against its own Kurdish citizens during the war with Iran.

In postwar Iraq, the Kurdish-Arab split remains im-

Ceerwan Aziz/Reuters/CORBIS

Shiite cleric Muqtada al-Sadr leads Friday prayers in the town of Kufa, some 160 km south of Baghdad on 16 April 2004 at the height of Shiite resistance to the U.S.-led occupation.

portant. Many Kurds are unwilling to live under a government dominated by Arabs and want at least autonomy over their own region if not outright independence. Meeting Kurdish demand for more freedom from Baghdad while maintaining the territorial integrity of Iraq will be a major challenge for the transitional parliament, whose primary task is to write a new constitution for a permanent regime.

The split between the Arab Shiite and Sunni communities is likely to prove even more intense as the United States and Iraqi authorities try to reconstruct the country. Their antagonism stems more from political, social, and economic differences than from theological disagreement. There are differences of faith, as there are between Catholics and Protestants in Northern Ireland. However, religion has become more a symbol of communal identity, and a way for Shiites to express their grievances over the inequalities in wealth and power that have characterized Iraq since it was created.

In the late 1960s there was not a single Shiite in the **Revolutionary Command Council (RCC),** which was the top level of the Baath Party leadership. By the late 1980s, however, more than 25 percent of those in the RCC and close to 30 percent of all party leaders were Shiites, and Shiites were represented in numbers roughly proportional to their share of the population at lower levels of the bureaucracy. Yet Shiites' sense they were discriminated against erupted in the first months after Saddam's overthrow in the insurgency led by the cleric, Muqtada al-Sadr.

The Shiites' sense of deprivation has also been fu-

eled by the perception that their community has been discriminated against economically. Living conditions in the predominantly Shiite areas of southern Iraq were so miserable in the 1940s and 1950s that tens of thousands of Shiite peasants migrated to Baghdad every year, where they formed the nucleus of a rapidly developing urban proletariat in what used to be known as Saddam City and is now Al-Sadr City.

The Baath regime worsened the already deep division. Initially this occurred because of the party's militantly secular orientation, which antagonized religious-minded Shiites, and by its long-standing rivalry with the Communist Party, which traditionally had recruited heavily in the Shiite community. Tensions deepened following the creation of a distinctly Shiite underground movement, al-Da'wa al-Islamiyya (the Islamic Call), which called for the establishment of an Islamic regime in the country.

The Baath government responded to this challenge in a particularly brutal manner in order to break the hold of religious leaders in the Shiite holy cities of Kerbala and Najaf. Clerics and theology students suspected of being affiliated with al-Da'wa were arrested and as many as forty thousand of them were deported to Iran.

The outbreak of the Iran-Iraq War, however, forced the regime to reconsider its strategy toward the Shiites. The fear that Shiites might defect and support their co-religionists to the east led Saddam Hussein to temper his repression with various measures designed to win them over.

But the moderation was not to last. When Shiites finally rose up in the wake of the first Gulf War, the brutal response from the authorities only heightened Shiite antagonism toward Baghdad. In order to flee the government, many Shiite rebels took refuge in the marshes in the southern part of the country, which were also a vital part of the regional economy. Saddam had the marshes drained in order to flush out the rebels and thus only reinforced the hatred many in the region felt toward the Sunni-led regime.

A Culture of Secrecy and Fear

Iraq has also often been described as having an inward-looking and secretive culture, which stems in part from the centuries of isolation after the Mongol and subsequent invasions. Mass and elite concerns about foreigners include not only the West, but their relations with two of their neighbors, Turkey and Iran. Neither is an Arab country. Both have vastly larger populations. In past centuries, empires based in those countries invaded and occupied Iraq.

Iraqis today have serious reasons for concern. For instance, many Turks still believe that Britain's decision to cede the Mosul region to Iraq in the early 1920s was illegal. Eighty percent of Iraq's water supply comes from Turkey and Syria, where both the Tigris and Euphrates have their origins. Turkey's pro-Western government allowed allied bombers to launch attacks from bases there during the first Gulf War. Saddam's regime had similar worries about Iran, epitomized by the dispute over the Shatt al-Arab River in southeastern Iraq, which we will see in more detail later in the chapter as we consider the events that gave rise to the Iran-Iraq War.

Some Iraqis, too, are concerned with what they see as the Western desire to dominate the region. They have not forgotten Britain's broken promises to Arab nationalists after World War I and continue to resent the way British colonial officials drew the country's borders. They remember, too, that Britain was the real power behind the monarchy and that it manipulated Iraqi affairs to further its colonial interests.

The bitterness toward Britain in particular and the West in general was compounded by the decisive role that Western countries played in the creation of Israel. To this day, many Iraqis regard Israel as an artificial entity imposed by the colonial powers to divide and weaken the Arab world.

After the Baath secured power, it actively encouraged distrust of the West. Saddam Hussein and his colleagues sought to limit the access of foreign visitors to Iraq, and those who were allowed in could not travel freely or easily come into contact with average Iraqis. Any Iraqi who did was likely to have a "visit" from one of the security forces that could put their careers—and even their lives—in jeopardy.

A Tradition of Political Violence

The last aspect of Iraqi popular culture is a propensity toward violence that is not matched in any of the other countries covered in this book. As early as the seventh century, the area was known for its turbulent nature, which coexists uneasily with its tradition of authoritarian rule.

During the 1940s and 1950s, the extreme polarization of wealth and the politicization of a new generation of Iraqis dissatisfied with the authoritarian nature of the monarchy resulted in numerous social and political upheavals. In July 1958 widespread popular discontent with the monarchy exploded in a particularly bloody fashion that led to its destruction.

The aftermath of the revolution was hardly more peaceful. In March 1959 local army commanders rose up

Conflict in Iraq

Conflict is the name of the game in Iraqi politics. Under Saddam Hussein's regime, conflict was largely suppressed. However, as the insurgencies since the end of major combat operations in April 2003 has shown, conflict among—and within—the three main religious and ethnic communities discussed in this section is likely to haunt Iraqi politics for years to come.

Very little is being done to address the root causes of the conflict. Those of us in the conflict resolution community think it could be decades before the generations of Kurdish versus Arab and Sunni versus Shiite disputes can be overcome, even if Iraqi and American forces can put down the insurrection that broke out within days of the overthrow of Saddam Hussein's regime.

against the government of General Qasim in the northern city of Mosul. For three days the city was engulfed in violence and bloodshed. Old personal grudges and family feuds were settled. Qasim's supporters were summarily executed. When it became clear that the coup had failed, the government allowed the Communist Party to go on a rampage and avenge the earlier killings.

When the Baath Party finally overthrew Qasim in 1963, his downfall turned into a particularly gruesome spectacle. His bullet-ridden corpse was shown for several days on Iraqi television.

When the Baath Party finally solidified their power in 1968, the government was able to put a lid on most public forms of violence—other than those it carried out itself. Nonetheless, when they fell, the conflict burst back into the open again and, along with the Kurdish/Arab divide, could well imperil the future of Iraq as a country.

Political Participation under the Baath

Public involvement in political life under Saddam Hussein was much like that in the Soviet Union before Mikhail Gorbachev came to power and opened up the system. There were next to no opportunities for Iraqi citizens to express their opinions, especially those that were at odds with the regime.

Instead, to the degree that members of the mass public were engaged in political life, they were mobilized to do so by the Baathist authorities. For instance, massive demonstrations were held in favor of the three wars the government fought before it was toppled. However, most Western observers were convinced that most peo-

ple participated in them because they were all but co-
erced into doing so by the party and the state.

We can see the lack of real democratic political participation in the last two presidential elections during
Saddam's reign. In 1995, 99.47 percent of the population
went to the polls, and, of them, 99.96 percent voted for
Saddam Hussein. In other words, no more than three
thousand people did not vote and no more than another
three thousand cast a ballot against Saddam. The regime
outdid itself seven years later when it reported a 100 percent turnout and 100 percent of the voters casting ballots
for Saddam. That may not have been terribly surprising
since participation was mandatory and voters had to
show their votes to poll watchers before depositing them
in the ballot boxes.

The limits on "demanding" public participation
were also evident in the extreme weakness of the Iraqi
opposition. It had no open support inside the country
and given the repressive power of the regime (see the
next section) it was forced to operate from abroad. Many
of those groups were funded by the United States, Iran,
and other opponents of the Baath Party that further undercut their potential support at home, something we
saw in the aftermath of the 2003 war.

The little opposition that existed was highly fragmented. Some of these divisions reflect the country's
ethnic and religious cleavages. Thus, the most outspoken critics of the regime were mostly Kurds or Shiites.
The one exception was the Iraqi Communist Party,
which protested the regime in all parts of Iraq, but like
the Tudeh in Iran, it had been all but completely destroyed by the 1990s.

After the first Gulf War, there was a Western-led attempt to create a broadly based opposition coalition—
the **Iraqi National Congress (INC),** which was headed by
Adnan Chalabi and all but completely funded by the
United States. Chalabi, a Shiite, has since been accused
of secretly passing information to the Iranian government and is all but completely discredited in the United
States and Iraq. The second-largest group was the Iraqi
National Accord, led by **Ayad Alawi,** who became the
interim prime minister as the United States began the
transfer of power to Iraqis in 2004.

The State under Saddam Hussein

Most third world countries have governmental institutions that are elaborately laid out in their constitutions.
In some cases, such as India, those provisions define political life roughly to the degree that they do in industrialized democracies. In many others, however, power rests

primarily with a single leader or a small group that is not
constrained by constitutional language or conventional
laws. That was particularly true in Iraq, which was dominated by one man and his personal entourage for a
quarter century.

A Party State

As in the Soviet Union, we have to start with the single
party that controlled the state. The Baath Party was
founded in the early 1940s by two French-educated Syrian teachers—Michel Aflaq, a Greek Orthodox Christian,
and Salah al-Din al-Bitar, a Sunni Muslim. Soon afterward, the party established branches in Iraq, Jordan, and
Lebanon.

Its ideology was always an ill-defined and abstract
mixture of pan-Arabism and non-Marxist socialism.
The key to its political philosophy was the premise that
nation-states in the Arab world were artificial entities
created by colonial powers who wanted to divide and
weaken the region. Therefore, the party's founders argued that only the unification of the various Arab states
would enable them to overcome underdevelopment and
foreign domination. Their goals were reflected in the
very name of their party, since the word *Baath* in Arabic
means "resurgence" or "renaissance."

Because Baathist leaders saw Arab countries as mere
parts of a wider Arab nation, the party's highest decision-
making body, the National Command, was a supranational institution. Subordinated to it were the party's
Regional Commands, which made up the leadership of
the Baath in each Arab country.

However, the notion that the Baath was a party that
transcended existing state boundaries soon became a
fiction, as country-based organizations asserted their
independence from the National Command. In 1966 an
important split took place between the Syrian and Iraqi
branches. From then on Syria and Iraq each had their
own "National Command" that put national interests
well above those of the "Arab nation."

After the Baath Party seized control in Baghdad in
1968, anyone who posed a potential threat to its monopoly of power was retired, jailed, executed, dismissed, or
reassigned to less-influential positions. All strategic positions in the state machinery were given to trusted or
long-standing party members.

Saddam Hussein, then head of the party's security apparatus, orchestrated and directed this thorough
"Baathization" of the state. At the same time, he revamped the Baath itself, transforming it from a small,
underground party into a mass-based organization. Full
membership was reserved for individuals who, after

years of service, finally proved their dedication to the regime. Membership in the party was for life, and defection was punishable by death.

Like other totalitarian parties, the Baath relied on political indoctrination to foster a sense of Iraqi nationalism and unconditional loyalty. The party tightly controlled the media, the curriculum at schools at all educational levels, and entry into the teaching profession.

Thus, in the mid-1980s, when Iraq's leadership was courting U.S. support in its war with Iran, teachers in Baghdad's schools taught their students that Americans were friends of the Iraqi people and that American visitors deserved a particularly warm welcome. During the 1990–91 Gulf crisis, the same teachers taught children that Americans were imperialists bent on dominating the Middle East and destroying Iraq.

The Baath also helped the authorities control the population. It could do so because it literally was everywhere—from small "cells" in neighborhoods and villages all the way up to its national authorities. Party units were called "divisions" at the level of towns or urban neighborhoods, "sections" that combined several divisions in a large city or a region, and "branches" for the eighteen provinces plus three for Baghdad.

The party was present in factories, universities, and government offices. It monitored the activities of journalists, lawyers, doctors, peasants, and workers through unions and professional organizations that the party itself controlled. Party members reported on their colleagues' and superiors' performance and loyalty.

Therefore, there were really two distinct chains of authority in the Iraqi state: the official, bureaucratic one and the one associated with the Baath Party. State and party were often played against one another in an attempt to weaken both and to diminish the possibility that either could provide potential enemies of the regime with a power base. The confusion and delays that this phenomenon generated are logical consequences of a system that valued political control more than bureaucratic efficiency.

As such, two parts of the former Iraqi state—the Council of Ministers (or cabinet) and the National Assembly—might seem familiar at first glance, because they have the same names as institutions frequently found in democratic political systems. In fact, they had little in common with their Western counterparts because they had next to no influence over policy making.

The cabinet did little more than implement policies that had already been adopted by the president and the Revolutionary Command Council (RCC), which will be discussed shortly. The National Assembly's 250 members were only allowed to run for election after being hand picked by a special committee controlled by Saddam Hussein and thus had even less power.

In practice, all power was concentrated in the hands of the Baath party leadership from 1968. And once Saddam took definitive control a decade later, the distinction between the party and his personal power all but evaporated.

The Cult of Personality

As also was the case in most totalitarian regimes, power was increasingly concentrated in the hands of a single leader in what is referred to as a **cult of personality.** When Elaine Sciolino arrived to cover Iraqi politics after the invasion of Kuwait in 1990, she asked her taxicab driver what he thought about Saddam Hussein. His answer was short but to the point. He tapped the dashboard of his car and said, "this is car, but if Saddam Hussein says it is bicycle, it is bicycle." In October 1991 Izzat Ibrahim, then vice chairman of the Revolutionary Command Council, summed it up more briefly: "Saddam Hussein is Iraq, and Iraq is Saddam Hussein."

Huge billboards throughout the country portrayed him in different guises—Saddam in a military uniform, Saddam in a tailor-made Italian suit, Saddam praying, Saddam wearing a Bedouin headdress and robe, Saddam as a shepherd tending his flock, or Saddam wearing the green fatigues favored by Baath leaders. His portrait was everywhere—in taxicabs, in stores, in government buildings, in homes (especially those of government employees), and on bus windows. There were Saddam t-shirts, watches with his face on the dial, and notebooks and calendars adorned with his image. Throughout the country, one found placards with quotes attributed to Saddam and others praising the president.

In the mid-1980s one of the very few jokes against the regime that made the rounds went like this:

"What is the population of Iraq?"

"Twenty-eight million. Fourteen million Iraqis and fourteen million pictures of Saddam Hussein."

Saddam Hussein's birthday was a national holiday. Schoolchildren memorized his sayings as well as poems and songs exalting him. News broadcasts focused on his activities. Television anchors read the dozens of congratulatory telegrams sent to him every day by government officials, artists, and leaders of professional, women's, and youth associations.

The most striking example of the personality cult is probably the set of two monuments called "Victory

SADDAM HUSSEIN

Ceerwan Aziz/CORBIS

A best-selling watch during the 1991 war, with Saddam Hussein pictured on the dial. Many wrist- and pocket-watches, as well as a wide selection of Saddam t-shirts, were available.

Saddam Hussein was born in 1937 and grew up in Tikrit, a poor city one hundred miles north of Baghdad. His mother was a widow, and there are rumors that he was abused by several of the relatives who helped raise him.

Saddam Hussein moved to Baghdad in 1955 and quickly became active in politics. He was wounded in the Baathists' attempt to assassinate Qasim in 1959 and fled to Cairo, where he studied law but never earned a degree. He returned to Iraq when the Baath Party first came to power in 1963.

After the Baath seized power for good in July 1968, he served as second-in-command to the new president, Major General Ahmad Hassan al-Bakr. In practice, however, he quickly became the driving force behind the new regime, and by the mid-1970s he had emerged as the de facto leader of Iraq. In July 1979 he forced al-Bakr to resign and assumed the presidency himself. Through repeated purges of the ruling elite, he rapidly turned Iraqi politics into one-man rule. He has been aptly described by *New York Times* journalist Thomas Friedman as a thirteenth-century tyrant whose unrelenting desire to acquire weapons of mass destruction make him the archetypical twenty-first-century threat (www.emergency.com/hussein1.htm). He was captured by American troops on 12 December 2003 and was awaiting trial for crimes against humanity when this book went to press.

Arches" that Saddam Hussein had built to celebrate Iraq's "victory" over Iran. These identical monuments are at opposite ends of a huge field in Baghdad. Each consists of two enormous, twenty-ton bronze forearms, which are giant replicas of Saddam's. The arms burst from the ground, each holding a giant sword. When they meet, the swords and the arms form an arch. Next to the base of the arches are some five thousand battle-scarred helmets of dead Iranian soldiers. The symbolism is obvious: Iraq's victory was achieved through the military genius and valiant leadership of Saddam, who will continue to usher his nation to ever greater successes.

The cult of personality reinforced two opposing images of Saddam Hussein: as benefactor and as ruthless leader. Thus, welfare programs and development projects are presented as personal gifts that Saddam showered on his people. In the 1970s and 1980s, for instance, he frequently handed out television sets while visiting Kurdish or Shiite villages. But if Saddam was the one who handed out benefits, he also was the one who handed

out the punishment. After the village of Dujayl, known to be a hotbed of Shiite fundamentalism, was the site of an assassination attempt against the Iraqi leader, he ordered the village razed. Almost immediately afterward, the government rebuilt it.

Through such displays, Saddam Hussein projected the image of a leader who was omnipresent, omnipotent, and omniscient. The message sent through such dramatic and seemingly contradictory actions was simple: Saddam Hussein alone decided who would live and who would die. And although many of the stories circulating in Iraq and in the Arab world about his brutality were true, many more were fabricated and spread by the regime to add to his aura of invincibility.

The Informal Chain of Command

Saddam's ability to maintain his privileged position rested largely on his personal control over a vast network of subordinates who managed the party and state. Trusted aides who reported directly to him and who were

A military procession passing under the famous giant arches made up of swords held in replicas of Saddam Hussein's hands.

Chris North; Cordaiy Photo Library Ltd./CORBIS

kept relatively uninformed of each other's activities headed every institution that mattered.

In so doing, Saddam Hussein made it unlikely that he would ever face a concerted challenge to his rule, especially given that he was also highly skilled at playing these men against one another. The concentration of power in Saddam's hands had two essential implications for the exercise of political power in Iraq.

First, the influence of any member of the Iraqi political elite was primarily a function of his personal access to the leader. Thus, men who do not belong to any of the official government bodies but who were particularly close to Saddam often exerted more power than those in formal positions of authority. Second, the real chain of authority in Iraq was exercised through a series of concentric circles emanating from Saddam. Such personalization of power, and the fluidity of institutional arrangements it implies, makes it all but impossible to present the kind of diagram of decision making included in the other chapters of this book.

The inner circle made up of Saddam Hussein's relatives largely ran Iraq from behind the scenes. In 1990 this group included eight of his family members: his two sons, **Uday** and **Qusay;** three cousins on his father's side (two of whom were also his sons-in-law); and three half-brothers.

However, the number of reliable family members declined significantly afterward as a result of all but com-

pletely open disputes among them. Although there are several such examples, one stands out. In August 1995 Saddam Hussein's two sons-in-law, who had been number two in the regime and head of Saddam's personal security guard, respectively, defected to Jordan, where they called for the overthrow of their father-in-law. When they finally returned to Baghdad after being granted a presidential pardon, they were killed together with all those who had shared their brief exile (except for Saddam's two daughters, who, with their mother, were placed under house arrest).

A second circle consisted of a handful of Saddam Hussein's close associates, who had been connected to him since the Baath's underground days. Although these men had some real influence, they lacked any kind of independent power base and owed everything to Saddam. This circle included Vice President Taha Yassin Ramadan, Foreign Minister Tariq Aziz, and others who were not as visible to observers in the West.

A third circle was composed of Saddam Hussein's relatives and others who hail from his hometown, Tikrit. It used to be customary for last names to refer to a person's place of origin, as in "Saddam Hussein al-Tikriti" (that is, "from Tikrit"). In 1976 the Baath Party suddenly abolished this practice on the grounds that it encouraged people to think of themselves not as Iraqis but as members of the parochial groups discussed earlier. Many observers believe that the real reason behind the decision

Saddam Hussein and his family during happier times. The photo includes his two brothers-in-law, who defected in 1995 and then were killed the following February.

AP/Wide World Photos

was that the leadership did not want to call attention to the fact that an embarrassingly large proportion of Iraq's political establishment had roots in Tikrit and were related to Saddam.

Other Institutions

At one time, a single institution did matter—the Revolutionary Command Council (RCC) of the Baath Party. Like a Communist country's central committee, the RCC was the highest de facto authority. It was chaired by Saddam Hussein who was also president of the republic, commander in chief of the armed forces, and secretary general of the Baath Party.

The RCC functioned as a collective decision-making body during much of the decade after the Baath Party seized power. The situation changed dramatically in July 1979 when al-Bakr was replaced by Saddam Hussein. By 1982 the new president had forced out all RCC members with an independent base of support and replaced them with people loyal to him personally. During the next twenty years, he reduced by the size and influence of the RCC.

One of the most important challenges facing the RCC and the party as a whole was control over the military. Considering the military's tradition of intervention in Iraqi politics, the leadership's suspicion of it was not unjustified.

The importance of the military was reflected in the composition of the first RCC, the five members of which were all career officers, and in the domination of the initial Baathist cabinet by individuals closely associated with prominent military figures. From the very moment the new regime assumed power, therefore, civilian party activists were fearful of the power that senior military commanders wielded in the state bureaucracy. "Turf" rivalries between the civilian and the military wings of the party were compounded by ideological differences between the two groups, with the professional soldiers tending to be more moderate and pragmatic than the more doctrinaire and ideologically oriented Baathists.

Only days after the 1968 coup, the civilian wing of the party, led by Saddam Hussein, moved to neutralize the most prominent military figures. Within a few years, most senior officers had been removed from positions of influence in the government and been replaced by civilian party functionaries. Significantly, the proportion of army officers in the RCC declined from 100 percent in the immediate aftermath of the 1968 coup to 40 percent in the second RCC established in November 1969. In the late 1970s and early 1980s, it fell to about 20 percent.

The armed forces underwent repeated purges as scores of officers were dismissed, forced to retire, and even executed. Political loyalty to the regime became a much more important consideration than professional competence in determining promotions. Only party members were allowed into the military academies. Soldiers were informed that belonging to non-Baathist organizations was a crime punishable by death.

The outbreak of the war with Iran in 1980 revived latent tensions and animosities between the political and military leaderships. After Iraqi forces suffered serious defeats in 1982, senior army commanders were reported to be highly resentful of the excessive centralization of decision making in Saddam Hussein's hands. After an aborted attempt to force Saddam to step down in 1982, he launched a major purge of the military and executed scores of high-ranking officers whom he suspected of agitating for his removal.

In an attempt to undermine the ability of army officers to develop their own power bases, the government accelerated their rotation from one branch of the military to another. In addition, officers blamed for defeats on the battlefield were executed for treason as a lesson to their colleagues. In several instances, successful officers were summoned to Baghdad after being told that they were going to be awarded medals for their performance at the front. Upon reaching the capital, they were arrested, and some were executed.

Saddam Hussein also tried to buy the officer corps' loyalty. Military spending was increased, and officers were given special benefits and privileges, including better housing, higher salaries, and access to government-controlled stores filled with imported goods unavailable to the majority of Iraqis.

This mixture of carrot and stick, combined with the frightening prospect of an Iranian victory, succeeded in ensuring the army's loyalty throughout the war. Yet after the war ended in 1988, there were once again rumors of coup attempts, followed by the execution of scores of officers.

With Iraq's defeat in 1991, many analysts hoped that the military might finally topple the regime. Saddam understood the threat and took steps to foil possible coup attempts during the summer and fall of 1991. He appointed a new army chief of staff, replaced the heads of the air force and the elite **Republican Guard,** and increased the rotation of senior military commanders.

Despite these and other precautionary measures, four officers in the Republican Guard attempted a coup in June 1992. Shortly afterward, two hundred officers were purged, and many of them were executed. During the course of the next decade, reports and rumors of attempted coups surfaced on a regular basis. The most serious, in mid-1995, was organized by a senior general who had been close to Saddam. Afterward, the general's mutilated body was delivered to his family—one of Saddam's favorite ways of publicizing the cost of "treason" against his regime.

The last major component of the regime was its collection of intelligence agencies that rivaled those of any other totalitarian regime in terms of the reach and brutality. The secret police was made up of not one but four distinct organizations. The most powerful was the **General Intelligence Apparatus,** which developed out of the Baathist secret police created by Saddam Hussein when the party was still underground. It handled both internal security and overseas operations but focused on monitoring the army, the bureaucracy, the Baath Party, and the "popular organizations" affiliated to it. The **General Security Directorate** was primarily in charge of domestic operations. **Military Intelligence** was set up to spy on the Iraqi armed forces, gather intelligence on foreign countries, monitor the activities of Iraqis living abroad, and arrange assassinations of Iraqi dissidents in exile. Finally, **Special Security** was directly attached to the presidential palace and provided Saddam Hussein with information on key government officials.

The existence of these distinct security services points to the leadership's paranoia and obsession with political control. It also reflects Saddam Hussein's reliance on divide-and-rule tactics as a way of preventing any single institution from becoming a threat to his personal power. Thus, the various intelligence agencies were given overlapping responsibilities, and they were instructed to spy not only on the population, the bureaucracy, the party, the army, and foreign countries, but on one another.

Public Policy

Because of its oil, Iraq has a greater economic potential than most third world countries. Unfortunately, Iraq's resources were squandered by a leadership that chose to use them to try to establish Iraq as the single most important force in the Arab world. To fulfill this ambition, Saddam Hussein led Iraq into three disastrous wars that ultimately destroyed his regime and devastated the country. Thus, Iraqis have suffered not only defeat in war but also continued poverty, both of which could have been avoided.

Economic Reform

When the Baath Party seized power in 1968, its vaguely socialist rhetoric offered no strategy for stimulating economic growth. Yet the absence of a concrete economic agenda was not really disturbing to the new elite, whose first priority was neither economic nor social, but political.

During the Baath's first decade in power, the leadership used economic policy primarily as a tool to consolidate its power. It is in this light that we should examine the tremendous increase in the state's economic role. By the late 1970s about 25 percent of the economically active population worked in government-related jobs.

By having the public sector serve as an employer of last resort, the leadership hoped to eliminate unemployment and increase popular support for the regime. In addition, the nationalization of many key businesses, the tightening of state regulations over industry and trade, and the extensive land reform measures of 1970 were all designed to increase the regime's control over the population.

The expansion of the public sector, however, was expensive. Financing it was made possible by the quadrupling of oil prices in world markets in 1973 and the nationalization of the oil industry the year before. The regime suddenly found itself the beneficiary of unprecedented oil revenues, which it used not only to increase state control but also to modernize the country and to extend basic social services to most of the population.

During the 1970s and 1980s, the state's modernizing policies radically changed the face of Iraq. In two short decades the country's infrastructure was drastically upgraded and expanded. Modern highways, bridges, airports, and hotels were built. Irrigation systems were developed, and electricity and running water were provided in rural areas whose residents could only have dreamed of having such services just a few years before. Suddenly, people in the countryside had television sets and refrigerators, sometimes handed out by the government.

The increased oil revenues also enabled the Baath leadership to provide the population with an impressive array of social services. Glaring poverty was considerably reduced. University graduates were guaranteed a job in the bureaucracy. The middle class grew. The state made large tracts of government-owned land available at low prices. Unemployment all but disappeared. Comprehensive social legislation was enacted to benefit workers. Rent controls were put into effect to guarantee access to housing. Basic commodities were heavily subsidized by the state.

The leadership also improved the condition of women in a country in which they traditionally have suffered fewer social constraints than in the rest of the Persian Gulf. Day-care centers were built. Legislation was passed to prevent discrimination against women in the workplace and to provide for the same salaries men received and paid maternity leave. By the late 1970s these measures had yielded significant results, with more women employed in the professions and the civil service than ever before. Further, following the outbreak

Liberalization in Iraq

AS NOTED IN THE TEXT, the regime allowed some liberalization of the economy in the 1970s and during a brief period between the Iranian and first Gulf wars. However, by the time the Baath regime fell in 2003, it probably had more de facto control over the economy than at any time after it came to power.

Therefore, any significant movement toward a more open and competitive economy will have to come with the transition to a new regime and the reconstruction of an economy that has been stymied by the insurgency, especially in Sunni-dominated parts of the country. Liberalization might also be made problematic by the fact that the vast majority of the money committed to rebuilding the country's infrastructure—a necessary precondition for any program for economic development—has gone to American firms.

of the war with Iran, women joined the labor force to replace men sent to the front.

The government also sought to improve educational and health services, which were provided free of charge. It spent an unprecedented amount of money to train nurses and physicians, and it expanded the number of clinics and hospitals in rural areas that had been neglected by the preceding governments. These efforts produced significant improvements in public health. Iraqis born in 1984 could expect to live an average of eight to nine years longer than those born two decades earlier. Meanwhile, infant mortality rates decreased from 140 to 80 per 1,000 live births between 1960 and 1981.

Similarly, schools, universities, and technical institutes were built or expanded. As a result, the number of graduates from primary schools doubled between 1973 and 1979. During the same period, the number of graduates from secondary schools tripled, and the number of graduates from universities and technical institutes jumped to eighteen thousand a year. The efforts made at the level of secondary education were particularly remarkable, because the percentage of the eligible Iraqis enrolled in secondary schools rose from 38 percent in 1976 to 67 percent in 1984.

Realizing that adult illiteracy rates remained high, the government also launched a massive literacy campaign in 1978. In its characteristically heavy-handed style, the regime forced all illiterates between the ages of fifteen and forty-five to participate. Public buildings were put at the disposal of the literacy campaign, and efforts were made to reach the most remote corners of Iraq. Marsh dwellers were forced to attend "floating schools," while nomads were assigned to "traveling schools" with special facilities that could be moved. To facilitate participation by mothers, hundreds of new nurseries were built. This massive effort paid off. Many women received their first formal education. Within just a few years hundreds of thousands of Iraqis learned to read and write.

Thus, during its first decade in power, the Baath contributed substantially to the socioeconomic development of Iraq. Unfortunately, these results were achieved through rigid repression and systematic political indoctrination akin to that practiced by the Soviets during the Stalinist era. Moreover, Saddam Hussein could have improved the living standards of his people even more had it not been for his diversion of Iraq's resources to the development of domestic agencies of repression and a massive arms buildup that consumed more than 40 percent of the budget from the 1980s onward.

Most importantly, the prosperity of the 1970s had been due not to an increase in productivity or to a diversification or expansion of the economy, but to the massive injection of oil revenues. Oil money, however, could not indefinitely compensate for the structural weaknesses of the economy that were increasingly apparent by the end of the decade.

In an effort to address these problems and improve economic performance, the authorities moved toward economic liberalization at the time that Saddam Hussein became president. Many farms and state-owned service industries were sold. The government encouraged foreign investment and reduced the bureaucracy's cumbersome controls.

Unfortunately, economic liberalization mostly benefited a group of speculators and wheeler-dealers with connections to the regime. Industrial production stagnated, shortages of essential goods continued to plague the country, and black markets in products and currencies flourished.

Even more importantly, after the invasion of Kuwait, it was impossible to talk about any kind of coherent economic policy in Iraq. The country spent at least 40 percent of its total income on the military. It also had to endure the sanctions (to be discussed shortly) that largely kept it out of global markets and sharply limited the amount of oil it could sell. Last but by no means least, Saddam and his entourage diverted as much as half of the income that was brought in through the United Nations *oil for food program* to the pocketbooks of the elite.

The Iran-Iraq War of 1980–88

The subordination of Iraq's welfare to its leaders' personal ambitions was not limited to domestic policy. Even more important were the decisions that took the country to war three times in fifteen years. (See table 14.3.) Because it is so important for politics in Iraq today, we will put off discussion of the U.S.-led invasion of 2003 until the next section.

Iran and Iraq have long been rivals. To some extent, this stems from the religious and ethnic differences discussed. However, tensions between the two countries also exist because of their competition for power in the Persian Gulf and the Middle East as a whole.

Until the late 1960s, the British military presence in the Gulf had helped prevent the hostility between the two countries from degenerating into open warfare. However, when the British announced that they would withdraw their military forces east of Suez by 1971, the rivalry between Iran and Iraq was suddenly renewed.

By that time, Iran had emerged as the more powerful of the two countries. Its population was about three

▌**TABLE 14.3** Iraq's First Two Wars under Saddam Hussein: A Chronology

22 September 1980	Iraq invades Iran.
June 1982	Iran drives Iraqi army back into Iraq. Saddam expresses willingness to end conflict, but Iran refuses.
July 1982	The war is now being waged in Iraqi territory, and develops into increasingly bloody stalemate.
26 November 1984	Desperate for improved relations with West, Iraq restores diplomatic relations with United States.
10 February 1986	Iranian troops capture Fao Peninsula.
April 1988	Iraqi forces push Iranian army back across border. The war finally turns in Iraq's favor.
20 August 1988	Cease-fire with Iran is signed.
2 August 1990	Iraq invades Kuwait.
29 November 1990	UN Security Council authorizes anti-Iraq coalition to drive Iraqi forces out of Kuwait if Saddam has not pulled out by 15 January 1991.
17 January 1991	U.S.-led coalition forces launch massive air campaign against Iraq. Devastating raids continue for six weeks.
24 February 1991	Coalition forces begin ground war that lasts only one hundred hours. Iraqi army is routed.
27 February 1991	Ground offensive is halted after Kuwait is liberated.
3 March 1991	Baghdad accepts coalition's cease-fire terms.

times and its area almost four times that of Iraq. It was also wealthier and more developed. Perhaps most importantly of all, the Shah had benefited from military and economic support from a succession of American administrations that had decided to use his regime as the pillar of its policy in the Gulf.

In the late 1960s the shah reignited a long-standing border conflict with Iraq. Since 1937 the internationally recognized border between Iran and Iraq had been set on the Iranian bank of the Shatt al-Arab River, which gave Iraq exclusive control over it. In 1969 the shah unilaterally abrogated the 1937 treaty and announced that Iran would now recognize the border as lying along the middle of the waterway's main channel, in effect claiming sovereignty over half the river.

Tensions between Iran and Iraq continued to build. In 1970 an Iranian-sponsored coup was foiled in Baghdad. Meanwhile, with direct encouragement from the United States, the shah began to project himself as the policeman of the Gulf. In November 1971 Iran occupied three islands strategically located at the entrance of the Strait of Hormuz, off the coast of the United Arab Emirates (UAE). In retaliation, Iraq cut off diplomatic relations with Tehran.

Much more threatening to Baghdad, however, was Iranian support for a Kurdish uprising within Iraq. The rebellion proved so effective that it became a major threat to the Baghdad government, which was forced to make a major concession to Iran. At an **Organization for Petroleum Exporting Countries (OPEC)** meeting in Algiers in March 1975, Saddam Hussein negotiated an agreement with the shah that called for an end to Iranian support for the Iraqi Kurds in exchange for Baghdad's recognition of Iran's claim to half the Shatt al-Arab.

In 1979, however, Iranian-Iraqi relations had taken a turn for the worse. The overthrow of the shah and the establishment of the Islamic Republic headed by Ayatollah Khomeini in Tehran had created an entirely new situation in the Persian Gulf (see Chapter 13). Soon, Iraqi authorities were accusing the Islamic Republic of interference in its political life—claims that were not unfounded. Meddling by Tehran was all the more threatening to the Baathist regime because Iraqi Shiites were increasingly alienated from the government in Baghdad.

Yet despite clear evidence of Iranian involvement, it is difficult to accept Iraq's claim that it started the Iran-Iraq War in self-defense. To a large extent, the war represented a bid for regional hegemony by Saddam Hussein.

The 1979 Camp David Accords and Egyptian president Anwar al-Sadat's peace treaty with Israel had left Egypt—traditionally the most influential country in Arab politics—ostracized by the rest of the Arab world. Saddam Hussein, who had led the opposition to the normalization of relations between Israel and Egypt, must have realized that oil-rich Iraq now had a unique opportunity to establish itself as the leading Arab power. He also had to have noticed the effects of the ongoing revolutionary turmoil in Tehran. The Iranian officer corps had been decimated in the wave of purges and executions that followed the shah's downfall. Given reports about the declining morale in and organization of the Iranian military, Saddam must have assumed that a sudden Iraqi attack could provoke the fall of the Iranian government.

Whatever the exact set of motivations, the Iraqi army invaded Iran in September 1980. Unfortunately for Iraq, the Iranian army did not disintegrate, and the Islamic Republic in Tehran survived by gaining the enthusiastic support of most Iranians who rallied around the regime to defend it against the invasion. Far from being the short campaign that Saddam Hussein had envisioned, the war turned into a protracted and extremely costly stalemate.

The Iran-Iraq War lasted almost eight years. It was the bloodiest conflict in the history of the modern Middle East and the most devastating military confrontation to date between two third world nations. As many as a million Iraqis and Iranians died in the war, and hundreds of thousands more were disabled for life. Virtually no Iraqi family was spared, and all-too-many parents had several children die at the front.

The Iran-Iraq War was also one of the most futile conflicts in history. It was largely caused by the personal hatred between two tyrants, each aspiring for regional leadership and imbued with a messianic conception of himself. Saddam Hussein saw Khomeini's revolutionary zeal and mixture of religion and politics as a dangerous threat that could be eliminated only through the annihilation of the man and the regime he had created. Khomeini, in turn, perceived Saddam as the archetypical modernizing, secular leader who had betrayed Islam and who had to be eradicated. Khomeini also had personal accounts to settle with Saddam, who in 1978, at the shah's request, had expelled him from the Shiite holy city of Najaf, where Khomeini had lived and taught for fourteen years. By 1981 Khomeini had made the ouster of Saddam from power one of the preconditions for a cease-fire. His refusal to compromise on that point, combined with Saddam's refusal to step down, largely explains why the war lasted so long.

To justify this senseless and increasingly bloody war, both regimes engaged in extravagant and self-serving rhetoric. Thus, Baghdad described the war as a valiant defense of the "Arab homeland" against the "fanatic Persians," the "Persian racists," or the "fire-eating Persians."

A scene of devastation from the Iran-Iraq War.

For its part, Tehran depicted it as a religious crusade or jihad (holy war) against "Baathist infidels" who had betrayed Islam and were oppressing Iran's Shiite brethren in Iraq.

After almost eight years of fighting, Iranian and Iraqi forces were located almost exactly where they had been when the war started. Neither country had achieved its war aims. Exhausted and lacking viable alternatives, the Islamic Republic finally agreed to sign the cease-fire for which Iraq had long been pleading.

The First Gulf War

Upon its seizure of power, the Baathist regime immediately launched a propaganda campaign against Israel and the United States. Then, in 1972, feeling increasingly threatened by the pro-Western regime of the shah, Iraq signed a Treaty of Friendship and Cooperation with the Soviet Union. This development caused great alarm in Washington, where it was interpreted as a sign that Iraq had become a Soviet client state, giving it a foothold in the strategically important and oil-rich Gulf region. Meanwhile, Baghdad also offered support to extremist Palestinian factions and adopted a confrontational stance toward the moderate, pro-Western Arab states in the Gulf.

From the mid-1970s onward, however, Iraq's relations with the Arab Gulf states improved significantly.

Iraq also distanced itself from the Soviet Union because of the latter's invasion of Afghanistan in 1979. It also developed closer ties with a few Western European countries—in particular France, which had become its major arms supplier.

The outbreak of the Iran-Iraq War changed things even more. Desperate for financial, political, and military support from Arab and Western states, the Iraqi regime toned down its militant rhetoric and began portraying itself as a bulwark against Iran's attempt to export its fundamentalist revolution to the Arab world. Within a few months, relations with Egypt, Jordan, Saudi Arabia, and the smaller Gulf states improved dramatically. Weapons, spare parts, munitions, military advisers, and migrant workers began to flow in. Even more decisive was the $40 billion in aid for Iraq's war effort sent by the Gulf states.

Even relations with the United States improved. For its part, the Reagan administration was interested in bettering relations with Baghdad out of fear that an Iranian victory would result in the spread of Khomeini's brand of Islamic fundamentalism throughout the Arab world. In one of history's many ironies, the man who was most responsible for smoothing American-Iraqi relations was Donald Rumsfeld, who would spearhead the third war almost exactly twenty years later. The United States provided a limited amount of ostensibly nonmilitary aid, although computers, for instance, could be used for military as well as civilian purposes. By 1987 Baghdad had become the world's largest recipient of U.S. government–guaranteed agricultural loans, the biggest single overseas buyer of American rice, and one of the largest importers of American wheat and corn. Washington also supplied intelligence information on the movement of Iranian troops.

When hostilities between Iran and Iraq came to an end in summer 1988, the prevailing view was that Iraq was now led by a reformed, moderate, and pragmatic regime. Further, from Washington's perspective, Iraq was seen as a necessary counterweight to the militantly anti-American Islamic Republic of Iran. Thus, for the next two years, Western governments were willing to ignore the continuing repression and human rights violations inside Iraq and the mounting indications that the country was still governed by a dangerous and expansionist regime.

But only for two years. The beginning of 1990 was marked by a return to the sort of belligerent rhetoric that the Baathist regime had not used since the early 1970s. Iraq seemed to be launching a new bid for leadership of the Arab world. As in the past, this was most evident in the upsurge in anti-Western and anti-Israeli rhetoric.

At a meeting of Arab states that February, Saddam Hussein gave his most virulent anti-American speech in more than a decade. He pointed out that the end of the cold war, the collapse of Communist regimes in Eastern Europe, and the weakening of the Soviet Union had left the United States in an unprecedented position of influence in the Arab world. He then predicted that the U.S. government would use its new power to try to impose American hegemony over the Gulf and to encourage Israeli aggression against Arab states.

Barely a month later, an Iranian-born journalist working for a British weekly was arrested by Iraqi authorities while investigating an explosion at a missile plant near Baghdad. Accused of spying for Israel and forced into making a confession, he was tried, convicted, and hanged within a week, despite pleas from the British government and the international community as a whole.

Throughout the spring of 1990, there was mounting evidence of Iraqi efforts to smuggle nuclear weapons technology from the West, accelerate the development of biological and chemical weapons facilities, and build a long-range artillery piece dubbed the "Supergun." On 1 April, fearful that the Israeli government was planning strikes against Iraqi nuclear or chemical facilities, as it had done ten years earlier, Saddam Hussein made a fiery speech in which he declared that, should Israel attack Iraq, Baghdad would retaliate with a chemical attack that would "burn half of Israel."

After April 1990 Saddam Hussein reserved his sharpest attacks for the Arab states in the Gulf. For eight years, he argued, Iraq had shed "rivers of blood" to protect the Gulf dynasties and the "Arab homeland" against Khomeini's revolutionary zeal. Yet, despite Baghdad's repeated requests, the oil-rich Arab states in the Gulf remained unwilling to cancel Iraq's war debt or provide it with additional funds to rebuild its economy. Such intransigence, Saddam contended, was an insult to Iraq and its war dead.

Meanwhile, Kuwait and the UAE continued to exceed their oil production quotas, driving down prices and depriving Iraq of much-needed revenues. Saddam claimed that excess pumping by the Gulf states had already cost Iraq $84 billion, which he took to be evidence that the small Gulf states were engaged in a plot against Iraq hatched by "imperialist and Zionist forces." In June and July, infuriated by what he saw as the arrogance of the Gulf rulers, Saddam pressed them even further, asking for $30 billion in additional grants.

He also charged Kuwait with stealing Iraq's oil by pumping excessive quantities from the Rumaila oil field, which lies mostly beneath Iraqi territory but stretches just across the border into Kuwait. Finally, Iraq revived its old demand to be given or leased the two Kuwaiti islands of Warbah and Bubiyan as a way of providing Iraq with a deep-water port in the Gulf. The Kuwaiti emir failed to take Iraq's threats very seriously and worded his refusal of Saddam's demands in language that was highly critical of Iraq. This, combined with Saddam's belief that the United States would not be able to reverse an Iraqi takeover of Kuwait, sealed the tiny nation's fate. Saddam appears to have believed that Saudi Arabia would never allow U.S. troops on Saudi soil, leaving the United States with no way of forcing Iraq out of Kuwait.

On 2 August 1990, 100,000 Iraqi troops invaded Kuwait and occupied the country in a mere six hours. By seizing its neighbor, Iraq would not only automatically eliminate its debt to it but also suddenly own about 20 percent of the world's proven oil reserves, placing itself in a much better position to influence oil prices. Control over Kuwait's wealth also would enable Iraq to repay its debt to Western European countries and to launch ambitious new development programs. Given the disastrous state of the Iraqi economy, Saddam Hussein may well have believed that his long-term political future depended on his ability to gain access to Kuwait's resources. Saddam's regional position also would be greatly enhanced by an Iraqi annexation of Kuwait, which the Iraqi leader could present as a successful

Globalization and Iraq

IRAQ IS ONE of the few countries in the world where the impact of globalization has been felt more as a result of political than economic forces.

Of course, globalization has had an economic impact. The United Nations imposed sanctions before the first Gulf war that continued for the most part until the 2003 defeat, which meant that most Iraqis did not have access, for instance, to adequate medical care. Many, too, had at most marginally acceptable diets. Estimates vary, but somewhere between a hundred thousand and a million Iraqis died as a result of easily treatable diseases and malnutrition during that twelve-year period.

"reconquest" of lands that Iraq had long claimed were rightly its own. Finally, by providing Iraq with a major port on the Gulf, the takeover of Kuwait would reduce its economic and military vulnerability especially vis-à-vis Iran.

Yet, contrary to what Saddam had anticipated, the world community demonstrated an unusual degree of unity in demanding the immediate, unconditional withdrawal of Iraqi forces from Kuwait. The United States, far from limiting itself to a verbal condemnation, took the lead in the international campaign against Baghdad. To Saddam's even greater surprise, the Soviet Union, Iraq's traditional patron, joined Washington in condemning Baghdad. France, the European country closest to Iraq, also insisted on an Iraqi withdrawal. The Arabs were split. Saddam, who had hoped that the Arab world would rally behind him, suddenly faced an alliance that included several key Arab states, including Egypt and Syria. Over three-quarters of a million allied troops, including 500,000 Americans, were sent to the region as part of *Operation Desert Shield* in an attempt to convince Iraq to pull out of Kuwait.

At this point, however, he still could have backed down. Instead, he decided to leave his forces in Kuwait, confident that the United States would not go to war with Iraq over the emirate, that Arab states would never dare ally with the United States against "Brotherly Iraq," and that, if they did, the masses throughout the Arab world would rise up in Baghdad's support. He turned out to be wrong on all three counts.

Repeated attempts to reach a negotiated settlement failed in part because of Saddam Hussein's belief in the primacy of coercion and intimidation over diplomacy and negotiation. Unlike those who see the use of force as a last resort, the Baathist top leadership was composed of individuals who saw concessions as signs of weakness and who consequently believed that compromise should be resisted unless one has absolutely no other option.

The United States launched *Operation Desert Storm* and went to war on 17 January 1991. They were backed by a broad coalition of the world's most powerful nations, including many in the Gulf region. The Arab masses did

A typical scene of the destruction in Baghdad during the first Gulf War.

Reuters/Bettmann/CORBIS

not rise up in defense of Iraq. By early March, less than a year after Iraqi tanks had rolled into Kuwait and only forty days after the beginning of the war, Iraq had been transformed from a major regional power into a devastated country, subject to the dictates of the United Nations and the U.S.-led coalition.

After that, the Iraqi regime complied only grudgingly and incompletely with UN resolutions that compelled it to fully disclose its weapons of mass destruction programs and to dismantle them. It allegedly tried to assassinate former U.S. president George H. W. Bush during his visit to Kuwait in April 1993. It interfered repeatedly with the work of inspection teams sent to monitor Iraqi compliance with UN resolutions. And it has continued to support terror as an instrument of state policy and failed to cease its brutal repression of the Iraqi people as required by UN Security Council Resolution 688.

All these issues would help lead to the third war, the regime's destruction, and the chaotic transition that followed in its wake.

The Third War and the New Iraq

The first Gulf War settled little more than the liberation of Kuwait. It would be another dozen years before one dramatic act in Iraq's political history—Baath rule—ended and another equally dramatic one—the transition to a new regime—began.

When Iraqi forces withdrew from Kuwait and surrendered several days later, the Allies were faced with a choice. They could suspend their own offensive operations, or they could push forward to Baghdad and force Saddam Hussein from power.

The first President Bush and his colleagues chose the former option. There are three generally accepted reasons for their decision. First, the mandate given for the use of force by the coalition was limited to freeing Kuwait, and Bush did not, therefore, feel he had the legal authority to continue the fight. Second, Bush's advisors told him that the drive to reach and capture Baghdad would be far bloodier than the war had been so far, which had claimed fewer than two hundred American lives, many of them through accidents or friendly fire. From what we have seen since the end of major hostilities in May 2003, Bush's advisors were probably correct. Third and probably most important, the Bush administration expected Kurds and Shiites, if not Sunni Arabs, to rise up and topple the regime.

Bush's hoped-for rebellions did break out, but they did not have the result he had wanted. Saddam's forces responded with the kind of brutality the world had come to expect of it. Iraqi troops battled Kurdish insurgents and recovered large parts of their protected region until allied forces returned to create **safe havens** and turned the area into an autonomous region that largely remained beyond Baghdad's control until the 2003 war. If anything, Saddam's troops were even crueler in the south. Among other things, they drained the swamps, which were a vital part of the ecology and economy on which millions of Shiites depended. Eventually, a bombing campaign forced the regime's troops to leave the region. A **no-fly zone** was established over the Shiite and Kurdish regions where Iraqi military planes could no longer operate.

Nonetheless, Saddam remained in power. His military, of course, was now much weaker. But there seemed to be few signs that he could be overthrown, despite explicit attempts by the West to create a viable opposition in the exile community.

A Decade of Tension

As we saw in the last chapter on Iran, sometimes the origins of a country's political difficulties lie outside its borders. That was also true for Iraq, especially after the terrorist attacks of 11 September 2001 and the Bush administration's response to them. But even in the decade before 9/11 when a full-blown war with Iraq was rarely on anyone's political agenda, pressures from Washington and elsewhere made economic and political life difficult in Iraq (see Table 14.4).

The West pursued what international relations scholars would call an active policy of containment against the regime. Economic sanctions remained in place, denying Iraq the ability to sell oil or buy almost anything in global markets. Those rules were eased a bit in 1996 when Iraq was permitted to sell a limited amount of oil, ostensibly to buy food, medicine, and other humanitarian supplies.

Allied forces also flew hundreds of thousands of sorties over Iraqi airspace. Any time an Iraqi antiaircraft locked onto an allied aircraft, the allied plane would launch tons of bombs, even though there was next to no chance that the Iraqi batteries could hit one of the planes. The bombing was particularly severe anytime the regime did something the West found unacceptable, such as the allegation that it planned to assassinate George H. W. Bush when he visited Kuwait shortly after he left office in 1993.

Of all the issues roiling Iraq's relations with the rest of the world, nothing was more important or more indicative of the cat-and-mouse game the regime played with the international community about its **weapons of**

▌**TABLE 14.4** Events in Iraq: 1990–2005

YEAR	EVENT
1990	Iraq occupies Kuwait
1991	First Gulf War
1992	Iraqis allegedly try to assassinate former U.S. President George W. Bush
1994	Iraq drains water from marshes in the south, endangering the livelihood of many Shiites
1996	Oil for food program authorized by the United Nations
1997–98	UNSCOM forced to leave, allowed back, finds Iraq in breach of UN agreements, forced to leave permanently
1999	Weekly and often daily bombings of Iraqi targets continue by primarily American and British air forces
2001	9/11 terrorist attacks
2002	George W. Bush implicates Iraq in his "axis of evil" State of the Union Speech
2003	U.S.-led invasion topples Saddam Hussein's regime; insurgency breaks out almost immediately and continues
2005	Provisional government elected primarily to draft a constitution for a permanent regime slated to take office in late 2005 or early 2006

mass destruction (WMD) program. The **United Nations Special Commission (UNSCOM)** was created in the wake of the 1991 Gulf War to monitor Iraq's compliance with the cease-fire resolution that called for the elimination of its entire WMD program, including missiles and other delivery systems. According to the terms of this resolution, the embargo on Iraq would be lifted once UNSCOM certified that Iraq had been fully disarmed.

UNSCOM relied on spot inspections of sites suspected of being the location for the manufacturing or stockpiling of WMD. Once inspected, these sites would remain closely monitored through sophisticated surveillance equipment.

Between 1991 and 1998, UNSCOM proved quite effective. Tons of chemical and biological weapons were located and destroyed. And yet, in late 1998, UNSCOM's job was far from over, as Iraq was still believed to be hiding biological and chemical stocks. In December 1998 Baghdad finally suspended cooperation with UNSCOM. It claimed that some of UNSCOM's members were acting as spies for the United States and that the commission's leader, Australian diplomat Richard Butler, was an American client (both of which could possibly have been true). In addition, the regime argued that, even if UNSCOM certified that all Iraqi WMD had been eliminated, the United States would still refuse to lift the sanctions on Iraq as long as Saddam Hussein remained in power.

The Iraqi government's refusal to allow UNSCOM to operate prompted a four-day bombing campaign of Iraq by American and British forces. Shortly thereafter, Baghdad announced that UNSCOM inspectors would never be allowed back into the country (UNSCOM's weapons inspectors had left Iraq a few days before the U.S. and British attacks began). UNSCOM was dead, and the UN

UNSCOM inspectors examine suspected chemical and biological warheads.

Security Council and the Iraqi government were unable to agree on a new way of inspecting that either could accept (www.un.org/Depts/unscom).

When UNSCOM was forced out, many outside observers thought Iraq still possessed some chemical and biological weapons, had the capacity to make many more of them quickly, and that their ongoing nuclear program had led Iraq to be dangerously close to developing a bomb at the time of the first Gulf War. Saddam Hussein said or did nothing to indicate otherwise, which, as we will see in a moment, contributed heavily to his ultimate defeat.

But it is safe to say that Iraq was not seen as one of the world's most dangerous places until 9/11. And, even then, the reaction that led to war came only from Washington and London, not the other major Western capitals.

It is also important to note that by 9/11, the coalition had already begun to unravel. Some of the allies thought the policy of containment was working well enough that Iraq was no longer a threat to its neighbors or anyone else. Others, most notably France and Russia, wanted to ease or even eliminate sanctions because of their economic ties to Iraq that had been interrupted following the invasion of Kuwait.

The Third War

The terrorist attacks on the World Trade Center and the Pentagon changed everything as far as the new George W. Bush administration was concerned. They had already been critical of what they saw as the weakness of a number of Clinton policies, including the containment of Iraq. But the day before the attacks, there was no reason to believe that major changes in policies toward Iraq were forthcoming.

Bush's response to the attacks was surprising, at least to his critics. After a few hours of uncertainty, his first public statements reflected a resolve and a firmness few thought he could provide. That was evident in the massive support given to the decision to go to war to topple the Taliban regime and undermine the al-Qaeda networks it harbored less than a month after 9/11.

There are also rumors that President Bush and Vice President Dick Cheney decided on the night of 9/11 or the next morning that war with Iraq was all but inevitable. As the stories go, neither looked forward to attacking Baghdad again, but it seems that both assumed that no war against terrorism could be won as long as Saddam Hussein and the Baath remained in power.

We may never know when the most critical decisions about Iraq were made. Nonetheless, it was clear by the time that Bush gave his 2002 State of the Union speech

President Bush giving his "axis of evil" speech in 2002.

that Iraq was his next highest priority (www.whitehouse.gov/news/releases/2002/01/20020129-11.html).

Bush certainly did not mince his words when discussing North Korea, Iran, and Iraq, which he labeled an "axis of evil." Regarding Iraq, he stated:

> Iraq continues to flaunt its hostility toward America and to support terror. The Iraqi regime has plotted to develop anthrax, and nerve gas, and nuclear weapons for over a decade. This is a regime that has already used poison to murder thousands of its own citizens—leaving the bodies of mothers huddled over their dead children. This is a regime that agreed to international inspections—then kicked out the inspectors. This is a regime that has something to hide from the civilized world.
>
> States like these, and their terrorist allies, constitute an axis of evil, arming to threaten the peace of the world. By seeking weapons of mass destruction, these regimes pose a grave and growing danger. They could provide these arms to terrorists, giving them the means to match their hatred. They could attack our allies or attempt to blackmail the United States. In any of these cases, the price of indifference would be catastrophic.

As Bush's speech indicated, American claims about Iraq revolved around three main themes.

- Iraq still had a stockpile of weapons of mass destruction. It may have had fewer than it did in 1991, but it not only had weapons but had the capacity to add new ones to its arsenal, possibly including primitive nuclear bombs.

- It had close ties to terrorist organizations that it had frequently supported over the years and to which it could supply such weapons.

■ Therefore, Iraq was a threat not only to the existence of Israel and the stability of the Middle East but to global security as a whole.

Each of those claims was questioned by Bush's critics in the United States, Iraq, and beyond.

■ Even if Iraq had weapons of mass destruction, its stockpiles were but a shadow of what they had been in 1990 and 1991. It was also not clear that the material they had tried to buy illegally abroad were for these and other weapons programs. And perhaps most importantly of all, there were no signs that Iraq had any plans to transfer those weapons to terrorist or other dangerous organizations.

■ There was no doubt that Iraq had supported and harbored some of the militant Palestinian terrorists who were committed to destroying the state of Israel. But these were not the same individuals or organizations who were responsible for the 9/11 attacks. There were reports that one of the leaders of the hijackings had met with Iraqi intelligence officials in the Czech Republic, but that was never confirmed. What's more, the kinds of people who joined al-Qaeda networks were highly critical of secular leaders like Saddam Hussein.

■ Few observers doubted that Saddam Hussein still harbored hopes that his Iraq could become a regional power. However, most intelligence reports indicated that Iraq's military capacity had been seriously eroded by the 1991 war and its aftermath and probably did not pose a serious threat to its neighbors, let alone Israel and the rest of the world.

It is far beyond the scope of this book to speculate on why the Bush administration continued to rely on the worst possible estimates of Iraqi capabilities and intentions (though see the article by James Fallows listed in InfoTrac College Edition Sources listed at the end of the chapter). Neither the Bush administration nor the authorities in Baghdad showed any serious interest in cooperation or even negotiation.

Tensions continued to mount. In May 2002 the United States was preventing the transfer of $5 billion of goods from entering Iraq. Four months later, Bush used his address to the General Assembly of the United Nations to attack what he called the "grave and gathering danger" of Iraq. He charged that if the United Nations did not do so, it would become "irrelevant."

A month later, the U.S. Congress overwhelmingly voted to authorize the use of force if need be. In November, the United Nations Security Council passed Resolution 1441, which found Iraq to be in "material breach" of its resolutions on WMD, and inspectors were allowed into the country once again. In early December, Iraq submitted an all but indecipherable report that claimed it had no such weapons.

Just before Christmas, President Bush approved sending troops to the region, a deployment that was expected to reach 200,000 by March 2003. But this time

On 2 December 2003, U.S. helicopters flew over the area as workers dismantle one of the four giant bronze busts of Saddam Hussein that long dominated Baghdad's skyline, in yet another move aimed at eradicating the former leader's influence in Baghdad.

Anja Niedringhaus/AP/Wide World Photos

the coalition was not holding. France, Germany, Russia, China, and others refused to cooperate on deploying troops at that time. Furthermore, the three powers with vetoes on the Security Council made it clear that they would block any authorization of the use of force until and unless it was completely clear that inspectors could not defuse the crisis.

President Bush would not wait (nor would President Saddam Hussein). In early 2003, the United States was leading a much smaller coalition than it had thirteen years earlier. The only other major power willing to commit a significant number of troops was the United Kingdom.

During late February and the first half of March, the United States and Great Britain lobbied for a new United Nations resolution allowing the use of force. In order for the resolution to pass, they needed nine of the fifteen members of the Security Council to vote in favor of using force against Iraq, and they would also have to convince every permanent member of the Security Council not to veto the action. When it became clear that they would not come close to getting the necessary votes, the United States abandoned its efforts at the UN on 14 March. Three days later, the British ambassador declared diplomatic efforts had failed. Bush gave Saddam and his family forty-eight hours to leave the country. They did not.

Two days later, the military offense dubbed **Operation Iraqi Freedom** began without UN authorization. It began with three days of air attacks on Baghdad and other high priority targets aimed at "decapitating" the Iraqi leadership. Unlike the first Gulf War, the air-only phase of this struggle was very brief. On 21 March, troops began to move toward Baghdad, which fell on 9 April. On 1 May, after flying a plane onto an aircraft carrier himself, Bush declared the end of major combat operations.

Occupation and Insurgency

The end of the formal war did not turn out the way the Bush administration had hoped. They expected that American and allied troops would be cheered as liberators and that they could all but immediately begin the transition to a new and more democratic Iraq.

In fact, only one of the coalition's major goals for the war had been accomplished: Saddam Hussein was out of power. Otherwise, the administration found itself in a political and military quagmire that at least some observers likened to Vietnam. Saddam and most of his colleagues were still on the loose. Less than ten days after the fall of Baghdad, the first demonstration against the presence of coalition (but really American) troops occurred. It was

already becoming clear that while most Iraqis were glad to be rid of Saddam Hussein, they were anything but overjoyed by the prospect of having close to 150,000 American troops on their soil for the indefinite future.

After a few missteps, the United States appointed a veteran diplomat, **Paul Bremer,** to head the civil administration in Iraq. Ironically, the headquarters of Bremer's operation was in one of Saddam's lavish palaces.

From the beginning it was clear that the occupation forces were in for a hard time. At first, they faced widespread lawlessness that included looting of banks and even of historical treasures from Baghdad's museums. British and other troops in the Shiite south faced less widespread, but still serious, discontent. Only in the Kurdish-dominated north were things reasonably calm.

The occupation forces also tried to track down, capture, or kill the remaining leaders from the old regime. After Baghdad fell, the U.S. Department of Defense issued its "deck of cards" that listed the top fifty-two leaders still at large. Saddam Hussein, of course, was the ace of spades (www.defenselink.mil/news/Apr2003/pipc10042003.html).

The cards were not just a publicity stunt. They were

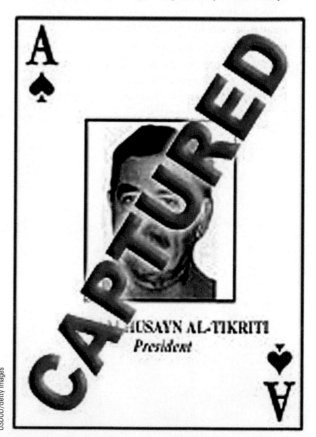

USDOD/Getty Images

Saddam Hussein's "card" from the "deck" of leading Baathists. This version was issued shortly after his capture.

given to troops in the field so that they would have a reasonable chance of identifying Baathists on the run. This was the one area where the occupation forces were reasonably successful, although the hunt absorbed tremendous amounts of time and energy. By late 2004, only four of them were still at large, and the highest ranking of them was the "king of hearts."

On the three other fronts, the occupation forces and civil administrators had a much harder time.

First, in part because of the civil unrest and in part because of the extent of the destruction, it took much longer than expected to rebuild even the most basic components of Iraq's infrastructure. In late 2004 when the main electrical generation plant was returned to Iraqi control, Baghdad still did not have a reliable electrical supply for the entire city.

Second, the United States was never able to find any weapons of mass destruction or even any evidence that the government had been working on them in the months before the invasion. At the end of 2004, the State Department announced that the search was over.

The Insurrection

The third and most vexing problem facing the occupation and the transitional government was the insurrection, which was far more violent and far more disruptive than even the strongest critics of the Bush administration had expected. To cite but two of the most obvious statistics, of the more than 1,350 Americans who had died in Iraq by the end of January 2004, more than 1,000 had been killed after Bush declared that major combat was over; another 15–20,000 have been wounded. No official figures have been kept on the number of Iraqis killed, but the best guess is between 30,000 and 100,000, most of whom were civilians.

The first major wave of the insurrection broke out in the south and was most frequently associated with the Shiite cleric Muqtada al-Sadr. Al-Sadr's father had been one of the four leading Shiite clerics in Iraq and had been killed in 1980. Although he was no supporter of the Baath regime, the younger al-Sadr opposed the presence of coalition forces in the south and in the holy cities of Kerbala and Najaf from the beginning. In summer 2003, he announced plans to create a shadow government whose goal would be turn postwar Iraq into a Muslim state. In so doing, he gathered a loose organization, the Imam Al-Mahdi Army, which engaged in anti-American protests that reached a peak in spring 2004 after the authorities closed down a newspaper al-Sadr edited. At its peak, the forces loyal to him had as many as twenty thousand men, but relatively few arms. Still, they engaged in regular battles in the Shiite cities in the south and in the massive, Shiite dominated Sadr City slum in Baghdad. The

Mohammed Khodor/Reuters/CORBIS

Masked Iraqi insurgents wield rocket-propelled grenade launchers near a burning U.S. Humvee vehicle in the embattled town of Falluja.

insurrections led by al-Sadr and other Shiites were also troublesome to the authorities because many suspect that Iran has been helping them, especially those forces led by clerics.

Al-Sadr joined many leaders who agreed to dissolve their private militias or have them join the official police and security services in summer 2004. While relatively few occupation soldiers were killed in the south, resentment remains intense enough that it is not safe for them to enter cities alone or at night.

The insurgency has been far more intractable in the area that has come to be known as the **Sunni Triangle.** This is the area where Saddam Hussein had his strongest support and includes his hometown and former power base of Tikrit as well as Baghdad, Falluja, and other cities. It is also where most of the fighting has occurred since summer 2004.

Indeed, the term "insurgent" used by the Western media understates the severity of the situation that amounts to what should probably be called a civil war or at least a guerilla war. To the degree that we understand who they are, the insurgents fall into three main categories—supporters of the Baath regime, other Iraqis opposed to the American-led occupation, and some foreign fighters with some sort of connection to al-Qaeda.

The fighting has been far worse than anything that occurred during the formal war. American troops cannot leave their camps without risking being blown up by a bomb left on the road or by an improvised missile sent by a hidden insurgent. The risks are even greater for Iraqis who are thought to be collaborating with the Americans. On 28 February 2005, for instance, more than 120 Iraqis were killed by a suicide bomber at a clinic in Hilla where they were lined up to take the physical exams needed before they could be hired into the new Iraqi security forces.

As these lines were written in March 2005, there were no signs that the insurgency would end at any time in the foreseeable future.

The New Iraq?

One of the ironies of modern warfare is that the victor often ends with major responsibilities for rebuilding the country it defeated. Whatever you think of the merits of the U.S.-led invasion or of the policies since the Baath regime was ousted, it is quite clear that the Bush administration knew from the beginning that after the fighting was over, it had to commit itself to building a stable and democratic Iraq. Where they may have been misguided was in thinking that a new Iraq could be created easily and quickly.

The **Coalition Provisional Authority (CPA)** was created as soon as the Baath were ousted from power. Within a few weeks Paul Bremer was named its administrator. Indications that the United States intended this to be a *provisional* organization are clear from its website that ended in .org rather than .gov, and the site will disappear from the Internet before this book is published. Unlike the war, most of the work of CPA and its successors has been authorized by the United Nations, which has played an active role in helping shape the transition.

After consulting fairly widely, the CPA appointed an Interim Governing Council in June that, in turn, appointed a cabinet in September. The CPA wanted to create a body that was broadly representative of Iraq's three main ethnic groups and ideological factions. But there was little illusion that the council was an independent body. Its main job was to draft an interim constitution, which went into effect in March 2004, and to pave the way for the creation of an **interim government** to which the CPA transferred at least legal sovereignty on 30 June 2004.

At that point, Bremer left. The leading American civilian official became the new ambassador, Michael Negroponte, who had been the U.S. ambassador to the United Nations and became National Director of Intelligence in April 2005. In most respects, however, the handover of sovereignty was more symbolic than real. Virtually none of the members of the interim government were critical of the United States. And more importantly, the fact that this government is being put together under the eye of almost 150,000 occupying troops makes any real claims for its independence more than a little illusory.

Nonetheless, the interim government led by Prime Minister Ayad Alawi took its work seriously. Several of his colleagues paid for their hard work with their lives as victims of the insurgency.

Their most important task was to prepare for Iraq's first ever free election, which was held on 30 January 2005. More than two hundred political parties ran candidates in an election that would be run according to proportional representation (see Chapter 2). In practice, few of those parties had any hope of winning seats, and as voting day neared they came together in three broad coalitions that for all intents and purposes mirrored the country's ethnic and religious divisions.

Like everything else in Iraq, the election proved controversial. President Bush, the interim government, and their supporters lauded the vote and the relative calm associated with it. Critics noted that most Sunni Muslims boycotted the election either out of opposition to the occupation or out of fear that insurgents might kill them. In the end, 58 percent of Iraqis voted, a total that compares favorably with all recent presidential elections in the United States other than 2004. The UN election advisor probably summed up the situation best when he told the press, "The elections were not perfect, they were never meant to be, but they were extremely successful."

It took two weeks for the votes to be counted. The results were not surprising. (See table 14.5.) The United Iraqi Alliance, a loose coalition of Shiite groups, won 140 seats in the provision parliament. An almost equally loose group, the Kurdistan Alliance, came in second with 75 seats. In part because of the Sunni boycott, the ticket headed by Interim Prime Minister Ayad Alawi came in a distant third with only 40 seats. Candidates who were not affiliated with the three main coalitions won the remaining 20 seats.

As these lines were written, the complex negotiations about who would become prime minister were still going on. The United Iraqi Alliance was certain to get the post, and its leaders had agreed on Ibrahim al-Jafari over Adnan Chalabi (a former Pentagon favorite) and others. Al-Jafari had been a leading member of the opposition movement in the exile community for many years and had close ties both to Iran and to the leading Shiite cleric, Grand Ayatollah Ali al-Sistani. However, Jafari will not be able to govern with ease, since his own coalition is fragmented, and most decisions to be made on the constitution will require a two-thirds vote, and thus agreement with the Kurds.

Feedback

One of the sources of Saddam Hussein's power was his all but total control of the mass media that was mentioned earlier. This power was not limited to the regime's domination of newspapers, radio, and television news. Foreign newspapers and magazines were banned, and it was illegal for Iraqis to watch television or listen to radio programs beamed in from abroad. Iraqis began tuning in to networks like al-Jazeera (www .aljazeera.com), based out of the UAE, in the last few years, although one suspects that anyone who had a satellite dish did so with the knowledge and acceptance of the authorities.

A lot of this has changed since Saddam was captured. There are now at least one hundred privately owned newspapers and a couple of dozen radio and television stations. The American authorities claim that these are all privately owned and independently run, which does seem to be the case.

However, at least through the end of 2004, none of those media outlets was more than slightly critical of the occupying forces or the interim government. The cre-

▌ TABLE 14.5 Seats in the Provisional Parliament: 2005

COALITION	NUMBER OF SEATS
United Iraqi Alliance	140
Kurdistan Alliance	75
Iraq List	40
Others	20

Voters lining up outside a polling station in Baghdad, Sunday, 30 January 2005

Msgt. Dave Ahlschwede, USAF/AP/Wide World Photos

ation of a truly free and vibrant press will be a major challenge for the regime that comes to power in late 2005 or 2006.

Key Terms

Concepts

Cult of personality	Shiite
Kurds	Sunni
Nation building	Weapons of mass
No-fly zone	destruction
Safe haven	

People

Al-Bakr, Ahmad Hassan	Faisal I
Alawi, Ayad	Hussein, Saddam
Bremer, Paul	Hussein, Qusay
Bush, George W.	Hussein, Uday

Acronyms

CPA	PUK	UNSCOM
INC	RCC	WMD
OPEC		

Organizations, Places, and Events

Baath Party
Coalition Provisional Authority
General Intelligence Apparatus
General Security Directorate
Gulf War
Interim Government
Iraqi National Congress
Military Intelligence
Operation Iraqi Freedom
Organization of Petroleum Exporting Countries
Ottoman Empire
Patriotic Union of Kurdistan
Republican Guard
Revolutionary Command Council
Special Security
Sunni Triangle
United Nations Special Commission

Critical Thinking Exercises

1. Much has changed in the world since this book was finished in early 2005. Does the analysis of Iraq presented in this chapter still make sense? In what ways? Why (not)?

2. In which respects does Iraq have very shallow roots as a nation? Explain how this feature has constituted an obstacle to the country's political and economic development.

3. What has been the impact of oil on Iraqi politics?

4. What do you see as the main accomplishments of the Baath regime? At what cost were these accomplishments realized?

5. In what respects did the very nature of Saddam Hussein's regime make it difficult to reach a peaceful solution to the international crisis generated by Iraq's invasion of Kuwait in August 1990?

6. Why did Iraq's rulers lead the country into three disastrous wars in the last quarter century? What impact did those conflicts have on the country's domestic politics?

7. Was the U.S.-led coalition justified in launching the invasion of Iraq in 2003?

8. Why was the situation so volatile in Iraq after the United States declared the end of major combat operations in 2003?

9. What are the prospects for democracy or even stability in Iraq given the fact that occupation forces are likely to be there for years and also given the fact that they are likely to face a protracted insurgency?

 ## Useful Websites

During this time of transition, websites on Iraq are likely to change more rapidly than those for other chapters in this book. There will, for example, be sites created for the transitional government and permanent regime that follows it. So don't be surprised if some of these links no longer work.

The best source on the Middle East in general and Iraq in particular is the University of Texas's MENIC project, which is also the virtual library site for the region. The site maintained by Columbia University's Middle East and Jewish Studies Program is almost as good.

menic.utexas.edu/menic/Countries_and_Regions/ Iraq/

www.columbia.edu/cu/lweb/indiv/mideast/cuvlm/ Iraq.html

Arabic News is one of several good sites that offer news feeds for the Middle East.

www.arabicnews.com

The Middle East Research and Information Project (MERIP) is a nonpartisan, Washington-based think tank that focuses on Iraq and the Gulf region as a whole. Its site includes its own reports and links to other good information.

www.merip.org

The Council on Foreign Relations has probably done the most consistent and unbiased work on Iraq since 9/11. Its website archives almost everything its scholars have written, but its URL has changed a number of times. Your best bet is to go to the Council's home page and navigate from there.

www.cfr.org

InfoTrac College Edition Sources

Assouly, Jeanne, and Christian Hoche. "Sanctions, Shortages, and Savagery: Suffering for Saddam."

Bhatiya, Shyam. "How Long Can Saddam Survive?"

Biddle, Stephen. "Victory Misunderstood: What the Gulf War Tells Us about the Future of Conflict."

Diamond, Larry. "What Went Wrong in Iraq."

Fallows, James. "Blind into Baghdad."

Goulding, Marrack. "No Shortcuts with Saddam."

Kay, David. "Iraq beyond the Crisis du Jour."

Muravchick, Joshua. "What to Do about Saddam Hussein."

Pollack, Kenneth. "What Went Wrong: Spies Lies and Weapons: How Could We Have Been So Far Off on Saddam Hussein's Weapons Program."

Wright, Robin. "America's Iraq Policy: How Did It Come to This?"

Further Reading

Batatu, Hanna. *The Old Social Classes and the Revolutionary Movements of Iraq: A Study of Iraq's Old Landed and Commercial Classes, and of Its Communists, Ba'athists, and Free Officers.* Princeton, N.J.: Princeton University Press, 1978. Although very academic in both style and substance, a first-rate, pathbreaking study of Iraqi political movements until the 1968 takeover by the Baath.

Bengio, Ofra. *Saddam's Word: Political Discourse in Iraq.* New York: Oxford University Press, 1998. An excellent analysis of Baathist indoctrination methods, drawing on a broad variety of primary sources, including Saddam Hussein's speeches and writings, Iraqi newspapers, Baathist publications, and Iraqi government documents.

Cockburn, Andrew and Patrick. *Out of the Ashes: The Resurrection of Saddam Hussein.* New York: Harper-Collins, 1999. A solid and critical treatment of Saddam Hussein's ability to survive in the aftermath of the Gulf War.

Gordon, Michael, and Bernard Trainor. *The Generals' War.* Boston: Little, Brown, 1995. A thorough account of the military politics of the Gulf War; somewhat critical of Colin Powell.

Karsh, Efraim, and Inari Rautsi. *Saddam Hussein: A Political Biography.* New York: Free Press, 1991. One of the best of many books on Iraq that appeared after the invasion of Kuwait, this one focuses on Saddam himself.

Kelly, Michael. *Martyr's Day: Chronicle of a Small War.* New York: Random House, 1993. The best book on the war and its aftermath for Iraqi society by a journalist who spent 1990–91 in the region and then lost his life as an embedded correspondent in 2003.

al-Khalil, Samir. *Republic of Fear: The Inside Story of Saddam's Iraq.* New York: Pantheon Books, 1990. A masterly treatment of the origins and functioning of Baathist totalitarianism in Iraq. A difficult but powerful and rewarding book.

Marr, Phebe. *The Modern History of Iraq.* Boulder, Colo.: Westview Press, 1985. One of the best brief histories of Iraq in this century; part of a series of such books published by Westview.

Pollack, Kenneth. *The Threatening Storm.* New York: Random House/Council on Foreign Relations, 2002. By far the best book by a liberal and veteran Iraq watcher on why war was inevitable. Pollack has since written about why some of his analysis was wrong, especially on WMD issues. His article on that is listed in the InfoTrac College Edition Sources section.

Sciolino, Elaine. *The Outlaw State: Saddam Hussein's Quest for Power and the Gulf Crisis.* New York: Wiley, 1991. Probably the most accessible general introduction to contemporary Iraq and the Gulf War. A pleasure to read.

The trouble with Nigeria is simply
and squarely a failure of leadership.
There is nothing basically wrong
with the Nigerian character. There is
nothing wrong with the Nigerian
land or climate or water or air
or anything else.

CHINUA ACHEBE

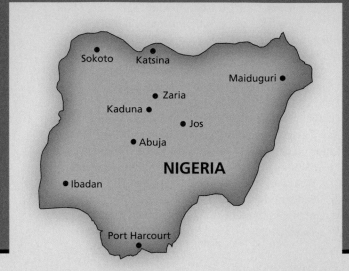

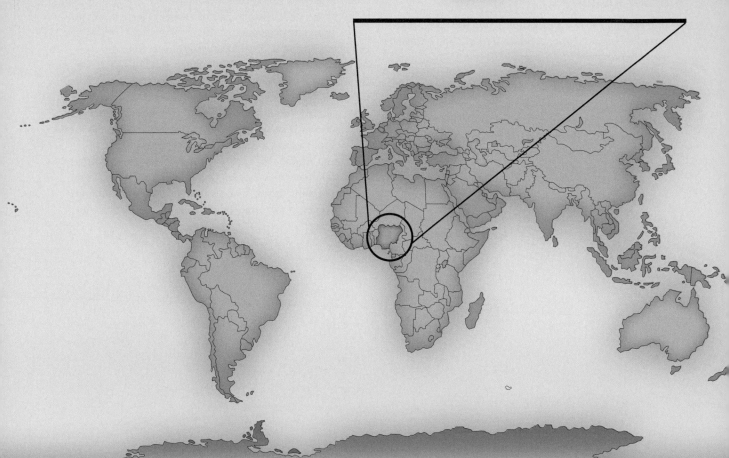

Chapter 15

NIGERIA

The Basics: Nigeria

Size	823,770 km^2 (about twice the size of California)
Population growth	2.4% (2004 est.)
Infant mortality	70.5 per 1,000 births
Life expectancy	50.5 years
Literacy	67%
Major religions	50% Muslim, 40% Christian, 10% indigenous religions
GDP per capita	$300 (2003 est.)
Economic growth	3.4% (2003 est.)
Currency	137 Naira = $1 (15 July 2004)

A New Democracy?

On 29 May 2003, **Olusegun Obasanjo** (1937–) was sworn in for his second term as president of Nigeria. Only once before in Nigeria's forty years of independence had an elected leader been re-elected or, for that matter, had an elected leader succeeded another elected leader.

A year later, President Obasanjo, a Christian, donned the robes of an Islamic emir to speak at the bicentennial of the Sokoto caliphate, a center and symbol of Nigeria's Muslim culture.

Optimists saw both events as harbingers of a successful start for the most recent attempt at creating a Nigerian democracy that began when Obasanjo was first elected in 1999. They also pointed to the indictments of government officials, one a former high-ranking Obasanjo associate, charged with corruption and the return of tens of millions of dollars from the Swiss bank accounts of former military ruler, **Sani Abacha.**

But there was also good reason to be pessimistic. Both the First and Second Republics had been overthrown by military leaders within a year of their second elections. Pessimists noted, too, that President Obasanjo, like President **Shehu Shagari** thirty years before him, had removed a state governor—and foe—in the

AP/Wide World Photos

New Nigerian President Olusegun Obasanjo, left, shakes hands with outgoing military ruler Gen. Abdulsalami Abubakar after a ceremony to hand over power to civilian rule in Abuja, Nigeria on Saturday, 29 May 1999. Promising that "we shall not fail," Obasanjo became Nigeria's first civilian president in fifteen years, ending a string of military regimes that crippled this west African nation.

months following his reelection as president ostensibly for an inability to keep the peace. Pessimists also pointed to thousands of people killed in ethnic and sectarian violence during Obasanjo's presidency. The Nobel Prize winner Wole Soyinka argued that such protests reflect the fact that Nigeria's "national contract," represented by the constitution, had never been legitimately adopted.

There is nothing new to such debates between optimists and pessimists about Nigeria. They have been around for at least the century since present-day Nigeria fully came under British colonial rule. Some British officials despaired at making anything out of the lands that became Nigeria. Others, like Sir George Goldie, saw great potential for cobbling together Islamic emirates, merchant kingdoms, and thousands of delta villages to form a great African adjunct to British mercantilism.

Upon independence in 1960, The U.S. Department of State published a report extolling the natural wealth, educated populace, agricultural potential, and bright future of Nigeria. In London, old-school imperialists shook their heads in despair (and a bit of racism) at the thought of such a backward place being "set free."

Nigeria is Africa's largest country with over 130 million people. Everyone agrees that Nigeria's oil and natural gas wealth should make it one of the richest countries on the continent.

Instead average income has fallen consistently over

the last forty years. Amazingly, not only food but gasoline must be imported because oil revenues are all too often diverted into the bank accounts of the leadership and thus do little to help average citizens, most of whom live on about $300 a year.

The problems are not just economic. As the statement by award-winning novelist, Chinua Achebe, suggests, Nigeria's history has been plagued by political problems that start with that very same leadership. On the day of Obasanjo's inauguration, the country had been ruled by the military for more than half of its forty-three years as an independent country. That makes it the country included in this book that has had the longest periods of military rule and in which the military has had the deepest impact on political life, by far.

Nigeria's political problems were never worse than in the six years before Obasanjo's election. In 1993, then-military strongman **Ibrahim Babangida** and his fellow officers refused to accept the results of an election that apparently had been fairly won by the business executive, **Moshood Abiola,** who was subsequently arrested. Babangida stepped aside, but he was replaced shortly thereafter by the far more ruthless and corrupt General Sani Abacha, who treated the country as all but his personal fiefdom. The regime cracked down on dissidents—real and imagined—culminating in the execution of the author and environmental activist **Ken Saro-Wiwa** in 1996.

Suddenly, in summer 1998, Abacha died. The presidency was handed to yet another general, **Abdulsalami Abubakar.** In the face of considerable pressure at home and from abroad, Abubakar announced plans for a speedy return to democratic rule, which was to begin with the release of Abiola. Abiola, then, unexpectedly died. Riots broke out, which only intensified the pressure on the new military rulers to cede power—so they did. The extent of the change is perhaps best symbolized in the presidential election that pitted two recently freed political prisoners against each other—Obasanjo and Olu Falae, a former civil servant and finance minister.

Obasanjo took office with a degree of popular support and enthusiasm the country hadn't seen since the first heady days after gaining its independence. Interviews with average Nigerian citizens by Western journalists showed widespread support for democracy and the new president, something no Nigerian government had enjoyed in thirty years.

Though once a military ruler of the country in the 1970s, Obasanjo had become one of the continent's leading advocates for reform and democracy in the twenty years after he had turned over power to the civilian second republic. He was head of Transparency International (www.transparency.org), a leading nongovernmental organization (NGO) that advocates openness in government. Indeed, Obasanjo had been so outspoken in his criticism of the outgoing military regime that he had been put in prison for treason and had faced the death penalty.

In his first term in office, Obasanjo offered evidence for optimists and pessimists alike. Several northern states adopted **Sharia,** the Islamic legal system, despite opposition from the non-Muslim half of the population. The army bloodily suppressed ethnic fighting in the state of Benue. Rioting in Lagos, the country's largest city, resulted in hundreds of deaths. The Miss World pageant, scheduled for the Muslim-dominated city of Kaduna, was forced out of Nigeria by protesters who found a beauty contest an insult to Islam. The pessimists also argue that old problems continue in the new Nigeria. In particular, corruption remains so widespread that civil servants are often referred to as lootocrats.

Optimists saw hope in the fact that ethnic divisions had not played much of a role in either the 1993 or 2003 elections. There was hope, too, in the formation of the New Partnership for African Development by the Nigerian, Algerian, and South African presidents. They pointed to the judicial resolution (and reversal) of a Sharia court's death sentence of a woman convicted of adultery. Nigeria and Cameroon negotiated the settlement of a land dispute after the International Court of Justice ruled against Nigeria. Nigerian forces have also played a major role in easing violent conflicts in many countries throughout the continent, including its own neighbors. With all the uncertainties in the Middle East (see the preceding two chapters), we may be entering a period in which Nigeria's petrochemical resources can truly be turned into an asset. Russian and Chinese oil companies now compete with European and American companies in Nigeria to explore new oil fields, create a natural gas industry, and build refineries.

But as we will see in the rest of the chapter, it is probably too early to tell whether the optimists or pessimists are right. Both see important parts of Nigeria's present—and its past. Which will shape the country's future is pretty much anybody's guess.

Thinking about Nigeria

Nigeria has a lot going for it. Almost one in every five Africans is a Nigerian. It is blessed with some of the most fertile soil on the continent. Compared with the rest of Africa, it has a well-educated population, including at least two million citizens with university degrees. Vast oil and gas deposits have brought it more money than most other African nations can dream of.

Those assets (except for the oil) were obvious before Nigeria gained its independence in 1960. Therefore, most observers expected Nigeria to help lead the continent in building strong states, democratic regimes, and modern economies.

Yet, as Achebe suggests in the statement that begins the chapter, Nigeria has had more than its share of trouble. Whether run by civilians or the military, the state has not lived up to expectations. There have been times, as during the civil war of 1967–1970 over **Biafra,** when it could be argued that there was no viable Nigerian state, if by that we mean an entity that can maintain basic law and order.

Those troubles begin with the basic social and economic conditions under which Nigerian citizens and their leaders live.

Poverty

Despite all of its resources, Nigeria remains desperately poor. According to the World Bank's calculations, it is in one hundred sixty-fourth place out of the 190 members of the United Nations.

From 1965 until 1980, Nigeria's GNP grew by an average of 6.9 percent per year because of the income it was able to realize from some low-level industrial development and the export of oil. From 1980 to 1987, however, the economy shrank by over 40 percent as its industries ceased being productive and oil prices collapsed. In the decade between 1992 and 2002, the shrinkage continued at a pace of about half a percent per year.

That decline took a human toll. When oil prices were at their peak in the early 1980s, GNP per capita averaged around $700 per year. By 1990 it had been cut by more than half. Today, it is little more than $300. Even at the more generous Purchasing Power Parity rate, it is still below $1,000. There has been some real improvement in the way many people live. Nonetheless, the average Nigerian leads an appallingly difficult life that is worse in most respects than the situations in the other third world countries covered in this book.

About 7 percent of all Nigerian children do not reach the age of one; 18 percent die before their fifth birthday. Most of those children succumb to malnutrition or diseases like diarrhea that could easily be treated or prevented if the country could afford some simple basic medications that can be bought over the counter in the West.

People who do survive childhood can only expect to live to fifty. The average Nigerian only consumes between 85 and 90 percent of the calories required to maintain a healthy life, a figure that has actually declined from 95 percent in the mid-1960s. Only 38 percent have access to safe drinking water. There are about 5,263 Nigerians for every doctor. In Mexico, the comparable figure is 613. About two-thirds of the population as a whole is literate, but only half the women can read and write.

Like most of Africa, Nigeria also remains a largely rural country with only about 30 percent of its population living in cities. But its cities are booming as millions of young people flee the countryside seeking jobs. The population of Lagos, for instance, reached a million by the mid-1970s and is probably over thirteen million now.

AP/Wide World Photos

Pedestrians and shoppers make their way through a crowded street in Lagos.

HIV/AIDS in Nigeria

Nigeria has one of the world's highest rates of HIV infection. The best estimate is that at least three million people have been infected, including eight hundred thousand children.

The struggle against HIV/AIDS has been hampered by two main problems. First, Nigeria's health care system in general is among the worst in the world. Second, HIV/AIDS carries a greater social stigma in Nigeria than in most other countries. Indeed, the situation was so bad that the government could not meet a minimal goal of treating ten thousand people in one hundred hospitals in the late 1990s and early 2000s.

Therefore, in 2003, President Obasanjo announced a new policy that had two main components. First, it will take advantage of the growing help from the international community to dramatically increase the number of people who have access to medication. Second, it has launched a massive educational campaign to provide more people with information about how to avoid getting infected and to reduce the disdain with which people who have the disease are commonly treated (www.nigeria-aids.org).

Lagos also provides a good picture of the twin realities of urban life in many third world countries. Miles of shantytowns surround a central city of wide boulevards and gleaming skyscrapers that remind one of New York or London. But for most urban Nigerians, the shantytown is their reality: ethnically segregated neighborhoods; houses without running water, electricity, or sewers; dead-end jobs, if they have jobs at all; endless traffic jams (called "go slows"); conflict with other neighborhoods. Residents of other cities with populations of over one million, like Kano, Ibadan, Abuja, Kaduna, Port Harcourt, and Benin, live in similar circumstances.

As is also the case in most of Africa, Nigeria has to cope with population growth of monstrous proportions. During most of the 1980s it averaged a growth rate of over 3 percent per year and has dipped just below that figure since the 1990s. Those statistics mean that 45 percent of the Nigerian population is under fifteen, while only 3 percent is over sixty-five. At an average growth rate of 3 percent, the population will double every twenty-four years. At that rate, Nigeria will have nearly 500 million inhabitants by the middle of the twenty-first century. That would be far more than the United States or Russia combined and roughly one and a half times the total African population today. Such population pressures are likely to make Nigeria even poorer as it is forced to spread its already limited resources even further.

Ethnicity

Ethnic differences and the conflict they engender plague many countries, especially in the third world. In Nigeria, no other political force comes close to it in importance. In all, Nigeria has about four hundred ethnic groups, each with its own language and customs.

Politically, the three largest ones matter most. The largest of these are the **Hausa-Fulani,** who live in the north and are mostly orthodox Muslims. The Fulani, who had some Northern African or even Arabian roots, gradually moved into the north and, beginning in 1804, began gaining control of the region and its predominantly Hausa-speaking population. Since then, the two have intermarried to the point that they are virtually indistinguishable. The region to the west of the Niger and Benue rivers is dominated by the **Yoruba,** that on the east by the **Igbo** (sometimes called the Ibo by American analysts). Many Yoruba and Igbo have converted to Christianity, and there are sizable Muslim and non-Christian minorities among the Yoruba.

Together, they account for 60–65 percent of the population, have produced most of the country's leading politicians, and served as the support base for all the political parties both before and after independence.

In the center of the country lies the **middle belt** in which there is no single dominant ethnic group or religion. As a result, the middle belt has produced some of its most nationally oriented leaders. In an attempt to create a symbol of national unity, during the 1980s the government moved the capital from Lagos in the heart of Yoruba territory to a new city in the middle belt, Abuja.

About half the country is Muslim and 40 percent is Christian. The rest of the population practices religions that antedate the arrival of the Arabs and Europeans.

Interethnic difficulties begin with the seemingly simple question of the way people communicate with each other. In the rather homogeneous rural areas, almost everyone still uses the local group's traditional language. The elite usually speak English, which is the official language of the national government and most mass media. In the cities where poorly educated people from different groups have to communicate with each other, new languages have emerged that combine simple English terms and African grammatical structures. *Washington Post* correspondent Blaine Harden provides the following example from a rap song about corrupt politi-

cians: "If him bring you money, take am and chop. Make you no vote for am." Which means, "If he tries to buy your vote, take the money and buy food. Then vote for somebody else." "*Chop-chop politics*" is the common Nigerian term to describe what Americans call "log rolling" or "pork barrel" politics.

As we will see in the rest of the chapter, Nigeria's ethnic problems go far beyond the trouble people have in communicating with each other. More than anything else, ethnicity structures life in the country: where people live, what they believe in, how they conduct their lives, how jobs are allocated, and whom they support politically. And, more than any other factor, ethnicity has made democratic government difficult and led to the coups of 1966, 1983, 1993, countless riots, and the civil war of 1967–1970.

High Stakes Politics

These problems and more have turned politics in Nigeria into a very high-stakes game. More people have been killed by repressive regimes elsewhere. Nonetheless, Nigeria's politics is highly charged because people have great and growing expectations about what their government could and should do, expectations that leaders are rarely able to meet.

In Chapter 5, we saw that Third and Fourth Republic France suffered from an interconnected syndrome that left it unable to effectively meet the domestic and international challenges the country faced. Similarly, Nigeria has seemed locked in a deteriorating spiral of social, economic, and political difficulties that, at best, reinforce and, at worst, feed off each other.

The most obvious manifestation of Nigeria's ills is the alternation between civilian and military governments, neither of which have been able to make much headway on any front. Whatever institutional forms it takes, Nigerian politics is a struggle in which all the key groups desperately want to win or, at the very least, keep their adversaries from winning. The spoils of office are high, as the rampant corruption attests. No one—elected or self-appointed—seems able to make decisions based on national interests.

The uncertainties of Nigerian political life also make Nigeria harder to study than most of the other countries covered in this book. Because of the shifts back and forth between civilian and military rule, Nigeria has very few established institutions to structure political life, whoever is in power. As a result, the sections on state structures and parties will be shorter than those in other chapters simply because there has been so little continuity in any part of Nigerian politics. On the other hand, the next section, which uses the history of the alternation between civilian and military rule to illustrate the rising stakes of Nigeria's politics, has to be relatively long, because without understanding those twists and turns you will not be able to make sense of the weakness of its institutions.

Key Questions

In short, we will be asking two sets of questions about Nigerian politics. The first will mirror those used in the other chapters on third world countries. The other will focus on conditions and problems unique to Nigeria.

- How is the legacy of imperialism still reflected in Nigerian politics?

- What role does ethnicity play in reinforcing the country's difficulties?

- Why does Nigeria remain one of the poorest countries in the world despite its massive oil and natural gas reserves?

- How have the frequent shifts from civilian to military rule and back again exacerbated the country's many social and economic problems?

The Evolution of the Nigerian State

Critics are quick to point to the flaws and corruption of Nigeria's post-independence leaders in assessing the country's problems. To a large extent they are right, since leaders of all political stripes have made damaging mistakes, many of which seem in retrospect to have been easily avoidable. However, the incompetence and/or venality of these men is by no means the entire story. Whatever the leaders of independent Nigeria had been like, they would have faced a tremendous burden of problems inherited from colonial times. In that history, three trends have played an important role in the shaping of modern Nigeria and continue to trouble it today:

- The slave trade cost the Nigerians and their fellow Africans countless millions of people from the sixteenth through the nineteenth centuries.

- Later, colonization disrupted traditional social and political systems and created new ones because Europeans created borders that suited their own purposes that did not take root very well. Moreover, the very drawing of the boundaries, as well as the

nature of colonial administration, made ethnic conflict all but inevitable after independence.

- The anticolonial struggle, the political arrangements made at the time the former colonies became independent states, and the largely informal pattern of neocolonial relations that were established afterward left the new state in a poor position to develop politically, socially, and economically.

Before the British

For many years, the conventional wisdom was that precolonial Africa was "primitive" and lacked anything approaching civilization or government. In fact, that was not the case (africanhistory.about.com).

There were a number of rather advanced civilizations in the area that is today's Nigeria. None had a written language, but, otherwise, many of them had well-developed political, cultural, and economic systems.

Outside influence in Nigerian life actually began before the Europeans arrived in the late fifteenth century. The spread of both the Sahara Desert and Islam brought at least the Hausa-speaking peoples into contact with the Arab world about a thousand years ago when it, not Europe, was the center of world civilization. By the thirteenth century, most had converted to Islam, although their practice was infused with their earlier beliefs.

By the thirteenth century, a king, or mai, had been able to consolidate his rule over a wide region, bringing together dozens of Hausa states. Although the regime's power ebbed and flowed over the centuries, it had well-developed bureaucratic, judicial, and imperial institutions. Political control was further centralized in the early nineteenth century when Usman Dan Fodio led a Fulani takeover of the northern region, established a caliphate under Islamic law (Sharia), and transformed the old Hausa states into emirates.

They were part of an elaborate trading network that extended at least as far as Baghdad. When the British arrived, they found extensive mines, manufacturing operations that made elaborate ceramics, and over thirty types of cloth along merchants who had established extensive financial and monetary systems.

The Yoruba developed a very different—but no less sophisticated—political system. There, one man, Oduduwa, brought together the thirteen settlements of Ile-Ife and created the first Yoruba kingdom—and with it, the first real sense of being Yoruba. Over the centuries, people spread out from Ile-Ife and established at least sixteen other kingdoms, all patterned along the same basic lines. By the end of the eighteenth century, a single kingdom covered what is now the Yoruba regions of Nigeria and virtually the entire country of Benin.

The Igbo had a different, but still elaborate, social and political system. Little attempt was made to forge a centralized regime. Instead, individual villages were largely self-governing, though all used essentially the same practices. As Chinua Achebe so brilliantly describes it in *Things Fall Apart*, the Igbo had a widely accepted, if unwritten, constitution. There were clearly defined policy-making, administrative, judicial, and military roles. The society was based on households led by men. Power and prestige went to those elders who had accumulated the most wealth, shown the most bravery in battle, and demonstrated the strongest commitment to the village's values. In short, life among the Igbo was based more on merit and less on the accident of birth than it was for the British who colonized them.

The Portuguese began the European influence on Nigeria in the late fifteenth century when its explorers landed on the coast, and its merchants started exchanging gold for slaves. The slave trade began to take a significant toll during the seventeenth century when huge sugar plantations were established on the Caribbean Islands for which labor had to be imported. At that point, British, French, Dutch, Spanish, and Swedish "merchants" joined the Portuguese, and by the middle of the eighteenth century, the booming slave trade was centered along what is now the Nigerian coast.

The Europeans did not establish many permanent settlements there at that time. African rulers were too strong and malaria and other diseases too deadly. Instead, they traded with African merchants, who were rich and powerful enough to kidnap, purchase, or otherwise obtain millions of people. In exchange, the merchants obtained textiles, firearms, liquor, iron, salt, and tools.

At least 200,000 slaves a year were sent westward from 1827 to 1834 from one port alone, the Bight of Bonny. No one knows for sure how many people were enslaved before slavery was finally ended in Brazil in the 1880s, but the most reliable estimates range between eleven million and twenty million. Of those, upwards of a million were Nigerian. But the cost of slavery cannot be measured simply in numbers of people alone. As the Nigerian historian Richard Olaniyan has put it:

> In assessing the impact of the Atlantic slave trade on the Nigerian societies, it is strongly tempting to think largely of the quantifiable, tangible costs—the number of prime-age individuals forcibly removed, for example—leaving aside the intangible social, psychological and political effects. Both the

Migration Today

In a curious twist of fate, U.S. immigration officials announced in early 2005 that more Africans voluntary moved to the United States in the 1990s than those forced to come to the Americas during any decade of the slave trade. The current wave of migrants, which is obvious to anyone who lives in or near a major metropolitan area in the United States or Europe, reflects a desire by young Africans, in particular, to escape the poverty and underemployment that they assume would be their lot back home.

> victims and the beneficiaries of the nefarious traffic suffered from it; as Professor Ryder holds, "on those who lived by it as well as those who suffered it the slave trade wrought havoc and debasement."[1]

But the costs of slavery go much farther. At that historical moment when new discoveries sparked by human initiative and curiosity were propelling European civilization forward, African development was being stunted as generations of its best and brightest youth were ripped out of society and sold into slavery.

Colonization

The slave trade wound down after its elimination in the British Empire in 1833 and in the United States after the Civil War. That did not mean that European involvement in Africa came to an end. Quite the contrary.

The industrial revolution and the rise of capitalism led Britain and the other European powers to seek new supplies of raw materials and markets for finished goods. (See table 15.1.) In Nigeria, the most important product it exported was palm oil, which was used to lubricate the machines in the new British factories. Between 1814 and 1834, annual sales of palm oil grew from 450 to 14,000 tons per year.

The end of the slave trade and the new relationships elicited more resistance from African traders and rulers, leading the British to establish a permanent colony at Lagos and a base at Lokoja where the Niger and Benue rivers come together. A more permanent European presence was also made easier when it was discovered that quinine cured malaria. Still, there was little thought of

[1] Richard Olaniyan, "The Atlantic Slave Trade." In Richard Olaniyan, ed., *Nigerian History and Culture* (London: Longman, 1985), 120.

▌ TABLE 15.1 Events in Nigeria before Independence

YEAR	EVENT
11th century	Arrival of Arabs
16th century	Beginning of slave trade
1884–85	Berlin Conference on Africa
1914	Unification of Nigeria as a single colony
1920	Creation of National Congress of British West Africa
1923	Formation of Nigerian National Democratic Party
1938	Nigerian Youth Charter issued
1948	Nigerianization of civil service begins
1951 and 1954	Interim constitutions go into effect
1960	Independence

colonizing all of Nigeria or the rest of Africa. Instead, in 1865, a British parliamentary commission went so far as to advocate phasing out all British activity along the Nigerian coast.

The European geopolitical situation was to change all that. The 1870s were a tumultuous time in Europe. The newly unified Germany and Italy disrupted the balance of power that had been so delicately carved out after the Napoleonic Wars in 1815. Those pent-up pressures had to be released somewhere, and that somewhere turned out to be Africa, setting off what is commonly known as the scramble for Africa.

Explorers and soldiers spread all over the continent staking claims to territories for their governments back in Europe. Often, representatives of two or more countries claimed the same territory.

The German government convened the International Berlin West Africa Conference, which lasted from November 1884 to February 1885. For all intents and purposes, the Berlin Conference merely finalized the carving up of the continent that was already well under way.

There was more than the pursuit of national glory and balance of power politics involved in the colonization of Africa. The industrialists and merchants spawned by the industrial revolution needed new markets to keep expanding their businesses. That led them to erect stiff tariff barriers to protect their own industries and sought colonial markets in which they would have the exclusive right to sell manufactured goods.

Meanwhile, missionaries were appalled by the values and customs of Africans now that they were sent "out" to the colonies in large numbers. The new sense of nationalism combined with the Europeans' moral certainty to create an unfortunate arrogance and ignorance. The Europeans failed to even notice that there were well-developed—albeit very different—civilizations all over the continent, prompting religious and educational leaders to try to convert the "heathens."

The British conquest of Nigeria was conducted through its existing coastal enclaves. They launched pacification campaigns designed to destroy the power of local leaders and, in the process, undermined popular belief in the various indigenous cultures. Though vastly outnumbered, the British were aided by their technical superiority and by the divisions among the Africans that made any kind of unified resistance impossible. Thus, the British manipulated warfare taking place among the Yoruba to take over the western region and establish a protectorate in Ibadan in 1893.

The British also used economic pretexts to justify their actions. In 1885, they fabricated a charge of obstructing free trade against Jaja of Opobo, a local merchant and strongman. Jaja was arrested, paving the way for British occupation of the territory previously under his control. By 1902, the British had solidified their hold over what is now eastern and western Nigeria. The British also took over the north during that same time period. Here, the central character was an adventurer and trader, Sir George Goldie. At the age of thirty, Goldie first visited the north, realized that there was too much competition among the British traders already operating there, and brought them all together into the United African Company. Goldie also was a fierce nationalist who feared that France had designs on the north. In short, Goldie realized that British trade and political control had to go hand in hand. His quest for "gold" and "glory" led him to convince the Foreign Office to appoint him chief agent and vice-consul of the Niger, which allowed him to offer British military protection on behalf of the UAC. By the time of the Berlin Conference, Goldie had negotiated more than two hundred treaties, which the British government used as the basis for its claim to the north.

In reality, British rule was anything but secure, especially away from the towns and the navigable rivers. Over the next fifteen years, they overcame stiff, if sporadic, resistance and gradually extended their control over more and more of the region. Finally, in 1906, British forces destroyed the remnants of the Fulani Empire and established British authority in the north. Eight years later the British combined the north with the south and east to create the single entity that then came to be called Nigeria. This was not even an African term, but one coined by the British. It was, in short, an artificial name to describe an artificial entity that had nothing in common with traditional regional alignments.

Things Fall Apart

The cultural, economic, and political disruption caused by colonialism probably went a lot further in Nigeria than it did in either India or Iraq. No one has expressed that impact any better than Chinua Achebe in *Things Fall Apart*. Most of us would not want to have lived in traditional Igbo society. Women were truly second-class citizens. Twins were killed. But it was also a society with its own culture and values in which people led lives of dignity as portrayed in the successes and failures of Okonkwo, the novel's protagonist and one of the village leaders. Toward the end of the book, British missionaries arrive and try to convert the residents of his village. They start with its weakest links, including one of Okonkwo's children who cannot or will not live up to the culture's demand that men prove themselves as warriors. The first missionary is relatively kind, but soon he is replaced by a less tolerant and less patient colleague who tries to convert the village in a far less tactful manner. Seeing his way of life slipping away, Okonkwo ultimately kills the minister, knowing full well that his act will bring soldiers in. Knowing, too, that not only his life, but the very way of life his people had always known, were about to be destroyed, Okonkwo kills himself in a final act of desperation. The novel ends with a British soldier writing his memoirs, tentatively entitled "The Pacification of the Primitive Tribes of the Lower Niger."

Colonial Rule

In comparative terms, British rule was relatively benign, especially in colonies like Nigeria where there were very few European settlers. Nonetheless, colonization had a devastating impact. As Basil Davidson put it:

> All the systems, in essential ways, operated with the same assumptions and for the same purposes. Each of them was racist and exploitative. They used colonial power to treat Africans as inferior to Europeans, justifying this by a whole range of myths about a supposed "white superiority." The purpose of using colonial power in this way was to make Africans serve the interests of European colony-owners.[2]

In 1914, the British created a single Nigerian colony but administered the north and south separately until the very end of the colonial period. Thus began the often-conscious practice of deepening already existing divisions, thereby magnifying the problems the Africans would have to deal with once the country gained its independence.

As one expert put it, "if the British 'created' Nigeria, British colonial policy largely contributed to its remaining a mere geographical expression."

In the north, the British relied purely on **indirect rule** in which local leaders continued to rule subject only to the limited supervision of imperial officials. In the south, they established a traditional colonial regime in which expatriate British bureaucrats governed directly. Even there, the British had to depend on local officials since they were so vastly outnumbered. As late as 1938, there were no more than 1,500 officials in the entire colony.

Frederick Lugard, the first British governor of northern Nigeria, referred to Britain's **dual mandate.** On the one hand, colonial administrators had to serve the interests of imperialists and industrialists back home. On the other hand, it had to promote members of the "native races" for many clerical and other administrative positions. The British chose to rule through traditional local leaders, the "kings" and "emirs" of the north and "chiefs" of the south. But it cannot be stressed strongly enough that these local leaders had no role in determining colonial policies, which were set by white men in London and Lagos.

There was one area in which colonial rule did benefit Nigerian society—education. Missionaries opened schools that were supported by grants from the British government. By 1926, there were about 4,000 elementary and 18 secondary schools. Of those, however, only 125 of the elementary and none of the secondary schools were in the north. In 1934, the first "higher college" that concentrated on technical education was opened, followed by a full-fledged university in Ibadan in 1948.

Only a tiny fraction of the colonial population received even an elementary education. Nonetheless, the establishment of this rudimentary system had two important and unintended side effects that were to hasten independence and a third side effect that would trouble the new country. First, it created a new elite separate from the traditional authorities that would form the core of the independence movement beginning in the 1930s. Second, the growing number of literate Nigerians made it possible for an active and often critical press to begin operations. Lastly, the unequal attendance at English-style schools gave advantages to those groups that sent the most children to them. Southerners—especially those from the southeast—went to school at much higher rates than northerners. When the new Nigerian

---

[2] Basil Davidson, *Modern Africa* (New York: Longman, 1983), 4.

government needed bureaucrats literate in English and familiar with Western-style administration, southerners filled most of the jobs throughout the country, which bred considerable resentment in the north.

Economically, the picture was decidedly less positive. The British assumed from the beginning that their colonies should pay for themselves while aiding industrial development at home. That was not possible given the economic systems the British inherited with the consolidation of colonial rule.

Therefore, as in India, they embarked on a series of changes that "undeveloped" Nigeria. Up to that point, Nigeria produced enough food to feed all its people and had the systems of trade and manufacturing noted earlier. The British destroyed almost all of that. They introduced cash crops that could be exported to help cover the costs of administering the colony. Each region specialized in a different crop: palm oil in the east, cocoa in the west, and peanuts in the north. As a result, Nigerian agriculture no longer produced enough for local consumption, and the colony had to begin importing food.

To make matters worse for the Nigerians, the Royal Niger Company was awarded a monopoly on trade and the profit that accrued from it. The British seized the tin mines in the Jos plateau that Nigerians had worked for more than two thousand years. The British expanded the mining operations, introduced modem machinery, and by 1928 were employing upwards of forty thousand Nigerians, but now the Nigerians were poorly paid wage laborers, not independent producers. Taxes and customs duties were imposed on imported goods. Thus, economic policy made Nigeria dependent on Great Britain and at the same time heightened the regional differences within the colony. As that happened, people began to consciously define themselves as Yoruba or Igbo or northerners. That sense of self-identification was especially pronounced in the north where development lagged, and more and more people began to fear becoming permanently poorer as well as politically weaker than residents of the south.

Independence

However powerful and destructive it may have been, British colonialism began sowing the seeds of its own destruction virtually from the beginning in Nigeria as it had in India. The British may have conquered Nigeria, but they could not forever keep it in submission. If nothing else, there were too few British and too many Nigerians. The British had to educate Nigerians to help manage the colony. Moreover, the British "civilizing" mission also led Nigerians not just to read and write and pray to the Christian God, but to learn about what the British claimed to be their values, including freedom and democracy.

From the moment the unified colony of Nigeria was created, events began to unfold that would lead to independence barely a half century later. The beginning of the drive toward independence came with World War I. The British imposed heavy taxes on Nigeria and the other African colonies to help pay for the war. Some Nigerians were drafted into the British army, where they served primarily as porters. The war and the reasons the British gave for fighting it do not seem to have had much of an impact on the Africans who served in the army. On the other hand, they did help a few members of the still tiny educated elite see the contradiction between the colonizers' democratic principles and the harsh realities of their rule.

Meanwhile, the vastly outnumbered British found they had to rely on Africans more and more in administering Nigeria. No Africans occupied decision-making positions during the interwar period. Nonetheless, the colonial rulers had to employ thousands of interpreters, clerks, and police officers.

Colonial rule in the 1920s had an unintended side effect that did neither the British nor the Nigerians much good in the long run. As noted earlier, the British were convinced that Africans lived in tribes. That belief led the British to assume that indirect rule should be conducted through tribal chiefs and that if a chief did not exist, they had to create one. Gradually, the practice worked. Chiefs began to consolidate their authority over communities that came to see themselves as unified peoples.

In short, the British created tribes in many places where no such institution existed. With time, those "tribes" became vehicles Africans could use to see and defend their common interests and, later, serve as the base of support for the parties that were to steer the path to independence and the tumultuous politics afterward.

At about this time, organized opposition to colonial rule appeared. In the first years of the last century, the American Marcus Garvey and others created a pan-African movement designed to bring Africans and African-Americans together to work for common goals, including colonial independence.

During the 1920s, pan-Africanism gradually gave way to the idea of a West African and then to Nigerian nationalism. In 1920, the **National Congress of British West Africa (NCBWA)** was formed by representatives from all the British colonies in the region. As with the other early African efforts, the NCBWA advocated limited reforms, such as the granting of some African representation in the colonial assemblies the British had created by then.

The first purely Nigerian political movement emerged with the formation in 1923 of the Nigerian National Democratic Party (NNDP) by **Herbert Macaulay** (1864–1946) who is frequently seen as the founder of Nigerian nationalism. For the most part, the NNDP and groups like it gained their support from the still small group of Western-educated lawyers, teachers, and merchants in Lagos. Only a few members of the old elite like Ahmadu Bello, the Sardauna (ruler) of Sokoto, supported these movements and thus helped build bridges between the new and traditional elites.

Although Macaulay took a more militant line than earlier opponents of colonial rule, his movement stopped short of demanding independence. During the 1930s, support for Nigerian political groups began to broaden with the formation of the **Nigerian Youth Movement (NYM).** Now critics went beyond attacking specific colonial institutions, such as the educational system that did not provide Africans with the skills that would allow them to become leaders, and began talking about a united and free Nigeria.

In 1938, the NYM issued the Nigerian Youth Charter, which was the first call for self-government. The document was largely ignored by the British, but it heartened and radicalized the educated elite, which now included a growing number of young people living outside of Lagos. Perceptive British observers also realized that irreversible changes were occurring in Nigeria and many other colonies that, sooner or later, would lead to the end of colonial rule.

Dissatisfaction continued to mount. Colonial rule had made Nigerians dependent on international markets. That was tolerable as long as the outside world was buying Nigerian goods and paying reasonable prices for them. But after the October 1929 stock market crash in New York, the demand for colonial goods evaporated. That left not just the Nigerian elite but Nigerian workers more painfully aware of what colonial rule was costing them. Nigerians paid nearly £1 million in taxes in 1934, but only about a quarter of the colonial budget went to social service, educational, or economic programs that would benefit them.

World War II made independence inevitable. This time, around one hundred thousand Nigerians served in the British army. Many saw combat. Unlike their parents in 1914, these soldiers returned with a heightened desire for independence, democracy, and equality—all those things they supposedly had been fighting for.

The war that had begun as an antifascist struggle became an anticolonial and antiracist one as well. In 1944, Macaulay and **Nnamdi Azikiwe** (1904–1996) formed the **National Council of Nigeria and the Cameroons (NCNC),** which went beyond the small steps advocated by earlier nationalists and demanded independence. As Azikiwe, who was to become the most important nationalist leader during the next generation, put it:

> We who live in this blessed country know that until we are in control of political power, we would continue to be the footstool of imperialist nations. We are fed up with being governed as a crown colony. We are nauseated by the existence of an untrammeled bureaucracy which is a challenge to our manhood.[3]

Meanwhile, the social changes that had begun before the war continued at an ever more rapid rate. The closure of many European and American markets deepened poverty in the countryside. The cities filled with un- and underemployed young men. Hundreds of new schools and a few universities were opened. Trade unions were formed. All were to become fertile ground for nationalist organizers over the next fifteen years. They were, after all, the first bits

Events outside Nigeria also hastened independence. In 1941, American President Franklin Delano Roosevelt and British Prime Minister Winston Churchill issued the Atlantic Charter, which declared that the Allies would "respect the right of all peoples to choose the form of government under which they will live" after the war. Shortly after the war, Britain granted India, Pakistan, Burma, and Ceylon (now Sri Lanka) their independence. Those landmark events gave the Nigerians new hope for their own future, especially because it was more developed than Sri Lanka. Meanwhile, the war had weakened the British, leading many politicians to conclude that they could no longer afford the colonies. In 1946, the new Labour government committed itself to reforms that would give colonies like Nigeria "responsible government" without either defining what that meant or establishing any kind of timetable for the transition to self-government.

Nigerians joined their fellow Africans in stepping up the pressure for independence sooner rather than later. Everywhere on the continent, nationalist movements garnered new support and radicalized their demands. Nigerian leaders raised the stakes by demanding meaningful political power immediately and indepen-

---

[3]Cited in Davidson, *Modern Africa.* 73.

dence in the not very distant future. They recognized that if they were to build a mass movement that would extend beyond the urban intellectuals, it would be easiest to do so on a regional level, which led to formation parties that recruited support largely along ethnic lines.

Nationalist leaders also were able to gather support among the "old boy" networks of high school and university graduates and the ethnic associations that emerged, among the new urban migrants. They also used a relatively free press to publicize their attacks on British policy and to claim that they would do a better job if they were in charge of an independent Nigeria.

The British did not reject their demands out of hand. As early as 1946, they began the transition to self-government by promulgating a constitution that established elected assemblies in each region, solidifying the borders that would create problems for the independent Nigeria. In 1948, the British started the "Nigerianization" of the civil service. By the early 1950s, the British had decided that they were going to have to speed up the move toward self-government, if not grant outright independence. That led to two more constitutions, which allowed each region to elect its own representatives and draft its own laws, gave them equal representation in the national legislature, and established a federal structure in which the national government shared power with the three regions.

Elsewhere, the drive toward freedom was moving even faster, especially after Ghana (formerly the Gold Coast) became sub-Saharan Africa's first independent state in 1957. Throughout this period, representatives of the British government and all the major Nigerian forces met in a series of sessions in London and Lagos to determine further constitutional reforms. By that time, electoral politics had already taken on a decidedly regional and ethnic tone. The National Council of Nigeria and the Cameroons (NCNC) organized the Igbo, including some in the neighboring French colony of the Cameroons. The relatively conservative **Northern People's Congress (NPC)** and more radical **Northern Elements Progressive Union (NEPU)** did well among the Hausa-Fulani. The **Action Group (AG)** dominated among the Yoruba, while the **United Middle Belt Congress (UMBC)** organized the various groups in the center of the country.

A federal election under universal suffrage (except for women in the Muslim north) was held in 1959. Final provisions for independence called for representation to be determined on the basis of population, which was to work to the benefit of the north that then accounted for about 40 percent to 45 percent of the total population. Nigeria finally became an independent country within the British Commonwealth of Nations on 1 October 1960

with **Tafawa Balewa** (1912–1966) as prime minister and Azikiwe as governor-general. Azikiwe would later become the symbolic president when Nigeria declared itself a republic three years later.

But as independence neared, two of the problems of high-stakes politics that were to plague the new country emerged as well. In their desire to spur development and to gain the support of voters, politicians began dispensing "favors," the first step toward the corruption that no Nigerian regime has been able to overcome. Similarly, the evolution of shared power within a largely regional framework intensified the already serious ethnic differences. Until it became clear that Nigeria was going to become independent, its people had a common enemy—the British. But once independence was assured, their internal differences began taking center stage. By the time independence officially came, Nigeria was united in name only.

The First Republic

Like most former British colonies, Nigeria started out with a standard parliamentary system. It had a bicameral parliament, but only the lower chamber, the House of Representatives, was directly elected and had any real power. Executive authority was vested in a cabinet and prime minister drawn from the ranks of the majority party in parliament. The government remained in office until its five-year term ended as long as it maintained the support or confidence of that majority. (See table 15.2.) There also was a ceremonial but powerless head of state, the governor-general until 1963 and the president thereafter.

The new Nigerian system only differed from classical parliamentary arrangements in one significant way. It was a federal system in which the national government

❚ TABLE 15.2 Nigerian Regimes and Leaders since Independence

YEARS	HEAD OF STATE	TYPE OF REGIME
1960–66	Tafawa Balewa	First Republic
1966	J. T. U. Aguiyu Ironsi	Military
1966–75	Yakubu Gowon	Military
1975–76	Murtala Muhammed	Military
1976–79	Olusegun Obasanjo	Military
1979–83	Shehu Shagari	Second Republic
1984–85	Muhammadu Buhari	Military
1985–93	Ibrahim Babangida	Military
1993	Ernest Shonekan	Third Republic and Military
1993–98	Sani Abacha	Military
1998–99	Abdulsalami Abubakar	Military
1999–	Olusegun Obasanjo	Fourth Republic

shared power with three (later four) regional ones that roughly coincided with the territories in which the largest ethnic groups lived. These governments, too, were structured along classical parliamentary lines. The creation of a federal system marked the early recognition that high-stakes politics in this highly diverse country would make governing exclusively from the center impossible without fanning ethnic tensions that long antedated the arrival of the British in the nineteenth century. In retrospect, it is easy to see why that type of system did not work. In parliamentary regimes, politics tends to be adversarial, pitting a unified majority against an equally united opposition. It "works" in a country like Great Britain because everyone accepts the rules of the game and the ideological differences between government and opposition are limited. The opposition accepts the fact that it is not going to have much influence on the shaping of legislation and that its main role is to criticize the government as vociferously as possible as part of its attempt to turn the tables at the next election.

In Nigeria, those conditions were not met by any stretch of the imagination. Early public opinion polls showed considerable hope for the new regime. Subsequent events, however, showed that whatever legitimacy the regime started with evaporated quickly.

Instead, political life turned into a vicious circle. Politicians were convinced that every contest was a **zero-sum** game in which the perceived costs of losing were potentially catastrophic. The government feared that a loss to the opposition would entail far more than simply spending a few years out of office. The opposition, in turn, resented its powerlessness and grew more convinced that the incumbents would do everything possible to stay in control.

It was clear that partisan politics was going to have a strong ethnic base. The main parties produced the four main leaders of those years—Nnamdi Azikiwe (NCNC), **Obafemi Awolowo** (AG), **Aminu Kano** (NEPU), and Sir **Ahmadu Bello** (NPC). Although they all tried to gain support throughout the country, they enjoyed next to no success outside their own ethnic community (the very confusing material on parties and elections in the first two republics is summarized in tables 15.3, 15.4, and 15.5). Each scored major victories in its "home" region. The Muslim-based NPC came in way ahead of the other parties but fell nineteen seats short of an absolute majority and therefore had to form a coalition with the Igbo-based NCNC with which it had had a loose alliance during the election campaign.

In other words, the first government of the new Nigeria represented some of its groups, but only some of them. From the beginning, democracy was on shaky

■ **TABLE 15.3** Political Parties and Leaders in the First and Second Republics

REGION	FIRST REPUBLIC PARTY	SECOND REPUBLIC PARTY	LEADER
North	Northern People's Congress	National Party of Nigeria	Ahmadu Bello
West	Action Group	United Party of Nigeria	Tafawa Balewa
East	National Council of Nigeria and the Cameroons	Nigerian People's Party	Nnamdi Azikiwe

ground. At the regional level, Nigeria was a collection of one-party fiefdoms where leaders bullied their opponents, which only served to heighten ethnic conflict and raise the stakes of national politics.

The new state had a lot of responsibility and a lot of resources to distribute, including the aid money that poured in after independence. Each faction sought to control the government so that it could distribute the lion's share of those resources to itself and its clients. Meanwhile, politicians began making choices about where they were going to operate. The most powerful northern politician, Sir Ahmadu Bello (1909–1906), chose to stay home and serve as premier of the northern region, while his deputy, Balewa, became prime minister of the federal government. Awolowo (1909–1987), the AG's leader, decided to lead the opposition in Lagos, leaving Chief Samuel Ladoke Akintola to head the regional government in the west. Azikiwe left the east to become the governor-general and then president.

Only one thing united these politicians: the pursuit of power. Leading politicians became enthralled with the wealth, status, and privileges holding office produced. To make matters more complicated, while the north dominated politically, it lagged way behind economically. Traditional Islamic rulers and values remained important, which led to limited educational development (only 2.5 percent of northern children were attending school), the exclusion of women from civil and economic life, and something approaching the rejection of "modern" society. Nonetheless, the south feared and resented the north's political power.

The first crisis occurred in the west. Awolowo had gradually moved to the left politically and began criticizing the fancy lifestyles politicians were beginning to lead. In the process he threatened and alienated both the national government and the regional one headed by his colleague and now-rival Akintola. Awolowo provoked a confrontation within the AG that culminated in the regional assembly's vote of no confidence in the Akintola government. Four days later, the federal government declared a state of emergency in the region. Akintola was returned to office, and Awolowo was arrested on trumped-up treason charges and sentenced to serve ten years in prison. The AG was irrevocably split.

Those same problems burst back onto the political scene shortly thereafter when the government tried to conduct a census in 1963. In most countries, the census does not provoke deep divisions. In Nigeria, the census was an example of high-stakes politics because the results would determine how many parliamentary seats would be allocated to each region and how government revenues and outside development aid would be distributed.

Each region's leadership doctored the results. Preliminary results showed that the populations of the east and west grew by 72.2 percent and 69.5 percent respectively in the ten years since the last census was conducted. Demographers easily showed that such growth was impossible given the rate at which women can physically bear children. Meanwhile, the north reported a more or less accurate increase of 33.6 percent, which meant it would see some of its political power eroded. Therefore, northern officials mysteriously "found" 8.5 million people who had been left out of the initial count, which restored them to the same share of the population they had had before the census began. The government threw out these figures and tried again the next year. The results were no different. But because the northern-dominated leadership then used the wildly inaccurate results in allocating seats for that year's parliamentary elections, the census did little more than fuel the antagonism between north and south.

The census debacle fed the next crisis over the parliamentary and regional elections of 1964 and 1965. On the surface, the party system seemed to be realigning into two broad coalitions. On the one hand, the losers in the earlier crisis—the NCNC and Awolowo's wing of the AG—came together with some minor groups to form the slightly left-of-center United Progressive Grand Alliance (UPGA). Meanwhile, the NPC allied with Akintola and others in the southern minority who themselves had created a slightly more conservative **Nigerian National Democratic Party (NNDP).**

In fact, the two were little more than collections of separate, ethnically based organizations, each of which was dominant in its own region. The politicians expressed lofty goals during the campaign. In reality, the campaign was marked by fraud, intimidation, and outright violence, which made a mockery of the democratic process.

Even though a candidate only needed the support of two fellow citizens to get on the ballot, sixty-one seats in the north were uncontested as NPC operatives "convinced" their opponents to withdraw. Violence during the campaign was so widespread that the vote had to be delayed in fifty-nine constituencies. Contests in many others were rigged to such a degree that district-by-district results were never published and would not have been believed had they been. In the end, the NPC-led coalition swept to victory, winning 198 of the 253 seats contested in a first round of voting. Although it did poorly in later elections to fill the other fifty-nine, it still had an overwhelming majority.

The results confirmed the regionalization of Nigerian politics. The NPC won 162 of 167 seats in the north and none anywhere else. All the NNDP victories were in the west, where it won 36 of 57 seats. The opposition carried every seat in the east, in the new mid-western state, and in Lagos. President Azikiwe called on his adversary, Prime Minister Balewa, to form a new government.

Regional elections in the West proved to be the last straw. The campaign was so violent that the federal government banned all public gatherings and sent half the federal police into the region. When results came in, they showed an overwhelming NNDP (Akintola) victory, even though most experts thought the UPGA (Awolowo) had actually won. Akintola returned to power and turned on his opponents, ordering the assassination of two popular UPGA organizers. The UPGA, in turn, decided that it had no legal way to redress its grievances, and it, too, turned to violence that included "wetting" its opponents by drenching them with gasoline and setting them on fire.

On the night of 14 January 1966, Akintola met with Ahmadu Bello and Tafawa Balewa in a desperate attempt to try to restore order. By morning, the military had intervened, overthrown the republic, and killed all three of them.

Military Rule I

What happened that night in Nigeria was, unfortunately, not all that uncommon. At one point or another, well over half of the sub-Saharan African countries have had military rulers, and almost all the rest have had some other type of authoritarian regime.

Nigeria's case was typical, too, in that the military had two reasons for intervening. The obvious one was the one they spoke about—the need to restore order. But there were ethnic reasons as well, for the Nigerian military was by no means neutral in the ethnopartisan battle that was the downfall of the republic.

Like everything else in Nigeria, the army changed rapidly after independence. In 1960, 90 percent of the

Four starving Biafran children sit and lie around a bowl of food in the dirt during the Nigerian-Biafran civil war.

Hulton Archive/Getty Images

officers were British expatriates. By 1966, 90 percent were Africans. Most of the officers, in other words, were young and had risen through the ranks very quickly. A disproportionate number of them, too, were Igbo and resented the way easterners had been treated.

After some initial confusion, Maj. Gen. J. T. U. **Aguiyi Ironsi,** an Igbo, took control of the new military regime. He moved quickly against corrupt officials and promised a rapid return to civilian rule. Ironsi also suppressed civil liberties and established a Supreme Military command (SMC) and a **Federal Executive Council (FEC)** of leading civilian civil servants that were to govern the country for the next thirteen years.

On 24 May 1966, however, Ironsi made a terrible mistake. He announced plans for a new, centralized constitution. This confirmed northerners' worst fears that the coup had, in fact, been carried out to secure Igbo control over the entire country. Hundreds of Igbos, who had been recruited to northern cities because of their educations, were killed in riots that broke out throughout the north.

In July, another set of officers staged a coup that brought the thirty-two-year-old Lt. Col. Yakubu Gowon (1934–) to power. Gowon was chosen in part because he was a "compromise" ethnically—he was a northerner but a Christian.

Now the task was not simply containing the conflict but keeping the country itself intact. The first serious talk of secession came from the north, but the second coup ended it. The SMC divided the country into twelve states in an attempt to reduce the ethnic and regional polariza-

tion, but nothing Gowon and his supporters did could stem the anger and violence.

The eastern region's governor and military commander, Col. Chukwuemeka Ojukwu, refused to recognize Gowon's government and demanded more autonomy for his region. More riots broke out. A million Igbo refugees hastily returned to the region, and Ojukwu ordered all noneasterners to leave the region.

The east then attempted to secede, creating the independent Republic of Biafra, which plunged Nigeria into a bloody civil war. Over the next thirty months, hundreds of thousands of Nigerians died before federal troops finally put down the revolt.

In sharp contrast with the events of the preceding decade, Gowon and the SMC were generous in victory. He announced that the military would remain in power another six years and then hand the government back to civilians. Moreover, oil revenues, especially after the price increases following the 1973–1974 OPEC embargo, left the government with unprecedented resources to use in smoothing the reintegration of the east. Nigeria began to cultivate its image as a continental leader, even entertaining some global pretensions, including the possibility of building an atomic bomb.

By 1974, it had become clear that things were not going well. Many officers proved to be as corrupt and arrogant as their civilian predecessors. In October, Gowon announced that the return to civilian rule would be delayed indefinitely.

Finally, nine years to the day after he seized power,

Gowon was overthrown in a bloodless coup and replaced by General Murtala Muhammed and a group of fellow officers who claimed they were committed to reform. The first day he was in power, General Murtala removed the twelve state governors and quickly moved on to fire 10,000 government officials and 150 officers. On 1 October 1975, he took the most important step of all, outlining a four-year plan for the restoration of democracy. Unfortunately, Murtala also incurred the wrath of many of his fellow officers, who assassinated him during a failed coup attempt on 13 February 1976.

He was replaced by Lt. Gen. Olusegun Obasanjo, who continued preparations for the return to civilian rule. Over the next three years, Obasanjo was a model of integrity and made certain that progress toward the new regime went smoothly. Press and other freedoms were extended, a new constitution was drafted, and seven more states were created to help ease ethnic tensions. A powerful **Federal Electoral Commission (FEDECO)** was established to remove the conduct of elections and the counting of ballots from the partisan process. In July 1978, civilians replaced military officers as governors of the now nineteen states. In 1979, Obasanjo gracefully gave up power.

The Second Republic

Like the Gaullists in France, Obasanjo and his colleagues tried to draft a constitution that they felt would give the country the best chance of avoiding a repeat of the catastrophe for 1966. Parliamentary institutions were rejected in favor of a presidential system modeled quite closely on the United States.

They hoped that a directly elected president would provide the country with an office around which its unity could be rebuilt. The president and vice president would be eligible to serve two four-year terms. In a measure designed to break down the ethnic stranglehold on the parties, a candidate needed to win a majority of the vote and at least a quarter of the ballots cast in at least two-thirds of the states to get elected.

The president appointed a cabinet that was neither drawn from nor responsible to the parliament, which had two houses with equal powers. The House of Representatives would have 449 members elected from single-member districts drawn up on a one-person-one-vote basis (although, of course, no census had been conducted to provide accurate population figures). There would also be a Senate with ninety-five members, five for each state.

FEDECO had to officially license all parties. All First Republic parties were banned. To be licensed, a new party had to demonstrate that it had a national and not just a regional organization.

Problems began before the new republic came into existence. The military government waited until September 1979 to lift its ban on partisan politics. That meant that the new bodies would only have three months to organize, establish national offices, and file the required papers with FEDECO.

Not surprisingly, only nineteen of the fifty or so potential parties were able to comply, and, of those, only five were finally licensed. Not surprisingly, too, four of the five were quite similar to First Republic parties, in large part because only the surviving politicians had well-established networks that would allow them to put together even the appearance of a national organization in so short a period. Thus, the **National Party of Nigeria (NPN)** succeeded the NPC and was based largely in the north and led by Alhaji Shehu Shagari (1925–), a former First Republic minister. Awolowo headed the **United Party of Nigeria (UPN),** whose Yoruba base of support coincided with that of his faction of the old AG. Azikiwe headed an Igbo-based replacement of the NCDC, the **Nigerian People's Party (NPP).** The **People's Redemption Party (PRP)** appealed to the same radical minority in the north as the old NEPU. Only the small Great Nigerian People's Party (GNPP), itself the result of a schism within the NPP, had no clear First Republic roots. Each party tried to broaden its base of support, and each had some success in doing so. Nonetheless, since they had so little time to prepare for the first elections, all the politicians found it easy to return to the rhetoric and style of First Republic days.

Five separate elections for state and federal offices were held in July and August 1979. (See tables 15.4 and 15.5.) Although there were quite a few charges of fraud and unfair campaign practices, the first elections were conducted relatively freely and honestly. The NPN won 37.8 percent of the House and 37.4 percent of the Senate vote respectively. Its candidate, Shagari, won 33.8 percent of the presidential vote, 4.6 percentage points more than his chief rival, Chief Awolowo.

The ethnic tensions that plagued the first republic were rekindled before the second formally began. Awolowo challenged the results, claiming that because Shagari had only won 25 percent of the vote in twelve of the nineteen states, he had not met the constitutional requirements for victory. FEDECO ruled that Shagari had won the 25 percent in twelve and two-thirds states, thereby giving him the minimum required.

Dissatisfaction with the new regime spread quickly once it became clear that the politicians were not going to be any more honest this time. Ministers were accused

▌ TABLE 15.4 Presidential Elections
in the Nigerian Second Republic

NAME	PARTY	PERCENT OF VOTE 1979	PERCENT OF VOTE 2003
Shagari, Shehu	NPN	33.8	47.5
Awolowo, Obafemi	UPN	29.2	37.1
Azikiwe, Nnamdi	NPP	16.7	14.0
Kano, Aminu	PRP	10.3	—
Yusuf, Hassan	PRP	—	3.8
Ibrahim, Izzat	GNPP	10.0	2.5
Braithwaite, Tunji	NAP	—	1.1

▌ TABLE 15.5 Seats in Parliament: 1979–1983

PARTY	HOUSE OF REPRESENTATIVES	SENATE
GNPP	43	8
UPN	111	28
NPN	168	36
PRP	49	7
NPP	78	16
Total	449	95

of taking bribes. A governor was arrested for allegedly trying to smuggle millions of naira into his private British bank account. The national telecommunications center was burned down to keep evidence about fraud and mismanagement from being made public.

Meanwhile, world oil prices collapsed. Well over 90 percent of Nigeria's foreign earnings came from oil sales, so when its income dropped by nearly 60 percent from 1980 to 1983, the government found itself in desperate straits. The federal and state governments no longer had enough money to pay civil service salaries or complete development projects. "Still," as Larry Diamond put it, "the politicians and contractors continued to bribe, steal, smuggle, and speculate, accumulating vast illicit fortunes and displaying them lavishly in stunning disregard for public sensitivities. By its third anniversary, disenchantment with the Second Republic was acute, overt, and remarkably broad-based."[4]

The second round of elections was held in 1983. All observers assumed that they would be a make-it-or-break-it event for the republic. Unfortunately, the campaign proved even more violent and fraudulent than the earlier ones.

There was blatant manipulation of the voter registration lists, which showed an unbelievable 34 per-

cent increase in the size of the electorate in just four years, most of which occurred in the north. Meanwhile, millions of names were missing altogether in the south and east.

Both Awolowo and Azikiwe insisted on running for president. Most observers expected that the thus-divided opposition would guarantee Shagari's reelection. But fearing the worst, the NPN passed out thousands of ballots that had already been filled out, bribed election officials, and refused to allow opposition poll watchers to do their jobs. When the votes were counted, Shagari and the NPN had won a landslide victory. The official—and unbelievable—figures gave him nearly 48 percent of the presidential vote, an almost 50 percent improvement over his 1979 tally. Even more amazingly, not only did all the corrupt NPN incumbent governors win, but the party won in six more states, giving it control of thirteen in all. And, despite all the evidence of growing dissatisfaction with the government and the NPN, it turned its slim plurality into a two-thirds majority in the House of Representatives.

To no one's surprise, the military stepped in again on New Year's Eve 1983. Like its predecessor, the Second Republic was not to survive its second election.

Military Rule II

At first, the military coup was widely accepted as inevitable given the level of corruption. As a former army leader put it, "[d]emocracy had been in jeopardy for the past four years. It died with the election. The army only buried it."

The new military regime, led by Muhammadu Buhari, was a lot like the old one. The Supreme Military Command was reconstituted. The military rulers cracked down, arresting hundreds of civil servants and politicians, including the president, vice president, and numerous ministers and governors. Soldiers found vast quantities of cash in the homes and offices of those arrested, lending even more credence to the rumors of corruption in high places.

Decree Number 2 gave the government broad powers to arrest anyone thought to be a security risk. The military interpreted this to mean anyone who criticized the regime. Decree Number 3 established military tribunals to try former politicians and government officials. Decree Number 4 banned any publication or broadcast that inaccurately criticized any government official or policy.

Support for the regime was not to last. It soon became clear that the officers were far less vigilant in prosecuting former NPN leaders than other politicians.

[4] Larry Diamond, "Nigeria: Pluralism, Statism, and the Struggle for Democracy." In Larry Diamond, Juan J. Linz, and Seymour Martin Lipset, eds. *Democracy in Developing Countries, vol. 2, Africa* (Boulder, Colo.: Lynne Rienner, 1988), 53.

Moreover, the economy continued to founder as the oil-induced crisis sent unemployment, inflation, and foreign debt skyrocketing. And, the government gave indications that it would not prepare a transition back to democracy.

Few were surprised when Buhari was, in turn, overthrown on 25 August 1985 in yet another coup, led by General Ibrahim Babangida (1941–) who was the first general who actually assumed the title of president. In his first months in power, Babangida sent mixed messages. On the one hand, he immediately repealed Decree Number 4 and declared that his government "does not intend to lead a country where individuals are under the fear of expressing themselves." Journalists were released from jail, and the detention centers created to hold those arrested under Buhari were opened for public inspection. On the other hand, Babangida continued the crackdown, banning serving politicians from public life for a decade. Babangida renamed the SMC the *Armed Forces Ruling Council (AFRC)*, but in practice there was little difference between the two.

In 1986, however, the regime embarked in two new directions that made Babangida's rule seem much like Obasanjo's and will be explored in more depth in the section on public policy that follows. First, the AFRC accepted a new economic policy of **structural adjustment,** including fiscal austerity and the support of market and other capitalist practices. Second, it announced a phased transition back to democracy to be completed by 1990.

The latter was greeted skeptically by critics who had come to doubt any general's commitment to civilian rule. Their skepticism grew as the government announced a series of delays in its plans to hand over power.

Nonetheless, the military plugged ahead with its reform effort, guiding a constituent assembly through the process of writing a constitution for a third republic in 1988. The next year, it began rebuilding the political parties. All politicians who held office in the First and Second republics were prohibited from running in at least the first set of elections. Thirteen groups asked to be certified as political parties, but all were rejected. Instead, the government created two new ones, the **National Republican Convention (NRC)** and **Social Democratic Party (SDP),** which were, in Babangida's own terms, "one a little to the left, and the other a little to the right of center."

Once presidential elections were finally scheduled for 1993, both parties nominated rich business leaders with close ties to the military regime to be their candidates. And, despite the regime's attempt to cast politics in national and economic terms, ethnicity remained on center stage. The NRC's candidate, Bashir Tofa, a Hausa-Fulani banker, assiduously chose an Igbo Christian as his running mate. The SDP, in turn, nominated Yoruba Moshood Abiola (1937–96), a well-known shipping magnate, publisher, and sponsor of soccer teams. Because he was a Muslim they thought Abiola might appeal in the north as well.

Neither candidate would have made an American campaign manager happy. Tofa was so unknown he did not even appear in Nigeria's *Who's Who.* His commitment to democracy was suspect, since he had publicly urged Babangida to stay in power until the turn of the century. Abiola was better-known in part because of Afro-Beat star Fela Kuti's song about him and the publicity he received in 1992 for demanding that Britain and the other colonial powers pay reparations for the damage they did to Nigeria and the rest of Africa.

The election campaign had little of the violence that marred earlier campaigns. But that is about the only positive thing that one can say about it. Only about 30 percent of the population turned out to vote. Voting patterns once again broke along ethnic lines, as Abiola ran far better in the east and west and Tofa in the north.

Unofficial results showed that Abiola had won easily with 55 percent of the vote. But even before the election occurred, a shadowy group close to Babangida, the Association for a Better Nigeria, called on the general to stay in power. As the results began coming in, the association went to court, citing rampant corruption in an attempt to get the publication of election returns overturned.

Finally, on 23 June, the military nullified the vote. It issued a decree claiming, "These steps were taken to save our judiciary from being ridiculed and politicized locally and internationally." Babangida insisted the military still intended to return the country to democratic and civilian rule in August, but it was hard to see how that could happen.

In turn, Abiola and his supporters went to court and took to the airwaves to defend what they clearly saw as a victory at the polls and to proclaim their boycott of any subsequent elections. More protests, some of which turned violent, took place, especially in Lagos, Abiola's base of support. On 26 August, Babangida decided to forgo another election and turned power over to a hand-picked civilian government, headed by Ernest Shonekan, the former chief executive officer of Nigeria's largest business conglomerate. Although Shonekan claimed otherwise, he was little more than a pawn for Babangida and the military.

This attempt at civilian rule was to last but eighty-three days. In November, the Supreme Court ruled that the Shonekan government had been put in office illegally. Within days, he was forced out of power by yet

SANI ABACHA

Issouf Sanogo/Getty Images

Sani Abacha was the military ruler of Nigeria from 1993 until his death in 1998.

Abacha was born in the northern city of Kano in 1943. After graduating from high school in his hometown, he joined the army and received further training at some of the most prestigious military academies in Great Britain. He then rose through the ranks very quickly and was promoted to general in 1980, at which point he received further training in Monterrey, California.

There is some debate about how large a role Abacha played in General Babangida's coup in 1983 or in his subsequent government. By the early 1990s, he had certainly become one of the regime's most vocal "insider" critics. When the 1993 election led to another coup, he was the obvious person to lead the next military government.

It was probably the most ruthless and certainly most corrupt of Nigeria's military governments. It is estimated that Abacha's family alone spirited $5 billion out of the country, a sum probably equaled by his colleagues.

Abacha died at his villa in June 1998. Rumors about his death still abound. The most credible one is that he suffered a heart attack after taking Viagra as part of an encounter with four Indian prostitutes.

His legacy continues. As we will see, one of the most popular Nigerian web scams purportedly comes from his widow who seeks help in obtaining their funds, which are supposedly frozen in foreign bank accounts.

Nigerian President General Sani Abacha at the airport of Abuja shortly before he died of cardiac arrest

another military leader, Sani Abacha, who had been a co-conspirator with Babangida in 1983 but had since become one of his fiercest critics.

This attempt at civilian rule lasted a mere eighty-three days. Even though the winners of that summer's elections never took offices in institutions that were never formally created, it is commonly referred as the Third Republic.

Military Rule III

Abacha appointed a number of civilians to his cabinet, including Abiola's running mate, a leading civil rights lawyer, and the editor of the largest independent newspaper. Nonetheless, Abacha's rule turned out to be the most repressive and the most corrupt in Nigerian history.

In summer 1994, Abiola declared himself president.

The government responded by arresting him and dozens of others. Abacha noted that "choosing the path of confrontation and subversion at this time of our national history will not be tolerated. Such acts will be sternly punished." All civilian political organizations were officially disbanded by the Provisional Ruling Council made up exclusively of officers.

Opposition continued with a long series of strikes, concentrated in the petroleum industry located mostly in the southwestern part of the country where Abiola came from. The regime cracked down on dissidents—real and imagined—culminating in the execution of the author and environmental activist Ken Saro-Wiwa in 1995.

The government cracked down harder than ever to keep its real and potential opposition cowed. In late summer 1995, Abacha purged the cabinet and fired the heads of the trade unions, the army and navy, and all the government institutions except for the elementary school system. More worrisome for most is the repression against dissidents, including the Nobel Prize–winning author Wole Soyinka who had his passport seized and was forced into exile. Other opponents like radical lawyer Gani Fawehinmi spent time in jail under a new law that allows the government to detain people without trial. Other detainees included leaders of the National Democratic Coalition and the Campaign for Democracy, as well as former President Obasanjo who was sentenced to death shortly before the military government fell.

The government gained some international support for sending its troops to neighboring countries on peacekeeping missions, but took more criticism for its human rights and economic policies. It got to the point that one joke put it that Abacha's Nigeria exported what it didn't have (prodemocratic troops) and imported what it already had (oil).

In other respects, the military was losing its grip on power. That grip literally came to an end in 1998 when Abacha died under mysterious circumstances at one of his villas (see the box on Abacha) shortly after Abiola died under equally mysterious circumstances while he was in prison awaiting trial.

We could consider why military rule unraveled under Abacha and how that helped pave the way for the creation of the Fourth Republic. But it makes more sense to see those details in the context of the broader prospects for **democratization** included in the section on public policy that follows.

Political Culture

Any country's political culture reflects the impact of its history on the way people think about politics and society as a whole. In Nigeria's case, the lack of unity and support for the regime and, at times, for the very existence of Nigeria have plagued it since independence. If anything, the actions of the elites since then have left the country more alienated and polarized than it was forty years ago.

Mass Political Culture

As with most third world countries, there have been no systematic studies of Nigerian political culture even though most observers are convinced that it is one of the most important causes of its fluid, unstable politics.

Therefore, all we can do here is outline the broad themes those observers point to.

First and most obviously, there is little that most Nigerians like about their political system. Things did not start that way. Polls conducted in the early 1960s suggested that Nigerians had a greater sense of national identity and pride than did most third world peoples. One 1962 survey, for example, found that only 16 percent of those sampled had trouble thinking of Nigeria in national terms. Similarly, three quarters of that same sample felt that Nigeria had "made progress" over the past five years and two-thirds thought it would continue to do so in the five years to come.

An Afroscope survey done forty years later found that 68 percent of Nigerians believed that "democracy is preferable to any other kind of government." The same poll reported that half of Nigerians supported a free-market economy while 41 percent thought the government should plan production and distribution of goods and services. However, neither the early optimism nor the more recent sentiments in favor of democracy has turned into sustained support for any of the country's regimes. If anything, Nigerians have grown more skeptical and cynical. The recent Afroscope poll showed that 20 percent of Nigerians thought that in "some circumstances, a non-democratic government can be preferable."

Part of the problem is that Nigeria is one of the most fragmented countries in the world along overlapping religious and ethnic lines. The more naive observers assumed that ethnic identification would give way to a national one soon after independence, not just in Nigeria but in the newly independent states in general. That has not been the case. If anything, ethnicity has become more, not less, important.

The limited evidence available to us suggests that most Nigerians do in some way think of themselves as Nigerians. However, their ethnic identification matters more as a source of pride (e.g., we Igbo) and even more importantly as a source of dislike and division (e.g., you Yoruba).

The three largest groups have virtually nothing in common politically, socially, or historically. The overwhelming majority of Nigerians only speak their "home" language, and if they learn another, it is invariably English and not one of the other indigenous tongues. The different groups live separately, either in their traditional regions or in ethnic enclaves called "sabon gari," literally strangers' quarters.

Closely paralleling ethnicity is religion. Religion is nowhere near as important as ethnicity in most of the south, where, for instance, Yoruba Muslims tend to act politically as Yorubas more often than as Muslims. In the north, however, it is hard to disentangle the impact of religion and ethnicity because so much of Hausa-Fulani culture is defined in terms of Islam. Traditional political and religious officials (who are often one and the same) have resisted attempts to "Westernize" the region, often with considerable success. Women in the north have only voted under limited circumstances and then only in voting booths that are separate from and perpendicular to those for men. The northern desire to use a separate legal system based on Sharia or Islamic law held up the drafting of the constitutions for every republic although northern states have been allowed to implement versions of it since Obasanjo returned to power.

Finally, there is the region itself, which to some degree transcends both religion and ethnicity in even broader fears the north has about the south and vice versa. As we saw earlier, many northerners are afraid that southern (or modern) cultural values and economic practices will undermine their way of life. Southerners, by contrast, fear that a northern majority could seize power and leave them a permanent and aggrieved minority.

Nigeria is by no means the only country divided along such lines. The problem is that Nigeria is not just fragmented, it is polarized as well. Under the best of circumstances, it is hard for people to reach compromises about identity-based issues. The use of Sharia in some parts of a country but not in others is seen as a win-lose conflict. Any concession is viewed by many people as total defeat. In Nigeria, the politicians who have fanned the flames of ethnic, religious, and regional hatred also failed to address the country's real social and economic shortcomings. Therefore, it was just a matter of time until the violence that had been primarily orchestrated by the elites started breaking out among an increasingly embittered public.

The importance of this alienation has been magnified by other aspects of Nigerian political culture, not the least of which has been the failure of class issues to take root. Most Nigerians live in abject poverty, one of the few things most Nigerians share. Moreover, the gap between rich and poor has grown dramatically, in particular as the corrupt political elite siphoned off public funds to support its lavish lifestyle. Had economic issues become more important in defining basic values and assumptions about politics, Nigeria might have found itself in a better position to mute the divisions across ethnic, religious, and regional lines.

There are also sharp differences between rural and urban cultures. In the countryside, where about two-thirds of all Nigerians still live, many "traditional" structures and values remain strong. In particular, rural elites have found it relatively easy to turn the power the British handed them as emirs or chiefs into powerful patron-client relations.

In a 1988 study of politics in rural Nigeria, William Miles showed that the traditional distinction between nobles and commoners has been carried over into the politics of modern Nigeria. Virtually everyone seems to accept the hierarchical relationships in which clients defer to their patrons when it comes to politics or advice in general.

Moreover, most seem to reject such notions as "all men are created equal" or a world in which one's rank or status does not matter. To the degree that it is understood, democracy is sharply at odds with values that remain strong in most areas of rural Nigeria. One herder defined democracy this way in talking with Miles: "Men wander around like cattle, without any direction. They make all kinds of excited noises, but there's no sense to it. Each goes his own way, lost, until there's no more herd." [5]

In addition, illiteracy remains the highest in the countryside. Not surprisingly, local studies have shown that most rural residents have at most a fuzzy idea of what national political processes and issues are all about. For instance, on the morning after the 1983 coup, Nigerian radio began playing Western classical music, which residents in one typical village assume is military music because it is only played before the announcement of a coup. When the announcement itself was made, it was done in English, which very few people in the countryside understand. Only two days later was it broadcast in Hausa. Perhaps because of their isolation, rural residents rarely get deeply involved in national politics. Rather, they tend either to follow the initiatives of their local patrons or be swayed by the outsiders who appear during crises or election campaigns.

The booming cities are a different story altogether. There, observers find highly politicized people who seem willing to take a stand on almost any issue at almost any time. They also find large numbers of highly dissatisfied people, alienated from a government that cannot provide jobs, housing, or health care.

That cynicism is not simply an urban phenomenon. The peasants Miles lived with were convinced that politicians are by their very nature dishonest and that it makes no sense whatsoever to trust them. And since cul-

---

[5] William Miles, *Elections in Nigeria: A Grassroots Perspective* (Boulder, Colo: Lynn Rienner, 1988), 86.

tures change slowly under the best of circumstances, it seems unlikely that these values will erode any time soon.

Elite Culture

In every country, elites think and act differently from average citizens. In few places, however, are the differences as pronounced and as politically important as they are in Nigeria.

The political and economic elite has been what amounts to a bourgeois class, if not quite in the way Marx anticipated. Its wealth stems from its control of the state. This has given rise to a category of political and bureaucratic officials who have used their positions for personal gain and who, like the European bourgeoisie Marx wrote about, have been able to protect their wealth and power under civilian and military rule alike.

Consequently, with but a few exceptions, members of the Nigerian elite were willing to violate the rules of the democratic game under the first two republics and overstepped normal bounds of authority when the military was in power. That greed and the willingness to subvert the democratic process that went along with it were shared by the elite as a whole and were not the province of any particular ethnic, religious, or regional group.

Nonelectoral Participation

If we looked at culture alone, it would be tempting to conclude that Nigeria is a disastrous civil war or revolution waiting to happen. Neither seems imminent in Nigeria today, ironically, precisely because the long history of military rule has neither provided many outlets for protest nor created widespread expectations that mass involvement of any sort can accomplish much. Thus, while there have been episodes of spontaneous, violent protest as recently as 2004, they have been few and far between in comparison with India or many other ethnically divided societies.

As with political culture, there have been sharp differences in patterns of political participation between rural and urban Nigeria. If the anthropologists are to be believed, there is little ongoing political life in the countryside other than during election campaigns. There have been a few times, however, when major protests broke out in the countryside. Activists from the Ijwa and Itsekeri peoples had been engaged in years of near–civil war over ethnic differences and access to the oil wealth of the Niger delta region. In August of 2003, more than one hundred people were killed. This ongoing conflict has shut down oil wells and reduced Nigeria's production by more than 10 percent. In another part of the country,

journalists estimated that more than eight hundred people died fighting in the middle belt state of Plateau during June 2004.

Most of the largest and often violent protests that have wracked Nigeria have occurred primarily in the cities, often in the former capital, Lagos. In 2004, violence broke out in the northern city of Kano resulting in the destruction of many churches. Observers note that such violence, urban and rural, has been more frequent under democratic regimes than under the more authoritarian military governments that were more intent on quashing all forms of mass participation. Nonetheless, in the early 1990s, Lagos rioters burned cars, looted stores, and trashed government offices to protest against the government's acceptance of an IMF-imposed austerity program to be discussed in the policy section that follows. In urban areas, we also find a wide variety of groups representing doctors, lawyers, students, and more. Informal groups of business leaders or ethnic associations seem to be far more influential in large part because they can work more effectively within the patron-client networks revolving around religious, linguistic, and regional affiliations that still largely dominate Nigerian politics.

There is one other issue that transcends ethnicity that could provoke intense conflict in the future—youth. For most readers of this book, the term "youth" covers people in their teens before they head off to university education or careers. In Nigeria, youth can include young people—especially men—into their thirties who have yet to make enough money to move away from home. There are millions of young men in that category, and in the years to come, they could pose the greatest danger to the stability of any regime. Already, young men and women in the oil fields in the south have taken the lead in protesting outside oil companies and the Muslim communities of the north have supported the imposition of Sharia law.

On the other hand, we should not confuse military rule in Nigeria with some of the extremely ruthless dictatorships the world has seen in this century, such as Saddam Hussein's in Iraq. During most periods of military rule, the press has remained reasonably free and has frequently criticized governments and their policies. Many interest groups were allowed to remain in existence, though, as with the press, those critical of military rule itself were often suppressed.

Though they have been few and far between, there have also been a number of interest groups that were not organized along ethnic lines. In particular, they had an important role in pushing for legal and constitutional reform when military rule began to weaken after execution of Saro-Wiwa and his colleagues. Thus, today's People's

Conflict in Nigeria

Almost every instance of protest politics in Nigeria since independence has revolved around religious, linguistic, and regional issues.

No single incident reflects that better than a bizarre series of protests that broke out in the northern city of Kaduna in November 2002 and ultimately killed more than one hundred people and injured five hundred more.

For reasons that defy belief, the leaders of the Miss World Pageant decided to hold the 2002 finals in this city populated largely by devout Muslims. Many of them were deeply offended by the notion of scantily clad young women parading across the stage of their local civic center. Anger mounted when an English language newspaper jokingly criticized the anti–Miss World activists by writing that the Prophet Muhammad would probably have chosen a woman like these for his wife.

The protests started out calmly enough. Crowds chanted "Allahu Akhbar" (God is great) or "Miss World is sin." Quickly and without much warning things turned violent. People the mob thought were Christians were pulled from cars, beaten, and often killed. Churches were burned; Christians later retaliated and burned mosques.

The organizers of the Miss World contest moved it to London. A Muslim Turk won.

One of the few recent incidents of conflict that did not involve ethnicity occurred in summer 2004 when urban residents (pretty much the only people who own cars) rioted after the government announced that gasoline prices would be set by the market and not fixed at an arbitrarily low level by the government.

Democratic Party (PDP) is an outgrowth of the earlier People's Democratic Movement that was founded by General Shehu Yar'Adua and other former officials who had been imprisoned under Babangida (Yar'Adua died in prison in 1996). Similarly, the sixty-three human rights organizations that made up the Transition Monitoring Group (TMG) brought to light a number of violations of the electoral law during the 1999 legislative and presidential campaign.

Political Parties and Elections

Political parties and competitive elections are accorded a privileged place in analyses of democracy. Their very existence is part of the definition of liberal democracy itself. How they operate in practice goes a long way in determining whether or not democracy will endure.

At this point, it should come as no surprise that at least until 1999, political parties and elections instead contributed to Nigeria's problems because they magnified existing ethnic tensions. Therefore, after the ill-fated presidential election of 1993, the Abacha government banned all partisan activity. Indeed, it was only after Abacha's death in June 1998 that the government authorized the creation of new political parties.

Unlike the parties created along with the Second Republic, the parties that sprang to life in late 1998 had little in common with earlier institutions. In all, nine political parties gained legal recognition. Each tried to ensure victory in one area of the country and gather support in other parts. Thus, the successful parties tended to be large coalitions. Of the nine, only three did well enough in state and local elections to be eligible to run in the 1999 legislative and presidential elections.

The two most prominent of them had close links to the military. Obasanjo and others who had come to oppose the Abacha government in the mid-1990s (though only after many of them had been sent to prison) formed the **People's Democratic Party (PDP).** The smaller All People's Party (APP) (now the **All Nigeria People's Party, ANPP**) was led by politicians who were close to Abacha. Only the small **Alliance for Democracy (AD)** had anything approaching unambiguous democratic credentials, since it was led by people who had been close to Abiola.

Perhaps even more significantly, all the parties had loose but noticeable links to the ethnically based parties dating back to the First Republic. Although he was personally a Yoruba, Obasanjo's PDP's roots could be traced back to the dominant Muslim-based parties of the north from the 1960s onward. Similarly, the APP had an Igbo stronghold, while the AD drew support from a handful of Igbo and the bulk of the Yoruba population. That said, all of the parties do a bit better than their predecessors in building support across ethnic lines.

Even after two national elections, it is hard to tell what the parties stand for since their goals and ideologies are rarely mentioned in their own literature or in the press. Only the AD has a website, and it has not been updated since 2001. For readers looking for more detailed information on the parties, visit www.nigeriamasterweb .com/Politics.html.

The Elections of 1999

The 1999 elections largely lived up to the mixed expectations of most observers. On the one hand, Obasanjo and the PDP did about as well as expected. The party handily won the legislative elections, totaling just under 60 percent of the vote and the seats for both houses. Their poor

■ **TABLE 15.6** Elections in Nigeria: 1999 and 2003

PARTY	HOUSE OF REPRESEN-TATIVES VOTE 1999	PRESI-DENTIAL VOTE 1999	HOUSE OF REPRESEN-TATIVES VOTE 1999	PRESI-DENTIAL VOTE 2003
PDP	58(%)	63	55	63
APP/ANPP	19	37	27	32
AD	21	—	9	—
Others	7	—	8	5

Note: The APP and ANPP ran a single candidate for president in 1999 and AD did not run one in 2003.

showing in the legislative elections prompted the AD and APP to run a single candidate, Olu Falae, in the presidential election. Obasanjo, however, did slightly better than his party had in that two-way race, winning nearly 63 percent of the vote, though he ran poorly in his native Yoruba-dominated west. (See table 15.6.)

On the other hand, there were the all-too-frequent charges of electoral fraud that prompted Falae to challenge the outcome in the courts. International and domestic monitors agreed that there had been considerable abuse. The most flagrant examples included instances in which the polls never opened because local officials arrived at the voting stations with ballot papers that had already been filled out. Nonetheless, most impartial observers felt that there were abuses on all sides, and that they were not extensive enough to have altered the outcome of the election. The courts then threw out Falae's challenge and Obasanjo took office on schedule.

The Elections of 2003

In some ways, the 2003 elections were more important for the new republic's success than those held four years earlier. The first vote marked an important transition away from military rule. The second one gave us more insights into whether it could last, something we will expect to see even more clearly when the third round of voting occurs in 2007 (www.cdd.org.uk/Briefing_Nig _Elections.htm#Whynigeria).

The results were as ambiguous as they had been four years earlier. The campaign and balloting progressed reasonably honestly. Nonetheless, there were signs of Nigeria's difficult past in this relatively placid election.

In particular, the main candidates were all eerily familiar because of their military backgrounds. President Obasanjo ran for reelection atop the PDP ticket. Former military ruler Buhari led the **ANPP** (formerly the APP). The third candidate to win a noticeable number of votes was Chukwuemeka Odumegwu Ojukwu who had led the secession attempt by Biafra in the 1960s. The presiden-

tial candidates, in a practice dating back to the Second Republic, chose running mates to ethnically balance their parties' tickets. At legislative, state, and local levels these parties competed with twenty-seven smaller, more parochial groups.

Legislative elections were held on 12 April 2003. Presidential and gubernatorial elections were held 19 April. The recently established **Independent National Electoral Commission (INEC)** (www.inecnigeria.org) ran the election without significant political interference and reported that more than two-thirds of registered voters turned out for the presidential ballot.

The Electoral Act of 2002 and a number of court decisions meant political parties could more easily gain recognition and run candidates. Therefore thirty parties were able to run candidates. In spite of the massive increase in the number of parties, the results were not very different from those in 1999. (See table 15.6 again.) If anything, the PDP solidified its control of the executive and legislative branches.

The reactions of the losing parties were also similar to what occurred in 1999. The opposition challenged the results, alleging administrative incompetence by INEC and massive voter fraud. The courts threw most of the objections out. International observers noted as many irregularities as seen in 1999, but none that seemed likely to affect the outcome except perhaps for governors' races in a handful of states where INEC forced the states to hold new elections.

The Fragile Nigerian State

Of the countries we have considered so far in Part 4, Nigeria comes closest to the general model presented in Chapter 11 where I suggested that the weakness of third world states is best reflected in their ineffectual central institutions. That might seem surprising at first glance. Military rulers, in particular, ran the state with an iron fist. They tolerated little or no organized opposition. Thus, when Abacha and his colleagues seized power in November 1993, they dissolved the parliament and all the other governmental institutions that would have been part of the Third Republic. In other words, with the exception of the civil service, the institutions of Nigerian government have rarely lasted more than a few years, and, at any given moment, their structures and operations have reflected the views of whichever group happened to be in power.

Whoever is in charge, the weakness of the state is obvious. Neither the military nor civilian authorities have been able assure basic law and order in Lagos and other cities. Foreign diplomats and business executives rarely leave their homes without armed escorts. It's not just the rich and powerful. The bodies of people killed in traffic accidents are frequently left by the side of the road, because the people who are supposed to collect them are afraid of being attacked by gang members or being held until they pay a bribe to the police.

The one civilian institution that has had a continuous existence since independence is the bureaucracy. Yet civil servants are often unpaid, and when they do get their salaries, they do not take home enough money to live on. As a result, many are corrupt.

To complicate matters further, the Nigerian state does not have many resources. A full 82 percent of its revenue comes from either the sale of oil or taxes on the profits of the operations of multinational petroleum companies operating in the country. While such statistics are reflected in the country's poverty, they also mean that winning control of government is more of a high-stakes contest than it would be in any of the countries covered earlier in this book because control of the state allows the leadership to put friends, relatives, and clients on government payrolls and to direct development projects to favored villages and neighborhoods.

The Fourth Republic

President Obasanjo and his colleagues hope to end nearly half a century in which Nigeria had a weak, corrupt, and often repressive state and replace it with one that is both more effective and responsive to the expectations of most of Nigeria's people. The initial signs were not all that encouraging. For example, the new constitution was not published until after the 1999 legislative elections took place and many of its provisions were not known until after Obasanjo was inaugurated. In the years since then, however, the new institutions have at least demonstrated considerable staying power if not the capacity to create a state that can enact and implement public policy nationwide (www.nigeria.gov.ng).

The centerpiece of the new state is its American-style presidency, which is not responsible to the National Assembly (www.nigeria-law.org/ConstitutionOf TheFederalRepublicOfNigeria.htm). It, in turn, has two houses, a 360-member House of Representatives elected from single-member districts and a 109-member Senate composed of three people elected from each state plus a single official from the capital region of Abuja.

For the moment, at least, the presidency is the most important institution in Nigeria, largely because of Obasanjo himself. The president is responsible for managing the day-to-day operations of the state and is also com-mander in chief of the armed forces, an important power in a country with such a long history of coups and military rule. As is the case in most such systems, the president is not a member of the legislature, but he (or she, presumably, at some point in the future) can go before the legislature to make statements on basic public policy issues on the initiative of either body.

The National Assembly's powers are quite similar to those of the Congress in the United States. Each house must agree on the same version of a bill before it is submitted to the president. While the president does not have a formal veto power, he must give his assent to it before it becomes law. If he refuses to do so or fails to act within thirty days, the bill is then returned to the two houses of the legislature. If each house passes it again with at least a two-thirds majority, it becomes law without any further action from the president.

The constitution also put in place a fairly standard judicial system for a country with such strong Anglo-American legal roots. It retains the earlier regimes' network of local and state courts and reinforced the power of a Supreme Court whose authority was often honored in the breach during Nigeria's first thirty years of independence. The one important new feature is an appellate court for Sharia law in Abuja and any other state that chooses to establish one. If a case involves issues that touch on Islam, either the plaintiff or the defendant can refer it to these religious courts rather than to a secular one.

The Personalization of Power

As is the case in much of the third world, one should not read too much into the formal language of the constitution and other legal documents because they tend to suggest that offices have more power than the individuals who occupy them. Doing so is misleading.

In a country like Nigeria, however, in which most institutions are weak, the person who occupies a position of authority is often far more important than the formal responsibilities and rules of the office itself. That emphasis on the individual politician may turn out well when he or she is someone of integrity and talent, as seems to be the case for President Obasanjo. But it also opens the door for abuse of power when the individuals involved lack either the ethical principles or the ability he and a handful of other Nigerian politicians have demonstrated over the years.

Not all observers are so optimistic about Obasanjo's presidency because of his continuing relationship with many senior officers. Nonetheless, he has spent the bulk of his presidency trying to reduce the impact of any indi-

OLUSEGUN OBASANJO

Olusegun Obasanjo was born in 1937 in Abeokuta in the largely Yoruba region in the southeast. Like many soldiers of his generation, he won swift promotion in part because leaders after independence had to replace the British expatriate officers who had run the military during the colonial era.

At age 33, he was already a general and was the officer who accepted the surrender of Biafran forces that ended the bloody civil war. Six years later, he was part of the group that staged a military coup that made him the country's *de facto* ruler for the next three years.

Unlike most other military rulers around the world, Obasanjo relatively willingly and relatively graciously presided over the return to civilian rule with the creation of the Second Republic in 1979, at which point he retired from active political life. At that point he returned to his home region to set up a poultry and pig farm.

He never fully withdrew from political life, serving on a number of ad hoc groups dealing with broader African issues, including apartheid in South Africa. He also was the founding president of Transparency International.

In 1995, he and forty-three other former soldiers were arrested by the Abacha government. Obasanjo, himself, was sentenced to death and expected to be executed when Abacha suddenly died in 1998 and all political prisoners were released. He instantly became the favorite to win the presidency of the new republic, an election he won in a landslide the next year.

Most observers think that Obasanjo has been one of the most honest and effective elected leaders in recent African history. His critics, on the other hand, point to the fact that at least ten thousand Nigerians have died in the first five years of his presidency.

---

vidual (including himself) and the likelihood that the military could ever come back to power. As he stated shortly after his first election, "we need someone who can act as a bridge for a gradual disengagement of the military. If we don't have someone who can understand them, then I think we will have problems."

Corruption

The weakness of Nigeria's state is most evident in the corruption that has plagued the country since independence. Of course, there is much we do not know about the magnitude of the problem since corrupt officials rarely talk about their ill-gotten gains. There is no doubt, however, that corruption is widespread. There was thus little surprise when a 1996 poll of international business executives rated Nigeria the most corrupt country in the world. Along those same lines, President Obasanjo built much of his political base for his return to power as head of Transparency International, an NGO that works to uncover corruption in the relations between businesses and governments.

Corruption takes many forms. In 1995, *60 Minutes* broadcast a program on scams run by Nigerian "businessmen" seeking investment capital from naive, rich foreigners. Charges (a euphemism for bribes) are exacted for ignoring environmental regulations on imported goods or even getting a boarding card for an air-

plane flight. The customs system is especially notorious. According to one importer, "No one pays the full customs duty. The going rate is to pay the customs officer a third of the difference between the official rate of duty and what you actually pay in duty (usually nothing)."

Under the military, the government encouraged foreign investment, but official approval for a contract typically only came when the officers in charge get their "personal interests" satisfied. Those interests came in the form of cars, offshore bank accounts, or tuition fees for their children's schooling abroad.

In 1992, the Nigerian National Petroleum Company (NNPC) had a gap of $2.7 billion, equal to 10 percent of the country's total GNP, between what international experts say it earned and what it claims it took in. The assumption is that the money had been diverted to the military leaders' offshore bank accounts.

The corruption is typified in the actions of the most recent governments to retrieve money allegedly spirited abroad by the Abacha family. Before he turned power over to Obasanjo, Abubakar obtained about $750 million from those accounts. The Obasanjo government has convinced Swiss banking authorities to freeze more than $600 million in Abacha deposits and to return nearly $140 million. Banks on the island of Jersey have returned $149 million to the Nigerian government. If government estimates are correct, the Abachas still have $3 billion in foreign bank accounts, and who knows how much

Most observers think that petrochemical products are Nigeria's leading export. Those of who live much of our lives on the Internet know otherwise. Nigeria is the home of the most egregious e-mail financial scam.

They come in many forms. In all cases, if you just send a few thousand dollars, the remaining balance will be wired to your account.

(Alleged) Nigerians started these scams. Here is an excerpt of the first and most infamous of them all, supposedly from Sani Abacha's widow. Of course, I have NOT included her email address.

> It gives me great pleasure to contact you. I am Mrs. Mariam Abacha, widow of the former Nigerian Military President who died mysteriously of a heart attack in 1998.
>
> I decided to contact you so that we can arrange for favorable terms of trade for the possibility of moving some family funds to your possession.
>
> Since the death of my husband, our family has not been allowed to move freely by the current government because of the enmity that existed between General Abacha and the current civilian president. Consequently, our joint bank accounts here in Nigeria and abroad have been frozen in a very wicked manner. In all, frozen accounts have made our family to have lost over $2 billion.
>
> All these losses were mainly due the fact that we mistakenly operated these accounts with Abacha family names which made it possible for the authorities to locate these funds.
>
> We are appealing for your urgent assistance to move the fund to your private or company bank account in any country you believe the money would be safe. Please contact my personal representative, who will arrange for the transfer of funds. Please, you are required to treat this letter as very confidential as no other person knows about this money except me, my son, Mohammed, and your very self.
>
> May God bless you as you help us at this difficult time.
>
> Mrs. Mariam S. Abacha

other members of the former military regime have in addition.

The Obasanjo government has made a major attempt to reduce corruption. The ninety-three top generals who served under Abacha were replaced as soon as Obasanjo took office. He also revoked all appointments and contracts made by the military after 1 January 1999. During his October 1999 visit to Washington and in almost all his other public statements for domestic as well as international audiences he stressed the new regime's commitment to honesty.

An investigation in 2004 caused the American company Halliburton to fire several of its top executives. A government white paper issued at about the same time charged 130 contractors, including a former presidential advisor, of accepting over 7 billion naira for projects that were never completed. Meanwhile, the National Electrical Power Authority set up a series of anticorruption, pro-transparency committees at its offices across the county and fired more than one hundred people charged with corruption.

Despite all these efforts it will take years if not decades before the Nigerian state can end its justified reputation for corruption that leads many analysts to call its civil servants "lootocrats."

Federalism

The last important—and troublesome—part of the Nigerian state is its federal structure. At independence, the country was divided into three regions in a way that maximized the influence of the leading ethnic groups. Since then, the country has been subdivided in an attempt to blunt the impact of ethnic conflict to the point that there are now 36 states and 449 municipalities, which, as in India, means that every substantial ethnic group can control the government of its "home" territory.

On one level, the creation of so many local government bodies has been a success. If nothing else, the creation of so many smaller states has made local politics less a part of the all-or-nothing game played at the national level.

In the 1970s and again in the 1990s, state and local governments played a vital role in forging the return to democracy. It was hoped that holding elections first at the subnational level would smooth the way toward peaceful democratic practices in Abuja as well.

In other ways, however, the federal system has been an impediment to democracy and stability. There has always been considerable uncertainty about what the respective responsibilities of the central and regional authorities should be. If nothing else, the inevitable duplication of services between the two levels drains the resources of a country that is so poor to begin with.

But most important of all, **federalism** has reinforced ethnicity as the most disruptive force in Nigerian political life. At the same time that it created places where each of the major ethnic groups could govern, it has made ethnic identity the most important stepping-stone to political power under both civilian and military rule.

Public Policy

Two issues have dominated public policy making in Nigeria since independence—democratization and development. No government—civilian or military—has made much lasting progress on either front, giving rise to the widespread futility and dissatisfaction that characterizes political life there today.

Democratization

Nigeria is the only country discussed in Part 4 of this book that has explicitly tried to build a democracy after years of authoritarian rule. And it has tried to do so twice.

In that sense, Nigeria is like much of Africa, which has lagged behind the rest of the world in creating democratic regimes. In fact, some would argue that no African country has fared worse at it than Nigeria.

The difficulties start with the First Republic and the difficult years after independence. Development economists often refer to factories that are built by outsiders and then handed over to third world executives as turnkey operations because the new operations literally only have to "turn the key" to get them to work. Such operations are rarely successful because the designers have not adapted the facility to local conditions. If nothing else, they have trained technicians who can keep the factory working when, as inevitably happens, something breaks down. In that sense, the First Republic, like most of the initial African regimes, was a "turnkey government." The Second Republic was, by contrast, "home grown," but it fared no better, not surviving its second election.

Since then, there have been two more attempts to build a democracy, both of which we will explore in some detail here, because they show us the difficulties of doing so in a country as divided as Nigeria.

Babangida's Failure

After he seized power in 1985, General Babangida decided to make democratization the centerpiece of what he claimed would be a brief period of military rule. Many observers are convinced that he was never strongly committed to democracy or civilian government. Researchers have yet to get access to documentary and other evidence about what really happened inside his govern-

Former military ruler Ibrahim Babangida at a meeting on democratization and economic development in 2002. He is about to introduce former U.S. President William Clinton.

ment, so we simply do not know how seriously to take those charges. Here, I have chosen to take his government at its word, because even given the best assumptions about his government's motivations, the failure of democratization in the late 1980s and early 1990s tells us a lot about both Nigeria and the third world as a whole.

Babangida endorsed what he called the "custodial theory," which holds that military government can only be justified on a temporary basis and only to prepare the return to civilian rule. Therefore, one of the first things his government did was to assess what had gone wrong in the First and Second Republics, in particular the way that ethnicity gave rise to conflict and corruption.

The seventeen-member team he designated to create the Third Republic therefore sought to engineer institutions through which a more cooperative, if not consensual, politics could operate. They started by banning all leading politicians and parties from the First and Second Republics on the assumption that they had twice demonstrated that they could not run the country. Then they laid out a phased transition that was scheduled to last four years. During that time, the next generation of politicians who lacked practical experience would learn on the job at the local level.

Their plan called for a decentralized system in which each of the main ethnic groups would dominate in at least one of the then thirty-one states. Just as important was the conclusion that the party and electoral systems had to be rebuilt from scratch. The government would license new political parties that could not succeed with narrowly based, ethnic support. The federal government would also fund the parties so that they would not be dependent on local bosses or corrupt officials. A neutral federal election commission would be set up to regulate the conduct of elections. In March 1987, the bureau submitted its report to the military authorities who accepted its basic provisions but pushed the planned date for the elections from 1990 to 1992.

Later that year, the government issued decrees setting up the official plans for the transition. Realizing that democracy requires a more enlightened population than Nigeria had, the government created a Directorate for Social Mobilization whose head described its mission: "If you want democratic government to be sustained over time, then the people have to be enlightened, mobilized, and properly educated."

The problems with the plan surfaced almost immediately. The government rejected all thirteen of the potential parties that emerged from grassroots organizational efforts and created two of its own practically out of thin air. Then it rejected the presidential candidates the two parties initially nominated and sent them back to the drawing boards.

When the 1993 presidential election actually occurred, it was the most honest and least violent in Nigerian history up to that point. Nonetheless, the government rejected the results and arrested the apparent winner, Abiola, thereby setting in motion the events that culminated in the coup led by Abacha later that fall.

Abubakar and Obasanjo

A more successful (so far at least) move toward democracy began in 1999, as we saw earlier. Ironically, this shift occurred with far less prior planning and only after Abacha's sudden death the year before.

After Ken Saro-Wiwa and seven of his colleagues were executed in 1995, almost forty countries withdrew their ambassadors from Abuja. Leaders throughout the Western world threatened to cancel all pending trade and aid deals, although in the end only military and certain other kinds of assistance were cut. Along with the international pressure, new protest groups developed at home, sparked both by the repression, the corruption, and the country's ongoing economic difficulties. Much of the protest focused on the release of Abiola and the establishment of the government that had been elected in 1993.

No one knows what would have happened had Abacha and Abiola not both died in rapid succession in

Democratization in Nigeria

NIGERIA IS ONE of many countries that has tried to make the transition from authoritarian to democratic rule, though few have had as many frustrations along the way.

Although many of the signs are positive for the Fourth Republic, as political scientists have learned in other countries it still has many hurdles to get past before we can feel reasonably certain that it will endure. First, it has only had a single, highly popular leader who will have to leave office in 2007 because he is limited to two terms. Second, there has obviously not been a transition in which one group of leaders peacefully and gracefully hands over power to the opposition. Third, it is by no means certain that the military will stay as politically neutral as it has been since Obasanjo (a former general himself) took office. Finally, it is hard to imagine democracy gaining widespread public support unless the government can address many of the social and economic problems that plague the country.

the summer of 1998. Their deaths, however, opened the door to a remarkably rapid chain of events that made the Fourth Republic possible less than a year later.

Abacha's successor, General Abdulsalami Abubakar, made it clear that he was not planning to perpetuate military rule and announced a timetable for the recreation of political parties and the holding of elections. At the Economic Council of West African States (ECOWAS) summit in late 1998, he announced that this was the one and only time that he would be addressing the delegates. In the end, Abubakar held true to his word and retired on 29 May 1999.

The election and reelection of Obasanjo in 1999 and 2003 seemingly provide evidence for the beginnings of stability, if not national unity. For instance, President Obasanjo made a speech extolling unity at the celebration marking the two hundredth anniversary of the accomplishments of Islamic scholar and warrior Usman Dan Fodio. Less than a week later, a group of northern governors issued a statement pledging loyalty to Nigeria as a single nation.

However, the regime will face a stern test in 2007 when Obasanjo has to step down. The potential candidate most frequently discussed in early 2005 was Ibrahim Babangida. There is concern, too, growing out of one of the most important conclusions to emerge from the literature on democratization. No amount of constitutional engineering or tinkering with established institutions can eliminate the debilitating effects of a situation in which people tend to view all issues and all conflict as **zero-sum** in nature.

Economic Development and Structural Adjustment

As you saw at the beginning of this chapter, the Nigerian economy is in shambles. While there have been moments when the economy was growing at a respectable rate and the future seemed promising, the country has not been able to take any significant steps that would dramatically improve the living conditions of its mostly impoverished population. Moreover, its economy has declined dramatically for most of the past decade, and the signs currently point to an uncertain but also unpromising future that is fraught with political implications.

In many respects, Nigeria has a typical economy for a third world country. Most Nigerians live in utter poverty. Also, like most countries in the third world, Nigeria's economy is largely based on the export of "primary" products and the import of some food, most manufactured goods, and almost all investment capital. That pattern invariably leaves the third world vulnerable because it is so reliant on at most a few commodities whose prices fluctuate on world markets.

In Nigeria's case, the situation might not seem so bad because its largest export by far is oil. Indeed, many observers expected oil revenues to turn Nigeria into one of Africa's, and perhaps even the world's, leading economic powers.

Instead, most of Nigeria's attempts at development have fallen flat on their face. The economy went into a tailspin in the mid-1980s from which it has yet to recover, despite having adopted the structural adjustment policies all but forced on Nigeria by the **International Monetary Fund, World Bank,** and other financial institutions.

In part, that failure reflects the corruption and mismanagement discussed earlier. It also reflects forces beyond the Nigerian government's control. Until the start of the crisis that led to the invasion of Iraq, oil prices had not stayed anywhere near as high as they were after the price shocks of 1973 and 1979. In 1989 alone, for example, the price of oil on the spot market dropped from about $21 to $14 a barrel in one six-month period. That decline cost the Nigerian government almost a third of the export revenues it had been counting on to pay for its import bills and to finance industrial and other development projects.

When combined with all its other problems, the drop in oil prices produced a crisis of massive proportions. In the second half of the 1980s alone, plummeting oil prices led to a more than 80 percent fall in GNP. Per capita income stood at about $1,000 per year but dropped by roughly 80 percent during the course of the decade and only rebounded slightly in the early 1990s. Graphing oil price changes is like drawing the side view of roller coaster. The price went from $21 a barrel in 1996 to about $12 in 1998. In 2000 the price had risen to over $30 a barrel, but by 2001 it was down to $16. The Gulf War caused prices to increase to $50 a barrel (May 2005), but production was hampered by strikes brought on by government attempts to raise gasoline prices and violence in the delta region, which led Shell and Total to shut down oil production operations for extended periods because of threats to their facilities and personnel.

The official value of its currency has never been a terribly good indicator of its real value, since most urban Nigerians choose to trade on the black market in which the naira is worth quite a bit less than the official exchange rate. Nonetheless, its value dropped by about half in the 1980s, a decline that continued through the 1990s. In October 1999, the U.S. dollar was worth 95 naira; the official exchange rate was 50 naira to the dollar. This gap had allowed military government insiders to buy naira at the official rate and sell them on the black market for quick and guaranteed profits. By 2003, when the last edition of *Comparative Politics* was published, a dollar could purchase about 140 naira. This fall in the value of the currency was due to reforms demanded by the IMF and to a 2002 crackdown on banks' international exchange business. By the middle of 2004, the value of the naira had stabilized between 135 and 140 for a dollar. The drop in the naira's value is one of the reasons why the country's total debt had gone up by about 1,000 percent during the last twenty years. Politically, it created real problems for the political leaders trying to manage the economy and maintain international support for Nigeria.

These are not just statistical abstractions. At the everyday level, the economic changes took a terrible toll on people's lives. The cost of basic foodstuffs increased by a minimum of 250 percent in the second half of the 1980s alone. The price of imported goods has risen even faster.

Until the late 1980s Nigerian leaders, civilian and military alike, pursued the then-common development strategy of important substitution. In the 1960s and 1970s they focused on developing Nigeria's industrial base so it could reduce its reliance on imported goods. That, in turn, mean relying heavily on foreign aid and loans for the investment capital for the start-up money that Nigeria could not provide on its own. Thus, right after independence, the U.S. government gave Nigeria a $225-million grant for roads, water supply, and education.

Over the years, Nigeria received considerable aid from both governmental and private sources, which it used to help build universities, factories, and modern urban amenities in Lagos, Abuja, and its other major cities.

Typical was the Delta steel complex in Aladja in Bendel state, which opened in 1982. Creating a locally run, integrated steel and iron industry has always been a high priority for the Nigerian or any third world government because they are components of almost all modern industrial products. The Aladja mill was to provide steel rods and other products for factories that would produce finished "rolling" steel. The Nigerian government played a major role in this and other development projects. Normally, it was the recipient of the foreign aid or loans. Either on its own or through the more than ninety partially private and partially public organizations known as **parastatals,** it determined how and where those funds would be invested.

Typical, too, is the fact that the Aladja mill did not live up to expectations. It never operated at more than 20 percent of capacity, which means that other factories that depend on its products were underutilized as well. Another project, the Adjaokuta steel mill, was projected to be Africa's largest steel factory when it was conceived in the boom years of the 1970s, but it was a decade late in coming on line and ended up costing $4 billion more than originally budgeted to complete.

There are lots of reasons for the problems with the iron, steel, and most other industrial sectors. Skilled labor is in short supply. Replacement parts and repairs in general are too expensive. Nigeria's legendary corruption extends into the economic arena as well as the political. There has also been far less foreign aid than Nigerians expected, far less than the 0.7 percent of GNP annually that the Organization for Economic Cooperation and Development (OECD) countries initially pledged a generation ago.

Whatever the reasons, the bottom line is clear. Two decades after these ambitious projects were conceived, Nigeria could not meet its own industrial demand. In iron and steel, that reached about six million metric tons in 1990, but even if all its plants that were either in operation or under construction worked at full capacity, it would only have been able to produce 1.3 million metric tons. The same was true in every other industrial sector.

There were problems with agriculture as well. As noted earlier, until colonization, the territory that became Nigeria could easily feed its people. Nigeria was a major exporter of agricultural products. But after independence, Nigerian officials emphasized industrial development at the expense of agriculture. In the 1980s, agricultural products made up only 3 percent of total exports. Moreover, Nigeria also was heavily dependent on imported food. Despite the grandiose "Operation Feed the Nation" (1976–1979) and "Green Revolution" (1979–1983) schemes, most farmers still use traditional agricultural techniques.

Even though there are now more roads into farming regions, and there are more support services, irrigation, and machinery available to farmers, agricultural production has not increased appreciably. Furthermore, there is very little quality control in what is produced and marketed. And, as with everything else in Nigerian life, corrupt trading practices take a lot of the potential profit and best produce out of the market.

In keeping with its general policy of **import substitution,** the Shagari government introduced higher tariffs in 1982 and other policies that would make imports more expensive and thus give a boost to domestic producers. Economic conditions did not improve, which was one of the reasons why the military stepped in the next year. The new Buhari administration strengthened the existing import restrictions and offered businesses incentives to encourage them to buy needed goods domestically.

Government spending was cut and new projects frozen, which led to the forced layoffs of thousands of workers. Meanwhile, the price of oil continued to plummet. As it did the country's debt spiraled upward, at which point the international financial institutions that "owned" the debt stepped in. The Buhari government had to apply to the International Monetary Fund's Extended Fund Facility for a loan to cover its immediate problems and restructure its long-term debt. The IMF only agreed to grant the money and negotiate new terms for the outstanding loans if the government agreed to a very different set of macroeconomic policies, conditions that have come to be known as conditionality. The IMF's conditions were part of the reason for Babangida's 1985 coup, leading the new government to declare an economic state of emergency that October. A massive public debate ensued. Ultimately, the government decided to reject the IMF loans under the proposed terms, but it did agree to do whatever was necessary to restructure Nigeria's economy in a more profitable direction, which, in the end, meant acceding to Northern demands.

Late that year, Babangida announced a two-year structural adjustment program, which has been extended in one form or another ever since. Its goal was to expand exports other than oil, reduce the import of goods that could be manufactured locally, achieve self-sufficiency in food production, and, most notably, increase the role of the private sector. Strategically, Babangida sought to reduce the state's economic involvement. Tariffs were reduced and import-license procedures simplified or, in some cases, eliminated altogether. In 1986 alone, seventeen parastatals were privatized, and by 1990, sixteen more had been as well. Another thirty have been sold since then.

After Abacha's death, the Abubakar government planned to set a new privatization plan in motion in 1999. By 2004, vice president Abdulsalami Abubakar was in charge of the National Council on Privatization and paper mills, auto assembly plants, fertilizer factories, railroads, airports, and even the Abuja Environmental Protection Board were slated to be sold.

So far, structural adjustment's record is mixed. There is more investment capital available, including $170 million from the private wing of the World Bank, to help fund the development of a natural gas field. Foreign investors can now own a 50-percent share of existing enterprises and a controlling ownership or, in some cases, even total ownership of new ones.

On balance, however, the transition has been difficult. Debt remains high, and interest on those loans continues to eat up about a third of the government's annual budget. The official inflation rate increased from 12 percent in 1987 to nearly 50 percent in 1989 before it began to level off. After 2000, inflation fell back to a 10–12 percent level. That did not help unemployment, which is es-

Liberalization and Globalization in Nigeria

NIGERIA SHARES many of the problems third world countries are facing as they struggle to integrate their economies into the increasingly integrated world economy. That has been true since before Nigeria gained its independence, but it has become particularly burdensome in the last twenty years when the debt crisis and other problems led the international financial leaders to require that governments adopt structural adjustment plans in order to receive loans and aid. These programs typically include reductions in tariffs, the encouragement of foreign investment, the greater use of markets in domestic economic life, privatization of state-owned enterprises, and fiscal restraint on the part of the government.

The logic behind structural adjustment is that, in time, third world economies will find profitable niches that will stimulate rapid growth in general. The problem is "in time." So far, the benefits of structural adjustment have gone to relatively few Nigerians, most of whom were wealthy to begin with.

In other words, the gap between rich and poor have widened considerably in the last generation. There is no better example of this than the riots that occurred when the government tried to change gasoline prices so that they better reflected market conditions. In fact, the protests were so intense that the government had to cancel many of the price changes it had intended to implement.

A man runs to safety as police fire tear gas at opposition demonstrators during an antigovernment rally protesting the government's decision to raise oil prices in 2004.

Pius Utomi Ekpei /AFP/Getty Images

timated to be at least 30 percent. Whatever the benefits of structural adjustment, economic control has shifted either outside the country altogether or to a small, increasingly wealthy domestic elite. Economic inequalities have increased, and structural adjustment plans in general provide few, if any, incentives for the beneficiaries of economic growth to deal with poverty and other social problems.

Progress under structural adjustment or any other economic strategy was also hindered by the bribes and other corrupt practices that were a central feature of Nigerian political life at least until Obasanjo was elected. Thus, in 2001, the Nigerian authorities were only able to meet four of the eleven conditions laid out by the IMF in granting the country a loan three years earlier.

The situation as of this writing is rather confusing. Obasanjo has refused to bow to demands by the IMF, but he has pledged to continue the structural adjustment policies. Still, his close links with officials from the Babangida government and the delays and difficulties in privatization projects give many observers pause on this front as well.

Feedback

As is the case almost everywhere, most Nigerians learn about political life primarily through the mass media.

For most of its history, Nigeria has had a reasonably free press. Its hundreds of newspapers and magazines have reflected a wide range of opinions on almost every issue. To be sure, the various military regimes have cracked down on the press and even closed some outlets at moments of the highest tensions, as was the case after Ken Saro-Wiwa was executed.

The problem is that relatively few Nigerians are literate enough to read a newspaper or wealthy enough to afford to buy one. Therefore, the key to feedback in Nigeria is radio and television, which civilian and military authorities have tried to control through the Nigerian Broadcast Commission (NBC).

Since the creation of the Fourth Republic, the NBC has struggled to find a balance between a desire to foster national unity and the new constitution's provision that states could establish and even own radio and television stations. The contradiction between those two positions became clear in 2001 when the state of Zamfara created a radio station, Voice of Islam, that infuriated Christians already worried about what they saw as the extreme use of Sharia in the state. Zamfara's leadership, for example, had authorized the beating of a woman who conceived a child out of wedlock and banned soccer for women as un-Islamic.

Nigeria and the Plight of the Third World

At this point you might well be asking a question that has lurked below the surface throughout this chapter. Why should there even be a Nigeria? After all, Nigeria as we know it began as an artificial creation of the colonial powers, and its history has at best been a rocky one ever since. It has never come close to creating an effective government or a modern economy despite all the human and natural resources Achebe alluded to in the statement that begins this chapter. In other words, it may well be the case that the Nigerian people would be better off if the country split up into at least three parts representing the main geographical and ethnic divisions of the First Republic.

That question is well worth asking of many other countries, which are also suffering from the combined effects of ethnic strife, corruption, military rule, underdevelopment, environmental decay, and the like. But all the signs are that it is a question that is not likely to be asked by the people who will be determining the future of Nigeria and similar countries.

For good or ill, most modern nation states and their boundaries seem set in stone for the foreseeable future, especially in Africa. In short, whatever scenarios might seem more plausible to outside observers, Nigerians and Liberians and Kenyans and South Africans probably do not have the Soviet or Yugoslavian option. They are stuck with each other and seem consigned to trying to find workable solutions within the limits imposed by existing national boundaries.

Key Terms

Concepts

Democratization	Indirect rule
Dual mandate	Mass political culture
Federalism	Sharia
Hausa-Fulani	Structural adjustment
Igbo	Yoruba
Import substitution	Zero-sum

People

Abacha, Sani	Azikiwe, Nnamdi
Abiola, Moshood	Babangida, Ibrahim
Abubakar, Abdulsalami	Bello, Ahmadu
Awolowo, Obafemi	Balewa, Tafawa

Ironsi, Aguiyi

Kano, Aminu

Macaulay, Herbert

Obasanjo, Olusegun

Saro-Wiwa, Ken

Shagari, Shehu

Acronyms

AD (Alliance for Democracy)

AG (Action Group)

ANPP (All Nigeria Middle Belt People's Party)

FEC (Federal Executive Council)

FEDECO (Federal Electoral Commission)

INEC (Independent National Electoral Commission)

NCBWA (National Congress of British West Africa)

NCNC (National Council of Nigeria and the Cameroons)

NEPU (Northern Elements Progressive Union)

NNDP (Nigerian National Democratic Party)

NPC (Northern People's Congress)

NPN (National Party of Nigeria)

NPP (Nigerian People's Party)

NRC (National Republican Convention)

NYM (Nigerian Youth Movement)

PDP (People's Democratic Party)

PRP (People's Redemption Party)

SDP (Social Democratic Party)

UMBC (United Middle Belt Congress)

UPN (United Party of Nigeria)

Organizations, Places, and Events

Biafra

International Monetary Fund

World Bank

Critical Thinking Exercises

1 Much has changed in Nigeria since this book was finished in early 2005. How have more recent events reshaped Nigerian politics?

2 Public opinion pollsters routinely ask questions about whether people think that their country is headed in the "right direction" or is on the "wrong track." If you were asked such a question about Nigeria, what would your answer be? Why did you reach this conclusion?

3 How have ethnic differences made the establishment of democracy so difficult in Nigeria? What could be done about that?

4 Leftist scholars often argue that outside forces dating from the colonial period onward are more responsible for the problems a country like Nigeria faces than its own domestic political forces are. Do you agree? Why (not)?

5 How has structural adjustment altered Nigerian politics?

6 Why is Nigeria's poverty such an obstacle to political stability, let alone democracy?

 ## Useful Websites

The Nigerian government now has a very good portal with links to its main offices and departments:

www.nigeria.gov.ng

The Library of Congress has commissioned a series of country studies over the years, all of which are now available online. One of the most useful and most recent is:

countrystudies.us/Nigeria

There are now a number of portals that include general information about Nigeria and its politics. These include:

www.nigeriamasterweb.com/Politics.html

www.nigeriaworld.com

There are also a number of sources of news on Africa, including Nigeria. The first to be owned by Africans based in the United States is:

www.usafricaonline.com

The Washington-based Fund for Peace has done an excellent analysis of the 2003 election.

www.fundforpeace.org/pathways/nigeria/elections.php

InfoTrac College Edition Sources

Bogaards, Matthijs. "Electoral Choices for Divided Societies."

Elaigwu, J. Isawa, and Habu Galadima. "The Shadow of Sharia over Nigerian Federalism."

Miles, William. "African Islamism from Below."

Okafor, Theresa. "Ethnocentrism in Africa."

Smith, Daniel Jordan. "Premarital Sex, Procreation, and HIV Risk in Nigeria."

Unegbu, O. Carl. "Nigeria: Bellwether of African Democracy."

Further Reading

Aborisade, Oladimeji, and Robert Mundt. *Politics in Nigeria.* 2nd ed. New York: Addison-Wesley, 2002. The best textbook on Nigeria.

Achebe, Chinua. *The Trouble With Nigeria.* London: Heinemann, 1984. Although very dated, this book addresses many of the problems Nigeria still faces today, especially its leadership.

Davidson, Basil. *Modern Africa*. New York: Longman, 1983. One of the best overviews of modern African history that puts Nigeria in perspective.

Dike, Victor. *Nigeria and the Politics of Unreason*. London: Adonis-Abbey, 2003. One of the highly critical books on the Obasanjo government.

Maier, Karl. *This House Has Fallen*. Boulder: Westview, 2000. An outstanding account of military rule in the 1990s.

Schwab, Peter. *Designing West Africa*. London: Palgrave, 2004. This book provides a historical overview for most major West African countries and thus puts Nigeria in perspective.

The Fox win means that Mexico has accomplished the rare feat of ending an authoritarian regime by voting it out of office, an event that comes at the end of a process of building an electoral opposition to the former ruling party that stretches back nearly a quarter century.

JOSEPH KLESNER

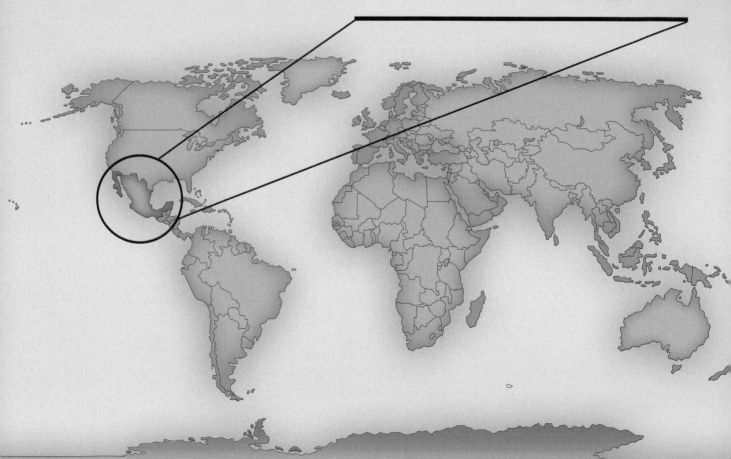

Chapter 16

MEXICO

The Basics: Mexico

Size	1,972,550 sq. km (roughly three times the size of Texas)
Population	More than 101 million
GNP per capita	$5,910
Out migration	2.77 people per 100,000 per year
Currency	11.14 pesos = $1
Religion	89% Catholic, 6 % Protestant, 5% Other or none
Capital	Mexico City, Federal District
President	Vicente Fox (2000)

A Failing Presidency?

The statement by Joseph Klesner that begins this chapter was written in 2001, when it made sense to view the unprecedented victory by President **Vicente Fox** as a major turning point in Mexican politics. Three years later, it was no longer so clear.

On 6 July 2004, the *New York Times* carried two very short but very revealing stories reflecting the disappointment many Mexicans felt about the presidency of Vicente Fox, the first person in over seventy years to be elected president who was not a member of the **PRI (Institutional Revolutionary Party).**

The first article told the story of Amalia Garcia, of the **Party of the Democratic Revolution (PRD).** Two days earlier, she had been elected governor of the northern state of Zacatecas. She was the first woman elected governor of one of the country's thirty-three states since 1989; she was also the first woman ever to head a Mexican political party when she ran the left-of-center PRD in the 1990s. Garcia attributed her victory in part to the fact that women made up most of the electorate, since half of the state's 1.5 million people were living in the United States, the vast majority of whom were men. That same day, two "migrants" were elected mayors of big cities, one of whom had made a fortune growing tomatoes in California, the other running a furniture factory in Texas.

Alfonso Murillo/AP/Wide World Photos

Mexico's President Vicente Fox and his bride and then chief presidential spokeswoman Martha Sahagún smile as they pose during a private wedding ceremony at the presidential residence Los Pinos in Mexico City, Monday, 2 July 2 2001.

Andrés Bermúdez, dubbed the tomato king, claimed "my victory opens the door to a lot of migrants. Just like we left in droves, a wave of immigrants will come back in droves and help their towns out of poverty."[1]

The second story announced the resignation of Fox's chief spokesperson, Alfonso Durazo. According to Durazo, he had grown disenchanted not only with Fox's public policies but with the fact that he seemed to be grooming his wife, Martha Sahagún, to run for the presidency when Fox's term expires in 2006. Sahagún subsequently decided not to run, but yet more damage was done to Fox's image.

These two stories took up no more than eight column inches of that morning's paper. Nonetheless, between them, they reveal three overlapping issues that define Mexican politics in these first years of the twenty-first century.

The first is Mexico's poverty. As the basics table shows, Mexico is by no means as poor as India or Nigeria. Nonetheless, many Mexicans live spartan existences. Sixteen percent of Mexicans live on less than a dollar a day. Ten percent of its adults are functionally illiterate. Almost that large a proportion of its children will not live

[1] "Mexico Elects a Woman as Governor." *New York Times.* 6 July 2004, A6.

to the age of five, are chronically underweight, or both. Moreover, the gap between rich and poor has widened significantly since the government started implementing market-oriented economic reforms in the 1980s, which we will examine in the policy section of this chapter.

The second is the impact of the United States. Mexican governments no longer consult the American ambassador before making major decisions as they did for a half century or more after the country gained its independence in 1810. Nonetheless, the United States still exerts a profound influence over its southern neighbor in a number of ways. Mexico's government and the financial institutions run by its citizens were largely responsible for the adoption of those economic reforms.

And, as these articles suggest, at least ten million Mexicans have moved to the United States. No one knows for sure how many there are because many entered the United States illegally, and it is thus impossible to get an accurate count of them. Many immigrants from other countries come to the United States to flee political oppression. Almost all Mexicans go there to flee poverty.

The third is Fox's controversial presidency. From 1927 until 2000, the PRI did not lose a single presidential election and only lost a handful of congressional and gubernatorial races. Sometimes it won elections honestly; sometimes (as in 1988) it controlled the vote count to turn defeat into "victory." More importantly, the PRI was able to control the country because it built an elaborate system of **patron-client** networks through which it determined who ran for office and then mobilized a loyal electorate. In short, they ran a system known for its corruption, much of which occurred plainly and openly.

Many observers inside and outside of Mexico hoped that Fox's victory would usher in a new era. Most of them have been disappointed. To begin with, Fox never enjoyed a majority in either house of congress. As a result, he had a hard time getting reform legislation passed. Moreover, many think that this farmer and Coca-Cola executive turned politician lacked the skills needed to turn his country around. And, as rumors started to swirl that he was laying the groundwork for his wife's presidential bid (Mexican politicians may not run for reelection), some worried that he was resorting to PRI-style tactics to build his own political empire.

Thinking about Mexico

Most readers of this book will be from the United States. That means that most of them will care more about Mexico than about other third world countries. But just because people in the United

States and Mexico share a long border, that does not mean that Americans know much about their southern neighbor. That ignorance often leads to stereotypical images about what Mexico is like, which can lead to misguided conclusions about it and what public policy toward it should be.

The Basics

Mexico is not as poor as most third world countries. Although it is not usually considered one of the **newly industrializing countries (NICs),** the World Bank's *World Development Report* ranks Mexico's economy ahead of Russia's. It has a middle class whose lifestyle rivals what we find in the United States or among South Africa's white population. Similarly, some Mexican analysts point out that their country is one of the world's fifteen leading industrial powers. And, until the sharp decline in world oil prices in the early 1980s, Mexico's growth rate had been quite high, averaging 6.5 percent per year between 1965 and 1980.

In fact, such statistics miss the part of the story that leads most observers to put Mexico in the third world. For much of the past twenty years, stagnation rather than growth has been the economic norm. Thus, growth averaged only about 1 percent per year in the 1980s, though it is higher now, especially since the **North American Free Trade Agreement (NAFTA)** went into effect in 1994. By contrast, inflation typically topped 50 percent per year in the 1980s and stood at nearly 30 percent before the government began to get it under control in the late 1990s.

This translates to continued poverty for most Mexicans. Housing and health care are not very good. Some 50 percent of Mexicans do not have access to either safe drinking water or a toilet. Only about one in ten has a telephone or television. Officially, unemployment is quite low, but a much higher proportion of Mexicans cannot find jobs that provide themselves and their families with more than a subsistence income, which contributes to the steady flow of immigrants to the United States. In the decade since NAFTA went into effect, the number of people in extreme poverty (income that is 25 percent below the poverty line) grew from 17 to 26 million. The cities are overcrowded, and Mexico City is so polluted that most experts doubt that its air can ever be made safe to breathe again.

Mexico's economic difficulties are compounded by its massive debt. Like many third world countries, Mexico borrowed heavily during the 1960s and 1970s on the assumption that it could use oil revenues to pay back the banks and governments that had made the loans. When prices fell after the oil crisis of 1979, Mexico's debt sky-

HIV/AIDS in Mexico

Mexico does not have a large number of people infected with HIV. As of late 2003, only about 0.3 percent of the population was infected with the disease and only about 160,000 people were living with fully developed cases of AIDS. According to official statistics, about five thousand people died of the disease that year and perhaps as many more died of it without have AIDS reported as the cause of death.

Do not be mistaken in concluding that HIV/AIDS is not a big issue in Mexico. Since the disease is spread mostly by sex workers and long-haul truck drivers, people not only in Mexico but in the United States are at risk.

Mexico embarked on a unique approach to addressing HIV/AIDS in late February 20005. With the support of the United States Agency for International Development, a coalition of leading Mexican businesses was formed to combat discrimination against HIV/AIDS sufferers at the workplace. The group, CONAES, hoped to enlist half of Mexico's largest employers by the end of 2005 and then launch a wider program to educate people about the risk of HIV/AIDS and other sexually transmitted diseases.

rocketed, reaching more than $100 billion in the late 1980s. Although it declined somewhat in the early 1990s, total debt leaped back toward the levels of the late 1980s as a result of the peso crisis in 1995. At the end of 2003, the debt stood at $159 billion, or almost 17 percent of Mexico's total GNP.

Diversity

Mexico is also a remarkably diverse country, which may not be apparent to generations of Americans raised on Westerns with their scenes of an arid, wide-open country of mountains and deserts. That image applies only to the northern part of the country. Southern coastal regions are hot and humid, but as you move inland and into the mountains, the climate turns more temperate.

The stereotypes are right in one respect: Mexico is a rugged country. Between the mountains, deserts, and jungles, only about 12 percent of its land is arable, and much of that land is marginal at best. But Mexico does have natural resources in two areas: minerals and petroleum. Mining has been an important industry practically since the day the Aztecs met Hernán Cortés and his fellow Spaniards with what seemed like mountains of gold artifacts. In the twentieth century, the discovery of substantial petroleum reserves turned Mexico into one of the world's leading oil and natural gas producers.

Mexican Names and Places

There are two linguistic issues to keep in mind while studying Mexico. First, names again. As in most Spanish-speaking countries, Mexican names have the following structure: first or Christian name, father's family name, mother's maiden name. Some Mexicans (for example, President Fox) do not routinely include their mother's family name. It can be confusing, but it will be clear from the usage which is which. If there are three names, it is the middle one that denotes the family, as in Carlos Salinas de Gortari.

Also, like most writers, I will regretfully use the term *American* to refer to the United States. Anyone who lives in either North or South America is, of course, an American. However, the way the English language has evolved there is no other stylistically acceptable adjective to describe things and people from the United States.

The Mexican population is also extremely diverse. Relatively few Spanish women came to New Spain, as Mexico was called after the conquest in the sixteenth century. Moreover, unlike the situation in the British colonies to the north, the Spaniards did not kill off most of the people they encountered when they arrived. In short, marriages and nonmarital sexual relations between Spanish men and Indian women were common, so that now the largest group of Mexicans is the **mestizos**—part Indian and part white. A substantial number of blacks also were brought to Mexico as slaves, especially in the state of Veracruz along the Gulf coast, which many observers think still feels more Caribbean than Mexican.

Currently, terms like *Indian* or *mestizo* are not primarily used to describe people's physical appearance. Instead, they describe the culture they were raised in. Thus, an Indian is not someone who is at least part Indian, for that describes a huge proportion of the Mexican population, but someone whose culture and identity are primarily Indian. Generally, Mexicans are less sensitive to (or perhaps less prejudiced about) race than are citizens of the United States.

Between 5 and 10 percent of Mexicans still speak only native Indian languages and are thus not very well integrated into what is a predominantly Spanish-speaking national culture. That said, the Indian influence is far more noticeable and valued than it is in the United States. The very name *Mexico* is derived from either Mexica, one of the Aztec tribes, or Mexitl, an Aztec epithet for God. Native influences can be seen in everything from the way many Mexicans dress, to the food they eat, to the way they practice Catholicism.

Big Brother Is *Watching*

All third world countries have had a long and not always pleasant relationship with one or more of the industrialized democracies. The one between Mexico and the United States is a bit different in two seemingly contradictory respects. On the one hand, the United States never colonized Mexico, although it did seize one-third of its territory after the Mexican-American War of 1848. On the other hand, the United States exerts more influence over Mexico than any single country has on any of the others covered in this book.

The two countries really are not as "close" as the length of their borders might imply. The United States and Canada share the world's longest unguarded border. The U.S.-Mexican border, in contrast, is one of the most closely patrolled, as the United States tries to stem the flow of illegal immigrants and drugs into its country. Indeed, some pundits refer to it as the border between the first and third worlds.

The United States and Mexico are increasingly dependent on each other economically. Mexico is the United States' third leading trading partner, trailing only Japan and Canada. The United States is even more important for Mexico, because two-thirds of all Mexican exports are sent north. Even prior to NAFTA, there was significant U.S. investment, especially in the **maquiladora** factories that dot the border and that produce goods for foreign markets using low-priced Mexican labor.

More important politically is the migration of Mexicans to the United States. There is nothing new to this. The American southwest has long been a "safety valve" providing jobs for unemployed Mexicans, who, had they not traveled north, might have fomented protest at home. There could be as many as three million Mexicans living illegally in the United States, and they send about $9 billion a year back to family members at home, adding more money to the economy than Mexico makes from its agricultural exports.

Many people in the United States believe that Mexican immigrants are a burden, a belief that led to the passage of the federal **Immigration Reform and Control Act** of 1986 and California's restrictive Proposition 187, which denied illegal aliens access to public services, in 1994. Many Americans, too, are worried that the presence of so many Spanish-speaking immigrants (not all of whom are from Mexico, of course) is diluting and threatening American culture.

Immigration is not the only thing Americans fear regarding Mexico. Much of the cocaine and marijuana destined for the western United States comes through Mexico.

American fears notwithstanding, this is a highly unequal relationship in which the United States is by far the more powerful partner. For the nearly two centuries that Mexico has been an independent country, the United States has exerted a powerful and often unwanted influence on its politics. This began with the first U.S. ambassador to Mexico, Joel Poinsett, who insisted that the new Mexican government heed Washington's wishes. Incidentally, Poinsett brought back from Mexico the Christmas plant that bears his family name, the poinsettia.

As recently as 1914, American troops invaded Mexico. And, although the United States no longer engages in that kind of direct intervention, its indirect leverage—ranging from the tens of billions of dollars Mexico had to borrow in recent years to the impact of its popular culture—may be no less overwhelming. Many Mexicans speak of their "dependent psychology," or the sense that the American big brother is always watching. With its wealth and freedom, the United States is highly regarded by most average Mexicans. At the same time, many are envious of what the North Americans have and resent their often arrogant, high-handed interference in Mexican affairs—most recently, with NAFTA and the conditions imposed on loan guarantees in 1995.

Key Questions

The most important question about Mexican politics cannot be answered here. As these lines were written, President Fox had been in office for more than four years, and it is still simply too early to tell how much Mexican politics will change as a result of his tenure for reasons that will be discussed below. What does seem certain is that the era of PRI domination is over. The party may well win future elections, but there seems to be no chance that it could ever again become the hegemonic party it was from the late 1920s through the late 1990s.

This leads us to five main questions about domestic politics in Mexico:

- Why did the PRI win so consistently, and how could it stay in power so long?

- How and why did forces undermining PRI rule emerge, culminating in Fox's victory?

- Why did three successive administrations in the 1980s and 1990s embrace structural adjustment as fully as any leaders in the third world?

Royalty-Free/CORBIS

A typical lineup of cars waiting to cross the border between Mexico and the United States just south of San Diego. Delays can last as long as four hours.

- How much have those reforms addressed Mexico's poverty and other pressing needs?

- How have the events of the last two or three decades affected Mexico's all-important relationship with the United States?

The Evolution of Mexican Politics

The evolution of Mexican politics has a lot in common with most other Central and South American countries—Spanish or Portuguese colonization, independence in the early nineteenth century, and a rather tumultuous history afterward. (See table 16.1.)

There is one way in which Mexico's political history is dramatically different. As should be clear from the

▌ **TABLE 16.1** Key Events in Mexican History

YEAR	EVENT
1519	Arrival of Cortés
1810	Declaration of independence
1836	Loss of Texas
1848	Mexican–American War
1864	Emperor Maximilian installed
1876	Beginning of Porfirio Diaz's reign
1910	Revolution
1929	Formation of PNR, which renames itself PRI in 1946
1934	Election of Cárdenas

preceding section, the United States has played a more important role in shaping Mexican political and economic life from its first years as an independent country than it has for most other countries of the region (www.mexconnect.com/mex_/history.html).

The Colonial Era

There is much uncertainty about the "Indians" who inhabited what is now Mexico before the Spaniards arrived. A thousand years ago the Mayans who lived along the Gulf coast had one of the most advanced civilizations in the world, but by the sixteenth century it had already begun to decline for reasons no one fully understands. By that time the Aztecs had come to dominate dozens of other tribes from their capital of Tenochtitlán (now Mexico City). The Aztecs were able to establish a centralized empire with an elaborate system of courts, tax collectors, and political-military administrators.

Ironically, the Aztecs believed that white gods in strange ships would one day appear on their shores. Despite fierce resistance from Moctezuma (Mexicans prefer this spelling rather than the Montezuma one usually seen in English) and, later, his nephew Cuautémoc, Cortés was able to use his superior weaponry to defeat the Aztecs and gradually extend Spanish control over a territory that stretched from what is now northern California into Central America.

Spanish colonial practices differed dramatically from those of the British. The Spaniards encountered well-established civilizations, not nomadic tribes. They thus had to incorporate the native population into the colonial system in an elaborate hierarchy that placed native Spaniards at the top, their mixed offspring below them, and the massive Indian population at the bottom. New Spain, as Mexico was then known, became part of an exploitative mercantilist empire that sent resources back to Spain but gave little, politically or economically, to the colonies. The Spaniards also brought the Catholic Church, which, in addition to trying to convert the natives, became an integral part of the colony's government. Perhaps most importantly, New Spain lacked the degree of self-government that was well established in British North America long before the revolutionary war.

Hints of problems to come appeared under Spanish rule. The church, for example, ended up owning one-third of the country while forcing Catholicism on virtually the entire population. Similarly, by the seventeenth century huge estates, or haciendas, had been created. Typically, land originally given to the Indians was seized, and the prior owners became peons or indentured servants to their Spanish overlords.

Ultimately, the Spanish were not very effective colonial administrators and were never able to secure their rule throughout the country. Nonetheless, late in the seventeenth century they tried to take firmer control of the colonies, thereby antagonizing the growing Mexican-born elite.

Independence

Although Americans tend not to think about it in this way, the thirteen colonies gained their independence in large part because the British were preoccupied elsewhere and could not commit the resources needed to hold onto a distant, troublesome, and not very important part of their empire. Independence for Spain's American colonies, too, became possible when Spain was weakened by the Napoleonic Wars that swept Europe in the first two decades of the nineteenth century and could not or would not pay the price to hold onto them.

In Mexico, the bloody, decade-long struggle for independence began in 1810 when the Creole priest Miguel Hidalgo y Castillo first proclaimed Mexican independence and quickly raised an army of more than 100,000. Hidalgo proved to be something less than a brilliant military strategist when his forces were slaughtered at Guanajuato. Within a year he was captured and executed, a fate that befell many others who took up the cause before the decade was out. But Hidalgo's forces were never fully defeated, and those who survived took to the countryside, beginning a tradition of guerrilla warfare that continues to this day.

In the end, it was the lay and clerical elite that finally forged an independent Mexico, deciding that it might be able to maintain its wealth and power against Hidalgo's followers and successors if it was independent of Spain. But its victory settled very little.

For more than a hundred years, Mexico careened from crisis to crisis and from caudillo (strongman) to caudillo while its social and economic problems festered. To solve them, Mexico needed outside help, but this was not forthcoming due to the political instability the country experienced during a tumultuous century.

No historical figure exemplifies independent Mexico's difficulties any better than one of its first leaders, Augustin de Iturbide. Iturbide was a rather unscrupulous opportunist who manipulated Spanish emissaries into granting Mexico its independence and making him the head of the first government. But pressures quickly mounted. When Spain rejected the agreement that gave Mexico its independence because the Mexican government was bankrupt, Iturbide responded by having himself declared Emperor Augustin I. In fact, Iturbide proved unable to rule other than through tyrannical means and, by the end of 1823, had been overthrown. It should be pointed out that U.S. intervention in Mexican politics began in these years, too, when its emissary, Joel Poinsett, made it abundantly clear that the Monroe administration did not approve of the Iturbide regime and left it financially ruined.

The most important political figure over the next thirty years was General **Antonio López de Santa Anna,** best known in the United States for his victory at the Alamo at San Antonio, Texas, in 1836. At home, Santa Anna has a considerably worse reputation, which Daniel Levy and Gabriel Székely describe as follows:

> In 1848, Mexico's most despised, traitorous, duplicitous native son presided over the loss of roughly half of Mexico's territory in a war with the United States. Santa Anna's most consistent preoccupation was self interest. Among his favorite self-designations were Most Serene Highness, Father of the Country, Savior, and Perpetual Victor. It is a sad commentary on Mexico's political instability from the 1820s to the 1950s that the last title had some validity. Almost no one could establish a viable government and a viable economic base.[2]

Santa Anna first appeared on the political scene in 1823 when he forced Iturbide into exile and then had him executed when he tried to return. Santa Anna dominated Mexican politics for the quarter-century that followed. Most of the time he operated behind the scenes as a series of weak elected presidents and military officers tried to govern. Meanwhile, the country was torn by conflict between liberals and conservatives, largely over the economic and other powers of the church.

Santa Anna held on primarily because of his reputation for defending Mexico's threatened sovereignty, though it must be said that he was not very good at it. He led Mexican troops in overcoming Spanish forces attempting to regain their lost colony in 1830, but after that he fared less well. Despite having defeated the Americans at the Alamo, he proved unable to win the war and keep Texas from gaining its independence. He also could not prevent the United States from seizing Texas and most of northern Mexico during the Mexican-American War in 1848. After the war, Santa Anna was exiled to Jamaica. Remarkably, he was asked back five years later to help restore order. This time he sold parts of what are now Arizona and New Mexico to the United States and used the money to support his repressive regime for two

more years before the liberals finally overthrew him and exiled him for good. For their part, the liberals were unable to secure their hold over Mexico City or much of the rest of the country. Nonetheless, they tried to promulgate a new constitution in 1857, launching the period of—and the war for—reform. In particular, they stripped the church of virtually all its wealth and civil power. In 1861, liberal forces led by the Indian General Benito Juarez finally entered Mexico City and took control of the entire country.

They were not, however, able to enact many of their other reforms. The years of war, intrigue, and chaos had taken their toll. Moreover, now that the American Civil War was under way, it was impossible for the United States to continue supporting Juarez. British, Spanish, and French forces saw this as an ideal opportunity to intervene, ostensibly to extract payment for their financial losses over the years. At first, Mexican forces defeated the invaders at Puebla on 5 May 1862. But the Europeans eventually forced President Juarez out of Mexico City and in 1864 installed the Austrian prince Maximilian and his Belgian wife, Carlotta, as emperor and empress. Quickly, the puppet emperor and the French forces that really held power realized that there were few riches to be had and that the Mexicans were not going to accept new foreign rulers. Within three years Juarez was back in Mexico City. Maximilian was executed, and Carlotta was sent into exile.

By the time of the 1871 election, political leaders were looking for someone to replace the aging and less-than-effective Juarez. Attention shifted to one of his most successful generals, **Porfirio Diaz** (1830–1915), whose campaign for the presidency was based on the idea that no president should be allowed to be reelected. When no one won a majority of the votes, the nation turned to Juarez yet again. But he died the next year, touching off another period of violence and instability that culminated in a military coup by Diaz in 1876.

Thus began the longest period of dictatorship in Mexican history, led, ironically, by the man who had introduced the principle of **nonreelection** to political life. To his credit, Diaz brought more than thirty years of stable government after a half-century of chaos. With the stability came considerable foreign investment and the first steps in the development of a modern economic infrastructure. Thousands of miles of railroads were built, as were oil refineries, sugar mills, and electrical generation facilities. But the growth came with a price. Order in the countryside was maintained by the ruthless mercenary *rurales.* Perhaps as many as five million peasants were forced back into servitude on the haciendas, many of which were now owned by foreigners. And, perhaps

---

[2] Daniel Levy and Gabriel Székely, *Mexico: Paradoxes of Stability and Change,* 2nd ed. (Boulder, Colo.: Westview Press, 1987), 23.

most importantly, the poor benefited little if at all from the country's economic progress.

The Revolution

By the early 1900s, Diaz's rule had sparked the same kind of broad-based opposition that toppled earlier strongmen. In the countryside, loosely coordinated bands of peasants took up arms, including groups headed by the legendary Emiliano Zapata (1879–1919) and Pancho Villa (1878–1923). In the cities, liberals, too, found themselves increasingly frustrated. In 1910 the anti-Diaz forces found a rallying point in the meek Francisco Madero, who published *The Presidential Succession of 1910*, in which he pointedly used Diaz's own theme of effective suffrage and nonreelection against the aging dictator. Meanwhile, the new labor movement organized a series of crippling and often violent strikes in the mines and mills.

All the tensions came to a head with the 1910 presidential election. Madero easily won the nomination of his newly created Anti-Reelectionist Party. As the campaign neared its end, however, Madero was arrested on trumped-up sedition charges. Diaz was declared the winner even though there was considerable evidence that the election was rigged.

Right after the election, Madero's family bribed the government to secure his release on the condition that he stay out of Mexico City. He took to the countryside, gathering supporters and evidence about electoral fraud along the way. On 25 October Madero and his growing band of supporters issued the Plan de San Luis Potosi, which was a de facto call for rebellion against the Diaz dictatorship.

Madero received strong support from the United States and from populist leaders like Zapata and Villa. In early 1911 he left his base in Texas and waged a series of battles against a surprisingly weak federal army, which ended with the 21 May 1911 agreement that Diaz would abdicate and be replaced by Madero.

The revolution, however, was far from over. Madero proved to be a weak leader and he quickly lost the support of most of the other populist leaders, including Zapata, who rebelled only two and a half weeks after the new president was installed. He faced an uprising, too, from the old dictator's nephew, Felix Diaz.

Madero's rule came to an end after the so-called Ten Tragic Days and the coup staged by the manipulative General Victoriano Huerta in February 1913. Pitched fighting had broken out between forces loyal to Diaz and to Madero. After his initial military leader was wounded, Madero appointed the untrustworthy Huerta as his new commander in chief. Before the ten bloody days were

over, Huerta had defeated both Diaz and Madero. Madero was arrested on 18 February, resigned the next day, and was shot three days later. U.S. Ambassador Henry Lane Wilson played a major role in these events, including the assassination of Madero.

Despite the American machinations, Huerta, too, was not to survive. A number of regional leaders, including Venustiano Carranza, refused to accept his presidency and took up arms along with Villa and others. Meanwhile, the Woodrow Wilson administration in Washington grew increasingly concerned with the European influence in Mexico—especially in the oil industry—and ended up attacking as well, occupying Veracruz for most of 1914. Between them, the U.S. invaders and Mexican rebels drove Huerta from office before the year was out, leaving yet another power vacuum in the capital. Marauding armies ravaged the countryside, ultimately resulting in the deaths of about 1.5 million people in a country that at the time had only 14 million inhabitants.

By 1916 Carranza, Zapata, and Villa were all forming massive armies of landless peasants, poor industrial workers, and others whose grievances were unmet and whose lives had been disrupted if not destroyed. Finally, by mid-1916, Carranza had defeated both Villa and Zapata and occupied Mexico City, forcing President Wilson to recognize his government. That fall, elections were held to choose a new constitutional assembly, which brought the bloodiest six years of the country's bloodiest hundred years to an end.

Institutionalizing the Revolution

On several occasions in the course of this book, we have seen that new constitutions do not necessarily lead to sweeping political change. And, given the instability and violence of Mexican history in the century after 1810, there was no reason to believe that the new constitution of 1917 would do so, either.

Surprisingly, the constitution has lasted and has structured Mexican political life ever since. None of the problems have disappeared, but Mexico has largely been spared the widespread violence that characterized its first century of independence and that plagues many other third world countries today.

The new constitution drew heavily on the principles underlying the largely ineffective but popular 1857 document. Presidents and most other officeholders were denied the right to run for reelection. The power of the church was sharply limited. Foreigners were no longer allowed to own Mexican land or mineral resources. Articles 27 and 123 endorsed the principle that the huge haciendas could be broken up, though not without compensation for their owners.

At first, there did not seem to be much of a chance that this constitution would be any more successful than the earlier ones. Carranza understood the importance of making reforms but proved reluctant to put them into effect. Moreover, the new regime was quickly beset by many of the same problems as the old one, and its leaders proved only marginally less corrupt than their predecessors. The Carranza government turned on its opponents, assassinating Zapata in 1919 after luring him to a meeting supposedly to discuss peace. Zapata's forces, in turn, assassinated President Carranza the following year.

Carranza was succeeded by another general, Alvaro Obregón, who had risen to prominence by defeating Villa in 1915. Obregón undertook an ambitious program to expand public education and attempted to implement land reform, though only about three million acres of land, about half of which was arable, was turned over to the peasantry. After putting down a rebellion by Huerta's forces in 1923, Obregón turned power over to President-elect Plutarco Elias Calles when his term ended in 1924. Calles, in turn, attacked the church, provoking a right-wing and clerical counterrevolution from 1926 to 1929.

Then the succession issue reared its ugly head once again. Without Calles's support, Obregón chose to run for the presidency again in 1928 in clear violation of Article 23. He won the almost certainly rigged election anyway, but he, too, was assassinated before he could assume office for another term.

Outgoing President Calles displayed an all-too-rare sense of tact and commitment to democratic practices, and, for once, an assassination did not spark another wave of violence. More importantly, having realized that presidential succession was not going to be possible, Calles and his supporters found another way to provide continuity from one presidency to the next: create a political party that could control the nomination (and hence the election) of the next president. The first convention of their National Revolutionary Party (PNR) was held in 1929, and, after several name changes, it became the PRI in 1946. Calles and the men who succeeded him until 1934 also put the brakes on social reform. Land reform, in particular, ground to a halt even though Mexico still had the largest number of rich landowners in the world. In short, despite the revolution, most Mexicans still lived in misery, albeit less violent misery.

These were important years, nonetheless, precisely because Calles and his colleagues accomplished something that had eluded their predecessors—regularizing who governed in general and how the process of succession would occur in particular. Previously, time and time again, uncertainties about and divisions over the succession had plunged Mexico into turmoil and civil war.

Although the specific practices continued to evolve over the next decade or so, the basic principles that were in use until 2000 were set by the end of the 1920s. The single party would control access to all political offices, but the various groups within the party would all win some of them. No president could serve more than a single six-year term. The outgoing president would consult widely within the party, but he would ultimately select the candidate to succeed himself.

Cárdenas and His Legacy

The Great Depression that began with the U.S. stock market crash in October 1929 was to result in one more wave of reform. Not surprisingly, the depression hit Mexico extremely hard, provoking new demands for economic reform and new pressures from below. Disgruntled party leaders convinced Calles (who remained the behind-the-scenes political kingmaker) not to select another conservative as the next presidential candidate in 1934, but to turn instead to the populist Indian leader and minister of war **Lazaro Cárdenas** (1895–1970).

Cárdenas had developed the ability to reach out to the Mexican masses when he was governor of Michoacan in the 1920s. He drew heavily on populist and even Marxist themes in blaming Mexico's problems on capitalism and greed at home and abroad. In this, he was not terribly different from many of his contemporaries. Unlike them, however, he was able to translate the rhetoric into concrete accomplishments. The highlight of his **sexeño** (six-year term) was agrarian reform, in which his government redistributed more land than all his predecessors combined. In all, about 15,000 villages and a quarter of the population benefited from the reform. Roughly half the cropland was taken from the hacendados and given not to individual peasants but to collective or cooperative farms known as *ejidos.* Typically, an individual family farmed but did not own its own plot of land, and the *ejido* could take it back if it were inefficiently or dishonestly run.

Cárdenas is also known for nationalizing the oil industry. Mexico produced about a quarter of the world's oil in the 1920s, most of which was controlled by foreign firms despite the earlier nationalization of other natural resources. In 1938 Mexico took over the oil wells and refineries, placing them under the control of a single nationalized firm, **PEMEX.** This was not simply a nationalist act. Until the 1950s about three-quarters of the oil was sold to businesses at subsidized prices, which helped make rapid industrialization and economic growth possible.

Cárdenas was by no means the radical revolutionary the American press often portrayed him to be. However, he was not all that democratic a president, either. The radical policy initiatives came from the government, and not as a result of pressures from below. Potential opponents, including former president Calles and a top labor leader, were exiled to the United States. Moreover, it was during the Cárdenas presidency that the party established an official trade union, the **Confederation of Mexican Workers (CTM),** and two peasant organizations, which became the main cogs in the PRI's corporatist machine.

Problems mounted during the second half of his term in office. The nationalizations cost the Mexican government considerable support from Britain, the United States, and other countries. Most ominously of all, the reforms provoked enough opposition at home that there was talk of another armed uprising. Perhaps as a result, Cárdenas slowed down the pace of reform and turned his attention to building the party and planning for his own succession. Because of the problems looming at home and abroad, he chose the moderate Catholic minister of war Manuel Avila Camacho to succeed him instead of another reformer. And, unlike many of his predecessors, Cárdenas withdrew from politics after he left office, thereby strengthening the principle that all subsequent Mexican presidents have followed: The end of a president's term in office also marks his retirement from any kind of active role in political life.

Cárdenas's reforms were by no means an unqualified success. Land redistribution and the other reforms did little to eliminate poverty or inequality. The hacendados, for instance, were able to use loopholes in the law to hold onto almost all of the most productive land. Still, considerable progress was made toward some of the goals espoused during the revolution, and Cárdenas richly deserves his place as one of the most revered leaders in Mexican history.

Cárdenas's retirement is normally viewed as the end of the revolutionary period in Mexican history. Since then, Mexican politics has been dominated by conservatives, albeit acting in the name of a revolution now eighty years in the past. The key to this process is what Fox's first foreign minister (and political scientist), Jorge Castañeda, calls the "peaceful and well-choreographed transfer of power."[3] In this system, the outgoing president chose the next PRI candidate for president, who, of

course, was bound to win. And, as we will see in more detail, because the president determined who held every office in the country that was controlled by the PRI, he had tremendous leverage over what came next.

An Institutional Revolutionary Party

It was through this process, in turn, that Mexico's revolution was institutionalized. Since 1940 Mexico has had eleven presidents. (See table 16.2.) The first two, Manuel Avila Camacho in 1940 and Miguel Alemán in 1946, were far more conservative than Cárdenas. Avila Camacho successfully cooled revolutionary enthusiasm and is known today mostly for introducing the country's first social security system. Alemán, however, shifted away from Cárdenas's policies and leadership style. Placing land reform on the back burner, he pursued rapid economic growth through industrialization, assuming that such progress would eventually provide a better standard of living to all Mexicans through what is called the trickle-down theory. The Alemánista model was not based on market forces, however. Rather, Alemán's approach stressed state ownership of a few key industries such as PEMEX and substantial state control over the private sector, which was largely controlled by the PRI. He was followed by the rather bland Adolfo Ruiz Cortines, who claimed to be trying to strike a balance between the Cárdenistas and Alemánistas but who is often called the Mexican Eisenhower because so little happened during his administration.

Then, in 1958, the pendulum swung marginally leftward with the next three presidents, Adolfo López Mateos, Gustavo Díaz Ordaz, and Luis Echeverria. Although

---

[3] Jorge Castañeda, *Perpetuating Power: How Mexican Presidents Were Chosen* (New York: Free Press, 2000), xi.

▌TABLE 16.2 Presidents of Mexico

NAME	START OF TERM
Venustiano Carranza	1917
Adolfo de la Huerta	1920
Alvaro Obregón	1920
Plutarco Elías Calles	1924
Emilio Portes Gil	1928
Pascual Ortiz Rubio	1930
Abelardo Rodriguez	1932
Lázaro Cárdenas	1934
Manuel Avila Camacho	1940
Miguel Alemán	1946
Adolfo Ruiz Cortines	1952
Adolfo López Mateos	1958
Gustavo Díaz Ordaz	1964
Luis Echeverría	1970
Jose López Portillo	1976
Miguel de la Madrid	1982
Carlos Salinas de Gortari	1988
Ernesto Zedillo	1994
Vicente Fox	2000

López Mateos called himself a leftist "within the revolution," there was not much substance to his leftism. Echeverria tried to limit the cost of food and housing and to increase government control over some key industrial sectors. But, on balance, all three adopted the Alemánista approach to economic development. Even more importantly for our purposes, each proved willing to repress groups that raised objections to PRI rule, including the bloody crackdown on student demonstrators in 1968.

Many Western countries experienced major turmoil in 1968, as we saw in Chapter 5 on France. The same was true in Mexico. Although many of the protesters involved in the demonstrations that swept the country that year returned to the PRI fold as adults, widespread disillusionment with the system set in for the first time. Since then, the PRI has had to face growing pressures for democratic and other reforms from outside the core of the system it controlled.

Under Echeverria, too, economic problems began to mount in the 1970s. Growth slowed, debt accumulated, and the peso had to be devalued. His successor, Jose López Portillo, stabilized the economy for most of his administration. The effects of the post–OPEC slump had begun to wear off, and economic growth picked up again. Political freedoms were expanded, making his one of the most open administrations since the revolution.

But the turnaround came in large part because López Portillo was able to impose wage controls and other austerity measures that kept labor costs down and increased the profits of middle-class and foreign investors. Moreover, there was ever more government corruption, and reports began to implicate the office of the president.

It was in López Portillo's final year that the Alemánista model collapsed. With the steep drop in oil prices, Mexican debt skyrocketed from not quite $49 billion in 1980 to over $72 billion the following year. The government had to cut its budget and subsidies to industry and consumers alike. Conflict over wages and prices broke out, as government, business, and labor all found themselves strapped. The flight of capital out of the country accelerated.

The government had no choice but to turn to the International Monetary Fund and private banks for $8 billion in loans. These agencies, of course, attached conditions to the loans, including pressuring the Mexican government to shift away from its state-dominated approach to industrial and overall economic development. The next presidential election was due in 1982, right in the midst of the debt crisis.

As it had done so many times in the past, the PRI followed the shifting political and economic winds, and in 1982 nominated a new kind of presidential candidate, **Miguel de la Madrid.** Previously, most prominent PRI politicians had built their careers in the military, labor, or the interior ministry. De la Madrid represented a new generation of politicians, dubbed the "tecnicos," most of whom had studied business or economics at prestigious American universities and had previously worked in one of the economics ministries. He spoke of "moral renovation," democratic reform, and a shift toward a more market-based economy, but only in the latter did he make any significant progress. Foreign investment was encouraged. Public enterprises were sold off, especially those that were losing money. Public subsidies were cut, and thousands of bureaucrats were fired. Unfortunately, because interest rates remained high and the price of oil low, very little economic growth occurred, especially after the middle of his term.

Congressional and state elections during the second half of de la Madrid's term showed that the PRI's electoral grip was loosening. The conservative, business-oriented **National Action Party (PAN)** grew rapidly, won some local elections, and probably won two governorships that the PRI ultimately held onto through fraud.

Nonetheless, the de la Madrid administration continued to pay lip service to democratic and economic reform, which it claimed to have fostered with the selection of another young tecnico, **Carlos Salinas de Gortari,** as presidential candidate for 1988—an election he won only through fraud and deceit. Salinas continued the generational change begun under de la Madrid. Eight of his twenty-two cabinet secretaries, for instance, had advanced degrees in economics or management and were in their early forties or younger, earning them the nickname "smurfs" to contrast them to the older "dinosaurs."

The new market-oriented policies de la Madrid and Salinas so enthusiastically endorsed were as far removed as one could get from the egalitarian ideals of the revolution or of the Cárdenas years. So, too, were the corruption and the repression, which some observers believe included the regular use of torture and occasional killings by the authorities. The Salinas administration was able to keep a lid on the most serious problems. However, his retirement served to open the proverbial floodgates.

Ernesto Zedillo almost certainly won his 1994 presidential election fair and square. As soon as he took office, however, he was greeted by another financial crisis that required even more foreign loans. Soon, scandals reached the top ranks of the party, including the Salinas family. His government's and the PRI's popularity soon plummeted.

The most important recent event demonstrating that Mexico was nearing the end of a political era came

Damian Doverganes /AP / Wide World Photos

Former president Carlos Salinas de Gortari.

with the 1997 congressional election. The PRI won only 38 percent of the vote and 48 percent of the seats. **Cuautémoc Cárdenas,** of the Party of the Democratic Revolution (PRD), was chosen mayor of Mexico City in the first election for that post.

Then came the 2000 election. This time, the electoral reforms (to be discussed in the section on political parties) had progressed too far for the PRI to be able to steal another victory at the polls. Fox won the presidency handily, but his supporters fell far short of a majority in the Chamber of Deputies and actually trailed the PRI in the less powerful Senate.

Political Culture

Mexico has an important place in the history of scholarship on political culture. It was the only third world country included in Gabriel Almond and Sidney Verba's path-breaking study of the relationship between culture and democracy, whose findings were discussed in the chapters on Britain and

An Intriguing Parallel

This overview of Mexican presidencies since 1940 allows us to see a country whose evolution in many respects parallels that of the Soviet Union prior to Gorbachev. To be sure, the two countries had very different institutional arrangements, and Mexico never had anything approaching Stalinism. Nonetheless, the five most important themes in Mexican politics after Cárdenas mirror those we saw in the Soviet Union under Brezhnev, Andropov, and Chernenko.

First, the Mexican system was stable. No leader has been willing to pursue policies that might undermine the regime or even provoke serious opposition. The practice of one president choosing his successor and the generally cooptive nature of the PRI were designed to maximize continuity in a country that had been in turmoil for decades.

Second, as the regime grew more stable and the PRI solidified its rule, social reform and the other goals of the revolution receded from center stage. As in Brezhnev's Soviet Union, official statements were always couched in revolutionary rhetoric, but the elite's primary goals lay elsewhere.

This concern with power brings us to the third, and perhaps the most important, theme—the elitism of Mexico's party state. The PRI was nowhere near as brutal as the old Communist Party of the Soviet Union. Nonetheless, the PRI was the only institution that counted.

Fourth, the stranglehold on power was accompanied by quite a bit of corruption, though in the Mexican case it went far beyond the opulent living conditions of its equivalent with the *nomenklatura*. Most notably, PRI officials turned the rigging of elections into an art form, something they had to do in the 1980s and 1990s as their popularity declined.

Fifth, like the centralized planning of the command economy, the Alemánista model of state-sponsored development no longer seemed to work very well. And, like Gorbachev, the PRI may have waited too long to begin to change.

Germany. Mexico was also one of ten countries covered in a mid-1960s anthology on the link between political culture and political development.

Since then, unfortunately, the study of Mexican political culture has gone into eclipse. This probably is the case because the liberal democratic biases in traditional studies of political culture make Mexico hard to understand in at least two respects. First, analyses based on individual attitudes about authority and the regime have not yielded useful descriptions of Mexican culture itself.

Second, to the degree that we understand it, political culture in Mexico has not been as important as those in Britain or the United States in determining what is politically acceptable.

But it would be a serious intellectual mistake to avoid the topic of Mexican political culture on two levels. First, when viewed in ways akin to what anthropologists mean by "culture," it was a major force sustaining PRI rule. Second, we will also see that social and economic changes eroded some of these traditional values, and helped produce the more democratic Mexico that elected Vicente Fox.

In stark contrast to Iraq, there is a very real sense of national identification and identity among almost all Mexicans. There is a common language, mass culture, and history from which only a few non-Spanish-speaking Indians are excluded. And even they share a common religion with the rest of the country that, despite the anticlericalism of many Mexican regimes, is a powerful unifying force bridging all the subcultures.

This national identity rests, too, on what some scholars have more speculatively seen as the blending of Spanish and Aztec cultures starting in the sixteenth century. Both had strong doses of authoritarianism and corruption that became part of the Mexican political landscape from the beginning.

In many, often surprising, respects, most Mexicans believe that the regime is legitimate. In particular, the revolution of 1910–17 remains a source of pride for almost all Mexicans, no matter how they react to the way its institutionalizers have ruled since then. And the more populist and revolutionary figures in Mexico's past—Hidalgo, Juarez, Zapata, Villa, and Cárdenas—are still widely viewed as heroes. The term *revolution* is used to describe almost anything positive, and the PRI tries to associate everything it does with a revolutionary mythology. Nationally approved textbooks speak positively of revolutions in the Soviet Union and Cuba, not because the PRI is in any way Marxist but because this helps to legitimize Mexico's revolution by linking it to "great revolutions" elsewhere.

Although anthropologists warn us not to exaggerate their importance, there have been trends toward authoritarian leadership throughout much of Mexican history. The revolutionary process, with its frequent turns to charismatic and, according to some, even messianic leaders, has at the very least reinforced those broader cultural traditions. Undoubtedly, all this made it easier for the PRI to build support for a strong presidency that, though shorn of the messianic, repressive, and even charismatic aspects, is highly reminiscent of these deeply rooted leadership styles.

■ **TABLE 16.3** Satisfaction with Democracy and Respect for Human Rights (percentage saying they were very or somewhat satisfied with democracy, and human rights matters a lot or some)

COUNTRY/REGION	SATISFACTION WITH DEMOCRACY	RESPECT FOR HUMAN RIGHTS
MEXICO	37	43
ADVANCED DEMOCRACIES	63	74
LATIN AMERICA AND CARIBBEAN	53	41
AFRICA	50	54
EAST ASIA	45	59
POST-COMMUNIST SOCIETIES	35	45

Source: Adapted from Moreno, Alejandro and Patricia Mendez, "Attitudes toward Democracy: Mexico in Comparative Perspective." *International Journal of Comparative Sociology* 29 (December 2002), 350–369.

Some of these trends are reflected in recent versions of the World Values Survey, which tracks people's commitment to democracy and other beliefs around the world. As table 16.3 suggests, Mexicans tend to have less respect for either democracy or human rights than people in all major parts of the world except for the post-Communist societies.

Mexico (along with most of Latin America) is known for male dominance in all areas of life, not just politics. Historians debate why this side of Mexican culture exists. Some cite the Spanish conquistadors, and others stress aspects of precolonial social structures. Whatever the cause, women have historically played a relatively minor role in Mexican politics (they only got the vote for federal elections in 1953), which many observers are convinced is a sign of how strong values associated with machismo still are.

But, as is so often the case with stereotypes, the reality is much more complicated. As Mexico urbanizes, as women get more education and increasingly enter the workforce (they currently make up only 30 percent of it), and as social conditions deteriorate, more and more women are beginning to reject the macho side of Mexican culture and to demand a more equal role in social, economic, and cultural as well as political life. Also, other societies that rarely get labeled macho have similar track records at keeping political life a predominantly male preserve.

Mexican society is also noted for strong patron-client relations, or **camarillas.** The PRI depends heavily on patron-client networks extending down from the party elite to vote-mobilizing organizations all around the country. We will return to these in the section on how the president dominates the state. As we will see in the next section, as Mexico urbanizes and Mexicans get more education, the influence of the camarillas has eroded, taking with it much of the support for the PRI.

Along with these general trends, we can talk about at least four distinct Mexican political subcultures. To begin with, there are some people—certainly less than 10 percent of the total population—who would fit into Almond and Verba's parochial category. Most of them are rural Indians who, as noted earlier, do not speak Spanish well, have not been integrated into the dominant national culture, and have not traditionally been active in politics. However, small groups of them have been involved in on-again/off-again uprisings in such poor states as Chiapas and Guerrero (which surrounds Acapulco).

Impressionistic evidence suggests that most Mexicans are what Almond and Verba called "subjects." That is, they are reasonably aware of what the government is doing. But these Mexicans probably are not as disinterested in the system or as unaware of their potential to influence decisions as are archetypical subjects. Rather, they tolerate the system, assuming and/or knowing that there is little they can do to change what they take to be a powerful, corrupt, or evil government. In one observer's words, they are "stoically fatalistic." They are disproportionately older, poorly educated, rural, lower class, and female—precisely those groups that have benefited very little from the system and have the least well-developed ideas about alternatives to it.

There are also quite a few people who clearly support the PRI and the system as a whole, just as there were in Brezhnev's Soviet Union. Some Mexicans undoubtedly still believe in the revolution and the party's commitment to carrying out its ideals. But they are probably few and far between. Rather, the regime's supporters tend to be those people who benefit from it. However large or small this subculture is, it is the one from which the leadership is selected.

Finally, there is an emerging anti-PRI subculture. The regime has always had its critics. Although very few people are willing to take up arms, anti-PRI opposition is growing, as is evident in the growing support for other political parties and the few interest groups not controlled by the PRI.

Most scholars also are convinced that broad-based support for the regime is eroding. This is not to suggest that cultural change is putting it in jeopardy. Indeed, there are no signs from the Fox administration's first year in power that it intends any sort of drastic constitutional reform. What's more, the PRI still has considerable support from the first three subcultures, even if this support is gained more for the careers and benefits it used to offer than as a result of the values and beliefs of the citizenry.

Political Participation

A generation ago, the focus here would have been on how the PRI was able to manipulate the way people participated in political life. Then, as now, there were few legal restrictions on what people could do. The Mexican constitution grants the basic freedoms of a liberal democracy and universal suffrage for everyone over age eighteen. There is little or no interference with an individual's ability to exercise a religion, travel, own property, or choose a school for his or her children. There also is open and often heated debate in the press and on the floor of the legislature on almost every significant issue that comes along.

The regime violated human rights more than we would expect in a true democracy. Strikes by railroad engineers in the 1950s and by telephone workers in the 1970s were forcibly suppressed. The government expelled peasants from land they had occupied in the 1970s. Most notoriously, government forces killed at least three hundred students in the so-called Tlatelolco massacre of 1968. During the infamous "battle of the streets" in 1980, Mexico City police officials "convinced" dissidents that their demonstrations clogged traffic and posed a danger to public safety, and so had to be stopped. Everyone understood that traffic was not the real problem and that if the protesters did not accept this ruse the police would be willing to use more drastic means. Some even claim that elements of the PRI were responsible for the assassination of its own candidate in the early stages of the 1994 presidential election. Because the government has been willing to resort to violence often enough, even veiled threats to use coercion usually work.

In comparative terms, however, the Mexican regime was not all that repressive after the revolution was institutionalized. Instead, the PRI was able to maintain its power by turning the clientelistic social structure into an umbrella organization that shaped what people did politically most of the time. It usually did not have to rely on force to keep the opposition at bay and out of office. If it needed to, it could simply stuff the ballot box or resort to other forms of fraud to ensure that it "won" every election that mattered.

It is because of this distinction between the relative freedom of individual expression and the sharply limited opportunities to turn dissent into political power that political scientists were reluctant to call Mexico a de-

▌ TABLE 16.4 Mexican Chamber of Deputies Election
Results, 1976–2000 (percentage of valid votes)

YEAR	PRI	PAN	PRD AND ITS PREDECESSORS	OTHERS
1976	85.2	8.9	—	5.9
1979	74.2	11.4	5.3	9.0
1982	69.3	17.5	4.4	8.6
1985	68.2	16.3	3.4	12.2
1988	50.4	18.0	4.5	27.3
1991	61.4	17.7	8.3	12.6
1994	50.3	26.8	16.7	6.2
1997	38.0	25.8	25.0	11.2
2000	36.9	36.9	18.7	6.1
2003	48.0	23.1	17.6	11.3

mocracy prior to 2000. The link between the free expression of political views and democracy is crucial because it is through elections and participation in interest groups that individual citizens have some control over who governs and what they do. It is this link between an autonomous civil society and the individuals in power that has largely been missing in Mexico.

To be sure, this civil society has grown considerably over the past generation. The PRI was also forced to accept reforms designed to make elections fairer and vote counts more honest and transparent. Together, these changes have produced a political landslide. In 1976 the PRI won fully 85 percent of the vote in the Chamber of Deputies election; in 2000 it only won 36.9 percent. (See table 16.4.)

It is because of the changes to be discussed next that political scientists are now more willing to think of Mexico as on its way to democracy.

The PRI and Its Hold on Power

Mexico was sometimes called "semidemocratic" because the PRI violated democratic principles in order to keep itself in power. Elections were always officially competitive. However, everything from its willingness to buy votes to its stuffing of ballot boxes made it impossible to think of Mexico as anything like the kind of democracy we saw in South Africa, let alone in the countries discussed in Part 2 (www.pri.org.mx).

The PRI was also a different kind of political party from any of those covered in the chapters on functioning democracies. Although the PRI has a formal institutional structure and holds regular meetings at which national issues are debated, it is not really a classical democratic party whose main goal is to build support for a particular viewpoint at the polls.

Instead, the PRI is an elaborate network of camari-

llas enrolling some fifteen million members. These patrons and their clients are drawn to politics less by their ideological views and more by their desire for power and, sometimes, wealth.

At the grassroots level, the PRI's organizers rarely talk about the "high politics" of government or national issues. Votes are won—or manufactured—in ways reminiscent of an American urban political machine of the early twentieth century. Votes are often bought either directly or through the provision of benefits for a given neighborhood, village, or social group. Fully 5 percent of the people who voted in the first-ever primary election to choose the PRI's candidate for the 2000 presidential campaign told pollsters they had received payment for their votes. Loyal and effective party workers are rewarded with jobs that are abundantly available given the rules on nonreelection.

The PRI probably won most of its elections fairly. But it was also able to win even when it stood a chance of losing. Because the party also controlled the **Federal Election Commission (CFE),** which was responsible for counting and validating election returns, it was easy for it to manipulate the results. Polling places were moved during the middle of election day, and, mysteriously, only likely PRI voters knew where they had gone. Some people voted more than once, and PRI supporters stuffed the ballot box with fistfuls of premarked votes. The vote count often bore little or no resemblance to the actual tally. Once the votes were in, *alquimia electoral*—literally, **electoral alchemy**—took place. A few days later, the CFE would report the official election results, which were widely viewed as fraudulent. As one recently "elected" PRI governor put it, "If it is fraud, it is patriotic fraud."

Electoral fraud became a serious political issue in 1988 when, it is all but universally assumed, the PRI stole the presidential election. From 1985 to 1988, the opposition staged over nine hundred demonstrations to protest the cheating. After the 1989 municipal elections, opposition groups seized over a hundred town halls to protest alleged electoral fraud. In the demonstrations that followed, at least twenty protesters were killed by police.

Since then, elections have been conducted more honestly, but the corruption has hardly disappeared. In the months before the 1991 elections, about 8 percent of the voters (or 3.1 million people) registered to vote, but the CFE "lost" their enrollment cards. In the state of Guanajuato, Fox, then the PAN's gubernatorial candidate, claimed that more PRI votes were cast than there were registered voters at several hundred polling stations. He also alleged that voting credentials were withheld from his supporters and used by others to cast multiple ballots for his PRI opponent. In this case, the

▌TABLE 16.5 The 2000 Mexican Election

CANDIDATE/PARTY	PERCENTAGE VOTE FOR PRESIDENT	PERCENTAGE VOTE FOR CHAMBER OF DEPUTIES	NUMBER OF SEATS IN CHAMBER OF DEPUTIES	PERCENTAGE VOTE FOR SENATE	NUMBER OF SEATS IN SENATE
Vicente Fox/PAN	42.5	36.9	223	36.7	51
Francisco Labastida/PRI	36.1	36.9	209	36.7	60
Cuautémoc Cárdenas/PRD	16.6	18.7	68	18.9	17
Other/spoiled ballots	4.8	6.1	—	5.4	—

corruption was so blatant that the PRI candidate had to step aside and cede the state to the opposition.

That said, the PRI campaigns are not merely pork barrel politics in action. Prior to 2000 the PRI used them to legitimize its rule, not simply by maximizing its vote but also by building broader awareness and support. In 1982 de la Madrid made nearly two thousand public appearances during his campaign. PRI symbols were everywhere—on posters, walls, t-shirts, and plastic shopping bags. Party leaders in Oaxaca gave prizes to workers who did the most to make the party known. Opposition parties had neither the money nor the activists to match PRI's efforts.

The bottom line is that the PRI always won—at least until the 1997 congressional election. Prior to 1988 it had never won less than 72 percent of the reported presidential vote or less than 65 percent of that for the Chamber of Deputies, the lower house of the legislature. It had never lost a presidential election. Through the 1985 elections, it had never lost a governorship and had failed to win only a single Senate seat. Even after its support began to erode in the 1980s, it was still able to maintain control of more than 95 percent of the country's two thousand municipalities.

Like Germany, Mexico now has an electoral law that combines single-member districts and proportional representation for the Chamber of Deputies. It has a total of 500 seats, 300 of which are elected from single-member districts. The rest are selected from party lists following a complex formula that brings each party's representation closer to its share of the vote. Prior to 1997 no opposition party ever won more than nine single-member districts, which meant that the proportional side of the voting had no practical effect, because the PRI had already won an overwhelming majority of the seats before the last 200 were allocated. By the mid-1990s the PRI had been forced to accept sweeping reforms that made the 1997 elections by far the most honest since the revolution. A truly independent **Federal Electoral Institute (IFE)** was created to supervise the balloting. Voters were given registration cards with their pictures on them. Workers at polling places were given at least rudimentary training, and in-

dependent officials monitored the voting at most of them. Most importantly, the IFE developed a mechanism for reporting the vote tallies the night of the election, leaving the ruling party with little time to engage in its electoral shenanigans.

This new sense of fairness, combined with the social and economic problems facing the country, produced the most dramatic change in Mexican electoral history in the twentieth century. In 1997 the PRI lost its majority in the Chamber of Deputies. The PRI was still the largest party, but the PAN and PRD together won significantly more votes and slightly more seats.

The first election of the twenty-first century finally saw the PRI defeated. (See table 16.5.) The campaign went badly from the beginning. The outgoing president, Ernesto Zedillo, did not handpick his successor, although it was fairly clear that he supported Francisco Labastida, who ultimately won the nomination (see the section on the state). Labastida turned out to be a lackluster candidate who had to support an administration that had had little success in dealing with Mexico's economic difficulties or with the rebellion in Chiapas, both of which reached crisis stage in the first days after Zedillo took office. As we will see shortly, the PRI also faced a formidable opponent in Fox, who had been on the political scene for more than a decade and had been running informally for the presidency since 1997. Although many observers called Fox's victory an upset, it probably was not, because the polls showed that voters were looking for change.

Even before its first partial defeat in 1997, the PRI had weakened considerably. In part, this reflected the changes in the electoral system that made voting more honest, gave opposition parties more seats, and so provided people with more of an incentive to vote for them. This weakness also grew out of its policy failures, which we will discuss toward the end of the chapter. Most importantly of all, its base of support was rooted in Mexico's version of **corporatism,** which had been eroding for decades. In Germany, we saw that corporatism was used to smooth economic policy making. In Mexico, the PRI used it, instead, to secure its control.

Recall that an official trade union and two peasant

organizations were created during the Cárdenas administration. Since then, other unions have been created for railroad, electrical, and telecommunications workers. Even journalists and photographers have their official PRI associations. Until recently, nearly all workers or peasants belonged to one or another of these quasi-official organizations, which blanket Mexican society and have played an important role in solidifying PRI support in three main ways.

First, they have provided Mexicans with tangible benefits that some theorists think are more powerful than the attitudes we normally associate with legitimacy. For example, more than two million families benefited from land redistribution during the 1950s alone. Government-sponsored health-care programs are often administered through these organizations. Photographers could buy inexpensive film only through their professional—and PRI-sponsored—association. Rest assured that the PRI made certain that people remembered who was responsible for providing such benefits.

Second, by tying Mexicans who were poor and powerless to the regime, the PRI was probably able to reduce the amount and severity of the protest it might otherwise have faced. Put simply, these organizations provided another example of the "causal arrow" running "downward" from state to society.

Third, these organizations gave the PRI a pool from which to recruit grassroots leaders and candidates. This, in turn, means that workers or peasants who saw themselves as potential leaders built their careers more by being part of the larger PRI machine than by being advocates for those they supposedly represented.

The PRI's hold on these organizations and their control of their constituents began to erode as the economic crisis deepened and its own policies became more market oriented. In the late 1980s, in particular, the CTM engaged in a series of strikes at some of the maquiladora factories, apparently against government wishes. More importantly, as civil society expanded, the PRI found it harder to incorporate well-educated urban voters into any of these networks.

All this suggests that the PRI entered the twenty-first century in trouble. After more than seventy years in power, it has to start from scratch and create a new identity for itself as a party of opposition. This means, in turn, that it will have to develop new ideals and policy proposals it can use to rebuild support. Shortly after its defeat, it was fined $92 million for illegal campaign practices and had to lay off two-thirds of its staff. And perhaps most damaging of all for the PRI, it has to do so with a declining base of support in Mexico's rural areas and among most traditional voters.

Conflict in Mexico

Observers who call Mexico democratic often cite the relative lack of violent, antisystem conflict to support their claim. It is true that by third world standards Mexico has relatively little "outside-the-system" protest and little of the racial, linguistic, and ethnic strife that is now so common in the third world.

However, there are two countertrends. First, there has not been very much of it in part because the state has made it hard for potential opponents to organize, let alone express their discontent. Second, the amount of dissatisfaction with the PRI regime has been mounting for years, whether measured in the number of attacks by guerrillas in Chiapas or Guerrero or in the number of votes won by opposition parties.

By early 2002, the PRI had begun something of a political comeback. It staged a hotly contested election for its new leader in which Roberto Madrazo edged out Beatriz Paredes in a ballot that was open to all Mexican voters. After forming broader alliances than ever before, the PRI won close to half of the votes in the 2003 election for the Chamber of Deputies and continued to do well in state elections through 2004. The PRI has also abandoned its obstructionist tactics in both houses of Congress on the assumption that cooperating with the government will help it in the future. Polls suggested that Madrazo (the presumptive candidate for 2006) would get about one-third of the votes in the presidential election, which might be just enough for him to win.

The Other Parties

Unlike the former Soviet Union, Mexico has always had more than one party. However, until 1988, no opposition group posed a credible threat to the PRI. Some parties that were supposedly in opposition were actually funded by the PRI in a peculiar attempt to give the outside world the impression that Mexico was a viable democracy.

The PAN

Until the late 1980s only one opposition party really mattered—the PAN (National Action Party). It was formed in 1939, mostly by people drawn from the Catholic Church and the business community who found Cárdenas's reforms too radical. During its first half-century the PAN was nowhere near strong enough to be able to beat the PRI. Its support was concentrated in the north and other

VICENTE FOX QUESADA

AFP/CORBIS

Fox holding a press conference wearing traditional Indian clothing.

Fox's victory forced the PRI from office for the first time in seventy-one years. Born in 1942 to a wealthy farmer and devout Catholic, Vicente was educated at a Catholic university in Mexico City and then at Harvard. He returned home to work for Coca-Cola, helping the company beat out Pepsi for the number one spot in the Mexican soft drink market. Today, he manages a 1,200-acre ranch where he grows vegetables and raises cattle and ostriches for export. When he ran for president, he was divorced, but shortly after taking office he married his public relations adviser.

Fox is a political veteran. He was first elected to the Chamber of Deputies in 1988. He ran for governor of Guanajuato in 1991 and probably would have won had the votes been counted honestly. He did win the seat four years later and almost immediately began his campaign for the presidency.

Fox is both charismatic and controversial. Although he claims to admire "third way" politicians such as Bill Clinton and Tony Blair, Fox has strong right-wing roots. He also tries to strike an earthy, populist tone despite his family's wealth. He rarely wears a suit, preferring blue jeans and a belt with a massive belt buckle bearing his name. He also does not shy away from controversial statements. During the campaign he referred to his opponent, Francisco Labastida, as a sissy and a transvestite.

---

relatively affluent areas of the country. There were questions, too, about whether the PAN was one of the parties that accepted support from the PRI (www.pan.org.mx).

By the 1980s, however, the PAN was a viable opposition party, though it was still too weak to mount a credible challenge to the PRI. Nonetheless, it had staked out a strongly probusiness position and gained some verbal support from the Reagan administration. Most importantly, it had demonstrated that it could consistently win one vote out of six, even according to the official figures.

The PAN's first real breakthrough came with the 1983 local elections, when its candidate was elected governor of Baja California Norte. Its progress and image were blunted somewhat by the PRD's arrival on the scene in 1988 (to be discussed shortly), though even then the PAN's vote at worst held steady and, given the fraud that year, probably actually increased marginally.

The PAN has been the biggest beneficiary of anti-PRI

sentiment since then. It won a full quarter of the vote in 1994 and 1997, which set the stage for its breakthrough in 2000.

The PAN's ultimate success cannot be separated from the personality of its current leader. The six-foot-five-inch Fox is one of the most charismatic leaders Mexico has seen since Lazaro Cárdenas. He has a broad appeal because he can present himself as an earthy farmer (he has been known to give the finger to PRI politicians) and a savvy business executive given his U.S. education and career at Coca-Cola. And in 2000 he made a conscious decision to try to unify the opposition by appealing both to the left and to traditionally conservative, Catholic PAN supporters. He did this, for instance, by allying with Mexico's small Green Party to form the Alliance for Change and by associating himself with left-of-center intellectuals such as Jorge Castañeda and Adolfo Aguilar Zinser, who became his foreign minister and chief economic adviser respectively. The reforms of the 1990s also made elections largely publicly funded, which meant that the telegenic Fox had plenty of money to run Mexico's first "modern" campaign.

The bottom line is that Fox scored a resounding victory. He won an overwhelming majority among those who claimed that their primary reason for voting was to produce change. He also did extremely well among middle-class voters, women, and others who are at the core of the growing civil society. Finally, he convinced about 30 percent of the people who had voted for Cárdenas in 1994 to switch, thereby eliminating the possibility that the PRI could squeak into power again against a divided opposition.

By late 2004, things were not looking as good for the PAN. The year before it had only won 23 percent of the vote in the congressional election, not even half the PRI's total. With less than eighteen months to go until the 2006 election, it was not even close to choosing a candidate—in a country where the national winner is usually known that far in advance. Nonetheless, most observers assumed that the PAN, PRI, and PRD candidates would run close to neck-to-neck and that Mexico would have highly competitive politics for the foreseeable future.

The PRD

In 1988 it looked as if the more serious challenge to the PRI's hegemony would come from a new and unlikely source—Cuautémoc Cárdenas, son of the last radical president, who had named him for the symbol of Indian resistance to the Spanish conquest. The elder Cárdenas had criticized the PRI's conservative, antirevolutionary turn in diaries that were published after his death in 1970, which served to crystallize left-wing dissatisfaction with the government. This dissatisfaction continued to mount, especially after Miguel de la Madrid introduced his "liberal" reforms in the 1980s. Meanwhile, the younger Cárdenas emerged as the leading advocate of this new left.

In 1986 many of the leftists organized their own faction within the PRI. As soon as Carlos Salinas's nomination was made public, Cárdenas and labor leader Porfirio Muñoz Ledo dropped out of the PRI to form the PRD (Party of the Democratic Revolution). Cárdenas declared his own presidential candidacy and stressed many of the same populist themes raised by his father nearly a half-century earlier.

The PRD did surprisingly well in 1988. Cárdenas claimed that it actually won the election, which it was denied only because of the most extensive voting fraud in Mexican history. Almost all outside observers were convinced that Cárdenas won a plurality among the votes

Cuauhtémoc Cárdenas, former mayor of Mexico City and one of the founders of the PRD.

Omar Torres/AFP/Getty Images

actually cast, but in the days before the results were announced, the PRI "manufactured" or "discovered" enough votes to deny him his victory.

The PRD was unable to maintain that strength during the 1990s. The PRI adopted new welfare and social service programs that ate away at some of the PRD's support. Some observers also claimed that it was too left-wing for the 1990s, a claim that may come back to haunt the party in the future as well.

The PRD staged an impressive comeback in 1997 and finished in a dead heat with the PAN. Perhaps more importantly, Cárdenas scored a landslide victory in the Mexico City mayoral election with 47 percent of the vote, or more than 20 percent more than his closest rival. He did poorly in 2000, however, as the PAN was able to appeal to the left as well as the right. Still, it has a major delegation in Congress and in many ways holds the balance of power, given that the PAN has to cooperate either with it or with the PRI to get legislation through. It also controls a number of cities, including Mexico City, and states, including Michoacan, which was won by Lazaro Cárdenas, the grandson of the famous president, which makes him the third member of his family to have been governor there.

As of late 2004, the PRD had not settled on a candidate for the 2006 election. The front runner was the highly popular mayor of Mexico City, Andres Manuel Ló-pez Obrador, who was running ahead of all other potential candidates in the early polls. However, López Obrador was caught up in a real estate and road construction scandal and could possibly be stripped of his legal right to run, which would make the 2006 outcome even more uncertain than when these lines were written.

The People, the PRI, and Civil Society

What we can say with some certainty is that Mexico is unlikely to return to the corporatist, camarilla-based rule of the PRI. This will probably be the case even if the PRI works out its internal difficulties and does not splinter, as some observers predict. Rather, this style of politics is not likely to succeed because of the changes in Mexican society that have led to the emergence of a viable civil society.

I could list the dozens of human rights, environmental, labor, and other associations that have made the front pages since the 1980s as evidence of this trend. Given the macho aspect of Mexican culture discussed earlier, however, there probably is no better single example to illustrate how much the country is changing than its burgeoning women's movement.

The modern Mexican women's movement is new. In the 1960s and 1970s it was limited almost exclusively to wealthy, educated women who had been influenced, among other things, by feminists from the United States and Europe.

Since the late 1980s the women's movement has broadened its appeal considerably. It started with a "historical accident," which so often plays an important role in political change. In 1975 Mexico City hosted a UN-sponsored conference to kick off International Women's Year, itself the beginning of a decade-long effort. It was hard for either the foreign participants or Mexican women to ignore the inequalities between men and women in Mexico when such an event was taking place there.

About that time, the earlier, rather elitist, women's movement began to lose support and largely gave way to what has been called "popular feminism," which organizes poor and middle-class women in both the cities and the countryside. There is no single popular feminist movement. Rather, it consists primarily of organizations that come together around mostly local issues, ranging from the aftermath of the 1985 Mexico City earthquake to the lack of potable water or decent schools in small towns.

These organizations combined protests over the kinds of issues we see in feminist movements in most

Democratization in Mexico

UNDER THE PRI, Mexico was what political scientists call a "semiauthoritarian state." It had the trappings of democracy, including competitive elections and constitutional guarantees of basic civil liberties. In practice, access to power was highly limited because power itself was concentrated in very few hands, mostly those of the national PRI leadership, which was itself a self-perpetuating oligarchy. There were concerns, too, about how much those civil liberties were honored, especially with the upsurge in crime and corruption involving the police in recent years.

As a result, the 2000 election that swept the PRI from power for the first time since the 1920s marked a sea of change in Mexican politics. However, it will take a few years of expanding democratic practices, lasting at least until the next presidential election, before we can state that Mexico has become democratic with any degree of certainty.

countries (for example, abortion, violence against women, and unequal pay) with concerns for the poor in general. Meanwhile, the economic changes of the past generation have created more employment opportunities for women at all levels, from manual and clerical workers to corporate executives. No one knows how strong these loosely organized movements are, though they certainly pale in comparison with the PRI and its officially sponsored women's organization. Nonetheless, it does seem safe to assume that, as Mexico democratizes and as economic developments further erode traditional social structures, these women's groups—along with other non-PRI movements—will grow dramatically.

The Mexican State

This section on the Mexican state has two main goals.

First, it describes the way the Mexican state operated under the PRI, and how it has changed under Fox. It should be pointed out from the outset that there have been no basic changes in state structures and procedures since Fox took office on 30 November 2000. Nor has Fox given many signs that he wants to change the formal rules of the game. Besides, he lacks the votes in Congress he would need to pass constitutional amendments. There is little doubt that the government is more open under Fox, but it remains to be seen how much of a long-term difference this will make in terms of holding it accountable, changing policies, and the like (historicaltextarchive.com/sections.php?op=viewarticle &artid=93).

Second, the material on the Mexican state will also provide one final example of the fact that constitutional theory and political reality are often not the same. As the revolution was drawing to a close in 1917, the men who would later form the PRI wrote a new constitution that they supposedly patterned after the one used in the United States. Indeed, there are a fair number of parallels between the two—at least on paper. Like the United States, Mexico has a bicameral legislature, with a lower house that, until recently, elected members from single-member districts of roughly equal size and an upper house giving each state two seats. Both are federal systems in which state and national governments are supposed to share power. Both are supposed to have a clear separation of powers, so that the legislative, executive, and judicial branches of the national government can "check and balance" each other.

In practice, the Mexican state has not been anything like the American. The constitution is not a sham document, as it was in the Soviet Union, written with the knowledge that it would never determine the way politics operated. Rather, the system turned into a semi-authoritarian and, until recently, highly stable one-party state because of a number of mostly informal and supposedly temporary arrangements that became a lasting part of the Mexican landscape as part of the way the PRI institutionalized the revolution.

Nonreelection and Presidential Domination

One parallel with the Soviet Union was that real power over policy making was held in relatively few hands. Rank-and-file PRI activists and elected officials had little influence over who made those decisions, let alone what they decided to do. (See figure 16.1.)

The PRI's hegemony itself had two vital and overlapping components above and beyond its ability to "win" every election that mattered, neither of which has changed with the election of a non-PRI government. The first is the principle of nonreelection; the second is the concentration of power primarily in the hands of the president.

The principle of nonreelection, which exists at practically every level, means that a new president faces inexperienced members of Congress and state officeholders (many of whom are also dependent on him for their positions) and appoints people to all key bureaucratic and

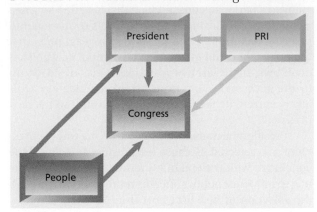

■ FIGURE 16.1 Traditional Decision Making in Mexico

judicial positions upon taking office. In other words, any new president can bring in a whole new team and embark in new policy directions in ways that happen only during rare periods of realignment in more fully democratic systems.

The principle of nonreelection has another, equally important implication. Like everyone else, presidents cannot stand for reelection and are expected to leave political life completely at the end of their term. As Frank Brandenburg pithily put it, Mexico has been able to "avoid personal dictatorship by retiring their dictators every six years."[4]

No recent president has had the unquestioned power of a true dictator. That said, any Mexican president is far more influential than his American counterpart, who, as we saw in Chapter 3, has little more than the power to try to persuade people, who do not have to agree with him.

The constitution gives the president considerable leverage. He is allowed to initiate legislation, and virtually all bills of any importance originate in the executive branch. He can issue decrees on a wide variety of subjects, including the way a law is implemented, the transfer of funds from one account to another, and even the authorization of expenditures above original appropriations. But the president's real sources of power are informal, in the way the system has evolved over the years.

Although there was considerable variation in the way PRI presidents led, they all followed a common pattern driven by the constraints of the single, six-year term. For all intents and purposes, the president's term began before he took office, with the nomination and election campaign in which the candidate started to lay out his

---

[4] Frank Branderburg, *The Making of Modern Mexico* (Englewood Cliffs, N.J.: Prentice-Hall, 1964), 141.

own agenda and style. Upon taking office, the president enjoyed a period of consolidation that lasted as long as a year and a half, during which he put his own team into place. It was primarily in the next two years or so that the president could implement substantial new policies of his own. In the last two years, his attention had to turn to the succession, and even before the election actually occurred, de facto power began to shift to the next president.

Presidential domination hinged on the way the president was selected. Because the president's political life concluded with the end of his term, the only chance he had to influence politics after his retirement was through the selection of his successor. Until Zedillo's administration, the outgoing president chose the next PRI candidate (and hence the next president) from the cabinet secretaries in office during the middle of his sexeño. The president was thus drawn from a very small and narrow pool of candidates. Beginning in the 1980s, most of them were relatively young men who were sons of PRI politicians, Mexico City–based, American-educated in economics or public administration, and part of the outgoing president's personal network of supporters. Salinas, for example, had been associated with de la Madrid since his student days, when he took a course from the future president.

A little more than a year before the election, the party chair (himself a client of the president) released a list of perhaps a half dozen possible candidates to the press. Supposedly, the list was the result of a wide consultation within the party (though it is not clear that the president consulted at all widely) so that it could be subject to considerably broader scrutiny in the population as a whole (which it also was not). Within a few months, the president made his final choice known (though he usually knew it before the short list was presented), and all the other potential candidates jumped on his bandwagon. Only then did the party hold a convention to officially nominate the president's choice. The president-designate then began his campaign by exercising the first of his many informal powers: determining who the party's candidates for the Chamber of Deputies and the Senate would be.

The incoming president had tremendous latitude in filling other posts. The president directly appointed thousands of people to posts in the twenty-four cabinet-level departments and the hundreds of quasi-independent agencies and public corporations. Normally, only about 35 percent of those appointees held high office in any preceding administration, thereby providing the new president with an ample opportunity to assert his independence. He also selected the next chair and other leading officials of the party, thereby giving himself effective control over nominations for all lower elected offices.

The system of all-but-total presidential dominance may not continue even if the PRI returns to office. In March 1999 President Zedillo announced that he would not personally designate his successor. Instead, the PRI would hold an American-style campaign with debates among the contenders and then a primary election. Jorge Castañeda, who published a book on presidential transitions shortly before being named foreign minister by Fox, claims that Zedillo made it abundantly clear that he wanted Labastida to win the nomination and that, as a result, the party machine fell into step behind his candidacy.

It is still not clear how Fox will handle the succession, though it almost certainly will not be the same old *destape* (unveiling) or *el dedazo* (finger tapping). Fox may still be able to determine who gets the PAN nomination, but even that is not a foregone conclusion, because he does not have the best relationship with the party's organizational leadership. Even if he does select someone, that candidate will almost certainly be in a very competitive race, one that he (or conceivably she) might not win.

The Cabinet, the Bureaucracy, and the Judiciary

The president's appointive power extends to the entire state, which means he has tremendous leverage over the way policy is implemented as well. Under the PRI, most important positions in the cabinet and bureaucracy were filled either from his personal camarilla or from a small group of other politicians who had the new president's trust. Others were chosen less on the basis of their positions on the issues the new government would face than on their personal connections (www.mexonline.com/mexagncy.htm).

What this meant was that, even more than the society as a whole, the government was based on patron-client relations. Virtually everyone in office owed his or her position to someone higher up in the hierarchy and thus, ultimately, to the president. Ambitious politicians enhanced their careers by exchanging favors with their patrons and clients, not by campaigning on their record or the issues.

There have been some changes over the years. At first, the PRI was little more than a loose coalition of revolutionary leaders held together by military officers turned politicians. Not surprisingly, the most important cabinet position and the source of future presidents was the minister of defense. As the regime indeed became institutionalized, the center of gravity shifted to **Gobernación,** the ministry responsible for internal security and the administration of elections. With the growth in the foreign debt and the emergence and other complex economic issues, the tecnicos came to dominate the PRI, and the various economic ministries became the most important stepping-stone. But this should not obscure the basic point being made here: The tecnicos, like everyone else, rose to positions of prominence because of their personal connections in the shifting PRI constellation of patron-client relations.

Fox seems to want to break this pattern. His original cabinet consisted of prominent politicians and business leaders, many of whom had spent years opposing the PRI. Many of them, however, do not have a long prior history with the PAN or with Fox himself. Many of the more prominent members, including former Foreign Minister Jorge Castañeda left the cabinet during the middle of the term, and Fox has consistently had trouble forging a coherent team to lead his administration.

It wasn't just the cabinet, however. The rest of the vast government bureaucracy, which employs about one out of every five Mexicans, was also part of the PRI machine. The Mexican bureaucracy bears less resemblance to a classic civil service than any of the others considered in this book. No country in Latin America has traditionally had a strong, professional civil service that is recruited by merit, that willingly serves any government no matter what its ideology, and that provides career-long opportunities to the men and women who join it. Mexico's, however, may be the least professional of them all.

Individual civil servants tend to move from agency to agency with their bosses, who, in turn, move more frequently than politicians in any other Latin American country. As with the Congress, there is so much turnover that it is hard for anyone to develop the expertise that comes from extended experience.

These bureaucratic weaknesses may not have been a serious problem when the demands on Mexican government were not very great. Now, however, they are a major contributor to Mexico's woes.

Mexico also has a Supreme Court with the power (on paper) of judicial review. But, unlike its counterpart in Washington, it almost never overruled an important government action or policy under the PRI. This is the case because even the judiciary is subject to presidential control. As in the United States, judges are officially appointed for life. In practice, judges, too, resigned at the beginning of each sexeño, allowing the incoming president to place his loyalists on the bench, as well as in the state houses, bureaucratic offices, and party headquarters. There are some signs that the court has become a bit more independent and aggressive since Zedillo, but it is far too early to tell if it can become an institution that regularly challenges any government's authority.

Congress and the Legislative Process

As noted earlier, the constitution established a bicameral legislature roughly paralleling the American system. Members of the Chamber of Deputies are elected for three-year terms. Senate terms last six years, with half its members elected every three years.

Although the Congress has to approve all legislation, it has rarely been anything more than a rubber stamp. There was no Mexican version of cabinet responsibility that obliged the PRI's members in the Chamber of Deputies and Senate to fall in line behind their president, but they consistently did so because of the way power politics traditionally worked in Mexico.

The roots of congressional weakness lie in the same peculiarities of Mexican presidentialism that have been at the heart of this section so far. Members of each house can serve only a single term at a time. Therefore, it is impossible for them to develop the expertise or the seniority that make U.S. congressional committee chairs, for instance, so important.

Even more importantly, PRI members of Congress were subservient to the president, who selected all its nominees. In the longer run, career advancement came only from building personal connections with more influential power brokers, not from making one's own mark in the legislature. Moreover, with the rise of the tecnicos, a congressional seat was no longer much of a stepping-stone for reaching the elite. Most members, instead, were PRI loyalists whose seats were rewards for years of party work.

As a result, prior to 1997 all significant legislation was initiated by the president and passed the Congress as easily as in parliamentary systems. Thus, the PRI voted as a bloc to confirm the questionable results of the 1988 election. The next year, it again voted unanimously to endorse President Salinas's bill to privatize the banks.

The 1997 election changed all that. Even though the PRI still held the presidency and a majority in the Senate, the PAN and the PRD held the balance of power. Because they did not agree on much and were not able to develop an alternative to the PRI's program, Mexico developed its own version of gridlock that students of the U.S. Congress should find familiar. And this remains the case today despite the Fox/PAN victory in 2000. There still is no majority in either house, and the country has no tradition of compromise decision making. The midterm elections in 2003 again deprived Fox of a legislative majority. In late 2004, there were some tentative signs that the PRI was at least willing not to block some of Fox's legislative initiatives. But it will take years before any regular pattern of interparty cooperation in policy making can take root.

The Federal System

Much the same can be said for state and local governments. Mexico is a federal system, officially known as the United Mexican States. The country is divided into thirty-one states plus the Federal District (Mexico City). The states, in turn, are subdivided into more than two thousand municipalities, which are more like American counties than cities. Each state has a governor and unicameral legislature. Each municipality has a mayor and municipal council.

In practice, the states and municipalities have little or no power because the PRI dominated there as well. Despite the increase in support for other parties in recent years, the opposition controls only about 15 percent of the municipalities and a quarter of the governorships. In other words, state and local government has, for all intents and purposes, been another appendage of presidential power. Not only did the president select the PRI's candidates, but he could remove governors or mayors from office. Again as with the members of Congress, governors and mayors could build their careers only by strengthening their position in the PRI's network of patron-client relationships, something that rarely happened with a politician who rocked the party boat. In addition, each national ministry maintained a federal delegate in each state to deal with overlapping jurisdictions and to make certain that the president's preferences were carried out.

Here, too, there were changes afoot even before 2000. By the mid-1990s it was no longer surprising when the PRI lost a state or local election. The PAN and the PRD have been developing enduring bases of support. By far the most important events here were the succession of PRD victories in Mexico City, which gave it control over the Federal District, in which roughly one out of every six Mexicans lives. The PAN, too, has taken more or less permanent control of a number of northern states. And its governors, in particular, have begun trying to promote investment in their states, reflecting the party's roots in the business community and their proximity to the United States.

The Military

There is only one area in which the PRI's long-term control of the government has won nearly universal approval: curbing the political power of the military. The military repeatedly intervened in Mexican politics well into the twentieth century. Similarly, it remains an important and often uncontrollable political force in much of Latin America.

In Mexico, however, the military has been effectively depoliticized. The original PRI politicians were all generals, and in 1946 Miguel Alemán became the first civilian president in thirty years. However, over the past half-century, the military has been turned into a relatively disciplined force with a professional officer corps. The military plays a role in issues of defense and national security, which includes internal as well as external threats. But otherwise, unlike what we saw in Iraq, it stays out of politics.

There is now some concern about the military, though not with any threat of a coup. Rather, there is little doubt that at least some high-ranking officers are corrupt, including more than a few who have close ties to the drug lords.

Corporatism and Corruption

Mexican politicians have never stressed individualism or the need to give the people as such access to the decision-making process. Rather, the emphasis has been on incorporating groups in a version of corporatism similar to that which helped create the integrated elite in France and Germany.

Mexicans have taken corporatism further and turned it into something quite different. As we saw earlier, the government created and/or legitimized organizations that at first glance looked much like the interest groups we find in industrialized democracies but that existed primarily to keep the PRI in office.

As such, they are part of the elaborate spoils system that is responsible for much of Mexico's corruption. Every political system (and, for that matter, just about every organization of any sort) has some degree of corruption. It is, however, an especially serious problem in Mexico, where it is built into the very logic of the system.

It is impossible to determine exactly how much corruption there is in Mexico. Most analysts believe there are few totally honest PRI officials anywhere in the country. During the last year of a presidency—the so-called *año del hidalgo*—the outgoing president bestowed lucrative jobs and other favors on the faithful.

Most public enterprises have been mismanaged.

The *Economist*'s depiction of the PRI "dinosaurs" who are still prominent in Mexican political life.

Racketeering and embezzlement are commonplace. Before oil prices plummeted, PEMEX officials routinely accepted kickbacks from their suppliers, many of which they partially owned. Petrochemical union officials, in turn, demanded a share of workers' salaries as a condition of employment. The best estimate is that over the past half-century elites siphoned off about $90 billion for their foreign bank accounts and investments, a sum roughly equal to the total Mexican debt.

Recent presidents have tried to crack down on some of these corrupt practices. De la Madrid had Echeverria's minister of agriculture arrested and the former head of PEMEX imprisoned. The former police chief of Mexico City was accused of involvement in the narcotics trade and, possibly, in the death of U.S. Drug Enforcement Agency officer Enrique Camarena Salazar. Antonio Zorilla Perez, the former head of a since-disbanded federal police force and a former PRI congressional candidate, was arrested in 1985 for his involvement in the murder of Mexico's leading journalist, Manuel Buendia. The former director of Mexico's largest mine, which had gone bankrupt, was also arrested, and charged with organizing a multimillion-dollar fraud.

Similarly, Salinas ordered the arrest of four leading stockbrokers, one of whom was among the PRI's leading contributors. He also promised free elections and released more than four hundred political prisoners the government had never even acknowledged were being held.

The crackdown went further under Zedillo. Dozens of people at or near the top of the PRI power structure have been implicated, including Salinas's brother, who was accused of ordering the assassination of the PRI's secretary general, Jose Ruiz Massieu. This, and accusations that the family had made tens of millions of dollars, forced former president Salinas to flee the country and live in exile in Ireland. Another of his brothers was murdered in Mexico City in December 2004 under mysterious circumstances.

Even more appalling may be the case of another member of the PRI elite, Carlos Hank Gonzales, who played a critical role in getting Zedillo the PRI nomination. Hank had used his years in public life to become a billionaire, stating that "a politician who is poor is a poor politician." One of his sons was caught trying to import ivory and skins of endangered species into the country. The Hanks are reportedly deeply involved in the drug trade and have been implicated in a number of murders, including that of the Catholic cardinal of Guadalajara in 1994. Nonetheless, the Hank family remains at the center of Mexican politics. In 2004, Jorge Hank Rhon was elected mayor of Tijuana despite allegations that he is not only one of the PRI's "dinosaurs" but deeply involved in the drug trade.

Needless to say, the likes of Salinas and Hank could only have gotten away with it because of their connections. Zedillo may have been more committed than his predecessors to the eradication of corruption. However, with the exception of Salinas, he did not break the unwritten rule that no member of the top elite can be indicted.

Public Policy

Debt and Development

Had this book been written twenty-five years ago, we probably would have been viewing Mexico through a very different and far more optimistic lens. Its stable government had smoothed the transition from revolutionary egalitarianism to state-sponsored industrialization. An annual average growth rate of 6.5 percent was being translated into new enterprises, some owned by the state and some by the private sector, and into an improved standard of living for most people. Moreover, Mexico seemed to be breaking the bonds of dependency by building its own industrial base and relying less on imports.

This Mexican model of stable development is long gone. The sharp decline in oil prices in the early 1980s sparked a general decline that left no part of the economy untouched. Even more importantly, the last three PRI presidents abandoned what were essentially autarkic policies and adopted new ones more in keeping with the structural adjustment policies demanded by the World Bank, International Monetary Fund (IMF), and other northern financial institutions.

It is far too early to tell if that will stimulate the rapid economic growth their advocates claim, let alone deal with poverty, inequality, and other issues that are low on their lists of priorities. In the short run, they have done little to stop the decline and have probably widened the gap between rich and poor. No government can do a lot to address such issues in its first four or five years in office, and Fox has been hampered here—as elsewhere—by his lack of legislative support and the overall poverty of the country.

Early Success

Industrialization was aided in the 1940s by high wartime demand for Mexican manufactured goods, minerals, and labor in the United States. More importantly for our purposes, it also was the product of a series of government policies that development economists call **import substitution.**

Despite the government's revolutionary origins and the huge role it was to play in industrial development, this was not a socialist policy. Rather, the government saw public ownership as providing it with more leverage over the economy, which it could use to stimulate growth. The government stepped in where the private sector could not or would not act—for instance, in extending the railroad, highway, electricity, and telephone networks or in keeping troubled industries afloat. Rarely did it take a private enterprise over for ideological reasons. We should not underestimate the state's power, because it did incorporate most of the major privately owned industries into the corporatist system. This made most of their owners and employees almost as dependent on the state as they would have been had their industries been publicly owned.

At the heart of these efforts was NAFINSA, the National Development Bank, which supplied about half the total investment funds. Much of that money went to the public sector, beginning with the nationalization of the railroads and PEMEX in the 1930s. The expansion of the state sector continued over the decades. By the end of the 1970s, the government owned all or part of more than a thousand companies, including smelters, sugar refineries, hotels, grocery stores, and even a shampoo factory. The wave of nationalizations ended in 1982 when the banks were taken over during the last weeks of López Portillo's presidency.

Taxes were kept low, and the prices of such key commodities as oil were subsidized to spur investment. Tariffs, in contrast, were kept high, averaging about 45 percent of the cost of the product being imported. Almost 95 percent of all imported goods required expensive government licenses and, as with everything else involving the government, entailed lots of red tape and often substantial bribes.

The combined public and private sector efforts paid off. The economy as a whole grew by more than 6 percent per year from 1940 to 1980. Industrial production rose even faster, averaging nearly 9 percent for most of the 1960s. Agriculture's share of total production dropped from 25 percent to 11 percent, while that of manufacturing rose from 25 percent to 34 percent. Development was concentrated in relatively labor-intensive, low-technology industries, such as food, tobacco, textiles, machinery, iron and steel, and chemicals. Exports grew tenfold, and manufactured goods came to account for a quarter of the total. The peso was one of the world's most stable currencies because the government kept it pegged at 12.5 to the dollar from 1954 to 1976. All this growth occurred without much of the inflation that was plaguing many other Latin American economies.

Don't let this picture mislead you into thinking

Mexicans outside the world's largest Wal-Mart, with its own McDonald's.

everything was fine. Relatively little attention was paid to the equality and social justice issues that had led to the revolution in the first place. Social services programs were limited at best. For example, there was no unemployment insurance of any kind. Mexico's income distribution was (and still is) among the most unequal in the third world. Rapid industrialization brought with it congestion and pollution.

Nonetheless, when compared with the rest of the third world, Mexico was doing rather well.

The Crisis

Although few economists or politicians realized it at the time, the economic boom began to slow during the 1970s. Neither the private nor the public sector proved able to spark the next stage in Mexico's industrial revolution, in which it would make more sophisticated, higher-technology products.

Moreover, at this point, the mismanagement of key industries became a problem. It was estimated, for instance, that PEMEX employed three or four times the number of workers it needed. Rapid population growth meant that more workers were entering the workforce than there were jobs for. There was a dramatic increase in government spending brought on by the last wave of nationalizations and a belated attempt to deal with social problems. To make matters worse, government revenues did not keep up with spending, creating budget deficits that, in turn, led to the key external problem, the accumulating national debt.

The budgetary and investment fund shortfalls were filled by heavy borrowing, mostly from northern banks and governments. Because of the heavy debt load and ensuing political problems during prerevolutionary times, PRI governments had borrowed very little early on. In 1970 the total debt was only $6 billion. But by the beginning of the López Portillo presidency in 1976, the debt was already $26 billion, and it would reach $80 billion by the time he left office six years later. Ultimately, the total debt would reach a peak of over $107 billion in 1987, making Mexico one of the most heavily indebted countries in the world. Debt already accounted for 16 percent of its annual GNP in 1970. By 1987 its share was up to 70 percent, making Mexico a leader in the world's **debt crisis.**

The borrowing was just the tip of the iceberg. Whether it wanted to or not, Mexico was being drawn into the global economy, which made it harder and harder to retain import substitution. The artificially low rate at which the peso was kept made it difficult for Mexico to import the new technologies it needed to continue its development. This, in turn, made investment abroad ever more lucrative, leading to massive capital flight to the United States and elsewhere in the second half of the 1970s.

The government also made one extremely costly mistake. López Portillo based his economic strategy on the assumption that oil prices would remain high. The rapid price increases and supply uncertainties in the global market after the OPEC oil embargo of 1973–74 came just as Mexican production capacity increased. Then, after the Iranian revolution in 1979, oil prices shot up again. Therefore, Mexico began selling massive amounts of oil. From 1979 to 1981 alone, Mexican oil revenues increased from $3.9 billion to $14.5 billion and accounted for almost 75 percent of all exports and for 45 percent of all government revenues.

Oil revenues thus papered over many of the underlying economic problems. Nonetheless, budget deficits and overseas borrowing continued to mount. Increased imports of consumer goods outpaced the growth in exports. Inflation broke the 20 percent barrier for the first time. The low value of the peso and high interest rates abroad accelerated capital flight by the so-called *saca-dolares* (dollar plunderers).

When oil prices began to drop in 1981, the government assumed that the decline would be temporary. It was wrong. By the summer of 1982 the Mexican economy was on the verge of collapse.

The government responded by closing the foreign exchange markets in August and nationalizing the banks in September. But the economy reeled out of control. By 1983 inflation had topped 100 percent, and it remained high, reaching a peak of 159 percent in 1987. The economy actually shrank for three of the five years from 1982 to 1986. The peso was allowed to float freely, and the exchange rate went from 56.5 pesos to the dollar in 1982 to 1,460 in 1987. This had devastating consequences for a country that was so dependent on imports, most of which had to be paid for in ever more expensive dollars.

The economy suffered yet another jolt in 1985. A devastating earthquake in Mexico City cost the government somewhere between $4 billion and $5 billion, an amount it could not afford. Meanwhile, the price of a barrel of oil dropped another 50 percent, which cut export earnings from $16 billion in 1985 to only $9 billion the following year.

Reform

The onset of the economic crisis led to two fundamental shifts in Mexican politics: the election of Miguel de la Madrid, and his government's agreement to debt reduction plans demanded by the country's public and private creditors.

The PRI has never been ideologically homogeneous. Rather, like other dominant political parties around the world, it is a loose collection of factions that support a variety of ideological positions. This diversity has given the PRI valuable flexibility, because on a number of occasions it opted for a presidential candidate who would set the country off in a new direction. Prior to 1982 this **pendulum effect** led to alternation between presidents who emphasized social reform and those who stressed economic development. But not until the election of de la Madrid had a president pursued policies that would increase the importance of market forces.

López Portillo thus chose someone with radically different ideas. To some degree, the outgoing president must have realized that policies like his would no longer work. De la Madrid's nomination also reflected the emergence of the tecnicos as a force in Mexican politics. Finally, his nomination was at least partially based on his reputation for honesty and competence.

Liberalization and Globalization in Mexico

THE TRENDS BUFFETING Mexico are not unique. Indeed, as we saw in the previous three chapters, globalization is a major factor in political life throughout the third world, and one of its most important effects has been toward a more liberal or market-oriented economy.

What makes Mexico unusual is the speed with which those forces hit the country and the directness with which its government reacted. Long one of the most autarkic of governments, the PRI all but overnight switched from import substitution to structural adjustment, rather than making the more typical and gradual transformation as we saw in Chapter 12 on India.

Whatever the exact reasons behind his nomination, de la Madrid took office in what amounted to a power vacuum. López Portillo's policies and his entourage were so discredited that de la Madrid started with a clean political slate and more latitude than most of his predecessors in recruiting his team, which included a disproportionate number of fellow tecnicos.

Despite forty years of import substitution and other policies designed to maximize Mexican economic autonomy, the country found itself more dependent on the outside world than ever. Under the best of circumstances, Mexico would have had trouble competing in the global market with its inefficient industries, limited investment capital, and overvalued currency.

The crisis made this difficult situation all but impossible. Moreover, it occurred at precisely the time that import substitution models were losing favor in international circles and being replaced by **structural adjustment,** with its emphasis on unrestricted trade in free markets as the best "engine" for economic growth.

Thus, the policies pursued by the last Mexican governments of the twentieth century had a lot in common with what we saw in India and South Africa. The one key difference was that Mexico adopted them earlier and more wholeheartedly.

No foreign bank or government dictated what Mexican policy had to be. Rather, the extent of the debt and the need for outside help in repaying it left the Mexican government in a far weaker position with far fewer options to choose from than it had had prior to 1982. It is only a slight exaggeration to say that the massive borrowing left the Mexican economy hostage to its creditors, who held the upper hand in negotiating deals to restructure the debt.

In short, the combination of the values held by the new generation of leaders and the crisis conditions led to one of the most dramatic economic turnarounds in modern history. Quickly, the government adopted four overlapping sets of policies that the Salinas and Zedillo administrations continued and added to:

- **Debt reduction.** Even before he took office, de la Madrid began negotiations about debt repayment with the IMF, the World Bank, northern governments, and private banks. The most sweeping measure was part of U.S. Secretary of the Treasury Nicholas Brady's multinational plan that consolidated some loans, turned others into bonds, and reduced Mexico's annual interest payments to banks by one-third. The agreement also offered incentives designed to keep up to $7 billion in capital in the country for future investment. Mexico still was paying an average of $10 billion a year in debt service, reducing the interest but not the principal on most of its loans. Mexico suffered a second fiscal crisis in the first weeks of Zedillo's term in office when portfolio investors removed about $5 billion in capital from the Mexican market, which sparked a run on the peso and forced Mexico to accept another expensive bailout package brokered by the United States. In other words, even with the Brady plan, past borrowing continued to plague the Mexican economy, forcing the government to take out yet more loans to pay off yesterday's debt and siphoning off money it could desperately use for other, more productive purposes.

- **Sharp cuts in government spending.** By early 1983 Mexico and the IMF had reached basic agreement on a severe austerity plan. Government spending would be sharply reduced to cut the deficit by half within three years. Subsidies would be cut and the prices charged by such government agencies as CONASUPO, which provided basic foodstuffs at below-market prices, would be increased. The Salinas and Zedillo administrations cut government spending and raised taxes even further. They were able to keep the deficit low (4 percent in 2003) and bring inflation under control. However, the social service programs, which were never very good to begin with, were seriously compromised.

- **Privatization.** To give market forces a major role in the Mexican economy, the government decided to give up much of its economic power by privatizing public enterprises, especially those that were a drain on public finances. In February 1985 the government made an initial announcement that 237 parastatals would be sold, and privatization has continued apace. Of the 1,155 firms the government controlled in the mid-1980s, only about 100 remain in state hands today. The government does, however, retain control of some of the largest and most important ones, including most of PEMEX.

The most significant privatization came in 1990 when the Salinas government returned the banks to the private sector. Actually, the first steps in that direction had begun within months of the initial nationalization, when the de la Madrid government allowed Mexican investors to buy 34 percent of the shares in any bank and foreign investors to purchase some nonvoting shares. With the 1990 decision, the state sold off most of its remaining stake in eighteen commercial banks, retaining only a limited, minority interest in some of them. The $6.5 billion it raised was supposed to be used to provide basic services, including drinking water, sewers, electricity, schools, housing, and health care, but little of it ended up there. All the signs are that PRI insiders were able to gain control of these companies and become wealthy overnight. According to one measure of wealth, Mexico had twenty-four billionaires in 2000, more than half of whom earned their wealth in the newly privatized banking system.

- **Opening up the economy.** The United States and the other creditors also insisted that Mexico open up its economy to more foreign investment. This began as early as the 1980s, but reached its peak with the 1994 implementation of NAFTA, which will remove all barriers to trade by 2010. The government also agreed to join GATT (General Agreement on Tariffs and Trade) and its successor, the WTO (World Trade Organization), the body that shapes international trade policy and requires free-market policies. Policies designed to make the economy more market oriented removed many of the rules on imports, which made it easier to import needed new technologies. Only 6 percent of imports now require government licenses. Tariffs have been reduced to an average of 10 percent, the lowest rate in Latin America.

In some ways, the opening of the economy has clearly paid off. A mini-"silicon valley" is developing in Guadalajara, where IBM, Hewlett-Packard, and other high-tech U.S. firms are assembling computers for the Mexican market and even for export. Most of the new industrial development originally was concentrated in the north, where special laws have long allowed foreign firms to open maquiladora factories that use duty-free imported components, assemble intermediate or final products, and then export what they manufacture. In 1990 more than fifteen hundred of these maquiladora plants were making such products as GI Joes and Barbie dolls, televisions, and automobiles for American and Japanese firms. The rules have since been loosened so that similar establishments have been opened elsewhere in the country. Mexico is attractive to these firms because wages are about an eighth of what they are north of the border. In fact, wage costs are so low that some Nissans built there are actually being shipped back to Japan. One American consultant estimated that it would make sense for any American firm that spends as little as 30 percent of its total expenditures on wages to relocate the manufacturing parts of its business to Mexico.

Economists who focus on conventional measures of success and failure tend to rate the reforms fairly highly. Inflation is down, and, in some years, so is debt. Growth rates have often been respectable, and there is a more visible middle class.

Scholars who focus on other issues, such as equity, are less optimistic. There has been something approaching a 50 percent decline in real wages. A total of 40 percent of the workforce is either unemployed or underemployed, and jobs have to be found for the million or so people who enter the workforce each year. About 40 percent of the population suffers from some form of malnutrition. Mexico's income distribution remains, in the World Bank's estimation, one of the world's worst.

While Mexico's yuppies are driving BMWs, watching DVDs on their home entertainment systems, and buying Pampers for their children, millions of poor people still lack indoor plumbing, hot water, health care, and adequate housing. The government tried to soften the impact of the economic reforms on the poor through the creation of the Program for National Solidarity (PRONASOL) during the Salinas administration. PRONASOL provided federal grants to local groups that develop plans to alleviate poverty in their regions. In classic Mexican corporatist style, however, the program was administered through the president's office and was used as a way to solidify support for the PRI's reformist wing. In many people's eyes, it turned into little more than another body to distribute pork barrel benefits. It has since been abandoned.

It also is not clear how much development the policies will lead to if by development we mean sustained, long-term growth. Some especially optimistic analysts think Mexico could be one of the next NICs, the South Korea of the early twenty-first century. Such develop-

ment, however, works on the assumption that global markets will continue to grow and that trading patterns will favor a country with Mexico's location, pattern of industrial development, and labor force, none of which seems certain in these uncertain economic times. And even if Mexico does prosper, it is likely to have an exaggerated version of the distorted development we find in most of the supposedly successful third world economies.

In fact, only two things are clear. First, there will not be significant economic policy changes under Fox. There will not have to be. The preceding three PRI presidents had already done most of his work for him. Largely as a result of global pressures, the once revolutionary PRI had turned its back on egalitarian goals and adopted modern, market-oriented policies as fully and as quickly as any government in the world.

Second, Mexico is losing control of its own economy and development. It may turn out that the reforms lead to substantial growth and generate a lot of wealth. But much of the new wealth—and concomitant political power—will lie in the hands of the foreign investors who supply the capital and the foreign bankers who attach conditions to their loans. For instance, U.S., not Mexican, telecommunications firms were lined up to buy the lion's share of Telefonos de Mexico. The U.S. government and private American firms are putting pressure on the government to allow outside investment in PEMEX and to increase the amount of oil it can sell in the United States even though the petrochemical giant is seen as a symbol of Mexican national independence and pride. Although the high-tech firms that have built factories in Guadalajara provide jobs and other benefits for people in the area, it is also true that the Americans control how those factories are run and repatriate almost all their profits back to the United States—just as they do with all the maquiladoras along the border.

After more than a decade of NAFTA, dependency on the United States has probably increased, although the impact of the trade agreement is a subject of tremendous controversy on both sides of the border. As NAFTA's supporters projected, trade between the United States and Mexico grew by a factor of four after the agreement went into effect. However, it also exacerbated differences within Mexico as the states closest to the U.S. border saw their economies expand while those elsewhere in the country grew poorer.

U.S.-Mexican Relations

Leftist scholars who study the third world often write about the impact of the "north" and the leverage it exercises over the "south." But they often have a hard time pinning down that impact because there is no single actor called the "north." Rather, they are actually talking about a mixture of states, corporations, and financial institutions whose individual effects are often difficult to sort out.

This is not the case for Mexico, where the impact of a single country to the north, its corporations, and the international financial institutions it dominates is all that really matters. Ever since 1821, the United States has had a tremendous influence on the way Mexicans live. And power does not flow only in that one direction. As we will see, Mexico retains considerable freedom to act as it wants in global affairs. Certain aspects of U.S.-Mexican relations can even work to the detriment of some Americans, as will probably be the case for workers in heavy industry under NAFTA.

Nonetheless, when all is said and done, the relationship is much the same as it always has been. The United States rarely tries to dictate Mexican domestic or foreign policy. But because of its size, wealth, and geopolitical power, Mexican policymakers follow U.S. wishes, far more often than not, especially when the issue at hand matters a lot to their counterparts in Washington.

Mexican foreign policy involves far more than its relations with the United States. However, the United States is a presence in Mexican affairs to a degree that far exceeds the impact of one country on any other considered in this book.

One former U.S. ambassador recently remarked that he had once apologized to the Mexican foreign minister for having to raise a trivial matter. The minister told him not to worry because about 85 percent of his time was devoted to U.S.-Mexican relations anyway.

In other words, as we already saw with the economy, the United States plays a vital role in Mexican affairs. The same can hardly be said for Mexico's influence on American politics. To take trade as an indicator again, Mexico may be the United States's third-most-important trading partner, but exports to and imports from Mexico account for only about 5 percent of the U.S. total as compared with U.S. exports and imports accounting for about two-thirds of Mexico's total.

Similarly, when U.S. officials visit Mexico, they can count on working with the most important leaders in the country. Conversely, when Mexican leaders come to the United States, they normally spend the bulk of their time with relatively low-ranking officials, such as the undersecretary of state for Latin American affairs.

Recent U.S.-Mexican relations have been fairly peaceful and even cooperative, but historically there have been moments of intense tension and conflict. In fact, in one form or another, those tensions have existed

Avocados?

On 14 July 2004, the *Washington Post* and the *New York Times* both ran a full page ad by APEAM, the Association of Producers and Exporters of Avocados from Michoacan. Their concern was that only thirty-one states in the United States allowed Mexican-grown Hass avocados to be imported during six months of the year. The rest banned them altogether.

APEAM claimed that California avocado growers were limiting the import of the Mexican salad ingredient to protect their own market, especially since their fruit cost American consumers 50 percent more than the Mexican version.

The point here is not to debate the relative quality of the two types of avocados (I live in a state where both are available, and they seem the same to me), but to see the importance of trade issues in the U.S./Mexico relationship.

from the beginning. U.S. intervention affected the course of the Mexican revolutions of 1810 and 1910, and almost everything in between. As the nationalist journalist Gastón Garcia Cantú put it:

> From the end of the eighteenth century through 1918, there were 285 invasions, incidents of intimidation, challenges, bombardments of ports, and subtractions of territory out of which seven American states were carved. No people in the world have had their territory, wealth, and security as plundered by anybody as Mexico has by the United States.[5]

With the consolidation of the PRI regime, relations improved to the point that the United States no longer contemplated direct intervention in Mexican affairs. Still, by the time Cárdenas took over in 1934, U.S. interests controlled more of the Mexican economy than ever. His reforms did strain relations some, but not as much as they might have a generation earlier, in large part because the United States found itself facing far more serious threats elsewhere.

During World War II, U.S.-Mexican relations took a decided turn for the better when Mexico declared war against the Axis powers. Although few of its troops fought, Mexico supplied the United States with oil, food, and other raw materials that it could no longer get from its traditional suppliers. Moreover, the so-called bracero

---

[5] Cited in Robert Pastor and Jorge Castañeda, *Limits to Friendship: The United States and Mexico* (New York: Vintage Books, 1988), 123.

program brought Mexican labor to U.S. factories and fields, freeing Americans for military service.

After the war, the United States found itself with a global role for the first time as it became preoccupied with the Communist threat. Given Mexico's stable, non-Communist regime, it receded from center stage in U.S. foreign policy concerns.

This is not to say that tensions completely disappeared. Mexico frequently criticized U.S. foreign policy, especially the interventions in Latin America prompted by U.S. fears of communism. Mexico opposed the CIA-backed overthrow of leftist governments in Guatemala in 1954 and Chile in 1973. It similarly supported Cuba's right to have a Communist government while opposing such U.S. attempts to topple it as the Bay of Pigs invasion in 1961. The Mexicans were among the first to break with the Somoza family dictatorship and to support the leftist Sandinistas in Nicaragua. Later, they were among the most strident critics of the Reagan administration's support for the Contra counterrevolutionary movement after the Sandinistas won.

Antagonisms between the two countries increased during the 1980s. In part this had to do with the Mexican economic crisis and its resentment of the U.S. role in forcing debt negotiations and other policy shifts discussed earlier. In part, too, it had to do with the Reagan administration's dissatisfaction with Mexico's Central American policy and its open courtship of the PAN, which it saw as a conservative, procapitalist, and realistic alternative to the PRI.

U.S.-Mexican relations have improved considerably since the election of de la Madrid. Mexico's new pro-market policies meshed nicely with those of the Reagan, Clinton, and both Bush administrations.

These improved relations, however, should not obscure the main point being made here. At all times this has been an unequal relationship dominated by a United States that has actively pursued its own interests, often without paying much attention to what the Mexicans wanted.

In this overview, then, we can see four key themes in Mexican foreign policy in general and in its relations with the United States in particular.

First, Mexican rhetoric under the PRI often was nationalistic. On one level, this is true of all countries, which naturally pursue what they perceive to be their own interests in international relations. But, perhaps because it has lived under the American shadow for so long, national pride is particularly important in Mexico whether expressed in formal policy or in textbooks.

Second, in the Estrada Doctrine of 1930, Mexico

American Fears of Mexico

In a peculiar way, many Americans live in fear of Mexico, as we saw most visibly in the 1992 and 1996 presidential campaigns of Ross Perot and Pat Buchanan.

To get a first glimpse at this fear, consider the following incident. During the summer of 1991, the U.S. Immigration and Naturalization Service began constructing a fourteen-foot-high wall along the border between San Diego and Tijuana. Ironically, the wall was made of metal slabs originally manufactured to serve as temporary runways during the Gulf War to liberate Kuwait. Even more ironically, at precisely that moment in history when we celebrated the collapse of a Berlin Wall built to keep East Germans from fleeing to freedom, the U.S. government was building what many Mexicans called a Berlin Wall to keep their citizens out of the United States.

On the one hand, Perot and Buchanan focused on the obvious fear of what many take to be uncontrolled illegal migration of Mexicans into the United States. Just below the surface lie other fears—of drugs, the economic drain many believe the third world countries impose on rich countries, the global population explosion, and the like.

On the other hand, these fears tend to blind people in the north to their own power, to their ability to determine what happens on the other side of the more often invisible wall that divides north from south.

committed itself to opening and maintaining diplomatic and other relations with all countries, including those whose policies it did not support. At least rhetorically, it has consistently championed the equality of all nations, nonintervention in other nations' affairs, national self-determination, and peaceful conflict resolution. It has also been one of the few countries willing to grant political asylum to refugees of almost all political stripes.

Third, from a U.S. perspective, Mexico has pursued a somewhat left-wing foreign policy. As we saw earlier, it has been willing to criticize U.S. intervention in the third world and has generally supported what it takes to be the interests of the third world as a whole. This was evident, for example, in its sponsorship of the Delhi Declaration in which the leaders of India, Tanzania, Argentina, Sweden, and Greece, as well as President de la Madrid, came out against further expansion of the nuclear arms race. However, Mexico's leftism has always been pragmatic, especially when there was any danger of serious opposition from the United States. Thus, it never advocated a

Sandinista victory over the Contras or gave more than to-ken support to leftist rebels in El Salvador.

Finally, there is a strong undercurrent of wariness regarding the United States both in Mexican public opinion and in its foreign policy. On the one hand, Mexican leaders realize that they must get along with their powerful neighbor to the north, and life in the United States is attractive to most Mexicans. On the other hand, most Mexicans remain highly suspicious of U.S. policies and intentions. One recent poll found that 59 percent of those sampled thought of the United States as an "enemy country," and 47 percent claimed that their opinion of the United States had worsened during the 1980s.

Virtually no Mexicans take U.S. declarations that its policies are altruistic seriously. Instead, Mexican leaders realize that the U.S. presence and its influence over foreign policy are facts of life. Their protests and seeming intransigence have been on issues that are not terribly important or in ways that are not very threatening to the United States. In fact, to cynical observers, they have been designed to placate Mexican voters rather than to demonstrate any real Mexican autonomy.

Immigration

In recent years no issue has revealed the unequal power in U.S.-Mexican relations more than the migration of millions of Mexicans to the United States. Migration between the two countries is not a new phenomenon. People have been moving from Mexico to the United States since colonial times.

It only became a serious political issue, however, after World War II. As we saw earlier, the United States actually encouraged Mexican migration during the war. However, with the defeat of Germany and Japan and the demobilization of millions of U.S. soldiers, the Mexicans became "excess" labor, and the United States began sending them home.

For the next forty years, U.S. policy followed a similar pattern. During times of economic expansion, immigration policies were loosened and/or U.S. officials turned a blind eye to the hiring of illegal or "undocumented" aliens. But when unemployment rose and Americans began to complain that illegal Mexicans were taking "their" jobs, the U.S. government tended to force the immigrants back out again.

In all, there were four major crackdowns—in 1947, 1954, 1964, and 1986. Whether economically justified or not, each was handled in a way that was bound to anger Mexicans. The 1954 program, for instance, was known as Operation Wetback and was directed by an army general as a military operation.

In 1986 Congress passed the Immigration Reform and Control Act, which created an amnesty program for Mexicans who had been in the United States illegally for five years, limited further immigration, and, for the first time, imposed penalties on U.S. employers who knowingly hired undocumented workers. The act, of course, applied to all illegal immigrants, but it was widely perceived as an anti-Mexican act because something on the order of two-thirds of all undocumented immigrants were Mexican.

Despite the law and the efforts of the Immigration and Naturalization Service (INS) to close off the border, the flow of people continues. The INS stops about 200,000 people a year trying to cross the U.S.-Mexican border illegally, but to little or no avail. No one knows how many people pay "coyotes" (men who try to sneak people across the border) to get them into the United States and, sometimes, find them a job. Not surprisingly, a huge black market in counterfeit and stolen "green cards" and other documents has sprung up. Although any estimate has to be treated with more than a few grains of salt, somewhere between 150,000 and 200,000 Mexicans move to the United States each year, of whom only 50,000 or 60,000 do so legally.

Concerns now extend beyond immigration itself to its impact on U.S. society as a whole. For example, California has immigrants from dozens of countries, but the bulk of them are Mexican. Fears about the cost of providing them welfare, education, and other social services, and about the "dilution" of American culture, were key reasons behind Proposition 187, which passed in a referendum in 1994, and the various attempts to make English the only language to be used in official state business and in education. None of these policies have had much of an effect—the immigrants keep coming.

To most Mexicans, U.S. immigration policy is biased and shortsighted. They note that many Americans believe that the roots of migration lie exclusively in Mexico, in the lack of jobs. Although most Mexicans will admit that migration strains U.S. educational, social service, and health-care systems, they argue that U.S. politicians overstate the problem. They point out that few undocumented Mexicans are taking jobs from Americans. Instead, most have taken jobs that Americans are no longer willing to do. They also point out that the migrants themselves are not the riffraff they are frequently portrayed as being in the media. The immigrants disproportionately come from the most talented and dynamic sectors of Mexican society and include 10,000–15,000 professionals a year.

Similarly, they note that the United States has never fully acknowledged the benefits it gets from the migration or the role that its businesses have played in perpetuating the problem by hiring people they know are there illegally. And they complain that the racism and indignity that everyone of Mexican origin is subjected to are not even on the U.S. policy-making agenda. Further, they charge that U.S. policy does not address the root cause of the problem in Mexico itself. The Mexican government would prefer not to have migration serve as a safety valve for the discontent that might erupt if the migrants had to stay at home unemployed or underemployed. However, to deal with the social and economic problems they feel are at the roots of the waves of migration, Mexican leaders would rather see the United States invest billions of dollars to provide more jobs in Mexico rather than in trying to close the border.

After Presidents Fox and Bush took office within two months of each other, there was considerable optimism that progress could be made regarding immigration. Bush was open to proposals that would have allowed Mexicans to move to the United States and work legally for a limited period of time. Fox hoped to add as many as two million illegal immigrants in the United States to the Mexican electoral rolls. In fact, Fox made his first state visit to the United States in the week before the 9/11 terrorist attacks. American concerns about the security of its borders ended serious discussion of immigration reform in ways Mexicans could support. The second Bush administration and the end of Fox's term in office could allow for some movement on this front.

Drugs

There is no question that the United States has a serious drug problem. There is also no question that many of the drugs Americans consume enter the country from Mexico. Marijuana probably generates more income in the poor state of Sinaloa than all legal crops (though it should be pointed out that marijuana is also the leading cash crop in California). In recent years, U.S. drug enforcement efforts have made it harder to import drugs along the east coast. Thus, as much as 70 percent of Colombian and Peruvian cocaine enters the United States across the Mexican border.

During the 1980s the U.S. government decided that it would concentrate less on reducing the demand for drugs and more on cutting the supply in what the first Bush and Reagan administrations called the "war on drugs." And, as with immigration, this has led some Americans to blame Mexico for much of the drug problem. Also, after the murder of U.S. Drug Enforcement Agency (DEA) agent Enrique Camarena Salazar, U.S. officials were highly critical of Mexican authorities for their failure to do much about the problem and for their in-

Marijuana seized by Mexican authorities in 1996. Many Americans argue that the Mexican government is not doing enough in the war on drugs.

Jose Luis Magna/AP / Wide World Photos

volvement in drug trafficking itself. Such criticisms surfaced again in the mid-1990s with the scandals implicating the Salinas, Hank, and other PRI families in the drug trade.

There is now considerable cooperation between policymakers and enforcement agencies on drug issues on both sides of the border. The CIA, FBI, and other U.S. agencies train Mexican officials, though they are also skeptical of the commitment south of the border.

In this case, the tension emerges less from misunderstanding than from the different national interests in the drug issue. Mexico itself does not have much of a drug problem; few Mexicans use marijuana, heroin, or cocaine. Moreover, even though the money is never included in official statistics and is never taxed, the profits from the drug trade amount to at least $2 billion in additional income for Mexicans. In this regard, the Mexican government has good reason to resist Washington's more drastic and invasive demands.

As with immigration, the point is not that U.S. policy is wrong per se. Rather, the problem is that it has contributed to the weakening of effective Mexican sovereignty. The Mexican government really has had no choice but to allow the DEA to operate inside Mexican territory, something Americans cannot ever imagine allowing another government to do on their soil. The Mexicans have been able to block some U.S. proposals, including one that would have allowed Air Force jets to pursue drug suspects into Mexican air space. But U.S. policymakers have largely turned a deaf ear to Mexican requests to pursue policies that address Mexican needs, particularly ones that would provide marijuana and poppy growers with the opportunity to make a decent living raising other crops.

Feedback

The same ambiguity regarding democracy and Mexico that we have seen throughout this chapter exists with the press as well. Mexican newspapers, magazines, and television stations are ostensibly independent of government control. The mass market press, however, rarely took PRI governments on, failing to report on electoral fraud and other flagrant violations of the law and democratic principles because the government has considerable leverage over it. The PRI had a virtual monopoly over the sale of newsprint. It also provided chronically underfunded and understaffed newspapers with much of their information, which often found

its way onto the front pages with next-to-no investigation or even editing. The largest newspaper chain and, until recently, the one television network with a national audience were controlled by PRI loyalists.

Occasionally, the government did clamp down, as when it engineered the firing of the editorial team at the independent and often critical magazine *Excelsior* in 1976. But more often, the press censored itself. Mass circulation dailies and television news provided bland coverage and tended to avoid controversial stories altogether. Instead, they presented government proclamations and covered the actions of its leaders in ways that made them seem little more than propaganda outlets for the PRI.

That said, pressures to open up the media have been building for years and have already had an impact. There are more independent outlets, though most of these still only reach the relatively well educated and affluent. Now, of course, the PRI-dominated media are critical of the Fox administration. Similarly, the opening up of the economy and the technological revolution have brought in more media that are not controllable by the government, including satellite access to CNN and the U.S. networks' Spanish-language services.

Conclusion: Mexico and the Third World

The most important theme in these pages on Mexico is the erosion of national sovereignty. Erosion of real national sovereignty is occurring everywhere, but it is especially evident in Mexico and the other third world countries considered in this book.

Mexican governments are less and less masters of their own destiny. I don't want to overstate this point. Few countries are giving up their *legal* sovereignty. Still, as this and the other four chapters on the third world show, the growing interdependence of the world's economic and other systems is sapping all countries of at least some of the ability to determine their own destinies. This trend is especially marked in the third world, where governments lack the wealth and other resources of the liberal democracies in the north.

It may be that this "globalization" is inevitable and irreversible. This should not, however, keep us from thinking about the ways in which it is reinforcing existing imbalances in the distribution of wealth and power or from worrying about what the consequences might be as globalization continues.

Key Terms

Concepts

Camarilla

Corporatism

Debt crisis

Electoral alchemy

Import substitution

Maquiladora

Mestizo

Newly industrializing country

Nonreelection

Patron-client relations

Pendulum effect

Sexeño

Structural adjustment

People

Cárdenas, Cuautémoc

Cárdenas, Lazaro

De la Madrid, Miguel

Diaz, Porfirio

Fox, Vicente

Salinas, Carlos de Gortari

Santa Anna, Antonio López de

Zedillo, Ernesto

Acronyms

CFE	NAFTA	PEMEX
CTM	NIC	PRD
IFE	PAN	PRI

Organizations, Places, and Events

Confederation of Mexican Workers

Federal Election Commission

Federal Electoral Institute

Gobernación

Immigration Reform and Control Act

Institutional Revolutionary Party

National Action Party

North American Free Trade Agreement

Party of the Democratic Revolution

Critical Thinking Exercises

1 Much has changed since this book was finished in early 2005. Does the analysis of Mexican politics presented here still make sense? Why (not)?

2 Public opinion pollsters routinely ask questions about whether people think their country is heading in the "right direction" or is on the "wrong track." If you were asked such a question about Mexico, how would you answer? Why did you reach this conclusion?

3 How did Spanish imperialism and the U.S. influence shape Mexican political life before, during, and after the revolution?

4 Why did the PRI emerge as the dominant political force in Mexico? How was it able to stay in power for so long?

5 What is the evidence for and against claims that Mexico is democratic? Which do you find more compelling?

6 Why has support for the PRI declined in recent years? What implications does that have for democratization in Mexico?

7 Mexico has been among the countries that have most fully adopted structural adjustment after having been among those to have most rigorously followed import substitution. Why was this the case? What impact has the shift in economic policy had on Mexican politics?

8 What impact does the United States have on Mexico?

9 Mexico entered new and uncharted territory with the election of Vicente Fox in 2000. What patterns in its political life do you think will be most likely to change? To stay the same?

Useful Websites

There are plenty of websites on Mexican politics. The problem is that surprisingly few of them have English language material, including those of the Mexican government and political parties. The sites listed here all have at least some material in English.

The President's Office now has a fairly extensive website in English, though there is far more in Spanish. The Chamber of Deputies' site is only in Spanish, but I have included it anyway on the assumption that many readers of this book will speak some Spanish.

envivo.presidencia.gob.mx/?NLang=en

www.cddhcu.gob.mx/

MexicoOnline is by far the best portal on politics and related issues in that country.

www.mexicoonline.com

George Grayson has written an interesting article in anticipation of the 2006 elections for Washington's Center for Strategic and International Studies.

www.csis.org/press/pr03_69.pdf

The left-of-center North American Conference on Latin America (NACLA) provides periodic analyses of events in Mexico and throughout the region.

The Latin American Network Information Center (LANIC) at the University of Texas has the best set of links to all aspects of Mexican life for academic use. Alex López-Ortiz maintains a remarkable database of online articles and other documents on Mexican politics and the University of Waterloo in Canada.

lanic.utexas.edu/la/mexico

db.uwaterloo.ca/~alopez-o/polind.html

InfoTrac College Edition Sources

Baer, M. Delal. "Mexico at Impasse."

Camp, Roderic Ai. "Performing on the Mexican Democratic Stage."

Castañeda, Jorge. "A Leader Failed by an Old System."

Celarier, Michelle. "Privatization: A Case Study in Corruption."

Dominguez, Jorge, and James McCann. "Shaping Mexico's Electoral Arena."

Klesner, Joseph. "The End of Mexico's One Party Regime."

Moreno, Alejandro, and Patricia Mendez. "Attitudes toward Democracy: Mexico in Comparative Perspective."

Pastor, Robert. "North America's Second Decade."

Peters, Enrique Dussel. "Mexico's Liberalization Strategy: Ten Years On."

Reding, Andrew. "Facing Political Reality in Mexico."

Schedler, Andreas. "Common Sense without Common Ground."

Further Reading

Barkin, David. *Distorted Development: Mexico in the World Economy.* Boulder, Colo.: Westview Press, 1990. A first-rate analysis of the uneven and, in some ways, unhealthy way the Mexican economy has evolved.

Bazant, Jan. *A Concise History of Mexico: From Hidalgo to Cárdenas.* New York: Cambridge University Press, 1977. The best short history concentrating on the century and a half when Mexican politics was most turbulent.

Camp, Roderic Ai. *Politics in Mexico.* New York: Oxford University Press, 1999. The best short book introducing Mexican politics for a mostly undergraduate audience.

Castañeda, Jorge. *Perpetuating Power: How Mexican Presidents Were Chosen.* New York: New Press, 2000. An overview by Mexico's preeminent political scientist, who is now foreign minister in Fox's government.

Domínguez, Jorge, and James McCann. *Democratizing Mexico: Public Opinion and Electoral Choices.* Baltimore: Johns Hopkins University Press, 1996. The first thorough analysis of the subject in Mexico. Unfortunately, there is little on the events after 1991.

Joseph, Gilbert M., and Timothy Henderson. *The Mexico Reader.* Durham, N.C.: Duke University Press, 2002. A massive volume covering almost all aspects of Mexican political, social, and economic life.

Levy, Daniel C., and Gabriel Székely. *Mexico: Paradoxes of Stability and Change.* 2nd ed. Boulder, Colo.: Westview Press, 1987. A thorough account of the strengths and weaknesses of the Mexican system; still worth reading more than a decade after it was written.

Levy, Daniel C., and Kathleen Bruhn, with Emilio Zebadua. *Mexico: The Struggle for Democratic Development.* Berkeley: University of California Press, 2001. A good overview of Mexican history focusing on the obstacles preventing the development of democracy.

Reavis, Dick. *Conversations with Moctezuma: The Soul of Modern Mexico.* New York: Quill/William Morrow, 1990. The best account of the "bottom side" of the Mexican situation in English, by an American journalist who lived in Mexico for many years.

Warnock, John. *The Other Mexico: The North American Triangle Completed.* Montreal: Black Rose Books, 1995. The best left-of-center critique of the PRI and structural adjustment.

EXPLORING WITH THE WORLD WIDE WEB

The third world has the largest number of countries of the three main types covered in the book. Not surprisingly, the countries differ among themselves far more than those covered in either part 2 or part 3.

The MicroCase data provide you with quantitative evidence of how difficult life is in most of the third world. As with parts 2 and 3, the exercise begins by guiding you through a series of maps that demonstrate how much poorer and less democratic the third world is than the industrialized democracies and most of the current and former communist regimes. The exercise then takes you "inside the third world" to explore the links between interethnic conflict, the fighting of civil wars, continued poverty, and the difficulty in establishing stable democracies in Africa in particular and the third world in general.

The third world, however, is also home to some promising innovations, including microcredit, which is helping millions of families escape poverty. South Africa has a new constitution, and its Truth and Reconciliation Commission is an institution that has been adapted for use in at least fifteen other countries. The website contains both the constitution and the executive summary of the commission's final report. Read them to see how the leaders of the "new" South Africa have tried to use the law to create and support their multiracial democracy.

Finally, readers who were shocked by the conditions in most third world countries may also find Charles William Maynes' article "America's Fading Commitments" unsettling. Maynes is one of the leading mainstream analysts of U.S. foreign policy. In this article, he chronicles the declining support for foreign aid and other forms of development assistance in the United States. Although other developed countries have not followed Washington's lead, the size of the United States means that its cutbacks have had a significant impact on the third world. Written in 1999, Maynes' article and others like it deserve our renewed attention in the wake of the events of September 11.

Part 5

CONCLUSION

Sometimes I wonder if we put all the problems on a circular board, all the proposed solutions on an outer wheel, and just spun away, and implemented each solution wherever it stopped on the wheel, whether we wouldn't do as well.

RICHARD FEINBERG

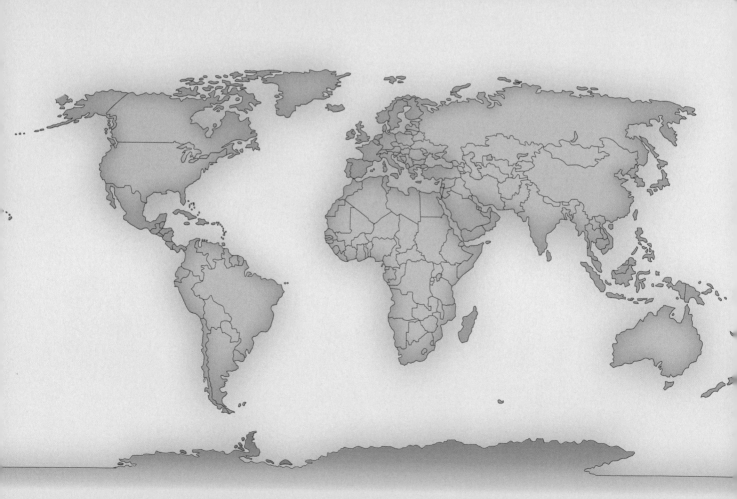

DANGER . . . AND OPPORTUNITY

Crisis

I began this book with a discussion of September 11. I will end it by returning briefly to the events surrounding the terrorist attacks and emphasize one of the concepts I introduced in those first few pages and have intentionally not returned to until now—crisis.

The events of 9/11 began one of the most important political crises of recent years. The unexpected and previously unimaginable magnitude of the attack amounted to a political wake-up call. So, too, did the later anthrax scares and the growing realization that the United States and other countries could readily be the targets of biological, chemical, and radiological attacks.

These were by no means the world's first serious terrorist attacks. And, as we will see in more detail in this chapter, they were certainly not the first or even the most intellectually compelling evidence that **globalization** is a phenomenon we need to take seriously. Nonetheless, the attacks were a powerful, visible, and unavoidable symbol of the dangers we all face.

In the aftermath of 9/11, few saw any alternative to war against the Taliban in Afghanistan and the terrorists they hosted. There was more criticism of plans to go to war with Iraq, but most observers agreed—including the war's opponents—that the world would be a far safer place if Saddam Hussein weren't in power. Those conflicts have reached some of the aims the Bush administration laid out for them, but they have resulted in even more turmoil and precious little success beyond such immediate short-terms goals as overthrowing the Taliban and Saddam Hussein. To see that, consider the political controversy around these two issues in a bit more detail.

In the days and weeks after 9/11, there were signs that something good could come out of the catastrophe. The United States cooperated more than ever with its traditional allies and made great strides with other countries with which it had had less amicable relations, including Russia and China. Those relationships foundered during the run-up to the war against Iraq, but in dealings with North Korea, American ties to its historical rivals have strengthened, not weakened.

And it wasn't just the United States. There is ample evidence, for instance, that the horrors of 9/11 finally convinced the Irish Republican Army that it had to begin handing in its weapons as part of the next major step toward peace in Northern Ireland. The allies were also able to convince Libya to abandon its weapons of mass destruction program. Last but by no means least, the addition of Eastern European members to NATO and the European Union signal an important expansion of stable democracy well beyond the old iron curtain.

But this conclusion is not simply a list of "good

Tom Hanson /AP/Wide World Photos

The last standing fragment of the World Trade Center towers in New York.

news/bad news" examples from the book and beyond. Rather, I want to take this discussion to another level so that you can put the two themes of its subtitle—global challenges and their domestic responses—in perspective. To do so, we have to think of them as part of an interconnected global **crisis.**

I use the word *crisis* in a particular way that has its origins in both the Greek and the Chinese languages. The English word *crisis* has its etymological roots in the Greek *krisis,* which literally means "a turning point." Doctors use the term in this way to define the moment when a patient is in a life-or-death situation. The ancient Chinese brought together two characters to convey what we mean by crisis. The first is the part of a crisis we in the West pay the most attention to—danger—and the second has to do with opportunity. In the paragraphs that follow, *crisis* will be used in both senses of the term.

People have dealt with crises since time immemorial. Our ancestors faced and overcame them time and time again. Today's evolutionary theorists are convinced that all life (and not just humanity) made major strides forward whenever it adapted effectively to a radical new change in its environment, something the dinosaurs were

not able to do during a period of global cooling some sixty million years ago.

Many things happen in a crisis. However, the "success stories" all have one common characteristic. To understand the dangers and seize the opportunities, people had to think "outside the box," to develop new and creative ways of understanding their problems and then solving them.

This was certainly true in the aftermath of 9/11. Many people who work, as I do, in the field of conflict resolution had to grapple with the need to bring the perpetrators of those horrific acts to justice, which seemed to require the use of force. Many hawks in the national security agencies of Western governments had to grapple just as hard with the realization that there was no purely military way of eliminating terrorism.

From this perspective, the terrorist attacks and the war against terrorism are but the "tip" of a much larger political "iceberg." This chapter, then, will give you a first glimpse at some new ways of thinking about political life. The picture that follows in the rest of this chapter is an ambiguous one. Just as in the sixteen chapters that came before it, it conveys a mixed message. Some parts of it will strike you as reflecting some of the world's more ominous problems. Other parts will strike you as indicating real rays of hope and—even more importantly— tangible accomplishments.

I don't mean to be confusing. Rather, as I will suggest throughout the chapter, any period of dramatic change brings with it unexpected and unpredictable difficulties. But it also opens the door to new social, economic, and political possibilities.

Danger

As is often the case with a new and controversial issue, political scientists do not agree on the issues associated with globalization that we should be focusing on. You will therefore encounter dozens of equally insightful formulations of what globalization is and what impact it is having. What follows is simply one version, which revolves around four overlapping dangers.

This version, not surprisingly, also allows us to see the importance of aspects of table 1.1 and figure 1.2 which are also reproduced on the inside front cover of the book. The most obvious is of the growing impact of globalization itself, which is making it harder and harder for states and citizens to be masters of their own political, economic, and social destinies. We will also see that the global crisis is not just international. In country after country, especially those covered in Parts 3 and 4, it has added new social pressures and new domestic policy burdens that leaders struggle to cope with.

The Growing Cost of Violence and War

No one who has seen videotape of the planes slamming into the World Trade Center needs to be reminded of the cost of war. To be sure, there have been other and more brutal conflicts around the world. However, the image of the collapsing towers and the more than three thousand lives lost is as powerful a symbol as we have of the realities of violence.

But those tragic attacks pale in comparison with other conflicts of recent years. Far more lives have been lost in Afghanistan and Iraq. And these wars do not come close to matching the horror of Rwanda, where 10 percent of the population was massacred in less than two months, or in the Democratic Republic of Congo where at least 2.5 million people died in a civil war that spanned the end of the last century and the beginning of this one.

In this sense, the costs of war and violence are not new. Indeed, they have been a part of the human experience ever since the beginning of recorded history. However, over the past century or so, they have escalated for two central reasons. First, new technologies have led to the production of deadlier weapons. Second, interdependence and now globalization have turned many local disputes into regional conflicts and, in cases like the war on terrorism, even global ones.

During the cold war, most people were preoccupied with the threat of nuclear war because it could have meant the end of civilization as we know it. Millions would have died in the countries that fired missiles at each other. Millions more in "noncombatant" nations would have died as well from radiation-induced diseases in the months and years that followed. Global economic and communication networks would have been hopelessly disrupted, spreading even more chaos, illness, and death. Controversial studies about a possible "nuclear winter" showed that the explosions would have hurled enough dust and soot into the atmosphere to cause an extended period of dark skies and low temperatures leading to permanent and irreversible ecological effects— much like the climatic changes that scientists believe wiped out the dinosaurs.

With the end of the cold war, the chances of a major nuclear war have all but disappeared—at least for now. As a result, analysts have been able to focus on the impact conventional war, and even the preparation for it, has had on states and their citizens over the past half-century or so.

During the cold war, the United States and the former Soviet Union saw virtually every conflict in the third world as a **zero-sum game** that would end up with a single winner and loser. Each side feared that it would lose yet another country to the other's camp. Superpower conflict did not entirely explain why the many wars fought over the past half-century began. Their roots lie in long-standing economic and ethnic antagonisms. But the perception that regional war reflected East-West tensions meant that each superpower was willing to pour in billions of dollars in aid, and sometimes its own soldiers, so that "its" side didn't lose.

The consequences were wars of gargantuan proportions that, all too often, turned into bloody stalemates. Regional wars typically dragged on without a decisive victory for either side and without a resolution of the underlying differences that sparked the conflict in the first place. Even when wars did yield winners and losers in the conventional sense, the winners didn't really earn a lasting or clear-cut victory. For instance, a generation after the fighting ended, Vietnam, the nominal "winner" against the United States, remains a poor and devastated country. Even though international forces were able to oust Saddam Hussein after more than a decade of authoritarian rule, the devastation of the Iraqi population remains. Meanwhile, none of the issues that led to war, other than the occupation of Kuwait, have been settled. And now, global wars are being fought between well-armed, wealthy states and loosely organized, international bands of terrorists who seem willing to do anything in support of their cause—including killing themselves.

Of the countries considered in this book, Iraq has suffered the most from war and other forms of political violence in recent years. Few of the others, though, have been spared.

Meanwhile, vital social needs have gone unmet. The countries that gave rise to most of the terrorists in the al-Qaeda network share the poverty that is so widespread in the third world and that stand in such sharp contrast to the power and wealth symbolized by the Pentagon and World Trade Center, respectively.

Overall, the governments of the world spend approximately $2 million *per minute* on defense. During that same minute, thirty children die somewhere on the planet from lack of food or affordable medication.

Similarly, the nations of the world spend more than $1 trillion on military expenses each year. Although his figures are now outdated, Harry G. Schaffer once eloquently summed up how we could use that trillion dollars to meet social needs in this country. I leave it to you to figure out how that sum of money could be used elsewhere, where the needs are even greater:

> With that amount of money, we could build a $75,000 house, place it on $5,000 worth of land, furnish it with $10,000 worth of furniture, put a $10,000 car in the garage—and give all this to each and every family in Kansas, Missouri, Iowa, Nebraska, Oklahoma and Arkansas. After having done this, we would still have enough out of our trillion dollars to build a $10 million library for each of 250 cities and towns throughout the six-state region. After having done all that, we would still have enough money left out of our trillion to put aside, at 10 percent annual interest, a sum of money that would pay a salary of $25,000 per year for an army of 10,000 nurses, the same for an army of 10,000 teachers, and an annual cash allowance of $5,000 for each and every family throughout that six-state region—not just for one year but forever.[1]

Environmental Abuse

In the past few years, attention has been drawn to a second set of human actions that could also lead to an equally devastating, if more gradual, catastrophe—the abuse of the environment. There's nothing new to the assault on our physical surroundings. At least since the beginning of the industrial revolution, people have been worried about the consequences of our actions. Read a novel like Charles Dickens's *Bleak House,* and you'll see that even in Victorian England people were aware of the harm the soot from thousands of coal furnaces was doing. America's first environmental movement during the progressive years of the early twentieth century was in large part a response to the wretched conditions in the cities that the aptly named "muckraking" journalists wrote about. But it is only in the past few years that the destruction of the environment has reached dangerous proportions.

At the beginning of the twentieth century, there were only 1.6 billion people on the planet. Now there are more than 6 billion of us, and that number will reach 9 billion or more before population growth could even begin to level off in the middle of the twenty-first century (www.census.gov/cgi-bin/ipc/popclockw).

What's more, we wield technological powers that take a far greater toll on our surroundings than anything the muckrakers of Teddy Roosevelt's day could have imagined. Back then, people had little impact on the whole ecosystem. They could largely ignore the by-products of material progress. They could cut down trees, deplete the soil, pollute the rivers, and poison the air. People paid a price for those actions, but the system as a whole was able to replenish itself.

Now, there are far more of us, and our lifestyles have changed. We produce more and waste more, and we are taking a far greater toll on the environment. Since the late 1960s, dire warnings have drawn people's attention to a host of environmental concerns, some of which are global in scope. For our purposes, a brief consideration of two of them will be enough.

First is the depletion of the **ozone layer** in the stratosphere. Chlorofluorocarbon (CFC) molecules escape from a number of everyday products and rise until they reach the ozone layer, where their chlorine is released. The chlorine begins destroying the ozone, which, in turn, means that more harmful ultraviolet rays reach the earth. These rays not only cause skin cancer but also kill the single-celled organisms that live at the top of the oceans and that are essential to the entire food chain.

CFCs have destroyed an average of 0.5 percent of the available ozone each year since the late 1970s. There is already a substantial hole in the ozone layer above Antarctica, and periodically one appears above the Arctic and the northern United States as well. The major industrial nations of the world agreed to reduce rates of CFC emissions by at least half before the end of the twentieth century. But this will only slow down the damage, because CFC molecules already up there will continue destroying ozone for the next century.

The dangers are just as clear for the second environmental issue, which is receiving more attention now—climate change, also known as **global warming** or the greenhouse effect. As long as there have been animals, they have released lots of carbon dioxide (CO_2) into the atmosphere and oceans as one of their waste products. Until recently, nature's mechanisms were able to regulate the amount of CO_2 and other potentially toxic compounds within limits that would continue sustaining plant and animal life indefinitely.

Now, however, that balance is in jeopardy. The industrial and other activities humans engage in put almost as much CO_2 into the atmosphere as all those natural processes combined. CO_2 is a by-product of the burning of fossil fuels and the cutting down of trees in tropical rain forests, which removes CO_2 from the atmosphere. Then we compound the damage by burning

---

[1] Harry G. Shaffer, "What a Trillion Dollars Would Buy," *Republic Airlines Magazine,* October 1986, 24.

Burning the rain forest in the Amazon basin.

Janduari Simoes/AP/Wide World Photos

the trees, thereby creating even more CO_2 for the atmosphere to absorb.

As the CO_2 and other gases, such as methane, rise, they begin to act much like the glass walls of a greenhouse. They let the sun's rays in but don't let much heat out.

The surface of the planet is gradually heating up. Scientists are not sure how much of this warming is due to the greenhouse effect, nor do they agree about how much hotter it is going to get. Nonetheless, average global temperatures have already increased by one to two degrees Fahrenheit over the past century, more than they had changed over the previous ten million years.

If we continue emitting CO_2 at our current rate (and even if the Kyoto Protocol goes into effect there will not be much of a reduction), average temperatures could rise by somewhere between three and thirteen degrees by the middle of the twenty-first century.

No one knows exactly what will happen. Polar ice packs could melt, and the oceans could rise by as much as seven feet. Coastal areas along the U.S. Atlantic seaboard could be permanently flooded. The Great Plains might be too hot and dusty for people to inhabit, and they might flock to the Yukon and Siberia looking for jobs and a hospitable climate. As in the great ice ages, global warming could so disrupt things that untold numbers of species disappear, including many plants and animals that we depend on.

Climate change and the depletion of the ozone layer are two of the most visible examples of how human actions are destroying the fragile life support system that all life depends on. We are still gobbling up the fossil fuels that make the Middle East so politically important, as well as other nonrenewable resources. Emissions from industrial plants are being carried by winds and then reappearing as acid rain that is killing fish in Canadian lakes, destroying the Black Forest in Germany, and damaging medieval buildings in Poland—all hundreds of miles from the source of the pollution. Improper storage of toxic wastes and other industrial activities are leaving an ever-growing number of people without drinkable water everywhere from the Love Canal in Buffalo, New York, to much of Africa. Radiation from Chernobyl contaminated the reindeer herds the Lapps depend on for their food and income. The air in Mexico City is so filthy that it may never be healthy to breathe it again. No one yet knows what to do with nuclear and other hazardous wastes, or how we are going to replace petroleum and other nonrenewable resources when they run out.

The ecologists and atmospheric scientists who have been studying these phenomena have discovered that our planet is remarkably resilient. It has been able to absorb all kinds of changes over the millennia and still manages to sustain life. But, they worry, it can only "bend" so far. Sooner or later, they fear, we will take the earth beyond the point at which a sustainable environment, and hence much (if not all) life, is possible. We do not know for sure where that point lies. But we do know that we are approaching it faster and faster each day.

The Perilous Global Economy

Of all these trends, the most difficult to understand, and perhaps the most important for the near future, is the growing **interdependence** of the world's economy. To see just how much the rest of the world is part of our daily lives, look around your home. Identify where your clothes, electronic gear, athletic equipment, and everything else come from, and you'll undoubtedly end up with a long list of countries.

The **international political economy,** as academics call it, involves, of course, much more than the consumer goods you have in your house, apartment, or dorm room. In fact, unlike traditional international political and diplomatic relations, it is all but impossible to put our fingers on it in any kind of readily describable way. Still, the trends political scientists and economists have been following, particularly since the **OPEC oil embargo** of 1973, are as consequential as those regarding war or the environment. To be sure, not all the signs are negative. There is more wealth and more people lead better lives than at any previous point in human history. At the same time, the disparities between rich and poor nations and between the rich and poor within nations are growing. What's more, the global economy seems increasingly unpredictable and resistant to control or manipulation.

As we saw throughout Part 4, the most important of these global economic trends is the growing gap between the rich nations, mostly located in the Northern Hemisphere, and the poor ones, mostly located in the Southern Hemisphere. Whatever indicator of economic performance we choose—GNP, quality of life for average people, debt—we find tremendous imbalance. There is nothing new to the internationalization of economic life. It was in part his opposition to the subsidies the government was paying to the British East India and other trading companies that led Adam Smith to write *The Wealth of Nations* in 1776. "Gold" joined "guns" and "glory" as the three "g's" that sparked the colonization of much of Africa and Asia in the second half of the nineteenth century.

Now, however, for the first time, international economic forces may be on the verge of outstripping domestic ones in political importance. It is not easy for the United States, still the richest nation on earth, to address any of its pressing economic problems on its own. After their first victory at the polls in 1981, French Socialists set out to "reconquer the domestic market." But they failed miserably, graphically demonstrating that even the fourth-strongest capitalist economy could not successfully adopt policies sharply at odds with dominant global trends. Even Japan is referred to as a "fragile superpower" because its prosperity depends on the maintenance of existing markets, trading patterns, and energy supplies, any of which could be easily disrupted. Americans saw the relevance of these global pressures in the discussion of "outsourcing" of manufacturing and other jobs overseas, which cost the state of Ohio, alone, more than a quarter million jobs during the first three years George W. Bush was president.

It is not just Japan but the entire international economic order that is fragile. The "ups" and the more frequent "downs" since the OPEC oil embargo have shown just how vulnerable all countries are to global economic forces that seem beyond anyone's control.

And, again, the attack on the World Trade Center provides a powerful symbol of that integration. The dead were not all Americans. In fact, people from over forty countries were killed when the towers collapsed. What's more, the attacks led to a worsening of the recession that was already taking hold in the United States and Europe, because of a sharp drop in business confidence and consumer spending in the weeks that followed 9/11.

Lives without Dignity

The current international political economy is difficult to understand because its workings seem so abstract, filled with technically complex measures of growth or debt and open to many different interpretations.

But it is not merely an abstraction. The difficulties and uncertainties of the last three decades, coupled with the military spending and environmental decay, have taken their toll on the way people live. Put bluntly, a surprising—and to most observers, an unacceptable—number of people lead lives without dignity.

Even the most powerful nations are not free from life's indignities. Over the past few years, we have seen news reports of a drop in Russian life expectancy by ten years. Americans have grown painfully aware of the millions who are homeless, lack health insurance, or form part of an urban underclass that has no reasonable chance of escaping a generations-long cycle of poverty.

We do not yet know what the human costs of our environmental wastes are, let alone what they will be, because we have yet to begin keeping records of what are often subtle effects that only become clear after a period of years. Nonetheless, we do know that deforestation in Africa leaves an ever-growing number of families without wood to cook their food and contributes to the

A newly arrived refugee family from the Sudan region of Darfur crosses into Chad on 27 January 2004 in the direction of the three improvised refugee camps in Tine, Chad. Fifty thousand black Sudanese have been killed in a genocide by the ethnic Arab militia known as Janjaweed. Almost 200,000 have fled into Chad seeking safety.

Marco Longari /AFP/Getty Images

drought that covers a growing part of the continent. We know that it is unhealthy to breathe the air in Mexico City and Los Angeles, drink the water in Moscow and St. Petersburg, or eat produce grown near the nuclear power plants that have had accidents in the United States and the former Soviet Union.

This all boils down to a simple fact: A huge proportion of the world's people—in some areas as much as 40 percent—go through life without their basic human needs being met, however we define that concept.

Many of my students told me during the fall 2001 semester that the first pictures of the third world they had ever seen came from the post–9/11 coverage in Pakistan and Afghanistan. These students came to class and talked about how shocked they were by the poverty the people there endure and by the combination of hopelessness and anger they saw in so many of those people's expressions.

And this takes us back to where we began this section on the "danger" side of the global crisis, because it seems only reasonable to assume that such deprivation will spawn more and more conflict and will continue the cycle of war and violence. It may be that clerics in the religious schools along the border between Pakistan and Afghanistan are teaching a generation of Muslims to hate the West. It may be, too, that it is easy for them to do so because of indignities these young people have to put up with every day.

As this edition of *Comparative Politics* was being written, the most visible example of the ways the parts of the global crisis can build off of each other was the crisis in the Darfur region of Sudan. Darfur is a desperately poor part of that desperately poor country. Sudan's national government is dominated by Arab Muslims and has been in a decades-long civil war with black Christians in the south. The people of Darfur are caught in between because they are black and Muslim. The conflict escalated in 2003 when a number of groups demanded inclusion in the government and better economic conditions. At that point, the Muslim Janjaweed militia—a government ally—began systematically attacking targets in Darfur, including mosques. Thousands were killed, and as many as a quarter million people were forced to flee in a campaign of ethnic cleansing. The militia effectively kept most relief aid from reaching the refugee camps, and it is estimated that as many as half of them will have died from starvation and easily preventable diseases by the time this book is published.

The Wheel of Fortune

As we saw in the first sixteen chapters, these are the issues politicians and average citizens around the world are grappling with. So far, however, they have not had much success, prompting Richard Feinberg's statement at the beginning of the chapter likening policy making to some kind of depressing real-world equivalent of the popular television show *Wheel of Fortune.* (If you still need to be convinced that the world is shrinking and that life is increasingly interdependent, King Features, the producer of *Wheel,* has been syndicating the rights to the show around the world. Now about thirty countries have their own, locally produced versions of the show, their own equivalents of Pat and Vanna, and their own contestants shrieking "big money" in their own language as the wheel spins and simplistic phrases are gradually revealed on the board.)

There is no shortage of plausible solutions to some of these problems. In 1988, for instance, Lester Brown and Edward Wolf of the Worldwatch Institute concluded their annual *State of the World* volume with a detailed proposal for creating a sustainable environment and a thriving economy for the planet as a whole by the end of the century. The price tag was remarkably low. It would have cost under $200 billion a year for the rest of the twentieth century, though that figure would be about twice that today.[2] This may seem to be a lot of money, but it isn't much more than a drop in the global bucket. It is also more or less the same sum that the United States spends on defense each year.

Consider another example. Students of the late Buckminster Fuller have developed something called the World Game (which was also discussed in Chapter 11). On a gymnasium floor, they unroll a map of the earth that is about seventy feet long and forty feet across. The "players" are distributed around the world according to population. Thus, if one hundred people show up, about twenty will be Chinese, another twenty will be from the Indian subcontinent, and so on. The organizers then give the players from each region its share of such scarce global resources as food, energy, money, and weapons. During the course of an afternoon or evening session, the players try to improve their region's lot by trading these resources back and forth. In the process, they come to see that there are many alternatives to the current distribution of the resources, some of which seem a lot better. You can now also play a version of the game on the Internet (www.worldgame.org).

I am not trying to suggest that the Brown-Wolf plan would work or that solving the global crisis is no more complicated than playing a very large board game. Rather, I am simply pointing out that there is no shortage of policy alternatives for people and their governments to consider.

What gets in the way is largely politics—the process of making decisions about the allocation of power and resources. In this sense, politics has always been the problem, as we have seen throughout this book. And because both power and resources are in short supply, politics engenders conflict and all the difficulties that come with it.

That said, there are two other common denominators hindering our ability to make progress in confronting the broader issues raised in this chapter, as well as those emanating out of 9/11, that will be the focus of the rest of this chapter.

Constraints on States and Citizens

My reading of the evidence is that the first of these common denominators is expressed in the subtitle of this book. Increasingly, the problems we face are global in nature, yet, most of the time, most of us still try to find national solutions to them.

International issues have always been important in determining a nation's politics and policies. In some countries and under some circumstances, they may have more of an impact than domestic ones, although political scientists and economists have not yet developed sufficiently sophisticated research tools to determine whether this is true.

Nonetheless, the impact of international forces on domestic political life clearly is increasing all the time. Rather than repeating much of what you have already seen to drive this point home, let me concentrate on one example from each of the three types of countries we have been focusing on.

There is no better example of the everyday impact of international forces on national politics than the European Union (EU). In the half-century since the creation of the European Coal and Steel Community, member states have ceded more and more of their sovereignty to European institutions. As we saw in Chapter 7, these bodies now have an impact on everything from national taxation policy to the way sports leagues are run and even to the content of chocolate bars and liqueurs. Although national governments may slow down the pace of integration over the next few years, Brussels undoubtedly will remain a source of political power in Europe that will rival that of any national capital.

Most of the issues regarding European integration are highly technical and complex, but its larger implications can be illustrated in a single, seemingly simple example: government procurement. Governments buy at least 10 percent of everything that is sold in most

[2]Lester Brown and Edward C. Wolf, eds., *The State of the World 1988* (New York: W. W. Norton, 1988), 170–188.

EU countries: computers, paper, telecommunications equipment, sand and salt for snowy roads, and so on. And they almost always buy goods produced by companies based in their own countries. For example, virtually all American police cars are made by one of the big-three auto companies in Michigan. Similarly, the various planes that have served as Air Force One were built by Boeing. By contrast, French president Chirac and German chancellor Schröder always fly on Airbus planes, which are built by a consortium of European firms.

Governments buy from their own companies for a number of reasons, including patriotic ones that sometimes have real national security implications. More often, however, they do so to protect domestic industries from foreign competition by giving them what amounts to a guaranteed market. Thus, the French government kept part of its computer industry alive that would not have survived had it been forced to compete in an open market. Now, however, EU governments are losing much of their ability to bypass foreign firms. Chirac is unlikely to be chauffeured in a Mercedes, or Schröder in a Renault. Still, more and more of what these governments spend on goods and services will go to firms based in other countries.

It is even hard to tell what a "national firm" is these days. Most countries, for instance, have a rule that requires its civil servants to fly on a "national carrier." But, as airlines develop global alliances, you book a flight on United and end up on Lufthansa, or make a reservation with Continental but find yourself seated on a Virgin Atlantic plane.

For what used to be the Communist world, consider the end of the cold war and then the collapse of the Soviet Union. It will be quite a while before we fully understand why the cold war ended. To some degree, it reflected the realization on the part of Americans and Soviets that the cold war had gotten out of hand and that the risks of a thermonuclear holocaust were no longer worth running. To some degree, too, it reflected external pressures that the Soviet Union could no longer face. Late in the Carter administration, the United States began a massive arms buildup, which President Reagan took even further. In all, the U.S. government added something like a trillion dollars to what it would have spent on defense had the buildup not occurred, which prompted Harry Schaffer to make the calculations cited earlier. It introduced a whole new generation of technologically sophisticated weapons: MX and cruise missiles, Stealth bombers and fighters, the "smart" bombs used against Iraq and Afghanistan, and more. The increased military expenditures took their toll on the U.S. government budget, contributing to drastic reductions in some social service programs and a spiraling federal deficit.

The impact was far greater in the Soviet Union. The Soviets spent at least as much as the United States did on defense, but they did so in an economy that was no more than half and probably more like a seventh the size. Although there were many reasons for the Soviet economic decline of the 1980s, military expenditures obviously drained a growing share of the country's scarce resources from civilian production. Similarly, as the United States began building its new generation of high-tech weapons, the Soviets suffered because of the technological gap that existed between the two countries in particular and between the first and second world in general.

Finally, for the third world, consider once again the political and economic changes that have occurred in India since Rajiv Gandhi came to power in 1984. At that point, India was trying to pursue an autarkic economic policy through which it would rely on its own resources to chart its own economic development. Like most of the other countries that followed that path, India developed very slowly. As we saw in Chapter 12, in the 1950s India and South Korea were at roughly the same level of development. Currently, South Korea is at least four times wealthier than India.

No one held a gun to the Indian government's head, saying, in essence, "change your economic policies or else." Rather, by the time Rajiv Gandhi replaced his mother, it had become clear to many younger Indian politicians that the self-reliant and often prosocialist policy was not getting the country very far very fast. First Gandhi and later P. V. Narasimha Rao forged a new set of policies that encouraged more foreign investment and, with it, more foreign control over the economy. The point here is not to be critical of the Indian and other third world governments that have opened their doors to more foreign investment or to rehash the debates over whether this constitutes a new form of imperialism. Instead, I simply want to point out that, as countries such as India make the decision to seek more outside investment, the control the government and the people have over their economic destinies becomes increasingly limited—whatever the impact on the economy itself.

Opportunity: A Change in the Way We Think

The second common denominator is far more controversial. It is also where my interpretation diverges the most from the conventional wisdom about politics in the new millennium.

Ways of Thinking

To begin with, think about a famous sentence of Albert Einstein's that at first glance may seem to have little to do with the subject matter we've been exploring all term:

> **The unleashed power of the atom**
> **has changed everything**
> **save our modes of thinking,**
> **and we thus drift**
> **toward unparalleled catastrophe.**

When I first encountered this sentence, the people leading the seminar broke it up the same way I have presented it here, which led us to a pair of key insights. The first is that everything had changed, not just war or relations between the superpowers. The second is that everything has changed except for our mode, or **way of thinking,** about political issues. In Einstein's view, there is a huge gap between the problems of the nuclear age and the political mechanisms we use in dealing with them, as depicted in figure 17.1. He concluded that as a result we are drifting, all but out of control, toward the "unparalleled catastrophe" of a nuclear war.

After I thought about the sentence for a while, I began to realize that it spoke to a broader set of political issues. What is unusual about the deployment of nuclear weapons is that it occurred and changed the nature of international relations so quickly. There are plenty of other examples in which the change came more gradually but led to the same kind of gap as depicted in figure 17.2, the same kind of situation for which "business as usual" no longer seems to work.

We saw an obvious example of this with the Soviet Union. The USSR established its party state in the aftermath of the 1917 revolution and kept its basic institutions and practices intact until the Gorbachev era. However, the Soviet society and economy, not to mention the country's international environment, changed dramatically, if at first gradually. Within a few months of taking power, Gorbachev and his colleagues realized that there was no way the country's problems could be solved with piecemeal reforms.

One way of thinking about the material presented so far in this chapter is to recognize that much of the world is in, or perhaps is entering into, one of those periods today. No state is having much success in defining and meeting policy goals, especially in those areas that reflect the world's growing interdependence.

If this is the case (and it is a big "if"), then there must be some underlying theme to politics in such a wide variety of countries that leaves governments as rich as the United States or as poor as Afghanistan in such difficulty.

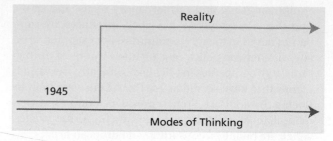

▌ FIGURE 17.1 Einstein: A Literal View

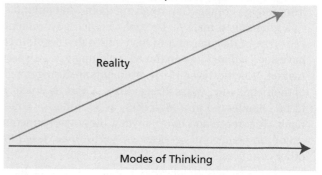

▌ FIGURE 17.2 Einstein: An Expanded View

If I'm right (another big "if"), this common denominator lies in the underlying way of thinking that shapes how we act politically.

To help students see this, I often have them do a simple but revealing exercise. I first have them discuss why some divisive international issue—such as U.S.-Iraqi relations—proved impossible to resolve. Then I have them discuss race relations in the United States. Finally, I have them discuss an interpersonal relationship they were involved in that fell apart.

I write what they say about each issue in two columns on the board. On the left side, I put the objective differences that gave rise to the conflict in the first place. Typically, I have a list of different histories or cultures for the political issues and different tastes and interests for the interpersonal ones. More interesting and important, however, are the themes that go in the right-hand column. There, I put the more subjective and controllable part of the problem: fear, miscommunication, anger, hatred, worries about losing a conflict that matters a lot. What's remarkable is that I get virtually the same list in the right-hand column for both the political and the interpersonal example.

Conventional Values

These results are not surprising. A significant body of research on conflict and its resolution stresses the similarities in the way we approach these kinds of problems at all levels, from the international to the interpersonal.

Scholars who work in this area focus on the often unspoken values and assumptions we use in analyzing the political world and then in determining how we act. (See table 17.1.) At the core of this value system is the belief that politics revolves around the allocation of scarce resources. The actors who take part in this political process—individuals, groups, classes, nations, and so on—are viewed as separate and autonomous. They are also thought to be pursuing their self-interest, which normally involves getting as much for themselves as possible in the short run.

Not surprisingly, if all participants are out to get as much as they can, it is hard to keep the competition courteous and respectful. Because I know you want what I want and we both can't have it, I have to be wary of your actions and intentions.

It is thus all but impossible to avoid thinking in adversarial "we" versus "they" terms, which psychologists call the "image of the enemy." "We" are good; "they" are dangerous. We turn the people or groups or nations we disagree with into objects of fear and hatred, and thus into caricatures of themselves (think about what Osama bin Laden had to say about President Bush, and vice versa). It is hard not to blow those differences far out of proportion. Effective dialogue becomes all but impossible.

We also view the political process in largely zero-sum or win-lose terms. We expect politics to be more or less like an athletic event, with clear winners and losers. And given the attitudes discussed in the preceding paragraphs, it should come as no surprise that we never want to lose. This way of thinking also leads to the assumption that the resolution of conflict will involve the use of **power,** which political scientists normally define as my ability to get you to do something you otherwise wouldn't do.

The last five words of that definition are crucial. Power is something I have to exert over you. In one form or another, power involves the use of force. For instance, I do not have to use physical force to get my students to hand in papers on time. But I do use another kind of force when I threaten to deduct points for each day a paper is late.

Violence remains the ultimate recourse we can—and may have to—turn to. If intense political struggles can have only one winner and one loser, and if we know that this will happen only if one side can force the other to go along, we know that violence is something we will have to employ from time to time. It is because we know that only one of us can win a struggle that we each consider to be of a life-and-death nature that we read the worst into each other's intentions. It is because we know we are competing for the same scarce resources that we assume power comes through strength. Violence is not an inevitable outcome. But, as the all-too-apt cliché puts it, when push comes to shove, force and violence are a frequent outcome.

Given all this, most of us view conflict as dangerous, and something to be avoided if possible. We are not evil or uncaring people, and it seems only natural that we would try to avoid situations that we assume will make things worse. But by putting conflict on the back burner rather than facing it, we actually are making matters worse. The anger, fears, and antagonisms do not disappear. Instead, they intensify; the chasms widen, and the costs we think we will incur by losing grow. So, when we finally do confront the problem, the stakes are higher and we are further apart than ever. And, in the most tragic moments, the anger and frustration produce events like those of 9/11.

Cooperative Problem Solving

My reading of the evidence presented in this book, and all the other research and teaching I've done, suggests that these are the values and assumptions that shape the way people and their governments act. They also are the ones that leave us relatively ill equipped to deal with the problems we face in this new century and millennium.

If you think back to the four issues I used to illustrate

▌ **TABLE 17.1** Contrasting Values and Ways of Thinking

CURRENT VALUES	NEW THINKING
Scarce resources	Scarce resources
Separate	Interdependent
Short term	Long term
Self-interest = "me" first	Self-interest = good of the whole
We versus they, or enemy thinking	We with they
Power over	Power with
Power = force and violence	Power = cooperation, working together
Conflict is bad	Conflict can be good

the dangers of the global crisis, you will see that they have one common characteristic. They do not seem amenable to "power-over" kinds of solutions. Instead, they seem to require some sort of cooperative approach.

To be sure, there was probably no way to destroy al-Qaeda and the people who made its operations possible without force. However, virtually everyone understands that terrorism will end only if the root causes that give rise to it are addressed, and this will require international cooperation. Similarly, there is probably no way of ending the destruction of the Brazilian rain forests without the rich countries of the north providing substantial aid to allow Brazil to develop without harming the global environment.

Today's problems may require cooperation across national borders and other lines of division, yet this is not how we normally go about dealing with them. Therefore, we will have to radically redefine the way we approach conflict. Research on conflict resolution suggests that the values and assumptions in the first column of table 17.1 can be changed. Indeed, these researchers have gathered a lot of evidence that conflict can be handled differently—and better—if we approach it with a set of values and assumptions more in keeping with the reality of life today.

These alternative values and assumptions are listed in the second column of the table. Like the traditional way of thinking, the new one is rooted in the fact that there are not enough resources to go around. However, the proper response to our difficulties rests on a different starting point: We are a single, interdependent people living on a single, interdependent planet.

If this is the case, everything we do directly or indirectly affects everything and everyone else (this point will be developed more fully in the next section). In other words, we really are not separate or autonomous actors. This, in turn, means that we have to rethink what we mean by self-interest. If, as another cliché has it, what goes around comes around, I am not maximizing my self-interest beyond the short term if doing so comes at your expense. If I grade you unfairly or treat you shabbily when you come to my office, it is going to come back to haunt me. You'll write me a bad course evaluation, gossip with your friends, drop the course, or complain to the chair of my department.

In this way of thinking, my self-interest and yours become the same, at least over the long haul. It is in both of our self-interests to work together on the paper I gave you a bad grade on. You'll do better next time, I'll become a better teacher because I can describe my expectations more clearly, and we'll both end up a lot happier.

This is also the dilemma the United States and its allies faced in the aftermath of 9/11. There seemed to be no way of bringing bin Laden and his colleagues to justice without the use of force. However, the bombing and the rest of the war also planted the seeds for more terrorism or other forms of violence later on. As everyone from President Bush to his harshest critics understood, a strategy will have to be found for turning victory in the shooting war into a very different kind of victory—one over the problems that leads thousands, if not millions, of Muslims to hate the West.

Recognizing our shared interests does not mean that conflict disappears. Far from it. If anything, there will be more, not less, conflict in the future. What could be different is the way we handle it. From this perspective, win-lose outcomes will always be counterproductive because they sow more animosity in the minds of the losers and so cause even more problems in the future.

Achieving our shared interests requires finding solutions we are both happy with, which are known as **positive-sum** or **win-win outcomes.** There are, in fact, relatively few instances in which political struggles have to result in winners and losers, as, for instance, may be the case with the debate over a woman's right to have an abortion.

In almost every other case, however, we can envision a solution that all parties benefit from beyond the short run. If you and I realize that we share a long-term common interest, we look at our differences in a new light. It makes absolutely no sense for me to treat you as an enemy (or vice versa), because this makes finding these win-win solutions all but impossible. Rather, our challenge is to find a way to overcome our differences in a mutually acceptable way.

But this cannot happen if violence and force are as commonly used as they are today. Power, from this perspective, is my ability to get you and me to do something that works for both of us. Power becomes something one exerts not "over" others but "with" them in trying to settle disagreements and reach win-win outcomes. In this sense, the very nature of conflict changes. It is no longer something to be feared, but a welcome opportunity to learn and improve the world we live in.

The use of these kinds of approaches in political life is in its infancy. We saw elements of it, however, in the remarkable changes in South Africa in the first half of the 1990s. After years of repression and struggle, the leaders of the National Party and the African National Congress realized they had to live together. Otherwise, the country would slide into deeper difficulties and, perhaps, fall apart. At that point, then-president F. W. de Klerk, Nelson Mandela, and their colleagues began the negotiations that led to power sharing, the transition to democratic rule, the creation of the Truth and Reconciliation Commission, and a whole series of less visible bridges between the white and black communities.

Curiously, Afghanistan provides us with one of the few political institutions that promote cooperative problem solving and conflict resolution. For centuries, Afghans have ended periods of turmoil by convening a *loya jirga,* in which tribal and other leaders come together and talk until they reach a consensus on what should happen next. Grassroots organizations such as the Foundation for Global Community (www.globalcommunity .org/index.shtml) and the Afghan Center (www.latimes .com/news/nationworld/nation/la-101401exhile.story), as well as a number of leaders in Afghanistan, were calling for one as these lines were being written.

I am not, by any stretch of the imagination, trying to suggest that such an approach to politics will become the norm anytime soon. There are few such institutions in any government. Thus, only ten states in the United States have consensus councils that make public policy by bringing all stakeholders together, helping them reach a win-win agreement, and then sending it to the state legislature for enactment. Some of the corporatist arrangements we saw in Europe and Japan promote cooperation between representatives of interest groups and the state.

However, such institutions and practices are by far the exception, not the norm. There is, thus, every reason to think that it will be difficult, if not impossible, to build a world in which cooperative problem solving for the long term becomes the norm.

Nonetheless, as we saw in the "evolution" sections in the preceding fifteen chapters, conventional wisdom can be changed and, indeed, must be changed when it outlives its utility. Throughout history, whenever a crisis became so overwhelming that it threatened what people held dear, they found a way to overcome it. This response never came easily. It always involved shedding ways of thinking and acting that were so deeply ingrained that many people were not even aware they existed. There always were doubters, but the fact of the matter is that, time and time again, people changed, and in so doing they changed the institutions that governed them.

I had reached this conclusion long before September 11. Indeed, the preceding paragraph is one of the few that has remained unchanged from the first edition of this book to the fifth. However, the events of that horrible day drove home for me the importance of making this kind of political paradigm shift more powerfully than anything else in my thirty years of teaching and writing.

Thinking Systemically

There are also empirical reasons for thinking that such new, more cooperative approaches to political problem solving could make sense. To see that, return to another of the points raised in Chapter 1 that has been off center stage for most of the book, though it has been used to structure parts of most chapters—systems theory. Figure 17.3 is a reproduction of figure 1.1 depicting a domestic political system that originally appeared on p. 12.

As noted in Chapter 1, systems theory is no longer very popular in political science. In the half century since it was introduced into our discipline, it has become the most widely used approach in the natural sciences, especially in ecology, which literally means the science of whole systems. Systems theory covers more than just domestic politics. It can be used profitably with any organization that is bounded (in other words, there are things outside it) and has a degree of internal structure. In short, almost any human institution.

It is particularly useful here because it can help us see the distinction between the two types of power we've

▌ FIGURE 17.3 The Political System

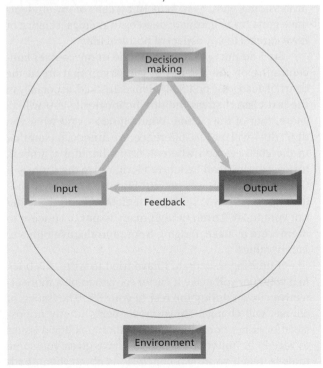

discussed. When people exert power by, say, making public policy, it can have three kinds of impact largely because of feedback. First, it can have a limited effect because people either do not hear about the policy or do not care much about it. Second, if it involves "power over" on an issue that matters to people who think their interests are harmed, they are likely to grow angrier and eventually place more demands on the system. On the other hand, "power with" tends to build bridges and what some scholars call social capital in which people become more and more likely to cooperate with each because their interests have been met in a system in which the stakes of politics seem lowered.

Conclusion: Student and Citizen

I always have a hard time figuring out how to end a book or plan the final class in my own introductory comparative politics courses. I struggle to find the right thing to say that will both sum up what I have covered and inspire readers to dig more deeply into political life.

One point I try to make is actually pretty easy and was already hinted at toward the end of Chapter 1. I am a political science professor and proud to be one. However, I know from nearly thirty years of teaching that less than one-tenth of 1 percent of my students will follow my professional path. Less than 10 percent of my students have gone on to graduate degrees in political science or have careers in any aspect of political life.

So, I do not spend a lot of time in my courses concentrating on the debates or the jargon that are at the heart of academic political science. Instead, especially in the last class, I stress the one political role you will all share, that of the citizen. What you do—and what you don't do—will make a difference. We Americans saw that in the 2000 election where a virtual handful of uncast, miscast, or misread ballots in Florida gave the contest to George W. Bush. It was not just Florida. About eight million women between the age of eighteen and thirty did not vote in 2000 even though many issues of concern to them were at stake, ranging from reproductive rights to family values.

If nothing else, then, I have tried to write this book in a way that will make it easier for you to be a more effective citizen during the rest of your life. The issues, of course, will change. However, it seems utterly impossible for either domestic or international political issues to recede in importance. I hope I have given you some tools to reach your own conclusions about them, both inside and outside of the voting booth.

In that last class, I also try to introduce a new topic that drives home at least one aspect of the global crisis discussed in this chapter. More often than not, I show part of a video on the Truth and Reconciliation Commission in South Africa, *Long Night's Journey Into Day* (www.irisfilms.org/longnight/).

The segment I show documents the reaction of Peter and Linda Biehl to the murder of their daughter, Amy, in an act of random violence in South Africa in 1993. Biehl had gone to South Africa to help in the transition from apartheid to democratic rule but was killed by four black teenagers who assumed she was a white South African.

The Biehls first made headlines by supporting the amnesty petition of the four young men who murdered their daughter. But this was just the beginning. They have since devoted all their time and effort to the Amy Biehl Foundation (www.amybiehl.org), which is continuing the work she started in South Africa. Even more remarkably, they have helped two of the young men complete their educations; the two now work for the foundation.

When the lights come back on and we start discussing the film, some students are shocked that parents are helping their daughter's murderers. Some disagree with that part of the foundation's work altogether. They ask me whether I would do what the Biehls did; I tell them I don't know, but I doubt it.

But as the discussion goes on, virtually all of them end up agreeing that the work these remarkable parents are doing is one powerful response to the issues discussed in this chapter and the sixteen before it. They also see that the Biehls were a lot like themselves and their parents before the murders. This helps them recognize that average people like their parents can make a huge difference.

And because it is also the last class of the semester, I show them the coffee mug that I use at the office. My stepdaughter gave it to me when I was struggling to write the conclusion for the first edition of this book.

Its caption, and the inspiration provided by the Biehls is the lesson I want to leave my own students and you with. Whatever our differences, I also think it is one we can all agree on. The mug shows a picture of a cat holding up a globe over the words "fragile, handle with care."

Key Terms

Concepts

Crisis	Interdependence
Global warming	International political
Globalization	economy

OPEC oil embargo
Ozone layer
Positive-sum outcomes
Power

Way of thinking
Win-win outcomes
Zero-sum game

Critical Thinking Exercises

1 Much has changed since this book was finished in early 2005. Does the analysis of the global crisis presented here still make sense? Why (not)?

2 Public opinion pollsters routinely ask questions about whether people think their country is heading in the "right direction" or is on the "wrong track." If you were asked such a question about the world as a whole, how would you answer? Why did you reach this conclusion?

3 Do you agree that the end of the cold war will be as important a turning point as suggested in this chapter? Why (not)?

4 What do the terms *new world order, globalization,* and *interdependence* mean to you? How much might things change for the better or for the worse in the next few years?

5 Do you think "ways of thinking" are as important as suggested here? If so, do you think they can be changed?

Useful Websites

There are literally thousands of useful websites that deal with the issues covered in this chapter. They fall into three main categories—those that deal with globalization, conflict resolution, and other issues that build out of either of them.

On globalization, Globalization 101, sponsored by the Center for Strategic and International Studies in Washington, is one of the few relatively unbiased and complete sources. Also useful is About.com's site on globalization, which provides a bevy of links and regular updates.

www.globalization101.org

globalization.about.com

On conflict resolution, the place to start is with the two sites run by the Conflict Resolution Consortium at the University of Colorado. Crinfo is a portal to the entire field; beyondintractability is an online handbook to the ways of understanding and addressing the most difficult disputes we face around the world. The International Security Network, based in Switzerland, is probably the best source on the academic material on all security issues, especially those involving ethnicity. Finally, most of the NGOs work-

ing on conflict resolution have their own websites. Search for Common Ground is the largest one in the field. It is part of the Alliance for International Conflict Prevention and Resolution that brings together most of the American-based NGOs and a few others located in Europe. Truth in advertising. I work on the two Conflict Resolution Consortium projects and am on the staff at Search for Common Ground.

www.crinfo.org

www.beyondintractability.org

www.isn.ethz.ch

www.sfcg.org

www.aicpr.org

Finally, there are sites that help visitors get beyond the specific issues of globalization or conflict resolution and see an even bigger picture. The Foundation for Global Community in Palo Alto, California, helps people see that the problems we face today grow out of all the centuries and millennia of human evolution. The Institute for Global Ethics in Camden, Maine, helps its clients see the costs individuals, organizations, or governments incur when they do not act ethically.

www.globalcommunity.org

www.globalethics.org

InfoTrac College Edition Sources

Barber, Benjamin. "Democracy at Risk: American Culture in a Global Culture."

Blechman, Barry. "The Intervention Dilemma."

Garrett, Geoffrey. "Globalization's Missing Middle."

Kelman, Herb. "Interactive Problem Solving."

Kidder, Rushworth. "Entering the Third Age of Ethics."

Last, David. "Peacekeeping Doctrine and Conflict Resolution Techniques."

Martinez, Ruben. "Globalization and the Social Sciences."

Moore, Rebecca. "Globalization and the Future of U.S. Human Rights Policy."

Schwartzman, Kathleen. "Globalization and Democracy."

Further Reading

Brown, Lester, ed. *The State of the World*. New York: Norton, published annually. The Worldwatch Institute's annual assessment of global trends, focusing on environmental issues and their broader impact.

Ellwood, Wayne. *The No-Nonsense Guide to Globalization*. London: Verso, 2001. Though written from an explicitly antiglobalization perspective, a book worth reading by us all because it contains one of the best short descriptions of what globalization entails and why it is happening.

Friedman, Thomas. *The Lexus and the Olive Tree*. New York: Farrar, Straus & Giroux, 1999. The most popular, optimistic, and, perhaps, best book on globalization.

Hauss, Charles. *Beyond Confrontation: Transforming the New World Order*. Westport, Conn.: Praeger, 1996. An attempt (which this author obviously likes) to consider the possibilities for change in the post–cold war era.

———. *International Conflict Resolution*. New York/London: Continuum Books, 2001. A more focused look at international conflict that blends theory with five contrasting case studies.

Horsman, Matthew, and Andrew Marshall. *Beyond the Nation-State*. London: HarperCollins, 1995. The most thorough analysis of the way global forces are altering and reducing the role of the state.

Kaplan, Robert. *The Coming Anarchy*. New York: Random House, 2000. The best criticism of globalization from a realist, right-of-center perspective.

Kidder, Rushworth. *How Good People Make Tough Choices*. New York: Morrow, 1995. An attempt by an ex-academic and ex-journalist, who is now head of the Institute for Global Ethics, to show the benefits of acting ethically and the costs of not doing so at everything from the interpersonal to the international level.

Klare, Michael, and Yogesh Chandrani, eds. *World Security: Challenges for a New Century*. New York: St Martin's, 1998. A collection of essays on various aspects of security above and beyond merely military ones.

Stone, Robert D. *The Nature of Development*. New York: Knopf, 1992. A wonderful book that traces the link between the environment and development mostly through the lives of individuals in the third world.

Glossary

Acronyms

AD Alliance for Democracy in Nigeria

AG Yoruba-based political party in postindependence Nigeria

ANC African National Congress

ANPP All Nigeria Middle Belt People's Party, the leading opposition party in Nigeria today

BDA Federation Association of German Employers

BDI Federation of German Industry

BJP Bhatriya Janata Party, India's fundamentalist party, in power from 1998 to 1999

BMS Bharatiya Mozdoon Sangh (Indian Union)

CAC CCP Central Advisory Committee

CAP Common Agricultural Policy of the EU

CBI Confederation of British Industry

CCP Chinese Communist Party

CDU Germany's Christian Democratic Union

CFC Chlorofluorocarbon

CFDT General Confederation of French Labor

CFE Former (and corrupt) Mexican electoral commission

CFSP Common Foreign and Security Policy of the EU

CGT French General Confederation of Labor

CITU Congress of Indian Trade Unions

CJD Creutzfeldt-Jakob Disease

CODESA Conference on a Democratic South Africa, constitution-drafting body after Mandela's release

COREPER EU Council of Permanent Representatives

COSATU Council of South African Trade Unions, affiliated with the ANC

CPSA Communist Party of South Africa

CPSU Communist Party of the Soviet Union

CSU German Christian Social Union Party

CTM The Confederation of Mexican Workers, Mexico's leading trade union

DDP German Protestant and Liberal People's Party under the Weimer Republic

DDR German Democratic Republic, the old East Germany

DGB Federation of German workers, its largest trade union body

DIHT German Chambers of Commerce and Industry

DNVP German National People's Party

DSP Japan's Democratic Socialist Party

EAGGF European Agricultural Guidance and Guarantee Fund

EC European Community, now the EU

ECJ European Court of Justice

ECSC European Coal and Steel Community, precursor of the EU

EEC European Economic Community, first official title of today's EU

EMS European Monetary System

EMU European Monetary Union, including the central bank and the euro

ENA National School of Administration, *grande école* for training France's bureaucratic elite

EP European Parliament

ERM European Rate Mechanism

EU European Union

Euratom European Atomic Energy Commission

EZLN Zapatista guerrilla movement in Chiapas, Mexico

FDP Germany's Free Democrat (or liberal) Party

FEC Federal Executive Council of Nigeria

FEDECO The national commission that monitored elections in earlier Nigerian republics

FN France's racist and right-wing National Front party

FY Fiscal year

GATT General Agreement on Tariffs and Trade

GDP Gross domestic product

GEAR Growth, Employment, and Redistribution program in South Africa

GNP Gross national product

HDI Human Development Index

IAS Indian Administrative Service

IFE Current and more autonomous electoral commission in Mexico

IFP Inkatha Freedom Party; opposition to the ANC, headed by Mangosuthu Buthelezi

IMF International Monetary Fund

INC Indian National Congress; Iraqi National Congress

INEC The commission monitoring elections in Nigeria

IPE International political economy

IRDP India's Integrated Rural Development Program

JCP Japanese Communist Party

KDP Kurdish Democratic Party

KGB Soviet secret police

KMT Chinese Nationalist Party; overthrown on mainland China by CCP; in power on Taiwan

KPD German Communist Party

LDP Japan's Liberal Democratic Party

MAC China's Military Affairs Committee

MITI Japan's Ministry for International Trade and Industry, now the Ministry of Economy, Trade, and Industry.

MNC Multinational corporation

MOF Japan's Ministry of Finance

MP Member of Parliament

NAFTA North American Free Trade Agreement, linking Mexico, Canada, and the United States

NBI National Business Initiative in South Africa

NCBWA National Congress of British West Africa; one of the leading groups advocating Nigerian independence.

NCNC National Council of Nigeria and the Cameroons; an Igbo-based movement for Nigerian independence.

NEDC Great Britain's National Economic Development Council

NEP New Economic Policy in USSR

NEPU Northern Elements Progressive Union; a left-of-center Muslim party in the Nigerian second republic.

NGO Nongovernmental organization

NHS Great Britain's National Health Service

NIC Newly industrializing country

NIMBY Not in my backyard

NNDP Nigerian National Democratic Party; one of the regionally based political parties in post-independence Nigeria.

NNP New National Party in South Africa

NP National Party in South Africa; dominated the apartheid years.

NPC Northern People's Congress; one of the Muslim-based political parties during postindependence Nigeria.

NPD Germany's neo-Nazi National Democratic Party of the 1960s

NPN National Party of Nigeria; a Muslim-based political party during the Nigerian Second Republic.

NPP Nigerian People's Party; one of the major parties in post-independence Nigeria.

NRC National Republican Convention; a leading independence movement in colonial Nigeria.

NSDAP Germany's Nazi Party

NYM Nigerian Youth Movement; a leading pro-independence movement in colonial Nigeria.

OECD Organization for Economic Cooperation and Development

OEEC Organization for European Economic Cooperation

OPEC Organization of Petroleum Exporting Countries

PAN National Action Party, the leading right-of-center opposition party in Mexico

PCF French Communist Party

PDP People's Democratic Party; President Obasanjo's party in Nigeria.

PDS Germany's Party of Democratic Socialism, successor to East German communists

PEMEX Mexico's nationalized petrochemical industry

PLA People's Liberation Army in China

PR French Republican Party; proportional representation.

PRC People's Republic of China

PRD Party of the Democratic Revolution, Mexico's main left-of-center opposition party

PRI Institutional Revolutionary Party, which ruled Mexico from 1927 to 2000

PRP A very left-of-center party in Northern Nigeria during the second republic

PS French Socialist Party

PUK One of the Kurdish opposition groups in Iraq and elsewhere

QUANGO Quasi-autonomous nongovernmental organization

RCC Revolutionary Command Council of the ruling Baath Party in Iraq

RDP South Africa's Reconstruction and Development Program

RI France's Independent Republican Party

RISA Reinvest in South Africa

RPR Most recent incarnation of the French Gaullist party

RSFSR Official title of the Russian federation of the old Soviet Union

RSS India's Rastriya Swayamsevak Sangh Party

SAVAK Iranian intelligence service under the shah

SDF Japan's Self-Defense Force

SDI South Africa's Special Development Initiative

SDLP Catholic Social Democratic Labour Party

SDP Britain's former Social Democratic Party; also, one of the political parties in Nigeria during the very short-lived third republic.

SDPJ Japan's leading Socialist Party

SEA The Single European Act

SED Socialist Unity Party of former East Germany

SEZ Special economic zone in China

SFIO French Socialist Party, until 1969

SNP Scottish National Party

SPD Germany's Social Democratic Party

TANU Tanzanian African National Union

TUC Trades Union Congress in Great Britain; United Democratic Front in South Africa.

UDF Union of French Democrats Party in France; Union of Democratic Forces in South Africa.

U.K. United Kingdom

UMBC United Middle Belt Congress; a powerful force during the Nigerian second republic.

UNSCOM United Nations Special Commission inspecting Iraqi compliance with UN arms limits

UPN United Party of Nigeria; the main Yoruba party in Nigeria's second republic.

VHP Vishwa Hindu Parishad, India's Worldwide Hindu Brotherhood

WMD Weapons of mass destruction (Iraq)

WTO World Trade Organization

Concepts

Acquis communautaires The body of laws and regulations new members of the EU must accept before gaining admission.

Afrikaner The portion of the South African white population with roots in Dutch culture. Primary architects and supporters of apartheid.

Amakudari Literally, "descent from heaven"; the Japanese practice of bureaucrats retiring at about fifty and taking prominent positions in the LDP or big business.

Anticlerical The belief that there should be no link between church and state.

Apartheid South African policy of racial separation from 1948 to 1994.

Autogestion A version of self-managed socialism popular in France in the 1970s and 1980s.

Backbenchers Members of a parliament who are not in the government or shadow cabinet.

Base Marxist term to describe class and other economic relations that define the "means of production" and the distribution of wealth and power.

Basic Law The German constitution.

Bloc vote French practice that requires a vote on an entire bill without amendments.

Bourgeoisie Among other things, a Marxist term to describe the capitalist class.

Broadening Support for expanding EU membership.

Bubble economy The Japanese economic boom that collapsed in the early 1990s.

Bureaucracy The part of the government composed of technical experts and others who remain from administration to administration.

Cabinet responsibility Principle that requires a prime minister and government to retain the support of a parliamentary majority.

Cadre Term used to define the permanent, professional members of a party, especially in the communist world.

Camarilla In Mexico and elsewhere in Latin America, a politician's personal following in a patron-client relationship.

Campaign In China (and to a lesser degree the former Soviet Union), policies in which the party seeks to reach its goals by mobilizing people.

Capitalist roader Derogatory term used to label moderate CCP leaders during the Cultural Revolution.

Carrying capacity The amount of development an ecosystem can bear.

Castes Groups into which Hindu society is divided, each with its own distinctive rules for all areas of social behavior.

Catch-all Term devised in the 1960s to describe a new type of political party that plays down ideology in favor of slogans, telegenic candidates, and the like.

Chador Full-body-covering garment that most Iranian women have to wear.

Chancellor democracy Germany's informal system of political domination by the prime minister.

Charisma A style of leadership that emphasizes the personal magnetism of a single individual.

Checks and balances In the United States, the informal designation of separation of powers.

Christian Democratic parties Political parties inspired by Catholic thought and ideals.

Civic culture Culture characterized by trust, legitimacy, and limited involvement, which some theorists believe is most conducive to democracy.

Civil society The web of membership in social and political groups that some analysts believe is needed to sustain democracy.

Class A societal group in which members share the same or similar economic roles and status.

Cleavage Deep and long-lasting political divisions.

Cohabitation In France, a period in which one party or coalition controls the Parliament and the other has the presidency.

Cold war Rivalry between the superpowers from the end of World War II to the collapse of the Soviet Union.

Collective responsibility The doctrine that all cabinet members must agree with all decisions.

Collectivist consensus Cross-party British support for the welfare state that lasted until the late 1970s.

Command economy A centrally planned and controlled economy. This kind of economy operated in the former Soviet Union and other communist countries.

Communal group Racial, ethnic, or linguistic groups that today are often the source of political violence.

Communism Theory developed by Marx and Engels that was adapted and used in such countries as China and the former Soviet Union.

Communist Party A political party inspired by Marxism-Leninism, usually as developed in the former Soviet Union.

Compromise Decision-making procedure in which all sides make concessions in order to reach an agreement.

Concerted action Cooperation involving the government, business, and labor in Germany.

Conditionality The imposition of stipulations before the granting of loans by the IMF, World Bank, and other international financial institutions.

Confucianism Chinese philosophical and religious tradition stressing, among other things, order and hierarchy.

Consensus policy making Decision-making procedures that emphasize win/win outcomes.

Constitution A basic political document that lays out the institutions and procedures a country follows.

Constructive vote of no confidence In Germany, means that a chancellor can be removed in a vote of confidence only if the Bundestag also agrees on a replacement.

Contradictions Marxist notion that all societies based on inequality have built-in flaws that will eventually lead to their destruction.

Corporatism In Europe, arrangements through which government, business, and labor leaders cooperatively set microeconomic or macroeconomic policy, normally outside of the regular electoral legislative process. In Mexico and elsewhere in the third world, another term to describe the way people are integrated into the system via patron-client relations.

Crisis A critical turning point.

Cult of personality In communist and other systems, the excessive adulation of a single leader.

Dalit Term to describe untouchables in India.

Debt crisis The massive accumulation of loans taken out by third world countries and owed to northern banks and governments from the 1970s onward.

Debt trap The inability of third world countries to pay back their loans to northern creditors.

Decision making The way governments (or other bodies) make policies.

Deep ecology Green belief that all social, economic, political, and environmental issues are connected to each other.

Deepening Expansion of the EU's powers.

Demand Inputs through which people and interest groups put pressure on the state for change.

Democratic centralism The Leninist organizational structure that concentrates power in the hands of the party elite.

Democratic deficit The lack of democratic procedures in the EU.

Democratization The process of developing democratic states.

Dependency A radical critique of mainstream economic theory that stresses the continued power the north has over the third world.

Devolution The process of decentralizing power from national governments that stops short of federalism.

Dialectic The belief that change occurs in dramatic bursts from one type of society to another.

Dirigisme French belief in a centrally planned and managed economy.

Division of powers U.S. notion that the levels of government have different responsibilities and power.

Dual Mandate In Nigeria and elsewhere, the notion that colonial powers had to rule on their own and through local leaders at the same time.

Electoral alchemy The way Mexican governments have used fraud to rig elections.

Electoral system Mechanisms through which votes are cast and tallied, and seats in the legislature are allotted.

Emergency Rule A provision in some constitutions that allows cabinets to rule in an all but dictatorial way for a brief period, as in India from 1975 to 1977.

Environment In systems theory, everything lying outside the political system.

Euroskeptic People opposed to expansion of the EU's power.

Extraterritoriality Portions of China, Japan, and Korea where European law operated during the late nineteenth and early twentieth centuries.

Faction A group organized on ideological or other lines operating inside a political party.

Failed state System in which the government loses the ability to provide even the most basic services.

Fascism Right-wing regimes, often drawing on racist philosophies in countries such as Germany and Japan between the two world wars.

Faulted society Germany from the late nineteenth century to the rise of Hitler, reflecting the unevenness of its social, economic, and political development.

Federalism Constitutional practice in which subnational units are granted considerable power.

Feedback How events today are communicated to people later on and shape what people do later on.

First past the post Electoral system based on single-member districts in which the candidate who receives the most votes wins.

Foreign aid Money or goods provided by richer countries to help poorer ones develop.

Four modernizations A policy first introduced by Zhou Enlai and championed by Deng Xiaoping, focusing on developing industry, the military, agriculture, and science in China.

Führer German term for "leader," used by Hitler.

Fundamentalism Religious beliefs of a literal nature that often lead to right-wing political views.

Glasnost Under Gorbachev, Soviet policies that opened up the political system and allowed for freedom of expression.

Global warming The well-supported theory that the earth is getting warmer due to the trapping of certain gases in the atmosphere.

Globalization Popular term used to describe how international economic, social, cultural, and technological forces are affecting events inside individual countries.

Government Either a generic term to describe the formal part of the state or the administration of the day.

Gradualism The belief that change should occur slowly or incrementally.

Grand coalition A cabinet that includes all the major parties, not just a bare majority.

Grandeur Gaullist goal for France.

Green Revolution In India and elsewhere, the technological improvements that drastically improved agricultural production and eliminated widespread starvation.

Greens Political parties that emphasize environmental and other "new" issues, and radical change.

Gridlock Term used in the United States and elsewhere to describe the paralysis of the legislative and executive branches.

Gross national product The total value of the goods and services produced in a society.

Groupism Japanese tendency for people to identify and base their behavior on group memberships rather than on individualism and personal preference.

Guardianship of the Jurist Developed by Ayatollah Khomeini, supports the notion that senior clerics have the best capacity to rule in a Muslim society.

Hard currency Currencies that can be traded openly on international markets.

Hausa-Fulani The leading Muslim group in northern Nigeria.

Historical materialism Marxist belief that the class divisions of a society determine everything else that matters.

Homelands Policy of the apartheid government in South Africa that created sham states for Africans.

Human Development Index The UN's best indicator of social development.

Hurting stalemate Theory that conflict resolution truly begins when both sides realize that they cannot win and that the costs of fighting have risen too high.

Igbo The leading ethnic group in southeastern Nigeria. Often also spelled Ibo.

Image of the enemy Psychological concept that focuses on stereotyping one's adversary.

Imperialism The policy of colonizing other countries—literally, establishing empires.

Import substitution Development strategy that uses tariffs and other barriers to imports, and therefore stimulates domestic industries.

Incompatibility clause French constitutional provision that bars people from holding a seat both in the National Assembly and in a cabinet.

Incremental Used to describe policies that make limited, marginal, or minor changes in existing practices.

Indirect rule British and other colonial procedures through which "natives" were used to carry out colonial rule.

Individualism The belief that emphasizes the role of the individual voter or consumer, typically associated with the rise of democracy in the West.

Industrialized democracy The richest countries with advanced economies and liberal states.

Input Support or demand from people to the state.

Integrated elite In Japan, France, and Germany, refers to cooperation among government, business, and other interest groups.

Interdependence The theory that all life is interconnected and that we are not independent or autonomous actors.

Interest group An organization formed to work for the views of a relatively narrow group of people, such as a trade union or business association.

Interim government Generically, any government that serves for a brief period as part of a transition. In Iraq, the government chosen in the 2005 election whose one main mission is to draft a new constitution.

International political economy The network of economic activity that transcends national boundaries.

Interventionist state Governments in industrialized democracies that pursue an active economic policy.

Iron triangle A variety of close relationships between business leaders, politicians, and civil servants.

Islamicists Muslims who are convinced that their faith should dominate politically.

Jati In India, a subcaste with its own rules, customs, and so forth.

Judicial review Power held by courts in some countries that allows them to rule on the constitutional merits of laws and other policies.

Keiretsu Japanese business conglomerates, often with political clout.

Koenkai Support organizations for Japanese politicians.

Kurds Minority ethnic group in Iraq and other countries in the region.

Laissez-faire Economic policy that stresses a limited government role.

Länder (land) German states.

Left Political groups favoring change, often of an egalitarian nature.

Legitimacy A key concept stressing the degree to which people accept and endorse their regime.

Manifesto In Britain and other parliamentary systems, another term for a party's platform in an election campaign.

Maquiladora Factory in Mexico (initially on the U.S. border, now anywhere) that operates tax-free in manufacturing goods for export.

Marxism-Leninism The philosophy adopted by ruling communist parties, which combined Marxist analysis with Leninist organizational structures and tactics.

Mass line Chinese Communist principle that stressed "learning from the masses."

Means of production Marxist term designating the dominant way goods are created in a given society.

Member of Parliament Elected members of the British or other parliament.

Mestizo Term used to describe Mexicans of mixed racial origin.

Microcredit Lending and development strategy that stresses small loans for new businesses, developed by the Grameen Bank in Bangladesh.

Modell Deutschland Term used to describe the political approach to German economic growth after World War II.

Money politics In Japan, an expression used to describe—and criticize—the high cost of running elections and the corruption it induces.

Multimember constituency Electoral district that elects more than one member of parliament.

Nation As used by political scientists, primarily a psychological term to describe attachment or identity rather than a geopolitical unit such as the state.

Nationalization Philosophies or attitudes that stress the importance of extending the power or support for a nation; government takeover of private business.

Nation building A process in which people develop a strong sense of identification with their country.

Near abroad Russian term to describe the other fourteen republics of the former Soviet Union.

New left Radicals from the 1960s.

New right Conservative political movements in industrialized democracies that have arisen since the 1960s and stress "traditional values," often with a racist overtone.

Newly industrializing countries The handful of countries, such as South Korea, that have developed a strong industrial base and grown faster than most of the third world.

No fly zone Regions in northern and southern Iraq where government airplanes are not allowed to fly.

Nomenklatura The Soviet system of lists that facilitated the CPSU's appointment of trusted people to key positions. Adopted by other communist regimes.

Nongovernmental organizations Private groups that are playing an increasingly important role in determining developmental and environmental policies.

Nonreelection Principle in Mexican political life that bars politicians from holding office for two consecutive terms.

Oligarch Business and political leaders with what some think is undue influence in Russia.

OPEC oil embargo The refusal by oil-producing countries to sell petroleum to Israel's allies in the aftermath of the 1973 war, which had sweeping ramifications for the global economy.

Output Public policy in systems theory.

Oyabun-kobun The Japanese system of patron-client relations.

Ozone layer Thin layer in the upper atmosphere that is being eroded by CFCs, which may have devastating environmental consequences.

Pantouflage The French practice of leaving the bureaucracy to take positions in big business or politics.

Parastatal Companies owned or controlled by the state in the third world.

Parliamentary party The members of parliament from a single party.

Party state The notion that the CPSU and other ruling communist parties dominated their entire political systems.

Patron-client relations Neofeudal relations in which "patrons" gain the support of "clients" through the mutual exchange of benefits and obligations.

Pendulum effect The notion that policies can shift from left to right as the balance of partisan power changes. In Mexico, reflects the fact that the PRI can move from one side to another on its own as circumstances warrant.

Perestroika Ill-fated program to reform the Soviet economy in the late 1980s.

Permit raj In India, the system of government rules and regulations that required state approval of most enterprises.

Political culture Basic values and assumptions that people have toward authority, the political system, and other overarching themes in political life.

Political party Organization that contests elections or otherwise contends for power.

Politics The process through which a community, state, or organization organizes and governs itself.

Positive-sum outcome Conflict resolution in which all parties benefit. Also known as win/win.

Postindustrial society Society in which the dominant industries are in the service and high-tech sectors.

Postmaterialism Theory that young middle-class voters are likely to support environmentalism, feminism, and other "new" issues.

Power As conventionally defined, the ability to get someone to do something he or she otherwise would not do.

Power ministries The most important departments in the Russian government.

Prefect Until 1981, the central government appointee who really ran France's departments.

Presidential Rule In India, the government's power to remove elected state officials and replace them with appointees from Delhi.

Privatization The selling off of state-owned companies.

Proletariat Marxist term for the working class.

Proportional representation Electoral system in which parties receive a number of seats in parliament proportionate to their share of the vote.

Public policy The decisions made by a state that define what it will do.

Purge The systematic removal of people from party, state, or other office; especially common in communist systems.

Qualified majority voting The EU voting system in which the Council of Ministers does not need to reach unanimity on most issues.

Radical French party that was radical by nineteenth-century standards, which is to say it favored democracy, capitalism, and anticlericalism.

Realignment A shift in the basic electoral balance of power in which substantial groups in a society change their long-term party identification.

Red Guard Radical students and other young supporters of Mao Zedong during the Cultural Revolution.

Regime The institutions and practices that endure from government to government, such as the constitutional order in a democracy.

Reparations Payments demanded of defeated powers after a war, especially important in Germany after World War I.

Restorative justice In South Africa and elsewhere, the attempt to forge reconciliation rather than seek revenge after the end of a conflict.

Right Political forces favoring the status quo or a return to earlier policies and values.

Rule of law In a democracy, the principle that legal rules rather than arbitrary and personal decisions determine what happens.

Safe haven Regions in northern Iraq where the United States and its allies guaranteed the safety of Kurds in the aftermath of the Gulf War.

Satellites The countries in eastern and central Europe that came under communist rule after World War II.

Securocrat Derogatory term used to describe the secret police and others in charge of enforcing apartheid laws in South Africa.

Separation of powers Formal term for checks and balances in a system like that of the United States.

Sexeño The six-year term of a Mexican president.

Shah Title of the rulers of Iran before the 1979 Islamic revolution.

Shadow cabinet In systems like Britain's, the official leadership of the opposition party that "shadows" the cabinet.

Sharia Islamic legal code that many argue should supersede civil law in countries such as Iran and Nigeria.

Shiite Minority Muslim sect, usually seen as more militant than the Sunnis.

Shock therapy Policies in formerly communist countries that envisage as rapid a shift to a market economy as possible.

Single-member district Electoral system in which only one representative is chosen from each constituency.

Single-member-district, two-ballot system In France, the electoral system in which a second, runoff ballot is held to determine the winner if no candidate gets a majority in the first round.

Social democracy Philosophy that rejects revolution and prefers moderate socialistic and other egalitarian reforms enacted through the parliamentary process.

Socialism A variety of beliefs in the public ownership of the means of production and an egalitarian distribution of wealth and income.

State All individuals and institutions that make public policy, whether they are in the government or not.

Strong state One with the capacity and the political will to make and implement effective public policy.

Structural adjustment Development strategy that stresses integration into global markets, privatization, and so on. Supported by the World Bank, IMF, and other major northern financial institutions.

Subsidiarity In the EU, policy that devolves decision making to the lowest appropriate level.

Subsistence economy One in which peasants predominate and grow food and other crops primarily for domestic consumption.

Sunni Majority Muslim sect, usually seen as more moderate than the Shiites.

Sunni triangle The region of Iraq in which Sunni Arabs make up the majority of the population.

Superstructure Marxist term for the government, religion, and other institutions whose primary role is to help support the dominance of the ruling class.

Support In systems analysis, popular input that tends to endorse the current leadership and its policies.

Supranational Authority that transcends national borders.

Swaraj The Indian movement for independence and self-rule.

Systems theory A model for understanding political life.

Taisho democracy The period after World War I in Japan in which it developed a liberal democratic regime similar to those in Europe at the time.

Third way A term used to describe the new and more central left-wing parties of the 1990s, most notably Britain's "New Labour."

Third world Informal term for the poorest countries in Asia, Africa, and Latin America.

Three-line whip In a parliamentary system, statements to MPs that they must vote according to the party's wishes.

Three pillars Informal term denoting the main areas in which the EU has worked since the Maastricht Treaty.

Totalitarian Regime in which the state has all but total power.

Tutelle In France, central government control over local authorities.

Two-party system Countries in which only two parties seriously compete for power.

Unanimity principle Formerly required for all decisions in the EU, now only for major new policies.

Unit The basic body assuring work, housing, and welfare to which most urban Chinese were assigned before economic reforms took hold.

Unitary state Regimes in which subnational units have little or no power.

Untouchables Indians outside of and "below" the caste system; abolished legally with independence.

Vote of confidence In a parliamentary system, a vote in which the members express their support for (or opposition to) the government's policies. If it loses, the government must resign.

Yoruba The leading ethnic group in southwestern Nigeria.

Warlord Prerevolutionary Chinese leaders who controlled a region or other relatively small part of the country.

Way of thinking The values or assumptions that shape the way people act.

Weak state One without the capacity and the political will to make and implement effective public policy.

Weapons of mass destruction Biological, chemical, and nuclear weapons.

White paper In Britain and elsewhere, a government statement that outlines proposed legislation; the last stage before the submission of a formal bill.

Win-win outcome Conflict resolution in which all parties benefit; also known as positive-sum game.

Zero-sum game Political outcome in which one side wins and the other loses.

People

Abacha, Sani The military ruler of Nigeria until his death in 1998.

Abiola, Mashood The apparent winner of the 1993 Nigerian presidential election of 1993; he died in prison of unexplained causes five years later.

Abubakar, Addulsalami Interim military leader of Nigeria in 1998.

Adenauer, Konrad First chancellor of the German Federal Republic (West Germany).

Al-Bakr, Ahmed Hassan First Baath president of Iraq, replaced by Saddam Hussein in 1979.

Alawi, Alar Prime Minister of interim Iraqi government.

Awolo, Obafemin A leading Igbo politician and head of Biafra during the civil war in Nigeria in the late 1960s.

Azikiwe, Nnamdi The leading Yoruba politician in post-independence Nigeria.

Babangida, Ibrahim Military ruler of Nigeria in the 1990s and potential candidate in 1997.

Balewam Tafawa One of the leaders of early independent Nigeria; killed in the first coup.

Bello, Ahmedu One of the leaders of early independent Nigeria; killed in the first coup.

Bhindranwale, Jarnail Singh Radical Sikh leader killed during the attack on the Golden Temple in 1984.

Biehl, Amy American student murdered during the transition to democracy in South Africa.

Biko, Steve Most important leader of South Africa's Black Consciousness movement; killed by the authorities while in prison in 1977.

Bismarck, Otto von Chancellor and most important founder of unified Germany in the last half of the nineteenth century.

Blair, Tony British prime minister since 1997 and architect of "New Labour."

Brandt, Willy First Socialist chancellor of the German Federal Republic.

Bremer, Paul Administrator of Iraq under the American occupation.

Brezhnev, Leonid General secretary of the CPSU from 1964 until 1982. Largely responsible for the stagnation of the USSR.

Cárdenas, Cuautémoc Son of Lazaro Cárdenas, founder of the PRD, and first elected mayor of Mexico City.

Cárdenas, Lazaro President of Mexico, 1934–40. The last radical reformer to hold the office.

Castro, Fidel President of Cuba since 1959.

Chalabi, Adnan Disgraced former leader of one wing of the Iraqi opposition.

Chen Duxiu Founder of the Chinese Communist Party.

Chernomyrdin, Viktor Prime minister of Russia, 1993–98.

Chiang Kai-shek Nationalist president of China before 1949 and later of the government in exile on Taiwan.

Chirac, Jacques Career French politician; president since 1995.

De Gaulle, Charles Hero of the French resistance against German occupation; founder and first president of the Fifth Republic.

De Klerk, F. W. The last president of South Africa under apartheid.

De la Madrid, Miguel President of Mexico, 1982–88; introduced structural adjustment reforms.

Debré, Michel Primary architect of the constitution of France's Fifth Republic; also its first prime minister, from 1958 to 1962.

Delors, Jacques Prominent French Socialist politician who was president of the European Commission, 1985–95.

Deng Xiaoping De facto ruler of China from the late 1970s to 1997.

Desai, Morarji First non-Congress prime minister of India.

Diaz, Porfirio Introduced the principle of nonreelection into Mexican politics; ironically, de facto dictator of the country for a quarter century in the late nineteenth and early twentieth centuries.

Duncan-Smith, Iain Current leader of the Conservative Party in Britain.

Engels, Friedrich With Karl Marx, the creator of communist theory.

Faisal I British-imposed king of newly independent Iraq after World War I.

Fang Lizhi Physicist and leading Chinese dissident, now living in exile in the United States.

Fischer, Joska Green member of parliament; foreign minister in the Schroeder government in Germany.

Fox, Vicente. First non-PRI president of Mexico, elected in 2000.

Gaidar, Yegor Reformist politician and acting prime minister of Russia in 1993.

Gandhi, Indira Prime minister of India, 1966–75 and 1979–84; daughter of Nehru and mother of Rajiv Gandhi; assassinated in 1984.

Gandhi, Mohandas Karamchand Leader of the Indian National Congress in the twenty years before independence.

Gandhi, Rajiv Prime minister of India, 1984–89, assassinated in 1991; son of Indira and grandson of Nehru.

Gandhi, Sonja Head of the Congress Party. Turned down the prime ministry in 2004.

Giscard d'Estaing, Valery Moderate president of France, 1974–81.

Gorbachev, Mikhail Head of the CPSU and last president of the Soviet Union.

Hashimoto Ryutaro Prime minister of Japan, 1995–98.

Hirohito Emperor of Japan during and after World War II.

Hitler, Adolf Nazi leader of the Third Reich, 1933–45.

Hobbes, Thomas British social theorist of the seventeenth century who emphasized a strong state.

Howard, Michael Leader of the British Conservative Party.

Hu Jintao President of China.

Hussein, Qusay Younger son of Saddam Hussein; probably the second-most-powerful person in Iraq when his father was deposed in 2002. Killed along with his brother by U.S. troops in 2003.

Hussein, Saddam President of Iraq from 1979 until 2002. Captured in December 2003 and currently awaiting trial.

Hussein, Uday Elder son of Saddam Hussein; thought of as the heir apparent until he was seriously wounded in a 1996 assassination attempt. Killed along with his brother by U.S. troops in 2003.

Ironsi, Aguiyi The military ruler of Nigeria during the Biafran war.

Jiang Qing Fourth (and last) wife of Mao Zedong and one of the leaders of the Gang of Four, a radical faction in the CCP during the Cultural Revolution.

Jiang Zemin President of China and successor to Deng Xiaoping.

Jospin, Lionel Socialist prime minister of France, 1997–2002.

Kano, Aminu A Muslim leader of early Nigeria.

Khamenei, Ayatollah Ali Supreme Leader of Iran since the death of Ayatollah Khomeini.

Khatami, Mohammed Reformist president of Iran, 1997–2005.

Khodorkovsky, Mikhail Russian tycoon arrested on corruption and tax evasion charges in 2003.

Khomeini, Ayatollah Ruhollah Muslim cleric who led the 1979 revolution in Iran and was leader of the country until his death in 1989.

Khrushchev, Nikita Successor of Josef Stalin as head of the CPSU and Soviet Union from 1953 until he was ousted in 1964.

Kohl, Helmut Longest-serving (1982–98) chancellor of Germany; oversaw unification.

Koizumi, Junichiro Prime minister of Japan, selected in 2001.

Le Pen, Jean-Marie Founder and main leader of France's racist National Front.

Lenin, V. I. Architect of the Bolshevik revolution and first leader of the Soviet Union.

Lin Biao Head of the PLA and designated successor to Mao Zedong; died in mysterious circumstances after a failed coup attempt in 1972.

Liu Shaoqi Moderate CCP politician and designated successor to Mao Zedong; died during the Cultural Revolution.

Locke, John Leading democratic and liberal theorist who stressed "life, liberty, and the pursuit of property."

MacArthur, Douglas U.S. army general who was SCAP in occupied Japan after World War II.

Macauley, Herbert The most important leader of the struggle for independence in Nigeria.

Madikizela-Mandela, Winnie Former wife of Nelson Mandela and an important, controversial leader of the ANC in her own right.

Malan, Daniel First National Party prime minister of South Africa after World War II; primary architect of apartheid.

Mandela, Nelson President of South Africa, 1994–99, and de facto leader of the ANC while in prison from 1964 to 1991.

Mao Zedong Chair of the CCP and head of the PRC from 1949 until his death in 1976.

Marx, Karl With Friedrich Engels, the leading nineteenth-century communist theorist.

Mbeki, Thabo President of South Africa since 1999.

Merkel, Angela Succeeded Helmut Kohl as head of the CDU; first woman to head a major party in Germany.

Mitterrand, François Resuscitated the French Socialist Party; president, 1981–95.

Miyazawa Kiichi First LDP prime minister to lose a vote of confidence, in 1993.

Monnet, Jean Primary architect of the EU and the French planning system.

Mossadeq, Mohammed Left-of-center prime minister of Iran, overthrown in a CIA-led coup in 1954.

Narasimha Rao, P. V. Prime minister of India, 1991–96.

Nehru, Jawaharlal Indian leader before independence, and prime minister, 1949–64.

Obasanjo, Olusegun President of Nigeria since 1999.

Ozawa Ichiro Chief kingmaker in Japanese politics in the 1990s.

Pompidou, Georges Second president of the Fifth Republic of France, from 1969 until his death in 1974.

Prodi, Romano President of the European Commission since 2001.

Putin, Vladimir President of Russia since 2000.

Rafsanjani, Akbar Hasemi Second president of Iran since the 1979 revolution. Running for reelection in 2005.

Salinas de Gortari, Carlos President of Mexico, 1988–94; continued structural adjustment reforms; currently living in exile because of his family's involvement in scandals.

Santa Anna, Antonio López de Nineteenth-century general and dictator responsible for Mexico's losing more than a third of its territory to the United States.

Saro-Wiwa, Ken Nigerian activist executed by the military government in 1996.

Schmidt, Helmut Chancellor of West Germany, 1974–92.

Schroeder, Gerhard SPD chancellor of Germany since 1998.

Shagari, Shehu President of Nigeria; overthrown in 1983 coup.

Shah, Mohammad Reza The second and last Pahlevi shah of Iran; deposed in 1979.

Shah, Reza First Pahlevi shah of Iran.

Singh, Manmohan Prime minister of India since 2004.

Spaak, Paul-Henri Belgian politician who was one of the leading architects of the early Common Market.

Stalin, Joseph Leader of the CPSU and Soviet Union, 1924–53.

Sun Yat-sen President of China after the 1911 revolution.

Suzman, Helen Liberal opponent of apartheid, often the only such opponent with a seat in the South African parliament during apartheid.

Takeshita Noboru Leading LDP politician and prime minister of Japan in the late 1980s.

Tanaka Kakuei Leading (and corrupt) LDP kingmaker in Japan in the 1970s and 1980s.

Thatcher, Margaret Conservative and first woman prime minister of Great Britain, 1979–90.

Trotsky, Leon Leading left-wing Bolshevik; purged in the 1920s and assassinated by Stalin's agents in 1940.

Tutu, Desmond Former Anglican archbishop of South Africa; leading opponent of apartheid, Nobel Peace Prize winner, and head of the Truth and Reconciliation Commission.

Vajpayee, Atal Bihari BJP prime minister of India, 1998–1999.

Verwoerd, Hendrik Leading creator of apartheid.

Walesa, Lech Most important leader of Solidarity and then president of Poland.

Wei Jingsheng Major Chinese dissident, now in exile in the United States.

Wen Jiabao Prime Minister of China.

Yeltsin, Boris Former reformist communist leader and president of Russia, 1991–2000.

Zedillo, Ernesto President of Mexico, 1994–2000.

Zhirinovsky, Vladimir Leader of the right-wing and racist Liberal Democratic Party in Russia.

Zhou Enlai Number two to Mao Zedong in China from 1949 until his death in 1975.

Zhu Rongji Currently prime minister of China.

Zyuganov, Gennady Head of the Russian Communist Party.

Organizations, Places, and Events

African National Congress Leading organization in the opposition to apartheid, now in power in South Africa.

Akali Dal The Sikh-based party in Punjab, India.

Alliance Coalition of British Liberals and Social Democrats in the 1980s that became the Liberal Democrats of today.

Article 9 The peace clause of the Japanese constitution that bans Japan from having an army for anything other than self-defense.

Assembly of Experts An informal body in Iran that has de facto veto power over all major political decisions.

Ayodhya Site of a disputed mosque/temple that sparked communal violence in India for much of the 1990s.

Baath Party Party in control of Iraq from the late 1960s until the U.S.-led invasion in 2002.

Beveridge Report Published in the 1940s; set the stage for the British welfare state.

Bharatiya Janata Party The Hindu party that won the 1998 election; often referred to as fundamentalist.

Black Consciousness movement An important, spontaneous group opposing apartheid in the 1970s, led by the late Steve Biko.

Blood River, Battle of During the Great Trek, a battle in which the Boers defeated the Africans, reinforcing their sense of being a chosen people.

Bolsheviks Lenin's faction of the Russian Social Democratic Party; later came to mean anyone who subscribed to his views and/or organization.

Bonyal Islamic charities in Iran, many of which are controlled by the government.

British East India Company Private company that colonized India until the 1850s.

Broederbond Secret Afrikaner organization, including many National Party and other supporters of apartheid.

Bundesbank Germany's central bank, replaced by the European Central Bank in 1999.

Bundesrat The upper house of the German parliament.

Bundestag The lower house of the German parliament.

Central Advisory Committee Informal group of senior Chinese Communist leaders in the 1980s.

Central Committee Supposedly the most important body in a communist party; its influence declined as it grew in size and the party needed daily leadership.

Cheka The Soviet Union's first secret police.

Chinese Communist Party (CCP) The only legal party in China, which has run the country since 1949.

Christian Democratic Party (CDU) Germany's leading right-of-center party; similar parties exist elsewhere where there is a large Catholic population.

Coalition Provisional Authority Official name of the U.S.-led occupation administration of Iraq.

Comintern The interwar coalition of communist parties directed from Moscow.

Commission, European The executive of the European Union.

Committee of Permanent Representatives European Union civil servants who are sent by and work for the member states rather than the EU itself.

Common Agricultural Policy The EU's agricultural policy, blamed for many of its economic troubles and likely to be changed as it adds new members.

Common Foreign and Security Policy EU goal of creating a single foreign policy for its fifteen member states; one of the three pillars.

Common Market Colloquial name used to describe the European Union, especially in its early years.

Communism Has many meanings, but usually used to describe policies and institutions derived from the works of Marx, Engels, and Lenin.

Communist Party (PCF) French Communist Party.

Communist Party of the Russian Federation The new incarnation of the CPSU for Russia.

Communist Party of the Soviet Union The party that ran the Soviet Union until its collapse in 1991.

Confederation of British Industry (CBI) The leading British business interest group.

Confederation of Mexican Workers The official trade union affiliated with the PRI.

Conference on a Democratic South Africa (CODESA) The constitution-writing body after 1991.

Congress of South African Trade Unions (COSATU) The most important trade union federation, affiliated with the ANC.

Conservative Party Britain's most important right-of-center party, in power more often than not for two centuries.

Constitutional Court In Germany, the court with powers roughly equivalent to those of the U.S. Supreme Court.

Constitutional Revolution Begun in 1906, the first attempt to bring anything like democracy to Iran.

Council of Ministers A generic term used to describe the cabinet in many countries.

Cultural Revolution The period of upheaval in China from the mid-1960s to the mid-1970s.

Daimyo Japanese feudal lords in the pre-Meiji period.

Democracy Movement Protests by Chinese students and others that culminated in the Tiananmen Square disaster of 1989 in Beijing.

Democracy Wall Literally, a wall on which Chinese dissidents wrote "big-character posters" in the late 1970s.

Democratic Socialist Party Japan's Social Democratic Party.

De-Stalinization The shift away from Stalinist policies and practices beginning with Khrushchev's secret speech in 1956.

Diet Japan's parliament.

Emergency Rule Provisions in the Indian constitution that allow a prime minister to rule by decree. Used by Indira Gandhi from 1975 to 1977.

ENArques Graduates of France's National School of Administration, many of whom become business and political leaders.

Euro The new European currency, introduced in 1999.

European Coal and Steel Community One of the precursors of the European Union, formed in 1951.

European Communities The formal name of what became the EU in the 1970s and 1980s.

European Court of Justice The EU's judicial body, with sweeping powers.

European Economic Community The precursor of the EU.

European Monetary System The first attempt to link the EU member states' currencies.

European Monetary Union Created in 1998; includes a central bank and the euro.

European Parliament The EU's legislature.

European Union The current name of the "Common Market."

Events of May 1968 French protest movements that almost toppled the Gaullist government.

Expediency Council A half lay and half clerical body designed to smooth relations between those two communities in Iran at the highest levels.

Falun Gong Chinese spiritual movement suppressed by the government since the late 1990s.

Fatherland–All Russia One of the leading opposition parties in Russia in the 1999 Duma elections.

Federal Election Commission The old (and corrupt) body that supervised elections in Mexico.

Federal Electoral Institute Created before the 1997 election to provide more honest management of elections in Mexico than its predecessor, the Federal Election Commission.

Federal Republic of Germany Formal name of the former West Germany and, now, the unified state.

Federalist Papers Key documents written in support of the U.S. Constitution during the debate on ratification in the 1780s.

Federation Council The largely powerless upper house of the Russian parliament.

Federation of German Labour (DGB) The leading German trade union.

Fifth Republic French regime since 1958.

Five-year plan In the former Soviet Union and other communist countries, the period for which Gosplan developed goals and quotas.

Force ouvrière Workers' Force, France's second largest and most dynamic trade union federation.

Fourth Republic French regime from 1946 to 1958.

Free Democratic Party (FDP) Germany's Liberal party.

Freedom Charter The ANC's proposals from the 1950s that led to its being banned.

Gang of Four Radical leaders in China during the Cultural Revolution, led by Jiang Ching, Mao's wife.

Gaullists General term used to describe supporters of General Charles de Gaulle and the parties created to back his vision for the Fifth Republic.

General Intelligence Apparatus One of Iraq's main intelligence agencies.

General secretary General term used to denote the head of a communist party.

General Security Directorate One of Iraq's main intelligence agencies.

Genro The small group of nobles who dominated Japanese politics after the Meiji Restoration.

German Democratic Republic (DDR) Formal name of the former East Germany.

Gobernación The ministry in charge of administration in Mexico; until recently, a post often held by politicians before becoming president.

Good Friday Agreement A practical peace agreement reached by the major parties in Northern Ireland with the British and Irish governments on, not surprisingly, Good Friday 1998.

Gosplan The Soviet central planning agency.

Government of India Act The 1858 law that turned most of India into a formal British colony.

Grandes écoles Highly selective French universities that train top civil servants and, hence, much of the elite.

Great Leap Forward Failed Chinese campaign of the late 1950s to speed up development.

Great Reform Act Law passed in 1832 that expanded the suffrage; widely seen as a key step toward democracy in Britain.

Great Trek Massive expedition by Boers to what is now the northeastern part of South Africa; symbolically important as a sign of Afrikaner power.

Green revolution The introduction of new seed varieties that helped reduce hunger dramatically in India.

Greens In Germany, the first major environmentally oriented party; now a junior partner in government.

Growth, Employment, and Redistribution Program (GEAR) South Africa's development strategy.

Guardian Council The leading theological body in Iran for political purposes.

Guerrero A poor province (although it includes Acapulco) in which rebels are fighting the Mexican government.

Gulf War The war between the UN coalition and Iraq following the latter's invasion of Kuwait in 1990.

House of Commons The all-important lower house of the British Parliament.

House of Councillors The upper house of the Japanese Diet.

House of Lords The weaker upper house of the British Parliament, slated for reform or abolition.

House of Representatives The lower house in the U.S., Mexican, and Japanese legislatures.

Hundred Flowers Campaign Reformist Chinese campaign in the mid-1950s.

Immigration Reform and Control Act U.S. law, passed in 1986, that limits the rights of immigrants, especially those from Mexico.

Indian Administrative Service The bureaucratic elite today.

Indian Civil Service The bureaucratic elite during colonial rule.

Indian National Congress The leader of the struggle for India's independence and the dominant party since then.

Inkatha Freedom Party The leading African-based opposition party in South Africa.

Institutional Revolutionary Party (PRI) The party that governed Mexico from 1927 to 2000.

International Monetary Fund International agency that provides loans and other forms of assistance to countries with fiscal problems.

Iraqi National Congress The leading exile-based opposition group to Baath rule.

Janata (Dal) Loose coalitions that unseated Congress in the late 1970s and 1980s in India.

Japan Communist Party (JCP) The most left-wing major party in Japan, and one of the most successful of the remaining communist parties in the industrialized world.

Komeito The Clean Government Party in Japan.

Kuomintang The Chinese Nationalist Party, which was nominally in power from 1911 to 1949; now in charge on Taiwan.

Kurdish Democratic Party The largest opposition group among Iraqi Kurds.

Labour Party The leading left-wing party in Britain, in power since 1997.

Law for Promoting Stability and Growth in the Economy Passed in 1967, a key provision in Germany's economic consensus.

Liberal Democratic Party In Britain, the number-three party and in some ways the most radical; in Japan, the dominant party since the 1950s; in Russia, the neofascist and racist opposition party led by Vladimir Zhirinovsky.

Lok Sabha The all-important lower house of the Indian parliament.

Long March Retreat by the CCP in the mid-1930s, which turned into one of its strengths in recruiting support.

Maastricht Treaty Created the EU and EMU; signed in 1992.

Majlis The Iranian parliament.

Marshall Plan U.S. funds provided for reconstruction of Europe after World War II.

May Fourth Movement Chinese protest movement triggered by opposition to the Treaty of Versailles; a major step on the path leading to the creation and victory of the CCP.

Meiji Restoration Political reform in Japan following the arrival of the West.

Mensheviks The smaller and more moderate faction of the Russian Social Democratic Party before World War I.

Military Affairs Committee One of the leading groups of the CCP under Deng Xiaoping.

Military Intelligence One of the leading intelligence agencies in Iraq.

Ministry of International Trade and Industry Japanese ministry that coordinates economic policy.

Mughals The Muslims who invaded and dominated India beginning in the sixteenth century.

Multinational corporation Company operating across national boundaries.

National Action Party (PAN) The leading right-of-center opposition party in Mexico.

National Assembly In France and South Africa, the lower house of parliament.

National Democratic Party Germany's most powerful neo-Nazi party since the end of World War II.

National Front France's racist right-wing party.

National Party The architect of apartheid in South Africa, in power from 1948 to 1994.

National Socialist Democratic Workers Party (NSDAP) Political party of Hitler in Germany.

Nationalist Party The Kuomintang, the ruling party in China before the CCP victory; in power on Taiwan.

Nazis Hitler's party, which ruled Germany from 1933 to 1945.

New National Party Successor to the apartheid-era National Party in South Africa.

Newly industrializing countries Countries in the third world that have made major strides toward industrialization.

Nongovernmental organization Nonprofit organizations that exert political influence around the world.

North American Free Trade Agreement (NAFTA) Agreement linking the economies of Canada, Mexico, and the United States.

Operation Iraqi Freedom Official name of the American-led invasion of Iraq in 2003.

Organization of Petroleum Exporting Countries (OPEC) Cartel of oil-producing countries; responsible for the 1973–74 embargo.

Ottoman Empire Islamic empire based in present-day Turkey; collapsed with World War I.

Our Home Is Russia New political party chaired by former prime minister Viktor Chernomyrdin.

Pahlevi dynasty The father and son who ruled Iran for most of the twentieth century, until the revolution of 1979.

Parity Law Recent French legislation guaranteeing seats in the parliament for women.

Party of Democratic Socialism (PDS) The successor to East Germany's Communist Party.

Party of the Democratic Revolution (PRD) The leading left-of-center opposition party in Mexico.

Patriotic Union of Kurdistan (PUK) One of the leading Kurdish opposition groups in Iraq and beyond.

Peace Clause Article 9 of the Japanese constitution, which denies it an offensive army.

People's Liberation Army China's military.

People's Republic of China Official name of the Chinese state.

Politburo Generic term used to describe the leadership of communist parties.

Popular Army The nonelite force in the Iraqi military.

Provisional government Generic term used to describe temporary governments formed until a new constitution is written; also, the government in Russia between the two 1917 revolutions.

Radicals People to the left of center; in France, the liberals who were radical only in nineteenth-century terms.

Rally for the Republic (RPR) The current name of the Gaullist Party in France.

Raja Sabha The weaker upper house of the Indian parliament.

Rashtriya Swayamsevah Sangh (RSS) A fundamentalist Hindu group and a precursor of the BJP.

Red Guard Students and others who supported Mao during the Cultural Revolution.

Red versus expert Debate in China pitting ideologues against supporters of economic development.

Republican Guard The elite military units in Iraq.

Revolution from above In Germany and Japan, elite-driven modernization efforts in the late nineteenth century.

Revolutionary Command Council The leadership of the ruling Baath Party in Iraq.

Russian Federation Formal name of Russia.

Second of Khordad Movement The political party organized to support the reform efforts of then-president Khatami in Iran. Named for the day he was first elected.

Secret speech Given by Khrushchev in 1957; seen as the start of the "thaw."

Secretariat Generic term used to denote the bureaucratic leaders of a communist party.

Senate Upper house of the legislature in the United States, France, Mexico, and South Africa.

Sharpeville Massacre Incident in 1966 in which nearly a hundred protesters were killed in South Africa.

Shinshinto The leading opposition party in Japan for a brief period in the late 1990s.

Shogun The de facto ruler of Japan before the Meiji Restoration.

Single European Act Act that created the truly common market in 1992.

Sino-Soviet split Tensions between the USSR and China that rocked the communist world.

Social Democratic Party (SDP) Germany's left-of-center party, in power since 1997.

Social Democratic Party of Japan The more important of Japan's two socialist parties.

Socialist Party (PS) France's new Socialist Party, created in 1971.

Solidarity The anticommunist union formed in Poland in the 1980s.

South African Communist Party Allied with the ANC during the apartheid years and now part of the government.

Soweto The slum/township outside Johannesburg that served as a key organizing point for protest against apartheid.

Special Economic Zones Cities and regions in China in which foreigners are allowed to invest.

Special Security One of the leading intelligence agencies in Iraq.

Standing Committee The subcommittee that runs the Politburo in China.

State Duma The lower house of the Russian parliament.

State Security Council The leading ministers of the Russian government; the coordinating body for secret police and other organs of repression in the later years of the apartheid regime in South Africa.

Supreme commander of the Allied powers (SCAP) General Douglas MacArthur, who ran the occupation of Japan following World War II.

Supreme Leader Title given to the ayatollah who sits atop all Iranian political institutions.

Syndicate Indian Congress leaders who ended up opposing Indira Gandhi.

Third International Moscow-dominated organization of communist parties around the world between the two world wars.

Tiananmen Square Symbolic heart of Chinese politics; site in Beijing of protests and a massacre in 1989.

Tokugawa shogunate The regime of mostly figurehead leaders who nominally ruled Japan from the beginning of the seventeenth century until the Meiji Restoration.

Tories Informal name for Britain's Conservative Party.

Trades Union Congress (TUC) Britain's leading trade union confederation.

Treaty of Amsterdam Minor 1998 agreement that added some limited powers to the EU.

Treaty of Rome Created the EEC in 1957.

Treuhand The agency responsible for selling off formerly state-owned East German companies.

Truth and Reconciliation Commission Official South African body looking into human rights violations under apartheid.

Twentieth Party Congress Occasion of Khrushchev's "secret speech" launching de-Stalinization.

Umkhonto we Sizwe Spear of the Nation; the ANC's revolutionary wing in South Africa.

Union for French Democracy The number-two right-of-center party in France.

United Democratic Front Above-ground unit created by the ANC in South Africa in 1983.

United Russia. The political party led by Russian president Vladimir Putin.

United States–Japan Security Treaty Controversial pact that tied the two countries together.

UNSCOM United Nations Special Commission that formerly conducted arms inspections in Iraq.

Warsaw Pact Alliance that was the communist world's equivalent of NATO.

Weimar Republic Germany's first and failed attempt at democracy.

White revolution The term used by the shah to describe reforms in Iran between the end of World War II and the downfall of his regime in 1979.

World Bank A major international lending agency for development projects based in Washington.

World Trade Organization International organization with wide jurisdiction over trade issues; replaced the General Agreement on Tariffs and Trade.

Yaboloko One of the leading reformist parties in Russia.

Zapatistas Informal name for Mexican revolutionaries in Chiapas.

PHOTO CREDITS

Chapter 1. 5: Carmen Taylor/AP/Wide World Photos **6:** Odd Andersen/Getty Images **7, top:** Reuters NewMedia Inc./Corbis **7, bottom:** Reuters/Corbis

Chapter 2. 24: Jacques Brinon/AP/Wide World Photos **31:** The Granger Collection **33:** Time Life Pictures/Getty Images **37:** Tony Harris/AP/Wide World Photos **39:** Antoine Serra/In Visu/Corbis **43:** Anthony Suau/Getty Images **45:** AFP/Corbis

Chapter 3. 50: AP/Wide World Photos **56:** Joe Raedle/Getty Images **58:** AFP/Getty Images **63:** Susan Walsh/AP/Wide World Photos

Chapter 4. 70: Ian Waldie/Getty Images **72:** Bettmann/Corbis **76:** Hulton Archive/Getty Images **79:** Steve Millar **80:** Joel W. Rogers/Corbis **81:** AFP/Corbis **83:** AFP/Getty Images **86:** Owen Humphrey/AP/Wide World Photos **91:** REX USA Ltd. **97:** Poster design by Iain Lanyon for David Hare's *The Permanent Way* **101:** Tom Sloan/Getty Images

Chapter 5. 112: Hulton Archive/Getty Images **115:** Luca Bruno/AP/Wide World Photos **120:** AP/Wide World Photos **123:** Reuters NewMedia Inc./Corbis **126:** Reuters/Corbis **135:** AP/Wide World Photos

Chapter 6. 144: Reuters/Corbis **145:** Reuters NewMedia Inc./Corbis **149:** Bettmann/Corbis **158:** Fritt Reiss/AP/Wide World Photos **164:** Sven Kaestner/AP/Wide World Photos **171:** Reuters/Bettmann/Corbis

Chapter 7. 178: Yves Herman/Corbis **181:** Bettmann/Corbis **184:** Reuters/Bettmann/Corbis **188:** Thierry Tronnel/Corbis **191:** AP/Wide World Photos

Chapter 8. 206: Paul B. Davies **209:** Bettmann/Corbis **213:** AP/Wide World Photos **218:** Reuters/Corbis

Chapter 9. 228: AFP/Getty Images **233:** Bettmann/Corbis **235:** Hulton Archive/Getty Images **241:** Peter Turnley/Corbis **243:** Reuters NewMedia Inc./Corbis **244:** Laski Diffusion/Getty Images **246:** AFP/Getty Images **251:** AP/Wide World Photos **257:** AFP/Getty Images

Chapter 10. 266: Li Xueren/XineHua/Corbis **271:** Hulton Archive/Getty Images **274:** Bettmann/Corbis **275:** AP/Wide World Photos **277:** Bettmann/Corbis **284:** AP/Wide World Photos **289:** Luke Frazza/AFP/Getty Images **290:** Bettmann/Corbis

Chapter 11. 308: Langevin Jaques/Corbis Sygma **317:** AFP/Getty Images **320:** C. Zlotnik/Woodfin Camp and Associates **321:** Jose Fuste Raga/Corbis **322:** John G. Mabanglo/AFP/Getty Images **325:** Grameen Communications **326:** Courtesy of Search for Common Ground

Chapter 12. 332: Robert Nickelsberg/Time Life Pictures/Getty Images **337:** The Mary Evans Picture Gallery/London **340:** Bettmann/Corbis **343:** Bettmann/Corbis **345:** Reuters NewMedia, Inc./Corbis **348:** Saurabh Das/AP/Wide World Photos **350:** Doug Curran/AFP/Getty Images **351:** AP/Wide World Photos **353:** Scott Barbour/Getty Images **360:** Kapoor Baldev/Sygma/Corbis **362:** © International Center for Religion and Diplomacy **365:** AP/Wide World Photos

Chapter 13. 372: Enric Marti/AP/Wide World Photos **376:** AFP/Getty Images **377:** Courtesy of Search for Common Ground **379:** Corbis Sygma **381:** AP/Wide World Photos **382:** AP/Wide World Photos **384:** Mohammad Syad/AP/Wide World Photos **385:** Peter Blakely/Corbis SABA **387:** Vahid Salemi/AP/Wide World Photos **390:** Vahid Salemi/AP/Wide World Photos **392:** Hasan Sarbakhshian/AP/Wide World Photos **397:** Atta Kenare/AFP/Getty Images

Chapter 14. 402: Karen Ballard/AP/Wide World Photos **407:** Barry Iverson/Woodfin Camp & Associates **408:** Ceerwan Aziz/Reuters/Corbis **412:** Ceerwan Aziz/Corbis **413:** Chris North; Cordaiy Photo Library Ltd./Corbis **414:** AP/Wide World Photos **419:** AP/Wide World Photos **421:** Scott Peterson/Getty Images **423:** UN/DPI Photo **424:** Reuters/Corbis **425:** Anja Niedringhaus/AP/Wide World Photos **426:** USDOD/Getty Images **427:** Mohammed Khodor/Reuters/Corbis **429:** Msgt. Dave Ahlschwede, USAF/AP/Wide World Photos

Chapter 15. 434: AP/Wide World Photos **436:** AP/Wide World Photos **447:** Hulton Archive/Getty Images **451:** Issouf Sanogo/Getty Images **460:** AFP/Getty Images **464:** Pius Utomi Ekpei/AFP/Getty Images

Chapter 16. 470: Alfonso Murillo/AP/Wide World Photos **473:** Royalty-Free/Corbis **480:** Damian Doverganes/AP/Wide World Photos **486:** AFP/Corbis **487:** Omar Torres/AFP/Getty Images **495:** Serge Attal/Getty Images **502:** Jose Luis Magna/AP/Wide World Photos

Chapter 17. 510: Tom Hanson/AP/Wide World Photos **513:** Januari Simoes/AP/Wide World Photos **515:** Marco Longari/AFP/Getty Images

Name Index

Italic page numbers refer to photographs, illustrations, tables, or figures. Boldfaced page numbers refer to biographical sketches.

SUBJECT INDEX

Italic page numbers refer to photographs, figures, and tables.